Professional JavaScript 2nd Edition

Mark Baartse
Stuart Conway
Jean-Luc David
Sing Li
Nigel McFarlane
Sean B. Palmer
Jon Stephens
Margie Virdell
Stephen Williams
Paul Wilton
Cliff Wootton
Jeff Yates

Wrox Press Ltd. ®

Professional JavaScript 2nd Edition

wrox

Published by Wrox Press Ltd,
Arden House, 1102 Warwick Road, Acocks Green,
Birmingham, B27 6BH, UK
Printed in the United States
ISBN 1-861005-53-9

Trademark Acknowledgements

Wrox has endeavored to provide trademark information about all the companies and products mentioned in this book by the appropriate use of capitals. However, Wrox cannot guarantee the accuracy of this information.

Credits

Authors
Mark Baartse
Stuart Conway
Jean-Luc David
Sing Li
Nigel McFarlane
Sean B. Palmer
Jon Stephens
Margie Virdell
Stephen Williams
Paul Wilton
Cliff Wootton
Jeff Yates

Category Manager
Dave Galloway

Technical Architect
Victoria Hudgson

Lead Technical Editor
Andy Polshaw

Technical Editors
M.K.L. Lau
Nick Manning
James Robinson

Author Agent
Trish Weir

Project Manager
Vicky Idiens

Indexing
John Collin

Technical Reviewers
Kapil Apshankar
Maxime Bombardier
David Emery
Joe Fawcett
Damien Foggon
Howard Freckleton
Gregory Griffiths
Martin Honnen
Israel Johnson
Alwyn Joy
Terry Joubert
Karen Little
Jim MacIntosh
Steve Parker
Alex Schiell
Stan Scott
Trevor Scott
Imar Spaanjaars
Andrew Watt
Steve Williams

Production Coordinator
Emma Eato

Production Manager
Liz Toy

Figures
Natalie O' Donnell

Cover
Chris Morris

Proof Reader
Miriam Robinson
Chris Smith

About the Authors

Mark Baartse

Mark Baartse works as a project manager and analyst on a range of Internet projects. He has worked for various companies including dotcom startups, web development houses, and Microsoft. He's interested in using technology to improve business efficiency, or just playing with the latest beta software for fun.

Stuart Conway

Stuart Conway is currently a Web Engineer at Redmond Technology Partners LLC in Bellevue, WA. He develops Internet and Intranet business applications for outsourced client development efforts. These applications include Intranet Communications, Advertising Sales, Sales Development, Knowledgebase, Collaboration Tools, B-2-B Web Applications, and others using ASP, XML/XSL, COM, and JavaScript.

He tries to spend most of his free time with his wife and kids, but has been found guilty of sneaking into his office from time to time to try out the recent advancements or download the latest SDK.

Stuart can be contacted at: s2conway@hotmail.com.

I would like to take a moment to remember all those who lost their lives in the recent terrorist attacks on the United States of America. My heart and prayers are with the families and friends of all the victims.

Jean-Luc David

Jean-Luc David is currently part of the IT team at CMRRA Ltd. in Toronto, Canada. In August 1999, he founded Stormpixel.com, a successful Internet development company specializing in interactive web applications. The client roster includes The Psychology Foundation of Canada, TheCyberKrib.com, and The Pickering Dragon Boat Challenge among many others. His programming experience spans from small business web sites, client-server applications, to database driven enterprise-level solutions.

In his leisure time, JL enjoys travel, music composition, and literary pursuits.
You can reach Jean-Luc at webmaster@stormpixel.com.

To my beautiful wife Miho for her love, patience, and understanding, while I was writing my chapter. Special thanks to my parents Brian and Sue for their generous help and support, my friend Stephan Doucet for his great advice and ice cold Coronas, my brothers Paul, JJ, and PPD for keeping me connected, Eiji and Toyoko for their encouragement and the best chicken teriyaki that I have ever tasted.

Sing Li

Sing Li is an active author, consultant, and entrepreneur. He has written for popular technical journals, and is the creator of the "Internet Global Phone", one of the very first Internet phones. His wide-ranging consulting expertise spans Internet and Intranet systems design, distributed architectures, digital convergence, embedded systems, real-time technologies, and cross platform software design. He is also an active participant in the Jini and JXTA communities.

Nigel McFarlane

Nigel lives in Melbourne, Australia, where he studies science, teaches, and consults in the programming industry and slips in the occasional bit of writing. At the moment he works from home, although that could change in an instant. Probably his best achievement occurred many years ago when he learned C++ on the job on a project already started, and still managed to get something working before the deadline hit. He's worked extensively with database, telecommunication, and of course, Web technology software. If there's a next wave to catch, it's probably at the beach, where he surfs very poorly. He also makes science posters. His computer interests include new user interface technologies and GNU/Linux-like data systems.

To Phil, yet again, for patience. Don't stress!

Sean B. Palmer

Born in England in 1982, Sean is an invited expert in three W3C Web Accessibility Initiative Working Groups, currently concentrating on accessibility applications of the Semantic Web, and the XML Accessibility Guidelines. Music and television aside, he also dabbles in, and occasionally develops, RDF, XHTML, URIs, and World Wide Web architecture in general, as well as being a member of the Working Group of the recently founded Semantic Web Agreement Group (SWAG).

Sean can be contacted at sean@blogspace.com.

Jon Stephens

Jon Stephens was a freelance Web developer/consultant for 4 years, until recently accepting a position with the Micro-Cap News Network, doing JavaScript and DHTML GUI programming and maintaining PHP/MySQL-based back ends for MCNN's sites. Previously, Jon worked with digital production and broadcast automation systems. He studied mathematics at East Tennessee State University, computer science at Northeast State Technical College, and is a Certified Master JavaScript and HTML Programmer. He is a long-time participant in the Builder Buzz developers' site, where he serves as a volunteer community leader. In his spare time, he enjoys driving his van around the Arizona desert with the radio turned up very loud.

I would like to thank all the editors and project managers at Wrox Press with whom I've been privileged to work, and who've offered me a great deal of encouragement over the last two years as a reviewer, and as an author. Thanks are also due to those "Buzzzers" who've provided me with invaluable feedback during the writing process: Jonny Axelson of Opera Software and Jody Kerr of RMI Consulting.

Margie Virdell

Margie Virdell has been a software engineer with IBM for over 14 years. After programming in Windows ever since its inception, she switched to working with IBM's software business partners two years ago. As an IBM Developer Relations e-business Architect, she promotes the use of Java and open standards, such as ECMAScript in Web application development.

Margie holds an MS in Computer Science (Business minor) and a BA in History (English minor), from Midwestern State University in Wichita Falls, Texas. She is a second-generation native Texan and loves living and working in the Silicon Hills of Austin, Texas.

Stephen Williams

Steve recently co-founded Chimera Digital Ltd., which operates in the streaming media and Internet application development environment. Prior to this he worked for Edison Interactive, where he was the lead developer for their Switch2 entertainment web site.

Steve has worked for over 7 years in the Internet Industry, and has been playing with JavaScript, since it was first released in Netscape 2. His interests in artificial life lead him from his Ph.D. in Molecular Microbiology, at The University of Birmingham, into object-oriented programming and the Internet. His experience is diverse, and encompasses client/server web/application development, database design, content management systems, IT training.

To my parents and sister for all their love and support. Special thanks to Vicky for her help over the years.

Paul Wilton

After an initial stint as a Visual Basic applications programmer at the Ministry of Defence in the UK, Paul found himself pulled into the Net. Having joined an Internet development company, he spent 3 years helping to create various Internet solutions, including an e-commerce web site for a major British bank. He is currently working freelance, and is busy trying to piece together the Microsoft .Net jigsaw.

Paul's main skills, are in developing web front ends using DHTML, JavaScript, VBScript, and Visual Basic, and back-end solutions with ASP, Visual Basic, and SQL Server.

Lots of love to my fiancée Catherine who ensures my sanity chip remains plugged in.

Cliff Wootton

Cliff Wootton lives in the south of England and works on multimedia systems and content management software for large data-driven web sites. Recent work, includes architectural design and development of components for several award-winning broadcast/entertainment websites, and the BBC News Interactive TV service. Before that, he spent several years developing geophysical software and drawing maps with computers for oil companies.

Cliff is married with three daughters, and a growing collection of bass guitars.

Sincere and heartfelt gratitude to Mike Smartt, John Angeli, and Andrew Godleman of BBC News Online for support and encouragement. It is a great privilege to work on projects with such an enthusiastic team.

Jeff Yates

Jeff Yates is currently employed by Lucent Technologies as an Industrial Electrician in Columbus, Ohio. During his free time, he works on his web site at: http://www.PBWizard.com/, which is explores the use of web standards in today's browsers. In the past, he has worked at Timken Roller Bearing as an Industrial Electrician and spent four years in the US Navy as a Sonar Technician.

Jeff holds an Associates Degree in Electronic Engineering Technologies from Columbus State Community College in Columbus, Ohio, and he is currently an on again, off again bachelors degree student at Devry Technical Institute of Technology.

His interests include Web Development, various programming languages, chess, reading sci-fi and fantasy novels, rollerblading, and white water rafting with his wife.

I would like to thank Cheryl, my wife, for her ongoing patience. All the hours I spend at the computer would drive most women to distraction, where she just claims "I always know were to find you when I need you." Without her support I would be lost.

Pro JavaScript 2nd Edition

Table of Contents

Table of Contents

Table of Contents

Table of Contents

Table of Contents

Table of Contents

Table of Contents

Pro JavaScript 2nd Edition

Introduction

JavaScript has come a long way since its inception as LiveScript in Netscape 2.0. Now one of the most popular and widely used programming languages around, JavaScript (or JScript as it is known when implemented in Internet Explorer) is used predominantly in web browsers for creating dynamic, interactive web pages. JavaScript can be used for server-side web development and administration, but we are focusing on its use in the web browser in this book. With the more recent versions of JavaScript, many new features are available to the web designer and we cover them in the following chapters.

Who Is This Book For?

This book is for anyone who needs to use JavaScript for client-side web development. You may already be familiar with JavaScript, and need an up-to-date guide covering the latest browsers and web standards. You may be an experienced programmer and need to pick up JavaScript as a new skill or you may have read *Beginning JavaScript* and want to further your knowledge. Whoever you are, if you want a practical guide to programming JavaScript in the browser for professional web sites, then this book is for you.

What Does This Book Cover?

This second edition of *Professional JavaScript* provides comprehensive coverage of the JavaScript language, its syntax, and its uses. We look at the latest web browsers and web standards, and move on to examine practical techniques in the form of short examples and more in-depth, fully worked case studies. This book will broadly focus on the use of JavaScript within the web browser since this is predominantly where it is used. The use of JavaScript on the serverside will not be covered, in this edition.

The book is divided into six sections, which are summarized below.

Section One: JavaScript for the Web

In the first section of the book, we concentrate on the core JavaScript language, and on the basic principles behind using JavaScript within the web browser.

Chapter 1: JavaScript, Browsers, and the Web
This chapter provides a bird's eye view of the JavaScript programming environment as it stands today, how it is used, what the major issues are, and the browser versions being used.

Chapter 2: Core JavaScript
As the title suggests, this chapter focuses on the core JavaScript language, providing a swift yet thorough tour from variables and data types, operators, expressions and statements, through to functions and objects.

Chapter 3: OO Techniques and JavaScript
In this chapter, we examine some of the concepts and principles of object-oriented programming, and see in what ways these are supported by JavaScript, and how we can apply such OO techniques to improve our JavaScript programming.

Chapter 4: Windows and Frames
Here, we examine how to manipulate frames and browser windows using JavaScript, concentrating on how to navigate framesets, how to access data and variables in one frame from another, and how to open and close new windows from JavaScript.

Chapter 5: Forms and Data
Interactive forms are an integral part of many web pages today. Here we learn how to use JavaScript with the various form elements, and how to manipulate, validate, and store form data.

Chapter 6: Multimedia and Plug-ins
This chapter looks at how to detect and control multimedia on a web page and includes coverage of some popular media formats such as Macromedia's Flash, Microsoft's Windows Media Player, RealNetwork's RealPlayer, and Apple's QuickTime.

Section Two: Towards Standardization

This section looks at the development of web standards and how they are changing the face of client-side web development. In particular, we look at XML and XHTML, Cascading Style Sheets, the W3C DOM, and at how to use JavaScript with these technologies.

Chapter 7: XML and XHTML
This chapter forms a basic introduction to the world of XML, the eXtensible Markup Llanguage, including some examples of well-formed and valid XML, how to display XML, and how we can access individual XML elements from JavaScript using the DOM. It concludes with a brief overview of some emerging XML applications, in particular XHTML.

Chapter 8: Cascading Style Sheets and JavaScript
This chapter includes a broad overview of cascading style sheets (CSS), but the focus is on how to access, modify and control CSS from JavaScript.

Chapter 9: The Document Object Model
The W3C Document Object Model (DOM) is a huge topic. Here, we start with an explanation of what it is and how much support there is for it in current browsers. The chapter's main focus is on how to use JavaScript to traverse and change the tree structure of a document. We finish up with a quick look at the DOM event model.

Chapter 10: Dynamic HTML
Here, we learn how to put all of these standards together – Dynamic HTML being a broad term covering the use of JavaScript together with HTML, CSS, and the DOM. The focus of this chapter is how to create cross-browser advanced dynamic effects.

Section Three: Development Strategies

Here we move on to look at a broad collection of issues important to anyone who is coding JavaScript for a professional and/or commercial web site.

Chapter 11: Establishing your Toolset
At this point, we take a quick break from JavaScript coding to take a look at some of the things we need to think about when setting up a development environment, such as which tools to use, and what resources are available to us as professional developers.

Chapter 12: Good Coding Practice
Rather than teaching any new JavaScript, this chapter focuses on how to write JavaScript well, providing a set of guidelines and strategies that help you to write clearer code with fewer bugs.

Chapter 13: Error Handling, Debugging, and Troubleshooting
In this chapter we examine the different types of JavaScript errors, what causes them, and how to find and fix them. It also includes coverage of two of the major script debugging programs: Microsoft Script Debugger and the Netscape JavaScript Console.

Section Four: Tips, Tricks, and Techniques

The purpose of this section is to gather together a collection of useful techniques along with some sample code for many of those smaller jobs that you will encounter time and again. Much of the code provided in this section is easily adaptable, and will provide a useful resource for you.

Chapter 14: Privacy, Security, and Cookies
We look at a variety of topics here, including how to keep your scripts hidden or private, how browser security is implemented, and how it impacts on how we write JavaScript. Finally, we look at how cookies work and how to control them from JavaScript.

Chapter 15: Regular Expressions
This chapter will examine the support for regular expressions in JavaScript, provide a thorough tutorial in regular expression syntax, and illustrate how to use them in JavaScript, with plenty of practical examples.

Chapter 16: Form Validation
Building on the coverage of the last chapter, this chapter illustrates how to use regular expressions to provide detailed and complex validation for diverse types of form data. All of this code is provided in the form of a reusable `Validate` class.

Chapter 17: Making Pages Dynamic
This chapter builds on the theory introduced in section two, and shows how to apply these techniques with a series of short standalone examples that illustrate the use of dynamic effects for showing and hiding data, navigation, working with tables, and much more.

Chapter 18: Internet Explorer Filters
This chapter teaches you how to use the filter effects available in version 5.5+ of Microsoft's Internet Explorer, and how to control them from JavaScript to create dramatic multimedia effects.

Chapter 19: Extension of Core and Browser Objects
Here, we illustrate how to use OO techniques to extend core JavaScript and browser objects. This is useful because it allows us to provide, for example, extra functionality on core objects, to create an ECMAScript-compliant object in a browser that implements it poorly, or to extend browser objects to allow us to write DHTML scripts accessible in older browsers.

Section Five: Case Studies

In this section, we see how some of the ideas covered so far in the book work in practice, with some more complex and in-depth case studies.

Chapter 20: BBC News Online Audio-Video Console

This case study details the development of a console streaming audio and video for the BBC News Online web site (http://news.bbc.co.uk/), which was launched in 1999. JavaScript is used extensively to control this multi-framed console.

Chapter 21: The BBC News Online Ticker

Also from the BCC News Online web site, this case study describes the news ticker available on the main page for the site, which was implemented in JavaScript for performance reasons, and to make it available in as many browsers as possible.

Chapter 22: Shopping Cart Application

This case study illustrates every aspect of developing the client-side end of an e-commerce application, from displaying a product list, adding items to a shopping cart, and displaying the cart's contents, through to the checkout. It does not, however, deal with the server-side details of taking credit card information and updating the database.

Chapter 23: JavaScript Family Tree Photo Album

Finally, this case study illustrates the use of dynamic HTML effects for an online family tree that includes photographs. In particular, this demonstrates the use of a reusable tree-controller.

Section Six: Current JavaScript Developments

In this final part of the book, we examine two different current JavaScript developments, one that is still at design stage, and the other a beta implementation.

Chapter 24: ECMAScript 4

Here, we look at the draft specification for the new ECMAScript version, and in particular the new language features that it proposes.

Chapter 25: .NET, Web Services, JScript.NET, and JavaScript

This final chapter examines the new .NET platform from Microsoft, and looks at the role that JScript has to play here. It explains what a web service is, and how we can access web services from Internet Explorer.

What You Need to Use this Book

A simple text editor is all you need to get going with JavaScript. This book does not rely on any particular tool. For most chapters, all you'll need is an editor for writing the code, and a browser for viewing the pages.

Much of the code works in version 4 browsers (Netscape and Internet Explorer) and later versions. Where this is not the case, we have flagged it up. For example, the chapters in Section 2 on web standards require a version 5 browser or above. Wherever possible, the code in this book is cross-browser compatible. Exceptions to this are Chapter 18 on filters and effects, which is Internet Explorer-specific, as is the final chapter of the book covering JScript.NET and web services. For Chapter 7 on XML, you'll need an XML-compliant browser, which means IE5+ or Netscape 6.1. One of the examples in that chapter is IE-specific. Note that if you're using Netscape 6, it's a good idea to make sure you have the latest version of the browser (6.1 at the time of writing), since bugs are being ironed out in each new version.

The code included in this book can be downloaded from http://www.wrox.com/. More details are given in the *Support, Errata, and P2P* section of this Introduction.

Conventions

To help you get the most from the text and keep track of what's happening, we've used a number of conventions throughout the book.

For instance:

> **These boxes hold important, not-to-be forgotten information, which is directly relevant to the surrounding text.**

While this style is used for asides to the current discussion.

As for styles in the text:

> When we introduce them, we **highlight** important words
>
> We show filenames, and code within the text like so: `example.js`
>
> Text on user interfaces is shown as: File | Save
>
> URLs are shown in a similar font, as so: http://www.w3.org/
>
> When referring to chapter sections or titles, we italicize them, as so: *Introduction*

We present code in two different ways. Code that is important is shown like this:

```
In our code examples, the code foreground style shows new, important, and
    pertinent code
```

Code that is an aside, or has been seen before is shown like this:

```
Code background shows code that's less important in the present context,
    or has been seen before.
```

In addition, when something is to be typed at a command-line interface (for example, a DOS/Command prompt), then we use the following style to show what is typed, and what is output:

> xsv regexp.xml

Support, Errata, and P2P

The printing and selling of this book was just the start of our contact with you. If there are any problems whatsoever with the code or any explanation in this book, we welcome any input. A mail to support@wrox.com should elicit a response within two to three days (depending on how busy the support team are).

In addition to this, we also publish any errata online, so that if you have a problem, you can check on the Wrox web site first to see if we have updated the text at all. First, pay a visit to http://www.wrox.com/, then, click on the Books | By Title(Z-A), or Books | By ISBN link on the left hand side of the page. See the screenshot overleaf:

Navigate to this book (the ISBN is 1861005539, if you choose to navigate this way) and then click on it. As well as giving some information about the book, it also provides options to download the code, view errata, and ask for support. Just click on the relevant link. All errata that we discover will be added to the site and so information on changes to the code that has to be made for newer versions of software may also be included here – as well as corrections to any printing or code errors.

All of the code for this book can be downloaded from our site. It is included in a zip file, and all of the code samples in this book can be found within, referenced by chapter number.

In addition, at http://p2p.wrox.com/, we have our free "Programmer to Programmer" discussion lists. There are already several JavaScript lists and either someone at Wrox, or someone else in the developer community should answer any questions that you post. Navigate to http://p2p.wrox.com/javascript, and subscribe to a discussion list from there. All lists are moderated and so no spam or irrelevant e-mails should come from us.

Tell Us What You Think

We've worked hard to make this book as useful to you as possible, so we'd like to know what you think. We're always keen to know what it is you want and need to know.

We appreciate feedback on our efforts and take both criticism and praise on board in our future editorial efforts. If you've anything to say, let us know via:

feedback@wrox.com

Or via the feedback links at:

http://www.wrox.com/

Pro JavaScript 2nd Editon

Section One

JavaScript for the Web

In this first section, we take a look at the basic principles behind using JavaScript for client-side web programming.

Starting with a broad overview of the current status of JavaScript and web programming in Chapter 1, we move on to an in-depth examination of the core JavaScript language in Chapter 2 – covering everything from variables and data types, through simple statement, and on to writing your own functions and working with objects. Chapter 3 takes a somewhat theoretical detour, examining some of the ideas and concepts behind object-oriented (OO) programming and how they apply to JavaScript. You'll see how OO principles such as inheritance are implemented in JavaScript, and how to use these in your own programs.

With Chapters 4, 5 and 6, we move on to the main topic of this book and start looking at how to use JavaScript within a web browser. We start with programming windows and frames, and then move on to examine one of the most common uses of JavaScript today – to script forms on web pages. The final chapter in this section focuses on the use of JavaScript with multimedia plug-ins, such as Flash.

Pro JavaScript 2nd Edition

1

JavaScript, Browsers, and the Web

JavaScript is one of the most widely used scripting languages in the world. Hardly a single commercial web page exists today that does not contain at least some JavaScript. It has an intuitive, accessible nature and is available pre-installed and free with most modern browsers. Today, it is seen as an integral part of web development toolsets, and was an early contributor to the fast growth of the Web and the Internet.

JavaScript is also a programming environment of sorts – the browser environment – one that has matured very rapidly. Go past the language's syntactic surface, and there is a wealth of complexity underneath, via the exposure of numerous Application Programming Interfaces (APIs) in the browser. It is not uncommon to use four or five different standards or component technologies in only a few lines of JavaScript. Although JavaScript can easily be programmed this way, in a seat-of-the-pants style, literate programming demands a firm grasp of these many APIs and the standards they emanate from.

We'll start in this chapter by giving a bird's eye view of the JavaScript territory before exploring it further. Some of what we start with is common industry knowledge, but there is method in briefly stating it. The computing world, and particularly the Web, has been changing so fast in the last few years that we really need to put a stake in the ground somewhere. So let's introduce JavaScript to you by first saying clearly in this chapter: what JavaScript is like now.

JavaScript and the Web

Although JavaScript has stretched itself beyond the web environment, for example it can be used in Microsoft's Windows Scripting Host (WSH), it is within the context of the Web that most of the action occurs, and that's what this book is about. So let's see how the Web and JavaScript get together. We call this client-side JavaScript (web browsers are web clients), to differentiate it from server-side JavaScript, or from standalone JavaScript. In this book, JavaScript always means client-side JavaScript.

A Technical Appetizer

Let's first have a quick example, for those who are coming in here without any previous JavaScript knowledge at all.

Hello World

The following web page includes a JavaScript <SCRIPT> block that prints "Hello World" in a web browser, by time-honored tradition a typical first program. Save this file as Taster.htm, and load it up into the web browser of your choice:

```
<!-- Taster.htm -->
<HTML>
<BODY>
   <SCRIPT LANGUAGE='JavaScript'>
      document.write("Hello, World!<BR>");
   </SCRIPT>
</BODY>
</HTML>
```

The output might look like this in Netscape 6 browsers:

Comparing the source page and the result, a couple of simple things can be immediately seen:

❑ JavaScript <SCRIPT> blocks look like HTML content, but aren't displayed like other content

❑ JavaScript can produce output in the browser that looks like normal HTML content output, but which comes from programmatic statements

Of course, the single line of script shown can be elaborated in numerous ways, and many tasks other than displaying a text string are possible. In general, in such a script we can:

❑ Insert, update, delete, or examine displayed HTML content and tags

❑ Capture and process user input from the keyboard or mouse

❑ Manage browser windows, images, animations, forms and cookies

❑ Query the browser to find out version and status information

❑ Perform general calculations typical of most programming languages

In short, scripts can be written to control many aspects of the browser environment that circumvent the normal processing steps associated with loading, viewing, and navigating between web pages.

Language Features

The JavaScript language is a third generation language (3GL), and a member of the C family of languages, with many of C's more difficult features taken out. Like C, it has no input or output of its own. Whereas C relies on the ever-present, but technically separate, `stdio.h` header, and `libc.a` or DLL library for input and output, JavaScript relies on facilities in the browser. Because JavaScript supports easy manipulation of objects, these browser facilities appear as functions (or procedures) and as object methods.

The main attributes of the language's design are:

❑ It's a third generation language, like C, Pascal, and BASIC

❑ It's free-formatted with C-like syntax, not line-by-line like FORTRAN

❑ It's interpreted and loosely-typed so no compiler is necessary

❑ It contains a garbage collector and there are no pointers (like Java)

❑ Basic types are floating-point numbers and Unicode strings – no precision choices, unlike C

❑ It supports arrays and objects, similar to Java or C++, but is not fully object-oriented as those languages are

❑ It has null and undefined special values, like Perl

❑ It has flexible statements and functions, and no `main()` is required

❑ It's hardware-independent and highly portable

❑ It embeds in other software, for example a web browser

And finally, like C, most of the used functionality is separated out into libraries and APIs. As a result, the code that supports the core language can be quite compact. This is a major design goal, intended to encourage the deployment of the anguage inside other software. We'll be covering most of the core language in the next chapter.

Support for Objects

One thorny JavaScript issue is its support for objects, where an object is defined as a group of named data items aggregated together into a single larger item. This issue exists because JavaScript's approach to objects is novel, at least compared to other languages whose object-enablement is more popularly known. The objects that JavaScript supports do not strictly match the traditional requirements for an object-oriented (OO) language. What passes for an inheritance mechanism is uniquely implemented, and encapsulation mechanisms barely exist. Although JavaScript supports type-like names for objects, there is no object type enforcement at all.

In order to stay clear of long arguments leading nowhere, it is best to characterize JavaScript's object support as object-based rather than object-oriented. By object-based, we mean that the inheritance features of a "true" OO language are missing. JavaScript does have a prototype feature that can be used to support some of the behavior you might expect of an OO language. For purists of OO, this is not enough to provide the "integrated language support" needed for a robustly OO language.

The objects that JavaScript does have, however, are extremely easy to use. For programmers who have yet to make the leap into OO-style development, JavaScript provides one of the most pain-free ways to pick this up. Object-oriented basics are covered in detail in Chapter 3, along with an in-depth examination of how JavaScript supports objects, and how you can work with them.

13

JavaScript Interpreter and Architecture

The code between the <SCRIPT> tags isn't shown on the page as normal text, since it is processed by the JavaScript interpreter, which sits inside the web browser. Sometimes this interpreter is called a script engine. When the browser reads a <SCRIPT> tag, all the content from that point until the matching end tag goes to the interpreter and not to the screen. We can compare how the browser manages this internally with how it processes plain HTML. Plain HTML is read from a web server using a networking library. The stream of textual characters read is parsed down (by an HTML parsing library) into tags and content, which in modern browsers is then stored in a large internal data structure. Normally, as this data structure is built, the content and tags discovered are scheduled for display with a graphics library called the renderer. Now, if <SCRIPT> tags are encountered, then the scheduling process halts. The subsequent content – the script – is passed instead to the JavaScript interpreter library. This library may restart the renderer with its own stream of HTML content if the script contains appropriate statements to do so. In any event, once the script ends, the process of feeding plain HTML to the internal data structure and renderer resumes.

The following diagram shows how the interpreter and the rest of the browser go together:

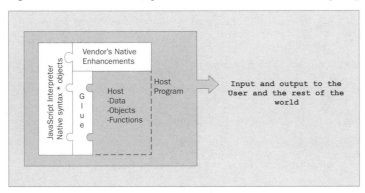

This diagram is from the point of view of the JavaScript interpreter. To the interpreter, the browser is just a host application. There are other host applications, such as web servers, but the focus of this book is the web browser. The JavaScript interpreter supports its own syntax separate from HTML, just like CSS style sheets have separate syntax from HTML. The interpreter has a few of its own objects available to the user, like the Date object. Then, because Microsoft and Netscape endlessly try to outdo each other, there are usually a few vendor-specific enhancements to the language. These are separate from the JavaScript language standard, which is called ECMAScript – more on that later. The most important feature, however, is the little bit of software glue that gives the JavaScript interpreter access to the guts of the browser (a set of APIs), which appear directly to the JavaScript programmer as objects. This is the programmer's access point to controlling both the browser for and the HTML that is displayed in the browser. From the diagram it's clear that the interpreter has no direct contact with the outside world. All its actions take place via facilities provided by the browser.

From the browser's point of view, the JavaScript interpreter should just be a consumer of the contents of <SCRIPT> tags. This is overly simplistic. In order for scripts to provide useful facilities to programmers, the glue shown in the above diagram must hook into many parts of the browser's architecture, providing the programmer with a kind of feedback loop to the browser's normal operation. Thus, the interpreter serves to lay bare many features of the browser that are otherwise hidden from the web page author. This is a deconstruction of the browser's otherwise seamless behavior.

From the programmer's point of view, scripts provide a point of control for the browser application, similar to the Visual Basic support available in Microsoft Word and Excel. With some limitations, the interpreter can be considered to "drive" the browser as though it were a big machine. Existing limitations to this approach mainly have to do with the design constraint that the browser user's ability to navigate where they wish cannot be entirely taken away by a script.

There are many facilities of the browser accessible from JavaScript, and for browser compatibility reasons, most of these are standardized. These standards are implemented as browser APIs exposed to the script writer. Various aspects of programming the browser and controlling content within the browser are the focus of Chapters 4, 5, and 6.

Browser Status and History

We can summarize the early era of JavaScript in one sentence: Netscape invented it in Navigator 2.0 and called it LiveScript, but convinced Sun Microsystems to agree to the name JavaScript for marketing reasons. Sun Microsystems actually owns the name. All the agonizing, buggy details about version 2.x and 3.x browsers can be pretty much forgotten now, and good riddance to them. They're so old now that they've universally been superseded.

One thing we can often forget about is whether JavaScript is turned on in the browser. Today, we basically assume it's on, or give up. What security concerns remain have either been bug-fixed, or never will be. Only for disabled users might we worry about use of JavaScript. This is because the equipment that the vision-impaired rely on cannot handle HTML pages whose content changes at the whim of a script. They rely on plain, static content. Elsewhere, JavaScript is almost a necessity, not an option.

The European Computer Manufacturers' Association (ECMA) standards body (http://www.ecma.ch/) has been working on a JavaScript standard called ECMAScript for several years. Version 1.0 is as complete as any standard gets, and version 2.0 is an extension, not a re-write of version 1.0. All modern browsers are compliant more-or-less with the standard, version 1.0 edition 2, at least. Version 1.0 has had three editions so far (changes to the standards document). Chapter 24 reviews of the history of ECMAScript so far, and looks to the future with an in-depth discussion of what the next edition is likely to hold.

Originally, an HTML tag or a JavaScript script working on one browser might not have worked on another. Although life's not perfect yet, the browser war is mostly over, with only side-skirmishes remaining. Just as Microsoft started beating Netscape to a pulp with its enhancements, the standards process caught up. We'll pay attention to those inconsistencies that remain in this book.

In a browser war, for user features and for desktop and developer integration features, Microsoft is probably ahead with its numerous ActiveX and .NET spins on the Internet Explorer browser. For sheer standards purity and portability, Netscape's Mozilla/Gecko 0.x, 1.x and Navigator 6.x might have the edge as an application GUI due to its XUL markup language and totally portable form controls. By using XUL, the whole user interface of the Netscape browser can be redesigned using a markup language. Portable form controls allow content shown in Netscape browsers to be (in theory) pixel-identical across platforms.

However, such a browser war for the web users is a war fought on media terms, not on browser terms. Fighting the war on media terms means that current tactics to earn or trap the user's loyalty do not necessarily involve browser improvements. Even so, large companies such as Microsoft and Netscape/AOL use every possible trick in the book, so the odd browser improvement still appears.

Some examples of successful non-browser technologies in the media war are traditional web add-ons such as Macromedia's Shockwave Flash, Apple's Quicktime, RealMedia's RealPlayer, Adobe PDF, and XML. Although JavaScript can interact with most of these, those interactions are not as important to JavaScript as interactions with the core web browser itself. Other aspects of the war don't require technology at all, but instead use business models drawn from publishing, telecasting, and other media enterprises. XML is a little different, because it is often used computer-to-computer rather than computer-to-user, although it can appear in the browser too.

History Summarized

Our view of JavaScript and the Web from today is a forward-looking one. We assume the technology is mostly compatible and mostly standard, at least for standards most intimately connected to HTML. We deal with incompatibilities as exceptions rather than as the common case. To assist us with these exceptions, we can consult a book such as this or a companion reference. We don't expect any radical upheavals in browser standards in the next few years.

Browser-specific Implementation Issues

As mentioned above, the version 5 and 6 browsers have been coalescing on a single JavaScript standard, the ECMAScript guidelines. Implementation of the HTML Document Object Model, which enables JavaScript to search and manipulate the HTML in a page, has also been coalescing on the HTML DOM specified by the World Wide Web Consortium (W3C). This should mean that over time, writing cross-platform JavaScript code would become easier.

In this book, we have ignored pre-version 4 browsers because these are on the whole obsolete, as they are 16-bit. We are talking about Internet Explorer and Netscape here, primarily, but as you will see, many of the more modern browsers are based on the Mozilla core, which is what Netscape 6 is built on.

Internet Explorer

Version 4 of Internet Explorer is fast becoming obsolete. However, as it shipped with Windows 95 and 98, there are still a few PCs with it installed, as the user has never upgraded the software. Upgrades to Internet Explorer have been provided on the cover disks of IT magazines, however, so its use has definitely been decreasing. Version 4 is not very standards-compliant; partially because many of the standards did not exist at the time it was created. Some of the features became standards, but not all, and many of the useful string methods were not implemented until later versions of the browser appeared. Some useful information, comparing versions of JScript (the MS-specific implementation of JavaScript), can be found at: http://msdn.microsoft.com/library/default.asp?url=/library/en-us/script56/html / js56jsoriversioninformation.asp. At time of editorial, one web site placed Internet Explorer 4 as only having a 4% share of the browser market. You would have to conduct your own research, however, before deciding whether or not to drop support for this browser.

Version 5 introduced many Dynamic HTML effects that later became integrated into the W3C's DOM standard. However, it was still using proprietary, non-standards based objects and methods, and so can still cause the JavaScript developer some grief in implementation. According to one site, it does still have a 35% share, however.

Version 5.5 is where IE rapidly converges on the standards and the developer should find little problems here. 50% of the browsers on the Web use version 5.5 of Internet Explorer 5.5 and so ensuring your code works for this browser is a good way to ensure that most of your site's visitors can execute the JavaScript code correctly.

Finally, version 6 has just been released at this time of editorial, and according to one estimate, it already has a 5% share. By the time this book hits the shops, it may have a 35% coverage or more. There are few differences between the JavaScript support between the two browsers; one difference is that it will be able to take advantage of JScript.NET, when it is released, which is the next incarnation of JavaScript for Internet Explorer and MS Windows.

There are some differences between JavaScript support with Internet Explorer 5.x on the Macintosh and that on the PC. Although the two browsers should have identical implementations, not everything has been ported across to the Macintosh platform correctly. Some recent statistics claimed that Macintosh users had only a 5%share of the desktop computer market. The percentage of Internet Explorer use on the Macintosh maybe lower, however, as many Mac users could use a Netscape product, or some other browser. We have pointed out in this book where code does not work on the Macintosh, however, and almost all of the code does work on both platforms.

Internet Explorer for MacOS X was only at a beta stage at the time of editorial. This platform brought up many more errors, but when it reaches final release, it may work identically to IE on MacOS 9 and earlier. We did no testing on Internet Explorer on Solaris, HP-UX, or the other UNIX platforms IE has been ported to.

Netscape

Netscape used to have 80%+ of the market share, but since Microsoft started bundling Internet Explorer with Windows, this has shrunk dramatically. A recent estimate gave Netscape 4.7 (their most popular browser) only a 5% share. However, until fairly recently, Netscape 4.7 was the only real graphical choice for users of Linux, BSD, and numerous UNIX platforms. The same went for users of BeOS. This means that numerous users will continue to browse with Netscape 4.x – even though it is a rather buggy piece of software. Netscape 4 has numerous proprietary features (in both HTML and JavaScript), and any code that utilizes the DOM could fail in Netscape 4, as any tag retrieval and manipulation has to occur using the `navigator` object, which is different from other browsers. Netscape 4.7 was the last large browser to perform simplistic HTML page display – all the others create an extra internal copy. This internal copy gives JavaScript a DOM to work with.

Netscape 6 has now been released, which is very standards-compliant, and is based on the open source Mozilla core – the Gecko HTML rendering engine in particular. At the time of editorial, no statistics could be found as to its rate of adoption, but it will be quite high. It is very resource-hungry, however, and so many users may prefer to continue to use Netscape 4. There are some differences between implementations in IE 5.5 and NS 6, but we will point them out in this book when they occur. Netscape brought out version 6.1 shortly after its launch of version 6. This is because Netscape 6 does have a number of bugs in its JavaScript implementation and so it would be advisable to recommend that visitors to your web site upgrade to the later version if they can.

A few other browsers are also based on the same Mozilla technologies as Netscape 6. Mozilla itself, when it finally reaches a stable release, is the obvious one, but the technology and the JavaScript language interpreter has been taken to other browsers. There are two JavaScript engines available through the Mozilla project; one called SpiderMonkey, written in C, and one called Rhino, written in Java. Other browser manufacturers have used this technology along with Mozilla's very fast Gecko HTML rendering engine. One browser that does use this technology is the small and lightweight Galeon browser, available for Linux.

Opera

At the time of writing, Opera's JavaScript support was very poor. Although it claims complete adherence to ECMAScript standards, it fails to correctly execute any code that references the DOM, and other code that it should have no problems with. You can assume that any code in this book will not work with Opera, unless it says otherwise in the text. However, Opera does appear have less than a 1% share of the market.

Maybe Opera will release a later version of its browser that supports the JavaScript standards as well as the other two major players, but they provide no such a browser available at this time.

Others

The other browsers form a very small share, and their implementations have not been tested in this book. However, some of these browsers (Konqueror for Linux) KDE, for example claim to follow the JavaScript and HTML standards, and as many are open source, they can easily be updated if it is found not to be the case. As long as their market share is small, and the other browsers are converging on the ECMAScript standard, then it is not in these smaller browsers' interests to deviate from these standards.

Current Uses of the Web

How much might we use JavaScript? Answer: how much we use depends on the goals of a given web site. We remarked earlier that media is a strong influence on the Web. Most web pages these days fall into one of a number of broad media categories. Graphic designers have introduced the word "modality" when talking about approaches to web site design. A modality is a particular method or approach used to tackle a problem; the point being that there are many, entirely different modalities. As an example, if you need to eat, you might buy food, beg for food, or visit a friend who cooks a lot – three different solutions to the same problem. The general web problem is how to effectively communicate information to the end user. There are a lot of different modalities used to solve that general problem, so let's look at a few.

Search Engines and Catalogs

We all need search facilities on the Web, and search engines and catalogs such as Google, Yahoo!, and LookSmart have been around for a long time. They are popular, although no longer stunningly profitable. Even Amazon.com is a catalog of sorts, albeit heavily pitched towards e-commerce. In principle, not much JavaScript is needed here as these sites are designed to perform at the back-end, not at the clientend in the browser.

Forms, Logins, and E-Commerce Sites

Without the <FORM> HTML tag, the Web would hardy be an interactive place. It seems like you can't get access to any high quality information anymore without creating yet another login identity using a form. You certainly can't buy anything anonymously – everyone wants return business from their customers. Even browsing a commercial web site without providing some kind of marketing-oriented information about yourself is becoming difficult.

Forms are an ideal place for the use of JavaScript, as the language allows immediate validation of the form without any submission being required. However, there is a big design decision here. Some web sites just submit your form information as is, and make the server do the validation work without JavaScript. Even so, JavaScript is still very useful for form-based environments. This is especially true for the drop-down navigation menus many sites use that aren't defined with <SELECT> tags. The menus at the top of Microsoft's own web site are classic example.

The successor to the simple form is the web-enabled application. The web server now often acts as Application Server Provider, or ASP (not to be confused with Microsoft's Active Server Pages). Big applications like Oracle Financials tend to require large volumes of JavaScript if they are to be web-enabled. ASPs are a growth area for web developers, since they allow businesses such as accountants to set up complex specialist computing systems and vend them to customers over the Web, service-style.

Control Panels and Consoles

One step to the left of forms is the idea of a Control Panel. The difference between a Control Panel or Console, and a traditional forms-and-menu application is that a console is less procedural in its use. This means a step-through-the-pages style doesn't suit the user's need. Instead, we have a complex page with lots of buttons to push and slide – a page that might update in real time from a server, or otherwise be quite active. A classic example is an alarm monitoring application such as MicroMuse's NetCool Web interface. There is minimal HyperText navigation in such a tool. Instead, information appears in real-time in the browser, via Java applets and HTML tied together with JavaScript. Although the general public might not see these applications too much, there are many technical fields such as telecommunications, factory automation, scientific equipment, energy, water, and traffic control where this kind of application is commonplace. Such technical fields are great places to stretch JavaScript muscles to their limits.

News and Discussions

Leaving aside the traditional newsgroups of the Internet, the Web contains a huge amount of news and discussion sites. Physical newspapers come in tabloid and broadsheet formats, and then we have magazines as well. Usually the Web uses a small sheet format that mimics a physical newspaper. They're easy to spot, with advertisements across the top and down the sides, like http://www.spacedaily.com/. An example that has typical JavaScript use is the American ABC network. At http://abc.go.com, scripting is used to extensively examine the user's browser and to manage popup windows.

For this news-casting style of web site, will we need our JavaScript? If the web site is book-like (see next item), then we definitely will. For compatibility checks and HTML adjustments, so that the largest possible audience is reached, we will also need it. As a brief example this next snippet of code will report some of the version information stored in the browser:

```
<HTML>
<BODY>
   <SCRIPT>
      var version = navigator.userAgent;
      alert(version);
   </SCRIPT>
</BODY>
</HTML>
```

For one particular Netscape browser, the resulting dialog is show below:

It's just as well that JavaScript has general-purpose programming functions, because we'll need a lot of string operations to detect and dig out the useful parts of this string.

E-Books

A true e-book industry, in which a viable electronic alternative to paperbacks would exist, has been slow to start up. Ordinary paper books are a very common metaphor used in web sites that are mostly informative. It is so common to see a clickable table of contents down the left side of a web page and detail to the right. A dynamic table of contents cannot be created without JavaScript, unless we resort to Java applets or a slower server-side solution. For sensible navigation within these very common online books, JavaScript is very useful.

Also in this category are government web sites with their hierarchically organized public information. However, if you bring up the subject of JavaScript technology, be sure that you're willing to defend yourself at strategy meetings, as public access to government information generally comes with a host of design constraints for accessibility reasons. Such design constraints can limit the use of JavaScript on government web sites.

Entertainment Portals

Another popular solution to the information communication problem is to entertain. For film and computer game sites this means heavy graphics and users with the very latest equipment and software, especially users who are gamers. If we can extract ourselves away from Shockwave Flash, we can do some really creative animated stuff with JavaScript. This use of JavaScript is the general topic of Dynamic HTML, in which an HTML page ceases to look like text, and instead looks like a bit like an arcade game. If we do use Shockwave Flash, we might find ourselves using JavaScript anyway, as we can interact with Flash animations from JavaScript scripts in the surrounding web page.

BrochureWare

For many small commercial companies, there's no need for an extensive online presence. The most that's required is that web-oriented customers are able to find some information about the company on the Web. Any business that results is delivered through traditional business channels. Although these web sites are often dull in the extreme (hence 'BrochureWare'), they can be great for web developers. This is due to a combination of factors. Firstly, they are small, so a developer can have more input into the design. Secondly, they are typically quick to do and varied, so the developer gains broad experience. But more importantly, their main goal might be to catch the viewer's attention, advertising-style. This is a great opportunity to use JavaScript more extensively to craft up some Dynamic HTML effect. This is fun creative programming that does not necessarily need a graphics designer.

Web Constraints and Trends

The Web is embedded in the real world, even if it sometimes seems an alternative world of its own. We'd really like to see our skills in demand. This isn't a Gartner Group report, for whatever they are worth, but perhaps we can project forward in time a little. First let's consider some technological aspects.

Because browser technology is mature and stable, we don't have the chaos at the moment that typified the early browser releases, and we can all catch up and draw breath. Any good technologist knows a stable point also means something really different must be on the horizon. It's not clear yet what that might be, perhaps one of the many Web standards still in development. In the meantime we think:

- ❑ Stable browser technology means that development tools like Dreamweaver have a chance to become more useful. Look for tools that do a lot of trivial JavaScript tasks for you. Non-trivial tasks still require that you have your own expertise.

- ❑ The mobile phone market is so fiercely competitive that it is merging with the palm-top market. We expect to see full HTML browsers, including JavaScript, on tiny screens quite soon. These browsers will require a different kind of tiny web site design.

- ❑ Getting high speed (at least 64kb/sec) Internet access to absolutely everyone is a difficult task. Web sites that want to reach everyone won't be able to assume high speeds for a long time, and so Web pages have a performance constraint for the foreseeable future. This obviously affects use of HTML and JavaScript, but particularly use of images. With the standards maturity we have now, we can actually do quite a lot with just JavaScript, HTML, and style sheets. We don't have to resort to images as much as we used to.

- ❑ Linux is only slowly reducing Microsoft's operating system near-monopoly, but Microsoft still seems to publicly decry it as a threatening competitor. Internet Explorer, probably with a chunk of the Microsoft.NET technology, will appear on Linux sooner or later. Like frequent flier programs for airlines, this is something Microsoft would like to hold off on until there's no alternative left. We don't know what affect the Sun Ray will have (a new computer consisting only of a software-free screen and a high-speed network card), but we've heard that schools absolutely love it.

- ❑ XML looks like being a killer technology for business-to-business data exchange. It's a modern, more flexible replacement for the old, old ANSI X.12 EDI standards. In fact, XML can be used for exchange between organizations of any kind of structured information. We're not sure how exciting it will be in the browser though, since that's a business-to-*consumer* environment. We can use JavaScript and XML within browsers to improve both data management and presentation, and form submission if we need to.

- ❑ Fragmentation of the Web user base is increasing. People surf the Web on their Palm Pilots; on the TV using WebTV and other set-top boxes; in different languages like Japanese, Russian and Arabic; or with WML, iMode, and other HTML alternatives. They also have vastly different access speeds from T1 connections right down to packet radio. In this book we aim at mainstream browsers, but a developer needs to be aware that there are a diverse variety of web devices out there. Although we can have compatibility within one platform, compatibility between *all* platforms is too difficult for now, except with the simplest possible web pages. A few more years of hardware *might* see convergence everywhere on the core JavaScript and XHTML standards, if nothing else.

At a more general technical community level, we see some trends:

- ❑ As the Internet boom slows, will governments start regulating the web environment more closely for purposes such as disabled access for the vision impaired? The US law known as Section 508 is already forcing US government Web sites in this direction. A lot of commercial web sites would have to change if this law was more broadly applied. There are many historical precedents for increased regulation: safety in the car industry, environmental monitoring of water, and financial disclosure, are all examples.

❑ How much longer will AOL fund the Mozilla developers, if Mozilla is nearly finished? Most of its developers are employees, not volunteers, and Mozilla is free, with open source code as well. At least it makes sense to fund the Netscape developers, since AOL wants to use that browser to retain its user base. Without Mozilla, there's only Internet Explorer, and Microsoft then effectively owns the Web.

❑ There are a lot of people with computer skills now, compared with a decade or two ago. If we hope to get the best jobs, we're going to have to skill up on technology more than before, or spend a lot more time selling ourselves. There are a lot of legacy web sites out there to maintain now, too. Who's going to do that?

Web Standards and JavaScript

A famous computer industry quote is that "the nice thing about standards is that there are so many to choose from". Of course, the ironic point is that a standard is supposed to remove choice, not add it. These days, for storing structured documents we have HTML, RTF (Rich Text Format), and PDF, plus many others, such as Microsoft Word versions, and the venerable original: plain ASCII text.

We are very fortunate as web developers that there are almost no competing standards in the web environment. Standards may go up a version, which is a headache, but generally we are spared two or more standards about the same thing. This means no canyon-sized rifts exist in the development community at the moment.

Compare this situation with network protocols. There are dozens of transport protocols, all different. Even today, if we log on to a network via Microsoft Windows, we may need both TCP/IP and IPX/SPX networks just to get our job done.

Types of Standards

There are so many standards at work on the Web; it's like a zoo. We can perhaps benefit from a simple classification system, to help us qualitatively understand a given standards parentage. When we think about standards, we just need to keep in mind that there are various types.

De facto standards are standards that became popular through no formal process. De jure ("as a matter of the law") standards are standards bashed out at a meeting. Laws made by the government are de jure standards. RTF is a de jure document format standard.

RFC (Request For Comment) standards are Internet standards developed by the IETF (Internet Engineering Task Force) as a technical note. A group of interested parties reviews the note for flaws and, after revision, if the note is popular, then it becomes a de facto standard. The RFC process can also be formal, so notes may tend towards de jure standards.

Predatory standards are standards with a strong political purpose. An expensive minimum dress standard at parties can be seen as a predatory standard. XSL was originally a predatory technical standard, designed to woo web page designers away from the simpler and less proprietary CSS.

Failed standards are standards that gain insufficient popular support or that lose out and are forgotten. Putting coats over puddles for women is a failed standard. The Betamax videocassette format is an example of a failed technical standard.

Finally, we have the dreaded non-standards, where no body of thought at all exists on how something is to be done.

Core Markup Standards

Although web pages started with HTML 1.0, or at least the tags that became HTML 1.0, today we think of the set of standards as a 'standards tree' starting with XML. Nearly all these standards are created and disseminated by the W3C consortium (www.w3.org).

21

❑ XML (a de jure standard) is a very general standard for marking up data. It can be limited in its use without a purpose-designed DTD (Document Type Definition) or XML Schema, which defines the structure of the allowed markup.

❑ XML is the basis for the XHTML DTD that lists tags for describing the structure of text documents. So XHTML is purpose-designed for document tags. Another, different DTD would be required to describe tags for the structure of accounting records, for example.

❑ XHTML 1.0 (a de jure standard) is an upgrade to the HTML standard (originally de facto, but in version 4.0, de jure). It is a translation of HTML 4.01, the latest version of HTML, into strict XML.

❑ HTML 3.2 is a deprecated and superceded standard. Some features of HTML 1.0 are still supported in all browsers, even though they aren't available in XHTML 1.0. This is because they are still popular, like <FONT> tags.

XHTML also provides features that support the use of style sheets within HTML pages:

❑ CSS1 and CSS2 are the massively popular (de jure) style sheet standards.

❑ JSSS is a failed JavaScript style sheet standard by Netscape.

❑ XSL (or XSLT), originally by Microsoft, was first a predatory style sheet standard extending style sheets beyond CSS 2. It has now been adopted for development by the W3C. It is a general transformation language for XML.

XHTML also provides features that support use of scripting languages within HTML pages:

❑ JavaScript, VBscript and PerlScript are languages that have been used to bring more interactivity and control to the static environment that HTML is restricted to. JavaScript has been the most successful of these.

❑ ECMAScript 1.0 edition 3 is the (de jure) standard for the JavaScript/ECMAScript language.

❑ DOM 0, 1, 2, and 3 (all except DOM 0 are de jure) standards provide an interface (API) between programming languages and all web page content within a browser. They also provide a standard binding to the JavaScript/ECMAScript language. This says exactly how the browser's interface must look in JavaScript. These DOM standards take some effort for the browser vendor to implement, so we expect a few incompatibilities here.

With so many standards, there's a lot to remember. Section 2 (Chapters 7 through 10) is focused on these web standards, beginning with a discussion of XML and XHTML, and moving on to look at scripting with style sheets and the W3C DOM, and how to put it all together with Dynamic HTML.

Ancillary Standards

There are always gaps in the most well-meaning and exhaustive standards. So it is with JavaScript and the Web generally. Here are the other (or at least, some of the other) important technical standards:

❑ HTTP is the RFC 2616 standard that specifies how web pages are transmitted and how forms are submitted. JavaScript can read a little of this protocol information in the browser.

❑ Cookies are special data items that travel between web browser and web server. The RFC 2109 standard defines cookies. They can be manipulated from JavaScript on the browser side.

❑ The Dublin Core (http://www.dublincore.org/) is a set of (de jure) recommendations for the data stored in the <META> tags in HTML pages. This data can be accessed from JavaScript, although web programmer uses are obscure.

❑ SOAP is a W3C standard that dictates how form-like, XML-structured data may be sent to and received from the browser. We'll need this standard if JavaScript is to be used to pull apart or put together such data and other applications.

❑ Netscape's NSAPI (de facto) plug-in standard provides a reliable way for JavaScript in the browser to work with plug-ins such as Shockwave Flash in all Netscape/Mozilla-based browsers.

The HTML and ECMAScript standards also make reference to a number of other standards in their descriptions, for example the IEEE 754 standard for floating-point numbers. There is no end to standards, really. There's even a recommendation for standard sizes for banner advertisements – at the Interactive Advertising Bureau (http://www.iab.net/). This is great, because we could use this info to write a CSS 2 default style sheet that will blank all these ads out.

Finally, there are the dreaded non-standards:

❑ Access to cookies from JavaScript is not standardized except by silent agreement, but seems to work.

❑ The BOM (Browser Object Model) of the web browser, consisting of many interesting objects available to JavaScript scripts, is really poorly standardized. There is de facto agreement between browsers for some aspects of it, but not all.

❑ The DOM Level 3 standard is not complete yet (in draft as we publish this). Until then, and maybe a bit beyond, there are a few small aspects of JavaScript access to web pages that are not quite covered by standards yet. Keyboard input is an example.

❑ XUL is an interesting standards attempt by Netscape. It is an XML DTD for describing user interfaces, and works in Netscape 6.x and Mozilla/Gecko only. Netscape's previous XML DTD attempts, JSB (JavaScript Beans) and <LAYER> tags, are failed standards.

❑ The set of fonts available to a web browser are not standardized. The use of standard realistic color models for web page display, such as the Pantone system, is not widespread either. Users do not use a standard screen resolution when surfing the web. And perhaps most influential of all, users themselves are not standard.

Standards Enforcement

Most web browsers are given away for free and there are very few police on the Internet or the Web. How on Earth can we make sure that the technical standards we rely on for JavaScript and HTML are faithfully implemented in browsers?

The only forces we really have at our disposal are communal ones. If we can't rely on vendors' idealism, or enlightened self-interest, then we'll have to shame them publicly, or as a last resort, banish their software from our computers. To see why even the most idealistic project requires community or consumer pressure, just take a look at http://bugzilla.mozilla.org/, the Mozilla project's bug database. If you use the query interface to select (say) all outstanding HTML bugs, you'll see it's a long list, even though that software is well polished. All software is like this. What the community perhaps hopes is that the developers get as far though the list as possible before collective exhaustion sets in, or before the world changes the rules.

There are a number of lobby groups working to ensure that browser vendors are sensitive about this.

❑ The Web Standards Project (http://www.webstandards.org/) is as near as you can hope to get to a peak body for consumer advocacy of standards. They are currently happy with the standards compliance of browsers, but unhappy with the way authoring tools like FrontPage create non-compliant HTML.

❑ Numerous enthusiasts have taken the standards testing challenge to heart and created exhaustive test cases, particularly of HTML. A good starting point is this enthusiast's site: http://www.robinlionheart.com/. These enthusiasts seem to find standards flaw after flaw, long after everyone else thought the party was over.

❑ Another place to look for standards tests is under the Projects, New Layout project, and under Testing, both on the (Netscape Mozilla project's) http://www.mozilla.org/ web site. If you download the whole Mozilla source code base, then there are thousands of regression tests contained therein, too.

❑ When the W3C publishes a new standard, they may also provide a demonstration implementation. This is a program that shows how the standard is supposed to work, but may not be otherwise useful (for example, a demonstrator of HTML may not be part of an Internet-enabled browser). This allows a direct comparison of what the ideal is with the reality of more commercial tools. The W3C's standards checking pages appear at http://validator.w3c.org.

❑ News services and written works (such as this!) are always keen to create a little public discussion by comparing the performance of well-known browsers against standards.

❑ If all else fails, you can download the appropriate standards for study and be infantry in the standards battle yourself. Anyone can enter a bug in the Mozilla bug database.

Of course, the other side of the coin is your own use (or abuse) of standards. When you make up your own HTML page, you should use a `<!DOCTYPE>` that is `"strict"`, so that the browser knows to be religious in its standards use. Your HTML and JavaScript should be written cleanly, and pass at least some kind of syntax check. If you care about standards, you should resist the temptation to use non-standard features promoted by different vendors. Put an "HTML-Compliant" image button from the W3C web site on your pages, and above all, avoid getting any press here: http://www.webpagesthatsuck.com/.

Developing with JavaScript

Thus far we've had a brief look at JavaScript from the technical, historical, and standards perspectives. We haven't said how this translated to the time you personally spend programming the language. Is it mostly design or testing? Who do you need to work with the most? We'll consider these issues now.

What Your Time is Spent On

JavaScript is a third generation, interpreted language; one of the Big Three (Perl, VBScript, and JavaScript). It's really this interpreted nature that defines JavaScript the most. Interpreted languages became very popular in the 90s, primarily because they typically don't let the programmer use pointers (memory addresses). One IBM study on defects (bugs) in software with direct memory access found that as much as 40% of all the later-identified defects were caused by pointer and memory problems. We must caution this is only one study. For garbage-collected languages like JavaScript and Perl, this 40% of defects is a potential saving. If so, that is efficient programming. With JavaScript, you don't need a compiler, header files, libraries, linker, project dependency files, and so on before you even get going. You just make an HTML page, add some scripting text, and load it into a browser. You don't even need a web server.

Now interpreted languages are usually slower to run than compiled ones. Because they are slower, they're not usually put to performance-critical tasks like creating new base technologies. Instead, they are often used to glue several technologies together ("integration"). Integration usually happens fast, like a building site, rather than carefully, like a master tradesman. Because interpreters have no compiler, fewer programmer-defects are automatically caught by the system at the development stage. That means more defects slip through to the deployment stage.

On the one hand, JavaScript programming is low-defect programming due to the lack of pointers. On the other hand, a sloppy programmer will end up littering the final product or web site with lots of scripting problems that have yet to be detected. On the Web, however, JavaScript scripts can be quite short. Short scripts are harder to make mistakes in, so for short scripts we get our 40% nearly without cost.

We don't get 40% savings on big jobs. It turns out that nearly all the browser technologies that JavaScript works with (HTML, HTTP, cookies, CSS) are interpreted too. So too are many of the common languages used on the web server-side (PHP, SSI, Perl, ASP, SQL). None of these languages have compilers automatically checking your code for basic mistakes. This means the "late defect" problem is particularly bad for large, complicated web sites; they can be developed fast, but they can take a long time to properly debug. So they retain problems long after the customer's received the "final" version. No wonder web sites crash. Software engineers should complement the shorter, faster, coding phase with a longer, more thorough, test phase. That'll be the day.

One other problem with a full client-server job is that you can find yourself working with a pair of client-server languages like JavaScript-Visual Basic or JavaScript-Perl. This is a headache because it's so easy to mix the two languages up. New variables are declared with my in Perl, but var in JavaScript, and so on.

The JavaScript interpreter is not the only place where one can save time. JavaScript comes with a big library of functions to work with. This library is the interface provided by the web browser. Most scripting involves working with these interfaces. This is hardly the "bare metal" programming that a Linux kernel developer might do in C or assembly. As JavaScripters, we'll be interface programmers instead, and learn how to re-program the browser or document. One problem we'll have with interfaces is that we endlessly need to look up the name of this or that object, or the special values for this-or-that, bit of data. There are too many to remember all at once. Maybe we can get close with experience.

In summary, our time will be spent on fast scripting jobs that roughly work straight away. If we're clean programmers, the work won't come back and bite us much. If we're sloppy, we will be sent back to the customer's web site over and over for months on end.

Whom Your Time is Spent With

Because JavaScript works in a browser, and the browser forms the user interface, the JavaScript programmer is quite close to the human side of computing. Lots of our defects will come from subjective human impressions. This means we will have to spend time on Human-Computer Interface tasks, such as prototypes, walk-throughs, focus groups, usability workshops, and so on. We certainly should prototype early and often to shake out the nasty user comments quickly. This is a great strength of both JavaScript and HTML, because of the quick way something can be thrown together and then torn apart again.

After users and graphic artists, the third part of our working environment will often be database administrators. We might avoid this if our work is very technology driven, or if the created web sites are small, but for any reasonably large job, a database backend will become necessary. We'll also have to deal with a database designer, or systems analyst occasionally to report that the schema has changed again. There's no need for SQL in the browser, but the data from the queries that occur on the server affect our page layout, processing, and especially validation if they change.

Unfortunately, as JavaScripters, we will never get invited to IBM for a seafood lunch courtesy of their power-dressing salespeople – there are no big sales in browsers. We are a mass-audience for browser vendors, so we have to wait for them to talk to us before we learn anything about their new products. Fortunately, newsgroup discussions on the subjects of JavaScript and browsers have very high participation rates.

Tools for Web Development

You're on the fairway of the 14th, 219 yards from the hole, with the golf ball deep in the rough. Now, whether to use an iron or a wedge? Such a decision faces every web developer when it comes to choosing the tools that are to assist with web development.

There is a very broad range of tools available. We'll look at some of the more popular ones in Chapter 11, at the start of Section 3, *Development Strategies Establishing your Toolset.* In this chapter we'll just point out the various types available. Generally, the tool you want is the one that supports your own skills the best. That said, it's also true that the HTML part of a web page's creation can be greatly sped up with the right tool.

Alas, we must report there are no tools that are really decent JavaScript helpers. There are a lot of gimmicky little tools out there that do one or two things, but nothing that's a complete answer. Microsoft and Netscape's visual debugging tools come pretty close, and we'll look at these in detail in Chapter 13.

Tools for Hand-Coding

The simplest way to proceed with JavaScript is just to create whole HTML pages using a simple text editor like Notepad, Emacs, or Vi. We recommend this approach for most of this book, because it gives the best 'hands on' learning experience. But once going at full steam, it's a slower solution than using a better tool. We'll find that even in high-end tools we'll end up typing our scripts in by hand anyway, but at least we might get HTML help, plus a bit of syntax highlighting and checking.

Tools for Editing

Better than hand coding is a WYSIWYG editor that saves us from typing in the HTML tags. These editors usually try to mimic word processors, and generally are focused on HTML only.

The simplest well-known WYSIWYG editor is probably Netscape's Composer. In Netscape Communicator 4.x, this tool was really awful – full of defects and limited in functionality. In version 6.x, it's much more reliable, and represents a simple, convenient, free editor for basic page creation. Add your JavaScript afterwards separately. Its main shortcoming is lack of good style sheet support – perhaps that's coming eventually.

There are lots of other tiny little HTML editors available for download on the Internet; just poke around. Some of them are pretty ordinary. Nevertheless, some people, especially UNIX people, are happier with a collection of small tools. To complement a plain HTML editor, you can add a style sheet creation tool like Style Master or Top Style – handy little tools that ease the struggle with style sheet syntax. No one (as we write this) yet supports the complicated behaviors that hook JavaScript into style sheets. For simple button images, perhaps try ButtonMania. However, all these are Windows tools.

At the high end, there are more famous editors like HotMeTaL, HotDog, and Microsoft's FrontPage 2002. These are all just big editors, basically. Some of the other tools mentioned later have menu options specifically designed to go through a FrontPage-generated page and rip out all the Microsoft-specific technology so that the page is portable again. FrontPage is recommended only where the pages are simple, or you're sure the environment is going to be Microsoft-dominated, like a corporate intranet.

One major limitation of editors is that they don't provide any proper support for sharing data between a server-based database and the end user.

Tools for Data Management

One step up from an editor is a tool that creates pages that can live happily with back-end applications on the web server. Macromedia's HomeSite product, and the NetObjects suite of tools accomplish this. They even contain facilities that speed the development of server-side functionality, although they are not server-focused themselves. We might call these tools client-server friendly. When we use these tools, we can hope that if we threw the tool away, the web pages we created with it will be manageable by some other tool.

Some tools go further than just being client-server friendly. Microsoft's Visual InterDev is a good example. This tool provides a full IDE with considerable database support provided by the tool, so using it we can create pages that connect to SQL Server and other databases. We can go even further and look at traditional client-server development tools like Oracle Forms that can now produce web-based output. Using these tools, when we press the Master Form Create button (or similar), the tool will generate much JavaScript automatically and put it inside the new page. This automates many mundane data type tasks for us.

For these big, complex, integrated tools, once we commit to one and use its proprietary features, we're really stuck with it. Our pages will never be manageable in an efficient way by anything else.

Tools for Designing

The problem with the database-like tools is that not everyone has a database background. The Web can be a highly visual medium, and that attracts a different kind of person altogether. For graphic designers, graphics programmers and the like, "design" doesn't mean suspension bridges, it means interestingly shaped coffee mugs. A tool that requires learning database theory is great for some, but not really aimed at this user base. These people need a tool that fits their mindset just as much as database people need an Entity-Relationship Diagrammer or an SQL Query Builder tool. Examples of these tools include Macromedia's Dreamweaver product and Adobe's GoLive!.

Summary

As part of the amazing growth of the Web, JavaScript has become a necessary part of web site development. Fortunately, we're mostly over the era when there were massive incompatibilities between browsers. We now have a fairly standard technology that is centered on an interpreter embedded in the web browser. By putting script statements into an HTML page, we can instruct the interpreter to change the behavior of the page.

Some uses of the Web are going to need more JavaScript than others. As the Web environment grows and matures within society, we also expect the technical constraints on our development will change a little. That's one to watch for the future. For the present, we've got our arms full with numerous standards. If we can't keep all the constraints and features these standards imply in our heads, then we're going to need a set of resources to refer to regularly.

When using JavaScript, we're dealing with the user interface part of computing, so we wear that hat a lot, and deal with user-interface people. Even though it's quite fast to make a page full of JavaScript, we have to watch out for the highly interpreted nature of the environment or else the defect rate will be high. Tools can help us here, whether they are simple popgun editors, or mighty cannon development environments, but our success will mostly be guided by our understanding of the technology.

Enough of generalities! Let's now leap into the guts of the JavaScript language and see how it all works, programmer to programmer.

2

Core JavaScript

The core language describes the basic constructions and features available in the IE and Netscape browsers. Here in Chapter 2, we'll specifically look at the following:

- ❑ Writing scripts and Unicode
- ❑ Functions
- ❑ Objects
- ❑ Control Loops
- ❑ Variables and Data Types
- ❑ Expressions
- ❑ Type Conversions

This may seem a little basic, but there are a few variations between versions and browser implementations, within even these rudimentary features. If you're new to JavaScript, then by the end of this chapter, you will be able to construct basic programs, although they won't be very sophisticated yet.

JavaScript 1.5 is the latest version of the core language to have been implemented by Netscape browsers, and it is to this version that this first part of the book will attend. It's supported in Netscape 6 and Microsoft's IE5.5 and IE6.

Writing Scripts and the Unicode Standard

JavaScript scripts are designed to be readable by humans. To make this as easy as possible, they're often stored in simple character-based files. This means that we don't need a special editor such as Microsoft Word in order to view the file's contents – Edit, Notepad, vi, Emacs, or any of many other text editors will do. So generally, we can just open a new file and start typing. However, let us pause for a minute and look at how the JavaScript language supports the text-based interface we have just described.

The primary problem with this is that different people type in different languages, and every computer has different support for the characters typed. A set of characters supported by a given computer and the values the computer gives each one are collected together into a character set encoding. If everyone agrees on the encoding, then there is common ground for communication. This is not always the case. **EBCDIC** (IBM) and **ASCII** (Standards USA) are different encodings for the same English characters – 26 letters, 10 numbers, and numerous punctuation marks and control characters. **JIT** is a very different character set, which represents Japanese characters. JavaScript in particular needs a solution to this problem, because it is most commonly used on the Web, which should be a highly international environment. English is still not the most common language in the world, even if it seems to be the common business language.

Enter the Unicode 3.0 standard, promoted and developed by the Unicode Consortium, http://www.unicode.org/. Their achievement has been to attempt to squeeze all the characters in the world into a single set, the Unicode set, with some space left over for future additions. Each character in Unicode has a 16-bit (two byte) value that is unique. JavaScript programs should be written in the Unicode character set. Since the first 128 characters match the ASCII character set – the one most English-speaking computer people have used for years – this is perfectly convenient for English speakers.

There is However one complexity. Unicode characters are 16 bits long. Most Western computers are based on 8-bit characters that follow the ASCII or the PC standard (that's the one that looks like ASCII but has little happy faces, lines, and corner symbols in it as well). Therefore, even if we have an editor that allows you to type in Unicode characters, we can't traditionally save the file as an ordinary text file. The solution to this is that the ECMAScript language allows any JavaScript program to be written using only the first 128 characters of Unicode, which is the same as ASCII. If we only need eight bits for a script, we can use all our familiar software tools, and the interpreter can convert what it reads to Unicode 16-bit when it interprets the script.

What would happen if we needed a non-English character such as χ or ε? There are two answers for 8-bit files. Outside of JavaScript strings and comments, the answer is: we can't do it. That's most of the script. Inside strings and comments, we can, by using the special sequence of characters \uXXXX where XXXX are hexadecimal digits for the Unicode number for the character needed. Therefore, we won't actually see the character we want, but we will be able to specify it.

To give a quick example, we mentioned earlier that ASCII corresponded to the first 128 characters in the Unicode set. The character "A" for example can be referenced as \u0041 in Unicode or 0x41 in 8-it character sets. Going back to the previous paragraph, the χ •character can be written as \u03C7. There's more on strings, comments, and hexadecimal numbers later in this chapter.

Finally, let's not confuse character set encodings with fonts. A font like Helvetica determines what a particular character looks like. A character set encoding number for a particular character just tells us which character the character is. Lexicographers are probably grinding their teeth in frustration at this simplistic explanation but it's enough for our purposes. Fonts have nothing to do with it.

In summary, if we read and script in English – a fair assumption for this book – just type the script as we would any text into a text file, and rely on the JavaScript interpreter to understand it all correctly. If we need special characters, we need to move to a computer with good Unicode support, or just use the escape sequence technique on the rare occasion when it's unavoidable. An escape sequence is a special series of characters that define one single character. For example, \n means newline and not a forward slash character and the letter n, the \ is an escape character.

Adding Our JavaScript to a Web Page

To add our JavaScript to the web page we need to use the HTML SCRIPT tag. This tells the browser that anything between the first SCRIPT tag and the closing /SCRIPT tag is script to be executed rather than plain text or HTML. By default, the browser assumes that script inside the script tag is JavaScript. We can specify this if we wish, for example, we can specify a particular version of JavaScript, using the SCRIPT tag's language attribute. If we specify a language or language version that the browser does not recognize or support, then the code won't be executed. A few examples are shown below:

```
<SCRIPT language='JavaScript'>// General JavaScript</SCRIPT>
<SCRIPT language='JavaScript1.2'>// NN4</SCRIPT>
<SCRIPT language='JavaScript1.5'>//NN6</SCRIPT>
<SCRIPT language='Jscript'>//IE4</SCRIPT>
```

The downside is that whereas IE recognizes JScript, it will only recognize some of the JavaScript, versions. Therefore, any version of IE would ignore a language attribute of JavaScript1.5, even though IE5.5 supports JScript 5.5, which is virtually the same. All versions of Netscape will ignore JScript but this is recognized by all versions of IE.

The language attribute can prove useful for stopping Netscape browsers from executing IE-only JavaScript or IE from executing NN6-only code. Often, we'll find it is the HTML and DHTML support in the browser that causes the majority of compatibility problems, rather than the JavaScript supported.

Another useful attribute of the SCRIPT tag is the SRC property. This tells the browser that the script to be executed is not contained inside the tags, but is instead inside a separate file. This file is a plain text file containing only JavaScript, no HTML is allowed. It's normally given the .js file extension so that we know that it contains JavaScript code. We'll see the SRC attribute in action later in the book.

Statements, Blocks and Comments

All JavaScript code consists of a sequence of statements. In simple terms, statements are processed top-to-bottom, one at a time, unless you organize it otherwise. Statements can be grouped together into a block, which behaves as a single statement, even though it contains many. Every statement also results in some action being made by the JavaScript engine, unless it is either a do-nothing statement or a comment.

Comments are notes made by the coder that should help readers understand how the series statements fit together. They can either span over several lines, in which case they are enclosed by a /* ... */ pair of delimiters, or they can be single-line comments, preceded by //. Single line comments will nest, meaning we can put a comment inside a comment, but multi-line ones will not. Additionally, single line comments can appear inside multi-line comments.

Here's an example program that prints out different text depending upon the value of the variable result. It also demonstrates the different types of comment:

```
//Example_01.htm
var result;
result = 15;   // for this test, set it to 15
result = 20;
result = 19;   // then set it again, final value is 19

if ( result == 15 )
{
    /* this bit won't be printed
       because it's not 15
    */
```

```
            document.write('The value is still 15<BR>');
    }
    else
    {
        /* this bit WILL be printed
           because it's not 15
        */
        document.write('The value has been changed to something else, ');
        document.write('namely ' + result + '<BR>');
    }
    /* end of example */
```

Ignore the lines reading if...else... for the moment. Notice how some lines end with a semi-colon (;) and some don't. In JavaScript, semi-colons are the official way of saying a statement has ended. JavaScript interpreters however let the script writer be carefree – if a statement looks like it has finished even though there's no semi-colon, and then the line ends, the JavaScript interpreter will assume you were lazy and act as though you did include one.

It's good practice to *always* put a semi-colon at the end of a statement, as it makes tracking down problems easier, and some fancy editing tools can cope better if the semi-colons are there.

There are two blocks in the example above. Blocks are started by a left curly brace ({) and ended by a right curly brace (}). In this example, the first block contains one statement (and a comment, but that's ignored), and the second contains two. An if statement only operates on one statement, so a block is used to make two statements behave like one. Notice that blocks break the rules: there is no need for a trailing semi-colon.

Note line 4. Line 4 has two statements: result = 20; and result = 19;. Also, the statement, result = 19; is split over to the next line. JavaScript is a free-format language. Provided we always use semi-colons, we can add as many spaces, tabs, and blank lines as we like (**whitespace**). All we need to ensure is that each statement is on a separate line, or divided with a semi colon.

This is similar to HTML. Just like HTML, using a spacing and indentation standard will make the code easier to understand in six months time when it is revisited. For example, the following code will not work:

```
var my_string = "first line
                 second line"   // no returns allowed in strings - use \n
/* You should use:
var my_string = "first line "
            + "second line";
*/
var copy = my_str ing;            // makes no sense. What does ing mean?
```

Variables and Constants

To declare a new variable in JavaScript, we use the keyword var. We can give our variables any names we like, so long as they:

❑   Are not reserved words, such as a JavaScript keyword like var itself.

❑   Have as their first character a letter or an underscore "_". A number cannot be used as the first character.

❑   Contain only letters, numbers, or underscores.

JavaScript is case sensitive, so a variable called `myName` is treated as a different variable to `MyName` or `myname`. As we'll see, JavaScript's case sensitivity covers keywords too, so `var` is correct, and not `Var` or `VAR`. In fact, all naming is case sensitive, which can be a source of many an annoying bug, so is something to bear in mind.

We can declare more than one variable at once using the `var` keyword, just as long as each variable name is separated by a comma. For example, if we wanted to declare variables named `myName` and `myAge`, we can declare it like this:

```
var myName;
var myAge;
```

Or put them on one line like this:

```
var myName, myAge;
```

When first declared, the variable contains no defined value (it is undefined). We'll see later how we can check if a variable contains a defined value. JavaScript allows us to initialize a variable at the time of declaration, something that is a good idea because initialized variables are another common source of bugs.

To initialize a variable, we use the = sign as an **assignment operator** to assign a value:

```
var myName = "Bob";
var myAge = 103;
```

We can also declare and initialize variables on one line as well:

```
var myName = "Bob", myAge=32;
```

As with other languages, variables in JavaScript have a certain **scope** or lifetime. This scope determines where the variable is accessible from and how long it retains its value. Variables defined within a function, (we'll learn about functions in JavaScript later in the chapter), are only accessible to code within the function itself and normally their value is lost once the function's execution stops. Variables declared outside of a function, for example, and defined in a block of code in a `SCRIPT` tag, are global variables, and are accessible by all code in the page.

Constants are new and are introduced in JavaScript 1.5; however, currently the only major browser to support them is Netscape 6. They are very similar to variables in that they can hold information, but the important difference is we must specify a value when we declare them, and that value can never change. The point of a variable that cannot be changed is that they can be useful for replacing literals that have special meaning. For example, `Pi` is a constant value. We could include it as a literal value in our code but if we assign it to a constant, it makes it much clearer to readers of our code what it represents; 3.141592653589793 is not just a number we plucked out of thin air, but actually represents something. To declare a constant we use the `const` keyword, specify a name for our constant and assign it a value:

```
const Pi = 3.14;  // Pi to 2 decimal places
const CompanyName = "Wrox Press Ltd";  // CompanyName is always Wrox Press
```

Something you may have noticed about variables and constants is that we don't declare what type of data they will be holding. This is because JavaScript is a weakly typed language meaning there is no way of specifying the type of data a variable must hold. As we'll see shortly, this does not mean JavaScript doesn't have data types.

Arrays

JavaScript has support for arrays. Essentially, these are like variables that can store many values. We'll see later that JavaScript's implementation of arrays is based on objects. As JavaScript's arrays are so closely linked with objects, we'll leave their discussion until we discuss objects.

Expressions and Conditions

With variables and statements, we can store as much data as we like, but eventually we'll want to manipulate it or check it. Expressions and conditions are used for these two tasks. Expressions combine values into a new value, whereas conditions compare values and return a Boolean true value. Conditions are a kind of expression most often concerned with testing logical values.

Expressions and conditions combine variables and constant data (and other expressions and conditions) together via operators. Except for string manipulation, the operators are mostly identical to those of the C and Java languages. An important matter is operator precedence, which is a set of rules dictating how expressions are interpreted when more then one operator is present. Parentheses, (and), can be used to force a different interpretation to that laid down by the precedence rules, which are detailed in Appendix B. For example:

```
a = 5 + 6 * 7 + 8;
a = (5 + 6) * (7 + 8);
```

In the operator precedence table, multiplication is performed before addition, so the top line gives a the value of 55. By adding parentheses, we force the additions to be evaluated first, and a becomes equal to 165 in the second expression.

An operator has to work with something in order to operate. Operators are divided into **unary** operators that operate on one piece of data, and **binary** operators that operate on two pieces of data, one on each side of the operator symbol. There is also a **ternary** operator that uses three pieces of data.

Arithmetic Operators

Arithmetic operators are the familiar mathematical ones, and are all binary operators: plus (+), minus (-), divide (/), multiply (*). There is also remainder (%), which gives the leftovers of a division. For example: 9 / 4 is 2.25, but 4 goes into 9 twice with one left over, so 9 % 4 is 1. This operator is also called **modulo**.

Let's have a look at examples of each of the operators:

```
a = 2 + 3;
b = 2 * 3;
c = 2 / 3;
d = 2 - 3;
e = 2 % 3;
```

The obvious results of these expressions are a=5, b=6, c=0.6666667, d=-1, and e=2.

For division of real numbers, not integers, the leftover is a real number. For example, 1.5 % 1.0 = 0.5. we need to be aware however of the limitations of real number operations. For example, 5.5 % 2.2 = 1.1, but in IE and Netscape browsers you will get 1.0999999999999996.

In some cases, operators can produce NaN or Infinity. NaN is Not a Number, and is a special value JavaScript uses to return a result of a calculation that has returned something that is not a number. For example:

```
a = 10 / "A"
```

This will return NaN. We can easily check to see if the result is NaN by using one of JavaScript's built in methods, isNaN(). We'll come back to this when we look at the Global object later in the chapter.

Infinity can also be a valid result of a calculation, for example:

```
b = 1 / 0;
```

Again, there is a special method in JavaScript to represent this, the isFinite() method, which we'll also look at when we come to the Global object.

Relational Operators

Relational operators are those used for comparisons and are all binary operators:

❑   less than (<)

❑   less than or equal to (<=)

❑   greater than (>)

❑   greater than or equal to (>=)

❑   equal (==)

❑   not equal (!=)

❑   strictly equal (===)

❑   not strictly equal (!==)

Discussion of what exactly *equals* and *strictly equals* mean is deferred for the moment, but it's safe to say if the two things compared are of the same type, then equal means 'the same as', in the common sense way you would expect:

```
a < b;
a >= b;
a == b;
(a + b) <= (c + d);
a === b;
c !== d;
```

The strictly equals operators === and !== were introduced in JavaScript 1.3 (IE5, NC4.06+), and are now part of the ECMAScript 3 specification.

If we wrap the above expressions in some code that tests for their truth or falsehood and generates code accordingly, then we might have an example that looks like this:

```
// Example_02.htm
var a=5;
var b=6;
var c=0.667;
var d=-1;
var arrResult = new Array(6);

if (a < b) {arrResult[0] = "a < b is True";} else
    {arrResult[0] = "a < b is False";}
if (a >= b) {arrResult[1] = "a >= b is True";} else
    {arrResult[1] = "a >= b is False";}
if (a == b) {arrResult[2] = "a == b is True";} else
```

```
        {arrResult[2] = "a == b is False";}
if ((a + b) <= (c + d)) {arrResult[3] = "(a + b) <= (c + d) is True";} else
        {arrResult[3] = "(a + b) <= (c + d) is False";}
if (a === b) {arrResult[4] = "a === b is True";} else
        {arrResult[4] = "a === b is False";}
if (c !== d) {arrResult[5] = "c !== d is True";} else
        {arrResult[5] = "c !== d is False";}

for (i=0; i<6; i++) {document.write("<p><b>" + arrResult[i]+ "</b></p>");}
document.write("<hr><b>Where:</b><br> a = " + a + "<br>b = " + b +
        "<br>c = " + c + "<br>d = " + d);
```

Inserting this code within some HTML tags and executing it in a web browser (Netscape 6), we see the following results:

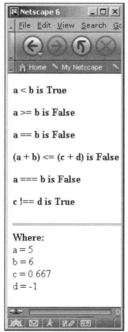

Logical Operators

Logical operators go hand-in-hand with relational ones. They are logical AND (&&), OR (||), NOT (!). The first two are binary, and the last one unary. These operators let us combine the truth-values of two variable tests into one result. AND only returns true if both sides are true, OR returns true if at least one side of the expression is true. NOT returns the reverse of the Boolean state of the value tested:

```
a && b;
a || b;
!a;
( a<=b ) && ( c > d );
(!a && b) || c;
```

Sometimes logical expressions can get quite complicated. It is best to use parentheses wherever possible, both to aid the reader's understanding, and to help avoid obscure bugs. Note that as these operators are evaluated left to right, so in the case of `false && aValue` and `true || aValue`, the expressions will return `false` and `true`, respectively, without evaluating `aValue`.

If a=true, b=false, c=true, and d=false in the examples above, using similar code to, we find the results are displayed as follows (Example_03.htm):

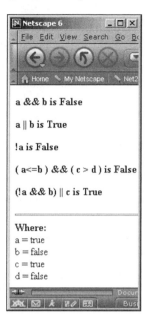

Miscellaneous Unary Operators

These are prefix and postfix increment (++), prefix and postfix decrement (--), unary plus (+), and unary minus (-). Here are examples:

```
// Example_05.htm
var a=1;

document.write("<B>");
document.write(a++ + "<BR>");
document.write(++a + "<BR>");
document.write(a-- + "<BR>");
document.write(--a + "<BR>");
document.write(+a + "<BR>");
b=-a; document.write(b + "<BR>");
b=2 * a++; document.write(b + "<BR>");
b=2 * ++a; document.write(b + "</B>");
```

The unary minus is the easiest to understand; it simply makes a negative number positive, and vice versa. All the rest are really as valuable for their side effects as much as for their main effect. This is because they often provide useful shorthand for longer expressions. The pre/post increment/decrement operators just gives us a fast way of saying a = a + 1 or a = a-1 – they increase or decrease the variable they are applied to by one, which is a very common operation.

When ++ is placed before the variable it works on, that variable is incremented and the new value is used in any expression it is part of. If ++ is placed after the variable it works on, however the variable's old value (before increment) is used in the expression and after that's over, the increment is applied. As the last statement in the example above shows, it can get confusing if overused.

If a=1 at the start of the example above, then by the end a=3, and b has been set to –1, 2, and 6 respectively. The value for a as the example proceeds is:

❑   2 – value of a incremented once and stored back in a

❑   3 – value of a incremented once and stored back in a

❑   2 – value of a decremented once and stored back in a

❑   1 – value of a decremented once and stored back in a

❑   1 – the value of a is converted to positive, though in this case it already is positive, but not stored back in a or anywhere else

❑   1 – the value of a is converted to negative (–1) and stored in b, not a

❑   2 – a is used in a multiplication (2 * 1) yielding 2, which is put in b, then a is incremented and stored back in a

❑   3 – a is incremented to 3, stored back in a and then used in a multiplication (2 * 3) yielding 6 which is stored in b.

Care has to be taken if these operators are mixed with other operators in an expression, or used in an assignment, as this next example shows:

```
a = 5; c = a++ + 2;      // c = 7, not 8;

b = 10; c = ++b + 2;     // c = 13, not 12;

a = 6; b = 11; c = ( ++a == b++ );
// Not obvious but c is false as 7 == 11 is false)
```

Unary plus won't change the sign of a number (unary minus does that) or its value, so you might think it's useless. Nevertheless, it does force any variable it is used with to undergo type conversion (discussed later), and on very rare occasions, that can be useful.

Assignment Operators

The assignment operators are the last general group of operators. Plain assignment (=) is the most obvious one. Usually, this operator is used to assign to the left hand side of the operator, the result of the right hand side. For example:

```
var leftHandSide = 23 + 2;
```

Here the left hand side is the variable named leftHandSide and it has assigned the result of the right hand side, the calculation 23 plus 2, (25). It could be the value of another variable or simply a piece of data. It may be looked at differently; if the copy of the value is a result, and storing that value is seen as a side-effect, then it looks like an operator that does nothing to a value, except pass it on untouched (and have a side-effect). If this doesn't sound plausible, consider this example:

```
var a = 2; b = 2; c = 2, d;
d = ( a + ( b + ( c + 3 ) ) );  // d becomes 9
d = ( a = ( b = ( c = 3 ) ) );  // d ( and a, b, and c) becomes 3
d = a = b = c = 3;  // d ( and a, b, and c) becomes 3
```

Line 2 is straightforward, it is just d=a+b+c+3, with more parentheses than are really needed. In Line 3, we can think like this: c is assigned 3, and passes 3 on, so (c = 3) is 3, then b is assigned that new 3, and so on. Finally, line 4 shows that the parentheses can be dropped, leaving us with a shorthand way of assigning the same value to numerous variables at once, note that evaluation occurs from right to left.

As often happens in C and other C-like languages, as well as JavaScript, mixing up = and == is a common source of bugs. See the Chapter 13, *Error Handling, Debugging, and Troubleshooting* for further discussion.

There are also compound assignment operators. All the arithmetic operators can be combined with = in a way which allows simple expressions to be written in a shorthand way, similar to ++ and --. Here is an example for plus:

```
a += 3;  // same as a = a + 3;
```

Other Operators

Three operators don't fit into any category. These are the ternary (meaning three-part) conditional operator (?:), the binary comma operator (,), and the binary string concatenation operator (+). Finally, some operators don't look much like operators.

Ternary Conditions

The ternary conditional operator is a quick way of assigning one of two values to a variable, depending on some test. It is just shorthand for a specific kind of if statement (ifs are described later), and it is often used in place of simple ifs for brevity. It works like this:

```
a = 1; b = 2; c = 3; d = 4;
x = ( a > b ) ? c : d;  // x becomes 4
/* The following is an if statement equivalent to the above line:
    if ( a > b) { x = c } else { x = d };
*/
```

If the expression before the ? (which should be a condition) is true, then the expression between the ? and the : is assigned to x, otherwise the expression to the right of : is assigned to x. This can become quite confusing if due care isn't taken. Any of the expressions can contain further ternary operators, so we can create a mess as well as confusion if we don't show enough restraint. As if...else statements are not that much more verbose and a lot more readable, it often makes sense to use them, rather then the ternary operator.

Void

Void is used for controlling expressions. All expressions calculate a value, normally the result of a comparison or a mathematical calculation. Sometimes it's preferable to just throw the result away, rather than storing it in a variable, particularly if the main aim of the expression is to achieve some side effect, such as changing a host object. Void causes the expression to report undefined, rather than what the expression's result would otherwise be.

Typeof

The typeof operator is used for identifying types. Given an expression or variable, it will return a string containing a word that describes the type of the expression's result or the variable's contents. Which word is returned is set down in full in Appendix C, but to demonstrate, here's a quick example:

```
// Example_06.htm
var a = 'anything';
var b = true;
var c;
document.write(typeof(a));  // displays "string"
document.write(typeof(b));  // displays "boolean"
document.write(typeof(c));  // displays "undefined"
document.write(typeof(d));  // displays "undefined"
```

The `typeof` operator will even work with a variable that has never been declared with `var`. We can do this without generating an error. This is especially useful, because we can check for the existence of variables with `typeof`.

For example, the following code will generate an error, because `myVariable` has not been defined:

```
<SCRIPT>
   document.write(myVariable)
</SCRIPT>
```

However, using `typeof` we can check to see whether the variable has been defined, if not we make sure our code does not attempt to access it:

```
if (typeof(myVariable) != "undefined")
{
    document.write(myVariable);
}
else
{
    document.write("myVariable undefined");
}
```

Data Types

We've seen how we can store data using variables, but we've not yet talked about the types of data JavaScript supports. In this section, we'll look at the various data types.

Primitive Types

The three primitive types, Boolean, Number, and String, are the simple building blocks of all data in JavaScript. After we've looked at the object data type, we'll see that each of the three primitive types has a corresponding object that provides additional functionality. For example, the String object allows us find out how many characters there are in the string. We'll see these objects in action in the Object section of this chapter.

Boolean

The Boolean type has only two values. The constants for these values are `true` and `false`, and are only used for truth-values. These constants are case-sensitive. Note that `null`, `undefined`, or an empty string, is interpreted as false and any other value is considered true.

Number

The Number type deals with strings of digits containing an optional decimal point, and an optional exponent. In effect, this means that it covers both floating-point numbers and integers, unlike with numbers in strongly typed languages. In fact, all numbers in JavaScript are stored as floating point numbers even though we may treat them as integers.

Floating-point numbers store fractional numbers like 123.456, 2.0, .4763 and 5.3e2. Integers here are dealt with as floating point numbers with no decimal point. Number constants can be written plainly in decimal, or in computer exponential, hexadecimal, or octal notation. For example, `result` is set to 255 in decimal in each line below:

```
result = 2.55e+2;   // Exponential
result = 0xFF;      // Hexadecimal   (0x added to front of number)
result = 0377;      // Octal   (0 added to front)
result = 255;       // Decimal
```

Note that only integer numbers can be specified in the octal or hex format. Therefore, the following is invalid due to the decimal point:

```
result = 0377.22;    // Octal   (0 added to front)
```

The Number type can cope with very large (or very small) values and negatives. Very large means the number can be as large as 10^{308}, and very small means down to 10^{-324}.

String

The String type consists of a series of zero or more text characters. Unlike some languages, there is no single character data type, just the String data type, which of course can store just one character if we wish.

A String is a row (not an array) of single characters, which means it cannot be accessed using array terminology, unlike with C. We'll see when we look at objects, later in the chapter, that there are ways of accessing individual characters in a string.

There are a few special characters, known as escape sequences, which can be stored in a String, all of which begin with a '\'. For example, '\n' in 'Hello, \n World!' would add a new line after the comma in Hello and mean World is placed on a separate line below Hello. There are eight escape sequences specified in the ECMAScript standard, besides \x and \u to indicate hexadecimal and Unicode sequences as we have seen previously. They are:

Escape Sequence	Unicode Equivalent	Produces
\b	\u0008	Backspace
\t	\u0009	Horizontal tab
\n	\u000A	Line feed (new line)
\f	\u000C	Form feed
\r	\u000D	Carriage return
\"	\u0022	Double quote
\'	\u0027	Single quote
\\	\u005C	Backslash

String Concatenation

The string concatenation operator takes two String values and creates a new String, which is the same as the two original strings run together. Some examples:

```
a = "Red";
b = "Blue";
c = a + b + "Yellow";   // c becomes "RedBlueYellow".
d = a + 5;              // d becomes "Red5".
```

However, since + is already used with Numbers as the addition operator, it can get a bit confusing. In the last line, one value is a String and one is a number, so how does + know whether to concatenate or to add them? JavaScript's simple rule of thumb is if one of the operand's is a string, then the + operator concatenates and does not add the two operands together. However, if we had this:

```
var numberInString = "55";
var result = numberInString + 5;
```

Then we'll get 555. We might actually want to add the two numbers together however rather than concatenate. In this case, we can convert the `numberInString` to a number type. We'll see how to do this in the section on conversion of data types. An alternative is to make it clear to JavaScript that we want `numberInString` to be considered as a number, even though it is a string data type. While the + operator has duel use, as concatenator of two strings and as addition of two numbers, other operators, such as the * for multiplication, has only one purpose which is to multiply two numbers. If we multiply `numberInString` by 1, which leaves it unchanged as a value, then JavaScript realizes that's only a valid operation for a number, and assumes we want `numberInString` to be treated as a number. If we change our code to:

```
var numberInString = "55";
var result = 1 * numberInString + 5;
```

We'll get the number 60 stored in result rather than the string 555.

No strings are damaged in the process of concatenation – in fact, a value that is a String type is always constant – unchangeable by any means. If we want to modify a String, we have to replace it fully with another string. When the + operator is used for string concatenation, it tries to perceive its two supplied values as strings.

Other Core Data Types

Aside from primitive types, JavaScript also defines a number of other core types, **Null**, **Undefined**, and **Object**.

Null and Undefined

Null is often commonly confused with 0, or an empty string as it's sometimes treated in other languages. JavaScript's `null` value means that there is no data or no known value, and it is used as a placeholder in a variable to let us know there's nothing useful in there. We can use `null` to clear our variables and in situations where we simply want to specify no data. Functions, which we'll see later, allow us to pass information in parameters. However, we can choose not to pass information by passing `null`. The method can then check for that using the `null` keyword. Examples of the use of null are shown below:

```
var myVariable = "Hello";
myVariable = null;
if (myVariable == null)
{
    // code for null situation
}
```

The code itself is pointless except to demonstrate `null` in use. On the second line, we set `myVariable` to `null`, which clears the string `"Hello"` stored in `myVariable`. This allows JavaScript's memory management to clear out the memory space allocated to `"Hello"` and free up memory, something termed garbage collection.

The `if` statement checks to see if `myVariable` is equal to `null`; which of course it is. Note that the `typeof` operator we saw earlier will report a variable which contains `null` as having a data type Object, so is best avoided when checking for `null`.

Sometimes `null` is confused with `undefined`. `Undefined` is the value held by a declared variable that has not been initialized to a value, or not yet set to hold any data. Although a newly declared variable holds no data, it does not hold a `null` value, but instead `undefined` as we can see from the example below:

```
var myVariable;
if (myVariable == undefined)
{
    // code that executes because myVariable is undefined
}
```

Unless you're doing something advanced, `undefined` is usually bad news meaning your script isn't working properly.

Object

We mention the Object data type here for completeness. It's complex enough to warrant its own section, however which we'll come to later in the chapter when we learn just how important objects are in JavaScript.

Flow Control

The flow control syntax features of JavaScript give the developer control over which JavaScript statements are executed and when. Without flow control, all scripts would start at the first statement, proceed rapidly to the last statement and then end immediately. This isn't very flexible if we want to do something repeatedly or execute particular statements.

Flow control statements involve checking the result of a condition to see if it equates to `true` or `false`. A condition can consist of calculations, relational operators, function calls, or simply a JavaScript data type. The section on *Relational Operators* which we saw earlier, contains the sort of common operators used in conditions, for example:

```
myAge > 100    // evaluates to true if myAge variable greater than 100

myAge > 18 && < 60    // evaluates to true if myAge variable greater than
                      // 18 and less than 60
myAge > = minAge(myAge * 2)    // evaluates to true if myAge is greater than
                               //or equal to value returned by function minAge
                               // which has been passed myAge multiplied by 2
```

if...else

The `if...else...` statement causes the interpreter to choose between one or two alternative statements and execute, at most, one set. The syntax is:

```
if ( condition )
{
    statements
}
```

Or alternatively:

```
if ( condition )
{
    statements
}
else
{
    statements
}
```

In the first form, if the condition is met, then the statement or statements are done, whereas otherwise it is skipped. In the second form, if the condition is met, then the first statement or block is done, whereas otherwise the second one is done. Each possible block is called a **branch**. Since a block uses braces, but a statement doesn't, it follows that braces are optional (but advised for clarity's sake) if there is only one statement in a branch. Some examples:

```
var x = 5, name = "Bob", a = 10, b = 12;

if ( x == 5 )              // first example
{
    y = 6;
}

var name = "Bob";

if ( name == "fred")       // second example
{
    y = 6;
}
else
{
    y = 7;
}

if ( x == y && a == b )   // third example
{
    x++;
    y++;
}
else
{
    a++;
    b++;
}
```

The statements making up each branch are indented only for ease of reading. Like HTML, it makes no difference to the result if there is extra whitespace included. One standard mistake to make is to begin the statement with if (x = 5) rather than if (x == 5) as in the first example. JavaScript will treat the assignment statement as always being true, so our code will always execute, even if x was 6. .

Finally, we can have a cascading if. This is an if statement that has multiple branches, as many as you like. The syntax is:

```
if ( condition )
{
    statements
}
else if ( another condition )  // repeat this middle part
{
    statements                 // as many times as you like
}
else
{
    statements
}
```

In this case, if the first condition is not met, then the second (and possibly, third, fourth, fifth, and so on) conditions are tested. If any become true, the accompanying block will be executed, and no others. If none of the conditions is met, then the else block is executed as for the simple case. If any of the conditions are met, then subsequent else if sections will not be evaluated. This is similar to short circuit Boolean evaluation, discussed in the *Expressions and Conditions* section. In this case, conditions are only evaluated until one yields a true result. Even if there are two conditions that are the same, which evaluate to true (difficult to see why we would want to do this), only the first will actually be tested.

while

The `while` statement repeats a statement or block based on a condition. Its syntax is:

```
while ( condition )
{
   statement or block
}
```

If the condition is met, one repetition occurs. After that, the condition is checked again to see if there should be another repetition, and so on. If the condition is initially false, then no repetitions at all occur. Care has to be taken that the condition eventually stops the cycle; otherwise, the loop will go on forever. Some examples:

```
// Example 07. Find the biggest factor of 134.
var num = 134 - 1;
var finished = false;

while (finished == false)
{
   if ( 134 % num == 0 )
   {
      document.write('The biggest factor of 134 is ' + num);
      finished = true;
   }
   num--;
}

// Example 2. Display all the numbers.
num = 0;
while (true)   // This loop never ends.
{
   document.write(++num + ' ');
   if (num > 20)
   {
      break;
   }
}
```

Note in the example, an `if` statement checks to see if num is greater than `20`, and if it is, the break statement is executed. This breaks out of the `while` loop so that it does not go on indefinitely and crash the browser. We'll discuss the `break` statement in more detail shortly. This example is just that, an example, generally speaking, the use of `while(true)` is best avoided as it too easily leads to infinite loops.

do...while

The `do...while` statement is a variant on the `while` statement. Its syntax is:

```
do
{
   statement
} while ( condition )
```

In this variant, the statement or block is always executed at least once. After that, the condition is checked again to see if there should be another repetition, and so on. This is sometimes more convenient than `while` on its own, because it more adequately matches the logic of the problem you are trying to solve. If the condition is never `true`, then only one repetition will occur. Care must still be taken to see that the condition eventually stops the cycle, or the loop will go on forever. Here is a previous example rewritten:

```
// example 07 again - biggest factor of 134.
var num = 134;
do {
    num--;
    if ( 134 % num == 0 ) {
        document.write('The biggest factor of 134 is ' + num);
    }
} while ( 134 % num != 0 )
```

This form of the while statement is supported by ECMAScript 3 and Netscape and Microsoft have both implemented it for IE4+ and Netscape 4+.

for

The for loop statement is similar to the while loop, but is more complicated. Like while, it also allows the same statement or block to be repeated, but in this case, a count is usually kept of the repetitions to make sure that the loop doesn't go on forever. The syntax is:

```
for ( setup; condition; change )
{
    statement
}
```

The block is the repeated part. The setup statement is a JavaScript statement that occurs before the first repetition occurs. The condition statement is a JavaScript expression (usually a condition) that is evaluated before the repeated part is started. If it evaluates to false right at the start, the statement or block is ignored. If it evaluates to true, then a repetition starts, or another repetition if one has already occurred. The change part of the for loop is a JavaScript statement that occurs just before the condition is re-checked, and which usually affects whether the condition will pass or not. These examples show a very common idiom using the 3 parts within the brackets of the for statement to set, test, and update a counter that controls the number of repetitions:

```
// Example_08.htm

// First example
var fruit = new Array(3);
fruit[0] = 'apple';
fruit[1] = 'pear';
fruit[2] = 'orange';
var count;

for (var count=0; count<=2; count++)  // display all fruit.
{
    document.write(fruit[count] + ' ');
}

// Second example
var new_line = '<BR>';
for (var loop1=0; loop1 < 5; loop1++) // display a triangle of T's.
{
    for (loop2=0; loop2 < loop1; loop2++)
    {
        document.write('T');
    }
    document.write(new_line);
}

// third example
for (;;)  // do nothing forever.
```

When loaded into MS Internet Explorer 6 Technology Preview, it brings up the following screen, and produces a warning box asking if we want to end the script, as it appears to be slowing Internet Explorer down. This is because the third example in the script is a never-ending loop:

Zero or more of the three parts of a `for` loop can be left out if they're not needed, but for this command, there must always be exactly two semicolons between the `for` parentheses with no carefree semicolon omissions allowed. Going towards the other extreme, if we want to evaluate more than one expression in such a statement, use a snippet of code such as this:

```
for (x=0; !x; exp1, exp2, exp3)
```

exp1, exp2, and exp3 are whole expressions or statements, as many or few as we want. Here, we are using the comma operator. When the third part of the `for` statement is evaluated (the bit after the second semicolon), each of exp1, exp2, and exp3 are evaluated in turn.

Finally, if we are not careful, we will end up with an infinite loop as in the case of the `while` statement. In the `for` case, this is very bad practice, because it can only really happen if the `loop` variable is messed around with a lot. The `loop` variable should just count up or down to some limit and not otherwise changed.

There is a second form of the `for` statement that is specifically for objects which we'll look at after we've looked at objects themselves.

break and continue

`break` and `continue` should only appear inside a block that is the repeated part of a `for`, `while`, `do..while`, or `switch` statement, (we discuss `switch` next). These statements give finer control over how a block of statements is repeated. `break` causes any repetition to stop immediately with no further repetitions. `continue` causes the current repetition to stop immediately, but the test for another repetition still goes ahead. Some examples:

```
// Example_09.htm

// Example 1. Display all multiples of 7 less than 200
var loop = 0;
while ( ++loop < 200 )
{
    if ( loop % 7 != 0 )
    {
```

```
        continue;
    }
    document.write(loop + ' ');
  }
document.write("<HR>");

// Example 2.
for (loop=1000; loop < 1099; loop++)
{
    if (loop % 99 == 0) break;   /* Find the first number bigger than 1000
                                    that is divisible by 99. */
}
document.write(loop);
```

In the while loop, the loop variable will increment through all the values from 0 to 199. The first thing that happens in the loop is the if test, which will succeed for all numbers not divisible by seven. Therefore, the branch or body of the if statement will execute. This is the continue statement, which sends control back to the while statement. Therefore, the number will only be written out if the if statement fails, which occurs when the number *is* divisible by seven.

In the for loop, the loop variable will increment through all the values from 1000 to 1098 in the ordinary case. However, if the if statement is ever satisfied, the break statement will execute. When that occurs, control will pass to the statement immediately following the for statement. Therefore, in this case, the last value of the loop variable is written out.

switch

Sometimes you are faced with many alternative paths through a script. The switch statement provides a neater mechanism for handling this problem than writing lots of if statements, provided the alternatives can be determined from the result of a single expression. An example:

```
switch (grade)
{
    case 'A':
        comment = 'Excellent';
        break;
    case 'B':
    case 'C':
    case 'D':
        comment = 'OK';
        break;
    default:
        comment = 'Not your day';
        break;
}
```

When the switch statement is executed, the expression in the brackets is evaluated and the interpreter starts searching for a case clause that has a matching value. When one is found, processing is resumed at that point. Notice that all the statements for a given case clause end with a break. This is to prevent the interpreter from blindly dropping through to the next case clause – switch is unusual in that respect. In addition, several case clauses can be 'stacked' so that if any of them match, the same group of statements will be executed. Finally, if none of them matches, then the default clause is picked for execution. If there is no default clause, then nothing is executed. It is good practice to always insert a default clause, even if it only breaks; that way we know that one of the switch alternatives will always be executed.

The value that follows the case clause is a little tricky. It can be any Number or String literal, or any expression that involves constants only (such as `10*6+4` or `Math.PI`). ECMAScript 3 and JScript 5.5/JavaScript 1.5 allow the value to be any expression at all, but for Netscape and IE 4, only constants are possible. It's possible to have different types of literals for different case values, although that has only obscure applications.

Functions

Functions group statements into a block and give that block a name, so that it can be referred to by that name each time that group of statements needs to be run. This saves us retyping the block each time we need it. In this section, we'll see how functions are implemented in JavaScript. We'll start by looking at our own functions and how to create and call them, before looking at some of the useful functions JavaScript has built in and available for our use.

Creating Our Own Functions

Let's look at the syntax involved in creating our own functions:

```
function functionName(parameters)
{
   //
   // function code
   //

   // optional return
}
```

Several points should be noted.

❏   `function` is a JavaScript keyword like `var`.

❏   `functionName` is the unique name given to the function, which follows the same rules as for variable names.

❏   `return` is a keyword similar to `break`, which is optional, and can only exist inside a function.

❏   `arguments` is an optional comma-separated list of variables that will be used inside the function.

❏   `parameters` are a comma-separated list of data items to be used by a function when it has been called. We can have no parameters at all if we wish, although then we must have an empty open and close bracket, `myFunctionName()`.

So if we wanted to write a function to add two numbers together:

```
function addNumbers(firstNumber, secondNumber)
{
   var result = firstNumber + secondNumber;
   return result;
}
```

We can give our function any name we like as long as it complies with the same rules as naming variables. Here, our function is named `addNumbers`. Our function takes two parameters, which we need to separate with commas. We then use those parameters to do the calculation. Finally, on the last line, we have the `return` keyword, which causes the function's execution to end, and in this instance, return the value stored in `result` to the calling code.

To use the function, it is simply a matter of using the function name, then passing any arguments required in brackets after it. Note that even if there are no arguments to be passed, we still need to have empty open and close brackets at the end:

```
var mySum = addNumber(1,2);
```

Here the code in the function will add 1 + 2 and return the result of 3, which is stored by the calling code in variable mySum. The two parameters, firstNumber and secondNumber, have been passed the values 1 and 2 respectively and will be available for use by the function code itself. Note that our function code is not executed when it's defined, only when we ask it to be executed by calling it as shown above.

Functions are a departure from the rule of executing a JavaScript statement as soon as we see it. The function definition (where the function's statements and name are described) is merely noted by the interpreter for later use – it doesn't actually run until the function is called elsewhere.

We don't need to return a value from a function. In fact, we don't even need to call return at all, in which case the function's execution will arrive at an end with the last line inside the code block defined with the curly brackets.

It's possible to have many return keywords in a function and, therefore, many places at which code execution ends and returns to the calling code:

```
function manyReturns(myParam1, myParam2, myParam3)
{
    if (myParam1)
{
    return 23;
}
else if (myParam2)
{
    return 24;
}
else if(myParam3)
{
    return 25;
}

return 26;
}
```

In the function above, there are four possible places at which the function's execution can stop and where control is returned to the calling code. For example, if param1 were true, then the function would end on the line return 23, with all other lines in the function never being called.

While JavaScript has no problems with many return values in a function, it's not generally good programming practice. Code is much more readable when we only need to deal with one entry and one exit point. Otherwise, it's easy to read over long routines, miss a return statement, and not realize that the code you're reading will never be called. We then spend a long while working out why we're not getting the return values expected.

Sometimes we do need to return different values, as in the above function. An alternative to many returns is to have a variable to hold the value and return this value at the end. For example, we could write the above function like this:

```
function manyReturns(myParam1, myParam2, myParam3)
{

    var result = 26;

    if (myParam1)
{
        result = 23;
```

```
}
else if (myParam2)
{
      result = 24;
}
else if(myParam3)
{
      result = 25;
}

return result;
}
```

Function Scoping of Variables

The scope of a variable is the part of the script over which the variable name can be referenced – that is, where we can use the variable in the program. Variables declared within a function are said to be local to that function, as they are accessible only within the body of the function in which they are declared. Remember though, that a variable does not exist before its declaration, so it is only available within a function from the point of its declaration until the end of the block in which it is defined. On the other side of the coin, we have global variables, which are available for the entire duration of the script.

This distinction between local and global scope is an attempt to reduce complexity by hiding variables from parts of the program where they would be irrelevant. If that was all, then complexity would indeed be reduced, but the scoping rules also make it possible for us to work with two variables that have the same name, provided they have different scopes. Should we choose to do so, then on referencing the name, the variable with the innermost or nearest scope with that name will be used. There is no way we can get at the outer variables, for example:

```
var stuff = 'outside';

function do_it()
{
   var stuff = 'inside';
   document.write(stuff);
}

document.write(stuff);   // display 'outside'
do_it();                 // display 'inside'
```

New scopes aren't created inside if branches or in while or for statement blocks. Those kinds of blocks will obey whatever scopes were at work just before they began.

Functions in Expressions

Earlier in the chapter, there was some discussion of operators that have side effects in expressions and conditions, such as the pre-increment operator (++). The main purpose of expressions and conditions is to return a value that is the result of a calculation. Not surprisingly then, we can nest function calls within function calls in much the same way as we can nest sums within sums. For example:

```
var sum = add_together( add_together(2,3) , add_together(4,5) );
```

This will initialize sum with a value of 14. When we perform such nesting, we want to ensure that they never return undefined values, or we'll get unexpected results.

Functions can do anything when called, including performing statements that are unrelated to the return value that they pass back. Since functions can participate in expressions and conditions, quite powerful side effects can occur as this optimistic example shows:

```
var tasks_complete = solve_all_world_problems() + keep_everyone_happy();
```

The return values for the two functions are added together and stored in the `tasks_complete` variable. Whatever the statements in these functions are, it's likely they are large and complex.

Native JavaScript Functions

The ECMAScript standard implemented by JavaScript comes with a few useful native functions. These are `parseInt()`, `parseFloat()`,`isNaN()`, `isFinite()`, `escape()`, `unescape()`, and `eval()`. All of these are for String and Number manipulation, except `eval()`, which is special.

Controlling Type Conversion – parseInt(), parseFloat()

`parseInt()` and `parseFloat()` are both used to extract Number type values from strings. As you can guess, the former will produce an integer and the latter, a floating point number. The following code will result in `wholeDollarsOnly` having `234` and `numericalValue` having `234.5`. With `parseInt()` there's no rounding, it simply chops off the fractional part:

```
var total = '234.50 dollars';
var wholeDollarsOnly = parseInt(total);   //Parse the number as a decimal
var numericalValue= parseFloat(total);   //Parse convert number to decimal
```

`parseInt()` works by taking the string passed to it, ignoring any initial whitespace and treating any integer that immediately follows as a number in the numerical base (`decimal`, `octal`, `hex`) specified in the second argument and returning a value in decimal. If it initially reads any non-whitespace character not considered a number in the specified base, it returns NaN. It also works with just the string argument by attempting to discern what base the number is in as it goes along. If there's a `0x` in front, it's treated as a `hex` number, and 0 in front is treated as an `octal` number. The strings "255", "0xFF" and "0377" would all return `255` through `parseInt()`.

`parseFloat()` works in much the same way as `parseInt()`, but also treats decimal points and exponents as valid characters and works only in decimal.

Detecting Odd Values – isNaN(), isFinite()

`isNaN()` and `isFinite()` do just what we'd expect – return `true` if a supplied number is NaN with `isNaN()`, and false if the number is +Infinity or -Infinity with `isFinite()`. Without these functions, it is awkward to attempt to detect these cases.

isNaN() was introduced in JavaScript 1.1 (NC3+,IE4+) and `isFinite()` *was introduced in JavaScript1.3 (NC4.06+, IE5+)*

Web Hacks – escape(), unescape(), URIencode(), and URIdecode()

The JavaScript language was born for use in web browsers. One consequence of this is that the `escape()` and `unescape()` functions appeared in the core language, as they are mostly useful for constructing URLs. The standard for valid URLs, RFC 1738, demands that if a URL contains non-alphanumeric characters with the exception of *, @, -, _, +, ., and / they should be encoded rather than used directly. A string passed to `escape()` returns a correctly encoded URL, and `unescape()` reverses the process.

These functions have been deprecated in ECMAScript 3 and replaced by `URIencode()` and `URIdecode()`. It's almost guaranteed that the older names will survive in software for a long time. However Here is an example of a URL before and after encoding by `escape()`. In case you're curious, file URLs just point to the local disk, in this case the `C:` drive.

Before:

```
file://C:/local/tmp/My Plan For World Domination!.doc
```

After:

```
file://C:/local/tmp/My%20Plan%20For%20World%20Domination%21.doc
```

The URIencode() and URIdecode() methods are only available in Netscape 6+ and IE5.5+ browsers. While they work in very much the same way as the escape() and unescape() methods, they do have the advantage of being compatible with URIs (Uniform Resource Identifiers), as well as the URLs (Uniform Resource Locators). URLs are actually one form of URI, a form used for locating resources, such as ftp and web sites on the Internet. The escape() function is described as not being URI safe, in that it may code characters that shouldn't be coded, and so if you're supporting Netscape 6+ and IE5.5 then URIencode() and URIdecode() are the recommended methods to use.

Evaluating Code – eval()

The function eval() takes a string, then examines and runs it as though it were a JavaScript script.

Objects

JavaScript is an object-based language, meaning almost everything we do is rooted in objects. Even things like parseInt() and parseFloat() actually turn out to be all part of a special JavaScript object, the Global object. Often, it hardly makes any difference that everything is object-based, and we can just carry on as normal. For example, although parseInt() is part of the Global object rather than strictly part of the language, we can still use it as such.

In this section, we'll look at what objects are. We'll then turn to the specifics of JavaScript's object support and look at all the special objects built into JavaScript. Finally, we'll look at object specific operators. We will not look at object oriented programming (OOP) with JavaScript here, as that will be covered in the next chapter.

What are Objects

We're comfortable with the idea of objects in the world outside of programming. We think of things such as a car, a table and a book as being objects (actual physical things). These things, or objects, all have commonality, such as certain properties and certain things we can do to them or with them. For example, a car might be red and have a 2-liter engine. We can do things with it, such as start its engine and drive somewhere. It's very easy to conceptualize a car as an object with properties and things it can do or have done to it.

So how is all this of any relevance to programming? Well, back in the 1950s and 60s, Kristen Nygaard was looking for a way to conceptualize real world problems when trying to design computer applications. This eventually led to the creation of SIMULA 67, a programming language with many of the object-oriented ideas in use today. Problems that computers needed to solve became more complex, and so did the code required to implement the solution. The idea behind object-oriented programming is modeling our problem on objects (the way we think normally anyway). Consequently, problems will be simplified and made more manageable. For example, if we were designing an online banking system, we would have a number of objects representing the various parts of the real world system. A bank account could be represented by a BankAccount object and it would have **properties** such as amount, account number, and customer number. It could provide us with functionality to do things with the account, something known as **methods** in OOP, such as PayInMoney(), WithdrawMoney() and DisplayFullStatement(). We'll be learning more about how this might work in JavaScript in the next chapter.

Vital to the understanding of objects is the concept of inheritance. Inheritance in OOP simply means that one class of objects can inherit the properties and methods of another class. So, lets take the class (or type), of things (objects) we call cars. Every car has certain things in common, such as an engine, wheels, and body. We mentioned above that if a car object and its other objects were to be any use, they would have methods, such as start engine and properties, such as engine size. While all cars might fit this basic type, however there are differences between cars that would cause problems. For example, some cars have an automatic gearbox and others a manual one. For our manual cars, we would want extra methods and properties, such as a ChangeGear() method and GearCarIn property. Given that manual and automatic cars have so much in common, it would make sense to have a car class defining all the basic properties and methods relating to every instance of a car we can imagine. Then for classes of car that don't fit that, such as manual and automatic cars, we can define a special class that inherits all the basic methods and properties from the car class.

This principle of inheritance has been applied to OOP. For example, the Object object in JavaScript is at the top of the inheritance hierarchy and the object from which all other objects inherit. We will now have a look at the Object object.

A central part of JavaScript's support for OOP is its object data type, as it is from this basic object that all other objects originate. It has two properties, prototype and constructor, and a number of methods: hasOwnProperty(), isPrototypeOf(), propertyIsEnumerable(), toLocaleString(), toString(), valueOf(). Most of these properties are of limited use in web programming, while some, such as the prototype and constructor properties, are very essential for object-oriented programming with JavaScript, which we'll come to in the next chapter.

Of all the methods, valueOf() is the most useful as it returns the primitive data type (if any) that is stored by the object. We'll see shortly that each of the primitive data types, Boolean, number and string, have an equivalent object representing them and providing extra functionality. To get the primitive value contained by these, we simply use the valueOf() method. As all other objects in JavaScript inherit from the Object data type, it means that they also all have its properties and methods.

Accessing properties and methods in JavaScript is very similar to accessing a variable or function. The difference is that we need to use the object name, then the period (.) character, and then the name of the property or method we want to access, noting that methods must always have parentheses after them. To create a new instance of a type of object, we use the new keyword and then specify the type of object we want to create. If we imagine that JavaScript had the Car type of object with the speed property and the setSpeed() method, the code we would use to create it and access its property and method would be:

```
var myCar = new Car();
document.write(myCar.speed);
myCar.setSpeed(100);
```

As we continue through the section on objects, we will look at actual objects supported by JavaScript and how they can be created and used.

Finally, before leaving this quick tour of objects in JavaScript, we need to take a look at **constructors**. When a new object is created or constructed we may have the option of passing information to the creation process. Each different type of object has different constructors, and often one type of object has two or more constructors. We'll see shortly that JavaScript has a Date object, where we can either pass no value when it's constructed, or we can pass the date and time for it to hold. When no value is passed to the Date object, it creates itself with the current date and time stored inside.

JavaScript's Native Objects

The real functionality of JavaScript comes from its native objects. While the core of the language so far has allowed us to store data and change the flow of code, native objects allow us to not just store a string, but also manipulate, search, and change it. In this section, we'll look briefly at all of the native objects and see how we can create and use each of them. We won't detail all of their properties and methods here as these can be found in Appendix D.

We'll see that there are two types of native objects; those created by JavaScript automatically and those we create ourselves. For example, the `Math` object is always present and provides a number of basic mathematical functions. The `String` object on the other hand, is something we create ourselves to store character information. It then provides a number of functions for manipulating characters stored by that object.

For objects that are not automatically created for us by JavaScript, we need to create them first. To do this, we use the `new` keyword and then specify the type of object we want to create. If we want to create a new `String` object, which we'll see shortly, we would write:

```
var myNewStringObjectInstance = new String();
```

The variable `myNewStringObjectInstance` holds a reference to the new instance of the String object. Note the brackets at the end of the `String` keyword. These are where we can pass arguments to the `String` object's constructor. We have left them blank in the example, but could have instead passed some text that is to be stored by the `String` object:

```
var myNewStringObjectInstance = new String("My text");
```

The Global Object

The `Global` object is one of the objects that we can't create. It's already created automatically by JavaScript for our use, even before the first line of our code is executed. In fact, the biggest secret to working with objects is that there's always one around you, the `Global` object. All the variables and functions we create, unless we say otherwise, are part of the `Global` object. Functions that we might have considered as part of the JavaScript language, such as `alert()`, are in fact simply part of the `Global` object. In many ways, although the `Global` object is the source of much of JavaScript's functionality, we generally just accept its presence, but carry on programming as normal.

Primitive Types Object Equivalents

Each of the three primitive data types has an equivalently named object type. These objects not only store the same data as the primitive types, but also provide functionality needed to manipulate the primitive data type.

> Note that although all the objects have the same name as the primitive type, they all also use an initial capital letter. As JavaScript is case sensitive, it is vital that we use an initial capital letter.

String Object

From all of primitive type representing objects, the `String` object has the most features. A quick look at the JavaScript reference in Appendix A will show you just how many. Chapter 15, *Regular Expressions* also covers some of the more advanced `String` object methods.

With the String object, we can search the string, match patterns of characters, find out its length, and examine individual and sets of characters inside it. In fact, it allows us to do pretty much all the stuff we want to do with strings. However, we can't change the value of the characters it stores, except when we first create the object. It is therefore important that the text we want to store is passed as an argument to the object's constructor:

```
var myString = new String("Hello World");
```

Many of its methods deal with characters and often return characters. For example, the indexOf() method will find a sub-string inside the string held by the String object and return an integer with the position of the matched string. The code below matches the word Hello and displays the position the match was made at:

```
var myString = new String("Hello World");
document.write(myString.indexOf("Hello"));
```

This would display 0 to the page, because the match has been found at the first character. It may seem odd that the first character is considered to be at position zero, but that's how all of the String methods operate. If no match were found, then -1 would be returned. Again, -1 is a common value in JavaScript for indicating no match.

Some methods will return a portion of the string contained in the String object. Let's say we have a String object stored in variable myString with the characters "0122 345678", and we wanted to change the string inside to store just the first four characters. We might think this is impossible, because we can't change the value of a string. It is, but we can create a new String object and store it in the same variable. The old String object will no longer be referenced or accessible to us, and will eventually be cleared out of the memory. Let's see the code for obtaining the first four characters:

```
var myString = "0122 345678";
myString = myString.slice(0,3);
```

The first thing that stands out is that no new operator has been used. This isn't a mistake; what we have done is create a string primitive in the first line and on the second line, we use this as if it was a String object. At this point, JavaScript assumes the only sane option is that the string primitive is converted (temporarily) to a String object. The method is run against the object and then myString is set back to a string primitive. On the second line, myString will continue to hold a string primitive consisting of the characters from the string starting at position 0 and continuing to position 3, the 0122. If we used the following piece of code:

```
var myString = new String("0122 345678");
myString = myString.slice(0,3);
```

Then the results would be the same, except that myString on the second line would hold a String object with "0122" stored inside it. If we wanted a string primitive, we would need to use the valueOf() method that all objects have. The primitive value of the object is then returned, if appropriate:

```
var myString = "0122 345678";
myString = myString.slice(0,3);
myString = myString.valueOf();
```

Number Object

The Number object represents the number primitive, just as with the string primitive and String object. The Number object contains few methods or properties however and is rarely used in web pages. All the useful mathematical functions are available in the Math object.

Boolean Object

Again, the Boolean object represents its primitive type of the same name. It has even less functionality than the Number object, and is extremely unlikely we would ever actually use it.

The Math Object

The `Math` object, like the `Global` object, is not an object we create ourselves, but instead, is already created for us by JavaScript. To access its methods and properties, we use its name. So to obtain the value of `PI` we would write:

```
document.write(Math.PI);
```

Most of the sort of functions found on a high school calculator are within the `Math` object, such as `cos` and `tan`. Also useful is the ability to generate a pseudo random number, (pseudo because nothing a computer does is really random). For this we use the `random()` method:

```
document.write("Today's random number is " + Math.random()");
```

That produces a fractional number between 0 and 1, which we need to multiply and round up. We can do this using the `Math` object's `round()` method to get a useful whole number.

For example, the following would write 44 to the page:

```
var myNumber = 44.49;
document.write(Math.round(myNumber));
```

The Date Object

The `Date` object is the key to date and time functionality in JavaScript. If we create it with no arguments passed to its constructor, it will contain the date and time of the user's computer. Alternatively, we can pass it a valid date and/or time. By valid we mean any of the commonly used formats, a few examples of which are shown below:

```
var myNowDateTime = new Date() // set to current date and time
var myDate = "1 Jan 2001" // 1 Jan 2001 - time left at default of 00:00
var myDate = "1/01/2001 11:39" 1 Jan 2001 - time 11:39
```

Given the different formats of date definition, particularly differentiations between US and UK formats, it's best to use the abbreviated month name rather than a number.

Having created our `Date` object, we find there are a vast number of methods that allow us to set the date and time, and retrieve parts of the date and time, such as month and year. It is worth being aware that the month value when using the `setMonth()` or `getMonth()` methods starts from 0 for January, 1 for February and so on up to 11 for December. Additionally, while the `setYear()` and `getYear()` methods are still available, they have been deprecated since the Y2K bug and `setFullYear()`, and `getFullYear()` have taken their place.

The `Date` object also provides a number of functions dealing with something called UTC time, previously known as GMT or Greenwich Mean Time.

The Error Object

The `Error` object was introduced in JScript 5, supported by IE5+ and JavaScript 1.5, supported by Netscape 6. It allows us to define our own errors, also known in JavaScript as **exceptions**, which we can generate if the situation arises. Some might wonder why we would need to deliberately generate errors when a few accidental typos will do the job just as well. Firstly, the `Error` object is for generating or **throwing** run time errors.

The sort of situations we might want to do this in are where the user has entered invalid data. We could throw an invalid data error in a function, which can be caught by code elsewhere. It has no methods, just two properties, `message` and `number` being the description we want to give to our error and the number we're providing. IE also supports the `description` property as an alternative to the `message` property, but they are identical. Netscape 6 only supports the `message` property.

In the code below, we create a new `Error` object, and pass to its constructor the number and message we want linked to that error:

```
var myError = new Error(101,"Darn it, I screwed up again");
document.write(myError.number);
document.write(myError.message);
```

To actually generate or throw the error we use the `throw` keyword:

```
throw myError;
```

We would normally do this within the context of a `try...catch` clause, like that shown below:

```
try
{
    throw myError;
}
catch(errorObj)
{
    document.write(errorObj.description);
}
```

The `try` clause allows us to try and run some code. We discuss `try...catch` in more detail in Chapter 13, *Error Handling, Debugging, and Troubleshooting*.

Array Object

We briefly mentioned arrays earlier in the chapter. We have saved the gory details until now because of the way JavaScript supports arrays, by having a special object called the `Array` object.

Let's start by looking at a simple array:

```
var myFriendsArray = new
Array("Monica","Joey","Chandler","Phoebe","Rachel","Ross");
document.write(myFriendsArray[0]);
```

First, we create a new `Array` object and pass the constructor all of the elements we want to initialize it with. We can pass as many or few arguments to the array as we wish and can add elements later on with code.

Arrays are zero-based in JavaScript, so when we want to write out `Monica`, the first array element, we use 0 in square brackets.

> Note the use of square brackets rather than round brackets (common in many programming languages). IE will accept square or round brackets, but not Netscape. If we want our code to be cross browser compatible then it is best to use only square brackets.

We can easily add new elements or modify existing elements simply by using the square brackets and supplying an index. So, to change element 1 containing "Joey" to "Janet", we would write:

```
myFriendsArray[1] = "Janet";
```

To add a whole new element:

```
myFriendsArray[99] = "Janet";
```

Note that we have not gone sequentially. We don't have to, although it can make accessing the elements marginally more tricky. If we stick to a sequence starting from 0 and going up one, then we can access elements using a `loop` and an index counter. Alternatively, we have to know the element number we want to access or we need to use a `for...in` loop which is specific to objects. We will revisit this later in the chapter.

So without having to keep count, we can tell how many elements we have, using the `Array` object's `length` property:

```
document.write(myFriendsArray.length);
```

`length` provides the next free element index in the array. So originally, our `Friends` array had six elements with index 0 to 5. `length` at this point which would be 6. When we added `Janet` at element index 99, this all changed. Now the next free element after the last index is `100` (99 + 1). This is another good reason for just sticking with arrays that go sequentially.

JavaScript arrays are very flexible. In fact, we can even use text rather numbers to index array elements. If we wanted, we could declare an array and then use text like that shown below:

```
var myFriendsArray = new Array();
myFriendsArray["TheFunnyOne"] = "Chandler";
myFriendsArray["TheDropDeadGorgeousOne"] = "Rachel"
```

So far, we have been storing strings in arrays, but we can store numbers, Booleans, or objects in array elements.

Strictly speaking, JavaScript does not support multi-dimensional arrays, but there is an easy way to fake them by storing an array inside an array. Let's say we want a two dimensional array. First, we need to declare our initial array:

```
var myMultiDimArray = new Array();
```

Then we need to store another `Array` object in the first array element:

```
myMultiDimArray[0] = new Array();
```

This allows us to use JavaScript's shorthand syntax and write:

```
myMultiDimArray[0][0] = "Some Value";
myMultiDimArray[0][1] = "Another Value";
```

If we want to write:

```
myMultiDimArray[1][0] = "Yet Another Value";
```

Then we first need to assign an array object `myMultiDimArray[1]`:

```
myMultiDimArray[1] = new Array();
```

For `myMultiDimArray[2][0]`, we need to assign `myMultiDimArray[2]` a new `Array` object. We can continue this as far as we like up to the maximum element index of 4 billion.

Using the same technique, we can have a three or more dimensional array. Here is a three dimensional array:

```
var myMultiDimArray[0] = new Array();
myMultiDimArray[0][0] = new Array();
myMultiDimArray[0][0][0] = "Some Value";
```

Object Based Operators and Flow Control

To round off our discussion of objects before we get to the more advanced object usage in the next chapter, we're going to take a brief look at the object-based operators and flow control statements we've not looked at yet.

for...in

Sometimes an object's contents are unknown. If it were an array, it would be easy to discover the contents by looking at the `length` property of the array and accessing all the elements starting at 0. It's not so easy for objects, because the properties of the object aren't neatly ordered and their names can be arbitrary strings.

The `for` statement discussed earlier has a variant designed for this job. Its syntax is:

```
for ( variable in object_variable )
{
    statements
}
```

An example:

```
var documentObj = window.document;
var prop;
for ( prop in documentObj )
{
    if ( typeof( documentObj[prop] ) == "string" )
        document.write("<BR>Property: " + prop + " has value: "
            + documentObj[prop]);
}
```

This example steps through all the properties of the `documentObj` variable containing a reference to the browser's document object and displays only those properties containing strings.

Unfortunately, the `for...in` statement is a potential trap for beginners. Ordinary properties are reported as you would expect, but some special properties never appear. This can be a source of confusion. Typical examples are methods of objects that are supplied by the host, not by the scriptwriter. The order in which properties are reported also varies between JavaScript vendors.

with...

The point has been made that every variable is part of an object, which we might call the current context, the current object, or the current scope. Sometimes (usually for typing convenience), we might want to change the current scope. The `with` statement does this and its syntax is:

```
with ( object )
{
    statements
}
```

An example:

```
var unrealistically_long_name = new Object();
unrealistically_long_name.sole_property = new Object();
unrealistically_long_name.sole_property.first = "Ready";
unrealistically_long_name.sole_property.second = "Set";
unrealistically_long_name.sole_property.third = "Go";

with ( unrealistically_long_name.sole_property )
{
```

```
    document.write( first + ',' + second + ',' + third + '!');
    // Ready, Set, Go!
}
```

To display the three deepest level properties would take very long lines of code, were it not for the use of with surrounding the line producing the output. Further work could be saved by putting the last three assignments inside the with statement as well.

in and instanceof

Both in and instanceof were introduced in JavaScript 1.4 and Jscript 5, so only Netscape 6 and IE5+ actually support them:

```
var a = ("PI" in Math);        //a holds true
var b = new String;
var c = (b instanceof String);  //c holds true
```

As the discussion of the for...in loop may have suggested, the in operator returns true if a specified property does exist with the specified object. In the example, the Math object does have a property called PI, so a is true. Similarly, instanceof returns true if the left hand side variable is an object of the type specified on the right. b is a String object in the example, so c is also true.

Functions Are Also Objects

Functions are objects and can be created like objects, as this fragment from the main example shows:

```
var data4 = new Function("a, b", "return (a<b) ? a : b;");
// return lesser value
data4(3, 5);
```

It's also the case that ordinary functions (ones that start with the function keyword) are objects:

```
function im_an_object()
{
   var prop1;
   var prop2;
   if ( arguments.length > 2) return "At least 3 properties";
}

var obj = im_an_object;
document.write(obj(1,2,3));   // do im_an_object
```

In this example, prop1, prop2, and the arguments array are all properties of the currently executing function object that corresponds to the function im_an_object(). Note it only applies to the currently executing function, and we can't use arguments outside the function itself. The syntax conveniently lets us overlook the fact that the function is an object, but as the penultimate line shows, we can assign and reference it from a variable just like other object types. We can even call the function using the assigned variable name as shown in the last line of the example.

Passing functions as parameters

Another advantage of functions being objects is that we can treat them like any other object when it comes to things like passing them inside other functions parameters. So, just as a Date object can be passed as an argument, so can one of our function objects as in the example below:

```
function addNumber(firstNumber, secondNumber)
{
   return firstNumber + secondNumber;
}

function subtractNumber(firstNumber, secondNumber)
{
   return firstNumber - secondNumber;
}

function doCalculation(myFunction)
{
   alert(myFunction(2,5));
}

var getUserCalcType = prompt("Enter + to add or - to subtract","");

if (getUserCalcType == "+")
{
   doCalculation(addNumber);
}
else if (getUserCalcType == "-")
{
   doCalculation(subtractNumber);
}
```

In the example, we have three functions. `addNumber()` and `subtractNumber()` are functions that we will pass as a parameter to the `doCalculation()` function, depending on whether the user enters " + " or " – " in the prompt box. Being able to pass functions like this enables stretus to leave it until the code is actually running before deciding what functions will be called.

Data Type Conversion and Equality

JavaScript is called a loosely typed language, because any variable or property can contain any type of data, but this flexibility doesn't come without conditions. Every piece of data still has a type, and there are several situations where decisions need to be made about how to handle those types. To save the developer the overhead of making those decisions (typically required in a strongly typed language like Java), the JavaScript interpreter follows a set of built-in rules. Obscure and hard to find bugs can occur if these rules aren't appreciated by the programmer, but for normal cases, it all works the way we would expect it to. The only time these rules apply is when type conversion happens – a piece of data of a given type needs to turn into another type. If you consider the following example, you'll see there are a number of ambiguities:

```
var u = String(5.35);   // 5.35 or "5.35" ?
var v = "10" + 23;   // "1023" or 33 ?
var w = ( "10.5" ==  10.5 );   // true or false ?

var x = new Object;
var y = x + 1;   // what ?
```

In the following sections, we'll develop enough rules for us to answer the questions posed in the comments of this example. First, the next bit cuts to the chase, and shows us how to avoid problems. After that, there's some minor agony covering the gritty details of the rules before we get to read something more palatable again.

Before we go into any of that however, we should return briefly to the question of the strictly equals operators, `===` and `!==`, that were introduced in JavaScript 1.3. These two operators compare not only the value of the variable but the type of the variable too. Two variables are strictly equal to one another if both their value and type are the same. Compare this with the `==` and `!=` operators in the rest of this section.

Quick and Safe Type Conversion

As you will see below, comparisons are the main bugbear. The safest way to proceed with comparisons without wasting time on bugs, compatibility problems, and obscure rules, is to stick to three simple guidelines:

- ❏ Compare same types only – don't mix Numbers and Strings
- ❏ If mixing is inevitable, force the conversion we want to happen
- ❏ Avoid comparing things with `null`; just rely on the fact that conversion to the Boolean type is reliable

This example illustrates these points:

```
var result = ( a+'' == b+'' );          // String comparison forced
    result = ( a-0 == b-0 );            // Number comparison forced
    result = ( !a == !b );              // Boolean comparison forced

if ( a != null ) { do_something(a); };  // possibly attracts bugs
if ( a ) { do_something(a); };          // more likely to avoid bugs

var message = "total errors: " + num_errors;     // always safe
```

Don't worry about concatenating Numbers and Strings together. It will work, because JavaScript always concatenates when one of the data types on the right or left of the + is a string.

Primitive Type Conversion

ECMAScript says that any piece of data can be converted to each of the three primitive types: Boolean, Number, and String. If the piece of data is an Object, then there is a mechanism to convert it to a Number or a String. If the piece of data isn't an Object, then the JavaScript interpreter does the job itself, internally.

JavaScript makes it easy for us to convert one type of data to the nearest equivalent primitive type. It makes it easy by providing three functions, all with the same name as the primitive type, which accept any type of data and convert that to the specified type.

Let's imagine we want to convert a string, `"54.56"` to a number:

```
var myString = "54.56";
var myNumber = Number(myString);
```

On the second line, we do the conversion explicitly from the string primitive to a number. Using the `String()`, `Number()`, and `Boolean()` methods to convert data is a bit like the constructor of the objects representing the data, but without the `new` keyword.

In the next three sections, we detail the rules that JavaScript uses when converting one type of data to another.

Conversion to Boolean

The conversion to Boolean is the easiest to grasp, as this table shows:

Original Type	Converted Boolean Value
Undefined	false
Null	false

Table continued on following page

Original Type	Converted Boolean Value
Number	`false` if -0, +0, or NaN, otherwise `true`
String	`false` if string length is zero, otherwise `true`
Object	`true`

Perhaps the most confusing is the conversion of a `Boolean` object as shown in the code below:

```
var myBoolean = new Boolean(false);
var myConvertedBoolean = Boolean(myBoolean)
document.write(myConvertedBoolean)
```

We would expect that `false` would be written out to the page as our original `Boolean` object was initialized to `false`. In fact, on the second line when we convert our `Boolean` object to a `Boolean` type, we actually get `true`. The reason being it is not the value the object contains that is converted, but simply the object. As we see in the table, an object data type is always converted to `true`.

Conversion to Number

Again, the conversion to `Number` is not too tricky, with two exceptions:

Original Type	Converted Number Value
Undefined	NaN
Null	+0
Boolean	1 if `true`, 0 if `false`
String	See below
Object	Returns the value of the object as a `Number` if `Boolean`, `Number`, or `String` object, otherwise returns NaN

Converting a `String` to a `Number` is tricky if we rely on the interpreter. We can do it ourselves with some object methods called `parseInt()` and `parseFloat()`, but we haven't covered objects yet, and in any case, the interpreter's own behavior needs to be stated.

To start with, either the `String` looks like a number or it doesn't. The latter case produces NaN, but the former case isn't simple. As the number type has a limit on the number of digits it can store, there is a special process the interpreter must go through to store the closest possible value to the number represented in the `String`. This is the business of rounding, and applies in the reverse situation as well – converting a `Number` to a `String`.

Conversion to String

As we've seen already, the major sticking point when converting to `Strings` is when the original type is `Number`:

Original Type	Converted String Value
Undefined	`"undefined"`
Null	`"null"`

Original Type	Converted String Value
Boolean	"true" if true
	"false" if false
Number	"NaN" if NaN
	"0" if +0 or -0
	"Infinity" if infinity, otherwise "xx" where xx is the number value. See above for discussion of rounding.
Object	Returns the value of the object as its built-in toString() method would, otherwise "undefined".

Operators and Mixed Data Types

Given the ability to convert between types at will, the following rules describe which conversions will occur when there is a mixture of types present. Step 1 is to identify what is a legal mixture and what isn't.

According to the ECMAScript standard, a mixture of types can only occur for binary operators. If a given binary operator only supports one type, then both pieces of data for that operator must either be of that type or be convertible to that type, otherwise an error results.

This takes care of most cases, such as multiplication, subtraction, and division. All those operators require two numeric (or numerically convertible) types.

Remove these cases and the **polymorphic** binary operators are left. Polymorphic means "many shapes" and polymorphic operators are those that work with more than one type of data. The assignment operators and the comma operator are examples, but they are straightforward. The assignment operators always change the contents of their left-hand data item to match their right-hand item, and the comma operator doesn't combine its two data types in any meaningful way at all.

The problematic operators are the relational operators (==, <, >, <=, =>) and the string concatenation operator (+), which is also used for addition. All these operators work with more than one type.

Some types (such as some objects) can be converted to either Numbers or Strings, the conversion rules for these hard cases come down to describing which way the two arguments will be converted in which circumstances. All else being equal, arguments that are Objects, have a preference as to which of String or Number they will convert to (usually Number, except for the Date type), and that preference can figure in the conversion decision as well.

The easiest case to understand is +, the addition/concatenation operator. The rule is:
For + operators, if either argument is a String then do String concatenation, not addition, otherwise do Number addition. A good rule of thumb is what would be the most sensible outcome where there are mixed data types. If a string is involved, it's most likely we are doing text-based operations, and so the interpreter converts all the values involved to strings. If no string is involved (only numbers), then it's sensible to assume that we're doing numerical operations. If it's hard to be sure what makes sense or otherwise, then use the three tables we saw earlier for definitions of conversion rules for Booleans, Strings, and Numbers. Let's take the example of adding two Booleans together:

```
var myBoolean = false;
var mySecondBoolean = true;
mySecondBoolean = mySecondBoolean + myBoolean;
document.write(mySecondBoolean);
```

The result that will be written out to the page is 1. When we look at the reasoning for this, let's consider the + operator, which indicates either concatenation or addition, depending on the situation. Neither is particularly logical here, but as no string data is involved, JavaScript assumes we mean numerical addition. We see that in the previous table, a Boolean converted to a number becomes 1 if true or 0 if false.

```
mySecondBoolean = mySecondBoolean + myBoolean;
```

This above line is treated by the JavaScript interpreter as:

```
mySecondBoolean = 1 + 0;
```

The mySecondBoolean variable will now hold a number data type, as we see if we add the following line to the code:

```
document.write(typeof(mySecondBoolean));
```

For the relational operators, the situation is similar, but the case for Strings is weaker.

For >, >=, <, <= operators, if neither argument can be converted to a Number, then perform string comparison, not numeric comparison. Otherwise, at least one argument can be converted to a Number, so do numeric comparison. If the non-numeric data converts to NaN, (not a value that can be converted to a valid number), then all comparisons will return false, except the != which will be true, as a number is not equal to NaN.

To apply this test to a specific example, ask yourself whether either argument could be a Number. If so, numeric comparison is in order. The interpreter does the same thing, but remembering what happens in these two cases can be tricky, because it can go either way (Number or String). A memory trick that can act as a rough guide, is to remember this:

String plus: either String, String compare: neither Number

As we can see, the rules regarding operators and conversion can get a little tricky. To make life easier for ourselves, it's best to convert any values where we feel there might be difficulties. We have already seen that methods such as String(), Number, and Boolean can be used to convert data, as shown below:

```
var myString = String("234");
var myNumber = Number("101");
var myBoolean = Boolean("true");
```

Summary

Datatypes, variables, and the basic language constructs that handle them lie at the core of JavaScript and are the details we use to screw everything else together. Support for basic mathematics and logic along with a systematic execution model are fundamental to JavaScript. Even within those simple features, there are a few incompatibilities and subtleties for which to watch out. We saw however, that JavaScript's core language goes further than this. Complex scripts using only the basic features of JavaScript are cumbersome and awash with trivial detail. It is when simple data items are conveniently aggregated together into objects, and simple series of statements are conveniently aggregated into functions, that the power of JavaScript comes into force.

Functions are a useful feature of JavaScript that allow us to reuse a piece of code without it having to appear more than once in our scripts. Objects allow the bundling of data and functions together into discrete lumps that are easy to manipulate and allow you to do cleaner and more organized design. The ease of use of JavaScript objects is one of the main appealing aspects of the language. Though object features are powerful, they often have a reputation for being too complex. No such reputation applies to ordinary JavaScript.

Objects in JavaScript go beyond mere utility; they are at the root of JavaScript's data manipulation model. It is important to develop an appreciation of how object-like most aspects of JavaScript are, because it helps when the problem gets tough. It leads to cleaner and more organized scripting, and that's how most features of the host that a JavaScript interpreter is embedded within make their appearance.

Having covered functions and objects, most of the features of the core JavaScript language have now been discussed. In the next chapter, we'll be taking a more detailed look at some of the more advanced aspects of objects in JavaScript.

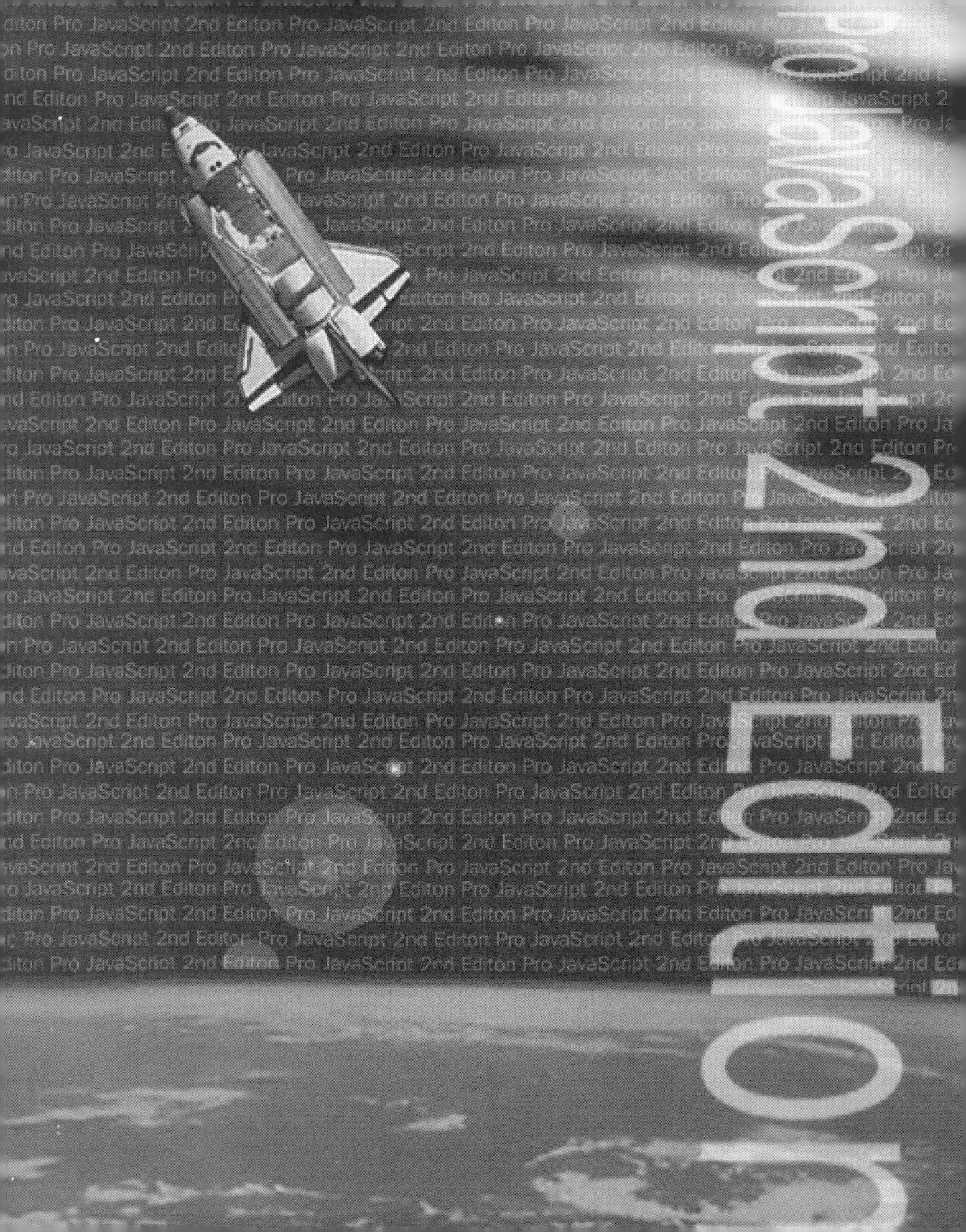
Pro JavaScript 2nd Edition
Pro JavaScript 2nd Editon

3

OO Techniques and JavaScript

Now that the basics of the language have been presented, it is time to dig into the creative side of JavaScript. If you are new to object-oriented (OO)programming languages, you can rest assured that you do not need to be a rocket scientist to use JavaScript. In fact, it is a great language to introduce OO programming, even though it isn't an OO language in a strict sense. If you come from a language such as C++ or Java, you will find JavaScript to be simplistic and flexible compared to what you are used to, but you can still apply most of what you already know. In this chapter, we'll look at:

❑ What objects are

❑ OOP techniques and JavaScript

❑ Object inheritance

❑ Adding protected data members to JavaScript

What are Objects?

Everything in JavaScript is an object or a primitive value that can be coerced into acting like an object (an example of primitive coercion is when we use `"STRING".toLowerCase()` to obtain `"string"`). Why did the creators of JavaScript make objects such an integral part of JavaScript? The quick answer is that manipulating objects in code is easier to understand, because it is closer to the way we see the world around us.

Look around the room you are in right now. You will most likely see at least a table, a chair, a light, and many other objects. You are definitely holding an object right now – this book. The human brain is geared to classify our surroundings into classifications. When we look at a kitchen chair and an office chair, we think of each as a chair, yet they have different shapes, different number of legs, one chair has wheels and armrests, and the other does not. We see the similarities and classify both types as a chair. We take our surroundings and develop associations of the objects we see around us. Objects bring this power to the world of programming.

We'll start with a short explanation of the theory behind object-orientated languages in general. Many of the terms used throughout this chapter will be defined within this section. If you are familiar with the theory, or if you wish to see how it applies to JavaScript, you can jump ahead to the section *OOP Techniques and JavaScript*.

Data Abstraction

One of the key concepts of OOP is data **abstraction**. Abstraction is the representation of a concept or information in a symbolic manner that can be manipulated. All programming languages use abstraction, but the difference is in what the language abstracts.

Assembly language abstracts the way a computer processor works. It is the programming language that is human readable for generating the computer binary instructions called machine language. This is a powerful abstraction in itself, as it allows the programmer to more readily understand and manipulate the fine details of every operation. The benefits of a low-level language like this are speed and control, but they also suffer from long development times and complexity.

High-level procedural programming languages, such as Basic and Pascal concentrate on the steps needed to solve a task. This style of programming vastly improved the development time over low-level programming languages. A disadvantage of procedural language, however, is that the program code describes the path to the solution, not the problem itself.

Along come OOP languages, which display the problem as objects with characteristics (called **properties**) and perform actions (called **methods**). These objects have interactions with other objects (such as an engine propelling a car) and associations with similar objects (a Mustang and a Celica are both cars). This type of abstraction allows the programmer to concentrate upon the problem, or subject, instead of concentrating upon the task.

Another benefit of using objects, is in the use of naming conventions. By giving the object a descriptive name, then the property names describe the object's characteristics and the methods describe its abilities. For example, if we have an object called `car` with a `color` property (`car.color`) and a `stop()` method (`car.stop()`), we can assume that the `color` property describes the color, and the `stop()` method makes the car stop.

Object Members

Objects are a unit of information together with the code for manipulating that information. Data is contained within properties. In JavaScript, this data can be any valid JavaScript value, including primitive values (strings and numbers) or an object reference. Code is contained within methods. Methods are functions which can use the `this` value in order to access other properties and methods of the object. An object's properties and methods are collectively referred to as the object's **data members**.

Interfaces

An **interface**, at its simplest level, is a mapping of member names (and any arguments that they may take) to their corresponding internal functions. It is a layer of code that separates an object from the rest of the computer environment, providing a means of I/O for communication. The major benefit behind using interfaces is **encapsulation**.

The many reasons for implementing interfaces for objects are beyond the scope of this book. For more information dealing with interfaces, any good OOP book should suffice.

> JavaScript does NOT implement user-defined interfaces. Care should be taken by the reader to understand that when the term interface is being used in relation to JavaScript user-defined objects, it is referring to a pre-determined set of properties and methods defined for that object class, not for interfaces as defined within this section.

Extensibility

Extensibility is the ability to expand upon or add to something. If you go to buy a car, you are not simply buying any car. The make, model, and color, are all properties of a car and these can be used to distinguish between different cars of the same type. However, cars come in a variety of types. The concept of a car (you get in, start it, and drive wherever you want to go) is expanded to include a specific type of car (a Ford Mustang that is souped up and goes very fast). The ability to expand the concept of a car to a specific type of car without re-creating the whole concept is called extensibility.

In order to implement extensibility in a flexible manner, we must be able to define and classify these concepts. A vehicle can be described as a mechanical means of transportation. An automobile is a vehicle that has four wheels, and is propelled by an engine. A Mustang is an automobile with a fast engine manufactured by Ford. Each of these concepts builds upon the concepts of the previous classification. In OO programming, this is called **inheritance**.

In order to use inheritance, we must have a way of defining the concepts that are to be inherited from. In the real world, the concepts are classifications; in OOP languages, we call them **classes** of objects. Every instance of an object has a class associated with it. This class describes what properties and methods the object has available to use and what, if any, class it inherits properties and methods from. There are two major advantages to extensibility: **code re-use** and **polymorphism**.

Class Hierarchy

There are a few terms that describe where in this inheritance chain a particular class belongs: **base** class, **derived** class, **child** class, **parent** class, **ancestor** class, and **descendant** class. What classes these refer to depend upon where in the inheritance chain, or inheritance hierarchy, the two classes being compared are.

In order to describe this hierarchy, let us assume that we have a chain of inheritance where class B inherits from class A, class C inherits from class B, and so on, to class F. The following can represent this:

A base class does not inherit from any other class. This is class A in the above diagram. A derived class is any class that inherits from another class. B, C, D, E, and F are derived classes.

> In JavaScript, all native objects inherit from the Object class. The Object class is the base class for all built-in object and user-defined objects, and conversely, all built-in and user defined objects are derived from the Object class.

The terms child class and parent class describe the relationship between two classes in which one class directly inherits from the other. In the diagram above, class D inherits from class C, so D is a child of class C, and C the parent of class D. Just because class D inherits from class C, this does not mean that another class cannot directly inherit from class C, but it does mean that class D *only* directly inherits from class C. This is called a one-to-many relationship.

The terms ancestor class and descendant class relate to inheritance anywhere along the inheritance chain. Class F in the diagram has five ancestor classes, classes E, D, C, B and A. Conversely, A has five descendant classes: B, C, D, E, and F. Therefore, an ancestor class is the parent class, the parent of a parent class, and so on until we return to the base class. Conversely, a descendant class is any class that is derived either directly or indirectly from another class.

Overriding Data Members

What happens when an ancestor class has a property or method with the same name as one of its ancestor classes? When we request that property or method, which one is used? The answer is the lowest descendant that declared that member is used. This process of a descendant class property superseding an ancestor class property is called **overriding**.

In a true OO language, not all properties and methods can be overridden. When a member is defined within the class, it must be explicitly set so that it can be overridden. In JavaScript, *any* property or method can be overridden.

Code Reuse

Code re-use is not copying and pasting code from a previous program into a current program, and then modifying the code to suit new needs. Code re-use in this case is including a script into your current program, and then extending its functionality without modifying the original file. Creating a new class and having that class inherit from the previous class accomplishes this. From our car example, the new class would be the Mustang class, and the previous class would be the automobile class.

There are two advantages of code re-use, which are a reduction in development time, and a reduction in bugs. Since we are using a lot of previously developed code, we are speeding up our development time. Less time writing new code means less development costs. In addition, since we are writing less code, by using old code that already work, we will be introducing fewer bugs.

Polymorphism

An advantage of using inheritance is that many classes of objects can inherit from the same class. This allows us to perform certain actions on all of the descendant classes of this class. Under some circumstances, we can treat all of the descendant classes as if they were of a common class. We can treat both a Mustang and a Celica as an automobile, since they both have wheels, can be steered, and can accelerate and decelerate. The ability to treat a class as if it were one of its ancestor classes is called **polymorphism**.

This is a very powerful tool. Let us assume that we have created the class `automobile` and have a library of routines for manipulating `automobile` objects, such as routines on how to drive, clean, and maintain automobiles. Polymorphism allows us to keep using these same routines on any class of object derived from `automobile`, without having to modify our code. As you can see, we have fallen back into the previous advantage, code reuse.

Encapsulation

An OOP language reduces the amount needed for the end user to be able to properly implement the object class to just its exposed properties and methods Since all of the data and code is contained *inside* of the object, it is said to encapsulate its data and implementation.

Data Encapsulation

There are three basic ways of exposing data and functions (object members) to JavaScript code. There are **public members**, **private members**, and **protected members**:

❑ Public members are the properties and methods of the object. These members are exposed to all code that has access to the object itself.

❑ Private members are variables and functions contained within the class's implementation code (code defined within the constructor function in JavaScript).

❑ Protected members are variables and functions that are accessible to all of the ancestor and descendant classes' implementation code, but not to other code.

JavaScript natively supports public members, and has its own version of private members, but does not support protected members. Later in this chapter, we will introduce a method to add support for protected members.

In this text, the term "object implementation code", when applied to JavaScript, is referring to constructor function code. Any code that is defined within the constructor, including function definitions, is considered part of the object's implementation code.

When we use private variables to hold all of the data for an object, and require all data access to be through the object's implementation code, we are encapsulating the data. This has two major benefits: **security** and **data integrity**. Data security simply means that the data is where we expect it to be. If the data was not encapsulated, it could be removed or deleted from the object by outside code, and the object's implementation code would not know where to find it. Data integrity, on the other hand, means making sure that the data is type checked and validated before storing. The chance of our code failing is reduced by making sure that the object's data is valid and always accessible through the correct channels, thus reducing bugs.

Implementation Hiding

Let us assume that we have created a class and have written the implementation code for it. We have distributed this code and a number of programs depend upon it. Time goes by, and we find that the code is unable to handle increased load demands or has a bug in it. It would be useful to be able to change our code without breaking the programs that depend upon it. In OO languages, we can readily do this.

The reason why it is easier to modify our code without worrying about breaking programs that depend upon it, is because the program is limited to the interface (properties and methods) that we expose for that object class. To the application, the object is a black box that we send information into and retrieve information from. How the object's code works is not important to the application, as long as it can find the properties and methods that it expects. In fact, the code is not even accessible to the program at all unless we make it so. This is called implementation hiding. Implementation hiding is not an integral part of JavaScript, since it does not implement formally defined interfaces, but the concepts of implementation hiding are just as valid as they are for other OO languages.

Why Are Objects so Important?

OO programming has the following major advantages over traditional programming languages:

❑ Reduced program development time and cost

❑ Ease of code reuse

❑ The code is easier to read, understand, maintain, and upgrade

JavaScript

Up until now, we have only been discussing the theory of OO languages, so now it is time to start applying this theory to JavaScript. In order to accomplish this, a few topics first need to be covered. These subjects include:

- ❑ JavaScript Objects
- ❑ Execution Contexts and Function Code
- ❑ Object Constructors
- ❑ Code Reuse

JavaScript Objects

JavaScript supports three types of objects: native, host, and user-defined. Native objects are objects supplied by the JavaScript language. Examples of these objects are `Object`, `Math`, `String`, and so on Host objects are supplied to JavaScript from the browser implementation, for interaction with the browser environment and the loaded document. Examples of these are `window`, `document`, `frames`, and so on User-defined objects are objects that you, the programmer, write implementation code for.

`Object`, with a capital "O", is a function that is used to create an object. Care should be taken when reading in that all object class names and constructor function names begin with a capital letter, and instances of an object all begin with a lower case letter. In most implementations host objects do not inherit from the `Object` class.

The Object Object

Object is the name of the base object class for all native objects, as well as the constructor function used to create an instance of the `Object` class. When we call the `Object` function as a constructor (`var x = new Object();`) without any arguments, it creates an object with the following properties:

- ❑ `constructor` – Contains a reference to constructor function used to create the object.
- ❑ `toString()` – A method that returns `"[object Class]"`, where the substring `Class` is replaced by the class name of the object (its constructor function's name).
- ❑ `toLocaleString()` – A method that acts similarly as `toString()` above.
- ❑ `valueOf()` – A method that returns the primitive value of the object. If the object does not have a primitive value associated with it then this method returns a reference to itself.
- ❑ `hasOwnProperty(propertyName)` – A method that returns `true` if the object has a property with the name `propertyName`, and `false` if it does not. Example: if an instance of an object named `myObject` has a property `myProperty`, then `myObject.hasOwnProperty("myProperty")` would return true.
- ❑ `isPrototypeOf(objectRef)` – If `objectRef` is an instance of this object, then this method returns `true`, else returns `false`.
- ❑ `propertyIsEnumerable(propertyName)` – If this object has a property with the name `propertyName`, and that property is able to be enumerated in a `for...in` loop, then this function returns `true`, else returns `false`.

There is another way of creating an object of the `Object` class. You can do so using an object constant. There is no difference between the two objects being created below in the example. They have the same properties, are of the same class (`Object`), and can be used for the same purpose:

```
var obj1 = new Object();
obj1.prop1 = "This is property 1";
obj1.prop2 = 2;

var obj2 = {prop1: "this is property 1", prop2:2};
```

The `Object` constructor is a special constructor that can create objects of another class, depending on what is passed into the constructor as its only argument. If the argument is a primitive value, then an object is created that corresponds to that primitive value. The string primitive value corresponds to the `String` class, the number primitive value corresponds to the `Number` class, and so on. Finally, if the argument passed in is already an object, then a reference to that object is returned unchanged.

The built-in JavaScript constructors can be called for type conversion. The same is true for the `Object` constructor. Calling `Object` as a function, will convert whatever is passed in into an object of the appropriate type (if it is not already an object), as described in the above paragraph, or creates a new object if no arguments are passed in.

Functions Are Objects Too

Functions are the basic unit of callable code in JavaScript. As such, they are considered a datatype and have a class associated with them, the `Function` class. They are objects and have properties and methods.

There are three ways of creating a `Function` object: with a named function, with an anonymous function, or using the `Function` constructor:

```
function functionName(arg1, arg2, arg3, ..., argN)
{
    //function body goes here
}
var functionName = function(arg1, arg2, arg3, ..., argN)
{
    //function body goes here
}
var functionName = new Function("arg1Name", "arg2Name", ..., "argNName",
    "function body as a string");
```

The first method shown above is the most commonly used and the easiest to recognize, read, and understand. The second method is commonly used for creating a method for an object. This can be hard to read at times and should be used with care. The last method of is the one that most readily demonstrates that a function is an object, since a constructor is explicitly being called to create one. This is the least commonly used method, but a good application for this is for adding code that cannot be compiled in older browsers when it is detected that the browser does support the syntax needed. For more information on functions and the `Function` constructor, see Chapter 2.

Execution Contexts, Function Code, and Scope

There are three types of executable code, and their related execution contexts: Global code, Eval code, and Function code. Global code is any code that is outside of a function. Eval code is code passed in as a string to the `eval()` function (such as `eval("alert('this is an Eval code generated alert')");`). Function code is code that is in the body of a function. The term execution context is just a formal name for the process of setting the variable scope and the `this` value to reflect our current position in code.

There is only one global execution context, but whenever a function is called or the eval() function is called, a new function or eval execution context is created. Understanding how the execution context is created when calling a function, specifically when calling a function with the new keyword, is important for object creation.

Entering a Function Execution Context

Every function call enters a new execution context, which ends when the function returns or is terminated by an exception (error). The execution context can be thought of as resolving the scope chain and setting two objects to contain values depending upon where in the code we are: the variable's object, and the this value.

Every execution context has a variable object associated with it. We cannot access this object; you can only access the variables that it contains as its properties. When we enter a function execution context, the variable object is initialized to contain only the formally declared arguments of the function, and is destroyed when the function finishes executing. Variables are added to the variable object, while the function code is executed by using the var keyword. These are the private variables for the function, and are accessible to the code within the function block. Variables lifetimes may be extended by the use of nested functions as described later in the next section.

The scope chain can be thought of as an object that contains references to all of the variables and objects that the currently executing code can directly see and manipulate. When first entering the function, the scope contains all of the defined function arguments, the arguments array, the global variables and, if the function is nested within other functions, each of the parent functions variables. When the function code is being executed, any variable declared, is added to the scope. You can think of a function as a block of code that can see any variable declared within its block of code and any variable declared in any block of code that contains the function's declaration.

The this value (or object) corresponds to the object that the currently executing code is attached too. The this value is set to the value of the global object (in browsers the global object is the window object) except under the following conditions. If the function is a method of an object, the this value is set to the object. If the function is called using the call() or apply() methods of a function object, then the this value is determined by the first argument passed into these methods.

Finally, if the function is called using the new keyword, then the this value is a newly created object that inherits all of the properties of this functions prototype property. No matter where we are in the code, there is a specific this value associated with it.

Below is an example that shows the this value and variable scope in practice within JavaScript:

```
// Extract from ExecutionContextTest.htm
var testString = "this string is defined in the global code";
var string1 = "a global string";

document.write( "<P>Testing Global Execution context<BR>");
document.write( "- The this value is " );
if( this != window ) document.write( "NOT " );
document.write( "the window object in global code <\/P>" );

function testScope(){
   document.write( "<P>Testing Function Execution context<BR>");

   var string1 = "a private string";

   document.write( "- the this value is " );
   if( this != window ) document.write( "NOT " );
```

```
      document.write( "the window object in function code <br>" );

      document.write( "- the global testString variable is " );
      if( !testString ) document.write( "NOT " );
      document.write( "within the scope of the function<br>");

      document.write( "- the string1 variable is " );
      if( string1 != "a private string" ) document.write( "NOT " );
      document.write( "a private variable of the function<\/P>");
}
testScope();


function testMethod(){
      document.write( "<P>Testing Function Execution context within a an object's
method<BR>");

      var string1 = "a private string";

      document.write( "- the this value is " );
      if( this != obj ) document.write( "NOT " );
      document.write( " the obj object within obj's method code <br>" );

      document.write( "- the global testString variable is " );
      if( !testString ) document.write( "NOT " );
      document.write( "within the scope of the method<br>");

      document.write( "- the string1 variable is " );
      if( string1 != "a private string" ) document.write( "NOT ");
      document.write( "a private variable of the method<\/P>");
}
var obj = new Object();
obj.method = testMethod;
obj.method();
```

The output for the above code is as follows:

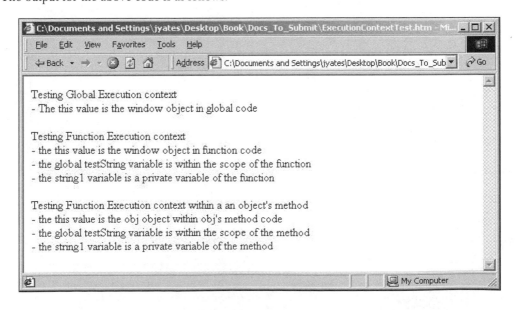

This example tests the value of the `this` value within three execution contexts by comparing it to the expected value of `this` following the steps outlined above. Within the global code and function code, it should be (and is) the window object, and from within an object's method code, it should be the object the method is attached too (and is). This example also illustrates that each of the three contexts have the `testString` global variable within their scope, but not the `string1` global variable. The reason why the function and the method do not have the `string1` variable within their scope is that they both declare a local variable with that name that supersedes it. For more information on variable scope, see Chapter 2.

The Power of Nested Functions

There are times when we will want to extend the lifetime of a function's private variables beyond the time when the function code terminates. Maybe the function calculates a value that is to be used later, but you want to restrict access to the value so that only private code will be able to access it. At this time, the reason is not important, but later on in this chapter, its importance will be made clear.

There are two methods of extending the lifetime of a function's variable. You can make it a property of a global object (such as window or the function itself), or you can use nested functions. Functions are objects of the `Function` class. They can be defined anywhere in code, and where they are defined determines their scope. If we define a function from *within* a function, the newly created function has access to the parent functions private variables.

Say we have two functions, one that performs a calculation on the arguments passed into it, and the other that recalls the results of the last calculation. This can be accomplished using nested functions with the benefit that there is no code that can modify the stored calculation, other than the two functions that we are creating. For example:

```
// Extract from NestedFunctions.htm
var doCalc, recallCalc;
function initCalculations(){
   var lastCalc;
   doCalc = function (x, y){
      lastCalc = x + y;
      return lastCalc;
   }
   recallCalc = function (){
      return lastCalc;
   }
}
initCalculations();

document.write( "<P>The sum of 3 + 7 is " + doCalc(3,7) + "</P>" );
document.write( "<P>The sum of 5 + 19 is " + doCalc(5,19) + "</P>" );
document.write( "<P>The last calculation had a result of " + recallCalc()
   + "</P>");
```

The output for this is as follows:

The sum of 3 + 7 is 10
The sum of 5 + 19 is 24
The last calculation had a result of 24

When the `initCalculations()` function is called, a local variable called `lastCalc` is created, and two functions are created and assigned to two global variables (`doCalc` and `recallCalc`). These two functions reference the `lastCalc` variable, thus keeping it from being destroyed when the `initCalculations()` function terminates. This can be seen when we call the `recallCalc()` function after calling the `doCalc()` function, which returns the value that `doCalc()` stored within it when last executed.

Notice that the only reason why the initCalculations() private variables are not destroyed is *only* because other code that they are within the scope of has not been terminated. Until the doCalc() and recallCalc() functions are destroyed (by deleting them or overwriting them), then the private variables will not be destroyed.

Object Constructors

Objects are constructed in code by calling a constructor function to create and initialize them. There are two types of constructor code: built-in constructors (those supplied by the implementation of JavaScript), and user-defined constructors.

Built-In Constructors

JavaScript comes with a several built in constructors. ECMAScript v3 defines a number of them, and individual implementations may define some additional ones. The objects that built-in constructors as defined by ECMAScript are Object, Function, Array, String, Boolean, Number, Date, RegExp, Error (with sub-classes of EvalError, RangeError, ReferenceError, SyntaxError, and TypeError). For more information on how to use these constructors, refer to Chapter 2.

User-Defined Constructors

Just like native JavaScript objects, user-defined objects have constructor functions. The difference is that you, the author, write the constructor. The constructor can be very simple or complex depending upon your needs. The constructor will both define a class of object and initialize it. The next section will introduce the mechanics of writing your own object constructors, and the different techniques available.

Code Reuse

In JavaScript, there are two methods of code reuse (with shades of gray in between). Of the two, the copy-and-paste method is most widely used (or abused). The other method is that each object implementation is stored in its own file to be included in a web page with an external <SCRIPT> tag. Each method has its strengths and weaknesses.

The copy-and-paste method is very simple. We can add new code or modify the existing code to suit. The main advantage is that the web page loads faster since it does not have to retrieve any external files. If our web page has many external files, whether script, style, or image, then the time that the page takes to load (upon a first visit) can be greatly extended. When an external script file is parsed in an HTML page, some parsers wait until the script file is loaded, parsed, and executed before rendering the rest of the page, inducing a significant delay to its loading time.

On the flip side, the upkeep of a site will be more difficult. Suppose we have an OO navigation menu system script on our site. In order to add a menu item to the site menu, we will then have to edit every page on the site to include this menu item. You may be thinking about storing the whole menu in one file that all of the pages access. This is the middle ground between the two methods. We are still cutting and pasting into one file, but sharing the file between different pages, which is a good compromise. We get pages that load relatively fast and decrease the upkeep requirements to help keep our site current.

What happens though if we add a sub-web to our site that uses the same menu code, but has different menu entries? The answer to this is to split the code into two files. The first file contains the code for generating the menu, and the second file holds the information for making the entries to the first file. The site is still easy to update and the cost is minor; our page takes just a little longer to load.

Now we decide that we want to change the way the second menu looks, or how it functions. Should we go back to storing it all in one file? No, instead we create a new menu object that inherits from the first menu object. This new menu object only modifies the original menu as needed for the desired effect. Now we have three files that we are loading.

If we follow this to its extreme, we have the second method of code reuse, one file for every constructor. The cost is that our page loads slower, and the benefit is that we do not have the same code floating around in different files. So, which method should be used?

Firstly, if you combine all of the constructors that are most commonly used throughout our site into one file, commonly called a script library, then one slightly larger file takes less time to load than a few smaller files. In addition, once the script is downloaded, it is stored in the browser's cache and can be quickly retrieved the next time it is needed. You will need to use some judgment. If the script is only used on one page, keep it inside the page, not as an external file. If multiple pages use the script, store it within an external file. If most of your pages use it, then store it in a library script file, with all of the other scripts that your site depends on. Only you can decide which is best for your needs.

OOP Techniques and JavaScript

In this section, we will be covering the basics of OO programming techniques as they apply to JavaScript, specifically constructors, classes, and inheritance.

Object Constructors, Classes and Instances

We'll start by clarifying the terms instance, class, and constructor. Let's look at an example. You want to buy a car, so you go to a car dealer and pick out a model that you want, and the dealer orders it from the factory. When the car arrives, the dealer calls you to collect it. In this example, the make and model of car is the **class,** the factory that makes it is the **constructor**, and the specific car that you drive away in is the **instance**.

Every object that we use in JavaScript is a class instance. They can be manipulated, modified, and used to perform their designed task. Whenever we create an object, we are creating an object that is an instance of a class. Object classes in JavaScript are defined as the constructor function used to create the instance of that object, and can be referenced via its constructor property.

Simple Object Creation

Now that we know the difference between objects, classes, and constructors, it is time to create our own instance of a class. We can do this by writing a function to initialize the properties of the objects that will be created by this class. The simplest constructor possible is shown below. The constructor does nothing at all; it does not initialize any property values. The objects created by this constructor will only have the properties and methods of the Object class, since all objects in JavaScript inherit from this. The only use for a constructor like this is to define it as a class of object for type checking using the instanceof operator:

```
function MyClass()
{
}
```

In order to create an instance of MyClass, we would use code similar to:

```
var myObject = new MyClass();
```

When we execute this code, a number of steps will be taken by the JavaScript engine. When the `MyClass()` function is called with the `new` keyword, a new object is created as if we called the native `Object` constructor using the `new` keyword, and assigned it to the `this` value. Its constructor property is set to `MyClass` and the newly created object is linked to the `MyClass.prototype` properties (see Chapter 2 for a description of the `prototype` property, and *Execution Contexts, Function Code, and Scope* in this chapter for the `this` value). Then the code within the `MyClass()` function is executed, which in this case is none. When the function code completes, the newly created object is returned and assigned to the `myObject` variable.

Let's create a more useful object that shows how the constructor can be used to initialize the object's values:

```
function Car(){
    this.speed = 0;
    this.accelerate = Car_Accelerate;
    this.decelerate = Car_Decelerate;
    this.getSpeed = Car_GetSpeed;
    this.purchased = false;
}
function Car_Accelerate ( ){
    this.speed++;
}
function Car_Decelerate ( ){
    this.speed--;
}
function Car_GetSpeed ( ){
    return this.speed;
}

var myCar = new Car();
```

The example above shows one of the many ways that you can design a constructor function for your class. This constructor creates a `Car` class of object that contains two properties and three methods. The properties are `speed` (how fast the car is traveling), and `purchased` (Boolean value indicating whether the car has been bought). The three methods are `accelerate()` (increase the speed property), `decelerate()` (decrease the speed property), and `getSpeed()` (returns the speed the car is traveling). All of these properties and methods are attached to the newly created object via the use of the `this` value from within the constructor.

One problem with this code is that the three functions that are to be assigned to the property methods are within the global scope. If someone writes a function with the same name somewhere else in code, it is possible that the constructor will use the wrong function(s) for its object's methods. In order to prevent this, we will move the functions out of the global scope as follows:

```
function Car()
{
    this.speed = 0;
    this.accelerate = Accelerate;
    this.decelerate = Decelerate;
    this.getSpeed = function(){ return this.speed };
    this.purchased = false;
    return;

    function Accelerate(){
        this.speed++;
    }
```

```
      function Decelerate(){
          this.speed--;
      }
  }

  var myCar = new Car();
```

This updated example shows how the same constructor can be written using private functions and anonymous functions. The private functions are the `Accelerate()` and `Decelerate()` functions that are located within the constructor. These functions are not within the global scope, so are safe from other functions or variables overwriting them. The anonymous function is the one assigned to the `getSpeed()` method of the newly created object. This is accomplished as shown by declaring a function without a function name. The same effect could have been accomplished using the `Function` constructor.

Those familiar with JavaScript may wonder why the functions used as methods were defined within the constructor. The first reason is that code outside of the constructor cannot access the function directly. Since the functions are designed to be methods, if they are called directly as functions instead of methods of an object, the `this` value will be an incorrect value. Another reason is that when reading the code, it is easier to visually associate the function with the constructor, which can help prevent coding errors. A third reason is that the function names are not placed in the global scope, thus more than one function can have the same name, so long as they are defined within different scopes.

An interesting side effect of the way JavaScript compiles its code is that you can declare a function within another function and use that function before its declaration. Notice how the `Accelerate()` function is assigned to the `accelerate` property before it is defined. In fact, in the above example the constructor's code *always* terminates before the nested functions are defined, due to the unconditional `return` statement. The code works because when the outer function is compiled the nested functions are compiled as well, thus the `Accelerate()` and `Decelerate()` functions are created within the constructors scope. This has the added benefit of separating the initialization code, the code before the `return` statement, from the implementation code, that after the return statement.

These two methods of object construction work, and meet our needs, can be slow and use up a lot of memory. There is a faster and a less memory intensive way of creating objects. Every function has a property called the `prototype` property, where if you add a property or method to it, then any object created by that function (when called as a constructor) will have access to these same properties and methods. Thus, every object will "get" the property and method if you attach them to it. An example of this is as follows (see *Extending a Class via the Prototype Object* later in this chapter for more information on the prototype property):

```
// Extract from SimpleObjectExample.htm
function Car() { };
Car.prototype.speed = 0;
Car.prototype.purchased = false;
Car.prototype.accelerate = function(){
    this.speed++;
}
Car.prototype.decelerate = function(){
    this.speed--;
}
Car.prototype.getSpeed = function(){
    return this.speed;
}

var myCar = new Car();
```

We have now seen three means of writing a constructor for creating the same type of object. It will receive the same properties and methods, and have the same functionality. The objects created by these three different constructors are almost indistinguishable for all practical purposes. Each of the three methods shown have their uses, which will become more apparent later on in this chapter, and you can also combine the different ways depending upon your needs.

The following example assumes that one of the above three versions of the `Car()` constructor has been defined, and shows how the objects created can be used:

```
var myCar = new Car();
var yourCar = new Car();

document.write( "<p>Two cars have been created, myCar and yourCar<\/p>");

myCar.speed = 25;
yourCar.speed = 35;

document.write( "<p>The initial speeds of the cars have been set" +
                " and are displayed below: <br>");
document.write("    myCar.getSpeed() = " +
                myCar.getSpeed() + "<BR>");
document.write("    yourCar.getSpeed() = " +
                yourCar.getSpeed()+ "<\/p>");

myCar.accelerate();
myCar.accelerate();
myCar.accelerate();

document.write("<p>myCar is accelerating and the cars are now going:<br>");
document.write("    myCar.getSpeed() = " +
                myCar.getSpeed() + "<BR>");
document.write("    yourCar.getSpeed() = " +
                yourCar.getSpeed()+ "<\/p>");

yourCar.decelerate();
yourCar.decelerate();
yourCar.decelerate();

document.write("<p>yourCar is decelerating and the cars are" +
                " now going:<br>");
document.write("    myCar.getSpeed() = " +
                myCar.getSpeed() + "<BR>");
document.write("    yourCar.getSpeed() = " +
                yourCar.getSpeed()+ "<\/p>");
```

When the code is run, you will get the following output:

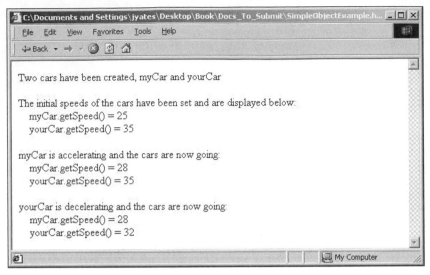

This code creates two objects of the Car class, myCar and yourCar. myCar is initialized with a speed of 25, and yourCar with a speed of 35. After displaying the speeds of the cars, myCar is then accelerated three times, and the speeds are displayed again. yourCar is decelerated three times and the speeds again displayed. This example shows that the instances of the Car class are independent of each other. When one car accelerates or decelerates, the other instances are not affected.

Note that all the properties and methods used so far are public members. There is no way to enforce the design on their actual use in other code. If the programmer wishes to, they could change the speed property to fast, although this means that afterwards, the accelerate() and decelerate() methods would not work properly.

Creating Objects That Implement Private Members

So far, the objects that we have created implement all data storage within public members (the properties of the object), which is how most JavaScript programmers store data. It is easy to get to and to modify. It also requires them to have intimate knowledge of how the object works, how it performs its calculations, and the types of data that it understands to be stored within its properties. This is perfectly acceptable if we are writing constructors for our own immediate use. However, the situation changes if the code is to be used by others (say, as part of a site library of objects), or if we expect there to be large gaps in times between our using the object and when we wrote the code for it, thus loosing the "feel" of the object.

The solution for this is to implement private members for data storage. The advantage here is the ability to protect your data from malicious code by preventing casual modification of the data by limiting its modification to public methods. These public methods can perform data typing and other validation upon the value before storing it within your data structure. This same method can throw an error if it is passed invalid data, thus aiding in the programmer in troubleshooting their code.

JavaScript does not have formal private members for objects, but it does have something that works just as well for our uses, private variables, and private functions. Remember that a function's private variables are not destroyed after the function terminates execution, as long as a nested function from within it still exists (say, as a method of an object). This enables us to be able to use the private variables to hold data that is accessible via the use of nested functions attached to the object as methods. It must be noted here that this precludes the programmer from attaching any of the methods that access the "private members" to the constructor's prototype property, but must instead attach the method from within the constructor's code.

The following constructor shows the how to implement private members (both a function and variable) with the use of public members attached within the constructor:

```
function MyClass()
{
    var privVar = "a private member";

    //the following methods are public members
    //that use private members
    this.setValue = function( value ){ return SetValue(value) };
    this.getValue = function (){ return privVar; }
    return;

    function SetValue(aNewValue)   //a private member
    {
        if (Object(aNewValue) instanceof String)
        {
            privVar = aNewValue;
        }
        return privVar;
    }
}

var myObject = new MyClass();
```

Here there are two public methods, setValue() and getValue(), which set and retrieve the value of the private variable privVar. getValue() directly accesses privVar and returns its value, while setValue() calls the private function SetValue() to perform data validation before the new value is placed in the privVar variable.

Each object created has its own copy of each private variable. This allows an object's methods to share information, but prevent access to these variables to code outside of the object's implementation code. Here, the value being set is limited to string values (either primitive or object) only. If nested functions were not used, then the value would have to be a property of the object and any code with access to the object could modify the property, thus bypassing this type checking. This is an example of implementing data encapsulation.

> **Make sure to document any methods that are dependent upon each other to prevent yourself or another author from overriding the methods; thus breaking the logic of your code. In the previous example, if the setValue() method is overridden, you have no means of modifying the privVar variable; thus breaking the logic of the getValue() method.**

Let's implement the Car class of objects using a private member for the speed of the car and rerun the acceleration and deceleration tests as we did before:

```
// Extract from, PrivateMemberExample.htm
function Car(initialSpeed){
    var speed = 0;
    if( !isNaN(Number(initialSpeed)) )
        speed = Number(initialSpeed);

    this.accelerate = function( ){ speed++; }
    this.decelerate = function( ){ speed--; }
    this.getSpeed = function( ){ return speed; }
}
```

```
Car.prototype.purchased = false;

var myCar = new Car(25);
var yourCar = new Car(35);

document.write( "<P>Two cars have been created, myCar and yourCar</P>");
document.write( "<P>The initial speeds of the cars have been set " +
                "and are displayed below: <BR>");
document.write("    myCar.getSpeed() = " +
                myCar.getSpeed() + "<BR>");
document.write("    yourCar.getSpeed() = " +
                yourCar.getSpeed()+ "</P>");

myCar.accelerate();
myCar.accelerate();
myCar.accelerate();

document.write("<P>myCar is accelerating and the cars are now going:<BR>");
document.write("    myCar.getSpeed() = " +
                myCar.getSpeed() + "<BR>");
document.write("    yourCar.getSpeed() = " +
                yourCar.getSpeed()+ "</P>");

yourCar.decelerate();
yourCar.decelerate();
yourCar.decelerate();

document.write("<P>yourCar is decelerating and the cars are " +
                "now going:<BR>");
document.write("    myCar.getSpeed() = " +
                myCar.getSpeed() + "<BR>");
document.write("    yourCar.getSpeed() = " +
                yourCar.getSpeed()+ "</P>");
```

The only major difference for using the Car constructor is that you are to now pass in the initial speed of the car for when you create it. The external code now does not have access to the speed data, thus it must be set from within the constructor. The only other way that you could explicitly set the speed would be to create a new method for doing so (since the accelerate and decelerate only modify the current value, not to set it to a specific value). After creating the two objects, and setting their initial speed during creation, we then run the same test on the objects. When you run this code, you will find that you will get the exact same output as you did in the previous example, because the same logic is being used, just two different means of implementing it.

JavaScript is designed to be a co-operative programming environment. This means that the author of a script is expected to understand the restrictions imposed by code upon arguments to functions and methods, as well as those for properties of the objects. *The language does not impose these requirements.* The method for data encapsulation presented here requires the programmer to send all values to a method of the object and to use (possibly) another method to retrieve it. This method is available for critical operations but, overall, we should just document a property's requirements and depend upon the programmer to only set the property's value to one that is valid.

Making Sure Constructors Always Create Objects

Nothing. A constructor *is* a function. A constructor can be called as a function by *not* using the new keyword. This is a bug that can, at times, be hard to find. In order to prevent this, we need a method of guaranteeing that a constructor always creates a new object. We can accomplish this by adding one line of code that detects if the this value within the constructor is an instance of the constructor's class using the instanceof operator. If it is not an instance of the constructor's class, then the constructor needs to be called using the new keyword, and the newly created object is returned:

```
function MyClass(arg1, arg2, arg3)
{
    if (! (this instanceof MyClass)) return new MyClass(arg1, arg2, arg3);
    //constructor code goes here
}

var myObject = MyClass();
```

The above code is not cross-browser compatible. Only use the `instanceof` operator when you are sure that the end user is running JavaScript version 1.4+ or JScript 5.5+ (Netscape 6+ or IE 5.5+). There are programming techniques that can be used for testing the browser to see what version it is, and running different code as necessary. The following example shows how the above code can be made backward compatible, but with a loss in functionality. This code assumes that a global variable called ECMA3 has been defined to true if the browser is IE5.5+ or Netscape 6+, false otherwise:

```
function MyClass(arg1, arg2, arg3)
{
    if (ECMA3 && !eval("this instanceof MyClass"))
        return new MyClass(arg1, arg2, arg3);
    //constructor code goes here
}

var myObject = MyClass();
```

This will run in older browsers as well as the newer browsers, but the `eval()` function is very slow to use since the string supplied must be compiled. The `eval()` function is necessary in this instance though, because without it, the whole script will not run due to a compiler error, because the older browser will not recognize the `instanceof` operator.

This covers the basics for creating user-defined objects. Next, we get into more complex object creation.

Object Inheritance

Recall that an object inherits all of the properties and methods of the `Object` class. The mechanism of this inheritance is the object's internal (not accessible) `prototype` property, which is set by its constructor's `prototype` property (which is accessible). The internal `prototype` property is an object, it also has an internal `prototype` property, whose members are inherited. This regression of prototypes continues until we get to the prototype of the `Object` class, the base class for all user-defined objects. The series of prototypes that an object inherits from is called the **prototype chain**.

You may have received the impression that when an object inherits a property it receives a copy of that property or in some way a separate value all of its own. This is not the case. The inherited property is just added to the lookup path (the prototype chain) for when the code requests the value of a property.

Extending a Class via the Prototype Object

When the value of a property is requested, the code first looks to the object to see if it has a property of that name that has been explicitly set (not inherited). If it does not, it then follows the prototype chain until it finds a property with that name and returns that value. If it does not find a property with the specified name, then the value returned for that property is undefined. Due to this mechanism, we can add a property to a constructor's prototype object and *all* objects derived from that constructor's prototype immediately inherit the added property, as long as a descendant class does not contain a property of that name.

Extending an object via its constructor's prototype can be very powerful. The following example shows how an object automatically acquires a property using this technique:

```
// Extract from ExtendingClassViaPrototypeExample.htm
function myObject()
{
    //this is just a bare constructor for this example
}
var obj1 = new myObject();
var obj2 = new myObject();

document.write("<P>Two instances of myObject have been "
   + "created, obj1 and obj2</P>");

// Test the adding of a property to an instance of the class

obj1.newProp = "This property is added to an instance of myObject class";

document.write("<P>obj1 has a property added to it called newProp<BR>");
document.write("The values for the newProp for each object is now:<BR>");
document.write("   obj1.newProp = "
                + obj1.newProp + "<BR>");
document.write("   obj2.newProp = "
                + obj2.newProp + "</P>");

//Test the adding of a property to the class prototype

myObject.prototype.newProp =
   "This property is an extension of the myObject class";

document.write("<P>The myObject constructor's prototype now has "
                + "a newProp property added to it<br>");
document.write("The values for the newProp for each object is now:<BR>");
document.write("   obj1.newProp = "
                + obj1.newProp + "<BR>");
document.write("   obj2.newProp = "
                + obj2.newProp + "</P>");
```

This example creates two instances of an object and adds a property to one of them. After displaying the value of that property for both instances, the code then adds a property to the class prototype with the same name, and displays the value of the property for both objects. The output of this code follows:

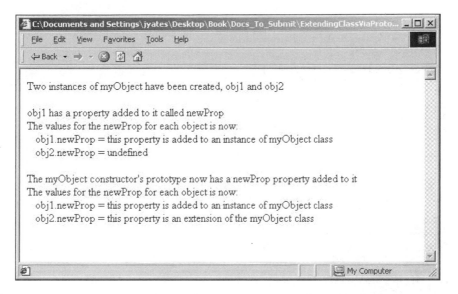

This illustrates two aspects of extending a class via its prototype object. Firstly, the property is immediately added to the prototype chain for all instances of the class. Secondly, if the property is overridden for a particular instance, then the overridden value is returned, not the value just added.

This technique is very useful for correcting a browser's implementation of a method. For example, Netscape's JavaScript 1.2 implementation of the Array.push() method is incorrectly per the ECMA standard. Chapter 19, *Extending JavaScript Objects*, shows numerous examples of extending classes via their prototype property. The next section shows how to add the call() and apply() methods to the Function object for older browsers, since they are used extensively in this chapter.

Upgrading Native Objects for Older Browsers

JavaScript 1.3 (Netscape Navigator 4.06+) introduced two very useful methods to the Function object, which are used frequently in this chapter: the call() and apply() methods, which are both used to call the function.

These two methods were including in the ECMAScript v3 standard, and Microsoft included them in Internet Explorer 5.5 (Jscript 5.5). They are very important to the implementation of inheritance as presented in this chapter. A means of providing these methods to older versions of JavaScript is presented below through the example of extending a class of objects via properties of the prototype of the Function constructor:

```
//Patch the apply method of the Function class of objects if needed
function _Apply_( thisObj, argArray )
{
   var str, i, len, retValue;
   if (thisObj + "" == "null" || thisObj + "" == "undefined")
      thisObj = window;
   if (argArray + "" == "null" || argArray + "" == "undefined")
      argArray = new Array();
   //make sure that the property getting the method is unique
   var index = 0;
   while( thisObj["temp" + index] + "" != "undefined" ) index++;

   thisObj["temp" + index] = this;
```

89

```
      str = "thisObj.temp" + index + "(";
      len = argArray.length;
      for(i=0; i<len; i++ )
      {
         str += "argArray[" + i + "]";
         if (i + 1 < len) str += ", ";
      }
      str += ");";
      retValue = eval(str);
      thisObj["temp" + index] = undefined;

      return retValue;
   }
   if (!Function.prototype.apply) Function.prototype.apply = _Apply_;

   //Patch the call method of the Function class of objects if needed
   function _Call_( thisObj, arg1, arg2, argN )
   {
      return this.apply(thisObj, Array.apply(null, arguments).slice(1));
   }
   if (!Function.prototype.call) Function.prototype.call = _Call_;

   //patch the undefined value for compatablility for older browsers
   var undefined;
```

The apply() method takes two arguments: an object reference to be used as the this value for the function call (thisObj) and an array containing the values to be passed to the function as its arguments (argArray). It creates a function call on the fly, as if the function were a method of the thisObj object. If the thisObj argument is null or undefined, then the this value for the function call is the global object (in browsers, the the window object). If the argArray argument is not provided (is null or undefined), then no arguments are passed to the function.

Creating the function (more specifically a method) call on the fly takes two steps. The first step is to find a property that is not being used. The following line of code accomplishes this:

```
      while( thisObj["temp" + index] + "" != "undefined" ) index++;
```

Notice how the return value of the property is converted to a string by adding a null string to it. This is so that it can be tested against "undefined", the string value of what is returned by a property request for a property that has not yet been defined. If the property is not undefined, then index is incremented, and the test is performed again. This is repeated until an unused property is found, at which point the this value (a Function object) is assigned to that property; making it a method of the object.

The next step is to construct the method call, using the eval() function, because we do not know how many arguments to pass into the method in advance. The following lines of code accomplish this:

```
      str = "thisObj.temp" + index + "(";
      len = argArray.length;
      for( i=0; i<len; i++ )
      {
         str += "argArray[" + i + "]";
         if (i + 1 < len) str += ", ";
      }
      str += ");";
      retValue = eval( str );
```

If `argArray` had three elements, and the `index` variable contains 3, then the `str` variable being constructed would contain the following code:

```
"thisObj.temp3(argArray[0], argArray[1], argArray[2]);"
```

This is the code string to be evaluated by the `eval()` function, which is the method call generated on the fly. The last step, before terminating the method, is to reset the value of the property back to `undefined`. Since some browsers do not define a global variable or property of `undefined`, we define it explicitly. using `var undefined`.

The `call()` method is very similar to `apply()`, so in the above code, `call()` uses `apply()` for its implementation. This method takes one or more arguments: the first argument is an object reference to be used as the `this` value for the function call, while the rest of the arguments are passed to the function as arguments for the function call.

Note how the arguments are passed to `apply()` from within this method. All of the arguments passed into `call()` are to be passed as the second argument to the apply method with the exception of the first argument, `thisObj`. A copy of the arguments array needs to be created, minus the first argument. The easiest way of doing this is to use the `Array.slice()` method, but this cannot be done directly, since the arguments array is not a native `Array` class of object. To get around this, we call the `Array`, using the already defined `apply()` method, to create an array that contains all of the elements within the arguments array, and then perform the `slice()` method.

Below are the two lines of code that attach the methods to the `Function` object:

```
if (!Function.prototype.apply)
   Function.prototype.apply = _Apply_;
...
if (!Function.prototype.call)
   Function.prototype.call = _Call_;
```

They first test to see if the `Function` object already has the method. If it does not, then the method is attached. The code above will work properly in version 4 and greater browsers (IE4+ and NN4+) and we recommend their inclusion in all OO scripts presented in this chapter.

Inheriting from an Instance

The simplest method of implementing class inheritance in JavaScript is to set the derived class constructor's prototype property to an instance of the parent class. The prototype will then contain all of the properties and methods of the parent class, because it is an instance of that parent class. The benefit of using this method is that the `instanceof` operator will return `true` for both the object class and all of its ancestor classes.

The following code shows inheriting via instance in a three-class inheritance chain. The `Mustang` class inherits from the `Ford` class, which inherits from the `Car` class. Each of these three constructors implements only public members in this example:

```
// Extract from InheritFromInstancePublicMembers.htm
function Car(initSpeed) {
   this.speed = 0;
   this.accelerate = Accelerate;
   this.decelerate = Decelerate;
   this.getSpeed = function(){ return this.speed };
   this.purchased = false;
```

```
      return;

      function Accelerate ( ){
         this.speed++;
      }
      function Decelerate ( ) {
         this.speed--;
      }
}

function Ford(initSpeed){
   this.make = "Ford";
}
Ford.prototype = new Car();

function Mustang(initSpeed){
   this.year = 2001;
   this.doors = 2;
}

Mustang.prototype = new Ford();

var myCar = new Mustang( );
var yourCar = new Mustang( );
var ourCar = new Car( );
```

Note that the `Car` constructor presented here is the same that was introduced earlier in this chapter. This constructor, and the other two presented here, will be used throughout the rest of the chapter to show the different inheritance techniques with modifications in order to properly discuss each of the techniques. Similarly, the test code below will also be used throughout the chapter. The only part of this code that will be modified from example to example will be the portion of the code that displays the expected values returned by the `getSpeed()` method of the objects, and thus will not be repeated throughout this chapter:

```
// Further extract from InheritFromInstancePublicMembers.htm
//Note: ECMA3 is true if the browser is IE5.5+ or Netscape 6+

document.write("<p>Creating three objects, myCar, yourCar "
   + "and ourCar.<br>");
document.write("myCar and yourCar are Mustang class objects, and ourCar "
   + "is a Car class object<br>");
document.write("All cars have been initialized with a speed of 0.<\/p>");

//start of test
document.write("<P>---- start of test ----</P>");

//display info about the objects created
document.write("<P>Testing objects using instanceof operator to test "
   + "for class and class inheritance.</P>");
if( ECMA3 )
{
   document.write( "<P>myCar <B>"
      + (eval("myCar instanceof Mustang")?"is":"is NOT")
      + "</B> a Mustang class object and <B>"
      + (eval("myCar instanceof Car")?"is":"is NOT")
      + "</B> a Car class object "
      + "(should be a Mustang and a Car class object).<BR>" );
```

```
        document.write("yourCar <B>"
            + (eval("yourCar instanceof Mustang")?"is":"is NOT")
            + "</B> a Mustang class object and <B>"
            + (eval("yourCar instanceof Car")?"is":"is NOT")
            + "</B> a Car class object "
            + "(should be a Mustang and a Car class object).<BR>" );
        document.write( "    ourCar <B>"
            + (eval("ourCar instanceof Mustang")?"is":"is NOT")
            + "</B> a Mustang class object and <B>"
            + (eval("ourCar instanceof Car")?"is":"is NOT")
            + "</B> a Car class object "
            + "(should only be a Car class object).</P>" );
    }
    else
    {
        document.write( "<P>   your browser does not support "
        + "the instanceof operator</P>");
    }

    //change car speeds (manipulate the objects)
    myCar.accelerate();
    myCar.accelerate();
    yourCar.accelerate();
    ourCar.accelerate();

    document.write("<P>Testing protected data members by manipulating "
        + "the speeds of myCar, yourCar and ourCar.<BR>");
    document.write("Results displayed below.</P>");

    //display the results of the object manipulation
    document.write("<P>The speed of myCar is <B>"
        + myCar.getSpeed() + "</B> (should be 2)<BR>");

    document.write("The speed of yourCar is <B>"
        + yourCar.getSpeed() + "</B> (should be 1)<BR>");

    document.write("The speed of ourCar is <B>"
        + ourCar.getSpeed() + "</B> (should be 1)</P>");

    //end of test
    document.write("<P>---- end of test ----</P>");
```

When the `InheritFromInstancePublicMembers.htm` file is viewed in a browser, you will see the following output:

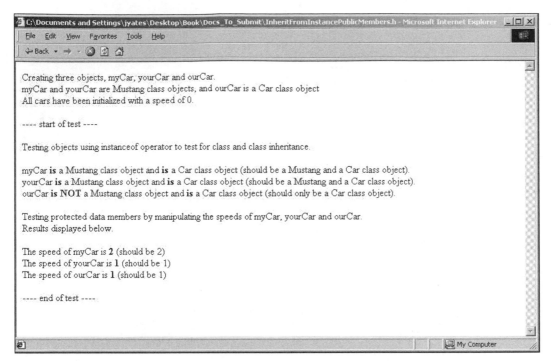

In this example, the Mustang class inherits from the Ford class by setting the Mustang's prototype property to an instance of the Ford class. The Ford class inherits from the Car class by setting the Ford's prototype property to an instance of the Car class. Because Ford inherits from Car, Mustang also inherits from Car. This is inheriting by object instance. Three objects are created: myCar, yourCar, and ourCar. myCar is a Mustang, as is yourCar, but ourCar is just of Car class. These three objects are tested for proper inheritance and the class implementation works properly.

As seen by the output above, myCar and yourCar are both a Mustang and a Car (which implies that they are both Ford class as well even though they were not tested as such). This first test is just to make sure that the internal prototype chain is verified, and that the instanceof operator works as expected.

The second test is to call their accelerate() method to show that the inherited methods are working properly. In the output the result of the method call, is displayed in bold, and the expected value follows within the parenthesis. Again, the output above shows that the results of this operation came back as expected.

Inheriting from an instance of a class requires only one line of code to be added per constructor that is inheriting from another class:

```
function Ford( initSpeed ){
    this.make = "Ford";
}
Ford.prototype = new Car();

function Mustang( initSpeed ){
    this.year = 2001;
    this.doors = 2;
}
Mustang.prototype = new Ford();
```

Most JavaScript programmers use this method of implementing inheritance, but there are requirements that must be met in order to use this technique. Specifically, all of the properties and methods of each of the inherited classes *must* be public. If any of the inherited classes use private methods that depend upon each other, such as a pair of set and get methods, then this means of inheritance will fail.

Let's look at an example. Note that this code is provided as an example showing that inheriting from an instance does not work when the class being inherited implements private members. This code will not work as expected, and it should not be expected to:

```
// Extract from InheritFromInstancePrivateMembers.htm
function Car()
{
    var speed = 0;
    this.accelerate = function (){ speed++ };
    this.decelerate = function (){ speed-- };
    this.getSpeed = function (){ return speed };
    this.purchased = false;
}
```

Here we can see that inheriting from an instance fails when one of the classes being inherited implements private members. The output indicates that the speed of myCar is 3 when it should be 2, and yourCar's speed is also 3 when it should be 1. This is because both of these objects are "sharing" the same instance of a Car class object within their prototype chain. The accelerate() method is called twice for myCar, and once for yourCar, for 3 calls that would set an instance of Car to have a speed of 3.

Whenever any instance of a Ford class (as well as Mustang, since it inherits from it) accelerates, *all* instances of the Ford class will accelerate. This not what we want, as we assume that each instance is independent of the others. In the above example, the only object that produced the expected output is ourCar, which is not an instance of a Ford class, and so is independent of that class.

There are two solutions for this problem. We can make all the members (properties and methods) of the classes public, or we can implement inheriting via class constructors, as described in the next section.

Inheriting from a Class Constructor

The above style of inheriting is fine for most applications, but not when one of the ancestor classes implements data hiding. The problem arises when we create more than one object that derives from a class implementing data hiding, since all instances of the class inherit from the *same* object instance. In the previous example, if we accelerate one car, we accelerate all cars. This is not the intended effect, so the code must be modified so that each instance has its own copy of the ancestors class's properties. The following code expands upon inheriting from an object instance to include inheriting from the class constructor as well:

```
// Extract from InheritFromConstructor.htm - with highlighted changes
function Ford(){
    Car.call(this);
    this.make = "Ford";
}
Ford.prototype = new Car();

function Mustang(){
    Ford.call( this );
    this.year = 2001;
    this.doors = 2;
}
...
```

Now when this modified code is run, we get the expected output. When `myCar` accelerates, `yourCar` does not. The key is that from within the `Ford` constructor, the `Car` constructor is called using the constructor function's `call()` method in order to re-initialize the private variables and the methods that access them. The same technique is used for the `Mustang` constructor. We must still set the prototype properties to an instance of the parent class (in order to keep the prototype chain intact), so that the `instanceof` operator operates properly.

> **Always call the parent class constructor before adding any properties to the object being constructed. If you do not then the parent class constructor may overwrite your property.**

This technique does have its disadvantages though: speed and memory consumption. Every call to the constructor causes a call to every one of its ancestor constructors. This can cause a dramatic increase in the amount of code run per object instance. In addition, each instance receives its own copy of each property and method, instead of inheriting them via the prototype property, which will increase the amount of memory used. In most cases, the speed and memory consumption difference is minor, but when a large number of objects are created, it may become significant.

Inheriting from a Class Constructor – Private Members and Overriding

In our examples so far, we have not overridden any of the private member access methods. The reason for this is that if any single method that uses the private data member is overridden, then all of the methods that access that data member must be overridden. Suppose we want our Mustang (a sports car) to accelerate faster than a normal car. To achieve this, we need to override the `accelerate()` method of the `Car` class within the `Mustang` classIn the following code, the speed is increased by 3 every time `accelerate()` is called, instead of by one:

```
/* Extract from InheritFromConstructorWithOverride.htm with highlighted
   changes */
function Mustang( initSpeed )
{
    var speed;
    Ford.call(this);
    this.year = 2001;
    this.doors = 2;
    this.accelerate = function (){ speed += 3; };
}
Mustang.prototype = new Ford();
```

Here we would expect the speed of `myCar` and `yourCar` to be 6 and 3 respectively. However, if you run this code, you'll see that they are both 0. This is because their `accelerate()` method is modifying the private `speed` variable within the `Mustang` constructor, but the `getSpeed()` method, which has not been overridden, is retrieving the value of the private `speed` variable from within the `Car` constructor. These two different variables have two different values.

There are two solutions to this dilemma. One solution is to do away with private data members and revert to using public data members (using only the properties and methods of the object for storing data), and so lose control over the value of our date. The other solution is to implement protected data members, which we'll look at next.

So far, we have covered how JavaScript implements objects, constructors, classes, inheritance, private variables, and public properties. The techniques you've learned should be sufficient for most of your user-defined object needs. The next section of this chapter is for those who wish to learn how to push JavaScript to its limits and see how much we can get away with by adding protected data member support for our class constructors.

Adding Protected Data Members to JavaScript

Within an object's code, JavaScript supports two types of data members, public and private. Public data members are the object's properties and methods. Any code that has access to the object can publicly access these data members. Private data members are also supported in the form of variables and functions defined within the object's constructor function, and are only accessible to methods defined within the constructor as nested functions.

In other OOP languages, there is another datatype, protected data members, which are variables and functions shared between a class implementation code and its derived class's implementation code. In JavaScript, this correlates to variables of one constructor being made accessible to another constructor, where one of the constructors inherits from the other. In the previous example, the Car class has three methods for manipulating the speed of the car. If any one of the methods is to be overridden, then they all must be overridden to prevent the other methods from being broken. If the private speed variable was made into a protected variable though, then each individual method could be overridden by different constructors, while retaining their functionality. Therefore, the use of protected data members can be used in order to overcome the limitations of using private members.

Since JavaScript does not directly support protected members, a mechanism must be created for doing so. There are two obstacles to be overcome when sharing a variable. Variables cannot be passed by reference – they are passed by value. This means that if code in one scope changes the value of the variable, code within another scope does not see this change. This problem can be overcome by storing the variables as properties of a private object. The other obstacle is security. A solution must be devised that will allow a constructor to retrieve the variables, but not outside of the code. Overcoming the limitations of JavaScript in order to use protected data members may add complexity to our code, and should be limited to only those variables that absolutely need to be shared between constructor codes.

In this section, we will cover a method of extending JavaScript to include protected data members, so that class implementation code can privately share information between them without exposing said information to outside code.

In this section, we will learn:

❑ What the protected method is

❑ How to use the protected method

❑ What the protected method does

❑ The internal workings of the protected method

The Protected Method

The goal of implementing protected members is to create a means for constructors to pass around a private object that contains all of the protected data members (the container object). One method of doing this is to extend the Object class to provide a means of sharing the private member container object.

It was discovered during the development of the protected method that any class implementing protected members needed to implement inheritance from a class constructor as well. Due to this, as well as timing issues, the protected member was designed to incorporate inheritance from a class constructor within itself. This has the added benefit of adding one line of code to our constructors, while at the same time eliminating one, with a net change of no added lines of code to our constructors. This can be a very attractive solution, since it does not add much more complexity to the code.

The syntax for implementing the protected method within a constructor is as follows:

```
var protect=this._protected_([ParentClass[, arg1, arg2, argN]]);
```

All tokens in the above should be replaced by names of your own choice. They are just placeholders for this description. All arguments within the square brackets are optional. A description of each part of the syntax follows:

- ❑ The *protect* variable is the variable that your constructor will use as it's private member container object.

- ❑ The *_protected_* method of the `this` value is the `protect()` method inherited from the `Object` class that this section is presenting.

- ❑ The *ParentClass* argument is a reference to the parent class constructor. This is the same constructor that we would normally use the `call()` method on when implementing inheritance from a class constructor; as was presented earlier in this chapter. If the current constructor does not inherit from another user-defined class, then the protected method should be called without any arguments.

- ❑ The optional arguments *arg1*, *arg2*, and *argN* represent the arguments to be sent to the parent class constructor from within the protected method.

The return value of the protected method is an object for your constructor to attach as properties all of its protected data members. All constructors of the current object will receive a reference to the same object, which means that any property you add to it will be available to all of the objects constructors.

For better understanding of how to use the protected method from within your constructor, the following section provides templates which you should follow when designing your constructors.

Constructor Templates for Implementing Protected Members

Below are the two templates to use for your constructors when implementing the protected members. Everything in italics is to be replaced by token names (function, variable, and argument names) of your own choice. The number and name of each argument is left to the discretion of the reader, depending upon the needs of your code.

This template, the `AncientClass` template that follows, is for use when the class constructor does NOT inherit from another user-defined class. Calling the protected method in this type of constructor is done in order to enable private members only:

```
// The below function is a template for a constructor for a class
// that DOES NOT inherit from another class other than the Object class.
function AncientClass(arg1, arg2, argN)
{
    var protect = this._protected_();

    /*Note: All protected variables and functions should be
            attached to the protect object */

    /////////////////////////////////////////////////////////
    // TODO:  constructor code goes here
}
```

The following template, the `DescendantClass` template, is for use when the class constructor inherits from another user-defined class. Calling the protected method in this type of constructor happens in order to enable private members and to implement inheritance from class constructors:

```
// The below function is a template for a constructor for a class
// that DOES inherit from another class.
function DescendantClass(arg1, arg2, argN)
{
   var protect = this._protected_(ParentClass, arg1, arg2, argN);

   /* Note:  All protected variables and functions should be
             attached to the protect object */

   ///////////////////////////////////////////////////////
   // TODO:  constructor code goes here
}
DescendantClass.prototype = new ParentClass();
```

By studying these two templates, you will see that protected members are implemented by using only one line of code per constructor:

```
var protect = this._protected_();
```

The above line is for the AncientClass constructor, and the following line:

```
var protect = this._protected_( ParentClass, arg1, arg2, argN );
```

is for the DescendantClass constructor.

For a better understanding of the implementation of the protected method, an example is presented below. This example modifies the example presented in the *Inheriting from a Class Constructor – Private Members and Overriding* section that did not work properly. This example corrects the prior example by implementing private members. The code used for implementing protected members is presented in bold:

```
// Extract from ProtectedExample.htm

//Car class constructor
function Car(initSpeed)
{
   var protect = this._protected_();
   protect.speed = 0;

   if(!isNaN(Number(initSpeed)))
      protect.speed = Number(initSpeed);

   this.accelerate = function() {protect.speed++};
   this.decelerate = function() {protect.speed--};
   this.getSpeed = function() {return protect.speed};
   this.purchased = false;
}

//Ford class constructor (extends Car class)
function Ford(initSpeed)
{
   var protect = this._protected_(Car, initSpeed);
   this.make = "Ford";
};
Ford.prototype = new Car();

//Mustang class constructor (extends Ford class)
```

```
function Mustang(initSpeed)
{
   var protect = this._protected_(Ford, initSpeed);
   this.year = 2001;
   this.doors = 2;
   this.accelerate = function() {protect.speed += 3};
}
Mustang.prototype = new Ford();

var myCar = new Mustang();
var yourCar = new Mustang();
var ourCar = new Car();
```

The Mustang class is overriding the Car class's accelerate() method with a method that increases the protected speed variable by 3. The original accelerate() method as implemented by the Car class, only increases it by 1.

The example creates three objects, two of which are of the Mustang class (myCar and yourCar). The code then calls myCar's accelerate() method twice, which should give it a speed of 6, and calls yourCar's accelerate() method once, which should give it a speed of 3. From viewing the output of the example, we can see that the expected values are returned, therefore protected data member access methods are shown to be overridable.

Source Code for the Protected Method

Now that we know to use the protected method, it is time to dig into the code behind it. The protected member attempts to perform three actions:

❑   Provide a means of security, so that the protected method can only be called from within an object's constructor

❑   Provide a means of creating and sharing an object to be used as the protected data member container.

❑   Provide support for inheriting from a class constructor

Below is the implementation of protected data members that was developed:

```
// Extract from ProtectedExample.htm

//extend the Object class to proved protected data members
function _Protected_(ParentClass, ParentClassConstructorArguments)
{
   /*make sure this function is called from within the objects
     constructor */
   if (ECMA3 && _Protected_.caller &&
      !eval("this instanceof _Protected_.caller"))
      eval('throw new Error("Protected Data Members can only be shared '
         + 'between related classes.");');
   if (ParentClass)
   {
      //the base class has to be pre-defined as a base class of this
      //object
      if (ECMA3 && !eval("this instanceof ParentClass"))
         eval('throw new Error("The base class constructor supplied'
            + ' was not pre-defined as the base class for this class.");');
      //reset the _protectedMembers_ property. It may have been modified.
```

```
      this._protectedMembers_ = Object.prototype._protectedMembers_;

      //re-initialize the base object of this class for this instance
      ParentClass.apply( this, Array.apply(null, arguments).slice(1));
   }
   var protect;
   var ACCESS_KEY = "Type here whatever you want to be the access key";
   function GetProtectedMembers(key)
   {
      var returnValue=this;
      if (key == ACCESS_KEY)
         returnValue=protected
      return returnValue;
   }
   protect = this._protectedMembers_(ACCESS_KEY);
   if (protect == this)
   {
      protect = new Object();
      this._protectedMembers_ = GetProtectedMembers;
   }
   return protect;
}
Object.prototype._protected_ = _Protected_;
Object.prototype._protectedMembers_ = function(){return this};
```

The above code was designed for backward compatablility. The ECMA3 variable was supplied by a browser detection script, which sets this variable to true if the browser supports the `instanceof` *operator and the* `throw...catch` *statement.*

This section contains a line-by-line description of the protected method whose source is provided above:

```
function _Protected_(ParentClass, ParentClassConstructorArguments)
```

This is the function declaration. There are two formally declared arguments, `ParentClass` and `ParentClassConstructorArguments`. `ParentClass` is an optionally supplied constructor reference to use when inheriting via an object constructor, to re-initialize the parent class properties of this object. If the constructor inherits, then this argument should always be supplied. `ParentClassConstructorArguments` is not a true argument, since it is not used within the code. Instead, it is a reminder to the programmer that any arguments the parent class requires for its constructor should be individually included there. This means that this function can be called with zero, one, or many arguments:

```
if (ECMA3 && _Protected_.caller &&
    !eval("this instanceof _Protected_.caller"))
   eval('throw new Error("Protected Data Members can only be shared '
      + 'between related classes.");');
```

Here is the first level of security for protecting our protected variables from external code. This code checks to make sure that the function only works when it is called from within one of the object's constructors.

The first check ensures that this line of code will run in the browser by testing the ECMA3 variable. The ECMA3 variable is supplied by a browser detection script discussed earlier in this chapter, which sets this variable to `true` if the browser supports the `instanceof` operator and the `throw...catch` statement. If this variable is `false`, that security is disabled.

If `ECMA3` is `true`, then the caller property of the function is tested to see if it is a constructor of the object. The `caller` property of a function holds a reference to the function that called it. If the calling function is not a constructor of the current object (tested using the `instanceof` operator), then an exception is thrown, stopping the execution of the code.

In order for this implementation to work properly, there must be a mechanism for calling the parent class constructors and to allow them to initialize the object before the current constructor does its initialization. When the function is called with a `ParentClass` argument, the following lines perform this action:

```
if(ParentClass)
{
    //the base class has to be pre-defined as a base class of this
    //object
    if (ECMA3 && !eval("this instanceof ParentClass"))
        eval('throw new Error("The base class constructor supplied'
            + ' was not pre-defined as the base class for this class.");');

    //reset the _protectedMembers_ property. It may have been modified.
    this._protectedMembers_ = Object.prototype._protectedMembers_;

    //re-initialize the base object of this class for this instance
    ParentClass.apply( this, Array.apply(null, arguments).slice(1));
}
```

Calling the `_Protected_` function with an invalid `ParentClass` argument can cause bugs in your code that are hard to trace. The above lines of code are designed to help you prevent this from happening, and to give you an idea of where the problem lies.

Part of the implementation of the protected method is expanding the `Object` class to have a method called `_protectedMembers_`, which returns a reference to the object to which it is attached. This method will be overridden later on in the code, but at this point in the code, it *must* be set to the original function. The following line of code guarantees this:

```
this._protectedMembers_ = Object.prototype._protectedMembers_;
```

This following line is for implementing inheritance via constructors. The parent class is called using the `apply` method of the constructor to give it its chance for initialization of the object:

```
ParentClass.apply(this, Array.apply(null, arguments).slice(1));
```

> *This code is not backward compliant due to the `apply()` method being used, but this can be overcome by implementing the `apply()` method yourself, using the `eval()` function. An example of this was provided earlier in the chapter in section: "Upgrading Native Objects for Older Browsers".*

The next variable declared is the `ACCESS_KEY` variable.

```
var ACCESS_KEY = "Type in whatever you want here to be the access key";
```

This variable holds the security key (a string that you can modify to whatever you wish) in order to limit the retrieval of the protected variable container to calls from within this function. This security can be easily bypassed by anyone understanding this code and is intended as a deterrent, not as a true security measure:

```
function GetProtectedMembers(key)
{
    var returnValue=this;
    if (key == ACCESS_KEY)
        returnValue=protect;
    return returnValue;
}
```

The `GetProtectedMembers()` nested function will become a method of the object being created. Its purpose is to pass the protected variable container between the constructors. This function references the variable `protect` that is in the `_Protected_` function, but since this function has only made a method of the object once, it only references *one* instance of this variable. This is the key to the functionality of protected members. The rest of this code is just to support these four lines:

```
protect = this._protectedMembers_(ACCESS_KEY);
```

This line of code retrieves the protected variable container. If this is the first time this code has been executed on the current object, then a reference to the current object will be returned:

```
if (protect == this)
{
    protect = new Object();
    this._protectedMembers_ = GetProtectedMembers;
}
```

If this is the first time this code has been run on the current object, then a new object is initialized to act as the protected members container. After a new container is made, a means of retrieving this container is implemented by overriding the original `_protectedMembers_` method (the one that returns a reference to the object) with the `GetProtectedMembers` function. This is only done once per object instance:

```
return protect;
```

Return the protected members container to the constructor:

```
Object.prototype._protected_ = _Protected_;
```

This line of code enables protected members for any object that wishes to implement it:

```
Object.prototype._protectedMembers_ = function(){ return this };
```

This line of code sets the `_protectedMembers_` method to its initial value, a function that returns a reference to its object.

The key to understanding this code is to realize that each constructor for each class for the object is calling this code with a reference to the next constructor to be called. The only constructor that does not pass in a constructor to be called is the lower-most user-defined class (the class that directly extends the `Object` class), and here is where the chain of function calls end. When the lower-most user defined class constructor calls this code, the protected member container is created and initialized. Then, in reverse order from the above, each constructor retrieves this container and keeps a reference to it for its own use.

This concludes the discussion of protected members. We have seen that there are three types of data used by object code

❑ Public data is stored as a property of the object itself and can be modified without restriction by any code that can get access to the object.

❑ Private data is stored as a private variable within the object constructor and can only be accessed via methods. If any of these methods are to be overridden, then all of the methods must be overridden.

❑ Protected data is stored in a container object that only the constructors of the object and their methods have access. Unlike using private data members, using protected data members eliminates the need for overriding all of the methods that access the data when only one of the methods are overridden. Which method we use to store and retrieve our object's data is dependent upon our needs when writing object code.

Summary

Here is a short review the features that most OO languages support:

❑ Interfaces – This is a cross language method for creating and accessing object members at run-time (a technique known as late binding). JavaScript does *not* support user-defined interfaces.

❑ Data Abstraction – The representation of information in a symbolic manner

❑ Extensibility – The ability to expand upon previously developed code

❑ Polymorphism – The ability to use and manipulate an object with only a partial understanding of the properties and methods that it supports

❑ Encapsulation – This is the ability to group data and code within a structure or entity. This is also referred to as information hiding.

JavaScript supports all of the above features, with the exception of interfaces. Interfaces allow objects created in one language to be accessible to programs written in almost any other language. This is a very powerful feature, but the nature of JavaScript as a loosely typed scripting language limits how useful this feature could be.

Data abstraction means concentrating upon the problem being solved, instead of the steps it takes to solve the problem. Creating an entity called an object and populating it with data, and methods for manipulating the data, help to accomplish this. In JavaScript, an object is seen as a unit of data and code for manipulating that data, thus data abstraction is a fundamental part of the JavaScript language.

Extensibility is the ability to readily expand upon existing code. In OOP languages, this is accomplished through inheritance. JavaScript natively implements a type of inheritance called prototype inheritance, or object-based inheritance. In this chapter, we covered the weaknesses of prototype inheritance and ways to overcome these weaknesses.

Polymorphism is the ability to use or manipulate an object as if it were an object of one of its ancestor classes. In JavaScript, all objects inherit from the base object class, Object. In this sense, we can say that JavaScript supports polymorphism to an extreme. With the addition of the instanceof operator, which allows the programmer to perform type checking, a more realistic application of polymorphism can be realized. Therefore, the answer to "does JavaScript support polymorphism" is yes, but the complete implementation of polymorphism requires the programmers to test and/or reject the object manually.

Encapsulation is the ability to contain data and code within an entity. Natively, JavaScript supports a form of encapsulation that we refer to as co-operative encapsulation. All of the object data and functionality is available for inspection and modification. This data and functionality is found in **public members**. Data encapsulation is the isolation or protection of data from casual modification from code external to the object code (information hiding). In JavaScript, this is not natively supported. With a little work by the programmer, using nested functions, we can use private and/or protected members to implement a more realistic form of data encapsulation. In conclusion, JavaScript does support a primitive form of encapsulation, and with a little work by the programmer, it can fully support all of the major forms of encapsulation.

In conclusion, we can say that although JavaScript is not a true OO language, it has, or can be made to act as though it has most of the features that identify an OO language. JavaScript is often referred to as an object-based language, because of the features it is lacking.

Pro JavaScript 2nd Edition

4

Windows and Frames

In this chapter, we will look at frames, browser windows, and how we manipulate them with JavaScript. Once we know how, it's straightforward, but it is something that can confuse at first, partly because frameset hierarchies can themselves get a little tricky.

We'll concentrate in this chapter on how to use code to access other windows and frames. We'll start by examining frames and look at the hierarchy we need to navigate using code when faced with framesets, and later IFRAMEs. We will then see how code in one frame can change, for example, the HTML in another frame, and also how functions and variables in one frame can be accessed by another frame. Finally, we'll see the possible pitfalls of the window object's load event and how to avoid them, and the security pitfalls of coding between frames.

In the second half of the chapter, we'll be turning to windows, in particular how to open and close new browser windows, how we can script between windows, and again the possible security pitfalls.

Frames

Frames have been available in HTML since the days of NN 2 and IE 3, and can be a great way of organizing web sites. They enable us to divide the page up into multiple areas, each area being generally independent of the other. It's quite common to have one frame with a list of menu options which when clicked, causes a larger second frame to change to a different page. We'll see later that placing JavaScript in the top frame allows us to store session information and define functions that will be used again and again in our website. As the top frameset page is not normally reloaded, it means that the browser only has to load these global functions once, thus reducing overall download times.

The only major downside to frames, is that for some browsers it makes it trickier for visitors to your web site to book mark a specific page. Instead, it's the main frameset-defining page that is bookmarked and whatever is the default for that frameset. This is not a problem for IE 5+ where framesets are correctly bookmarked, but is for earlier versions of IE and for all Netscape browsers. Another issue we also need to be aware of, is that security restrictions set by the browser will limit what our JavaScript can do when accessing frames. As we'll see later in the chapter, it's particularly restrictive where we load pages into our frameset, where the pages are not hosted on our domain. So if our web site, http://www.yourdomain.com, has a frameset which loads a page from http://www.google.com, then we'll find that JavaScript has very limited access to the http://www.google.com page.

To define framesets, we use the HTML FRAMESET tag. We can specify how much screen space inside the frameset each frame gets using the rows and cols attributes of the FRAMESET tag. So, cols='50%,50%' would divide the screen vertically into two columns with each taking 50% of the screen. To divide the screen into rows, we can use the row attribute, for example: rows='25%,25%,*'. Note here we have used the * to indicate that the remaining frame should take up whatever room is remaining, which in this case is 50% of the screen. If we don't use the % sign, then it's assumed by the browser we mean pixels.

Between the FRAMESET opening and closing tags, we insert FRAME tags for each frame we want to define. We give each a name using the tag's NAME attribute, which allows us to refer to the frames later in script. We can load blank frames, but more than likely we'll want to specify what page is loaded into the frame when the frameset is loaded. For this we use the SRC attribute of the FRAME tag. The following would create a frame that loads MyPage.htm into it:

```
<FRAME SRC='MyPage.htm' name='MyFrame'></FRAME>
```

Our coverage of frames will start with looking at how frameset definition determines the object hierarchy we need to navigate. We'll then look at how we can access one frame's document from another, before seeing how JavaScript functions and variables are available from different frames. We'll finish off by looking at the problems that occur with the window object's load event, and by looking at security issues.

How Framesets Are Structured

Each browser window we can see has a window object. This window object is created for us automatically by the browser and allows us to access and manipulate the browser window and the HTML document it contains. The window object has a number of different properties, methods, and events. It is via its properties that we gain access to the document object, which allows us to manipulate the page itself, using DHTML for example. Without framesets, we only have one window, with one window object representing that browser window.

If in our page, we define a frameset with two frames, what have we created? The answer is that we have created two more windows, each with its own window object. It might seem a little strange at first as you might not think of a frame as a separate window, but as one window divided into a number of parts. However, to the browser each frame is a separate window with a window object, which contains a document object representing the page.

Therefore, we need to think of each frame as a separate window with all the properties, events, and methods of a single window object. Questions raised now include:

❑ How are they organized?

❑ What is the relationship between one window and another?

❑ How do we access one window object from another?

Let's start with the structure, which will be explained with a simple example. Below, is a page (SimpleFrameset.htm) with a FRAMESET tag:

```
<!-- SimpleFrameset.htm -->
<HTML>
<FRAMESET COLS='50%,*'>
    <FRAME SRC='SimpleLeftFrame.htm' NAME='LeftFrame'>
    <FRAME SRC='SimpleRightFrame.htm' NAME='RightFrame'>
</FRAMESET>
</HTML>
```

Now, we create the two pages pointed to in the SRC properties, as shown below. The first is SimpleLeftFrame.htm:

```
<!-- SimpleLeftFrame.htm -->
<HTML>
<BODY>
    <H3>Left Frame</H3>
</BODY>
</HTML>
```

The second is SimpleRightFrame.htm:

```
<!-- SimpleRightFrame.htm -->
<HTML>
<BODY>
    <H3>Right Frame</H3>
</BODY>
</HTML>
```

Now, load the frameset page into a browser and you should see the page shown below:

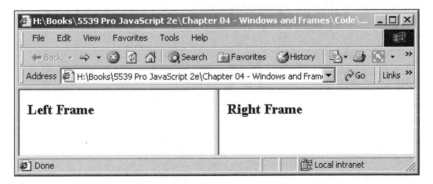

The frameset-defining page is the parent window, and each of the frames its children. We can't actually see this parent window; we just see the frames that are loaded inside it. It's still there, however, and viewing the page source with the browser will confirm this. The hierarchy created by this frameset is shown in the diagram below:

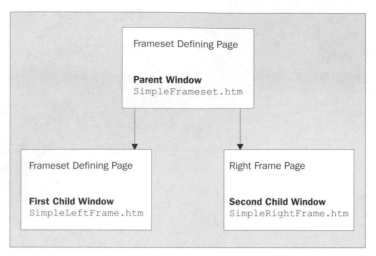

Like any family tree, the parent window is at the top of the hierarchy and each of its siblings is underneath, but at the same level as each other. The order of the children is based on the definition of the FRAME elements. So, the first FRAME element will create the first child frame, the second will create the second frame, and so on. That still leaves us the question of how we access one frame from another. The window object has some properties that help us out here. First, we have the frames collection, which is an array with each element containing the window object of each frame defined by a frameset in the current window. Remember that all arrays are zero based, so to access the first frame we need element zero:

```
var firstFrameWindow = window.frames[0];
```

If the code above were in the frameset-defining page, it would set variable firstFrameWindow to reference the first frame. To access the second frame:

```
var secondFrameWindow = window.frames[1];
```

If there had been a third frame, then that would be frames[2], a fourth would be frames[3], and so on. How do we know how many frames there are? Like any JavaScript array, we can use the length property. So the following code in our frameset page would display 2:

```
alert(window.frames.length);
```

We gave each of our frames a name, LeftFrame and RightFrame. We did this because it allows us to use the name in the frames array rather than a number. The main advantage of this is it makes it easier for us to remember that: window.frames["LeftFrame"] refers to the LeftFrame's window object. It is the same as window.frames[0]; it's just much easier to remember. Using the array index is handy where, for example, we wanted to loop through each frame in turn, or where our code doesn't know in advance how many frames there are, such as where we have a general purpose routine rather than one specific to the page.

Even easier still, as long as we have given our frames a name, we can just use the name without specifying the frames property:

```
window.LeftFrame;
```

All along, we've been using window (window.frames), where we can actually omit the window object and just use frames, because window is assumed by default in JavaScript. However, it makes it clear what we are referring to; it is the current page's window object that contains the frames, and is the parent to them.

Let's put all the above code snippets into a short example, using the code below to make `SimpleFrameset2.htm`:

```
<HTML>
<HEAD>
    <SCRIPT>
    function frameset_onload()
    {
        var leftFrameWindow = window.LeftFrame;
        var rightFrameWindow = window.frames[1];

        alert("Left frame is named " + leftFrameWindow.name)
        alert("Right frame is named " + rightFrameWindow.name)
        alert("Number of frames is " + window.frames.length);
    }

    </SCRIPT>
</HEAD>
<FRAMESET COLS='50%,*' onload='frameset_onload()'>
    <FRAME SRC='SimpleLeftFrame.htm' NAME='LeftFrame'>
    <FRAME SRC='SimpleRightFrame.htm' NAME='RightFrame'>
</FRAMESET>
</HTML>
```

At the top, we have added a script block and a function, `frameset_onload()`, inside it. As the function's name suggests, it's called by the FRAMESET tag's `onload()` event handler, which itself fires once the frameset has been loaded. It's important that our code is called by this event and not just directly in the script block, like this:

```
<SCRIPT>
    var leftFrameWindow = window.LeftFrame;
    var rightFrameWindow = window.frames[1];

    alert('Left frame is named ' + leftFrameWindow.name)
    alert('Right frame is named ' + rightFrameWindow.name)
    alert('Number of frames is ' + window.frames.length);
</SCRIPT>
```

If this were at the top of the page, prior to the FRAMESET tag, then our attempts to reference the frame's window objects would fail. This is, because at that point in the page when the script runs, the FRAMESET tag and its associated FRAME tags have not yet been parsed by the browser's HTML parser; they simply don't exist yet. If we try and access these non-existent frames then we'll get errors, as you would expect. However, by not running the code until the frameset's `load` event has fired we can be sure that the page has been parsed and the frames, will now exist. It's in the FRAMESET tag that we add the `onload` event handler and get it to call our `frameset_onload()` function.

We've seen that we can access any child frame from its parent using the `frames` array. To access the parent from the child, the window object has another property that helps us do this – its `parent` property. The `parent` property is a reference to the window object of this window object's parent, as you would expect. In our simple frameset, either of the two child windows will have their parent property reference the window object of the frameset-defining page. The parent frameset's parent is itself, so for the top page, `window.parent` and `window` are the same thing.

So, for example, to either the left or right frame pages we could add:

```
alert(window.parent.location.href);
```

This would display the URL of the frameset page.

We can now access a frame from its parent and the frameset page from its children, but how do we access one child frame's window object from another child window? We already know that the frame's `array` property of the parent window object contains all the window objects for each frame defined. We also know that we can access the parent window object from a child window using the `parent` property. So put the two together and we have our answer; we access the frame's property of the parent window and gain access to the frame we want using its `frames` property.

For example, to access the HREF of the first child window (the left frame) from the second child (the right frame), we would write:

```
alert(window.parent.frames[0].location.href);
```

We can also use the `name` instead:

```
alert(window.parent.frames["LeftFrame"].location.href);
```

A Complex Frameset

We have seen how accessing one frame from another works with simple framesets, but what about where we have more than one page defining a frameset. Let's say the left frame in the example we saw earlier wasn't a page, but another frameset-defining page, giving us the frame arrangement shown below:

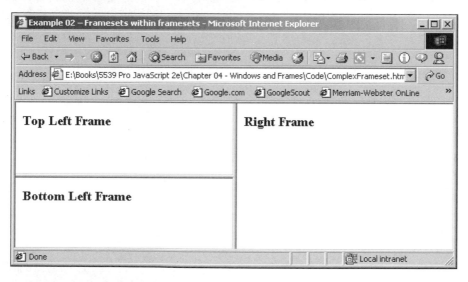

The main frameset page is now:

```
<!-- ComplexFrameset.htm -->
<HTML>
<HEAD><TITLE>Example 02 - Framesets within framesets</TITLE></HEAD>
<FRAMESET COLS='50%,*'>
    <FRAME SRC='ComplexLeftFrame.htm' NAME='LeftFrame'>
    <FRAME SRC='ComplexRightFrame.htm' NAME='RightFrame'>
</FRAMESET>
</HTML>
```

The left page has been changed to this:

```
<!-- ComplexLeftFrame.htm -->
<HTML>
<FRAMESET ROWS='50%,*'>
   <FRAME SRC='ComplexLeftTopFrame.htm' NAME='LeftTopFrame' >
   <FRAME SRC='ComplexLeftBottomFrame.htm' NAME='LeftBottomFrame' >
</FRAMESET>
</HTML>
```

The right page is the same as in the previous example, but with the name changed to
ComplexRightFrame.htm, and the two pages LeftTopFrame.htm and LeftBottomFrame.htm are:

```
<!-- ComplexLeftTopFrame.htm -->
<HTML>
<BODY>
   <H3>Top Left Frame</H3>
</BODY>
</HTML>
```

```
<!-- ComplexLeftBottomFrame.htm -->
<HTML>
<BODY>
   <H3>Bottom Left Frame</H3>
</BODY>
</HTML>
```

So where does that leave our hierarchy of frames? The diagram below shows the results:

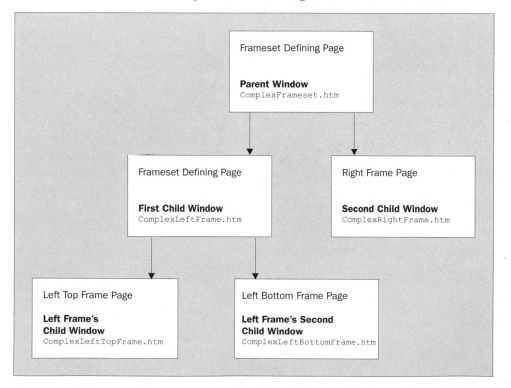

We can see that the hierarchy of the previous pages remains the same. The first frameset-defining page that we load into the browser is at the top of the family tree. We then have its two children, LeftFrame and RightFrame. The LeftFrame page has spawned two children, LeftTopFrame and LeftBottomFrame. The question now is how do we access these children from other frames and vice versa?

The principles remain the same – we still use the frames and parent properties, but it's just a slightly more complex family tree we need to navigate. Let's start from the LeftTop frame (ComplexLeftTopFrame.htm) and let's say we want to access the window object of the RightFrame, we need to walk the hierarchy. First, we need to get a reference to the LeftTopFrame's parent – this is simply:

```
window.parent
```

Now looking at the diagram, we can see we next need to get LeftTopFrame's parent's parent:

```
window.parent.parent
```

Now the RightFrame is one of the frames defined by the top page's frameset, so to get the RightFrame's window object, we need to use the top page in the hierarchy's frames array. We'll use the frame's number:

```
window.parent.parent.frames[1]
```

Remember the frames array is zero based, so the second child is in the element with index of 1. We could use the frame's name instead:

```
window.parent.parent.frames["RightFrame"]
```

So to get the URL of the RightFrame from the LeftTopFrame we would write:

```
alert(window.parent.parent.frames["RightFrame"].location.href);
```

When things get this long, it's better to use variables to store the references:

```
var rightFrame = window.parent.parent.frames["RightFrame"];
alert(rightFrame.location.href);
```

Things start to get quite long when we have window.parent.parent, and even worse if the LeftTopFrame was also a frameset-defining page. In this situation, we can use the window object's top property, which provides a reference to the window object at the very top of the hierarchy, which in our case is the first frameset-defining page, SimpleFrameset.htm. So we could change:

```
var rightFrame = window.parent.parent.frames["RightFrame"];
```

To:

```
var rightFrame = window.top.frames["RightFrame"];
```

Which would do the same thing.

As with the simple frameset example, it's important that we don't try and access frames before they are actually loaded, something that is only an issue where we want to execute code when a page loads. If we stick with using the FRAMESET elements onload() event handler or the onload event handler of the BODY elements, then we will be fairly safe, but still need to be careful. We'll talk about the order of frame loading shortly. Let's add this code to the ComplexLeftTopFrame.htm page that will display the URL of the right frame. We need to change ComplexLeftTopFrame.htm to look like that shown below, which we'll call ComplexLeftTopFrame2.htm:

```
<!-- ComplexLeftTopFrame2.htm -->
<HTML>
<SCRIPT>
   function window_onload()
   {
      var rightFrame = window.top.frames["RightFrame"];
      alert(rightFrame.location.href);
   }
</SCRIPT>
<BODY onload='window_onload()'>
   <H3>Top Left Frame</H3>
</BODY>
</HTML>
```

If you save the page and load into your browser, you will see an alert box appear displaying the location of the ComplexLeftTopFrame.htm page.

We have not added the code so that it is executed as the page is parsed, as we did with the previous example, because this would lead to an error. Instead, we have added it to the page's load event by adding the onload() event handler to the BODY element. This then calls our window_onload() function, which contains the line of code we saw earlier, and then sets variable rightFrame to reference the window object of the right frame. We then use this object to get the location.href property. We could dispense with setting a variable to hold the reference to the frame and just write:

```
alert(window.top.frames["RightFrame"].location.href);
```

This works just as well. The main disadvantage of this approach would be if we needed to access the right frame more than once, because the code would be slightly longer. Also by using a well named variable, it makes it very obvious what it is we are accessing, the rightFrame.

There are advantages and disadvantages with the top property. On the plus side, it will always refer to the top of the frame hierarchy regardless of the page we use it in. On the negative side, if we change our frameset, for example if the current top page was itself loaded into a frameset, then it would no longer be the top page and we would need to recode any references to it.

Before we leave this section, let's see how we would access the LeftBottomFrame from the RightFrame. We need to walk the hierarchy; first we need to get the parent window of the RightFrame:

```
window.parent;
```

Next, we want to get the window object of the LeftFrame, which is the first child frame of the RightFrame's parent. We can either use its index in the frames array, which is zero, or the name in the frames array, or just the name of the frame. Each approach is shown below:

```
window.parent.frames[0];
```

```
window.parent.frames["LeftFrame"];
```

```
window.parent.LeftFrame;
```

From here, the LeftBottomFrame is the LeftFrame's second child, so again we can use any of the three ways of accessing it:

```
var leftBottomFrame = window.parent.frames[0].frames[1];
```

```
var leftBottomFrame =
    window.parent.frames["LeftFrame"].frames["LeftBottomFrame"];
```

```
var leftBottomFrame = window.parent.LeftFrame.LeftBottomFrame;
```

Let's change the ComplexRightFrame.htm page so it looks like this:

```
<HTML>
<HEAD>
    <SCRIPT>
function window_onload()
    {
        var leftBottomFrame = window.parent.LeftFrame.LeftBottomFrame;
        alert(leftBottomFrame.location.href);
    }
</SCRIPT>
</HEAD>
<BODY onload='window_onload()'>
    <H3>Right Frame</H3>
</BODY>
</HTML>
```

We will see an alert box with the location and filename of ComplexRightFrame.htm. However, this example does not work properly on Netscape 6.01 due to how that browser handles deeply nested framesets.

That completes our coverage of how frameset hierarchies are structured and how we can navigate them. Before we leave this section, we'll take a brief look at the IFRAME type of frame.

The IFRAME

A frameset page simply defines frames – there is no other visible HTML and no BODY tag. However, the IFRAME tag allows us to define a frame inside a non-frameset defining page's body – it's a little like having a window in the page that looks out onto another page. The IFRAME has been supported by Internet Explorer since version 3, and is now also supported by Netscape 6+. As it is part of the HTML 4 standard, we can expect any new browsers to support it. The IFRAME is quite handy as it can be positioned anywhere in the page using stylesheets and acts like a window in our page. We can load a page into it like any other frame or write to its document directly, as we'll see shortly.

So in the simple page below, we have two IFRAMEs. Note this will not work on Netscape browsers before version 6:

```
<!--IFRAME FRAME Page-->
<HTML>
<HEAD>

<SCRIPT>
    function window_onload()
    {
        var IFrame1 = window.IFrame1;
        var IFrame2 = window.frames[1];

        alert(IFrame1.name);
        alert(IFrame2.name);

    }
</SCRIPT>
```

```
   </HEAD>
<BODY onload='window_onload()'>
   <IFRAME SRC='IFramePage.htm' NAME='IFrame1' STYLE=
      'position:absolute;width:150px;height:100px;top:10px;left:20px;'>
   </IFRAME>

   <IFRAME SRC='IFramePage.htm' NAME='IFrame2' STYLE=
      'position:absolute;width:250px;height:100px;top:250px;left:20px;'>
   </IFRAME>
</BODY>
</HTML>
```

We also need to create the page loaded by the IFRAME tag's SRC property called IFramePage.htm:

```
<!-- IFramePage.htm -->
<HTML>
<BODY>
   <H3>IFRAME FRAME PAGE</H3>
</BODY>
</HTML>
```

As it's just an example, we have used the same page for both the frames. The page will look like that below:

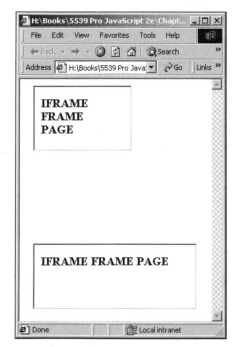

As the page loads, we will see two alert boxes appear, telling us the names of the IFRAMEs (IFrame1 and IFrame2).

The question is how does this fit into our hierarchy? The answer is that each IFRAME becomes a child frame of the page it's in, just as each frame defined in a page's frameset becomes a child frame of that page. The main difference, is that with IFRAME's we can have frames and HTML content in the same page, with framesets and no HTML content is allowed.

In the example, we add the `onload` event handler to the BODY tag which calls the `window_onload()` function we see below:

```
function window_onload()
{
   var IFrame1 = window.IFrame1;
   var IFrame2 = window.frames[1];

   alert(IFrame1.name);
   alert(IFrame2.name);
}
```

We have two examples of how we can access the child IFRAME windows of the current page, and we can see it's very much the same as how we accessed child frames when they were defined with FRAMESET and FRAME tags.

Let's turn to a more complex example and alter the `ComplexLeftBottomFrame.htm` page and add an IFRAME:

```
<!-- ComplexLeftBottomFramev2.htm -->
<HTML>
<BODY>
   <H3>Bottom Left Frame</H3>
   <IFRAME SRC='IFramePage.htm' NAME='IframeFrame' STYLE=
      'position:absolute;width:250px;height:100px;top:50px;left:20px;'>
   </IFRAME>
</BODY>
</HTML>
```

So how does that leave our hierarchy?

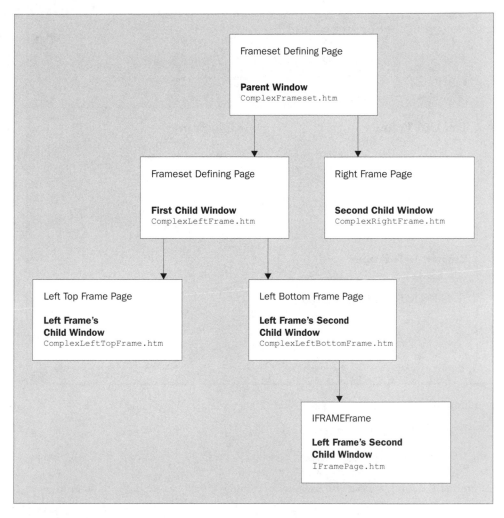

We can see that the `IFRAME` frame is `ComplexLeftBottomFramev2`'s first child. As with frames defined using framesets, the child's window object is available in the `ComplexLeftBottomFramev2`'s `frames` collection, or directly using its name. A screenshot is shown overleaf:

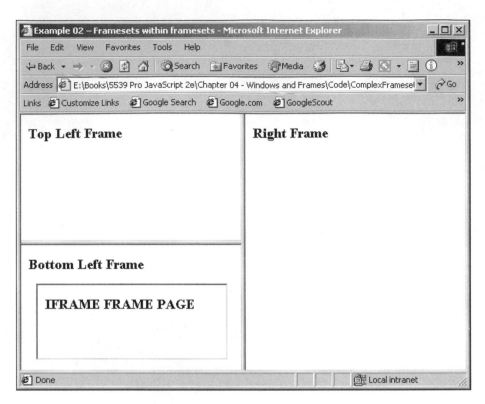

Code within the `ComplexLeftBottomFramev2` page can access the child like this:

```
var childIFrame = window.frames[0];
```

```
var childIFrame = window.frames["IFrameFrame"];
```

With Internet Explorer, we can also use the frame name directly as we did with other frames:

```
var childIFrame = window.IFrameFrame;
```

As with frames defined with FRAME tags, we can only access the iframes when they have been parsed, so as with frames, using the window's load event by adding the onload event handler to the BODY tag is the best option.

Finally, how would we access the IFRAME's window object from our RightFrame? As before, it's just a matter of walking the hierarchy, moving up using the parent property, and then back down the other side with the frames array:

```
var IFrameWindow =
parent.frames["LeftFrame"].frames["LeftBottomFrame"].frames["IFrameFrame"];
```

Note that because of the order in which the frames load, this will only work correctly if the code is executed after all the frames have loaded. For example, if it was added to a button's onClick. Shown below, is `ComplexRightFrame.htm`, but altered to include such a button:

```
<HTML>
<HTML>
<HEAD>
   <SCRIPT>
function button_onclick()
{
   var IFrameWindow =
   parent.frames["LeftFrame"].frames["LeftBottomFrame"].frames["IFrameFrame"];
   alert(IFrameWindow.name);
}
</SCRIPT>
</HEAD>
<BODY>
   <H3>Right Frame</H3>
   <FORM>
   <INPUT TYPE='button' VALUE='Show IFrame name' onclick='button_onclick()'>
</FORM>
</BODY>
</HTML>
```

The Frame Loading Order

If we're only accessing other frame's windows when the pages have loaded, for example when users press a button, then there's no need to worry about which page loaded when. However, if we are inserting script into the page that either runs as the page is loaded or is called by the window object's load event, then we need to be very careful when accessing the window object's of other frames, because there is a distinct possibility they may not have loaded yet.

If we take our example frameset we've been using. If we try and access the IFRAME's window object from the ComplexRightFrame.htm, then we'll get an error:

```
<HTML>
<HEAD>
  <SCRIPT>
      var IFrameWindow =
 parent.frames["LeftFrame"].frames["LeftBottomFrame"].frames["IFrameFrame"];
      alert(IFrameWindow.name);
  </SCRIPT>
</HEAD>
<BODY>
   <H3>Right Frame</H3>
</BODY>
</HTML>
```

The IFRAME hasn't yet been loaded into the LeftBottomFrame at the point at which the RightFrame tries to access it and we get an error. If we change so that the window's Load event calls the script, then this will work as, by co-incidence, the RightFrame's window onLoad fires after the LeftBottomFrame has loaded. Note this will not work in Netscape 6 due to the way it handles deeply nested framesets.

Let's see the order in which our frameset's frame pages are parsed and their window objects load events are raised. We can do this by adding the following to each of our pages:

```
<HEAD>
   <SCRIPT>
      function window_onload()
      {
```

```
            alert(window.name + " window onload event just fired");
        }

        alert(window.name + " frame's page is being parsed");
    </SCRIPT>
</HEAD>
```

For each non-frameset defining page, we need to alter the BODY tag to this:

```
<BODY onLoad=window_onload()'>
```

For each frameset page, that does'nt have BODY tags, we need to alter the script in the SCRIPT tag just, we added and add this after the function definition:

```
        window.onload = window_onload;
```

Doing this leads to the following event sequence in IE 5.5 on Windows 2000. Note this list is not the exact text you will see. For example, the top frameset page has no name to display:

1. Top Page parsed

2. LeftFrame parsed

3. RightFrame parsed

4. RightFrame window load event fires

5. LeftTopFrame parsed

6. LeftBottomFrame parsed

7. IFRAME parsed

8. Top Page's window load event fires

9. LeftFrame's window load event fires

10. LeftBottomFrame's window load event fires

11. IFRAME window load event fires

12. LeftTopFrame window load event fires

It is this order in Netscape 6 on Windows 2000:

1. Top Page parsed

2. LeftFrame parsed

3. RightFrame parsed

4. LeftTopFrame parsed

5. `LeftBottomFrame` parsed

6. `RightFrame` window load event fires

7. `LeftTopFrame` window load event fires

8. `IFRAME` parsed

9. `IFRAME`'s window load event fires

10. `LeftBottomFrame`'s window load event fires

11. `LeftFrame`'s window load event fires

12. Top Page's window load event fires

As we can see, the orders are different. Just to make it more complex, IE's order can actually vary and the alert boxes themselves can affect the order of events. It is also possible that the order you see will vary depending on your operating system as well as the version of IE you are running.

We can see that relying on an exact order of events, as regards the page being parsed and the window's `onLoad` being fired, is a potential recipe for disaster. Let's say we have a variable in one page, which is altered during another frame's parsing. We then rely on the value of this variable in a later event's `onLoad`, which in turn is relied on by yet another event's `onLoad`. This will cause problems, because firstly it will be very difficult to keep track of where a variable is being changed, and secondly because the order of events may not match our expectations and lead to a bug that is very difficult to track.

The answer to these problems is first to avoid reliance on the order of events – doing so is bad for your health and leaves you looking old before your time. Second, if we need global variables, then put them in the HEAD of the top frameset-defining page as that is always parsed first. Any initialization of the variables should also be done here, either at the time of declaring the variables, or by the window's load event. This then fires only after all the child frames have been parsed, so if we need to access code or the document objects of frames, we can do it here with less chance that the page is not yet parsed and therefore accessible. However, even then if the frame's page has failed to load we will face errors. As we'll see in the next section, we can avoid this by checking if what we want to use is actually available.

Coding Between Frames

Now we know how to access the window object of one frame, from code in another frame, we have the tricky stuff out the way. Using this knowledge for DHTML or for using variables or calling functions in other frames, is fairly easy and is the topic of this section.

DHTML Between Frames

As we'll be covering DHTML comprehensively in later chapters, we'll just look at very basic DHTML here. DHTML across frames is no different from DHTML in just one page; the thing that is different is the window object being used. Without frames it is the window object of the page that is being acted upon. In fact, as it's the default object, we often don't even use its name. In frames, it is not this page's window object, but that of another frame that is being acted upon.

We can demonstrate this easily with an example where we change the background color of a page.

Our page looks like this:

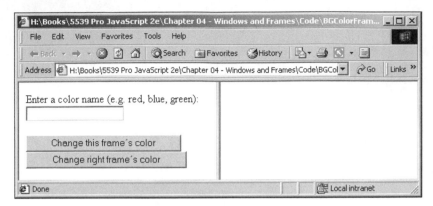

We can enter a color name in the text box, such as red, and then click the top button to change the background color of the same frame, or the bottom button to change the background color of the right frame.

We need just two pages for this, first the frameset defining top page:

```
<!-- BGColorFramesetTopPage.htm -->
<HTML>
<FRAMESET COLS='50%,*'>
   <FRAME SRC='BGColorLeftFrame.htm' NAME='LeftFrame'></FRAME>
   <FRAME SRC='about:blank' NAME='RightFrame'></FRAME>
</FRAMESET>
</HTML>
```

Second, we need a page for the left frame called `BGColorLeftFrame.htm`:

```
<!-- BGColorLeftFrame.htm -->
<HTML>
<HEAD>
   <SCRIPT LANGUAGE='JavaScript'>
      function cmdChangeLeftFrame_onclick()
      {
         var newBGColor = document.frmColorChanger.txtBGColor.value;
         document.bgColor = newBGColor;
      }

      function cmdChangeRightFrame_onclick()
      {
         var windowObject = window.parent.frames["RightFrame"];
         var newBGColor = document.frmColorChanger.txtBGColor.value;
         windowObject.document.bgColor = newBGColor;
      }
   </SCRIPT>
</HEAD>
<BODY>
   <FORM NAME='frmColorChanger'>
      <P>
         Enter a color name (e.g. red, blue, green):
         <INPUT TYPE='text' NAME='txtBGColor'></INPUT>
      </P>

      <INPUT TYPE='button' VALUE='Change this frame&acute;s color'
         NAME='cmdChangeLeftFrame'
```

```
                onClick='cmdChangeLeftFrame_onclick()'></INPUT>
          <INPUT TYPE='button' VALUE='Change right frame&acute;s color'
             NAME='cmdChangeRightFrame'
             onClick='cmdChangeRightFrame_onclick()'></INPUT>
      </FORM>
   </BODY>
   </HTML>
```

We can have a page loaded into the right frame, but we don't need one. The difference between the two functions, cmdChangeLeftFrame_onclick() to change the left frame's color, and cmdChangeRightFrame_onclick() to change the right frame, is simply which window object is referenced.

In the cmdChangeLeft_onclick() function shown below, we first obtain the color entered by the user in the form's text box. Then we use the window object (the window object of this frame) to reference the document object and change its bgColor property:

```
function cmdChangeLeft_onclick()
{
   var newBGColor = document.frmColorChanger.txtBGColor.value;
   window.document.bgColor = newBGColor;
}
```

In the second function, cmdChangeRight_onclick(), the principles are the same as far as changing the document's bgColor property goes, except we obtain a reference to the right frame's window object using the parent and frames properties to navigate the frame hierarchy:

```
function cmdChangeRight_onclick()
{
   var windowObject = window.parent.frames["RightFrame"];
   var newBGColor = document.frmColorChanger.txtBGColor.value;
   windowObject.document.bgColor = newBGColor;
}
```

Before we move on to look at accessing code in other frames, let's see how we can change our example so that instead of changing the background color, it changes the content loaded into the right frame. We can do this with the document object's open(), write(), writeln(), and close() methods. The open() method opens the document; basically it clears everything that went before. As is fairly obvious, the write() and writeln() methods write HTML to the page. The difference between them is that writeln() also writes a carriage return at the end of the line. Finally, the close() method closes the document to any further writing. Note that none of this changes the source page, but simply the HTML the browser displays.

Let's alter the cmdChangeRight_onclick() to write the text in the text box to the right frame rather than using it as a color value:

```
function cmdChangeRight_onclick()
{
   var windowObject = window.parent.frames["RightFrame"];
   var newText = document.frmColorChanger.txtBGColor.value;
   windowObject.document.open();
   windowObject.document.write(newText);
   windowObject.document.close();
}
```

Things start the same; we obtain a reference to the window object of the right frame. Then we obtain the text inside the text box, this text is our HTML that will be written to the document. Finally,, on the last three lines, we open the document for writing, write the HTML in newText to the document and finally close the document.

DHTML techniques will be studied in more depth in Chapter 10. When using DHTML and frames remember it is not the methods of DHTML that change, but simply which Window object and its associated document object that varies.

To finish, let's create a simple example to demonstrate where to access form controls in another frame and how to change the location of two pages at once.

First, we need to create the frameset-defining page; we'll name this AccessCrossFramesExample.htm:

```
<HTML>
<FRAMESET COLS='33%,33%,*'>
    <FRAME NAME='LeftFrame' SRC='GoPage.htm'></FRAME>
    <FRAME NAME='MidFrame' SRC='FormPage.htm'></FRAME>
    <FRAME NAME='RightFrame' SRC='FormPage.htm'></FRAME>
</FRAMESET>
</HTML>
```

Next, we need to create the GoPage.htm that will go in the left frame. It's this page that contains the code to change locations:

```
<HTML>
<HEAD>
    <SCRIPT>
        function cmdChangeLocations_onclick()
        {
            var midFrame = parent.frames[1];
            var rightFrame = parent.frames[2];

            var newMidFrameHref = midFrame.frmLocation.txtLocation.value;
            var newRightFrameHref = rightFrame.frmLocation.txtLocation.value;


            midFrame.location.href = newMidFrameHref;
            rightFrame.location.href = newRightFrameHref;
}
    </SCRIPT>
</HEAD>
<BODY>
<FORM>
    <INPUT type='button' VALUE='Change Page Locations'
      ONCLICK='cmdChangeLocations_onclick()'
      NAME='cmdChangeLocations'>
</FORM>
</BODY>
</HTML>
```

To save on typing, the mid and right frames actually load the same source page, FormPage.htm. Note the example would work exactly the same if we had two different pages loaded. Let's create the FormPage.htm page now:

```
<HTML>
<BODY>
<FORM NAME=frmLocation>
    <INPUT TYPE='text' NAME=txtLocation>
</FORM>
</BODY>
</HTML>
```

If we load `AccessCrossFramesExample.htm` into our browser we see the page below:

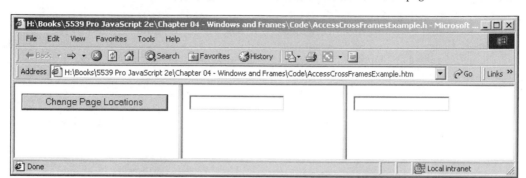

In the two text boxes, we enter the new page we want loaded into that frame when the Change Page Locations button is clicked. It can be a file location or a URL, and once we have done that, clicking the button will cause both pages to be loaded into the frames at once.

The code itself is quite simple. First, we created out frameset page and specified we wanted three columns, the first two taking up 33% of the page, and the final column on the right taking the remaining space, 34%.

The pages containing the text box are very simple, literally just the HTML of the page and one text box inside a form named `frmLocation`.

It's the first page (`GoPage.htm`) that contains all our code and in particular, the function `cmdChange Locations_onclick()` which we call in the page's `Change Page Locations onclick` event handler:

```
function cmdChangeLocations_onclick()
{
   var midFrame = parent.frames[1];
   var rightFrame = parent.frames[2];

   var newMidFrameHref = midFrame.frmLocation.txtLocation.value;
   var newRightFrameHref = rightFrame.frmLocation.txtLocation.value;

   midFrame.location.href = newMidFrameHref;
   rightFrame.location.href = newRightFrameHref;
}
```

The function first obtains references to the window objects of the frame's `MidFrame` and `RightFrame`, which in this case have our `FormPage.htm` loaded. This page's `parent` window (the frameset-defining window), contains the `frames` array, and we use this to access the other frames. Remember, that the `frames` array is zero based, so 0 is the first frame created in the HTML. In other words, we are referring to the frame on the left with `GoPage.htm` loaded, and 1 and 2 being `MidFrame` and `RightFrame` respectively.

Once we have the reference to the frames, we can then use these references to access the `frmLocation` form that is inside the pages. This enables us to access the `form` elements. In the next lines, we do just that, and set variables `newMidFrameHref` and `newRightFrameHref` to the values of `txtLocation` text box that is in each of the two frames (mid and right).

Finally, on the last two lines, we change the `location.href` of each of the frames to load in another page. Obviously, if we load a page without the `txtLocation` text box, then clicking the Change Page Locations button will throw an error. The concept of accessing forms in other frames and how to change the location of the page inside two or more frames at once is something that can be very useful.

Accessing Code in One Frame from Another Frame

As with DHTML across frames, once you've navigated the frame hierarchy and got the window object of the frame with the code in, then everything else is easy. In fact, it's not different from calling functions or using variables in the current page. Again, it's just whose window object we're accessing that changes. So if we are accessing a variable or function in the same page, in longhand:

```
window.variableName
window.functionName()
```

Or for short (and as we're familiar with), we normally just write the names as the window object is assumed by default:

```
varibleName
functionName()
```

When it's a variable or function in another frame, then it's simply a reference to the window object of that frame and then the function or variable name:

```
window.parent.frames["MyFrameName"].variableName
window.parent.frames["MyFrameName"].functionName()
```

Let's take our original simple frameset example with just the frameset defining page and the left and right frame pages. Let's add a script block with a single method and a single variable inside the top frame and the right frame of each of the page's HEAD tags. So for the top frameset page we add:

```
<!-- NewSimpleFrameset.htm -->
<HTML>
<HEAD>
   <SCRIPT LANGUAGE='JavaScript'>
      var frameName = "Top Frameset Defining Page";

      function sayWhoAmI()
      {
         return "I'm the " + frameName;
      }
   </SCRIPT>
</HEAD>
<FRAMESET cols='50%,*'>
   <FRAME SRC='NewSimpleLeftFrame.htm' NAME='LeftFrame'>
   <FRAME SRC='NewSimpleRightFrame.htm' NAME='RightFrame'>
</FRAMESET>
</HTML>
```

Then change the right frame's page to:

```
<HTML>
<HEAD>
   <SCRIPT LANGUAGE='JavaScript'>
      var frameName = "Right Frame Page";

      function sayWhoAmI()
      {
         return "I'm the " + frameName;
      }
   </SCRIPT>
</HEAD>
<BODY>
```

```
    <H3>Right Frame</H3>
</BODY>
</HTML>
```

Now, lets add a couple of buttons to the left frame's page that use the variables and call the functions. Change the left frame's page to that shown below:

```
<HTML>
<HEAD>
    <SCRIPT LANGUAGE='JavaScript'>
        function useOtherFrameCode(otherFrameWindowObject)
        {
            alert("Variable frameName is " + otherFrameWindowObject.frameName);
            alert("Return value of function sayWhoAmI is " +
                otherFrameWindowObject.sayWhoAmI());
        }
    </SCRIPT>
</HEAD>
<BODY>
    <H3>Left Frame</H3>

    <FORM NAME='form1'>
        <INPUT TYPE='button' VALUE='Use Right Frame Code'
            onClick='useOtherFrameCode(window.parent.frames["RightFrame"]);'
            NAME='cmdUseRightFrame'></INPUT>
        <INPUT TYPE='button' VALUE='Use Top Frame Code'
            onClick='useOtherFrameCode(window.parent);'
            NAME='cmdUseTopFrame'></INPUT>
    </FORM>
</BODY>
</HTML>
```

This page should look like this in IE 5.5+:

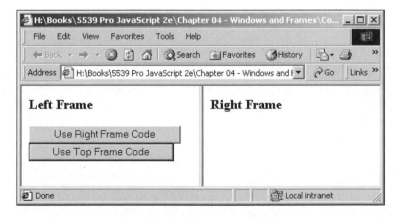

We have just one function in the page that's called by both the buttons' onClick event handler. The difference is which window object reference is passed. In the first button's onClick event handler, we call the useOtherFrameCode() function and pass the right frame's window object. In the second button, we pass the window object of the parent frameset-defining page. Either way, when it comes to using the code in the useOtherFrameCode() function, it is exactly the same – just use the variable and call the function as we would normally, but with just the window referenced being different.

Using the ScriptSpace of the Top Frame

What do we mean by the "ScriptSpace" of the top frame? We use it here to refer to JavaScript inside a SCRIPT tag, inserted into the head of the frameset-defining page at the very top of the frameset hierarchy. It is also assumed that this very top frameset page does not change when the user navigates the website, only the pages inside its frame change. We created a ScriptSpace in the top frameset page of our previous example.

So what's the big deal about the top frameset's ScriptSpace? There are two very big advantages of using the ScriptSpace in the top frame. First, as the page is never unloaded while browsing the website it means any page level variables created there don't get unloaded and retain their values. This makes the top frameset page's ScriptSpace a great way of persisting session state on the client machine. It's something that is used in the Chapter 22, *Shopping Cart Application* to keep track of items in the user's shopping cart while they browse the website. It means that we don't need to store information in cookies, unless of course we want to persist data after the user leaves the web site, closes the browser or moves out of the frameset.

The second advantage of the top frameset's ScriptSpace is that it gives us a place to put all our functions and variables which are used repeatedly throughout the website. In comparison to having them repeated in each page, this saves download time and keeps functions together in one place. Keeping functions in one place means that if we spot a bug in a function we only need to fix the bug once, we don't need to go through every page that has a copy of that function and fix it. Our code also becomes more maintainable and any changes or improvements involve changes to just the global functions and not to each place the function is used.

Frames and Browser Security

With frames containing pages from the same URL, we have the same access to the window and document object's properties and methods of other frames as we do when they are the window and document objects of the same page. This is because the pages are all from the same origin, based on domain name, sub domain name or file address. Then they are our own pages and we should be allowed to do what we like.

However, if the pages in frames are of different origins, then we find we're much more limited in what we can do. This is really for our own security, as it stops hackers loading our pages into their framesets and then accessing all the code and page elements that we can do ourselves. The restrictions are fairly severe, perhaps too severe, and mean that we should avoid scripting across frames where the pages are hosted on different servers or with different domain names.

In the previous example, we had the left frame calling code in the top or right frames. Imagine the pages are loaded from a server, rather than loaded directly using the local file system, and we leave the frameset page and left pages on one server and move the right frame page to a different server on a different domain. If we try our page and click the button to access the right page's code from the left page, we'll see this error in Internet Explorer:

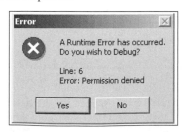

In Netscape 6, we need to use the JavaScript console to see the message, which is "Uncaught Exception: Null" – not especially helpful, but it's Netscape's way of saying "I can't access the object in question and am throwing an exception instead". We're not stopped completely from accessing the window object, but we are very restricted, essentially to doing things that are not very useful. In the next section, when we look at cross browser window scripting, we'll see the same security restrictions are in force.

There is no easy way around the restrictions in Internet Explorer, but Netscape browsers do support scripts that have been digitally signed to validate their origin. These scripts suffer less restriction than unsigned scripts, but it does mean that our pages won't be accessible from Internet Explorer, and the certificate required for signing is quite expensive.

Frame Events

Before we move onto windows, let's look at some of the more useful events specific to frames. The `frame` object has the load event and the frameset. The `FRAMESET` tag also has the load event, but also has an unload event.

To capture these events, we add event handlers to the `FRAME` and `FRAMESET` tags. In the code below which is taken from our `SimpleFrameset.htm` example, we have added these event handlers. Note this example only works in IE4+ and Netscape 6+:

```
<HTML>
<FRAMESET COLS='50%,*'
      onload='alert("FramesetLoaded")'
      onunload="alert('FramesetUnloaded')">

   <FRAME SRC='SimpleLeftFrame.htm'
      NAME='LeftFrame'
      onload='alert("LeftFrameLoaded")'>

   <FRAME SRC='SimpleRightFrame.htm' NAME='RightFrame'>
</FRAMESET>
</HTML>
```

The `load` event fires when the frame or frameset is first loaded into the browser, while the `unload` event fires when the browser window is closed or when the user navigates to another page.

Windows

In this section, we concentrate on creating new browser windows separate from the current one. We'll start by seeing how we can create simple pop-up boxes using the `alert()`, `confirm()` and `prompt()` methods. Then we'll look at how to create whole new browser windows. Once we have seen how to create a new window, we'll then look at how code can be used to communicate between them and change the contents of the new window's page. Finally, we'll see how to close the windows and check to see if the user has closed a window.

Basic Pop-Up Windows

The easiest windows to create are those we create with the `alert()`, `prompt()` and `confirm()` methods, which themselves are methods of the `window` object of the current browser window.

The `alert()` method displays a modal pop-up window, which contains the message we supply as its only parameter. By modal, we mean that the user must deal with the pop-up box before they can return to the page that opened it. Additionally, all execution and page loading halts until the user has closed the pop-up window.

So to display a message saying "So long and thanks for all the fish", we would write:

```
<HTML>
<BODY>
   <SCRIPT>
   alert("So long and thanks for all the fish");
   </SCRIPT>
</BODY>
</HTML>
```

This displays:

We can use the `alert()` method anywhere we can normally use JavaScript, such as inside the page as it is loaded or attached to an event handler. Note that using either the `alert()`, `prompt()` or `confirm()` method in the window's onunload event handler will not work in Netscape 4.

Next, we have the `prompt()` method, which like `alert()` displays the first argument passed to it, but it also has a text box for the user to enter information. When they close the box, whatever they have entered is returned to us. The method has a second option argument that is a default value to be displayed inside the text box. So for example:

```
<HTML>
<BODY>
   <SCRIPT>
   var userInput = prompt("What is the price of fish these days?",
       "Not Much");
   alert(userInput);
   </SCRIPT>
</BODY>
</HTML>
```

This will display:

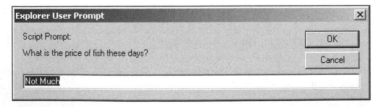

Note that if the user clicks Cancel then null will be returned, we can check for this:

```
if (userInput == null)
{
   // code to handle null
}
```

Finally, we have the `confirm()` method. This is similar to the `alert()` method, except that with this function, two buttons are displayed instead: OK and Cancel. If the user clicks OK then the Boolean value `true` is returned, otherwise `false` is returned. It's useful for situations where we want to confirm (hence its name) a certain course of action with the user, such as:

```
<HTML>
<BODY>
   <SCRIPT>
   var userInput = confirm("Do you wish to erase your hard drive?");
   if (userInput == true)
   {
      alert("Your hard drive is now erased");
   }
   else
   {
      alert("Your hard drive and your lovely data are still intact");
   }
   </SCRIPT>
</BODY>
</HTML>
```

This will show:

That completes our look at simple pop-up boxes. It's now time to turn to creating new browser windows.

Opening a New Browser Window

Opening a new window requires the use of the window object's open() method. Each window opened is independent of the window that opened it, the **opener** window. This means that if the opener window is closed, the opened windows remain open and vice versa. We'll see later how it's possible for opener and pop-up windows to access each other both in terms of code and DHTML.

The open() method takes four parameters although all of them are optional. So at its simplest, the following will open a new, blank window:

```
window.open();
```

No page will be loaded inside it, its size and appearance will be the default values, it does not have a name, and will not replace any existing windows previously opened. Its size and position will vary between browser type and platform.

Although the window will contain a blank page, we can write to the page and generally manipulate it through its window object. So, how do we get access to the window object of the newly opened window? When we open the window with the open() method, it returns a reference to the window object of the newly created window. It's up to us to store this reference in a variable, so that we can manipulate it later. If we want to manipulate the window outside of the function that created it, then clearly the variable must have page level scope:

```
var myWindowObject;

function openAWindow()
{
   myWindowObject = window.open();
}
```

We will see later in the chapter how to manipulate the window object.

Blank default sized and positioned windows are not very exciting, so how can we set things ourselves? This is where the four optional parameters of the open() method come in. The open() method's first parameter is the URL of the page to be loaded into the new window. The second parameter specifies a name for the window. However don't think this allows us to access the window by its name, but rather the name is used as the target attribute on FORM or A HTML elements. So if we want a hyperlink to open a page in our separate browser window, first we open the window:

```
var myWindow = window.open("MyURL","MyWindowName");
```

Then any hyperlink with its target attribute set to MyWindowName will open the page, not in the same browser window as the A element, but instead in our separate browser window:

```
<A HREF='SomePage.htm' TARGET='MyWindowName'>Click Me</A>
```

We will look at defining the look of the window in the next section, but before we do let's mention the fourth parameter, which is specific to IE 4+. The fourth parameter contains a Boolean, which determines whether the URL that is loaded into the new window should create a new entry in the window's browsing history, or replace the current entry in the browsing history. If it is set to true, then no new history entry is created. This clearly only applies if the window was already open and we are opening it again. This leads to the question of if open() opens a new browser window, then how can we possibly be opening the same window again?

When we give a window a name (specify a value for the second parameter of the open() method) and if we later open another window with the same name, then the first window is replaced by the second, rather than two windows with the same name co-existing. The only trouble is that in this circumstance, it's easy for the second window to become hidden behind the main window. In this case, after opening the window, use the focus() method to ensure it is brought to the front:

```
var myWindow = window.open("","MyWindowName");
myWindow.focus();
```

The myWindow.focus() method will ensure the window is in front of the opening window. Also note that if we don't want to specify a parameter for the window.open() method, we don't have to, unless of course we're passing later parameters, as we are in the example. In this case an empty string for the string parameters is necessary.

Specifying the Look of a New Window

A list of the more commonly used cross browser compatible features is shown below:

Window Feature	Possible Values	Description
directories	yes, no	Show directory buttons
height	Integer	Height of new window's content area in pixels
left	Integer	Window's left starting position in pixels
location	yes, no	Show location text field
menubar	yes, no	Show menubar
resizable	yes, no	User can re-size the window once opened

Window Feature	Possible Values	Description
scrollbars	yes, no	Show scrollbars if page too large to fit in window
status	yes, no	Show status bar
toolbar	yes, no	Show toolbar
top	Integer	Window's top start position in pixels
width	Integer	Width of new window's content area in pixels

Note that this is not an exhaustive list; there are other features specific only to IE or NN that are not covered here. You can find a complete list of JavaScript's window features at
http://www.webreference.com/js/tutorial1/features.html#alwaysLowered.

Inside the string passed to the third parameter of the open() method, we simply specify each attribute name, followed by an equals sign and the value it should be set to. Between each attribute name=value pair, we need to have a comma. We only have to set the attributes we want to change and don't need to specify them all. So let's say we want the new window to be opened in position 50 pixels left, 100 pixels down and with no toolbar:

```
var myWindow =
    window.open("MyPage.htm","MyWindowName","left=50,top=100,toolbar=no")
```

> **It is important to note that in order to gain the best browser compatibility, there must be no spaces after the commas that separate the attributes.**

Reopening Windows With Internet Explorer 4.0

Some IE 4, but not 5.0+, installations have a problem with reopening existing windows. If a window is already open, then attempting to reopen it gives an error instead of the expected result. In the following example, if loaded into IE 4, try clicking the first link, ignoring the new window, and clicking the second link in the original window:

```
<!-- ReopeningWindows.htm -->
<HTML>
<BODY>
    <A HREF='page2.html'
       ONCLICK='window.open("page2.html", "new_win"); return false;'>
       Page 2
    </A>
    <BR>
    <A HREF='page3.html'
       ONCLICK='window.open("page3.html", "new_win"); return false;'>
       Page 3
    </A>
</BODY>
</HTML>
```

The problem is that window.open() won't work properly if a window with the same name already exists, though this was remedied in Internet Explorer 5.0.

The work-around is to only open the new window if it doesn't already exist. We do this by checking a reference to the new window before we open it. We have to save that reference at some point too. Each of the onClick events above should be changed and have this bit of script instead, although the URLs will obviously be different for each link:

```
if (window.winref && !window.winref.closed)
    window.winref.replace("page2.html");
else
    window.winref = window.open("page2.html","new_win");
return false;
```

Of course, you may have to format it differently (or put it in a JavaScript function) in order to fit the code sensibly into the event handler.

Moving and Resizing Windows

Once you have opened a window, you can change its position on screen and its size using the window object's resizeTo() and moveTo() methods, both of which take two arguments in pixels.

Let's imagine that, having just opened a new window, we want to make it 350 pixels wide by 200 pixels high, and move it to a position 100 pixels from the left of the screen and 400 pixels from the top. The code needed would be:

```
var newWindow =
    window.open("myURL",myWindow,"width=125,height=150,resizable");
newWindow.resizeTo(350,200);
newWindow.moveTo(100,400);
```

You can see that, after opening our window in the first line, we then resize it to 350 pixels wide by 200 pixels high in the second line. Then in the third line, we move it so it is 100 pixels from the left of the screen and 400 pixels from the top of the screen.

> Note that whereas for IE 4+ and NN 6, the dimensions refer to the outside of the window, in NN4 it refers to the content of the window, (the page itself and not the browser's normal menu bars and frames).

In addition to resizeTo() and moveTo(), there are also the methods resizeBy() and moveBy(). These resize or move the window by a certain amount, for example resizeTo(200,200) would not make the window 200 pixels by 200 pixels, but instead would increase its current size by 200 pixels.

Opening a Dialog Window

All the windows we've created so far, act independently of each other. We can switch between windows, we can close one window and the rest remain open and so on. However, sometimes it's useful to be able to obtain information from a user, or even simply inform them of something and do so inside another window. Only once the user has read the message or entered the information do we want them to be able to close the pop-up dialog window and return to the main window. Only IE 4+ supports a special kind of window called a dialog window.

In fact, since IE 5, there are now two types of dialog window we can open, a **modal** dialog window, supported by IE 4+, and one the Microsoft documentation describes as **modeless**. A modeless window is essentially a window always floating above the opener window and is supported only by IE 5+. Both of them are identical in that that they open a new window, which always remains above the opening page. The difference is that the modal window won't let you return to the opening page until you have dealt with it and closed it. Also, execution of scripts and loading of pages comes to a halt and the opener window is frozen until the user closes the modal dialog window.

The modeless dialog window does allow the user to return to the opener window even though the modeless window will remain on top. Additionally, the opener window is not frozen and scripts still continue running and pages loading. If the user navigates the opener window away from the original page then associated modeless dialog windows are closed.

The window object has the two methods required to open the modal and modeless windows, showModalDialog() and showModelessDialog(). They each take up to three parameters; the URL of the page to be loaded into the dialog window, any information we want to be passed to the new window and finally, the features of the window.

The methods also return values; the showModelessDialog() method returns a reference to the window object of the new window, just as the window.open() method did. However, given that the execution of scripts stops on the line opening the modal dialog window, and doesn't continue until the user closes the window, there would be little point in showModalDialog() returning a reference to a window object. What it does return, is information set by the dialog window itself using the window object's returnValue property. The returnValue property only applies to modal dialog windows.

All the parameters, apart from the first that specifies the URL, are optional. Note there is no name property as there was with the window.open() method. So to open a modal dialog box, we write:

```
var returnValue = showModalDialog("MyPage.htm");
alert(returnValue);
```

The alert statement has been added at the end to emphasize that the alert statement will not execute until the user closes the modal dialog window. Note that returnValue will be empty unless we actually return a value from the opened page, something we'll see shortly.

To open a modeless dialog window:

```
var windowObjectRef = showModelessDialog("MyPage.htm");
alert(windowObjectRef.location.href);
```

Here, the alert line will execute immediately after the window has been shown and not wait until the user has closed the window.

The second and optional parameter of the dialog show methods is one that allows us to pass information to the dialog window. The data type can be any JavaScript data type, such as a string, number, object, or even an array of values. The dialog window can pick up the information using the read only dialogArguments property of the window object. So let's say we open a dialog window like this:

```
var windowObjectRef = showModelessDialog("MyPage.htm","Some Data");
```

In the page loaded into the dialog window, we could extract the data passed like this:

```
alert(window.dialogArguments);
```

This would display "Some Data". Note that only 4096 characters (4K) of string data can be passed and anything past that is discarded.

The third parameter is the features parameter, a little like the features parameter of the window.open() method we saw earlier, though there are two important differences. The first is that the list of feature attributes are different from the ones associated with window.open() and secondly, just as CSS attributes are separated with semi-colons, so are the attributes of dialog window features. This is in contrast to window.open() where its feature attributes were separated by commas. Also again like CSS, the value of an attribute is not specified after an equals sign but after a colon. The full list of possible features, taken from a table in the Wrox Press book *JavaScript Programmer's Reference*, by Cliff Wootton (ISBN: 1-861004-59-1), is shown below:

Feature	Range	Default	Description
center:	yes, no, 1, 0, on, off	yes	Controls dialog window centering within the desktop
dialogHeight:	height value	none	Sets the dialog window height
dialogLeft:	left position	none	Sets the left edge coordinate of the dialog window relative to the upper-left corner of the desktop
dialogTop:	top position	none	Sets the top edge coordinate of the dialog window relative to the upper-left corner of the desktop
dialogWidth:	width value	none	Sets the dialog window width
edge:	sunken, raised	raised	Defines the dialog window edge style
help:	yes, no, 1, 0, on, off	yes	Controls the context-sensitive Help icon
resizable:	yes, no, 1, 0, on, off	no	Controls the resize box. IE 5+
scroll:	yes, no, 1, 0, on, off	yes	Defines whether the dialog window has scrollbars. IE 5+ only
status:	yes, no, 1, 0, on, off	Varies	Defines whether the dialog window has a status bar

So to open a modal dialog window with no status bar, a left edge at 100 pixels, and the top at 50 pixels, we would write:

```
var returnValue = window.showModalDialog
    ("MyPage.htm","","status:no;dialogLeft:100px;dialogTop:50px")
```

Unfortunately, no version of Netscape supports the dialog methods, but they can be emulated using the focus() method and information passing by access of variables between windows, which we'll see shortly.

Coding Between Windows

We saw how coding between different frames involved obtaining a reference to the window object of the frame we wished to access. This involves using properties of the window object such as top, parent, and the frames array. We'll see in this section that the principles are the same, in that we need to obtain references to the window object of opened and opener windows. The difference compared to frames is the properties we need to use and the relationship of opener and opened windows.

Window Hierarchy

The hierarchy for new windows is much simpler than that for frames. When we open a separate window with window.open() it returns a reference to the window object of the opened window. We need to store this if we want to access the new window from the opener window.

If we want to access the opener window object from the opened window's page, then we need to use the opener property of the window object. So, we open a new window like this:

```
var openedWindowObject = window.open("SomePage.htm");
```

We access the new window using the reference to the window object returned into the openedWindowObject variable. In SomePage.htm, if we wanted to access the window object of the opener window, we would write this:

```
var openerWindowObject = window.opener;
```

The hierarchy is a simple vertical hierarchy. If in the opened window we opened yet another window our hierarchy would be:

There is no windows array, as there was a frames array when we looked at frames, so moving up and down the hierarchy is fairly easy. There is also no equivalent of the top property either.

DHTML Between Windows

As with frames, once we know how to access a particular window object, then everything else becomes easy. Everything said about cross-frame DHTML applies to cross-window DHTML. Let's look at an example where we open a new window, set its background color to red, and write the words "HELP!!!" inside it.

Our window-opening page looks like this:

```
<!--DHTML Between Windows-->
<HTML>
<HEAD>
   <SCRIPT LANGUAGE='JavaScript'>
      function openWindow()
      {
         var helpWindow = window.open();

         helpWindow.document.open();
         helpWindow.document.bgColor = "red";
         helpWindow.document.write("<H3>HELP!!!</H3>");
         helpWindow.document.close();
      }
   </SCRIPT>
</HEAD>
<BODY>
   <FORM>
      <INPUT TYPE='button' VALUE='Open Window'
         onClick='openWindow();'
         name='cmdOpenWindow'>
   </FORM>
</BODY>
</HTML>
```

This displays a page with a single button, shown below:

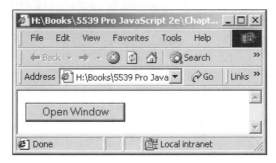

When the button is clicked, the openWindow() function is called. This starts by opening a blank window (a window with no page loaded). We store the reference to the new window's window object in the helpWindow variable.

With the window object reference in helpWindow, we can do similar things to what we can do to the current page's window. In this case, we clear the document by opening it. Then we change the bgColor to red. We need to do this after we clear the document; otherwise the bgColor change is cleared also. Then we write some HTML to the document before finally closing the document to new information.

Let's change our example so that the opener window has a form. The opened window will also contain a form that allows the user to enter a number and click a button to send the information to the opener's form. The opener window will then transfer this to the original form.

The page that opens the new window is this:

```
<!--Opener Window with Form -->
<HTML>
<HEAD>
```

```
<SCRIPT LANGUAGE='JavaScript'>
   function openWindow()
   {
      var helpWindow = window.open
         ("GetAge.htm","GetAge","toolbar=no,width=250,height=150,left=300");
      helpWindow.focus();
   }
</SCRIPT>
</HEAD>
<BODY>
   <FORM NAME='frmAge'>
      <INPUT TYPE='text' NAME='txtAge'></INPUT>
      <BR>
      <INPUT TYPE='button' VALUE='Open Window'
         onclick='openWindow()' NAME='cmdOpenWindow'>
   </FORM>
</BODY>
</HTML>
```

Now, we need to create the GetAge.htm page that opens in a new window:

```
<!--GetAge -->
<HTML>
<HEAD>
   <SCRIPT LANGUAGE='JavaScript'>
      function sendValue()
      {
         var age = window.document.frmAge.txtAge.value;
         window.opener.document.frmAge.txtAge.value = age;
      }
   </SCRIPT>
</HEAD>
<BODY>
   <FORM NAME='frmAge'>
      Enter Your Age:
      <BR>
      <INPUT TYPE='text' NAME='txtAge' VALUE='0'></INPUT>
      <BR>
      <INPUT TYPE='button' VALUE='Ok'
         NAME='cmdAge' onClick='sendValue();'></INPUT>
   </FORM>
</BODY>
</HTML>
```

Let's look at the function that opens the new window:

```
function openWindow()
{
   var helpWindow = window.open
   ("GetAge.htm","GetAge","toolbar=no,width=250,height=150,left=300");
   helpWindow.focus();
}
```

We've loaded the GetAge.htm in as the first parameter. For the second parameter, we have specified a name. If we don't include a name for our window, each time the **Open Window** button is clicked the code will open a brand new window, leaving any existing windows open. If we give the window a name, clicking the **Open Window** button will replace any window opened with the same name, hence we don't end up with lots of open windows. We've also switched off the toolbar to make the window more dialog box-like.

In the second line, we use the window object's `focus()` method to make sure that the opened window always appears in front of the current window. This is especially important when the same window (a window with the same name) is opened repeatedly.

Lets turn to the `GetAge.htm` page and see how it passes the information entered by the user back to the opener window's form.

When the button is clicked the `sendValue()` function is called:

```
function sendValue()
{
    var age = window.document.frmAge.txtAge.value;
    window.opener.document.frmAge.txtAge.value = age;
}
```

This obtains the age from the form and then uses the `window.opener` property to get a reference to the `window` object that opened this window and the form element contained in that window.

Accessing Code In One Window From Another Window

As with frames, all a window needs to do to call functions and access variables in other windows is get a reference to the window object of the window with the functions and variables in. We've seen that the key to doing this is storing the window object returned by `window.open()` and using the `window.opener` property to gain a reference to the window object that opened this window. Once we've done that, the rest is easy. For example, if we open a new window like this:

```
var windowObject = window.open("MyPage.htm");
```

`MyPage.htm` has a variable with page scope called `myVar`, and a function called `myFunction()`. To make use of them we just write:

```
windowObject.myVar;
windowObject.myFunction();
```

If `MyPage.htm` wants to call variables and functions in the opener window, it just uses `window.opener`:

```
window.opener.myVar;
window.opener.myFunction();
```

Windows and Browser Security

Everything said about frames and browser security applies to windows. If the page loaded into a new window is from the same URL as the page doing the opening, then we are free to manipulate the window and its document. However, if the URL of the new window is different, then although we can access its window object, we will find ourselves very restricted as to what we can do. Access to DHTML and code inside the new window is not possible, although NN4 is an exception and does allow access to code inside the other window.

Closing Windows

In this final section, we'll look at how we can close a window, how to check if a window is closed, and also mention the objects' `unload` event.

Closing a window requires use of the `window.close()` method. With IE, however if we close a window that was opened by the user rather than by our code, we get a message stating that the web page we are viewing is trying to close the window. We then have the option whether or not to close the window by clicking **Yes** or **No**.

Although this does not make for a major problem it does make our interface look a little less professional, and it does mean we can't be sure that a `window.close()` will actually have the desired effect, the user may have clicked No. Remember, this only applies to windows not opened by our own code.

How can we tell if a browser window is still open? We can be sure when our code has closed it, but there's nothing to stop the user closing a window. In an earlier example, we had an opened window passing back information entered in a form to the opener window. If the user closes the opener window, but leaves the other window open, then our code will throw an error. One way around this is to use the `window.closed` property to see if it is still in existence. Let's alter the example, `GetAge.htm`, to cope with the user closing the parent window:

```
<!-- GetAge2.htm -->
<HTML>
<HEAD>
    <SCRIPT LANGUAGE='JavaScript'>
        function sendValue()
        {
            if (window.opener.closed)
            {
                alert("Someone has stolen the window");
            }
            else
            {
                var age = window.document.frmAge.txtAge.value;
                window.opener.document.frmAge.txtAge.value = age;
            }
        }
    </SCRIPT>
</HEAD>
<BODY>
    <FORM NAME='frmAge'>
        Enter Your Age:
        <BR>
        <INPUT TYPE='text' NAME='txtAge' VALUE='0'></INPUT>
        <BR>
        <INPUT TYPE='button' VALUE='Ok' NAME='cmdAge'
            onClick='sendValue();'></INPUT>
    </FORM>
</BODY>
</HTML>
```

This time, we check to see if the window is actually still there by using `window.opener.closed`.

Finally, we'll briefly mention the `window` object's `unload` event. This event fires when the user either browses to another page, or closes the browser window. To capture it we need to add the onunload event handler to the BODY tag:

```
<BODY onunload='myFunction()'>
```

Note that with Netscape 4 any attempts to use `alert()`, `prompt()` *or* `confirm()` *will fail.*

Summary

In this chapter, we looked at how JavaScript interacts with HTML frames and new browser windows. We saw that framesets are organized into an almost family tree like parent/child structure. Each child window object of a frameset-defining page is contained inside the `frames` array and accessible by either its index or name. Each child frame has access to its parent via the `window` object's `parent` and `top` properties.

We also looked at creating new browser windows using JavaScript. Creating a standard browser window required use of the window object's open() method. We also saw that IE allows us to create dialog windows, essentially windows that always remain above the opener window. As with frames, child and parent windows can access each other. A child window can access the window object of the window that opened it using the opener property. In the case of a parent window, accessing a child was necessary to ensure that the reference to the child window object returned by the window.open() method was stored in a variable for access later.

For both frames and windows, we saw that once we obtained a reference to the window object of the frame or window we wanted to access, then access to code inside the frame/window and DHTML manipulation of the document was fairly easy. However, we did learn that it's only possible to fully manipulate a frame or window where the page loaded inside is from our website (shares the same domain name).

In the next chapter, we turn our attention to JavaScript scripting with forms and data.

Pro JavaScript 2nd Edition

5

Forms and Data

Without client-side scripting, a web browser can't do much other than display information. HTML form elements by themselves aren't that flexible – all that plain HTML form elements can do, is to send any user data directly to a web server. With the addition of JavaScript, a web browser's form elements take on some of the attributes of more data-oriented software tools, such as 4GL form-building packages and spreadsheets. Without JavaScript or an alternate scripting language, some HTML tags such as `<INPUT TYPE='button'>` are entirely useless, without an `onClick` event handler and code inside it, the button won't do anything when clicked.

Once data input is possible in a web browser, a browser page starts to look like the front end of a database client. However, the form support built into HTML doesn't supply many options for storing data. If web pages with forms are going to take on some of the attributes of database clients, then more flexible options are required. Once JavaScript enters the picture, there are several places in a browser where data can be placed apart from inside HTML fields, for example in the URL itself, using cookies, using framesets, and putting JavaScript in the top frame, as we did in Chapter 4 – Windows and Frames.

The main problem with forms in an HTML document, is that if the form is submitted, the data has to go somewhere to be processed. This chapter describes only the management of forms and data on the client side.

Forms

JavaScript can interact with HTML forms directly in a number of ways. It can:

- ❑ Write out `<FORM>` element tags with inline JavaScript, as for other HTML tags
- ❑ Act as event handlers for `FORM` elements, via HTML tag attributes or host object properties
- ❑ Read and modify the values of most `FORM` elements
- ❑ Access and change form attributes, for example disable a button using the IE's `disabled` property
- ❑ Construct `FORM` elements in a limited way, or more flexibly if Dynamic HTML is used

It is beyond these basic tasks however that JavaScript adds real value to forms and HTML. The higher-level tasks that JavaScript can achieve are:

❑ Validating and correcting user data

❑ Performing calculations on user data

❑ Storing and forwarding user data

❑ Controlling user navigation through the data input process

All these tasks can happen solely inside the browser, without any need for network requests resulting in smoother form operation results. Without JavaScript, every form check or change requires that a form's details be passed to a web server for a response, which can slow processing down considerably.

Form Objects

HTML forms are part of HTML documents, so it's no surprise that form-style tags are reflected in JavaScript as objects that are properties of the document object.

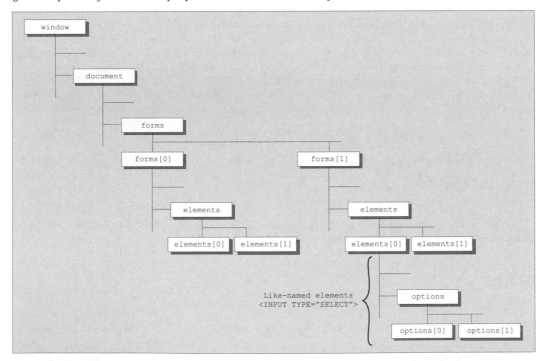

This diagram shows the basic structure of the forms part of the Document Object Model (DOM). The specific methods and properties are listed in Appendix F. Key features are described in this chapter.

In addition to the objects in the above diagram, there are several miscellaneous features of web browsers that can assist with forms. These are also described in this chapter.

Form Objects Explained

An HTML document can contain more than one form; to allow us to access it we have the `document` object's `forms` property, which contains an array of all the forms inside the page. Each array element contains a reference to each form object, and these objects have as properties all the important attributes of the corresponding `<FORM>` tag. We'll see shortly that as well as being able to access each form using the `document.forms` property, we can also use `document.frmName` and also the DOM method `getElementById()` if we give the form an ID. We'll talk about the alternative methods shortly.

Internet Explorer and Netscape 6+ HTML documents can have text fields and buttons without any `<FORM>` tag, for Netscape 4 they must be inside a form. One exception to this, is if form controls exist both within and outside a `<FORM>` tag, then the ones outside the tag are ignored. For Netscape 4, `form` elements must always be inside a `<FORM>` tag, or else they won't appear to the user or the JavaScript processor at all.

Each `form` object has an `elements` property that is an array. Each array element is one of the form controls in the HTML form. The form controls populate the array in the same order that they appear in the HTML document's source, not as they appear on the screen. `<INPUT>`, `<BUTTON>`, `<TEXTAREA>`, and `<SELECT>` tags, are all the form controls available and are represented as a `forms` array element, one for each instance in the document. This includes `<INPUT TYPE='HIDDEN'>`. Effectively, a form control and a form element are equivalent – the former emphasizes what the user visibly sees, the latter emphasizes an object the scriptwriter sees.

It's best to think of the individual element objects as being of a generic input type of object, rather than being specifically a `checkbox` or `textarea` object. This is because these objects have in common several properties such as `type`, `value`, `name`, and `form`. The `type` property allows us to discover from within JavaScript, which HTML tag was used to create the element we are examining. It reflects the `TYPE` attribute of the `<INPUT>` tag, as well as covering the `<SELECT>` tag and the `<TEXTAREA>` tag. The `value` property is the current data value held by the control. The `name` property reflects the `NAME` attribute of the corresponding tag. The `form` property refers back to the `forms` array element that this form control is a part of. In addition to these basic properties, there are properties that only apply to some types of control, and properties for event handlers (described further on). See the Appendices for complete lists of object properties.

In the simple example below, we have various form elements inside a form. We then use JavaScript to loop through the elements and write their name, index in form, and type to the page:

```
<!-- Example_01.htm -->
<HTML>
<BODY>
<FORM NAME=form1>
    <INPUT TYPE="text" NAME=text1><BR>
    <INPUT TYPE="password" NAME=password1><BR>
    <INPUT TYPE="file" NAME=file1><BR>
    <TEXTAREA rows=2 cols=20 NAME=textarea1>
    </TEXTAREA><BR>
    <INPUT TYPE="checkbox" NAME=checkbox1><BR>
    <INPUT TYPE="radio" NAME=radio1>
    <INPUT TYPE="radio" NAME=radio1>
    <INPUT TYPE="radio" NAME=radio1><BR>
    <SELECT id=select1 NAME=select1>
        <OPTION VALUE=Option1>Option1</OPTION>
        <OPTION VALUE=Option2>Option2</OPTION>
        <OPTION VALUE=Option3>Option3</OPTION>
    </SELECT><BR>
    <INPUT TYPE="submit" VALUE="Submit" NAME=submit1>
    <INPUT TYPE="reset" VALUE="Reset" NAME=reset1>
    <INPUT TYPE="button" VALUE="Button" NAME=button2><BR>
</FORM>
```

```
<SCRIPT>
   var numFormElements = document.form1.elements.length;
   for (var elementIndex = 0; elementIndex < numFormElements;
      elementIndex++)
   {
      var formElement = document.form1.elements[elementIndex];
      document.write("<P>Element Name is " + formElement.name + ", ");
      document.write("Element Index is " + elementIndex + ", and ");
      document.write("Element Type is " + formElement.type + "</P>");
   }
</SCRIPT>

</BODY>
</HTML>
```

If we start by looking at the script block, we see that the first thing we do is to find out how many elements there are in the form. We've used the `elements` array property of the form and accessed its `length` property:

```
var numFormElements = document.form1.elements.length;
```

We could also have used the form's `length` property, which gives us exactly the same information:

```
var numFormElements = document.form1.length;
```

In our `for` loop, we loop through each form element in the `form.elements` array. We write out to the page the form's name, its index inside the elements array, and finally, what type of element it is. We obtain the reference to each `element` with the `elements` array and an index:

```
var formElement = document.form1.elements[elementIndex];
```

We can also shorten this to:

```
var formElement = document.form1[elementIndex];
```

This is obviously a bit easier to use, and does exactly the same thing. We're using the elements array and an index to access the form elements, because we're accessing them via a loop, but of course we could just use their actual name:

```
var formElement = document.form1.text1;
```

For most form element types, this two-level hierarchy of forms and form elements covers it all. The `<SELECT>` form control is the exception, as we saw in the example above the `elements` array does not include the `<OPTION>` elements. Within the `element` object for each `<SELECT>` tag is a property options. This is an array of further objects, one for each `<OPTION>` tag within the `<SELECT>` tag. The type of these `<OPTION>` tag objects is `Option`. `Option` objects can replace existing objects in the options array of a `<SELECT>` element, which means menu items can be changed. We'll see how to do this in more detail shortly.

Naming Form Elements

When there is more than one form, or one form with many elements, using array indices quickly becomes confusing, as the above example shows. Fortunately, form and element tags are accessible via their names as well. The value of the NAME attribute of the appropriate tag is used as the property name. So, if our form is this:

```
<FORM NAME='frmPersonalDetails'>
   <INPUT TYPE='text' NAME='txtAge'>
</FORM>
```

Then we can access the form like this:

```
var myForm = document.frmPersonalDetails;
```

Similarly, we can access the textbox like this:

```
var myTextBox = document.frmPersonalDetails.txtAge;
```

The named notation is a lot clearer structurally and almost identical. There is one catch, as we can see in the form below:

```
<FORM NAME='frmPersonalDetails'>
    <INPUT TYPE="radio" NAME=radio1>
    <INPUT TYPE="radio" NAME=radio1>
    <INPUT TYPE="radio" NAME=radio1>
</FORM>
```

In the HTML above, the NAME attribute for the three radio buttons is identical, indeed to group radio buttons it must be. If the radio buttons are referred to by array indices, there is no problem. Referring to the checkboxes via properties presents a difficulty, however: An object can't have two properties with the same name, whether it is a form element or not. If you wish to use property names, there must be some other solution.

The key to this problem is that, for like-named radio buttons, the property name no longer refers to just one of the elements. Instead, it refers to a new, intermediate object. In Netscape Navigator and IE4+, this object is of the type InputArray, and it is a JavaScript array, though strictly speaking, IE uses a collection, which is very similar to an array. Each identically named element is then a member of the InputArray array. This array can cryptically appear when bug-ridden scripts are run with Netscape browsers. It helps to remember that each form element is just a type of input item, and therefore an InputArray is just an array of such items. In the example shown below, we access each radio button in a radio button group using the InputArray object:

```
<!-- Example_02.htm -->
<HTML>
<BODY>

<FORM NAME='frmPersonalDetails'>
    <INPUT TYPE="radio" NAME=radio1 VALUE="One">
    <INPUT TYPE="radio" NAME=radio1 VALUE="Two">
    <INPUT TYPE="radio" NAME=radio1 VALUE="Three">
</FORM>
<SCRIPT>

    var inputArray = document.frmPersonalDetails.radio1;
    var arrayLength = inputArray.length;
    for (var elementIndex = 0; elementIndex < arrayLength; elementIndex++)
    {
        var formElement = inputArray[elementIndex];
        document.write("Element Index is " + elementIndex + " and ");
        document.write("Element Value is " + formElement.value);
        document.write("</P>");
    }
</SCRIPT>
</BODY>
</HTML>
```

In the script block, we start by obtaining a reference to the `InputArray` object for the radio button group called `radio1`. Then we find the number of radio buttons in the group by using the `length` property of the `arrayInput` object. Finally, we loop through each radio button element in the group, and output its `index` in the array and also its `value`, just to prove which one we are accessing.

Using names can make life a lot easier, especially if they are short and descriptive. It's best to avoid names like `form1`, as it doesn't give much of a clue what the form is all about, whereas `frmPersonalDetails` makes it much clearer.

Form Object Events

The form object has just two events specific to it, namely `reset` and `submit`.

The `reset` event triggers when the form is reset, either by the user clicking a reset button, or by our code calling the `reset()` method. It's useful where we want to allow the user to completely clear the form. The `form` object also has a `reset()` method, however, in NN6 this does not cause the `reset` event to fire, although it does in NN4 and IE4+.

The `submit` event fires when the form is submitted by the user clicking a submit button. Note that if the form is submitted due to the use of the forms `submit()` method, then no browsers will fire the `submit` event. The `submit` event is a great place to perform all the form validation. The `onSubmit` event allows us to return a `true` value if we want the form submission to allow the POST or GET to go ahead, and `false` if we want to stop it. So, if we define our form `onSubmit` event handler like this:

```
<FORM onSubmit='return isFormValid(this);'
    ACTION='SomePage.htm'
    METHOD='POST'
    NAME='frmPersonalDetails'>
```

If the `isFormValid()` function returns `false`, the form POST will not continue. Note we pass this to the `isFormValid()` function. Here, this is a keyword that provides a reference to the object that caused the event to fire, in other words our `form` object. While passing it is optional, it does mean that the `isFormValid()` function doesn't have to obtain a reference to the form, but simply uses the `form` object passed as a parameter. If we are writing generic form checkers, in other words ones designed to be re-used in different pages, then this is essential as it does not tie the code in the routine to any particular form. We put this into a simple example below:

```
<!-- Example_03.htm -->
<HTML>
<HEAD>
<SCRIPT language="JavaScript">
    function isFormValid(formToValidate)
    {
        var formIsValid = true;
        if (formToValidate.txtName.value == "")
        {
            formIsValid = false;
            alert("Please enter your name");
        }

        return formIsValid;
    }
</SCRIPT>
</HEAD>
<BODY>
    <FORM onSubmit='return isFormValid(this);'
        ACTION='SomePage.htm'
        METHOD='POST'
```

```
            NAME='frmPersonalDetails'>
            Please enter your name:<BR>
            <INPUT TYPE="text" NAME=txtName>
            <INPUT TYPE="submit" VALUE="Send Form" NAME=subSendForm>
      </FORM>
   </BODY>
</HTML>
```

This displays a page with a text box for the user to enter their name and a submit button for them to send it. When the user hits submit, the `onSubmit` event handler fires and our `isFormValid` routine called. If the text box is empty, then we notify the user of their mistake, and set `formIsValid` to `false` to stop the form POST, as that variable's `value` is returned at the end of the function. As we are working client-side and don't have a page to submit to, we'll find a successful submit will lead to a page not found error.

We'll see later that individual form elements have events such as `focus` and `blur`, which fire when a form element gets the focus (the focus of the users actions), and when the form element loses focus, the `blur` event.

These are useful events, but they have disadvantages. Firstly, as we'll see, it's easy to get into an infinite event loop of `focus`/`blur`. Secondly, often more than one element is involved in obtaining data. For example, we might obtain the date using three drop down boxes. Actually, checking the whole data using `focus`/`blur` events gets a little tricky in these circumstances, we are best waiting until the user is ready to submit the form and then check that it's valid.

Form Elements

Once you've got your web page set up to receive data, you will want to do something with that data. There are several common tasks.

Extracting Data from Form Elements

For some elements, obtaining data is not the point, for example buttons are there just to be clicked, not to allow the user to enter data, they are simply a way of interacting with the user. For many other `form` elements, such as text boxes, password boxes, and text areas, the extracting of data from them is easy, and just involves the control's `value` property, which we saw earlier. In this section, we'll look at how to get the selected values from the slightly more tricky elements, such as `<SELECT>` elements, radio button groups, and checkboxes.

We'll start by looking at the `SELECT` element.

Select Element

We learnt earlier, that the `select` control is unusual in that it consists of the outer `<SELECT>` tag and between its open and close tags are `<OPTION>` tags, one for each menu option. So, it's not the `<SELECT>` element that contains the value, but whichever options the user selected.

If multiple selects are not allowed (its size is 1, or the `multiple` attribute is not set), then we simply need to work out which option element has been selected, and get its value. The key to this is the `selectedIndex` property of the `<SELECT>` element's object, which returns the index of the first option selected. This is demonstrated in the following example:

```
<!-- Example_04.htm -->
<HTML>
<HEAD>
<SCRIPT language="JavaScript">
   function showSelection()
   {
      var selectedIndex = document.myForm.mySelectControl.selectedIndex;
```

```
            var selectedOptionValue =
                document.myForm.mySelectControl.options[selectedIndex].value;
            alert(selectedOptionValue);
        }
</SCRIPT>
</HEAD>
<BODY>
<FORM NAME="myForm">
    <SELECT NAME=mySelectControl size=1>
        <OPTION VALUE=OneValue>One</OPTION>
        <OPTION VALUE=TwoValue>Two</OPTION>
        <OPTION VALUE=ThreeValue>Three</OPTION>
    </SELECT>
    <INPUT TYPE="button"
        VALUE="Show Selection"
        onclick="showSelection()"
        NAME=cmdShow>
    </FORM>
</BODY>
</HTML>
```

If the <SELECT> element has a size of more than 1, then it will be a listbox, and then we need to check that an option has been selected before trying to retrieve the value. If no option is selected, then -1 is returned by selectedIndex. An alternative, would be to ensure an option is selected when the page loads, or when the form is reset, by adding the selected attribute to one of the <OPTION> tag's definitions. What if however multiple selections are allowed? In this case, selectedIndex will return the index of the first of the options selected.

If we want to obtain all the values selected and put them in an array, then we need to loop through the options array property of the <SELECT> element. The option object for each <OPTION> element has the selected property, which is true if the element is selected, or false otherwise. This can be demonstrated by modifying the previous example to use a listbox, which can have more then one item selected:

```
<!-- Example_05.htm -->
<HTML>
<HEAD>
<SCRIPT language="JavaScript">

    function getSelectedValues(selectElement)
    {
        var selectedValues = new Array();
        var optionElement;
        var valueIndex = 0;

        for(var optionIndex = 0;
            optionIndex < selectElement.options.length; optionIndex++)
        {
            optionElement = selectElement.options[optionIndex];
            if (optionElement.selected)
            {
                selectedValues[valueIndex] = optionElement.value;
                valueIndex++;
            }
        }

        return selectedValues;
    }
```

```
        function showSelection()
        {
           var selectedValues =
              getSelectedValues(document.myForm.mySelectControl);
           var arrayElement;

           for (arrayElement in selectedValues)
           {
              alert(selectedValues[arrayElement]);
           }
        }
</SCRIPT>
</HEAD>
<BODY>
<FORM NAME="myForm">
    <SELECT NAME=mySelectControl SIZE=3 multiple>
        <OPTION VALUE=OneValue>One</OPTION>
        <OPTION VALUE=TwoValue>Two</OPTION>
        <OPTION VALUE=ThreeValue>Three</OPTION>
    </SELECT>
    <INPUT TYPE="button"
        VALUE="Show Selection"
        onclick="showSelection()"
        NAME=cmdShow>
</FORM>
</BODY>
</HTML>
```

The `getSelectedValues()` function takes just one parameter, the `<SELECT>` element's object whose selected values we want to obtain. We then have a `for` loop that goes through each `option` object in the `options` array to check whether it has been selected. If it has been, we add the value to the `selectedValues` array. Finally, at the end, we return our array populated with all the values of options selected by the user.

Our `showSelection()` function has been altered. It first gets the selected values, which are returned as an array. Then the `for..in` loop goes through each item in the array, or none, if there were no options selected.

Radio Buttons

The good news is that unlike `<SELECT>` elements, only one radio button in a group can be selected at any one time. The bad news is that a radio button group has no `selectedIndex` property, so we need to employ a similar looping technique as to the one used previously to find out which radio button in the group has been selected and what its value is. This is demonstrated in the following example:

```
<!-- Example_06.htm -->
<HTML>
<HEAD>
<SCRIPT language="JavaScript">

    function getSelectedRadioValue(radioGroup)
    {
        var selectedRadioValue = "";
        var radIndex;

        for (radIndex = 0; radIndex < radioGroup.length; radIndex++)
        {
```

```
            if (radioGroup[radIndex].checked)
            {
                selectedRadioValue = radioGroup[radIndex].value;
                break;
            }
        }

        return selectedRadioValue;
    }

    function showSelection()
    {
        var selectedValue =
            getSelectedRadioValue(document.myForm.myRadioButton);
        alert(selectedValue);
    }
</SCRIPT>
</HEAD>
<BODY>
    <FORM NAME="myForm">
        One
        <INPUT TYPE="radio" NAME=myRadioButton VALUE="One">
        <BR>
        Two
        <INPUT TYPE="radio" NAME=myRadioButton VALUE="Two">
        <BR>
        Three
        <INPUT TYPE="radio" NAME=myRadioButton VALUE="Three">
        <BR>
        <INPUT TYPE="button"
            VALUE="Show Selection"
            onclick="showSelection()"
            NAME=cmdShow>
    </FORM>
</BODY>
</HTML>
```

The getSelectedRadioValue() function takes the InputArray object representing our radio button group as its parameter. The function itself loops through each radio button object in the group until it hits the radio button selected, if any, by the user. It then obtains its value, which is stored in variable selectedRadioButtonValue for later return from the function.

Checkbox

Obtaining the value of a checkbox is simply a matter of reading its value property. However, this doesn't tell us whether the user has checked the checkbox, but simply what value we gave the checkbox. To see if the checkbox is checked, we need to use its checked property. This returns true if the box is checked, or false otherwise, as we see in the code below:

```
var isChecked = document.myForm.checked;
```

Dynamically Changing Select Elements

The good news is that with IE4+ and Netscape 6, adding and deleting options to the list control after the page has been loaded is very easy. These browsers have a <SELECT> element that support the add() and remove() methods. The bad news is that a bug in Netscape 6.0 prevents the add() method from working. Also Netscape 4 does not support the add() or remove() methods, but we'll see that there's a way around that.

Let's look first at how IE4+ and Netscape 6, when the bug is fixed, can add new options. The first task is to actually create a new option object. The option object's constructor takes four parameters, all of which are optional:

❑   The text to be displayed to the user

❑   The value the option is to have

❑   The default selected state

❑   The currently selected state

Shown below, we have set just the first two parameters:

```
var myNewOption = new Option("Text User Sees", "Option's Value");
```

The second parameter, the value of the option, can be textual or numeric data. This part of the code is identical whether we're using IE4+ or Netscape 4+.

Now we need to add the option to the SELECT element using the SELECT element's add() method. All options are actually stored in the options array property of the SELECT element, all that add() method does, is add it to the array at the position we specify. The add() method takes two parameters, the option object we just created, and the index indicating where in the option's array we want this option to be inserted. So, if we wanted it to be added to the very beginning, our code needs to be:

```
document.myForm.mySelectElement.add(myNewOption,0);
```

To add it to the second from top position, we would write:

```
document.myForm.mySelectElement.add(myNewOption,1);
```

To add it to the end, we could use the option array's length property:

```
var lastIndex = document.myForm.mySelectElement.options.length;
document.myForm.mySelectElement.add(myNewOption,lastIndex);
```

Removing an option is even easier, we use the remove() method and pass the index of the option to be removed:

```
document.myForm.mySelectElement.remove(0);
```

Let's now see how we do the same thing under Netscape 4, and 6 until the add() bug is fixed. The key is the options array property of the <SELECT> element. To remove an option from that array, we need to remove it from that array by setting the array element to null. So if we want to remove the first option (the option with index 0 in the options array):

```
document.myForm.mySelectElement.options[0] = null;
```

To add an option, we need to first create a new option object, as we did with IE, and then insert it into the options array:

```
var myNewOption = new Option("Text User Sees", "Option's value");
document.myForm.mySelectElement.options[0] = myNewOption;
```

However, unlike the add() method, this doesn't actually add a new option, but rather it replaces an existing option, the one with the index specified, with our new option. What about if we want to insert new options rather than replace existing ones?

157

In this instance, we need to first move all the array elements up one in the `options` array whose `index` is higher than our insertion point. So, if we want to insert a new option into the array at `index` 1, then our code would be:

```
var optionsArray = document.myForm.mySelectElement.options;
var indexCounter = optionsArray.length;
var insertAtIndex = 1;

for (; indexCounter >= insertAtIndex; indexCounter--)
{
   optionsArray[indexCounter] = optionsArray[indexCounter - 1];
}

var myNewOption = new Option("Text User Sees", "Option's value");
optionsArray[insertAtIndex] = myNewOption;
```

We start by setting the `optionsArray` variable to reference our `SELECT` control's options array. This is just for convenient shorthand, as it saves typing the full reference and it makes our code that bit more readable.

Then, in the `for` loop, we move the `option` objects in each element of the `options` array to a position one above their current index. We start with the last element, and continue until we reach the element we'll be inserting into.

Finally, on the last lines, we create the new `option` object and insert it into the now vacant element of the `options` array. Unfortunately, while this method of adding elements is Netscape 4 compatible, it's not IE compatible, as IE does not allow `OPTION` elements to be moved like this. This is easily remedied by changing the above code, so that instead of moving `option` objects around the array, instead we just change the text option's display and their value:

```
var optionsArray = document.myForm.mySelectElement.options;
var indexCounter = optionsArray.length;
var insertAtIndex = 1;

optionsArray[indexCounter] = new Option();

for (; indexCounter >= insertAtIndex; indexCounter--)
{
   optionsArray[indexCounter].text =
      optionsArray[indexCounter - 1].text;
   optionsArray[indexCounter].value =
      optionsArray[indexCounter - 1].value;
   optionsArray[indexCounter].defaultSelected =
      optionsArray[indexCounter - 1].defaultSelected;
}

var myNewOption = new Option("Text User Sees", "Option's value");
optionsArray[insertAtIndex] = myNewOption;
```

This will work on IE4+ and Netscape 4+. Note that we also make sure that the default selected element remains the default selected element by also setting the `defaultSelected` property of moved elements.

Let's put this into a fuller example, in which we allow the user to add new options by entering the text and value for the new option, then clicking a button to add it to the `SELECT` control.

```
<!-- Example_07.htm -->
<HTML>
<HEAD>
<SCRIPT language="JavaScript">
```

```
        function addOption(optionsArray, insertAtIndex, optionText, optionValue)
        {
            var indexCounter = optionsArray.length;

            optionsArray[indexCounter] = new Option();

            for (; indexCounter >= insertAtIndex; indexCounter--)
            {
                optionsArray[indexCounter].text =
                    optionsArray[indexCounter - 1].text;
                optionsArray[indexCounter].value =
                    optionsArray[indexCounter -1].value;
                optionsArray[indexCounter].defaultSelected =
                    optionsArray[indexCounter - 1].defaultSelected;
            }

            var myNewOption = new Option(optionText, optionValue);
            optionsArray[insertAtIndex] = myNewOption;

        }

        function cmdAddOption_onclick()
        {
            var form = document.myForm;
            var insertAtIndex = form.mySelectControl.selectedIndex + 1;
            var optionText = form.txtOptionText.value;
            var optionValue = form.txtOptionValue.value;
            var optionsArray = form.mySelectControl.options;
            addOption(optionsArray, insertAtIndex, optionText, optionValue);
        }
    </SCRIPT>

    </HEAD>
    <BODY>
        <FORM NAME="myForm">
            New Option Text:
            <INPUT TYPE="text" NAME=txtOptionText>
            <BR>
            New Option Value:
            <INPUT TYPE="text" NAME=txtOptionValue>
            <BR>
            <INPUT TYPE="button"
                VALUE="Add New Option"
                onclick="cmdAddOption_onclick()"
                NAME=cmdAddOption>
            <BR><BR>
            <SELECT NAME=mySelectControl size=3 multiple>
                <OPTION VALUE=OneValue>One</OPTION>
                <OPTION VALUE=TwoValue>Two</OPTION>
                <OPTION VALUE=ThreeValue>Three</OPTION>
            </SELECT>
        </FORM>
    </BODY>
</HTML>
```

For the most part, we've reused the code described previously. However one important change is that we have created a new function called addOption(), which will add a new option to any options array. It takes four parameters. The first parameter, is the options array of the select control. Then we have the array index position that the new option is to be inserted into the array. Third parameter is the text to be displayed to the user in the option, and finally, we have the value to be given to the new option element.

When the **Add New Option** button is pressed, the buttons, `onClick` event handler calls our `cmdAddOption_onclick()` function. This obtains the text and value for the new option from the values entered by the user in the text boxes. It also sets `optionsArray` to the options array and `insertAtIndex` to the next option element after the currently selected option. If none are selected, then –1 is returned by `selectedIndex` property and, with 1 added to it gives zero, resulting in the new option being added at the top of the control. Then, using the information gathered, it then calls `addOption()` to add a new option.

Obtaining Data Without Forms

It's possible to collect user-input without using `<FORM>`, `<INPUT>`, `<SELECT>`, or `<TEXTAREA>` HTML tags. Usually, forms are good enough, but a number of obscure possibilities present themselves that traditional HTML forms can't help with. For example:

- ❑ You need to prompt the user before the whole HTML page is loaded
- ❑ You want to collect input from a narrow or hidden frame
- ❑ The user has no keyboard, perhaps in an information kiosk or WebTV

In summary, the other features you might want to bring to bear on data input problems are:

- ❑ Message boxes: `confirm()` and `prompt()`, allow simple input
- ❑ Dynamic HTML: you can mockup any kind of input you want with Dynamic HTML and receive input via events

HTML Hyperlinks can be used to capture a single item of data if the user clicks on them. If the user has no keyboard, then an image map of a keyboard can allow us to collect keyboard input anyway.

Let's look at each of these in turn.

confirm() and prompt()

We looked in detail at the `alert()`, `confirm()`, and `prompt()` methods in the windows and frames chapter. The `confirm()` and `prompt()` functions are built into client-side JavaScript, and give a very simple way to obtain information. The `confirm()` method asks the user to confirm an action, hence the name. The message passed to the function in its only parameter is displayed in a message box along with **OK** and **Cancel** buttons. If the user clicks the **OK** button, then the function returns `true`, otherwise it returns `false`. For example:

```
if (confirm("Do you want to continue?"))
{
    // The user clicked OK button
}
else
{
    // The user clicked Cancel button/
}
```

The `prompt()` function allows the user to enter characters into a message box, this string being returned to us when the user clicks **OK**. If the `Cancel` button is clicked, then `null` is returned. As with `confirm()` a string with the message to be displayed to the user is passed as the function's first parameter. The functions second parameter is the default value to be displayed in the prompt box's text box when it's displayed. Note if the user clicks the Cancel button then null is returned, something we need to check for with an if statement:

```
    var userInput = prompt("Enter your date of birth", "");
    if (userInput == null)
    {
        // user hit cancel button
    }
```

Input with DHTML

We look at the nuts and bolts of how DHTML works later in Chapter 10, so for now, we'll just look at a very basic example of using DHTML to obtain user information.

The example is a very simple way to obtain numbers in something looking like a calculator, although the usual calculator functions are not present.

Clicking any of the numbers, causes them to be shown in the display, and clicking **AC** clears the display. Unfortunately, to keep the example simple, it only works in IE5+ and Netscape 6+, in other words. JScript 5 and JavaScript 1.5. Once you've read the DHTML chapter, you'll find it easy to make it work with version 4 browsers and extend its currently not very useful functionality, although NN4's lack of a click event handler for <TD> tag and poor ability to change tables, may make this trickier than with IE4:

```
<!-- Example_08.htm -->
<HTML>
<HEAD>
    <STYLE>
        .buttonTD
        {
            width: 25px;
            height: 25px;
            font-weight: bold;
            font-size: 14pt;
            background-color: lightgrey;
            text-align:center;
        }

        .displayTD
        {
            width: 100px;
            height: 30px;
            font-weight: bold;
            font-size: 14pt;
            background-color: lightblue;
            text-align:right;
        }
    </STYLE>
    <SCRIPT LANGUAGE='JavaScript'>
        var displayNumber = "";

        function displayDigit(digit)
        {
            displayNumber = displayNumber + digit;
            var displayTD = document.getElementById("displayTD");
            displayTD.innerHTML = displayNumber;
        }

        function clearDisplay()
        {
            displayNumber = "";
            var displayTD = document.getElementById("displayTD");
            displayTD.innerHTML = " ";
```

```
            }
       </SCRIPT>
   </HEAD>
   <BODY BGCOLOR='white'>
      <TABLE>
         <TR>
            <TD COLSPAN=3 CLASS='displayTD' ID='displayTD'> </TD>
         </TR>
         <TR>
            <TD CLASS='buttonTD' onclick='displayDigit("7")'>7</TD>
            <TD CLASS='buttonTD' onclick='displayDigit("8")'>8</TD>
            <TD CLASS='buttonTD' onclick='displayDigit("9")'>9</TD>
         </TR>
         <TR>
            <TD CLASS='buttonTD' onclick='displayDigit("4")'>4</TD>
            <TD CLASS='buttonTD' onclick='displayDigit("5")'>5</TD>
            <TD CLASS='buttonTD' onclick='displayDigit("6")'>6</TD>
         </TR>
         <TR>
            <TD CLASS='buttonTD' onclick='displayDigit("1")'>1</TD>
            <TD CLASS='buttonTD' onclick='displayDigit("2")'>2</TD>
            <TD CLASS='buttonTD' onclick='displayDigit("3")'>3</TD>
         </TR>
         <TR>
            <TD CLASS='buttonTD' onclick='displayDigit("0")'>0</TD>
            <TD CLASS='buttonTD' onclick='displayDigit(".")'>.</TD>
            <TD CLASS='buttonTD' onclick='clearDisplay()'>AC</TD>
         </TR>
      </TABLE>
   </BODY>
</HTML>
```

As we'll be looking at DHTML and CSS in later chapters, we'll just look at the principles of the code above. Each of the numbers is simply a table cell with the `onClick` event handler calling the `displayDigit()` function, and passing the number to be displayed.

The `displayDigit()` function first concatenates the number passed as a parameter to the variable `displayNumber`, which actually holds the data input. Then it writes the number to the light blue table row at the top of the calculator, by setting that element's `innerHTML` property.

This example is very rudimentary, but we can see how DHTML, rather than forms, can be used to input data. This is particularly useful if we want more inventive and attractive interfaces than that which a standard `form` element provides.

Input with Hyperlinks

We can use hyperlinks to pass information from page to page. We do this using the same method that forms use with the GET method, rather than POST; they simply add the information after the URL. When we want to add data to the URL, we need to add "?" after the end of the URL, so that the browser knows that what comes after is not part of the web address, but data to be processed. For example:

```
<A HREF='ReceiveInfo.htm?Paul'>My Name Is Paul</A>
```

When the user clicks the link, it will take them to the page `ReceiveInfo.htm` and pass the data `"Paul"`. The question is how do we retrieve the information? The key to getting our hands on data in a URL, is the `window.location.search` property. This contains everything from and including the "?". So, in our case:

```
document.write("Info Sent is " + window.location.search);
```

Will write to the receiving page:

"Info Sent is ?Paul"

We can trim off the "?" by using JavaScript's string functions, for example:

```
var infoPassed = window.location.search.substring(1);
```

This will take a slice of the string starting from the second character. As we've not specified the last character to form part of the slice, the `slice()` method will return everything all the way to the end of the string.

There are limitations. First, is that a maximum of 4000 characters are allowed to be used, although in these 4000 characters, we must allow for the web site address itself. The second is that any characters, except letters of the alphabet and numbers, can't be passed as they are in a URL. If we changed our URL to:

```
<A HREF='ReceiveInfo.htm?Paul Wilton'>My Name Is Paul</A>
```

We'll find that:

```
var infoPassed = window.location.search.substring(1);
```

In IE and Netscape 6 will be:

Paul%20Wilton

Netscape 4 however would return Paul Wilton.

We mentioned that only alphanumeric characters can appear in URL data, any other characters need to be encoded before being used in URL data, and decoded again when we want to extract the data. The built-in methods `escape()` and `unescape()` will encode and decode URL data respectively. For example, the following code will encode the string "Paul Wilton" ready to add onto a URL:

```
var myData = escape("Paul Wilton");
```

This code will extract it and decode it:

```
unescape(window.location.search);
```

Data

The purpose of HTML form elements, is to collect data and, if you're interested in JavaScript, then you'll want to work on that data. Beyond accepting the user's input and fiddling with the data immediately afterwards, there are some larger issues to consider. Some of these are:

❑   What format does input data have?

❑   Where is the data stored?

❑   How long does the data last?

Persisting Web Site Data

The fundamental problem with HTML and browsers is that, when the user surfs around the World Wide Web, documents viewed, appear and disappear from the browser. What if you want some of the document information to hang around after a document has long gone? It's not so obvious how or where. Isn't there somewhere else within a browser to store information apart from HTML documents? Sometimes the answer is No. However, there are several possibilities made available by the browser that are good candidates for storing data and these are discussed below.

HTML Form Fields

The most obvious place to store data, is in HTML form fields. The user can type information into the visible fields, and the scriptwriter can get and set this data via the appropriate value property of the FORM element. Form fields are just JavaScript host objects, so they act like other JavaScript objects in most other respects.

Form fields have some other useful behaviors. If a form is submitted, there's no work required by the scriptwriter – the browser does all the conversion and submission for you. The <INPUT TYPE ='HIDDEN'> field is priceless for scriptwriters who want to include extra, user-invisible information in a form.

Forms can have as many form elements as you like, and text fields can generally be as big as you like. There is a form-wide limit of 4096 bytes (4KB) on form GET operations, but POST operations have no limit. There are limits however to how much data individual text elements will reliably hold. For example, there is an approximate 30,000-character limit on reading the contents of a <TEXTAREA> tag. This is very similar to a defect in Netscape version 3.0 that couldn't manage scripts much bigger than 30,000 characters. Somewhere in the browsers, there is a 16-bit limit in this textarea respect. Recall that the METHOD attribute of the <FORM> tag defines whether GET or POST is the method used for sending the data.

Forms have other limitations, too. The main one is that forms are part of an HTML document. If the document disappears, then the form data generally disappears. If your browser is Netscape Navigator 3.0+ or Internet Explorer 4.0+, then you can rescue the data if you navigate back through the history to the document in question. If the browser shuts down, however, the data is gone.

Form data also suffers from performance problems. If a web page is slow to load, then the tags containing a form may take some time to appear and the scriptwriter has to coordinate this. Also, data stored in a form can be slow to work with. If you have a complex script that manipulates form data in a repetitive way, your script can run inefficiently.

JavaScript Variables and Objects

JavaScript variables are another obvious place to store data. Since each script fragment is part of a given document that is part of a browser window, JavaScript variables are by default properties of some window object. It is also possible to store them as properties of most browser objects, though. JavaScript properties are a great place to store data, since you have the full flexibility of JavaScript at hand. All other data storage methods are restricted to strings, whereas JavaScript variables can be numbers or objects.

However, JavaScript variables have limitations. If browser windows close or the browser entirely closes down, then JavaScript variable data is lost. Unlike form element data, if you navigate back through history to old documents, you don't get any JavaScript variables back that the document might have contained. You may find some variables are reconstructed when the document is redisplayed, but strictly speaking, they're new variables with the same name as old ones. We did see, in chapter 4 *Windows and Frames*, that one way round this was to have variables in a frameset defining page that didn't change, something we termed script space. We use this technique again, in chapter 22 Shopping Cart Application, to hold details of the customers shopping cart while they browse the web site.

Attached to Document Object Model Objects

Sometimes it's handy to decorate parts of a document with extra information. This example illustrates:

```
<!-- Example_09.htm -->
<HTML>
<BODY>
   <FORM>
      Mystery button page<BR>
      <INPUT TYPE="button" VALUE="One"></INPUT>
      <INPUT TYPE="button" VALUE="Two"></INPUT>
      <INPUT TYPE="button" VALUE="Three"></INPUT>
   </FORM>
   <SCRIPT LANGUAGE='JavaScript'>
      var messages = [ "10 seconds to detonation", "Don't touch",
         "Elevator ready" ];
      var increment;

      for (increment=0; increment<3; increment++)
      {
         document.forms[0].elements[increment].details
            = messages[increment];
         document.forms[0].elements[increment].onclick
            = function (increment){alert(this.details);};
      }
   </SCRIPT>
</BODY>
</HTML>
```

None of the buttons in this example have explanatory labels. Instead, a property is added to each button object with a description of that object. When the button event handler fires, this new property is handy and available. Clearly, any amount of data can be attached to existing objects in this way. The data will still disappear when the containing document disappears. The book, *JavaScript Objects*, Wrox Press (ISBN:1-861001-89-4), illustrates this technique extensively.

A side effect of this strategy, might be obscurely useful at some point. If the property name you use clashes with an existing property of the object, then that existing property is replaced. This might be useful if, for some reason, you want to disable an object property, such as the `window` object's `open` property. It's very simple:

```
<!-- Example_10.htm -->
<HTML>
<BODY>
   <SCRIPT LANGUAGE='JavaScript'>
      window.open = null;
   </SCRIPT>
</BODY>
</HTML>
```

Internet Explorer 4+ has easy HTML syntax for extra attributes:

```
<!-- Example_11.htm -->
<HTML>
<BODY>
   <FORM>
```

```
        <INPUT TYPE='text' NAME='myname' VALUE='myvalue'
          MYATTRIBUTE='myatt'></INPUT>
    </FORM>
    <SCRIPT LANGUAGE='JavaScript'>
      alert(document.forms[0].myname.MYATTRIBUTE);
    </SCRIPT>
  </BODY>
  </HTML>
```

As expected, this displays **myatt** inside the dialog popped up by `alert()`. Although Netscape 4 will let you add new attributes to HTML tags, the information won't appear inside JavaScript when those tags are rendered.

In Netscape 6, we can use JavaScript to access our attributes, but must use `getAttribute()` method:

```
<!-- Example_12.htm --><HTML>
<BODY>
  <FORM>
    <INPUT TYPE='text' NAME='myname' VALUE='myvalue'
      MYATTRIBUTE='myatt'></INPUT>
  </FORM>
  <SCRIPT LANGUAGE='JavaScript'>
    alert(document.forms[0].myname.getAttribute("MYATTRIBUTE"));
  </SCRIPT>
</BODY>
</HTML>
```

The good news, is this also works with IE4+.

Cookies

Chapter 14, on Privacy, Security, and Cookies, explains cookies, and is recommended reading if you want to do anything at all with them. Within this chapter, you only need to know that cookies allow us to store small amounts of data on the user's computer. In fact, they are not a JavaScript feature, but part of the browser:

❑   They are more tedious to access from a script

❑   They are automatically submitted to web servers with all URL requests, which is very convenient

❑   They can be shared between multiple windows in a browser

❑   They can survive window, full browser, and computer shutdown

Cookies are limited to storing strings of less than 4096 bytes each.

URLs

It might seem odd, but URLs are a potential place for storing data. We saw earlier in the chapter, how data could be added to the end of a URL. If a web page is retrieved with a GET-style request, data is pinned to the end of the URL when the web server responds to an initial GET request from the browser. That URL then goes into the browser's history list. From JavaScript, you can look through the history list and extract that data again. This is a read-only storage method – you can't change an historical URL. The size limit is 4096 bytes, as for URLs.

An alternative method, is to simply make sure that whenever the user browses to another page in our web site, the data we want to persist is added to the end of the URL. We can do this in the `window` object's `unload` event handler, which fires whenever another page is browsed to.

HTML/XML Tags and Content

Provided you have a browser that supports the DOM level 1 standard, it's possible to see the full text of an HTML document as data. Therefore, it is also possible to store data inside the HTML document itself. Put another way, we can create extra HTML objects and insert them into the document for future access. Internet Explorer 5+ and Netscape 6+ are the only browser to support this feature so far:

```
<!-- Example_13.htm -->
<HTML>
<BODY>
    <DIV ID='astro' STYLE='display:none'>
        <SPAN ID='sun'>Apollo, the sun king</SPAN>
        <SPAN ID='moon'>Luna, the mad woman</SPAN>
        <SPAN ID='earth'>Gaea, the provider</SPAN>
    </DIV>
    <SCRIPT LANGUAGE='JavaScript'>
        var astroElement = document.getElementById('astro');
alert(astroElement.getElementsByTagName('span')[0].firstChild.nodeValue);
    </SCRIPT>
</BODY>
</HTML>
```

In this example, there are three astronomical entries: sun, moon, and earth. None of the detail shows due to the STYLE of the <DIV> tag, which is set to display: none. Using the DOM of Internet Explorer 5.0+, you can treat these three items like an array of records. The alert box extracts the description for sun. Chapter 9, DOM covers this technique in more detail.

Internet Explorer 5.0+ supports XML as well as HTML, therfore this approach can be used in either markup language. Data stored by this method won't be submitted with form submissions and disappears when the document is no longer viewed in the browser, since the data is effectively part of the document. There is another benefit to this approach. If there is a lot of data, the HTML document will be quite large. In this approach, the data is stored directly in HTML, so the document will be efficient to load.

Java, Plugins, and Elsewhere

There are other places you can put your data using client-side JavaScript. When all else fails, you can escape out of the HTML environment entirely and store your variables somewhere else. The remaining candidates are the <OBJECT>, <APPLET>, and <EMBED> tags. Only the first of these is supported by HTML 4 spec.

Given sufficient security, <OBJECT> embedded objects, applets, and plug-ins in a web page might store data anywhere: to local disk, across the network, or maybe within their own context inside the browser. Details really depend on the specific object, applet, or plug-in.

Java is an interesting case, because the contents of Java applets are readily available from inline JavaScript within the same HTML document, and the lifetime of a Java applet can be longer than that of the parent HTML document.

Finally, we can always submit our data to a web server for storage via a GET or POST URL request, in true database style. In that case, we need to organize the server so that it doesn't wipe out the page the client-side script is within with its response.

Storage Comparisons

The table below contrasts the different client-side storage techniques available. all are accessible from JavaScript within the browser, therefore there's no obstacle to moving data around. Just use a bit of JavaScript to copy the data from one type of storage to another:

Storage Type	Lifetime of Storage Type	Capacity of Storage	Automatically Sent to Servers?
HTML FORM elements	HTML document & pages stored in history	Unlimited, but maximum of 4KB when sent in a GET request	Yes
JavaScript variables	HTML document	Unlimited	No
Cookies	Specified: up to forever	At least 20 at 4KB each	Yes
URLs	Browser session	Up to 4KB per URL	Yes
HTML/XML tags	HTML document	Unlimited	No
Java	Browser session – can be extended with appropriate security in place	Unlimited	No

For the remainder of this chapter, we'll be mostly considering plain form elements, since that is where 90% of the action is.

Validation

Using JavaScript to check user-entered data in a browser can give the user better feedback. If the data is ever submitted, some program on the web server side will have to consume that data. If there are checks to be done on that data, and they can be performed in the browser, then the user will get a faster response. If the server program knows that the browser has already done some validation, life becomes a lot less complex at the server end, probably reducing the amount of information passed back and forth between the server and client. So validation benefits both the user and the web site maintainer, by reducing the number of packets that are sent/requested by the server/client. This effectively frees network bandwidth and allows the server more processor cycles and memory to spend on other tasks.

However, the World Wide Web is a public place with folk of all kinds and, as we'll see shortly, there's really no escape from validation at the server. Therefore, validation in the browser is of primary benefit to the user. In this section we'll look at the basics of form validation, however a much more sophisticated approach using regular expressions is discussed in Chapter 15.

Validation Models

Deciding when to check the data the user enters is a design issue for validation. The options are form level validation, field level validation, and key level validation.

Form level validation is the easiest. When the user attempts to submit the data, use an onSubmit or onClick event handler to check the user's work and reject the submission if there are problems, perhaps with an alert() pop-up. If two fields depend on each other and the user picks a bad combination, a form level check can sometimes warn the user too late.

Field level validation isn't any harder, except more handlers are required. When the user leaves a field, or changes its state, a handler fires and a warning occurs if there is a problem. Unless the handlers are carefully organized to prevent the user from moving on when an error has occurred, a form-level recheck is required as well. This careful organization can be very time consuming if portability and backwards compatibility are issues, because of the complexities of event models, as discussed earlier in this chapter.

Key level validation is an attempt to stop users from typing forbidden things at all. Trying to guarantee only uppercase alphabetic letters in a text field is an example. An event captures each keystroke the user types and either allows it or ignores it. This degree of control has little to recommend it for forms, unless you are trying to implement your own keyboard shortcuts. It has its uses with Dynamic HTML, discussed in Chapter 10.

A simple example showing a mixture of form-level validation and additional field level checks is shown below:

```
<!-- Example_14.htm -->
<HTML>
<HEAD>
    <SCRIPT LANGUAGE='JavaScript'>
        function validate(formToCheck)
        {
            var formIsValid = true;
            var parseZipCode = parseInt(formToCheck.postal.value);
            if (formToCheck.country.value.length != 2
                || isNaN(parseZipCode)
                || parseZipCode < 0)
            {
                alert("Evidently you're lost.");
                formIsValid = false;
            }

            return formIsValid;
        }
    </SCRIPT>
</HEAD>
<BODY>
    <FORM METHOD='POST' ACTION="SomeFormProcessor.htm"
        ONSUBMIT='return validate(this);'>
        <H3>Where are you? </H3>
        <BR>Enter your two letter country code:
        <INPUT TYPE='text' NAME='country'
            ONCHANGE='this.value=this.value.toLowerCase();'></INPUT>
        <BR>Enter your postal code:
        <INPUT TYPE='text' NAME='postal'></INPUT>
        <BR><INPUT TYPE='submit'></INPUT>
    </FORM>
</BODY>
</HTML>
```

This example does most validation in the form's `onSubmit` event handler. A minor correction is applied in the first `<INPUT>` tag to provide the user with some quick and harmless feedback for that particular input item.

Regular Expressions

A regular expression is like a formula for a JavaScript string that must follow a specific pattern. Regular expressions use this pattern to describe another string pattern. When a normal string is examined with a regular expression, a conclusion is drawn about whether, or how, that normal string matches the pattern of the regular expression. So, regular expressions are a matching tool for strings – very handy for user input.

Regular expressions occupy two parts of the JavaScript language places: as methods of the String object, and in their own right in the form of the RegExp object. The critical detail for validation is that the test(regexp) method of a RegExp object returns true if the string is of the pattern dictated by the regexp regular expression, otherwise it is false.

These regular expressions are delimited by / characters, instead of quotes in JavaScript source, so they're not strings themselves.

Here's how to use it:

```
var str = "Eany Meany Miny Mo";
var bool = null;
bool = /Meany/.test(str);          // true - contains 'Meany'
bool = /^E/.test(str);             // true - starts with 'E'
bool = /[Nn][^yY]/.test(str);      /* false - all n's and N's have a
                                      trailing y or Y */
```

Regular expressions can get quite complex. Their syntax is copied exactly from the same feature in the Perl language. Chapter 15 covers regular expressions in depth, and Chapter 16 has details of how they can be used to validate complex types of form data.

Numbers

text, textarea, and password form controls return strings. If the form demands a number from the user, it needs to be converted. One method of doing this, is to use two built-in JavaScript functions: parseInt() and parseFloat(). Both take strings and attempt to read numbers from them, either an integer, or a floating point number. This can be somewhat successful, especially parseInt(), which can read numbers in bases other than 10 if necessary. For example:

```
var num1 = parseInt('23', 10);      // decimal
var num2 = parseInt('1AB2', 16);    // hexadecimal
var num3 = parseFloat('garbage');   // returns NaN
var num4 = parseFloat('123.45');
```

Unfortunately, these functions have a failing. Both functions stop trying to read the string as soon as a number is successfully read. This example doesn't fail:

```
var num5 = parseFloat('3.1415926junk');    // num5 = Math.PI (roughly).
```

More irritatingly, neither does this:

```
var num6 = parseFloat('11.22.33');         // num6 = 11.22
```

There are four alternatives:

❑   Accept the first thing typed and discard the rest

❑   Rely on having a Netscape 4+ or Internet Explorer 4+ browser and use the handy isNaN() function

❑   Examine the user data thoroughly, for example using regular expressions as we do in Chapter 16: Form Validation

❑   Use the Number() method which converts the string passed in its parameter to a number, with any non-digit characters resulting in NaN, in other words var myNum = Number('11.22.33') will result in myNum holding the value NaN

Dates

Dates can be awkward to validate in a web browser if you insist on the user typing the whole date in. Users of relational databases will know that there are a million ways to represent the same date. Which to choose? The key to easy date validation, is to not give the user choice in the first place.

The best solution for validating dates is to use international date format. This format spells the month out into three letters and keeps the rest of the date in digits as below:

04-Jan-1998
29-Feb-2001

With this format, there's no confusion about what is a year or a month, or which century applies. The examples show an English interpretation of the standard; for other languages it's different. Try to do dates this way:

```
<!-- Example_15.htm -->
<HTML>
<BODY>
   <FORM>
      <INPUT TYPE='text' MAXLENGTH='2' SIZE='2'></INPUT>-
      <SELECT SIZE='1'>
         <OPTION VALUE='1'>Jan</OPTION>
         <OPTION VALUE='2'>Feb</OPTION>
         <!-- and so on -->
      </SELECT>-
      <INPUT TYPE='text' MAXLENGTH='4' SIZE='4'></INPUT>
   </FORM>
</BODY>
</HTML>
```

With this design, the user can't get the month wrong. We'll still need to check the year and day are sensible number values or we could use `select` controls for them as well. The `selectedIndex` property of the `<FORM>` element will also give us the number of the month the user has chosen, but the months will be numbered from zero, not 1. Therefore, it is possibly less error prone to include `VALUE` attributes, as is done in the above example, and lookup those after we've worked out which element is selected. To tell if a year is a leap year, try this function:

```
function isLeapYear(year)
{
   return (year % 4 == 0 && (year % 100 !=0 || year % 400 == 0));
   /* Years that are multiples of 100 are not leap years, unless they are
      also multiples of 400 */
}
```

The Netscape validation library, described a bit further on, has some very useful date validation routines. Another wonderful resource for dates, is the "Date and Time Articles" at http://www.irt.org/.

Layout

There are several display techniques using JavaScript that build on the basic `<FORM>` tags of HTML, and we shall examine these now.

Read-Only Fields and Boilerplate

Sometimes, form data in a document shouldn't be changeable by the user. Boilerplate text and read-only form fields can achieve this.

Boilerplate text is just all the content of a document that doesn't change. If a document is dynamically produced, such as the results of a search query, then plain HTML text can be displayed. The catch with displaying form data in this way is that JavaScript cannot change it, unless Dynamic HTML techniques are exploited. If form content displays a mixture of form controls and boilerplate text, and that form needs to be submitted, then there should be a hidden field duplicating each boilerplate data item, or else those items won't be submitted with the rest of the data.

To make existing form controls read-only, there are three alternatives: don't let the user get near the control; change the control's state back as soon as the user changes it; or use the `readOnly` attribute. The first possibility is covered under Form Events and is perhaps a better approach for `text`, `password`, and `textarea` fields. Alternatively, to change a field back to what it was before the user touched it try these various tricks:

```
<!-- Example_16.htm -->
<HTML>
<BODY>
<FORM NAME="frmReadOnly">
   <!-- This works for "text", "textarea" and "password" types -->
   <INPUT TYPE='text' NAME='first' VALUE='Important'
      ONBLUR="this.value=this.real"></INPUT>
   <SCRIPT LANGUAGE='JavaScript'>
      document.frmReadOnly.first.real = document.frmReadOnly.first.value;
   </SCRIPT>

   <!-- This works for all checkboxes and radio button groups of one -->
   <INPUT TYPE='checkbox' NAME='second'
      ONCLICK='this.checked=!this.checked;'></INPUT>

   <!-- This works for radio button groups of more than one button -->
   <INPUT TYPE='radio' NAME='third' CHECKED></INPUT>
   <INPUT TYPE='radio' NAME='third'
      ONCLICK='this.form.third[0].click()'></INPUT>
   <INPUT TYPE='radio' NAME='third'
      ONCLICK='this.form.third[0].click()'></INPUT>

   <!-- This case is solely for SELECT -->
   <SELECT NAME="fourth" ONCHANGE="this.selectedIndex=this.realIndex">
      <OPTION SELECTED VALUE="A"> Apples</OPTION>
      <OPTION VALUE="B"> Banana</OPTION>
   </SELECT>
   <SCRIPT>
      document.frmReadOnly.fourth.realIndex =
         document.frmReadOnly.fourth.selectedIndex;
   </SCRIPT>
</FORM>
</BODY>
</HTML>
```

Let's briefly look at these tricks, necessary only for Netscape 4, as Netscape 6+ and IE4+ support the `readOnly` attribute.

First, we have a way to ensure the value of a text box never changes:

```
<!-- This works for "text", "textarea" and "password" types -->
<INPUT TYPE='text' NAME='first' VALUE='Important'
   ONBLUR="this.value=this.real"></INPUT>
<SCRIPT LANGUAGE='JavaScript'>
   document.frmReadOnly.first.real = document.frmReadOnly.first.value;
</SCRIPT>
```

The script block immediately after the control will execute as the page is parsed. It sets the property `real` of the text control to that text controls value. The text control doesn't have a built-in property called `real`. We just added it to this particular text control's object, simply by using it. We can do this with all objects in JavaScript. Now, when the text control's change event fires, in other words when the user finishes making changes to the contents of the text box and moves to another part of the page, the event handler code will set the text box's value back to that contained in its `real` property that we set when the page was parsed.

Next, we have a way to make a checkbox read only:

```
<!-- This works for all checkboxes and radio button groups of one -->
<INPUT TYPE='checkbox' NAME='second'
    ONCLICK='this.checked=!this.checked;'></INPUT>
```

When the user clicks the checkbox they reverse its value, in other words from checked to not checked or vice versa. What we do is, in the click event, we reverse the changes made by the user.

Next, we see how to ensure a radio button group can't have its default value changed:

```
<!-- This works for radio button groups of more than one button -->
<INPUT TYPE='radio' NAME='third' CHECKED></INPUT>
<INPUT TYPE='radio' NAME='third'
    ONCLICK='this.form.third[0].click()'></INPUT>
<INPUT TYPE='radio' NAME='third'
    ONCLICK='this.form.third[0].click()'></INPUT>
```

We've decided to make the first radio button the checked one, and the one that must remain checked. When the user clicks one of the other radio buttons in the group, the `onClick` event handler code for that button clicks the first radio button, so whatever the user does, the first radio button remains checked. Note we use the `form` property that all form element controls have. This gives us a reference to the `form` object within which the control is contained. From there we can access the first radio button, in other words index of zero, of the radio button group called `third`.

Finally, we have our `SELECT` control, which always returns to its default value:

```
<!-- This case is solely for SELECT -->
<SELECT NAME="fourth" ONCHANGE="this.selectedIndex=this.realIndex">
    <OPTION SELECTED VALUE="A"> Apples</OPTION>
    <OPTION VALUE="B"> Banana</OPTION>
</SELECT>
<SCRIPT>
    document.frmReadOnly.fourth.realIndex =
        document.frmReadOnly.fourth.selectedIndex;
</SCRIPT>
```

The script block immediately following the control is executed as the page is first loaded and parsed. As with the textbox example, it creates a property, `realIndex`, which contains the `index` of the default selected option. In the `onchange` event handler, which will be called whenever the user changes the selected option, the code sets the selected `index` to that specified in the `realIndex` property we created and set when the page first loaded. So, whatever the user does, when they leave the control it will be changed back to its default selected option.

Submit, reset, button, hidden, and image input types can't have their values set directly by the user at all, so they are ignored. Their normal action can be disabled with an `onClick` handler if desired.

There are other solutions. HTML 4.0 has a READONLY attribute for FORM elements, which is the ultimate solution, but it is only supported in Internet Explorer 4+ and Netscape 6+. For example:

```
<INPUT TYPE="text" READONLY NAME="myTextBox">
```

Or via JavaScript:

```
myControl.readOnly = true;
```

A Java applet that displays a single piece of text can be exploited from JavaScript. A normal <INPUT> form control of type button, reset, or submit can have its displayed value changed via JavaScript – although the user can still push the button, they can't change the displayed value.

For the ultimate results in managing read-only screen data, one needs only to consider Dynamic HTML's ability to manage all the boilerplate text on a web page in intimate detail. See Chapter 10 for more details of Dynamic HTML.

Multi-Record Forms

There are several approaches to displaying more than one record at a time in a document. The simplest is to have a <FORM> container for each record, which is straightforward. If all the records are to be part of a single form, however some other approach is necessary.

Repeating Controls

A form can have multiple elements with the same name, so a simple solution is to use the same form elements repeatedly. Ten records with a street and suburb field, each means ten text fields named street and ten named suburbs. This may only require plain HTML. The main disadvantage is that many form elements lined up in a document can be hard on the eyes. This approach makes adding records difficult, unless extra spare fields are supplied. When the data is submitted, a large amount of data is sent, which can exceed the limits of some CGI systems and which can take some effort to extract in the receiving program.

List Viewers

A flexible approach is to store records in a set away from the user's view and only display the current record. The following example demonstrates this:

```
<!-- Example_17.htm -->
<HTML>
<HEAD>
  <SCRIPT>
    function Horse(kind) // constructor, add other parameters as required
    {
        this.kind = kind;
    }

    var list = new Array(); // the list of records, each an object.
    var current = 0;
    list[current++] = new Horse("Arab");
    list[current++] = new Horse("Quarterhorse");
    list[current++] = new Horse("Palamino");
    list[current++] = new Horse("Gelding");
    list[current++] = new Horse("Shetland Pony");
    list[current++] = new Horse("Hack");
    list[current++] = new Horse("Mule");

    function next(form)
    {
        if ( current + 1 < list.length )
            form.kind.value = list[++current].kind;
    }

    function previous(form)
    {
```

```
            if ( current > 0 )
                form.kind.value = list[--current].kind;
        }
    </SCRIPT>
</HEAD>
<BODY>
    <FORM>
        <INPUT TYPE='text' NAME='kind'></INPUT>
        <INPUT TYPE='button' VALUE='Next' ONCLICK='next(this.form);'></INPUT>
        <INPUT TYPE='button' VALUE='Previous'
            ONCLICK='previous(this.form);'></INPUT>
    </FORM>
    <SCRIPT LANGUAGE='JavaScript'>
        current=0;
        document.forms[0].kind.value=list[0].kind;
    </SCRIPT>
</BODY>
</HTML>
```

It is easy to see how insert, delete, and update operations could work on the JavaScript list array via user buttons. The one visible record acts as like a "letterbox slot" into the list. More than one row at a time could be displayed using this approach.

Let's take a look at how the code works.

First, we define a function that will be used as the constructor for our Horse object. The constructor takes just one parameter, the kind of horse this Horse object represents:

```
function Horse(kind) // constructor - add other parameters as required
{
    this.kind = kind;
}
```

In the next lines, which are executed when the page is parsed, we create a new Array object and insert various new Horse objects into its elements. This is the data we'll be navigating through later:

```
var list = new Array(); // the list of records, each an object.
var current = 0;
list[current++] = new Horse("Arab");
list[current++] = new Horse("Quarterhorse");
list[current++] = new Horse("Palamino");
list[current++] = new Horse("Gelding");
list[current++] = new Horse("Shetland Pony");
list[current++] = new Horse("Hack");
list[current++] = new Horse("Mule");
```

Finally, in the next script block, we have our next() and previous() functions, which are called when the user clicks the Next and Previous buttons in our form. These update the value property of the INPUT element named kind:

```
function next(form)
{
    if ( current + 1 < list.length )
        form.kind.value = list[++current].kind;

}

function previous(form)
{
    if ( current > 0 )
        form.kind.value = list[--current].kind;
```

175

```
        }
```

In our `next` function, we take the form containing the text box used to display the `kind` value, as a parameter. Our `if` statement checks to see if `current + 1`, in other words the current array index + 1, is less than the total number of `Horse` objects in our array, in other words the `list.length` property. This is to ensure that we've not moved past the last item in the array. If we've not then current variable is incremented and used to extract the data from the list array. The `previous` function works the same but in reverse, in other words we go back through the list array.

In the second script block, we ensure that the text box is filled with the `kind` value of the first `Horse` object in the list array:

```
<SCRIPT LANGUAGE='JavaScript'>
    current=0;
    document.forms[0].kind.value=list[0].kind;
</SCRIPT>
```

Selectable HTML

HTML form controls don't provide very flexible layout options. If visual display is an issue, it may be better to render the records in boilerplate HTML, with only minimal form controls. This example reuses the data of the previous example:

```
<!-- Example_18.htm -->
<HTML>
<HEAD>
    <SCRIPT>
        function Horse(kind) // constructor, add other parameters as required
        {
            this.kind = kind;
        }

        var list = new Array(); // the list of records, each an object.
        var current = 0;
        list[current++] = new Horse("Arab");
        list[current++] = new Horse("Quarterhorse");
        list[current++] = new Horse("Palamino");
        list[current++] = new Horse("Gelding");
        list[current++] = new Horse("Shetland Pony");
        list[current++] = new Horse("Hack");
        list[current++] = new Horse("Mule");

    </SCRIPT>
</HEAD>
<BODY>
    <FORM>
        <TABLE BORDER=1>
            <SCRIPT>
                var i;
                for (i=0; i < list.length; i++)
                {
                    document.write('<TR><TD>'+
                        '<INPUT TYPE="radio" NAME="horse" VALUE="'+i+'">');
                    document.write('<TD>'+list[i].kind+
                        '<TD>Other horsing around</TR>\n');
                }
            </SCRIPT>
        </TABLE>
    </FORM>
</BODY>
</HTML>
```

This example looks better, but lacks any editable fields. Any record can be selected by checking its radio button. The value of the radio button contains enough information to identify the record – seed data again. In this case, the seed is the index of the list array. If that array didn't exist, perhaps because the page was the output of some search query, the seed data is sufficient to use as a query used to display the record in an editable form. We could make the example more useful by attaching event handlers to each of the radio buttons, for example the onClick event handler.

TEXTAREA

<TEXTAREA> tags provide a form control for multi-line input, which sounds perfect for multiple records. Their only obvious restriction is that their content must only be plain text, which is rather primitive.

For display only of multi-record data, you may find <TEXTAREA> tags to be of limited use. There are two traps. The first is that Windows, UNIX, and MacOS differ over the end-of-line character, the first two requiring \r\n, the other just \n. As far as we're aware, this incompatibility is restricted to <TEXTAREA> tags. Fortunately, the \r\n combination works in both places, so use that. The following is a portable example displaying three lines:

```
<TEXTAREA ROWS=3 ONCHANGE='this.value="ten\r\ngreen\r\nbottles";'>
    No bottles yet
</TEXTAREA>
```

Unfortunately, the Macintosh requires just \r. If you want portability on all three platforms, you will have to avoid literal characters altogether. Instead, test the operating system using one of the compatibility techniques, set a variable to the correct characters, and use that variable instead.

The second trap is the auto wrap feature of the <TEXTAREA>. If a line extends past the physical width of the <TEXTAREA>, and the COLS attribute is set to a value, then the line will be broken unpredictably into two, spoiling the display. You can deal with this by setting the WRAP attribute to off, but then you must live with the possibility that all your text might not all appear – the user might need to scroll the TEXTAREA. A compromise is the virtual setting, this wraps the text, but sends the text with only the new lines added by the user.

If the user can change the <TEXTAREA> tag's contents, the situation is much worse. <TEXTAREA> tags were designed for plain text, not formatted information. Their word-wrapping behavior formats plain text nicely, but makes data entry of line-oriented information very difficult. You can't stop the user adding additional lines beyond the value of the ROWS attribute, and, if the COLS attribute is set, you can't stop the user from entering a long line that gets word wrapped, and that is then indistinguishable from two separate, smaller lines.

With careful processing of the <TEXTAREA> tag's value, you can reformat user input, but really this is so limited, it is not recommended. Desperate tactics: use a 4.0 browser and capture each keystroke the user makes over the TEXTAREA control and insert it into the <TEXTAREA> tag's value yourself from the scripting side.

Custom Form Elements

Sometimes, the various HTML tags that make up form elements seem a bit limited. If you really want to do something else, there's always a way.

Clickable Elements

Any HTML element that's clickable can be used to store simple form data. Usually, that data just amounts to a flag that says 'I was picked'. The most traditional clickable elements are hypertext links (<A> tags) and images. With the Dynamic HTML support in Internet Explorer 4+ and Netscape 6, however virtually any tag will do.

This example shows how to use links to simulate a simple radio button set arrangement. When a link is clicked, a URL request that is effectively a GET form request is sent with a single form element, called dress. Although in this case each item's full description is linked, there's nothing stopping you from making some other bit of HTML the link, leaving each item's description stated near it:

```
<!-- Example_19.htm -->
<HTML>
<BODY>
    Dressing for Dinner? Choose your attire:<BR>
    <A HREF='answer.html?dress=white_tie'>Top Hat and Tails</A><BR>
    <A HREF='answer.html?dress=black_tie'>Tuxedo</A><BR>
    <A HREF='answer.html?dress=casual'>Slacks and Coat</A><BR>
    <A HREF='answer.html?dress=punk'>Safety Pins</A>
</BODY>
<HTML>
```

The next Internet Explorer 4+/Netscape 6+ example is a little more sophisticated. Information is collected from the user's clicks until the submit link is clicked. When the user clicks on one of the color bars, a note is made. Then, when they click the I'm the pot ! link, this information is added to the URL. The example is very limited in its current form, but the principles could be used and adapted for something more sophisticated:

```
<!-- Example_20.htm -->
<HTML>
<BODY>
    <SCRIPT LANGUAGE='JavaScript'>
        var palette="?palette=A";
    </SCRIPT>
    Click on the colors of the rainbow that appeal, and then click on the
    pot of gold to have your preference registered.<BR>
    <DIV STYLE='background : red'
        ONCLICK='window.palette+="&col=red"'>
        Color 1
    </DIV>
    <DIV STYLE='background : orange'
        ONCLICK='window.palette+="&col=orange"'>
        Color 2
    </DIV>
    <!-- ... and so on ... -->
    <DIV STYLE='background : violet'
        ONCLICK='window.palette+="&col=violet"'>
        Color 3
    </DIV>
    <A HREF='#'
        ONCLICK='window.location.href+=palette; return false'>
        I'm the Pot!
    </A>
</BODY>
</HTML>
```

In the first line of script, we're creating a dummy variable called palette which is initialized to a value that we're not really interested in. We do this because we can then add zero or more items to the string that it begins in a consistent way, as shown in the <DIV> onclick events. Otherwise, we'd need tricky logic to test whether each item added was the first one or not – the first item must be preceded by ?, and not by &.

Q&A Sessions

The prompt() and confirm() functions, described earlier in this chapter, are the simplest way to get data from the user. We can even put these functions in the head of a document, so that we can gather data before any of the document is displayed:

```
<!-- Example_21.htm -->
<HTML>
<HEAD>
   <SCRIPT LANGUAGE='JavaScript'>
      var polite = confirm("Be nice?");
   </SCRIPT>
</HEAD>
<BODY>
   <SCRIPT LANGUAGE='JavaScript'>
      if (polite)
         document.write("Welcome to my home page");
      else
         document.write("Waddaya want?");
   </SCRIPT>
</BODY>
</HTML>
```

A second use of message boxes is when we want to implement a simple Question-and-Answer session, similar to a Microsoft Wizard dialog box. For such a system, we can use a shopping cart arrangement with a separate HTML page for each stage of the Q&A, but for very simple uses, a few simple dialog boxes may be enough:

```
<!-- Example_22.htm -->
<HTML>
<BODY>
   Budget Examiner<BR>
   <SCRIPT LANGUAGE='JavaScript'>
      var income =   prompt("Enter your annual income",'');
      var expenses = prompt("Enter your annual expenses",'');
      var tax = prompt("Enter your tax % as 2 digits",'');
      if (income * (1 - tax/100) > expenses)
         document.write("You still have spending money");
      else
         document.write("You're broke!");
   </SCRIPT>
</BODY>
</HTML>
```

In a real application (where you are doing more than just illustrating a point of design), when reading data from the user, you should include all the proper input validation checking that has been discussed earlier in this chapter.

Adding a Little Style to Controls

If we don't like the look of plain, boring old HTML controls, then we can always use CSS style to spice them up, as in the example below:

```
<!-- Example_23.htm -->
<HTML>
<HEAD>
   <TITLE>
      input css control
   </TITLE>
</HEAD>
<BODY style="background-color: lightgrey;">
   <input TYPE="text" style="border-width: 0; background-color: blue;
      color: white; font-family: Arial; font-size: 24pt;"
      VALUE="Type in here">
   <BR>
   <input TYPE="text" style="background-color: transparent;
      color: white; font-family: 'Times New Roman'; font-size:16pt;"
```

```
          VALUE="Type in here">
   <BR>
</BODY>
</HTML>
```

Without any JavaScript and just a little CSS, at all the text boxes look quite different, Chapter 10 has more details about how CSS works. If we want something radically different then we can use DHTML and create our own controls, a very simple example is shown below:

```
<!-- Example_24.htm -->
<HTML>
<BODY>
<!--  add styles as required  -->
Click on yellow and type away:
<SPAN ID="TextBox"
    STYLE="background: yellow; width: 2em; clip: rect(0 100 32 auto)"
    ONKEYPRESS="this.innerText+=String.fromCharCode(window.event.keyCode)">
</SPAN>
</BODY>
</HTML>
```

In this example, the <SPAN> tag acts as a textarea. Whenever a key is pressed while the mouse is over the <SPAN>, the key character is added to the <SPAN> contents, although you have to click once on the span to give it the input focus to start with. Because all of the style properties are exposed to JavaScript for this tag, we have fine control over the textarea's fonts, size and appearance. This rather crude and simple example can be enhanced quite a bit to support character deletion by backspacing or highlighting to show input focus and so on. It could also be constrained on the screen by clip regions and so on.

This example only works in Internet Explorer 4.0+.

Tree Menus

A common control that isn't provided by the HTML form element tags is a tree menu or tree menu controller. This kind of control allows the user to navigate hierarchical data within a web document in a similar way to the Macintosh's Finder or Microsoft Window's Windows Explorer.

The book, *JavaScript Objects* (Wrox Press, ISBN: 1-861001-89-4) discusses tree-controllers at length, but in the meantime you might like to have a look at some tree controllers available on the World Wide Web. A fairly well documented Dynamic HTML controller is available at http://www.treemenu.com/. A controller that is less well documented but mimics Windows Explorer more closely is available at: http://www.geocities.com/Paris/LeftBank/2178/foldertree.html.

Zones

Zones are a design technique for forms that don't require any JavaScript. Don't get confused with Internet Explorer security zones – we're talking about a design technique, not a browser feature here.

Zones are so useful that they're worth a mention anyway. A zone is just a rectangle of a web page used to collect similar information together and are usually separated by blank space. This arrangement makes a page or form easier for the eye to read and the brain to make sense of. There's no rocket science involved, usually just some appropriate HTML (such as <FIELDSET> and <LEGEND> tags of HTML 4.0) or simply some layout and design before you even touch the keyboard. Thinking in terms of zones is a good design strategy.

If you have a look around the web at some of the more expensive, corporate web sites, you'll see how zones are used to divide and draw the user's attention to different parts of the web page.

Summary

Just like the other parts of an HTML document, HTML form elements make an appearance as host objects accessible from a browser-embedded JavaScript interpreter. From the JavaScript perspective, there are some complexities with HTML forms that aren't obvious from the equivalent HTML tags, and the scriptwriter needs to beware of these. Furthermore, although HTML forms are an obvious and logical place to store user or developer data in a web document, they are not the only place.

JavaScript allows the scriptwriter to add intelligence to forms. The two main possibilities are smarter processing via scripting in validation, and better form element layout. When traditional HTML forms are too limited, JavaScript can exploit Dynamic HTML where it's available to escape right out of the box and innovate more flexible form elements from scratch.

The flexibility provided by JavaScript makes a number of more complex form designs possible. Shopping carts, multi-record forms, and master-detail forms, are all examples. With client-side JavaScript, a web browser starts to look a bit like a traditional 4GL database client and some of the processing of those tools is possible, provided the scripter is wary of a number of design issues.

Finally, the main bugbear of forms is the question of where the data should be sent. There are a few browser escape hatches, but in general, scripting at the web server is required.

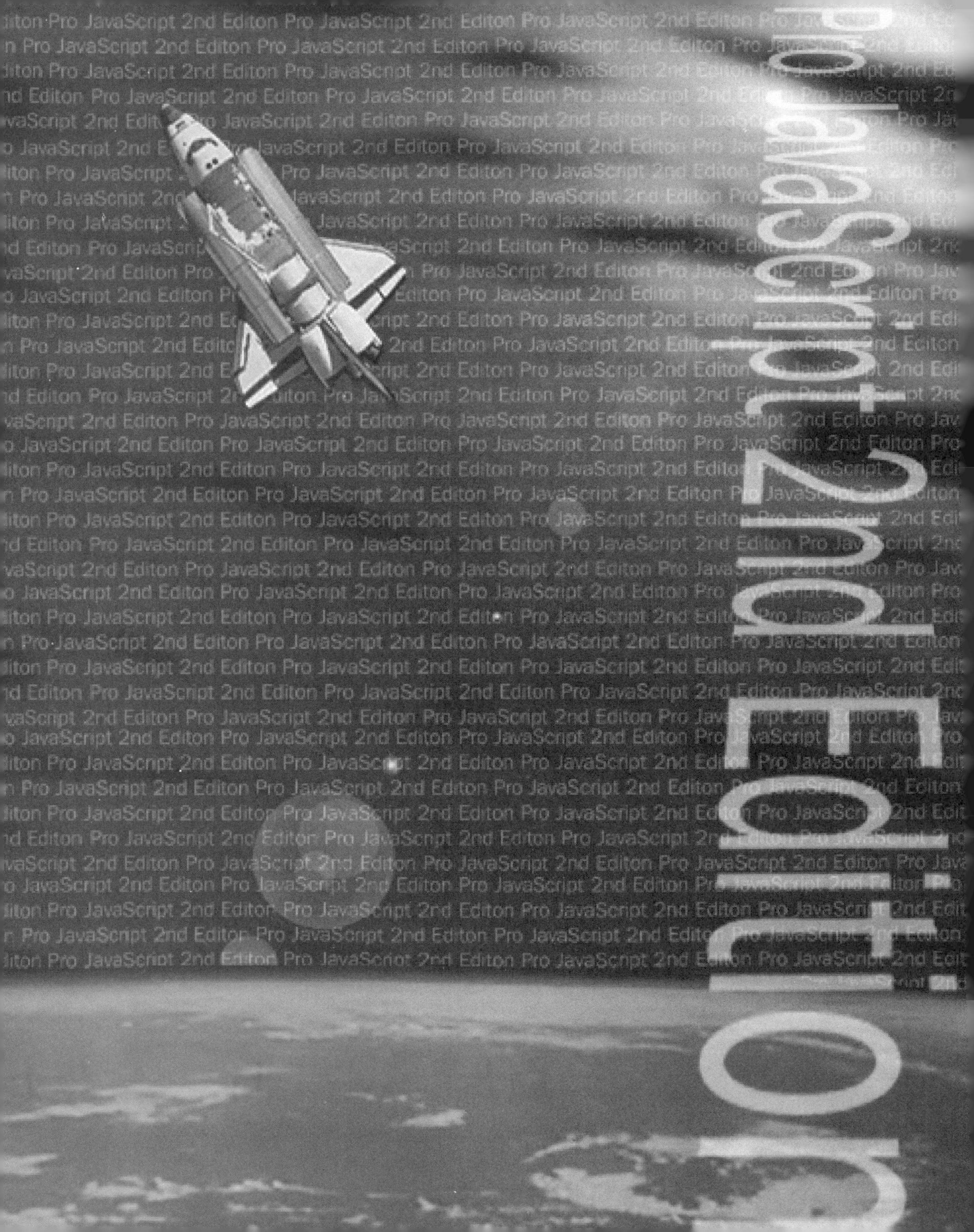
Pro JavaScript 2nd Edition

6

Multimedia and Plug-Ins

Multimedia is at the forefront of the Internet revolution. New interactive web sites are quickly replacing old static web pages, with broadband high-speed access now available to a mass market. This underscores the feasibility of real-time high quality audio and video on the Web.

JavaScript is a powerful client-side tool for delivering multimedia. The recent proliferation of multimedia API libraries and development tools simplifies greatly the production and integration of rich content on the Web. Combining the strengths of JavaScript and embedded multimedia, developers can now devise custom media players, presentations and full-featured web applications.

This chapter will cover in detail how JavaScript can be used to detect and control multimedia on a web page. We will also examine how to solve compatibility problems and implement practical real-world solutions. Finally, we will look into developments and standards that will shape the future landscape of the Web.

A Brief History Of Web Multimedia

It is important to understand how rich media has evolved on the Web. This section will present a brief historical overview of the rapid development of interactive multimedia and present a *behind the scenes* look at the fundamental integration of multimedia and the browser.

The inclusion of rich media on the Web has only been around since 1994. Netscape was unleashed on the world thanks to the work of Jim Clark and Marc Andreessen. In Netscape 2.0 they included the unique functionality of displaying **hypermedia**. The term hypermedia was coined in the 1960s by futurist Ted Nelson to describe the concept of establishing non-linear electronic links between text, video, sound, and music. Initially, Netscape 1.0 and Mosaic 1.0 could only display sound and graphics using external helper applications. The integration of the helper applications into the browser led to the development of the **plug-in**.

A plug-in is simply a program that extends the capabilities of a web browser. These programs rely on Multipurpose Internet Mail Extensions (MIME)-types associations to determine which plug-ins to launch. They are also highly dependent on the client platform and operating system. This technology was spearheaded by Netscape to allow third party developers to add extra graphics and sound functionality to be integrated in the browser.

It is interesting to note that IE was able to handle Netscape style plug-ins up until Version 5.5 Service Pack 1. Netscape has never supported ActiveX.

IE 5.5 Service Pack 2 and IE 6 no longer support plug-ins. Microsoft has announced that developers should use equivalent ActiveX components for creating content geared specifically for their new browsers. Despite shifting away from Netscape's technologies, Microsoft has made the surprising move to openly support the use of the EMBED element (a proprietary HTML extension developed by Netscape) for adding ActiveX controls on web pages.

Microsoft invented ActiveX controls as reworked OLE controls that are optimized for the Web. ActiveX controls are independent of the IE browser, and are portable to other Microsoft/Windows-based systems. For example, the controls can allow you to embed Excel spreadsheets onto a web page (as long as Excel is installed on the client machine). ActiveX is based on the Component Object Model (COM). It utilizes the operating system's resources to run. They are self-contained pre-compiled programs that add functionality to a web page as opposed to the browser.

ActiveX has its share of disadvantages. The controls are highly integrated into the Windows operating system. This has led to the proliferation of ActiveX hacks and vulnerabilities. For example, Eyedog is an obscure control that serves as a system diagnostic tool. However, if not properly patched it can be used to query a person's registry via Internet Explorer. As a result of these attacks, many users entirely disable the ActiveX functionality in their browsers, which is bad news for web developers. On top of that, ActiveX controls cannot easily be ported to other platforms.

Microsoft has devised many interesting solutions to tackle the shortcomings of ActiveX in the development of the .NET platform. The Webform component deployed along with ASP+ solves the problem of browser incompatibility by pre-rendering custom content on the server before it is delivered to the client browser. Unlike ActiveX, Webforms do not require to be installed on the client machine, and they are tailored to every browser (with a definite bias towards Microsoft-based technologies).

Microsoft is also slowly shifting from COM/ActiveX to .NET components. The advantage of the .NET architecture is that it is compatible with all computer languages and platforms (that support the .NET runtime).

Incorporating Multimedia Into a Web Page

This part of the chapter will outline the practical approaches on how to incorporate audio, video, and animation on a web page. Every browser reacts uniquely to multimedia. We will examine the particularities of the interactions between browsers and plug-ins, placing a special emphasis on the latest browsers and technologies.

There are two fundamental elements used to incorporate multimedia on a web page: EMBED and OBJECT.

EMBED

EMBED is a proprietary Netscape element introduced as an extension of HTML 3.2. EMBED is primarily used to incorporate Netscape style plug-ins on web pages. However, it can also be used to add other types of file formats such as text files. This tag is compatible on IE 3.0 through to version 6.0. IE 4.0 introduced additional JScript support.

Certain vendors recommend the use of EMBED to integrate their plug-ins on the Web. An example of this is Adobe and their SVG plug-in and until recently, QuickTime. The EMBED element has been kept in use due to its broad implementation and compatibility on multiple platforms.

Note that HTML 4.0 recommends the use of the OBJECT element instead of EMBED. EMBED is unofficially deprecated from the standard (along with the APPLET element) primarily because APPLET and EMBED are proprietary standards developed to embrace specific technologies (respectively Java and Netscape). On the other hand, the OBJECT element can be used to embed anything on a web page; it can encompass both current and future technologies by any vendor.

All current versions of Netscape support the EMBED element. Here is a typical example of its use:

```
<EMBED SRC='movie.asf' NAME='movie'></EMBED>
```

The EMBED element has many attributes, allowing web developers to control how the multimedia is presented on a web page. In fact, every single media format has a customized set of attributes. Here is a list of some of the core EMBED attributes:

Attributes	Description
ALIGN	Specifies how text will be aligned beside the embedded element. Possible values are: Top, Bottom, Right, Left, Right Texttop, Middle, Absmiddle, Baseline Absbottom.
BORDER	The BORDER attribute defines the size of the border around the plug-in.
FRAMEBORDER	Specifies the thickness of the frame around the EMBED.
HEIGHT	Specifies the height of the embedded element on the page. Values include absolute pixel sizes or percentages.
HIDDEN	Embeds a media file on the page, although the interface is not visible to the user. Note that the object is still accessible using JavaScript.
HSPACE	This attribute specifies the amount of padding to include on the left and right sides of the embedded object. Usually measured in pixels.
NAME	Provides a unique label for the embedded element on the page so that it may be referenced and manipulated using JavaScript.
PALETTE	PALETTE only works on the Windows platform. There are two possible values for this attribute: FOREGROUND and BACKGROUND. A setting of FOREGROUND will make the plug-in use the foreground colors. The BACKGROUND setting will make the plug-in use the background colors.
PLUGINSPAGE	Specifies a URL for a page containing the appropriate plug-in if it is not available to the client's browser.
PLUGINURL	Specifies a direct URL for the desired plug-in. This attribute will override PLUGINSPAGE.
SRC	Specifies the location of the media file to be embedded into the web page.
TYPE	Defines the MIME type of the embedded object.

Table continued on following page

Attributes	Description
UNITS	Defines in what units the HEIGHT/WIDTH or VSPACE/HSPACE elements should be measured. Possible values include:
	PIXELS – The default UNITS setting in Netscape. This value indicates that HEIGHT and WIDTH attributes should be measured using the number of pixels.
	EN – This value indicates that HEIGHT and WIDTH attributes should equal half the current font's point size. EM and EN are used in typography to determine font spacing.
VSPACE	This attribute specifies the amount of padding to include on the top and bottom sides of the embedded object. Usually measured in pixels.
WIDTH	Specifies the width of the embedded element on the page. Values include absolute pixel sizes or percentages.

You can access the IE specific EMBED attributes at:
http://msdn.microsoft.com/workshop/author/dhtml/reference/objects/embed.asp

NOEMBED

What if the users are running older browsers or don't have the appropriate plug-ins? Compatibility and accessibility are the key objectives in providing the optimal experience to your intended audience. This element provides a simple alternative message to your users in the event they are unable to experience rich media content.

The content contained between the NOEMBED tags will display when a Netscape-compatible browser is unable to instantiate the plug-in object. Note that IE does not support this tag.

Here is an example of a generic use of NOEMBED:

```
<EMBED SRC='coolcontent.mov' NAME='coolcontent' WIDTH='100' HEIGHT='100'>
<NOEMBED>Sorry, you need the appropriate player to view this presentation.
</NOEMBED></EMBED>
```

Netscape 6

Mozilla has redesigned the implementation of plug-ins in their new browser. They have removed the dependencies on the Java Virtual Machine (JVM) and have changed the underlying architecture of their plug-ins, from the **LiveConnect /Netscape Plug-In API** to the **Mozilla Plug-In API**. It is important to note that some of the major multimedia applications vendors have not yet released new Mozilla based plug-ins for this new browser. Hopefully, support for this browser will increase to facilitate the creation of compatible web media applications.

OBJECT

The OBJECT element has gone through many permutations before settling on its current state. The APPLET element was originally introduced along with the HTML 3.2 specifications. The objective was to allow developers to have Java Applets download and execute automatically in HTML documents, a novel idea at the time.

APPLET was deprecated in HTML 4.0 in favor of the OBJECT element. There are several reasons for this: the APPLET element does not take into account new media types, it only works with Java based Applets and it has accessibility issues. The OBJECT element was designed to replace the EMBED, APPLET, SOUND, BGSOUND, and IMG elements.

OBJECT support has been available in HTML since IE 3.0 and in script since IE 4.0. The only Netscape browser that supports the OBJECT element is Netscape 6+. Note that IE cannot embed images (as per the W3C standards) using the OBJECT element while Netscape 6+ can do this without any problems.

The OBJECT element is commonly used to incorporate Microsoft ActiveX controls into a HTML page. Much like EMBED, we can assign certain attributes to this element in order to gain more control over the display and behavior of the components. These attributes are assigned to the embedded object using the parameter (PARAM) tags.

Here is a short-listing of core attributes for the OBJECT element:

Attributes	Description
ARCHIVE	ARCHIVE can contain a space delimited listing of URIs with archived resources relating to the object. You can also include the URI from the DATA and CLASSID attributes. Objects require less time to load in the browser when you pre-load the archive files. Relative URI listings are relative to CODEBASE.
CLASSID	CLASSID can be used to indicate the implementation of an object with a URI. This attribute can be used standalone or in conjunction with the DATA attribute, (it depends on the nature of the object). On the Microsoft platform, the CLASSID attribute is used to uniquely identify ActiveX components. The browser can then cross-reference the registry and load-in the appropriate component.
CODEBASE	CODEBASE lists the base path of the URI indicators found in the DATA, CLASSID, and ARCHIVE attributes. The default value for this attribute is the same path as the parent document containing the object embed.
CODETYPE	CODETYPE contains an indicator of what type of data is accepted for the object defined in the CLASSID.
DATA	DATA is used to specify the location where the object's data is stored. URIs are resolved as per the path established in the CODEBASE.
DECLARE	This attribute declares, but doesn't instantiate the object in question. The object can later be instantiated by referring to the declaration.
HEIGHT	Specifies the height of the embedded element on the HTML page. Values are listed in pixels.
NAME	NAME assigns a label to the instantiated object. ID is also supported as an alternate attribute.
STANDBY	This attribute may contain a short message that is displayed while the object is loading in the browser.
TYPE	TYPE indicates the type of data specified in the DATA attribute, such as a MIME-type. This attribute is usually set to avoid the delivery of incompatible file formats to the object.
USEMAP	This attribute specifies the URL of a client-side image map that is to be tied in with the OBJECT. The name of the client-side map and USEMAP must match to work effectively.
WIDTH	Specifies the width of the embedded element on the page. Values are listed in pixels.

The IE specific OBJECT attributes can be found on the MSDN site at:
http://msdn.microsoft.com/workshop/author/dhtml/reference/objects/OBJECT.asp

The Netscape specific attributes can be found at:
http://developer.netscape.com/docs/manuals/htmlguid/index.htm

The W3C page for the OBJECT element can be found at:
http://www.w3.org/TR/html401/struct/objects.html

Here is a typical example of how OBJECT can be used to embed a media file into a HTML document:

```
<OBJECT CLASSID='clsid:6BF52A52-394A-11D3-B153-00C04F79FAA6' ID='movie'>
<PARAM NAME='SRC' VALUE='movie.asf'>
</OBJECT>
```

Alternative Browsers

Here is a list of some of the leading alternative browsers. Each has distinctive characteristics to keep in mind, especially if you are investigating compatibility issues regarding the wide implementation of rich media content.

Opera

Alongside IE and Netscape, Opera 5.0 is becoming increasingly popular due to its speed, compact size, and adherence to standards.

Note that Opera supports the OBJECT element. The browser however does not support the ALIGN, CLASSID, CODEBASE, CODETYPE, and STANDBY attributes. Opera also does not support the LiveConnect Plug-In specifications. Opera 4+ contain the Sun Java Runtime Environment to handle Java applets. If you are using an earlier version of the Opera browser, you must manually download the JRE from Sun's website to get Java support.

Opera also has its own Plug-In API, which is derived from Netscape's specifications. Therefore, all pre-Netscape 6 plug-ins will function in Opera. Opera's documentation advises developers to build plug-ins that are compatible with both Netscape's plug-in specifications and Mozilla's new Plug-In API. Note that ActiveX or VBScript will not run in this browser.

Opera currently supports Flash, Shockwave, QuickTime, and RealMedia using Netscape plug-ins. If you want to create a multimedia page for Opera, be sure to follow the Netscape specifications – use the EMBED element.

You can get more information about the Opera browser at http://www.opera.com.

NeoPlanet

NeoPlanet uses the IE 5.0 browsing engine at the core. Therefore, the browser is ActiveX compatible. Furthermore, NeoPlanet has integrated the Gecko Mozilla engine in their browser for greater cross-browser compatibility. This also means that the browser can embed rich media using plug-ins, as long as they are based on the new Mozilla Plug-In API.

Special Considerations

There are few important details to remember regarding the incorporation of rich media on a HTML page.

From a practical standpoint, both the EMBED and OBJECT elements should be used in conjunction to make sure that your content is cross-browser compatible. Netscape does not natively accept ActiveX controls, and will ignore the OBJECT elements that reference the ActiveX controls.

The parameter (PARAM) tags are an important component of the OBJECT element. They contain the attributes and values that should be applied to the embedded OBJECT. Note that the EMBED tags nested between the OBJECT tags should follow the PARAM declarations. Here is an example:

```
<OBJECT>
<PARAM>
<PARAM>
<EMBED>
</EMBED>
</OBJECT>
```

If you are using IE, it will attempt to access the application referenced in the CLASSID to render the media. If the application cannot be found, it will look for the "alternative" content between the OBJECT tags. In this case, we have used EMBED to display the media using the browser's default media player as defined by the associated MIME-type.

Accessibility guidelines dictate that alternative content should be presented if required plug-ins or controls are not available on the client machine. Embedding the plug-in or component within a TABLE element is a useful technique to accomplish this. Here is an example:

```
<TABLE CELLPADDING='0' CELLSPACING='0' BORDER='0' WIDTH='500' HEIGHT='500'>
   <TR><TD BACKGROUND='alternativeimage.jpg'>
      <OBJECT CLASSID='clsid:22d6f312-b0f6-11d0-94ab-0080c74c7e95'
         ID='greatcontent' WIDTH='500' HEIGHT='500'>
         <PARAM NAME='FileName' VALUE='greatcontent.asf'>
         <EMBED SRC='greatcontent.asf' NAME='greatcontent' WIDTH='500'
         HEIGHT='500'></EMBED>
      </OBJECT>
   </TD></TR>
</TABLE>
```

As shown above, a background image (alternativeimage.jpg) is defined as the background of the table. If the embedded object executes, it will overlay the background image you have defined in the table. However, if the plug-in or component is not present, the background image will show in the place of an empty object placeholder. Be sure to add the HEIGHT and WIDTH attributes to the table to match the HEIGHT and WIDTH of the embedded media.

Detecting Plug-Ins and Controls Using JavaScript

A factor that is often overlooked when designing multimedia rich pages is the user experience. Many developers fall into the trap of assuming that their intended audiences possess the required plug-ins. As an end user, there is nothing more frustrating than arriving at a page with a plug-in placeholder or being unable to view content when you know you have the necessary tools installed on your computer.

Admittedly, detecting the presence of multimedia on the client can be tricky. In the case of Netscape, it is relatively easy. JavaScript 1.1 and above includes the navigator object that can be used to detect these capabilities. However, IE is a different story altogether.

There has been a general lack of information on the Web regarding the effective detection of IE controls and components. As a result, many detection routines in use today are inadequate in certain circumstances. For example, you may have a plug-in installed, but a website's detection routine will not find it and lead you to error pages or a blank screen. This is especially true with many Flash driven pages. Most experienced users know to look at the HTML source to find the desired content pages. Unfortunately, this is far from an effective solution.

In this section, we will explore the strategies that will help you build a robust detection routine that can help your users get the best experience from your media-rich web pages.

Component Detection using IE 5.0+

Microsoft has added a new set of DOM behaviors to IE 5 and above that allows developers to detect and manipulate browser-based components. The Client Capture (`clientCaps`) behavior provides information about supported features in IE as well as a way for installing browser components on demand. This behavior is accessible using IE 5+ on Windows or Unix based platforms.

To make use of this behavior, we must create an XML namespace. It is important that the namespace declaration is placed in the HEAD of the HTML document or you will get an error. This declaration will make the entire browser (including tags and elements) accessible to `clientCaps`:

```
<xml:namespace ns='http://www.microsoft.com/ie' prefix='MSIE'/>
```

Alternatively, you can use the following tag to replace the HTML with the same effect:

```
<HTML xmlns:MSIE>
```

Then we define the `clientCaps` behavior and object within the browser namespace. The following should be placed between the HEAD tags:

```
<STYLE>
    @media all {MSIE\: clientCaps {behavior: url #default#clientcaps);}}
</STYLE>
<MSIE:CLIENTCAPS ID="oClientCaps" />
```

This is the actual JavaScript code that detects the presence of a component on a user's system. The `comVersion` variable contains the current version number of the application in question. The browser cross-references the registry using the `ComponentID` (`cID`) value. If the component is found, the variable `comInstalled` is set to `TRUE`. If the component is not found, the value is returned as either `FALSE` or `Undefined`.

In some cases, if the component is not found the browser will generate a runtime error and your JavaScript program will stop in its tracks. When detecting components, it is important to add error checking to eliminate the possibility of this happening. If you look at our detection program (located at the end of this section), we will outline effective methods of avoiding detection errors.

Here is the code used to detect the components in the registry through the browser:

```
<SCRIPT LANGUAGE="JavaScript">
    comInstalled=oClientCaps.isComponentInstalled(cID,"ComponentID");
    comVersion-oClientCaps.getComponentVersion(cID,"ComponentID");
</SCRIPT>
```

Note that this routine will not work on a Mac, because a Mac has no registry to reference, and Microsoft components are not compatible with the Mac OS.

Here is a listing of non-version specific component identifiers for most popular multimedia types:

Name Of Multimedia	Unique Component Identifiers (cID)
Macromedia Flash Player	{D27CDB6E-AE6D-11cf-96B8-444553540000}
Macromedia Shockwave Flash Player	{166B1BCA-3F9C-11CF-8075-444553540000}

Name Of Multimedia	Unique Component Identifiers (cID)
Windows Media Player 6.4	{22D6F312-B0F6-11D0-94AB-0080C74C7E95}
Windows Media Player 7/8	{6BF52A52-394A-11D3-B153-00C04F79FAA6}
RealNetworks RealPlayer G2	{CFCDAA03-8BE4-11CF-B84B-020AFBBCCFA}
Apple QuickTime	{02BF25D5-8C17-4B23-BC80-D3488ABDDC6B}

Using Object Instantiation to Detect ActiveX Objects

This method is the most effective way of detecting the presence of ActiveX controls registered in the IE 4+. However, be aware that many users choose to disable ActiveX in their browsers for security reasons.

The JavaScript code to detect the presence of ActiveX components is as follows:

```
<SCRIPT LANGUAGE='JScript'>
    var activexDetect = new ActiveXObject(ProgID);
</SCRIPT>
```

In the above code, we create an instance in the ActiveX object. If the object was successfully created, then the component is installed on the client's machine and it will be available as a resource. If not, then the value of the object will be NULL or generate a runtime error. For a discussion on coping with these errors, please refer to our detection program at the end of this section.

Here is a listing of the multimedia types that can be detected using this method and their corresponding Program Identification Strings:

Name Of Multimedia	Program ID (ProgID)
Macromedia Flash	ShockwaveFlash.ShockwaveFlash
Macromedia Shockwave	SWCtl.SWCtl
Windows Media Player 6.4/7/8	MediaPlayer.MediaPlayer.1
RealNetworks RealPlayer G2	rmocx.RealPlayer G2 Control.1
Apple QuickTime 5.0.2	QuickTimeCheckObject.QuickTimeCheck.1

As you may have noticed, most of the values listed in the ProgID column in the table contain a 1 appended to the end of the string. These Program IDs can be used to generically determine if an ActiveX component is installed on the client machine. Please keep in mind however that the code will not determine the versions of the applications in question.

Detecting ActiveX Version Information Using IE

Detecting the version information in an ActiveX control can be a little complicated. Most of the version detection routines available are written in VBScript.

Software vendors frequently implement proprietary versioning standards for their ActiveX controls. For example, Shockwave distinguishes each ActiveX control by appending a version number at the end of the Program ID. The plug-ins listed above also do this. You can detect the version by instantiating each version of the player, starting from the highest version to the lowest.

The following table contains the Program ID and the corresponding version information for the Shockwave player:

Program ID	Description
SWCtl.SWCtl	The generic ActiveX control.
SWCtl.SWCtl.1	Shockwave Player, version 6
SWCtl.SWCtl.7	Shockwave Player, version 7
SWCtl.SWCtl.8	Shockwave Player, version 8

The values listed in this table can be found on Macromedia's website at:
http://www.macromedia.com/support/director/ts/documents/shockwave_player_detect.htm

The following snippet of code tests the existence of the SWCtl.SWCtl.7 object that would confirm the presence of the Shockwave Player Version 7 on the client's browser:

```
<SCRIPT LANGUAGE='JScript'>
    var shockwave7Installed = new ActiveXObject("SWCtl.SWCtl.7");
</SCRIPT>
```

The best place to find information regarding Class Names and Program Identification strings is in the Windows Registry.

The OLE/COM Object Viewer

The OLE/COM Object Viewer is a useful interface to find information about the objects and components installed on your computer. You can obtain a free copy at:
http://www.microsoft.com/com/resources/oleview.asp.

As an alternative, you can use the Registry Editor to look up these values by clicking the Start Menu | Run, and then typing regedit. Type in the name of the application you are looking for using the Find option. The information should be located under the HKEY_CLASSES_ROOT folder in the Registry list.

Detection Problems – IE on the Mac

Note that the ActiveX detection scripts listed above will not work on the Mac platform. Microsoft has added little to no ActiveX functionality in their implementation of IE for the Mac. With the release of IE 5, Microsoft added plug-in detection functionality to MacIE. The browser can now detect Netscape-type plug-ins through the JavaScript navigator.plugins object.

Other than this, there is no documented way to detect ActiveX or Plug-Ins on IE 4.0 on the Mac platform.

Using Browser Objects – The navigator Object

Fortunately for developers, the Netscape browser has JavaScript objects that can be accessed to help find out the availability of plug-ins. Here is a list of the relevant methods for the navigator object:

The navigator.plugins() Method

Possibly the easiest way of ascertaining the existence of a plug-in, this method is effective with Netscape based browsers (including Opera) and IE 5 on the Mac platform.

The Windows version of IE has access to the plug-ins collection, but it functions completely differently. It will not detect plug-ins, but rather objects placed on the page using the EMBED tags.

Note that if you use the `autoComplete()` function in Visual Interdev, it will retrieve the properties of the `navigator` object, and no errors will appear at run time. However, IE will not be able to detect plug-ins using the object (as explained above).

The following JavaScript program called `pluginNSDetect.html` will generate a list of all the plug-ins contained in the browser by accessing the `navigator.plugins()` method. In particular, the program will list the name, filename, and description:

```
<!--DetectPlugins.htm -->
<HTML>
<BODY>
   <SCRIPT LANGUAGE='JavaScript'>
      if (navigator.plugins)
      {
         for (i=0; i < navigator.plugins.length; i++)
         {
            document.writeln("Plugin Name: "
               + navigator.plugins[i].name + "<BR>");
            document.writeln("Plugin Filename: "
               + navigator.plugins[i].filename + "<BR>");
            if (navigator.plugins[i].description)
            {
               document.writeln("Plugin Description: "
                  + navigator.plugins[i].description + "<BR><BR>");
            }
            else
            {
               document.writeln("No description available.<BR><BR>");
            }
         }
      }
   </SCRIPT>
</BODY>
</HTML>
```

The output on Netscape 6.1 looks like this:

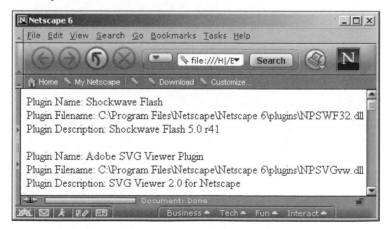

Please refer below for a list of the `navigator.plugins` object methods and properties:

Properties and Elements	Description
length	This property will indicate the number of plug-ins available to the browser
name	This property will return the value of the plug-in object's name
filename	This property will return the plug-in object's file name
description	This element of the navigator.plugins array will return a description of each plug-in

Methods	Description
refresh()	This method refreshes all of the plug-ins installed in the browser. It makes available newly installed plug-ins without the need to restart the browser.

The navigator.mimeTypes() Method

Netscape has access to two resources to render multimedia: plug-ins and helper applications. Note that navigator.mimeTypes() will not work on any version of IE. The helper application is a designated application registered in Windows to handle specific file types. The execution of helper applications is determined by the embedded file's MIME-Type.

The navigator.mimeTypes() method will help you determine whether the browser recognizes the MIME-Type tied in to a particular application, thus confirming its existence and availability to the browser. It even can provide you with the name of the plug-in associated to a particular MIME-Type. Here is a mini-JavaScript program called mimeNSDetect.html that will generate a list of all the accessible MIME-Types for Netscape (and other compatible browsers):

```
<!-- MimeTypes.htm -->
<HTML>
<BODY>
    <SCRIPT LANGUAGE='JavaScript'>
        if (navigator.mimeTypes)
        {
            for (i=0; i < navigator.mimeTypes.length; i++)
            {
                document.writeln("MIME Type: " + navigator.mimeTypes[i].type
                    + "<BR>");
                document.writeln("MIME Suffixes: "
                    + navigator.mimeTypes[i].suffixes + "<BR>");
                document.writeln("MIME Type: "
                    + navigator.mimeTypes[i].description + "<BR>");
                if (navigator.mimeTypes[i].enabledPlugin==null)
                {
                    document.writeln("No plug-in found<BR><BR>");
                }
                else
                {
                    document.writeln("Plug-in Name: "
                        + navigator.mimeTypes[i].enabledPlugin.name + "<BR><BR>");
                }
            }
        }
    </SCRIPT>
</BODY>
</HTML>
```

Note that with Mozilla/Netscape 6, this program yields quite different results compared to Netscape 4. While Netscape 4 lists all MIME types registered in Windows, Mozilla only lists the MIME types for which plug-ins are installed.

Here is a list of elements associated to the `navigator.mimeTypes` array:

Elements	Description
description	This element provides a description for a specified MIME-Type.
Type	This element returns a MIME-Type name. For example: `image/jpg`, `video/mpg`.
Suffixes	This element returns a list of file name extensions associated with a specific MIME-Type. For example: `mpg`, `mpeg`.
enabledPlugin	This element references the plug-in name associated with a particular MIME-Type.
Length	This element returns the number of MIME-Types available to the browser.

The Whole Enchilada – A Generic Plug-in Detection Module

To apply all of these techniques, we will create a generic JavaScript detection module called `detectMM.js`. This module will permit you to detect the existence of all current popular media formats. The particulars of how this module will interact with each application will be covered in the code explanations below.

Here is the source for `detectMM.html`. First it adds in the functions defined in `detectMM.js`, then uses the component detection routine to discover all the components in the browser (if applicable). Once the results have been determined, the program will populate an array called `resultsGrid`:

```
<HTML>
<HEAD>
<TITLE>WROX Multimedia Detection Test</TITLE>
<xml:namespace ns='http://www.microsoft.com/ie' prefix='MSIE' />
    <STYLE>@media all{ MSIE\:clientCaps
        {behavior:url(#default#clientcaps);} }
    </STYLE>
<MSIE:CLIENTCAPS ID="oClientCaps" />
<SCRIPT LANGUAGE="JavaScript" type="text/javascript" SRC="detectMM.js"></SCRIPT>
```

The following section of the program detects the components. In order to avoid runtime errors, we used the `try...catch` statements to silently trap the errors instead of displaying them. The `try...catch` statements are only available in JavaScript 1.5, so only Netscape 6 and IE 5+ can process them.

Notice that we define the block of code as JScript rather than JavaScript. JScript is Microsoft's implementation of JavaScript. Both languages are based on the ECMA standards and have minor differences between them. If this block of code were declared as JavaScript, it would generate errors in Netscape 4.7 and below. The reason for this is because try and catch are reserved words within that browser. By declaring it JScript rather than JavaScript, Netscape will ignore the code and no errors will appear:

```
<SCRIPT LANGUAGE="JScript">
if ((ie5 || ie6) && (win)){
for(d = 0; d < 5; d++){
errorStatus=0;
try { comInstalled=oClientCaps.isComponentInstalled(iecomDetect[d],"ComponentID");
}
```

195

```
catch(err){ errorStatus=1;
            comInstalled="False"; }
if (errorStatus==0){
comInstalled=oClientCaps.isComponentInstalled(iecomDetect[d],"ComponentID"); }
if (comInstalled){ resultsGrid[0][d]="True"; }
                  else
                  { resultsGrid[0][d]="False"; }
}}
</SCRIPT>
</HEAD>
<BODY>
<SCRIPT LANGUAGE="JavaScript" TYPE="text/javascript">detectMM();</SCRIPT>
<SCRIPT LANGUAGE="JavaScript" TYPE="text/javascript">makeGrid();</SCRIPT >
</BODY>
</HTML>
```

Here is the source for detectMM.js. Before we can start examining the plug-ins and controls in the browser, we must first determine the user's browser and platform:

```
// Define Primary Variables
var pluginsLength;
var pluginsCurrent;
var mimeLength;
var mimeCurrent;
var axDetect;
var errorStatus=0;

// Set up Navigator Variables
var navMime=navigator.mimeTypes;
var navPlug=navigator.plugins;
var userAgt=navigator.userAgent.toLowerCase();
var appNam=navigator.appName.toLowerCase();
var appVer=navigator.appVersion.toLowerCase();
var appMajor=parseInt(navigator.appVersion);
var appMinor=parseFloat(navigator.appVersion);

// Detect Browsers and Platforms
var mac=(appVer.indexOf("mac")!=-1);
var win=(userAgt.indexOf('win')!=-1);
var nix=(userAgt.indexOf("inux")!=-1);
var bsd=(userAgt.indexOf("bsd")!=-1);
var ie=(appNam=="microsoft internet explorer");
var ie5=(appVer.indexOf('msie 5')!=-1);
var ie6=(appVer.indexOf('msie 6')!=-1);
var ns=(appNam=="netscape");
var moz=(appNam=="gecko");
var aol=(appNam=="aol" && appMajor>4);
var opera=(userAgt.indexOf('opera')!=-1);
```

The next step is to create a multi-dimensional array that will contain all the plug-in information in a grid generated by the program:

```
var gridHeader = new Array(3);
var resultsGrid =
   new Array(new Array(5), new Array(5), new Array(5), new Array(5));
```

We will then create arrays to hold the information needed about each media format that will be used to query the browser:

```
    // Set up the CLASSID and Pointers for ActiveX
    iecomDetect[0] = "{D27CDB6E-AE6D-11cf-96B8-444553540000}";
    iecomDetect[1] = "{166B1BCA-3F9C-11CF-8075-444553540000}";
    iecomDetect[2] = "{22D6F312-B0F6-11D0-94AB-0080C74C7E95}";
    iecomDetect[3] = "{CFCDAA03-8BE4-11CF-B84B-0020AFBBCCFA}";
    iecomDetect[4] = "{02BF25D5-8C17-4B23-BC80-D3488ABDDC6B}";
    activexDetect[0] = "ShockwaveFlash.ShockwaveFlash";
    activexDetect[1] = "SWCtl.SWCtl.1";
    activexDetect[2] = "MediaPlayer.MediaPlayer.1";
    activexDetect[3] = "rmocx.RealPlayer G2 Control.1";
    activexDetect[4] = "QuickTimeCheckObject.QuickTimeCheck.1";
    navplugDetect[0] = "Flash";
    navplugDetect[1] = "Shockwave";
    navplugDetect[2] = "Windows Media Player";
    navplugDetect[3] = "RealPlayer";
    navplugDetect[4] = "QuickTime";
    navmimeDetect[0] = "flash";
    navmimeDetect[1] = "shockwave";
    navmimeDetect[2] = "mplayer";
    navmimeDetect[3] = "realaudio";
    navmimeDetect[4] = "quicktime";

    // Set up table headers
    gridHeader[0] = "Detection: IE Component";
    gridHeader[1] = "Detection: IE ActiveX";
    gridHeader[2] = "Detection: NS Plug-Ins";
    gridHeader[3] = "Detection: NS Mime-Types";
```

Here is the main function of our program. It will use all the techniques indicated at the beginning of the chapter. There are three components to this function. First, the program will check for the existence of ActiveX controls by looping through the `activexDetect[]` array. If the control is found, the program adds the value of `true` into the `resultsGrid[]` array. The same process is used to find the existence of plug-ins and MIME-Types.

The ActiveX detection routine incorporates a bit of VBScript in order to avoid run-time errors. The reason for doing this is that IE 4 does not have sufficient resources to do error checking using JavaScript alone. The mini-VBScript function first checks whether the VBScript engine installed on the client machine is higher than 2.0. Then, the function `detectAX()` instantiates the multimedia ActiveX objects to check for its existence. If it is found, `detectAX()` will have a value of TRUE. The `on error resume next` statement makes sure that no ugly errors pop up during the ActiveX detection. Errors are known to happen if the ActiveX control is not found on the client.

You will notice that the VBScript is embedded into our JavaScript routine using `document.writeln()` in order to streamline our code. The closing SCRIPT tags are split up in two halves in order to prevent errors. The browser would otherwise confuse the ending tag as the end of the JavaScript code rather than the VBScript code:

```
function detectMM()
{
   if (ie && win)
   {
   document.writeln('<script language="VBscript">');
   document.writeln('vbDetect=false');
   document.writeln('if ScriptEngineMajorVersion>=2 then');
   document.writeln('vbDetect=true');
   document.writeln('end if');
   document.writeln('function detectAX(ax)');
   document.writeln('on error resume next');
   document.writeln('detectAX=false');
```

```
    document.writeln('if vbDetect then');
    document.writeln('detectAX=IsObject(CreateObject(ax))');
    document.writeln('end if');
    document.writeln('end function');
    document.writeln('</scr' + 'ipt>');
for (i = 0; i < 5; i++)
    {
    axDetect = detectAX(activexDetect[i]);
    if (axDetect){ resultsGrid[1][i]="True";
    }
else
    {
    resultsGrid[1][i]="False";
    }
    }
}
```

Then, the program checks for the existence of plug-ins using the navigator.Plugins and navigator.MimeTypes objects:

```
if (navPlug && navPlug.length>0)
{
pluginsLength = navPlug.length;
if (pluginsLength > 0) {
for (t = 0; t < 5; t++){
resultsGrid[2][t]="False";
for (i = 0; i < pluginsLength; i++){
pluginsCurrent = navPlug[i];
if (pluginsCurrent.name.indexOf(navplugDetect[t]) != -1){
resultsGrid[2][t]="True"; }
}}}}else
{ for (d = 0; d < 5; d++){ resultsGrid[2][d]="NS Compatible Only"; }}

if (navMime && navMime.length>0){
mimeLength = navMime.length;
if (mimeLength > 0) {
for (t = 0; t < 5; t++){
resultsGrid[3][t]="False";
for (i = 0; i < mimeLength; i++){
mimeCurrent = navMime[i];
if (mimeCurrent.type.indexOf(navmimeDetect[t]) != -1){ resultsGrid[3][t]="True"; }
}}}}else
{ for (i = 0; i < 5; i++){ resultsGrid[3][i]="NS Compatible Only"; }}

if (!((ie5 || ie6) && win)){ for (i = 0; i < 5; i++){ resultsGrid[0][i]="WinIE5+
Only"; } }
if (!(ie && win)){ for (i = 0; i < 5; i++){ resultsGrid[1][i]="WinIE Only"; } }
}
```

The function makeGrid() creates a table that lists all of the results of our detection schemes stored in the resultsGrid[] array:

```
function makeGrid()
{
document.write('<table border="1" cellpadding="1" cellspacing="0"><tr><td>File
Types > <\/td><td>Flash<\/td><td>Shockwave<\/td><td>Windows
Media<\/td><td>RealAudio<\/td><td>Quicktime<\/td><\/tr>');
for (i = 0; i < 4; i++)
    {
    document.write('<tr><td>'+gridHeader[i]+'<\/td>');
    for (t = 0; t < 5; t++)
```

```
        {
        document.write('<td>'+resultsGrid[i][t]+'<\/td>');
        }
    document.write('<\/tr>');
    }
    document.write('<\/table>');
}
```

Controlling Popular Media Formats Using JavaScript

At this point, we have learned how to effectively add multimedia to a web page and detect the plug-ins and components to deliver the optimal user experience to our audience. The next step, is to learn how to control the delivery of rich media on the Web. Fortunately for us, most vendors have provided developers with JavaScript API functions to access and manipulate most media applications. In this section, we will explore the popular media types available on the Web and the JavaScript objects, properties, methods and events that control them.

Macromedia

In 1984, a small company called MacroMind (later changed to Macromedia) developed the Shockwave file format, a technology that has left an indelible mark on the Web. Flash and Shockwave are some of the most popular multimedia formats in use today. Macromedia uses vector technology to deliver dazzling compact animations on the Internet. According to their marketing, 35% of the 50 top websites use Flash. Flash is installed in 90% of browsers according to a survey of 250 million people.

Macromedia Shockwave and Flash Formats

For the sake of simplicity, we will focus primarily on Flash. Flash was developed as a vector-based lightweight version of Shockwave optimized for the Web. Shockwave content is created using Macromedia Director and is primarily intended for Multimedia CD-ROM applications, interactive presentations, and games. Shockwave can also accommodate proper graphics such as bitmaps. One of the great features is that Flash and Shockwave movies behave and display consistently on both Macs and PCs and many browser configurations.

Embedding Flash on a Web Page

Here is a typical example of how a Flash movie can be embedded into a web page:

```
<OBJECT ID='spacemovie' CLASSID='clsid:D27CDB6E-AE6D-11cf-96B8-444553540000'
   CODEBASE='http://active.Macromedia.com/flash2/cabs/swflash.cab
   #version=2,0,0,11' WIDTH='500' HEIGHT='500'>
     <PARAM TYPE='movie' SRC='spacemovie.swf'>
     <EMBED NAME='spacemovie' SRC='spacemovie.swf' WIDTH='500' HEIGHT='500'
     PLUGINSPAGE='http://www.Macromedia.com/shockwave/download/index.cgi
     ?P1_Prod_Version=ShockwaveFlash'>
   </EMBED>
</OBJECT>
```

Controlling Flash Using JavaScript

Macromedia has developed a very good API that allows us to control the delivery of Flash on the Web. The `FSCommand` is a special command that can be used by Flash developers to trigger JavaScript events from within the Flash environment. There is a very limited range of communication that can be sent from JavaScript to the Flash scripting engine using this interface (commands include: `ShowMenu()`, `Quit()`, `AllowScale()` and `FullScreen()`). You can learn more about the discrete interaction between browser JavaScript code and Flash at: http://www.macromedia.com/support/flash/ts/documents/tn4160.html

More information regarding the Macromedia Flash API can be found at:
http://www.macromedia.com/support/flash/ts/documents/tn4160.html

Putting It All Into Practice – Integrating JavaScript and Flash

In order to demonstrate the practical application of the Macromedia API, we will create a small program that controls a Flash movie in the browser using JavaScript.

Here is the source for `flashPlayer.html`:

```
<HTML>
<HEAD>
<SCRIPT LANGUAGE="JavaScript">
    function flashPlay(){ document.wrox.Play(); }
    function flashStop(){ document.wrox.Stop(); }
    function frameJump(x){ document.wrox.GotoFrame(x); }
</SCRIPT>
<TITLE>WROX flashPlayer</TITLE>
</HEAD>
<BODY BGCOLOR='#000000'>
<P ALIGN='CENTER'>
    <OBJECT CLASSID='clsid:D27CDB6E-AE6D-11cf-96B8-444553540000' ID='wrox'
        WIDTH='300' HEIGHT='300'>
      <PARAM NAME='movie' value='wrox.swf'>
      <PARAM NAME='loop' value='true'>
      <PARAM NAME='wrox' src='wrox.swf' swLiveConnect='true' width='300'
        HEIGHT='300' LOOP='true'>
    <BR>
      <A HREF='Javascript:flashPlay()'>Play</A> 
      <A HREF='Javascript:flashStop()'>Stop</A> 
      <A HREF='Javascript:frameJump(25)'>Jump to Frame 25</A> 
      <A HREF='Javascript:frameJump(50)'>Jump to Frame 50</A> 
      <A HREF='Javascript:frameJump(75)'>Jump to Frame 75</A>
</P>
</BODY>
</HTML>
```

RealNetworks

RealNetworks is one of the leading companies offering streaming media solutions on the Web. Previous to 1996, the only multimedia formats available online were MIDI, WAV, and Audio files (AU). RealNetworks changed the landscape of the Web by introducing the RealPlayer, one of the first streaming audio solutions.

A Streaming Media Primer

There are currently two methods of streaming multimedia using RealNetworks technology. The Real-Time Streaming Protocol (**RTSP**) is a protocol to deliver real-time multimedia delivery to the client's computer. It is currently a proposed standard with the Internet Engineering Task Force (IETF). Media streams are delivered in RTSP format via dedicated servers such as the RealSystem Server or the RealSystem iQ. This type of streaming is ideal for live broadcasts. It takes up hardly any storage space on the client's computer and essentially allows *on-demand* access to multimedia streams.

HTTP streaming also has its advantages: The quality of the streams is higher than when using the RTSP protocol and the streams are cached on the client side meaning no dedicated server is required; the streams are delivered via your web server. Using HTTP will also mean that you can only deliver a handful of streams at a time and you will not be able to take advantage of advanced capabilities such as dynamic client bandwidth detection.

Embedding RealMedia

With the release of RealPlayer G2, developers now have JavaScript access to the RealPlayer ActiveX control in IE, or plug-in for Netscape. In order to expose the functionality of this type of media, we must first embed the Real file on a HTML page. It should look something like this:

```
<OBJECT CLASSID='clsid:CFCDAA03-8BE4-11cf-B84B-0020AFBBCCFA'
   ID='media'>
   <PARAM NAME='SRC' VALUE='media.rm'>
   <EMBED SRC='media.rm' NAME='media'></EMBED>
</OBJECT>
```

Then we can access the embedded media using syntax such as:

```
<INPUT TYPE='image' SRC='play.gif' onClick='document.media.DoPlay(); return
false;'>
```

The RealNetworks JavaScript API allows developers to create incredible web applications using customized graphics instead of the default player. RealNetworks has produced a mind-boggling quantity of controls to allow developers to manipulate every facet of the interactive experience, from complex error handling protocols to player controls and packet transmissions.

Using MetaFiles

Most streaming formats rely on **MetaFiles**. A MetaFile is simply a text file that points to a URL containing the source of a multimedia stream. Here's essentially how RealPlayer handles the delivery of media streams: The .RAM MetaFile is processed through the appropriate plug-in or component. The plug-in then knows to initialize a stream and access the media source (the .RM file). The same applies to the Windows Media Player and QuickTime (with different file extensions of course).

Creating a Custom Interface For RealPlayer

In order to demonstrate the integration between JavaScript and RealPlayer, we will create a very simple custom audio player. The first step in creating the player involves correctly embedding the media. The second part will involve creating a custom form to control the player using JavaScript object calls.

Here is the code for customRP.htm. The program simply embeds the RealPlayer clip onto the web page and defines a form to control the player's API.

```
<HTML>
<HEAD>
<TITLE>WROX RealAudio Player</TITLE>
<SCRIPT LANGUAGE="JavaScript" type="text/javascript"
   SRC="customRP.js"></SCRIPT>
</HEAD>
   <BODY BGCOLOR='#000000' TEXT='#c0c0c0' LINK='#c0c0c0' ALINK='#c0c0c0'
      VLINK='#c0c0c0'>
      <P ALIGN='CENTER'>
         WROX RealAudio Player<BR><BR>
         <SCRIPT LANGUAGE="JavaScript">embedPlayer();</SCRIPT>
         <FORM NAME='customRP'>
            <A HREF='Javascript:doPlay()'>Play</A> 
            <A HREF='Javascript:doStop()'>Stop</A> 
            <A HREF='Javascript:doPause()'>Pause</A> 
         </FORM>
      </P>
   </BODY>
</HTML>
```

We define the functions to control RealPlayer using the API. Note that we didn't use the OBJECT tag in the embedPlayer() function. Instead, we are using the RealPlayer Java plug-in, which is compatible with both IE and Netscape. The reason we used the plug-in is because it loads quickly onto the HTML page. However, the program may not work on browsers that don't support LiveConnect – namely Netscape 6+ and Opera. In order to get around this problem, you should add a browser/platform checking routine before execution.

```
// Audio Player Functions
function doPlay(){ document.javaPlug1.DoPlay(); }
function doPause(){ document.javaPlug1.DoPause(); }
function doStop(){ document.javaPlug1.DoStop(); }
function embedPlayer(){document.write('<embed name="javaPlug1" type="audio/x-pn-
realaudio-plugin" border=0 height=30 width=330 src="victory.ra"
controls="StatusBar" autostart="false">');}
```

The Embedded RealPlayer Functionality Guide

The Embedded RealPlayer Extended Functionality Guide is an invaluable tool available on the www.real.com website. It contains the complete listing of all the JavaScript methods accessible to developers to effectively control content delivered via RealPlayer. You can access the guide at: http://service.real.com/help/library/guides/extend/embed.htm

For more information about RealAudio and RealVideo development, go to the Development Zone at RealNetworks: http://www.realnetworks.com/devzone/

Microsoft Windows Media Player

The Windows Media Format is one of the most popular file types on the Web. Most of the major companies online use Microsoft Advanced Streaming Format (ASF) files to deliver everything from live concerts to corporate presentations. Microsoft is really pushing the incorporation of digital rights management within this format in order to make it appealing to the major record companies and movie studios.

From a development standpoint, it is important to note that they have drastically revamped the Windows Media API for Windows Media Player 7.1. Here are some of the changes they have implemented:

❑   The ActiveX object differs from Version 6.4. (Note that backwards compatibility is possible).

❑   The Player control has been sub-divided into sub-controls.

❑   The new version of the Media Player no longer supports a number of parameters and controls available to the Media Player version 6.4. This leaves the developer the task of detecting which version is installed on the client machine.

Embedding Windows Media Files on a Web Page

A complete list of parameters that can be added to the OBJECT tag can be found in the Windows Media Player SDK, which is available at: http://msdn.microsoft.com/library/default.asp?url=/library/en-us/wmplay/mmp_sdk/default.asp

The Windows Media Player does not support Real Networks or QuickTime content with one special exception: if the user has upgraded Windows Media Player from an earlier version to version 7, they will be able to view QuickTime 2.0 encoded media.

The Player Object Model (POM)

Microsoft has built a robust API for controlling the Windows Media Player version 7 and 8 via the Player Object Model. It is the primary object for the Media Player ActiveX. Here is a diagram of the model:

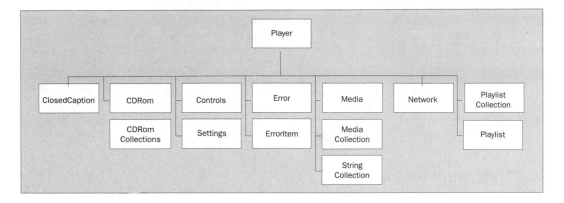

Syntax

The syntax for writing JScript objects for the WMP control is `Player.Object.Method`:

❑ `Player` refers to the value of the `ID` tag in the embedded object on the web page. You can also refer to the `Player` object as a global attribute.

❑ `Object` refers to one of the objects from the `Player` collection.

❑ `Method` actually tells player to do something. The method may contain properties that can give developers finite control over the execution of the commands on the player.

For example:

```
player.Controls.play()
```

Compatibility Issues

In order to maintain backwards compatibility, Microsoft decided to bundle the Windows Media 6.4 ActiveX control (`Msdxm.ocx`) along with the new 7.0 ActiveX control. Therefore, if a web page requests the older control, the content will still play through the new player. Have a look at the `WMplayer.html` file in the code download.

Apple QuickTime

QuickTime is one of the major players with regard to the streaming media formats. The latest version, QuickTime Player 5.0.2 is compatible with an impressive array of file types. Apple also has powerful Virtual Reality Modeling Language (VRML) tools for their Mac platform.

From version 2.5, QuickTime has offered HTTP streaming. HTTP streaming is ideal for delivering short high quality media clips on low bandwidth sites. A web server is typically used to deliver the streams to a client multimedia application. In this case, the multimedia application primarily handles the bulk of the communication between client and server. The limitations of HTTP streaming are that this type of streaming is not scalable – a web server has a limited capacity for delivering multimedia using this method. Additionally, in order to view the stream, you must start at the beginning of the clip. There is no way to start a clip from the middle, for example.

A new feature of QuickTime version 4+ is the ability to deliver streaming media using the Real-Time Streaming Protocol (RTSP). RTSP is equivalent to the "On-Demand" streaming. It requires a dedicated server to deliver long play media such as full-length movies. The server primarily handles the exchanges between client and server. RTSP servers have large-scale multi-threading capabilities, making RTSP ideal for enterprise-level or high bandwidth websites.

The QuickTime Format

The latest version of QuickTime is based on the excellent Sorenson video compression scheme that got the attention of the major Hollywood film studios. On Apple's site, hundreds of movie trailers are available to download or stream. Another QuickTime strength is the Virtual Reality support. Using free Mac tools on the site, you can quickly and professionally create QuickTime Panoramic or Object movies. An object movie consists of a movie presenting an inanimate object that can be rotated in place at any angle. A product demo on an e-commerce site is a practical example of this kind of movie; the movie allows potential customers to view products at all angles before purchasing it. Alternatively, panoramic movies contain 360-degree views of particular locations. Museums and art galleries frequently use them on websites to give their users the opportunity to take a virtual tour of their premises.

Embedding QuickTime Movies

Apple has recently created a QuickTime 5.0.2 ActiveX as a companion to the QuickTime plug-in. The development of the new control was prompted by Microsoft's announcement that IE 5.5 and 6 would no longer support Netscape-style plug-ins.

For compatibility with the new ActiveX control, Apple suggests using a combination of the OBJECT and EMBED tags. Here is an example script of an embedded movie using the new QuickTime ActiveX:

```
<OBJECT CLASSID='clsid:02BF25D5-8C17-4B23-BC80-D3488ABDDC6B'
    WIDTH='500' HEIGHT='500'
    CODEBASE='http://www.apple.com/qtactivex/qtplugin.cab'>
<PARAM NAME='src' VALUE='earth.qt'>
<PARAM NAME='autoplay' VALUE='true'>
<PARAM NAME='controller' VALUE='false'>
    <EMBED SRC='earth.qt' WIDTH='500' HEIGHT='500' AUTOPLAY='TRUE'
        CONTROLLER='FALSE'
        PLUGINSPAGE='http://www.apple.com/quicktime/download/'
        ENABLEJAVASCRIPT='TRUE' NAME='movie1'>
    </EMBED>
</OBJECT>
```

You can view a complete list of attributes for the EMBED element specific to QuickTime at:
http://www.apple.com/quicktime/authoring/embed2.html

The QuickTime Object Model (QOM)

With the release of QuickTime 4.1, Apple enabled control of their plug-in using JavaScript. This functionality is activated when you set the ENABLEJAVASCRIPT attribute to TRUE in the EMBED element.

The QuickTime Object Model comprises of seven sets of properties and commands. These include:

- ❏ Movie Properties
- ❏ Movie Commands
- ❏ Track Properties
- ❏ Sprite Track Properties
- ❏ QuickTime VR Movie Properties
- ❏ Plug-in Properties
- ❏ QuickTime Properties

Note that JavaScript control of QuickTime is only available in Netscape 4.7 and below. The plug-in relies on LiveConnect to communicate with the JavaScript code. To improve the compatibility of QuickTime on the Web, Apple has developed a version of QuickTime that works with IE 6.0. Unfortunately for developers, the new ActiveX control does not allow for JavaScript functionality.

If you try to view a QuickTime movie using Netscape 6 on MacOS, the movie will not appear where it is supposed to, and it may be offset on the page. Netscape 6 will also generate blank dialog boxes if you try to perform tasks when a QuickTime or Flash movie is playing.

Apple has developed a Java interface that allows communication between QuickTime and IE without relying on LiveConnect. The JScript Applet allows calls between JavaScript to access the applet, which in turn communicates with QuickTime. The applet must be developed using the QuickTime Java Application Development API at:

http://developer.apple.com/samplecode/Sample_Code/QuickTime/QuickTime_for_Java/JScriptApplet.htm

The QuickTime JavaScript API can be found at:

http://developer.apple.com/techpubs/quicktime/qtdevdocs/REF/QT41_HTML/QT41WhatsNew-72.html

QuickTime In Action

Here is an example of an application that applies the QuickTime JavaScript API. The program first checks if the user has a LiveConnect enabled browser before displaying the controls in order to avoid JavaScript compatibility errors:

```
<HTML>
    <HEAD>
        <TITLE>WROX QuickTime Player</TITLE>
    </HEAD>
<BODY>
<P ALIGN='CENTER'>
    <OBJECT CLASSID="clsid:02BF25D5-8C17-4B23-BC80-D3488ABDDC6B"
        WIDTH="160" HEIGHT="144"
        CODEBASE="http://www.apple.com/qtactivex/qtplugin.cab">
    <PARAM NAME="src" VALUE="earth.qt">
    <PARAM NAME="autoplay" VALUE="true">
    <PARAM NAME="id" VALUE="movie1">
    <PARAM NAME="enablejavascript" VALUE="true">
    <PARAM NAME="controller" VALUE="false">
    <PARAM NAME="loop" VALUE="true">
        <EMBED SRC="earth.qt" WIDTH="160" HEIGHT="144" AUTOPLAY="true"
            CONTROLLER="false" NAME="movie1" enablejavascript="true"
            pluginspage=http://www.apple.com/quicktime/download/ loop="true">
        </EMBED>
    </OBJECT>
</P>
<SCRIPT LANGUAGE="JavaScript">
    var ns=(navigator.appName.toLowerCase()=="netscape");
    var ns6=(navigator.userAgent.indexOf("Netscape6")!=-1);
    if(ns && !(ns6))
{
    document.write('<p align="center">');
    document.write('<a
        href="javascript:document.movie1.Play();">Play<\/a> ');
    document.write('<a
        href="javascript:document.movie1.Stop();">Stop<\/a> ');
    document.write('<\/p>');
}
    </SCRIPT>
</BODY>
</HTML>
```

When you run this example, you will be prompted to download QuickTime. Upon installation, choose the Recommended version. After installing QuickTime, you will also be prompted to install an additional plug-in. It is also important to keep in mind that the QuickTime JavaScript API only functions in Netscape 4.7 and below. It will not work on any version of IE or Netscape 6, which means that all you will see in the browser window is the running movie, without the Play and Stop controls.

Further information and development tools can be found at: http://developer.apple.com/quicktime/.

JavaScript and Java

In terms of flexibility, Java has an edge over many other programming languages. It has no external dependencies, works on almost every computing platform, and is extremely well documented. Microsoft has de-emphasized the use of Java by removing the Microsoft (Java) Virtual Machine (VM) from the default install of Windows XP and IE 6.

As a result, Sun is currently working on its own JVM that will integrate the latest version of Java in IE 6. The Mozilla Organization is also working on an ActiveX control that will give IE 6 the ability to support Java. Mozilla has currently integrated the Sun JVM in Netscape 6. The challenge that lies ahead is to make these components easy to install, widely accessible to consumers and most importantly, to showcase and promote the use of client-side Java.

Java is a useful cross-platform tool to extend the functionality of JavaScript and the web browser. This part of the chapter will focus on the basics of developing Java applets and the relationship and integration of JavaScript with Java.

Compare and Contrast

Java and JavaScript differ in more ways than they are similar. JavaScript is an interpreted language that is limited by the rules imposed on the browser. Java applications on the other hand are byte code-compiled and executed within a virtual machine. Java offers more discrete controls beyond the capabilities of the browser. Graphics & multimedia, file operations and network functionality are all missing from native client-side JavaScript.

Getting Started

Both Microsoft and Netscape have undergone different implementations of Java in their respective browsers. In order to gain the optimal browser support for the Java language, we recommend that you install the latest version of the Java Runtime Environment (JRE) from the Sun Microsystems website. The current version is 1.3.1, with a beta version (1.4.1) currently in the works. This will give your Netscape compatible browser the ability to run most Java applications. The current Sun JRE is available at http://java.sun.com/j2se/.

As a result of Sun's litigation settlement, Microsoft can distribute the Microsoft JVM for the next seven years. This Java Virtual Machine is compatible with all versions of IE (including version 6). You can download the Microsoft JVM and documentation at http://www.microsoft.com/java/.

If you are planning on developing applets on a Mac, be sure to download the Mac OS Runtime for Java (MRJ). The current version, MRJ 2.2.5, is based on Sun's Java Development Kit (JDK) version 1.1.8. The Mac OS X contains an integrated implementation of the Java2 JDK Standard Edition v.1.3 and the HotSpot VM version 3.1. More information is available at http://www.apple.com/java/.

The Java code included in this chapter was tested using the Java2 Platform SDK, Standard Edition v.1.3.1. You can download a copy of the SDK at: http://java.sun.com/j2se/.

The APPLET Element

The APPLET element was introduced with HTML 3.2 to allow developers to embed Java applets on web pages. This element has been deprecated in HTML 4.0 in favor of the OBJECT element. The APPLET element is compatible with Netscape browsers, but note that there are several documented bugs in Netscape 6.1. A comprehensive list can be found in the Netscape 6.1 Release Notes at http://home.netscape.com/eng/mozilla/ns6/relnotes/pv6-1.html.

The APPLET element is supported by IE 4.0 and above. IE 6 will render Java content using the APPLET element, only if the Microsoft JVM is installed on the client machine.

Here is an example of a typical use of APPLET:

```
<APPLET code='ShowMovie.class' width='500' height='500'>
Alternate Text
</APPLET>
```

Here is a list of the parameters that can be applied to the APPLET element:

Attributes	Description
CODEBASE	This attribute specifies the directory that contains the applet's code. The default value is the document's base URL. CODEBASE is an optional attribute.
ARCHIVE	This attribute describes what resources and classes should be preloaded. The classes are loaded using an instance of an AppletClassLoader with the given CODEBASE. A comma separates the archives if more than one archive is referenced. ARCHIVE is an optional attribute.
CODE	This is a mandatory attribute. It contains the filename of the compiled Applet class file. The filename should be contained in the same directory as defined by the CODEBASE. Either the CODE or OBJECT attributes must be defined within the APPLET element.
ALT	This attribute contains text that will displayed if the browser is able to interpret the APPLET element, but cannot run Java-based applets. ALT is an optional attribute.
NAME	This attribute names the instance of the applet. This facilitates the referencing of the Java applet through other applets and JavaScript. NAME is an optional attribute.
WIDTH / HEIGHT	These attributes define in pixels the initial height and width of the display area for the instantiated applet. These are mandatory attributes.
ALIGN	This attribute specifies the alignment of the applet. Possible values include: LEFT, RIGHT, TOP, TEXTTOP, MIDDLE, ABSMIDDLE, BASELINE, BOTTOM, ABSBOTTOM. ALIGN is an optional attribute.
VSPACE / HSPACE	These attributes define in pixels the amount of horizontal and vertical whitespace around the applet's display area. VSPACE / HSPACE are optional attributes.

Scripting Basic Java Applets

All you really require to code basic Java applets is a text editor and a copy of the Java Development Kit (JDK).

The JDK has many useful tools. The main tools you will use are **Javac** (a Java compiler) and **appletviewer** (a mini web browser used to execute your Java code). If you want to store your Java classes into a `.jar` file, the JDK also contains the `.jar` packager for that purpose.

The next step involves setting up your development environment. Your tools need to be on your path variable. Next, you must set up the location of your `.jar` files and classes in your classpath variable. Finally, your compiled class must have the same filename as your class (minus the file extension of course). All of the startup details are included in the JDK. *Beginning Java 2,* by Ivor Horton (ISBN: 1861003668) is also a good resource for developers wanting to learn the particulars of Java.

In order to understand the Java syntax and code, we will design a simple applet called `HelloWROX.java`:

```java
// HelloWROX.java
import java.applet.Applet;
import java.awt.*;

public class HelloWROX extends Applet
{
    String myGreeting;

    public void paint(Graphics g)
    {
        myGreeting = "Hello WROX!";
        g.drawString(myGreeting, 30, 30);
    }
}
```

As you can see, all of the variables in the example have been declared and every programming element has been declared in a class. The `import` statement is useful to add rich class libraries into your code. Object inheritance is supported and used heavily throughout.

To complete your first applet, compile the `.java` file into a binary file by typing the following command in a command prompt box:

> javac HelloWROX.java

A file called `HelloWROX.class` will be created. The next step is to integrate the applet into a web page:

```html
<!-- HelloWROX.htm -->
<HTML>
<HEAD>
   <TITLE>Hello WROX</TITLE>
</HEAD>
<BODY>
   <APPLET CODE='HelloWROX' WIDTH='300' HEIGHT='300'></APPLET>
</BODY>
</HTML>
```

Integrating Your Custom Applets with JavaScript

We will now examine the methodologies involved in integrating JavaScript with Java applets. The first involves using JavaScript to control events occurring within the applet. The second involves the applet controlling your JavaScript code.

Calling Java from JavaScript

The key to integrating JavaScript and Java, is the creation of publicly accessible Java classes and methods within the applet. We will demonstrate how we can pass data from JavaScript into a Java applet by creating an application called the WROX Color Selector.

Here is the source for `ColorPick.java`. The first step involves adding the applet and AWT (Abstract Windows Toolkit) libraries to our code. The applet libraries will allow our code to be integrated into a Java applet. The AWT libraries are typically used to add graphics and GUI functionality, such as scrollbars, windows, and buttons:

```
import java.applet.Applet;
import java.awt.*;
```

The next step involves defining the primary class `ColorPick`, making it publicly accessible and setting default values for the variables:

```
public class ColorPick extends Applet {

// Define Variables
   String TextMessage;
   int C1 = 0;
   int C2 = 0;
   int C3 = 255;
   Font fnt = new Font("Arial", Font.BOLD, 15);
   Color tColor;

 // Set up Default Message
   public void init()
   {
      TextMessage="Please Select A Color";
      repaint();
   }
```

We will now create a method called `SetTextColor()`. Note that we have also made this method publicly accessible (therefore accessible to JavaScript). Four arguments are allowed to pass within this method; the first, `MsgText`, will contain the name of the color. The next three arguments will respectively contain RGB (Red/Green/Blue) values ranging from 0-255:

```
// Set up Method Accessible to Javascript
 public void SetTextColor(String MsgText, int Color1, int Color2, int Color3)
{
   TextMessage = "The color is now "+MsgText;
   C1 = Color1;
   C2 = Color2;
   C3 = Color3;
   repaint();
}
```

Next, the `paint()` method will be used to refresh the applet window with the updated values culled from the `SetTextColor()` method:

```
// Refresh Applet Window with User Selection
  public void paint(Graphics g) {
  tColor = new Color(C1,C2,C3);
  g.setColor(tColor);
  g.setFont(fnt);
  g.drawString(TextMessage, 10, 30);
  }
}
```

If you look at the source code for `ColorPick.html` that is included in the code download for this book, you will notice it contains two distinct parts; a form that will be used as an interface and the embedded applet. We have named the instance of the applet `ColorPick` to make it accessible to JavaScript. The buttons in our form contain the `onClick` event handler, which passes the appropriate values via the `SetTextColor()` method as defined in our applet.

Before we can access the applet, we must call `isActive()` to figure out if the applet has been fully loaded and initialized. In order to accomplish this, we have created a JavaScript function called `appletInit()`, which checks whether the applet has been fully instantiated before we attempt to communicate with it using JavaScript.

Calling JavaScript From Java Applets

Java applets are not given easy access to your JavaScript code. The `MAYSCRIPT` attribute of the `APPLET` tag and the Java `JSObject` and `JSException` classes provide the mechanism for communicating with JavaScript.

Unfortunately, there is no true cross-browser method of accessing JavaScript using Java. Most of the Java to JavaScript communication is accomplished using LiveConnect supported in Netscape 4.7 and below. LiveConnect functionality is available (but limited) in IE 4 and 5. Keep in mind that Microsoft is no longer integrating Java technology in their new products. Opera and Netscape 6.1 do not contain practical LiveConnect functionality.

The MAYSCRIPT Attribute

The `MAYSCRIPT` attribute is used to allow Java to contact your JavaScript code. You must place the `MAYSCRIPT` attribute inside the `APPLET` tags. Here is an example:

```
<APPLET NAME='myApp CODE='SimpleBanner.class' HEIGHT='60' WIDTH='468' MAYSCRIPT>
```

JSObject

Java relies on objects from the `netscape.javascript.JSObject` Java class to communicate with JavaScript. Using the `getWindow()` method, you can create an object which has access to all the JavaScript in your code. The `getMember()` method will allow further access to particular elements on the web page. Here is an example:

```
JSObject win = JSObject.getWindow(this);
JSObject doc = (JSObject)win.getMember("document");
JSObject.getWindow(this).eval("window.alert('Java to Javascript…The Eagle Has
Landed')");
```

The Java Security Model

The Java Security Model is built around the premise that there are malicious users that may want to arbitrarily run harmful code in a browser. Both Microsoft and Netscape use this model as the security basis for the whole browser, not only the JVM.

The Java Sandbox Model

The Java Sandbox concept is simple. If an applet is downloaded and is standalone, then it is allowed to have access to system resources and write files to your hard drive. However, if an applet is downloaded from a network such as the Internet into your browser, it is not trusted by default. The applet will have very limited access to your system. While this approach is inherently secure, the tradeoff for developers is a lack of functionality.

In Java 1.0, the `SecurityManager` class could be added to a project in order to create a custom security policy and extend the class security privileges. With Java 1.1, Sun Microsystems added the ability to digitally sign an applet to verify its authenticity and creation date before it is executed. The advantage is that it permitted designers to add applets to the Web that could perform useful tasks and extend the functionality.

Java 2 v.1.2 introduced the least privilege concept. It is a versatile and configurable system which, implements a security policy based on the origin of the applet and the permission status of the person accessing it.

As web developers, we always seek new ways to extend the functionality of our applications. Java has proven to be a useful tool on the Web. It can be found in countless chat, messaging, and multimedia applications. Java effectively pushes the boundaries outside the limitations of the browser and enhances the capabilities of JavaScript.

Emerging Technologies

This section will contain a general survey of four new standards, SMIL, HTML+TIME, SVG, and XUL.

The trend towards integration has begun, with many companies merging technologies in order to expand their scope of influence. For example, RealNetworks has incorporated a Mozilla component into RealPlayer so that it can browse and process HTML files and Apple has added support into their new QuickTime player to accommodate a wide variety of multimedia formats. Additionally, RealNetworks has recently collaborated with Macromedia in the development of RealFlash. This combines the strength of the streaming RealAudio format with the compelling visuals of Flash, as well as a dash of a new standard called SMIL.

SMIL

SMIL (pronounced "SMILE") is an acronym for Synchronized Multimedia Integration Language. It is a standard developed by the W3C as an initiative to promote the interaction between divergent multimedia technologies. Currently, some of the major companies supporting SMIL include RealNetworks and Apple. RealNetworks has added cross-compatible SMIL in their player versions 5.0 and G2.

Microsoft has added full support for the SMIL 2.0 Recommendation into IE 6 through an expanded implementation called HTML+TIME. More information on SMIL can be found at: http://www.w3c.org /TR/REC-smil/ and also at http://www.w3c.org/TR/smil20/ now that version 2 is a Recommendation.

HTML+TIME

This technology is Microsoft's enhancement of SMIL. Although they recognize that SMIL is perfect for delivering offline multimedia, Microsoft has independently instituted 'improvements' to SMIL in order to make it functional on the Web. The enhancements are:

❑   It supports the ability to add `TIME` attributes to any web element in order to make them appear and disappear according to a timeline. Conceptually, this will give SMIL similar capabilities to the Shockwave and Flash file formats. In addition, developers will have access to new temporal objects that can be manipulated with JavaScript.

❑   HTML+TIME gives developers an unparalleled degree of control with regard to the triggered synchronization and timing of these elements using a few lines of code. This makes it easy to create dynamic content such as slide shows and presentations.

IE 5.5 and 6.0 support HTML+TIME 2.0 and SMIL 2.0. In order to make sure the code functions correctly in the browser, you must have the component installed, otherwise the time-coded elements will appear all at once.

HTML+TIME is currently only a W3C Note and details of it can be found at: http://www.w3c.org/TR/NOTE-HTMLplusTIME. Gradually, there will be many changes made to this new standard, but its current status offers an exciting glimpse into what we can expect in the future.

HTML+TIME Applied

We've created an application called the WROX Quiz Show using HTML+TIME that demonstrates the cool functionality encapsulated in this technology. Note that this program will only function at present on IE 5.5+.

Here is the source code for `quizshow.html`:

```
<HTML>
<TITLE>WROX Quiz Show</TITLE>
```

First, we must declare an XML namespace that will make available to our application the temporal functionality of HTML+TIME. We then create classes that define the behaviors used in our program. For example, the SEQ class tells the browser that the HTML assigned to this behavior should be displayed in sequence. The PAR class is used to display HTML at the same time as other temporal events:

```
<XML:NAMESPACE PREFIX="t"/>
<STYLE>
    .time { behavior: url(#DEFAULT#TIME); }
    t\:IMG { behavior: url(#DEFAULT#TIME); }
    t\:PAR { behavior: url(#DEFAULT#TIME); }
    t\:SEQ { behavior: url(#DEFAULT#TIME); }
</STYLE>
<BODY BGCOLOR="#FFFFFF">
<DIV STYLE="color: #0000ff; text-align: center; width: 100%; height: 100%;"
border="1" id="mainscreen">
```

The next part of our application displays an opening message. The HTML contained within the SPAN element inherits the HTML+TIME functionality with the attribute CLASS="time". t:TIMEACTION is used to determine what the browser should do within the event defined between the SPAN tags. In this case, we are instructing the browser to display the HTML content. t:ENDEVENT uses a JavaScript event handler, onclick, to determine when to move on to the next event. We created a SPAN containing the message click to begin. Once the user clicks on the message, the program moves on to the next event:

```
<SPAN CLASS="time" ID="title" t:TIMEACTION="display" t:ENDEVENT="click.onclick"
STYLE="font: 20pt Verdana; COLOR:#000000; font-weight:bold;"><IMG
SRC="wroxlogo.gif" ALT="wroxlogo"> WROX Quiz Show</SPAN>

<SPAN CLASS="time" ID="click" t:TIMEACTION="display" t:ENDEVENT="click.onclick"
STYLE="font: 9pt Verdana; text-decoration: none; cursor: hand;"><BR><BR>click to
begin</SPAN>
```

The next part of our program is split into three parts. Each part contains:

❑ A "Ready Set Go" countdown

❑ A question with three possible choices while a timer counts down from 10 to 1

❑ Notification of whether the answer given is correct or not

The t:BEGINEVENT waits for the user to click on click to begin before starting the new event. The t:PAR attribute is used to tell the browser that the HTML contained within can be shown in parallel or simultaneously to other events.

```
<t:PAR t:BEGINEVENT="click.onclick"
t:ENDEVENT="bad.onclick;wrong.onclick;right.onclick;">
<DIV STYLE="font: 16pt Verdana; color:#000ff; font-weight:bold;" ID="countdown1">
```

The t:BEGIN and t:DUR attributes tell the browser at which point each HTML element should be shown and for how long it should appear in the browser window. This section prepares the user for the first question. Notice that the last message, "GO!" will display for 2 seconds after 6 seconds of the countdown have passed:

```
<P ID="count1" CLASS="time" t:BEGIN="0"  t:DUR="2"
    t:TIMEACTION="display">Welcome to the WROX Quiz Show</P>
<P ID="count2" CLASS="time" t:BEGIN="2"  t:DUR="2"
    t:TIMEACTION="display">Prepare to test your knowledge of Javascript</P>
<P ID="count3" CLASS="time" t:BEGIN="4"  t:DUR="1"
    t:TIMEACTION="display">Ready?</P>
<P ID="count4" CLASS="time" t:BEGIN="5"  t:DUR="1"
    t:TIMEACTION="display">Set...</P>
<P ID="count5" CLASS="time" t:BEGIN="6"  t:DUR="2"
    t:TIMEACTION="display">GO!</P>
</DIV>
</t:PAR>
```

The following event occurs simultaneously or parallel to the above countdown. This event will show the question and three possible answers after waiting 8 seconds for the countdown to complete. The questions and answers will display on screen for exactly 20 seconds. An onclick handler will be tied into each of the answers:

```
<t:PAR t:BEGINEVENT="click.onclick"
t:ENDEVENT="bad.onclick;wrong.onclick;right.onclick;">
<DIV STYLE="font: 16pt Verdana; color:#000ff; font-weight:bold;" ID="question1">
<P ID="q1" CLASS="time" t:BEGIN="8" t:DUR="20" t:TIMEACTION="display">What element
is used to embed an ActiveX on a webpage?</P>

<SPAN CLASS="time" t:BEGIN="8" t:DUR="20" ID="bad" t:TIMEACTION="display"
t:ENDEVENT="bad.onclick" STYLE="font: 9pt Verdana; text-decoration: none; cursor:
hand;">EMBED</SPAN>

<SPAN CLASS="time" t:BEGIN="8" t:DUR="20" ID="wrong" t:TIMEACTION="display"
t:ENDEVENT="wrong.onclick" STYLE="font: 9pt Verdana; text-decoration: none;
cursor: hand;">APPLET</SPAN>

<SPAN CLASS="time" t:BEGIN="8" t:DUR="20" ID="right" t:TIMEACTION="display"
t:ENDEVENT="right.onclick" STYLE="font: 9pt Verdana; text-decoration: none;
cursor: hand;">OBJECT</SPAN>
</DIV>
</t:PAR>
```

While the questions and answers are displayed, the following event will provide a 20 second timer on screen. If the user does not click on one of the answers, the timer will end and a link will appear to the next event:

```
<t:PAR t:BEGINEVENT="click.onclick"
t:ENDEVENT="bad.onclick;wrong.onclick;right.onclick;">
<DIV STYLE="font: 16pt Verdana; color:#ff0000; font-weight:bold;">

<P ID="timer" CLASS="time" t:BEGIN="8" t:DUR="20" t:TIMEACTION="display"
    STYLE="font: 12pt Verdana; color:#000000; font-weight:bold;">Timer</P>
<P ID="timer" CLASS="time" t:BEGIN="8"  t:DUR="2"
    t:TIMEACTION="display">10</P>
<P ID="timer" CLASS="time" t:BEGIN="10" t:DUR="2"
    t:TIMEACTION="display">9</P>
```

```
<P ID="timer" CLASS="time" t:BEGIN="12" t:DUR="2"
    t:TIMEACTION="display">8</P>
<P ID="timer" CLASS="time" t:BEGIN="14" t:DUR="2"
    t:TIMEACTION="display">7</P>
<P ID="timer" CLASS="time" t:BEGIN="16" t:DUR="2"
    t:TIMEACTION="display">6</P>
<P ID="timer" CLASS="time" t:BEGIN="18" t:DUR="2"
    t:TIMEACTION="display">5</P>
<P ID="timer" CLASS="time" t:BEGIN="20" t:DUR="2"
    t:TIMEACTION="display">4</P>
<P ID="timer" CLASS="time" t:BEGIN="22" t:DUR="2"
    t:TIMEACTION="display">3</P>
<P ID="timer" CLASS="time" t:BEGIN="24" t:DUR="2"
    t:TIMEACTION="display">2</P>
<P ID="timer" CLASS="time" t:BEGIN="26" t:DUR="2"
    t:TIMEACTION="display">1</P>
<SPAN CLASS="time" t:BEGIN="28" ID="ctimeout" t:TIMEACTION="display" STYLE="font:
9pt Verdana; text-decoration: none; cursor: hand;">
<BR>Continue >></SPAN>
</DIV>
</t:PAR>
```

We have defined two events to handle the two possible outcomes of the question – whether the user has guessed correctly or not. The program will then go to a new countdown event and the process will continue for two more questions. The code below shows the events for the first question. You can view the rest of the code by looking at quizshow.html included in the code download.

```
<t:PAR t:BEGINEVENT="bad.onclick;ctimeout.onclick;wrong.onclick"
    t:ENDEVENT="cwrong.onclick" STYLE="font: 16pt Verdana; color:#000ff;
    font-weight:bold;">
<P ID="w1" CLASS="time" t:BEGIN="0" t:TIMEACTION="display">I'm sorry...you
    picked the WRONG answer.</P>
<P ID="w2" CLASS="time" t:BEGIN="0" t:TIMEACTION="display">The Correct
    Answer is OBJECT.</P>
<SPAN CLASS="time" t:BEGIN="0" ID="cwrong" t:TIMEACTION="display" STYLE="font: 9pt
Verdana; text-decoration: none; cursor: hand;"><BR>Next Question >></SPAN>
</t:PAR>
<t:PAR t:BEGINEVENT="right.onclick" t:ENDEVENT="cright.onclick" STYLE="font:
    16pt Verdana; color:#000ff; font-weight:bold;">
<P ID="w1" CLASS="time" t:BEGIN="0" t:TIMEACTION="display">OBJECT is the
    right answer!</P>
<SPAN CLASS="time" t:BEGIN="0" ID="cright" t:TIMEACTION="display"
    STYLE="font: 9pt Verdana; text-decoration: none; cursor: hand;"><BR>Next
Question >></SPAN>
</t:PAR>
<t:SEQ t:BEGINEVENT="cwrong.onclick;cright.onclick;">
<DIV STYLE="font: 16pt Verdana; color:#000ff; font-weight:bold;">
    <P ID="p2" CLASS="time" t:DUR="4" t:TIMEACTION="display">Now for Question
        Number 2.</P>
    <P ID="p3" CLASS="time" t:DUR="1" t:TIMEACTION="display">Ready?</P>
    <P ID="p4" CLASS="time" t:DUR="1" t:TIMEACTION="display">Set...</P>
    <P ID="p5" CLASS="time" t:DUR="2" t:TIMEACTION="display">GO!</P>
</DIV>
</t:SEQ>
<t:PAR t:BEGINEVENT="cwrong.onclick;cright.onclick;"
t:ENDEVENT="bad1.onclick;wrong1.onclick;right1.onclick;">
```

An interesting point to consider is that regular JavaScript functions and variables appear to ignore all TIME attributes. JavaScript behaves as it would on regular HTML pages. This severely limits the programmability of HTML+TIME. Hopefully, this standard will be extended in the future to give programmers more discrete control on timed events.

Scalable Vector Graphics (SVG)

Scalable Vector Graphics (SVG) is a vocabulary used to describe vector based two-dimensional images using XML. SVG can be used to describe geometric shapes, alphanumeric characters and images. One of the fantastic features of SVG is the ability to quickly generate animations and dynamic filter effects using DOM and XML based code. The SVG objects can be assigned JavaScript event handlers that transform these animations into interactive experiences. The promise of SVG is a standardized cross-browser, rich multimedia environment for developers. Vector graphics are ideal for the Web due to their inherent small file sizes and perfect graphical rendering at any resolution.

SVG was made a Recommendation with the W3C on September 5 2001. You can find out more at http://www.w3.org/TR/SVG/.

Adobe have been instrumental in the initiative to make SVG an official standard. They have released a plug-in that allows users to view, develop, and test SVG-compliant code. Other companies that have incorporated SVG into their products currently include Corel and JASC.

Putting SVG Into Practice

None of the current browsers natively support the SVG at this time, but now that the standard has been given Recommendation status by the W3C, SVG support will likely be integrated into future browser versions. In 1998, Microsoft proposed a similar technology called the Vector Modeling Language (VML), for which they integrated support for in IE 5. As far as the W3C is concerned, SVG is a more complete standard. It is easier to learn and seems to be more consistently implemented.

If you wish to experiment with this technology, you must download the SVG Viewer from Adobe. Note that at the time of writing, the plug-in will not function under Netscape 6 or IE on a Mac. There are a few determined Mozilla developers building versions of Netscape that incorporate limited support for SVG. You can find more information at http://www.croczilla.com/svg/.

We've created an application that will show the application of web vector graphics using SVG. The program, WROX SVG Olympic Rings, displays the Olympic rings using SVG and XML. If the user clicks on a link indicating a color, the program will display the meaning of the ring in the SVG window.

The program has two components, `olympix.html` and `olympix.svgz`. Here is the source code for `olympix.svgz`:

```
<?xml version="1.0" encoding="iso-8859-1"?>
<!DOCTYPE svg PUBLIC "-//W3C//DTD SVG 20000303 Stylable//EN"
"http://www.w3.org/TR/2000/03/WD-SVG-20000303/DTD/svg-20000303-stylable.dtd">
<svg xml:space="preserve" width="5.5in" height="2in">
```

First, we define this as an XML document. The SVG window is set at a width of 3.3 inches by 2 inches. Then we define the placement and color of each Olympic ring by using the `circle` element defined in the SVG Recommendation. The `text` element is used to display the geographical area that corresponds to each ring. Notice that we have filled each circle with color using the `fill:color` command, but the fill will not show because we have set the `fill-opacity:` to zero:

```
<g id="blue" transform="translate(30, 20)" style="fill-opacity:0;">
    <circle style="fill:blue;stroke:blue;stroke-width:2;" cx="50" cy="50"
        r="15" />
    <text x="153" y="75" style="font-family:Verdana; font-weight:800; font-
size:40; fill:white; writing-mode:tb; text-anchor:middle">Europe</text>
    </g>
<g id="black" transform="translate(63, 20)" style="fill-opacity:0;">
    <circle style="fill:black;;stroke:black;stroke-width:2;" cx="50"
```

```
              cy="50" r="15" />
         <text x="119" y="60" style="font-family:Verdana; font-weight:800;
font-size:40; fill:white; writing-mode:tb; text-anchor:middle">Africa</text>
      </g>
      <g id="red" transform="translate(96, 20)" style="fill-opacity:0;">
         <circle style="fill:red;stroke:red;stroke-width:2;" cx="50" cy="50"
            r="15" />
         <text x="86" y="75" style="font-family:Verdana; font-weight:800; font-
size:40; fill:white; writing-mode:tb; text-anchor:middle">America</text>
      </g>
      <g id="yellow" transform="translate(45, 38)" style="fill-opacity:0;">
         <circle style="fill:yellow;stroke:yellow;stroke-width:2;" cx="50"
            cy="50" r="15" />
         <text x="138" y="40" style="font-family:Verdana; font-weight:800; font-
size:40; fill:white; writing-mode:tb; text-anchor:middle">Asia</text>
      </g>
      <g id="green" transform="translate(80, 38)" style="fill-opacity:0;">
         <circle style="fill:green;stroke:green;stroke-width:2;" cx="50"
            cy="50" r="15" />
         <text x="104" y="60" style="font-family:Verdana; font-weight:800; font-
size:40; fill:white; writing-mode:tb; text-anchor:middle">Australia</text>
      </g>
   </svg>
```

Here is the source code for `olympix.html`. The JavaScript functions `ringDisplay()` and `ringHide()` first attempts to determine whether a SVG document is embedded into the HTML using the `getSVGDocument()` method. `svgObj` is referenced to the embedded document if it is found. Then, using the `getStyle()` method, we set the `fill-opacity:` of the individual rings (as defined in our `.svgz` file). The EMBED element was used as indicated by the SVG documentation provided by Adobe.

```
<HTML>
<HEAD>
<TITLE>WROX SVG Olympic Rings</TITLE>
<SCRIPT LANGUAGE="JavaScript1.2">
function ringDisplay(RingID)
{
   var svgReference = document.olympix.getSVGDocument();
   var svgObj = svgReference.getElementById(RingID);
if (svgObj != null)
   {
      var svgStyle = svgObj.getStyle();
      svgStyle.setProperty ('fill-opacity', .7);
   }
return true;
}

function ringHide (RingID)
{
   var svgReference = document.olympix.getSVGDocument();
   var svgObj = svgReference.getElementById(RingID);
if (svgObj != null)
   {
      var svgStyle = svgObj.getStyle();
      svgStyle.setProperty ('fill-opacity', 0);
   }
return true;
}
</SCRIPT>
```

```
</HEAD>
<BODY BGCOLOR="#DEDFFE">
<P ALIGN="CENTER">
<FONT COLOR="#000000" FACE="verdana" SIZE="2">
<B>The Meaning of the Olympic Rings</B><BR></FONT>
<EMBED NAME="olympix" WIDTH="250" HEIGHT="200" SRC="olympix.svgz"
    pluginspage="http://www.adobe.com/svg/viewer/install/"><BR>

<A HREF="javascript:void()" ID="blue" onMouseOver="return
     ringDisplay('blue')" onMouseOut="ringHide('blue')" onClick="return
     false;">blue</A> 

<A HREF="javascript:void()" ID="black" onMouseOver="return
     ringDisplay('black')" onMouseOut="ringHide('black')" onClick="return
     false;">black</A> 

<A HREF="javascript:void()" ID="red" onMouseOver="return ringDisplay('red')"
     onMouseOut="ringHide('red')" onClick="return false;">red</A> 

<A HREF="javascript:void()" ID="yellow" onMouseOver="return
    ringDisplay('yellow')" onMouseOut="ringHide('yellow')" onClick="return
    false;">yellow</A> 

<A HREF="javascript:void()" ID="green" onMouseOver="return
    ringDisplay('green')" onMouseOut="ringHide('green')" onClick="return
    false;">green</A> 

</P>
</BODY>
</HTML>
```

The SVG application may not display correctly unless you use the Adobe SVG Plug-In. You can download the plug-in from: http://www.adobe.com/svg/main.html.

XML-Based User-Interface Language (XUL)

The XML-based User-interface Language (**XUL**) is a standard developed by Mozilla. From a technical standpoint, the browser user interface (UI) is displayed and managed by the same engine that manages HTML content in the browser. UI descriptions are structured much like HTML. XUL utilizes XML to describe and build custom UI constructs.

XUL (pronounced **Zool**) was conceived to give developers a means to deliver Internet applications that look and feel like desktop applications. XUL is in direct competition with Microsoft's core application interface tools such as Visual Basic and Visual C++. In a nutshell, XUL is an XML-based GUI construction language.

There are currently no plans for Microsoft to support XUL. The language is an integral component in the Mozilla application development framework. Unfortunately, at the time of writing the only browser that fully supports XUL is Netscape 6+.

XUL has many advantages: first and foremost, it's intended to be a standardized cross-browser solution for UI design, substituting the use of Java and DHTML. Additionally, XUL can integrate with other XML-based languages. It's versatile, transportable, well documented, and easy to learn.

XUL Basics

UI design is an art form in itself. XUL provides the basic building blocks to construct effective designs including toolbars, buttons, menus, keyboard shortcuts, tree-views, input controls, and various dialog boxes.

XUL uses four primary components to describe a user interface: the Layout and Elements, Style Sheet, Entity Declarations, and Localization Information.

217

JavaScript is used with XUL to provide functionality to the design elements. Event-based programming keeps track of each button click and scrolling menu bars, etc.

You can find updated resources at http://www.mozilla.org/projects/xul/ and http://www.xulplanet.com/.

Summary

In this chapter, we have discussed the origins of rich media and its implementation on the Web. We've seen:

❑   How to incorporate plug-ins and ActiveX controls using the EMBED and OBJECT elements

❑   How to detect plug-ins and controls using JavaScript, taking into consideration compatibility issues and error handling

We also examined the major multimedia platforms (RealAudio, Flash, Windows Media Player, and QuickTime). We learned how to implement their respective API tools to create web applications and also how to control the plug-ins or ActiveX controls using JavaScript.

We then analyzed the relationship between Java and JavaScript and found out how to create simple applets that allow two-way communication between these different languages.

Finally, we examined some of the newer multimedia standards. These promise to be powerful tools for web developers once the standards become more stable and browser vendors implement native support.

The next chapter will take a look at HTML, XML, and XHTML.

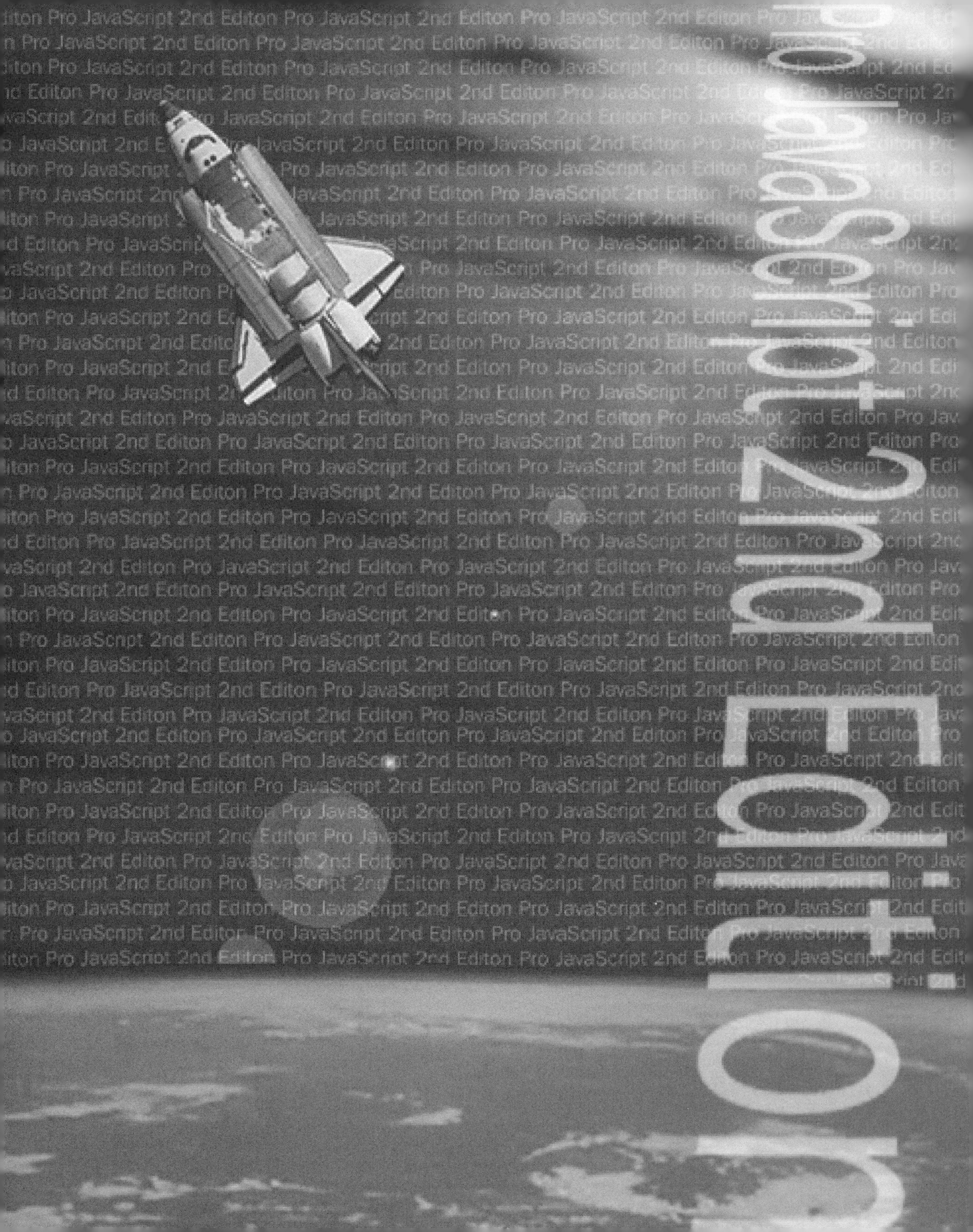
Pro JavaScript 2nd Edition
Pro JavaScript 2nd Editon

Section Two

Towards Standardization

One of the biggest problems developers face when working with JavaScript in web browsers is the variety of different implementations. For the first time with version 4 browsers, we were able to use JavaScript with the browser's object model to create sophisticated dynamic effects. The cross-browser problems, however, became worse.

The development of web standards is an attempt to deal with problems such as these. The World Wide Web Consortium (W3C) is an organization that aims to promote interoperability on the Web by the development of web standards. By choosing a standards-based approach, you can develop more robust browser-independent web pages. There are many different types of standard that the W3C is involved with, but in this chapter, we'll just look at those relevant to the client-side web programmer.

The best known of these standards is, of course, HTML, but in this section, we'll be focusing on some of the standards built on top of this, such as Cascading Style Sheets (CSS) for presentation effects, and the Document Object Model (DOM), which defines a standard mechanism allowing programmatic access to every element in a HTML document. We'll see how to script these with JavaScript, creating Dynamic HTML pages. Before we get stuck into these, however we'll start off with a quick overview of XML, the eXtensible Markup Language, which unlike HTML, is designed for marking up *data*, rather than content for *display*.

Pro JavaScript 2nd Edition

7

XML and XHTML

In this chapter, we shall explore the world of XML (the Extensible Markup Language), explain its relationship to other languages, such as SGML and HTML, discuss how it can be used, and detail specific implementations. If you are already familiar with XML, you may wish to just skim through this chapter.

Introducing XML

Angular brackets, such as those used in HTML, are part of what is called a **markup language**. The most well-known markup specifications are SGML, XML, and HTML:

❑ **SGML** is a **meta-language**: a language that defines a few things, such as what the angular brackets mean, and roughly where they can go, but then lets other people decide the exact details of the angular brackets. In other words, it's a language for creating languages.

❑ **HTML** is not a meta-language (it doesn't allow you to create other languages), but it is an application of SGML. HTML is a language that is built as an SGML language, conforming to the rules that SGML sets out.

❑ **XML**, on the other hand, is a meta-language that is derived from SGML, a subset of SGML. We can create languages as applications of XML, which are both cost effective and usable on the World Wide Web. XML however, doesn't have to be used exclusively on the Web. For example, it is also widely put to use in corporate databases. **XHTML** (which we shall cover in more detail later on), is just a re-drafting of HTML as an XML language. Because XML was derived from SGML, XHTML is both an application of XML and SGML.

History of XML

The history of XML and how it evolved from SGML is very interesting, and will give us a better idea of its potential and use. It is not crucial to understanding what XML is, however so readers may want to skip to the section titled *Well Formed XML,* which explains more about XML's syntax.

SGML

In 1986, the ISO 8879 **SGML (Standard Generalized Markup Language)** specification was published, paving the way for a myriad of technologies, that would eventually form the basis for the majority of Web formats.

As already mentioned, SGML is a meta-language; that is, a language for creating other languages. Before the World Wide Web came along, SGML was mainly used in complex documentation systems, such as **TEI (Text Encoding Initiative** – http://www.uic.edu/orgs/tei/). For more information on SGML, try Robin Cover's excellent resource at: http://www.oasis-open.org/cover.

SGML soon developed an aura of mystery due to its complexity and enormous diversity. SGML's complexity was both its most valuable asset, and its greatest threat. However, there was also a real need for a simpler subset of SGML, because in practice developers often only used a subset of the constructs that SGML provided, and building parsers to cope with all that SGML had to offer was too difficult.

HTML and the Web

HTML was invented in 1990 by Tim Berners-Lee, then of CERN, while experimenting with his new universal information system, the World Wide Web. It was designed to be a simple and interoperable **hypertext** language, for which programs (browsers) could be written. He decided that the language should be as recognizable as possible by the CERN employees of the time, so he made it look like an internal SGML language that CERN was using at the time called **SGMLGuid**. Early HTML looks a lot like SGMLGuid, which was a complex document formatting language, except for a reduction in the amount of tags, and the addition of the all-important anchor tag (`<A>`), which is used to embed hypertext links within the document.

Although early HTML (before the SGML experts got to it) looked like SGML, there was actually no strict definition of the language, other then Tim's early notes. Therefore, programs that were created to parse and display the HTML were often filled with bugs, and often tried to render incorrect HTML as best as they could, without validating it against a strict definition.

This went on until about early 1992, when SGML programmers, such as Dan Connolly, were introduced to the WWW, and decided to create proper **Document Type Definitions** for HTML against which it could be validated. However, by then it was too late – people had begun to create invalid code, and write browsers which parsed that code. The HTML developers resented SGML's complexity, and the SGML developers resented HTML's apparent lack of structure and non-adherence to the SGML specification. The SGML community was often filled with arguments between various parties, and this was something that the Web community wanted to avoid if possible.

Meanwhile, more and more people were creating HTML documents, and more and more programs were being written to display them. The popular Mosaic browser came on the scene, bringing the Web to hundreds of thousands of people for the first time, which boosted the development of the Web, but had a downside in that it would still attempt to fix invalid code for rendering. Mosaic also introduced new features such as embedded images.

Soon, people were adding tags to HTML on a whim. Microsoft added support for tags, such as `<MARQUEE>`, and Netscape added support for `<BLINK>`, creating a divide in the market, and a dangerous instability that left HTML (which was always a language with little architectural stability), in a state of pure pandemonium, with presentational tags galore, and proprietary features being added on a regular basis.

The **World Wide Web Consortium (W3C)**, directed by Tim Berners-Lee, aimed to put an end to the confusion by issuing a series of HTML specifications, in the hope that software manufacturers (including Microsoft and Netscape, both members of the W3C) would adhere to them. Dave Raggett, an instrumental figure in the development of HTML since 1993, helped to develop many of the early specifications, including HTML+, HTML 3.0 (both of which were later abandoned), and HTML 3.2. He also helped develop the latest versions of the HTML Recommendation with HTML 4.0/4.01.

Extensions were still being added, however, and people were still not creating valid HTML documents. Something needed to be done.

Data and XML

SGML's complexity spurred a group of people to wonder what would happen if a subset of SGML were created, a language built for the Web, built for any purpose, but that had a simple structure that could easily be processed without necessarily looking at a definition for that language. Jon Bosak, Dan Connolly, Tim Bray, and many others at the World Wide Web Consortium, picked up the idea of XML and turned it into a reality. By 1997, it was being introduced in Web conferences, and by 1998, it was a W3C Recommendation.

Well-Formed XML

So, what is XML? One of the key features of XML, is that the specification defines it well enough so that it can be parsed without necessarily being validated. That is, all applications of XML have to conform to a set of simple, but strict rules, to be **well-formed** XML. However, to build the applications themselves, we have to have **valid** XML, which we can think of as being a restriction on well-formedness. We shall look at XML validity later on, but for now, we shall give a general introduction to well-formed XML.

The definitive specification for XML is available on the Web at: http://www.w3.org/TR/REC-xml. The XML homepage is at: http://www.w3.org/XML/.

Tags, Attributes, and Elements

These are the core parts of any XML instance.

Tags

As is the case with SGML, XML is just data that is delimited by instructions in angle brackets. These instructions are called **tags**. Tags in XML are just like tags in HTML or any other SGML application, except that XML defines them as being case-sensitive. In other words, <tag> and <TAG> are not the same.

Tags in XML must always start with an alphabetic character, and may not start with the three-letter character sequence xml, in any combination of upper and lower case.

Elements

An **element** consists of a set of two tags: an **opening tag**, and a **closing tag,** and the content in between. Closing tags always have a "/" character before the tag name, as in HTML, for example:

```
<tag>
   My element data
</tag>
```

XML can only consist of a set of elements, in other words all tags must be closed. Elements can also be nested within one another. This means that we can place one element inside another element, for example:

```
<tag>
   <anotherTag>
      data
   </anotherTag>
   more data
</tag>
```

Elements cannot overlap. The following example is *not* well-formed XML:

```
<tag>
    <a>
        blargh
        <b>
            2
    </a>
            3
        </b>
</tag>
```

Instead, we should ensure that the tags nest correctly, for example:

```
<tag>
    <a>
        blargh
        <b>
            2
        </b>
    </a>
    <b>
        3
    </b>
</tag>
```

Elements can also be "**empty**":

```
<tag></tag>
```

XML introduces a shorthand for empty tags by using a single tag, but to show that it is closed, we put a "/" character before the ">" character. Here is an example of shorthand for an empty tag:

```
<tag />
```

Remember, that the above is just shorthand for `<tag></tag>`, so the rules about all tags having to close still applies. An XML document itself must consist of exactly one **root element**. The root element is simply the topmost element in the document – an example is the `<HTML>` tag in HTML.

Attributes

An element may also have a set of **attributes**. These are the same as in HTML, except that there are formal rules that define how they must appear in the opening tag. They consist of a set of name and value pairs. Here is an example of an empty element with an attribute:

```
<tag myAttribute='my attribute value' />
```

Elements can have any number of attributes, from none to unbounded. Attribute names (for example, the `myAttribute` part in the example above) are case sensitive, and cannot contain spaces. Attribute values are always joined to the attribute name with an "=" character, and enclosed in quotation marks. These can either be single quotes or double quotes, but not a mixture of each. For example, the following is not well-formed XML:

```
<tag myattribute='my attribute value"/>
```

Both of the following, however, are valid:

```
<tag myattribute='my attribute value'/>
<tag myattribute="my attribute value"/>
```

Attribute minimization (a feature of SGML, whereby attributes could consist of a name only, rather than a name and value pair), is no longer allowed in XML. Note that both element and attribute names must comply to the following XML specification rules:

❑ All names must start with a letter, an underscore, or a colon, and may contain any combination of letters, digits, ".", "-", "_", or ":"

```
NameChar ::= Letter | Digit | '.' | '-' | '_' | ':' | CombiningChar |
Extender

Name ::= (Letter | '_' | ':') (NameChar)*
```

❑ When creating an XML file with namespaces (discussed later), to conform to the XML Namespaces specification, names cannot contain the ":" character, because this is reserved.

```
NCName ::= (Letter | '_') (NCNameChar)*
```

❑ No name may start with the three-letter character combination xml in any case, as these are reserved for use in future XML specifications.

The XML Document Declaration

XML documents often come with a little bit of code at the very beginning to identify themselves to processors as XML documents. When present, this declaration must be the first thing present in the document – before any characters including whitespace, other character data, and markup. The XML Declaration is also sometimes referred to as the **XML prolog**. Here's what it looks like:

```
<?xml version='1.0'?>
```

This tells the processor that "this in an XML document of version 1.0". Version 1.0 is the only version of XML to date.

The XML declaration can also contain details about character encoding of the document. Indeed, if the character encoding of the document is anything other than UTF-8 or UTF-16, the declaration must be included. For example, here is the declaration that would be put at the very beginning of an ISO-8859-1 encoded document:

```
<?xml version-'1.0' encoding='ISO-8859-1'?>
```

Generally, it is a good idea to include the XML declaration even if you are sending your XML as UTF-8/UTF-16, but there are some exceptions to this rule. Note that if the XML document is to contain special characters, such as acutes, graves, and umlauts (for example, if it contained a list of names that could potentially contain such characters), then it does need to be encoded as ISO-8859-1, or some equivalent encoding.

Processing Instructions

XML also has a set of **Processing Instructions**, or **PI**s for short. These give specific instructions to processors. All PIs start with the characters "<?" and end with "?>", just like the declaration above. The most common use for PIs, is to attach **XSLT stylesheets** to XML documents, the use of which we shall look at in more detail later.

Comments, Entities, and Other XML Paraphernalia

XML can also contain a number of other constructs, including **comments**, and **CDATA** sections. A comment simply looks like it does in HTML:

```
<!-- This is a comment -->
```

Comments always start with `<!--`, end with `-->`, and cannot contain the character sequence `"--"` anywhere within itself. It is also illegal to end the comment with a `"-"`, so `<!-- my comment --->` is illegal.

Comments are part of an XML tree, but are often not parsed (they cannot be parsed by any of the XML stylesheet technologies that we shall be introduced to later on in this chapter). If you want something to be accessible by code, it's best not to include it in a comment tag.

Entities, similar to character entities in HTML, allow us to use certain characters that XML disallows. For example, we can't use the `"<"` character between tags, otherwise the processor would think that it was the start of a new tag. Therefore, we can use the `&lt;` entity (`"lt"` stands for less than). The entities available for an XML document are:

❑ `&lt;` A less than sign: (<)

❑ `&gt;` A greater than sign: (>)

❑ `&amp;` An ampersand: (&)

❑ `&quot;` A Double quotation mark: (")

❑ `&apos;` A single quotation mark: (')

Note that XML does not declare the ` ` entity, commonly used in HTML. We should use ` ` instead.

To use an entity, we simply write it in our XML instance. For example:

```
<myElement>And some &lt;text/&gt; with entities.</myElement>
```

CDATA sections simply mark up some character data, reducing the need for entities. Here's an example of a CDATA section:

```
<myElement><![CDATA[
This section will render as <characterData />, not displaying
any of the markup inside. A CDATA section simply converts any of the data within
it to entity escaped character data, eliminating the need for entities.]]>
</myElement>
```

The only restriction on CDATA sections, is that they cannot contain the character sequence `"]]"`.

Another important detail to note is that all elements and attributes starting with the three letter sequence xml, with any case used for any character, are reserved by the XML specification, and as such are prohibited. We shall see an example of why this is in the next section about namespaces.

Namespaces

XML as a meta-language is a great idea, but the problem is, that it is impossible to recognize what an element means in a given context. For example, let's say that we come up with a language that contains an element called `"<s>"`, and we specify that the element means `"strong"`. Now, let's say that someone else comes up with a totally different language that also has an `"<s>"` element in it, but that means `"sale"`. This would mean that our languages cannot be mixed or otherwise interact. This was the greatest problem that XML had to face, and was the reason for the creation of **XML Namespaces**.

A specific set of elements and attributes with a particular use, is called an **XML vocabulary**. There are numerous XML vocabularies, and the way to distinguish one from the other,, is by specifying that the vocabulary belongs to a specific **namespace**. For instance, **MathML** is a vocabulary that allows a compliant parser to render mathematical content on the screen. This vocabulary has been given the namespace: `http://www.w3.org/1998/Math/MathML`, and if the `xmlns` attribute is set to this on the root node, the parser knows that all the markup therein, is to be interpreted as MathML. An XML namespace name is simply a **URI (Universal Resource Identifier)**, or rather, a URI Reference, (see http://www.ietf.org/rfc/rfc2396.txt).

Here's an example of an XML document with a namespace:

```
<s xmlns="http://example.org/2001/test/"/>
```

Here's another:

```
<s xmlns="http://example.org/2001/anothertest/"/>
```

Note how the namespaces are different, and yet the root element is the same. Now parsers can tell the two `<s>` elements apart. A namespace declaration applies to the element it appears in and all of the children of that element.

The thing that confuses many people about namespaces, is the use of URIs for the namespace names, and more specifically URLs. There is no guarantee that any web page is going to be at the URLs used above, although there could be. The namespace name is simply a unique name that we can use in XML documents. Some people have gone so far as to accuse namespaces as being a broken piece of Web architecture, because it means that URLs are being used for two different things, but it should be noted that as the use of URLs (and all URIs) are contextual, this doesn't matter a great deal. In other words, we know that if a URL is being used as a namespace, then it might not be a reference to any particular web page, but that if it's in a link on some HTML page, then it probably does refer to a web page.

In any case, a URL identifies a resource, and the web page returned from it is simply a representation of that resource. Therefore, it's legal to return an HTML representation of a resource that is a namespace.

XML Namespaces also allow you to define prefixes, so that we can mix elements in different namespaces. To declare a namespace prefix, you simply use the `xmlns` attribute, but add something along the lines of `:myprefix` after it. For example:

```
<myElement xmlns:myprefix="http://example.org/#"/>
```

The prefix `myprefix` has now been assigned to the `example.org` namespace name, so that every time we start an element or attribute with that prefix and a colon, we know that it belongs to that namespace. For example:

```
<a xmlns:pre="http://example.org/pre#">
   <pre:b pre:c="abcxyz"/>
   <d/>
</a>
```

Note how elements `a` and `d` are not in the `http://example.org/pre#` namespace, but that element `b` and the attribute `c` are. It is also important to note that it doesn't matter what prefix we use for a given namespace, and that even if we use two different prefixes, as long as they use the same namespace, they are taken to be equivalent. For example:

```
<a xmlns:abc="http://example.org/test#"
   xmlns:xyz="http://example.org/test#">
   <abc:b/>
   <xyz:b/>
</a>
```

Here, the b element with the abc prefix is exactly the same element as the b element with the xyz prefix.

XML Example

Here, we shall come up with an example of XML that we shall be using later to demonstrate how XML can be processed and displayed. It's a simple order form in XML, that we can type out, and save as order.xml:

```
<?xml version='1.0' encoding='UTF-8'?>
<OnlineOrder xmlns='http://infomesh.net/2001/order/'
   ID='123456'>
   <CustomerName>
      <FirstName>Arnold</FirstName>
      <LastName>Williams</LastName>
   </CustomerName>
   <Address>
      <Street>32, Elm Street</Street>
      <Town>AnyTown</Town>
      <State>Texas</State>
      <Country>USA</Country>
   </Address>
   <Items>
      <Item>
         <Book ISBN='1861005539' Title='Professional JavaScript'>
            <Price>49.99</Price>
         </Book>
      </Item>
      <Item>
         <CD Artist='Bob Dylan' Title='Highway 61 Revisited'>
            <Price>15.99</Price>
         </CD>
      </Item>
   </Items>
   <CreditCard Type='Visa'>
      <Number>1234 4567 1234</Number>
      <ExpiryDate>03-04</ExpiryDate>
   </CreditCard>
</OnlineOrder>
```

Valid XML

XML is great in that anyone can define a new set of elements, but what happens if we want to create an entirely new language based upon XML? We need some way of restricting well-formed XML to specify what tag names are valid, the attributes that they can contain, and the allowed or required content of each element and attribute.

We can do this using a type of document called a **schema**. This is simply a document that controls the ordering, positioning, and other details of the markup in a language, based on XML (which is technically, but less commonly, called an **application** of XML). There are generally two types of schemas: **DTDs** (**Document Type Definitions**, based upon the DTDs that SGML had), and **XML schemas**, which are themselves well-formed XML. There is only one XML DTD language detailed in the XML specification, but there are a few XML schema languages being developed. One of them, is the W3C's XML Schema language, which many people simply refer to as "XML Schema". We should be careful not to confuse "XML Schema" with "XML schemas" (small "s") in general. Another schema language, which has been used by Microsoft, is **XDR – XML Data Reduced**.

XML DTDs

As we have already mentioned, XML DTDs are a particular way of constraining XML to create your own language. They do so by stating what an element is, and what it can contain (in terms of other elements, attributes, and character data). They also allow us to specify what kind of character data an attribute may contain.

For example, let's say we want to create a language that has three elements: <document> (the root element), <para>, and <emph>. We want <document> to be the root element, and to contain one or more <para> elements, and we want those <para> elements to represent a paragraph of text. We shall let <para> include character data and <emph> elements (which we'll use to define emphasized text). Here is the DTD fragment that does this for us:

```
<!ELEMENT document (para)+ >
<!ELEMENT para (#PCDATA|emph)* >
```

The "*" character simply specifies that it may occur zero or more times, and the "+" character indicates that it may occur one or more times. The parentheses indicate a group, and the pipe character "|", indicates logical OR. We shall learn some other important characters later on.

Therefore, we can read this declaration as: "The <para> element can contain zero or more occurrences of either #PCDATA or the element <emph>". #PCDATA simply indicates that the element can contain character data as well as elements. If we left out #PCDATA, we could not have character data as direct children of the element, only other elements.

We'll now define the <emph> element, by saying that we cannot nest <emph> elements, and so <emph> can only have character data inside. Here's the DTD fragment for that:

```
<!ELEMENT emph (#PCDATA) >
```

Now, let's define some attributes. We'll define an id attribute for both the <para> and <emph> elements:

```
<!ATTLIST para
    id  ID  #IMPLIED >
<!ATTLIST emph
    id  ID  #IMPLIED >
```

The id ID #IMPLIED line declares that this element can have an id attribute, that its content must be of type ID (a data type set out by the XML specification), and that its use is optional; that's what the #IMPLIED token denotes. If we wanted to require the id attribute to be used, we would have used #REQUIRED instead.

Here is an example of a document that conforms to this DTD (assuming that the DTD was saved as document.dtd):

```
<!DOCTYPE document SYSTEM "document.dtd" >
<document>
    <para>Here is some <emph>text</emph>.</para>
</document>
```

As we have already seen, DTDs use special characters to indicate how often a group may occur, and what kind of ordering the group can have. Here, is a run through of those characters:

❑   A* – Pattern A can occur 0 or more times

❑   A+ – Pattern A can occur 1 or more times

❑   A? – Pattern A can occur 0 or 1 times

❑   A,B – Pattern A must occur, followed by pattern B

❑   A|B – Pattern A or pattern B must occur

A pattern could be either a group, or an element. You can see how it is very easy for us to come up with quite complex data structures and describe them tersely using the DTD syntax.

Attribute types can be any one of the following:

- ID
- CDATA
- IDREF
- IDREFS
- ENTITY
- ENTITIES
- NMTOKEN
- NMTOKENS

So, how do we reference XML DTDs from the XML files that we create using the DTD? We do so by including a piece of code at the top of our XML files called a **document type declaration**. Although the initials are the same as for Document Type Definitions, we usually avoid using the acronym DTD to stand for document type declaration for obvious reasons!

Here is an example of an XML document with a DTD:

```
<?xml version="1.0" encoding="UTF-8"?>
<!DOCTYPE html PUBLIC "-//W3C//DTD XHTML 1.1//EN"
    "http://www.w3.org/TR/xhtml11/DTD/xhtml11.dtd" >
<html xmlns="http://www.w3.org/1999/xhtml" xml:lang="en" >
<head>
    <title>My title</title>
</head>
<body>
    <p>My document.</p>
</body>
</html>
```

As you can see, the document type declaration always goes at the top of the document (although after the XML declaration) and consists of a number of parts. <!DOCTYPE lets the processor know that this is a document type declaration. html lets the processor know that we are validating the root element, html. The next two pieces, PUBLIC and '-//W3C//DTD XHTML 1.1//EN' are optional parts that specify a **Formal Public Identifier** (**FPI**) for the language. Such identifiers should be globally unique, but there is no way to guarantee this. Each language should have a different FPI.

The next bit is simply a URL to the location of the DTD itself, in this case http://www.w3.org/TR/xhtml11/DTD/xhtml11.dtd. If you go to that location with your browser, you will indeed find a DTD there, for XHTML 1.1 (a language that we shall cover in more detail later in this chapter).

W3C XML Schema

XML DTDs were primarily based upon SGML DTDs, and as such, they weren't as specifically geared towards validating XML as they might have been. For example, it is difficult to enforce namespace mixing and data types in XML DTDs. The solution was to come up with a new grammar for validating XML that allowed all of this, and that was itself an XML language. The W3C took this on, and W3C XML Schema was released as a Recommendation.

Let's take the DTD example from the previous section.

```
<!ELEMENT para (#PCDATA|emph)* >
<!ELEMENT emph (#PCDATA) >
<!ATTLIST para
   id  ID  #IMPLIED >
<!ATTLIST emph
   id  ID  #IMPLIED >
```

Then re-draft it as an XML Schema:

```
<xs:schema xmlns:xs="http://www.w3.org/2001/XMLSchema">
<xs:element name="document">
   <xs:complexType>
     <xs:sequence>
       <xs:element ref="para" minOccurs="1" maxOccurs="unbounded" />
     </xs:sequence>
   </xs:complexType>
</xs:element>

<xs:element xs:name="para">
   <xs:complexType mixed="true">
     <xs:attribute name="id" type="xs:ID" use="optional" />
     <xs:sequence>
       <xs:element ref="emph" minOccurs="0" maxOccurs="unbounded" />
     </xs:sequence>
   </xs:complexType>

</xs:element><xs:element xs:name="emph">
   <xs:complexType mixed="true">
     <xs:attribute name="id" type="xs:ID" use="optional" />
   </xs:complexType>
</xs:element>
</xs:schema>
```

As you can see, many of the elements follow the DTD fragments. xs:element is used to declare an element in much the same way as <!ELEMENT ... in DTD notation. The name attribute of xs:element sets the name of the element being defined, and the type attribute references a content type for the element. The xs:complexType element takes the place of a content type. It can contain a mixture of xs:attribute elements (which set what attributes an element can have), and group elements: xs:group, xs:all (which we won't cover here), xs:choice, and xs:sequence. xs:group is used a little like parentheses in DTDs, in that it denotes a sub content group. xs:choice is much like a group that uses the | syntax inside it: it makes you choose one element from within it. xs:sequence is much like the "," syntax in DTDs – it denotes that all of the elements must occur in sequence.

Inside complex types and groups, elements are referenced using xs:element again, but instead of the name attribute, we use the ref attribute to show that we are not redefining the elements, merely referencing them.

The mixed attribute on a complexType simply denotes whether or not the element that references that complexType can contain #PCDATA or not. It is set to false by default, and once set to true allows #PCDATA.

We shan't go into too much detail about XML Schema, because the specification can get quite complex in some places. We shall, however, go through another example. Here, is an XML Schema for our order.xml file:

```
<xs:schema xmlns:xs="http://www.w3.org/2001/XMLSchema">
   <xs:element name="Address">
      <xs:complexType>
         <xs:sequence>
```

```
                <xs:element ref="Street"/>
                <xs:element ref="Town"/>
                <xs:element ref="State"/>
                <xs:element ref="Country"/>
            </xs:sequence>
        </xs:complexType>
    </xs:element>
    <xs:element name="Book">
        <xs:complexType>
            <xs:sequence>
                <xs:element ref="Price"/>
            </xs:sequence>
            <xs:attribute name="ISBN" type="type.ISBN" use="required"/>
            <xs:attribute name="Title" type="xs:string"
                use="required"/>
        </xs:complexType>
        <xs:complexType name='type.ISBN'>
            <xs:simpleContent>
                <xs:restriction base='xs:string'>
                    <xs:pattern match='[0-9]{9}[0-9X]' />
                </xs:restriction>
            </xs:simpleContent>
        </xs:complexType>
    </xs:element>
    <xs:element name="CD">
        <xs:complexType>
            <xs:sequence>
                <xs:element ref="Price"/>
            </xs:sequence>
            <xs:attribute name="Artist" type="xs:string"
                use="required"/>
            <xs:attribute name="Title" type="xs:string"
                use="required"/>
        </xs:complexType>
    </xs:element>
    <xs:element name="Country" type="xs:string"/>
    <xs:element name="CreditCard">
        <xs:complexType>
            <xs:sequence>
                <xs:element ref="Number"/>
                <xs:element ref="ExpiryDate"/>
            </xs:sequence>
            <xs:attribute name="Type" type="xs:string" use="required"/>
        </xs:complexType>
    </xs:element>
    <xs:element name="CustomerName">
        <xs:complexType>
            <xs:sequence>
                <xs:element ref="FirstName"/>
                <xs:element ref="LastName"/>
            </xs:sequence>
        </xs:complexType>
    </xs:element>
    <xs:element name="ExpiryDate" type="xs:string"/>
    <xs:element name="FirstName" type="xs:string"/>
    <xs:element name="Item">
        <xs:complexType>
            <xs:choice>
                <xs:element ref="Book"/>
                <xs:element ref="CD"/>
            </xs:choice>
        </xs:complexType>
```

```
      </xs:element>
      <xs:element name="Items">
        <xs:complexType>
          <xs:sequence>
            <xs:element ref="Item" maxOccurs="unbounded"/>
          </xs:sequence>
        </xs:complexType>
      </xs:element>
      <xs:element name="LastName" type="xs:string"/>
      <xs:element name="Number" type="xs:string"/>
      <xs:element name="OnlineOrder">
        <xs:complexType>
          <xs:sequence>
            <xs:element ref="CustomerName"/>
            <xs:element ref="Address"/>
            <xs:element ref="Items"/>
            <xs:element ref="CreditCard"/>
          </xs:sequence>
          <xs:attribute name="ID" type="xs:ID" use="required"/>
        </xs:complexType>
      </xs:element>
      <xs:element name="Price" type='xs:decimal' />
      <xs:element name="State" type="xs:string"/>
      <xs:element name="Street" type="xs:string"/>
      <xs:element name="Town" type="xs:string"/>
   </xs:schema>
```

For more information on W3C XML Schema, try the W3C's XML Schema site, at:
http://www.w3.org/XML/Schema.

Other Schema Technologies

Another XML schema language in development, is **RELAX-NG**. This is a relatively new language being developed under the aegis of OASIS (an XML interoperability standards group). More information about RELAX-NG, is available from http://relaxng.org/. Basically, it is XML DTDs drafted in XML, with none of the additional features that W3C XML Schema introduces (such as data types, and substitution groups, both of which are beyond the scope of this chapter). This makes it ideal for lightweight XML validation that does not use these features.

Another XML schem,a is **Schematron** by Rick Jelliffe. Schematron works differently from most of the 'traditional' schema languages, in that it can match patterns of elements. To quote the Schematron homepage:

> *"The Schematron differs in basic concept from other schema languages in that it" (is) "not based on grammars but on finding tree patterns in the parsed document. This approach allows many kinds of structures to be represented which are inconvenient and difficult in grammar-based schema languages."*

The Schematron homepage is at:

http://www.ascc.net/xml/resource/schematron/schematron.html

There are a number of implementations for Schematron, including validating parsers that will use Schematron patterns found in W3C XML Schema files.

Parsers and Validation

There are two types of XML parsers: **validating parsers**, and **non-validating parsers**. A validating parser confirms that an XML document complies with the appropriate schema, while a non-validating parser just checks for well-formedness. IE 5 onward and Netscape 6 have XML parsers built into them. MSIE, however, has a built in 'XSLT stylesheet' that enables you to view the XML tree. Netscape does not have this feature yet, but can display XML styled with CSS.

IE uses Microsoft's own MSXML parser to parse the XML, which is a validating parser. Earlier versions of MSXML contained a number of bugs, especially when validating, although the latest version (MSXML4) is quite good. There are a number of validating parsers, including:

❑   Xerces (Java, C++, and Perl versions)

see: http://xml.apache.org/xerces-j/index.html

❑   MSXML – see: http://msdn.microsoft.com/xml

❑   SXP (Java) – see: http://www.loria.fr/projets/XSilfide/EN/sxp/

Non-validating parsers:

❑   XP (Java) – http://www.jclark.com/xml/xp/index.html

❑   Expat (C) – http://www.jclark.com/xml/expat.html

(James Clark's XML tools are very popular!)

Displaying XML

XML can be rendered using style sheet technologies. The two main style sheet technologies that are used to style XML, are **XSLT** (**Extensible Stylesheet Language Transformations**), and **CSS** (**Cascading Style Sheets**).

Displaying XML with CSS

CSS is a language that was developed by the W3C to style HTML and XML documents. Originally proposed by Hakon Wium-Lie (formerly of CERN, then W3C, and currently Opera Software), CSS went to recommendation in 1996, followed by CSS2 in 1998. The CSS Working Group is currently working on CSS3.

A CSS style sheet is simply a set of rules that tell the user agent (browser) how to render the XML document by giving characteristics to the elements. The basic syntax is a selector, and then a declaration block. The selector selects a range of elements, based on their name, or one of their attribute values, and so on. The declaration block (which is in curly braces: "{}"), is then applied to all elements that match that selector.

Here is an example of a CSS:

```
document { font-family: arial, sans-serif;
    font-size: 1em; margin: 1.5em; }
heading, para { display: block; }
heading { font-family: tahoma, sans-serif; font-size: 2em; font-weight: bold; }
para { margin: 2em; }
para important { font-style: italic;
    font-weight: bold; color: #b05000; }
```

Type it out and save it as `style.css`. Now, if we type out the following file and load it into a browser (IE5.5+, or Netscape 6):

```
<?xml-stylesheet type="text/css" href="style.css"?>
<document>
   <heading>My Heading</heading>
   <para>Some <important>important</important> text.</para>
</document>
```

Then we get the document rendered according to the style sheet:

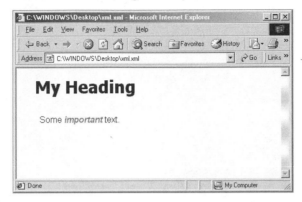

Note how the style sheet is referenced from the processing instruction at the top of the file. CSS is covered in more detail (with respect to manipulating with JavaScript) in the next chapter.

More information on CSS can be found from the W3C's CSS homepage (http://www.w3.org/Style/CSS/), and the style page at: http://www.w3.org/Style/.

Displaying XML with XSLT

XSLT (**Extensible Stylesheet Language Transformations**) works by changing the structure of an XML document according to some rules, and then outputting it. In other words, XSLT is very powerful, as it lets us transform the structure of an XML document, changing the elements and data in one document into a new document. XSLT has proven itself an incredibly useful technology, because it makes it possible to convert from any XML language into any other XML language. It also allows output as HTML (where it expands empty tags, such as <tag /> into <tag></tag>), or text.

Note that XSLT does not allow one to say how a document should be rendered – that's for CSS. In other words, it does not allow us to tell a browser to style a particular element in a certain color, although it does let us transform that element into (for example), a final form markup language that might contain a set of elements for expressing color.

XSLT documents are themselves XML. Let's take a quick look at a practical example of an XSLT document: a stylesheet that can convert our order.xml example into XHTML:

```
<xsl:stylesheet
   xmlns="http://www.w3.org/1999/html" version="1.0"
   xmlns:xsl ="http://www.w3.org/1999/XSL/Transform"
   xmlns:o="http://infomesh.net/2001/order/"
   xml:lang="en" >

<xsl:template match="/">
   <html xmlns="http://www.w3.org/1999/html">
     <head>
        <title>Your Order</title>
        <link rel="stylesheet" type="text/css" href="style.css" />
```

```
            </head>
            <body>
                <h1>Order</h1>
                <xsl:apply-templates/>
                <address>
                    <a href="http://example.org/">example.org</a>
                </address>
            </body>
        </html>
</xsl:template>

<xsl:template match="//o:CustomerName">
 <h2>Customer Name</h2>
 <dl>
 <xsl:for-each select=".//o:FirstName">
    <dt>First Name</dt>
        <dd><xsl:value-of select="." /></dd>
 </xsl:for-each>
 <xsl:for-each select=".//o:LastName">
    <dt>Last Name</dt>
        <dd><xsl:value-of select="." /></dd>
 </xsl:for-each>
 </dl>
</xsl:template>

<xsl:template match="//o:Address">
 <h2>Customer Address</h2>
 <dl>
 <xsl:for-each select=".//o:Street">
    <dt>Street</dt>
        <dd><xsl:value-of select="." /></dd>
 </xsl:for-each>
 <xsl:for-each select=".//o:Town">
    <dt>Town</dt>
        <dd><xsl:value-of select="." /></dd>
 </xsl:for-each>
 <xsl:for-each select=".//o:State">
    <dt>State</dt>
        <dd><xsl:value-of select="." /></dd>
 </xsl:for-each>
 <xsl:for-each select=".//o:Country">
    <dt>Country</dt>
        <dd><xsl:value-of select="." /></dd>
 </xsl:for-each>
 </dl>
</xsl:template>

<xsl:template match="//o:Items">
<h2>Items</h2>
<xsl:apply-templates/>
</xsl:template>

<xsl:template match="//o:Item">
 <xsl:for-each select=".//o:Book">
    <h3>Book</h3>
<dl>
    <dt>ISBN</dt>
        <dd><xsl:value-of select="(@ISBN)"/></dd>
    <dt>Title</dt>
        <dd><xsl:value-of select="(@Title)"/></dd>
    <dt>Price</dt>
        <dd><xsl:value-of select="(.)" /></dd>
```

```
    </dl>
  </xsl:for-each>
  <xsl:for-each select=".//o:CD">
    <h3>CD</h3>
<dl>
    <dt>Artist</dt>
        <dd><xsl:value-of select="(@Artist)"/></dd>
    <dt>Title</dt>
        <dd><xsl:value-of select="(@Title)"/></dd>
    <dt>Price</dt>
        <dd><xsl:value-of select="." /></dd>
</dl>
  </xsl:for-each>
</xsl:template>

<xsl:template match="//o:CreditCard">
  <h2>Credit Card</h2>
  <dl>
  <dt>Type</dt>
    <dd><xsl:value-of select="(@Type)"/></dd>
  <xsl:for-each select=".//o:Number">
    <dt>Number</dt>
        <dd><xsl:value-of select="." /></dd>
  </xsl:for-each>
  <xsl:for-each select=".//o:ExpiryDate">
    <dt>Expiry Date</dt>
        <dd><xsl:value-of select="." /></dd>
  </xsl:for-each>
  </dl>
</xsl:template>
</xsl:stylesheet>
```

Save this file as `style.xsl` in the same directory as the `order.xml` file. You should be able to view the output by adding the following line to `order.xml` (underneath the XML declaration):

```
<?xml-stylesheet href="style.xsl" type="text/xsl"?>
```

You'll need to have IE5.5 with MSXML3, IE6, or Netscape 6.1 for this to work. Netscape 6 has some bugs, in that it won't correctly display selections based on attribute values. The output appears like this:

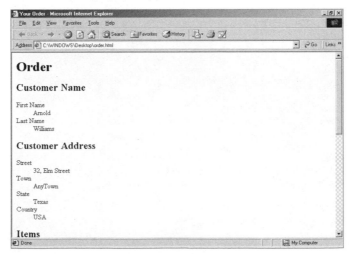

So, how does it work? The style sheet itself is comprised of a series of templates (the contents of the `xsl:template` elements), and the expressions inside those templates. The first tag of importance in the stylesheet is:

```
<xsl:template match="/">
```

The `match` attribute tells the XSLT processor what elements in the source document (`order.xml`) we are applying the stylesheet to match the template to; `"/"` means the root of the document in this case. XML trees will be explained later on in the section *XML and JavaScript*. All you need to know, is that the value of the `match` attribute has a special syntax for pointing to XML documents. This syntax, called **XPath**, is very easy to learn:

❑   / means the root element

❑   /abc means the element abc directly under the root

❑   /abc/def means the element def directly under abc directly under the root

❑   //abc means any abc element in the document

❑   /abc//def means any def element as a descendant of abc, directly under the root

These types of expressions can get very complicated, but for most tasks, you only need to learn the basics outlined above.

When the XSLT processor finds an element that matches the value of the `match` element, it outputs everything that is in that template, unless it contains some XSLT elements, which have special purposes. So, for example, the following template:

```
<xsl:template match="/">
    <a>
        <b/>
    </a>
</xsl:template>
```

Would output `<a><b/></a>`, when it came to the root element. The next important element that we come across is the `apply-templates` element.

```
<xsl:apply-templates/>
```

This applies all the other templates in the document to that particular position. So, for example:

```
<xsl:template match="/">
    <a><xsl:apply-templates/></a>
</xsl:template>
<xsl:template match="//c">
    <b/>
</xsl:template>
```

This would match the root element, and output `<a></a>`. Then, it would carry on doing the other templates, and put the results in between the `<a>` and `</a>` tags. Here, we have a template that matches any c element and converts it into a b element.

Another useful XSLT element is `for-each`. This matches every occurrence of a particular element within a template, no matter how many times it occurs. For example:

```
<xsl:template match="/">
    <xsl:for-each select=".//c">
        <b/>
    </xsl:for-each>
</xsl:template>
```

This matches *every* c element that occurs under the root element and converts it into a b element.

The next element that we have used in the example is the `value-of` element. This takes a certain piece of the element, for example its content, or an attribute value, and returns it. For example:

```
<xsl:template match="//c">
    <b>
        <xsl:value-of select="."/>
    </b>
</xsl:template>
```

This would take a c element, and return a b element that includes the content of c. For example, it would convert.

```
<c>My text.</c>
```

Into:

```
<b>My text.</b>
```

For more information on XSLT, take a look at the W3C XSL style site (http://www.w3.org/Style/XSL/) and the XSLT specification at: http://www.w3.org/TR/xslt.

XML and JavaScript

Due to its structuring, XML can easily be accessed and manipulated from JavaScript code.

The XML DOM

The **DOM** (**Document Object Model**) enables us to access parts of a document as objects for use in our JavaScript. The XML DOM is simply a Document Object Model for XML, allowing us to access parts of XML documents in our JavaScript code.

XML Trees

To XML parsers, an XML document looks like a tree. It's difficult to explain what an XML document tree is without illustrating it, so lets do that. We'll use the following document as the example:

```
<myDocument xmlns="http://example.org/myLanguage"
    xml:lang="en" >
    <title>My Document Title</title>
    <para>
        Here is a simple example of XML! Note that the things
        in angular brackets, e.g. <myElement/> can be made up
        by anyone, giving XML its power.
    </para>
</myDocument>
```

Here's what the tree for this document looks like:

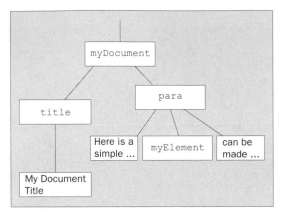

XML document trees have special terminologies to describe their component parts. For example, an element that occurs directly within another element, is said to be a **child** of that element. The enclosing element is, logically, called the **parent** element. The table below describes the terms used:

Term	Description
Node	An element, a text node, a comment, or version
Root node	The first element in the XML document tree
Parent node	The relationship between an node and its immediate enclosing element
Child node	The relationship between an element, and its immediate internal nodes (inverse of parent)
Grandparent node	The parent of the parent of a node
Grandchild node	The child of a child of a node
Ancestor node	The parent of a node to any level
Descendant node	The child of a node to any level
Sibling node	A node that has the same parent as another node (like brothers and sisters!)
Leaf node	Nodes with no further nested nodes

Because these terms are common words, their usage should be easy to remember.

JavaScript API

The XML DOM contains a number of methods to manipulate XML documents. The best way to illustrate how the JavaScript API works on the XML DOM, and to show its power is by providing an example. We shall use `order.xml` as our test file once again. Note that this code will only work on IE5+.

Here is a simple example that finds the first items node in an `order.xml` file, gets the values of the price elements of the item children, uses these to display the total price, and offers a discount if more than three items have been purchased. The tags below are shown in lower case, as the XHTML Recommendation (that we discuss later) specifies that. The code below is broken up with explanatory text:

```
<!-- DOM_Example.html -->
<html xmlns="http://www.w3.org/1999/xhtml"
   xml:lang="en">
<head>
   <title>Your Invoice Details</title>
</head>
<body>
   <h1>Invoice Details</h1>
   <script type="text/jscript">
   <!--
       var msXML=new ActiveXObject("microsoft.xmldom");
       msXML.async = false;
```

Here, we create a new ActiveX Object, the MS XML DOM that we will use to handle our XML. With IE5+ on Windows there are a couple of other ways of handling XML from JavaScript embedded in XHTML, namely using embedded XML islands, or processed XML islands, but we'll just concentrate on using ActiveX for now.

```
       msXML.load('order.xml');
```

Here, we load the order.xml file into the ActiveX Object, which enables us to access it according to the XML DOM. In other words, it has processed the file in such a way that we can now access it using the standard JavaScript methods for the XML DOM.

```
       var items = msXML.documentElement.firstChild.nextSibling.nextSibling;
```

Now we get into the main part of the code. msXML is the document object into which we loaded the order.xml file. The documentElement object is the root element of that document, in our case OnlineOrder.

Now, we need to go down the tree in order to access the items element. If you go through the order.xml file, you can see exactly where we are going: the first child element of OnlineOrder is CustomerName. The nextSibling to this is Address, and then the nextSibling to that is the Items element. Therefore, we have now stored the Items element as an object into the items variable:

```
       var itemList = items.childNodes;
```

Now, we want to create a list of all Item elements within the Items element. As you can see from order.xml, there are two childNodes of the Items element. childNodes creates an array (starting from 0) of all of the elements that are child nodes of the Items element, so now they are all stored in itemList:

```
       var priceTotal = 0;
```

Here, we assign the value 0 to the variable priceTotal. We shall use this later on in the code to store the total price of the items.

```
       for(count=0;count<=itemList.length-1;count++)
```

Here we create a for loop. We initially set count to 0 because we are going to be selecting each of the elements in the item list, the array of which starts at 0. We shall continue doing this for loop until count is equal to the length of the itemList minus 1.

```
       {
           var myItem = itemList.item(count);
           var Price = myItem.firstChild.firstChild.firstChild.data;
           numericPrice = Number(Price);
           priceTotal += numericPrice;
       };
```

243

This is the main part of the `for` loop. For each time we have `count`, we assign the variable `myItem` to the particular item in the list. The `item()` method should not be confused with the `Item` element, even though it returns it: that is coincidence! The `item(count)` method is a general method that returns any given object in an array at the position indicated by `count`.

Once we have stored the `Item` element in the `myItem` variable, we can search for the `Price` element that lies within it. Referring once again to `order.xml`, we see that the first child of the `Item` element is either `Book` or `CD` (or, presumably, something else). Then, the first child of that element is the `Price` element. However, we don't want the `Price` element itself, but the data that's contained inside the price element. The text inside the element is considered a node itself, so we use another `firstChild()` method, and finally the `data()` method to retrieve the data within that text node. We store this data in the variable `Price`.

Then, we simply cast the string to a number by taking 0 away from it, and store it in `numericPrice`. Then, each time we get a price, we add it to our grand total, `priceTotal`.

```
document.write("<p>Total value of your items is: ")
document.write("<strong>" + priceTotal + "</strong></p>");
```

Here, we simply print out the grand total to the current document.

```
            if(itemList.length >= 3)
            {
                document.write("<p>Because you purchased three items or more, \n");
                document.write(" you get a discount!</p>");
                var newPrice = priceTotal * 0.9;
                document.write("<p>Price you pay: <strong>"+b+"</strong></p>");
            };
        // -->
        </script>
    </body>
    </html>
```

In this part of the script, we create a conditional `if` statement such that if there are three or more list items, then we get a discount. Because we're using JavaScript, we can even calculate the discount that one gets by multiplying `priceTotal` by a percentage (a number between 0 and 1).

XHTML

As we mentioned earlier in this chapter, HTML was greatly hindered by a lack of decent parsers, and proprietary extensions. XHTML is a language that was devised as a simple reformulation of HTML as an application of XML.

We have already used XHTML once in this chapter – for the JavaScript example. Note how the example follows the well-formedness rules of XML. Note also that it doesn't have a `DOCTYPE` declaration with which to specify a schema for the language, but one may be derived from the namespace.

The Working Group of the W3C responsible for the development of XHTML is the HTML WG. More information on them and (X)HTML in general can be found at: http://www.w3.org/MarkUp/.

Types of XHTML

The HTML WG recently issued four specifications that are central to XHTML:

❑   XHTML 1.0: The Extensible Hypertext Markup Language (A Reformulation of HTML 4 in XML 1.0), W3C Recommendation 26 January 2000, http://www.w3.org/TR/xhtml1/

❑   XHTML Basic, W3C Recommendation 19 December 2000, http://www.w3.org/TR/xhtml-basic/

❑   XHTML m12n – Modularization of XHTML, W3C Recommendation 10 April 2001,
http://www.w3.org/TR/xhtml-modularization/

❑   XHTML 1.1 – Module-based XHTML, W3C Recommendation 31 May 2001,
http://www.w3.org/TR/xhtml11/

XHTML 1.0

XHTML 1.0 was the first specification to be issued, and simply re-drafted the previous work on HTML
(namely, the HTML 4.01 specification – http://www.w3.org/TR/html401) into XML.

*Interestingly, XHTML is a rarely used standard, because people are so used to not having code that
can be validated, and the benefits of using XML aren't obvious to many when they have used SGML
tag soup for so long. However, XHTML does have two main benefits: 1) we can transform into and
out of it using XSLT, and 2) it is extensible thanks to XML and XML Namespaces.*

XHTML Basic and XHTML 1.1

XHTML Basic and XHTML 1.1 were produced by the HTML WG as implementations of XHTML
m12n (which we shall discuss in the next section). XHTML Basic was, as the name suggests, a small
language consisting of a few core modules, for use on devices that don't have a large amount of
memory, such as hand-held mobile Internet devices.

XHTML 1.1, on the other hand, was meant to be a language for the common Web, or computers with plenty of
memory. In fact, XHTML 1.1 is very close to the Strict version of XHTML 1.0 (which corresponds to the Strict
version of HTML 4.01, a particular version of it that uses less presentational markup).

XHTML m12n: Modularizing XHTML

XHTML m12n was a specification that was worked on for quite some time before XHTML Basic and
1.1, although it was released as a recommendation *after* XHTML Basic and before XHTML 1.1.

The theory behind XHTML m12n, is that all of the basic components of XHTML (such as forms, images,
and phrasing), could be broken into smaller parts called **modules**, so that people could then stick these
parts together to create new languages. The HTML Working Group first had to categorize each of the
elements in XHTML 1.0 into modules – for example, the <a> element goes in the Hypertext module,
<ul> and <ol> go into the List module, and so on. We can then create our own languages based upon
these modules, either by selecting a certain amount of modules (for example, we might want to create a
language which consists of only text, hypertext, lists, and forms), adding some elements in a new module
(for example, adding the <embed> element into XHTML), modifying existing modules (perhaps by taking
elements out that we don't like, such as <b>), or modifying existing languages which utilize the modules,
such as XHTML 1.1 and XHTML Basic. In other words, XHTML modularization lets us create
customized languages based upon XHTML, perhaps letting us merge it with other languages (such as SVG
and MathML, which we shall be covering in the next section, *XML and Emerging Specifications).*

The reason for this modularity, was to promote XHTML's use over a wide range of devices, including
(but not limited to) wireless Internet devices, such as mobile phones. XHTML was lacking this
interoperability aspect until XHTML m12n came around. The biggest advantage that XHTML has is its
extensibility. However, in version 1.0 of XHTML, extensions could only be made by making
proprietary extensions to the DTD, which wasn't very easy to do.

Here is a list of some of the modules and the elements that they contain. Required indicates that a
module is required in every customized XHTML language that is created, and Deprecated indicates that
the module is out of date and not recommended for XHTML languages:

Module	Required/ Deprecated	Elements
Structure	Required	`<noscript>`, `<script>`
Stylesheet		`<style>`
Style Attribute	Deprecated	*Style attribute*
Link		`<link>`
Base		`<base>`
Name Identification	Deprecated	*Adds the* `name` *attribute to certain elements*
Legacy	Deprecated	`<basefont>`, `<center>`, `<dir>`, `<font>`, `<isindex>`, `<menu>`, `<s>`, `<strike>`, `<u>` *and certain deprecated attributes*

We don't have the space available to explain the modularization in depth here, but you can find an example XHTML module online at:

http://www.w3.org/TR/xhtml-modularization/DTD/xhtml-basic-table-1.mod

Modularization makes heavy use of DTD constructs called **entities**. These simply reference a piece of DTD code that is found elsewhere in the file, or in another file. They can also be used to import external files. This is useful because it allows us to create a new DTD simply by referencing an existing XHTML DTD (for example, the XHTML 1.1 DTD), and making a few modifications to it. For example:

```
<!ENTITY % xhtml-form.module "IGNORE" >
<!ENTITY % xhtml-table.module "IGNORE" >
<!-- Bring in the basic tables module -->
<!ENTITY % xhtml-basic-table.mod
    PUBLIC "-//W3C//ELEMENTS XHTML Basic Tables 1.0//EN"
        "http://www.w3.org/TR/xhtml-modularization/DTD/xhtml-basic-table-1.mod"
>
%xhtml-basic-table.mod;
<!ENTITY % xhtml11.mod
    PUBLIC "-//W3C//DTD XHTML 1.1//EN"
            "http://www.w3.org/TR/xhtml11/DTD/xhtml11.dtd" >
%xhtml11.mod;
```

What this does is build upon the XHTML 1.1 DTD, by importing it, ignoring the Form and Table modules, and adding the Basic Table module. This file could then be saved to the Web, and then referenced as usual by any conforming instance of the new language.

Note that a version of XHTML m12n using W3C XML Schema is being developed by the HTML WG, a draft for which is available from:

http://www.w3.org/TR/xhtml-m12n-schema/

XML and Emerging Specifications

We have already looked at some applications of XML, including XML schemas and XHTML. There are many more applications of XML, however; let's take a look at some of these here.

SVG – Scalable Vector Graphics

SVG is a format that allows people to create with vector graphics and animations using XML syntax. Developed by the W3C, the SVG specification went to Recommendation status on 5th September 2001, and is available at http://www.w3.org/TR/SVG/. It already has a number of excellent implementations, notably by Adobe, who have created a plug in for SVG that works in Internet Explorer and Netscape 4.x.

Here is a short example of SVG, excerpted from a W3C Note on accessible SVG (http://www.w3.org/TR/SVG-access/) by Charles McCathieNevile and Marja-Riitta Koivunen (the italicized text has been added to replace the relative URL for the style sheet):

```
<?xml version="1.0"?>
<!-- box.svg -->
<?xml-stylesheet href="http://www.w3.org/1999/09/SVG-access/svg-basic-style.css"
type="text/css"?>
<!DOCTYPE svg PUBLIC "-//W3C//DTD SVG 20000802//EN"
    "http://www.w3.org/TR/2000/CR-SVG-20000802/DTD/svg-20000802.dtd">
<svg width="6in" height="4.5in" viewBox="0 0 600 450">
    <g transform="translate(10 10)">
        <title>Hub</title>
        <desc>A typical 10BaseT/100BaseTX network hub</desc>
        <rect width="253" height="84"/>
        <rect width="230" height="44" x="12" y="10"/>
        <circle cx="227" cy="71" r="7"/>
    </g>
</svg>
```

SVG has been widely praised, due to its usability and accessibility features, and everyone concerned with the technology is hoping for even more implementations in the future.

SMIL

SMIL (pronounced "smile") **2.0** – the **Synchronized Multimedia Language** version 2.0, was released as a W3C Recommendation on 7 August 2001 (available from http://www.w3.org/TR/smil20/). It provides a comprehensive language for creating multimedia presentations for the Web. SMIL includes audio, video, and captions capabilities, and can be used for a wide range of purposes, such as slideshow presentations, streaming videos, and newscasts.

SMIL is broken into a set of modules, for example timing, layout, metadata, and so on. Here is a short example of SMIL:

```
<smil xmlns="http://www.w3.org/2001/SMIL20/">
<head>
    <layout>
        <root-layout width='200' height='100'/>
        <region id='abc' z-index='1' left='0' top='0' width='200'
            height='100'/>
    </layout>
</head>
<body>
    <seq repeat='10'>
        <img src='frame1.gif' region='abc' dur='500ms'/>
        <img src='frame2.gif' region='abc' dur='500ms'/>
        <img src='frame3.gif' region='abc' dur='500ms'/>
        <img src='frame4.gif' region='abc' dur='500ms'/>
        <img src='frame5.gif' region='abc' dur='500ms'/>
        <img src='frame6.gif' region='abc' dur='500ms'/>
        <img src='frame7.gif' region='abc' dur='500ms'/>
```

```
                <img src='frame8.gif' region='abc' dur='500ms'/>
                <img src='frame9.gif' region='abc' dur='500ms'/>
                <img src='frame10.gif' region='abc' dur='500ms'/>
        </seq>
    </body>
</smil>
```

This file, when played in a SMIL user agent, would render the frames (`<img src.../>`), in sequence (`<seq>`), 500 milliseconds at a time (`dur='500ms''`), in the designated viewing window (`<region id...`), 10 times (`repeat='10'`).

More information on SMIL can be found on the SMIL homepage at: http://www.w3.org/AudioVideo/.

RDF – Resource Description Framework

RDF is one of the most incredible uses for XML to date, in that it is one of the foundation blocks for the **Semantic Web**, a concept invented by Tim Berners-Lee where all pieces of data are called **resources**, and can be identified by a URI. Essentially, it's a huge global database, in much the same way that the WWW is a huge global documentation system.

As far as XML is concerned, the Semantic Web raises a number of simple issues that all XML developers would do well to understand. XML by itself has no inherent semantics. Some people think that by putting their data into XML form, it somehow becomes magically useful. What actually happens, is that the data gains a higher potential for being useful. The meaning of any data in XML is hinted at by the designers of the language, and then embodied by the implementations. For example, XHTML would be nothing if there were no web browsers to use it, and there would be no web browsers to use it if there wasn't a definition of what HTML is somewhere.

RDF is just a format that contains details about which parts of the document are data, and which aren't. It's a meta-language, in that it allows us to create our own languages on top of it. It gains its power by using URIs to communicate that data. Indeed, our `order.xml` example could have been drafted in RDF. RDF can be processed easily by any RDF processor, which can then send it to a Semantic Web agent to try to gauge the meaning of the data. It takes the guesswork out of the XML. Here is an example of XML RDF:

```
<rdf:RDF xmlns:dc="http://purl.org/dc/elements/1.1/"
    xmlns:foaf="http://xmlns.com/foaf/0.1/"
    xmlns:rdf="http://www.w3.org/1999/02/22-rdf-syntax-ns#">
    <rdf:Description>
        <rdf:type rdf:resource="tag:infomesh.net,2001-09-10:test:Chapter"/>
        <dc:creator rdf:parseType="Resource">
            <foaf:name>Sean</foaf:name>
        </dc:creator>
        <dc:title>XML and XHTML</dc:title>
    </rdf:Description>
</rdf:RDF>
```

This simply means that: "there exists a Chapter which has the title *XML and XHTML*, and was written by something which has the name 'Sean'".

More information on RDF is available from: http://www.w3.org/RDF/, and the Semantic Web at: http://www.w3.org/2001/sw/.

MathML

The goal of **MathML** (**Mathematical Markup Language**) is to enable mathematics to be served, received, and processed on the World Wide Web, just as HTML has enabled this functionality for text. The W3C page for MathML is at: http://www.w3.org/Math/.

Here is an example of MathML 2.0, expressing the definite integral between 0 and Pi of the expression x to the (natural number) e:

```
<!-- MathML.xml -->
<math xmlns="http://www.w3.org/1998/Math/MathML">
<mrow>
  <msubsup>
   <mo>&int;</mo>
   <mn>0</mn>
   <mn>&Pi;</mn>
  </msubsup>
  <mrow>
    <msup>
       <mi>x</mi>
       <mi>&ExponentialE;</mi>
    </msup>
    <mo>&InvisibleTimes;</mo>
    <mrow>
       <mo>&DifferentialD;</mo>
       <mi>x</mi>
    </mrow>
  </mrow>
</mrow>
</math>
```

This renders, in a MathML-aware browser, such as Amaya, as:

$$\int_0^\Pi x^e \delta x$$

The specification for MathML 2.0 is available from http://www.w3.org/TR/MathML2/. The MathML group state, on the homepage, that:

> "Combined with a style sheet to specify other aspects of layout, MathML should eventually be used by browsers without the use of plug-ins."

There are a number of MathML implementations available that work at the time of writing, However which include:

❑   Maple7: http://www.maplesoft.com/products/Maple7/index.shtml

❑   Mozilla: http://www.mozilla.org/projects/mathml/

❑   The W3C's Amaya browser: http://www.w3.org/Amaya/

Summary

We discussed the history and usage of XML, including how it arose from the need for a simple meta-language based upon SGML. We saw how HTML had evolved alongside XML, to be eventually drafted as an XML language called XHTML.

We also went through the structure of XML: how it works, what makes it tick, and even how to create our own languages using XML. We saw how to render XML using one of the XML styling technologies, and how to access and manipulate parts of the XML tree using JavaScript and the XML DOM. We've seen that XML is a very powerful language with many implementations in the form of browsers, editors, and parsers.

XML has inspired a Web revolution that looks set to continue for a long time to come.

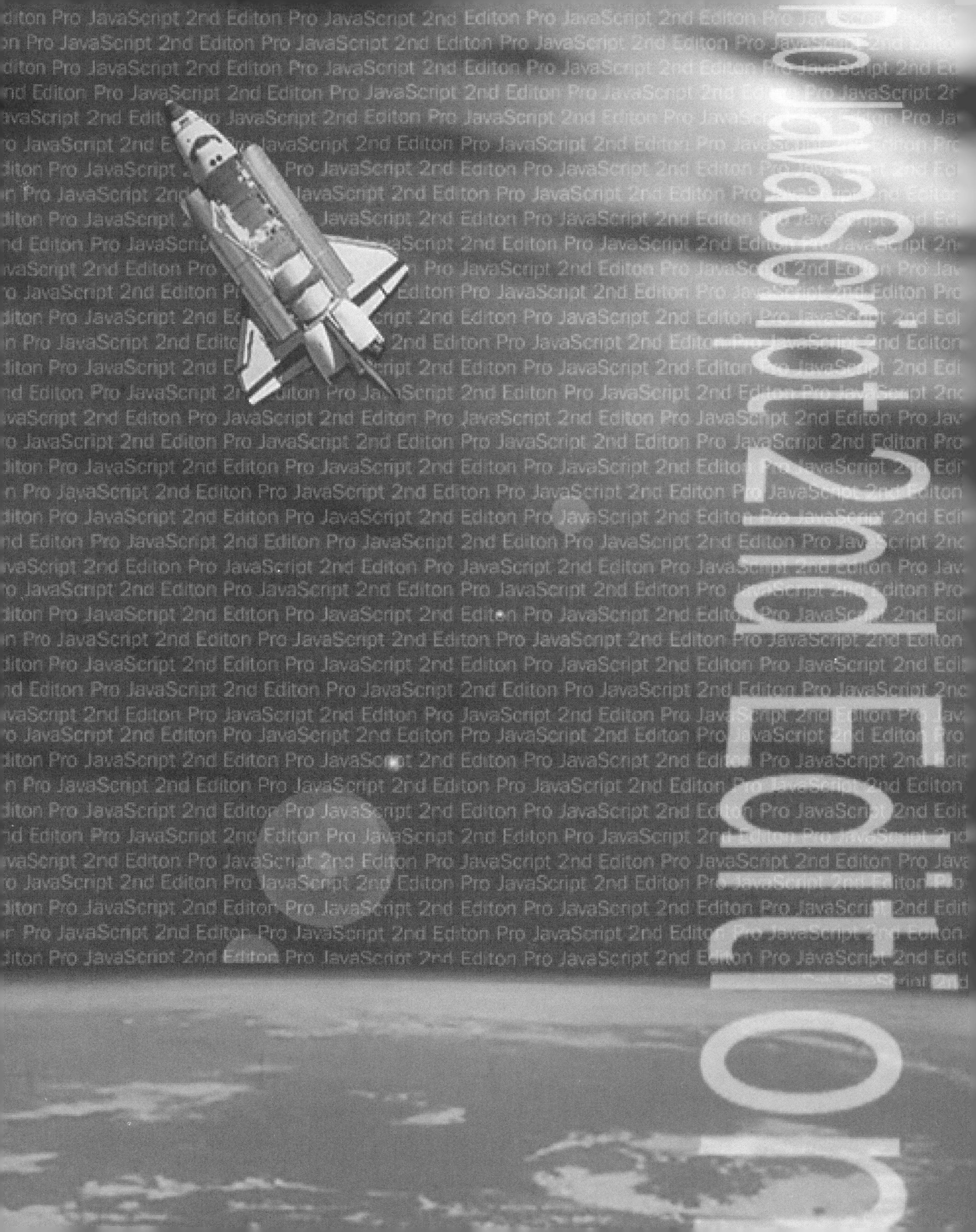
ProJavaScript2ndEdition

8

Cascading Style Sheets and JavaScript

From the JavaScript developer's point of view, CSS, DOM, and DHTML are inextricably linked. We must navigate the DOM organization of the document to dynamically alter the HTML. Likewise, to control and access CSS style objects from JavaScript, we must use the DOM level 2 bindings to locate and modify the style rules that control how the document is rendered on different media. Some of these renderings are non-visual and so the perceived appearance of the document may not change in any visible way. At the time of writing though, none of the browsers completely implements the DOM level 2 CSS model. Netscape Navigator (NN) version 6 offers the most complete implementation at present, but even that lacks significant features such as aural styles.

In this chapter, we look in particular at CSS style objects and style sheets, as well as how to access them from JavaScript. We will see a little DHTML and quite a lot of DOM, but the focus will be on CSS control from JavaScript. That means we are not going to exhaustively cover CSS, but the principles of how we can operate on CSS controlled styling.

Cascading Style Sheets represent a flexible way to control presentation style and appearance of a web page way beyond what we can accomplish with pure HTML, and it is the method of presenting HTML being pushed by the W3C. Style sheets also allow the content and presentational style to be separated from one another largely so that we can deploy the same content across a variety of different platforms. CSS also allows quite a lot of HTML to become deprecated. For example, the <FONT> tags are no longer necessary, and so are deprecated, unless we are planning to present our web pages on older non-CSS compliant browsers. Thankfully, these are becoming less popular as the general public is installing the more recent versions of the web browsers.

CSS style control also allows us to save a lot of work. One area that was particularly frustrating for web content producers was that table cells did not inherit any of the page styling that was present at the point where the <TABLE> tag initiated the table content. By defining a default style for the table cells using CSS, we only need to define this once in the document.

As a baseline, this chapter is written on the assumption that we are interested in versions of Microsoft Internet Explorer (MSIE) from 5.0 upwards and NN from version 6.01 upwards. NN version 6.00 is functionally identical, but version 6.01 is recommended due to minor bug fixes in its CSS support. Versions prior to these had some support for CSS control via JavaScript. There are significant omissions on some browser versions earlier than those mentioned, and since they are declining in use, we should be looking towards future browser implementations that are more standards compliant. Of the other browsers, Opera is noteworthy as a standards compliant browser. The CSS support in version 3.6 is partial, but is improved in versions that are more recent. Details of the Opera browser's support for standards (including CSS) can be found at http://www.opera.com/docs/specs/. This includes a helpful note on what CSS support is not available in Opera.

Design Goals for CSS

The design of CSS has to be seen against the context of the non-style sheet controlled background that persisted before CSS was implemented. As is the case with HTML, browsers should be able to discard safely those parts of the CSS style control that they cannot understand without the effects being overly detrimental.

Browsers should be able to present a meaningful rendering with no CSS support at all. A browser that can only support CSS level 1 should produce some output that is styled more closely to the designer's original intent. A CSS level 2 compliant browser should render something very close to the original design. Therefore, CSS has a major design goal of being forward and backward portable.

The history of work on the styling model we now know as CSS goes back to some early work at CERN in 1994. The original design work on HTML in 1990 could potentially use a style sheet but its syntax was never made public. Other early browsers also supported style languages but when the Netscape browser became dominant, style control had been quite restrained by its design. In the meantime, various groups were working on developing the style control languages and in November 1994, an initial proposal was put forward at the Web conference in Chicago. During 1995 and 1996, work proceeded on CSS and the W3C organization was founded. In December 1996, W3C published CSS level 1 as a Recommendation. This led to the formation of a CSS working group that commenced the development of CSS level 2. That was published as a Recommendation in May 1998. Work is currently proceeding on level 3, which is still undergoing some significant changes.

At the same time, the Document Object Models group is developing an object structure that the CSS style model can be stored in so that it can be operated on from languages such as Java and JavaScript. DOM level 1 did not support CSS, but an entire module within DOM level 2 is devoted to the CSS object model structures. DOM level 3 will add further capabilities in due course.

The abstraction of content and styled appearance controls means that CSS is complementary to HTML and XML. By separating the two, you can more easily alter the rendered output to suit a particular device. For example, web pages that are meant to be viewed on a PC screen may set the font sizes quite small. When viewed on a Web on TV browser, these fonts are difficult to read so a more suitable font size can be defined. This is most convenient if all you need to do is swap a style sheet description between the two platforms. The content authoring process should not need to be changed at all.

The CSS specification is designed to be independent of the browser vendor, the operating system platform, and the display device. Certainly, different presentational styles will be necessary if a page is to be viewed on a TV compatible browser, a mobile phone, PDA, or PC based web browser. The media selection allows styles to be defined according to how the document is presented and includes print and accessibility support for sight-impaired users by way of audible styles. however, the more esoteric of these however are not currently well supported.

Keeping the style sheets separate from the document content allows them to be maintained separately and to be shared amongst many documents. This greatly improves the ease of maintenance of a large and complex web site. Because a style sheet can be shared in this way, the network performance is improved overall as long as the browser properly caches the style sheet between pages. This is a good design approach to take from the outset when you are planning to build web sites with large amounts of dynamically generated content.

Although CSS Level 2 is more complex than Level 1, it is reasonably simple to learn and use. CSS Level 3 will introduce more functionality but will also provide a modular approach to the overall conceptual framework.

The inheritance mechanisms of CSS allow style control to be passed down from parent elements into their children. Having defined a font family for example, all elements contained within the object with that font definition should inherit the same font family, unless they override it with their own. This very flexible and provides a very rich choice of rendering alternatives and special effects that are very difficult or even impossible to reproduce with plain HTML. We illustrate this with an example based on table drawing later on in this chapter.

Although background color appears to be inherited from a parent object to its children, this is not actually, what is happening. By default, background color is set to be transparent. Therefore, if the background of a parent element is set to red, then all its child elements will appear to have the same background color because they have a clear background.

Although the CSS standard describes the various style attributes, it is bound to JavaScript through the DOM Level 2 style module. There is no formal specification for the bindings to HTML. A somewhat logical mapping in the implementations means that the DOM specified `backgroundColor` property maps to the `background-color` style declaration. This can sometimes be a little confusing and you can accidentally use the JavaScript property name in a style sheet. This will not flag an error, but the style will not appear the way you intend it to, and it can be frustrating to debug. Using style declarations in JavaScript will most likely lead to error messages and so they are easier to find.

CSS 1 and CSS 2

The authoritative source for information on CSS functionality is the W3C web site where you can find the Recommendations for completed standards such as CSS Levels 1 and 2, and the work in progress on CSS Level 3:

CSS Level 1 Recommendation - http://www.w3c.org/TR/REC-CSS1
CSS Level 2 Recommendation - http://www.w3.org/TR/REC-CSS2
CSS Level 3 work in progress - http://www.w3c.org/Style/CSS/current-work

The CSS Level 1 and 2 standards provide the present level of functionality although not all of the standard functionality has yet been deployed in current browser versions. Because this is changing so rapidly, the best place to look is on the W3C web site where they maintain a list of the latest developments in browser support for CSS. This page is at http://www.w3c.org/Style/CSS/ and you need scroll down to the section headed 'CSS Browsers'.

The following bullet list summarizes the CSS Level 1 support:

❑ Basic pseudo classes. These are a way to describe portions of a document that are not explicitly marked up, such as the first line or first character of a paragraph. Certain modes of behavior of an anchor are defined as pseudo classes (visited, link and active). CSS level does not mandate that they must be supported but that they may be supported.

❑ Attributes controlling background appearance. These sometimes look as if they are inherited, but this may be because the background of child objects is transparent.

- ❏ Border control attributes that provide control of line thickness, dash style and color.

- ❏ Margin control attributes for increasing the space around an object.

- ❏ Padding control attributes for offsetting the borders away from the object body.

- ❏ Simple float control to control the way that text flows round the object.

- ❏ Basic color control of foreground, such as the text color of a paragraph.

- ❏ Display control and object visibility so objects can be hidden or revealed at will.

- ❏ Font selection and metrics for detailed control of typographic effects.

- ❏ Textual content layout for justifying and flowing text.

- ❏ Object sizing, alignment and simple positioning to provide precise layout control.

- ❏ List appearance controls for stylizing lists and defining whether items are enumerated with roman numerals, numbers or bullet marks.

CSS Level 2 adds these capabilities, over and above those of CSS Level 1:

- ❏ Multiple media types to allow alternative style renderings for print and screen.

- ❏ Paged media such as laser printers.

- ❏ The inheritance value for all properties so that explicit inheritance can be defined.

- ❏ Audible styles to which date have not been implemented in any of the mainstream browsers.

- ❏ Better internationalization support by way of text directions and list style types. Additional pseudo class support with language selectors is also defined.

- ❏ More sophisticated font support. CSS Level 1 support is expended by the addition of font-size-adjust and font-stretch capabilities.

- ❏ Table formatting control.

- ❏ More flexible positioning controls, with relative, absolute and fixed being available.

- ❏ Additional box type.

- ❏ Content overflow controls, including clipping and visibility.

- ❏ Control of minimum and maximum dimensions.

- ❏ More sophisticated selector mechanisms, which are aware of children, siblings and attributes.

- ❏ Automatically generated content, such as counters.

- ❏ Text appearance control of shadowed effects.

- ❏ Additional pseudo classes. In Level 2, we now have a hover class for the anchor elements. We now have child and sibling object references and the ability to place content before and after an object using style sheet declarations.

- ❏ Improved system colors and fonts.

- ❏ Cursor support.

The Future – CSS 3

At the time of writing, CSS Level 1 and 2 standards work is largely complete, and the W3C is now putting some effort into the CSS Level 3 standard. The original intention was to progress to a Recommendation some time during 1999. Progress has slowed somewhat however and it may be some time before the work on CSS Level 3 is complete. The following areas are being worked on as part of this revision to CSS:

❑ A more modular design approach so that partial implementations can be delivered and still conform to the standard.

❑ Work on media support is taking place.

❑ The syntax rules in the HTML style attributes are being reorganized.

❑ Better color support is being provided.

❑ The Ruby alignment directives introduced into IE by Microsoft are being ratified. A Ruby is a small piece of text that can be displayed (rather like a tool tip) when complex oriental typography is being rendered.

❑ The use of CSS in mobile devices is evolving.

❑ Some work is being done on selectors. This adds namespace specifications to the selectors so that the same selector can have different meanings according to the namespace it is being used in. Some new simple sub-string selectors are being added and a few new pseudo classes and elements. Some additional quite complex grammar is being defined so that selectors can define attribute values as well so that they can be conditionally applied to elements. The authoritative source is at http://www.w3.org/TR/css3-selectors/.

❑ Better control for multiple column layouts is being added.

❑ Integration with DOM Level 2.

❑ A simple API for CSS that can be accessed from a variety of languages is being devised.

❑ Scalable Vector Graphics (SVG) is now being considered as an integral part of the CSS complex.

❑ User interface controls are being developed; facilities of this area available as XUL support in Netscape 6.

❑ Further work on media types that support paging (such as printed output) is taking place.

❑ Behavioral extensions are being investigated as a means of attaching event handlers to XML documents through the style rules.

❑ Disability access is being improved.

❑ Namespaces are being extended. This allows styles to be defined to render differently according to the namespace they are used in. Namespaces are described in a little more detail later on.

Using CSS

Style control can be applied in several different ways:

❑ Attached inline to the tags

❑ In a <STYLE> block at the top of the document

❑ In a separate document that is included via a <LINK> tag.

❑ Through a DOM structured interface that exposes the style attributes as properties and methods of some objects

Here are some short examples of each kind of styling attachment. Tag inline first:

```
<HTML>
<BODY>
    <P STYLE="color: red;">A styled paragraph</P>
</BODY>
</HTML>
```

Now exactly the same styling done with a <STYLE> tag:

```
<HTML>
<HEAD>
    <STYLE TYPE="text/css">
        P {color: red;}
    </STYLE>
</HEAD>
<BODY>
    <P>A styled paragraph</P>
</BODY>
</HTML>
```

Now, using an external document and a <LINK> tag. Style sheet document first:

```
P   {color: red;}
H1 {color: green;}
H2 {color: blue;}
```

Save the style sheet document in the filename `stylesheet.css` and insert a <LINK> tag into the original HTML document like this:

```
<HTML>
<HEAD>
    <LINK REL="stylesheet" TYPE="text/css" HREF="stylesheet.css"></LINK>
</HEAD>
<BODY>
    <P>A styled paragraph</P>
</BODY>
</HTML>
```

Now if we want to access the style of a paragraph object in the document from a JavaScript environment, we need to first find the paragraph and locate its `style` object. Here is a brief example of how to do that. Note the addition of the `ID=" "` attribute to the <P> tag. This helps us locate the object because the DOM organization of the document is different for almost every browser version and platform:

```
<HTML>
<BODY>
    <P ID="myPara">A styled paragraph</P>
    <SCRIPT LANGUAGE="JavaScript">
        document.myPara.style.color = "red";
    </SCRIPT>
</BODY>
</HTML>
```

It is that last possibility that is of most interest to us as JavaScript programmers. Whichever means we use to attach the styling to the objects, it is always CSS that performs the styling effects for us. The alternative ways to attach the styles are merely convenient mechanisms that provide different degrees of sharing of style definitions between objects in the same document and documents in the same web site.

The Current State of CSS Availability

In an ideal world, CSS would provide all the capabilities we need to control the style and appearance of our web pages on a variety of different platforms and media types. Right now, it does a reasonable job, but there are a few issues still to be resolved. There has been little evidence of widespread browser support for audible style attributes for example. These would be of great benefit to blind web users who might currently use a textual browser with its output being fed through a text to speech converter. Audible styles greatly expand the amount of control over the browsing experience for the sight-impaired.

The CSS style language is one of several alternatives in use by the web community. CSS is primarily designed for styling HTML but it can be used on XML documents too. The Extensible Stylesheet Language (XSL) is designed specifically for styling XML. They are not both trying to do the same job, however. In the case of XSL for example, it has transformation tools that can convert the XML into other formats such as HTML,. CSS Level 2 is designed to be used for styling XML documents without the transformation capabilities that XSL provides. however, CSS level 1 however is not powerful enough to do any of this at all. The W3C organization sees CSS and XSL as being complementary technologies.

Microsoft has supported various CSS capabilities in its Internet Explorer browser since version 5. Historically they have had incomplete support of CSS levels 1 and 2 but have also added many proprietary style controls. Some of these are in advance of standards proposals that they have put forward while others simply provide capabilities that are not supported in any other browser. So far they have not claimed to be standards compliant on CSS, but the support is generally quite good.

NN version 6 also has very good support for CSS. Netscape 4 browsers however are somewhat lacking. Netscape attempted to provide an alternative with the JavaScript Style Sheets (JSS) model in Netscape Navigator version 4. This was somewhat difficult to implement and was virtually guaranteed to fail from the outset, as Netscape would be the only browser manufacturer to support it. As of Netscape version 6, it has become deprecated and you should revise any projects that use it to remove what remaining JSS implementations you have.

Support for DOM Level 2 and hence the CSS object model in NN version 6 is excellent as the browser assiduously sticks to the DOM standard defined by W3C. Versions 3 and 4 of IE are a little patchier in their DOM and CSS support as far as the object model is concerned. It is significantly improved in versions 5.0 and 5.5. Versions of IE on the Windows platform are somewhat in advance of the implementation on the Macintosh platform. Certainly there are some shortcomings in the Macintosh version of IE 5, as far as correctly named properties of `document` objects are concerned. At least the style sheet is accessible with the same `styleSheets` array property in both IE and NN version 6, so if we are careful, we can build JavaScript code that works reasonably well across both browsers. Beware though that in IE there are some missing DOM specified methods for locating child HTML elements.

In general, the control of CSS from JavaScript is quite good for CSS Level 1 functionality. CSS Level 2 requires later browser versions, and is not as well supported. This means that our available controls are more limited than we would like. This will improve of course as browsers are revised to accommodate more of the W3C standards.

There is much subtlety to using CSS. For example, certain positioning controls only work when absolute positioning is defined. Examining all of the complexities of CSS is beyond the scope of this chapter, which is intended to introduce you to how JavaScript can access the CSS model.

CSS Syntax

We need to know a little CSS syntax to inform our script writing efforts. It helps to be able to visualize the relationship between the CSS source text and the DOM CSS model that is created from it.

The style sheet is composed of a collection of rules. Each rule consists of a selector and a declaration block. Within that declaration block, there will be one or more property specifiers.

For every HTML tag, there will be a selector having the same name. The selector names can be modified with a class name to allow several alternative selectors to be applied to elements as needed. The rules for defining selectors are quite complex so we will start off with a simplified syntax before delving into those complexities.

Let's assemble that set of components in an example. Here is a single property specifier:

```
font-size: 12pt
```

Now here are several property specifiers assembled into a declaration block:

```
{
    font-size:    12pt;
    color:        red;
    text-align:   center;
}
```

Aside from the fact that there must be at least one property specifier in the braces, the other aspects of the syntax are optional. Here is a simple declaration block with a selector for an HTML tag:

```
P { font-size: 14pt; }
```

Here the selector is extended to include a class name so that it applies only to those HTML <P> tags with a matching CLASS="special" attribute:

```
P.special { font-size: 14pt; }
```

This slightly different form applies to any HTML element with the CLASS="special" attribute:

```
.special { font-size: 14pt; }
```

Finally, the pseudo elements and classes are delimited with a colon character, so we can apply that styling only to the first character of a matching paragraph like this:

```
P.special:first-letter { font-size: 14pt; }
```

The syntax for describing a selector is very flexible. Here is a table summarizing the selector syntax for CSS Level 2. For illustrative purposes we have used imaginary tags to illustrate the relationship with HTML:

Pattern	Style effect applied to
*	All HTML elements.
T	Only those HTML elements of type <T> will be affected.
S T	Only those elements of type <T> that are inside an <S> tag.
S T U	Contextual selector. Only those elements of type <U> that are inside a <T> tag which itself is inside an <S> tag.
S > T	Child selector. Only the <T> tagged elements that are inside an <S> tag will be styled by this selector. This may be a different target element to that defined simply by the selector S T without the caret symbol.

Pattern	Style effect applied to
`S.X > T`	Child selector. Only the `<T>` tagged elements which are inside an `<S>` tag that has the `CLASS="X"` attribute will be styled by this selector. This may be a different target element to that defined simply by the selector `S.X T` without the caret symbol.
`S + T`	Sibling selector. This is useful when you have two adjacent paragraphs but you only want to operate any of them except the first one of them. Given that you may specify an indent only for second and subsequent paragraphs, this rule might be useful: `P + P { text-indent: 2em; }`
`.class`	Only those elements which have a `CLASS="class"` attribute will be affected.
`P.class`	Only those `<P>` elements which have a `CLASS="class"` attribute will be affected.
`#id`	Only those elements which have an `ID="id"` attribute will be affected. This is useful for applying style to specific instances of an HTML tag.
`:first-child`	This is complementary to the `S + T` selector because it will only operate on the first one of a series of sibling elements.
`:link`	This is intended for use with an `<A>` tag to indicate style that is to be applied to an unvisited link.
`:visited`	This is intended for use with an `<A>` tag to indicate style that is to be applied to a visited link.
`:active`	This is intended for use with an `<A>` tag to indicate style that is to be applied to a link while the pointer is over it and the mouse button is down.
`:hover`	This is intended for use with an `<A>` tag to indicate style that is to be applied to a link while the mouse rolls over it.
`:link:hover`	Pseudo classes can be compounded. This example will apply style to a link only when the mouse hovers over it and conditional on that link not having been visited before.
`:visited:hover`	This example will apply style to a link only when the mouse hovers over it and conditional on that link having been visited before.
`:focus`	This style applies to those elements that currently have focus.
`:lang(xx)`	This is an alternative technique for selecting style according to the language of the page or the element. One of the two letter country codes replaces the xx. This is a useful alternative to the `[LANG|="xx"]` attribute mapping selector. Language can be applied at the element level with the `LANG=""` attribute. When applied to the `<BODY>` tag, it defines the language for the whole page or the language is indicated in the HTTP headers.
`[attr]`	All HTML elements that have an `attr=""` attribute containing any value.
`[attr="value"]`	All HTML elements that have an `attr="value"` attribute. The attribute name and value must match.
`[attr~="value"]`	All HTML elements that have an `attr=""` attribute which contains the text "value" as a discrete word within the quoted string.

Table continued on following page

Pattern	Style effect applied to
[attr|="value"]	All HTML elements that have an `attr=""` attribute which contain any words that begin with the text "value". So in this case `attr="value1"` and `attr="value"` would match but `attr="val"` would not.
S, T	Grouping selector. This will match any elements in <S> or <T> tags.
T:first-letter	The first letter of all content within a <T> tag.
T:first-line	The first line of all content within a <T> tag.
T:before	The generated text specified in the declaration will be styled and inserted immediately before the <T> tag.
T:after	The generated text specified in the declaration will be styled and inserted immediately after the <T> tag.

Here are a few examples of rules that illustrate the selectors from the table:

```
.some { background-color: red }
```

Defines the background color of all HTML tags that have the CLASS="some" attribute set:

```
* { background-color: red }
```

Defines the background color of every HTML Element in the document:

```
H1 { background-color: red }
H1 { font-style: italic }
```

The above is the same as saying:

```
H1 { background-color: red; font-style: italic }
```

Moreover, the grouping rules apply like this:

```
H1 { background-color: red }
H2 { background-color: red }
H3 { background-color: red }
```

Is the same as saying:

```
H1, H2, H3 { background-color: red }
```

The nesting of elements allows tags to be set against a background effect that might negate their appearance. For example, defining exactly the same background color for an <H1> tag and an <EM> tag, then placing an <EM> block inside an <H1> block would render the <EM> tagging completely ineffective. This can be managed like this:

```
H1 { background-color: red }
EM { background-color: red }
H1 EM { background-color: blue }
```

This properly allows the <EM> block to stand out against its enclosing <H1> block when they are marked up like this:

```
<H1>This will be red <EM>then blue</EM> and red again</H1>
```

The design of special purpose selectors can become quite sophisticated. The CSS Level 2 specification allows for an element to have several classes defined by a space separated list. So with CSS Level 2 the selector H1.warning applies to those <H1> elements which have the word "warning" in their CLASS="" attribute value. This is generally denoted by a selector in the style sheet that looks like this:

```
H1[CLASS~="warning"]
```

That selector means: match any <H1> element whose CLASS attribute value is a space separated list of values one of which is exactly "warning".

So <H1 CLASS="error warning"> or <H1 CLASS="warning"> will both match the selector. As the attribute name is also specified, this selection mechanism need not depend on the CLASS="" attribute but some other attribute, that is user defined.

Other more complex rules allow tags to be styled according to their context when they are children of another tag or siblings of one another. Attribute selectors also provide sophisticated rules for matching attributes on HTML tags. You can gain a thorough description of these CSS rules and selectors from the W3C Recommendations at the following URLs:

- http://www.w3.org/TR/REC-CSS1
- http://www.w3.org/TR/REC-CSS2/

Measurement Units

The values we specify for style sheet attributes are used to indicate a large variety of different kinds of quantity. They can also be specified as relative or absolute values in some cases. There are symbolic names for some values too. This can be quite confusing and when you request a property value from a style object, you may or may not get back an indication of the unit of measure. Sometimes the unit of measure is stored and sometimes not. You will probably need to experiment with this somewhat.

The following data types are specified in the standard:

- Integer values
- Floating point numbers
- Absolute length values (mm, cm, in, pt, pc)
- Relative length values as a proportion of the font size (em) or the height of a small 'x' in the current font size (ex)
- Device specific pixels (px)
- Relative values as a percentage
- Universal Resource Identifiers
- Counters are defined as generated content and are useful for formatting lists with enumerated items
- Colors as symbolic names or hex coded triplets
- Angles in degrees, grads or radians
- Time values in milliseconds or seconds
- Frequencies measured in Hertz or kHz
- String literals

This table lists the various measurement units and any special points of interest:

Unit	Abbreviation	Type	Description
Integer		n/a	The styling engine is often smart enough to work out for itself the intent of the style designer when no units are specified. Some property values do not have a unit of measure as such, so the values can safely be specified as an integer.
Float		n/a	See integer. Much the same rules apply.
Millimeter	mm	Abs	Metric units. The display rendering software needs to take into account the screen resolution and apply algorithmic correction for the pixel density.
Centimeter	cm	Abs	Metric units. See mm description. 10 mm = 1 cm.
Inch	In	Abs	Imperial units. See mm description. 25.4 mm = 1 in.
Point	Pt	Abs	Traditional printing units. See mm description. 72 pt = 1 in.
Pica	Pc	Abs	Traditional printing units. See mm description. 1 pc = 12 pt.
M-width	Em	Rel	The width of an M character in the current font. This is generally taken to be the point size of the font with a letter M assumed to fill a square box.
X-height	Ex	Rel	The height of a small x character in the current font. Some fonts have a proportionally larger x-height than others do. This tends to yield an appearance that looks like the font is larger than it really is.
Pixel	Px	Abs	A pixel on the screen may not render the same size on a printer. No account of pixel density is made. Often, a printer will assume a density of 72 pixels per inch for purposes of rendering output according to CSS, but this is not reliable.
Percentage	%	Rel	A relative value computed according to the corresponding value in a parent element.
URI		n/a	A reference to another document. Neither absolute nor relative in the visual sense.
Color name		n/a	A pre-defined set of symbolic color names that the browser supports for HTML use can also be used for CSS.
Color value	#rrggbb	n/a	Color values can be specified as a triplet with a leading hash.
Keyword		n/a	Many CSS properties have a set of related symbolic keywords that can be used to specify relative values. In terms of font metrics, the x-small font should render at the same apparent size on all devices, platforms and screen resolutions. In fact, it tends to not scale very well on higher density pixel resolutions and is not very reliable across platforms or across browsers.

Unit	Abbreviation	Type	Description
Millisecond	ms	Abs	A thousandth of a second. Useful for aural styles. In the future, this might become useful to transitions if they become standardized.
Second	Sec	Abs	One second. This unit of measure is not often used. 1000 ms = 1 sec.
Degree	Deg	Abs	Angular measure is used in Aural styles. In due course, when CSS level 3 is standardized, it may be useful for describing skewing effects on fonts.
Radian	Rad	Abs	An alternative angular measure. Not very popular as it is not as intuitive as degrees.
Hertz	Hz	Abs	This unit of measure is implied in the specification but since its context is constrained mainly to aural styles, the unit of measure may be omitted.
Kilohertz	kHz	Abs	Vocal ranges will rarely require values to be specified in KHz so this unit of measure may not prove to be particularly useful.

We must obviously use a unit of measure that is correct for its context. For example, bounding box margins cannot be specified in milliseconds or with color values. They need to be indicated using a spatial unit of measure or one of the relative computed measurements.

The browsers are quite smart in their handling of JavaScript driven values. They will often assume an appropriate measurement unit according to the context you are applying it, but it is good practice to always indicate the measurement units explicitly.

CSS Modularization

The various stylistic controls in CSS are grouped in logical sets that help us to understand how they work. Later, when we develop some examples, we can use this modular structure to focus on particular aspects. CSS Level 3 standardizes this modular structure so that implementers can select sub-sets of CSS functionality for use in their products, without becoming non-compliant with the W3C standards. Here is a list of modules that the CSS Level 3 working group is currently developing. The list is not exhaustive as new modules are still appearing from time to time:

- ❑ Box module
- ❑ Pseudo classes and elements
- ❑ Values and units
- ❑ Cascading and inheritance
- ❑ Namespaces
- ❑ Actions and behaviors
- ❑ Font control
- ❑ Text control

- ❏   Multiple columns

- ❏   Ruby annotation

- ❏   Object positioning

- ❏   Color model and backgrounds

- ❏   Borders, margins and padding boxes

- ❏   List layout

- ❏   Table layout

- ❏   Paged media

- ❏   Automatically generated content

- ❏   Media typed (paged and scrolling)

- ❏   User interface control

- ❏   Speech and aural styles

- ❏   Visual filter effects

While these are somewhat logical, they may not correspond completely to the modularization scheme being developed for CSS Level 3. However, since that is currently incomplete, we need to wait until it is fully developed before we will know the outcome. The SVG specifications were part of the CSS Level 3 work but have now been separated into an independent working group. Some of their work is relevant, however in particular their implementation of visual filter effects that are attached to SVG objects via a `style` property.

The CSS level 3 working group summary at http://www.w3c.org/Style/CSS/current-work has further details.

The CSS Object Model

Just as the content of a document is represented using the Document Object Model (DOM), the styling of that content as defined by CSS is reflected into a styling model. The CSS object model is defined in DOM Level 2 by a styling module. A PDF document describing the style sheet extensions can be found on the W3C web site at: http://www.w3.org/TR/DOM-Level-2-Style.

As a document is parsed, an object tree is constructed. This process is standardized by the DOM. Here is a simple document that will become a tree structure:

```
<HTML>
<BODY>
    Some text
    <IMG SRC="image.gif"></IMG>
    <DIV>
        Some text
        <HR></HR>
        Some text
    </DIV>
</BODY>
</HTML>
```

The DOM organization for this (in a simplified form) becomes a tree like this:

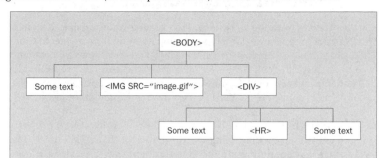

The nesting of these items can be presented visually as a series of boxes inside other boxes. So unless we invoke some positioning controls to physically move some of these items, they become contained within one another on the screen like this:

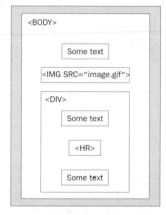

Style properties are applied beginning with the outer objects and cascading down to the inner objects provided the style properties are inherited. The style of the innermost <HR> object may depend on inherited style properties from the <DIV> or <BODY> objects.

Each of these objects has a `style` object that we can access from JavaScript. It is referred to by the `style` property of the owner element object.

Depending on how we locate the `style` object you want to operate on, you may affect the appearance of just one HTML Element object, several or even all HTML Elements objects of that same kind. To be able to do that from JavaScript requires a little exercise first. Over the next few pages, we shall develop some useful debugging and inspection techniques and explore how the browser maintains the style model as a collection of related objects. It is helpful to be able to do this before we start to manipulate the style model from script.

Most CSS style control will degenerate to a simple two-step process:

❑   Locate the `style` object controlling the style within the scope you want to control
❑   Modify one of the properties of that `style` object

Accessing the Element's Style Object

Browser support for CSS varies with the browser and the version you are using. Recent MSIE and NN browsers support CSS Level 1 quite well. CSS Level 2 support is still incomplete, but major parts of it are implemented. There are subtle variations between the MSIE and Netscape support that cause the appearance of styled content to be slightly different. Access to the `style` object and its properties depends on the DOM level 2 support. NN attempts to support DOM level 2 as accurately as possible. MSIE supports many important aspects of it, but is quite non-standard in the way it constructs an object model of a document.

Each HTML Element object has a `style` object attached through its `style` property. The appearance of the element can be controlled by modifying the properties of that style object. The initial values will be any inline style values that are defined in the HTML document. The MSIE browser supports two additional objects accessible as the `currentStyle` and the `runtimeStyle`. The `currentStyle` object contains properties that reflect the cascaded style. This includes inline and inherited values. The `runtimeStyle` object initially has the same values but as the style properties are modified, it is updated to reflect the style as you run your scripts. These are not standardized and for portability reasons you should avoid using them. The portable object relationship is shown in this diagram:

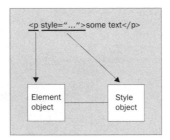

So the element and its `style` object have a one to one relationship. Whatever style is inherited by the element will be overridden by the values in its `style` object. The property values in this `style` object are defined by `STYLE=""` attributes in the HTML tags that instantiate the element. This is generally not a recommended way to add style because you can only affect one element at a time and the amount of style markup that is added to the document becomes unwieldy and hard to maintain.

Now we can begin to formulate a strategy in JavaScript for accessing the `style` objects. First, let's look at some ordinary HTML with no style controls applied to it at all. Any `style` object we locate can only contain default information. As we have given the `<P>` tag an `ID=""` attribute, we can use a DOM method to locate the object that represents the tag and then run an enumerator on it to see its properties. We'll present the properties in a simple table so they are easier to read. This works fine on MSIE and on NN version 6 across the different platforms:

```
<!-- Example_01.htm -->
<HTML>
<BODY>
   <P ID="myPara">
   A paragraph of plain text delimited by a single paragraph mark.
   </P>
   <HR></HR>
   <TABLE BORDER="1">
      <TR>
         <TH>Property</TH>
         <TH>Value</TH>
      </TR>
      <SCRIPT LANGUAGE="JavaScript">
```

```
                var myPara = document.getElementById("myPara");

                for(var myEnum in myPara.style)
                {
                    document.write("<TR><TD>");
                    document.write(myEnum);
                    document.write("</TD><TD>");
                    document.write(myPara.style[myEnum]);
                    document.write("</TD></TR>");
                }
            </SCRIPT>
        </TABLE>
    </BODY>
</HTML>
```

The results are variable across platforms and browsers. The most consistent fact is that in a default scenario like this, most of the properties are empty. A few have some default values specified.

The MSIE browser on different platforms yields a different list of properties. Many, but not all DOM defined properties of the style object are present. Aside from the `aural` style properties, some versions of MSIE do not support the `float` and `size` properties. As you would expect, the Windows version of MSIE supports more features than MSIE on other platforms. Microsoft provides some reference material regarding its implementation of the `style` object at the following URL. You should note however that some of the property names they describe do not always comply with the standards: http://msdn.microsoft.com/workshop/author/css/reference/attributes.asp.

NN attempts to provide DOM standard support and nearly all the CSS level properties are present, including the aural style properties. Some small inconsistencies are evident, such as the `float` property being called `cssFloat`, and there are a couple of additional non-standard properties that bear some resemblance to forthcoming features in CSS Level 3.

The full list of properties is summarized in the appendices with notes on browser variants that support them. Any property names not described in the DOM and CSS standards should be used with extreme caution for they will immediately render your scripts non-portable. In this respect, NN is a much truer representation of the CSS functionality than MSIE, although it is still incomplete. As long as we constrain our development processes to only use W3C defined standard functionality, we can largely avoid these sorts of problems as long as browser manufacturers adhere to the standards. To retain optimum portability, you should avoid using functionality that has not yet completed its development in the W3C Working Groups.

This fragment of script and its surrounding table might be useful if you are trying to debug some CSS problems and are not sure whether the style object for the Element is being set up correctly.

Modifying the Element's Style Object

Now that we can access a `style` object for our paragraph of text, we can experiment with some alterations of its appearance under script control.

`Example_02.htm` changes the background color of our `<P>` block to yellow:

```
<!-- Example_02.htm -->
<HTML>
<BODY>
    <P ID="myPara">
    A paragraph of plain text delimited by a single paragraph mark.
    </P>
    <HR></HR>
```

```
   <SCRIPT LANGUAGE="JavaScript">
      var myPara = document.getElementById("myPara");
      myPara.style.backgroundColor = "yellow";
   </SCRIPT>
</BODY>
</HTML>
```

Here are some further lines of script that can be added after the background color change. This sets the font size to 24 pixels high:

```
myPara.style.fontSize = "24px";
```

Now by changing the measurement units, we can use points instead of pixels:

```
myPara.style.fontSize = "24pt";
```

The results are a slightly larger font size on some displays, depending on the pixel resolution (dots per inch). Now if we change the measurement units to picas, we can draw some very large characters:

```
myPara.style.fontSize = "24pc";
```

Leaving the measurement units unspecified draws the text in an implementation specific size. Some browsers will assume you mean pixels but the results will be unpredictable.

Adding some more script let's alter the other font metrics, but we cannot access any styling that affects anything other than the whole element in one go. None of the Pseudo element access is possible because this `style` object is attached to the `Element` object that is instantiated from the `<P>` tag. Pseudo element styles are accessible from JavaScript, but we need to gain access another way because they will be controlled by a different object.

Reading values back from the `style` object will yield the same value, but the case of the value you might have stored earlier is not guaranteed to be preserved. NN seems to preserve the original string, but MSIE converts symbolic values to lower case if you read them back.

These example lines all specify the same color value (note they must all be specified in quotes):

```
myPara.style.backgroundColor = "yellow";
myPara.style.backgroundColor = "Yellow";
myPara.style.backgroundColor = "YELLOW";
myPara.style.backgroundColor = "#FFFF00";
myPara.style.backgroundColor = "rgb(255,255,0)";
```

You don't always get back what you put in though. These two lines can be used in the previous example to define a color and then retrieve it for examination:

```
myPara.style.backgroundColor = "yellow";
document.write(myPara.style.backgroundColor);
```

You can try assigning various different color values to see what your browser does with them.

On MSIE, the values will always be returned in lower case. NN returns the values you specified apart from when you describe a color triplet with a leading hash symbol. Then Netscape returns an `rgb()` function. That `rgb()` function will be lower case even if you specified it as `RGB()` when you assign it. MSIE is also a little smarter in that it can tell if you are specifying the same color in a different way. It will not replace "yellow" with "#FFFF00". If you assign the value "yellow" and then assign an equivalent `rgb()` function of hash color value, it will retain the value "yellow". If you specify a slightly different value, however it knows that "#FFFF01" and "rgb(255, 255, 01)" are not equivalent to "yellow" and it will replace the value in the `style` object's property. The results will still be returned in lower case later on.

This only becomes important if you specify a value and then later on perform some string comparison against it after reading it back from the `style` object's property. It may not match even though you expect it to.

The safe course is to stick to lower case symbolic color names and `rgb()` function specifications for colors.

The following table summarizes what you get back if you retrieve the value later:

Assigned value	MS Internet Explorer	Netscape Navigator
`"yellow"`	`"yellow"`	`"yellow"`
`"Yellow"`	`"yellow"`	`"Yellow"`
`"YELLOW"`	`"yellow"`	`"YELLOW"`
`"#FFFF00"`	`"#ffff00"`	`"rgb(255,255,0)"`
`"rgb(255,255,0)"`	`"rgb(255,255,0)"`	`"rgb(255,255,0)"`

Documents and Style Sheet Collections

Rather than apply style to individual elements, it is better to construct a style sheet and share the style definitions across many objects. This does not stop you from modifying elements individually, but if they share any common attributes, they do not need to be defined repetitively.

Style sheets can be embedded into the document with the `<STYLE>` tag or included from a shared document with a `<LINK>` tag.

The DOM Level 2 CSS support describes an object model for representing these collections of style rules and their selectors. At the lowest level, the same `style` objects are used. This facilitates the cascading down of a style from the document's globally available style sheet collection. Down through successive parent-child node relationships to a leaf node that has its own `style` object that can override all the cascaded and inherited styles for that single item.

Here is a diagram showing how the `<STYLE>` and `<LINK>` tags create `StyleSheet` objects in a collection that is linked to the `document` object:

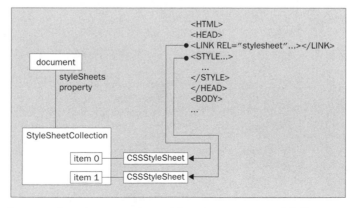

Based on the earlier experiments, we can now add a `<STYLE>` tag and define some simple rules. This is important because it will create a `styleSheet` object that we should be able to modify from within JavaScript. The same thing should happen if we use the `<LINK>` tag to refer to an external style sheet.

Similar to what we looked at earlier, `style` objects are also instantiated as a result of defining style rules in a style sheet. A document object model is constructed that maps that collection of rules to an object instantiated from a <STYLE> tag. That object is a `styleSheet` object and is one of a collection of such objects accessed from the `document.styleSheets` property.

This example displays the length of that collection and demonstrates that it grows according to how many <STYLE> tags there are:

```
<!-- Example_03.htm -->
<HTML>
<HEAD>
   <STYLE TYPE="text/css">
      P { color: blue }
   </STYLE>
</HEAD>
<BODY>
   <P ID="myPara">
   A paragraph of plain text delimited by a single paragraph mark.
   </P>
   <HR></HR>
   <SCRIPT LANGUAGE="JavaScript">
      document.write(document.styleSheets.length);
   </SCRIPT>
</BODY>
</HTML>
```

Now add another <STYLE> block immediately below the previous one and run the example again:

```
<STYLE TYPE="text/css">
   P { background-color: red }
</STYLE>
```

The first time this collection contained one object representation of a style sheet, the second it contained two.

DOM describes this collection as a `StyleSheetCollection` class. None of the browsers use this class name for the object and in that respect they are non-compliant, although they do implement the correct behavior. After all, it's just a collection object.

StyleSheet Objects

When examining the objects in a `document` object's `StyleSheetCollection`, we find that again none of the browsers adheres strictly to the DOM Recommendation. The objects have the wrong class name. They should be `CSSStyleSheet` objects. NN implements a more compliant set of properties for this object, but it has one incorrectly named property. MSIE implements many useful properties that resemble the DOM specification, but it is also incorrect. Oddly, the version 5.0 MSIE browser on the Macintosh has a slightly more compliant list of properties than the version 5.5 MSIE browser does on Windows.

Taking a single style sheet, we can start to unwrap the model in a little more detail. For portability, the property names used in the diagram will be the DOM standard ones that you can map to browser specific names using the table below:

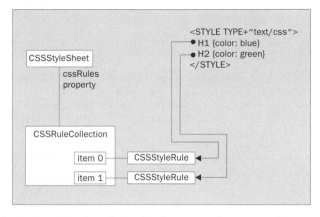

Note how similar this structure is to the relationship between a `document` object and its `styleSheets` collection.

The following table lists the DOM property names and the nearest equivalent property names for these style sheet objects in MSIE and NN. From the table, you should see which ones are reasonably safe to use. The object properties are described in more detail in the appendices. You can see that there is a document hierarchy implied by the `owningNode` and `parentStyleSheet` properties. This is not fully supported by the browsers yet and the property name differences makes it quite difficult to use:

DOM name	MSIE 5.0 (Mac)	MSIE 5.5 (Win)	Netscape
cssRules	cssRules	rules	cssRules
Type	type	type	type
Disabled	disabled	disabled	disabled
owningNode	owningNode	owningElement	ownerNode
parentStyleSheet	parentStyleSheet	parentStyleSheet	parentStyleSheet
href	href	href	href
title	title	title	title
media		media	media
		pages	
	id	id	
	cssText	cssText	
	readOnly	readOnly	
	imports	imports	
	owningElement		
	rules		
			ownerRule

We can fix the incorrectly named properties by creating aliases for them. Given that we have a reference to a `styleSheet` object in a variable, we can test whether a property exists and fix it. This corrects the missing `cssRules` property for MSIE version 5.5 on Windows:

```
if(!myStyleSheet.cssRules)
{
    myStyleSheet.cssRules = myStyleSheet.rules;
}
```

DOM also specifies that these objects should support the deletion and addition of rules within the style sheet. Unfortunately, While the `deleteRule()` method works on MSIE version 5.0 (Mac) and NN version 6, it does not work on MSIE version 5.5 on Windows. The `insertRule()` method does not appear to work properly at all anywhere, although it does appear to overwrite.

This suggests that for now, structural alterations to the style sheet contents may not be possible. A useful work around however may be to create some rules in the source style sheet to act as placeholders that you can then modify later if necessary.

Style Rules

We are close to locating the style objects we are looking for. Let's examine one of the style sheet rule collections. DOM calls these objects `CSSRuleCollection` objects. Accessing a single `CSSStyleRule` object from the collection and enumerating its properties again tells us how different the browsers are from one another and the DOM specification.

This diagram shows the linkage between a `CSSStyleRule` and its `style` object:

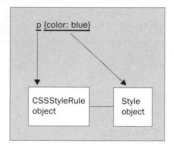

Note again the similarity with the relationship between an element object and its `style` object and how they are instantiated. In this case, the selector instantiates the `CSSRuleObject` where an equivalently named tag instantiated the element. The contents of the style rule define the properties of the `style` object as do the contents of the `STYLE=" "` HTML tag attribute for an element style.

Let's once more summarize the property naming differences for the `CSSStyleRule` object to see if there is any commonality that we can usefully exploit:

DOM name	MSIE 5.0 (Mac)	MSIE 5.5 (Win)	Netscape
type			Type
cssText	cssText		cssText
parentStyleSheet	parentStyleSheet		parentStyleSheet
selectorText	selectorText	selectorText	selectorText
Style	style	style	Style
	readOnly	readOnly	
			parentRule

Again, you can see significant differences in the strategy for supporting DOM and CSS by MSIE across the different platforms. The support for standards based models is apparently superior on the Macintosh platform. NN gets this object very close to the specification and even gets the correct class name.

We are fortunate, however, that all browsers on all platforms support the `style` property at this level and they all use the correct name. This gives us a clear and consistent way to access the `style` object for a particular rule in a portable manner.

We demonstrate that in this example by defining a paragraph style and modifying it with script. We should see that all the paragraphs in the document reflect that styling change. This also includes the fix for the missing `cssRules` property on MSIE version 5.5 (Win):

```
<!-- Example_04.htm -->
<HTML>
<HEAD>
   <STYLE TYPE="text/css">
      p { color: blue }
   </STYLE>
</HEAD>
<BODY>
   <P>First paragraph</P>
   <P>Second paragraph</P>
   <P>Third paragraph</P>
   <HR></HR>
   <SCRIPT LANGUAGE="JavaScript">
      var myStyleSheet = document.styleSheets[0];

      if(!myStyleSheet.cssRules)
      {
         myStyleSheet.cssRules = myStyleSheet.rules;
      }

      var myStyle = myStyleSheet.cssRules[0].style;

      myStyle.backgroundColor = "rgb(255, 128, 128)";
   </SCRIPT>
</BODY>
</HTML>
```

Therefore, now we can modify the individual style of a specific object and the style settings that are shared by a variety of similar objects – all from JavaScript.

Note that in the example, the accessor for the style sheet is a numeric index within the style sheets collection. There is some risk to this technique because the items may move if additional <STYLE> tags are placed into the document. You cannot use the `ID=""` mechanism with a `getElementById()` method call because in some browsers you will get back something that looks like an HTML element object. It certainly does not have a `cssRules` property so you cannot traverse the style sheet model to manipulate the rules. You can access the `innerHTML` of this Element object, but that is not a portable approach either.

Scope of CSS Style Control

Depending on how you define your selectors, where you specify your inline styles and whether you access `style` objects that are part of a style sheet or child objects of an Element, will all affect the resulting display.

Controlling Individual Element Styles

Earlier, we mentioned that depending upon the style object we operate on, we might affect just one instance of all HTML element objects of a particular kind, or several, or all.

Let's explore that with some examples. First, we will create a short fragment of HTML with three instances of the <H1> HTML Element object class. Like this:

```
<!-- Example_05.htm -->
<HTML>
<BODY>
    <HR></HR>
    <H1 ID="H1_1">Heading object 1</H1>
    <HR></HR>
    <H1 ID="H1_2">Heading object 2</H1>
    <HR></HR>
    <H1 ID="H1_3">Heading object 3</H1>
    <HR></HR>
    <SCRIPT language='JavaScript'>
        var myObject = document.getElementById("H1_1");
        myObject.style.backgroundColor = "red"
    </SCRIPT>
</BODY>
</HTML>
```

There are some portability issues with older browsers, but let's try to remain on the right path and retain DOM standards compliance. This will ultimately be beneficial as it means our scripts will likely run on NN version 6 as well. At the end of the chapter, we discuss portability, old browsers and some workarounds.

Controlling Shared Styles

Now we will create a style sheet and attach that style to several objects. Note that we define the styles as being available to HTML elements of all kinds and not specifically just <H1> tags. If we access the single style object that is associated with the .H1STYLE rule, we will affect the appearance of all HTML elements that use that style, but not the elements that use the .OTHER style. We use the trick that fixes the missing cssRules property on MSIE version 5.5 (Win) to cure a minor portability problem:

```
<!-- Example_06.htm -->
<HTML>
<HEAD>
    <STYLE>
        .H1STYLE { font-style: italic }
        .OTHER   { font-style: bold   }
    </STYLE>
</HEAD>
<BODY>
    <HR></HR>
    <H1 CLASS="H1STYLE">Heading object 1</H1>
    <HR CLASS="H1STYLE"></HR>
    <H1 CLASS="H1STYLE">Heading object 2</H1>
    <HR></HR>
    <H1 CLASS="OTHER">Heading object 3</H1>
    <HR></HR>
    <SCRIPT LANGUAGE="JavaScript">
        var myStyleSheet;
        var myStyleObject;

        myStyleSheet = document.styleSheets[0];

        if(!myStyleSheet.cssRules)
        {
            myStyleSheet.cssRules = myStyleSheet.rules;
        }
        myStyleObject = myStyleSheet.cssRules[0].style;
```

```
         myStyleObject.backgroundColor = "red"
      </SCRIPT>
   </BODY>
   </HTML>
```

Executing this fragment of script will color the background of the first two <H1> tags **and** the <HR> rule
tag, which is set to the same styling class. So careful grouping of style classes and their association with
HTML elements can simplify your script design if you want to modify several items at once.

Tag Specific Styles

Now let's modify the appearance based on a global change to all <H1> tags, but not affecting any non
<H1> HTML element objects. Note that we define a style for a tag name and we don't need to associate
it explicitly because CSS does an implicit join between the rule name and the appropriate tags. The
fragment of script will change the background color of all <H1> tags leaving all other HTML elements
unchanged. This colors all of the <H1> blocks in the document red.

```
   <!-- Example_07.htm -->
   <HTML>
   <HEAD>
      <STYLE>
         H1 { font-style: italic }
         h2 { font-style: bold  }
      </STYLE>
   </HEAD>
   <BODY>
      <HR></HR>
      <H1>Heading object 1</H1>
      <HR></HR>
      <H1>Heading object 2</H1>
      <HR></HR>
      <H1>Heading object 3</H1>
      <HR></HR>
      <SCRIPT LANGUAGE="JavaScript">
         var myStyleSheet;
         var myStyleObject;

         myStyleSheet = document.styleSheets[0];

         if(!myStyleSheet.cssRules)
         {
            myStyleSheet.cssRules = myStyleSheet.rules;
         }
         myStyleObject = myStyleSheet.cssRules[0].style;
         myStyleObject.backgroundColor = "red"
      </SCRIPT>
   </BODY>
   </HTML>
```

Local Style Overrides

One final experiment is to see what happens if we explicitly associate a style with one of the <H1>
blocks. Would that override its style settings and block the global change we just tried?

Modify the HTML one further time like this. Without running any script code on this, the middle <H1>
tag now would have a green background and the other two would be red:

```
   <!-- Example_08.htm -->
   <HTML>
   <HEAD>
```

```
    <STYLE>
        H1 { font-style: italic }
        .H1_ODDBALL { background-color: green}
    </STYLE>
</HEAD>
<BODY>
    <HR></HR>
    <H1>Heading object 1</H1>
    <HR></HR>
    <H1 class='H1_ODDBALL'>Heading object 2</H1>
    <HR></HR>
    <H1>Heading object 3</H1>
    <HR></HR>
    <SCRIPT LANGUAGE="JavaScript">
        var myStyleSheet;
        var myStyleObject;

        myStyleSheet = document.styleSheets[0];

        if(!myStyleSheet.cssRules)
        {
            myStyleSheet.cssRules = myStyleSheet.rules;
        }
        myStyleObject = myStyleSheet.cssRules[0].style;
        myStyleObject.backgroundColor = "red"
    </SCRIPT>
</BODY>
</HTML>
```

On MSIE, the middle <H1> tag inherits the same font style as the other <H1> tags by virtue of the H1 CSS rule. Its background color is defined separately however and we can modify the values belonging to the style object it inherits from, without affecting the values it overrides. It looks like everything behaves predictably after all.

Unfortunately, NN version 6.01 renders all three <H1> tags with a red background. It appears to have a bug in its support for the CLASS="" attribute.

Pseudo Classes and Elements

CSS implements some pseudo classes and elements to aid our document styling control. These don't actually exist, but provide a symbolic representation that can be used to grasp some otherwise abstract concepts.

The following pseudo elements and classes are provided in compliant implementations:

Name	Description	Class or Element
:link	Unclicked link color	Class
:visited	Visited link color	Class
:hover	Mouse over color	Class
:active	Mouse clicked on color	Class
:focus	Color when element has focus	Class
:lang(code)	Conditionally styles according to the language code	Class
:first-child	The first child element of a containing element.	Class

Name	Description	Class or Element
`:first-line`	Selects the first line of an element.	Element
`:first-letter`	Selects the first letter of an element.	Element
`:before`	The interstitial space immediately prior to the element.	Element
`:after`	The interstitial space immediately following the element.	Element

Now that we know what the pseudo classes and elements are, we can look at manufacturing some scripts to access them. We have to find the `style` object that carries their attributes however so we can modify them. As pseudo elements and classes do not actually exist as objects, we cannot traverse the DOM to find them. We need to track down the relevant `style` object that instantiated the rule from the style sheet that we are studying.

Example: Link Pseudo Classes

This fragment of HTML defines the pseudo classes that can associate with an anchor object created by an `<A>` tag:

```
<!-- Example_09.htm -->
<HTML>
<HEAD>
   <STYLE>
      A:link    {color: red    }
      A:visited {color: green  }
      A:hover   {color: blue   }
      A:active  {color: yellow }
   </STYLE>
</HEAD>
<BODY>
   <A ID='AnAnchor' HREF='somepage.htm'>Click me</A>
</BODY>
</HTML>
```

We can refer to the CSS rules array in the `styleSheet` object containing these pseudo class rules with an accessor like this:

```
myObject = document.styleSheets[0].cssRules;
```

That array in this example is four elements long and so our rules are instantiated into these style objects:

```
myLinkStyle    = document.styleSheets[0].cssRules[0].style;
myVisitedStyle = document.styleSheets[0].cssRules[1].style;
myHoverStyle   = document.styleSheets[0].cssRules[2].style;
myActiveStyle  = document.styleSheets[0].cssRules[3].style;
```

Now we can change the hover color like this:

```
myHoverStyle.color = "black";
```

Although the hover color was defined as blue in the style sheet, placing a `<SCRIPT>` block so that it is executed inline in the body will override the current setting. So, let's add a little interactive hover color selector to finish this example:

277

```
<!-- Example_10.htm -->
<HTML>
<HEAD>
   <STYLE>
      A:link    {color: red    }
      A:visited {color: green  }
      A:hover   {color: blue   }
      A:active  {color: yellow }
   </STYLE>
</HEAD>
<BODY>
   <A ID="AnAnchor" HREF="somepage.htm">Click me</A>
   <HR></HR>
   <SCRIPT LANGUAGE="JavaScript">
      var myStyleSheet = document.styleSheets[0];

      if(!myStyleSheet.cssRules)
      {
         myStyleSheet.cssRules = myStyleSheet.rules;
      }

      var myLinkStyle    = myStyleSheet.cssRules[0].style;
      var myVisitedStyle = myStyleSheet.cssRules[1].style;
      var myHoverStyle   = myStyleSheet.cssRules[2].style;
      var myActiveStyle  = myStyleSheet.cssRules[3].style;
   </SCRIPT>
   <FORM>
      <INPUT TYPE='button' VALUE='yellow'
         onClick='myHoverStyle.color = "yellow";'></INPUT>
      <INPUT TYPE='button' VALUE='black'
         onClick='myHoverStyle.color = "black";'></INPUT>
   </FORM>
</BODY>
</HTML>
```

Initially, the hover color for the <A> tag is blue, but clicking on either button selects yellow or black as the hover color accordingly.

Example: Pseudo Elements

Note that CSS only allows us to apply styling effects to pseudo elements. This is specifically **not** a way to extract the first line or first character of a <P> element, only a way to change its appearance. We must traverse the DOM if we want to modify the content of an element.

The pseudo elements in the selectors each instantiate a CSS rule object with its own private style object that we can access from JavaScript. There is no HTML markup that indicates the first character or line of a paragraph, but this style sheet behaves as if there were. As CSS does the work of finding and internally managing the first character and first paragraph, we don't need to write any complex JavaScript to do that:

```
<!-- Example_11.htm -->
<HTML>
<HEAD>
   <STYLE>
      P {color: red}
      P:first-line {color: green}
      P:first-letter {color: blue}
   </STYLE>
</HEAD>
<BODY>
   <P>
```

```
    This is an example paragraph that we want to apply some pseudo element
    styling control to. Obviously, we need to make the paragraph content
    long enough so that there is a first line to denote as something
    distinct from the rest of the paragraph.
</P>
<HR></HR>
<SCRIPT LANGUAGE="JavaScript">
    var myStyleSheet = document.styleSheets[0];

    if(!myStyleSheet.cssRules)
    {
        myStyleSheet.cssRules = myStyleSheet.rules;
    }

    var myParaStyle = myStyleSheet.cssRules[0].style;
    var myLineStyle = myStyleSheet.cssRules[1].style;
    var myCharStyle = myStyleSheet.cssRules[2].style;
</SCRIPT>
<FORM>
    First letter:
    <INPUT TYPE='button' VALUE='yellow'
        onClick='myCharStyle.color = "yellow";'></INPUT>
    <INPUT TYPE='button' VALUE='black'
        onClick='myCharStyle.color = "black";'></INPUT>
    <INPUT TYPE='button' VALUE='blue'
        onClick='myCharStyle.color = "blue";'></INPUT>
    <BR></BR>
    First line:
    <INPUT TYPE='button' VALUE='yellow'
        onClick='myLineStyle.color = "yellow";'></INPUT>
    <INPUT TYPE='button' VALUE='black'
        onClick='myLineStyle.color = "black";'></INPUT>
    <INPUT TYPE='button' VALUE='blue'
        onClick='myLineStyle.color = "blue";'></INPUT>
    <BR></BR>
    Paragraph default
    <INPUT TYPE='button' VALUE='yellow'
        onClick='myParaStyle.color = "yellow";'></INPUT>
    <INPUT TYPE='button' VALUE='black'
        onClick='myParaStyle.color = "black";'>
    <INPUT TYPE='button' VALUE='blue'
        onClick='myParaStyle.color = "blue";'></INPUT>
    <BR></BR>
    </FORM>
</BODY>
</HTML>
```

Of course, we can modify any attribute of the `style` object that we care to. We can modify `fontSize` or `fontStyle`, for example. Note that the window width determines how much of the paragraph wraps, and therefore the extent of the first line may not be predictable unless we are controlling the rectangular box in which the paragraph is contained. Even then, platform specific font metrics may still cause problems. Beware that this may just be an approximation.

Adding Content Before and After

In the previous example, we made the assertion that you cannot change the content of the styled element. In a literal sense, that much is true. The DOM CSS standards say however we can modify the appearance in such a way that it looks as if the content has been changed. We can place style sheet generated content before and after the element being styled, but it is not structurally part of the DOM object collection, only part of the view of the DOM that we are rendering. This is done with the `:before` and `:after` pseudo elements.

These pseudo elements are only supported by NN version 6 at present. The subtlest aspect of accessing the `style` objects for these pseudo elements is the quoting of your text strings. You must make sure there are leading and trailing quote marks when you assign a new value to the `content` property of the `style` object. This won't work:

```
myStyle.content = "new value";
```

However, this will work:

```
myStyle.content = '"new value"';
```

Note how the double quotes are enclosed inside another matching pair of single quotes.

A working example for NN version 6 is shown below:

```
<!-- Example_12.htm -->
<HTML>
<HEAD>
   <STYLE>
      P:before {content: "BEFORE|"}
      P:after {content: "|AFTER"}
   </STYLE>
</HEAD>
<BODY>
   <P>This text is in HTML.</P>
   <HR></HR>
   <SCRIPT LANGUAGE="JavaScript">
      var myStyleSheet = document.styleSheets[0];

      if(!myStyleSheet.cssRules)
      {
         myStyleSheet.cssRules = myStyleSheet.rules;
      }

      var myBeforeStyle = myStyleSheet.cssRules[0].style;
      var myAfterStyle = myStyleSheet.cssRules[1].style;

      myBeforeStyle.content = '"PRE|"';
      myAfterStyle.content = '"|POST"';
   </SCRIPT>
</BODY>
</HTML>
```

Font Control

For font attributes, we can control the font, character size, and styling of the characters. Other font display metrics can also be altered. The properties can be set to symbolically named values or sizes measured in percentages or points when altering the size of the characters.

Here is a list of the font and leading control properties belonging to the `style` object:

Property Name	Range of Values
Font	A compound rule containing a variety of font property specifications each, accessible individually below.
fontFamily	A font family name or list of names in order of precedence. The list depends on the browser and platform and may include additional installed fonts.

Property Name	Range of Values
fontSize	An absolute or relative font size or the symbolic value: inherit.
fontSizeAdjust	An adjustment factor or a symbolic value none or inherit.
fontStretch	One of: normal, wider, narrower, ultra-condensed, extra-condensed, condensed, semi-condensed, semi-expanded, expanded, extra-expanded, ultra-expanded or inherit. Not yet supported by MSIE or NN.
fontStyle	One of: normal, italic, oblique or inherit. There is no visible difference between italic and oblique in most cases. Where there is a difference, it is in the subtleties of replacing one or two character glyphs that look less attractive when they are slanted. The effect is most noticeable with a serif font and the small letter a. Set the font to Times, 24 and toggle between normal and italic in the example. Oblique looks the same as italic for this font.
fontVariant	One of: normal, small-caps or inherit.
fontWeight	One of: normal, bold, bolder, lighter, 100, 200, 300, 400, 500, 600, 700, 800, 900 or inherit.
letterSpacing	A relative or absolute length value or one of these symbolic values: normal or inherit.
lineHeight	A relative or absolute length value or one of these symbolic values: normal or inherit.

Here is an example showing how we might manipulate the font properties of a style object. The <FORM> elements define values that are applied to the properties of the style object for the paragraph. Here we interact with font family, font size and style:

```
<!-- Example_13.htm -->
<HTML>
<HEAD>
   <STYLE>
      P {color: red;
        font-stretch: ultra-expanded;


         }
      P:first-line {color: green}
      P:first-letter {color: blue}
   </STYLE>
</HEAD>
<BODY>
   <P>
      This is an example paragraph that we want to apply some pseudo element
      styling control to. Obviously, we need to make the paragraph
      content long enough so that there is a first line to denote as
      something distinct from the rest of the paragraph.
   </P>
   <HR></HR>
   <SCRIPT LANGUAGE="JavaScript">
      var myStyleSheet = document.styleSheets[0];

      if(!myStyleSheet.cssRules)
      {
         myStyleSheet.cssRules = myStyleSheet.rules;
      }
```

```
        var myParaStyle = myStyleSheet.cssRules[0].style;

        function chooseFont()
        {
           myFontMenu = document.myForm.myFont;
           myParaStyle.fontFamily =
           myFontMenu[myFontMenu.selectedIndex].text;
        }

        function chooseFontStyle()
        {
           myFontStyleMenu = document.myForm.myFontStyle;
           myParaStyle.fontStyle =
              myFontStyleMenu[myFontStyleMenu.selectedIndex].text;
        }
</SCRIPT>
<FORM NAME='myForm'>
   Font name:
   <SELECT NAME='myFont' onChange='chooseFont()'>
      <OPTION>Times</OPTION>
      <OPTION>Arial</OPTION>
      <OPTION>Verdana</OPTION>
      <OPTION>Helvetica</OPTION>
   </SELECT>
   <BR></BR><BR></BR>
   Font size:
   <INPUT TYPE='button' VALUE='9'
      onClick='myParaStyle.fontSize = "9px";'></INPUT>
   <INPUT TYPE='button' VALUE='18'
      onClick='myParaStyle.fontSize = "18px";'></INPUT>
   <INPUT TYPE='button' VALUE='24'
      onClick='myParaStyle.fontSize = "24px";'></INPUT>
   <BR></BR><BR></BR>
   Font style:
   <SELECT name ='myFontStyle' onChange='chooseFontStyle()'>
      <OPTION>normal</OPTION>
      <OPTION>italic</OPTION>
      <OPTION>oblique</OPTION>
   </SELECT>
   <BR></BR><BR></BR>
</FORM>
</BODY>
</HTML>
```

The example is portable across NN version 6 and MSIE version 5 upwards.

Box and Text Flow Control

The table below contains a list of the box and text flow controlling properties belonging to the `style` object:

Property Name	Range of Values
Clear	One of: none, left, right, both, or inherit
Direction	One of: ltr, rtl, or inherit
Float	One of: left, right, none, or inherit
orphans	Either an integer value, or the symbolic value: inherit

Property Name	Range of Values
overflow	One of: `visible`, `hidden`, `scroll`, `auto`, or `inherit`
quotes	Either some string literals to describe the quotes or one of the values: `none` or `inherit`
textAlign	A text alignment string or one of: `left`, `right`, `center`, `justify`, or `inherit`
textDecoration	A combination of: `underline`, `overline`, `line-through`, `blink`, or exclusively one of `none` or `inherit`. On NN version 6, setting the decoration for text to blink is ignored until some other change causes the page to be redrawn. Deactivating the blink effect behaves the same way. The blink value is not supported by MSIE.
textIndent	An absolute or relative value, or `inherit`
textShadow	The value: `none` or `inherit`, or a series of shadow effects cast by a light source. This is not currently supported by any browser, although a similar effect is possible in MSIE using its filter effects.
textTransform	One of: `capitalize`, `uppercase`, `lowercase`, `none`, or `inherit`
unicodeBidi	One of: `normal`, `embed`, `bidi-override`, or `inherit`
whitespace	One of: `normal`, `pre`, `nowrap`, or `inherit`
widows	Either an integer value or the symbolic value: `inherit`
wordSpacing	A length value or one of: `normal` or `inherit`. Not supported on MSIE version 5.5 (Win).

The example demonstrates some of the text transformations that can be applied. However, please do Note that not all of these are functional in all versions of browsers across every platform, so we are still some way from a completely portable solution:

```
<!-- Example_14.htm -->
<HTML>
<HEAD>
   <STYLE>
      P {color: red     }
      P:first-line {color: green    }
      P:first-letter {color: blue    }
   </STYLE>
</HEAD>
<BODY>
   <P>
      This is an example paragraph that we want to apply some pseudo element
      styling control to. Obviously, we need to make the paragraph
      content long enough so that there is a first line to denote as
      something distinct from the rest of the paragraph
   </P>
   <HR></HR>
   <SCRIPT LANGUAGE="JavaScript">
      var myStyleSheet = document.styleSheets[0];

      if(!myStyleSheet.cssRules)
      {
         myStyleSheet.cssRules = myStyleSheet.rules;
      }
```

```
            var myParaStyle    = myStyleSheet.cssRules[0].style;

        function chooseDecor()
        {
            myDecorMenu = document.myForm.myDecor;
            myParaStyle.textDecoration =
                myDecorMenu[myDecorMenu.selectedIndex].text;
        }

        function chooseTrans()
        {
            myTransMenu = document.myForm.myTrans;
            myParaStyle.textTransform =
                myTransMenu[myTransMenu.selectedIndex].text;
        }
    </SCRIPT>
    <FORM NAME='myForm'>
        Text alignment:
        <INPUT TYPE='button' VALUE='left'
            onClick='myParaStyle.textAlign = "left";'></INPUT>
        <INPUT TYPE='button' VALUE='right'
            onClick='myParaStyle.textAlign = "right";'></INPUT>
        <INPUT TYPE='button' VALUE='center'
            onClick='myParaStyle.textAlign = "center";'></INPUT>
        <INPUT TYPE='button' VALUE='justify'
            onClick='myParaStyle.textAlign = "justify";'></INPUT>
        <BR></BR>
        <BR></BR>
        Text decorations:
        <SELECT NAME='myDecor' onChange='chooseDecor()'>
            <OPTION>none</OPTION>
            <OPTION>underline</OPTION>
            <OPTION>overline</OPTION>
            <OPTION>line-through</OPTION>
            <OPTION>blink</OPTION>
        </SELECT>
        <BR></BR>
        <BR></BR>
        Transform:
        <SELECT NAME='myTrans' onChange='chooseTrans()'>
            <OPTION>none</OPTION>
            <OPTION>capitalize</OPTION>
            <OPTION>uppercase</OPTION>
            <OPTION>lowercase</OPTION>
        </SELECT>
        <BR></BR>
        <BR></BR>
        Word spacing:
        <INPUT TYPE='button' VALUE='-10'
            onClick='myParaStyle.wordSpacing = "-10";'></INPUT>
        <INPUT TYPE='button' VALUE='0'
            onClick='myParaStyle.wordSpacing = "0";'></INPUT>
        <INPUT TYPE='button' VALUE='10'
            onClick='myParaStyle.wordSpacing = "10";'></INPUT>
        <INPUT TYPE='button' VALUE='50'
            onClick='myParaStyle.wordSpacing = "50";'></INPUT>
        <BR></BR>
        <BR></BR>
    </FORM>
</BODY>
</HTML>
```

Object Size and Positioning

Here is a list of the object size and positioning control properties belonging to the `style` object:

Property Name	Range of Values
Bottom	A length value, percentage, or symbolic value: `inherit` or `auto`
Height	A length value, percentage, or symbolic value: `inherit` or `auto`
Left	A length value, percentage, or symbolic value: `inherit` or `auto`
maxHeight	A length value, percentage, or symbolic value: `none` or `inherit`
maxWidth	A length value, percentage, or symbolic value: `none` or `inherit`
minHeight	A length value, percentage, or symbolic value: `inherit`
minWidth	A length value, percentage, or symbolic value: `inherit`
position	One of: `static`, `relative`, `absolute`, `fixed`, or `inherit`
Right	A length value, percentage, or symbolic value: `inherit` or `auto`
Top	A length value, percentage, or symbolic value: `inherit` or `auto`
verticalAlign	A relative or absolute line height reference or one of: `baseline`, `sub`, `super`, `top`, `text-top`, `middle`, `bottom`, `text-bottom`, or `inherit`
Width	A length value, percentage or symbolic value: `inherit` or `auto`
zIndex	A z index value or one of: `auto` or `inherit`

Here is an example showing how to access a style associated with a single image and another that is globally applied. To try out the example, you will need to supply an image file called `picture.gif`, or modify the example to use an image you have available:

```
<!-- Example_15.htm -->
<HTML>
<HEAD>
   <STYLE>
      IMG {width: 300px }
   </STYLE>
</HEAD>
<BODY>
   Image 1:
   <IMG NAME='myImage1' SRC='picture.gif'></IMG>
   <BR></BR>
   <BR></BR>

   Image 2:
   <IMG NAME='myImage2' SRC='picture.gif'></IMG>
   <BR></BR>
   <BR></BR>

   Image 3:
   <IMG NAME='myImage3' SRC='picture.gif'></IMG>
   <BR></BR>
   <BR></BR>
```

285

```
    Image 4:
    <IMG NAME='myImage4' SRC='picture.gif'></IMG>
    <BR></BR>
    <BR></BR>

    <SCRIPT LANGUAGE="JavaScript">
        var myStyleSheet = document.styleSheets[0];

        if(!myStyleSheet.cssRules)
        {
            myStyleSheet.cssRules = myStyleSheet.rules;
        }
        var imgStyleGlobal = myStyleSheet.cssRules[0].style;

        var myImages = document.getElementsByName('myImage1');

        var imgStyleLocal  = myImages[0].style;

        // This line affects the specific image owning this style
        imgStyleLocal.width  = '60px';

        // This line affects all other images through the global style
        imgStyleGlobal.width = '40px';
    </SCRIPT>
</BODY>
</HTML>
```

The final size and aspect ratio of the image may not be what you expect because in this example, we are applying some scaling on a global basis and some by means of JavaScript. The scaling we apply from JavaScript is also affecting global and local values. This can get quite complex if you set the height globally and the width locally or if you use percentage scaling factors.

Color Model and Backgrounds

Here is a list of the color model and background properties belonging to the `style` object:

Property Name	Range of Values
background	Optionally the background color, image, repeat, attachment and position or the symbolic value: inherit
backgroundAttachment	One of: scroll, fixed, or inherit
backgroundColor	A color, transparent, or inherit
backgroundImage	An image URI, none or inherit
backgroundPosition	A percentage, length or x/y coordinate, or symbolic reference to align top, center, bottom with left center, or right edge
backgroundRepeat	One of: repeat, repeat-x, repeat-y, no-repeat, or inherit
color	A color name, hex value or the symbolic value: inherit

The example shows how you can modify the origin position of a background image using form-based controls:

```
<!-- Example_16.htm -->
<HTML>
<HEAD>
```

```
      <STYLE>
         body { background: url(picture.gif) }
      </STYLE>
   </HEAD>
   <BODY>
      <SCRIPT LANGUAGE="JavaScript">
         var myStyleSheet = document.styleSheets[0];

         if(!myStyleSheet.cssRules)
         {
            myStyleSheet.cssRules = myStyleSheet.rules;
         }
         var myBodyStyle = myStyleSheet.cssRules[0].style;

         var myHoriz = 0;
         var myVert = 0;

         function moveLeft()
         {
            myHoriz--;
            update();
         }

         function moveRight()
         {
            myHoriz++;
            update();
         }

         function moveUp()
         {
            myVert--;
            update();
         }

         function moveDown()
         {
            myVert++;
            update();
         }

         function update()
         {
            myBodyStyle.backgroundPosition = myHoriz+"px "+myVert+"px";
         }
      </SCRIPT>

      <FORM>
         <INPUT TYPE='button' VALUE='left' onClick='moveLeft();'></INPUT>
         <INPUT TYPE='button' VALUE='right' onClick='moveRight();'></INPUT>
         <INPUT TYPE='button' VALUE='up' onClick='moveUp();'></INPUT>
         <INPUT TYPE='button' VALUE='down' onClick='moveDown();'></INPUT>
      </FORM>
   </BODY>
</HTML>
```

Box Model – Borders, Margins, and Padding

Here is a list of the border, margin, and padding control properties belonging to the style object:

Property Name	Range of Values
Border	Optionally the border width, style color, or the symbolic value: inherit
borderColor	Up to 4 colors, transparent, or inherit symbols
borderStyle	UP to 4 border styles or the symbolic value: inherit
borderTop	Optionally the border width, style, color or the symbolic value: inherit to be applied to just one side
borderRight	Optionally the border width, style, color or the symbolic value: inherit to be applied to just one side
borderBottom	Optionally the border width, style, color or the symbolic value: inherit to be applied to just one side
borderLeft	Optionally the border width, style, color or the symbolic value: inherit to be applied to just one side
borderTopColor	A color or the value: inherit for this side
borderRightColor	A color or the value: inherit for this side
borderBottomColor	A color or the value: inherit for this side
borderLeftColor	A color or the value: inherit for this side
borderTopStyle	The style or the value: inherit to be applied to just this side
borderRightStyle	The style or the value: inherit to be applied to just this side
borderBottomStyle	The style or the value: inherit to be applied to just this side
borderLeftStyle	The style or the value: inherit to be applied to just this side
borderTopWidth	The border width or the value: inherit to be applied just to this side
borderRightWidth	The border width or the value: inherit to be applied just to this side
borderBottomWidth	The border width or the value: inherit to be applied just to this side
borderLeftWidth	The border width or the value: inherit to be applied just to this side
borderWidth	Up to 4 width values or the symbolic value: inherit
margin	Up to 4 margin width values or the symbolic value: inherit
marginTop	The margin width or the symbolic value: inherit
marginRight	The margin width or the symbolic value: inherit
marginBottom	The margin width or the symbolic value: inherit
marginLeft	The margin width or the symbolic value: inherit
padding	Up to 4 padding width values or the symbolic value: inherit. The padding property is not supported on MSIE version 5.5 (Windows).
PaddingTop	The padding width or the symbolic value: inherit
paddingRight	The padding width or the symbolic value: inherit
paddingBottom	The padding width or the symbolic value: inherit
paddingLeft	The padding width or the symbolic value: inherit

This diagram illustrates how the elements is enclosed in padding, then border, and finally a margin to separate it from adjacent elements:

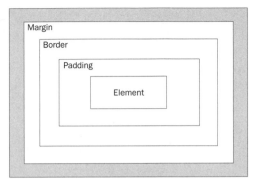

CSS allows us to set all four sides of these items at once, but that makes for rather awkward scripting of the attributes. It is may be more convenient to adjust each side independently if you want to control them separately. You should always remember that the values you assign to the properties of a DOM CSS style object are strings. The CSS mechanisms inside the browser will parse them as such.

We would not normally have such thick borders, margins and padding as is shown in the illustration, but there is nothing to stop us setting the width of these items to overly large values.

Here is an example that exercises the border styles. Note that this example works on NN version 6 due to the DOM traversal model and the way the <SELECT> menu is handled. Other examples show how to traverse the DOM in ways specific to MSIE. Certain traversals to access form contents and popup values are still somewhat platform and browser version specific.

```
<!-- Example_17.htm -->
<HTML>
<HEAD>
   <STYLE>
      IMG { width: 30px }
   </STYLE>
</HEAD>
<BODY>
   <IMG NAME='ONE'   SRC='picture.gif'></IMG>
   <IMG NAME='TWO'   SRC='picture.gif'></IMG>
   <IMG NAME='THREE' SRC='picture.gif'></IMG>
   <IMG NAME='FOUR'  SRC='picture.gif'></IMG>
   <BR><BR></BR>
      <BR></BR>
</BR>
   <SCRIPT LANGUAGE="JavaScript">
      var myStyleSheet = document.styleSheets[0];

      if(!myStyleSheet.cssRules)
      {
         myStyleSheet.cssRules = myStyleSheet.rules;
      }

      var myImageStyle = myStyleSheet.cssRules[0].style;
      myImageStyle.borderColor = 'red green blue yellow';

      function chooseStyle()
      {
         myStyleMenu = document.myForm.myStyle;
         myImageStyle.borderStyle =
```

```
                    myStyleMenu[myStyleMenu.selectedIndex].text;
        }
    </SCRIPT>
    <FORM NAME='myForm' ID='myForm'>
        Border style:
        <SELECT NAME='myStyle' onChange='chooseStyle()'>
            <OPTION>none</OPTION>
            <OPTION>dashed</OPTION>
            <OPTION>dotted</OPTION>
            <OPTION>double</OPTION>
            <OPTION>inset</OPTION>
            <OPTION>groove</OPTION>
            <OPTION>outset</OPTION>
            <OPTION>ridge</OPTION>
            <OPTION>solid</OPTION>
        </SELECT>
        <BR></BR>

        Border width:
        <INPUT TYPE='button' VALUE='0'
            onClick='myImageStyle.borderWidth = "0px";'></INPUT>
        <INPUT TYPE='button' VALUE='1'
            onClick='myImageStyle.borderWidth = "1px";'></INPUT>
        <INPUT TYPE='button' VALUE='5'
            onClick='myImageStyle.borderWidth = "5px";'></INPUT>
        <INPUT TYPE='button' VALUE='10'
            onClick='myImageStyle.borderWidth = "10px";'></INPUT>
        <INPUT TYPE='button' VALUE='25'
            onClick='myImageStyle.borderWidth = "25px";'></INPUT>
        <BR></BR>

        Margin:
        <INPUT TYPE='button' VALUE='0'
            onClick='myImageStyle.margin = "0px";'></INPUT>
        <INPUT TYPE='button' VALUE='1'
            onClick='myImageStyle.margin = "1px";'></INPUT>
        <INPUT TYPE='button' VALUE='5'
            onClick='myImageStyle.margin = "5px";'></INPUT>
        <INPUT TYPE='button' VALUE='10'
            onClick='myImageStyle.margin = "10px";'></INPUT>
        <INPUT TYPE='button' VALUE='25'
            onClick='myImageStyle.margin = "25px";'></INPUT>
        <BR></BR>

        Padding:
        <INPUT TYPE='button' VALUE='0'
            onClick='myImageStyle.padding = "0px";'></INPUT>
        <INPUT TYPE='button' VALUE='1'
            onClick='myImageStyle.padding = "1px";'></INPUT>
        <INPUT TYPE='button' VALUE='5'
            onClick='myImageStyle.padding = "5px";'></INPUT>
        <INPUT TYPE='button' VALUE='10'
            onClick='myImageStyle.padding = "10px";'></INPUT>
        <INPUT TYPE='button' VALUE='25'
            onClick='myImageStyle.padding = "25px";'></INPUT>
        <BR></BR>
    </FORM>
</BODY>
</HTML>
```

List Layout

Here is a list of the list layout control properties belonging to the `style` object:

Property Name	Range of Values
listStyle	A compound setting of several of the list style attributes in one property
listStyleImage	An image URI, the value: none or inherit
listStylePosition	One of: inside, outside, or inherit
listStyleType	One of: disc, circle, square, decimal, decimal-leading-zero, lower-roman, upper-roman, lower-greek, lower-alpha, lower-latin, upper-alpha, upper-latin, hebrew, armenian, georgian, cjk-ideographic, hiragana, katakana, hiragana-iroha, katakana-iroha, none, or inherit
markerOffset	A length value or one of the symbolic values: auto or inherit

This example illustrates how we can see the various different list style types interactively. Not all of them are supported and the list style type should default to something sensible if an unsupported option is chosen. Note in particular we have installed an error trap function and assigned it to the `window.onerror` property. This nicely avoids causing MSIE version 5.5 (Windows) to crash when unsupported list style types are defined:

```
<!-- Example_18.htm -->
<HTML>
<HEAD>
   <STYLE>
      LI {color: red    }
   </STYLE>
</HEAD>
<BODY>
   <OL>
      <LI>Item one</LI>
      <LI>Item two</LI>
      <LI>Item three</LI>
      <LI>Item four</LI>
      <LI>Item five</LI>
      <LI>Item six</LI>
      <LI>Item seven</LI>
      <LI>Item eight</LI>
      <LI>Item nine</LI>
      <LI>Item ten</LI>
      <LI>Item eleven</LI>
   </OL>
   <SCRIPT LANGUAGE="JavaScript">
      var myStyleSheet = document.styleSheets[0];

      if(!myStyleSheet.cssRules)
      {
         myStyleSheet.cssRules = myStyleSheet.rules;
      }

      var myListStyle = myStyleSheet.cssRules[0].style;

      function chooseDecor()
      {
         myListStyleTypeMenu = document.myForm.myListStyleType;
         myListStyle.listStyleType =
```

```
                    myListStyleTypeMenu[myListStyleTypeMenu.selectedIndex].text;
        }


        // Special error trap for MSIE version 5.5 (Win)
        function trapError()
        {
            return true;
        }

        window.onerror = trapError;
    </SCRIPT>
    <FORM NAME='myForm'>
        List style type:
        <SELECT NAME='myListStyleType' onChange='chooseDecor()'>
            <OPTION>none</OPTION>
            <OPTION>disc</OPTION>
            <OPTION>circle</OPTION>
            <OPTION>square</OPTION>
            <OPTION>decimal</OPTION>
            <OPTION>decimal-leading-zero</OPTION>
            <OPTION>lower-roman</OPTION>
            <OPTION>upper-roman</OPTION>
            <OPTION>lower-greek</OPTION>
            <OPTION>lower-alpha</OPTION>
            <OPTION>lower-latin</OPTION>
            <OPTION>upper-alpha</OPTION>
            <OPTION>upper-latin</OPTION>
            <OPTION>hebrew</OPTION>
            <OPTION>armenian</OPTION>
            <OPTION>georgian</OPTION>
            <OPTION>cjk-ideographic</OPTION>
            <OPTION>hiragana</OPTION>
            <OPTION>katakana</OPTION>
            <OPTION>hiragana-iroha</OPTION>
            <OPTION>katakana-iroha</OPTION>
        </SELECT>
    </FORM>
    <BR></BR>
    <BR></BR>
</BODY>
</HTML>
```

As the list is textual, all the usual text manipulations that we used before can be applied to the style object associated with the list element.

Table Layout

Here is a list of the table layout control properties belonging to the style object:

Property Name	Range of Values
borderCollapse	One of: collapse, separate, or inherit
borderSpacing	A horizontal and vertical length value or the symbolic value: inherit. Note that the vertical length value is optional.
captionSide	One of: top, bottom, left, right, or inherit
emptyCells	One of: show, hide, or inherit
tableLayout	One of: auto, fixed, or inherit

Other stylistic effects can be used to access table cells, but these are not yet very well supported from JavaScript. Changing the background of a table cell is still best done with the `bgColor` property of the `TD` object, rather than accessing its `style` and `backgroundColor` or `color` properties for portability. We can manipulate table appearances however as shown in this example:

```
<!-- Example_19.htm -->
<HTML>
<HEAD>
   <STYLE>
      TABLE {background-color: ivory   }
      TR {background-color: green }
      TH {background-color: blue  }
      TD {background-color: cyan  }
   </STYLE>
</HEAD>
<BODY>
   <TABLE border='1'>
      <TR><TH>Heading 1</TH><TH>Heading 2</TH></TR>
      <TR><TD>Row 1 cell 1</TD><TD>Row 1 cell 2</TD></TR>
      <TR><TD>Row 2 cell 1</TD><TD>Row 2 cell 2</TD></TR>
      <TR><TD>Row 3 cell 1</TD><TD>Row 3 cell 2</TD></TR>
      <TR><TD>Row 3 cell 1</TD><TD></TD></TR>
      <TR><TD>Row 5 cell 1</TD><TD>Row 5 cell 2</TD></TR>
   </TABLE>
   <SCRIPT LANGUAGE="JavaScript">
      var myStyleSheet = document.styleSheets[0];

      if(!myStyleSheet.cssRules)
      {
         myStyleSheet.cssRules = myStyleSheet.rules;
      }

      var myTableStyle = myStyleSheet.cssRules[0].style;
      var myTRStyle    = myStyleSheet.cssRules[1].style;
      var myTHStyle    = myStyleSheet.cssRules[2].style;
      var myTDStyle    = myStyleSheet.cssRules[3].style;

      function errorTrap()
      {
         return true;
      }

      window.onerror = errorTrap;
   </SCRIPT>
   <FORM NAME='myForm'>
      <BR></BR>

      Empty cells:
      <INPUT TYPE='button' VALUE='SHOW'
         onClick='myTableStyle.emptyCells = "show";'></INPUT>
      <INPUT TYPE='button' VALUE='HIDE'
         onClick='myTableStyle.emptyCells = "hide";'></INPUT>
      <BR></BR>

      TR style:
      <INPUT TYPE='button' VALUE='BLANK'
         onClick='myTRStyle.backgroundColor = "";'></INPUT>
      <INPUT TYPE='button' VALUE='INHERIT'
         onClick='myTRStyle.backgroundColor = "inherit";'></INPUT>
      <INPUT TYPE='button' VALUE='GREEN'
         onClick='myTRStyle.backgroundColor = "green";'></INPUT>
      <INPUT TYPE='button' VALUE='BLUE'
```

```
                onClick='myTRStyle.backgroundColor = "blue";'></INPUT>
        <BR></BR>

        TH style:
        <INPUT TYPE='button' VALUE='BLANK'
            onClick='myTHStyle.backgroundColor = "";'></INPUT>
        <INPUT TYPE='button' VALUE='INHERIT'
            onClick='myTHStyle.backgroundColor = "inherit";'></INPUT>
        <INPUT TYPE='button' VALUE='YELLOW'
            onClick='myTHStyle.backgroundColor = "yellow";'></INPUT>
        <INPUT TYPE='button' VALUE='RED'
            onClick='myTHStyle.backgroundColor = "red";'></INPUT>
        <BR></BR>

        TD style:
        <INPUT TYPE='button' VALUE='BLANK'
            onClick='myTDStyle.backgroundColor = "";'></INPUT>
        <INPUT TYPE='button' VALUE='INHERIT'
            onClick='myTDStyle.backgroundColor = "inherit";'></INPUT>
        <INPUT TYPE='button' VALUE='CYAN'
            onClick='myTDStyle.backgroundColor = "cyan";'></INPUT>
        <INPUT TYPE='button' VALUE='MAGENTA'
            onClick='myTDStyle.backgroundColor = "magenta";'></INPUT>
        <BR></BR>
    </FORM>
  </BODY>
</HTML>
```

In this example, the <TABLE> background color is overridden by the <TR> background. That in turn is overridden by the <TD> and <TH> background colors. The example turns these on and off by using the inherit value. On NN version 6, if you look closely, the shadow color of the table cells is defined by the background color of the <TR> style. If the <TR> style is set to inherit, then the red background color defined by the <TABLE> style comes in to action.

This inheritance technique works on NN version 6 and MSIE version 5, but the empty cells switch does not work on all versions of MSIE. MSIE on Windows does not recognize the keyword inherit and throws an error. The error trap function is installed to deal with that. Setting the property to be an empty string accomplishes the same thing. NN version 6 operates properly with the inherit keyword, but when the blank value is used, screen updates are held pending until some other change triggers them. This is a bug in the CSS style change trigger code. There is no platform neutral way to do this that is guaranteed to work, so browser detection will be necessary. That should be put in the initialization code to define a variable to contain the value for the inherit effect. Then that variable can be used as an indirect reference.

Visual Effects

Here is a list of the element display controlling properties belonging to the style object:

Property Name	Range of Values
clip	A shape name or one of the symbolic values: auto or inherit
display	One of: inline, block, list-item, run-in, compact, marker, table, inline-table, table-row-group, table-header-group, table-footer-group, table-row, table-column-group, table-column, table-cell, table-caption, none, inherit
visibility	One of: visible, hidden, collapse, or inherit

These properties are generally useful for organizing and grouping content within the page. The visibility control allows objects to be hidden. Another way to hide objects is to set their display property to none. That should collapse the layout and reflow the surrounding content too. That is useful because the collapse keyword does not work when applied to the visibility property.

```
<!-- Example_20.htm -->
<HTML>
<HEAD>
   <STYLE>
      IMG {border: 10px    }
   </STYLE>
</HEAD>
<BODY>
PRE:<IMG SRC="picture.gif">:POST

   <SCRIPT LANGUAGE="JavaScript">
      var myStyleSheet = document.styleSheets[0];

      if(!myStyleSheet.cssRules)
      {
         myStyleSheet.cssRules = myStyleSheet.rules;
      }

      var myImageStyle = myStyleSheet.cssRules[0].style;
   </SCRIPT>
   <FORM NAME='myForm'>
      <BR></BR>

      Display:
      <INPUT TYPE='button' VALUE='NONE'
         onClick='myImageStyle.display = "none";'></INPUT>
      <INPUT TYPE='button' VALUE='INHERIT'
         onClick='myImageStyle.display = "inherit";'></INPUT>
      <INPUT TYPE='button' VALUE='INLINE'
         onClick='myImageStyle.display = "inline";'></INPUT>
      <INPUT TYPE='button' VALUE='BLANK'
         onClick='myImageStyle.display = "";'></INPUT>
      <BR></BR>

      Visibility:
      <INPUT TYPE='button' VALUE='VISIBLE'
         onClick='myImageStyle.visibility = "visible";'></INPUT>
      <INPUT TYPE='button' VALUE='HIDDEN'
         onClick='myImageStyle.visibility = "hidden";'></INPUT>
      <INPUT TYPE='button' VALUE='COLLAPSE'
         onClick='myImageStyle.visibility = "collapse";'></INPUT>
      <BR></BR>
   </FORM>
</BODY>
</HTML>
```

In NN version 6, setting the display property to inline may have a different effect to inherit. That is because the parent that the inherit comes from might be a block structured element. That means an image that was inline becomes block formatted. You must explicitly set it to inline rather than hoping that it inherits an inline value.

MSIE behaves slightly differently. While it may not honor all the inline, inherit or blank values, at least they negate the effect of setting the display property to none.

In all cases, setting the visibility merely hides the object and the content is not reflowed. You must use display = none to accomplish that.

On MSIE version 5.5 (Windows), the unsupported `display: inherit` and `visibility: collapse` cases will throw an error. You can use the same error-trapping trick as was implemented in an earlier example.

Automatically Generated Content

Here is a list of the automatically generated content properties belonging to the `style` object:

Property Name	Range of Values
content	One of: a string literal, a URI, a counter, an `attr()` function denoting a tag attribute name, or a symbolic value from: `open-quote`, `close-quote`, `no-open-quote`, `no-close-quote`, or `inherit`
counterIncrement	A counter identifier, an integer or the symbolic value: `none` or `inherit`
counterReset	A counter identifier, an integer or the symbolic value: `none` or `inherit`

This area is only partially functional at present. Some browsers exhibit very strange values in the properties belonging to the `style` object that is instantiated by rules containing counters. This suggests that we should wait a while before trying to drive this kind of style effect from JavaScript.

An example of how to operate on the content property was given earlier when discussing pseudo elements.

Media Types (Paged and Scrolling)

Here is a list of the media type properties belonging to the `style` object:

Property Name	Range of Values
Marks	One of: `crop`, `cross`, `none`, or `inherit`
Page	A page identifier or the symbolic value: `auto`
pageBreakAfter	One of: `auto`, `always`, `avoid`, `left`, `right`, or `inherit`
pageBreakBefore	One of: `auto`, `always`, `avoid`, `left`, `right`, or `inherit`
pageBreakInside	One of: `auto`, `avoid`, or `inherit`
Size	Up to two page dimensions (width and height or one of the symbolic values: `auto`, `portrait`, `landscape`, or `inherit`

Typically, we would want to reformat the page content significantly for use on a printer instead of a display screen. That may be a non-trivial exercise and, because the whole page is being rendered differently, the imperative for having JavaScript adding any dynamism may depend very much on the kind of media platform being targeted.

Rules for printing are set up in the style sheet like this:

```
@media print { … rules here … }
```

Or in a separate style sheet linked in for specific media types like this:

```
<LINK MEDIA="print" HREF="printStyle.css" TYPE="text/css" />
```

User Interface Control

Here is a list of the user interface related properties belonging to the `style` object:

Property Name	Range of Values
cursor	One of these cursor types: a URI, auto, crosshair, default, pointer, move, e-resize, ne-resize, nw-resize, n-resize, se-resize, sw-resize, s-resize, w-resize, text, wait, help, or inherit
outline	A compounded set of color, style and width values
outlineColor	A color value (name or hex) or symbolic value: invert, or inherit
outlineStyle	A border style, name, or inherit
outlineWidth	A width value, or inherit

These styles might be very useful when designing user interfaces for Web-On-TV applications. Typically, much more use is made of tabbed and highlighted user interface elements on a TV oriented page. This is because the user is probably interacting with a remote control handset that has arrow keys, and there is no interactive mouse driven cursor being used.

These are not yet widely supported in all browser versions and platforms.

Speech and Aural Styles

The speech and aural style properties are provided to support sight-impaired users. With these properties, you can define speech patterns, voice characteristics and locate the sound sources in a spatial context.

These are not yet well supported in browsers. Control of this category of styling is accomplished with the following properties of the `style` object:

Property Name	Range of Values
azimuth	Used for defining the position of a sound source. It is a direction on the horizontal plane surrounding the listener. An angle, or one of these symbolic values: center, center-right, right, far-right, right-side, far-rightbehind, rightbehind, center-rightbehind, centerbehind, center-leftbehind, left-behind, far-leftbehind, left-side, far-left, left, center-left
cue	Optionally, the specifications for: cue-before, cue-after, or inherit
cueAfter	Specifies a sound to be played after a spoken item. One of: a URI, none, or inherit
cueBefore	Specifies a sound to be played before a spoken item. One of: a URI, none, or inherit
elevation	Used with the azimuth value to specify a spatial position in 3D space. An angle or one of these symbolic values: below, level, above, higher, lower, or inherit
pause	One or two pause times expressed in absolute or relative terms, or the value: inherit

Table continued on following page

Property Name	Range of Values
pauseAfter	The duration of a pause after a spoken item. A pause time expressed in absolute or relative terms, or the value: inherit
pauseBefore	The duration of a pause before a spoken item. A pause time expressed in absolute or relative terms, or the value: inherit
pitch	The basic pitch of the voice synthesizer. A frequency, or one of the symbolic values: x-low, low, medium, high, x-high, or inherit
pitchRange	A range over which the synthesizer can modulate the speech to make it more or less interesting. A pitch range, or the value: inherit
playDuring	A URI with optional mix and repeat modifiers or one of the symbolic values: auto, none, or inherit
richness	Either a richness value, or inherit
speak	One of: normal, none, spell-out, or inherit
speakHeader	Defines how the headings are spoken. One of: once, always, or inherit
speakNumeral	Formats the way that numeric values are spoken. One of: digits, continuous, or inherit
speakPunctuation	Indicates how to speak punctuation symbols. One of: code, none, or inherit
speechRate	The speech can be played at a variety of speeds according the circumstances. A speech rate value or one of the symbolic values: x-slow, slow, medium, fast, x-fast, faster, slower, or inherit
stress	Controls how the voice sounds. A stress value, or inherit
voiceFamily	Selects a voice in much the same way that a font is chosen. A series of voice names (like a font selector) or the value: inherit
volume	An absolute or relative volume level, or one of: silent, x-soft, soft, medium, loud, x-loud, or inherit

The aural styles are hardly supported in any browser. NN version 6 does provide style properties to contain the values, but neither NN nor MSIE has properly integrated this capability with the underlying speech capabilities of the platform. This is strange because both MacOS and Windows both support spoken text capabilities.

Proposed CSS Level 3 Namespaces

The CSS Level 3 working document on namespaces is located at http://www.w3c.org/1999/06/25/WD-css3-namespace-19990625/. The source document referred to by the CSS work is the XML Namespaces document can be found at http://www.w3.org/TR/REC-xml-names/. This short extract from the CSS Level 3 Namespaces module illustrates how namespaces might be used in a compliant implementation:

```
@namespace foo url(http://www.foo.com);

foo|H1 { color: blue }

foo|* { color: yellow }

|H1 { color: red }
```

```
*|H1 { color: green }

H1 { color: green }
```

The @namespace declaration defines the URL and gives it a symbolic name. This greatly eases the use of namespaces and makes them much more convenient. Without this declaration, the URL would have to be placed in front of every rule. Then:

The first rule will match only <H1> elements in the "http://www.foo.com" namespace.

The second rule will match all elements in the "http://www.foo.com" namespace.

The third rule will match only <H1> elements without any declared namespace.

The last two rules are equivalent and will match <H1> elements in any namespace (including those without any declared namespace).

Other Practical Applications

Here are several other experimental applications. Sometimes thinking laterally and applying a very small amount of JavaScript can solve an otherwise very difficult problem.

Portable Font Sizes

Onc of the quite difficult issues with using style driven font sizes is that the font metrics in different platforms do not map to the same visual appearance. In particular, NN on Macintosh and Linux exhibits a consistently smaller font size than MSIE on the Macintosh or NN on Windows.

Perhaps if we can locate the style rule that defines the font size and we can detect the platform, we might make an adjustment only on that platform with a fragment of in-lined JavaScript.

Here is an example where we are only testing for the presence of the MacOS platform, but we can make the test as sophisticated as you need to. This is enough to demonstrate the principle:

```
<!-- Example_21.htm -->
<HTML>
<HEAD>
   <STYLE>
      p { font-size: small }
   </STYLE>
</HEAD>
<BODY>
   <P>
      Here is some example text drawn in the specified font size for this
      platform.
   </P>
   <SCRIPT LANGUAGE="JavaScript">
      var myStyleSheet = document.styleSheets[0];

      if(!myStyleSheet.cssRules)
      {
         myStyleSheet.cssRules = myStyleSheet.rules;
      }
      var myParaStyle = myStyleSheet.cssRules[0].style;

      if ((navigator.userAgent.indexOf('Macintosh')) > 0)
      {
```

```
                    myParaStyle.fontSize = 'large';
            }
    </SCRIPT>
</BODY>
</HTML>
```

Changing the Appearance of Input Objects

Perhaps you want to accomplish some different button appearance effects. The style controls can be applied to HTML elements that are usually rendered in a somewhat fixed manner. The buttons displayed with an `<INPUT>` tag can be modified like this:

```
<!-- Example_22.htm -->
<HTML>
<HEAD>
    <STYLE>
        INPUT { width: 350px }
    </STYLE>
</HEAD>
<BODY>
    <FORM NAME='myForm' ID='myForm'>
        <INPUT TYPE='button' VALUE='Example button'></INPUT>
    </FORM>
    <BR></BR>
    <SCRIPT LANGUAGE="JavaScript">
        var myStyleSheet = document.styleSheets[0];

        if(!myStyleSheet.cssRules)
        {
            myStyleSheet.cssRules = myStyleSheet.rules;
        }

        var myButtonStyle = myStyleSheet.cssRules[0].style;

        myButtonStyle.color            = 'red';
        myButtonStyle.backgroundColor  = 'yellow';
        myButtonStyle.borderColor      = 'blue magenta cyan green';
        myButtonStyle.borderWidth      = '5px';
        myButtonStyle.height           = '50px';
        myButtonStyle.borderStyle      = 'groove';
        myButtonStyle.lineHeight       = '32px';
        myButtonStyle.cursor           = 'help';
        myButtonStyle.fontFamily       = 'sans-serif';
        myButtonStyle.fontSize         = '24pt';
        myButtonStyle.fontStyle        = 'italic';
        myButtonStyle.fontVariant      = 'small-caps';
        myButtonStyle.fontWeight       = '800';
        myButtonStyle.textDecoration   =
            'blink overline underline line-through';
    </SCRIPT>
</BODY>
</HTML>
```

The example illustrates a static effect that you could easily implement just with rules in a style sheet. The main point is show how to drive the values in from JavaScript. Adding some dynamism to select the values is a simple extension that we have already demonstrated in other examples.

In a real scenario, you may want to change the appearance of the button during some event handler to simulate hover and activation effects. There are ways we can easily apply this effect to text in an anchor, but not so easily to a button.

Even with this level of control, we still lack some capabilities such as being able to change the shape of the button. That is likely a limitation of the platform the browser runs in and, in the not too distant future, buttons might be manufactured with Scalable Vector Graphics in which case they can be any shape you want. For now, many of the effects that we might have had to use an image replacement technique for can be accomplished like this.

Note that this degree of control works in NN version 6 and most of it is functional in IE 5 with the exception of the `blink` attribute on some platforms. The above example looks amazingly similar on both browsers. There are some minor differences in the font metrics, which change the scaling slightly.

Event Driven Style Changes

This borders closely on the subject of DHTML that is closely related when you are creating dynamic effects with JavaScript. It is likely you will employ a mixture of Dynamic HTML and Dynamic CSS through a DOM driven model, which explains why the three areas are so closely linked. This example tracks the mouse X and Y coordinates through an event handler and uses them to generate two complementary colors that are applied to a paragraph of text through its `style` object:

```
<!-- Example_23.htm -->
<HTML>
<HEAD>
   <STYLE>
      SPAN { border-style: groove;
         border-color: gray;
         margin: 20px;
         padding: 5px;
         background-color: yellow;
         width: 50px;
         text-align: right }
   </STYLE>
</HEAD>
<body onMouseMove='mouseMove(event)'>
   <SPAN ID='AAA'>00</SPAN>:<SPAN ID='BBB'>00</SPAN>:
   <P ID="CCC">Some text whose background is being colored</P>
   <BR></BR>
   <SCRIPT LANGUAGE="JavaScript">
      var mySpanAAA = document.getElementById("AAA");
      var mySpanBBB = document.getElementById("BBB");
      var myParaCCC = document.getElementById("CCC");

      function mouseMove(anEvent)
      {
         if(!window.event)
         {
            myEvent = anEvent;
         }
         else
         {
            myEvent = window.event;
         }

         myX = Math.floor(myEvent.screenX/3);
         myY = Math.floor(myEvent.screenY/3);
         if(myX > 255)
         {
            myX = 255;
         }
         if(myY > 255)
         {
```

```
            myY = 255;
        }

        myHexX = myX.toString(16);
        myHexY = myY.toString(16);

        if(myX < 16)
        {
            myHexX = '0' + myHexX;
        }

        if(myY < 16)
        {
            myHexY = '0' + myHexY;
        }

        mySpanAAA.innerHTML = myHexX;
        mySpanBBB.innerHTML = myHexY;

        myBackColor = '#88' + myHexX + myHexY;
        myTextColor = '#' + myHexX + myHexY + '88';

        myParaCCC.style.backgroundColor = myBackColor;
        myParaCCC.style.color           = myTextColor;
        return true;
    }
    </SCRIPT>
</BODY>
</HTML>
```

Note how the <SPAN> blocks are driven dynamically to display the current mouse coordinates after they have been hex coded.

Mouse Event Driven Positioning

Objects can be repositioned under event control driven by the mouse. This is actually quite simple to accomplish, but there is a very subtle pitfall. If we do not set the position property of the `style` object to `"absolute"` in either the <STYLE> block or in the JavaScript, then the object will not track the mouse movement. In that case, it will stay where it was when the page was first rendered.

Here is a simple example that you can embellish in many ways:

```
<!-- Example_24.htm -->
<HTML>
<HEAD>
    <STYLE>
        IMG { position: absolute}
    </STYLE>
</HEAD>
<body onMouseMove="mouseMove(event)">
    <IMG ID="myImage" SRC="picture.gif"></IMG>
    <SCRIPT LANGUAGE="JavaScript">

        function mouseMove(anEvent)
        {
            if(!window.event)
            {
                myX = anEvent.pageX;
                myY = anEvent.pageY;
            }
            else
```

```
            {
                myX = anEvent.x;
                myY = anEvent.y;
            }

            window.status = myX;

            myImageObject = document.getElementById("myImage");

            myImageObject.style.top = myY-15;
            myImageObject.style.left = myX-15;
            return true;
        }
    </SCRIPT>
</BODY>
</HTML>
```

Portability and Very Old Browsers

Take this example section of code that we used earlier:

```
<!-- Example_05.htm -->
<HTML>
<BODY>
    <HR></HR>
    <H1 ID="H1_1">Heading object 1</H1>
    <HR></HR>
    <H1 ID="H1_2">Heading object 2</H1>
    <HR></HR>
    <H1 ID="H1_3">Heading object 3</H1>
    <HR></HR>
    <SCRIPT LANGUAGE="JavaScript">
        var myObject = document.getElementById("H1_1");
        myObject.style.backgroundColor = "red"
    </SCRIPT>
</BODY>
</HTML>
```

MSIE does not support the DOM method getElementById() on the Windows CE operating system, so on that platform you will have to use an alternative. MSIE does support several non-portable mechanisms for accessing child elements, but let's try to remain on the right path and retain DOM standards compliance. This will ultimately be beneficial as it means our scripts will likely run on NN version 6 as well.

Getting this to run on MSIE version 4 is certainly going to be problematic. MSIE version 4 does not support either getElementById() or getElementsByTagName(). You can try using document.H1_1 to access the first <H1> Element. That does work on MSIE version 4.5 for Macintosh, but it breaks on version 5.0 and later on both Macintosh and Windows. Using document.all.H1_1 does locate the correct object on more versions of MSIE, but the all property is not present on NN. Using the same trick we deployed earlier to fix a missing property in MSIE version 5.5 (Windows), we can fool NN into thinking it has a document.all property. This only comes into play on Netscape browsers. Replace the script block in the previous example with this code and it will work across a very wide selection of browsers, platforms and legacy versions of browsers:

```
<!-- Example_25.htm -->
<HTML>
<BODY>
    <HR></HR>
```

```
<H1 ID="H1_1">Heading object 1</H1>
<HR></HR>
<H1 ID="H1_2">Heading object 2</H1>
<HR></HR>
<H1 ID="H1_3">Heading object 3</H1>
<HR></HR>
<SCRIPT LANGUAGE="JavaScript">
    if(!document.all)
    {
        document.all = document.getElementsByTagName('*');
    }

    myObject = document.all.H1_1;
    myObject.style.backgroundColor = "red"
</SCRIPT>
</BODY>
</HTML>
```

Another technique uses the conditional operator to access a CSS rule object either by the `rules` or `cssRules` property.

```
var myParaStyle = document.all ?
document.styleSheets[0].rules[0].style :
document.styleSheets[0].cssRules[0].style;
```

Trying to get a portable script design working is likely to add complexity. You could consider it as a series of compromise decisions that you have to make. Each one falling back to a less desirable position. They are:

Preference	Description
1	The Holy Grail. Total portability with no special code taking account of different browser versions.
2	Coding carefully but sub-optimally because it is more portable. The perfect coding solution may not be portable, but a less elegant form may work.
3	Simulating missing functionality by adding object properties that are only available in some browsers for example. This is a little harder with methods, but not impossible.
4	Setting up initial conditions using browser matching and conditional blocks of code.
5	Completely reorganising the code and executing radically different code designs after selecting them through a browser match.
6	Including different JavaScript script insert files according to browser versions with the <SCRIPT SRC=""> attribute.
7	Least desirable of all is to serve a different version of the page based on the server identifying the browser type. From the client end, this is quite desirable, but is very hard to maintain on a large scale.
8	Worst case scenario is just to let it break. This is unfortunate, but if out of several hundred thousand users, only one has a browser that is too many versions out of date, there has to be a point at which you simply have to let it go.

Some browsers (notably MSIE version 5.5 on Windows) will throw an error on receipt of an invalid value for a style property. You can trap this out by executing the following script source in the global code. Putting it inline in the document as it loads is probably sufficient:

```
function errorTrap()
{
   return true;
}

window.onerror = errorTrap;
```

Working on these examples revealed another interesting bug in MSIE. You cannot use the getElementById() method to assign a value to a variable with the same name as the ID you are searching for. This causes an error:

```
myImage = document.getElementById("myImage");
```

This is however fine:

```
myImageObject = document.getElementById("myImage");
```

Summary

In this chapter, we have learned that we can explore the CSS object model that is standardized by the DOM specification and which the browsers partially implement. They do implement it at least well enough that the version 5 and 6 browsers should support scripting that will work in a portable fashion.

We can largely accomplish everything we need to do without needing to write large amounts of browser specific code. One of the best ways to solve this is to fix the missing functionality in a browser by adding a couple of lines of script. That restores the browser's internal object model to something close to what is supported by the other browsers.

We have also learned that CSS is a constantly moving target. As soon as the browser manufacturers catch up with the standard, the working groups have moved on and defined new functionality. This is as we would expect. Regrettably, however, browser manufacturers are still keen to introduce special features that no one else supports.

We can accomplish some very interactive things with CSS. It is a lot more powerful than some of the former DHTML techniques that we used where all kinds of massive document content changes were necessary to achieve simple effects.

In the future, CSS will evolve further and in due course, we shall be able to do even more with it.

Pro JavaScript 2nd Edition

The Document Object Model

The Document Object Model (DOM) is a standard application-programming interface (API) designed by the W3C explicitly for accessing the content of HTML and XML documents.

DOM defines the logical structure of documents using a system of Node objects arranged into a tree-like organization. DOM also specifies the way a document is accessed and manipulated from a variety of programming languages. Here, we shall focus on access via JavaScript, although work is underway to operate on DOM structures from Java and C languages among others.

In this chapter, we are mainly concerned with the basic DOM Level 1 nodal tree model. DOM standardization work is also going on in other groups, and there are similar initiatives in the Synchronized Multimedia Integration Language (SMIL), Mathematical Markup Language (MathML), and Scalable Vector Graphics (SVG) groups who are all working closely with the DOM group to ensure interoperability. Other mark up languages and XML based groups are also looking at the DOM and how to access it from JavaScript and other languages.

In the DOM Recommendation, the model is based on the content of a document. However, that document could contain XML that is being widely used for interchanging data between different systems. In the context of a web browser, that document would contain HTML.

Given access to a DOM representation of a document, a software developer can construct new documents or modify existing ones. Typically, within a web browser we are concerned more with modification. In general, the creation of document content supported by web browsers is weak.

In this chapter, we shall explore the Document Object Model and discover how to operate on it with JavaScript, and what strengths and weaknesses it has. The chapter is broken down as follows:

❑ Overview of theory and practice.

❑ DOM Levels 0, 1, 2 and 3 and how they are organized.

- ❏ DOM tree structure – including Node Objects, Parent-Child Relationships and different types of nodes. DOM Utility Methods and access to CSS will also be covered although CSS is covered extensively in the previous chapter.

- ❏ Browser implementations.

- ❏ Modularization of the DOM.

- ❏ DOM standardized event models.

The DOM standard is now so large that to try and cover it all in a single chapter of a book will hardly do it justice at all. We shall cover the most prominent aspects of it, focussing on traversing documents, the tree structure, capabilities that are currently implemented, and how well they are implemented.

We must deal with the theoretical side of things first to get an overall feel for how it all hangs together. We'll then look at writing some scripts to dig more deeply into the nodal structure, before exploring other aspects such as the event model with some practical work.

> **If you are trying to learn about DOM, Netscape 6 is probably the best one to experiment with. The support for DOM methods is much weaker in the other browsers, although IE 5 on the Macintosh is better than IE 5.5 on Windows in respect of its DOM support. IE 6 on Windows resolves some (but not all) of these issues. Netscape 4 is not suitable for running the examples in this chapter as it does not have support for DOM.**

In the examples we give here, there are notes regarding what works where, but with the situation changing all the time, it may be possible to install parts of your Windows operating system and upgrade the DOM support without realizing it.

The general caveat is, try it and see if it works on your target platforms. If it doesn't, then develop a minimal work around that you can discard later when the functionality is made available more widely.

Theory and Practice

It is necessary to consider the Document Object Model from both a theoretical point of view and a practical one.

The theoretical approach is necessary, because DOM is a work in progress as far as the standards development is concerned and the browser manufacturers are a long way behind W3C in their implementations. Progress is being made on standardization with the current work being referred to as Level 3.

The practical side of this, is to see what progress the browser manufacturers have made in implementing the DOM capabilities. Broadly, that means DOM Level 1 with some small portion of Level 2 event handling.

Simply referring to DOM is not sufficient. DOM can mean XML or HTML document structures. Traversing a DOM representation of a document can mean navigating a nodal tree structure or accessing components using HTML tag attributes, such as ID=" " to pick out an individual HTMLElement object.

We shall concentrate primarily on the DOM representation of a HTML document in a web browser context. We will make some reference to the standard, but the support for the capabilities defined in the standard is somewhat incomplete and quite inconsistent, even within a browser family such as IE.

The Document Object Model is the means by which the browser maps the document content in a single HTML web page to a structure that you can access from your JavaScript code. Through the DOM API, we can access individual HTMLElement objects, CSS style sheets also handle events triggered by user interaction. The DOM organizes the document into a tree structure, where HTML elements are nested within one another in a reflection of the way that tags are contained (nested within another) in the document source.

The DOM standards developed by the W3C are language independent. Techniques that work in JavaScript may well work in Java (assuming a similar and compliant implementation exists for both languages). The W3C standards include bindings for JavaScript and Java in the appendices, while other groups are developing language bindings for different languages.

All of this suggests that without the DOM standards, we would be nowhere at all. In fact, document content was being modelled within the browsers well before the DOM standard was created. In the early days, the browser implementations led the way, but the W3C is now much further ahead.

The situation now, is that each browser supports its own particular DOM representation. They are converging with one another by adding capabilities described by the W3C, but you still have to write DOM access code very carefully to work around the shortcomings in the various implementations. Occasionally, a DOM specified feature helps you out, but generally the traversal support is implemented so differently in each browser, that you may still have to write browser specific code.

Your web browser is an application that supports a DOM implementation. The implementation is what creates the model, while the application aspects of the browser allow us to add, modify, or delete portions of the DOM representation of our web page with JavaScript or Java code.

The DOM lets us access the document to obtain a collection of objects that reflect the contents of all tags of a particular name. For example, it could collect all h1 tags to generate a table of contents. We could gather a collection of objects to which the same CSS style class has been associated. These need not be the same HTML element types.

Although up to this point in the book we have not gone to great lengths to talk about DOM, many of the examples in other chapters in fact, rely on DOM facilities provided by the API to manipulate the HTML content from JavaScript.

DOM Levels 0, 1, 2, and 3

DOM originated from a desire to give access to the document from the JavaScript and Java environments. The immediate benefit of this was Dynamic HTML. That was not really a DOM implementation at all, but was a founding influence of the DOM initiative. DHTML was fundamentally a browser based script interface. The W3C DOM group was formed from a variety of people from a DHTML persuasion and others who had worked on XML, SGML, and other environments. All of that influenced what eventually became what we now know as DOM.

W3C mandates that there is DOM Level 0 functionality, but that it is not standardized. It is assumed as the de facto state of affairs with some very early (and now obsolete) browser versions. Those would typically be Netscape 2 and 3 and IE 3 browsers, which evolved into DHTML with version 4 browsers. However, DHTML has become far more sophisticated and the distinctions between DHTML techniques and DOM techniques are quite subtle. Some contrasts between them are covered in Chapter 10, *Dynamic HTML*.

DOM Level 1 functionality is primarily concerned with traversing a static document, extracting components from it, and modifying the DOM structure. DOM Level 1 is somewhat monolithic. The standard is defined in a single document, although there are two editions. The second edition is logically the only one we should consider, and it can be obtained in various forms at http://www.w3.org/TR/2000/WD-DOM-Level-1-20000929. DOM Level 1 capabilities are broadly supported by IE 5and Netscape 6, although Microsoft do not make great claims about their DOM compliance, and seem to favor the DHTML approach in their example scripts. Only certain event handling aspects of Level 2 are addressed by any browser, and then only in Netscape 6 at present. DOM Level 3 is not yet stable enough for any implementation, although no doubt any DOM Level 3 capabilities that are being submitted or promoted by web browser manufacturers will make it into their browsers at the earliest opportunity.

The capabilities offered by each version of the DOM generally build on the functionality of the earlier version. This can be illustrated with a diagram:

Level 0	Level 1	Level 2	Level 3
Everything in one module	Everything in one module	Core	Core
		HTML	HTML
		Style	Style
		Events	Events
		Traversal & Range	Traversal & Range
		Views	Views
			Content models, Load & Save

In the illustration, you can see that the DOM Level 1 capabilities were split in Level 2. The darker rectangles indicate the modules that are supported at least in part by current browsers. Nevertheless, Level 2 support is somewhat incomplete.

The DOM Level 1 functionality is enhanced in Level 2, but the major improvement in Level 2 is that it supports a rich event model that allows documents to be completely interactive as well as a style model that reflects the CSS styling of the document.

DOM Level 2 also adds a range model for manipulating sections of text and a traversal model for viewing a subset of the document content. This provides iteration tools and filter mechanisms that should go a long way to addressing the major shortcomings in the current DOM implementations that browsers support at present. Level 2 is also modularized, which is quite helpful as it is about three times the size of Level 1. Documents describing Level 2 can be found at the same location at the W3C web server (http://www.w3.org/TR/2000/ DOM-Level-2-Core/).

DOM Level 3 is not yet fully standardized (indeed, the HTML module of DOM Level 2 remains at draft stage) and there is still much work to be done. The DOM requirements document (at http://www.w3.org/TR/DOM-Requirements/) enumerates the work being done on the DOM Level 3 core module. Extensive changes to the event handling capabilities are also taking place. The loading and saving external XML based documents and a path based location mechanism for accessing nodes is also being considered. This would be extremely useful, as it is quite a computationally expensive task to walk a DOM tree to locate an item because it requires iteration through unwanted nodes and a means of filtering to locate the ones you want. It is also risk prone due to browser implementations not being exactly equal.

DOM Tree Structure

In this part of the chapter, we shall focus primarily on Node objects and their descendents. There are other object classes of course in the DOM Recommendation, which we'll visit later. Typically, they deal with events for example. Other special object types are provided to gather groups of nodes into collections.

The DOM Recommendation documents describe an ideal world where the tree-structured organization of the document is as laid down in the W3C documents. Unfortunately, significant parts of that functionality are missing. In this discussion, we shall approach it from a theoretical point of view, illustrating the concepts with short fragments of JavaScript. However, you must be aware that these are example code fragments that will likely throw errors in the current (as of 2001) browsers.

The Document Object Model is a representation of XML, HTML, or indeed any kind of structured document, using objects to encapsulate various component parts of that document. As long as the document can be constructed with a nodal tree structure, you can manufacture a DOM representation. The basic Node organization is not intended to pre-suppose any particular document type. A layer that sits on top of the basic DOM organization imposes HTML functionality. In object-oriented terms, the HTMLElement objects are sub-classes of the fundamental DOM Nodes. As XML is a more generic document format, it can be realized with fundamental DOM objects.

The DOM is quite distinct from the Browser Object Model. They impinge on one another at the global document property (window.document). The browser object model is a container within which the ECMA Core object model and the DOM lives. The illustration shows how they descend from the global object:

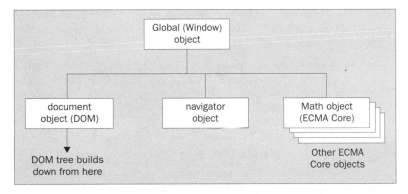

There are basically four kinds of entity here:

❏ The global object is the top-level container and root of the entire hierarchy

❏ The document object is the head of the DOM tree

❏ The navigator object is an implementation specific object (there may be others depending on the browser.)

❏ The Math object and the collection of objects adjacent to it are those defined by ECMA and considered to be part of the core language

The document parser manufactures the DOM tree structure. This breaks the document into components on a logical basis according to whatever mark up is present. Each mark up tag becomes an Element node. It may contain some content between the beginning and ending tags. All of that content would be considered to be a child of the Element object. Between the tags at any particular level in the hierarchy, there would be some interstitial content that was not considered to be mark up. That would be stored in a Text node. Text nodes may contain whitespace or even null data where two mark up tags are placed immediately next to one another.

The eventual result is a tree of related nodes of different types. Let's look at a diagram that illustrates that parsing process:

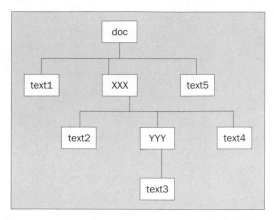

Using object references from one to another, a tree structure is built that represents the whole document. The parser reduces the document down to indivisible components, represented by objects that can have properties that are accessible from the scripting environment. Note in the diagram how textual content inside the XXX and /XXX tags is placed one level down from the XXX object. The YYY object also has some text contained inside its tags.

Documents will largely be composed of HTMLElement objects, alternating with Text node objects. A HTMLElement corresponds to a HTML tag and a Text node object corresponds to the text between tags. These are both based on the fundamental DOM Node object class. Other node types allow us to store arbitrary data, attributes, and some active components. The range of node types and their content is summarized in the table:

Node type	Introduced	Description
Node	Core 1	The primary data type on which all objects within a DOM is based.
Document	Core 1	The root of the document tree giving primary access to the DOM representation.
DocumentFragment	Core 2	A lightweight document node. Provided as a means of extracting part of a document tree as a whole. Useful in cut and paste type operations.
HTMLDocument	HTML 1	A sub-class of the Document node representing a HTML document.
DocumentType	Core 1	A container for DTD entities that is not yet rigorously standardised.
Element	Core 1	An element within a HTML or XML document. However, HTML elements are instantiated as HTMLElement objects, which are a sub-class of the Element object. XML based Element objects may need to be examined to access the correct Attribute object while these attributes are generally presented as simple named properties of a HTMLElement object.

Table continued on following page

Node type	Introduced	Description
HTMLElement	HTML 1	A sub-class of the Element object that represents a HTML tag in a document. The HTML module also defines a sub-class of the HTMLElement object for each kind of HTML tag specified in the HTML 4.0 standard.
Attribute	Core 1	Contains the attribute data for an Element object. Many attribute objects may be associated with a single element. For a HTML document, these objects represent the content of HTML tag attributes.
CharacterData	Core 1	A Node object that has been extended to support character data. This is not generally instantiated as such, but is sub-classed by any nodes that need to contain character data such as comments and Text node objects.
Text	Core 1	A sub-class of the CharacterData object that represents textual content between mark up tags (Element objects).
Comment	Core 1	A sub-class of the CharacterData object to contain the text within the comment delimiters.
CDATASection	Core 1	A special container for escaped text that contains characters that might be interpreted as mark up.
Entity	Core 1	A parsed or unparsed entity within a XML document.
EntityReference	Core 1	A reference to a XML entity object.
Notation	Core 1	An object that represents a notation declared within a DTD. This is covered in the XML 1.0 Recommendation.
Processing Instruction	Core 1	Part of the XML functionality to hold processing instructions within the document.

Later on, we shall work through a variety of examples, looking at these different kinds of nodes, how they relate to one another, and how we can read or write their various property values to achieve some dynamic effects.

This nodal structure is independent of the HTML nature of the document. This is because the fundamental tree structure can be constructed just with Document and Element objects (both of which are Node object sub-classes), and they have no particular flavor of mark up language implied at all. The HTML document is parsed into object classes that are descendents of Element and Document and are called HTMLElement and HTMLDocument. These new classes add functionality related to the HTML document mark up.

We won't explore all of the different node types here, but just those that are most relevant to creating dynamic effects on a web page written in HTML.

Node Objects

We showed in the previous section, how a document tree is constructed from a document having been parsed into individual nodes. A single node is considered a parent and may have several child nodes. Each of those child nodes has a common parent referenced via a parentNode property and they are siblings of one another. There is one node at the root of the tree. That is the Document node. Below that, the child nodes are ordered in the sequence that they appear in the document, but additional nodes can be inserted under script control.

The properties belonging to the node object vary according to the type of node that is instantiated.

The basic DOM node supports a few properties that are useful when navigating the DOM structure. These help us to find out about the node and what it represents. They are useful, but possibly not as likely to be commonly used unless you are developing very sophisticated DOM oriented scripts:

Property	Description
nodeName	The value depends on the kind of node being examined. Element nodes place the HTML tag type that instantiated the object in this property. That is not the same value as the NAME="" HTML tag attribute. Attribute objects have a HTML tag attribute name as their nodeName value. Others are assigned according to the type of node.
nodeType	The nodeType property determines the kind of node this object represents. However, in browser implementations, the object is instantiated as a sub-class of DOM Node object and its class type distinguishes how it actually behaves. Nevertheless, from the DOM perspective, if a subset of the properties is taken, the object can be seen as a simple DOM node.
nodeValue	For attributes and Text node objects, this is the value or content of the attribute or Text node. For most other node types, this value is null apart from comments, processing instructions and CDATA nodes. Comment nodes use this to store the text within the comment delimiters. ProcessingInstruction nodes store information about how to process the XML data in the document. CDATA nodes are containers to store XML content that may have mark up embedded in them. They escape the content in such a way that it won't be accidentally parsed.
childNodes	A collection of node objects that are immediate children of the owning node.
firstChild	The first item in the childNodes collection.
lastChild	The last item in the childNodes collection.
parentNode	A reference to the node whose childNodes collection this node belongs to.
previousSibling	The node immediately before the current node in the childNodes collection belonging to their joint parent node.
nextSibling	The node immediately after the current node in the childNodes collection belonging to their joint parent node.
attributes	A collection of Attribute node objects belonging to this node.
ownerDocument	A reference to the root of the DOM tree structure.

These are the most useful methods of the DOM Node object for operating on the DOM tree:

Method	Description
createElement(tagName)	Creates a new instance of an Element node based on the tag name provided. In a HTML context, there is the implication that this should suitably sub-class the created Element. The standard is ambiguous here, and this method belongs to the Document node definition and not to the HTMLDocument node definition. The results may well be browser specific, since they support different class names.

Table continued on following page

Method	Description
createTextNode(aText)	Creates a new instance of a Text node containing the specified text as its data.
cloneNode(aRecursive)	Clone an existing node, potentially copying recursively down into its own tree structure. Note that if we do clone a node, any attached event handlers associated with the node being copied will not be cloned with it. We will need to re-attach them if necessary.
importNode (aNode, aRecursive)	Import a node from another childNodes collection potentially copying recursively down into its own tree structure.
appendChild(aNode)	Append a node to the receiving Node object's childNodes collection.
insertBefore (newNode, oldNode)	Insert a new node into the childNodes collection of the receiving node immediately before the indicated oldNode.
removeChild(aNode)	Remove a node from the receiving node's childNodes collection.
replaceChild (newNode, oldNode)	Replace an old node with a new one in the receiving nodes' childNodes collection.
getElementsByTagName (tagName)	Returns a collection of objects having been instantiated from the specified tag name.
getElementById(anId)	This is a HTMLDocument extension that locates an object according to its unique ID value. Therefore, it refers to a singular HTMLElement object.
getElementsByName(aName)	Returns a collection of HTMLElement nodes that share the same name. NAME="" attributes need not be unique within the document. This is also an extension provided by the HTMLDocument sub-class.
hasChildNodes()	Return Boolean true if the Node owns any children.
hasAttributes()	Return Boolean true if the Node has some attribute nodes belonging to it.

The scope of these depends where in the DOM we are sending the method request. If we apply it to the document object at the top of the DOM, then the search scope includes the entire document. Alternatively, if we just apply it to an object that reflects a table tag, only the objects within that table will be examined for a match.

Parent-Child Relationships

Locating an object may involve walking some kind of DOM hierarchy and navigating through various parent/child node relationships. Some other quite convenient techniques involve the use of methods to walk the DOM tree or sub-tree downwards from a target object and locate objects according to some search criteria.

The properties that maintain the relationships between parents, children, and sibling objects need to be maintained carefully and consistently by the DOM implementation.

Here is a simple familial group of DOM nodes showing the relational links between them:

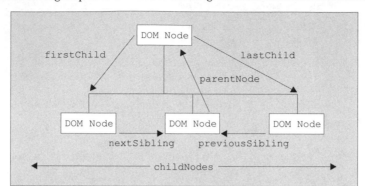

The childNodes property refers to a collection of object references that refer to all the immediate child nodes contained within a parent. This is slightly different to the children property supported by IE. While childNodes returns a collection containing Element nodes and Text nodes, the children collection only returns the Element nodes. The all property in IE walks the tree and makes a collection of all descendents as many generations deep as it needs to go.

The firstChild and lastChild properties merely point at the head and tail of the childNodes collection. The nextSibling and previousSibling properties can be used to index one node left or right through the childNodes collection. The parentNode property is a reference further up the tree, which can be walked upwards to the owning document node. That root node is always referred to by the ownerDocument property of any Node object.

Document Nodes

There is one DOM node having the nodeType value 9 that represents a Document object. This is at the top of the DOM tree. It may be possible to have more than one Document object in an implementation, but they will generally correlate one per window, frame or layer.

As this is the owner node for the whole document, all factory methods for creating new child objects are also associated with this object. These factory and utility methods are particularly useful (others are listed in the appendices)

If we examine the properties of a Document object in a browser window, there are a lot more properties than it appears should belong to the DOM Document object. This is because what we are really looking at is a DOM HTMLDocument object and we need to understand the object as a HTMLDocument sub-class of the Document object class.

This area can be confusing because some browsers display DOM class names, some use DOM HTML class names, and in the case of IE on Windows, they simply don't tell you at all. We can usually work out what the class really is by looking at the nodeName, nodeType or data property values, so you can usually work it out with some additional scripting. That is, if it is at all important to your script that it knows the correct class names. Most of the time it doesn't matter, but it's good to know these things when we are trying to diagnose a problem.

DOM abstracts the capabilities of a Document object by describing a generic document node object that is of no particular flavor. This can be used to reflect the contents of XML documents, but lacks important properties that HTML documents require. So, DOM specified a sub-class called the HTMLDocument Node. Browsers implement the HTMLDocument class and do not make the Document class accessible. However, some browsers refer to the object type as a Document while others call it a HTMLDocument. Also beware of these inconsistencies if you write scripts that need to inspect objects to determine what class they are.

DOM Level 2 introduces the concept of a `DocumentFragment` node, which is a lightweight `Document` object. It defines enough of the document structure to be able to carry a portion of a document tree as if it had been cut or copied to the clipboard.

Element Nodes

In the same way that a `Document` and `HTMLDocument` class are supported, there is also an `Element` class and a `HTMLElement` class.

HTML tags are encapsulated or reflected into a sub-class of the DOM node object. However, the browser will instantiate `HTMLElement` objects of a sub-class that is appropriate to the HTML tag being represented. This is necessary because apart from the common attributes and methods that all node objects need to support, each tag also supports a variety of special properties based on the HTML tag attributes it supports.

For example, the `IMG` tag supports a `src=""` HTML tag attribute, but the `HR` tag doesn't. Therefore, these two would be instantiated as members of the `HTMLImageElement` and `HTMLHRElement` sub-classes respectively. These would inherit common properties from the `HTMLElement` object that in turn inherits from the DOM `Element` object. The `Element` object is of course a sub-class of the DOM `Node` object and inherits some of its behavior from that.

In accordance with the DOM standard, the HTML tag attribute values are reflected into `Attribute` nodes, which we will look at shortly. Historically, DHTML techniques have operated on properties that belong directly to the parent object, rather than navigate a DOM structure to find a related node. Although you can use the DOM structure to find an attribute, the property access technique is far simpler.

Generally, the DOM node properties are widely supported as they are defined in the standards document.

Attribute Nodes

When a document mark up tag is reflected into an object there needs to be a way of representing the tag attributes in a way that can be related to the `Element` object. However, not all tags support the same subset of attributes and it just isn't sensible to develop a superset of all tag attributes and define them all as properties. Each tag attribute is encapsulated in an object and then they are all assembled into a collection. A reference to that collection is stored in the `attributes` property.

In the case of a HTML document, the tags are still reflected into objects but are `HTMLElement` objects or sub-classes of `HTMLElement`. Although the HTML tag attributes are reflected into `Attribute` objects to provide a compliant implementation, they are also available directly as properties of the `HTMLElement` object. This necessitates there being a sub-class of `HTMLElement` for each type of HTML tag. Indeed, the DOM Recommendation allows for this and defines a set of classes for that purpose.

Other DOM structures are being proposed, such as the one for Scalable Vector Graphics. In due course, we shall be able to operate on vector drawings with JavaScript.

The relationship between a line of HTML and the DOM nodes that it instantiated is shown here:

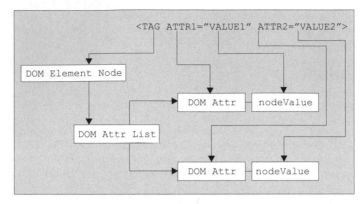

While these `Attribute` nodes will be useful for developing XML applications for the scripting of HTML, we can use the properties belonging to the `HTMLElement` objects themselves to make our scripting simpler.

CharacterData Nodes

The DOM standard describes a sub-class of the `Node` object for managing textual content. All text oriented node classes are grouped together and sub-classed from this `CharacterData` node class. This class is generally not exposed for script access directly.

This allows some common functionality to be shared between all textual nodes. Essentially, this class provides access to the internal data and length of a textual object by means of the data and length properties.

There are some useful utility functions provided for editing the textual content of the node. These allow you to extract any portion as a sub-string, append more data, insert at any point, delete or replace some of the data. These properties and methods are enumerated in the appendices.

The sub-classes of the `CharacterData` class are:

❏   `Text` nodes

❏   `Comment` nodes

❏   `CDATASection` nodes

Text Nodes

`Text` nodes were not available in any portable form before DOM standardized the way a document is converted to a collection of objects. Before the DOM was standardized, Microsoft did provide some access to textual content with proprietary COM objects such as `Microsoft.XMLDOM`. DHTML did not require access to `Text` nodes since (in IE at least) the `innerHTML` and `innerText` properties yielded something functionally similar.

The way DOM organizes a document representation requires that a `Text` node object be placed between two adjacent `HTMLElement` objects if there is some text in between them.

So, this fragment of HTML:

```
<BR></BR>
Some text
<BR></BR>
```

Theoretically produces this group of objects:

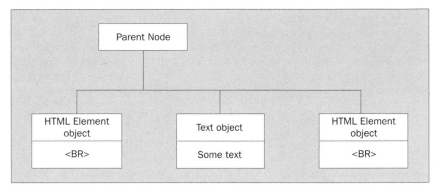

The word 'theoretically' was used on purpose because the /br tags may instantiate additional HTMLElement objects in some browsers and there may be extra Text nodes placed in the tree contained in this document fragment.

Alternatively, this fragment of HTML:

```
<P>Some text <IMG…></IMG> and some more.</P>
```

Theoretically produces this group of objects:

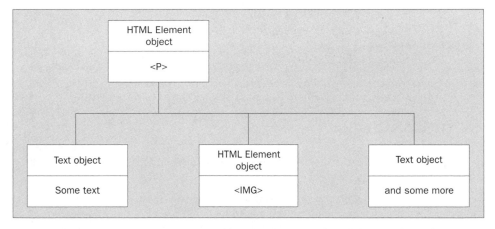

The Text nodes may be present in some implementations, whether the text either side of the IMG tag was present in the document or not. This is dependent on the browser, as we shall see when we examine some real-world scenarios.

When a document is parsed from a HTML source, the HTMLElement nodes are generally interposed between Text nodes. This is an area where the browser manufacturers are allowed some leeway and if the HTML mark up has no textual content between one HTMLElement and another, the parser may omit the interstitial Text node (as is the case with IE). This is the one thing that renders the childNodes collection of a Document object virtually unusable without writing filter scripts of your own.

Even if the browser retains all of the candidate Text nodes, many of them are likely to be empty. After modifying a DOM tree by removing an Element, several Text nodes may end up being adjacent to one another. This might happen if a DIV were removed, or perhaps an IMG object. If there are several Text nodes next to one another, the DOM tree can be normalized, so that adjacent Text nodes are merged into a single node and empty Text nodes are removed. This somewhat flexible nature of the DOM gives browser manufacturers some maneuverability in how they represent the DOM tree when it reflects the contents of a HTML document source. This normalization sometimes happens without you needing to intervene, or you can force normalization by calling a method to activate it. We will be looking at some examples of this in a few pages time. In the meantime, here is a sequence of objects showing how normalization is applied:

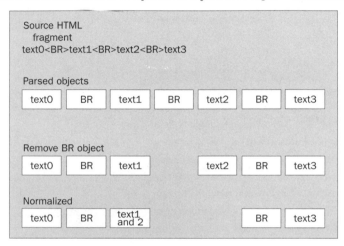

Now, we can work through some of the properties and methods belonging to the DOM Node objects to see how they can be used to manipulate the DOM representation of the document. We'll try to do that without being overly concerned with the fact that the document is marked up and parsed with HTML. In principle, a DOM can be parsed from a variety of different kinds of documents.

Access to CSS Styles

In the chapter on CSS, there are several illustrations of how we could access and operate on the CSS styling model from JavaScript. That access mechanism rather depends on the DOM Level 2 style module for its support of styleSheet and style objects.

The style and styleSheet objects introduced at DOM Level 2 are attached to instances of the HTMLDocument via a collection object referenced by the styleSheets property of the document object. These provide locally defined or globally cascaded and inherited styling effects. Although they aren't based on the Node object, they can be located in a similar way by navigating an object representation of the style sheet or as a child object of a HTMLElement.

Supporting Actors

We shall look at the event handling and modularization support later. Those two aspects of DOM are built around the DOMImplementation object and the various event-handling objects.

In support of our activity with the nodal tree structure, we will encounter the following additional object types, as well as the different kinds of nodes we have already discussed:

Class	Description
DOMException	These objects help to manage error situations when you try to operate on the DOM structure inappropriately. The browser should incorporate them into its exception handling mechanisms so you can trap the errors more easily.
NodeList	A list of nodes presented as a collection. This is essentially an array and is presented when you request the childNodes collection from an object.
NamedNodeMap	This is another way of presenting a collection of names. However, it is more like a dictionary than an array. Although you may access the objects by numeric index, this is simply to aid enumeration. You would normally expect to access the objects by name. It is specifically stated in the standard that this is NOT a sub-class of the NodeList object.

Studying the Browser Implementations

We need to get comfortable with the way our browsers maintain a DOM structure. Some simple exercises to understand a little bit about how the browsers implement the DOM and its component objects will help with that.

We need some tools to help us examine the internal structure of the DOM implementation and how it constructs the tree structure from the document we give it. As the tools are written in JavaScript, we learn more as we build them.

Inspection Tools

To examine the contents of a web page without having to add code to that web page is the most desirable goal for our tool design. If we have to add some inspection code to the page we are examining, then we will change the DOM tree for that document and our inspection scripts will become an integral part of the document we are trying to look at. This gives rise to several problems:

❑   We may find that adding our code changes the page so much that it no longer works

❑   Outputting the results may cause further DOM modification

❑   We can very easily create recursion loops causing a browser crash

Our inspection tools should, therefore, try to avoid any detrimental effects if possible

It would be helpful if we can build a test harness (or framework) in which we can mount the document we want to probe unchanged, and then provide the debugging capabilities around that. One likely candidate for being able to do that is the use of framesets. We must try and keep the inspection tools simple, so that they are very portable, otherwise we won't be able to inspect the behavior of our target document on multiple platforms.

As a result of that, we won't build sophisticated user interface mechanisms into the test harness for now. However, these examples should always be considered to be just a starting point for your own experimentation so that you can build more sophisticated tools once the basic inspection tool is working.

We'll keep it simple for now. Just two frames in a frameset with predefined file names of target.htm for the file we are going to inspect and inspector.htm for the small fragment of code that probes the DOM structure and produces the output. Sitting around them in the test harness will be a library of 0

This technique is modelled on the multiple frame session storage approach described in the chapter covering the BBC News Online Video Console that also uses multiple frames and provides utilities for communicating between them. See Chapter 20, *Online News Site Audio-Video Console* for details of that case study.

Here is a diagram showing the structural relationship:

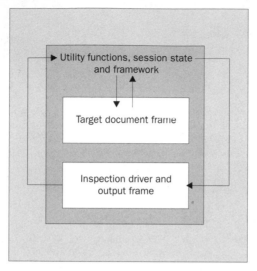

The arrows in the diagram signify the call sequence from the inspection driver, invoking utility functions that drill down into the DOM in the target frame. The results return via the utility functions and are output in the inspection driver frame.

To use this inspection tool, go through these steps:

1. Create a folder to work in

2. Locate your candidate document that you want to examine and copy it to the folder

3. Rename it to be called `target.htm`

4. Clone a new copy of `harness.htm` into the folder you are working in

5. Create or copy the `inspector.htm` file

6. Modify the `inspector.htm` file to locate the object you want to examine

7. Add a call to the inspector function that you want to invoke

8. Load `harness.htm` into your browser

We see that the target document appears in the upper frame, while the inspection output appears in the lower frame.

We haven't provided any interlocking or checking for load states so if your target document takes a long time to load, the inspector may attempt to examine it before it is ready. Simply reload the lower frame once the upper frame has completed its load cycle. This is a rare occurrence and less likely because of the placement of the frames relative to one another.

As this is only a starting point, you can enhance the test harness in many ways. For example, in Chapter 18, *IE Filters and Effects*, there are example code fragments that solve the same interlocking scenarios by checking for ready state values to avoid filter collisions. You could add some code using the same ideas to implement interlock scenarios and prevent the need for a manual reload if you need it.

Since we refer internally to the target document using the frame name therefore, you don't necessarily need to modify or clone the target document – you could operate on it in place by modifying the FRAME tag for the targetFrame to point at it. You must observe the 'same-server' or 'same-domain' security requirements that are intentionally provided to stop you hacking documents unless you own them. If the target is remote you could place the inspection tools on the same web server, rather than store them locally on your own file system.

Example Test Target Document

Here is an example very simple target we will examine:

```
<HTML>
<BODY>
<IMG ID='fred' SRC='fred.gif' ALT='Alternative Text'
     BORDER='10' HEIGHT='50' WIDTH='50' HSPACE='10'
     VSPACE='10'></IMG>
</BODY>
</HTML>
```

You can place any image you like in here for test purposes.

Containing Frameset

Here is the frameset container. This is contained in a file called harness.htm:

```
<HTML>
<HEAD>
<SCRIPT LANGUAGE='JavaScript'>
… Utility functions here …
</SCRIPT>
</HEAD>
<FRAMESET FRAMESPACING='0' FRAMEBORDER='1' BORDER='1' ROWS='*,50%'>
   <FRAME SRC='target.htm' NAME='targetFrame' FRAMEBORDER='1'
               MARGINHEIGHT='10' MARGINWIDTH='10' SCROLLING='auto'>
   <FRAME SRC='inspector.htm' NAME='inspectFrame' FRAMEBORDER='1'
               MARGINHEIGHT='10' MARGINWIDTH='10' SCROLLING='auto'>
</FRAMESET>
</HTML>
```

It contains two frames, one has a document file called target.htm, which is the content we want to inspect. The other is the inspection script that looks 'over wall' into the other frame and displays what it finds.

We put the inspection scripts in the top-level frameset to avoid duplicating them each time in the inspector.htm file.

We'll discuss the utility functions one by one now. They need to be placed in the SCRIPT block at the head of the harness.htm file.

Object Inspector Function

This inspector uses a for(… in …) enumerator to examine all the enumerable properties of the object. This does not guarantee that all properties will be visible because some are marked internally with a "Don't enum" attribute.

323

Note that all the `document.write()` calls have the `inspectorFrame` prefix. This ensures that the output is written to the correct target. Without this, the output gets written to the top-level frameset, replacing the frameset containment and test harness:

```
function inspectObject(anObject)
{
    var myIndex = 0;

    inspectFrame.document.write("Object: ");
    inspectFrame.document.write(whatClass(anObject));
    inspectFrame.document.write("<br><br>");

    inspectFrame.document.write("<table border='1'><tr>");
    inspectFrame.document.write("<td>Index</td>");
    inspectFrame.document.write("<td>Property</td>");
    inspectFrame.document.write("<td>Value</td>");
    inspectFrame.document.write("</tr>");
    for(myEnum in anObject)
    {
        inspectFrame.document.write("<tr>");
        inspectFrame.document.write("<td>");
        inspectFrame.document.write(myIndex);
        inspectFrame.document.write("</td>");
        inspectFrame.document.write("<td>");
        inspectFrame.document.write(myEnum);
        inspectFrame.document.write("</td>");
        inspectFrame.document.write("<td>");
        inspectFrame.document.write(trapHTML (myEnum, anObject[myEnum]));
        inspectFrame.document.write("</td>");
        inspectFrame.document.write("</tr>");
        myIndex++;
    }
    inspectFrame.document.write("</TABLE>");
}
```

HTML Recursion Trap

It is important to note that the `innerHTML`, `outerHTML`, `innerText`, and `outerText`, as well as the `text` properties of an object are caught via the `trapHTML()` function so that they are not output as raw HTML. This is to avoid recursion loops if the inspector is used within the same document that it is inspecting.

The trapping is based on a `switch(...)` case selector based on the passed in property name.

You could arrange to pass back the value after processing it with the `escape()` function if you would like to see the contents of these properties or you could make a more sophisticated filter yourself:

```
function trapHTML(aProperty, aValue)
{
    switch(aProperty)
    {
    case "innerHTML" :
    case "outerHTML" :
    case "innerText" :
    case "outerText" :
    case "text"      : return("{target." + aProperty + "}");
                       break;
    }
    return(whatClass(aValue));
}
```

Object Class Extractor

On some browser and platform combinations, putting a reference to an object in a `document.write()` call, results in a string describing the object class name. On IE in Windows, you just get the string `[object]` and nothing more. This function attempts to dig a little deeper to ascertain the class name or at least some indication of what kind of object we have. This is quite useful when enumerating the properties of an object because we can see what kind of object is related through the property value.

This function is called at the heading of the inspectors when the object type is displayed and also from within the HTML recursion trap, which is a sensible central location through which all object property values are passed.

Here is the object class extractor. It is quite simple, but can be made more sophisticated if you need it to be:

```
function whatClass(anObject)
{
   if(!anObject)
   {
      return("null");
   }

   if(toString(anObject) == "[object]")
   {
      if(anObject.nodeName)
      {
         return "[object "+anObject.nodeName+"]";
      }
   }

   return(anObject);
}
```

Collection Inspector

This is a simple enumerator. It creates a stream of HTML using `document.write()` calls and plays them out inline as the BODY is parsed. The enumeration is built inside a table so that the output is neatly arranged. For cross platform use, any objects belonging to the collection are checked to see if they are `Text` or `Element` nodes and a third column is generated that helps determine what kind of object is being accessed. This is necessary because on the Windows platform, IE is not so ready to tell us the object class unless we dig for it somewhat. Here is the source code for the collection inspector:

```
function inspectCollection(aCollection)
{
   inspectFrame.document.write("Object: ");
   inspectFrame.document.write(whatClass(aCollection));
   inspectFrame.document.write("<br>");
   inspectFrame.document.write("Length: ");
   inspectFrame.document.write(aCollection.length);
   inspectFrame.document.write("<br><br>");

   inspectFrame.document.write("<table border='1'><tr>");
   inspectFrame.document.write("<td>Index</td>");
   inspectFrame.document.write("<td>Object</td>");
   inspectFrame.document.write("<td>Content</td>");
   inspectFrame.document.write("</tr>");
   for(myEnum=0; myEnum<aCollection.length; myEnum++)
   {
      inspectFrame.document.write("<tr>");
      inspectFrame.document.write("<td>");
      inspectFrame.document.write(myEnum);
      inspectFrame.document.write("</td>");
```

```
      inspectFrame.document.write("<td>");
      inspectFrame.document.write(aCollection[myEnum]);
      inspectFrame.document.write("</td>");
      inspectFrame.document.write("<td>");
      if(aCollection[myEnum].data)
      {
         inspectFrame.document.write(aCollection[myEnum].data);
      }
      else
      {
         inspectFrame.document.write(aCollection[myEnum].tagName);
      }
      inspectFrame.document.write("</td>");
      inspectFrame.document.write("</tr>");
   }
   inspectFrame.document.write("</table>");
}
```

Attributes Inspector

This is structurally very similar to the other inspectors. In this case, we display the nodeName and nodeValue of the objects in the collection. There is a small conditional test to prevent crashes when the nodeValue is not present, as is the case on some items in the attributes collection in IE:

```
function inspectAttributes(aCollection)
{
   inspectFrame.document.write("Object: ");
   inspectFrame.document.write(whatClass(aCollection));
   inspectFrame.document.write("<br>");
   inspectFrame.document.write("Length: ");
   inspectFrame.document.write(aCollection.length);
   inspectFrame.document.write("<br><br>");

   inspectFrame.document.write("<table border='1'><tr>");
   inspectFrame.document.write("<td>Index:</td>");
   inspectFrame.document.write("<td>nodeName:</td>");
   inspectFrame.document.write("<td>nodeValue:</td>");
   inspectFrame.document.write("</tr>");
   for(myEnum=0; myEnum<aCollection.length; myEnum++)
   {
      inspectFrame.document.write("<tr>");
      inspectFrame.document.write("<td>");
      inspectFrame.document.write(myEnum);
      inspectFrame.document.write("</td>");
      inspectFrame.document.write("<td>");
      inspectFrame.document.write(aCollection[myEnum].nodeName);
      inspectFrame.document.write("</td>");
      inspectFrame.document.write("<td>");
      if(aCollection[myEnum].nodeValue)
      {
         inspectFrame.document.write(aCollection[myEnum].nodeValue);
      }
      else
      {
         inspectFrame.document.write("not supported");
      }
      inspectFrame.document.write("</td>");
      inspectFrame.document.write("</tr>");
   }
   inspectFrame.document.write("</table>");
}
```

Inspector Document

The inspection steering code is in the file inspector.htm that looks structurally like this:

```
<HTML>
<BODY>
<SCRIPT LANGUAGE='JavaScript'>
   ... inspection code here ...
</SCRIPT>
</BODY>
</HTML>
```

The code that drives the inspection is executed inline in the script block in the BODY area. The inspection driver script to examine the sample target.htm file shown earlier looks like this:

```
<HTML>
<BODY>
<SCRIPT LANGUAGE='JavaScript'>
// Add the top frame to our scope chain
// This saves us having to use the 'top' prefix on
// every call to the harness utilities.
with(top)
{
   // Locate the target document to examine
   var targetDocument = targetFrame.document;


   // Locate the target object to be examined
   var myTarget = targetDocument.getElementById("fred");


   // Call the inspector
   inspectObject(myTarget);
}
</SCRIPT>
</BODY>
</HTML>
```

Note how we use the with() statement to reduce the complexity of the inspection calls, by bringing the utility library within the scope chain of the inspection script.

Other Useful Inspection Techniques

Adding alert() calls in your scripts is similar to using the printf() function when debugging C language programs. You may find it worthwhile writing supporting functions to format the text before passing it to the alert(). You can push amazingly large amounts of debugging output through an alert() box.

If you wish, you can create additional frames or open extra popup windows for the output. As long as you maintain a handle to refer to these external frames and windows, you can ensure the document.write() calls are targeted correctly.

To make a truly amazing and useful trick, we could make it into a **Bookmarklet**. This is a fragment of JavaScript code that is stored in your bookmarks file and invoked directly from the Favorites menu. You need to write these concisely, as there may be space limitations in what you can store. After all, you are actually doing code inside a URL.

Here is a useful Bookmarklet that pops a window and displays the contents of a form. This will work with forms that you have loaded from remote servers. The 'same-server' security rules seem not to be applied at this level:

```
// Provided for our enjoyment by Jon Stephens
// Note, the line breaks and space have been added to aid
// readability.  You should omit the line breaks when
// inserting this into the bookmark Any unnecessary spaces
// can also be removed to prevent URL buffer overruns.
// This also works fine when wrapped in a function
// declaration and called from a button on the form page.

javascript:
var output = "";
for(var i = 0; i < document.forms.length; i++)
{
    for(var j = 0; j < document.forms[i].elements.length; j++)
    {
        output += "Form "
                + i
                + " -- # "
                + j
                + " -- Type: "
                + document.forms[i].elements[j].type
                + "; "
                + document.forms[i].elements[j].name
                + ": "
                + document.forms[i].elements[j].value
                + "<br>"
    }
};
var newWin = window.open("","newWin","width=350,height=350");
with(newWin.document)
{
    open();
    write(output);
    close();
}
```

When condensed, the Bookmarklet looks like this:

```
javascript:var output="";for(var i=0;i<document.forms.length;i++){for(var
j=0;j<document.forms[i].elements.length;j++){output+="Form "+i+" -- # "+j+" --
Type:
"+document.forms[i].elements[j].type+";"+document.forms[i].elements[j].name+":
"+document.forms[i].elements[j].value+"<br>"}};var
newWin=window.open("","newWin","width=350,height=350");with(newWin.document){open(
);write(output);close();}
```

DOM Implementations in IE and Netscape

Currently, we should expect to find DOM Level 1, plus DOM Level 2 events implemented quite widely. However, the Mozilla browser is the only one attempting to support the DOM Level 2 event model and therefore it is available in Netscape 6. IE supports a bubbling event model that is similar to the one defined by DOM Level 2 but lacks the capture phase support. IE also lacks some of the supporting methods that DOM Level 2 specifies. Some of the other modules in DOM Level 2 are supported in new or expected versions of browsers, but the support may not be complete. Some modules are hardly supported at all, such as the Traversal and Views modules, for example. We look in more detail at the modularization strategy and how to detect the available modules in an implementation later on in this chapter.

The Driving Forces

Perhaps it is coincidence, but modules that have some active participation from Microsoft and Netscape seem to be better supported by way of implementations. However, they have both publicly stated that they do intend to support the standards fully and completely in due course, and they will prioritize resources where they are perceived to be most useful at present.

As is the case with all other areas of web content, the DOM is not implemented the same way in all browsers, and we still find that we need to design our pages carefully if we want them to work in all the available browsers. This is gradually improving, but there are still some minor ambiguities in the standards that allow the browser manufacturers freedom in interpreting them, though this is not the major issue.

Looking at things from a commercial perspective, it is more a matter of Microsoft having established a de facto standard by means of their dominant position. The capabilities of the IE browser are very advanced and capable.

Microsoft has a working event bubbling mechanism that is not standards compliant, but offers the developer a very powerful platform to create new content. There is very little advantage to Microsoft in adopting standards and dropping proprietary features that differentiate their browser from the rest of them. Certainly, it would not increase their market share to do that. Indeed, Microsoft would have to invest significant effort to become standards compliant in the sure knowledge that to do so would probably erode their market share in the long term. No company is going to do that willingly. Arguably, the standard is different, but possibly no more powerful than the existing support in IE (with respect to event handling at least).

If total standards compliance is your preference, the best chance you have is with Netscape Navigator. The Mozilla project on which it is based is attempting to honor the standards as accurately as possible. However, they are currently focussed on offering solid DOM Level 1 functionality with CSS and DOM Level 2 event capabilities added on top of that. The more esoteric DOM Level 2 support is some way off. DOM Level 3 is further in the future, possibly so far over the horizon as far as implementations are concerned that we may as well ignore it for now.

Evaluating the Implementations

In the chapter covering CSS, we use inspection techniques to examine the DOM models that the browsers construct. We have provided a more sophisticated and flexible inspection tool in this chapter so we can dig more deeply into the DOM structures. We can run this inspector in several different browsers to confirm that we are accessing the same component within the DOM.

We will restrict our testing to IE 5+ and Netscape 6. Some techniques will work in older browsers and we will look at them as special cases later on. The Opera browser at present does not offer a dynamic and script driven rendering capability although doubtless this is something they plan to add in due course. We need to deal with some basic principles, first and that's much easier if we choose some browsers that are close (although not exactly identical) in the way they parse the HTML into a DOM tree.

Even W3C Uses DOM & JavaScript

Interestingly, when we go and examine the W3C documents at http://www.w3.org/DOM/, we will find that the page there contains calls to JavaScript that construct a table of contents at the start of the page. It is an example of how to use JavaScript to access DOM Level 1 constructs within our HTML document.

The JavaScript code that does this is included from a file called demo.js in the same directory as the document. You can download and examine this page by adding demo.js to the URL for the document, and then telling the browser to fetch and then save the content into a file on your local hard disk.

The filename seems to change from time to time, so access the page at http://www.w3.org/DOM/ and then use the View|Source menu item in your browser to look for the SCRIPT tag that includes the JavaScript insert. Note its name and append it to the URL in the location bar of your browser and press return to load it. Depending on how your browser is configured to cope with different file types, it may display the URL as text or may ask if you want to save it.

What the Standard Says

The starting point should be the DOM Level 2 core standard document. During the introduction, a short fragment of HTML containing a table is presented.

Here it is with the necessary HTML and BODY tags and some minor changes added to help us view it in a web browser:

```
<HTML>
<HEAD>
    <TITLE>DOM Example</TITLE>
</HEAD>
<BODY>
    <TABLE BORDER='1'>
        <TBODY>
            <TR>
                <TD>Shady Grove</TD>
                <TD>Aeolian</TD>
            </TR>
            <TR>
                <TD>Over the River, Charlie</TD>
                <TD>Dorian</TD>
            </TR>
        </TBODY>
    </TABLE>
</BODY>
</HTML>
```

The DOM example document looks like this in both IE and Netscape 6:

| Shady Grove | Aeolian |
| Over the River, Charlie | Dorian |

The DOM parsing process looks for significant token character strings in the document source and uses them to delimit fragments of content that it can then digest and reflect into objects. In HTML and XML, the left caret (<) and right caret (>) characters are significant as are ampersand (&) and semi-colon (;) when they describe a character entity. In between the balanced pair of < and > characters, the parser looks for further significant characters such as space, equals (=), double-quote (") and single-quote (') to determine how to separate HTML tag attributes. Within certain quoted strings, other language parsing comes into play, though that may be deferred until run time. For example, onEvent handlers contain a fragment of JavaScript, but this is not evaluated until the event is triggered.

The hierarchical nature comes from the parser determining that text contained within the < and > characters is a tag and that there should be a corresponding closing tag that balances it symmetrically. Between those two corresponding tags, further content is considered to be a child or descendent and a tree structure is built using the parsed tag as a root node.

The standard says that the table fragment of HTML should create a DOM node tree like this. We have placed it in top context so you can see how it relates to the HTML, HEAD, and BODY tags that represent the document root:

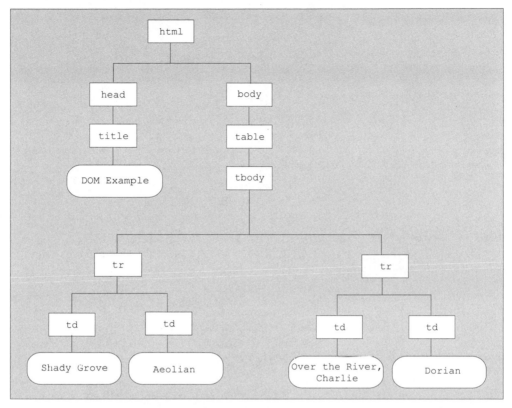

The rounded boxes in the diagram represent leaf nodes. These are nodes which are not extended any further. Generally, they will be some kind of data or textual content. The square boxes illustrate the branching structure which is a navigational path to reach the leaf nodes.

This is actually described in two parts of the DOM Recommendation. The DOM Core module is the foundation on which the rest of DOM is constructed. The second part we are interested in here is the DOM HTML module. DOM specifies that there is a generic Document object class and that there is a sub-class of that, providing a HTML specific document (HTMLDocument). Some functionlity is therefore generic, while some is available only in HTML documents.

The structuring of a DOM tree is described in the generic document structures. Nevertheless, the HTML module is useful because it provides a great deal of useful functionality that we can use to operate on objects that reflect the HTML tags. The separation of Core and HTML functionality into different modules of the DOM standard is not immediately obvious when we approach the document from JavaScript running in a browser. The browser provides us with a HTML centric view that obscures the DOM core capabilities and makes them look as if they are part of the DOM HTML functionality. It helps to make the standard more portable across markup languages. The generally useful navigation and structural definitions reside in the Core module. Only those aspects that pertain to parsed HTML need to be in the HTML module. We could just as easily define an SVG module to sit on top of the Core module to describe specialized aspects of a Scalable Vector Graphic image. We could illustrate this showing a Core Foundation module with parsed language support sitting on top like this:

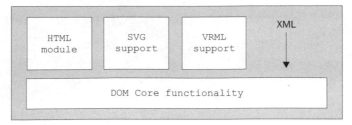

With IE 5, you can create and load an XML document with something like this:

```
var xmlDoc = new ActiveXObject('Microsoft.XMLDOM')
xmlDoc.load('whatever.xml');
```

Then you can operate on it with JavaScript using only the core DOM methods.

Finding the Target Object

Let's look again at what we expect to see if we load the example from the DOM standard. It should look like this in both IE and Netscape 6:

Shady Grove	Aeolian
Over the River, Charlie	Dorian

Using JavaScript, we can locate the table in the DOM and then examine it, but first we have to find it.

There is a shortcut to that using getElementById(), but we won't learn anything about the way that DOM is implemented in the browsers if we take the 'easy path' straight away. In any case, that short cut is useful for jumping to a well defined point in our document but it is only useful for wholesale access to objects if we are prepared to give all of them a unique ID, which is impractical. We should, therefore, study the DOM structure more closely so that we can use these technques once getElementById() has got us near to where we want to be.

We can use the inspector tools that were described a little while ago. To start with, make yourself a folder to work in and create a copy of all the inspector components.

Our starting point will be the document object at the top of the DOM tree structure – the root document node. This is accessible from JavaScript as the document property belonging to the global (window) object. It corresponds to the box labelled 'html' in the previous tree diagram. The rest of the DOM is constructed as a tree-like series of connected nodes with the root of the tree attached as a property to the document object.

Let's set up the inspector. Put this into the target.htm file and save it in the work folder:

```
<HTML>
<HEAD>
   <TITLE>DOM Example</TITLE>
</HEAD>
<BODY>
   <TABLE BORDER='1'>
      <TBODY>
         <TR>
            <TD>Shady Grove</TD>
            <TD>Aeolian</TD>
         </TR>
         <TR>
```

```
                <TD>Over the River, Charlie</TD>
                <TD>Dorian</TD>
            </TR>
        </TBODY>
    </TABLE>
</BODY>
</HTML>
```

Now we can define the inspection probe by putting this into the `inspector.htm` file:

```
<HTML>
<BODY>
<SCRIPT LANGUAGE='JavaScript'>
with(top)
{
    inspectObject(targetFrame.document);
}
</SCRIPT>
</BODY>
</HTML>
```

By running the inspector, then editing the `inspector.htm` file and rerunning the example again, we can manually walk through the DOM representation, examining objects as we go. We need to do that anyway to locate the top of the `TABLE` described in the DOM standard.

If we run the inspection now by loading the `harness.htm` file into our various browsers we can examine the properties of the `document` object.

Performing this inspection in Netscape 6 shows good correlation between the output and what you would expect based on the DOM standard. We see objects having class names, such as `HTMLCollection` or `HTMLElement` for instance.

With IE 5 on the Macintosh, the output is structurally right, but object class names are not correct. Here we see class names such as `HTML` and `ImageArray`.

With IE on Windows, the output reflects the massively larger number of properties, amongst which is something that resembles the DOM required properties. However, they may not have the correct names and object class names are difficult to distinguish on this platform as we only see the string `"[object]"`. The inspector tool goes some way to helping us with that, but it uses `nodeName` properties that indicate which HTML tag the object represents though that is not necessarily its true class name.

The differences between the browsers that might affect our DOM activities are summarized in this table. We show the actual values returned by the browsers, not the corrected ones that the inspector tool provides:

Property	Netscape 6 Value	IE 5 (Mac) Value	IE 5.5 (Win) Value
attributes	null	null	n/s
body	[object HTMLBodyElement]	[object BODY]	[object]
childNodes	[object NodeList]	[object ChildNodes]	[object]
document Element	[object HTMLHtmlElement]	[object HTML]	[object]
firstChild	[object HTMLHtmlElement]	[object HTML]	n/s
implement -ation	[object DOMImplementation]	[object Implementation]	n/s

Table continued on following page

333

Property	Netscape 6 Value	IE 5 (Mac) Value	IE 5.5 (Win) Value
lastChild	[object HTMLHtmlElement]	[object HTML]	n/s
next Sibling	null	null	n/s
nodeName	#document	#document	n/s
nodeType	9	9	n/s
node Value		null	n/s
owner Document	null	null	n/s
parent Node	null	null	n/s
previous Sibling	null	null	n/s
style Sheets	[object StyleSheetList]	[object styleSheets]	[object]

(n/s *means Not Supported*)

We'll now go back to our search for the table defined in the DOM standard. Each node in a DOM structure has a collection, referred to by the childNodes property. This is a list of objects, which are contained within the document node owning that childNodes collection. In theory, traversing the DOM from the top to the bottom is a process of walking the tree of nested childNodes collections. We can visit every node in the DOM with a tree-walking algorithm. At the end of each branch is a leaf node often implemented as a Text node object. Since Text nodes are considered atomic, they cannot have children, so even if the DOM implementation constructs a childNodes collection for them, it should be empty. Image objects are also leaf nodes.

If we need to modify the DOM structure, we can split the Text nodes to insert an additional HTMLElement or join them by removing HTML and normalizing the two adjacent Text node objects. We'll deal with that later on as it becomes quite complex – obviously, we can't do that to an image object.

Sitting at the top of the document tree, our document object has a childNodes collection that we want to inspect. If we modify the inspector.htm file, we can re-run the example to examine the collection of child nodes. Note that this time we invoke the collection inspector rather than the object inspector:

```
<HTML>
<BODY>
<SCRIPT LANGUAGE='JavaScript'>
with(top)
{
    var myTarget = targetFrame.document.childNodes;
    inspectCollection(myTarget);
}
</SCRIPT>
</BODY>
</HTML>
```

All of our three browsers reveal they have a collection with just one object in it that represents the HTML tag. The class names (or what we can detect as class names) are all different, but navigationally we are still safe.

Now modify the line that locates the childNodes collection so that it refers to the first item in the collection and call the object inspector instead of the collection inspector like this and re-run the example. Note that childNodes[0] is the same as using the firstChild property:

```
var myTarget = targetFrame.document.childNodes[0];
inspectObject(myTarget);
```

We start to reveal some interesting differences. On IE 5 (Mac), we see the firstChild and lastChild properties belonging to this child object. The firstChild points at a Text node. On the other two browsers – IE (Win) and Navigator, this property points at an object reflecting the HEAD tag.

We should see this more obviously if we examine the childNodes collection for the HTMLElement. Both browsers correctly refer to a BODY element with their lastChild property. When we have finished examining the DOM example, we can look a little more at this familial relationship and study firstChild, lastChild, parentNode, and sibling object references. To enumerate the childNodes for the HTML object, modify the inspector.htm file to use this call:

```
var myTarget = targetFrame.document.childNodes[0].childNodes;
inspectCollection(myTarget);
```

Running the inspector with IE 5 (Mac) presents this output (note the Content column shows the data property for Text node objects and the nodeName property for others that support it):

Object: [object ChildNodes]
Length: 3

Index	Object	Content
0	[object Text]	
1	[object HEAD]	HEAD
2	[object BODY]	BODY

Netscape 6 presents this output:

Object: [object NodeList]
Length: 3

Index	Object	Content
0	[object HTML HeadElement]	HEAD
1	[object Text]	
2	[object HTML BodyElement]	BODY

IE 5.5+ (Win) presents this output:

Object: [object]
Length: 2

Index	Object	Content
0	[object HEAD]	HEAD
1	[object BODY]	BODY

If we use the `inspectObject()` function to look at the `Text` node object (when it is present), we see that it is virtually identical, but the ordering of the nodes in the collection is different and presents us with some difficulties when writing portable code to access the `HEAD` element. There are ways round this with some of the DOM convenience methods that we'll look at later.

Fortunately, we are interested in the `BODY` element, and there is a shortcut to it using `document.body`. Already we can probably conclude that the `childNodes` collection is not the way to navigate document structures. Let's persevere for a little longer, because we need to locate the table object at least. We'll take a shortcut and use `document.body` for now. So, modify the `inspector.htm` file to locate and inspect a target object like this:

```
var myTarget = targetFrame.document.body;
inspectObject(myTarget);
```

The objects that represent the `BODY` element are quite different between browsers. IE has almost four times as many enumerable properties as Netscape. However, it looks like Netscape contains a sub-set of IE's properties and the properties defined by the DOM standard capabilities are similar enough to be useful.

We should expect to be quite close to our DOM table example now, so let's examine the `childNodes` collection belonging to the `BODY` element:

```
var myTarget = targetFrame.document.childNodes[0].childNodes;
inspectCollection(myTarget);
```

We get three different collections and, although they all have the `TABLE` object referred to, they also have different combinations of `Text` nodes wrapped around it:

- ❑ In IE 5.5+ (Win), we just see one `TABLE` object in the collection
- ❑ In Netscape 6, an empty `Text` node prefixes it
- ❑ In IE 5 (Mac) an empty trailing `Text` node is added

At least the trailing `Text` node doesn't cause us any grief, but the lack of a leading `Text` node offsets the index of the `table` object so that we can't reliably index the `childNodes` collection if we want portability.

IE provides a `children` collection that might help solve this. That collection is not portable to Netscape, but we may be able to manufacture a `children` object for that browser.

Modify your `inspector.htm` so it looks like this. The changes introduce a `for()` loop that manufactures a `children` array in those browsers that do not already have one:

```
<HTML>
<BODY>
<SCRIPT LANGUAGE='JavaScript'>
with(top)
{
    var myEnum;
    var myChildren = new Array();
    var myIndex = 0;

    var myTarget = targetFrame.document.body.childNodes;
```

```
    if(!targetFrame.document.body.children)
    {
        for(myEnum=0;myEnum<myTarget.length; myEnum++)
        {
            if(myTarget[myEnum].nodeType != 3)
            {
                myChildren[myIndex] = myTarget[myEnum];
                myIndex++;
            }
        }
    }
    else
    {
        myChildren = targetFrame.document.body.children;
    }

    inspectCollection(myChildren);
}
</SCRIPT>
</BODY>
</HTML>
```

The script code checks for the existence of a `children` collection and if there is not one, it manufacturers one by processing the `childNodes` collection and discarding any `Text` nodes it finds. It does depend on the `nodeType` value to detect the different kinds of DOM `Node` objects that it might encounter.

This kind of filtering capability is being standardized as part of the DOM Level 3 work, but its implementation in browsers is a long way off.

In the early days of JavaScript usage, before DOM standardization became widely used, DHTML scripting paid little attention to the text content between HTML elements, and was mainly concerned with altering the HTML appearance. With DOM, we now have a means of radically altering the content of the document. We shall look at some `Text` node modifications shortly.

So, we have a workable solution in filtering the `childNodes` collections and then navigating them. It isn't ideal, but we could generalize the filter and also take advantage of the `children` collection if it is available, for performance reasons.

All of this tree walking and traversal seems to be a lot of hard work. Maybe there is an easier way to do this?

Of course there is! Not that we have wasted our time so far. Its important to understand this DOM tree structure to manage the fine points of the navigation, but you can dive straight at some major 'landmark' objects using search functions that DOM specifies, and which the browsers support in a portable manner.

The most useful of these is probably `getElementById()`. This is a function that belongs to the root level document object, and as long as the ID values are unique within the document (as specified by HTML 4.01), then this is a very useful function indeed.

If we modify the `TABLE` tag so it looks like this:

```
<TABLE BORDER='1' ID='fred'>
```

Then we can locate it with this line of script:

```
var myTable = document.getElementById("fred");
```

Let's just apply that to the inspector. Add the `ID` value to the `TABLE` tag in the `target.htm` file.

Then modify the code inside the `inspector.htm` file so it looks like this:

```
var myTarget = targetFrame.document.getElementById("fred");
inspectObject(myTarget);
```

When we run the inspector, we see that an object representing the root of the table hierarchy is presented.

Traversing the DOM Representation of a Table

So, now we can study the internals of a table. This also can be navigated using the `childNodes` collection, but suffers from the same issues regarding `Text` nodes. HTML rules dictate that we should not place any text inside a `TABLE` block unless it is inside `TD` or `TH` blocks.

As a basis for our table examination, we need to create a reference to it and store that in a variable. This will accomplish what we need (in the context of our inspector tool):

```
var myTable = targetFrame.document.getElementById("fred");
```

For the sake of curiosity, we can examine the `childNodes` that belong to the `TABLE` object like this:

```
inspectCollection(myTable.childNodes);
```

We can see the difference immediately. IE has just one object in the collection. It represents the `TBODY` tag.

Netscape includes some whitespace `Text` node objects:

Index	Object	Content
0	[object Text]	
1	[object HTMLTableSectionElement]	TBODY
2	[object Text]	

Let's step back one level and look at the object representing the `TABLE`. Modify the code inside `inspector.htm` so it looks like this:

```
var myTable = targetFrame.document.getElementById("fred");
inspectObject(myTable);
```

Running this example, reveals that the `rows` collection is available on all browsers. We can examine that collection like this:

```
inspectCollection(myTable.rows);
```

We get an object representing each `TR` tag in the table. If we examine those two `row` objects, we find that each has a `cells` property. So we can examine a single `cell` and see if there is a leaf node at the end by looking at its `childNodes` collection we would use:

```
inspectObject(myTable.rows[0].cells[0].childNodes[0]);
```

The inspector tool already checks the `data` property of a `Text` node, we now see the text "Shady Grove", which comes from the original HTML document we started with.

DOM Traversal – Basic Conclusions

We have traversed a document and found the object tree we want. We have also discovered that document trees and the internal structure of tables are stored differently in IE and Netscape. If we remove all the whitespace from the DOM representation, we can access the DOM in a portable manner. Fortunately, we also find that DOM and the HTML properties provide helpful ways to work around that.

Tables can be very usefully accessed using row and column index values like this:

```
myTable.rows[myRow].cells[myColumn];
```

This is constrained by the fact that we may need to replace `myTable` with `myTBody` or `myTHead` if there is more than one in the table. We also find that we can easily access the contents of a cell with DOM traversal like this:

```
myTable.rows[myRow].cells[myColumn].childNodes;
```

This is somewhat better than the `innerHTML` property that yields a textual representation of the cell contents with no navigable structure.

There are many ways to traverse the DOM tree. In the examples here, we have used the `childNodes` approach in most cases. We can shortcut some of that by searching for tag names, `ID` values, or by using the convenience properties such as the `document.body and myTable.rows` value. The important rule is to refer back to the DOM standards to ensure the technique you are using is robust and portable, and to test it on your target browser and platform to ensure portability.

Modifying the Tree

The DOM Recommendation specifies some utility methods for modifying the familial relationships. We can experiment with these to see if they work consistently enough across the browser implementations. Before we do that, lets just see what kind of baseline we are starting from. We'll create a simple single layer tree and see what it looks like in several different browsers on different platforms.

The Starting Line

We'll base all our operations on the same starting point and use the inspector tool again, so we can analyze the structures if we want to. Below is a simple fragment of HTML containing some text separated by `hr` tags. Put this into the file called `target.htm`:

```
<HTML>
<BODY>
   One
   <hr></hr>
   Two
   <hr></hr>
   Three
   <hr></hr>
   Four
   <br></br>
</BODY>
</HTML>
```

Here is the inspection driver code that lists the `childNodes` belonging to the body of the document in the `target.htm` file. Put this in the `inspection.htm` file:

```
<HTML>
<BODY>
<SCRIPT LANGUAGE="JavaScript">
with(top)
{
    var myTarget = targetFrame.document.body;
    inspectCollection(myTarget.childNodes);
}
</SCRIPT>
</BODY>
</HTML>
```

Here is an illustration of what we might hope for given the following assumptions:

❑   Empty whitespace does not create a Text node (although we suspect it will sometimes)

❑   Closing br tags with /br should not cause any problems

❑   Closing hr tags with /hr should not cause any problems

❑   Browsers behave consistently

❑   XHTML is supported

We expect a DOM tree to be created like this:

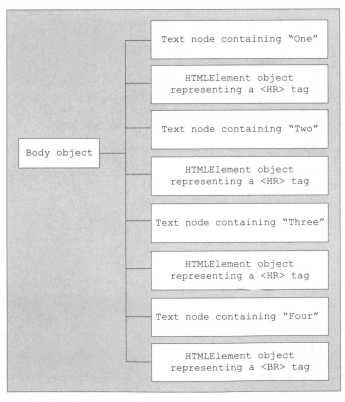

On a Macintosh running IE 5, the inspector generates this output – listing the items in the document.body.childNodes collection:

Index	Description
0	A Text node containing "One".
1	An HR object based on the hr tag.
2	A Text node containing "Two".
3	An HR object based on the hr tag.
4	A Text node containing "Three".
5	An HR object based on the hr tag.
6	A Text node containing "Four".
7	A BR object based on the br tag.
8	A BR object based on the /br tag.
9	A Text node containing nothing. This is always present.

Note that items 7 and 8 are both [object BR] items. The item 8 is actually a closing /br tag in the document. IE seems to treat this as a plain br tag, and obviously doesn't honor the strict XHTML rules correctly. Item 0 is a leading Text node. An empty trailing Text node is placed at item 9.

Oddly enough, Netscape Navigator does exactly the same thing with empty Text nodes, and treats the /br tag in the same way although the object class names are the correct DOM specified class names. The only difference is that Netscape 6 always places the null Text node object at the end, while IE only puts it there if there is a /br tag. Here is the Netscape 6 output:

Index	Description
0	A Text node containing "One".
1	An HTMLHRElement object based on the hr tag.
2	A Text node containing "Two".
3	An HTMLHRElement object based on the hr tag.
4	A Text node containing "Three".
5	An HTMLHRElement object based on the hr tag.
6	A Text node containing "Four".
7	An HTMLBRElement object based on the br tag.
8	An HTMLBRElement object based on the /br tag.
9	A Text node containing nothing. This is present only when the /br tag is present otherwise it's not added to the collection.

On IE 5.5 under Windows, we get a quite different picture. This table summarizes the childNodes collection on that platform:

Index	Description
0	A Text node containing "One".
1	An HR object based on the hr tag.
2	A /HR object based on the /hr tag.
3	A Text node containing "Two".
4	An HR object based on the hr tag.
5	A /HR object based on the /hr tag.
6	A Text node containing "Three".
7	An HR object based on the hr tag.
8	A /HR object based on the /hr tag.
9	A Text node containing "Four".
10	A BR object based on the br tag.
11	A BR object based on the /br tag. Yes, there is no leading slash symbol on the tagName value for the object.

Note the even worse situation where the /hr tags are creating objects in the DOM too. Additionally, there is no trailing Text node with null content as there is on the Macintosh platform.

This craziness makes a total nonsense of trying to use the DOM childNodes property for anything meaningful. Every time you acquire a childNodes collection, you are going to need to filter it to create a smaller set of objects that are a sub-set of what's available on all platforms. Of course, that's possible, but it is rather cumbersome. With this XHTML closure tag behavior, it's no longer even safe to assume that we can just remove the Text nodes from the childNodes collection. Now we must remove Element nodes whose class name starts with a slash character.

It is also very perverse that IE and Netscape on the Macintosh platform should be so near to one another in behavior, while IE across the Macintosh and Windows platforms is so radically different in behavior.

These differences between browsers also calls into question the sense of adopting strict XHTML closing tags for browsers that don't anticipate seeing closures on what they normally expect to be unary tags. This is especially the case on those occasions where we would expect to traverse a DOM representation of the document.

Branching Out and Pruning Down

Okay, so we have just established beyond reasonable doubt that the DOM hierarchy our document is parsed into is somewhat problematic and less than perfect when we try to move our code from browser to browser. While that is bad news for us, it is helpful to know the limitations of something like that.

Even so, we can still modify the tree structure and move nodes around if we are careful with how we do it. Let's try to add a new node to the document. We need to be able to create our new node so we shall need a constructor. Luckily, DOM specifies that the necessary construction functions for manufacturing new nodes be provided by the document object in a compliant implementation. So to create a new Text node, we call:

```
document. createTextNode("Data")
```

Adding a Text Node

We can now put that to work with a simple example that adds a new `Text` node every time the form button is clicked. Here's the example code:

```
<!-- appendToDOM.htm -->
<HTML>
<HEAD>
    <SCRIPT LANGUAGE="JavaScript">
        function appendToDOM()
        {
            // Now manufacture a new node
            var myNewNode = document.createTextNode("New Text Node. ");

            // Now append the child object
            document.body.appendChild(myNewNode);
        }
    </SCRIPT>
</HEAD>
<BODY>
    One
    <HR></HR>
    Two
    <HR></HR>
    Three
    <HR></HR>
    Four
    <BR></BR>
    <FORM NAME="myForm">
        <INPUT TYPE="Button" VALUE="Append to DOM"
        onClick="appendToDOM();"></INPUT>
    </FORM>
</BODY>
</HTML>
```

Inserting a Text Node

We'll try something a little more difficult now. We'll create a new `Text` node and add it to the DOM tree, adjacent to one of the existing `Text` nodes. That way we can search for the `Text` node we want by inspecting the `data` property, and while we shall need to scan the whole `childNodes` collection to find it, the code should work on all the browsers that support the DOM editing we need (IE 5 and Netscape 6):

```
<!-- BetterappendToDOM.htm -->
<HTML>
<HEAD>
    <SCRIPT LANGUAGE="JavaScript">
        function appendToDOM()
        {
            var myCollection = document.body.childNodes;
            var myTargetNode;
            var myNewNode;

            // Locate the target node in a portable way
            for(var myEnum=0; myEnum<myCollection.length; myEnum++)
            {
                if(myCollection.item(myEnum).nodeType == 3)
                {
                    if(myCollection.item(myEnum).data.indexOf("Two") != -1)
                    {
                        myTargetNode = myCollection.item(myEnum);
                break;
                    }
```

```
            }
        }

        // Now manufacture a new node
        myNewNode = document.createTextNode("New Text Node.");

        // Now insert the child object just in front of the target
        document.body.insertBefore(myNewNode, myTargetNode);
    }
    </SCRIPT>
</HEAD>
<BODY>
    One
    <HR></HR>
    Two
    <HR></HR>
    Three
    <HR></HR>
    Four
    <BR></BR>
    <FORM NAME='myForm'>
        <INPUT TYPE='Button' VALUE='Insert into DOM'
        onClick='appendToDOM();'></INPUT>
    </FORM>
</BODY>
</HTML>
```

When we run this example, the text is inserted just in front of the word "Two" on the screen. However, IE keeps the text on the same line, while Netscape maintains a line break at the front of the target Text node. You may need to eliminate that line break to get the portable effect you want. This suggests a bug somewhere in the page renderer because there is no HTML markup creating those line breaks, so they shouldn't be there.

Moving a Text Node

The appendChild() method can also be used to move an item. Like this:

```
<!-- FurtherAppendToDOM.htm -->
<HTML>
<HEAD>
    <SCRIPT LANGUAGE="JavaScript">
        function appendToDOM()
        {
            var myCollection = document.body.childNodes;
            var myTargetNode;

            // Locate the target node in a portable way
            for(var myEnum=0; myEnum<myCollection.length; myEnum++)
            {
                if(myCollection.item(myEnum).nodeType == 3)
                {
                    if(myCollection.item(myEnum).data.indexOf("Two") != -1)
                    {
                        myTargetNode = myCollection.item(myEnum);
                        break;
                    }
                }
            }

        // Now append the target node to the end of the document
        // Moving it from its previous location
        document.body.appendChild(myTargetNode);
```

```
        }
      </SCRIPT>
   </HEAD>
   <BODY>
      One
      <HR></HR>
      Two
      <HR></HR>
      Three
      <HR></HR>
      Four
      <BR></BR>
      <FORM NAME='myForm'>
         <INPUT TYPE='Button' VALUE='Append/move within DOM'
         onClick='appendToDOM();'></INPUT>
      </FORM>
   </BODY>
   </HTML>
```

Here is the screen before clicking the button:

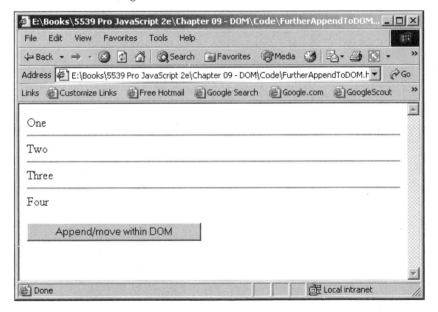

Here it is afterwards:

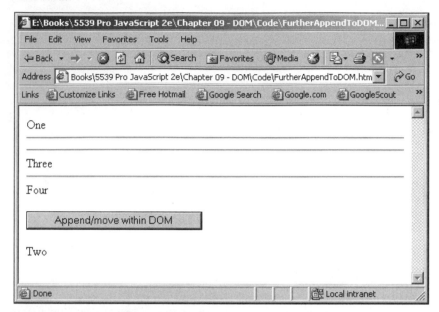

The result is that the text "Two" has relocated to the bottom of the page.

Removing a Node

We can just remove a child like this:

```
myOldObject = document.body.removeChild(document.body.childNodes[2]);
```

Beware that when we have removed a node, the childNodes collection will be shuffled to remove the empty slot. Subsequent index positions may have altered so you might want to create variables that refer to the specific objects before altering the collection. All of this is complicated because if you are operating on the childNodes collection it's going to look different on each browser and platform as we discovered earlier.

Modifying the document structure will also trigger Document Mutation Events if the DOM Events module is fully supported. We shall look at DOM events in more detail later on. However, a mutation event signifies that the document content has been altered. If this is important, you can add an event handler to intercept this action and take some measures if necessary.

When you have two adjacent Text nodes, the DOM tree should be normalized.

Normalizing Text Nodes

Performing any Text node splitting, appending, insertion, moving or deletion can lead to us having two adjacent Text nodes with no intervening HTMLElement node. This is not structurally wrong, but if the document had been saved and then loaded, those two Text nodes would have become one. We can accomplish this by applying the normalize() method call to the parent object.

Let's run a short experiment to see Text node normalization in action. This fragment of HTML will create an appropriate node structure using HR tags and Text nodes so put this into the target2.htm file:

```
<HTML>
<BODY>
   One
   <hr></hr>
   Two
   <hr></hr>
   Three
   <hr></hr>
   Four
   <br></br>
</BODY>
</HTML>
```

The inspection script to display this should be put into the `inspector2.htm` file, which should look like this:

```
<HTML>
<BODY>
<SCRIPT LANGUAGE="JavaScript">
   with(top)
   {
      var myObject = targetFrame.document.body.childNodes;
      inspectCollection(myObject);
   }
</SCRIPT>
</BODY>
</HTML>
```

Earlier on, we discovered that we got different structures on the various browsers. Broadly, they are similar enough that our example will still work. Setting aside the differences between browsers, the `childNodes` collection contains something similar to this:

Index	Description
0	A Text node containing "One"
1	A HR object based on the hr tag
2	A Text node containing "Two"
3	A HR object based on the hr tag
4	A Text node containing "Three"
5	A HR object based on the hr tag
6	A Text node containing "Four"
7	A BR object based on the br tag

We will now alter the collection so that we only have the Text nodes left and then normalize whatever is left. We will enumerate through the `childNodes` collection and remove any nodes that are not type 3 (Text nodes). Bear in mind that we need to do this carefully, as we are going to alter the collection we are enumerating. By enumerating from the highest index and moving towards the beginning of the collection, we can avoid problems with nodes slipping under the index pointer. The `childNodes` collection looks like this after stripping out all but the Text nodes:

Index	Description
0	A Text node containing "One".
1	A Text node containing "Two".
2	A Text node containing "Three".
3	A Text node containing "Four".

After removing the unwanted nodes, we call the normalize() method on the owner node that the childNodes array belongs to. After that stage the childNodes collection should look like this:

Index	Description
0	A Text node containing "One Two Three Four".

Our nodal structure is now reduced to a single Text node object.

We'll implement code to demonstrate the normalization in the inspector.htm script, which should be changed so it looks like this. Note that we call the inspector several times to take a snapshot of the childNodes collection. Note that not all versions of IE support the normalize() method, and some will throw an error. Testing for the presence of the normalize property on the target object avoids this problem, but does not allow the normalization to take place:

```
<!-- inspector-normalize.htm -->
<HTML>
<BODY>
   <SCRIPT LANGUAGE='JavaScript'>
      with(top)
      {
         var myObject = targetFrame.document.body;

         // Snapshot at start
         inspectFrame.document.write("<h2>Before deleting</h2>");
         inspectCollection(myObject.childNodes);

         // Locate and remove non text nodes
         for(var myEnum=myObject.childNodes.length-1; myEnum>-1; myEnum--)
         {
            if(myObject.childNodes.item(myEnum).nodeType != 3)
            {
               myObject.removeChild(myObject.childNodes.item(myEnum));
            }
         }

         // Snapshot after deleting nodes
         inspectFrame.document.write("<h2>After deleting</h2>");
         inspectCollection(myObject.childNodes);

         // Normalize the childNodes
         if (myObject.normalize)
         {
            myObject.normalize();

            // Snapshot after normalizing nodes
            inspectFrame.document.write("<h2>After normalizing</h2>");
```

```
                 inspectCollection(myObject.childNodes);
         }
     }
   </SCRIPT>
 </BODY>
 </HTML>
```

There are several important caveats to this.

The example works as expected in IE 5 on Macintosh and Netscape 6. On IE 5.5 for Windows, the `normalize()` method is not supported and the script throws an error at that point if you don't test for its availability before calling it. However, the node removal has taken place and the second snapshot inspection shows that there are only four `Text` nodes remaining.

Some versions of IE have been reported to do the normalization automatically on deletion of the `hr` nodes and do not need the `normalize()` method to be called explicitly. This particular area of behavior is likely to change, and so you should check whether it is available in your target browser or not. This behavior may be observed in version 6 or later IE browsers.

Safety Measures

You may want to enclose the modifications to your DOM tree based on the `childNodes` property on a test for the existence of some child nodes. You can use a test such as this one (shown in pseudo code):

```
if(document.body.hasChildNodes())
{
    ... some code operating on the childNodes collection ...
}
```

This returns the value true if the `Node` has any child nodes of its own. This is equivalent to checking the length of the `childNodes` collection for a zero value. The value `false` is returned if there are no children.

Namespace Issues

Reading the DOM Level 2 Core standard document (section 1.1.8 XML Namespaces) suggests that we must be aware of namespaces when normalizing `Text` nodes. However, from a HTML standpoint this is not likely to worry us. Mostly because its not very likely that we will have created objects belonging to different namespaces from a single HTML document. This whole area is more for the benefit of XML application developers.

However, the issue is that if you do have nodes belonging to different namespaces, you cannot normalize them into a single node. So you may have a document that contains adjacent `Text` nodes even after normalization.

This may lead to problems with load and save activities but since they are part of DOM Level 3, they won't affect us for some time either.

The general warning is to not mix calls to the DOM Level 1 `create...()` methods and the DOM Level 2 `create...NS()` methods within a single application.

Splitting Text Nodes

The complementary operation to joining `Text` node objects together is dividing them at a specified location so that a new `HTMLElement` or other `Text` node can be inserted.

Here is an example that moves a HR element into the middle of a `Text` node. Start with this fragment of HTML that draws a horizontal line, some text, and a BR tag at the end:

```
<HTML>
<BODY>
   <HR></HR>
   One Two
```

```
      <BR></BR>
   </BODY>
   </HTML>
```

The interesting portion of the node map is:

```
[object HR]
[object Text]
[object BR]
```

Now we can use the `splitText()` method to break the text into two fragments, and the `insertBeforeObject()` method to relocate the HR object between them like this:

```
<!-- splitText.htm -->
<HTML>
<HEAD>
<SCRIPT LANGUAGE="JavaScript">
function splitter()
{
    var myTextNode;
    var myObject = document.body.childNodes;

    // Locate target HR node
    var myHRNode = document.getElementById("myHR");

    var aRegExp = /One\wTwo/;
    // Locate target text node
    for(var myEnum=0; myEnum<myObject.length; myEnum++)
    {
        if(myObject[myEnum].nodeType == 3)
        {
            if(myObject[myEnum].length > 6)
            {
                myTextNode = myObject[myEnum];
            }
        }
    }


    // Split the text node and get a pointer to the second half
    var myTarget = myTextNode.splitText(4);

    // Insert the HR before the second half
    document.body.insertBefore(myHRNode, myTarget);
}
</SCRIPT>
</HEAD>
<BODY onLoad="splitter()"><HR ID="myHR"></HR>One Two<BR></BR></BODY>
</HTML>
```

The `splitText()` method returns a pointer to the second half of the text so you can `insertBeforeObject()` using that as a reference point. The enumeration loop is necessary to locate the Text node that we want. Maybe there are other ways to locate your desired Text node, but in this case, we know it is the only one that has a `length` value greater than 6, because of the text string that must be maintained in its `data` property.

This works in all the required browsers we are basing our tests on. Note that the body element is condensed, and does not have the carriage returns and indents that we usually use to make our code more readable. This is because Netscape 6 includes these when it is looking for Text nodes, so we have removed them because the page will not display correctly if it comes across a section of whitespace longer than six characters.

Leading and Trailing Whitespace

Arbitrary whitespace is added to the data value of a Text node. This is done inconsistently across the different browsers, so you need to process the value yielded by the data property to take this into account. For example, a Text node that you think should contain "ABC" may actually contain " ABC " or may even have new-line characters embedded in it. Placing the property extraction in an escape() function and passing that to an alert() box illustrates this:

```
alert(escape(myTextNode.data));
```

Playing with Attributes

We have done a lot of work up to now with the nodal structure of the document. Now we shall look at the attribute mechanisms. Note that this mode of access is primarily for XML oriented projects, although it works for HTML at the expense of a little more work on the script. In general however, HTML oriented JavaScript developers will just access the properties directly as members of the Element object rather than traverse its attributes collection.

Examining the Attributes

Let's create a small fragment of HTML and try examining the results with some JavaScript. Back up a working copy of the inspector tool and put this into the target.htm file:

```
<HTML>
<BODY>
   <IMG ID='fred' SRC='fred.gif' ALT='Alternative Text'
        BORDER='10' HEIGHT='50' WIDTH='50' HSPACE='10'
        VSPACE='10'></IMG>
   <BR></BR>
</BODY>
</HTML>
```

Note that we have created an IMG tag with eight attributes. Now put this into the inspector.htm file:

```
<HTML>
<BODY>
<SCRIPT LANGUAGE="JavaScript">
with(top)
{
   var myImage = targetFrame.document.getElementById("fred");
   inspectAttributes(myImage.attributes);
}
</SCRIPT>
</BODY>
</HTML>
```

When we run this example in Netscape 6, it yields a short list of attributes. Note that only the eight cited in the IMG tag are enumerated:

351

Index	Attribute	Value
0	id	fred
1	src	fred.gif
2	alt	Alternative Text
3	border	10
4	height	50
5	width	50
6	hspace	10
7	vspace	10

When we run the same script on IE, we do see these items listed, but we also see a lot of others. IE enumerates its `attributes` collection as if every conceivable image attribute had been defined, even though some have a `null` value. This means that positional access to `Attribute` nodes in these collections is not viable and an associative mechanism of some kind needs to be used.

For some browsers, you may have to build that associative mechanism yourself with an enumeration loop. We show how to do that shortly, when we modify the `alt` text on an image via the DOM `Attribute` node collection.

Modifying Attribute Values - alt text

If we can locate the correct `Attribute` node for a property, we can use DOM techniques to alter it. Most of these values are accessible through named properties of the owner object and there is usually no need to resort to this kind of access. However, knowing it is available may solve a problem for you if there is no other way to access the attribute value:

```
<HTML>
<HEAD>
<SCRIPT LANGUAGE="JavaScript">
function changeAltText()
{
    var myImage   = document.getElementById("fred");

    var myAlt = myImage.attributes.getNamedItem("alt");

    myAlt.nodeValue = "New alt text value.";
}

function mouseOver()
{
    var myImage   = document.getElementById("fred");

    window.status = myImage.alt;
}

</SCRIPT>
</HEAD>
<BODY>
    <IMG ID='fred' SRC='fred.gif' ALT='Alternative Text'
        BORDER='10' HEIGHT='50' WIDTH='50' HSPACE='10'
        VSPACE='10' onMouseOver="mouseOver()"
        onMouseOut="window.status=''"></IMG>
```

```
        <BR></BR>
        <FORM NAME='myForm'>
            <INPUT TYPE='Button' VALUE='Change Alt Text'
            onClick="changeAltText();"></INPUT>
        </FORM>
    </BODY>
</HTML>
```

When you run this example in Netscape 6, rolling the mouse over the image displays the alt text in the window status message area. Rolling off the image clears the status area back to its default value.

After clicking on the form button, you should see a different alt text when you roll over the image. The example demonstrates access to the alt text using DOM to set it and HTML access via a simple property in the rollover handler.

The example works as it is in IE 5 on the Macintosh, but throws an error in IE 5.5 on Windows, because the getNamedItem() method is not supported. Here is an alternative version that scans the attributes collection with a for() loop to emulate the getNamedItem() method. This is what we referred to a little while ago as a "Roll your own associative access mechanism". This slightly more complicated version also works on IE 5.5 in Windows without throwing an error:

```
<HTML>
<HEAD>
    <SCRIPT LANGUAGE="JavaScript">
        function scanForNamedItem(aCollection, aName)
        {
            for(var myEnum=0; myEnum<aCollection.length; myEnum++)
            {
                if(aCollection[myEnum].nodeName == aName)
                {
                    return aCollection[myEnum];
                }
            }
            return(null);
        }

        function changeAltText()
        {
            var myAlt;
            var myImage   = document.getElementById("fred");

            if(!myImage.attributes.getNamedItem)
            {
                myAlt = scanForNamedItem(myImage.attributes, "alt");
            }
            else
            {
                myAlt = myImage.attributes.getNamedItem("alt");
            }

            myAlt.nodeValue = "New alt text value.";
        }

        function mouseOver()
        {
            var myImage   = document.getElementById("fred");
            window.status = myImage.alt;
        }
    </SCRIPT>
</HEAD>
<BODY>
```

```
<IMG ID="fred" SRC='fred.gif' ALT='Alternative Text'
    BORDER='10' HEIGHT='50' WIDTH='50' HSPACE='10'
    VSPACE='10' onMouseOver="mouseOver()" onMouseOut="window.status=''"></IMG>
<BR></BR>
<FORM NAME='myForm'>
<INPUT TYPE='Button' VALUE="Change Alt Text" onClick="changeAltText();"></INPUT>
</FORM>
</BODY>
</HTML>
```

The getNamedItem() method is supported in IE 6, so you will be able to use the simpler version on that browser.

Modifying Attribute Values – Image Size

Now we can try to modify another attribute using the DOM attribute interface. This will not alter the HTML, but it should change the appearance on screen. Here is a short script that locates the attribute's objects for image size and modifies them. It is based on the portable example for modifying the alt text. This time we are going to try to change the height and width of the image on screen:

```
<HTML>
<HEAD>
    <SCRIPT LANGUAGE="JavaScript">
        function scanForNamedItem(aCollection, aName)
        {
            for(var myEnum=0; myEnum<aCollection.length; myEnum++)
            {
                if(aCollection[myEnum].nodeName == aName)
                {
                    return aCollection[myEnum];
                }
            }
            return(null);
        }

        function changeSize()
        {
            var myHeight;
            var myWidth;
            var myImage   = document.getElementById("fred");

            if(!myImage.attributes.getNamedItem)
            {
                myHeight = scanForNamedItem(myImage.attributes, "height");
                myWidth  = scanForNamedItem(myImage.attributes, "width");
            }
            else
            {
                myHeight = myImage.attributes.getNamedItem("height");
                myWidth  = myImage.attributes.getNamedItem("width");
            }

            myHeight.nodeValue =  myWidth.nodeValue  = 200;
        }
    </SCRIPT>
</HEAD>
<BODY>
    <IMG ID='fred' SRC='fred.gif' ALT='Alternative Text'
      BORDER='10' HEIGHT='50' WIDTH='50' HSPACE='10'
      VSPACE='10'></IMG>
    <BR></BR>
    <FORM NAME='myForm'>
```

```
            <INPUT TYPE='Button' VALUE='Change Alt Text'
            onClick='changeSize();'></INPUT>
      </FORM>
   </BODY>
   </HTML>
```

That works on all our target browsers – IE 5 (Mac), IE 5.5 (Win) and Netscape 6.

HTMLElement objects

If we inspect the object created by an IMG tag, we find that there are just 43 properties supported by Netscape. A few of those are redundant and some are not supported anywhere else.

The property list for the image object is almost twice as long on IE 5 for the Mac, while there are more than 150 in the latest version of IE on Windows. Can this many properties really be that necessary? If you do choose to take advantage of the more than 100 additional Microsoft proprietary properties, you are just locking your web site into IE.

As the node represents a HTMLElement, its nodeValue cannot hold a simple primitive data type. Ideally, we might want to get at the binary data for the image, but that isn't possible using standard JavaScript for security reasons. Note that the nodeType is set to 1, which indicates an Element object.

There are limits to what we can change here, and if we wanted to replace the image with another kind of HTMLElement, we ought to be operating on the childNodes collection belonging to its parent object. This is because you cannot change the class of an object. So to replace an img object with an hr object, you must delete one and create a new one to replace it.

Here is an example where we create a new hr object and replace an existing image object in the document with an object we have totally manufactured inside the scripting environment. This works in all the browsers we are interested in for test purposes – IE 5 (Mac), IE 5.5 (Win), and Netscape 6:

```
<HTML>
<HEAD>
   <SCRIPT LANGUAGE="JavaScript">
   function switchObject()
   {
      var myImage   = document.getElementById("fred");

      // Create a new Element object
      var myNewNode = document.createElement("HR");


      // Now append the child object
      var myOldImage = document.body.replaceChild(myNewNode, myImage);
   }
   </SCRIPT>
</HEAD>
<BODY>
   <IMG ID="fred" SRC='fred.gif' ALT='Alternative Text'
      BORDER='10' HEIGHT='50' WIDTH='50' HSPACE='10'
      VSPACE='10'></IMG>
   <BR></BR>
   <FORM NAME='myForm'>
      <INPUT TYPE='Button' VALUE='Switch object'
      onClick='switchObject();'></INPUT>
   </FORM>
</BODY>
</HTML>
```

When you click on the button, the `document.createElement()` method is called and the substitution is made with the `replaceChild()` method.

What Happens to Character Entities in Text Nodes?

In HTML documents, certain characters need to be encoded so that they do not confuse the HTML parser. Such escape mechanisms are commonplace in programming and markup languages, since we need to reserve certain characters to indicate syntactic rules. If we then want to include those characters, then we have to represent them in some way that does not break those syntactic rules. It's a common problem.

The parsing process can all become very confusing, because in a document, at least three (and maybe four) different parsers are working co-operatively on the content:

❑ HTML is processing everything in the document but delegating the content inside some tags to the other two parsers.

❑ JavaScript or JScript is parsing everything inside the SCRIPT tags unless the LANGUAGE="" tag attribute calls in a further parser such as VBScript.

❑ VBScript can be invoked if the browser and platform support it for the content inside SCRIPT tags where the LANGUAGE="VBScript" attribute is defined.

❑ CSS parsing takes place on the content inside the STYLE tags if the TYPE="text/css" tag attribute is present. Other styling parsers are potentially available but in practice this is the main one.

In HTML, the less than and greater than symbols (< and >) are meaningful, and we cannot simply place them into the text flow. They are commonly escaped using a character entity. However, these character entities are introduced themselves by a meaningful character, the ampersand (&), which should also be escaped since it is the leading symbol of a character entity definition. Some parsers may be smart enough to check the second character of an entity but it is better to be safe than sorry. Our minimum set of character entities are the following three, though there are many more :

❑ < – (<)

❑ > – (>)

❑ & – (&)

Note that the character entities in the HTML portion of the document (those parts which are outside of the SCRIPT tags) are trailed by a semi-colon (;), but because this is not a control-sequence-introducer character, it can safely be used in text as it stands.

So, what does this look like from a JavaScript point of view? Let's create a small document and inspect its content. We shall use the JavaScript `alert()` function to look at the result. If we had used `document.write()`, the HTML parser would see the character entity and render it as an ampersand character. Without the `alert()` function, we won't be able to tell whether we get back "&" or just "&" from the `innerHTML` property:

```
<HTML>
<BODY>
   <P ID='myPara'>Here is an ampersand (&amp;) character.</P>
   <HR></HR>
   <SCRIPT LANGUAGE='JavaScript'>
      var myDOMPara = document.getElementById("myPara");
      alert(myDOMPara.innerHTML);
   </SCRIPT>
</BODY>
</HTML>
```

In the first example, we use the `innerHTML` property to extract the HTML. This yields the source HTML with the escape character sequence intact. We actually get this back in the alert box:

Here is an ampersand (&) character

In IE, we can use the `innerText` property like this:

```
alert(myDOMPara.innerText);
```

We then get this back:

Here is an ampersand (&) character

Now we need to traverse the DOM a little further to locate the leaf node containing the text and look at its `data` property. Like this:

```
alert(myDOMPara.childNodes[0].data);
```

In both IE 6 and Netscape 6, this yields the result:

Here is an ampersand (&) character

There are also two properties, reflecting the value in IE and Netscape 6. They are `data` and `nodeValue`. Both return the same thing, so they are equivalent to the `innerText` mechanism in IE when we use them on Netscape 6.

So, if it is important to preserve character entities, examine the `innerHTML` property of the parent object, or extract the `nodeValue` of the leaf node containing the text if you want the character entity rendered down. The difference is subtle, but important, because the raw character entity is the input data to the HTML parser while the rendered-down ampersand character is the output of the HTML parser.

When storing values back into the `Text` node, you need to store the rendered version of the character as it would appear at the HTML parser output, but the character entity should be used when storing into the `innerHTML` property of its parent. The DOM should be immediately updated and so writing a change into `innerHTML` should be reflected in the leaf node immediately.

Modularization of the DOM

With DOM Level 1, there is practically no modularization of the standard. Significant complexity was added at DOM Level 2 to make it necessary to group the functionality into manageable sections. Further modules are being worked on at Level 3. If we refer back to the first diagram in this chapter, it shows the gradual migration of modules. Those marked in gray are those that some support is offered for in contemporary browsers:

DOM Modules

The DOM Level 1 functionality has evolved principally into the **DOM Core** and **HTML** modules. This is similar to Core JavaScript in the sense that it provides basic foundational organization, and the rest of the standard is built upon it. With the DOM Core module, we can build an object representation of any document but it has no real sense of what kind of document that is. It could be a HTML page or an XML data file. Many of our examples in the rest of this chapter will use this DOM Core functionality to manipulate the document. This diagram shows how the component modules relate to one another, and build on one another's capabilities:

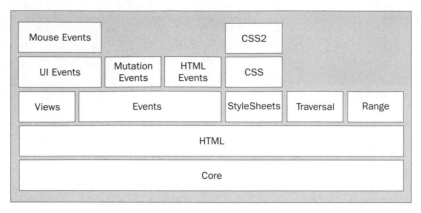

Although the diagram only shows HTML sitting above the core, the XML module can be used in its place. However, if that is the case the **HTML Events** module must be removed, as it can only be present when the underlying HTML module is present too.

Some DOM Level 1 functionality was moved into a separate module called **DOM HTML**. This embodies all of the HTML specific functionality of a document and sits on top of the DOM Core module from which most of its objects are sub-classed. This is a representation of the content of the document with very little knowledge of its relational structure or stylistic appearance since those aspects of DOM are covered in the Core and CSS modules. This abstraction of content and presentation control helps us to re-purpose the content for different display platforms. By marking up the text to indicate the classification of the content fragments, we can define the stylistic appearance centrally, and provide a consistent viewing experience. From the outset, HTML did that, but with the introduction of tags that control specific font, color and layout, the abstraction of content and style from one another becomes difficult.

The **DOM CSS** module describes how the document appearance is rendered and controlled. This is of course related to the CSS standard and includes an object representation (the `style` object) of all the functionality that CSS defines.

The **Traversal** and **Range** module is quite a large part of the DOM Level 2 Recommendation changes. This module describes a `NodeIterator`, which can be used for enumerating a collection of nodes, and a `TreeWalker`, which visits all the nodes in a tree structure. A tree-walking algorithm is quite a complicated thing to write in JavaScript, and having one built into the interpreter is very helpful because you can reconstruct a new version of the document by walking through the tree and processing the `Node` data at the leaves. The `TreeWalker` should maintain the correct ordering of the serialized source document.

The Traversal and Range module also describes the functionality of a `NodeFilter`. This is the one thing that would perhaps make the `childNodes` collections useful and portable. The filter would select a sub-set of the nodes in the collection and provide a collection that has been filtered for you. You can do this in JavaScript, but you have to enumerate through the entire collection and build an array of items that you have filtered. We now know that is non-trivial due to the treatment of whitespace `Text` nodes and XHTML closure tags.

This level of traversal functionality is quite sophisticated, and most script developers will be unaware of its existence. Indeed, it is not widely implemented in browsers yet.

The **DOM Events** module is quite important as it removes a major area of incompatibility between the Netscape and Microsoft browsers. If they both supported the same standardized events model, then we could develop much more portable event handling script designs than we have been able to.

The **DOM Views** module allows documents to be rendered in a variety of different ways, but to be simultaneously represented in all of them if desired. For example, alternative views might be presented in different frames in a browser. The source document may be the same, but its appearance may be quite different in each case.

The DOM Views module documentation doesn't give much in the way of examples of how this might be applied, but it does mention that a view can be the result of computing the appearance, possibly by applying different CSS Style Sheets. We can speculate that you could construct an index menu to a document and place that in a side bar and an expanded view of the document in the main page area. Both of these could be taken from the same document source. The CSS Style Sheets in each case would be different. To realize this capability in a useful way, there needs to be a means of attaching behaviors or events to the items in the side bar to make it into a navigation controller for the main page.

Views can be static snapshots or dynamically updated **live views**. Support of this module is based on DOM Core, and is related to the handling of user interface events as well. It is quite a small module, and may become more important later. For now, browsers do not support its functionality. However, we can place a document into multiple frames and we could possibly write some JavaScript to modify the style objects according to which frame the document is loaded to accomplish some of the multiple view capabilities.

Modularization Strategy

The DOM Level 2 Recommendation is now extremely large and complex, containing around 500 pages. Some of this is mandatory for a compliant implementation. Without DOM Core support for example, none of the other modules can be implemented. The DOM HTML module is fundamental to a DOM implementation in a web browser.

Some parts of the standard describe multiple modules. For example, the DOM style document describes DOM StyleSheets, DOM CSS and DOM CSS2 modules.

As some modules will not be required in all implementations, you need a way to find out if the module you need is available. A compliant implementation should provide enquiry mechanisms to establish if a functional module is supported. The feature names for this enquiry mechanism are noted here as well, and shortly we'll look at an example that tests them:

Module	Identifier	Document
Core	Core	DOM2-Core
XML	XML	DOM2-Core
HTML	HTML	DOM2-HTML
Views	Views	DOM2-Views
Style Sheets	StyleSheets	DOM2-Style
CSS	CSS	DOM2-Style
CSS2	CSS2	DOM2-Style
Events	Events	DOM2-Events
User interface Events	UIEvents	DOM2-Events
Mouse Events	MouseEvents	DOM2-Events

Table continued on following page

Module	Identifier	Document
Mutation Events	`MutationEvents`	DOM2-Events
HTML Events	`HTMLEvents`	DOM2-Events
Range	`Range`	DOM2-Traversal-Range
Traversal	`Traversal`	DOM2-Traversal-Range

The documents are available at the following URLs:

❑ http://www.w3.org/TR/DOM-Level-2-Core/

❑ http://www.w3.org/TR/DOM-Level-2-HTML/

❑ http://www.w3.org/TR/DOM-Level-2-Views/

❑ http://www.w3.org/TR/DOM-Level-2-Style/

❑ http://www.w3.org/TR/DOM-Level-2-Events/

❑ http://www.w3.org/TR/DOM-Level-2-Traversal-Range/

Detecting What Features are Available

Most DOM implementations that you will encounter from a JavaScript perspective will be found in a web browser. Some may be implemented in a server side context. In the future, DOM and JavaScript are likely to be available to a variety of different kinds of system. JavaScript is becoming more modularized, and the standard may allow implementers to support a sub-set of the functionality so long as they implement a complete module. This means that it may be important to know what modules are currently available.

The DOM standard provides enquiry mechanisms for us to determine what functionality is available. Certain modules require that other modules be available to satisfy dependencies between them. Here is a fragment of code that tests for the availability of the HTML module at version 1.0. It locates a DOM Implementation object and requests the information using its hasFeature() method:

```
<SCRIPT LANGUAGE='JavaScript'>
   var myDOMImplementation = document.implementation;
   var myState = myDOMImplementation.hasFeature("HTML", "1.0");
   document.write(myState);
</SCRIPT>
```

Use these feature name and version number values with the implementation.hasFeature() method call to determine what features are implemented:

Feature	Version	Description
CSS	2.0	DOM Level 2 CSS support
CSS2	2.0	DOM Level support for CSS extended interfaces
Events	2.0	DOM Level 2 event model
HTML	1.0	DOM Level 1 HTML model
HTML	2.0	DOM Level 2 HTML model

Table continued on following page

Feature	Version	Description
HTMLEvents	2.0	DOM Level 2 HTML event support
KeyEvents	3.0	DOM Level 3 key event support (part of Events)
MouseEvents	2.0	DOM Level 2 mouse event support (part of Events)
Mutation Events	2.0	DOM Level 2 mutation event support (part of Events)
Range	2.0	DOM Level 2 text range module
StyleSheets	2.0	DOM Level 2 StyleSheets module
Traversal	2.0	DOM Level 2 document traversal module
UIEvents	2.0	DOM Level 2 user interface event support (part of Events)
Views	2.0	DOM Level 2 views module
XML	1.0	DOM Level 1 XML extended interfaces
XML	2.0	DOM Level 2 XML extended interfaces

The following script, will list all the features defined at version 2.0 of the DOM standard, and tell us whether the browser supports them as version 1.0 or 2.0 functionality. This implementation object is well supported on Netscape 6. In IE 5 for Macintosh, it reports true only for DOM Level 1 HTML and XML, even though significant amounts of DOM Level 2 support are available. IE on windows does not support the document.implementation property until version 6, where it only reports true for HTML at DOM Level 1:

```
<!-- feature_list.htm -->
<HTML>
<HEAD>
   <TITLE>DOM Feature Test</TITLE>
</HEAD>
<BODY>
   <TABLE BORDER='1'>
      <TR><TH>Feature</TH><TH>1.0</TH><TH>2.0</TH></TR>
      <SCRIPT LANGUAGE='JavaScript'>
         checkFeature("XML");
         checkFeature("IITML");
         checkFeature("Views");
         checkFeature("StyleSheets");
         checkFeature("CSS");
         checkFeature("CSS2");
         checkFeature("Events");
         checkFeature("UIEvents");
         checkFeature("MouseEvents");
         checkFeature("MutationEvents");
         checkFeature("HTMLEvents");
         checkFeature("Traversal");
         checkFeature("Range");

         function checkFeature(aFeature)
         {

            document.write("<tr>");
```

```
                document.write("<td>"+aFeature+"</td>");
                document.write("<td>");
                document.write(portableHasFeature(aFeature, "1.0"));
                document.write("</td>");
                document.write("<td>");
                document.write(portableHasFeature(aFeature, "2.0"));
                document.write("</td>");
                document.write("</tr>");
            }


            function portableHasFeature(aFeature, aVersion)
            {
                if(document.implementation)
                {
                    return(document.implementation.hasFeature(aFeature,
                    aVersion));
                }
                else
                {
                    return("undefined");
                }
            }
        </SCRIPT>
    </TABLE>
</BODY>
</HTML>
```

DOM Event Models

Event handling is covered in various chapters elsewhere:

❑   Chapter 10, *Dynamic HTML* shows how DHTML event handling illustrates many dynamic document effects that are triggered by events.

❑   Chapter 8, *Cascading Style Sheets and JavaScript* shows how event handling can be used with CSS to alter the appearance of the document.

❑   Chapter 18, *Internet Explorer Filters* discusses IE filter effects and the events that are related to them.

❑   Chapter 21, *The BBC News Online Ticker* shows in a case study how to create event driven text play out using an animated effect.

All of the above typically use the classic technique of assigning an event handler function to a property of the Element that is to trap the event. Alternatively, they show how to attach events using the HTML tag attributes.

Here we shall examine an alternative way to manage event handlers and how they are attached to elements.

The W3C documentation states that the DOM Events module standardizes an event driven interface to objects within the document. It builds on the DOM Core module but also interacts with the DOM Views module.

The event complex needs to support registration of handlers against objects and for particular event types. It also needs to cope with user interface needs so that some events are not attached to an object at all, but to the client interface. The event complex also needs to be able to respond to document mutations. Our earlier examples have shown a variety of ways in which a script can mutate a document. This document modification itself can trigger events and it may be important to your overall design to track these events. Generally however, mutations are considered to apply to changes in the document structure and might not be triggered simply by changing the color of an on-screen element.

Combining the Capture and Bubble Phases

We discuss the event capture and event bubble phases in more detail in the next chapter. Basically, event capturing refers to incoming objects propagating downwards from the browser window object to the object that the event was triggered on. Any object in the document hierarchy can "capture" the event on its way down to the target object. Meanwhile, event bubbling refers to the event reaching the bottom of the DOM tree and returning to the top. Events "bubble" upward from the target object towards the topmost object that represents the browser window.

The DOM Event standard attempts to tidy up a complex situation, where the two main browsers have each offered a completely different model for processing events. In fact, they don't even respond to the same set of events. This is considered the DOM Level 0 scenario and without mincing words, it is rather a mess. The event model has stabilized in DOM Level 2, but only Netscape attempts to support it completely.

There are two phases to event handling in DOM Level 2:

❑ Capturing events as they propagate down from the window to the target object. This is the original "classic" Netscape model.

❑ Responding to events as they bubble up from the target object to the outer containing objects in the DOM tree. This is the "classic" IE model.

The event commences its downward journey from the browser window object until it reaches the target object. Then it rebounds and bubbles back upwards to the window object again. We can specify when to intercept the event. We can specify this either on its downward journey (during its capture phase), or as it rebounds upward (in its bubbling phase). If an event handler is defined as a capturing handler, it will not be invoked again during the bubbling phase.

The advantages of this are for event processing that needs to be exploded out and delegated to several different objects, we can use the capturing and routing technique. Alternatively, event handling that involves a degree of common behavior for many objects can be trapped with a single assignment of an error handler to a container that grabs the events as they bubble upwards. Specialized handlers can be introduced at lower levels if necessary.

The older browsers let you trap only one event to a handler, but DOM exceeds this capability, because it has the ability to specify more than one handler per event type. DOM compliant browsers must support this capability, so it should be available in all browsers as they support the standards more effectively. This feature may be useful if you have a selection of several possible actions that need to be performed in a different order or only by particular kinds of events.

The final exit status of the event handler defines whether the browser continues with any additional handling of the event after the handler scripts have done their work. Normally, there will be only one handler attached at a suitable point in the document hierarchy. If handlers are attached to several objects that (from an event handling perspective) are logically contained within one another, then the outermost handlers can be inhibited using the bubble-canceling feature.

Event Objects

We may already be somewhat familiar with Event objects from earlier versions of the browsers. IE maintains a single Event object while Netscape manufacturers a different one for each event being triggered. In the DOM, there is a separate and discrete Event object created for each trigger, and these are passed to the listener in its argument.

These DOM Event objects have a few additional attributes over and above the older IE and Netscape Event objects that they replace, (see Appendix D for details). However, for backwards compatibility, it is likely that the browsers may continue to support some legacy functionality that is browser specific. The minimum required support should be DOM compliant.

The DOM standard states that new Event objects can be manufactured by calling document.createEvent(), which should be followed, by a call to initEvent() being sent to the newly created Event object. Here, is an example:

```
myEvent = document.createEvent('click');
myEvent.initEvent('click', true, true);
```

The createEvent() method shown in the example takes one parameter. It is the event name in lower case without any "on" prefix.

The initEvent() method takes three parameters. The first is the event name, just like the createEvent() method. The second parameter is a Boolean value indicating whether it can bubble (true). The third argument (also Boolean) allows the event to be cancelled (true) or inhibits canceling (false).

Unfortunately, none of the browsers support this yet.

The properties and methods supported by the DOM Event object are summarized in Appendix D.

Event Types

DOM standardizes the following kinds of events, though more can be added by the implementation, and later versions of DOM may provide additional ones:

Event type	Event Name	Notes
HTMLEvent	abort	Raised when page loading is halted before an image has completely loaded. This applies to OBJECT elements.
HTMLEvent	blur	Occurs when an Element loses focus either by pointing at something else with the mouse or by using the tab key. Valid only for the LABEL, INPUT, SELECT, TEXTAREA, and BUTTON elements.
HTMLEvent	change	This event is raised when a form control loses focus but has changed its value since it last gained focus. This applies to INPUT, SELECT, and TEXTAREA elements.
HTMLEvent	error	Raised when a loading fault occurs. Applies to OBJECT, BODY, and FRAMESET elements.
HTMLEvent	focus	Occurs when an Element receives focus either by pointing at it with the mouse or by using the tab key. Valid only for the LABEL, INPUT, SELECT, TEXTAREA, and BUTTON elements.
HTMLEvent	load	An object has completed loading. Applies to BODY, FRAMESET, and OBJECT elements.
HTMLEvent	reset	Occurs when a form is reset to its initial data state. Only applies to FORM elements.

Event type	Event Name	Notes
HTMLEvent	resize	This event is triggered when a document view is resized.
HTMLEvent	scroll	This event is triggered when a document view is scrolled.
HTMLEvent	select	The user has selected some text in a field. Valid for INPUT and TEXTAREA elements.
HTMLEvent	submit	Occurs when a form is submitted. Only applies to FORM elements.
HTMLEvent	unload	An object is about to be unloaded from the window. This applies to BODY and FRAMESET elements.
KeyEvent	To be defined in a later DOM Level	These events are subject to DOM Level 3 standards work.
MouseEvent	click	The mouse pointer is over an object and the button has been clicked down and up.
MouseEvent	mousedown	The mouse pointer is over an object and the button has been clicked down.
MouseEvent	mousemove	The mouse has moved while it was over the receiving object. These events can only happen after a mouseover and before a mouseout.
MouseEvent	mouseout	The mouse has just left the active area for the object and has just crossed the edge.
MouseEvent	mouseover	The mouse has just crossed the boundary of the receiving object moving from outside its active area to a position just inside.
MouseEvent	mouseup	The mouse pointer is over an object and the button has been released after having been pressed down.
Mutation Event	DOMAttr Modified	This event is raised when a Node's attributes are altered.
Mutation Event	DOMCharacter DataModified	This event is raised if the content data of a node has been altered, but no nodes have been removed or added.
Mutation Event	DOMNode Inserted	A node has been added as a child of another node in the document. This is sent to the specific node being inserted.
Mutation Event	DOMNode InsertedInto Document	A node has been added as a child of another node in the document. This is sent to all nodes that are implicitly being inserted when a sub-tree is added.
Mutation Event	DOMNode Removed	A node has been removed from the childNodes collection of another node. This is sent to the specific node being removed.

Table continued on following page

Event type	Event Name	Notes
Mutation Event	DOMNode RemovedFrom Document	A node has been removed from the childNodes collection of another node. This is sent to all nodes that are implicitly being removed when a sub-tree is deleted.
Mutation Event	DOMSubtree Modified	Raised after a small change to the document has taken place. This is fired after other more specific events have been raised.
UIEvent	DOMActivate	Mouse clicks or presses activate an object and raise this event.
UIEvent	DOMFocusIn	Raised when an event target receives focus. The object need not be a form control item.
UIEvent	DOMFocusOut	Raised when an event target loses focus. The object need not be a form control item. This is similar to the blur event for an HTML form control.

IE and Netscape will also support other event names through their existing HTML event handling interfaces. As long as the target browser supports them, we should attempt to use DOM event names if possible.

Attaching Event Handlers – Classic Style

In HTML 4.0, events can be registered simply by assigning a function handler to an event handler property. This works fine in IE and Netscape 6. Here is a simple example with a click handler attached to a h1 element node though a simple JavaScript assignment:

```
<HTML>
<HEAD>
   <TITLE>DOM Example</TITLE>
   <SCRIPT LANGUAGE='JavaScript'>
      function eventHandler()
      {
         alert("An event was triggered.");
      }
   </SCRIPT>
</HEAD>
<BODY>
   <H1 ID='myH1'>A heading text</H1>
   <P>A paragraph of plain text</P>
   <HR></HR>
   <SCRIPT LANGUAGE='JavaScript'>
   var myH1Object = document.getElementById("myH1");
   myH1Object.onclick = eventHandler;
   </SCRIPT>
</BODY>
</HTML>
```

Event Listeners

DOM introduces the event listener concept. This is related to the attachEvent() method in IE. As we can attach several listeners to an object, it can respond to a variety of events and call up different handlers accordingly. However, we can also define several handlers for the same event. This means that we can have some generic event handling that needs to be applied to many objects, and we can have some specific handling just for some of them. As we can factor our event handlers into smaller components, we may accomplish much better code reuse with this approach.

These event listeners are attached by calling the addEventListener() method, which has a call syntax like this:

```
myObject.addEventListener(aType, aFunction, aPhase)
```

The three arguments are defined as follows:

❑ aType is the event type that the object will listen for. This is just the name of the event without the 'on' prefixing text and without capitalization. For example, use mouseOver and not onmouseOver.

❑ aFunction is a reference to the function object to be called when the event is triggered. We can pass parameters to the function by placing them in brackets as if the function were being called normally: aFunction(arg1, arg2).

❑ aPhase indicates whether to capture the event on its way down, or intercept it as it bubbles up. It is a Boolean variable (true or false). The capture phase is indicated with the true value, and the bubbling phase with false.

Attaching DOM Event Listeners

Now we can build an example using an event listener with a DIV block. Of course, we can implement this same apparent behavior using simpler techniques that have been around for a while. The point of this example is to explore the use of the DOM event handling mechanisms, as these are likely to be the long-term solution to a portable design.

In this case, we can accomplish something that works quite well in Netscape, but is problematic in versions of IE because they don't completely support the DOM event model and the addEventListener() method prior to version 6. Even then, some DOM event names are not supported and may throw an error if you use them in an addEventListener() call:

```
<!-- EventHandler1.htm -->
<HTML>
<HEAD>
    <STYLE>
        DIV
        {
            color: blue;
            background-color: #CCCCFF;
        }
    </STYLE>
    <SCRIPT LANGUAGE='JavaScript'>
        var myObject;

        function postLoadInit()
        {
            myObject = document.body.childNodes[1];

            myObject.addEventListener("mouseover", makeItHot,  false);
            myObject.addEventListener("mouseout",  makeItCold, false);
        }

        function makeItHot()
        {
            myObject.style.color           = "red";
            myObject.style.backgroundColor = "#FFCCCC";
        }

        function makeItCold()
```

```
            {
                myObject.style.color            = "blue";
                myObject.style.backgroundColor = "#CCCCFF";
            }
        </SCRIPT>
    </HEAD>
    <BODY onLoad='postLoadInit()'>
        <DIV>Goodbye Cruel World</DIV>
    </BODY>
    </HTML>
```

Note that if you attach event handlers to a node and then that node is later cloned or imported to another childNodes collection, the attached handlers will not be cloned. You will need to reattach them if necessary.

Detaching Event Listeners

Given you have identified your event target object, you register a new event handler with the addEventListener() method call. Calling this again will add multiple listeners. If you want to un-register that handler and not assign a new one, then the removeEventListener() method call should suffice.

Event listeners are detached from event targets with the following method:

```
removeEventListener(eventName, handlerFunction, captureFlag)
```

The three parameters above have the same syntax and meaning as for the attachEventListener() method. All three values taken together make a compound key for locating and removing the correct handler in case there are several that have been attached in a chain.

Here is a variation on the example that registered events. In this one, we remove the event handlers the very first time they are called. After that, the mouse rollover ceases to work at all because it has been disengaged:

```
<!-- EventListener2 -->
<HTML>
<HEAD>
    <STYLE>
        DIV
        {
            color: blue;
            background-color: #CCCCFF;
        }
    </STYLE>
    <SCRIPT LANGUAGE='JavaScript'>
        var myObject;

        function postLoadInit()
        {
            myObject = document.body.childNodes[1];

            myObject.addEventListener("mouseover", makeItHot,  false);
            myObject.addEventListener("mouseout",  makeItCold, false);
        }

        function makeItHot()
        {
            myObject.style.color            = "red";
            myObject.style.backgroundColor = "#FFCCCC";
            myObject.removeEventListener("mouseover", makeItHot,  false);
        }

        function makeItCold()
        {
```

```
        myObject.style.color            = "blue";
        myObject.style.backgroundColor = "#CCCCFF";
        myObject.removeEventListener("mouseout",  makeItCold, false);
     }
   </SCRIPT>
</HEAD>
<BODY onLoad='postLoadInit()'>
   <DIV>Goodbye Cruel World</DIV>
</BODY>
</HTML>
```

Note how the `removeEventListener()` method calls are the exact complement of the `addEventListener()` calls.

Manually Dispatching Events

The DOM Level 2 standard defines a means of dispatching events manually to other objects. To do this you really need to be able to create new `Event` objects of your own, and this is not yet supported in any browser. The event dispatch takes place through this method:

```
dispatchEvent(anEventObject)
```

The parameter is the new event object that has been created and initialized.

However, this example assumes that one day it will work in a browser and you might use this technique to create an object that you can then dispatch to an event target, like this:

```
myEvent = document.createEvent("click");
myEvent.initEvent("click", true, true);
myTargetObject.dispatchEvent(myEvent);
```

Here it is in context in a larger example script. In this example, the `init()` function fires a timer that waits for 4 seconds. In that timer handler, a new `Event` object is created, initialized, and dispatched to the target object:

```
<!-- EventDispatch.htm -->
<HTML>
<HEAD>
<TITLE>Manual Event Dispatching Example</TITLE>
<SCRIPT LANGUAGE='JavaScript'>
   var myH1Object;

   function init()
   {
      myH1Object = document.getElementById("myH1");
      myH1Object.addEventListener("mouseover", eventHandler,  false);
      setTimeout("fireAnEvent()", 4000);
   }

   function eventHandler()
   {
      alert("An event was triggered.");
   }

   // As of Netscape Navigator 6.01, the createEvent() throws an exception
   // so we must wait for a later version that corrects this problem.  None
   // of the other browsers support the DOM event  module at this time
   // either.
   function fireAnEvent()
   {
```

```
        var myEvent = document.createEvent("mouseover");
        myEvent.initEvent("click", true, true);
        myH1Object.dispatchEvent(myEvent);
    }
</SCRIPT>
</HEAD>
<BODY onLoad='init();'>
    <H1 ID='myH1'>A heading text</H1>
    <P>A paragraph of plain text</P>
    <HR></HR>
</BODY>
</HTML>
```

Handling Multiple Actions

To handle multiple actions, you have to do some neat programming tricks with your JavaScript code. For example, rather than build a switch case mechanism inside a general-purpose event handler to create your own dispatcher, you can call the component functions by attaching them to the browsers own dispatcher mechanism. This might be helpful if you have an indicator mechanism that has a common universal reset, followed by a specific highlight for each kind of event. Building your own dispatcher might look like this (in pseudo-code):

```
function clearAllIndicators()
{
    ... some code ...
}

function setIndicator1()
{
    ... some code ...
}

function setIndicator2()
{
    ... some code ...
}

function setIndicator3()
{
    ... some code ...
}

function myDispatch(anEvent)
{
  clearAllIndicators();

   switch(anEvent.which)
   {
      case type1: setIndicator1()
      break;

      case type2: setIndicator2()
      break;

      case type3: setIndicator3()
      break;
   }
}

target1.onevent = myDispatch;
target2.onevent = myDispatch;
target3.onevent = myDispatch;
```

If we build the same thing around the browser's DOM event dispatcher, the initialization code assigns handler functions to events like this:

```
target1.addEventListener('eventname', clearAllIndicators, false);
target1.addEventListener('eventname', setIndicator1, false);

target2.addEventListener('eventname', clearAllIndicators, false);
target2.addEventListener('eventname', setIndicator2, false);

target3.addEventListener('eventname', clearAllIndicators, false);
target3.addEventListener('eventname', setIndicator3, false);
```

We no longer need the `myDispatch()` function. Note that the `false` value is simply there to define whether event capturing (`true`) or bubbling (`false`) is required. Setting them `true` renders them invisible during the bubbling phase.

XML Namespace Support

DOM Level 2 provides some support for XML Namespaces. This applies to the `Element` and `Attribute` objects and comprises some additional properties and methods.

These properties relate to the XML namespace support:

Property	Description
namespaceURI	This is an XML Namespace definition. It is granted when the object is created and cannot be modified. It only applies to `Element` and Attribute nodes.
localName	The `localName` property is that part of the fully qualified name, minus the namespace prefix component. Therefore, this is unique within a namespace, but may not be unique across namespaces. This is a DOM Level 2 feature and not yet widely supported. This only applies to `Element` and `Attribute` nodes.
prefix	This provides a means (when permitted) of modifying the namespace prefix of the object. It will cause a mutation of `nodeName`, `tagName`, and `name` properties, and only applies to `Element` and `Attribute` nodes. Changing the `prefix` value does not alter the `namespaceURI` and `localName` properties. Attributes do not inherit namespace values from their owning elements and unless the namespaces are specified, the objects simply have no namespace defined.

DOM Level 2 also introduces some variations on methods, which have the letters 'NS' as a suffix to the method name. These are part of a scheme of namespace management. This allows elements to be created and owned by a particular namespace. These methods are summarized in the appendices.

Namespace support is provided for the benefit of XML developers who intend to use XML Namespaces. At present, there is some evidence that Netscape has some support for namespaces by virtue of the `prefix`, `publicId`, `systemId`, and `namespaceURI` properties on some `Element` objects. It is likely to be some time before enough browsers support this for it to become popular and, therefore, useful. The DOM standard states that HTML-only implementations need not support namespaces, so since our focus is on HTML, rather than XML we can safely ignore them for now.

Coming Later – What's Not Available Yet

Probably the best thing we could hope for is more-widespread support for the standards across more browsers. Whether Microsoft can be persuaded to do this is the biggest hurdle, considering IE remains the dominant choice in deployed browsers.

In the meantime, the working groups are developing the next generation of DOM standards. Progress grinds slowly forward, and it will be some time before all the browsers can be driven with a wholly standards compliant approach to manipulating the Document Object Model.

In DOM Level 2

There is still yet more to be implemented from DOM Level 2. The traversal and range capabilities are sorely needed if we are ever going to find a practical use for the `childNodes` collection. The lack of these capabilities is a serious impairment to what we might do to dynamically alter the DOM tree structure.

Although the Netscape 6 supposedly provides support for the Views module, this has so far proved to be of little practical use.

In DOM Level 3

The core module in DOM Level 3, adds some support to documents and entities for encoding schemes but more importantly, adds much needed support for node tree management. Comparing nodes against one another and comparing sequences of nodes will be possible. The support for namespaces is also rounded out with some additional methods. These are not likely to be used in HTML situations but will enable more sophisticated XML projects to be tackled.

The DOM Level 3 event module standard adds some more support for keyboard handling. A range of constant values so specific keys can be detected means you can create some interesting event handlers to provide function key support.

DOM Level 3 introduces a content model for access to the content rather than the object organization or style. This suggests some intriguing possibilities for documents having much more dynamic content. This module also covers load and save capabilities, which suggests some archiving capabilities may be defined if the implementations need to provide them.

Summary

This has been a very code heavy chapter to work through. DOM concepts aspire to accomplish a lot, but the available implementations are not mature enough for us to use them easily. Those available capabilities are useful, and we should be grateful. However, we can anticipate further advances still to come.

In this chapter, we have explored some of the problematic areas of DOM. This is not so much to take a critical view, but more so that you can see where the pitfalls are and how to avoid them.

Possibly, the most significant issue is that of the `childNodes` collection. This suffers from several portability problems:

- ❑ Whitespace `Text` nodes
- ❑ XHTML closure tags instantiated as `Elements`
- ❑ Different object class names (or none at all)

These all make it harder to mandate and adhere to a standards based approach to script design.

Even so, there is also much to be encouraged by and many of the examples only required small adjustments to solve cross platform issues. This is generally down to missing or incorrectly named properties, which can be corrected with small fragments of script.

There is also more new DOM related functionality on the horizon.

Pro JavaScript 2nd Edition

10

Dynamic HTML

The topic of Dynamic HTML covers a very wide area. It is concerned with the modification of the content once it has been received by the client browser. Some dynamic changes may take place at the server with pages being rendered according to user input; search engines are probably the most common example of this. However, that is not Dynamic HTML, but **dynamically generated HTML**, a quite different process that may involve server side parsed <SCRIPT> tags.

There is a variety of strategies for adding dynamics to received HTML. Dynamic HTML has been in existence since version 2 of Netscape Navigator, well before any standards were evolved to describe it. Now, it is embodied in several important standards, each one dealing with a discrete aspect of dynamic content. Dynamic HTML is the sum of these and more.

What is the difference between Dynamic HTML (DHTML) and the DOM? The quotation below is taken from the DOM FAQ, and it describes the differences from the point of view of the W3C organization. You can obtain the DOM FAQ at: http://www.w3.org/DOM/faq.html.

❑ "Dynamic HTML (DHTML) is a term used by some vendors to describe the combination of HTML, style sheets and scripts that allows documents to be animated. The scripting interfaces provided in DHTML have a significant overlap with the DOM, particularly with the HTML module. Compatibility with DHTML was a motivating factor in the development of the DOM. The DOM, however, is more than DHTML. It is a platform- and language-neutral interface that will allow programs and scripts to dynamically access and update the content, structure and style of documents, both HTML and XML."

The differences between the ways DOM and DHTML arrange the structure of a document are summarized below:

Component	DOM Access Technique	DHTML Access Technique
Parent	The object hierarchy is based on DOM `Node` objects and the tree is walked upwards by inspecting the `Node.parentNode` property.	The object hierarchy is based on `HTMLElement` objects represented as sub-classes of DOM `Node` objects and the tree is walked upwards by inspecting the `Node.parentElement` property.
Siblings	Sibling nodes can be accessed by means of the `previousSibling` and `nextSibling` properties of a `Node` object.	Locating sibling elements requires that your script traverses upwards to a parent `HTMLElement` and accesses its `children` collection. However, that only works in MSIE. A `children` collection can be constructed in other browsers by taking the DOM parent Node's `childNodes` collection and removing any text node objects and then locating the original target node by its index to access its immediate siblings. This is non-trivial and DOM navigation is far superior to DHTML navigation in this respect.
Content	The data value of a DOM `Node` is accessible through the `nodeValue` property of the Node object. The values are also accessible as a child `textNode`, which represents a leaf of the DOM tree.	DHTML object values are accessed through the `innerHTML` property of the `HTMLElement` object. MSIE provides additional, non-portable access with `innerText`, `outerText` and `outerHTML` properties.

In Chapters 8 and 9, which discussed CSS and DOM respectively, we looked at how the appearance of a document is controlled through a styling object model (CSS), and how documents are modeled so that we can access the content in an organized manner (DOM). Now we can integrate these together with some additional JavaScript and explore the result – this is otherwise known as Dynamic HTML.

In fact, if you have looked at the CSS and DOM chapters, you will already have been studying some DHTML techniques, because that's how the inspector functions are implemented.

Although the browser-based implementations of the DHTML standard are still incomplete in some areas, the recommended approach is to adhere to the standard where possible. That way, as browsers provide more support for the standard, your scripts are more likely to continue to work. This is the optimal approach to portable software design.

A Historical Perspective

Dynamic HTML has been around since JavaScript was first incorporated into the Netscape 2 browser as the LiveScript interpreter. Over the next few years, the MSIE and Netscape browsers each offered enhancements to the language, and there was much confusion about what was available in each version. The functionality that was common to both browsers was often used to enhance the dynamism of page content.

In the very early stages, however, we could use core JavaScript, such as `document.write()` and image replacement techniques, but not much else was available to make HTML dynamic. The `global` object was there of course, which in the context of a web browser is the same thing as the `window` object. In other hosted implementations of JavaScript, there must be a `global` object, but it need not be the `window` object. That object contained information about the window content; the `navigator` object was there too. Events were primitive if they were even available at all in the earliest browsers.

DHTML did not appear in a useful form until the version 4 browsers were released. Internet Explorer surged ahead aggressively with the version 5 browsers, which further developed CSS and DOM support, but this was a little patchy in Netscape Navigator, which remained at version 4 for some time.

Navigator is now in version 6, which attempts to provide a very standards-compliant implementation with excellent DOM and CSS support. It's not completely up to date with the latest standards, but what is available is mostly implemented correctly, apart from a few misnamed properties and object classes. Attaining 100% compliance is difficult because standards are evolving all the time.

Internet Explorer version 5 is functionally compliant with the W3C standards in many areas, such as the structural organization of a document into related objects. It lacks compliance in the area of property names and object class names. There are many additional properties that MSIE implements, but its biggest drawback is its inconsistent support for DHTML across browser versions, and inconsistencies between the same versions across platforms. The Macintosh and Windows versions of MSIE implement such radically different collections of objects when a document is parsed that DOM features such as the `childNodes` collection are very difficult to use. The version 5.5 browser supports more features, and the version 6 browser that is on beta release at the time of writing is reputed to also support DOM and CSS in a very standards-compliant manner.

Netscape Navigator has implemented and discarded several approaches to dynamic HTML. **JavaScript Style Sheets** (**JSS**), for example, was a complete dead end. JSS never caught on with other browser manufacturers, and should have remained an internal Netscape technology, since it supported (to some extent) the standardized CSS styling model. Layers are another example of an approach that has fallen by the wayside. Again, they work in such a restricted environment that they are of little use for practical web site building, so they're not going to be covered in this chapter.

An area where Internet Explorer excels is in the provision of **filters** and **transitions**. These are covered in Chapter 18. This support may become more standardized as a CSS capability, but for now, it is only implemented on MSIE, and then only on the Windows platform.

DHTML Techniques

Now we can begin to look at some techniques for Dynamic HTML that are well known and widely available enough to be safe and easy to use. They fall into several logical groups:

- Using `document.write()` to create dynamic HTML inline and on the fly, possibly even while the page is loading

- Image replacement to accomplish simple script-driven animation

- Using `innerHTML` to modify blocks of content in a structured manner after page loading is complete

- Object positioning to control layout to satisfy requirements of accuracy or to animate effects

- Reorganizing content by moving blocks of HTML from one part of the document to another

- Using transition effects to ease the user from one page to another with a graceful change to the content

- Using event handling to make the HTML responsive to what happens in the environment it is being displayed in

We shall examine each of these techniques and work through some examples that illustrate how you can deploy them. These examples can be downloaded from http://www.wrox.com/.

document.write()

The simplest way to create Dynamic HTML is to use document.write() methods. These can be placed inline and executed as the document is parsed during page loading.

In some browsers, because the HTML is created dynamically, the binding of the objects being instantiated is somewhat looser than when they are instantiated from static HTML. This can lead to some stability problems if you add event handling to them, or use exotic HTML tags. This concept is somewhat esoteric, so we need to explore what it means.

When the browser parses some HTML, it creates an object of whatever class it thinks best represents that HTML and populates its property values from the HTML that it examines. Generally, the tag will select an object class and any tag attributes will become properties. If the tag is a block tag with some HTML inside it, further objects may need to be created by the parser. Here is an illustration of that instantiation:

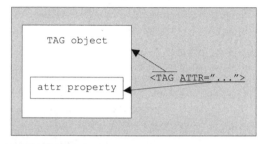

Once the parser has traversed the HTML from beginning to end, it knows what objects need to have been created, but it cannot make any final decisions about the relational links between them until it reaches a closure tag. During document loading the <BODY> tag is usually open, and it is not until the parser encounters the </BODY> tag that it can resolve things such as the length of the childNodes collection. Taking a fragment of HTML:

```
<BODY>
<H1>...</H1>
<P>...</P>
<HR>
<H1>...</H1>
<P>...</P>
</BODY>
```

While not all parsers operate in a two-phase manner, conceptually, the technique is to perform a first pass to build a collection of objects and then a second pass to link them together. It is that second pass that joins parentElement to childNodes. Other relationships, such as firstChild and nextSibling are also resolved. These relationships cannot be satisfactorily resolved until closure. This second pass is sometimes called a **fixup process** and is triggered by closure tags. Here is our collection of objects ordered and related:

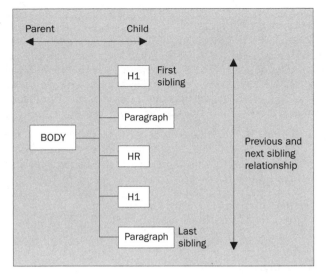

Because the objects may either be incomplete, unspecified or may actually change as the document grows, trying to access them using `document.write()` calls can lead to problems. If we then change the document content using `document.write()`, a situation can arise where the objects are instantiated from HTML that is ephemeral. That is to say, viewing the source will yield the original downloaded document source. It will not display the buffered and modified source which the browser holds internally either in an explicit form or through re-evaluating some JavaScript.

If an internal buffer is used to construct some ephemeral HTML, and then modify it, and finally parse it to create objects, we get strong linking between that HTML and the instantiated objects. If a fragment of JavaScript has to be evaluated to produce the HTML to be parsed, the parentage of the object is not so reliable. If some change then happens to the document that moves or destroys that fragment of instantiating JavaScript, then you can no longer recreate the object from it. This is a big problem if you have referred to the internals of that document elsewhere or if it is displayed on screen.

Here is an example that explores this problem:

```
<BODY>
   <SCRIPT LANGUAGE='JavaScript'>
      document.write("<IMG ID='ABC' SRC='myimage.gif'");
   </SCRIPT>

   ...

   <SCRIPT LANGUAGE="JavaScript">
      myImage = document.getElementById("ABC");
      myImage.src = "newimage.gif";
   </SCRIPT>
</BODY>
```

The risk here is that the second script block attempts to traverse the document tree to pick up a reference to the image. This might work in some browsers if the HTML parser operates in an incremental fashion and fixes up the DOM structures at the end of every line of script. There's a significant performance hit if you try to do that sort of thing. If that fix up only happens at closure, when the parser reaches the `</BODY>` tag, then the second block of script is likely to fail. It may fail in such a way that the `myImage` variable contains the undefined value, but then `myImage.src` will throw an error. That second fragment of script should really be called during an `onLoad=""` event handler.

An example of where this is extremely problematic is with the <OBJECT> tag, which we cannot reliably add to a document with an inline `document.write()` method when using Internet Explorer. The object needs to be bound to a BODY object, but this is not fully rendered until the </BODY> closure tag. It is therefore not instantiated completely when an inline <script> block is encountered. The <object> tag created with a `document.write()`, can instantiate a new object, but it cannot attach it to the incomplete BODY object, since the necessary hooks do not exist until the BODY object instantiation is complete. You can make the item during an onload event handler but it then becomes an innerHTML operation rather than a `document.write()` operation.

We can use the `document.write()` technique to just insert a small piece of text or HTML into the page, or we can write the entire page. Generally, it is probably not a good idea to write the entire body in this way, as it's very difficult to get it to work properly if you overwrite some static HTML containing the script that generated the content later on.

There are also risks with using `document.open()` and `document.close()` methods, which are related to `document.write()`. These will close the current document being written to and open a fresh empty one. They are best avoided for inline use, but might be useful for clearing down the page content during some later script-driven process.

Example document.write() calls

The following technique is useful when we want to place some content into the page that depends on the time of day at the client side. Another scenario where it might be useful is where the content may change from time to time, but needs to take into account some aspect of the receiving client without us needing to have client specific versions of the page being served.

In this example, the inline JavaScript uses a for loop to list all of the properties of the navigator object and also shows their present value:

```
<!-- docwrite_01.html -->
<HTML>
<BODY>
    This page contains some dynamically generated HTML using
    document.write() calls.<BR></BR>
    <BR></BR>
    The following text between the rules is dynamically generated:<BR></BR>
    <BR></BR>
    <HR></HR>
    <SCRIPT LANGUAGE='JavaScript'>
        for(myEnum in navigator)
        {
            document.write(myEnum);
            document.write(" = ");
            document.write(navigator[myEnum]);
            document.write("<BR>");
        }
    </SCRIPT>
    <HR></HR>
    <BR></BR>
    And now we are back to statically written HTML.
</BODY>
</HTML>
```

Note that we separate each line with a <BR> tag that needs to be written. We are writing to the input of the HTML parser, so our output is processed in the same way that any other HTML is processed within the page. Recall the discussion on binding and parsing earlier in the chapter. This means that we can build a table, but do not need to dynamically write all of its tags.

If the browser you are testing this on does not have a navigator object, or if it marks the properties with the "Don't Enum" attribute, the same technique should work with other kinds of objects. The beta version of Opera 5.12 will not execute the example correctly due to a problem in the for(... in ...) enumerator. Try building a simple index counting loop to see the effect of inline dynamically generated HTML instead if that is the case. The navigator object was chosen for reasons of safety. Because it doesn't contain any HTML, it isn't likely to set up a recursive loop.

Enumerating the document object may cause problems if you don't prevent the value of the innerHTML property from being echoed back through the document.write() method. If that happens, the document acquires a large fragment of new HTML at the point where the document.write() occurs, the list of properties suddenly expands, and the enumeration will start to traverse those new items. This will yield yet more innerHTML, which again is added. This has a recursive effect and the interpreter goes into an endless loop. You can only stop this by crashing out of the browser, which might bring down the whole operating system on some platforms. You can avoid this by putting a test for the innerHTML property name or by using the escape() function on the line that outputs the property value.

The previous example can be recast like this to show a mixture of dynamically generated and static HTML:

```
<!-- docwrite_02.html -->
<HTML>
<BODY>
    This page contains some dynamically generated HTML using
    document.write() calls.<BR></BR>
    <BR></BR>
    The table content is dynamically generated but the heading and containing
    table is not:<BR></BR>
    <BR></BR>
    <TABLE BORDER='1'>
        <TR>
            <TH>Property</TH>
            <TH>Value</TH>
        </TR>
        <SCRIPT LANGUAGE='JavaScript'>
            for(myEnum in navigator)
            {
                document.write("<tr>");
                document.write("<td>");
                document.write(myEnum);
                document.write("</td>");
                document.write("<td>");
                document.write(navigator[myEnum]);
                document.write("</td>");
                document.write("</tr>");
            }
        </SCRIPT>
    </TABLE>
    <BR></BR>
    And now we are back to statically written HTML.
</BODY>
</HTML>
```

We could just as easily have written the whole table or placed an image or <FONT> tag into the output. Although with CSS capabilities, we should use the styling object model rather than put <FONT> tags into the HTML. Both of these examples work fine across MSIE and Netscape Navigator browsers. Because this technique is so simple, portable, and easy to deploy, it gets used a lot. A screenshot from Netscape 6 reading Example_02.htm is shown below: In this example you can see it was run on Windows NT. The texts will change slightly if this is run on a different operating system or browser.

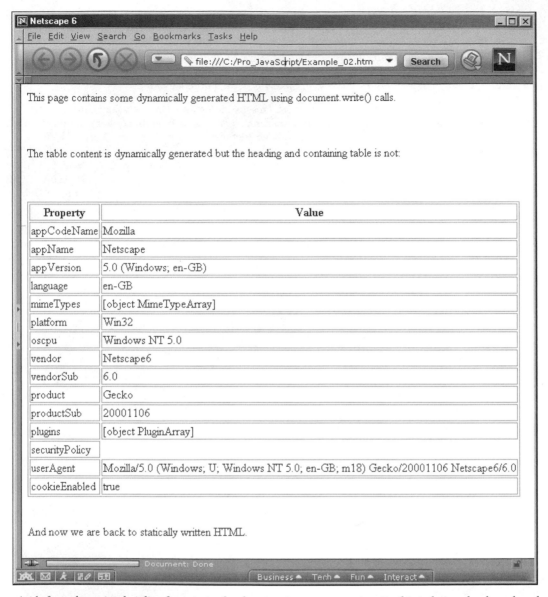

Aside from these simple inline fragments of code using `document.write()`, this technique has been largely superseded by using the DOM and object model access to the text within a leaf node of the document tree.

Image Replacement Techniques

After web page developers had discovered the delights of dynamically generated HTML courtesy of the `document.write()` call, the next most popular use was image replacement. Buttons automatically highlight as the mouse pointer moves over them in this useful user interface feedback technique. This is called a **rollover**.

Getting this to wok involves locating an object that represents an image defined by an <IMG> tag, and modifying the value in the SRC HTML tag attribute. This all works much better if the image has already been loaded into the browser's file cache. This is accomplished by instantiating some invisible IMAGE objects, and loading the images without displaying them. As long as they are not purged from the cache, the dynamic image animation looks fine.

Here is an example showing how to do a rollover. First, without any smart caching:

```
<!-- rollover.html -->
<HTML>
<HEAD>
    <SCRIPT LANGUAGE='JavaScript'>
        function rollOn()
        {
            event.srcElement.src = "hot.gif";
        }

        function rollOff()
        {
            event.srcElement.src = "cold.gif";
        }
    </SCRIPT>
</HEAD>
<BODY>
    <IMG SRC='cold.gif' onMouseOver='rollOn()' onMouseOut='rollOff()'></IMG>
</BODY>
</HTML>
```

If you are loading all the components (the HTML, and the images) from the local file system, this works very quickly. Over the Internet with a dial up connection, it looks clunky the first time the mouse rolls over the image.

In the example, the image object is located using the srcElement property. This property is supported by the MSIE event object. In other browsers (and according to the DOM standard), you should use the target property to accomplish the same thing. The srcElement property is less standards-compliant but more widely supported because of the dominance of the MSIE browser. You can add a fragment of script to fix this. It will test for the existence of a target property and use the srcElement instead. It assumes you have already located the event object and stored a reference to it in the myEvent variable:

```
if(!myEvent.target)
{
    myEvent.target = myEvent.srcElement
}
```

This fragment of script simply creates a target property by duplicating the srcElement property. There is another example later on in the discussion about DOM events, which demonstrates a different solution.

The event handling used in this example is appropriate for Internet Explorer and Opera 5, but does not work in Netscape Navigator earlier than version 6:

```
<!-- rollover2.html -->
<HTML>
<HEAD>
    <SCRIPT LANGUAGE='JavaScript'>
        function rollOn()
        {
            document.images[0].src = "hot.gif";
        }
```

```
            function rollOff()
            {
                document.images[0].src = "cold.gif";
            }
        </SCRIPT>
    </HEAD>
    <BODY>
        <IMG SRC='cold.gif' onMouseOver='rollOn()' onMouseOut='rollOff()'>
    </BODY>
    </HTML>
```

The reason older Netscape Navigator browsers don't support this example is that images don't respond to events in the same way and must be wrapped in an HTML element that does honor the event. To get this to work in older versions of Netscape Navigator, modify the line containing the image tag to this:

```
<A HREF='doc.html' onMouseOver='rollOn(event)' onMouseOut='rollOff(event)'><img
border=0 src='cold.gif'></A>
```

In the code above, the file doc.html is just a dummy link - exactly what the A element links to is unimportant. Ideally, we want a generalized approach that doesn't require us to locate images by index number and that works across every possible browser we could encounter. Here's a candidate that is functionally the same as before, but has some interesting differences:

```
<!-- rollover3.html -->
<HTML>
<HEAD>
    <SCRIPT LANGUAGE='JavaScript'>
        function replaceImage(anImageName, anImageFile)
        {
            document.images[anImageName].src = anImageFile;
        }
    </SCRIPT>
</HEAD>
<BODY>
    <A HREF='doc.html'
        onMouseOver='replaceImage("ABC", "hot.gif")'
        onMouseOut='replaceImage("ABC", "cold.gif")'>
    <IMG NAME='ABC' SRC='cold.gif' BORDER='0'></A>
</BODY>
</HTML>
```

This works fine on a variety of browsers. Also of note is the fact that we have reduced the number of functions to one and that we are passing parameters to JavaScript from HTML. Because the image is wrapped in an <A> tag, it works on Netscape 4 and the newer browsers don't really care about that additional wrapper even though they would happily work without it.

For performance reasons we can pre-cache the images by requesting them from the web server. Creating a new instance of the Image object, and setting its src value, causes the image to be requested from the server. The cache should remember all of the images requested if they are simply called in one at a time with a <SCRIPT> block like this in the <HEAD> of the document:

```
<SCRIPT>
    myImage1 = new Image();

    myImage1.src = "hot.gif";
    myImage1.src = "cold.gif";
</SCRIPT>
```

You might prefer to create a different instance of the `Image` object for each one so you can maintain a handle on them and keep them in an array. That way, you wouldn't have to remember the `src` value, you could just copy it from object to object. We can enhance our portable example one more time to show that in action:

```
<!-- rollover4.html -->
<HTML>
<HEAD>
    <SCRIPT LANGUAGE='JavaScript'>
        var myArray = new Array();

        myArray[0] = new Image();
        myArray[1] = new Image();

        myArray[0].src = "hot.gif";
        myArray[1].src = "cold.gif";

        function replaceImage(anImageName, cacheIndex)
        {
            document.images[anImageName].src = myArray[cacheIndex].src;
        }
    </SCRIPT>
</HEAD>
<BODY>
    <A HREF='doc.html'
        onMouseOver='replaceImage("ABC", "0")'
        onMouseOut='replaceImage("ABC", "1")'>
    <IMG NAME='ABC' src='cold.gif' BORDER='0'></A>
</BODY>
</HTML>
```

This may be the optimum technique, because in busy loading situations, the cache purging may be inhibited by the fact that an object still has a pending handle on the image in the cache. This depends on the internal workings of the browser, but it seems as if it should work, given the way memory allocation is often implemented in object-oriented systems. Keeping a reference open on an object means that its reference count is more than zero, and that should inhibit any garbage collection.

innerHTML and Friends

Let's explore this in two parts. First, we need to locate our target object. There are many ways to do this, some of which are more portable than others. Some of these methods are efficient and some are impossible to use without extremely large amounts of supporting code.

Finding The Target

The method that we use to locate an object we want to operate on depends on our starting point. If we just have a simple familial relationship, we can use DOM to find a child node, a sibling, or even a parent node. It's a bit more complicated if we are trying to locate a specific object from amongst all the objects in a document.

The DOM standard is supposed to make our lives easier in this respect. One method of access that it offers is the `childNodes` collection. This is a list of all immediate descendants from a particular object. However, the browser manufacturers populate the `childNodes` collection in so many different ways that it is virtually impossible to use without writing some fairly complex script to filter the objects we want from the ones we don't. In particular, the `childNodes` collection may contain miscellaneous text nodes that are placed between the objects representing the HTML tags. Prior to DOM, the browser ignored these text nodes. The price for being able to gain access to them (and that is very useful indeed) is some increased complexity.

If we name our tags with `NAME=" "` attributes we can locate them associatively in the various collections. Earlier we used this to find an image object. It works for forms and form elements too.

If we don't have a collection that contains the tags we want, we can manufacture one with the `document.getElementsByTagName()` method. We can then traverse that with an enumerator of some kind.

If we apply `ID=""` attributes to the tags, we can use `document.getElementById()` methods to extract the one we want. Be careful not to duplicate the ID values. The results are unpredictable. You may get a collection instead of a single object or you may get either the first or the last item with the requested ID. The results may be version and platform dependent even within the same browser family.

There is an interesting bug with this method on MSIE. You must not use the same name for the ID and the JavaScript variable to which you assign the results. The following code throws an error:

```
myImage = document.getElementById("myImage");
```

However, this is okay:

```
myImage1 = document.getElementById("myImage");
```

We can still accomplish many Dynamic HTML effects without using any of the new DOM standardized functionality. For example, the objects in the document can be walked in a tree-like manner using the ID values. This is illustrated in the code below, which will only work in Internet Explorer:

```
<!-- tree.html -->
<HTML>
<BODY>
    <DIV ID='ONE'>
        <IMG ID='TWO' SRC='cold.gif'></IMG>
    </DIV>
    <SCRIPT LANGUAGE='JavaScript'>
        document.all.ONE.all.TWO.src = "hot.gif";
    </SCRIPT>
</BODY>
</HTML>
```

In this example, the page should have been displaying the `cold.gif` image, but we walk the document content using ID values and replace the source image with another. The `all` property is only available in MSIE, and is wasteful of programming resources since it walks the entire tree and builds a collection of all objects in it. The DOM `childNodes` collection allows a much more efficient traversal but it has some serious portability problems and requires a lot of extra script to support it. This should be improved further in DOM Level 3 with the addition of some new traversal mechanisms.

The `<DIV>` tag allows the content of the document to be organized with some structure imposed on it. The HTML `<DIV>` tag is a block level component, whereas an HTML `<SPAN>` tag is inline. This results in a line break above and below a `<DIV>`, which behaves as if there were an implied `<BR>`, tag either side of it. This doesn't happen with a `<SPAN>`, which can be used within a line of text. CSS style classes can be applied to `<DIV>` and `<SPAN>` blocks. As a result, they are often used to add structure to large text blocks.

Getting At the Content

The `<DIV>` and `<SPAN>` tags are especially useful to the DHTML developer because the HTML inside them can be accessed using the `innerHTML` property.

The `innerHTML` property is a member of a family of properties that MSIE introduced at version 3. However, they are not all supported in Netscape Navigator and only `innerHTML` has made it into Netscape Navigator 6.

You can access the inner or outer content as either HTML or text. This gives rise to four properties:

- ❏ innerHTML
- ❏ outerHTML
- ❏ innerText
- ❏ outerText

The innerHTML and outerHTML properties are illustrated in the diagram:

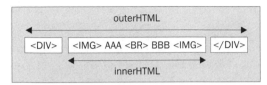

Note that the outerHTML property includes the <DIV> tags as well. This means that if we replace the outerHTML of a <DIV> tag, the <DIV> itself is overwritten. We will need to add that <DIV> mark-up to the replacing content if we want to preserve the structure. Otherwise, innerHTML should be used.

The innerText and outerText properties are for most purposes identical, and in this case yield the string "AAABBB" with no internal HTML tags. The difference becomes apparent when you try to write to the property. The innerText property replaces the content between the tags with the text you assign to the property. The outerText property obliterates the containing tags too. It corresponds to the innerHTML and outerHTML shown in the diagram.

Only the innerHTML property is portable enough across browsers to be of any practical use, and has largely been superseded by the DOM content replacement tools described in Chapter 9, *DOM*.

Here is a very simple example that works in MSIE 5 and Netscape 6 that replaces the HTML inside a <SPAN> block:

```
<!-- span.html -->
<HTML>
<BODY>
<SPAN ID='mySpan'>100</SPAN>
    <SCRIPT LANGUAGE='JavaScript'>
        myTarget = document.getElementById("mySpan");
        alert("Click to continue");
        myTarget.innerHTML = "One hundred";
    </SCRIPT>
</BODY>
</HTML>
```

Here is a more complex example where we use the innerHTML property to modify the page content using an interval timer. This example just increments a counter in MSIE 5 and Netscape 6, and continues to count as long as the page is open:

```
<!-- counter.html -->
<HTML>
<BODY>
    <DIV ID='ABC'>
    </DIV>
    <SCRIPT LANGUAGE='JavaScript'>
        myTarget = document.getElementById("ABC");
```

```
        myIndex = 0;

        setInterval("incrementor()", 100);

        function incrementor()
        {
            myTarget.innerHTML = myIndex++;
        }
      </SCRIPT>
   </BODY>
</HTML>
```

The interval timer is necessary to give the browser an opportunity to update the screen display. Just putting the `incrementor` function into a `for()` loop as shown in the following fragment of code will not allow the display to refresh between loop cycles, and you will only see the final state:

```
myTarget = document.getElementById("ABC");
for(value=0; value<100; value++)
{
myTarget.innerHTML = value;
}
```

Positioning Objects

With DHTML, we can achieve a very fine degree of control over the positions of objects on the screen. We can move them around the screen using X and Y coordinates. We can also place them on top of one another using the Z-Ordering attribute.

This is all quite difficult to do with plain HTML. With CSS, it becomes a lot easier and with a combination of DOM to locate the object, CSS properties to control its appearance and position, and JavaScript to manage the whole process, we can accomplish almost anything we want to. Prior to DHTML, there were all kinds of somewhat non-portable approaches to this kind of layout problem.

It's always good to illustrate this sort of thing with some examples, so let's create an example with several objects that we can control independently. This fragment of HTML defines those three objects using <DIV> tags.

```
<!-- dance.html -->
<HTML>
<HEAD>
</HEAD>
<BODY>
    <DIV ID='A1' CLASS='red'>RED</DIV>
    <DIV ID='B2' CLASS='green'>GREEN</DIV>
    <DIV ID='C3' CLASS='blue'>BLUE</DIV>
</BODY>
</HTML>
```

Since the <DIV> tag is considered a block element, a line break is placed between each item automatically. Now let's add a little style to make the text larger and colored differently. Add this <STYLE> block inside the <HEAD> tags:

```
<STYLE>
    BODY
    {
        font-family: Arial;
```

```
            font-size: 64px;
        }

        .red
        {
            color: red;
            position: absolute;
        }

        .green
        {
            color: green;
            position: absolute;
        }

        .blue
        {
            color: blue;
            position: absolute;
        }
    </STYLE>
```

When we reload the page, we should see that the text is now colored in a bigger font and takes on a sans-serif appearance. Because we haven't given it any position control, it's also all jumbled up in the same place.

Let's add some JavaScript to make the text dance around the screen. We can do that by calling a function to move the text intermittently. We'll generate a random number for the position each time.

Add this <SCRIPT> block just after the style sheet, also in the <HEAD> block:

```
<SCRIPT LANGUAGE='JavaScript'>
  myArray = new Array();

  function init()
  {
      myArray[0] = document.getElementById("A1");
      myArray[1] = document.getElementById("B2");
      myArray[2] = document.getElementById("C3");

      setTimeout("dancingText()", 1000);
  }

  function dancingText()
  {
      for(myIndex=0; myIndex<3; myIndex++)
      {
         myArray[myIndex].style.left = Math.random()*400;
         myArray[myIndex].style.top  = Math.random()*400;
      }
      setTimeout("dancingText()", 1000);
  }
</SCRIPT>
```

To activate this, we can call it when the body has finished loading by changing the <BODY> tag to this:

```
<BODY onLoad='init()'>
```

OK, that was a simple example. We are moving text blocks around in the X and Y-axis, but not changing their Z-ordering yet.

Lets, add a little more style and color to the background of each <DIV> block, and modify the script a little so it only moves one text block at a time. We can arrange things so that the movement happens within a smaller distance so they are likely to overlap. This will ensure that the moved item is always placed on top of the others. Here's the final page of HTML, with its CSS styling and JavaScript code:

Replace the <STYLE> block with this new one:

```
<STYLE>
    BODY
    {
        font-family: Arial;
        font-size: 64px;
    }

    .red
    {
        color: red;
        background-color: #FFCCCC;
        position: absolute;
    }

    .green
    {
        color: green;
        background-color: #CCFFCC;
        position: absolute;
    }

    .blue
    {
        color: blue;
        background-color: #CCCCFF;
        position: absolute;
    }
</STYLE>
```

Now replace the <SCRIPT> block with this new one:

```
<SCRIPT LANGUAGE='JavaScript'>
    var myArray = new Array();
    var myIndex = 0;

    function init()
    {
        myArray[0] = document.getElementById("A1");
        myArray[1] = document.getElementById("B2");
        myArray[2] = document.getElementById("C3");

        setTimeout("dancingText()", 1000);
    }

    function dancingText()
    {
        // Move all the objects back one Z position
        myArray[0].style.zIndex--;
        myArray[1].style.zIndex--;
        myArray[2].style.zIndex--;

        // Move selected item to the front
        myArray[myIndex].style.zIndex = 3;
```

```
                 myArray[myIndex].style.left = Math.random()*80;
                 myArray[myIndex].style.top  = Math.random()*80;

                 // Point to next item
                 myIndex = ((myIndex + 1) % 3);

                 setTimeout("dancingText()", 1000);
              }
        </SCRIPT>
```

This example works on Internet Explorer and on Netscape Navigator 6. To accomplish the same on Netscape Navigator 4 we'll have to use layers. However, that is a severely deprecated capability. Most of the DOM capabilities are not supported as effectively in Netscape Navigator version 4 in any case, and usage statistics suggest that its use is rapidly declining.

If this capability is required in Netscape version 4, here is a small example showing some layer moving code:

```
<!-- dance2.html -->
<HTML>
<HEAD>
   <STYLE>
      body
      {
         font-family: Arial;
         font-size: 64px;
      }

      .red
      {
         color: red;
         background-color: #FFCCCC;
      }

      .green
      {
         color: green;
         background-color: #CCFFCC;
      }

      .blue
      {
         color: blue;
         background-color: #CCCCFF;
      }
   </STYLE>
   <SCRIPT LANGUAGE='JavaScript'>
      var theScrollValue = 1;
      var theMaxScroll   = 400;

      function nav4_scrollPage()
      {
         self.document.layer1.moveTo(0,theScrollValue);
         self.document.layer2.moveTo(theScrollValue,0);
         self.document.layer3.moveTo(theScrollValue,theScrollValue);

         theScrollValue++;

         if(theScrollValue == theMaxScroll)
         {
            theScrollValue = 0;
         }
```

```
            setTimeout("nav4_scrollPage()", 20);
        }
    </SCRIPT>
</HEAD>
<BODY onLoad='nav4_scrollPage()'>
    <LAYER TOP='0' LEFT='0' NAME='layer1' CLASS='red'>
        RED
    </layer>
    <LAYER TOP='0' LEFT='0' NAME='layer2' CLASS='green'>
        GREEN
    </LAYER>
    <LAYER TOP='0' LEFT='0' NAME='layer3' CLASS='blue'>
        BLUE
    </LAYER>
</BODY>
</HTML>
```

The <DIV> tags are now <LAYER> tags and the CSS position property no longer needs to be set to absolute because we aren't using CSS to do the scrolling; we are moving the whole layer. It works well enough, but it is not as flexible. Oddly enough, scrolling moves in the opposite vertical direction on Internet Explorer and Netscape Navigator. Layers are the only way to scroll page content on Netscape Navigator unless you want a visible scrollbar. Turning off the scrollbar in Navigator 4 stops the page from scrolling as a whole – although its layers are still free to move.

Changing Content Ordering

Sometimes we want to move content from one part of a document to another. Perhaps we have contrived to hide some content **below the fold**. That is, lower down the page so that it disappears off the bottom of the window. Perhaps the window has been rendered non-scrolling, so this content cannot be made visible unless we want it to be.

Here is an example where we use dynamic techniques to display one of four possible text blocks in a visible region. We won't worry about the window setup. That happens outside of this fragment of HTML in the page that invoked it. In any case, it may be useful for the purposes of experimentation to be able to scroll the content for now.

With CSS, another possibility presents itself. That is the visibility property. Setting the value of this to hidden will obscure the data text. Here is the basic HTML and CSS style to define four <DIV> blocks, only one of which is on display. We can add a fragment of JavaScript to move the text of <DIV> blocks B2, C3, and D4 into block A1 in a cyclical manner. Here is the code, which will work on MSIE 5 and Netscape 6:

```
<!-- cycle.html -->
<HTML>
<HEAD>
    <STYLE>
        body
        {
            font-size: 24px;
        }

        .data
        {
            visibility: hidden;
        }

    </STYLE>
<SCRIPT LANGUAGE='JavaScript'>
        var myArray = new Array();
```

```
      var myIndex = 1;

      function init()
      {
          myArray[0] = document.getElementById("A1");
          myArray[1] = document.getElementById("B2");
          myArray[2] = document.getElementById("C3");
          myArray[3] = document.getElementById("D4");

          setTimeout("movingText()", 1000);
      }


      function movingText()
      {
          myArray[0].innerHTML = myArray[myIndex].innerHTML;

          myIndex++;
          if(myIndex == 4)
          {
              myIndex = 1;
          }

          setTimeout("movingText()", 1000);
      }
   </SCRIPT>
 </HEAD>
 <BODY onLoad="init()">
    <DIV ID="A1" CLASS='show'>Default text content.</DIV>
    <DIV ID="B2" CLASS='data'>The first paragraph of text.</DIV>
    <DIV ID="C3" CLASS='data'>The second paragraph of text.</DIV>
    <DIV ID="D4" CLASS='data'>The third paragraph of text.</DIV>
 </BODY>
 </HTML>
```

Transition Effects

One of the most powerful capabilities of Internet Explorer on the Windows platform is its Filters and Transitions support. This is covered in a Chapter 18, but it is so useful that maybe we can accomplish some of the effects in a portable manner.

Microsoft added a filter property to the CSS implementation in MSIE 4. This invokes a process when the content of the display changes. It requires that a pixel buffer of equal size to the changed area be set aside. This can be as large as the whole page on display, so the memory requirements can be quite demanding. The new page content is rendered into this off-screen pixel map and is then displayed using a transition reminiscent of PowerPoint.

MSIE also supports some static filter effects that can be applied to text and images to distort them in various ways, such as blurring.

These ideas were put forward in an enhancement proposal, but the CSS working group decided to reject this and consider instead what the Scalable Vector Graphics group were doing. The SVG group has described how a filter property belonging to a style object might work. Until the outcome of the ongoing work of the SVG group is known, the only way to get transition effects is to use Microsoft proprietary filters or to roll your own with JavaScript. There is also some interesting work in this area under the SMIL standards group, which Microsoft are also contributing to, although they implement something called HTML+TIME in the MSIE browser, which is a superset of the functionality.

In the tradition of experimenting with our own scripted approach to solving a problem, let's see if we can accomplish a simple fade based on the previous example:

```
<!-- fade.html -->
<HTML>
<HEAD>
    <STYLE>
        body
        {
          font-size: 24px;
        }

        .data
        {
          visibility: hidden;
        }

        .data
        {
          color: rgb(255, 255, 255);
        }

    </STYLE>
    <SCRIPT LANGUAGE='JavaScript'>
        var myArray = new Array();
        var myIndex = 1;
        var myGray = 0;
        var myIncrement = 1;

        function init()
        {
            myArray[0] = document.getElementById("A1");
            myArray[1] = document.getElementById("B2");
            myArray[2] = document.getElementById("C3");
            myArray[3] = document.getElementById("D4");

            setTimeout("movingText()", 5);
        }


        function movingText()
        {
            myArray[0].style.color = "rgb("+myGray+", "+myGray+", "+myGray+")";

            myGray += myIncrement;

            if(myGray > 255)
            {
                // Switch text content when faded out
                myArray[0].innerHTML = myArray[myIndex].innerHTML;

                myIndex++;
                if(myIndex == 4)
                {
                    myIndex = 1;
                }

                myIncrement *= (-1);
                setTimeout("movingText()", 0);
            }
            else if (myGray < 0)
            {
```

```
                // Display a little longer when faded in
                myIncrement *= (-1);
                setTimeout("movingText()", 3000);
            }
            else
            {
                // Routine 5 ms delay for fade
                setTimeout("movingText()", 5);
            }
        }
    </SCRIPT>
</HEAD>
<BODY BGCOLOR="white" onLoad="init()">
    <DIV ID="A1" CLASS='show'>Default text content.</DIV>
    <DIV ID="B2" CLASS='data'>The first paragraph of text.</DIV>
    <DIV ID="C3" CLASS='data'>The second paragraph of text.</DIV>
    <DIV ID="D4" CLASS='data'>The third paragraph of text.</DIV>
</BODY>
</HTML>
```

The real bonus is that it works on Netscape Navigator version 6 and MSIE 5.0 on Macintosh, as well as MSIE 5.5 on Windows. We see that we can accomplish some transitions in a portable manner.

Color Selector Example

Here is a quite complex example, showing the use of various traversal mechanisms, DOM, CSS, and the innerHTML capabilities. We will create a table and use the column and row addresses to set the red, green, and blue values of a color register. We will then set the background color of a table cell accordingly.

This kind of event programming is quite complex and difficult to get working across multiple browsers, and so this is a very MSIE specific solution for now. Later, we'll see how to get it working on Netscape Navigator 6:

```
<!-- MSIE_color_select.html -->
<HTML>
<HEAD>
    <SCRIPT LANGUAGE='JavaScript'>
        // Define initial states
        var myOldSrcElement;
        var myRed   = "00";
        var myGreen = "00";
        var myBlue  = "00";

        // Handle clicks in the table
        function clicked()
        {
            var myValue;
            var myColumn;
            var myRow;

            myEvent = event;

            // Indicate what was clicked on
            if(myOldSrcElement)
            {
                myOldSrcElement.bgColor = "white";
            }

            // Work out click column and row
            myColumn = (myEvent.srcElement.cellIndex) + 1;
            myRow    = myEvent.srcElement.parentElement.rowIndex;
```

395

```
            // Set color intensity
            switch(myRow)
            {
                case 1: myValue = "FF";
                        break;

                case 2: myValue = "CC";
                        break;

                case 3: myValue = "99";
                        break;

                case 4: myValue = "66";
                        break;

                case 5: myValue = "33";
                        break;

                case 6: myValue = "00";
                        break;

                default: myValue = "";
                        break;
            }

            // Set colour to change
            if(myValue != "")
            {
                myEvent.srcElement.bgColor = "red";

                switch(myColumn)
                {
                    case 1: myRed = myValue;
                            break;

                    case 2: myGreen = myValue;
                            break;

                    case 3: myBlue = myValue;
                            break;
                }

                myColour = "#" + myRed + myGreen + myBlue;

                myTarget = document.getElementById("COLORCELL");
                myTarget.bgColor = myColour;

                myResult = document.getElementById("OUTPUT");
                myResult.innerHTML = myColour;

                myOldSrcElement = myEvent.srcElement;
            }
        }
    </SCRIPT>
    <STYLE>
        td {text-align: right }
    </STYLE>
</HEAD>
<BODY>
    Selected color: <SPAN ID="OUTPUT"></SPAN>
    <BR></BR>
    <TABLE BORDER='1'>
        <TR><TD ID='COLORCELL'> </TD></TR>
```

```
        <TR><TD>
            <TABLE BORDER='1' onClick='clicked()'>
            <TR><TH>Red</TH><TH>Green</TH><TH>Blue</TH></TR>
            <TR><TD>100</TD><TD>100</TD><TD>100</TD></TR>
            <TR><TD>80</TD><TD>80</TD><TD>80</TD></TR>
            <TR><TD>60</TD><TD>60</TD><TD>60</TD></TR>
            <TR><TD>40</TD><TD>40</TD><TD>40</TD></TR>
            <TR><TD>20</TD><TD>20</TD><TD>20</TD></TR>
            <TR><TD>0</TD><TD>0</TD><TD>0</TD></TR>
        </TABLE>
    </TD></TR>
    </TABLE>
</BODY>
</HTML>
```

The color table functionality is built around an event handler that figures out what row and column is used. The row number defines a value and column number defines whether it applies to red, green, or blue. Then the persistent values for the other two of the RGB triplet are combined with the new value and the background color of a target cell is modified. At the same time, the color value is stored in a `<SPAN>` block. On receipt of the click, the persistent storage also blanks out the previous item that was clicked on, and sets the new item to red.

Dynamic HTML and the New Event Models

The new event model in Netscape Navigator 6 is supposed to be DOM Level 2 compliant. Therefore, if we can get things working in this browser, we'll likely be well set up for the future.

The event models in Internet Explorer and versions of Netscape Navigator prior to version 6 are fairly well understood. Netscape Navigator 6 introduces a DOM standardized event model that is somewhat difficult to understand at first because it appears to implement an MSIE and a classic Navigator event model simultaneously.

Simple things like attaching event handlers to objects using HTML tag attributes work as we would expect. Some of our earlier examples have already used that technique.

The most portable technique available is to attach the event handler with an HTML tag attribute and to include the `event` keyword as a place-holding parameter. The parameter is interpreted in different ways by various browsers. MSIE substitutes its global `event` object and passes a reference to it as a value. Netscape and other browsers don't support a global `event` object, as it is not specified by W3C and is not considered part of the core language by ECMA. Netscape Navigator overrides the parameter specified in the HTML tag attribute. The value is replaced by a reference to an `event` object that describes the event that has just been triggered.

Here is an example of a highly portable event handler that works on Macintosh and PC platforms, and on current and earlier versions of the MSIE, Netscape, and Opera browsers:

```
<!-- port_event.html -->
<HTML>
<HEAD>
<SCRIPT>
    function rollOn(anEvent)
    {
        alert(anEvent.type);
    }
</SCRIPT>
</HEAD>
<BODY>
<A HREF='doc.html' onMouseOver='rollOn(event)'>Roll over me</A>
</BODY>
</HTML>
```

The Event Capturing Model

Events in older versions of Navigator propagate downwards from the browser window object to the object that the event was triggered on. Any object in the document hierarchy can capture the event on its way down to the target object. This generally applies to window.document and layer objects in the version 4 Navigator browser. Here is an illustration showing the direction of event propagation:

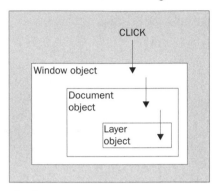

Events resulting from a user action for example will be passed to the topmost window object. That object has the opportunity to capture the event or ignore it. If the event is ignored, it will be passed to the document object instantiated from the document in the window. If the window object has a handler registered for the event and captures the event as it passes, the event will never reach the document object (even if it does have a handler), unless the window object's handler passes on the event. The same happens with respect to the document and layer objects. The layer object only receives the event if the document object allows it to.

The handlers are attached by assigning a function reference to the property of the window, document, or layer that corresponds to the event to be handled. Thus:

```
function myHandler(anEvent)
{
...
}

document.onmouseover = myHandler;
document.onmouseout  = myHandler;
```

On its own though, this will not capture any events. You must add a captureEvents() method call to define which events are to be captured by the target object. This line is required to capture mouse events that are indicated using some pre-defined constants:

```
document.captureEvents(Event.MOUSEOVER | Event.MOUSEOUT);
```

The releaseEvents() method complements the captureEvents() method and provides a way to stop capturing events individually. It is called in a similar way with an event mask specifying which events to discontinue capturing.

If the event is to be propagated, the routeEvent() method should be called, passing the incoming event object as a parameter:

```
function myHandler(anEvent)
{
...
document.routeEvent(anEvent);
}
```

If you don't route the event, then you can pass the event to another object that has handlers registered and capturing enabled by means of the `handleEvent()` method call. That may be necessary if you need to deviate from the normal propagation route for the event. Such as this:

```
function myHandler(anEvent)
{
...
someObject.handleEvent(anEvent);
}
```

It is important that you understand that the event handler is called from the event that is propagating the event onwards, but that the handler associated with the target object is invoked.

The Event Bubbling Model

Event handling is quite different on MSIE, where events propagate in the opposite direction to Netscape Navigator prior to version 6. Events bubble upward from the target object towards the topmost object that represents the browser window. In this scenario, any object can process the event on its way up, but the events may be inhibited according to the exit status or internal script activity of any intervening handlers. This is a much simpler model to understand and use.

Using a similar diagram, the event propagation is quite different:

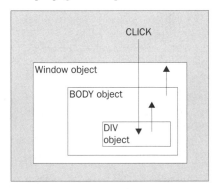

In this model, we can define an event handler for each of the objects or just the outermost that we think should handle the event. If we only define a handler for the `window` object, then the event will not be taken and handled by the `DIV` or `BODY` objects unless they too have handlers defined. Events will only reach the outer container objects if the event handler for an inner object allows them to.

The final exit status of the event handler defines whether the browser continues with any additional handling of the event after the handler scripts have done their work. Normally, there will be only one handler attached at a suitable point in the document hierarchy. If handlers are attached to several objects that are logically contained within one another (from an event handling point of view), then the outermost handlers can be inhibited by using the bubble-canceling feature.

This is accessible to the script developer through the `cancelBubble` property of the `event` object. Since the `event` object is owned globally by the `window` object, this line of script will inhibit any higher order event handlers from seeing the event:

```
window.event.cancelBubbble = true;
```

It won't halt the current event handler though, and that should at some stage return `true` if the browser should honor the event, or `false` to inhibit any browser event handling.

Setting the `cancelBubble` property to `true` in the handler associated with the `<DIV>` block stops the event from being processed by the document's handler:

```
function myHandler()
{
    ...
    window.event.cancelBubble = true;

    return false;
}

myDiv.onClick    = myHandler;
document.onClick = myHandler;
```

The bubbling needs to be cancelled in this case otherwise the event handler would be invoked more than once as it bubbles up through the document content model. In this example, the handler returns `false` to inhibit any browser activity as well.

The DOM Event Model

The event model in Netscape Navigator 6 combines the Netscape Navigator 4.x event model with the one found in MSIE. Netscape Navigator 6 supports event handling in both directions. The event commences its downward journey from the browser `window` object until it reaches the `target` object. Then it rebounds and bubbles back upwards to the `window` object again. What makes Netscape Navigator 6 so interesting is that we can specify when to intercept the event. This can either be on its downward journey (during its capture phase), or as it rebounds upward (in its bubbling phase). If an event handler is defined as a capturing handler, it will not be invoked again during the bubbling phase.

The advantages of this are that for event processing that needs to be delegated to several different objects, we can use the capturing and routing technique. Alternatively, event handling that involves a degree of common behavior for many objects can be trapped with a single assignment of an error handler to a container that grabs the events as they bubble upwards. Specialized handlers can be introduced at lower levels if necessary.

Older browsers let you trap an event to a handler, but Netscape Navigator 6 exceeds this capability because it has the ability to specify more than one handler per event type. Netscape Navigator 4.x can only support one action for an event. DOM compliant browsers must support this capability, so it should be available in all browsers as they support the standards more effectively. This feature may be useful if you have a selection of several possible actions that need to be performed in a different order or only by certain kinds of events.

To handle multiple actions, you have to do some neat programming tricks with your JavaScript code. For example, rather than build a switch case mechanism inside a general-purpose event handler to create your own dispatcher, you can call the component functions by attaching them to the browsers own dispatcher mechanism. This might be helpful if you have an indicator mechanism that has a common universal reset followed by a specific highlight for each kind of event. Building your own dispatcher might look like this (in pseudo-code):

```
function clearAllIndicators()
{
...
}

function setIndicator1()
{
...
```

```
    }

    function setIndicator2()
    {
    ...
    }

    function setIndicator3()
    {
    ...
    }

    function myDispatch(anEvent)
    {
      clearAllIndicators();

      switch(anEvent.which)
      {
        case type1: setIndicator1()
        break;

        case type2: setIndicator2()
        break;

        case type3: setIndicator3()
        break;
      }
    }

target1.onevent = myDispatch;
target2.onevent = myDispatch;
target3.onevent = myDispatch;
```

If we build the same thing around the browser's event dispatcher, the initialization code assigns handler functions to events like this:

```
target1.addEventListener('eventname', clearAllIndicators, false);
target1.addEventListener('eventname', setIndicator1, false);

target2.addEventListener('eventname', clearAllIndicators, false);
target2.addEventListener('eventname', setIndicator2, false);

target3.addEventListener('eventname', clearAllIndicators, false);
target3.addEventListener('eventname', setIndicator3, false);
```

We no longer need the myDispatch function. Note the false value is simply there to define whether event capturing (true) or bubbling (false) is required. Setting them to true renders them invisible during the bubbling phase.

We'll come back to look at event listeners again shortly.

Implementing Simple Event Handlers

Here is how to attach a simple event handler using an HTML tag attribute:

```
<!-- event.html -->
<HTML>
<HEAD>
   <SCRIPT LANGUAGE='JavaScript'>
      function clickHandler()
      {
```

```
            alert("You clicked?");
        }
    </SCRIPT>
</HEAD>
<BODY>
    <IMG SRC='cold.gif' onClick='clickHandler()'></IMG>
</BODY>
</HTML>
```

This is the most straightforward and portable way to do it. It is quite limited, but it works on both MSIE 5 and Netscape 6.

We can accomplish the same thing with JavaScript, but it may be inconvenient to do it inline and we may need to wait until the </BODY> closure so that we can assign the handler to the event hook like this instead:

```
<!-- event2.html -->
<HTML>
<HEAD>
    <SCRIPT LANGUAGE='JavaScript'>
        function clickHandler()
        {
            alert("You clicked?");
        }

        function init()
        {
            document.images[0].onclick = clickHandler;
        }

    </SCRIPT>
</HEAD>
<BODY onLoad="init()">
    <IMG SRC='cold.gif'></IMG>
</BODY>
</HTML>
```

Note that we refer to the function as if it were an object. This means we leave off the brackets.

In this example, we have two event handlers, which change places with one another when they are called:

```
<!-- event3.html -->
<HTML>
<HEAD>
    <SCRIPT LANGUAGE='JavaScript'>
        function clickHandler1()
        {
            alert("Handler 1 - You clicked?");
            document.images[0].onclick = clickHandler2;
        }

        function clickHandler2()
        {
            alert("Handler 2 - You clicked?");
            document.images[0].onclick = clickHandler1;
        }
    </SCRIPT>
</HEAD>
<BODY>
    <IMG SRC='cold.gif'></IMG>
    <SCRIPT LANGUAGE='JavaScript'>
        document.images[0].onclick = clickHandler1;
```

```
        </SCRIPT>
    </BODY>
    </HTML>
```

This technique allows a little more sophistication. We have to assume the target object is the one to which we attached the handler because the handlers refer to the same image object using a specific reference.

During the handling of an event, we may be able to determine the target object using a more indirect and general-purpose approach. This exposes further differences between the Netscape Navigator and MSIE event objects, but the DOM standard definition of an event object defines a common approach that all browsers should eventually adopt.

The object that received the action and triggered the event is indicated in the `target` property of a DOM compliant `event` object. The `currentTarget` property indicates which object owns the listener that invoked the handler. They may be the same object when an event handler is first invoked, but should indicate different objects once bubbling comes into play or events have been delegated with the `dispatchEvent()` method.

In the MSIE browser, the `event` object indicates the target object with the `srcElement` property while Netscape Navigator supports the `target` property on its `event` object. This example works around those portability issues:

```
<!-- event4.html -->
<HTML>
<HEAD>
    <SCRIPT LANGUAGE='JavaScript'>
        function clickHandler1(anEvent)
        {
            myTarget = whatTarget(anEvent);
            alert("Handler 1 - You clicked?");
            myTarget.onclick = clickHandler2;
        }

        function clickHandler2(anEvent)
        {
            myTarget = whatTarget(anEvent);
            alert("Handler 2 - You clicked?");
            myTarget.onclick = clickHandler1;
        }

        function whatTarget(anEvent)
        {
            if(!anEvent)
            {
                return(window.event.srcElement);
            }
                        return(anEvent.target);
        }
    </SCRIPT>
</HEAD>
<BODY>
    <IMG SRC='cold.gif'></IMG>
    <SCRIPT LANGUAGE='JavaScript'>
        document.images[0].onclick = clickHandler1;
    </SCRIPT>
</BODY>
</HTML>
```

Note the addition of the `whatTarget()` function in this example. It checks for the existence of the `event` object being passed as a parameter to the event handler. If the object passed in that parameter is `undefined`, it assumes we are in an MSIE browser and works out the target object accordingly from the `srcElement` property and returns that value. Otherwise, it inspects the `event` object and returns the value of its `target` property.

As we are assigning the event handler using JavaScript, we don't get the opportunity to force the browser to pass an event object as a parameter value. That event object passing which happens when we include an HTML tag attribute like this:

```
onClick="handler(event)"
```

This technique works in a very portable manner because Netscape Navigator passes its own event object as the parameter and ignores the value you define in the tag attribute. MSIE however, picks up the `window.event` property value and places that in the event handler call as an argument. You cannot replicate this behavior however when assigning handlers from JavaScript.

Event Listeners

Netscape Navigator 6 introduces the **event listener** concept. This is related to the `attachEvent()` method in Internet Explorer. As we can attach several listeners to an object, it can respond to a variety of events and call up different handlers accordingly. We can however also define several handlers for the same event. This means that we can have some generic event handling that needs to be applied to many objects, and we can have some specific handling just for some of them. As we can factor our event handlers into smaller components, we may accomplish much better code reuse with this approach.

These event listeners are attached by calling the `addEventListener()` method, which has a call syntax like this:

```
myObject.addEventListener(aType, aFunction, aPhase)
```

The three arguments are defined as follows:

❏   `aType` is the event type that the object will listen for. This is just the name of the event without the on prefixing text and without capitalization. For example, use `mouseover`, not `onmouseover`.

❏   `aFunction` is a reference to the function object to be called when the event is triggered. We can pass parameters to the function by placing them in brackets as if the function were being called normally: `myFunction(arg1, arg2)`.

❏   `aPhase` indicates whether to capture the event on its way down, or intercept it as it bubbles up. It is a Boolean variable (`true` or `false`). The capture phase is indicated with the `true` value, and the bubbling phase with `false`.

Using DOM Event Listeners

Now we can build an example using an event listener with a `<DIV>` block. Of course, we can implement this same apparent behavior using simpler techniques that have been around for a while. The point of this example is to explore the use of the DOM event handling mechanisms, as these are likely to be the long-term solution to a portable design.

In this case, we can accomplish something that works quite well in Netscape Navigator 6 but is problematic in versions of Internet Explorer because they don't completely support the DOM event model and the `addEventListener()` method prior to version 6. Even then some DOM event names are not supported and may throw an error if you use them in an `addEventListener()` call although this may be fixed in future versions of MSIE:

```
<!-- listener.html -->
<HTML>
<HEAD>
   <STYLE>
      div
      {
         color: blue;
         background-color: #CCCCFF;
      }
   </STYLE>
</HEAD>
<BODY onLoad='postLoadInit()'>
   <DIV>Goodbye Cruel World</DIV>
   <SCRIPT LANGUAGE='JavaScript'>
      var myObject;

      function postLoadInit()
      {
         myObject = document.body.childNodes[1];

         myObject.addEventListener("mouseover", makeItHot,  false);
         myObject.addEventListener("mouseout",  makeItCold, false);
      }

      function makeItHot()
      {
         myObject.style.color           = "red";
         myObject.style.backgroundColor = "#FFCCCC";
      }

      function makeItCold()
      {
         myObject.style.color           = "blue";
         myObject.style.backgroundColor = "#CCCCFF";
      }
   </SCRIPT>
</BODY>
</HTML>
```

In some earlier examples, we relied on some inline code to pick up the object reference. In this case, we call an initializer once the body has completed loading. This is possibly a better technique as the body and its child object relationships should be correctly joined up. That may not be the case before the closing </BODY> tag.

Navigator 6 Color Selector

Now that we have explored some of the simpler aspects of the new DOM event model capabilities, perhaps we can go back to the earlier MSIE-specific color selector example and make it work with Netscape Navigator 6.

We won't worry about making it work on both browsers for now. That just comes down to some browser detection tricks to choose the right code at the right time and it will make our example needlessly complex:

```
<!-- NN_color_select.html -->
<HTML>
<HEAD>
   <SCRIPT LANGUAGE='JavaScript'>
      // Define initial states
      var myOldSrcElement;
      var myRed   = "00";
      var myGreen = "00";
      var myBlue  = "00";
```

```
// Attach an event handler function to each table cell
function init()
{
   myTable = document.getElementById("UI");

   for(myRow=1; myRow<7; myRow++)
   {
      for(myCell=0; myCell<3; myCell++)
      {
         myTable.rows[myRow].cells[myCell].addEventListener("click",
            clicked, false);
         myTable.rows[myRow].cells[myCell].bgColor = "white";
      }
   }

}

// Handle clicks in the table
function clicked(anEvent)
{
   var myValue;
   var myColumn;
   var myRow;

   // Fixup clicks on cell & row objects
   if(anEvent.target.cellIndex)
   {
      myCellObject = anEvent.target;
   }
   else
   {
      myCellObject = anEvent.target.parentNode;
   }
   myRowObject = myCellObject.parentNode;

   // Indicate what was clicked on
   if(myOldSrcElement)
   {
      myOldSrcElement.bgColor = "white";
   }
   myCellObject.bgColor = "red";
   myOldSrcElement = myCellObject;

   // Work out click column and row
   myColumn = (myCellObject.cellIndex) + 1;
   myRow    = myRowObject.rowIndex;

   // Set colour intesity
   switch(myRow)
   {
      case 1: myValue = "FF";
         break;

      case 2: myValue = "CC";
         break;

      case 3: myValue = "99";
         break;

      case 4: myValue = "66";
         break;
```

```
                        case 5: myValue = "33";
                            break;

                        case 6: myValue = "00";
                            break;

                    }

                    // Set colour to change
                    switch(myColumn)
                    {
                        case 1: myRed = myValue;
                            break;

                        case 2: myGreen = myValue;
                            break;

                        case 3: myBlue = myValue;
                            break;
                    }

                    myColour = "#" + myRed + myGreen + myBlue;

                    myTarget = document.getElementById("COLORCELL");
                    myTarget.bgColor = myColour;

                    myResult = document.getElementById("RESULT");
                    myResult.innerHTML = myColour;


                }
        </SCRIPT>
        <STYLE>
            td {text-align: right }
        </STYLE>
    </HEAD>
    <BODY onLoad="init()">
        <TABLE BORDER='1'>
            <TR><TD ID='COLORCELL'> </TD></TR>
            <TR><TD>
                <TABLE BORDER='1'>
                    <TBODY ID="UI">
                        <TR><TH>Red</TH><TH>Green</TH><TH>Blue</TH></TR>
                        <TR><TD>100</TD><TD>100</TD><TD>100</TD></TR>
                        <TR><TD>080</TD><TD>080</TD><TD>080</TD></TR>
                        <TR><TD>060</TD><TD>060</TD><TD>060</TD></TR>
                        <TR><TD>040</TD><TD>040</TD><TD>040</TD></TR>
                        <TR><TD>020</TD><TD>020</TD><TD>020</TD></TR>
                        <TR><TD>000</TD><TD>000</TD><TD>000</TD></TR>
                    </TBODY>
                </TABLE>
            </TD></TR>
        </TABLE>
        <BR></BR>
        Selected color: <SPAN ID="RESULT"></SPAN>
    </BODY>
</HTML>
```

This works on Netscape Navigator version 6. To get it to work, we had to change quite a few things from the MSIE version of the page. Here are the changes and why:

The table cells now contain zero padded values. These help to fix a problem in the event capture code in Netscape Navigator that sometimes routes the event to a table row object rather than a cell object. We also have some additional fix-up code that helps to cure this. It's not 100% reliable, but it is helpful. It is indicated with a comment in the example code and checks for the existence of a `cellIndex` property. That is only present on cell objects. The `if()` block selects one of two alternative ways to determine the cell object that was clicked on.

We used `getElementById()` here. We might still walk the DOM tree to locate objects but that technique is unreliable across different browsers and platforms due to the variety of ways in which browsers treat whitespace and text nodes. We now have an `init()` handler, which walks the cells in the table and attaches the same event handler to them all. By rights, this should mean the `row` objects do not detect the events but they sometimes do. This might be a bug in the way that `row` and `cell` objects are mapped within a table.

The event handler now accesses the target object as a property of the `event` object, passed in to the handler rather than the globally shared event handler that Internet Explorer uses. As the `event` object carries this contextual information, the event handler can be simplified somewhat.

Color value calculation is the same as before and so is the session state persistence, but in general, the object location is tighter apart from the event triggering object location. On the whole, this is because we attach rather more event handlers to objects, which means the event handler only has to deal with a single target object rather than having to traverse a portion of the DOM tree to find the item that was clicked on.

Summary

It is difficult to completely separate DOM, CSS, and JavaScript when we are looking at Dynamic HTML. They are so interrelated that to do any meaningful work requires that we use a little of each. Significant amounts of dynamism can be accomplished with very simple techniques.

The newer browsers are improving with regard to their W3C standards compliance. This will improve in the future. There is still much to look forward to, with DOM Level 3 and CSS 3 work being still done. The working groups are certainly considering further developments beyond those releases.

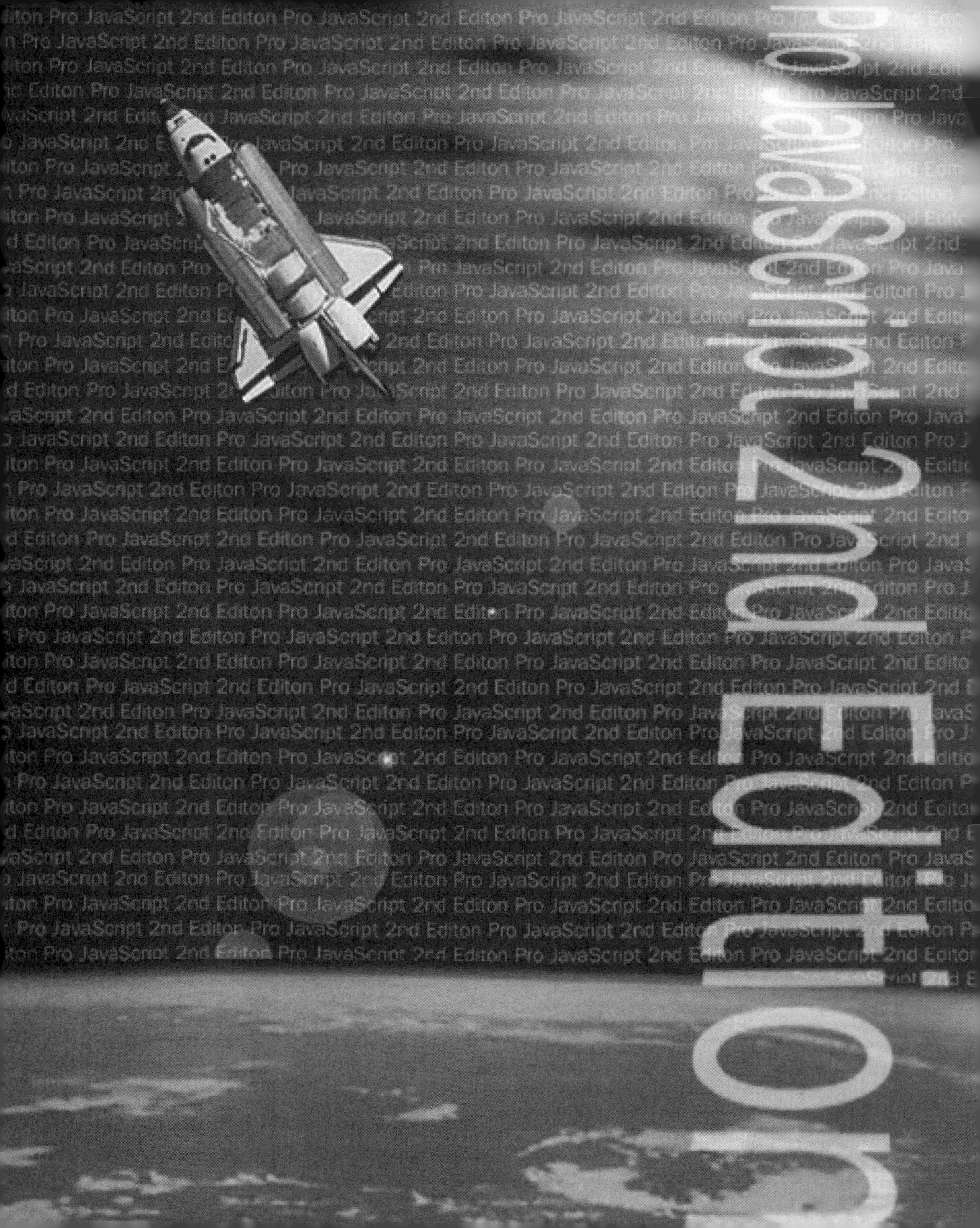
ProJavaScript2ndEdition
Pro JavaScript 2nd Editon

Section Three

Development Strategies

So far in this book, we've seen a lot of theory. In the first section, we covered the core JavaScript language and how to use it to program in the web browser. In the previous section, we moved on to look at some more advanced techniques using JavaScript with the latest web standards to create dynamic cross-browser pages.

In this section, we'll take a bit of a detour, and look at some related issues important to anyone taking on JavaScript programming in a professional environment. If you're programming for a living, rather than just for fun, then you're going to have to think about what tools you use, how to set up platforms for development and testing, how to code well to avoid as many bugs as possible, how to debug your code when necessary, and how to include proper error handling in your code to deal with those unexpected situations. Over the next three chapters, we'll be focusing on these issues.

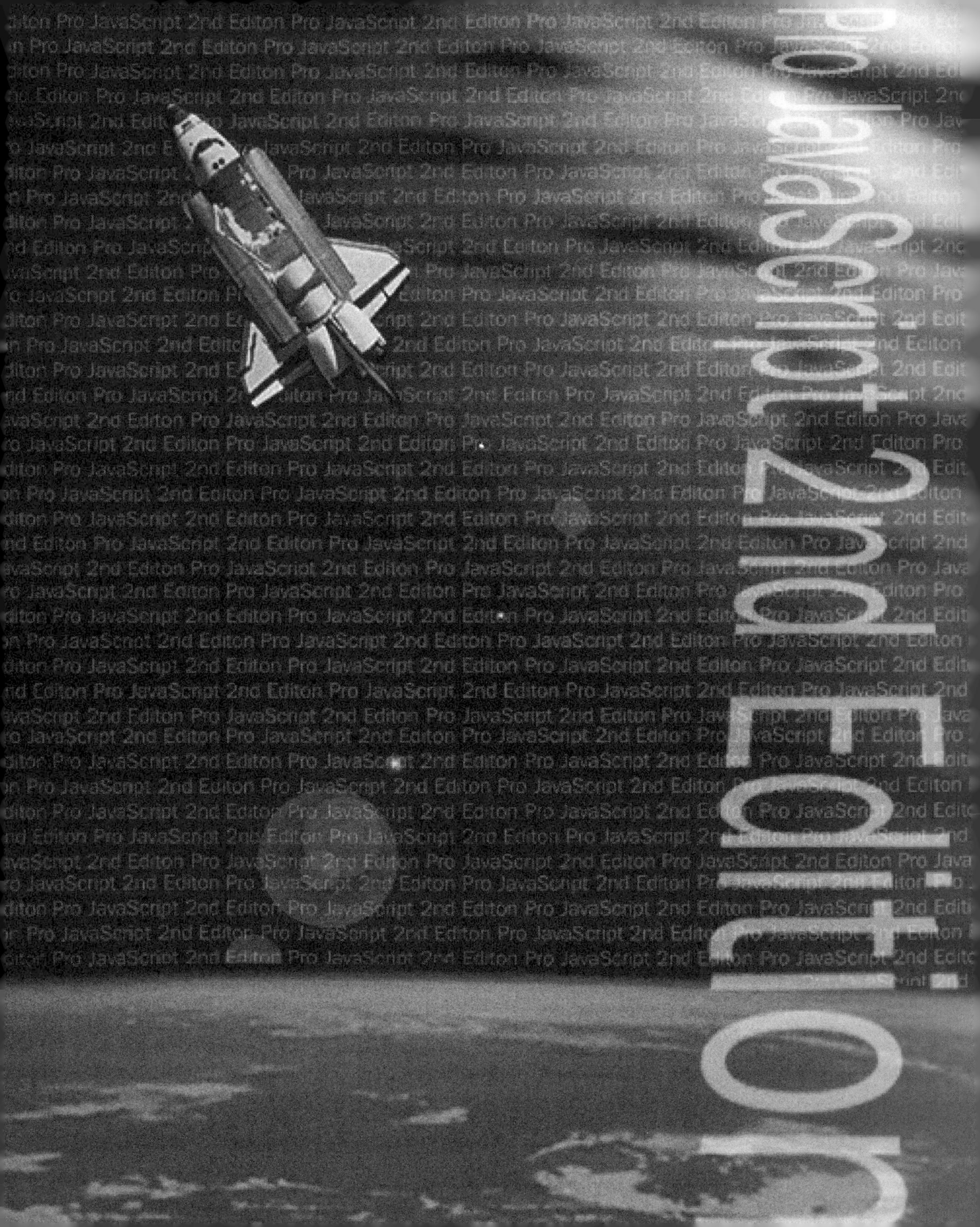
Pro JavaScript 2nd Edition

11

Establishing Your Toolset

It's easy to develop a web site in a vacuum. All you need is a text editor and a Web browser. A basic web page can be made in less than an hour, and dumped onto the global Web in a minute. Why is it then, that some web projects are such a mess? Live web sites can be buggy, work on only one or two browsers, and take forever to update. All these things can cost customers an unbudgeted fortune to have rectified, unless they are particularly good at writing contracts. Somewhere along the line, pure scripting knowledge stops being enough for quality web sites. In this chapter, we take a break from looking at coding issues, and explore the technologies and processes that you need to keep the quality, value, and efficiency of your JavaScript work high.

How do we increase efficiency? There is an old adage: "the right tool for the right job". Compare JavaScript with a compiled language such as C. C programmers require a tool set or tool chain before they can do anything. This tool set consists of compilers, pre-processors, linkers, libraries, debuggers, dependency tools, and so on. In JavaScript programming, we've been blinded so far by the simplicity of the browser environment. We've used few tools other than a simplistic text editor. For bigger, more professional tasks, we need a suitable tool set, or the limits we work under will drive us crazy with frustration.

Some parts of the Web development process are quite complicated, such as coding standards and debugging, which are treated in subsequent chapters. In this chapter, we'll look at the overall development process – which tools to use where, why, and when. We'll look at the development problem that creates the need for more tools. We explore what is required for a professional test bed and examine a number of tools. Next, we look at the benefits that source code control tools can bring to our development process. Finally, we examine how existing libraries of source code written by others can speed up our development.

The Scripting Production Problem

When we add JavaScript to a web page, the overall quality of the produced page can go down very quickly. The main reasons for this are:

❑ Invisible scripting effects: We can't just visually confirm the page is fine as we did with plain HTML. In simple cases, we might be able to, but in general, we can't. Our testing now requires planning and analysis, and is a non-trivial burden.

❑ Unexecuted scripts: When an HTML page loads, all the HTML content is rendered, but not all of the JavaScript scripts necessarily execute straight away – many may only execute after user input. Defective event handlers, functions, and objects can sit in the page for a long time before they are ever used. Their defects might ultimately be revealed only by end-users or customers.

❑ Stateful pages: The existence of JavaScript variables means that a page might act differently depending on what values those variables hold. This further increases the testing complexity.

❑ Functional versus aesthetic failure: If a script has a defect, generally it is not usable at all. If HTML has a defect, it may be ugly, but it will probably be tolerable. JavaScript is less forgiving than HTML when it comes to defects – most JavaScript defects translate to complete failure of the code.

❑ Finally, there are many different browsers and browser versions, all implemented differently.

For these reasons, during a large web project, using JavaScript is going to cost time and effort. We need a reliable system that will minimize the amount of testing and re-testing we need to do, just like any programming activity.

Building a Production Line

In this section, we explain how to get your equipment together to a professional standard, if it's not already. To reduce the development defect rate, and therefore the amount of testing, we just use standard engineering practices. This means we identify the production steps and support each one with equipment designed to prevent defects that could be introduced in that step. We make sure that each step is reasonably separate, so that it doesn't interfere with other steps.

For web development, the steps are well known, although they go by many names. A typical list for a non-trivial project might be:

❑ Conceptual design

❑ Prototyping

❑ Engineering design

❑ Code and unit testing

❑ System testing (and fixing found defects)

❑ Browser compatibility testing (and fixing found defects)

❑ Release (or go live)

At any stage we might need to backtrack to earlier stages – there are many approaches here. The conceptual design stage is where the overall site's *feel* is determined; engineering design is where the developer thinks about how technology should be best used to solve the problem. For the uninitiated, "Code and unit test" means writing needed scripts and testing individual pieces, rather than testing the whole site as one. We're not overly concerned about the names of the stages here; they're familiar to most programmers. We just want to see what technologies can be applied where.

We might build our web site production line standalone, or in an office where there's already some infrastructure, such as a LAN or a server room. We will describe a system useful for a sole operator. If you have a LAN and a network administrator to work with, then we'll indicate at appropriate points what they could do for you.

In this chapter, we're focusing purely on client-side web development, since the development of web pages dynamically generated by server-side technologies is beyond the scope of this book. If we had infinite time and resources, or worked for a large corporation, then we might choose the following production line. We've chosen a Microsoft Windows-based approach, but Linux servers/clients or Apple Macs could be substituted at most points in this diagram:

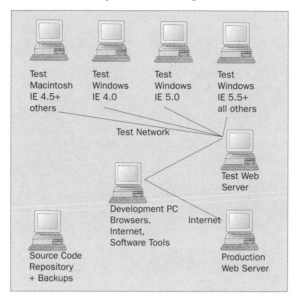

In the above diagram, we have the three main functions of development, test, and live production separate. We never test on the production web server. The finished web site is uploaded via FTP and we access the web site like any external user. The test web server is our crash-and-burn machine, on which we do all the basic testing. If we're lucky, we'll have two test web servers – one in good condition holding the last fully tested version, and one for spot tests and messy experiments. We use FTP to put files on these servers as well. Avoid drag-and-drop copying across a LAN because it re-introduces informal behavior that we're trying to avoid. The other test computers need web browsers only, and make client-server pairs with the test web servers. We need one test client for Macintosh users. We need two or more test clients for IE because Windows won't allow multiple versions of IE to co-exist on one computer. IE 5.0 does have a 4.0 "compatibility mode", reducing the requirements by one. (This compatibility mode is an IE 5.0 install time option and appears as a menu item in the Start menu hierarchy – a starting point is to read this article in Microsoft's online knowledge base: Q197311.) All the other browsers, including all Netscape versions, can be installed on a single PC. We also have a PC responsible for holding the official source of the developed web pages – a repository. A repository is just a very simple database that holds a set of files and directories. This computer provides version control, backups, and lets us share our work with other developers. Finally, our own Development PC is the one on our desk that is full of the useful tools that we use to create the web pages, script them, and possibly debug them.

With this setup, each production step is independently supported. In particular, neither your own PC nor the "live" production PC is the final authority for the web site, meaning that neither of these hosts are the "bible" for the website's files. Our own development PC is too unreliable (accidents happen), and the live machine is too critical for such a task. In addition, the places we test at are well away from any development or live system. Finally, we use formal mechanisms for copying our work between the computers. We use FTP to get to Web servers, even test ones. On the source code repository computer, we will use a proper "deposit and withdrawal" mechanism (discussed later under *Tools for Managing the Codebase*) to get a copy of any web site needing further work.

This might all sound very formal, but all we're really trying to do is discourage the temptation to make fixes that are done on the live site and forgotten. If we lose control over which fixes have been applied where, we're not professional anymore. We want to be able to track and reproduce every change ever made, because we can't spot all changes visually as we might have done with plain HTML.

If we want access to the test machines without cluttering our desks or having to live in a test room, then there are a number of solutions. One solution is to use the multi-boot / multi-partition features of Windows, on the Wintel hardware architecture. In our view, this is not practical because it takes too long to reboot the computer each time we want to use another operating system. An alternative is to install VMware (http://www.vmware.com). In a computer with sufficient memory, VMware allows several operating systems to run at the same time. They can be used alternately simply at the press of a key, and programs can be run in both simultaneously. The main drawback of VMware is that some Windows drivers are imperfectly supported, so that advanced access to printers and so on can be unreliable. The best solution is probably to install VNC (http://www.uk.research.att.com/vnc/) or pcAnywhere (http://www.symantec.com) on the test machines and access them that way from our own desk. These tools provide facilities that allow a remote PC to run its display within a window on your PC. This window acts like a whole computer monitor, responding to your keyboard and mouse as a real console would. Unfortunately, the VNC server for MS Windows, although free, is slow to update, as it has to install the equivalent of a UNIX X Server on top.

For a standalone setup, such a system is not practical – too many computers are required. What we will do in this chapter is use a much simpler system that mimics the ideal, but doubles up some of the tasks:

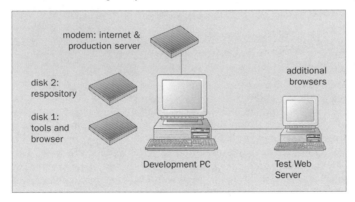

Our development PC is the same as before, but now we use our ISP to reach the production web server, which is probably at some server farm. Our development PC is the same, except that we have a drive allocated to the sole purpose of being the repository for all our web sites' source code. Using two disks, we might still remember to do proper version control when we check out and check in versions from one disk to the other. If we destroy our main disk accidentally (it's the one we use all the time after all), the precious official versions of our web site are still safe on the repository disk. If we have a CD burner or tape drive, then we have a backup system as well. The only thing we should ever need to backup is the repository disk.

Our real investment is in a test web server. We simply must keep our testing environment separate to the development environment. The test web server also has a total of three IE versions installed if we include "4.0 compatibility mode" (assuming it's running Windows). This means that we put the browsers and the server on the same machine. Because of this, you might also want to get hints from your network administrator on how to setup a local DNS server so that you can give the server the same name as your production machine, e.g. www.wrox.com. That's better than posting our web site onto newsgroups and begging someone to compatibility test it for us. We can put all the Netscape, Opera, and other browsers on any host, since they support multiple installs. We want to keep the installed web site separate to prevent us from working directly on it. We'll always make our changes on the development host. All this caution is because of the defects we can introduce with JavaScript and other web programming technologies such as PHP and ASP.

Choosing Development Tools

In this section, we'll look at two strategies: tools to assist with writing scripts, and tools to assist with managing scripts. The subject of debugging tools is left to Chapter 13, where we discuss debugging techniques in detail.

Tools to Speed Up Scripting

We are going to look at web development from two different perspectives: learner and engineer. In both cases, the more complex, fancier tools are more useful in the end than a text editor such as Notepad is. However, the programmer's own knowledge and experience of the technology is always the final limit on scripting, and when we first learn, we want to expand that limit as much as possible. Small tools keep you closer to the underlying technology, especially when you're still learning basics. We want to deliver quality code fast, but to be professional we must work through the learning process by hand first. Therefore, we'll take the two sets of tools one at a time. Firstly the smaller tools for point solutions, and secondly, tools for integrated development.

It isn't possible to cover every useful tool here, but we will cover some of the more popular tools and you can make an informed decision as to whether to use these tools or not.

Tools for Point Solutions

We'll start by looking at the simplest and most common tool, the text editor, used by novices and experts alike. Then we'll move on to look at a couple of other simple tools that have popped up to meet non-editing requirements: TopStyle and ButtonMania. These are point solution tools, each aimed at solving a narrow problem. Between them, we'll have most of our common development requirements met.

Choosing a Text Editor

How are we to choose between all of the text editors currently available? All we need to look at is the editor's support for three things: mouse, keyboard, and smarts. Programmers spend a long time in editors, and if there's no mouse support, forget it. For the same reason, the choice of keyboard commands can become personal to the point of religious fervor. The main choices are:

❑ Simple keys: Originally, from Apple or Xerox, cut, copy and paste are implemented as *Ctrl+X, C* and *V*. *Ctrl+S* means Save. Perhaps the sequence *Alt F S Alt F X* means, "save and quit", to many programmers. Examples of tools are Notepad, EDIT, and most Microsoft-like products. These tools typically need frequent mouse work when in use, but this key set is popular. Usually it includes the WordPerfect-like special keys – the arrow keys, Insert, Home, and so on.

❑ WordStar keys: Common in programmer tools such as Borland's IDEs, for example, TurboPascal, but originally from the WordStar word processor, this key set is familiar to anyone who remembers that "*Ctrl+K B Ctrl+K K*" is a block select sequence. These keys are not so common any more.

❑ Vi keys: This editor of UNIX origin still has a hold on many peoples hearts, but can deeply offend those that grew up on GUIs. It is very fast to use, once the obscure commands are learned, very flexible, and extensible.

❑ Emacs keys: Endless combinations of *Alt* and *Ctrl* are sometime very obscure to the uninitiated, but grant access to a massively powerful "Swiss-army knife" of an editor. The right combination of keys and world domination, or a copy of Hamlet, may well be the result.

In this section we'll look very briefly at two Windows editors: NoteTab Pro, which originates from Windows programming land and uses the simple key set, and gVIM, originating from UNIX programming land, which is a drastically enhanced version of UNIX's vi that also supports the mouse. What are noteworthy about these two editors are their extensibility, flexibility, and the little JavaScript they each support.

NoteTab Pro is backed by its own scripting language that allows, amongst other things, extensive control over cutting and pasting text. Each of the buttons at the bottom of the window is actually a library of features that are only three clicks away. We will illustrate their use with a JavaScript library, which we downloaded from the many libraries available at http://www.notetab.com/. This particular library is a single file named `javascripts.clb` (there are several JavaScript ones to choose from), which can be found at http://www.notetab.com/java.htm#JavaScript and has the name javascripts.zip. This can be put into `C:\Program Files\NoteTab\Libraries` and NoteTab automatically detected this file without needing to be restarted. This next screenshot shows a new button at the bottom, representing this new library. We've clicked it once to expose the tasks the library can perform:

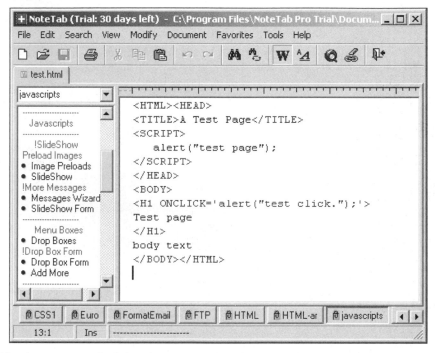

Each of the dot-points on the left indicates a job this library will do for us, much like a menu option. If we move the insertion point to just before the `</SCRIPT>` tag and double-click **Image Preloads** on the left, then the following new JavaScript code is automatically pasted in for us inside the `<SCRIPT>` tags:

```
<!--Begin preloading images-->
{
image_name = new Image(width,height);
image_name.src = "image_name.gif";
image_name2 = new Image(width,height);
image_name2.src = "image_name2.gif";
}
```

This is clearly a laborsaving arrangement. The NoteTab libraries are fully user-customizable, so there's plenty of scope for automating repetitive tasks with this editor. NoteTab easily beats NotePad.

The second editor we'll briefly look at is gVIM. The installation process for this editor is a bit fiddly, and is not helped by an incomprehensible web site at http://www.vim.org. The latest version as we write this is 5.8. The steps for installing that version are:

❑ Follow the Download Vim link near the top of the web site, choosing options that lead to a PC version of gVIM, until you have navigated to a mirrored download directory similar to ftp://ftp.au.vim.org/pub/vim/pc/.

❑ Download `gvim58.zip` and `vim58rt.zip`. No other files are required.

❑ Unzip these files to an install directory, we chose C:\local\install. The individual files should appear in C:\local\install\vim\vim58.

❑ Start an MS-DOS emulation window and type:

> **cd \local\install\vim\vim58**

❑ Type install and answer the questions that follow the same way as in this screenshot of the complete install. The user input is shown below, so the user responses are: y, 2, 3, y, 1, and y.

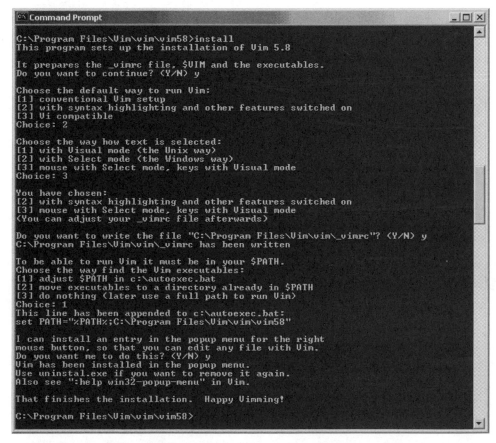

Until you reboot, you'll have to run gVIM by double-clicking the `C:\Program Files\Vim\vim\vim58\gvim.exe` icon.

Be warned that without a tutorial or prior experience, you might find gVIM nearly unusable! A beginning is to note that *i* and *a* put you into "insert" mode, while *Escape* stops insert mode. The simplest navigation keys are *h, j, k, l*. Type :help and *Enter* for assistance. UNIX programmers often love VIM.

gVIM has both JavaScript and HTML syntax coloring. Although it does not have the extensive libraries of NoteTab, it does come with a huge bundle of useful macros written in its terse and cryptic, but extremely powerful macro language. One of the best features of gVIM and vi in general is its various bits of support for C-like languages such as JavaScript. An example is automatic indenting and parentheses matching. Perhaps the most powerful example is the **ctags** functionality, suitable for very large developments. This requires a small, separate program executes and examines the entire source code for a given development effort at night and creates a special keyword file that gVIM understands. From gVIM, a single keyboard command can send the programmer to any function in any file in the whole development tree. This feature provides a very fast way of navigating through code shared over large numbers of files. The gVIM help describes these and millions of other features extensively.

Highly configurable, it is possible to spend as much time piecing together special enhancements to NoteTab or gVIM as is spent developing websites. Fortunately, others have created these libraries for you.

TopStyle

TopStyle (available from http://www.bradsoft.com/topstyle/download/index.asp) is a graphical tool for constructing CSS style sheets. Alas, it's yet to support JavaScript stylesheet behaviors, which are a CSS3 thing, although you can type them in by hand. This screenshot illustrates the main features of the tool:

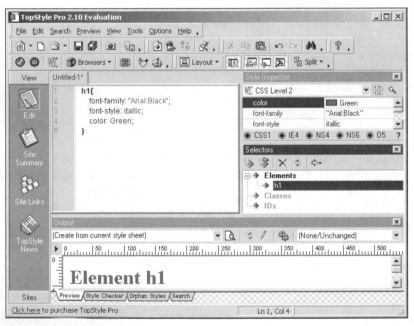

There are many incidental user interface elements shown here, which we'll ignore. The important bits to study are the four small windows that make up 80% of the viewing area. They are named Untitled-1*, Style Inspector, Output, and Selectors. The first is the raw style sheet code under construction – in this case, font information about <H1> tags. The Style Inspector window is a list of all the style sheet attributes that exist. It can easily be seen that attributes in the text of the first window appear here as well. The Selectors window is just a handy organizer for all the styles created so far – a single h1 selector is the only one in this case. The Output window shows what the built style looks like – visual feedback for you. There's a mass of menu options and icons to examine when first learning this tool, which can be confusing. To get started, just click the purple New Selector button in the Selectors window, choose Simple or Class at the top of the popup wizard, choose a tag, click Add, click OK. Now you can add whatever style attributes you want from the Style Inspector window.

This tool's value is simple: no syntax errors, no looking up style attributes elsewhere, and instant feedback on style choices. This tool is a good way for a learner to properly grasp the technology. If you are busy with numerous other tasks, a small tool like this is a great thing to play with, in the free time you don't have. Nothing can really replace basic style sheet expertise, however – for more information on style sheets, see Chapter 8.

ButtonMania

The second point solution tool we'll look at is ButtonMania (available from http://w1.321.telia.com/~u32102551/). This little tool creates decorative button-like images: both pressed and unpressed versions. It also creates menu tabs. Both are perfect for use in web sites. The interface is a little odd, and takes a while to get used to. The three main windows are shown here:

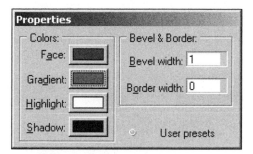

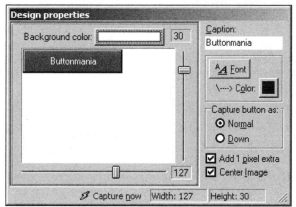

The first window is the final captured image or button – the other windows are used to design it. The Properties window is specific to the type of button you choose (there are a number of types). The Design properties window is where general aspects of the button are picked, such as font. This is a very simple and handy tool for web images; it is one that picks up where styles, or Microsoft Paint, leave off. What is particularly interesting for JavaScript users is the menu item under the Create Button menu named JavaScript Helping Hand. When selected, a new window is revealed, and after a few clicks plus the Edit, Generate Code menu item; that window looks like this:

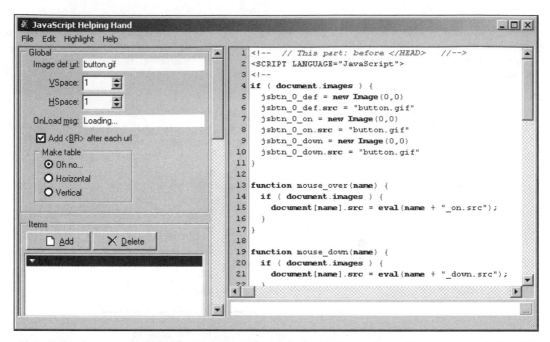

This window has generated JavaScript code automatically for the frequently used image swap technique. We discuss this technique in Chapter 10. Once the buttons are created, just cut and paste the script into the HTML page – no hand coding required. That is very efficient, if we understand what's going on, and don't just blindly use it from the start. This is not the last code generator we'll see in this chapter. Generated code can also be of very poor quality, which is arguably the case here. At least it's a fast starting point.

Sticking to a plain text editor is the practice that's probably holding efficiency back the most now. A major shortcoming of a plain text editor is its lack of support for HTML, CSS, and JavaScript help on syntax, standards, and compatibility issues. Up until now, we have to rely on books or industry web sites like http://www.webmonkey.com.

Tools for Integrated Development

If we were to write a small computer program, we'd need a text editor. If we were to write a very large one, we'd need a programming environment – a software facility that supports all the development needs we have at once, such as the Unix shell, EMACS, or Visual C++. Such tools exist for web programmers as well. These are referred to as Integrated Development Environments, or IDEs.

In this section, we'll look at five: HotDog, Allaire/Macromedia's HomeSite, Dreamweaver, and Microsoft's Visual InterDev. This last tool is undergoing name changes as Microsoft aligns existing tools with their .NET strategy. We chose these tools because, apart from being popular, they provide a simple way for us to see how the JavaScript support of point-solution tools scales up for larger tools.

HotDog

HotDog (available from http://www.sausagetools.com/), is best described as a plain text editor on steroids. Its goal is to assist the HTML author with HTML tags in every possible way, and that includes help with JavaScript. Here is a screenshot of a sample session:

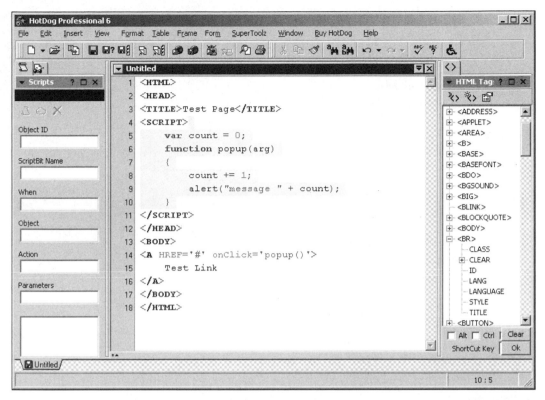

The main part of the window shown is occupied by three panes or sub-windows. There's a lot of advanced text editor functionality. The obvious benefit of HotDog, and half of its original success, is the syntax support for HTML and JavaScript shown in the center window. HTML text and JavaScript keywords are highlighted in various colors, and finder and wizard features help us out when our memory lapses as we type. Clearly, this is better than a simple text editor is. HotDog also includes a built-in CSS style sheet creator.

The left pane above shows part of HotDog's limited JavaScript support. Using this pane, individual event handler scripts (called actions) can be configured or saved in template files for future use. Therefore, we could build a handler library and get some JavaScript reuse across pages or projects.

A second bit of JavaScript support is to be found under the menu item Format | Dynamic HTML Animation. This opens a window similar to the JavaScript code-generating facilities of ButtonMania. It allows you to insert pre-existing scripts into the web page, to create simple animation of a HTML tag, for example. If we do use HotDog's JavaScript support, then we might notice something unusual – instead of seeing references to `alert()`, we may see references to `hdscrAlert()`. This is because HotDog includes a set of its own JavaScript functions in the page. The `hdscrAlert()` function is a HotDog function that eventually calls the normal `alert()` function. It does this for both browser-compatibility reasons and as an attempt to provide a standard set of commonly used functions. We'll see this is a common strategy for the bigger tools. As developers we need to decide whether to commit to these function libraries or not. Such a library is okay if we can extract it from the tool. Since the library is always published with the web site, this isn't usually a problem. In HotDog's case, some attempt has additionally been made to "shroud" the code. Shrouding means that the JavaScript code provided by HotDog is unreadable when casually reviewed, due to petty formatting and encrypting tricks. That was a brief fashion in about 1997, but these days is considered a pointless trick, since no real protection is granted, and the code's purpose is usually trivial anyway.

For plain HTML users, HotDog might be a good choice. For script developers, however, it falls short on two counts: its syntax support for JavaScript is quite limited, and it doesn't help us with the production process as much as we'd like. For those more oriented towards GUIs, its interface is quite clunky too. However, it does represent an important step in the evolution of Web development tools, which is why we look at it here. In summary: if you already have HTML knowledge and are now adding scripting to your skills, you'll be held back if you continue to use HotDog.

HomeSite

A step up from HotDog in terms of programmer support is HomeSite 4.5.2 (available from http://www.macromedia.com/software/homesite/trial/). Its current reputation is that it is arguably the best tool for cross-browser, client-server oriented, web sites. Its age means that it may lose that crown unless it gets a major upgrade, however. HomeSite also has the problem that it has been eclipsed by Dreamweaver, which we'll look at next. Here's a brief look at HomeSite in action:

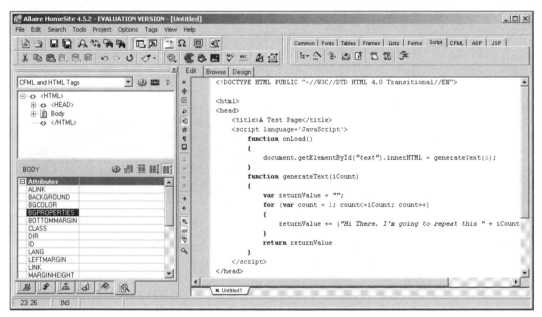

Just as for HotDog, HomeSite provides syntax coloring for HTML and JavaScript, and many buttons and menu items. The panes on the left of this screenshot show HomeSite tag support. Not shown are HomeSite's neat, popup attribute hints for HTML tags. These remind you of the correct HTML syntax as you type. The Drop-down menu to the right is the "JavaScript Tree", which provides us with a reminder of the general Browser Object Model (henceforth BOM), and DOM objects available in browsers. This is great for script writers. It does not provide, however the parameters and types of the methods, functions, and properties it lists. Next to the JavaScript Tree button is a JavaScript Wizard button that provides six common tricks for which code is automatically generated, similar to the ButtonMania example. Finally, TopStyle is integrated into HomeSite, so we don't need to learn yet another CSS creation tool.

Two things set HomeSite apart from HotDog: the Project menu and integration with source code control systems. These features are designed to assist the development production process.

424

The concept of a project is familiar to most Windows programmers and is common in IDEs. We bundle up a web site into a single, recognizable, development unit. A master file lists all the contents of the web site, and it's up to us to maintain it. Unfortunately, there is a big hole in HomeSite's conception of a project. We should create a project with physical, manual attributes, not with the HomeSite default of virtual attributes. The former case demands that all the files for the web site are gathered together in the same directory tree. The latter case allows us to put items into the project from anywhere (for example, from across the corporate LAN). Unless we're extremely careful about what we're doing, the virtual approach would make our web site's version control far worse than for no project at all.

The source code control features of HomeSite allow us to automatically copy our web site into and out of a source code repository that is usually provided by another tool. The repository and HomeSite are connected by a Windows API.

HomeSite provides us with a built in FTP client that lets us publish our web site directly to any FTP-enabled web site host. It provides a kind of control center from which we can collect together files, plan versions, save, restore, and publish our web site, in addition to merely developing it. In theory, we can go through most of the steps in the production process using this one tool. HomeSite and tools like it provide good support for the development cycle. That means more stability and less JavaScript testing.

Finally, if we need it, HomeSite provides support for back-end web server scripting tasks that are driven from embedded scripts in an HTML page. Examples are tags and scripts for the ColdFusion application server, JSP, and Microsoft ASP `<SCRIPT RUNAT='server'>` scripts. Therefore, we needn't leave HomeSite even for these tasks.

Dreamweaver

If you are approaching JavaScript programming from a layout, graphics design or animation point of view, then the very popular, highly integrated tool Dreamweaver might be better for you. Dreamweaver (available from http://www.macromedia.com/software/dreamweaver/trial/) is a web development tool aimed more at visual design than programming. Web programming and web design overlap in a number of places: in layout, style sheets, and in animations to cite just a few. Therefore, Dreamweaver has many design-oriented features familiar to the web developer, plus extensive JavaScript support. The emphasis, however, is on providing a shortcut means to an end, rather than on finding the most convenient way to access the enabling technologies, such as HTML and JavaScript. This means that Dreamweaver does its best to hide the technology from you. Here is a screenshot of the tool showing a web page in early development:

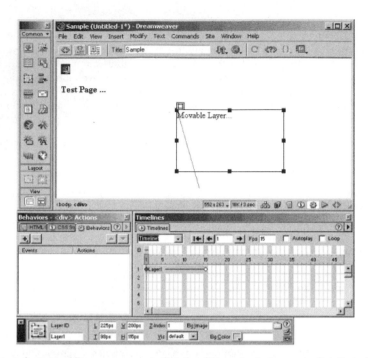

The most obvious feature of Dreamweaver is that the different windows are distributed on the desktop in a very similar manner to traditional graphic design tools such as Adobe Illustrator. Only a few of the windows are shown here. Let us examine the many windows shown, starting clockwise from the top left. In order the windows are as follows: a small floating toolbar of common tasks; the large main editing window in "Design view"; the middle-sized Timelines animation planner; a wide object properties window for the currently selected object; and lastly, the small Assets window, currently showing the scripted behaviors in the page. Just one behavior appears consisting of an onFrame1 event and a Drag Layer action.

The design view, rather than the code view is the most convenient for developing content in Dreamweaver – HTML and scripts are only obvious in the code view, however. Therefore, there's less need to learn HTML tags in this tool. There is much drag-and-drop support for arbitrary placement of page elements. When creating styles, there's very little mention of the CSS attribute names – instead there are plainly named form controls and menu items from which to select values.

The power of Dreamweaver for the script writer is in its behaviors and timelines, which together allow animation. The Timelines window shows a "film strip" which states which JavaScript scripts run on which HTML objects in the page at what times. What does this have to do with JavaScript? Timelines, animations, behaviors, actions, and all the rest are just an alternative set of terms for Dynamic HTML. Dreamweaver will create some Dynamic HTML for you. It supplies some complex JavaScript functions that make up a simple time-based scheduler. This scheduler is just a more sophisticated version of the setTimeout() and setInterval() browser functions. Using this scheduler and a choice of pre-supplied JavaScript functions, you can piece together sophisticated DHTML effects without much thought at all. Looking back at the last screenshot, the diagonal line in the main editing window indicates the track along which the movable layer will travel. Of course, the layer can contain any kind of content.

The Dreamweaver JavaScript scheduler is not particularly unique or sophisticated. An alternate, freely available scheduler exists in the JavaScript animation library at http://www.javascript-games.org/. Using any such library does a lot for you.

All tools have their shortcomings, and one of Dreamweaver's is that it doesn't help us with our engineering-oriented production problems much – there are no project concepts or source code control features. For highly animated pages, however, it is definitely the biggest gun we can bring to bear, and is a worth point solution tool for those tasks. With deadline pressures and the other real world constraints on our work, Dreamweaver can save us time by doing a lot of scripting for us. As for all code generators, we have to live with generated scripts that aren't finely tuned for our specific purpose.

Visual InterDev and .NET

Now let's have a look at Microsoft's Visual InterDev. It is rather biased towards Microsoft and Internet Explorer, but it has the best JavaScript support of the tools we are looking at. Here is a typical screenshot of InterDev 6:

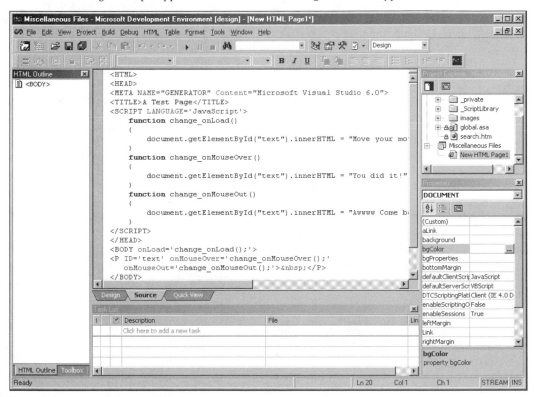

Many of its features are similar to those of the other tools we've looked at. It is rather more sophisticated than the other tools, and can provide a fully JavaScript-oriented view of web pages, as shown above. In this kind of view, the tool works primarily with the JavaScript scripts, rather than primarily with HTML that happens to contain JavaScript. The left pane above provides the developer with a structured view of all the script handlers that can potentially be embedded in a given web page. This can be used as an architectural or navigational aid, as well as providing an easy way to find and add the right event handler for the right HTML element. The bottom right pane allows lookup of the BOM/DOM object model (as does the JavaScript Tree in HomeSite), but also provides extensive support for selecting values for object properties as well as simply listing the properties. These object models are documented from a Microsoft perspective. Where Visual InterDev excels, though, is in its syntax assistance. For example, standard browser object names are auto-detected and the object properties provided as a dropdown hint menu, a feature known as **IntelliSense**. Just keep typing if the required property is known, or select from the list if it has slipped from the mind. This should be very familiar to any programmer who has used a Microsoft IDE. The syntax hints extend to reminders of function and object parameters including allowed values.

427

Such tightly integrated language help is quite seductive, and easy to get used to. If we really want highly portable web pages, however, we're best steering clear of Visual InterDev because we're sure to be tempted into Microsoft-only features. Like all the Microsoft "Visual" products, Visual InterDev is highly integrated with Microsoft Windows and other Microsoft products such as debuggers, web servers, and so on. For a Microsoft-centric web development project, we can't beat the efficiency of the Microsoft products, once we've spent a moment working out how best to use them together. Visual InterDev supports backend, project, FTP, and source code control features just as HomeSite does. It is almost a complete solution for JavaScript development.

Visual Studio.NET, the next incarnation of their developer tools, doesn't have Visual InterDev as such. All programming languages have an identical IDE, and this IDE is very similar to InterDev. The language used is specified on startup, and if you specify that you are creating a web site, then it will look for HTML, JavaScript and ASP on the pages, and you are able to use IntelliSense on all of the languages. The IDE's main difference from InterDev 6 is its Context Help on the right hand side. This will give help on whatever native object, method, or property you are using at the time.

FrontPage

FrontPage is the web-designing package provided by Microsoft with their Office suite. FrontPage has very limited functionality; it is targeted mainly at your average Office user, and so it covers the middle ground in terms of ease of use and power. Most developers dislike FrontPage, but it is already installed on many PCs, so it is worth a mention here. The first thing to note is that it has no JavaScript support built in. If you use FrontPage, and a script fails to execute correctly in the Preview pane, then it gives the option of loading up Microsoft Script Debugger, or Visual Interdev if it is installed and the whole HTML page is debugged inside this application instead. This section will therefore cover its HTML generation abilities. Let's see how it looks first:

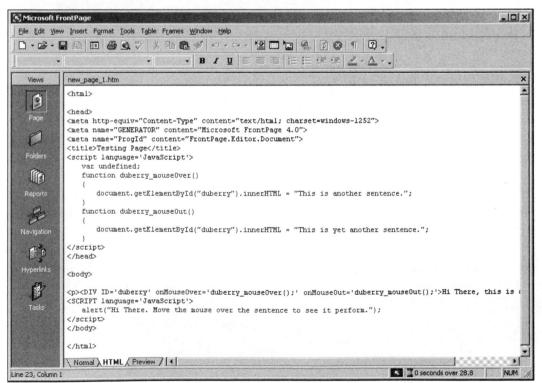

Above is the HTML view. The Preview view is the equivalent of loading the page into a browser, whereas the Normal view is where the commands and buttons of FrontPage can be utilized to add features to the web site, and the text content can be entered just by typing. One main use is its ability to add components to the web page. It enables you to add Excel Spreadsheets, for instance, so that as long as the surfer has MS Excel installed, then they can read the spreadsheet embedded into the page. It also allows the reader to add some other useful objects, such as a hit counter. Unfortunately, many of the components that can be added are ActiveX components and so are limited to Internet Explorer on Windows.

FrontPage, in Normal view, works in a similar way to that you would expect a word processor to behave. We can set the alignment of text or objects with the click of a button, and we can select numerous things and change the properties all at once. In Format | Style we can specify a stylesheet for the document in a simple and straightforward manner. We just specify the HTML elements we would like the styling applied to and then set the font, paragraph, border, and numbering for it. We can also specify style changes to user-defined tags (buy use of the ID attribute).

Because of its lack of JavaScript support, Microsoft-bias, and its limited web designing features, we would not recommend using this product. The latest version of FrontPage that is shipped with Office XP has no support for JavaScript either, and has very few extra features included. Visual InterDev is a much better IDE and tools such as Dreamweaver are much more competent at building up a web page. FrontPage Express (which is a free download that is available with IE 5) is a very restricted version of FrontPage and so even that option isn't worthwhile. As a developer, it is likely that you would prefer to use a text editor rather than this tool.

The one feature of FrontPage that does make it especially appealing to new users is the FrontPage extensions, which can be built into a web server (and are built into IIS 5 by default). These enable the content of a site designed in FrontPage to be uploaded to the web server, without the use of FTP (which many users find primitive). However, there have been a number of security scares with these FrontPage extensions, and the feature is not good enough to warrant a changeover.

Tools for Managing the Codebase

If you have worked with a source control system before, you may want to skip to the next section, as this section serves as a broad introduction and overview. The source code of our website, any related files, the directory structure they reside in and all other bits and pieces is collectively called a **codebase**. Making these files is not like making bricks. Once you've made a brick, it stays a brick for the much of the future. Our files can be damaged, modified, lost, or accidentally deleted. Worse, we can forget what they do, why they do it, whether they work properly or not, or even if they ever worked. Everyone's been through an accidental deletion tragedy. We need something to cut down the angst. Source code control, in which we limit the damage we can do to our own files, is a piece of our production armory just like other development tools. Why are we talking about source code control in a JavaScript book? JavaScript can cause many defects in web pages as we said at the start of this chapter, and source code control is going to help. We will also illustrate how to restore control of a web site that has had emergency, undocumented, unknown fixes applied. This is a common JavaScript scenario.

In our simple equipment setup, our development PC has a disk drive separate to the one we use for all development. This is where we will put controlled versions of our codebase. We certainly wouldn't install any software on it. That disk is for long-term storage only.

Minimum Safe Behavior

If you don't wish to invest in a source code control system, then you can get away with a minimal approach. This approach consists of regularly backing up files *before* embarking on each phase of development, not after. This way you can always go back to the last known version if things go wrong. You could rely on a simple archiving tool such as WinZip. Every time you embark on a new task, you zip up the whole web site in whatever state it might be, and store it on the repository disk with a date and version marked. Provided the backup is made regularly, you now have a simple system of time stamped versions you can refer back to if required. Such a simple approach is good enough for one person, but doesn't coordinate web site work with others. It also doesn't provide us with any source code diagnosis or management tools. There are better ways.

CVS

CVS, the Concurrent Version System, is a free and open-source source control tool whose technology underlies many source code control systems. It is called "concurrent" because it has multi-user support. Microsoft's and MetroWerks' Visual SourceSafe is based on CVS technology, as are many other tools such as WinCVS and tkCVS. The example below uses WinCVS, which can be downloaded from http://www.wincvs.org/download.html. For any software job where the software is to be deployed and maintained over the long term, CVS is essential. Other versioning tools available include RCS and SCCS (which are very primitive), and ClearCase (which is more advanced than CVS, but expensive – $3000 a seat at time of editorial).

For those new to CVS, the "man page", or help page, is vital – you'll read it many times. Even with a GUI interface, knowing the command line options can still be important. An online copy of the help is available here: http://www.die.net/doc/linux/man/man1/cvs.1.html.

The problem with CVS is that it requires a little practice before everything makes sense. Some of the concepts are a little strange compared to other programming tools. A huge amount of time can be spent learning CVS's finer points, which we'll avoid in this section. We'll just explain the simplest CVS concepts, set up a working repository, and do a simple exercise.

The CVS system is simple in concept. Users check out (extract from the repository) files and work on them in a workspace, making and saving changes in the workspace. If the changes are valuable, they are committed back (saved permanently) to the repository. If they are simply experimental or otherwise not required, the workspace is simply deleted. If a user commits changes, then other users can bring those changes into their workspaces. A user can review what the differences are between their workspace files and the repository files at any time. It is this last feature that allows every single change to be tracked. Furthermore, when changes are committed, a name, date, and optional comment are recorded. CVS commands can be used to recall this information, so that a record is automatically kept of who changed the files at what time. Ideally, all users of the system write meaningful comments when they commit changes. "Commit early, commit often" is a CVS catch cry, since no changes are safe until committed. In the rare event that changes from two users conflict, that is, they both change the same file in the same place, CVS makes the person slowest to commit responsible for cleaning up the clash.

Here is a conceptual diagram of how CVS works:

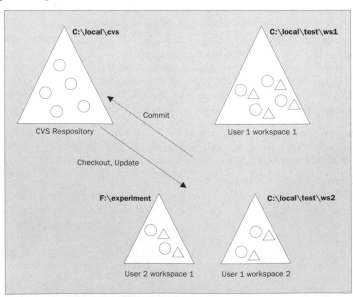

Each big triangle represents a directory tree. Each circle represents a **module**. A module in CVS is a collection of files. Modules can be complicated, but they can also be just a directory name, which is how we operate here. The small triangles are CVS configuration information, also called housekeeping information. This information is stored on a per-directory basis. It has its own sub-directory that's always named CVS - this keeps it separate to our precious source files. Finally, the module with a spot in it is a special module named CVSROOT. This contains housekeeping information for the entire CVS repository. This is similar to a data dictionary in a database or the registry in Microsoft Windows.

In the diagram above, the CVS repository on the left contains the official source file copies of the work at hand, in our case a web site that we will dub the "Kaos" web site. Two users are currently developing the scripts for it and using the CVS repository. User 1 has checked out (extracted copies of) all the files except for CVSROOT from the repository into C:\local\test\ws1. The CVSROOT module is rarely checked out, so this is normal. User 1 has also checked out a second copy of two modules, into C:\local\test\ws2. User 2 has checked out two modules into F:\experiment. So, there are three **workspaces** – a CVS term that just means a directory structure that includes some CVS housekeeping files as well as source code from the repository. The housekeeping information is stored in the workspace not in the repository, therefore the repository can't be damaged or become confused by accidental deletions in the workspace. The repository doesn't actually know what workspaces exist, although the workspaces all know (from the housekeeping files) where the repository is. In fact, any workspace can be entirely deleted, or partially deleted, at any time. However, the repository can be damaged badly by careless use of the CVS commands, so care is required – this is not an RDBMS system where you can use the transaction log to recover from most mistakes.

In our example, we'll just have one user and one workspace.

Here is a screenshot of WinCVS 1.2 (At this time, 1.3 is in beta testing):

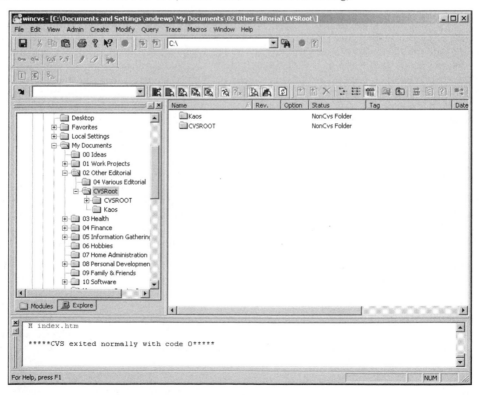

431

The top two panes shown look a bit like Windows Explorer, but they're not. They represent views or reports, rather than displaying all the contents of the C: drive. Of the two tabs on the top left pane, only the Modules tab is interesting to us here. Although it shows most of the PC's directory hierarchy, its real purpose is to identify CVS-related directories and allow us to set the current directory. The top right pane shows how WinCVS identifies a CVS-related directory – it has a check mark in the folder icon. The bottom pane is a command line interface; irritatingly it doesn't yet have a command prompt like C:\>, or $ for UNIX users. We can use the menus and see output appear in this command line pane. If all else fails, we can type commands here, starting at the first blank line.

First, let's install the needed software. WinCVS and Tcl install just like any developed-for-Windows software: download and fire-up the supplied installer. Tcl is required to make the bottom pane of WinCVS work, and is available from http://dev.scriptics.com/. To configure WinCVS, choose Admin | Preferences from the WinCVS menu bar. Going through all the tabs and fields of the resulting dialog box, enter the CVSROOT as a folder outside the installation directory of WinCVS. Set Authentication to Local mounted directory. Uncheck everything else, except under the WinCVS tab enter another, temporary, directory in the HOME folder box. Next, under View | File Filter, make sure that all filters are selected. This is the case when the filter menu items all show depressed icons - choose each item to see the state of the icons change. Finally, under View | Toolbars, ensure all toolbars are selected. These last few steps are just to ensure all the features of WinCVS are exposed to view as we experiment. We are now ready to set up a source code controlled development environment.

Let's make a CVS repository first. We should only ever need one. Make sure that the CVSROOT directory exists and is empty. From the WinCVS menu bar choose Create | Create a new Repository. Choose C:\local\cvs as the repository location. Click OK. You can explore what's been put here with Windows Explorer but it is strongly recommended that you avoid manual changes to this area. All changes should be made indirectly via CVS tools.

Now for a workspace, recall this is just a normal directory plus some CVS housekeeping files. Using Windows Explorer, make sure that a folder called C:\local\test exists and is empty. The workspace directory will not be a proper workspace until CVS provides it with housekeeping configuration files containing workspace information. Fortunately, there is a special module name, ".", (period,) which means "everything, even if its nothing". Unfortunately, WinCVS has a defect and the Create | Checkout modules menu item can't handle ".". To get around this, first make sure that in the upper left pane of WinCVS, the Modules tab is selected, and the C:\local\test folder icon is selected. Then, in the lower command line pane, on the first blank line, type the following command and press Enter:

```
cvs checkout .
```

You should see output in the lower pane with files flagged with a U, indicating that they have been Updated. CVS always uses a single letter to indicate how the status of a file in a workspace has changed. Using Windows Explorer you can examine how CVS has added to the directory structure under C:\local\test, making it a proper workspace. None of the files are new source code files. Finally, delete the C:\local\test\CVSROOT directory using Windows Explorer. We're not interested in this module, and we don't want to make any accidental changes to it. We now have a workspace.

Now we will create our own module for the Kaos web site. It will have two HTML files and a Windows bitmap image. The contents of these files are unimportant, so just use anything. In the workspace, create a directory called Kaos – C:\local\test\Kaos. It should then appear in the top right pane in WinCVS, with the words "NonCvs Folder" next to it. Using Windows Explorer, put two HTML files and one .bmp file in this directory. If you open the Kaos folder in WinCVS, you should see these three files listed with blue question mark icons to the left and NonCVS File to the right. The CVS workspace knows that it doesn't control these files yet. We have now started the process of web site development.

Committing source files to the CVS repository is a two-step process if the files are new. First we must `cvs add` the files to the repository, then we must `cvs commit` them. If directories, rather than files are added, the `commit` step happens automatically. Adding of directories is required because the CVS repository must understand the full hierarchical structure of the source code.

To add files to the repository, note the small bright icons with a plus sign in them (bottom right menu bar in this image, but they could be elsewhere on the toolbars on your machine). These are `cvs add` icons. One is for text files and directories, the other for binary files. The one that is marked **01** is for binaries. These allow you to add individual files and folders to the repository. It is very important to use the correct one on a given file, or else your files will always come out of the repository damaged. Select the `test` directory on the left, then single click the `Kaos` folder on the right. Click the **Add** icon – at this stage, only one should be available. The folder is added to the repository, as reported in the output in the bottom pane. Open the `Kaos` folder in the left pane, which displays the three web site files on the right. Click each one in turn, and add them with the correct **Add** toolbar icon – use the binary icon for the image. Now all the new files are added, but the addition is not yet permanent. They can now be committed individually or together. To commit all of them at once, click the `test` directory in the top left pane and select the `Kaos` directory on the right. From the menu bar choose **Modify | Commit selection**, and type **New Kaos web site** when asked for a log message.

Now the web site is saved safely in the repository. At this point you could experiment with making changes to the content of the three files in the `Kaos` directory and see what is reported if you commit again. This is the CVS development cycle: modify files, commit, modify, commit.

That concludes our lightning tour of CVS. CVS is quite complex, and we have brushed over some matters in order to get through a concrete example. In particular, we haven't dealt with the subject of versioning. CVS can also help us to have a rock solid release cycle, via its ability to "`cvs tag`" a coordinated set of repository files.

A Production Sample Run

So far, we have looked at a variety of development tools. Here, we'll pause for a moment and show how to tie everything together into a series of steps, and see exactly how a project might develop up until the final release stage.

At the start of the project, we might have some informal files that have been used as a demo, prototype, or presentation tool for a new customer. We have all the equipment and software installed for the simple set up described earlier. We have CVS installed, with the repository on a separate disk or on a shared file server. We also have our personal development environment. Using WinCVS, or the source code control features of a tool such as Visual InterDev, we can create a workspace on a development PC in which we'll work from now on.

We make a directory for the new web site in the workspace, fill it with the prototype files, and commit it to CVS using WinCVS or our IDE tool. We've had a chance to properly read up on CVS, and so now we understand how to "brand" a set of files with a version number. At this point, we may gain a development deadline and other people may become involved. We make the location of the CVS repository known so that other developers, or web designers, can add their material. Everyone is warned to `cvs commit` their material in a timely manner.

Now we can clean up the prototype for proper development without forcing it to be unavailable for sales staff. We FTP it onto a test site and see what needs fixing. We make fixes in the workspace, which we can access from any development tool such as HomeSite. We might also create a project for the web site, and commit project files to CVS as well. We test trivial changes using a browser on the development PC that just loads the files in the workspace for viewing. When we're happy, we commit everything to CVS again. This committed version is an improved version of the prototype, ready for system test.

We are now ready for formal testing. We clean out the test web site PC, and FTP the prototype from the workspace onto it. This way, we are sure of what we're testing. Now we test with all required browsers. We note the defects we find, and go back to the development hosts for a fix cycle. All developers with fixes to address agree to a time by which they will commit their files again. When this commitment occurs, we can tell using reports available from CVS the amount of code changed since the last release. In this case, that's the amount of defects introduced by the requirement for cross-browser portability. We can use this measurement to adjust our estimates the next time management needs a quote on a job; that makes the estimates more accurate. It also tells us the cost in labor of cross-platform support. There are many such statistics that CVS will provide for us. We can clean out the test website again, FTP this last committed version onto it, and test again to ensure that all the required changes have indeed been captured.

A second prototype might be required for usability studies or further requirements development. We can use the "branch" functionality of CVS to split off a copy of the current prototype version. In the branched copy (still stored in the CVS repository), we can do all the temporary scripting required to illustrate the points the customer wants to see in the second prototype. Therefore changes to a branch version don't affect the main version normal development can continue on the main version. After the usability study, we can compare the main and branch versions with the CVS tools, and then merge them together automatically if it's justified. This is a mechanism that stops multiple, slightly different copies of a web site from floating around in an unmanaged way.

When we finish development, we can tag the latest committed version of every file and call it a beta release. Now we can clean out the test PC again and drop the beta release on it for more rigorous testing.

Finally, at production release, we apply a last CVS tag and FTP the release onto the production site. If all the developers interested in cutting-edge development now move on, then we have the repository, its files, version, and release information, dates and comments on the changes committed. Subsequent maintenance programmers can use this as a reliable source of information about how the software was created.

In addition, at any time, we can FTP the production or test web site onto our development PC and use CVS to see if there are any changes compared with the repository version. Since everyone uses the repository, this checks all work associated with the web site, not just our own.

Reusing Existing Code

Another way to increase efficiency in development is to use someone else's code. In this section, we'll look at several examples of libraries that can be used by JavaScript.

When using someone else's code, the question of ownership is always the first issue. For JavaScript, a rough guide is as follows (this is not legal advice). All written works, including software, automatically carry an international copyright, even without a copyright statement. People are supposed to make a legal agreement with copyright owners before using their code. This is almost never done for JavaScript, because theft is unpolicable, scripts are unprotectable or trivial in content, and the script owners often don't mind anyway.

In general, there is no practical reason why our scripting should not benefit from study or use of other people's scripts. If a given script is unique, we might pause for a minute and consider the implications of using it. If the owner were a large commercial company with long, complicated license agreements, we'd perhaps do well to be a little cautious.

The Netscape Validation Library

The Netscape validation library is a single JavaScript .js file containing numerous validation routines for string values. These values are typically user input supplied to HTML forms. There are two versions of the library, one that is highly backwards compatible, and one that is shorter, more up to date, and uses JavaScript regular expressions. They are highly portable, browser friendly scripts. The first version is available here: http://developer.netscape.com/docs/examples/javascript/formval/overview.html, and the regular expression version is available here: http://developer.netscape.com/docs/examples/javascript/regexp/overview.html

These libraries are recommended for a number of trivial validation techniques and can save a lot of time. In Chapter 16 we've described in more depth the issues surrounding validation, but in general, if user input goes into a JavaScript string, we want to be able to diagnose what the user's typed by looking at the string. We will examine the use of the Netscape validation library with an example.

In this example, a web marketing company has given up on subtle approaches designed to extract personal information from web surfers, and instead is trying something more straightforward. Their web site asks directly for intimate details of the surfer's life, in return for which they state that you may win a trip into space. The company is expecting a somewhat naive clientele, so validating their input is important.

Here is the very simple web page to which we will add validation scripts:

The source code for this file is just plain HTML, with a simple <FORM>, so there's no need to repeat it all here. In order to best illustrate the validation library, we've made all form elements <INPUT TYPE="text"> fields – obviously, this could be more sophisticated. To use the validation library, we add this to the <HEAD> section:

```
<SCRIPT SRC='FormChek.js'></SCRIPT>
```

In this page, we implement validation very simply. We prevent the user from submitting an incomplete form by preventing navigation out of a field that hasn't been filled in correctly yet. After the first <INPUT> tag, we insert the following script:

```
<SCRIPT>
document.forms[0].elements[0].focus();
</SCRIPT>
```

All that remains is to enforce navigation. We add an onChange event handler for each field, one that performs validation, and if the validation fails, we cancel the navigation that caused the onChange event. We pluck these validation functions straight from the Netscape library, so the <INPUT> tags appear as follows:

```
<BR>Enter your full name:  
<INPUT TYPE='text'
    onChange='return isAlphabetic(this.value);'>
<BR>Enter your age in years:  
<INPUT TYPE='text' SIZE=3 MAXLENGTH=3
    onChange='return isNonnegativeInteger(this.value);'>
<BR>Enter your sex:  
<INPUT TYPE='text' SIZE=1 MAXLENGTH=1
    onChange='return isLetter(this.value);'>
<BR>Tell us your credit card number:  
<INPUT TYPE='text'
    onChange='return isAnyCard(this.value);'>
<BR>Tell us your phone number:  
<INPUT TYPE='text'
    onChange='return isInternationalPhoneNumber(this.value);'>
<BR>Tell us your real email address:  
<INPUT TYPE='text'
    onChange='return isEmail(this.value);'>
<BR>Tell us a personal weakness we can exploit:  
<INPUT TYPE='text'
    onChange='return !isWhiteSpace(this.value)';>
```

The library obviously provides many convenient functions. Of course, nothing's perfect, and we still need to hand-code some validation logic if, for example, the user enters "O" for Other in the "enter your sex" field. The library also provides some companion string formatting functions, so that if the user's entered international phone number is not in a standard format, for example, we have a handy function to rewrite it correctly.

One constraint of this library is that many functions are interrelated in the file, so it's not possible to just cut a single function out and use it. Therefore, you may still find cause to make or clone your own validation routines, or at least tailor them from this library. These libraries are highly portable, but there are other portability traps to fall into. Beta versions of Netscape 6 in particular have a number of problems correctly firing event handlers.

Cookie Libraries

The `cookie` property of the browser `window.document` object has a particularly annoying implementation, which has led to JavaScript libraries that ease the use of this property. Firstly, data written to the `cookie` property must be encoded using the global `escape()` or `encodeURL()` method, since it is eventually transported over HTTP to the web server. Secondly, data read from the cookie must be separated out from a concatenated string of cookies.

Rather than struggle with these annoyances, it's much easier to just use some simple accessor functions that have well chosen arguments. There are many such libraries, and they are mostly the same. The one examined here comes from http://www.dithered.com/javascript/cookies/. There are five extremely simple functions provided that can be dropped straight into any web page:

- ❑   void setCookie(name, value, expires, path, domain, secure);
- ❑   String getCookie(name);
- ❑   String deleteCookie(name, path, domain);
- ❑   Date fixDate(date);
- ❑   Boolean supportsCookie();

The first three functions are all you really need. Arguments to `setCookie()` are optional after the first 'name' argument, which matches the requirements of the RFC cookie standard. The `fixDate()` function is a workaround for an ancient Netscape date bug, now long gone. The `supportsCookie()` function allows you to check if the browser supports the cookie interface or not. In this case, that function is rather poorly implemented, as it creates a fake cookie property where one shouldn't be. We could easily improve its implementation from:

```
function supportsCookies() {
   setCookie('checking_for_cookie_support', 'testing123');
   if (getCookie('checking_for_cookie_support')) return true;
   else return false;
```

To:

```
function supportsCookies() {
   setCookie('checking_for_cookie_support', 'testing123');
   if (getCookie('checking_for_cookie_support'))
   {
      deleteCookie('checking_for_cookie_support');
      return true;
   }
   else
   {
      delete window.document.cookie;
      return false;
   }
```

For IE 4+ and Netscape 6+, the `window.navigator.cookieEnabled` property (it holds a Boolean value) can be used instead of this routine entirely. Otherwise, these cookie routines are very simple and convenient. Always have a copy lying around. Cookies and JavaScript are discussed in more detail in Chapter 14, but third party libraries will be covered here.

The HierMenus Library

The HierMenus library is a very popular piece of Dynamic HTML that provides an interactive, multi-level menu with some similarities to the right-click Context menu available in browsers and Microsoft Windows. According to the comments in the source code, any site using this menu can only do so free of charge if a link back to the HierMenus web site is included in the built page. Many sites seem to use this library without displaying such a link, so perhaps there are alternate arrangements as well. The HierMenus library is available at http://www.webreference.com/dhtml/hiermenus/.

An Example Menu

The Palm web site (http://www.palm.com/) and the HierMenus web site itself are examples of the HierMenus library in use. Here is the Palm homepage:

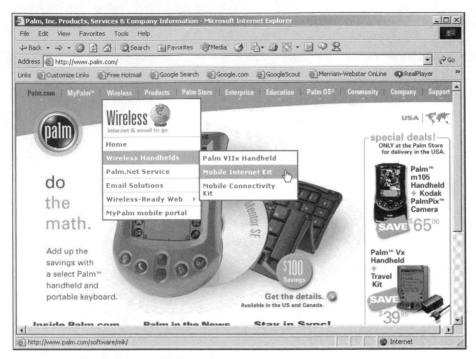

In this screenshot, the Palm web site shows two levels of pop-up, hierarchical menu that appear when the mouse moves over the Wireless item in the menu bar at the very top of the page. This is entirely a Dynamic HTML effect. One of the great strengths of the HierMenus library is that it is portable across browser versions and brands, although the list is currently restricted to Netscape 4+ and IE 4+.

The highlighting of menu items in the menus is due to the HierMenu features. It also allows embedding of images in the menus. Colors, fonts, and other formatting properties are fully configurable.

In order to use the HierMenus library, download the ZIP file from the web site noted above. The remarks here are based on version 4.0.14 of the menu. Minor versions seem to change almost weekly, but the basic structure of the scripts doesn't change much. Most of the files in the download are just small images used as navigation hints inside any created menu items. LoadMe.html is a demonstration page showing four examples of the HierMenus library at work.

The two most important files in the distribution are HM_Loader.js and HM_Arrays.js. The former is the one you must include with a <SCRIPT SRC='...'> tag. It does not need to be modified and contains scripting that performs essential initialization tasks.

Summary

You need to be aware that for all the advantages the addition of JavaScript to your web pages brings, it also dramatically increases the number of possible defects of the web site production process. In order to produce professional quality pages, a toolset is required that assists in mitigating and detecting defects.

The key to reducing defects is to recognize the temptations inherent in an interpreted development environment such as JavaScript. Therefore no compiler transforms the source code into unreadable binary form such source is available for in-place modification on every production, test, and development host. In the worst cases, in-place modification makes version control and deployment unmanageable.

To reduce the temptation to make in-place changes, a set of tools is required that creates staging points in the production process. The most vital requirement is a dedicated test host separate to production and development hosts. Integrated development tools provide reference information and assisted-completion features that serve as a crutch when programmer's memory fails. Some tools can auto-generate sophisticated scripts that also save considerable programming time. Source code control tools such as CVS are crucial when trying to track down web site changes and versions.

Finally, sometimes writing your own scripts is unnecessary. A number of common scripting tasks are embodied in publicly available libraries, ranging from humble cookie libraries to sophisticated Dynamic HTML effects.

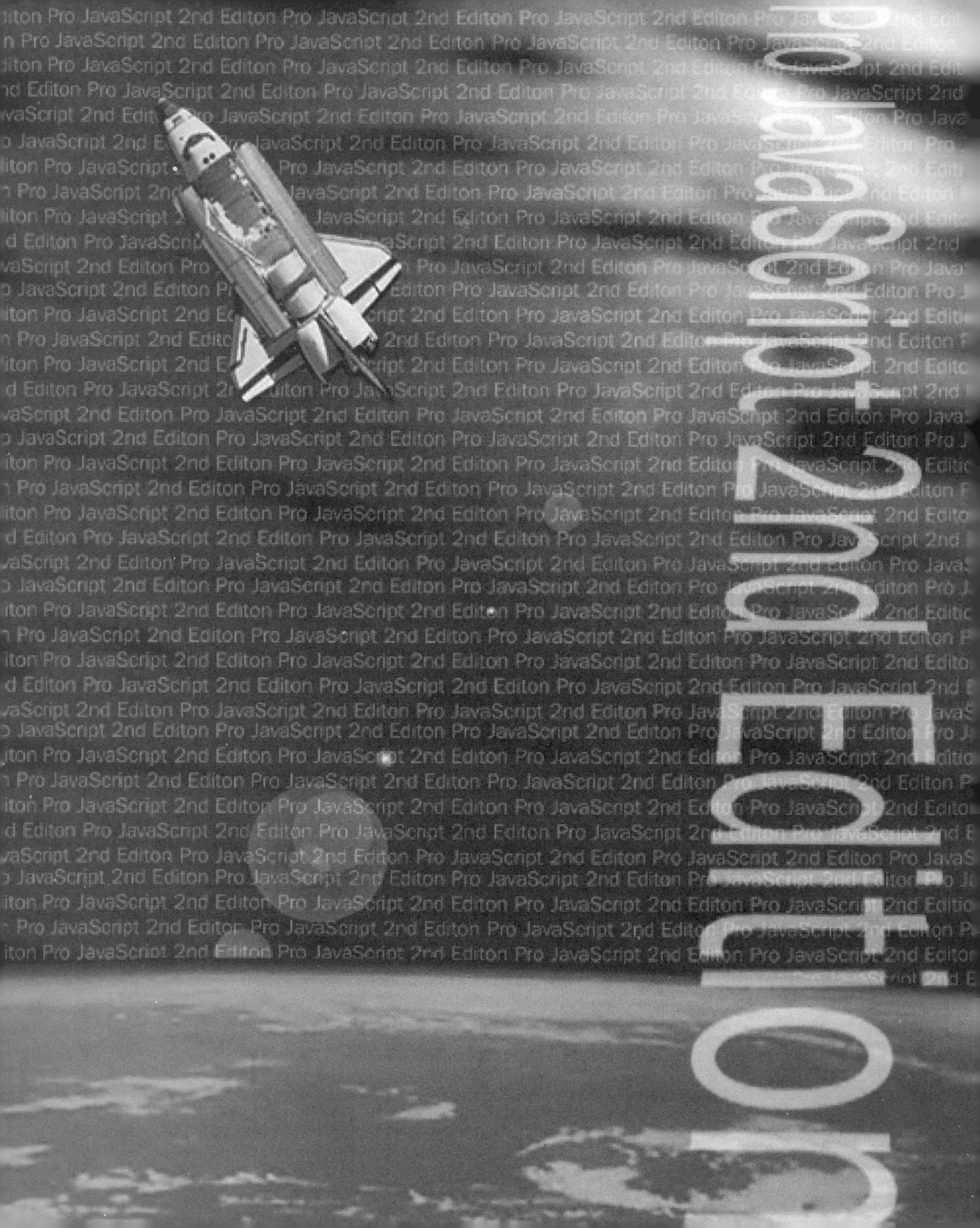
Pro JavaScript 2nd Edition
Pro JavaScript 2nd Editon

Good Coding Practice

In this chapter, we'll be seeing how we can make life easier for ourselves and other people by adopting effective coding standards when developing web applications with JavaScript. The aim is not to set rigid rules, but rather to show that by following fairly simple guidelines we can increase our efficiency, so that more time can be dedicated to creating great web applications and less time working out why our code is not working.

Why We Need Coding Standards

Coding standards are a set of guidelines whose aim is to make our code more consistent, more readable, more manageable, and as a result more efficient. By efficient, we don't mean that the code runs faster but mean that the code is easy to edit, to debug, to modify and to extend. These coding guidelines are based on learning from the mistakes of others. Organizations like IBM and NASA, for example, have done much research into why some code and projects succeed, and why others don't. Imagine the consequences of a bug in the millions and millions of lines of code involved in space shuttle launches. Our code might only launch a web page, but that's no reason why we can't learn from NASA's mistakes! They examined how even some ways of laying out code causes programmers problems and results in bugs, while other ways result in code that's easy to understand and has less bugs as a result. Code that is easier to understand is also code that is easier to update and extend when the time comes.

In fact, in many ways, coding standards are even more important because JavaScript is a relatively forgiving language. For example, it's not a typed language – we don't declare what types of data a variable will hold. It will allow you to reference variables that haven't been declared and you can add properties to an object just by using them. While in the short term this makes things quicker, it can lead to problems later. For example, the following code won't raise any errors, but won't work as we expect:

```
var myObject = new Object;
myObject.myNum = 100;
if (myObject.mynum == 100)
alert("MyNum was 100");
```

We declare myObject and set it to reference a new Object. We then set its myNum property to 100; JavaScript allows us to create properties like this simply by using them. Our mistake however is that in the if statement, we use mynum with a lower case n. We should use myNum with upper case N. It is a simple mistake and in four lines of code easy to spot, but in 100+ lines of code it's a different matter and JavaScript raise an error, so it is down to us to spot it.

It's surprising how large the JavaScript code in web pages can become. Often, what starts out as a few lines of code attached to an event becomes a mammoth 500-line monster that is difficult to handle. It's therefore best to build in good design and use coding standards, even when it might not initially seem important. In fact, with poorly written or designed code, it can often be easier to start from scratch. This doubles the required effort when it could all be avoided if things were well written in a way that was manageable by someone other than the original coder. In 6 months time, you can bet that no one will remember what variables named a or b were used for.

General Good Practice

We'll start by looking in this section at general good practice that applies to all coding. In the next section, we'll be looking at coding practices specific to variables and functions.

Good Layout

Good layout should be about making your code more readable. For example, look at the following code, which would output the twelve times multiplication tables (1 * 12 = 12, and so on):

```
var a = 12;
var b;
if (a == 12)
for (b = 1; b < 13; b++) document.write(b + " * " + a + " = " +
   b * a + "<BR>");
alert("Complete");
```

On first glance it's not obvious that the for loop is inside the if statement, but that alert("Complete") is not. When it's just a few lines it's not hard to work out, but hide it in a great mass of code with a similar lack of layout, and suddenly life becomes that much harder.

Indenting code makes it so much easier to follow and therefore understand and debug. There are many differing opinions on where to correctly indent if statements, loops, functions, and so on. More importantly, whatever method we use must be logical and we must stick to it. For example, the code above could be indented like this:

```
var a = 12;
var b;
if (a == 12)
{
   for (b = 1; b < 13; b++)
   {
      document.write(b + " * " + a + " = " + b * a + "<BR>");
   }
}

alert("Complete");
```

It is now much clearer that the loop will only be executed if the if statement's condition is true, now that the loop's body of code is clearly marked out. We've also enclosed the code inside the if statement and the for loop inside the curly brackets, even though when code is just one statement it is optional. Doing this helps clarify what code belongs to which if statement or loop.

This way of laying out the curly brackets is not the only way, an common alternative, which the author finds confusing, is called the K&R coding style; after its use by Kernighan and Ritchie, who created the C programming language. They suggest putting the braces at the end of lines like this:

```
if (a == b) {
    doSomething();
} else {
    doSomethingElse();
}
```

Rather than the style suggested above like this:

```
if (a == b)
{
    doSomething();
}
else
{
    doSomethingElse();
}
```

There's no hard and fast rule, but the second way shown above is much easier to read.

Use Descriptive Names

Variable and function names should tell us, without having to run through the code in our mind, exactly what they do. For example:

```
var myVariable = 7.8;
```

This tells us nothing about what the variable might be used for. Only by carefully examining the context of the surrounding code would we be able to glean its purpose. However if we use:

```
var currentAPRRate = 7.8;
```

Then this tells us what the variable is used for, meaning that we do not need to examine the surrounding code. If we apply this principle to the 12 times multiplication table example, we saw earlier:

```
var timesTable = 12;
var timesBy;

for (timesBy = 1; timesBy < 13; timesBy++)
{
    document.write(timesBy + " * " + timesTable+ " = "
        + timesBy * timesTable + "<BR>");
}

alert("Complete");
```

We can guess what this does without having to go through it line by line. If we apply this practice to all our code's methods, variables, objects, and functions, it will allow us to easily skim read the code.

Obviously there is a trade off between being descriptive, and using names that make a small pamphlet look like a novel! To keep things short, we can use abbreviations such as num for number, desc for description, and so on. It doesn't matter what we use so long as we maintain consistency and use abbreviations that are commonly understood. In other words, if we use num for number, we should stick to that rather than using no or numb.

As well as being descriptive, names should also give an idea of what type of values are involved. For example:

```
var userValidity;
```

This tells us that the variable is something to do with users and their validity, but alternatively:

```
var userIsValid;
```

If we are used to the convention, this would tell us that this variable lets us know whether a user is valid and will contain either `true` if they are and `false` otherwise.

Use Naming Conventions

In some ways, this follows on from use descriptive names above. A naming convention is simply a rule for specifying what details we should include in our variable names and how the names should be formatted. There is quite a wide range of different conventions and there's no overall best one to use, it really depends on personal choice. The important thing is to stick with whichever one you choose.

A common convention used with JavaScript is the Camel Convention. In short, it states that all variable and functions should start with a lower case letter and then have each word in the name start with an upper case letter, for example:

```
userIsValid
sendEmail
loadCookie
```

The alternative to this is the Pascal Convention, where every word in the variable or function name is capitalized:

```
UserIsValid
SendEmail
LoadCookie
```

The final convention we'll look at is the Hungarian Notation. If your wondering why the strange name, its because the person who devised it was Hungarian.

The idea behind Hungarian Notation, is that every variable should have letters put in front of its name to indicate its scope and its datatype. We can also use it and apply it to things like the names we give HTML form elements and even to the IDs of HTML tags. There's not a strict notation, we can use what letters we like to indicate data type, but shown in the table below are some suggestions based on a modified version of that used by Microsoft VB programmers, and found at http://support.microsoft.com/support/kb/articles/Q110/2/64.asp:

Prefix	Data Type/Object Type	Example
str	String Data Type or String Object	strUserName
num	Number Data Type or Number Object	numInterestRate
obj	Object Data Type	objMyObject
bln	Boolean Data Type or Boolean Object	blnIsUserReady
rxp	Regular Expression Object	rxpMatchNames
dat	Date Object	datNowDateTime
arr	Array Data Type	arrMyPhoneNumbers

Prefix	Data Type/Object Type	Example
cbo	Combo box and drop down list	cboEnglish
chk	Checkbox	chkReadOnly
cmd	Button	cmdOk
fil	File Input type	filSource
frm	HTML Form	frmEntry
fra	HTML Frame	fraStyle
img	Image Element	imgIcon
lst	List box Element (SELECT element with more than one list item showing, for example, size=2)	lstPolicyCodes
opt	Option element in SELECT control	optRed
txt	Text Input Element	txtLastName
pwd	Password Input element	pwdUserPassword
sub	Form Submit Button	subSendForm
rst	Form Reset Button	rstClearForm
rad	Radio Button Element	radMale

This is not a complete list but, it gives the general idea. We can easily make our own up, for example par for a HTML <P> tag object, win for a window object, doc for a document object. So long as we stick with something that other programmers might recognize, and use it consistently.

We also mentioned that the variable name can also indicate the variable's scope, for example, a local. Variable is one only accessible inside a function and a global variable being one that is accessible anywhere in the page. The convention for this is to add l_ for local variable and g_ for global. The other option is to only add g_ to the front of the variable name when it's global, otherwise adding nothing means it's local.

Okay, let's put it all together and create a few variables that follow the Hungarian Notation:

```
<SCRIPT>
    var l_dat = New Date();  // local variable containing Date object
    var g_str = "My String"; // global variable containing a string;
</SCRIPT
<BUTTON NAME='cmdOk' VALUE='Ok'><!-- HTML button element ->
<FRAME NAME='fraLeftFrame' SRC='LeftPage.htm'><!-- HTML FRAME element ->
```

One of the downsides to the Hungarian Notation is that if we change the type of value a variable contains, then we are left with a misleading variable name, or we have to go through our code and change all instances of the name. In fact, the naming convention is probably most useful when applied to HTML elements, as these don't normally change.

Use Variables for Special Values

We will often have constant values that crop up a number of times in our code. As the values don't change, we use the literal value rather than a variable. However, if we instead use a well named variable it makes our code that bit more readable. It might be slightly less efficient, but in most cases, the extra overhead of using a variable rather than a literal is worthwhile for the sake of readability.

Take the example below:

```
var userIncome = 6000;
var totalTax = 0;

if (userIncome >= 5000 && userIncome <= 10000)
{
   totalTax = userIncome * 0.1;
   alert(totalTax);
}
```

What are 5000 and 10000 signifying? Why is 0.1 used? Look at the code below:

```
var lowerTaxBandStart = 5000
var lowerTaxBandEnd = 10000;
var lowerTaxRate = 0.1;
var userIncome = 6000;
var totalTax = 0;

if (userIncome >= lowerTaxBandStart && userIncome <= lowerTaxBandEnd)
{
   totalTax = userIncome * lowerTaxRate;
   alert(totalTax);
}
```

Now there is no need to guess or try and work things out. 5000 is the start of the lower tax band, 10000 the end and 0.1 is the lower tax band's tax rate. Maybe when you write the code you think that you'll remember what the values mean, but in 6 months time, unless your memory is perfect they will be just numbers and you will have to figure out what they mean.

In other programming languages, a constant could be used; a constant being a variable that cannot be changed, unfortunately only JavaScript 1.5, as supported by Netscape 6, supports constants via the const keyword. To make things clearer, we could add the prefix const to the name, or make all constant variables upper case (anything that will make obvious that these variables should never be changed).

Comments

Script comments should be used to describe the script, its variables, functions, and any intrinsic logic; such as any business rules or formulas included. Use JavaScript comments liberally throughout your code. Comments help explain what the script is doing, especially to other programmers. In some cases, the code you wrote six months ago, which made perfect sense at the time, may seem confusing and foreign when you have to go back and debug it. A comment here or there, explaining a function or loop, can save a lot of time. Following is an example of an amply commented script:

```
/************************
includedJavaScript.js

Purpose: Contains global JavaScript functions used on
         multiple pages of the XXXXXX application.
Author: Skrip T. Reiter - skriptr@xyzz.com
Date: 6/10/2001
Revision History:
Date:            Change:                          By:
------------------------------------------------------------
6/11/2001        Added divide() function.         Martin
************************/

//Declare global variables
var nAmps; //Amperage of the given circuit
```

```
    //End declaring global variables

    /*************************
    Function: calculateCurrent
    Purpose: Calculates circuit current based on Ohm's Law
            (circuit current = (voltage / resistance)
    Inputs: nVolts - number representing circuit voltage
            nResistance - number representing circuit resistance
    Output: Sets variable nAmps = nVolts/nResistance
    *************************/
    function calculateCurrent(nVolts, nResistance)
    {
        nAmps = divideNumbers(nVolts,nResistance);
    }
```

While admittedly, the preceding script contains quite a few (possibly too many) comments, which, in fact, are unnecessary text lines that must be downloaded to the client, it does illustrate the type of information and organization that would be useful, should other programmers need to modify or debug your code. Remember, the amount of commenting needed is inversely proportional to the amount of your code that is self-documenting with descriptive variable and function names.

Keep it Clear and Simple

In this section, we will look at how to make our code clear simple. Some programmers take great delight in creating code so concise that it is virtually impossible to fathom. For example, take the code snippet below:

```
    x = (b>>2?(a%2):(a%3))+a++;
```

What does it do? In 6 months time after this has been written, we'll be scratching our heads and spending a few minutes working it out. Code such as this stops us and other programmers from being able to skim read the code, and as a consequence makes debugging difficult and extending the code a nightmare. We could simplify it:

```
    rightShiftValue = b >> 2;
    if (rightShiftValue == true)
    {
        remainder = a % 2;
    }
    else
    {
        remainder = a % 3;
    }

    remainder = remainder + a;
    a++;
```

This may not be perfect (partly due to the a and b variable values) and the code is much longer, but it's easier to understand and therefore debug, and with programmer time being at a premium, reducing the time it takes to write code is often the number one priority. Let's look at the principles of simplifying code.

Simplify Conditions

When we have very complex or lengthy conditions in our if statements or loops, we can simplify them and make the code more readable by using variables. Take the following example:

```
    if (userIncome > lowerBandStart && userIncome < lowerBandEnd
        && userAge > retirementAge && userLocation == "Florida")
    {
```

```
    // do something
}
```

We could simplify this to:

```
var isLowerTaxBand =
    userIncome > lowerBandStart && userIncome < lowerBandEnd;

if (isLowerTaxBand && userAge > retirementAge && userLocation == "Florida")
{
    // do something
}
```

While slightly slower, it makes it just that bit easier to understand. How far we need to go to simplify depends on the circumstances. For example, if a pensioner in the lower tax band was something we used again, then we could change our code to:

```
var isLowerTaxBandPensioner = userIncome > lowerBandStart
    && userIncome < lowerBandEnd && userAge > retirementAge;

if (isLowerTaxBandPensioner && userLocation == "Florida")
{
    // do something
}
```

Without needing to understand the whole code, we can see that the code in the if statement relates to lower tax band pensioners living in Florida.

Using Arrays as Lookup Tables

We can sometimes use arrays as a replacement for if statements in our war on complexity.

For example, the Date object's getMonth() method only returns a number, from 0 to 11, representing the month. There is no Date object method to return just the month name. We could use an if or a case statement:

```
<!-- 04_months_long.htm -->
<HTML>
<HEAD><TITLE>Month Example using switch</TITLE></HEAD>
<BODY>
    <SCRIPT LANGUAGE='JavaScript'>
        var monthName = "";
        var monthNumber = new Date().getMonth();

        switch (monthNumber)
        {
            case 0:
                monthName = "January";
                break;
            case 1:
                monthName = "February";
                break;
            case 2:
                monthName = "March";
                break;
            case 3:
                monthName = "April";
                break;
            case 4:
                monthName = "May";
```

```
            break;
        case 5:
            monthName = "June";
            break;
        case 6:
            monthName = "July";
            break;
        case 7:
            monthName = "August";
            break;
        case 8:
            monthName = "September";
            break;
        case 9:
            monthName = "October";
            break;
        case 10:
            monthName = "November";
            break;
        case 11:
            monthName = "December";
            break;
        }

        alert(monthName);
    </SCRIPT>
</BODY>
</HTML>
```

While not particularly complex, the code above is lengthy. The code below uses an array to do the lookup:

```
<!-- 04_months_short.htm -->
<HTML>
<HEAD><TITLE>Month Example using arrays</TITLE></HEAD>
<BODY>
    <SCRIPT LANGUAGE='JavaScript'>>
        var monthName = "";
        var monthNumber = new Date().getMonth();
        var monthNames = new Array("January","February","March","April","May",
            "June","July","August","September","October","November",
            "December");

        alert(monthNames[monthNumber]);
    </SCRIPT>
</BODY>
</HTML>
```

We can see it is now much smaller.

JavaScript allows us to access array elements using text rather than numbers. Let's imagine we want to calculate the APR of a loan based on the user's credit rating, and the number of months the loan is for.

We could use a series of if statements:

```
<HTML>
<BODY>
    <SCRIPT LANGUAGE='JavaScript'>
        var userCreditRating = "Embarrassing";
        var loanTerm = 24;

        if (userCreditRating == "Good")
```

```
        {
            if (loanTerm == 12)
            {
                loanAPR = 5.5;
            }
            else if (loanTerm == 24)
            {
                loanAPR = 5.8;
            }
            else if (loanTerm == 36)
            {
                loanAPR = 5.9;
            }
        }
        else if (userCreditRating == "Poor")
        {
            if (loanTerm == 12)
            {
                loanAPR = 6.5;
            }
            else if (loanTerm == 24)
            {
                loanAPR = 6.8;
            }
            else if (loanTerm == 36)
            {
                loanAPR = 6.9;
            }
        }
        else if (userCreditRating == "Embarrassing")
        {
            if (loanTerm == 12)
            {
                loanAPR = 9.5;
            }
            else if (loanTerm == 24)
            {
                loanAPR = 9.8;
            }
            else if (loanTerm == 36)
            {
                loanAPR = 9.9;
            }
        }
    </SCRIPT>
</BODY>
</HTML>
```

We could replace this with an array like this:

```
<!-- 05_loan.htm -->
<HTML>
<HEAD><TITLE>Loan Rate Calculator</TITLE></HEAD>
<BODY>
    <SCRIPT LANGUAGE='JavaScript'>
        var userCreditRating = "Embarrassing";
        var loanTerm = 24;
        var loanAPRs = new Array();
        loanAPRs["Good"] = new Array();
        loanAPRs["Good"][12] = 5.5;
        loanAPRs["Good"][24] = 5.8;
        loanAPRs["Good"][36] = 5.9;
```

```
        loanAPRs["Poor"] = new Array();
        loanAPRs["Poor"][12] = 6.5;
        loanAPRs["Poor"][24] = 6.8;
        loanAPRs["Poor"][36] = 6.9;

        loanAPRs["Embarrassing"] = new Array();
        loanAPRs["Embarrassing"][12] = 9.5;
        loanAPRs["Embarrassing"][24] = 9.8;
        loanAPRs["Embarrassing"][36] = 9.9;

        loanAPR = loanAPRs[userCreditRating][loanTerm];
        alert(loanAPR);
    </SCRIPT>
</BODY>
</HTML>
```

This is not only shorter, but also easier to follow than the `if` statement example. It is particularly good if we need to obtain a number of `loanAPRs`. With the second method, it now just takes one line for each lookup, rather than another series of `if` statements.

An additional advantage is that we can loop through the array elements; let's say with the loan example above that we wanted to display all the APRs for someone whose credit rating is perhaps embarrassing:

```
<!-- 05_loan_cycle.htm -->
<HTML>
<BODY>
    <SCRIPT LANGUAGE='JavaScript'>
        var userCreditRating = "Embarrassing";
        var loanTerm = 24;
        var loanAPRs = new Array();
        loanAPRs["Good"] = new Array();
        loanAPRs["Good"][12] = 5.5;
        loanAPRs["Good"][24] = 5.8;
        loanAPRs["Good"][36] = 5.9;

        loanAPRs["Poor"] = new Array();
        loanAPRs["Poor"][12] = 6.5;
        loanAPRs["Poor"][24] = 6.8;
        loanAPRs["Poor"][36] = 6.9;

        loanAPRs["Embarrassing"] = new Array();
        loanAPRs["Embarrassing"][12] = 9.5;
        loanAPRs["Embarrassing"][24] = 9.8;
        loanAPRs["Embarrassing"][36] = 9.9;

        var loanTerm;
        for (loanTerm in loanAPRs["Embarrassing"])
        {
            document.write("A term of " + loanTerm + " months is "
                + loanAPRs["Embarrassing"][loanTerm] + "% apr<BR>");
        }
    </SCRIPT>
</BODY>
</HTML>
```

We have used a `for...in` statement to loop through the loan terms.

451

There is one pitfall with using arrays like this and that's case sensitivity. For example:

```
loanAPR = loanAPRs["embarrassing][12];
```

This would fail, as it should be "Embarrassing", with a capital "E". One way around this would to be to use a function, or have a class with a method that converts the string to lower case.

Keep the Number of Exit Points in a Loop to a Minimum

It makes a loop difficult to follow if there are numerous possible exit points by use of the break statement. Sometimes break statements are necessary, but they should be minimized and used as the exception rather than the rule.

Simplify Complex Nested Ifs

One way of simplifying ifs is by using switch statements; however, with very deeply nested ifs we can simplify using functions. Take the following nested if statements:

```
var isSuitableBrowser = false;

if (browserName == "Netscape" || browserName == "Microsoft")
{
   if (browserName == "Microsoft" && browserVersion > 3)
   {
      isSuitableBrowser = true;
   }
   else if (browserVersion >= 6)
   {
      isSuitableBrowser = true;
   }
}
```

On its own, the code is not that bad, but inside a larger amount of code, it makes things more difficult to read. If we converted it to a function:

```
function isBrowserSuitable(browserName, browserVersion)
{
   var isSuitableBrowser = false;

   if (browserName == "Netscape" || browserName == "Microsoft")
   {
      if (browserName == "Microsoft" && browserVersion > 3)
      {
         isSuitableBrowser = true;
      }
      else if (browserVersion >= 6)
      {
         isSuitableBrowser = true;
      }
   }

   return isSuitableBrowser;
}
```

We could call this inside code like this:

```
if (isBrowserSuitable(browserName, browserVersion))
{
   // some code
}
```

Our `if` statement, here, is not nested particularly deeply, and when it is just a few lines we can cope; but in 50 or 100 lines of code, and if we have the `if` statement nested 3 or 4 levels deep, then this technique makes the code much more readable. By splitting code into small packages like this, it reduces the complexity of its appearance – something we'll appreciate when it comes to fixing bugs.

The only downside with using functions like this is the code will run slower, however we'd need to loop through a million times to see even a small difference. While saving millionths of a second may be important in time-critical applications, for example on a server, it's not generally the case in client-side JavaScript.

Keep Related Code Together

If we keep lines of related code together, it avoids us having to make mental leaps throughout the code. It also means we are less likely to overlook something if we cut and paste the code elsewhere later. For example:

```
var degCelsius = prompt("Enter the degrees in Celsius",0);
...
// Lots of unrelated code
...
var degFahrenheit = 9 / 5 * degCelsius + 32;
```

It would be very easy if the code was 100 lines, for us to make changes to the `degCelsius` variable between its declaration and its value being set and the line in which we actually first use it. In addition, if we wanted to use the degrees Celsius to Fahrenheit code line, we could easily overlook the fact that the first line is also needed. What we should have done is this:

```
...
// Lots of unrelated code
...
var degCelsius = prompt("Enter the degrees in Celsius",0);
var degFahrenheit = 9 / 5 * degCelsius + 32;
```

With regard to the line 'Lots of unrelated code', it is worth noting that a variable or function should not figure in the code, unless you can make a good case for its presence.

Organize Your Code

Good code organization not only makes things easier to understand and manage, but can also make code re-use easier. We'll now look at two ways we can organize code. The first is by using JavaScript files and inserting them into the page, while the second is by using JavaScript classes.

Use .JS Script files

A JavaScript file that usually has a `.js` file extension is simply a plain text file that contains only JavaScript. The advantages of this approach are that:

❑   It is maintainable

❑   There is segregation of logic and presentation

❑   We can add in a different function later on without the page breaking down

❑   In general, it is less likely to go wrong

For example, we could have a file named `MathFunctions.js` containing the following:

```
// MathFunctions.js
function fixDecimalPlaces(fixNumber, decimalPlaces)
{
```

```
    var lDiv = Math.pow(10,decimalPlaces);
    fixNumber = new String((Math.round(fixNumber * (lDiv)))/lDiv);

    var zerosRequired;
    var decimalPointLocation = fixNumber.lastIndexOf(".");
    if (decimalPointLocation == -1)
    {
        fixNumber = fixNumber + ".";
        zerosRequired = decimalPlaces;
    }
    else
    {
        zerosRequired = decimalPlaces -
            (fixNumber.length - decimalPointLocation - 1);
    }

    for (; zerosRequired > 0; zerosRequired--)
        fixNumber = fixNumber + "0";

    return fixNumber;
}
```

This function fixes a number to a specific number of decimal places. It is used in the shopping cart application in Chapter 22 for the rounding and fixing of money values to two decimal places.

To insert this code into a web page we use the <SCRIPT> tag as normal, except we set the <SCRIPT> tag's SRC property to the URL of the file. So assuming our .js file was in the same directory as our web page it would be:

```
<SCRIPT SRC='MathFunctions.js'></SCRIPT>
```

If we were keeping all .js files in a common directory in order to make scripts easier to organize, we might have:

```
<SCRIPT SRC='/JavaScripts/MathFunctions.js'></SCRIPT>
```

Let's put this into a simple page:

```
<!-- 07_fix_decimal_places.htm -->
<HTML>
<HEAD><TITLE>Displays 1.2544 to 2 decimal places</TITLE></HEAD>
<BODY>
    <SCRIPT LANGUAGE='JavaScript' SRC='MathFunctions.js'></SCRIPT>
    <SCRIPT LANGUAGE='JavaScript'>
        alert(fixDecimalPlaces(1.2544, 2))
    </SCRIPT>
</BODY>
</HTML>
```

This assumes that the MathFunctions.js file and the page are in the same directory.

Use Classes

We learnt about JavaScript's object and prototype support in Chapter 3, *JavaScript OOP Techniques*. From the point of view of making code more manageable and re-usable, JavaScript's class support is very useful, particularly when coupled with the use of .js files mentioned above. In Chapter 16, *Form Validation* and Chapter 22, *Shopping Cart Application* we will see this put into practical use. In those chapters, we create various classes that map to various ideas or concepts involved in the applications. For example, in the shopping cart application, we have a class representing a shopping cart, a class representing an item that goes in a shopping cart, a class that represents the customer, and a class representing a credit card.

With classes, and instances of objects based on them, we can encapsulate methods and properties that relate to something in particular, such as a shopping basket. Obvious methods for a shopping basket are addItem(), removeItem() and getShoppingBasket(). If we later choose to enhance the functionality of the shopping basket, we simply add more methods to its class. We can then simply add the functionality of a shopping basket to our web pages by inserting the class using the SRC property of a <SCRIPT> tag, and create an object based on the class in our page.

Another advantage of using classes inside .js files is maintainability. Firstly, if we just have one class per file, it makes it easier to enhance the class and we don't need to go searching through lots of code to find the class because it's nicely wrapped up in a .js file. Secondly, if we do spot and fix a bug, then all pages using the class will instantly take advantage of the bug fix (so long as we don't introduce any new errors).

Let's look at a simple example where we want to create an online message board. We could start by creating a MessageBoard class. This would have methods such as addMessage(), deleteMessage(), and displayMessage(). However, what does a message board consist of? Messages. Therefore, we could create a class to represent an individual message, the Message class. We could store these messages inside the MessageBoard class itself. Let's create the outline code for these classes, first the Message class:

```
function Message(subject, body)
{
    this.subject = subject;
    this.body = body;
}

Message.prototype.setSubject(subject)
{
    this.subject = subject;
}

Message.prototype.getSubject()
{
    return this.subject;
}

Message.prototype.setBody(body)
{
    this.body = body;
}

Message.prototype.getBody()
{
    this.subject = subject;
}
```

We start by defining the constructor, which stores the subject and body inside the class. We then have a series of get and set statements that allow us to read and write the properties of the class (our subject and body properties).

Now let's create the message board class:

```
function MessageBoard()
{
    this.messages = new Object();
}

MessageBoard.prototype.createNewMessage= function(subject, body)
{
    var newMessage = new Message(subject, body);
    this.messages[subject] = newMessage;
```

```
    }

    MessageBoard.prototype.getMessage = function(subject)
    {
        return this.messages[subject];
    }

    MessageBoard.prototype.displayMessages()
    {
        // code to iterate through the messages property and display messages
    }
```

This code is far from complete, but hopefully gives an idea of how we can go about designing classes and putting them into action, Chapters 2 and 3 have more details, and the shopping cart application sees these principles put into practice.

Specifics

In this section, we look at coding practice that is specific to variables and functions.

Variables

In this section, we'll look at coding standards that are specific only to variable usage.

Initialize Variables

It is easy to declare a variable at the top of a function and make assumptions about the values it contains later on. To avoid this it is best to initialize variables to a default value that avoids errors. For example, in the code below, we should return true if the data is valid, or false otherwise:

```
function isDataValid(dataToValidate)
{
    var isValidData;
    if (someCondition)
    {
        isValidData = false;
    }
    else if (anotherCondition)
    {
        isValidData = false;
    }
    else if (yetAnotherCondition)
    {
        isValidData = false;
    }

    return isValidData;
}
```

However, the problem is that we are checking for invalid data and setting isValidData to false when some is found. At the end, we return isValidData, but as we forgot to set isValidData to true and never initialized it to true, then we are returning an undefined value.

If we then use the function like this:

```
if (isDataValid(someData))
{
    alert("Data Valid");
}
else
```

```
{
    alert("Data Invalid");
}
```

This will always be invalid. It's harder to track down because JavaScript will not notify us of this error. All this could be avoided by initializing the variable in the function, for example:

```
var isValidData = true;
```

Minimize Variable Scope

Variables should have local scope (be restricted to a function) unless it is impossible or makes coding very inefficient to do. This is because it is very difficult to keep track of the value of a variable if we have a global variable that can be accessed and changed by any function in the page, or even worse in a frameset by any code in any page loaded into the frameset. Often we find that we expect a global variable to have a certain value at a point in a function, but for some reason it doesn't. We then have to trace through each line of code to see where the global variable has been altered. If we have a lot of code, this can be quite a task and makes development time longer than necessary compared to if we used a local variable. Sometimes of course we need to use global variables so it's more a matter of avoiding their use unless necessary, rather than never using them at all.

Having many functions accessing a global variable make it hard to work out which functions are using the global variable, which aren't, which of them are changing the global variable's value, and which are leaving it unchanged. An alternative to this is to have a global variable, but not use it in any of the functions, rather pass the global variable to the function as a parameter. This allows us to still use a global variable, but means it is made much clearer which functions are making use of it. In addition, as it's passed as a parameter the function gets its own local copy, it therefore doesn't change the global value. We'll see an example of using function parameters rather than global variables in our *Cleaning Up a Coding Disaster* section at the end of this chapter.

Use for One Purpose

It can be tempting sometimes to save on the number of variables created by using them repeatedly for different situations. Either this can result in miscellaneous non-descriptive names, such as `tempNumber` or `tempVal`, or it means we have names that are misleading. It may seem a little wasteful to declare a variable for each different calculation but it does make our code clearer and easy to read.

For example:

```
var tempVal = prompt("Enter the degrees in Celsius",0);
tempVal = 9 / 5 * tempVal + 32;
```

What does the previous code do? the following code, despite no extra explanation makes it clear:

```
var degCelsius = prompt("Enter the degrees in Celsius",0);
var degFahrenheit = 9 / 5 * degCelsius + 32;
```

The second version of the code is clearer and we can see that it is converting degrees Celsius into degrees Fahrenheit.

Another way in which it can be tempting to use variables for more than one purpose is with flags. Let's say we have a variable that will contain a temperature measurement, except if it is -9999 and so flags up an error. For example, a function called `getTemperature()` could return the current outside temperature, unless there is an error, in which case would return -9999. We will probably remember this when we create the function, but if we come back to it much later, or if someone else is altering the code, then it will be less obvious without looking at the function's code and reading it line by line to see what -9999 signifies. It is better to make it clear by using exceptions – raise an exception in the function and handle it in the calling code using a `try...catch` clause. For more information, see Chapter 13, *Error Handling, Debugging, & Troubleshooting*.

Remove Unused Variables

When we are altering code, it is a good practice to remove any no longer used variables. If we don't do this and we come back to the code much later, we can find in lengthy pieces of code that we are never quite sure if a variable is still being used. This means that we leave it in just in case, or even worse, we use it thinking it will have the value we expect. The best way to do this is to just assign the value undefined to the variable. For older web browsers that do not allow us to assign the value of undefined to a variable, we can create an undefined variable called undefined first:

```
var undefined;
var strMessage = "Hi there";
strMessage=undefined;
```

Functions

In this section, we will look at coding standards that are specific to the use and creation of functions.

Functions Should Do One Thing and Do it Well

It makes functions easier to name and to understand if they have a single purpose. For example, there's no doubting what the Date object's getMonth() method does, so anywhere it is used in our code, we know exactly what it will do; this is the same for any methods or functions we create. It also means that it is more likely they can be re-used. Let's imagine the Date object didn't have a getMonth() method, but only a getDateAndTime() method, which returns the full day, month, year, hour, minute, and second information. As it's returning so much information, we can't just use it, but would have to write code to extract the month from its return value.

Functions should also be cohesive, that is they should be self-contained. There should be no reliance on some external global variable, instead if a variable is needed, it should be passed as a parameter; that way we can see all the external information the function needs. It's easier to create cohesive functions if we use a divide and conquer approach when deciding what functions we need. By this, I mean split the problem we have up into smaller and smaller chunks until we get to the point where we have functions that do just perform one function. For example, if we have an online banking system, we might start by looking at what functionality we need. Let's say that we decide we need the following functionality, where we want to be able to:

- ❏ Open and Close an account
- ❏ See the account balance
- ❏ View the last 10 transactions
- ❏ Put money in and take money out

From this we can then split it further:

- ❏ Function to open a new account
- ❏ Function to close an account
- ❏ Function to obtain account balance
- ❏ Function to display account balance

❑   Function to obtain last 10 transactions

❑   Function to display last 10 transactions

❑   Function to put money in

❑   Function to take money out

We may want to split even further. For example, creating a new account may involve a number of steps, not only creating a new account, but if you're a new customer, then adding you to a central database and so on. With divide and conquer, we keep dividing the problem into smaller chunks until we're happy we have the functionality down to small cohesive functions (functions that perform one specific task).

Don't Exit a Function in the Middle

If a function always ends at its natural finish (the last line of code in the function), it makes the overall code clearer. In particular, it's easy to overlook a `return` statement embedded inside a large block of code in a function and then wonder why only some of the function's code is being executed. In a small block of code, this is easier to spot, but code has a habit of growing, and before you know it, a return statement buried deep inside a nested `if` statement is overlooked. Here's an example of what to avoid:

```
function isDataValid(dataToValidate)
{
    if (someCondition)
    {
        // lots of code
        return false;
        // lots of code
    }
    else if (anotherCondition)
    {
        // lots of code
        return false;
        // lots of code
    }
    else if (yetAnotherCondition)
    {
        // lots of code
        return false;
        // lots of code
    }

    return true;
}
```

Obviously, in such a simple example, it's not really that much of a problem, it is when we start adding lots of code that things start to get tricky, and a return statement gets overlooked. Instead, we could write:

```
function isDataValid(dataToValidate)
{
   var isValidData = true;
   if (someCondition)
   {
      // lots of code
      isValidData = false;
      // lots of code
   }
   else if (anotherCondition)
   {
      // lots of code
      isValidData = false;
      // lots of code
   }
   else if (yetAnotherCondition)
   {
      // lots of code
      isValidData = false;
      // lots of code
   }

   return isValidData;
}
```

We use `isValidData` to store the value we will return, and only at the end of the function do we exit out of it.

In addition to having one return point from the function, it's also a good idea to avoid the use of labels to jump around the script, as it leads to spaghetti-like code, and makes reading it difficult to follow.

Function Names

Function names, like those of variables should be descriptive. In addition, in JavaScript the Camel Convention of starting names with lower case and then putting each word in the function name in upper case is generally followed. Developers do not normally use the Hungarian Notation for functions however as they could with variables. Unlike variables, however functions do things and so should start with a verb, followed by something that describes in more detail what the function does; for example, `get()` vs. `getEmployeeDetails()`, and they should not be vague, like `process()` vs. `saveEmployeeList()`.

It is also a good idea to use a naming standard for naming events. One common practice is to give a function called from an event handler a name that contains _eventName_ as its suffix. For example, let's say that we have a form with a button, and we add the `onClick` event handler and call a function from it. We should call this function, `cmdCheckUserId_onclick()`:

```
<BUTTON NAME='cmdCheckUserId' VALUE='Log On'
   onClick='cmdCheckUserId_onclick()'></BUTTON>
```

It means that when we look at the function we know exactly from where it will be called. Obviously, we shouldn't then go and use the function outside that event handler.

Cleaning Up a Coding Disaster

Let's look at an example of some code that can be described as the Three Mile Island/Chernobyl disaster of coding standards:

```
<HTML>
<BODY>
   <SCRIPT>
```

```
    var runningTotal;

    function findTax(money, rate)
    {
       runningTotal = 0 + (money * rate);
    }

    function calcLocalTax(money, rate)
    {
       runningTotal = runningTotal + (money * rate);
    }

    function showTotalDue(money, rate)
    {
       var tempVar = runningTotal + (money * rate);
       document.write("Tax is " + tempVar);
    }

    findTax(100,.1);
    calcLocalTax(100,.05);
    showTotalDue(100, .01);

    </SCRIPT>
</BODY>
</HTML>
```

The example has been kept simple, but its purpose is to calculate the total tax to be paid on a particular income. So, what's wrong with it?

The first problem is the global variable, `runningTotal`. What is it the running total of? as We wrote the example, We know that it's a running total of tax to be paid, so why don't We say that and call it something like `totalTaxDue`? We might also want to initialize it, for example as 0, because it's going to hold numerical values. In addition, the variable is right at the top of the script block, which is then followed by function declarations. It would be better to keep it together with the code that uses it.

The next problem is that the global variable is changed in each of the functions, something that is not obvious – particularly if the code were much longer and more complex. The function names don't help, as they don't necessarily suggest that one external variable will be changed. The `showTotalDue()` function is particularly bad as it suggests that its role is to display the total amount due, presumably the total tax due, and yet it also does a calculation that changes the tax before it is displayed; breaching the good coding practice of a function doing one thing and doing it well.

Another problem is with the names of the functions and their parameters. For example, I know that `findTax()` calculates the national tax due, so why not call it `calcNationalTaxDue()`. In addition, instead of money, it would be better to call it income; a small change, but it makes things slightly more precise. Also, instead of using the variable name `rate`, how about calling it `taxRate`, or even `nationalTaxRate`.

The next problem is with the following extract:

```
    findTax(100,.1);
    calcLocalTax(100,.05);
    showTotalDue(100, .01);
```

What is not obvious, without reading the functions, is that the order of the first two statements is important. In `findTax()` we set the running total to `0 + (money * rate)`. In the `calcLocalTax()` function, we rely on the fact that `runningTotal` has a number in it, otherwise:

```
runningTotal + (money * rate);
```

will concatenate `money * rate` to `runningTotal` and we'll end up with NaN, a value that is not a number.

Although it is not necessary, it would be a good idea to use a variable to store the 100, which represents total income, and possibly do the same for the tax rates. Doing so makes it easier to see what values like 100 and 0.05 represent.

Finally, we have a dodgy bit of coding in the function showTotalDue():

```
var tempVar = runningTotal + (money * rate);
```

What is this? What does the calculation represent? It represents miscellaneous taxes, so why not use a variable name that tells us that. Also, this code has nothing to do with showing the total tax due, and should be put in a function of its own; helping to ensure that our functions are cohesive and do one job well.

Lets see what an improved version of the code might look like:

```
<!-- 08_TaxCalc.htm -->
<HTML>
<BODY>
    <SCRIPT LANGUAGE='JavaScript'>
        function calcNationalTax(income, nationalTaxRatePercent)
        {
            return income * (nationalTaxRatePercent / 100);
        }

        function calcLocalTax(income, localTaxRatePercent)
        {
            return income * (localTaxRatePercent / 100);
        }

        function calcMiscTax(income, miscTaxRatePercent)
        {
            return income * (miscTaxRatePercent / 100);
        }

        function showTotalDue(totalTaxDue)
        {
            document.write("Tax due is " + totalTaxDue);
        }

        var totalTaxDue = 0;
        var totalIncomeForYear = 100;
        var nationalTaxRatePercent = 10;
        var localTaxRatePercent = 5;
        var miscTaxRatePercent = 1;

        totalTaxDue =
            calcNationalTax(totalIncomeForYear,nationalTaxRatePercent);
        totalTaxDue += calcLocalTax(totalIncomeForYear,localTaxRatePercent);
        totalTaxDue += calcMiscTax(totalIncomeForYear,miscTaxRatePercent);
        showTotalDue(totalTaxDue);
    </SCRIPT>
</BODY>
</HTML>
```

Briefly, the improvements we've made are:

- ❏ We've made variable and function names more descriptive and precise.

- ❏ Instead of each function accessing the global variable, they instead just do the tax calculations and return the result, which is then stored in a global variable. This way, no hidden activity is going on inside the functions.

- ❏ Each function does one thing – the function that displayed the amount due previously, also calculated miscellaneous taxes due. That calculation has been moved out to a separate function.

- ❏ Used variables store values such as total income and tax rates to make it clear what the numbers represent. In addition, we have converted the tax rates to actual percentages, these are then divided out by the functions to the fractional value we need.

It might be argued that for such a small amount of code we could get away with bad coding practice. However when we get to 400 lines of JavaScript, and we've being asked to debug 400 lines of poorly written JavaScript, and still have the scars to prove it, then good coding practice really pays off in terms of saving time and avoiding hair loss.

Summary

In this chapter, we have taken a brief look at how using good coding practice can make life a little easier for ourselves so that more time can be spent creating code, and less time on fixing it. We will now summarize some of the techniques fundamental to good coding practice in JavaScript:

- ❏ Layout your code so it is easy to follow. The start and end of blocks of code should be obvious.

- ❏ Use Descriptive Names – adopt naming conventions so that variable or function names describe what they actually do.

- ❏ Use Variables for Special Values – literal values keep you guessing, while using a well-named variable clarifies what the purpose is.

- ❏ Keep it clear and concise by:

  - ❏ Simplifying Conditions – use variables to store the results of length conditions.

  - ❏ Using arrays as lookup tables – as alternative to nested `if` statements or `switch` statements.

  - ❏ Keeping the number of exit points in a loop to a minimum – keeps it clear where a loop starts and ends.

  - ❏ Simplifying Complex Nested `if`s.

  - ❏ Keep Related Code Together.

- ❏ Organize Your Code using:

  - ❏ `.js` script files.

  - ❏ JavaScript classes.

- ❏ Variables:

  - ❏ Initialize Variables.

  - ❏ Minimize Variable Scope.

  - ❏ Use for one purpose.

  - ❏ Remove unused variables.

❑ Functions:

    ❑ Functions should do one thing and do it well.

    ❑ Don't exit a function in the middle and avoid the use of labels, which leads to difficult to follow spaghetti like code.

Pro JavaScript 2nd Edition

13

Error Handling, Debugging, and Troubleshooting

Because JavaScript is interpreted, the feedback we receive about our scripts' health is mostly limited to warnings about syntax problems. Once these are overcome, the available few run-time diagnostics generally translate into "I tried to do it, but something that I needed didn't exist."

JavaScript is intended to be a quick and easy interpreted and interactive language, often requiring only a few statements. There is no compiler rigorously checking scripts before allowing them to be used. Consequently, it is very easy to become sloppy in your programming habits. Many problems such as errors caused by not testing objects before use, not handling exceptions, or forgetting closing parentheses because of improper indentation are due to poor programming habits.

In this chapter, we will discuss the different types of JavaScript errors, what causes them, and how to find and fix them. Finally, we will discuss two of the major script debugging programs: Microsoft Script Debugger and the Netscape JavaScript Console.

Types of JavaScript Errors

JavaScript statements are interpreted as the interpreter in the host application (such as a web browser) loads them. During the loading of the script, a syntax check is performed. If any syntax errors are found, the script stops executing and an error is reported. After the syntax check completes, all global commands (those not contained within a function), such as declaring variables, are executed. At this point, a **run-time error** may occur, caused by anything from an undefined variable to an array index out of boundary. Run-time errors cause the function to stop executing, but allow other functions within the script to continue to operate. Functions or subroutines are parsed when the script is loaded, but not executed until called by other functions or events. During the execution of functions, run-time errors or **logical errors** (errors that generate results other than those expected) may be generated.

Load-Time Errors

JavaScript catches and reports **load-time** (or **syntax**) **errors** as the script is loaded. Load-time errors are generated by major mistakes in script syntax. Scripts that include load-time errors generate error messages when the script is loaded and do not execute. These errors are perhaps the easiest of all types of errors to catch and fix because they are generated each time the script is loaded, as opposed to run-time or logical errors, which are only generated when a function is called or a certain set of conditions are satisfied. Missing quotes, parentheses, or curly braces are among the most common causes of load-time errors. Take, for example the following snippet of code:

```
<!-- loadtime.html -->
<HTML>
<HEAD>
   <TITLE>Load time Errors</TITLE>
   <SCRIPT LANGUAGE='JavaScript'>
      alert('Hello, World'
   </SCRIPT>
</HEAD>
</HTML>
```

When the preceding code is loaded into Internet Explorer (IE) 5 (with script debugging disabled and script error notification enabled), the following error message is generated:

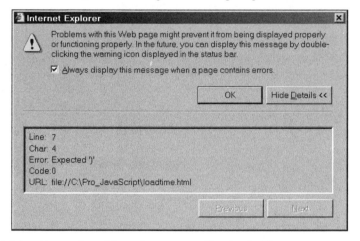

To disable script debugging and enable script error notification in IE:

1. Open an Internet Explorer browser window

2. Click Tools

3. Click Internet Options

4. Click the Advanced tab

5. Under the Browsing heading, check the Disable script debugging option

6. Check the Display a notification about every script error option

7. Click OK

Netscape 6 generates a similar error in the JavaScript console (Tasks, Tools, JavaScript Console):

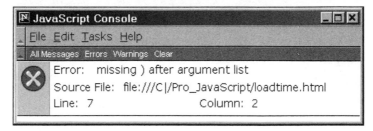

As you can see, both browsers display similar information about the error. They each list a description of the error encountered, the file (source file or URL) that caused the error, and the line and position of the error. It is important to note that the line and the column (or character position) of the error may not always represent the exact position of the error. Line numbers and character positions of errors are a little tricky to get used to. The reason is that the JavaScript interpreter displays the line number and position of the point at which it couldn't continue. In the IE example above, the JavaScript interpreter could not continue at line 5, character 5 – specifically the "<" in the </SCRIPT> line. In the Netscape 6 example, the JavaScript interpreter stopped at line 5, column 3. The differences in line, character, and column numbers are due to the difference in JavaScript interpreters and where they reach the point where they cannot continue. For this reason, it is helpful to use an IDE (for example: Microsoft Visual Interdev, Allaire HomeSite, Macromedia Ultradev, etc.) that displays line numbers.

Run-Time Errors

Run-time errors are errors that are caught after the script has been loaded and while the script is executing. A run-time error occurs when a script tries to perform an invalid action. If a script encounters a run-time error, an error message is displayed and the script stops executing. Other scripts can still be run, but each time the script with the error is called, the error message will be displayed. Some of the common causes for run-time errors occur when referencing undefined variables, misapplying objects, inserting type mismatches, and creating infinite loops. The following code generates an all too typical run-time error:

```
<!-- runtime.html -->
<HTML>
<HEAD>
    <TITLE>Example 2 - Run-time errors</TITLE>
    <SCRIPT LANGUAGE='JavaScript'>
        var sTestString = "Hello, World";
        alert(sTestStrings); //Note the trailing "s" in sTestStrings
    </SCRIPT>
</HEAD>
</HTML>
```

The error messages generated by IE5 and Netscape 6 are as follows:

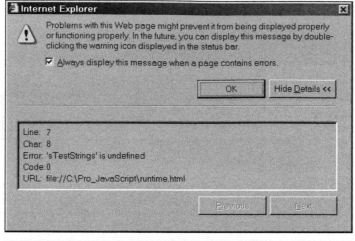

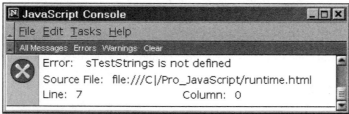

Each browser is informing the user that the variable sTestStrings is not defined. Because the browser does not know what to display in the alert() box, an error is returned.

Here is a more complex example of some code that generates a run-time error:

```
<!-- runtime2.html -->
<HTML>
<HEAD>
    <TITLE>A more complex run-time error</TITLE>
    <SCRIPT LANGUAGE='JavaScript'>
        document.getElementsByName("txtName").value = "XX"
    </SCRIPT>
</HEAD>
<BODY>
    <INPUT TYPE='text' name='txtName' value='Fred'></INPUT>
</BODY>
</HTML>
```

The errors generated by this script are as follows:

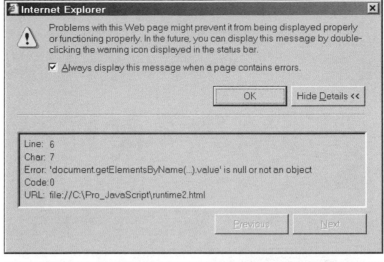

The reason this script generates errors is that it is executed before the text box is created. The script cannot assign a value to something that is not yet created. This script is perfectly valid and would generate no errors if executed after the text box has been created, or if it were placed in a function that is called after all the HTML is loaded.

Logical Errors

Logical errors are free from syntax and run-time errors, but generate incorrect results. Logical errors do not cause a script to stop executing unless the unintended results of a logical error, coupled with another command or script, generate a run-time error. Logical errors are often the hardest to debug and may require the programmer to trace the values of each variable at every step in the script. Some of the common causes for logical errors are using "=" instead of "==,"and mismatched data types. The following code illustrates how easy it is to generate a logical error:

```
<!-- logical.html -->
<HTML>
<HEAD>
   <SCRIPT LANGUAGE='JavaScript'>
     var value;
      for (counter=1; counter<6; counter++)
      {
         value=counter;   // Done to stop an infinite loop...
         if (value=3)
         {
            alert("We've reached the half way point\nvalue = 3");
         }
```

```
        else
        {
            alert("value = " + value);
        }
    }
  </SCRIPT>
 </HEAD>
 </HTML>
```

In the preceding example, the result is always as follows:

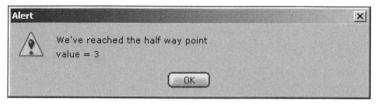

The first evaluation (the `if` statement) of the variable will always return `true`, because it sets the value of the variable to 3 every time by using the "=" operator instead of the comparison operator, "==." Since the `if` evaluates `true` (as it would only return `false` if `value` could not be changed for some reason), we will always get the alert pictured above. If we were to replace the "=" with "==" or "===", the results would be as intended, and the value in the `alert` box would represent the variable's expected value, in other words it starts with a value of 1 and increases each time you click OK until it reaches the value of 5.

Common JavaScript Errors

If you have worked with JavaScript for any length of time, you will doubtless have encountered or will at least be familiar with many of these problems. It is always helpful to have another look, though, in order to keep these issues in the front of your mind while coding.

Undefined Variables, Spelling, and Script Sequence

A variable can be defined in two ways in JavaScript: **implicitly** and **explicitly**. Implicit definition allows a variable to be defined simply by assigning it a value:

```
iNumber = 3;
```

Explicit variable definition uses the `var` keyword:

```
var iNumber = 3;
```

or:

```
var iNumber;//explicit variable definition
iNumber = 3; //variable initialization
```

The preceding lines all produce the same results (with a small deviance in relation to variable scope; variables implicitly declared within functions become global variables): a variable named `iNumber` is defined and its value is set to 3.

As you can see, it is easy to define a variable; all you have to do is assign it a value. The only time you really get an error is when the variable has not been defined at all.

Undefined variable errors are most often caused by misspelled and incorrectly capitalized variable names.

```
// typo.html
var goToTown = "go to town";
var staysHome = "stay home";

if (confirm("Click 'OK' if you want to go to town"))
{
    alert("I want to " + GoToTown);
}
else
{
    alert("I want to " + stayHome);
}
```

There are two major mistakes in the preceding script. The first mistake is the variable `goToTown` is improperly capitalized as `GoToTown`. The second mistake is the variable `staysHome` is spelt `stayHome`. Both of these mistakes cause similar undefined variable run-time errors:

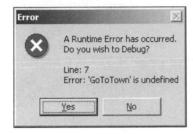

The error box above is the one displayed when Microsoft Script Debugger is installed and enabled. For more information, see the Microsoft Script Debugger section later on in this chapter.

As easy as it is to define variables in JavaScript, undefined variables are a very common cause of run-time errors. The error is not generally caused in *how* the variable was defined, but *when*. Take, for example the following code:

```
function doAlert()
{
    alert(sWrox);
}
doAlert();
var sWrox = "Wrox";
```

In this example, although it does not generate a run-time error, as above, it is very easy to see where the problem lies. The variable `sWrox` is defined after the `doAlert()` function is called, and is therefore returned as "undefined." In a real situation, this type of mistake may not be so easy to spot, especially as specific scripts are often included as `.js` files, so the actual code is sometimes not visible on the page.

Closing or Mismatched Parentheses and Braces

Another frustrating, real-world problem is forgetting to close out parentheses or adding an extra one where it is not needed. This type of mistake generates a load-time syntax error.

Missing curly braces are one of the most common mistakes. Take the following code:

```
function returnBit(bValue)
{
    var bReturnValue = false;
    if (bValue)
    {
```

```
        bReturnValue = true;
    return bReturnValue;
}
```

The `if` statement does not contain a closing curly brace and triggers the following error:

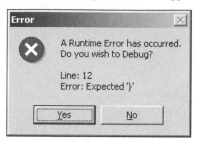

Proper indentation, as mentioned in the previous chapter, will greatly reduce the chances of making this mistake.

Another common mistake is forgetting that the argument for the `if` statement must be in parentheses. Here is an example:

```
function returnBit(bValue)
{
    var bReturnValue = false;
    if bValue
    {
        bReturnValue = true;
    }
    return bReturnValue ;
}
```

The `bReturnValue` in `if bReturnValue` is not in parentheses, therefore the following error occurs:

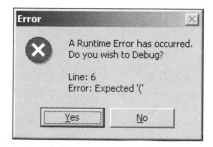

Using Methods the Object Does Not Support

Using a method that an object does not support is a common mistake, especially when working with the HTML DOM. This snippet generates a run-time error.

```
var iValue = 123;
nValue = iValue.replace(2,4);
return iValue;
```

The preceding code is trying to perform a string replacement on an integer, which returns the following error:

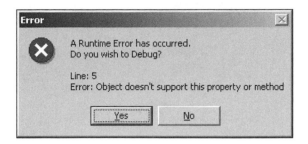

Using Reserved Words

There are words in JavaScript that are part of the JavaScript language syntax and therefore have predefined meanings in JavaScript. These are **reserved words**. Most reserved words are the keywords used by JavaScript itself. Others are reserved for expected future use. Reserved words may not be used as variable, function, object, or method names. If you attempt to use a reserved word, the JavaScript interpreter will generate a load-time error.

In the example below, we attempt to declare a variable name with the reserved keyword `case`:

```
var case;
```

The JavaScript interpreter then raises an error:

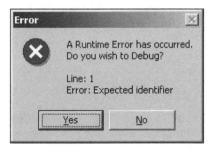

It is important to note that `Case` is a legal name, since JavaScript is case-sensitive (no pun intended). It is, however, bad practice to use keywords at all, no matter how they have been capitalized. A list of the reserved words in JavaScript is shown in Appendix A.

Quotes

Improperly placed or missing quotation marks are common mistakes in JavaScript, especially when JavaScript is being generated and escaped dynamically, or when a JavaScript string contains quotation marks.

Quotes Around Variable/Object Names

Inadvertently placing quotes around variable or object names causes JavaScript to view the name of the variable or object as a string. This can cause your script to return unexpected results. The following code...

```
var FirstName = "John";
var LastName = "Doe";

alert("Welcome, " + FirstName + " " + "LastName" + ".");
```

...gives this output:

No Quotes around Strings

Forgetting to place quotes around a string causes JavaScript to view the string as a variable or object, which can cause your script to produce a runtime error. This code...

```
var FirstName = John;
var LastName = "Doe";

alert("Welcome, " + FirstName + " " + LastName + ".");
```

...produces this error:

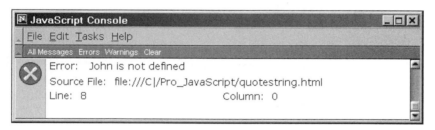

Mismatched Quotes

Mismatched quotation marks in a string can also generate JavaScript errors. It is important when working with strings in JavaScript that we escape all quotation marks within a string. Here is an example of a string that will generate errors:

```
var myString1 = "Then he said, "I will!""
```

Here is the error message:

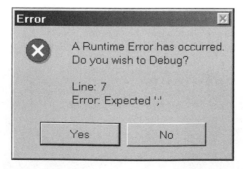

The string generates an error because the quotation marks within the string must be escaped, or at least alternated between single and double quotes. Here are some possible ways to fix it:

❑   Replace the double quotes within the string with single quotes:

```
var myString1 = "Then he said, 'I will!'";
```

❑   Use single quotes to enclose the string:

```
var myString1 = 'Then he said, "I will!"';
```

❑   The preferred way to handle quotes within the string is to escape them, rather than switching back and forth between single and double quotes:

```
var myString1 = "Then he said, \"I will!\"";
```

See Chapter 2, *Core JavaScript* for more on escaping characters in JavaScript.

Missing "+" Signs when Concatenating

When concatenating a string with a JavaScript variable or object, it is easy to forget to put the "+" between each string, variable, or object being concatenated. Missing "+" operators are very difficult to notice when you are trying to debug page after page of JavaScript. Here is a real-world example in which it is easy to forget the concatenation operator:

```
var userName = "Joe";
var itemNumber = 1234;
var sURL;

sURL = "formPost.htm?user=" + userName + "&itemNumber=" itemNumber

document.location.href = sURL
```

Here, there should be a "+" between "&itemNumber=" and itemNumber.

"=" vs. "==" vs. "==="

In JavaScript, "=" is an assignment operator that sets the value of whatever comes before it to whatever comes after it. "==" means "is equal to", and performs a comparison of the values on either side of it, returning a Boolean. "===" means "is strictly equal to", and performs a comparison of both the value and data type of the values on either side.

```
var i = 2;
alert(i=3)//returns 3
alert(i=="3")//returns true
alert(i==="3")//returns false
```

In this example, the variable i is declared with a value of 2. On the second line, the value of the variable is changed to 3, as reported with the alert. The i == "3" on the third line evaluates as true because the value of i was changed on line 2. The fourth line evaluates to false, because the variable i is of the numeric data type.

"<>" vs. "!="

For ASP or VB programmers, it is usual to use "<>" for "not equal to." This produces a syntax error in JavaScript. The JavaScript operator for inequality is "!=."

Methods as Properties and Vice-versa

In JavaScript, a set of parentheses must follow every method, whether or not that method accepts parameters. Properties never have a trailing set of parentheses.

In this example, the toLowerCase() method does not have a set of trailing parentheses; therefore, JavaScript is trying to interpret it as a property:

```
var myVar = "HELLO, WORLD!";
alert(myVar.toLowerCase);
```

This produces some interesting results:

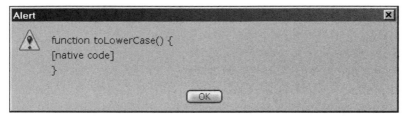

The results in the alert box are basically the prototype of the toLowerCase() method, the methods and properties of which are non-enumerable native code of the JavaScript toLowerCase() host object.

Similarly, when placing parentheses after a property, the JavaScript interpreter attempts to interpret the property as a method:

```
var myVar = "HELLO, WORLD!";
alert(myVar.length());
```

This generates a run-time error:

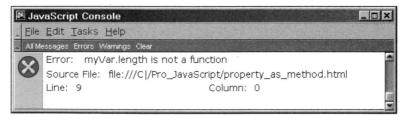

Dangling "else" statements

Sometimes it is not clear which if statement a given else statement belongs to. The following example has both bad formatting and bad logic:

```
if(result!="win")
    if(result=="lose")
        do_lose();
else
    do_win();
```

In this example, you never win. The else branch belongs to the second if statement. Use of curly braces (as described in the previous chapter) eliminates this error.

```
if(result!="win")
{
   if(result=="lose")
   {
      do_lose();
   }
}
else
{
   do_win();
}
```

Problems with for...in

As briefly described in Chapter 2, the for...in syntax is used to find the names of all the properties of a JavaScript object. The problem is that it does not always work as expected; some properties don't appear and some objects don't seem to have any properties at all. You can do little about this because it is a product decision made by the developers of the JavaScript interpreter. Usually this problem only occurs when you are hacking into the browser "off the beaten track" for your own ends.

Your only strategies are:

❑ To know the property names in advance

❑ To appreciate why they are hidden from inspection and accept it

To know an object's properties in advance, resort to documentation such as this book's Appendices. The only other possible tactic is to probe the object in question, one property at a time, using array syntax. This takes a very long time, and is a last resort.

According to the ECMAScript standard, a given property of an object has a few **attributes** describing that property, such as property name and property value. One such attribute is the DontEnum attribute. If this attribute is present, then the property won't be revealed by a for...in loop. This is how object properties are excluded in such loops.

There are several reasons why some host object properties have this DontEnum attribute. The simplest one is that some properties aren't interesting. Every method of an object is also a property of that object. It is pointless trying to interact with a method property if the object is a host object. An example for Navigator 4.0:

```
alert(document.open);
document.open = "Fruit Salad";
alert(document.open);
```

This script displays the following alerts, and messes up the document object in the process. The open() method is not accessible afterwards for creating new browser windows.

479

A second reason for non-enumerable properties is that some host objects don't follow the same rules as JavaScript. Java classes exposed as JavaScript host objects in a browser are an example. The JavaScript property `java.lang` isn't really an object, but a **package** of object types (also called a class library). `java.lang.io` is a sub package `java.lang`, but isn't an object either. A package is merely a group of related objects collected together. These classes are stored on disk and it isn't easy, efficient or even that useful to sift through them looking for `java.lang` members that might be objects. In any event, the browsers won't let you do it. Therefore, this item and the others relating to Java classes can't be enumerated at all from JavaScript.

Note that the above discussion relates to Java *classes* accessed from JavaScript only, not Java *objects* accessed from JavaScript. You can enumerate through a Java object from JavaScript as normal.

Falling Foul of Types

It is easy to create "quick and dirty" client-side JavaScript. A loosely typed language saves a lot time that would otherwise be spent organizing the right kind of data for the right kind of variables. Once finished, specially gifted people called users come along and expose gaping holes in your scripts. JavaScript may have un-typed variables, but all the data itself is fully typed, and users will find a way to make your script trip over this distinction.

Chapter 1 describes how type conversion works in JavaScript. The most common trap is to develop all your scripts with Netscape 4.0 browsers and then discover that it doesn't work on any other browsers because you rely on the special behavior of Netscape's JavaScript 1.2 `!=` and `==` operators. Don't use `<SCRIPT LANGUAGE='JavaScript 1.2'>` when developing, unless portability is not required. It's probably safest to leave the `LANGUAGE` attribute out altogether, since JavaScript is the default browser scripting language anyway. If you must specify it, use `LANGUAGE='JavaScript'`. If you are sure your users will only use a really recent browser, then `LANGUAGE='JavaScript 1.3'` or `LANGUAGE='JavaScript 1.4'` is also a good option, as you then have available the error handling events of those versions.

Converting user input into numbers can be problematic. If your CGI program is crashing, your e-mail is not arriving properly, or JavaScript is popping up errors on some obscure browser, first go back and check that all numeric values entered by the user are carefully validated. Form Validation is discussed in Chapter 16.

Finally, older browsers have limited JavaScript support for types (also described in Chapter 1). If you want to support those browsers, don't be fancy with `null`, `NaN`, `typeof()`, or `Array` objects.

String Truncation

Beware of string constants that are over 80 characters. Some earlier browsers can't handle them. Just break them up into smaller chunks – it is easier to read anyway. This example has only short strings but it illustrates the principle:

```
var big_string   = "first chunk "
                 + "second chunk "
                 + "third chunk ";
```

Beware of the null character problem in Netscape browsers. The value of `"xxx\000yyy".length` is 3 except for recent Netscape 4.0 releases; the y characters are lost to view. For all browsers, attempting to display such a string with `alert()` or `document.write()` is generally problematic as all will understand the string to be xxx only and not xxx\000yyy.

Unique Function Names

Each function and variable must have its own unique name. Duplicating variable or function names may not necessarily result in an error, but will generate some unexpected results:

```
function alert(s)
{
   document.write(s);
}
function myFunction()
{
   alert("The first function");
}
function myFunction()
{
   alert("The second function");
}

myFunction();
```

In the preceding code, the JavaScript core alert function is redefined to do a document write. Next a function is defined, and then redefined in the next block. The result illustrates the importance of unique function names:

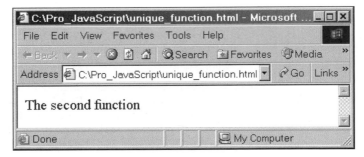

Using Exceptions

In JavaScript, anything that throws an error or attempts to perform an illegal operation is defined as an **exception**. Exceptions that are not handled within the code generate the familiar cryptic system error messages and cause the script to stop executing. By handling exceptions we can use our own custom error messages and launch our own custom error-handling functions.

When a function or method is called, the only mechanism described to date for passing information back to the script fragment that called the function of method is the `return` statement. What happens if something goes wrong? This example function illustrates:

```
function add_like_a_child(nOne, nTwo)
{
   var vReturnValue;
   if (nOne + nTwo > 20)
   {
```

```
            vReturnValue="Finger & toe limit passed!";
    }
    else if (nOne + nTwo >10)
    {
        vReturnValue = "Finger limit passed!";
    }
    else
    {
        vReturnValue = nOne + nTwo;
    }
    return vReturnValue;
}
```

The problem with this function is that every time it gets used, additional code is required to check the return value. One never knows until after that check whether the function has worked usefully or not. In this case, you may have to do two checks, one for each unusual case. If the function was complex, you may have to do many checks. Here's an example of using this function:

```
var vResult = add_like_a_child(3, 5)
if ( vResult == "Finger & toe limit passed!")
{
    // Do something to cope
}
else if ( vResult == "Finger limit passed!" )
{
    // Do something else to cope
}
// Carry on normally if we reach this point
```

In Java, this kind of difficult case is handled with exceptions. The general goal of exceptions is to provide a mechanism that reports when something unusual happens. With such a mechanism in place, one can rely on return values reporting only normal, successful output from the function. With extraordinary cases taken care of, there's no need for special, extra checks of the function's return value.

To a degree, JavaScript tries to mimic Java in its syntax. Exceptions are likely to become a major feature of JavaScript in the future. The reason for this is that if an object is to be used in a script, the script writer must have access points through which he can get at that object and its properties and methods. These access points combined make up the object's **interface**, or **signature**. In computer language terms, the three main features of object interfaces are properties (also called attributes), methods and exceptions. Therefore, there are exceptions in JavaScript.

In Java, we have to rigidly declare the type of thing that an exception is. True to form, in JavaScript an exception can be any old thing, such as an object or a string. Here's the official syntax for the JavaScript statements supporting exceptions. First, to create an exception:

```
throw expression;
```

Secondly, to handle an exception:

```
try
    statement-block
catch ( identifier )                    // variant1, can be repeated
    statement block
catch ( identifier if condition )       // variant2, can be repeated
    statement block
finally                                 // optional, at most one.
    statement block
```

Here is the previous finger counting function re-written:

```
function add_like_a_child(num1, num2)
{
    if ( num1 + num2 > 20 )
        throw "Finger & toe limit passed!";
    if ( num1 + num2 > 10 )
        throw "Finger limit passed!";
    return num1 + num2;
}
```

In this function, if a `throw` statement is ever executed, processing of the function stops, and the function returns immediately. No ordinary return value is returned. Instead, an exception is returned.

Here is the calling code rewritten (this will work in Netscape 6 and Internet Explorer 5):

```
var iResult;
try
{
    iResult=add_like_a_child(3,5);
    if (iResult == 8)
    {
        alert("Correct");
    }
    else
    {
        alert("Please try again");
    }
}
catch (sError)
{
    if ( sError == "Finger & toe limit passed!" )
    {
        alert("Finger & toe limit passed!");
    }
    if ( sError == "Finger limit passed!" )
    {
        alert("Finger limit passed!");
    }
}
finally
{
    alert(iResult);
}
```

In this script, the `iResult` variable might never be set in the fourth line. If the function returns an exception, processing immediately jumps straight to the `catch` statement, which has access to the exception in the error variable, and the statements in the block following the `catch` statement are executed instead. If there is no exception, and the function returns normally, then processing continues with the next statement in the `try` block, and when that block is finished, the `catch` block is stepped over entirely, similar to an unused branch of an `if` statement.

The whole explanation gets a lot easier once you know a little jargon. If something goes wrong, you say the function throws an exception. The function is called in a `try` block and exceptions are handled in `catch` blocks. The `finally` block is always executed if no exception is outstanding at the end.

The rules for how this process works are as follows:

❑   If a `throw` statement is reached in a function (or in any block of code), then that function will not continue. It will not return a value, and it will not return `void`. Instead, it will cease immediately and the exception will be created.

❑   If the statement or function causing the exception is not inside a `try` block, then a runtime interpreter error will occur and the script will stop. If the statement or function is called inside another function, method or `try` block, then that collection of statements will be aborted as well and the exception passed up to the next level of control until a `try` block is found or an error occurs.

❑   If the statement or function causing an exception is inside a `try` block, then any further statements in that block are ignored. The interpreter looks through any `catch` blocks that might be present. If one is found with satisfactory criteria, that `catch` block is executed. When all `try` and `catch` blocks have been executed according to the exception, the `finally` block is executed.

What are `catch` block criteria? There are two cases, illustrated here:

```
catch (error) {Execute error handling statements}
```

and:

```
catch (error if (error > "Error 1")) {Execute error handling statements}
```

In the first case, the `catch` block matches all exceptions. In the second case, the `catch` block only matches those exceptions that pass the `if` criteria. If there are multiple `catch` blocks, then the first case will catch everything, much like the `default:` clause of a `switch` statement, so it makes sense to put it last in the list of `catch` blocks. The `error` variable tracks the exception, and it acts within the `catch` block like a function parameter. The `catch` block treats the variable, `error`, in much the same way that the following script treats the variable `error2`:

```
function HandleError(error2)
{
    if(error == "ErrorType1")
    {
        //exception routine for condition 1
    }
    if(error == "ErrorType2")
    {
        //exception routine for condition 2
    }
}
```

Exception Syntax vs. "if"

If you've never used exceptions before, you're likely to be very skeptical about the syntax arrangements required to get them working. Common objections to the above example are:

❑   It's more verbose. There are actually more lines than the plain `if` case and so takes more effort.

❑   It looks pretty much like the first example structurally. Where's the improvement?

❑   The language is foreign. What's the matter with good old `if`?

For simple cases, it is true that the argument for exceptions is weak; the exception-style code can definitely be bigger. Scripts that just perform sequences of guaranteed operations really have no need of exceptions at all. More generally, the argument for using exception syntax goes like this:

❑   Exception syntax is clearer when many things go wrong.

❑   Once you're used to it, exception syntax is easier to read, because you learn to ignore `catch` blocks. `catch` blocks account for 1% of the code actually run (errors are rare) and contain 99% of the irrelevant detail (errors are messy to recover from).

❑   Exceptions are examples of "cleaner code" or "good programming style"

❑   Exceptions are one of the three major features of objects, the other two being attributes and methods.

Here is an example that shows exception syntax working for the script writer, rather than against:

```
// piece of code that could fail 20 different ways
try
{
   // might cause 1 of 5 exceptions
   dodgy_task_1();
   // might cause 1 of 4 exceptions
   dodgy_task_2();
   // might cause 1 of 7 exceptions
   dodgy_task_3();
   // might cause 1 of 4 exceptions
   dodgy_task_4();
}
catch (everything)
{
   // scream blue murder
}
```

Because a `throw` statement immediately aborts the `try` block, each function can come straight after the other, confident that if something goes wrong, the later ones will never be executed. We've saved using many `if` tests by using the `try` block in this case. Note that functions needn't have a non-`void` return value in order to make use of exceptions.

Finally, we needn't restrict ourselves to throwing primitive types. Here's some code that illustrates:

```
// throws an object
throw {err_string:"You're doomed", err_number: 23};
```

The above statement creates a two-property object and returns that as the thrown item. On the other hand, the statement below expects the exception to be an object with an `err_number` property, which clearly will be the case if the previous `throw` statement is responsible for the exception.

```
// catches only error number 23
catch (e if ( e.err_number == 23)) { ... }
```

Exceptions vs. Events vs. Errors

If you've played around with JavaScript in browsers, then you might be aware that there are triggers or **events** that can make JavaScript script fragments run, especially if a given web page contains forms. These kinds of events are not generally considered exceptions. Events, generally occurring as a form of input from a user or a network, are normal occurrences. They are usually handled in the same way as normal data. Exceptions are not considered normal, and are usually used for error conditions, where something went wrong that the script has been able to anticipate (with `try...catch` blocks), but can't really handle normally.

Sometimes it's possible to confuse events with exceptions. This is because the way a script prepares for events is typically somewhat different to the way it receives more basic kinds of user input, and can seem similar to the oddity of handling exceptions. However, they are separate and different. Chapter 5, *Forms and Data*, gives an idea of what ordinary events are like, and if you look there, you'll see that it does not mention JavaScript exception syntax.

Exceptions Make Sense for Host Objects

A further reason for exception handling support in JavaScript is to be found in host objects (or built-in objects and methods such as the `date` object or the `replace` method). Without host objects JavaScript is nearly useless. What if those host objects generate exceptions as part of their attribute/method/exception interface? There must be a mechanism in place in JavaScript to support this kind of communication.

Exceptions Make Sense for Interpreter Errors

Some terrible things can go wrong with JavaScript scripts. If the script writer has made a typographical error in some obscure part of a large script, it might never be detected until that script is installed in some critical place. That is the risk taken with interpreted languages.

If the interpreter comes to read the script and finds a typographical error, it would be useful if there were something that could be done about it, rather than the whole script just stopping dead. This is a future direction for the ECMAScript standard – scripting errors might be reported as exceptions and handled by the system that starts the JavaScript interpreter in the first place.

Writing Clean, Bug-Free Code

The quickest way to debug a script is to never introduce a bug in the first place. Writing clean code is the best way to avoid making coding mistakes. Clean code is well organized, self-documenting, indented, and commented. See the previous chapter for some solid guidelines for writing clean code.

Write Modular Code

When writing JavaScript, it is important to make your code as modular as possible. Modular code is divided into many different functions, with each function ideally performing one particular task. Modular code reduces duplication and overall script complexity. It also never makes direct reference to variables or HTML elements, but accepts them as inputs. The only variables declared in functions are local variables. External variables are not set directly by the functions, but by the value returned by the function. It is possible for modularization to go too far, especially when we begin to write scripts that perform or duplicate built in JavaScript functions.

Verify Existence of Objects

"... undefined" run-time errors are perhaps the most common errors that you will encounter when writing JavaScript. You can eliminate this error almost entirely by verifying that the object exists before trying to access its properties or methods. Generally, a block similar to the following should be included near the top of your script and/or near the top of each function in which an object is referenced:

```
try
{
    if(object or property)
    {
        //proceed as planned
    }
}
catch(error)
{
    //insert error handling here
}
```

Debugging Techniques

There are a number of effective debugging techniques available for JavaScript programs, ranging from the trivial to the comprehensive. Debugging techniques that involve new windows, writing to the current document or a new window, or alerts should be removed or commented out before the code goes live.

Client-Side JavaScript

For HTML-embedded JavaScript, the crudest debugging tool is `document.write()`. Even if it messes up an HTML document, at least we get some feedback while testing. Coupled with a `window.open()` command, we can send the output to another window if we desire. For example:

```
var newWindow = window.open("","newWindow"); newWindow.document.write("Hello,
World!");
```

JavaScript used for Internet connection proxy configuration files, or for browser preference files in Netscape browsers (such as `prefs.js`, discussed later on in this chapter), are not amenable to debugging – we have to test them using trial and error.

Alerts

Using `window.alert()` functions embedded in inline JavaScript scripts is the simplest way of stopping the JavaScript interpreter at a given point or points when a document is loading. The message in the alert box can reveal the value of any interesting data as well. This is the simplest way to debug complex logic that involves lots of `if` statements and function calls – just add an `alert()` to the suspect branch or function and you'll know whether it's being executed or not. Alerts are particularly effective with JavaScript URLs as well. The following example stops the script execution with an alert to check the value of the variable after each statement:

```
var myString = "Part One";
alert(myString);

var myString += ", Part Two";
alert(myString);
```

javascript: URLs

Once an HTML document is fully loaded, `document.write()` isn't of much use; inline alerts won't help if the script has finished running. `javascript:` URLs, which we can type in at any time in the browser window's address or location field, allow us to probe the browser and document and see what the current state is. This example shows a window's URL:

```
javascript:alert(top.location.href);
```

However, `javascript:` URLs can be used more generally. Provided you are patient and careful, any amount of JavaScript can be included. This example displays all the element numbers of the first form that have value properties:

```
javascript:var i; for (i=0;i< document.forms[0].elements.length;i++)
   { alert(i); }
```

Any function or method in the browser that is otherwise available to JavaScript can be called. This means we can force a form `submit()` directly, perform a `click()` on a button, or call any of our own functions. This example deletes a cookie using the popular routines, which are assumed to be included in the document somewhere:

```
javascript:DeleteCookie("biscuit3");
```

Java Console Logging

In Netscape Navigator, version 4+, if we don't want to disturb a document when it is loading, but we want a record of what happened, we can log information to the *Java* console. You can watch the console as the document loads, or examine it afterwards. The approach is very similar to `document.write()`; just embed statements as follows at strategic points in your script:

```
java.lang.System.out.println("Window name is: "+top.name);
```

This version does not write an end-of-line character to the console:

```
java.lang.System.out.print('more..');
```

File Logging

If logging output to the console is not permanent enough, the client-side JavaScript can write to files on the test computer's local disk. All that is required is that security features in the browser that prevent this type of behavior are turned off:

```
var err = "Some script error" ;
var oFSO = new ActiveXObject("Scripting.FileSystemObject") ;
var oFile = oFSO.CreateTextFile("C:\ErrLog.txt") ;
oFile.WriteLine(err);
```

Microsoft Script Debugger

The Microsoft Script Debugger is an impressive IDE-style debugging environment that tests for and corrects errors in scripts written in any ActiveX-enabled scripting language (such as JavaScript, VBScript, WSH, etc.). Microsoft Script Debugger works hand in hand with Internet Explorer to provide context-sensitive debugging information when a scripting error is encountered. Microsoft Script Debugger can also be used alone to create and debug scripts outside the browser.

Obtaining Microsoft Script Debugger

Microsoft script debugger is freely available from:

http://msdn.microsoft.com/scripting/default.htm?/scripting/debugger/default.htm

If the preceding URL is invalid, go to http://www.microsoft.com/ and search for Microsoft Script Debugger.

You may already have the debugger installed if any of the following are installed:

❑ Microsoft Visual Studio components (Visual Interdev, Visual Basic, Visual C++, etc.)

❑ Internet Information Services (IIS) or Microsoft PWS

❑ Windows 2000

The version of Microsoft Script Debugger installed with these applications is the advanced version. This performs the same functions as the basic version (available at the URL above), but has more features and a slightly different screen layout. Throughout the remainder of this chapter all screen shots and layout references will be for the basic version 1.0 (using IE 5.0), as it is freely available to all and can be installed alongside and run separately from the advanced version.

Enabling the Microsoft Script Debugger

After installation, the easiest way to determine whether or not the Microsoft Script Debugger is enabled is by starting up Microsoft Internet Explorer and clicking the View selection in the menu bar.

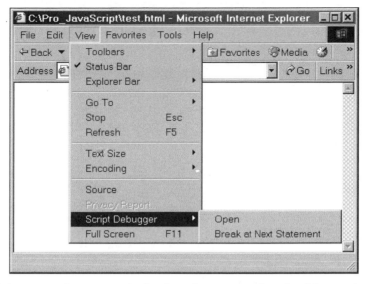

If the Script Debugger option appears in the drop-down menu, then the debugger is already enabled. Otherwise, to enable the script debugger, click the Tools option in the menu bar, and then select the Internet Options... option.

Select the Advanced tab on the Internet Options screen that appears. If the Disable script debugging option is checked under the Browsing heading, uncheck it, and click OK. Script Debugging is now enabled. Note that some systems require a restart of IE before the changes take effect.

Using Microsoft Script Debugger

Once the script debugger has been installed and enabled, you are ready to use it to aid you in debugging troublesome scripts. We are going to use the following document, saved as VBTrim.html for most of our debugging examples:

```
<!-- VBTrim.html -->
<HTML>
<HEAD>
    <TITLE>Using the Microsoft Script Debugger</TITLE>

    <SCRIPT LANGUAGE='JavaScript'>
    function VBTrim(txtInput)
    {
       //First, check to see if input string has at least one character
       if (txtInput.length > 0)
       {
          //Set local variable to value of input string
          var sToTrim = txtInput

          // Next, remove leading spaces
          while (sToTrim.substring(0,1) == ' ')
          {
             sToTrim = sToTrim.substring(1, sToTrim.length);
          }

          // Finally, remove trailing spaces
          while (sToTrim.substring(sToTrim.length-1,sToTrim.length) == ' ')
          {
```

```
            sToTrim = sToTrim.substring(0, sToTrim.length-1);
        }

        //return the trimmed string
        return sToTrim;

    }

    else //No characters have been entered in the text box
    {
        alert("You have not provided a string to trim!")
        return false;
    }

}
</SCRIPT>

</HEAD>
<BODY>
    Trim leading and trailing spaces: <BR><BR>
    <INPUT TYPE='text' name='txtValue'>
    <input type='button'
    onClick="txtValue.value = VBTrim(txtValue.value)" value="Trim">
</BODY>
</HTML>
```

Can you find the error? Hint: It is a logical error that is produced only under a certain conditions. The preceding code results in the following browser output:

Opening Microsoft Script Debugger

As with most software applications, there are several ways to perform tasks in Microsoft Script Debugger. There are four main ways to open the debugger:

❑   From the executable in the directory where the Script Debugger was installed. This loads up a new, blank script debugger instance. A document must be opened, or a new document must be created in order to use the debugger further.

❑   From Internet Explorer, by selecting View, Script Debugger, and then Open from the menu bar. This loads the current Internet Explorer document (as read-only) into the script debugger. You can also use the Break at Next Statement option in the same menu. The script debugger will open the next time a script is run.

❑   From within a script. Use the debugger keyword to open the Microsoft Script Debugger with the current document whenever script execution reaches that line (VBScript uses the stop keyword.)

❑ From a script error message. When the script debugger is enabled, any time a script encounters an error, you will see a screen similar to the following, providing you with an opportunity to debug:

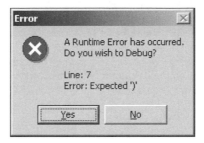

Now that we know the many ways in which the debugger can be opened, let's go ahead and open our test HTML document (above) in Internet Explorer 5. Once you have opened the document in IE, select **View** from the menu bar. Next, select **Script Debugger** and then **Break at Next Statement**. Finally, click the **Trim** button. (Refreshing the page does not work in this case, because no statements are executed when the HTML document is loaded.)

The debugger opens a window similar to the following, with the statement that triggered the debugger to open highlighted in yellow:

```
Read only: file://C:\Pro_JavaScript\VBTrim.html [break]                    _ □ ×
                    return sToTrim;

              }

              else //No characters have been entered in the text box
              {
                  alert("You have not provided a string to trim!")
                  return false;
              }

          }
       </SCRIPT>

   </HEAD>
   <BODY>
      Trim leading and trailing spaces: <BR><BR>
      <INPUT TYPE='text' name='txtValue'>
      <input type='button'
      onClick="txtValue.value = VBTrim(txtValue.value)" value="Trim">
   </BODY>
   </HTML>
```

Now would be a good time to explain the various buttons and menus contained in the Microsoft Script Debugger Window:

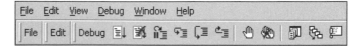

Function Name	Description	Icon	In Menu
Run	Starts or continues the execution of the currently selected script or document		Debug
Stop Debugging	Cancels the debugging of the currently selected script or document		Debug
Break at Next Statement	Breaks into the debugger when the next statement is executed		Debug
Step Into	Executes the next statement		Debug
Step Over	Skips the next statement		Debug
Step Out	Steps out of the current function		Debug
Toggle Breakpoint	Toggles a breakpoint on or off		Debug
Clear All Breakpoints	Removes all breakpoints		Debug
Running Documents	Toggles on or off the Running Documents window (discussed later)		View
Call Stack	Toggles on or off the Call Stack window (discussed later)		View
Command Window	Toggles on or off the Command window (discussed later)		View

Debugger Windows

In addition to the main window that is opened whenever the debugger is called, there are three smaller windows that can be opened to provide you with some additional debugging flexibility.

Running Documents Window

The Running Documents window displays a list of all applications hosting documents that contain active scripting. Click the "+" sign next to the application (Internet Explorer, for example) to expand the list of currently running documents. In the example below, Internet Explorer is running four different .htm documents.

Double-click a document to load it into the script debugger, or right-click on a document to set a breakpoint for the next statement.

Call Stack Window

The Call Stack window displays a list of all currently running threads and active procedure calls.

1. Load the following (rather pointless) HTML document into IE.

```
<!-- button.html -->
<HTML>
<HEAD>
    <SCRIPT>
        function doButtonClick(o)
        {
            o.click();
        }
    </SCRIPT>
</HEAD>
<BODY>
    <INPUT TYPE="button" onClick="doButtonClick(this)" VALUE="Click">
</BODY>
</HTML>
```

2. Select View | Script Debugger | Break at next statement from the IE menu bar

3. Click the Click button on the web page.

4. When the script debugger opens, click the Call Stack button to toggle on the Call Stack window (if it is not already open).

5. You should see the following in your debugger window: the onClick event that called the debugger should be highlighted and the Call Stack window should display Jscript – anonymous function – the value assigned to the onClick event:

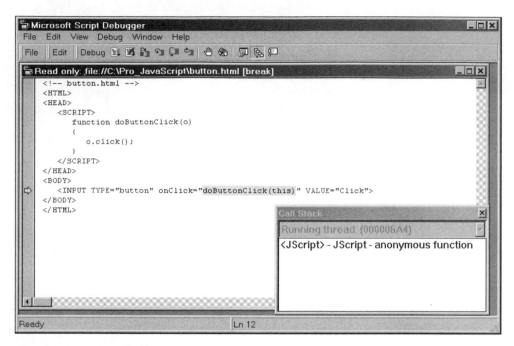

6. Click the Step Into button until the line containing `o.click();` is highlighted.

7. Your debugger should look like the screen captured below, with the line containing `o.click();` highlighted and the Call Stack window containing `doButtonClick()` (our custom function).

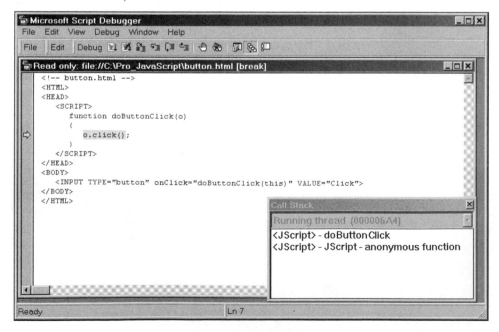

As each statement is executed, it is added to the top of the Call Stack window. It is removed once it finishes executing and returns control to the calling procedure. To go the line with the statement containing the function in the Call Stack window, simply double click that line. If there is more than one thread for a running document, individual threads can be selected from the drop-down list.

Command Window

The Command Window displays debugging information about the scripts based on debugging commands that you type. For example, load VBTrim.html into IE and click Break at next statement, enter " 5" (3 spaces followed by a five) into the text field, then click the Trim button. Toggle on the command window by clicking the Command Window button. Your debugger should appear as follows:

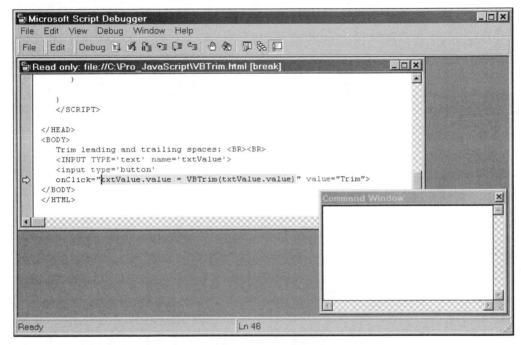

Type sToTrim (the name of our variable) into the command window and press Enter. You should get the following text in the command window:

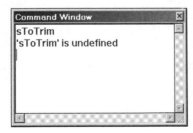

This tells us that the variable is undefined, because it only has function scope and the function has not been called yet.

Click the Step Into button until the statement:

```
while (sToTrim.substring(0,1) == ' ')
```

is highlighted. Place your cursor on the top line of the command window (which should read sToTrim), then press Enter. Your command window should appear as follows:

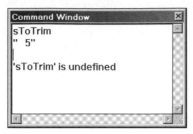

The value of sToTrim is now "   5", which is the value we passed in. Click the Step Into button twice more, until it returns to the first while line. Again, check the value of sToTrim. Your command window should display the following:

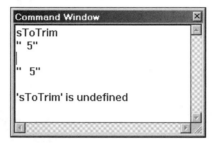

The first space has been removed, leaving the value of sToTrim as "   5" (two spaces followed by "5"). Repeat the steps of clicking the Step Into button twice until it returns to the first while line and checking the value of sToTrim, which will now be " 5". Repeat the sequence yet again. Your command window should display the following:

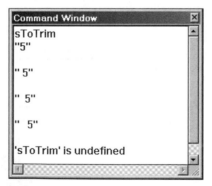

Now the sToTrim variable has been completely trimmed of all leading spaces. The next click of the Step Into button takes you to the while statement that checks for trailing spaces, of which there are none. Another click of the Step Into button takes you to the return statement. A final click of the Step Into button returns control to the document containing the script. Click the Stop Debugging button and then check the results of stepping through the code with the debugger in the IE window running the page. The value in the textbox has been successfully trimmed.

Setting Breakpoints

Breakpoints are an effective way of stopping a script executing when it reaches a certain point. For example, open the debugger with our VBTrim.html document, this time by placing the debugger keyword just before the function statement:

```
<SCRIPT LANGUAGE="JavaScript">
    debugger;
    function VBTrim(txtInput)
    {...
```

Next, open the document in IE. Notice the debugger opens right away (with the debugger statement highlighted). This is because the debugger statement has global scope, as it is not contained within a function, and is therefore executed as the page loads.

Now let's set some breakpoints. Place your cursor on the return sToTrim; line and click the **Toggle Breakpoint** button. Your debugger should like this:

The debugger highlights the breakpoint in red. The next step is to click the **Run** button in the debugger toolbar. This returns execution control to IE. Go back to the document in IE and enter "4" as a value in the text box. Click the **Trim** button. Again, the debugger opens, but this time it stops on the line where we just set our breakpoint:

497

```
Microsoft Script Debugger - [Read only: file://C:\Pro_JavaScript\VBTrim.html [break]]
 File  Edit  View  Debug  Window  Help

 File   Edit   Debug

        // Finally, remove trailing spaces
        while (sToTrim.substring(sToTrim.length-1,sToTrim.length) == ' ')
        {
            sToTrim = sToTrim.substring(0, sToTrim.length-1);
        }

        //return the trimmed string
        return sToTrim;

    }

    else //No characters have been entered in the text box
    {
        alert("You have not provided a string to trim!")
        return false;
    }

Ready                                        Ln 29
```

Setting breakpoints allows you to stop the script at any point in the execution. This allows you to easily find where errors occur and track variable values with each statement.

To clear breakpoints, position your cursor on the line that contains the breakpoint you wish to clear, then click the **Toggle Breakpoint** button. To clear one or more breakpoints, use the **Clear All Breakpoints** button (the position of the cursor does not matter in this case).

Code Stepping

The Microsoft Script Debugger makes the process of stepping through code relatively painless. The **Step Into** button (which we have been using above) allows the user to execute the next script statement relative to the cursor. To illustrate, lets load `VBTrim.html` document (with the `debugger` statement still at the beginning of the script) into IE. Again, in the debugger, open the document with the `debugger;` line highlighted.

To begin stepping into the script, click the **Step Into** button. The execution control is returned to IE, because the script is waiting for some kind of input. Enter " **s** " (space, "s", space) as a value, and then click the **Trim** button. The debugger has now highlighted the function call triggered by the button's `onClick` event in the HTML document. If you continue to click the **Step Into** button, the script runs its course and returns the desired results to the browser.

But what if we were to determine early on that a particular procedure is not the one causing the error? Is there a way to just execute the remaining statements within that procedure and return us to the next statement? The answer is yes, by using the **Step Out** and **Step Over** debugger functions. To demonstrate, we will need to change our `VBTrim.html` document. We are going to change it so that we have a function to trim the leading spaces and a separate function to trim the trailing spaces. So now `VBTrim.html` looks as follows:

```
<!-- VBTrim.html -->
<HTML>
<HEAD>
    <TITLE>Using the Microsoft Script Debugger</TITLE>

    <SCRIPT LANGUAGE="JavaScript">
    debugger;
    function VBTrim(txtInput)
    {
        //First, check to see if input string has at least one character
```

```
        if (txtInput.length > 0)
        {
            //Set local variable to value of input string
            var sToTrim = txtInput;

            //Call trimLeadingSpaces function for input string
            sToTrim = trimLeadingSpaces(sToTrim);

            //Call trimTrailingSpaces function for input string
            sToTrim = trimLeadingSpaces(sToTrim);

            //return the trimmed string
            return sToTrim;
        }
        else //No characters have been entered in the text box
        {
            alert("You have not provided a string to trim!");
            return false;
        }
    }
    function trimLeadingSpaces(sLeading)
    {
        while (sLeading.substring(0,1) == ' ')
        {
            sLeading = sLeading.substring(1, sLeading.length);
        }
            return sLeading;
    }

    function trimTrailingSpaces(sTrailing)
    {
        while (sToTrim.substring(sToTrim.length-1,sToTrim.length) == ' ')
        {
            sToTrim = sToTrim.substring(0, sToTrim.length-1);
        }
        return sTrailing;
    }

    </SCRIPT>

</HEAD>
<BODY>
    Trim leading and trailing spaces: <br><br>
    <input type="text" name="txtValue">
    <input type="button"
    onClick="txtValue.value = VBTrim(txtValue.value)" value="Trim">
</BODY>
</HTML>
```

Go ahead and load the changed document in IE. The Script Debugger should open right away, with the debugger statement in the document highlighted in yellow. Click the **Step Into** button one time, then enter " spaces " as a value in the text box and click the **Trim** button. The onClick event in the document is now highlighted. Click the **Step Into** button until the debugger moves within the trimLeadingSpaces() function (4 clicks).

```
🖥 Microsoft Script Debugger - [Read only: file://C:\Pro_JavaScript\VBTrim.html [break]]    _ □ ×
🖥 File   Edit   View   Debug   Window   Help                                              _ 🗗 ×
  File │ Edit │ Debug 🗐 🏧 🏚 ⛏ ⛏ ⛏ │ 🖐 👁 │ 🗐 🐾 🔲
         }
         function trimLeadingSpaces(sLeading)
         {
⇨           while (sLeading.substring(0,1) == ' ')
            {
                sLeading = sLeading.substring(1, sLeading.length);
            }
            return sLeading;
         }

         function trimTrailingSpaces(sTrailing)
         {
            while (sToTrim.substring(sToTrim.length-1,sToTrim.length) == ' ')
            {
                sToTrim = sToTrim.substring(0, sToTrim.length-1);
            }
            return sTrailing;
         }

Ready                                         │ Ln 33
```

At this point, the debugger has jumped out of the VBTrim() function and into the trimLeadingSpaces()
function. We will, for argument's sake, assume that there is nothing wrong with this function. In order to get out
of this function, yet still have it execute, we use the **Step Out** button. This allows the current procedure to finish
executing, and returns to the next statement in the calling procedure (VBTrim()). Your debugger should now
be on the next line of the VBTrim() function (trimTrailingSpaces()).

```
🖥 Microsoft Script Debugger - [Read only: file://C:\Pro_JavaScript\VBTrim.html [break]]    _ □ ×
🖥 File   Edit   View   Debug   Window   Help                                              _ 🗗 ×
  File │ Edit │ Debug 🗐 🏧 🏚 ⛏ ⛏ ⛏ │ 🖐 👁 │ 🗐 🐾 🔲
            if (txtInput.length > 0)
            {
                //Set local variable to value of input string
                var sToTrim = txtInput;

                //Call trimLeadingSpaces function for input string
                sToTrim = trimLeadingSpaces(sToTrim);

                //Call trimTrailingSpaces function for input string
⇨               sToTrim = trimLeadingSpaces(sToTrim);

                //return the trimmed string
                return sToTrim;
            }
            else //No characters have been entered in the text box
            {
                alert("You have not provided a string to trim!");
                return false;
            }

Ready                                         │ Ln 20
```

Let us also assume that the trimTrailingSpaces() function does not contain the errors. Use the
Step Over button to execute the function without stepping through it line by line. The **Step Over**
button, like the **Step Out** button, returns us to the next statement of the calling procedure.

500

```
Microsoft Script Debugger - [Read only: file://C:\Pro_JavaScript\VBTrim.html [break]]   _ □ ×
File   Edit   View   Debug   Window   Help                                               _ 8 ×

 File   Edit   Debug  ▤↓ ▨ ▥ ▥ ▥ ▥  🖑 ®  🗐 ₨ ▤

              var sToTrim = txtInput;

              //Call trimLeadingSpaces function for input string
              sToTrim = trimLeadingSpaces(sToTrim);

              //Call trimTrailingSpaces function for input string
              sToTrim = trimLeadingSpaces(sToTrim);

              //return the trimmed string
 ⇨            return sToTrim;
          }
          else //No characters have been entered in the text box
          {
              alert("You have not provided a string to trim!");
              return false;
          }
      }
      function trimLeadingSpaces(sLeading)
      {
 ◄                                                                                        ►
Ready                                           Ln 23
```

The **Step Out** and **Step Over** buttons allow us to save time by not having to step through each line of each function called by the main procedure. If you are positive that a certain function does not contain an error, step over the function call. If you want to test a value within a function, but not the entire function, step into it until you get to the statement where the value is set, test the value using the command window, and then step out.

Bookmarks

Bookmarks allow us to return to specific lines in the code more easily. When you get to a line that you would like to bookmark, just press CTRL + F2. The debugger will mark each bookmarked line as follows:

```
Microsoft Script Debugger - [Read only: file://C:\Pro_JavaScript\VBTrim.html [break]]   _ □ ×
File   Edit   View   Debug   Window   Help                                               _ 8 ×

 File   Edit   Debug  ▤↓ ▨ ▥ ▥ ▥ ▥  🖑 ®  🗐 ₨ ▤

☐         else //No characters have been entered in the text box
          {
              alert("You have not provided a string to trim!");
              return false;
          }
      }
☐     function trimLeadingSpaces(sLeading)
      {
          while (sLeading.substring(0,1) == ' ')
          {
              sLeading = sLeading.substring(1, sLeading.length);
          }
          return sLeading;
      }

☐     function trimTrailingSpaces(sTrailing)
      {
          while (sToTrim.substring(sToTrim.length-1,sToTrim.length) == ' ')
          {
 ◄                                                                                        ►
Ready                                           Ln 40
```

To move to the next bookmark, press F2. To move to the previous bookmark, press SHIFT + F2. To remove a bookmark, press CTRL + F2.

Exercise

Now that we have discussed the major features of the Microsoft Script Debugger, it is time to put that knowledge to some practical use. Let us take, for instance, our VBTrim.html document (the version with three functions).

Some of our fictitious users have reported to us that the VBTrim.html page places the word false in the text box every so often after the button is pressed. The first thing we as programmers do is to load the page into our debugger. Next, using the Command Window, supply a value to the function that would test the majority of the statements, such as a string with a beginning space, one or more characters and then a trailing space. This tests all of the script statements except for the else statement.

Not having found the anomaly with the previous input string, we need to generate an input that tests the else statement. This input is an empty string (txtInput.length = 0). We see now that the return statement is actually returning the string "false" to the text box. To fix the error, we should remove the return statement, or return the input string.

Netscape JavaScript Console

Netscape provides the JavaScript Console as a tool to aid in debugging JavaScript. The console displays a list of all errors generated by the currently loaded document. The JavaScript Console functions similarly to the Command Window in the Microsoft Script Debugger. It allows you to enter JavaScript commands and displays the results.

Opening the Console

Typing javascript: in the address bar of Netscape Navigator 4.x opens the JavaScript Console, which appears as follows:

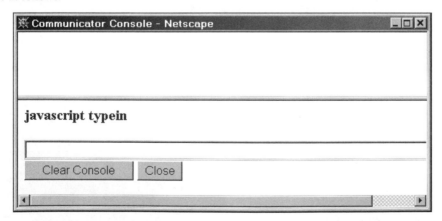

To open the JavaScript console in Netscape 6, go to the Tasks menu, select Tools, and then click JavaScript Console.

The JavaScript console for Netscape 6 appears as follows:

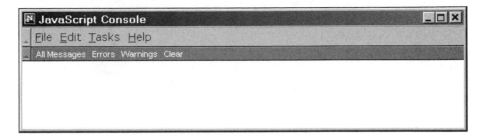

Evaluating Expressions with the Console

While the Netscape JavaScript Console is similar to the Microsoft Script Debugger command window in that it allows us to evaluate single line JavaScript expressions, it differs in that it does not allow you to interact with the code loaded into the browser. For example, load the following code into the NN 4.x browser:

```
<!-- alerti.html -->
<HTML>
<HEAD>
   <SCRIPT>
      var i = 3;
   </SCRIPT>
</HEAD>
</HTML>
```

Next, open the JavaScript console and type alert(i) into the javascript typein text box. This results in the following error:

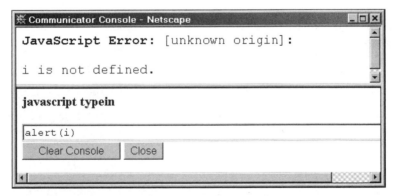

This is because the console is not interacting with any of the code on the page. In order to interact with the code on the page, use a javascript: URL in the address bar of the browser, such as javascript: alert(i).

To generate the proper results using the console, you must reproduce the entire script, or section of script required to generate the desired results.

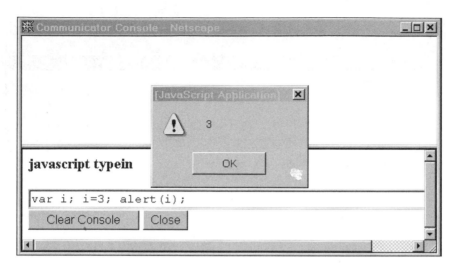

Calling the Console on Error

For Netscape 4.06+ browsers (excluding version 6+), the JavaScript Console can be scripted to appear whenever the page encounters an error. To script this functionality, you will need to change the prefs.js user preference file located in the Netscape program installation directory, under Users, then User Name (or default). For example:

```
C:\Program Files\Netscape\Users\default\prefs.js
```

Open the prefs.js file in your script editor of choice. You will need to add the following line to the end of this file:

```
user_pref("javascript.console.open_on_error",true);
```

You will need to save and close the prefs.js file and restart Netscape for the changes to take effect.

The functionality for opening the console automatically on error in Netscape 6 is currently not implemented.

Setting Watch Points

While the JavaScript console does not allow us to interactively step through our script, Netscape does provide **watch points** to help us follow variable values throughout a script. Watch points use the watch() and unwatch() methods to track properties of objects.

The watch() method accepts two parameters: the name of the property to watch, and the name of the function to execute when it changes. When the specified property is changed, the watch() method passes the name of the property, the previous value, and the current value to the specified function.

Note that it is important that the function return the current of the property, otherwise the property will become undefined.

The unwatch() method accepts the property name as a parameter and simply terminates the tracking of changes to that property.

The following script demonstrates the use of the watch() and unwatch() methods. The script "watches" the value of the myObj.myProp property until the counter reaches 3.

```
<!-- watchpoint.html -->
<HTML>
<HEAD>
    <SCRIPT>
        function showChange(propName,wasVal,isVal)
        {
            document.write('MyObj.' + propName + ' changed from <b>' + wasVal +
            '</b> to <b>' + isVal + '</b><br>');
            return isVal;
        }
        var myObj = new Object;

        myObj.watch('myProp',showChange);

        for (var i=1; i<=5; i++)
        {
            myObj.myProp = i
            if (i == 3)
            {
                myObj.unwatch('myProp')
            }
        }
    </SCRIPT>
</HEAD>
</HTML>
```

The result of the script is shown below:

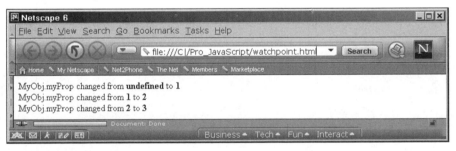

Summary

The interpreted and loosely typed nature of JavaScript means that errors are often reported without detailed explanations of what went wrong. There are plenty of ways to probe a given script's behavior, ranging from simple interactive inquiries to full-blown visual debugging environments. Simple techniques are often sufficient to pick up the commonest problem cases. For the rest, we must accept that the convenience of an interpreted language gives flexibility on one hand, but on the other puts the onus on the script writer to use an extra degree of care.

In this chapter we discussed:

❑   The three different type of JavaScript errors: load-time, run-time, and logical

❑   Some of the more common JavaScript errors

❑   Using exceptions

❑   Some of the more basic debugging techniques

❑   The Microsoft Script Debugger

❑   The Netscape JavaScript Console

Now that you have finished reading about and employing techniques discussed in this chapter you should be able to debug your script quite efficiently. By following the guidelines discussed in this and the previous chapter, you should generate fewer bugs in the first place. Even if not all of the information here was new to you, we hope that it served as a good reminder of the

Pro JavaScript 2nd Edition

Section Four

Tips, Tricks, and Techniques

When developing web applications with JavaScript, we often find that there are some problems and challenges that we encounter time and again. In these situations, we may adapt code used previously, gathering more and more useful code solutions as our experience increases. This section is something of a mixed bag – a collection of miscellaneous techniques and code examples that will provide a useful resource for you, for those smaller jobs that you often encounter. The code examples are re-usable and/or easily adaptable, and should help prevent you from having to re-invent the wheel each time.

In the first chapter in this section, we focus on how to keep your scripts hidden, or private, controlling cookies through the use of JavaScript, and how security issues affect our code. Next, we move on to look at how to use regular expressions in JavaScript, and how to use these for advanced form validation. In Chapter 16, we'll work through the development of a class for validation, which you will be able to apply to your own work. After that, we spend a couple of chapters looking at some dynamic effects, firstly using Internet Explorer filters, and then some more cross-browser techniques using DHTML and the W3C DOM, which was covered back in Section Two. Finally, we cover some extremely useful code that allows you to apply object-oriented techniques to extend core and browser JavaScript objects. This allows you to provide extra functionality on core objects, create ECMAScript-compliant objects in old browsers, or to extend browser objects to allow us to write DHTML scripts accessible in older browsers.

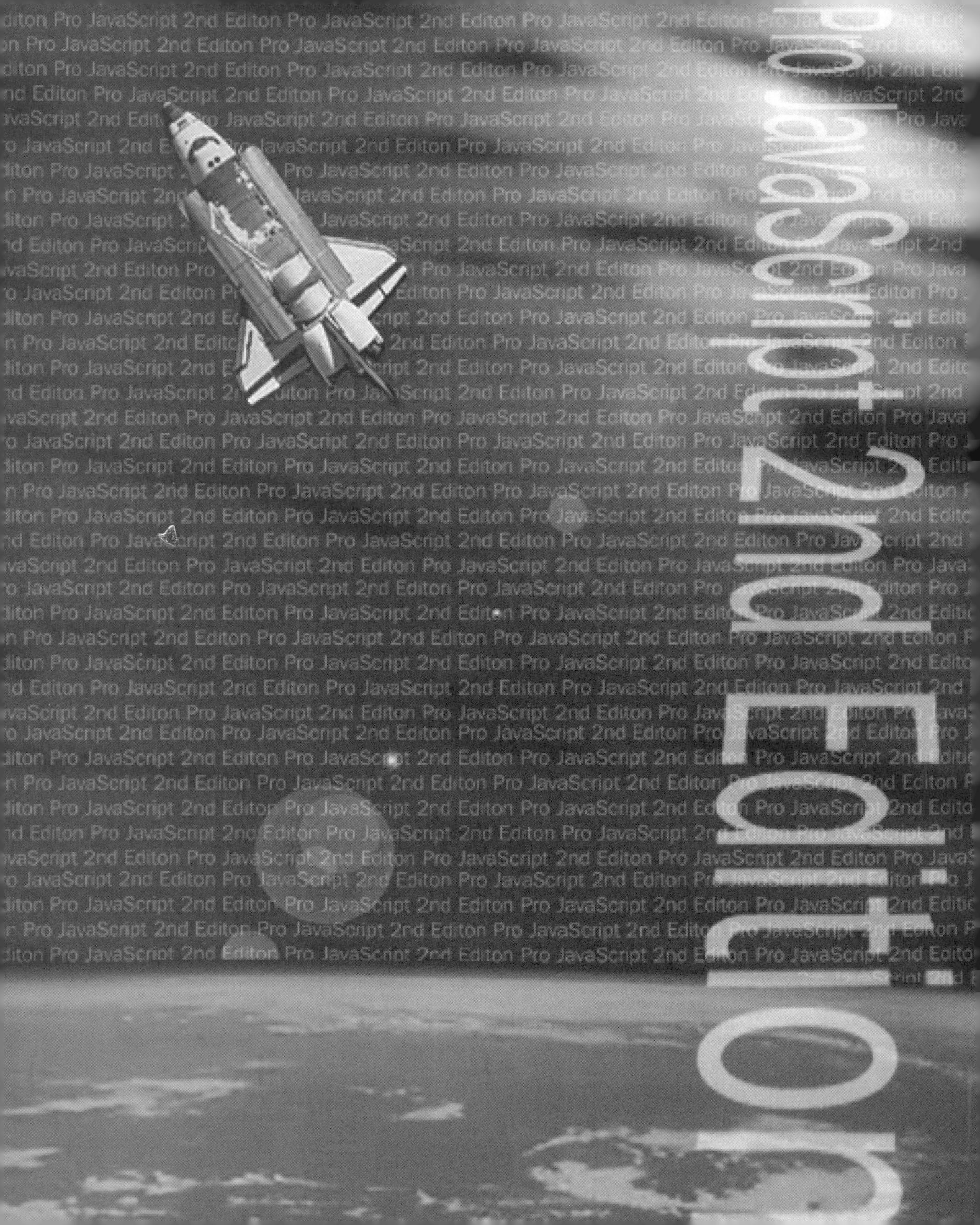
Pro JavaScript 2nd Edition
Pro JavaScript 2nd Editon

Privacy, Security, and Cookies

JavaScript scripts used on the Internet come with a number of risks. Allowing any script, possibly written by an anonymous scriptwriter, to do something unknown to a trusting person's computer, is a risk for that trusting person. On the other hand, to allow an anonymous person to obtain a script that is someone else's property, presents a risk to the owner of the script. There are numerous mechanisms available that help address these safety issues.

What your script does to your own property, is your own concern. It is when your property and scripts are mixed with other people's property and scripts, that risks arise and people are likely to become annoyed, upset, or even litigious. **Privacy** matters set the boundaries of what should not or cannot be shared. In our case, we're referring to sharing our script with anyone visiting our web site. **Security** matters set the boundaries of good behavior when there is a need to share. **Security hobbles** prevent scripts from crossing either kind of boundary without appropriate permission.

We'll see in this chapter, the pitfalls produced by security hobbles so we can avoid them in our scripting. We'll then look at how we can use **cookies** to store data in a web browser that persists beyond the user's current visit to our web pages. In the last part of the chapter, we'll create a JavaScript class that takes the bite out of programming cookies.

Privacy for Browser Scripters

For script writers, the two main privacy issues are preventing scripts from being stolen, and preventing scripts from being wrecked. The task is harder for JavaScript than it is for Java, or similar languages, because the script source and the executable code are one and the same.

For standalone scripts, neither issue is a problem, unless someone else has access to your computer or your account. If those scripts are used as CGI or ASP programs behind a web server, then there is also no problem, unless the web server has a security problem.

For server-side JavaScript, the scripts are stored and executed with the web server, so provided the server is secure, no web user can access them. HTML files sent to the user, should be stripped of any server-side JavaScript in the web server before delivery.

For client-side JavaScript, the situation is much worse. There is no way to systematically protect JavaScript code, except by entering into a security arrangement with the user. There are a few partial solutions.

Hiding Source Code

Client-side JavaScript has virtually no protection on the Web. If you need your web pages and its JavaScript to be publicly available, you might as well accept that the work you do, is there to be stolen and modified as any web user sees fit. It should be very difficult for someone to crack your web site and damage your original HTML and .js files, so at least the pages delivered by the web server are sent in good order, even if the user does something with it afterwards.

Once the JavaScript is in the web browser, there are only a few things that can be done to protect it. In particular, this code does not protect anything:

```
<HTML>
<HEAD>
    <SCRIPT SRC='secret.js'></SCRIPT>
</HEAD>
</HTML>
```

The JavaScript in the file secret.js may not appear when the user chooses to View Source for this document, but its URL is obvious. The user only needs to type the full URL for the file into the browser, retrieve the file, and then do View Source again. Browsers can display plain text files, as well as HTML files, and a .js file is typically a plain text file.

For a user on the Web who views publicly available HTML, there are few foolproof tactics for protecting or hiding client-side JavaScript. The nearest thing is to embed your JavaScript in a Java applet, using the Netscape LiveConnect features of Java, though of course this is for Netscape only. That is a lot of work for non-trivial JavaScript.

An easier, but less effective, tactic is to protect your scripts by making the job of copying them less palatable, rather than impossible.

Relying on Microsoft

Microsoft provides a tool called the Microsoft Script Encoder that makes JavaScript unreadable. This tool can be downloaded for free from http://msdn.microsoft.com/scripting/ as a component of the Microsoft Scripting Engine. It does a good job of hiding your precious scripts from lazy thieves, but isn't robust enough to entirely guarantee anything. In particular, a clever thief can decode the scripts encoded by this tool, so don't bet the family jewels on it.

To get encoding working, you need the Microsoft Script Encoder tool and at least version 5.0 of JScript, which now ships with IE.

Use of the encoder is restricted to Microsoft environments so cannot be used with Netscape.

The encoder tool is a simple command line driven one – run it from an MS-DOS window. The current version is version 1.0. Here is a simple example of using the encoder. First, a plain HTML file called before.htm:

```
<HTML>
<BODY>
<SCRIPT>
   alert('Page has started loading');
</SCRIPT>
<FORM>
Your information goes here:
<INPUT TYPE='text'
   onchange='this.value=this.value.toUpperCase()'
   WIDTH=10>
</FORM>
</BODY>
</HTML>
```

Here is the command that encodes the file:

```
C:\Program Files\Windows Script Encoder > screnc before.htm after.htm
```

When you run the downloaded file, `screnc.exe` is placed in a folder called **Windows Script Encoder**. Make sure you place `before.htm` in this folder before entering your command prompt. Here is the encoded file, created in `after.htm`:

```
<HTML>
<BODY>
<SCRIPT language = JScript.Encode>
   #@~^KgAAAA==@#@&ls•DD`BhlTnP4ldPkYC.D+N,sWmNkLv#p@#@&DgwAAA==^#~@
</SCRIPT>
<FORM>
Your information goes here:
<INPUT TYPE='text'
   ONCHANGE='this.value=this.value.toUpperCase()'
   WIDTH=10>
</FORM>
</BODY>
</HTML>
```

The encoder has translated the contents of the `SCRIPT` block from one language (JScript) to another (`JScript.Encode`), which is a special Microsoft variant of JavaScript that is designed to be readable by computers, not humans. As you can see, the first script block re-written in `JScript.Encode` cannot be identified as an `alert()` statement. The encoder doesn't hide JavaScript event handlers at all, so that code is still exposed. We can fix that by varying the original content to look like this:

```
<HTML>
<BODY>
<SCRIPT>
   .alert('Page has started loading');
</SCRIPT>
<FORM>
   Your information goes here: <INPUT TYPE='text' WIDTH=10>
</FORM>
<SCRIPT>
   function do_change()
   {
      this.value=this.value.toUpperCase();
   }
   document.forms[0].elements[0].onchange = do_change;
</SCRIPT>
</BODY>
</HTML>
```

The encoded copy now looks like this:

```
<HTML>
<BODY>
<SCRIPT language = JScript.Encode>
#@~^IgAAAA==C^+.D`EnlT+,4lkPdYmDOn9PVKCNbxoEbI^#~@
</SCRIPT>
<FORM>
    Your information goes here: <INPUT TYPE='text' WIDTH=10>
</FORM>
<SCRIPT language = JScript.Encode>
#@~^fwAAAA==@#@&P~6EmYbW~NK{^tmxLnv#PP~Y4k/c-
CV!+{Y4kd7lsE•YKj22•DZCd•`bi)@#@&P~9W1E:•xD0KDh/]!D•V+snxD/$ZDWm4lUon~{P[W|^tmxLnp
@#@&^#~@
</SCRIPT>
</BODY>
</HTML>
```

Now, the event handler source code is hidden as well.

Such an encoded page is loaded into a browser via a normal URL, and the JavaScript's effect is identical to the unencoded version, but there are a few restrictions:

❑   Using a source-level debugger on an encoded script is not practical

❑   Only Internet Explorer 4.0+ can handle an encoded script

Therefore, unless Microsoft ends up entirely dominating the browser market, encoding is only useful where you control the browser user's computer. Encoding applies to other uses of Microsoft JScript too, such as JScript in ASP. However, its benefit is easiest to see in the browser. Be mindful that the encoding scheme has been cracked, and that there are decoders available, so the system is not intended to have robust security.

Making it Too Much Effort

If you need your web pages to be viewable in all browsers, then Microsoft encoding isn't currently an option, and therefore your scripts must be *au naturel*. However, there are some simple barriers that will make the job harder, and encourage any thieving culprits to give up. Remember, that you will also find the code hard to read with barriers yourself, so keep in mind that you might need to return to adjust the code at some point.

Firstly, you could put the whole HTML or JavaScript file contents on one line. Many CGI programs that produce HTML don't put line breaks into the generated HTML file. This helps keep the file as small as possible, improving download performance. You can do the same with your JavaScript SCRIPT sections. The script stealer has to create a formatting program to fix this, or do it by hand. If your JavaScript code is CGI generated, it is easy to apply a filter to the output that removes all return characters.

Secondly, you could use obfuscation (confusion) techniques. It's possible, or even common, to write really unclear code that no one can understand. JavaScript has syntax related to C, therefore some research of the obfuscation techniques in C may help you create unreadable code.

Alternatively, you could use a code-shrouding program. Such a program takes your readable JavaScript source, and translates it to equivalent source, but with formatting removed and all symbolic names replaced with randomly generated names. You keep the original source, in case you need to make further changes, which are re-shrouded as needed. Here's an example showing a function before and after shrouding:

```
// before
function calculate_interest(principal, percent_rate, yearly_calculations, term)
{
    var factor = 1 + percent_rate/yearly_calculations/100;
```

```
    // one lot of interest
    return principal * Math.pow(factor, yearly_calculations * term);
}
```

```
// after
function a01(a02,a03,a04,a05){var a06=1+a03/a04;return a02*Math.pow(a06,a04*a05);}
```

The new function works the same as the original, but its meaning is a near mystery. JMyth is one such tool for JavaScript: http://www.geocities.com/SiliconValley/Vista/5233/jmyth.htm.

Unfortunately, such tools have severe limitations. Firstly, as the example shows, built-in objects, methods, and properties can't be renamed. These are often a large part of the code, and can give away the code's intent. Secondly, the translation is almost guaranteed to produce non-working code if `eval()`, `setTimeout()` or `setInterval()` are used, since their string arguments are actually code in disguise. Translators are usually too dumb to detect these more complex cases, so the arguments refer to original names, not translated ones. Finally, if the document is a frame, referring to functions or variables in another frame, the translator has the further job of coordinating all the changes across documents. Leaving aside these limitations, you may still find such a tool useful.

Making it Impolite

If you put a copyright statement in comments at the top of your code and ask that others should not use it, or at least if they do, attribute it back to you, people might just do that. If the information is published (exposed on the Web), then you automatically have some copyright rights in countries that respect the Berne convention (most countries), provided you identify yourself as the author.

The Most Practical Approach

In the end, worrying about theft is probably not productive. The main problem, is identifying when your script has been taken and used elsewhere, and by whom – almost impossible to enforce or police on the Web. Most client-side JavaScript code is small and uninspired, and uses well-known techniques that aren't new in any case.

Discouraging Onlookers

As a script writer interested in privacy, your main enemy might be thieving web surfers, but they're not the only enemy. Your JavaScript-enabled web pages and any responses from the browser user may pass through any number of intermediate computers as part of their delivery, which could be run by malignant server administrators. What to do about these people?

Hiding Downloaded Scripts

When a user requests a URL from a web server, everyone between the user and the web server has a chance to look at it. Most browsers now include support for a network protocol called the **Secure Sockets Layer (SSL)**. If support for this is turned on, then all data sent between the browser and any web servers with the same support will be hidden from intermediate systems. It can also deny all but your friends access to the web server that provides your scripts.

However, once the user has the data, such as a `.js` file, they may do anything with it without using secure means, such as forwarding it via e-mail. Therefore, even with SSL, files are only as safe as the recipient is. The main purpose of SSL is to extend the safety of web page delivery from the web server out beyond the browser to the browser user.

Simple JavaScript Password Checking

Using JavaScript, the following HTML document performs the most rudimentary password checking imaginable:

```
<HTML>
<BODY>
<SCRIPT>
    var passwd = prompt("Enter password:", "")
    this.location.href = passwd+".htm";
</SCRIPT>
</BODY>
</HTML>
```

If the user doesn't know the name of the entry page, then access fails. Even if the user looks at the JavaScript code, nothing secret is revealed. This simple kind of thing is more than enough to keep out ignorant passers-by. On another page, you would supply a form where the user would submit a request for access, and perhaps then you would e-mail them the password. It's like trying to get into a nightclub without being a member. However, this kind of system is not very secure, because a user can attempt as many times as they like to guess the file name, or even set up an automatic system to check all possibilities.

Security

In this section, we'll look at browser security and how it protects the browser user, but also how, as a consequence, it impacts on our creation of JavaScript in web pages, and limits to some extent what we can do.

Safety for Browser Users

For users of JavaScript enabled browsers, requesting a URL represents a risk if it contains JavaScript. Without security hobbles, a JavaScript script could seize control of the browser, or possibly the user's computer. The simplest form of safety for the user is to turn JavaScript support off in the browser via the browser preferences (though this means that only static HTML pages will work correctly). This can't be done from within an HTML embedded JavaScript script, except by special arrangement of the `navigator.preference` property in Netscape Navigator 4.0+. Even then, the browser must be shut down and re-started for it to take effect. It can be set in the `prefs.js` preference file for Netscape 3+.

JavaScript bugs that create security risks have been identified in all browsers. To avoid as many of these as possible, try to ensure that the user has the latest version of the browser available. The following web page is a good starting point for JavaScript security bug information: http://www.w3.org/Security/Faq/www-security-faq.html#contents.

There are several kinds of security hobbles that protect the browser user.

I/O Restrictions

The main input mechanism for a browser is via user interaction with the browser's graphical interface. The main output mechanism is the display of HTML to that graphical interface, or requesting documents over the Web via URLs. All of these can be done to a degree from JavaScript, as we've seen in earlier chapters. However, it is nearly always true that client-side JavaScript is restrained from doing any other input or output, like writing to the user's computer's disk or network without the user's permission. Generally, the user can be confident that no changes are occurring to the local computer outside of the browser. There is the odd exception, however. Writing to files, network connections, and to the display are the main sources of risk. Display related restrictions are discussed later. Writing to files or to network connections is generally impossible without special arrangements, and next we will look at local scripts along with Java and ActiveX controls.

Local Scripts

If a browser loads a script directly from the local computer without using a web server, then that script can do anything the language and host objects allow. The user may get a warning and an option to back out, depending on how the browser's security preferences are set up.

JScript 3.0 and later can take advantage of a pack of file system access objects. These objects are stored in a system file called scrrun.dll, supplied as part of the WSH, Jscript, or VBScript installation. You can get this file, available as part of the scripting engine downloads, at http://msdn.microsoft.com/scripting. It adds FileSystemObject, TextStream, File, and Folder objects which allow local files to be removed or renamed as well as created or changed, but this is only possible for Internet Explorer 3+, and browser security options must be lowered by the user for this to happen. The main purpose of this JavaScript add-on, is to make server-side JavaScript programs more useful.

Netscape JavaScript can also write to local files, but there is no direct support in the language. Instead, Java objects supply this functionality – those objects must be accessed from JavaScript via LiveConnect, which is a Netscape technology that allows Java applets and JavaScript to communicate with each other. Note that bugs in Netscape 6.0 and 6.01, prevent this approach from being used. Here is an example, which works only in Netscape 4, of writing a user-supplied string to a user-supplied filename:

```
<!-- NN4io.htm -->
<HTML>
<BODY>
<SCRIPT>
function save_it(jo_file, filedata)
{
  netscape.security.PrivilegeManager.enablePrivilege("UniversalFileAccess");
  var jo_writer = new java.io.FileWriter(jo_file);
  jo_writer.write(filedata,0,filedata.length);
  jo_writer.close();
  netscape.security.PrivilegeManager.disablePrivilege("UniversalFileAccess");
}
</SCRIPT>
<FORM>
    File Name: <INPUT TYPE='text' NAME='file'><BR>
    File Data: <INPUT TYPE='text' NAME='data'
                  ONCHANGE='save_it(this.form.file.value, this.value)'>
</FORM>
</BODY>
</HTML>
```

This example also requires some agreement from the user before it can go ahead. Microsoft browsers can also take advantage of Java to write to local files, but the security mechanisms are different. In particular, the netscape.security... permission request lines are not available to Microsoft browsers.

Java and ActiveX Connections

A browser that supports Java applets or ActiveX controls, can make network connections. These ActiveX controls and Java applets can be controlled via JavaScript scripts. ActiveX controls are subject to very few restrictions and, once downloaded, can have considerable access to your computer or other computers via a network.

Without a security agreement, however, the connections are of limited use. Java applets are downloaded via a URL in an APPLET or OBJECT HTML tag. Only the server supplying the page for that URL can be connected to. If the tag includes a CODEBASE URL, then the computer at that CODEBASE URL is the only possibility for connections. In either case, the applet can only contact the host that it came from.

A more subtle possibility stems from the fact that one Java applet may converse directly with another. However, the part of the Java system that loads applets also ensures that applets from different sites can't communicate with each other. This prevents one applet from exploiting the network connections available to another.

Window Limitations

The main form of output from client-side JavaScript, is not to files and network connections, but to the browser itself. JavaScript can affect windows in a browser in three ways:

❏   Write new content to browser windows

❏   Change window decorations such as toolbars and menus

❏   Modify JavaScript host objects and variables within windows

The user can have more than one browser window open at a time. The user can also have more than one URL per window if frames are present, and those URLs can come from different web sites. If it were not for a number of security hobbles, JavaScript could use its control over windows to:

❏   Forge or manipulate content displayed from other web sites, misrepresenting those sites

❏   Make the browser uncontrollable by the user

❏   Wreck the JavaScript data and objects stored in windows displaying other web sites

Two concepts are central to the window security features that prevent these things from happening.

Every Window is an Island

To understand JavaScript window security restrictions, first take a step back and reflect on the ECMAScript standard. If you skipped Chapter 4, *Windows and Frames*, it will help to go back and look at it before reading on here.

In ECMAScript terminology, an **execution environment** is a stage on which scripts can perform (execute), whether those scripts are standalone or in web client or server applications. When an execution environment is created, such as in a browser, a good question is "What is the current object?" The standard states that all built-in objects and built-in functions in a script are part of a special global object, which is the current scope when that script starts executing. Even functions like parseInt() can, therefore, be viewed as a method of an object.

However, there is not just one global object in a JavaScript-capable web browser. Instead, the browser has a global object for each browser window or frame currently in existence. These global objects each have a property window that refers back to that global object. This window property provides a named hook so that the scriptwriter can get access to that global object.

Each global object is like a bucket in which all the data specific to the window can be stored, making it easy to access. Therefore, the window property sits at the top of a hierarchy (or a pool) of data that includes all the JavaScript variables, objects, and host objects in that window. If the window is closed, everything owned directly or indirectly by the global object is tracked down and cleaned up. If a window is open, then all items within that one bucket are on the same footing – they can all access each other.

This makes each window fully self-contained and independent. It also makes it easy to keep scripts from interfering with other windows, since they can only ultimately belong to one global object. Viewed from the JavaScript perspective, the browser is not a single hierarchy or pool of objects and properties, it is a number of hierarchies or pools.

Unfortunately, life is rarely that simple. In reality, one window will often contain JavaScript variables that refer to objects or properties in other windows. A simple example is the window.open() method – the return value can be stored in a variable in the containing window, but refers to the global object in the newly created window. Similarly, the newly created window's global object has an opener property referring back to the old window.

The owner of a window is the host address of the window's main URL, for example: www.something.com:80. Attempts to work with properties or methods in a different window have to first pass checks based on the owners of the two windows. This script can be used to show the dynamic behavior involved:

```
<!-- windows.htm -->
<HTML>
<BODY>
<SCRIPT>
var win2 = null;

function open_local()
{
    top.win2=window.open(window.location.href,'test');
}

function open_remote()
{
    top.win2=window.open('http://www.wrox.com','test');
}

function show_it()
{
    window.document.forms[0].one.value = top.win2;
    window.document.forms[0].two.value = top.win2.name;
    window.document.forms[0].three.value = top.win2.location.href;
}
</SCRIPT>
<FORM>
<INPUT TYPE='button' VALUE='Open local window' ONCLICK='open_local()'>
<INPUT TYPE='button' VALUE='Open remote window' ONCLICK='open_remote()'>
<INPUT TYPE='button' VALUE='Show window details' ONCLICK='show_it()'>
<INPUT TYPE='button' VALUE='Go backwards' ONCLICK='window.history.go(-1)'>
<BR>
Type of win2: <INPUT NAME='one' TYPE='text'><BR>
Name of win2: <INPUT NAME='two' TYPE='text'><BR>
URL  of win2: <INPUT NAME='three' TYPE='text'><BR>
</FORM>
</BODY>
</HTML>
```

When displayed, the document looks like this:

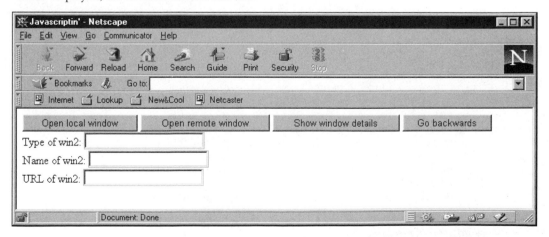

This HTML page has four purposes:

❑ To create a second window with a URL that is at the same web site as the main window

❑ To create a second window with a URL that is at a different web site as the main window

❑ To display some state information about the second window

❑ To provide content for the second window when the URL for that window is at the same web site as the original window

The Show window details button is used to report the current state of the auto-created window.

The following discussion pertains to Netscape behavior, but note that Netscape 6 operates slightly differently, and generally has more restrictions. Before pressing either of the open buttons, reporting the current state produces an error, because the second window is not open and, therefore, win2 is not yet an object. If a local window is opened, the name and URL will display correctly. If a remote window is opened, then an error results when trying to get its URL (assuming you don't own the Wrox web site). If you navigate with that new window back to a local web page, either via the Open local window button or directly using the window toolbars, the URL is accessible again.

When the window is off-limits, Netscape's error is: "Access disallowed from scripts at http://mysite.com/tests/remote_test.htm to documents in another domain." This message assumes that the mysite.com site is where you are doing the testing.

If the second window is closed, a number of obscure errors can occur, depending on the version, and whether Java is enabled or not. It is better not to examine a closed window object, except to test if the window is closed by looking at the Boolean value of `window.closed`.

Every Window is Free

Without security arrangements granting the script writer special privileges, some browser features can't be removed from the user's control. In this section, these features are merely characterized. Some typical features are:

❑ Generally, existing windows can't have toolbars or other window decorations removed or added. With Netscape 4, there is a work around to this using `window.open('', '_self', 'toolbar=no, status=no, menubar=no')` to set and remove features of an already opened window.

❑ Documents loaded into frames from other sites can't have their events stolen by the frameset .

❑ Windows smaller than 100x100 cannot be created to help ensure the user is able to read the content.

❑ Windows can't permanently obscure other windows, or grab the user's input focus and keep it, although IE does allow large modal windows to be opened, which make it difficult to swap to another window.

❑ Canvas and kiosk mode, in particular, in which a single window takes over the whole screen, requires special privileges for Netscape 4+ browsers. For these browsers, the user can drop the above restrictions on scripts by changing their browser. For full documentation on which methods require special privileges before they can be used refer to: http://developer.netscape.com/docs/manuals/index.html?content=security.html and in particular the download links titled 'Introduction to the Capabilities classes' (http://developer.netscape.com/docs/manuals/signedobj/capabilities/index.html), and 'Netscape System Targets' (http://developer.netscape.com/docs/manuals/signedobj/capabilities/index.html).

❑ IE has the full screen mode and allows Modal dialog boxes, neither of which require special security privileges.

Resource Limiting Features

Browsers are designed to limit the user to a fraction of the resources of the browser's computer:

❏ **Disk space.** Pages loaded from a given web server can't consume more than 80 Kilobytes of space in a Netscape browser's cookie file, however, more than that can be consumed with Internet Explorer. Creating new JavaScript Image objects, or writing new HTML pages is still subject to the caching restrictions that the browser user puts in place when setting the browser's preferences. If the user has all caching turned off, images or pages won't be cached if they are not part of a currently displayed window.

❏ **Memory.** Internet Explorer 4.0+ allows the user to place an upper limit on the amount of memory that a newly downloaded ActiveX control can consume. Otherwise, browsers can still consume large amounts of memory. The video memory used for graphics and windows is easy for most browsers to consume, especially if there are many windows, frames, and images displayed.

Such memory protection systems aren't foolproof. Even for normal memory and non-ActiveX controls, the following script fragment will bring most browsers quickly to their knees:

> **Don't try this script unless you're willing to lose any unsaved information and re-boot your PC**

```
<HTML>
<BODY>
<SCRIPT>
   var big_string = "double me up!";
   while (true)
   {
      big_string = big_string + big_string;
      // 20 iterations equals all your memory
   }
</SCRIPT>
</BODY>
</HTML>
```

Memory limitations also apply to Java applets in Netscape Navigator. Sometimes these applets are 'cleaned up' to save memory, which can also positively impact on JavaScript:

❏ **Network Connections.** JavaScript scripts may open many windows, but the maximum number of connections set by the user via preferences will still be observed. Any additional windows will have to wait for a free connection and may possibly time-out.

❏ **CPU.** Netscape 6 and Internet Explorer 4.0+ will abort any JavaScript script that executes more than one million 'instructions' (a vague term used by the vendors, probably meaning one JavaScript statement) before finishing. This is designed to prevent scripts from locking the user out of the browser permanently, not to prevent the browser from consuming large amounts of CPU time. In fact, IE5.5 will ask the user before the million instruction mark if they want to continue running a long running script. This feature can be annoying if you are trying to do long, complex calculations with the interpreter. The user still has access to window menus and toolbars. There is also a workaround: break the task into steps and only run one step at a time.

Other Potential Risks

There are other risks for the user when using a browser on the Internet, but not many of them involve JavaScript. A few do:

❏ Submitting HTML forms. The user's name or e-mail address cannot be obtained by a web site due to a form being submitted, unless the user has made special security arrangements. So submitting forms is generally safe for the user.

❏ Client-side JavaScript cannot silently e-mail a user when the user browses to a web page. The user always gets the opportunity to confirm or cancel the submission.

❏ The user can configure a helper application to run when a particular file type (MIME type) is fetched across the network. Configuring a standalone JavaScript interpreter to run when JavaScript files are received is a risky choice, unless the interpreter has a security system of its own. This is because a downloaded standalone script will then automatically run, doing who knows what.

❏ In modern browsers, the user can release all of the restrictions in the browser that require a security agreement. To do this in Internet Explorer, select the Tools|Internet Options menu and then click the Security tab. The details of each zone's security can be set here, set the Minimum Security level to None. In Netscape 4+ browsers, shut down all of the Netscape windows and modify by hand the `prefs.js` file. That file is stored in the Netscape installation area (there is one for each browser user and one for the default user). Add the following line and restart the browser: `user_pref("signed.applets.codebase_principal_support", true);` This line means that every computer that supplies a script to the browser can be trusted to supply safe scripts. Obviously, this is not realistic, and so this option is usually only needed in test environments. Even after supplying this line, the user is asked for every privilege requested to grant it, and if they do not click the checkbox to remember the decision, they will get asked again next time the privilege is requested.

Cookies

We learnt earlier that security restrictions prevent JavaScript from accessing the user's hard drive. This means that from client-side JavaScript, cookies are the only way of storing information once the user has left the web site. Cookies are a form of data passed both ways between web browsers and servers. The actual cookie data is just text and is stored in a special file on the user's computer. Although cookies can be sent from and received by a server, they are only permanently stored on the user's computer with nothing stored on the server. Cookies sent to a user's browser, have some insignificant implications for privacy. Cookies can be managed from JavaScript.

In this section, we'll look at the theory behind cookies, how we can control them with JavaScript, and the common uses of cookies, before finally creating a cookie toolkit. The cookie toolkit will take the form of a JavaScript class, which provides all the cookie based functionality you're likely to need and does so in an easy to use way. Let's start, however, by looking at the theory of cookies.

Cookie Theory

It might sound like an obscure branch of theoretical physics, and possibly have some similar looking enthusiasts, but the mysteries of cookies are quick to penetrate.

Cookies Enhance Web Requests

The communication between web browser and web server is defined by the HTTP network protocol. That protocol says that each URL request and the consequent response form a pair of messages independent of the past and the future. Cookies are an enhancement to HTTP that let state maintenance between subsequent requests happen. Originally proposed for standards consideration by Netscape Communications (their proposal is at http://www.netscape.com/newsref/std/cookie_spec.html), the most official specification can be found at: http://www.cis.ohio-state.edu/htbin/rfc/rfc2109.html. Most of the basic points of the specification are covered in the following sections.

Each URL or HTTP request made by a browser user is turned into lines of text called **headers** for sending to the web server. When the web server issues a response, the same happens. Cookies are just extra header lines containing cookie-style information. This is all invisible to the user, unless the user chooses a preference in their browser to be warned when cookies are sent. So, user requests and web server responses may occur with or without invisible cookies riding piggyback.

A key point is that the piggybacked cookies in the web server response get stored in the browser once received. Although a browser also reports its current cookies to the server when it makes requests, the server generally doesn't save them. This is almost the reverse of HTML form submissions: the browser has the long-term responsibility for the data, not the server (the server says what to change, not the browser). However, the browser can use JavaScript to set its own cookies as well. We can only send and read cookies to/from the domain they were created on.

Anatomy of a Cookie

A cookie is much like a JavaScript variable, with a name and a value. Unlike a variable, however, the existence of a cookie depends on several other attributes as well. This is because cookies can arrive at a browser from any web site in the world and need to be kept separate.

A cookie has `name`, `value`, `domain`, `path`, `expiry time`, and `secure flag` attributes, and we'll look at each attribute below.

name

A cookie name is a string of characters. The rules are different to JavaScript variable names, but common sense applies: use alphanumerics and underscores. Avoid using '$'. Cookie names are NOT case-sensitive. Although the standard says that they are case-insensitive, some browsers treat them as case-sensitive, which can create a real mess. Good advice is to just stick to lowercase. To really understand the naming rules, you can read the HTTP 1.1 standard at http://www.ietf.org/rfc/rfc2616. `'fred'`, `'my_big_cookie'`, and `'user66'` are all valid cookie names. There are no reserved words or variable name limits.

value

The value part of a cookie is a string of characters. That string must follow the rules for URLs, which means the `escape()` and `unescape()` functions should be applied if one is set by JavaScript. The `name` and `value` together should be less than 4095 bytes. There are no `undefined` or `null` values for cookies, but zero length strings are possible.

domain

If two different web sites are viewed in a browser, they should not be able to affect each other's cookies. Cookies have a `domain` property that restricts their visibility to one or more web sites.

Consider an example URL http://www.altavista.yellowpages.com.au/index.html. Any cookies with domain www.altavista.yellowpages.com.au, are readable from this page. Domains are also hierarchical, that is cookies with domains, such as altavista.yellowpages.com.au, yellowpages.com.au, and .com.au could all be picked up by that URL in the browser. The leading period is required for partial addresses. To prevent making a cookie visible to every web page in the world, at least two domain portions must be specified.

In practice, the `domain` attribute isn't used much, because it defaults to the domain of the document it piggybacked into the browser on (very sensible), and because it's unlikely that you would want to share a cookie with another web site anyway.

path

In a similar manner to domains, the path attribute of a cookie restricts a cookie's visibility to a particular part of a web-server's directory tree. A web page, such as http://www.microsoft.com/jscript might have a cookie with path /jscript, which is only relevant to the JScript pages of that site and any sub-directories contained in that directory. If a second cookie with the same name and domain also exists, but with a path of /, then the web page within the /jscript directory and its sub-directories would only see the first cookie, because its path is a closer match to the URL's path. However, the rest of the site outside the /jscript directory would see the second cookie.

Paths represent directories, not individual files, so /usr/local/tmp is correct, but /usr/local/tmp/myfile.htm is not. Forward slashes ('/' not '\') should be used. Trailing slashes as in /usr/local/tmp/ should be avoided. That is why the top-level path is a zero-length string, not '/'.

> The **name**, **domain**, and **path** combine to fully identify an individual cookie.

expiry time

The expiry time provides one of two cleanup mechanisms for cookies (see the next section for the other). Without such mechanisms, cookies might just build up in the browser forever, until the user's computer fills up.

The expiry time is optional. It is a moment in time. Without one, a cookie will survive only while the browser is running. With one, a cookie will survive even if the browser shuts down, but it will be discarded at the time dictated. If the time passes when the browser is down, the cookie is discarded when it next starts up. If the time dictated is zero or in the past, the cookie will be discarded immediately.

secure flag

This is a true/false attribute, which hints whether the cookie is too private for plain URL requests. The browser should only make secure (SSL) URL requests when sending this cookie. This attribute is less commonly used.

Browser Cookie Restrictions

Browsers place restrictions on the number of cookies that can be held at any one time, (although Netscape is more particular about this than IE) The restrictions are:

- ❑ 20 cookies maximum per domain
- ❑ 4096 bytes per cookie description
- ❑ 300 cookies overall maximum

The standard, RFC 2109 (http://www.w3.org/Protocols/rfc2109/rfc2109) sets these maximums. Netscape's specification and browsers state these maximums in an attempt to guarantee that all your disk space won't be consumed.

If you rely heavily on cookies, you will soon exceed the Netscape limit of 20. In that case, that browser will throw out one of the 20 when cookie 21 arrives. This is a source of obscure bugs. It is better to use only one cookie, and pack multi-variable data into it via JavaScript utility routines – 4096 bytes is quite a lot of space. Internet Explorer doesn't have the 20 cookies per domain limit.

The Netscape file that the cookie data resides in when the browser is shut down, is called `cookies.txt` on Windows and UNIX, and resides in the Netscape installation area (under each user for Netscape Communicator). It is a plain text file, automatically generated by the browser on shutdown, similar to the `prefs.js` file. The user can always delete this file if the browser is shut down, which removes all cookies from their system. An example file:

```
# Netscape HTTP Cookie File
# http://www.netscape.com/newsref/std/cookiespec.html
# This is a generated file!  Do not edit.
www.geocities.comFALSE  / FALSE      937972424      GeoId  2035695874900187870
.linkexchange.comTRUE   / FALSE      942191819      SAFE_COOKIE 3425efc81808cebe
www.macromedia.com      FALSE   FALSE     877627211      plugs      yes
```

The large number in the middle is expiry time in seconds from 1 January 1970. From this example, you can see that most web sites set one cookie only, and then it only contains a unique ID. Web sites often use this ID to look up their own records on the visitor holding the ID.

The equivalent files for Internet Explorer 4+ are stored by default in the `C:\WINDOWS\COOKIES` directory in `.txt` files with the user's name. These are almost readable. Ironically, if you copy the files to a UNIX computer, they are easily readable.

JavaScript and Cookies

Using JavaScript, cookies can be accessed from the browser, from a CGI program, and from server side JavaScript. Only the first method is examined here.

Cookies in the browser revolve around the JavaScript `window.document.cookie` property that first appeared in Netscape Navigator 2.0. This property is unlike other JavaScript object properties for a number of reasons:

❑ It isn't really related to its parent object, in this case the `document` object

❑ Although it's singular in name, it holds all the visible cookies, but it's not an array

❑ If you set the `cookie` property, its new value won't always match what you set it to

The `cookie` property is really just a service point for managing the browser's cookies. It doesn't directly represent the current cookie data. This is different to the other properties in JavaScript, such as the `forms` array that exactly matches each FORM tag

When you read the `cookie` property, you get a report in a single string of the cookies that are currently visible and unexpired for the current window's domain and path. Only name and value attributes are supplied in this report:

```
bookmark1=face.htm; my_id=541263; quote=Et%20tu,%20Brutus
```

This means that when looking for a specific cookie, you must pick the `cookie` property's string apart. You can't know when a cookie expires or will be visible without explicitly re-setting it

When setting a cookie, you must use a string in a specific format. That format is:

```
name=value; expires=date; path=directory; domain=domain-name; secure
```

Each semi-colon separated item is optional, except the first. The [value] part must be run through the `escape()` function first. The date for `expires` requires the exact format that the `toGMTString()` method of the `Date` object produces:

```
// example date: 'Mon, 13 Oct 1997 12:40:34 GMT'
```

Managing cookie strings can be maddening because of the way they work with `document.cookie`. Fortunately, the cookie toolkit, discussed later in the chapter, takes all of the pain out of using cookies, and can be easily incorporated in your own web pages.

Using Cookies

Cookies can be put to a number of simple uses. When cookie problems occur, this JavaScript URL is very useful for debugging. It effectively replaces all semi-colons with new lines and produces a readable report if many cookies are present:

```
javascript:alert(document.cookie.split(';').join('\n'))
```

Logging-in Users

Cookies can be used to force browser users to supply usernames and passwords before viewing web pages. Web servers already have a mechanism for doing this called HTTP Authentication, but if you don't like that system, you can use cookies instead. The steps are:

❑   Create an ordinary HTML form to accept username and password.

❑   Submit that form to a 'login' CGI program that validates the form details. The username and password might be validated against entries in a private file on the web server, like `/etc/passwd` on UNIX.

❑   Have the login CGI program return a failure page if the details are wrong.

❑   Have the login CGI program return the first real page if the details are right.

❑   Return a special cookie to the browser if the details are right. This cookie is used to track the user when browsing through pages of the web site.

❑   Each page on the site should be accessible through a second CGI program. This second program checks the cookie before delivering the requested page. This is because a user might try to get around the login screen by going directly to the URL of another page. The cookie created cannot be as simple as `login=true;`, because an expert user might see this cookie and just create it with a JavaScript: URL the next time s/he enters the web site, avoiding the login again. The cookie value should be different each time the user logs in (perhaps containing an encrypted time), so that subsequent checks can confirm that the value supplied is recent.

In general, this is not a highly secure login mechanism, but it does prevent unknown users from easily entering your web site. It is less efficient than HTTP Authentication.

If you don't have the opportunity to use CGI programs, you might think that the password can be checked in client-side JavaScript, and then proceed directly to the next page. Yes it can, but it's not secure, because the browser user can always view the JavaScript source and, therefore, work around the password-checking code.

Cookies as Bookmarks

In Netscape there is no way to automate the creation of bookmarks from JavaScript and there is no way to automatically navigate to a specific bookmark. Cookies can be used to workaround these restrictions. Note that with IE4+ we can use the `window.external.AddFavorite()` method which takes two parameters, the first being the URL and the second the name to be given to the favorite, for example:

```
window.external.AddFavorite(location.href, document.title);
```

A cookie with an expiry date set long into the future, will exist forever, effectively. A cookie whose value is a URL, can always be used as a bookmark. Provided the favorite cookie has been set at some time in the past, the user can be returned there automatically. This cookie could be set by client-side JavaScript either automatically, in response to some user input, or it could be set in the browser in the response from a CGI program.

More than one bookmark is possible by using more than one cookie, or, if the Netscape 20 cookie limit is close, concatenating all the bookmarks together into one cookie's value and unpacking them when needed.

User Preferences

Along with bookmarks, cookies can be used to store a limited range of user preferences. The range is limited, because of security hobbles. As for the last section, these can be set in a number of ways. Common preference choices might be:

- ❑ background color
- ❑ choice of frames or no-frames display
- ❑ choice of in-line images or text only display
- ❑ choice of navigation menu style
- ❑ font size

As the page is downloaded, inline JavaScript can check for special preference cookies and switch to the appropriate page, or adapt the page layout as required.

User Profiling

A web site can use a cookie to track a user's movements around the site. Web servers already have facilities for tracking the number of times each web page gets loaded, but cookies allow extra information to be supplied. Without the user's agreement, nothing can be stored in the cookie that exposes the real identity of the user, but the cookie can be used to show that the anonymous user is the same anonymous user as last time. Also see the Cookie Traps section below.

Visit Counter

Possibly the simplest use of a cookie is to store a number in it, and increment it each time the user loads a page that lies in the cookie's domain and path. This gives the HTML author a simple way of establishing familiarity with the user.

Shopping Carts

Shopping carts work around the limitation that HTML forms are restricted to one document. If you don't want to use a hidden frame and JavaScript variables to store the cart's contents, you can use cookies. There isn't much difference, but the main benefit is that cookies are easier to submit to a web server. You don't have to recreate a HTML form, they are submitted directly with every URL request. The main disadvantage is that you have to pack your cart items into and out of the cookie, which can be annoying.

Cookie Traps

From the point of view of security, the web site http://www.doubleclick.com is worth considering. As briefly discussed in the User Profiling section, cookies can't expose a user's true identity. This site has an advertising network that collects profiles of browser users by using cookies. The first time the user views an advertisement from this network, the cookie is set. Subsequently, when the user views a page anywhere in the network, the cookie is discovered and the user's presence is reported back to the network's data-collection service. Like tracking a wild animal, cookie footprints reveal the user's habits, which advertisers can then take advantage of. The next time the user views a page in the network, an advertisement appears tailored to the user's current habits. If you like tea, everywhere you go will eventually advertise tea bags.

Cookie Toolkit

Writing, reading, and deleting cookies is not difficult, however it is a bit monotonous to repeat the same code again and again for each of our web pages that uses cookies. So, to make life easy for ourselves, we'll create a cookie toolkit, which will take all the work out of using cookies.

The toolkit only works with IE4+ and Netscape 4.06+.

What is it and How Does it Work?

The cookie toolkit is seven functions (listed below) providing all the cookie functionality we're likely to ever need. All the functions are places in a single plain text file called `CookieToolkit.js`. Adding the toolkit to our web page is very easy, we simply use the SRC property of the SCRIPT tag to include it:

```
<SCRIPT SRC='CookieToolkit.js'></SCRIPT>
```

In the example above, we've assumed the file is in the same directory as our web page. However, the SRC property can be any valid path or full URL.

Once the .js file has been included in our page, using the functions is simply a matter of calling them, just as if they were in the page itself. Here are the seven methods of the Cookie Toolkit:

❑ writeCookie()

❑ readCookie()

❑ deleteCookie()

❑ writeMultiValueCookie()

❑ readMultiValueCookie()

❑ deleteMultiValueCookie()

❑ cookiesSupported()

The method names give away their purpose, and we'll be discussing them fully when we create them. However, it's worth just briefly taking an overview of the functionality provided. The first three methods deal with writing, reading and deleting whole cookies. Remember, we can have up to 20 of these whole cookies per domain with Netscape browsers. To get round this, we can store multiple values in one cookie and, as each cookie can have 4096 bytes, that provides a fair bit of space to store multiple values. To take the pain out of creating multi-value cookies, we have three appropriately named methods that are nice and easy to use. Finally, we have a method that will detect whether the browser supports cookies and, if so, whether they are turned on by the user.

It's important to note that the Cookie Toolkit only works with version 4 browsers and later. Given that in mid 2001 earlier browsers make up about 0.3% of the total browser user base, it's safe now to remove support for older browsers. It's advisable to have browser version checking code to take users of older browsers to a page telling them to upgrade.

Now, let's turn to the task of creating the Cookie Toolkit's code.

The writeCookie() Method

```
// Create a cookie
function writeCookie(cookieName, cookieValue, expires,
                     domain, path, secureFlag)
{
   if (cookieName)
   {
      var cookieDetails = cookieName + "=" + escape(cookieValue);
```

```
        cookieDetails += (expires ? "; expires=" +
            expires.toGMTString(): '');
        cookieDetails += (domain ? "; domain=" + domain: '');
        cookieDetails += (path ? "; path=" + path: '');
        cookieDetails += (secureFlag ? "; secure": '');
        document.cookie = cookieDetails;
    }
}
```

This method creates a whole cookie. It takes as its parameters all the cookie attributes we talked about earlier, such as the essential `cookieName` and `cookieValue`. JavaScript, being a chilled out sort of language, is quite happy if you don't include any of the parameters. In theory, they are all optional, though the `cookieName` and `cookieValue` are rather important. All the parameters except the `expires` and `secureFlag` are required to be strings. The `expires` parameter requires a `date` object and the `secureFlag` a Boolean. If we just want to set the cookie name and value:

```
writeCookie("Name","Paul");
```

If we want to set the expiry date to say a year from now, then:

```
var expireDate = new Date();
expireDate.setDate(expireDate.getFullYear() + 1) ;
writeCookie("Name","Paul", expireDate);
```

How about if we want to set the `name`, `value`, and `secure` flag parameters but none of the others? The following will return a syntax error:

```
writeCookie(cookieName,cookieValue,,,,true);
```

So instead, we need to have the `null` keyword for each parameter that we're not supplying:

```
writeCookie(cookieName,cookieValue,null,null,null,true);
```

Turning to the code of the function, we see that it's simply a matter of concatenating the parameters that are not `null` to form a string that we'll set the `document.cookie` property to. We used the conditional (trinary) operator (?) to do the checking. For example, in the line that deals with the `expires` date:

```
cookieDetails += (expires ? "; expires=" + expires.toGMTString(): '');
```

If `expires` contains a value, any value so long as it's not `null`, then the cookie `expires` attribute is set to the GMT value of the passed `date` object. Otherwise `''`, or an empty string, is concatenated. This principle applies to all the optional cookie parameters. Note that the `cookieValue` parameter is escaped before being concatenated to the string, this is so that characters that can't be stored in a cookie, punctuation for example, are converted to their character set number equivalent.

Having built up our cookie definition string in the `cookieDetails` variable, on the last line, we then actually set the cookie using the `document` object's `cookie` property.

The readCookie() Method

We've written a cookie, so now let's create the code that reads it back in again:

```
// Obtain a cookies unescaped value
function readUnescapedCookie(cookieName)
    {
    var cookieValue = document.cookie;
```

```
        var cookieRegExp = new RegExp("\\b" + cookieName + "=([^;]*)");
        cookieValue = cookieRegExp.exec(cookieValue);

        if (cookieValue != null)
        {
            cookieValue = cookieValue[1];
        }

        return cookieValue;
    }

    // Obtain a cookies value
    function readCookie(cookieName)
    {
        cookieValue = readUnescapedCookie(cookieName)

        if (cookieValue != null)
        {
            cookieValue = unescape(cookieValue);
        }

        return cookieValue;
    }
```

We can see that we have created two functions. The reason for this is that later on in our cookie toolkit, we need to read a cookie value before it has been unescaped (converted to document.cookie friendly encoded format with characters such as punctuation replaced by their character set number).

Let's start by looking at the readUnescapedCookie(cookieName) function. This makes use of a regular expression to extract the required cookie's value from the string of cookies returned by document.cookie. We'll look at regular expressions in more detail in the next chapter. The document object's cookie property returns all the cookies, for that domain, in the format cookieName=cookieValue;. So, an example cookie string might be:

AccountId=10199;AccountName=SavingsAccount;

Our regular expression, "\\b" + cookieName + "=([^;]+)", will match a word boundary, followed by the name of the cookie we want, followed by an equals sign (=). This is followed by a regular expression group, which matches one or more characters that are not a semi colon, (this group being the value part of the cookie that we want). Our code uses the exec() method to execute the regular expression against the cookie string, the results being the cookie name / cookie value pair of the cookie we want. Assuming that null has not been returned (there was a matching cookie name), then in our if statement block we set the cookieValue variable to the characters matched by our regular expressions only group (the cookie value characters). We unescape this value, remember that cookies can only hold letters and numbers, and store the result in cookieValue.

Finally, at the end we return cookieValue, which will be either null if no cookie is found, or the value of the cookie.

The first function is designed only for use by the Cookie Toolkit itself, it's the second function which is the one we use when reading a cookie. This reads the cookie using the function readUnescapedCookie(), and then unescapes it before returning its value to the calling code.

The deleteCookie() Method

So far, we have created and read cookies, now let's see how to delete them:

```
    // Deletes existing cookie
    function deleteCookie(cookieName)
    {
```

```
    var expiredDate = new Date();
    expiredDate.setMonth(-1);
    writeCookie(cookieName,"",expiredDate);
}
```

As we can see, deleting a cookie is very easy. Simply set its `expiry` value to a date that has already passed, which causes the cookie to immediately expire. We use the `Date` object to get the current date, and then set its `Month` to -1. As there is no such thing as the -1 month of the year, JavaScript instead assumes we mean -1 month from the first month of the year. The month before January is the previous year's December, and this is what the date is set to. This guarantees that the expiry date will be quite some time before whatever the current date is. Finally, we use the `writeCookie()` method in order to set a cookie with the expired date.

The writeMultiValueCookie() Method

Now that we've created all the methods necessary for writing, reading, and deleting a whole cookie, let's see how we can write a cookie with an embedded sub value. The advantage of having a multi-value cookie (of storing more than one discrete value inside one cookie), is that it gets over the 20 cookies per domain limit that browsers like Netscape specify. It also means we can store related information in one cookie, for example we might want to store information about a person, such as name, age, address and gender. With multi-value cookies, we could have a main cookie called Person and store the name, age, address, and gender as sub values inside it.

The process for identifying and delimiting sub values inside a cookie is that used by Microsoft's IIS (Internet Information Server). Active Server Pages (ASP) allows us to read and write multi-value cookies on the server. As we've adopted the same delimiters, it means any multi-values set on the client can be read by the server and vice versa. If you're using a different server that supports the reading and writing of multi-value cookies, then you may be able to change the delimiters so they match those expected by your server.

The delimiter we've adopted to mark the end of one multi-value and the beginning of another is the ampersand (`&`) character. So, if we have a whole cookie named `PersonalDetails` with the sub values `Name` and `Age` and `Gender` (`Bob`, `55`, and `Male` respectively), then our whole cookie would look like this:

```
PersonalDetails=Name=Bob&Age=55&Gender=Male
```

Let's create the function, to be added to `CookieToolkit.js`, which makes writing a multi-value cookie nice and easy:

```
// Create a cookie and specify a sub value
function writeMultiValueCookie( cookieName, multiValueName, value,
    expires, domain, path, secureFlag)
{
    var cookieValue = readUnescapedCookie(cookieName);
    if (cookieValue)
    {
        var stripAttributeRegExp = new RegExp("(^|&)" +
            multiValueName + "=[^&]*&?");
        cookieValue = cookieValue.replace(stripAttributeRegExp,"$1");
        if (cookieValue.length != 0)
        {
            cookieValue += "&";
        }
    }
    else
        cookieValue = "";

    cookieValue += multiValueName + "=" + escape(value);
    var cookieDetails = cookieName + "=" + cookieValue;
```

```
        cookieDetails += (expires ? "; expires=" + expires.toGMTString(): '');
        cookieDetails += (domain ? "; domain=" + domain: '');
        cookieDetails += (path ? "; path=" + path: '');
        cookieDetails += (secureFlag ? "; secure": '');
        document.cookie = cookieDetails;
}
```

The method takes exactly the same arguments as the `writeCookie()` method, but with the addition of the `multiValueName` parameter, which is the name by which we access the sub value. The first three parameters are essential, but the `expires`, `domain`, `path`, and `secureFlag` parameters are optional, just as with the `writeCookie()` method. Similar to that method, if we do decide to provide a value to a later argument, then the previous arguments must either have a value or we must pass `null`.

The function's first task is to get the whole cookie that contains the sub value. To do so, we use this toolkits `readUnescapedCookie()` function.

The task of the `if` statement and its code block is, if a value has been found for the whole cookie, to strip out the existing multi-value, if it exists, but not to change any existing multi-values. Once the multi-value cookie to be changed has been removed, all we need do to add it with its new value, is concatenate the sub value onto the end of the whole cookie.

So taking our previous example, let's say we have a cookie called `PersonalDetails` with three multi-value properties, `Name`, `Age`, and `Gender` with the values `Bob`, `55`, and `Male` respectively. When we read this cookie using `readCookie()` we get just the main cookie's value, in other words, `Name=Bob&Age=55&Gender=Male`, and not the `PersonalDetails=` part.

This would be the value stored in `cookieValue`. It might be the first time the whole cookie has been written, so the `if` statement checks to see if `cookieValue` contains a value. If it does then we remove the multi-value attribute we want to change by replacing it with an empty string, and this is the purpose of our regular expression and `replace()` method:

```
   var stripAttributeRegExp =   new RegExp("(^|&)" +
                       multiValueName + "=[^&]*&?");
   cookieValue = cookieValue.replace(stripAttributeRegExp,"$1");
```

We use a regular expression to do the matching of the multi-value name/value pair. Our regular expression looks for characters matching the multi-value name which are either at the beginning of the string or follow a `&` character. It then matches an equals sign and any characters following it until a `&` character is found, which indicates another multi-value pair. Finally, it matches the `&` character so that is removed as well. Notice in the `replace()` method, we replace the multi-value name/value pair with whatever was matched by the first regular expression group, (the `(^|&)`). So if a `&` was matched, then we don't want to remove it. Let's use our example and say we want to change the value of the `Age` sub value from `55` to `45`. Our regular expression will match:

`&Age=55&`

If we replace `Name=Bob&Age=55&Gender=Male` with a empty string we'd get:

`Name=BobGender=Male`

Where the delimiter between the sub values `Name` and `Gender` is lost, instead we want to replace with a `&` leaving us with the correct value of:

`Name=Bob&Gender=Male`

With any previous multi-value removed, adding the new value is just a matter of tacking the name/value pair onto the end of the existing whole cookie. First, we check to see if there are any other multi-values still left after the replacement, such as if the `cookieValue`'s length is greater than zero. If so, we need to add a `&` character to indicate the start of another multi-value name/value pair. Otherwise, if we were changing the `Age` value from 55 to 45 we would end up with:

```
Name=Bob&Gender=Male&Age=45
```

In the final lines of the method, we create the cookie string and add the cookie attributes, just as we did with the `writeCookie()` method. We only escape the multi-value's value and not the name and ampersand, so that it can be read back later. It's because we don't want to escape the ampersands that we don't use the `writeCookie()` method, as this would escape the whole multi-cookie, ampersands, and all, and mean we'd lose the sub value delimiters.

The readMultiValueCookie() Method

We've written a multi-value cookie, so let's create the method to read it back in again:

```
// Obtain sub value stored inside a cookie
function readMultiValueCookie(cookieName, multiValueName)
{
    var cookieValue = readUnescapedCookie(cookieName)
    var extractMultiValueCookieRegExp = new RegExp("\\b" +
        multiValueName + "=([^;&]*)");
    cookieValue = extractMultiValueCookieRegExp.exec(cookieValue);

    if (cookieValue != null)
    {
        cookieValue = unescape(cookieValue[1]);
    }

    return cookieValue;
}
```

The method's first task is to read the value of the whole cookie containing the sub value, which it does using the `readUnescapedCookie()` function. Then, in code very similar to that in `readCookie()`, we create a regular expression that will match the name/value pair of the multi-value. Our regular expression starts by matching a word boundary. This is so that multi-value names such as `FirstName` and `SecondName` are not confused. Then we match the name of the multi-value, followed by an equals sign and inside a regular expression group we match all characters until a `;` or `&` character is found, indicating the end of the cookie or the multi-value part. If it finds neither, then it simply matches until the end of the string.

The `exec()` method will then try to match our regular expression against the string passed in the variable `cookieValue`. It will either return `null` if no match is found, or a special array containing details of the match. The multi-value cookie's value part will be contained in the first and only regular expression group, which we can access using the second array element of the results array returned by `exec()`.

We finally return the multi-value, either the value found, or `null` if no such multi-value cookie is found.

The deleteMultiValueCookie() Method

The final functionality for dealing with multi-value cookies is to be able to delete one:

```
// Deletes sub value stored inside a cookie
function deleteMultiValueCookie(cookieName, multiValueName, expires,
                                domain, path, secureFlag)
{
    var cookieValue = readUnescapedCookie(cookieName);
    if (cookieValue)
```

```
        {
            var stripAttributeRegExp = new RegExp("(^|&)" +
                multiValueName + "=[^&]*&?");
            cookieValue = cookieValue.replace(stripAttributeRegExp,"$1");

            if (cookieValue.length != 0)
            {
                var cookieDetails = cookieName + "=" + cookieValue;
                cookieDetails += (expires ? "; expires=" +
                    expires.toGMTString(): '');
                cookieDetails += (domain ? "; domain=" + domain: '');
                cookieDetails += (path ? "; path=" + path: '');
                cookieDetails += (secureFlag ? "; secure": '');
                document.cookie = cookieDetails;
            }
            else
            {
                deleteCookie(cookieName);
            }
        }
    }
}
```

This method works in a very similar manner to the `writeMultiValueCookie()` function. The difference here is that, whereas that function first removed the existing multi-value, if any, to be written and then added the new multi-value pair to the end, this function does the removal part, but does not add any new multi-value name/value pair.

First, we read the whole cookie value using the `readUnescapedCookie()` function. If its value is not `null` then we create a regular expression identical to the one used in the `writeMultiValueCookie()` method. Its purpose is to remove the multi-value's name/value pair and any associated `&` signs. Then, using the `replace()` method, we strip out the existing multi-value name/value pair and replace it with whatever was matched by the first group of the regular expression, which will be the `&`. As in the `writeMultiValueCookie()` method we want to retain any leading `&` as it's the delimiter for multi-values after the one being deleted.

If the cookie string is not of zero length after the removal of the multi-value pair, then there must be another multi-value pair, so we need to write out the cookie and store the remaining multi-values. If `cookieValue` is zero length (the multi-value we just deleted was the only one in that cookie), then we might as well save cookie space and delete the whole cookie using this toolkit's `deleteCookie()` function.

The cookiesEnabled() Method

Our final function checks to see whether cookies are switched-on by the user. Some users are likely to have switched them off, so it is not enough to assume a user has cookie support just because they have a version 4+ browser. It's still advisable that we redirect users of pre version 4 browsers away from any pages using the `CookieToolkit`, due to the browsers' lack of support for some aspects of JavaScript classes, the `prototype` property, and the regular expression object used by this class:

```
// Returns true if cookies are supported by browser & switched on by user
function cookiesEnabled()
{
    var cookiesEnabled = window.navigator.cookieEnabled;

    if (!cookiesEnabled)
    {
        document.cookie = "cookiesEnabled=True";
        cookiesEnabled = new Boolean(document.cookie).valueOf();
    }
```

```
    return cookiesEnabled;
  }
```

IE4+ and Netscape 6+ have a `navigator` object with the `cookieEnable` property that returns `true` if cookies are enabled. This makes checking for cookies easy with those browsers. Unfortunately, Netscape 4 does not have this property, so we need to take a more convoluted approach. With Netscape 4, we need to write a test cookie and then read it back. If reading it back returns an empty string, then cookies are disabled (it's a crude method, but it works). We convert the value in `document.cookie` to a Boolean by creating a new `Boolean` object and passing the `document.cookie` to its constructor. The `valueOf()` method will return a native Boolean value, rather than an object. If you don't plan to support Netscape 4, then the `if` statement and code block is redundant.

On the final line, we return a Boolean value indicating whether cookies are supported.

Using the CookieToolkit

Let's take a brief look at an example that uses many of the functions in our toolkit. The example displays a form, shown below, that enables cookies to be written, read, and deleted. If just the cookie name is entered then only whole cookies will be written, read, or deleted. We can optionally enter a name for the multi-value attribute to read, write, and delete just multi-value cookies.

The expiry date box is optional, if no date is entered, then the cookie expiry date won't be set and any cookie created will expire when the browser window is closed. To keep the example short, no validation of the fields is made. The date field, if completed, needs to have any valid date inside it, such as 1 Jan 2010.

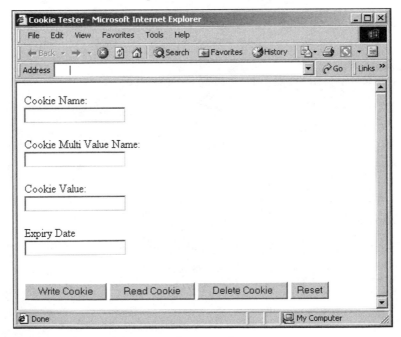

The code for the page is shown below, save the example as `CookieExample.htm`:

```
<!-- CookieExample.htm  -->
<HTML>
<HEAD>
<SCRIPT SRC="CookieToolkit.js"></SCRIPT>
```

```
<SCRIPT>

function window_onload()
{
   if (cookiesEnabled() == false)
   {
      alert("You'll need to enable cookies to use this page");
   }
}

function writeCookie_onclick()
{
   var form = document.frmCookie;
   var cookieName = form.txtCookieName.value;
   var cookieMultiValueName = form.txtCookieMultiValueName.value;
   var cookieValue = form.txtCookieValue.value;
   var expiryDate = form.txtCookieExpires.value;

   if (expiryDate != "")
   {
      expiryDate = new Date(expiryDate)
   }
   else
   {
      expiryDate = null;
   }

   if (cookieMultiValueName != "")
   {
      writeMultiValueCookie(cookieName,cookieMultiValueName,cookieValue,
         expiryDate);
   }
   else
   {
      writeCookie(cookieName,cookieValue,expiryDate);
   }
   alert("Cookie Set");

   form.txtCookieValue.value = "";
}

function readCookie_onclick()
{
   var form = document.frmCookie;
   var cookieName = form.txtCookieName.value;
   var cookieMultiValueName = form.txtCookieMultiValueName.value;
   var cookieValue = "";

   if (document.frmCookie.txtCookieMultiValueName.value != "")
   {
      cookieValue = readMultiValueCookie(cookieName,cookieMultiValueName);
   }
   else
   {
      cookieValue = readCookie(cookieName,cookieValue);
   }

   form.txtCookieValue.value = cookieValue;
}

function deleteCookie_onclick()
```

```
{
    var form = document.frmCookie;
    var cookieName = form.txtCookieName.value;
    var cookieMultiValueName = form.txtCookieMultiValueName.value;

    if (document.frmCookie.txtCookieMultiValueName.value != "")
    {
        var expiryDate = form.txtCookieExpires.value;

        if (expiryDate != "")
        {
            expiryDate = new Date(expiryDate)
        }
        else
        {
            expiryDate = null;
        }

        cookieValue = deleteMultiValueCookie(cookieName,cookieMultiValueName,
expiryDate);

    }
    else
    {
        cookieValue = deleteCookie(cookieName);
    }

    form.txtCookieValue.value = "";
}

</SCRIPT>
<TITLE>Cookie Tester</TITLE>
</HEAD>
<BODY onload="window_onload()">
<FORM name="frmCookie">
    <P>Cookie Name:<BR>
        <INPUT type="text" name=txtCookieName ></P>
    <P>Cookie Multi Value Name:<BR>
        <INPUT type="text" name=txtCookieMultiValueName ></P>
    <P>Cookie Value:<BR>
        <INPUT type="text" name=txtCookieValue ></P>
    <P>Expiry Date<BR>
        <INPUT type=text name=txtCookieExpires></P>
    <BR>
    <INPUT type="button" value="Write Cookie" name=cmdWriteCookie
        onclick="writeCookie_onclick()">
    <INPUT type="button" value="Read Cookie" name=cmdReadCookie
        onclick="readCookie_onclick()">
    <INPUT type="button" value="Delete Cookie" name=cmdDeleteCookie
        onclick="deleteCookie_onclick()">
    <INPUT type="reset" value="Reset" name=cmdReset>
</FORM>
</BODY>
</HTML>
```

Let's look at each of the four functions in turn, starting with window_onload().
This function, as the name suggests, is called by the window object's onload event handler added to the <BODY> tag. It uses the cookiesEnabled() function to check whether cookies have been enabled. If disabled, the user is alerted that the page is not going to work. In a real world situation, we would handle this much better by, for example, taking the user to a page not relying on cookies or a page informing them that without cookies this web site is simply not going to function properly.

Next, we come to the `writeCookie_onclick()` function, which, as its name suggests, writes a new cookie. At the top of the function, we obtain the cookie data entered into the form by the user. Our next task is to create a new `Date` object containing the expiry date of the cookie.

If the expiry date entered by the user is not empty, then we create a new `Date` object and store the reference in the variable `expiryDate`. Otherwise, we set `expiryDate` to `null`. When `expiryDate` is later passed to the Cookie Toolkit's `writeCookie()` method, we can be sure that if an expiry date was entered by the user then the method will act on it. If not, then `expiryDate` will be `null` and Cookie Toolkit's `writeCookie()` method will ignore the parameter.

We're now ready to write the cookie. Based on whether a value was entered in the `txtMultiValueName` text box, whose contents we have stored in the variable `cookieMultiValueName`, we decide whether to create a multi-value cookie or a whole one.

The difference is a matter of which write cookie function of the Cookie Toolkit we call, and the parameters passed. The `writeMultiValueCookie()` function requires one extra value, the multi-value's name. We finish at the end of the function by clearing the value box and notifying the user that the cookie has been sent.

Our next function, `readCookie_onclick()` works very much like the `writeCookie_onclick()` function, except the obvious difference that we're reading a cookie back rather than writing one. First, we initialize variables to the cookie name and multi-value name. Then, depending on whether a multi-value name has been entered, we read in a whole cookie or a multi-value cookie using the Cookie Toolkit's `readCookie()` and `readMultiValueCookie()` functions respectively. The variable `cookieValue` is used to store the cookie value obtained and the textbox, `txtCookieValue`, is set to `cookieValue`'s value.

Finally, we have the `deleteCookie()` function. As with the previous functions, first we read in the cookie name and multi-value name. Then, we delete either a whole cookie or multi-value cookie depending on whether a multi-value name was supplied by the user. A whole cookie can just be deleted using the Cookie Toolkit's `deleteCookie()` method and passing the cookie name. With multi-value cookies, we need to supply an expiry date to the `deleteMultiValueCookie()` method. This is because we don't want to expire the whole cookie, just one of the multi-values it contains. It's unfortunate that once a cookie has been set, it's not possible to recover its expiry date, we need to generate a new one every time.

Finally, the function clears the `value` property to make it clear something did just happen and the cookie has been deleted. It also makes it easy to check that the cookie name and multi-value names are still there. Clicking the Read Cookie button should display null in the value text box.

Summary

Privacy and security concerns serve to make client-side JavaScript a complex matter.

By default, the browser user is safe while the client-side JavaScript scriptwriter is not. The scriptwriter's activity is restricted by security hobbles, and the scripts are exposed to the user's whim. Half-hearted attempts at security, such as code shrouding may keep the ignorant and lazy at bay, but ultimately provide no security at all. In order to be properly secure, a complete solution involving digital certificates is required. This is not usually free, and requires extra organization and tools. Users may need to be educated as well, since they should not just accept every security alert the browser presents them with.

Cookies are a mechanism residing in the grey area between secure and insecure. Useful for maintaining data in the browser client and for tracking browser users, they have some slight implications on security. Their behavior in browsers is unusual compared with other browser features and can only be controlled from the browser via JavaScript. The Cookie Toolkit, a JavaScript class that we created, takes most of the difficulties out of using cookies. With the Cookie Toolkit, cookie programming is simply a matter of calling object methods and passing parameters.

To further investigate cookies, www.cookiecentral.com provides a good resource.

Pro JavaScript 2nd Edition

15

Regular Expressions

If you've come across regular expressions before, in Perl scripting for example, then you can skip these first few paragraphs and move straight onto *Regular Expressions in JavaScript*, on the next page. The name "regular expression" doesn't give much away about their use. In short, they are all about matching patterns of characters in strings. You may well have used methods such as indexOf() in the past to search for the existence of one string inside another. The problem with this is it's not very flexible. We can only search for a string of actual characters, such as "Pauline" or "Paula". If we wanted to search for the words Pauline or Paula, but not Paul, then indexOf() requires extra coding to handle this. As we'll find out in this chapter, using regular expressions makes this sort of problem more approachable.

A real world use for regular expressions is to check the validity of form data. For example, we might want to find out if the e-mail address entered by a user in a form does at least match the permitted format. If the user has entered "mind_your_own_business" as an e-mail address, we can see straight away that it's not one of the possible valid patterns, such as username@server.com. There are many variations of e-mail addresses, with all the following being valid: paul.wilton@mymailserver.co.uk, paul@my.mailserver.co.jp, and p@p.org. Without regular expressions, the code to check every possible combination would be quite lengthy and complex. As we'll see later in this chapter, it takes just three lines of code using regular expressions. Of course, we can only check the format is valid, not that the e-mail address actually exists.

Regular expressions are a very powerful tool for checking the validity of forms, but they have other uses as well, such as search and replace. Let's say a web site for small children has a message board and obviously they want to prevent swear words in messages. Rather than checking every message by hand, we could either stop the message being posted by searching for bad language, or allow it to be posted, but use regular expressions to search and then replace offending words with something more appropriate.

Regular expressions are undoubtedly very powerful, but that power comes at a price – complexity. Simple tasks such as searching for Pauline or Paula, but excluding Paul, isn't a problem with regular expressions; while checking e-mail validity, does require a little more skill and understanding. By the end of this chapter, you will be on the road to regular expression guru!

First, we'll look at how regular expressions are made available for our use in JavaScript. Then we'll look at the regular expression syntax before finally looking at some examples of how to actually use regular expressions in JavaScript.

Regular Expressions in JavaScript

Before we look at regular expression syntax, let's take a look at how regular expressions are implemented in JavaScript.

Creating Regular Expressions with the RegExp Object

Implementation of regular expressions in JavaScript revolves around the RegExp object. The RegExp is a type of object supplied by the browser, just like the String object. Just as a String object holds character data, a RegExp object holds a regular expression. Therefore, with a String object, we can create it and pass an initial value in its constructor like this:

```
var myString = new String("Some characters");
```

To create a new RegExp object we write:

```
var myRegExp = new RegExp("MyRegularExpression");
```

As with the String object, we've declared a variable myRegExp to hold a reference to the RegExp object we're about to create. On the right hand side, we create a new RegExp object and pass to its constructor a string of characters representing our regular expression.

There is, however, a second way of creating a RegExp object using a so-called regular expression literal, which is shown below:

```
var myRegExp = /MyRegularExpression/;
```

This does the same thing as the first above, but there are two important differences. First what is between the first forward slash and the close forward slash is not a string of characters representing a regular expression but the actual regular expression. You might be wondering, what the difference is , as surely a regular expression is a regular expression.

A string can have special characters that we call escape sequences. These escape sequences allow us to represent characters we can't actually type in our code such as \n for a new line or \b for a backspace. We'll learn shortly that regular expressions also have special character sequences and these sometimes conflict with the escape sequences in strings, so \b in a string is not the same as \b in regular expression syntax, which matches a boundary between a word and something that's not a word; we'll explain this fully later. When we declare a RegExp like this:

```
myRegExp = new RegExp("MyRegularExpressionAsAString");
```

We're actually passing a string value as a parameter to the RegExp object's constructor. As it's a string, it can contain the escape sequences that any string can contain, like \b. As \b conflicts with the \b in regular expression syntax, we need to specify that it's a \b of regular expression syntax by adding an extra back slash, so \b becomes \\b, but \b is still the string syntax version Now when we declare a RegExp object like this:

```
var myRegExp = /MyActualRegExpNotAString/;
```

Everything between the forward slashes is regular expression syntax and not a string, and so we do not use \\b to represent \b in regular expressions. So if our regular expression is "Hello\b World", where the \b is the regular expression word boundary matching character, then using the slashes we'd declare it like this:

```
var myRegExp = /Hello\b World/;
```

With the new operator it would be:

```
var myRegExp = new RegExp("Hello\\b World");
```

The only exception to this rule of having an extra \ for the RegExp's constructor is when we're passing values which are not string objects, but from say a text input box on a form, which can't contain string escape sequences. So if we have:

```
var myRegExp = new RegExp(document.myForm.myTextInputBox.value);
```

The user won't need to enter \\b or \\n, they can enter the syntax as it would be if we used:

```
var myRegExp = /MyRegularExpression/;
```

There is a second difference between the two ways of declaring a RegExp object. With the first way (using the new operator), the regular expression is not compiled, whereas when using the second way with the forward slashes, it is. What exactly do we mean by compiled? Well, before the JavaScript interpreter can use the regular expression, it has to convert it from the human readable regular expression pattern you'll soon come to know and love into a machine friendly internal format. A RegExp object created using new RegExp(), stores the regular expression pattern as a string inside the RegExp object and each time we use the RegExp object to do a pattern match it compiles the regular expression pattern to the efficient internal format before using it to pattern match.

With the second method using the forward slashes, the regular expression pattern is compiled as the RegExp object is created, so that each time it's used to pattern match, it's already compiled into the internal format. Being pre-compiled is generally more efficient and that is the best method to use, unless you have a regular expression pattern that will be changing, in which case you can create a RegExp object, set the regular expression pattern of it, and then compile it with a special method. We'll find out more about this later in the chapter.

Regular Expression Flags

When creating regular expressions and afterwards by setting properties of the RegExp object, we can set certain flags to specify whether our patterns are case sensitive, global and/or multi-line. If we create the RegExp object with the new operator then we specify the flags as an optional second parameter to the constructor like this:

```
var myRegExp = new RegExp("Catherine","ig");
```

With the second method, we add the flags after the closing forward slash:

```
var myRegExp = /Catherine/ig;
```

We can add any, all or none of the flags as we wish. Default matches are case sensitive and only match the first matching string.

Flag Type	Flag Character	Description
Case Sensitivity	i	Using the i flag makes character matching case insensitive. So Paul and paul are treated the same. By default, only same case characters are matched.
Global	g	Search for every occurrence of a matching pattern. By default, only the first matching pattern is found.
Multi-line (Only available in IE5.5+ and NN6+)	m	Determines how strings with more than one line, (with newline characters) are treated.

Let's start by looking at the case sensitivity flag, which is the i character, as in insensitive. If we define a RegExp object with the pattern Catherine:

```
var myRegExp = /Catherine/;
```

Then only the pattern, here a string of characters, Catherine with a capital 'C' and not catherine with a small 'c' will be matched. Add a case insensitive flag i:

```
var myRegExp = /Catherine/i;
```

Now both Catherine and catherine will be matched, as well as permutations that have a mix of both upper and lower case letters, such as CaTHerINE.

Normally the first matching pattern is looked for in a string and the rest ignored unless we use the global flag g, which says look for all matching patterns and not just the first. So:

```
myRegExp = /Catherine/;
```

Would match only the first Catherine in a string like that below:

```
var myString = "Catherine loved picking roses. Catherine put them in water";
```

To match the second one, we need to use the global flag like this:

```
myRegExp = /Catherine/g;
```

The final flag is the m, for 'treat as multi-line' and is only available with JavaScript 1.5 supported by Netscape 6+ and JScript 5.5 available in IE5.5+. We'll see later that regular expressions have special characters, ^ and $, which specify that the position of the match must be the beginning or end, the beginning or end of what depends on this m flag. If the flag is not set then the beginning is the start of the string and the end the end of the whole string. With the m flag set, the beginning is the beginning of the string, or of a new line, and the end is the end of the string, or the end of any line. So for example if string was:

Start of my string.
This is the End.

With no m flag, a ^ will match the beginning of the string, just before the S in Start, and the $ will match the end of the string, the point after the period. If the multi-line flag is set then there are now two matches for ^, the start of the string and the start of the second line. The $ will now match the point after the very last character, as before the point after the period, but before that the point just after the period in the first line. We will look at this flag later in the chapter when we've seen the relevant special characters, and things should become much clearer.

Using the RegExp Object with the test() Method

We'll be looking in detail at the RegExp object later in the chapter, once we've discussed regular expression syntax. However, to get us started and so that we can use examples to demonstrate regular expression patterns, we will look at the RegExp object's test() method.

The test() method takes one parameter, a string that the regular expression will be tested against to see if a match is made. If there is a match, then the method returns true.

```
var myRegExp = /pattern of characters/;
```

If we wanted to test to see if this pattern is found inside the sentence, "Regular expressions are all about matching a pattern of characters." then we would write:

```
var myRegExp = /pattern of characters/;

if (myRegExp.test("Regular expressions are all about matching a pattern of
characters."))
{
   alert("A matching pattern was found");
}
else
{
   alert("No matching pattern found");
}
```

There the pattern "pattern of characters" does exist inside the string we passed to the test() method, so the first alert() box will appear telling us a matching pattern was found. If we change the regular expression to:

```
var myRegExp = /pattern of numbers and letters/;
```

and try the code again, then no match is found and the second alert box appears telling us this.

Using the String Object's replace() Method

To help demonstrate multiple matches we're going to briefly look at the replace() method of the String object. The method takes two parameters, the first is the regular expression to be matched, and the second is the string to replace the patterns matched.

So to replace Catherine with Cathy in the following string:

```
var myString = "Catherine loved picking roses. Catherine put them in water";
```

We would need to write:

```
// 01 - Cathy alert box.htm
var myString = "Catherine loved picking roses. Catherine put them in water";
myRegExp = /Catherine/g;
myString = myString.replace(myRegExp,"Cathy");
alert(myString);
```

We've added the g for global match flag at the end so that it's not just the first occurrence of Catherine that is matched and replaced as we can see from the screenshot overleaf:

Now that we know how to create regular expressions in JavaScript and test if they work, let's move on to look at regular expression syntax.

Regular Expression Syntax

In this section, we will study the syntax of regular expressions, starting with very basic regular expressions and then moving onto the various special characters and group pattern matching, making sure along the way we take in plenty of examples.

Simple Regular Expressions

In the previous section, we had a taste of some very basic regular expressions. In its simplest form, a regular expression is simply just the actual characters we want to match. Therefore, if we want to match Catherine, we just create our regular expression:

```
var myRegExp = /Catherine/;
```

With the flags we discussed previously, we can also match without case-sensitivity, and globally.

How do we go about matching the non-printable characters such as tabs and newlines? Well as with strings, there are escape sequences that can be used to specify these characters. An escape sequence is a special command inside a string that tells the JavaScript interpreter that what follows is not a character, but a character indicating a different character. The \ is the character indicating that what follows is an escape sequence of characters. What follows indicates what character the escape sequence represents, so \t represents a tab. As some normal characters such as the ? and * also have special meaning in regular expression syntax, which we'll see in the next section, then these too need to be represented by escape sequences. A list of these are shown in the table below:

Escape Sequence	Description	Regular Expression Special Character
\/	Matches an actual / character.	No
\\	Matches actual \.	Yes
\.	Matches . character.	Yes
*	Matches * character.	Yes
\+	Matches + character.	Yes
\?	Matches ? character.	Yes
|	Matches | character.	Yes
\(	Matches (character.	Yes

Escape Sequence	Description	Regular Expression Special Character
\)	Matches) character.	Yes
\{	Matches { character.	Yes
\}	Matches } character.	Yes
\^	Matches ^ character.	Yes
\$	Matches $ character.	Yes
\n	Matches new line.	No
\r	Matches carriage return.	No
\t	Matches tab.	No
\v	Matches vertical tab.	No
\f	Matches form feed.	No
\nnn	Matches ASCII character specified by octal number nnn. So \103 matches an uppercase C	No
\xnn	Matches ASCII character specified by hexadecimal number nn. So \x43 matches C.	No
\unnnn	Matches the Unicode character specified by the four hexadecimal digits represented by nnnn.	No

So lets say we have the string, "The price is $1.95 and is available now." and want to match the $ and replace it with a £ – what regular expression would we need? As the $ sign is a special character, we can't just use it in our pattern, we must use the escape sequence \$ to tell JavaScript we mean a $ character and not the regular expression special character $.

```
var myString = "The price is $1.95 and is available now.";
var myRegExp = /\$/;
myString = myString.replace(myRegExp,"£");
document.write(myString);
```

Note if we have more than one $ then only the first will be matched, so we need to use the global flag to make sure all patterns matching are replaced:

```
var myRegExp = /\$/g;
```

Special Characters

If we could only match actual characters then this would be a very short chapter and regular expressions not exceptionally useful. What makes regular expressions powerful is the many special characters that allow us to match particular classes of characters, such as letters, digits, and whitespace characters (tabs, spaces, newlines and so on) to name just a few. These character classes allow us to match where we have a set pattern, but don't know or care what the actual character values are. For example, the pattern of a telephone number, e-mail, or ZIP code might be set, but the actual digits and characters vary.

We'll start by looking in this section at the various classes of characters, then we'll look at how regular expressions allow you to group character patterns and finally we'll see how its possible to match either one or another group of characters in a single regular expression.

Matching Classes of Characters

Shown below are the special character classes in JavaScript's regular expression syntax. These groups replace one single character. Therefore, a \d will match any one digit.

Character Class	Characters it matches	Example
\d	Any digit, includes 0-9	\d\d matches 72, but not aa or 7a.
\D	Any character that is not a digit	\D\D\D matches abc, but not 123.
\w	Any word character, such as A-Z, a-z, 0-9, and the underscore character _	\w\w\w\w matches Ab_2, but not £$%* or Ab_@.
\W	Any non-word character	\W matches @, but not the letter a.
\s	Any whitespace character, includes tab, newline, carriage return, form feed and vertical tab	
\S	Any non-white space character	
.	Any character	. matches any single character except a new-line character.
[...]	Any one of the characters between the brackets	[abc] will match a or b or c, but nothing else. [a-z] will match any character in the range a to z.
[^...]	Any character, but not one of those inside the brackets	[^abc] will match any character except a or b or c, but A or B or C could be matched by this pattern. [^a-z] will match any character which is not in the range a through z, but all uppercase letters could be matched by this pattern

So to match a telephone number in the format 1-800-888-5474, the regular expression would be

```
/\d-\d\d\d-\d\d\d-\d\d\d\d/
```

Any \d will match any character in the digit class and of course, the – matches just a dash. To test it works in code:

```
var myRegExp = /\d-\d\d\d-\d\d\d-\d\d\d\d/;
alert(myRegExp.test("1-800-888-5474"));
```

Try this and you'll see an alert box with true displayed to say it's true and valid. Change the string to be tested:

```
var myRegExp = /\d-\d\d\d-\d\d\d-\d\d\d\d/;
alert(myRegExp.test("X-800-888-5474"));
```

and we get **false** displayed. To match a date such as `Jul 31 2001`, our regular expression would be:

```
/[a-zA-Z][a-zA-Z][a-zA-Z] \d\d \d\d\d\d/
```

The `[a-zA-Z]` will match any character from small `a` to small `z` and capital `A` to capital `Z`. Therefore, what we are saying is match any pattern consisting of three letters which are in the range a-z or A-Z followed a space followed by two digits followed by another space and finally with four digits at the end.

A good idea in this situation is to use the `i` flag to say the match is case insensitive and just have `[a-z]` or `[A-Z]`, for example:

```
var myRegExp = /[a-z][a-z][a-z] \d\d \d\d\d\d/i;
```

If we wanted to allow dashes between date digits as well as spaces, such as `Jul -31 -2001`, we'd change our regular expression to:

```
/[a-z][a-z][a-z][ -]\d\d[ -]\d\d\d\d/i
```

Something you're probably starting to notice is there is a lot of repetition of characters. In the regular expression above, we have three instances of `[a-z]`, two of `\d` in the middle, and four `\d` characters at the end. To help us in this situation, regular expression syntax has special repetition characters and these are the topic of our next section.

Repetition Characters

Repetition characters not only make our regular expressions more compact but they also allow us to specify that a character or, as we'll see shortly a group of characters. Let's start by looking at the repetition characters available:

Special Character	Meaning	Example
`{n}`	Match n of the previous item.	`/x{2}/` matches xx, but not x or xxx
`{n,}`	Match n or more of the previous item.	`/x{2,}/` matches two or more x, that is xx, xxx, xxxx, xxxxx ...
`{n,m}`	Match at least n and at most m of the preceding item, if n is 0, this makes the character optional.	`/x{2,4}/` matches xx, xxx and xxxx, but not x or xxxxx
`?`	Match the previous item zero or one times, essentially making it optional.	`/x?/` matches x or xx
`+`	Match the previous item one or more times.	`/x+/` matches x, or xx or xxx or any number of x
`*`	Match the previous item zero or more times.	`/x*/` matches no x, x or xx or x with any number of x

In the light of this table, let's change our telephone and date regular expressions we saw earlier.

First, the telephone regular expression can be changed from:

```
/\d-\d\d\d-\d\d\d-\d\d\d\d/
```

to:

```
/\d-\d{3}-\d{3}-\d{4}/
```

The updated regular expression will match exactly the same pattern, reading a digit, followed by a dash, followed by a digit occurring three times followed by a dash, followed by a digit occurring three times, followed by a dash and finally followed by a digit occurring four times.

Let's update our short date matching expression from:

```
/[a-zA-Z][a-zA-Z][a-zA-Z][ -]\d\d[ -]\d\d\d\d/
```

to:

```
/[a-zA-Z]{3}[ -]\d\d[ -]\d{4}/
```

We haven't changed the \d\d in the middle to \d{2} as it adds an extra character, thus lengthening the expression rather than shortening it.

Even more useful than the shorthand of {n} are the ?, +, and * special repetition characters. Let's say we wanted to match a 16-digit credit card number. When users enter credit card numbers, they sometimes enter the whole number with no spaces, and sometimes they split it up into groups of four digits with spaces between the groups as it's printed on the card itself. This does present a problem as it means either we strip out spaces using a replace and then do our regular expression pattern match, or we have two regular expressions to match each situation, like this:

```
/\d{16}/
```

And:

```
/\d{4} \d{4} \d{4} \d{4}/
```

Using the ? repetition character which matches the previous character zero or one times, we can combine the two regular expressions like this:

```
/\d{4} ?\d{4} ?\d{4} ?\d{4}/
```

Now the ? after each space means the space must appear zero or one times. Let's create a simple example based on this in which a user enters their card number in a text box and hits a button to check its validity. In reality, we would use this as part of a form validation exercise and instead of telling the user whether it is valid or not, we would simply submit or not submit the form.

```
<HTML>
<HEAD>
   <SCRIPT LANGUAGE='JavaScript'>
      function isCCNumValid(ccNumber)
      {
         var ccNumRegExp = /\d{4} ?\d{4} ?\d{4} ?\d{4}/;
         return ccNumRegExp.test(ccNumber);
      }
   </SCRIPT>
</HEAD>
<BODY>
   <FORM ID='form1' NAME='form1'>
      Enter a 16 digit credit card number:
      <BR><INPUT TYPE='text' NAME='txtCCNum'><BR>
      <INPUT TYPE='button' VALUE='Is It Valid?'
```

```
                onClick='alert(isCCNumValid(document.form1.txtCCNum.value))'
                NAME='cmdCheckCCNum'></INPUT>
     </FORM>
   </BODY>
   </HTML>
```

We have attached code to the button's click event that calls the `isCCNumValid()` function, which uses the regular expression we've just looked at to check the credit card number text box for validity. Try it out and you will notice there is a fatal flaw, in that although the pattern matching defined by the regular expression must appear inside the string at some point, it can be anywhere. So if the user enters "My Phoney number is 2222 4444 5555 6666!!!!!!" then apparently that is valid:

In the next section, we'll look at how to specify whereabouts inside the string the matching pattern should be found.

Pattern Position Characters

The position characters allow us to specify where in a string the pattern should be found; this is called **anchoring** the pattern. By anchor, we mean that (at least) one end of the regular expression is fixed to a point in the string to be matched. Therefore, anchors stop the normal behavior of searching all along the string for any match.

There are four special position characters and these are shown in the table below:

Position Character	Description
^	The pattern must be at the start of the string, or if it's a multi-line string, then at the beginning of a line. For multi-line text, (a string that contains carriage returns) we need to set the multi-line flag, either when defining the regular expression or by writing *RegExp*.multiline = true, where RegExp is our instance of a RegExp object.
$	The pattern must be at the end of the string, or if multi-line string then at the end of a line. For multi-line text we need to write *RegExp*.multiline = true.

Table continued on following page

Position Character	Description
\b	This matches a word boundary, essentially the point between a word character and a non-word character (the start of a word).
\B	Match a position that is not a word boundary (not the start of a word).

To solve the problem we had earlier with the credit card number, we can use a ^ character at the start of the regular expression to ensure the card number is the first thing in the string, and the $ character to ensure that the pattern is also the end of the string. By using this method, we ensure that the card number pattern is the first, last, and only thing in the string. So now, our RegExp object declaration becomes:

```
var ccNumRegExp = /^\d{4} ?\d{4} ?\d{4} ?\d{4}$/;
```

It is with the ^ and $ special characters that the setting of the multi-line flag becomes important. If the m flag is set, for example /pattern/m, then ^ matches the position following a \n or \r as well as the position at the very beginning of the string and $ matches the position preceding \n or \r as well as the position at the very end of the string.

If the m flag is not set, then ^ matches the position at the beginning of a string, and $ matches the position at the end of a string. Let's look at a simple example to demonstrate the effect of the multi-line flag:

```
<HTML>
<BODY>
    <PRE>
    <SCRIPT LANGUAGE='JavaScript'>
        var myString = "First line of text.\nSecond line of text."
            + "\nThird and final line";
        var showMultiLineStartRegExp = /^/gm;
        var showMultiLineEndRegExp = /$/gm;

        var multiLineStringResult =
            myString.replace(showMultiLineStartRegExp,"^");
        multiLineStringResult =
            multiLineStringResult.replace(showMultiLineEndRegExp,"$");
        document.write("Mutli Line Flag Set");
        document.write(multiLineStringResult);

        var showStartRegExp = /^/g;
        var showEndRegExp = /$/g;

        var StringResult = myString.replace(showStartRegExp,"^");
        StringResult = StringResult.replace(showEndRegExp,"$");
        document.write("Mutli Line Flag NOT Set\n\n");
        document.write(StringResult);
    </SCRIPT>
    </PRE>
</BODY>
</HTML>
```

The code simply replaces all the positions matching the ^ or $ special characters, (start and end characters), with the equivalent character literal (an actual ^ or $). The results are shown overleaf:

We can see that the results of using the m flag, shown at the top, have meant the beginning and end of each line have been matched using the ^ and $ special characters respectively. In the second results block, we see that when the multi-line flag is not set, then only the start and end of the string are matched by ^ and $.

The final two entries in the table above, \b and \B, match word boundaries and non-word boundaries, and can cause confusion at first. A word boundary is the boundary between the class of characters defined by \w, such as any letter, number, or underscore characters, and any non-word character as defined by the class \W. A non-word boundary is simply the opposite of a word boundary so any boundary between two word characters or two non-word characters is a non-word boundary.

It's easiest to show this with an example, which allows you to explore the boundaries:

```
<!-- 04 - Boundaries of Text.htm -->
<HTML>
<HEAD>
   <SCRIPT LANGUAGE='JavaScript'>
      function cmdShow_onclick()
      {
         var displayResultsDiv;
         var boundaryRegExp;
         var resultsString = "";
         if (document.form1.radBoundaryType[0].checked)
         {
            boundaryRegExp = /\b/g;
         }
         else
         {
            boundaryRegExp = /\B/g;
         }

         if (document.all)
         {
            displayResultsDiv = document.all.divShowResults;
         }
         else
         {
           displayResultsDiv = document.getElementById("divShowResults");
         }
         resultsString = document.form1.txtTextString.value;
         resultsString = resultsString.replace
```

```
                        (boundaryRegExp, "<SPAN STYLE='color: red;'>|<\/SPAN>");
                displayResultsDiv.innerHTML = resultsString;
            }
        </SCRIPT>
    </HEAD>
    <BODY>
        <DIV ID='divShowResults'>
        </DIV>
        <FORM NAME='form1'>
            <TEXTAREA ROWS='10' COLS='40' NAME='txtTextString'></TEXTAREA>
            <P>
                Show Word Boundaries - \b
                <INPUT TYPE='radio' NAME='radBoundaryType' CHECKED></INPUT>
                <BR>
                Show Non-Word Boundaries - \B
                <INPUT TYPE='radio' NAME='radBoundaryType'></INPUT>
            </P>
            <BR>
            <INPUT TYPE='button' VALUE='Show Boundaries'
                onClick='cmdShow_onclick()' NAME=cmdShow></INPUT>
            <INPUT TYPE='reset' VALUE='Clear Form'></INPUT>
        </FORM>
    </BODY>
</HTML>
```

Save the page and load it into either IE4+ or Netscape 6 – this example is not compatible with Netscape 4 just to keep things simple. This script will not work with Netscape 4, because Netscape 4 does not support the innerHTML property. Type, "Explore the boundaries of your text" into the text box then hit the Show Boundaries button. As we can see from the screenshot below, the text appears above the text box with the word boundaries marked out by red lines. We can see that between the start of the string (a non-word) and the 'E' (a word character) is the word "boundaries". Next is the boundary between the "e" in "Explore" and the space that is a non-word character. Again, the between space and the "t" in "the" is another word boundary.

If you select the Show Non-Word Boundaries radio button and click the show button again, the text will now instead show non-word boundaries. Enter your own examples and test to see where the word and non-word boundaries appear:

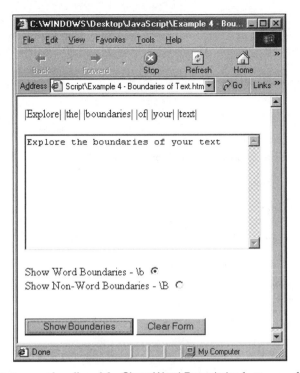

We connect the `onClick` event handler of the Show Word Boundaries button, so that it calls the `cmdShow_onclick()` function. In the function, we create a new regular expression object based on which of the two radio buttons is selected. If it is the first, then our regular expression is `/\b/g`, which will match word boundaries, and because we've set the global flag it will match all the word boundaries. If the second radio button is selected, we set our regular expression to `/\B/g` which will match all the non-word boundaries.

We then get the value of the text in the text box, and using the String object's `replace()` method, and our newly created RegExp object as its first parameter, we replace all the matching boundaries with a | character with the font set to red. Finally, we set the `innerHTML` property of the `divShowResults` to the results of our replacing word or non-word boundaries.

So when would we actually use word boundaries? Imagine we have the following string: "Pauline, Paul, and Paula", in which we want to replace "Paul" with "Ringo". We cannot use:

```
/Paul/g
```

This is because it would match Paul, which is what we want, and the Paul in Pauline, and in Paula. We want to replace Paul with Ringo only where Paul is a whole word on its own (the pattern is positioned between two word boundaries). Therefore, what we need is:

```
/\bPaul\b/g
```

Grouping Characters and Alternation

We are almost at the end of our brief journey through regular expression syntax in JavaScript, just grouping characters and alternation left to cover . We'll look at the | alternation character first.

Alternation Character

Lets say we wanted to match Paul or alternatively John in a regular expression. Without the alternation character, we would need two regular expressions and therefore two different comparisons, but with it we can write just one:

```
/Paul|John/
```

The alternation character becomes even more useful when coupled with grouping.

A Capturing Group – Capturing Parenthesis

In its simplest form, we can group a pattern by placing it inside parenthesis like this:

```
/Paul(a|ine)/
```

This groups the a|ine pattern, which will match the "a" in "Paula" or the "ine" in "Pauline". The Paul at the front obviously matches Paul and put together, the regular expression will match any pattern starting with "Paul" and ending with a pattern matching that grouped in brackets. Added to code, it looks like this:

```
var myRegExp = /Paul(a|ine)/g;
var myString = "Paul, Paula, Pauline.";
myString = myString.replace(myRegExp,"Ringo");
alert(myString);  // Displays Paul, Ringo, Ringo
```

This will display the alert box shown below:

If we wanted to match Paul as well, we use repetition characters, because they specify a certain number of repetitions of the last item, the last item being either a single character or a group:

```
/Paul(a|ine)?/
```

The example above would match Paul, Paula and Pauline because the ? repetition special character will match the group it follows zero or one times. The result with this would be:

If we wanted to match any single word starting with Paul, then that would be:

```
/\bPaul[a-z]*\b/i
```

This will match Paul, Paula, Pauline, Paulo and other permutations, but not the less common name Apaul, as we've added the word boundary characters to stop that. As you've probably spotted, the previous examples above would have matched Apaul due to a lack of boundary character – often the hard part with regular expressions is making sure you cover every possible pattern you want, but no more.

Grouping characters by enclosing them in capturing parenthesis has an additional benefit, in that it captures the characters matched by the group and allows us to use them again later using \groupNumber where groupNumber is the order of the group in the regular expression. This type of group is also known as a **capturing group** – it captures the results of matches made. It will become clearer if we look at an example. Let's imagine that we want to match cases where a word has been repeated, a common typing error. Our example string could be "One man and and his dog." First, we need to match a word:

```
/\b[a-zA-Z]+\b/
```

We start by specifying the pattern must be anchored between word boundaries. Then we define a pattern that will match one or more times the characters inside the square brackets (any letters between a-z or A-Z). Next, we add all of this into a group by wrapping it in parenthesis:

```
/(\b[a-zA-Z]+\b)/
```

Now we have a pattern inside a group that will match a single word. To match a second word that is identical to the pattern matched by the group, we add \s\1.

```
/(\b[a-zA-Z]+\b)\s\1/
```

The \s specifies any whitespace character and the \1 specifies to match the same characters as were matched by group 1. Let's put this in a simple example:

```
var myRegExp = /(\b[a-zA-Z]+\b)\s\1/;
if (myRegExp.test("One man and and his dog."))
{
    alert("There's a repeated word");
}
else
{
    alert("No repeated words");
}
```

A Non-Capturing Group – Non-Capturing Parenthesis (IE5.5+/NN6+ Only)

This groups a pattern in just the same way as the capturing group, except we won't be able to access the specific characters matched by each group, either inside the regular expression or via JavaScript later. However, in our /Paul(a|ine)?/ regular expression we saw earlier, this is not a problem. Indeed, because it's not capturing the matches, the non-capturing method is more efficient. To group without capturing we would write:

```
/Paul(?:a|ine)?/
```

The difference is simply that we've added ?: after the opening parenthesis. Apart from that, it works the same. As it is non-capturing, we cannot use it with, /(\b[a-zA-Z]+\b)\s\1/, our regular expression that matches duplicate words, because for that example to work, we rely on capturing the results of characters matched by a regular expression group.

Positive Look-Ahead Grouping (IE5.5+/NN6+ Only)

The regular expression syntax for this sort of group is (?=pattern). The difference between this type of grouping and the two we saw above is that the pattern matched by this type of group does not form part of the final results; that is, the result of the match is not captured. This will make more sense when we look at the RegExp and String object and their exec() and match() methods that allow us to access the characters of each match made.

Previously the characters matched by any group are captured and considered a part of the match, which we can access inside the regular expression with \groupNumber. Positive look-ahead grouping is non-capturing – although a match must be made on the group, the matches are not captured but instead thrown away and not be included in the results. Matching of the pattern continues from the after the last match and not after the match made by the group; it is like the pattern in the group was never there, even though it must be matched upon for a full pattern match to be made. It's handy for where we want to match something, but don't want the match to form part of the results. So for example, look at:

```
/ABC(?=123)\d/
```

This would match the pattern starting with ABC, which contains 123 in the middle, and ends with any digit. The 123 matched in the group is not actually captured and will not form part of the result strings. So

```
ABC12345
```

Will be matched by the regular expression but the match result would be:

```
ABC1
```

The question is, why is the match not:

```
ABC4
```

This type of group does its match, but then instead of matching of the \d continuing with the digit 4, the next character in the string after the group, the \d is matched with the character after the last match made by the consuming pattern, here the ABC pattern, before the group – in this case the digit 1. This is shown in the diagram below:

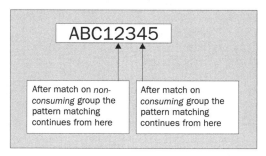

Let's look at a slightly more useful example where we have a string of names like this "The characters are Frasier Crane, Daphne Moon, Niles Crane, and Marty Crane" and we want to capture all the first names but don't want to capture the last names. Our regular expression could look like this:

```
/\b[A-Z][a-z]+(?= [A-Z][a-z]+\b)/g
```

Let's break the this down. We know that we need to match first names followed by second names, but we only want the first name part to form the results of the match. We have assumed that two words separated by a space and with both starting with capital letters are the first and last names of people. The first part of our pattern is \b[A-Z][a-z]+, which matches a word boundary followed by a capital letter of the range A–Z, then followed by one or more lower case letters.

The second part of the pattern is our positive look-ahead group; this matches a space and again a word starting with a capital letter followed, by one or more lower case letters, and ending at a word boundary. By placing the pattern in a positive look-ahead group, we force the pattern to be matched, but avoid having it as part of the result.

Let's put this together in a short example:

```
<!-- 07 Positive look ahead.htm -->
<HTML>
<BODY>
   <SCRIPT language='JavaScript'>
      var matchFirstNamesRegExp = /\b[A-Z][a-z]+(?= [A-Z][a-z]+\b)/g;
      var names = "The cast are Frasier Crane, Daphne Moon, Niles Crane ";
      names += "and Marty Crane.";
      var matchResultsArray = names.match(matchFirstNamesRegExp);
      var arrayIndex;

      for (arrayIndex = 0; arrayIndex < matchResultsArray.length;
         arrayIndex++)
      {
         document.write(matchResultsArray[arrayIndex] + "<BR>");
      }
   </SCRIPT>
</BODY>
</HTML>
```

This produces the results shown below:

We'll look at the String object's match() method later, but for now it's enough to know that it returns in an array all the matching strings based on the RegExp object passed as a parameter.

Negative Look-ahead Grouping (IE5.5+/NN6+ Only)

This works exactly like the positive look-ahead grouping, except that instead of matching the pattern inside the group, it matches any pattern that does not match the pattern specified inside the group. Its syntax is:

```
/(?!pattern)/
```

As an example, if we had the string "New England, New Hampshire, New Haven, New York" and wanted to match any place that started with "New" but didn't end in "Hampshire or "York", then our regular expression could be:

```
/\bNew (?!Hampshire|York)[a-zA-Z]+\b/g
```

Here we are matching a pattern that starts by matching a word boundary followed by New, followed by a space. Then comes our negative look-ahead group that will match anything as long as its not Hampshire or York. As this is also a non-consuming grouping, the `[a-zA-Z]+` will match from the first character after the space following New rather than after the end of the pattern matched by the group itself. Assuming no match is made on Hampshire or York it's the `[a-zA-Z]+` which matches the characters following the "New", in our example, England and Haven. Any pattern matched by the non-capturing group – like the positive look-ahead group any matching pattern is not returned as part of the results. Finally, we have a word boundary character.

Put in the context of some code, this gives us:

```
<!-- 08 - Negative look ahead.htm -->
<HTML>
<BODY>
    <SCRIPT LANGUAGE='JavaScript'>
        var matchPlaceNamesRegExp = /\bNew (?!Hampshire|York)[a-zA-Z]+\b/g;
        var names = "New England, New Hampshire, New Haven, New York";
        var matchResultsArray = names.match(matchPlaceNamesRegExp);
        var arrayIndex;

        for (arrayIndex = 0; arrayIndex < matchResultsArray.length;
            arrayIndex++)
        {
            document.write(matchResultsArray[arrayIndex] + "<BR>");
        }
    </SCRIPT>
</BODY>
</HTML>
```

The results of this are shown below:

As before, we have used the String object's `match()` method, and passed it the RegExp object we created on the first line.

That completes our look at regular expression syntax in JavaScript. Before we move on and look at the RegExp and String objects and their use of regular expressions, let's look at a couple of real world examples of regular expressions.

Each of the grouping method characters and the alternation character are shown in the table below:

Character	Description
|	Alternation character, for example /apples|pears/ will match either apples or pears in a string, for example: "The apples were lovely."

Character	Description
(pattern)	Capturing parenthesis – pattern inside parenthesis will be grouped and treated as a whole. Results of matched groups are captured and available for later use, for example via *groupnumber* (a so-called back-reference).
(?:pattern)	Non-capturing parenthesis – works as capturing parenthesis but results of matching groups not captured. Only supported in IE5.5+ and Netscape 6.
(?=pattern)	Positive look ahead grouping – pattern inside group must be found but is not captured for reference later, using *groupNumber* and won't be contained in the strings returned as part of the final results of matches made. So, /Wrox (?=Press|Press Ltd)/ will match "Wrox Press" and "Wrox Press Ltd", but only "Wrox" is returned as the match results, the "Press" and "Press Ltd" are discarded. Only supported in IE5.5+ and Netscape 6.
(?!pattern)	Negative look-ahead grouping – works as the Positive look-ahead grouping, except matches are made only where the pattern inside the group is not found. So /Wrox (?!Press|Press Ltd)/ will match "Wrox", but won't match where it is followed by "Press" or "Press Ltd". Only supported in IE5.5+ and Netscape 6.
\\groupNumber	*groupNumber* will match the same characters as were matched by the group, which is the *groupNumber* group in the regular expression. So \\1 will match the same characters as were matched by the first group in the regular expression, \\2 the second, and so on. This is called a back-reference. Only works with capturing parenthesis – (pattern) type group where matches made by the group are captured and available for use later in the regular expression.

We're going to take a brief look at some more useful examples of regular expressions. These will be then put into use in the next chapter, *Form Validation*. This itself will be put to good use in Chapter 22, *Shopping Cart Application*.

Validating a ZIP Code's Format

For our first example, we'll look at something simple – checking the format of a ZIP code. US ZIP codes come in two formats (12345 or 12345-1234), so we either need to match five digits or five digits with a dash, and another four digits at the end.

So, to match the five digits:

```
/\d{5}/
```

To match the dash and four digits, we use:

```
/-\d{4}\/
```

We can't just add it on the end of the previous match as it's optional, we need to put it in a non-capturing group and use the ? special character to specify that the group can appear zero or one times. This makes our whole expression:

```
/\d{5}(?:-\d{4})?/
```

If we try this, we will find that while it confirms valid results, such as "12345" or "12345-9876", it will also say that "12345-XXXX" and "!!!12345!!!!!" are valid. This is because we have not anchored the pattern to appear at any particular point in the string. We need to specify that the pattern is the only thing allowed in the string and we do this by specifying it must appear at the start and the end of the string using the ^ and $ special characters:

```
/^\d{5}(?:-\d{4})?$/
```

Validating an E-mail Address's Format

In this section, we'll look at checking the validity of e-mail addresses. We can't actually check the existence of the e-mail address, but at least we can check that it is valid.

The first task is to actually work out which patterns we want to match, and which ones we don't. Let's start by listing the sort of patterns we expect our e-mail addresses to take:

```
someone@mailserver.com

someone.something@mailserver.com

someone.something@subdomain.mailserver.com

someone@mailserver.co.uk

someone@subdomain.mailserver.co.uk

someone.something@mailserver.co.uk

someone@mailserver.org.uk

someone@subdomain.mailserver.org.uk
```

We could go on and list many more variations, but at least we have an idea of what to aim for in terms of valid patterns to match. Assuming we will have international customers, we also need to allow for things like .co.jp, .org.de, and so on.

To describe trying to write a regular expression that handles all of the above patterns is quite a challenge. The best thing to do is split it into manageable chunks, so let's start at the beginning and deal with the section before the @.

First, let's deal with someone@ – this is easy enough, as it is just one or more of the \w class of characters followed by a @.

```
/\w+@/
```

The problem with this is that something like "!!""££$$someone@" would be valid.

We need to ensure that either the e-mail address starts at a word boundary or even better that it is at the very start of the string – we're assuming that the string will contain only the e-mail address. Therefore, we need to add the ^ special character at the start to make sure it is positioned at the start of the string.

```
/^\w+@/
```

Now we need to handle "someone.something@" – Note the . is a special character in regular expressions and so normally needs to have a \ in front. In fact, inside the [] is an exception to the rule and the \ is optional.We could do this:

```
/^[\.\w]+@/
```

This would indeed match someone.something@, but it would also match someone..something@, which is not valid. To stop this, we need to prevent more than one . in succession. What we need is to say we want a group of characters whose pattern is zero or one . followed by one \w class character. We want one or more of these patterns, so let's change our expression:

```
/^(\.?\w)+@/
```

We've used a capturing group for reasons of backwards compatibility with Netscape 4 and IE4 and IE5. We're not interested in capturing the results of the group's match, so for efficiency a non-capturing group would work, but only with IE5.5 and Netscape 6. Our group can consist of a dot followed by a letter or just a letter, and this can appear one or more times. It prevents two dots together, but it does allow .someone@.

E-mail addresses cannot start with a dot. They must start with a \w class character so let's change our regular expression again:

```
/^\w(\.?\w)+@/
```

The only thing missing is support for the "-" character. To add it to our regular expression, we use the [] brackets to specify the \w and - characters:

```
/^\w(\.?[\w-])+@/
```

Dealing with the part after the @ is a little easier, because we already have some of the code written. After the @ part, we want to match mailserver or mailserver.subdomain, which is the same as someone and someone.something.

Therefore, we can make our regular expression:

```
/^\w(\.?[\w-])+@\w(\.?[\w-])+/
```

Now we need to add support for the .com, .co.uk and the .org.uk parts. The alternatives are three letters alone, or three letters followed by two letters. Another alternative is two letters followed by two letters. We can check for three letters followed by an optional dot and two letters like this:

```
/[a-z]{3}(\.[a-z]{2})?/
```

To match two letters followed by a dot and then two more letters requires this:

```
/[a-z]{2}\.[a-z]{2}/
```

Either of these two alternatives is acceptable, so we need to use the alternation character and add them at the end of the current regular expression, not forgetting the compulsory .:

```
/^\w(\.?\w)+@\w(\.?[-\w])+\.[a-z]{3}(?:\.[a-z]{2})?|[a-z]{2}\.[a-z]{2}/
```

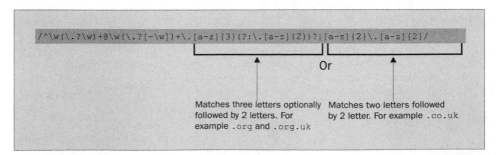

We still need to make sure that there is only an e-mail address in the string and nothing else. Currently, something like `someone.something@as.com.www!!!!!!` would be valid.

We need to add the `$` character to specify that the pattern should be at the end:

```
/^\w(\.?\w)+@\w(\.?[-\w])+\.[a-z]{3}(\.[a-z]{2})?|[a-z]{2}\.[a-z]{2}$/i
```

As case does not effect the validity, we have also added an `i` flag to make it case insensitive.

Now there's still one last mistake – the `$` at the end applies only to the pattern after the alternation character so `someone@something.co.uk!!!` would be invalid, but `someone@something.com!!!` would be valid, as it is the pattern to the left of the alternation character that is matching it. We need to group the parts that check for `.co.uk` and `.com`, and so on.

```
/^\w(\.?\w)*@\w(\.?[-\w])*\.([a-z]{3,4}
(\.[a-z]{2})?|[a-z]{2}(\.[a-z]{2})?)$/i
```

We have enclosed `\.[a-z]{2})?|[a-z]{2}\.[a-z]{2}` in a capturing group, so now one or the other of the patterns inside the group will be matched, but the `$` at the end is outside the group and is a compulsory part of the pattern.

That completes the look at the e-mail pattern matching regular expression. At first glance, it looks horrendous, but when the problem and regular expression is broken down into easy stages, we find it's not so bad at all. We'll see this regular expression in use in the next chapter and again in Chapter 22.

Using Regular Expressions in JavaScript

We've seen how to create regular expressions in JavaScript and the regular expression syntax supported. We'll now look at the objects in JavaScript that support regular expressions and examine their more commonly used properties and methods.

First, we'll look at the global RegExp object, then the RegExp object instance, and finally the String object. We've already talked about the RegExp object we can create using new `RegExp()` or with `/myPattern/`, but as we'll see shortly, there is a global RegExp object whose properties reflect matches made using RegExp objects we have created.

Global RegExp Object

There are two types of RegExp object. We've already seen the first, this is an instance of the RegExp type that we create ourselves using the new keyword or with `/regular expression/`. The browser also has a different RegExp, which is automatically created by the browser. We can't create a global RegExp object, but just like the Math object, we can use its static methods and properties. We'll refer to a RegExp we create ourselves as a RegExp instance, and the other as a global RegExp. Whenever a successful match is made on an instance of a RegExp object, the global RegExp object has its various properties updated. Values of the properties from a previous match are overridden from the latest successful match. Note it is only successful matches that will update the global RegExp object; as far as the global RegExp object is concerned, unsuccessful matches are ignored and it will continue to hold details of the last successful match. As the object is global, we don't need to create it, but simply use it, for example:

```
var inputValue = RegExp.input;
```

The global RegExp object has no methods, only properties, and we discuss each of them below. Note that all properties are read-only; although we can change them, there will be no effect. All of the properties are available in Netscape 4 and later, except the index property. IE5.5 supports all of the properties. IE4 and 5 only support the input, $1...9 and lastIndex properties. IE4 and 5 support on the Mac is even more limited, and use of the global RegExp is probably best avoided for that platform; most of the examples will not work on the Mac.

One situation to be aware of is when we have a frameset with a RegExp object instance in one frame that we are accessing from another frame. In this circumstance, the global RegExp, which will be affected by any successful matches, will be the one with the RegExp object instance in it, not the global RegExp of the page from which we're accessing it.

$1...$9 Properties

These return the characters matched by each capturing group. The number can be from 1 to 9 and is based on the order of the group inside the regular expression.

Suppose we have if the regular expression:

```
/\d\d (\w\w\w) \w\w (\s\s)/
```

If there was a successful match, then RegExp.$1 would return the characters matched by (\w\w\w) and RegExp.$2 would match the second group (\s\s). There are no more groups and so RegExp.$3 and above will return an empty string. Remember that only a capturing group returns sub-matches in groups.

In the example below, we create a regular expression that will check for one of three browser names, Microsoft, Netscape, and Opera. Using the test() method and passing the window object's navigator.appName, we check to see if this is one of our three supported browsers. If so, then we can obtain its name from the first and only group in the regular expression using the global RegExp object's $1. If there is no match, then browserName remains at its initialized value of Unknown.

```
<!-- 09 - Browser check.htm -->
<HTML>
<BODY>
    <SCRIPT LANGUAGE='JavaScript'>
        var browserName = "Unknown";
        var browserCheckRegExp = /(Microsoft|Netscape|Opera)/;
        if (browserCheckRegExp.test(navigator.appName))
        {
            browserName = RegExp.$1;
        }

        alert(browserName);
    </SCRIPT>
</BODY>
</HTML>
```

index Property

This returns the first character position in the last successful match. So, if our regular expression is:

```
/\d\d\d/
```

And our string is:

```
"007, also known as James Bond"
```

A successful match, for example using `exec()`, which we'll talk about shortly, or `test()`, would leave index with a value of zero, as we can see in the following code which works on IE4+:

```
var myRegExp = /\d\d\d/;
myRegExp.test("007, also known as James Bond");
alert(RegExp.index);
```

As with the other properties of the global RegExp object, only successful matches cause the index to change. In the code below for example, the second `alert()` shows 0, even though there is no match, it still holds the value from the previous successful match.

```
var myRegExp = /\d\d\d/;
myRegExp.test("007, also known as James Bond");
alert(RegExp.index);
myRegExp.test("James Bond licensed to kill");
alert(RegExp.index);
```

input Property

In IE4+ this returns the value of the string searched in the last successful match. In the example below, the `alert()` will display "007, also known as James Bond":

```
var myRegExp = /\d\d\d/;
myRegExp.test("007, also known as James Bond");
alert(RegExp.input);
```

This property is not fully supported by Netscape browsers; the example above will display an empty string.

lastIndex Property (IE4+ only)

This is the character position after the last matching character in the last successful match. As with the index property, it is a zero-based index, so the first character in a string is zero, the second 1, and so on. It is identical to the `lastIndex` we saw for a RegExp object instance, except it contains the value of the `lastIndex` of the last successful match of any RegExp object instance in the page, rather than that for a specific RegExp object. In the example below, the 007 will be matched. The character after the 7 has an index of 2 and the next character after it has a `lastIndex`, of 3. Remember that string indexing starts at zero (first character has index of 0, next of two, and so on).

```
var myRegExp = /\d\d\d/;
myRegExp.test("007, also known as James Bond");
alert(RegExp.lastIndex);
```

lastMatch Property

This contains the actual characters matched in the last successful match. In the example below, `lastMatch` is 007.

```
var myRegExp = /\d\d\d/;
myRegExp.test("007, also known as James Bond");
alert(RegExp.lastMatch);
```

lastParen Property

This property gives us the characters matched in the last capturing group in the last successful match. In the code below, `lastParen` will be 7. It is only the last capturing parenthesis whose match will be returned, while the non-capturing parenthesis will be ignored.

```
var myRegExp = /(\d\d)(\d)/;
myRegExp.test("007, also known as James Bond");
alert(RegExp.lastParen);
```

leftContext Property

This gives us the characters from the beginning of a searched string up to the position before the beginning of the last successful match. In the example below, this will return James Bond and a trailing space (everything apart from the 007 matched):

```
var myRegExp = /\d\d\d/;
myRegExp.test("James Bond 007");
alert(RegExp.leftContext);
```

rightContext Property

This returns the characters from the character following the successful last match to the end of the searched string. In the example below, this will return "James Bond", this time with the space before James Bond also being included, (everything to the right of the pattern matched):

```
var myRegExp = /\d\d\d/;
myRegExp.test("007 James Bond");
alert(RegExp.rightContext);
```

RegExp Object

We saw near the beginning of the chapter how we can create instances of the RegExp object using the new operator together with the constructor function:

```
var myRegExp = new RegExp("regular_expression_pattern");
```

Or with a regular expression literal:

```
var myRegExp = /regular_expression_pattern/
```

We also saw the test() method in use and as it's quite simple anyway, we won't cover it again. We'll start by looking at the compile() method.

compile() method

At the beginning of the chapter when we talked about the two ways of creating a RegExp object and setting the regular expression syntax, we mentioned that using: new RegExp() and passing the regular expression to the constructor was marginally less efficient then the method using /myRegularExpression/ because the second method compiled the regular expression pattern into a more efficient internal format.

If we want to test with a number of varying regular expressions, we can create just one RegExp object, use the compile() method to set its regular expression pattern, and change the pattern as much as we like, saving on the time required to create a RegExp object. The time saving is small and so only important if we are doing a vast number of regular expression matches or tests.

The first argument of the compile() method is the regular expression string itself. As the method name suggests, the pattern is compiled into the efficient internal format. Using compile() where we have a number of regular expression patterns, and plan to use each of them multiple times, is not only efficient as the regular expression is compiled, but also means only one RegExp object has to be created. This is more efficient than creating multiple objects.

The `compile()` method's second argument is the flags we want to set (the `i`, `g` and `m` flags). So to use the `compile()` method with our Zip Code checking regular expression, we would write:

```
<!-- 10 ZIP Validation.htm -->
<HTML>
<BODY>
   <SCRIPT LANGUAGE='JavaScript'>
      var myRegExp = new RegExp();
      myRegExp.compile("^\\d{5}(?:-\\d{4})?$","i");

      var myZipCode = prompt("Enter a Zip code","");
      if (myRegExp.test(myZipCode))
      {
         alert("Valid Zip");
      }
      else
      {
         alert("Invalid Zip");
      }
   </SCRIPT>
</BODY>
</HTML>
```

We start by creating a new RegExp object instance, then use `compile()` to set our Zip checking regular expression. Note that we've set the case insensitive flag as the compile method's second parameter. This is not necessary in this case and is included for example purposes only. To set the global and multi-line flags, we'd write:

```
myRegExp.compile("^\\d{5}(?:-\\d{4})?$","gmi");
```

The order the flags are set is not important. We obtain a Zip code from the user using the `prompt()` method, and then test to see if it matches our Zip matching regular expression and use the result in an `if` statement to let the user know if it is valid or not.

Here is the user prompt:

exec() Method

The `exec()` method executes a search of a matching pattern inside the string passed as the method's only argument. If there is no matching pattern then null is returned, otherwise it returns a special type of array with details of the last match made. This special array has the following properties:

Property	Accessed Using	Description
input	resultsArray.input resultsArray["input"]	Whole string that was searched on.
index	resultsArray.index resultsArray["index"]	The character index in the string from which the pattern match started.

Property	Accessed Using	Description
lastIndex	resultsArray.lastIndex resultsArray["lastIndex"]	The character index at which the next match will start.
[0]	resultsArray[0]	Value of the whole match made – combination of [1]...[n] concatenated.
[1]...[n]	resultsArray[1] resultsArray[2] ... resultsArray[n]	Value of each captured sub group.

Where exec() actually starts its pattern matching from is determined by the RegExp object instance's lastIndex property, which is automatically updated after each exec() performed on a RegExp object. We can also set its value ourselves. If the regular expression has its global flag set, then the next matching pattern starting from the character with index of lastIndex will be matched. If the global flag is not set, then searching for a pattern will always start at the beginning of the string. Either way, the results array won't contain details of all matching patterns.

As each exec() is called, its not just the properties of the RegExp object instance itself that are updated, but also of the global RegExp. We'll see what these properties are and how exec() affects them in the next section. For now let's look at an example in which we have a string containing a list of names separated by commas, such as "Homer Simpson, Ralph Wigam, Lisa Simpson, Apu Nahasapeemapetilon". Let's imagine we want to extract each persons name in the list, but have access to their first and last names separately.

Our regular expression syntax is:

```
/\b([a-z]*) ([a-z]+)/gi
```

This matches a word boundary, followed by one or more letters; this is the first name, and has been grouped so that we can obtain them as a subgroup in our code later. Then follows a space, and then the surname that is again one or more letters in a group so we can obtain them as a subgroup. We have set the g and i flags. If we didn't set the g flag, the search would always start at the beginning of the string regardless of the lastIndex value.

There is the code to do the search and display the results:

```
<!-- 11 - Exec Method.htm -->
<HTML>
<BODY>
    <DIV ID='resultsDiv'></DIV>
    <SCRIPT LANGUAGE='JavaScript'>
        var myRegExp = /\b([a-z]*) ([a-z]*)/gi;
        var myString = "Homer Simpson, Ralph Wigam, Lisa Simpson, "
            + "Apu Nahasapeemapetilon";
        var resultsHTML = "";
        var resultsArray;

        while ((resultsArray = myRegExp.exec(myString)) != null)
        {
            resultsHTML += "<P>Full name = " + resultsArray[0] + "<BR>";
            resultsHTML += "First name = " + resultsArray[1] + "<BR>";
```

```
            resultsHTML += "Last Name = " + resultsArray[2] + "<BR>";
            resultsHTML += "lastIndex = " + myRegExp.lastIndex + "</P>";
        }

        document.write(resultsHTML);
    </SCRIPT>
  </BODY>
</HTML>
```

The results of the code are shown in the screenshot below:

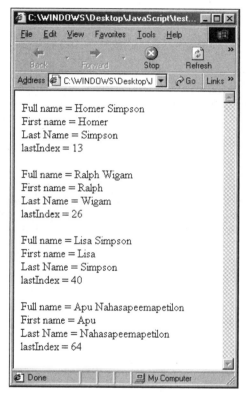

The loop continues while the return value from the exec() method is not null. Remember when there is no match, null is returned. Then we obtain from the results array the full match, the first sub match (our first group) and finally the second sub-match. Additionally, we obtain the value of lastIndex from our RegExp object instance. If we had a non-capturing match in our regular expression using (?:pattern), then the sub-values would not have been available to us in the array, only the full matching pattern.

Each time the exec() is called, we can see that lastIndex is set to the next character in the string after the pattern matched. The next time exec() is called, matching starts from there. This only happens if the global flag is set, otherwise matching always starts from the beginning and in this code, missing off the global flag would lead to an infinite loop – certainly an easy mistake to make and one to watch out for.

lastIndex Property

We have seen the lastIndex property in use above and discussed it when looking at the global RegExp object. We found that when the exec() or test() methods are executed, its value will be: 0, if there is no match, and if there is a match, then it is set to the next position following the most recent match.

If we set `lastIndex` to a value greater than the length of the string being searched, then 0 is returned and no match made. If it is equal to the length of the string, the regular expression matches if the pattern matches the empty string. Otherwise, there is no match and `lastIndex` is set to -1. It is important to note that in Netscape browsers, we must set the global flag for the `lastIndex` property to work, otherwise we'll find its value will always be undefined.

Regular Expression Support with the String Object

In this final section, we will look at the String object's methods that make use of regular expressions.

search() Method

The `search()` method searches the string in the String object for a pattern matching that specified by the RegExp passed as the methods only argument. If a match is found, then the character position of the first matching character is returned. As it is a zero-based index, the first character is 0, the second 1, and so on. If no match is made then -1 is returned.

If a successful match is made, then the global RegExp object will be updated and its properties accessed as shown in the example below:

```
var myRegExp = /\d\d\d/;
var myString = "Ah 007 we meet at last";
alert(myString.search(myRegExp));
alert(RegExp.lastMatch);
```

In this example `search()` will return 3 and the global RegExp object's `lastMatch` property will be 007.

split() Method

This method splits a string at each point where a match with the RegExp object, passed as a parameter, is made. It returns an array containing the results of the split. Unlike the methods we've seen previously, the `split()` method does not require the global flag to be set; it will match all the points to split at without the need for this flag.

The key to the `split()` method is making sure that your regular expression matches all the characters you want the string split on and those that you don't. If for example, we wanted to split a sentence into just the individual words, but didn't want the spaces, tabs, or any punctuation characters, then we would need a regular expression like this:

```
/\b[\s\W]*/
```

If we had a string like "The cat sat, with a big sigh, on the mat." and split just along word boundaries or spaces, we would have the punctuation left in. Shown below is an example of the code required to split the sentence and display the array with each word on a separate line without the punctuation:

```
var myRegExp = /\b[\s\W]*/;
var myString = "The cat sat, with a big sigh, on the mat.";
var resultsArray = myString.split(myRegExp);
var arrayItem;

for (arrayItem in resultsArray)
{
    document.write(resultsArray[arrayItem] + "<BR>");
}
```

match() Method

The match() method takes a RegExp object as the parameter and it returns an array if matches are found or null otherwise. If the global flag on the RegExp object instance is set, then the individual elements of the array will contain each of the pattern matches found inside the string. If the global flag is not set, then the first element of the array will contain the first matching characters; the remaining elements contain any capturing group matches, defined in the regular expression syntax, if any.

As well as the array's indexed elements, with the results the array has three properties: input, index, and lastIndex. These match properties of the same names in the global object, which is also updated if a successful match is made.

Input is the whole string searched, index is the character in the string in which the last successful match was made, and lastIndex is the character after the last successful match.

The differences made by setting the g flag is demonstrated in the code below:

```
<!-- 13 - Match Method.htm -->
<HTML>
<BODY>
   <SCRIPT LANGUAGE='JavaScript'>
      // Global match
      var zipCodes = "12345-6543, 90210, 99882, 11225-4455, 11223";
      var matchZipCodesRegExp = /\d{5}(-\d{4})?/;
      var matchResultsArray = zipCodes.match(matchZipCodesRegExp);
      var arrayIndex;

      document.write("<H4>Non Global Match</H4>");

      for (arrayIndex = 0; arrayIndex < matchResultsArray.length;
         arrayIndex++)
      {
         document.write(matchResultsArray[arrayIndex] + "<BR>");
      }

      document.write("<H4>Global Match</H4>");
      matchZipCodesRegExp = /\d{5}(-\d{4})?/g;
      matchResultsArray = zipCodes.match(matchZipCodesRegExp);
      for (arrayIndex = 0; arrayIndex < matchResultsArray.length;
         arrayIndex++)
      {
         document.write(matchResultsArray[arrayIndex] + "<BR>");
      }
   </SCRIPT>
</BODY>
</HTML>
```

This code writes the following to the page:

In the first regular expression, we are matching a Zip code using the same syntax as we saw earlier in the chapter, that is, matching 5 digits optionally followed by the pattern of a dash, followed by four digits contained in the first and only group in this pattern.

```
var matchZipCodesRegExp = /\d{5}(-\d{4})?/;
```

Note that in this first RegExp object, we are not setting the global flag. So when we obtain an array of matching values using the match() method, it contains just the matches; the first element contains the whole match made, and the second element contains the characters matched by the first and only group in this regular expression. These results are written out to the page using a for loop.

Then we create a second regular expression, identical to the first except the RegExp has its g flag set.

```
matchZipCodesRegExp = /\d{5}(-\d{4})?/g;
```

Using match() to obtain an array of resulting matches and looping through it, we see that the array does not contain one match and all the regular expression capturing-group matches, but instead, each individual array element contains each match found in the string.

replace() Method

The replace() method returns a string in which any patterns matching the regular expression contained in the RegExp object passed as the first parameter have been replaced with the string specified in the second parameter. If the g flag is set in the RegExp object then all matching patterns in the string will be replaced, otherwise only the first match. Note that the original string remains unchanged; it is the string returned which has been searched and replaced.

We saw this method earlier in the chapter, but what we didn't look at was the ability to use sub-group matches in the regular expression as part of the replacement string. We have seen that in regular expressions \n can be used to refer to the characters matched by the capturing group whose number is based on the position in the regular expression. We can use something similar in the replacement string, except instead of \n it is $n. For instance, $1 will replace the characters matched by group 1, $2 by group 2 and so on, up to $9 for group 9. Let's look at an example in which we want to update the year, but leave the month unchanged. Note it works in IE, but will need some modification to work in Netscape; we'll talk about that shortly:

```
var yearUpdateRegExp = /\b([A-Z][a-z]* )\d\d\d\d/g;
var myString = "Last year over 9000 people attended the events ";
myString += "which next time will be held in May 2000 and July 2000";
var myString = myString.replace(yearUpdateRegExp,"$12002");
alert(myString);
```

In the regular expression, we start by matching a word boundary, then comes our first group. This group will match the month, based on the assumption in this sentence that any word starting with a capital letter is a month. Then at the end, we match the four digits of the year.

When we use the `replace()` method, you'll notice in the second argument we have passed is `$12002` – the `$1` will be whatever characters were matched by the first group. When May 2000 is matched, it will be May and when it is June 2000, it will be June. If we try to run this example, we may hit problems due to this line:

```
var myString = myString.replace(yearUpdateRegExp,"$12002");
```

The problem is that Netscape thinks we mean group number 12002 and not group 1 and the digits 2002. We can easily correct this for Netscape 6 like this:

```
var myString = myString.replace(yearUpdateRegExp,"$012002");
```

In Netscape 6, the `$` can go up to 99, in compliance with the ECMAScript 3 standard. So now Netscape 6 knows we mean group 01 or 1 rather than group 12. This still won't work with Netscape 4, and we need to re-write our regular expression so that the space is out the group:

```
var yearUpdateRegExp = /\b([A-Z][a-z]*) \d\d\d\d/g;
```

Now our `replace()` method can include the space as well:

```
var myString = myString.replace(yearUpdateRegExp,"$1 2002");
```

This makes it quite clear to the browser that it is group 1 and the digits 2002. It's one of those cross browser, hair pulling out things we come across from time to time.

Summary

In this chapter, we have taken a rapid tour through the regular expression syntax, and objects that can use regular expressions in JavaScript. Though perhaps daunting at first, we saw that if broken down into easy steps, regular expressions are actually fairly straightforward and enable us to do complex form validation and string replacement, which would normally take 10 times the amount of code.

We covered:

❑ The regular expression syntax and flags

❑ Special characters within regular expressions

❑ Grouping characters

❑ The global RegExp object and its properties

❑ The RegExp instance object and its methods

❑ Regular expression support with the String object – covering its methods

Regular expression syntax in JavaScript 1.2/JScript is based on regular expressions in Perl 4 and JavaScript 1.5. JScript 5 is based on Perl 5. To find out more about regular expression syntax look out for books on Perl's regular expressions.

Pro JavaScript 2nd Edition

Form Validation

In Chapter 5, *Forms and Data*, we looked briefly at basic form validation. In this chapter we'll extend the form validation beyond just checking that fields have been filled in and that the information is basically valid. We'll be using the knowledge we gained in the previous chapter on regular expressions and seeing how they can be used to check that data supplied by the user contains only valid characters and is in a format applicable to the information. For example, if the user entered their e-mail address as "Not Telling!!!" then we can see it contains invalid characters and that its format is also incorrect.

As well as checking the characters and format of the data, we'll also see how we can apply logical rules to check validity. For example, credit card numbers can be checked against certain rules to see if they are valid. We can also set ranges to ensure only valid data is supplied. For example, if the user enters "May 23 3000" as their date of birth then it's possible that they have got it wrong.

As we go along, we will build up validation methods of a JavaScript form validation class. In the final part of the chapter, using the validation class, we will create a form validation system that automates much of the form validation process. You will see that it is very easy to incorporate it in your pages for an almost off-the-shelf form checker. In addition, it's been designed to be easily extensible, so if you find there is a type of information it does not check, it will be very easy to add it. A system like this means all your form checking code can be in one place and easily re-used to save time.

The Validate Class

In this section we will add a number of methods to our validation class so that it can carry out the following types of checks:

❑ **Validating Basic Information.** This is the most basic type of checking where we simply check that the data only consists of certain characters (for example ensuring that data contains only letter characters, and no numbers or punctuation characters). This type of checking is useful where the data does not fit any particular format, (unlike an e-mail address, where there is always a certain pattern), or the data cannot be validated using an algorithm. The methods we create here will be used later on in our validation class.

❑ **Validating Age.** A valid age consists only of number characters and must be within a certain range. For example, -1 is not a valid age, nor is 200 (at least not for any human being I've met). This method will check these sorts of parameters.

❑ **Validating Passwords.** This method does not check that a password is correct, but checks that any password entered by the user conforms to certain standards, for example, does it have the required minimum number of characters, is there any punctuation in it, and so on. There are many different possibilities as to what these parameters could be, but we can easily change these if we so wish.

❑ **Validating Telephone Numbers.** Telephone numbers can be validated in terms of what characters they contain and the pattern of those characters. As the pattern of characters varies from country to country, the method adopts a loose pattern checking approach.

❑ **Validating Zip/Post Codes.** As with telephone numbers, postal codes can be checked in terms of which characters they can contain and the format allowed. This method will check for a valid US Zip code or UK postcode.

❑ **Validating E-Mail Addresses.** We check that the e-mail address contains only valid characters and is in a valid format, for example me@me.com or me@me.co.uk .

❑ **Validating Dates.** We have two methods for validating dates. The first checks that a given day, month and year combination would be valid. For example, 29th February 1999 is not valid as that was not a leap year, but 29th February 2000 is valid, because 2000 was a leap year. We don't attempt to check that a date value contained in a string is valid because of the massive number of possible of valid date formats. Our second method extends the first by also checking that the date would be valid as a date of birth for a living person. This means dates in the future or way back in the past would be invalid.

❑ **Validating Credit Card Details.** For card validation, we have a number of methods for checking that the expiry date is valid and for checking that a given credit card number could be valid. We can check that the card number contains only valid characters, but we'll see that different card types must also conform to certain parameters, such as having a certain number of characters and starting with certain digits. We'll also see that a special algorithm, the **Luhn Formula**, can be used to check that a card number could be valid. We say *could be* valid because while the number could in theory be used by a credit card company, it doesn't necessarily mean they *have* used it. Only server-side processing can fully check a number, but at least with this method we can perform initial checks.

Before we turn to form validation and start adding methods to the validation class, we first need to create that class and look briefly at how we incorporate it in our pages to make use of it. The concepts behind classes in JavaScript were covered in Chapter 3, *JavaScript OOP Techniques*.

First, we need to create a .js file. You can use the text editor of your choice. Enter the code below and save the file as Validate.js. All the code examples in this chapter are available for download from http://www.wrox.com/.

```
//
//    Define Validate class Constructor
//

function Validate() {}
```

That's as far as the class goes for now until we extend it in the next section, when we add lots of methods for the validation of different types of information. The class constructor is called whenever a new object instance of our class is created. We don't have any code we need to execute in the constructor, so it is left blank.

We've used the term **object instance**. What do we mean by that? The class we'll be defining is like a template or blueprint, for an object. We can't use the class itself, instead, we ask JavaScript to create a new object based on this class blueprint, our `Validate` class. This new object is an **instance**, our class blueprint made real, as it were, and it's this object instance that we use. We'll see shortly how we create an instance of our class.

Let's take a look at how we use the class in a web page. First, we need to add the code to the header of every page in which we want to use the class by using the `<SCRIPT>` tag:

```
<SCRIPT SRC='Validate.js'></SCRIPT>
```

Using relative paths on the assumption that both files are in the same directory, we have added a `<SCRIPT>` tag and set the `src` to the location of the `Validation.js` file. We then need to create a new object of this class type:

```
var validator = new Validate();
```

We will now be able to access any methods of the `Validate` class by using this object instance of the class. So our web page could look something like this:

```
<HTML>
<HEAD>

<SCRIPT SRC='Validate.js'></SCRIPT>

<SCRIPT LANGUAGE='JavaScript'>
    var validator = new Validate();

    function cmdValidate_onclick()
    {
        // use validator object instance of Validate class
        // to check form
    }

</SCRIPT>

</HEAD>
<BODY>
<FORM NAME='frmValidate'>
    Enter the text to validate:
    <BR>
    <INPUT TYPE='text' name=txtValidate>
    <BR>
    <INPUT TYPE='button' VALUE='Check Form'
            onclick='cmdValidate_onclick()'
            NAME='cmdValidate'></INPUT>
</FORM>
</BODY>
</HTML>
```

Save this page as `TestValidatePage.html` – we'll be re-using it throughout this section to test our validation methods. Our page simply consists of a text box, which will have its contents validated, and a button that checks the validity when clicked.

It's important to note that the `<SCRIPT>` tag linking to the `.js` file should come before we actually try and use the class to create an object based on it, as the page needs the class template first before it can create the object. It's also important that the `SCRIPT` tag's `SRC` attribute should point to our new `Validate.js` page, or we'll get a "Validate is undefined" error. We'll see this test page example throughout the next section as we develop the `Validate class`'s information validation methods. In the chapter's final section, we will add extra functionality to the class so it can be used as an automatic system you can drop into your web pages to check forms. We'll also use it to validate an online purchase in the Shopping Cart case study in Chapter 22.

Validating Information

In this section we'll look at various types of information and see how we can ensure as far as possible that the information the user has entered is valid. We'll be using what we do here for the final section on the validation class.

Validating Basic Information

We'll start by looking at fairly simple validation which checks that data entered by the user contains only letters or that it contains only numbers and so on. For example, if we ask for the person's first name, we do not expect it to contain numbers or punctuation. This sort of validation is useful where there are no other rules to validate against and no particular format that would determine validity.

Letters, Numbers, and Spaces Only

We'll create a regular expression that will test for the existence of any characters that are not letters, numbers or a space:

```
/[^a-z\d ]/i
```

This regular expression will match any character that is not one of those in the square brackets, (not a letter in the range of a to z, the `\d` – a digit, or a space). We've added the `i` flag so the regular expression is case insensitive.

We'll now create a method that uses the expression and add it to our `Validate` class, just below the constructor:

```
Validate.prototype.isOnlyAlphaNumeric = function(string)
{
    var invalidCharactersRegExp = /[^a-z\d ]/i;
    var isValid = !(invalidCharactersRegExp.test(string));

    return isValid;
}
```

We add the method to our class in the same way we saw in Chapter 3, *JavaScript OOP Techniques*. First, we have the name of the class we are adding the method to, and then we reference its prototype before finally adding the name of the new method, `isOnlyAlphaNumeric`. We set this to reference the function we create on the lines below. This function has just one argument, the string we want to validate. Its return value is `true` if there are only alphanumeric characters, and `false` if any other character is found.

The method itself first creates a new RegExp object and sets the regular expression syntax to what we discussed earlier. Then we set the `isValid` variable to the inverse of the results of our RegExp object's `test()` method to which we pass our string to be validated. A successful match returns `true`, indicating invalid characters have been found and so `isOnlyAlphaNumeric` should return `false`.

Modifying the test page we saw briefly earlier in the section on the `Validate` class, we can test our new method:

```
<HTML>
<HEAD>

<SCRIPT SRC='Validate.js'></SCRIPT>

<SCRIPT LANGUAGE='JavaScript'>
    var validator = new Validate();

    function cmdValidate_onclick()
    {
        var stringToValidate = document.frmValidate.txtValidate.value;
        if (validator.isOnlyAlphaNumeric(stringToValidate))
        {
            alert("Valid form");
        }
        else
        {
            alert("Invalid form");
        }
    }
</SCRIPT>

</HEAD>
<BODY>
<FORM NAME='frmValidate'>
    Enter the text to validate:
    <BR>
    <INPUT TYPE='text' NAME='txtValidate'></INPUT>
    <BR>
    <INPUT TYPE='button' VALUE='Check Form'
            onclick='cmdValidate_onclick()'
            NAME='cmdValidate'></INPUT>
</FORM>
</BODY>
</HTML>
```

Enter some test characters into the text box and click the button to check the new method actually works.

As we saw earlier, we include our script in the page using a `SCRIPT` tag and by setting the `SRC` property to the `Validate.js` file. Then in the script block below, we create a new instance of an object based on the `Validate` class:

```
var validator = new Validate();
```

To test our new method, we have added code to the `cmdValidate_onclick()` function that is called when the button is clicked. The function itself makes use of a validator variable that contains the reference to an object instance of our `Validate` class. Using the `isOnlyAlphaNumeric()` method of the Validate object instance, we let the user know if the form checks our entries as valid or invalid.

Letters and Numbers Only, No Spaces

This is almost identical to the method above, except we don't allow spaces. This is quite a common requirement; for example, letters and numbers are fine for a password, but spaces rarely are:

```
Validate.prototype.isOnlyAlphaNumericNoSpace = function(string)
{
    var invalidCharactersRegExp = /[^a-z\d]/i;
```

```
        var isValid = !(invalidCharactersRegExp.test(string));

        return isValid;
    }
```

All that has changed is the method name and the regular expression. We've removed the space from the regular expression, so now spaces will come under the disallowed category of characters.

We can change our cmdValidate_onclick() function in the test page to check our new function:

```
function cmdValidate_onclick()
{
    var stringToValidate = document.frmValidate.txtValidate.value;
    if (validator.isOnlyAlphaNumericNoSpace(stringToValidate))
    {
        alert("Valid form");
    }
    else
    {
        alert("Invalid form");
    }
}
```

Letters Only

Here is the regular expression that checks for characters other than letters and the space:

```
/[^a-z ]/i
```

It's the same as the alphanumeric regular expression we just discussed, except the \d has been removed.

Next, we add it as a method of our Validate class:

```
Validate.prototype.isOnlyAlphabetic = function(string)
{
    var invalidCharactersRegExp = /[^a-z ]/I;
    var isValid = !(invalidCharactersRegExp.test(string));

    return isValid;
}
```

When we add it as a method of our Validate class, the code is the same as with the isOnlyAlphaNumeric() method, but with the regular expression changed. Our test page's function cmdValidate_onclick() can be changed to try out the new method:

```
function cmdValidate_onclick()
{
    var stringToValidate = document.frmValidate.txtValidate.value;
    if (validator.isOnlyAlphabetic(stringToValidate))
    {
        alert("Valid form");
    }
    else
    {
        alert("Invalid form");
    }
}
```

Numbers Only

The final information type that we will validate in this section is information that contains numbers only. Here's the regular expression that checks for anything that is not a number:

```
/[^\d]/
```

Our method to check for numeric characters only is:

```
Validate.prototype.isOnlyNumeric = function(string)
{
    var invalidCharactersRegExp = /[^\d]/;
    var isValid = !(invalidCharactersRegExp.test(string));

    return isValid;
}
```

To test this, just change the if statement in the test page's function to the following:

```
function cmdValidate_onclick()
{
    var stringToValidate = document.frmValidate.txtValidate.value;
    if (validator.isOnlyNumeric(stringToValidate))
    {
        alert("Valid form");
    }
    else
    {
        alert("Invalid form");
    }
}
```

So far we have only checked strings to see if they contain only numerical characters. If we were writing a financial application, we might want to go further and check for integers or floating point numbers, so let's add methods to do just that.

To check for integers, both positive and negative, we need the regular expression:

```
/[^\d-]/
```

The regular expression allows for the minus sign. Here's the method to add to our class definition:

```
Validate.prototype.isValidInteger = function(string)
{
    var invalidCharactersRegExp = /[^\d-]/;
    var isValid = !(invalidCharactersRegExp.test(string));

    return isValid;
}
```

To check for floating point numbers our regular expression is:

```
/[^\d\.-]/;
```

This checks for anything that is not a digit, decimal point or minus sign. To specify that the decimal point is not the regular expression special character (".") indicating any class of characters, we have added the "\" (although the square brackets are not strictly necessary). Our method to be added to the Validate class:

```
Validate.prototype.isValidFloatingPoint = function(string)
{
   var invalidCharactersRegExp = /[^\d\.-]/;
   var isValid = !(invalidCharactersRegExp.test(string));

   return isValid;
}
```

You'll now see that extending the Validate class in order to check new types of information is quite straightforward.

Validating Age

Checking the validity of an age requires that first, we check that only numbers have been entered, and secondly, we check that the range is valid. If someone enters their age as 513, they're either a vampire or lying.

We don't need to create a regular expression on this occasion – the isOnlyNumeric() method of the Validate class does that for us. What we do need to check is the age range, so let's call our method for validating ages isValidAge(), and add it to the Validate class:

```
Validate.prototype.isValidAge = function(age)
{
   var isValid = false;
   if (this.isOnlyNumeric(age))
   {
       isValid = (parseInt(age) >= 0 && parseInt(age) < 140)
   }

   return isValid;
}
```

We start by setting isValid to false – we'll set this to true only if we confirm it is actually valid. Then in our if statement we use the isOnlyNumeric() method of the Validate class to check that only number characters are present. We've used the this keyword to refer to the object instance before trying to access its isOnlyNumeric method. In the context of a class definition, this always refers to the object instance of that class.

If there are only number characters, we set isValid to the results of the Boolean expression that tests to see that the number entered is within the range of greater or equal to 0 and less that 140. 140 might be a bit optimistic about life expectancy, but let's look on the positive side!

Finally, we return the Boolean result of our character and range tests.

Save the changes to Validate.js and change the function cmdValidate_onclick() in our test page to check what we have added works:

```
function cmdValidate_onclick()
{
   var stringToValidate = document.frmValidate.txtValidate.value;
   if (validator.isValidAge(stringToValidate))
   {
       alert("Valid form");
   }
   else
   {
       alert("Invalid form");
   }
}
```

Validating Password Formats

With passwords, we usually do not only restrict the types of characters allowed, but also want to ensure the number of characters entered is within a certain range. A one-character password is not going to be hard to guess! Note that different sites may have different password requirements and so might different parts of the same site.

We'll allow just letters and numbers to be allowed for our passwords. This makes our regular expression:

```
/[^a-z\d]/i
```

If there are other characters we want to allow, we can easily change the regular expression to reflect this.

We also want to ensure passwords are of a reasonable length, say between 8 and 16 characters. Using our regular expression and range parameters, let's create the Validate class's isValidPassword method:

```
Validate.prototype.isValidPassword = function(password)
{
    var invalidCharactersRegExp = /[^a-z\d]/i;
    var isValid = !(invalidCharactersRegExp.test(password));
    if (isValid)
    {
        isValid = (password.length >= 8 && password.length <= 16);
    }

    return isValid;
}
```

As with previous validation methods, we start by creating a regular expression that will match any of the characters that are not allowed (any characters that are not in the range a to z or a digit). Our regular expression has the case-insensitive flag i set, so we don't need A-Z in the expression.

We then use our regular expression object to test for invalid characters and store the negated results in the isValid variable – remember this value is true if the test for invalid characters returned false, hence the need to negate the results of the test. If isValid is true (no invalid characters found), then we set isValid to the results of the Boolean expression, which checks to see the number of characters in our password is between 8 and 16. Finally, we return isValid.

We can modify our test page to check for valid passwords using our new method:

```
function cmdValidate_onclick()
{
    var stringToValidate = document.frmValidate.txtValidate.value;
    if (validator.isValidPassword(stringToValidate))
    {
        alert("Valid form");
    }
    else
    {
        alert("Invalid form");
    }
}
```

Validating Telephone Numbers

With all the previous validation methods we have only checked that the characters entered are valid and not that they are in any particular format. This time we'll check both for validity of characters entered by the user and that the format of the information supplied matches that of a valid telephone number.

Our first problem is working out which formats we want to allow. If we are restricting our user base to North America then we can be fairly restrictive as to what we consider a valid format. It's likely, however, that we'll want to allow international visitors to our website, and this makes defining an exact format virtually impossible.

We can create a fairly loose format that will prevent clearly ridiculous numbers but still allow most valid numbers through.

What we need to allow are numbers such as:

- ❏ +1 (123) 123 4567
- ❏ +1123123 456
- ❏ +44 (123) 123 4567
- ❏ +44 (123) 123 4567 ext 123
- ❏ +44 20 7893 4567

You can find more information on world telephone numbering systems at http://phonebooth.interocitor.net/wtng/.

We could allow many other variations, but here we are considering:

- ❏ The local area code – 2 to 5 digits, but sometimes in brackets (compulsory)
- ❏ The actual subscriber number – 3 to 10 digits, but sometimes with spaces (compulsory)
- ❏ The international number starting with + followed by 1 to 3 digits (optional)
- ❏ An extension number – 2 to 5 digits preceded by x, ext, extn, or extension, sometimes in brackets (optional)

Lets create our regular expression in stages and join it altogether at the end, starting with the international dialing code:

```
/(\+\d{1,3} ?)?/
```

So far, we're matching a "+" followed by 1 to 3 digits and an optional space. The plus has a "\" in front to specify we mean an actual "+" character, and not the regular expression special character. The characters are wrapped inside a group which we match zero or one times, as indicated by the "?" after the closing bracket of the group.

Next, we need a pattern that will match the area code:

```
/(\(\d{1,5}\)|\d{1,5})/
```

Here, we have added `(\(\d{1,5}\)|\d{1,5})`, which is a group whose pattern matches either 1 to 5 digits in brackets, or just 1 to 5 digits. Again, the brackets are special characters in regular expression syntax, so when we want to match actual brackets we need the "\" in front.

Next, we will match the subscriber number:

```
/ ?\d{3,4} ?\d{0,7}/
```

Note that there is a space before the "?", which matches zero or one space, followed by three digits, followed by zero or one space, and finally followed by between 0 and 7 digits.

Finally, let's add the part to cope with an optional extension number (here it is split across two lines, but must be one line in the actual code):

```
/( (?:x|xtn|extn?|extension)\.? ?\d{1,5})?/
```

The bit we have added is `( (?:x|xtn|extn?|extension)\.? ?\d{1,5})?`, which is a group that checks for a space, followed by an inner group will match either x, xtn, ext, extn or extension. Following this, the pattern is zero or one actual full stop (not the regular expression special character) followed by zero or one space followed by 1 to 5 digits. Outside the group we use the "?" to specify that the group can appear zero or one times (making it optional).

We also want to ensure there are no characters before or after the telephone number, so we add the "^" special character, meaning the pattern must be at the beginning, and the "$" to specify it must also be at the end. This completes our monster-sized regular expression:

```
/^(\+\d{1,3} ?)?(\(\d{1,5}\)|\d{1,5}) ?\d{3,4} ?\d{0,7}(
(x|xtn|extn?|extension)\.? ?\d{1,5})?$/i
```

We have also added the i flag to make the match case insensitive. The expression must actually go on one line, but the width of this book forces it onto two.

Let's put this together into a new method for our Validate class:

```
Validate.prototype.isValidTelephoneNum = function(telephoneNum)
{
    var validFormatRegExp = /^(\+\d{1,3} ?)?(\(\d{1,5}\)|\d{1,5}) ?\d{3,4}
        ?\d{0,7}(?: (x|xtn|extn?|extension)\.? ?\d{1,5})?$/i;
    //Remember to put this regular expression on one line.
    var isValid = validFormatRegExp.test(telephoneNum);
    return isValid;

}
```

After we have created our RegExp object, we use the test() method to check a matching pattern is found in the telephoneNum variable. We are not checking for invalid characters here, but for a valid format, so there's no need for the "!" negation operator, unlike previous in methods we have created. As the format defined by our regular expression doesn't allow for any invalid characters, there is no need to test for them. Finally, the result is returned.

As with the previous examples, you can change the code in the test page to test the new method:

```
function cmdValidate_onclick()
{
    var stringToValidate = document.frmValidate.txtValidate.value;
    if (validator.isValidTelephoneNum(stringToValidate))
    {
        alert("Valid form");
    }
    else
    {
        alert("Invalid form");
    }
}
```

An alternative to our "one size fits all" method of checking telephone numbers would be to ask the user which country they are from, and check for telephone number formats specific to that country. This would be tricky to do, however and requires much more complex code.

Validating ZIP/Postal Codes

We are going to split our checking of postal codes into two parts. First, we will create a regular expression to check US ZIP codes, and then we will create a regular expression to match UK postcodes. We'll then put these into a new method for the Validate class called `isValidPostalCode`. We will not attempt to create a regular expression that covers the world's postal codes because there is not enough commonality, unlike the telephone numbers where there was just about enough in common to use with just one pattern. If we did want to cover all the postal codes of the world, we'd need to have regular expressions specific for each country that we were concerned with validating, and for the rest have no validation at all. This method would, therefore, also need to be passed the country of the user. However, to keep things manageable, we'll stick with just the UK and USA.

ZIP codes can be in one of two formats, either five digits (12345) or five digits followed by a dash and four digits (12345-1234)

We saw the ZIP code regular expression that matches these in the last chapter, although we've used capturing groups so that it works with IE4+ and Netscape 4, as well as IE5.5 and Netscape 6:

```
/^\d{5}(-\d{4})?$/
```

This matches five digits followed by a non-capturing group that matches a dash followed by four digits. The group has the "?" special character after it, meaning it is to be matched zero or one time, making it optional. We have added the "^" at the start and "$" at the end to ensure there are no characters before or after the ZIP code.

For a regular expression that covers UK post codes, let's consider their various formats.

UK postcodes come in the format of two letters followed by one or two digits, a space (although this is optional), a digit, and then two letters. Valid examples include: CH3 9QZ, PE29 1WW, SW1V 2HX, and B27 3BH.

Based on this, our regular expression is:

```
/^[a-z]{1,2}[\da-z]{1,2} ?\d[a-z][a-z]$/i
```

Again, we have added the "^" at the start and "$" at the end of the pattern to be sure that the only information in the string is the postcode. Although postcodes should be upper case, it is still valid for them to be lower case, so we have set the case-insensitive flag `i`.

To validate both ZIP codes and UK postcodes in one expression, we can use the alternate regular expression special character:

```
/^(\d{5}(-\d{4})?|[a-z]{1,2}[\da-z]{1,2} ?\d[a-z][a-z])$/i
```

We have the ZIP and postcode matching regular expressions inside the group. On the left before the "|" we have the pattern to match the ZIP. On the right, we have the pattern to match a postcode. We have put them both in a group because of the "^" character at the start and "$" at the end, which were taken from the two separate regular expressions matching Zips and postcodes. These ensure that whatever pattern is matched in the group constitutes the only characters in the string. Without the grouping, the "^" would be on the left of the alternation character, so the ZIP code would have to be at the start and the "$" would be on the right of the alternation character. We don't want the pattern to be at either the start or the beginning of the string, but both.

Let's now add the `isValidPostalCode()` method to our `Validate` class:

```
Validate.prototype.isValidPostalCode = function(postalCode)
{
    var validFormat = /^(\d{5}(-\d{4})?|[a-z]{1,2}[\da-z]{1,2} ?\d[a-z]
        [a-z])$/i;
    // Put the above regular expression on one line
    var isValid = validFormat.test(postalCode);
    return isValid;
}
```

We create the RegExp with the regular expression syntax we just looked at, then we check that a matching pattern is found in the passed `postalCode` parameter and return the result.

We can alter our test page to check our new method actually works:

```
function cmdValidate_onclick()
{
    var stringToValidate = document.frmValidate.txtValidate.value;
    if (validator.isValidPostalCode(stringToValidate))
    {
        alert("Valid form");
    }
    else
    {
        alert("Invalid form");
    }
}
```

If we wanted to improve our postal code validator we could match ZIP codes to state. The same is not easily possible with UK postcodes, as there is no simple postcode and county match. Sophisticated postcode validation (checking that the address entered matches the postcode) is something that requires server side processing, a database, and a lot of free time!

Validating E-mail Addresses

In this section, we'll look at validating the format of an e-mail address. We can only check that the e-mail address is valid, not that it actually exists. We looked in detail at the regular expression required to match e-mail patterns in Chapter 15, *Regular Expressions*, so here we'll simply create the method to check e-mail addresses and add it to our `Validate` class. We saw in that chapter that the regular expression required was:

```
/^\w(\.?\w)*@\w(\.?[-\w])*\.([a-z]{3}(\.[a-z]{2})?|[a-z]{2}(\.[a-z]{2})?)$/i
```

There's only one change: we have changed the non-capturing groups to normal capturing groups. Only IE5.5+ and Netscape 6 support these groups, so to aid cross-browser compatibility they have been changed. This does not affect how the regular expression works, but simply means group matches are being captured when we never actually use them.

Let's use the regular expression and create our `isValidEmail` method to add to the `Validate` class:

```
Validate.prototype.isValidEmail = function(email)
{
    var validFormatRegExp = /^\w(\.?\w)*@\w(\.?[-\w])*\.([a-z]{3}(\.[a-
z]{2})?|[a-z]{2}(\.[a-z]{2})?)$/i
    var isValid = validFormatRegExp.test(email);
    return isValid;
}
```

Note that in your code the regular expression must go on one line.

Validating Dates

Dates can be a real problem because of the many possible valid formats and the difference between US and UK date formats. For example, all of the following are valid:

- ❏ 1/10/2001
- ❏ 10-01-2001
- ❏ 01-10-2001
- ❏ 10-Jan-2001
- ❏ Jan-10-2001
- ❏ January-10-2001
- ❏ 10th Jan 2001
- ❏ January 10th 2001

The list can go on and on. We could write a regular expression that could extract the date parts (or use a `Date` object) but it still leaves the problem about differences between US and UK date formats. For example, 10-01-2001 could be 10th of January 2001 or 1st October 2001, depending on whether it is a orUS UK, format. The easiest way round this is to use either select boxes or text boxes to input the date. Having one box for the day of the month, one for the month, and one for the year, would leave no room for ambiguity.

We can use the `navigator` object (in Netscape 4+) or the `userLanguage` (IE4+) property to tell us the language of the user's browser (whether its US English or UK English). Even this however is far from reliable. The Netscape Navigator 4 version only tells us it is EN (English) and so doesn't help much. The IE4 version tells us the installed language of the user's browser, but the IE5+ version tells us the installed language of the user's operating system. Therefore, what this actually returns may or may not reflect reality. For example, you might be in the UK, with regional settings defaulted to UK, but `userLanguage` on a IE5.5 browser running on Windows 2000 says EN-US. This actually reflects how the operating system was obtained, not where the user lives. `userLanguage` and language properties are therefire unreliable for our purposes.

Having made the decision to have separate form elements for each part of the date, we still need to validate the date itself. For example, 29th Feb 2001 is not valid, but 29th Feb 2000 is, because 2000 was a leap year. We deal with this using the `Date` object, an implicit object supplied by the browser. In particular, we will use the feature that causes the day of the `Date` object to roll over to the next month when you set the day of the month to an invalid value.

For example, if we create a new `Date` object like this:

```
var myDate = new Date("29 Feb 2001");
```

Then check the value of the day of the month using the `getDate()` method:

```
alert(myDate.getDate());
```

The value we get is not 29, because JavaScript has realized that there are only 28 days in February 2001 when creating the Date object, and sets the date to 1 March 2001. Instead of setting the date to 29, it has added 29 days onto the 1st of February to return the 1st of March.

Let's create an `isValidDate()` method to our `Validate` class based on what we've seen above:

```
Validate.prototype.isValidDate = function(day, month,year)
{
   var isValid = true;

   var enteredDate = new Date(day + " " + month + " " + year);
   if (enteredDate.getDate() != day)
   {
      isValid = false;
   }
   return isValid;
}
```

Our method is very simple. On the second line, we create a `Date` object and use the day, month, and year to create a date that we pass to the constructor. If that date is invalid, either due to leap years or because the user enters "XX" as the day or year, then in the `if` statement, `enteredDate.getDate()` will not be the same as the date parameter passed to the method. In this case, we set `isValid` to `false`.

To test this, we need to make significant alterations to our test page, so you might want to save it as `TestDate.html` rather than overwrite the existing version.

```
<HTML>
<HEAD>

<SCRIPT SRC='Validate.js'></SCRIPT>

<SCRIPT LANGUAGE='JavaScript'>
   var validator = new Validate();

   function cmdValidate_onclick()
   {
      var day = document.frmValidate.txtDay.value;
      var month =
         document.frmValidate.cboMonth[document.frmValidate.cboMonth.
         selectedIndex].value;
      var year = document.frmValidate.txtYear.value;

      if (validator.isValidDate(day,month,year))
      {
         alert("Valid form");
      }
      else
      {
         alert("Invalid form");
      }
   }
</SCRIPT>

</HEAD>
<BODY>
<FORM NAME='frmValidate'>
   <P>Day  / Month  / Year (yyyy)<BR>
   <INPUT ID='txtDay' NAME='txtDay' SIZE='2' MAXLENGTH='2' >  
   <SELECT ID=cboMonth NAME=cboMonth>
      <OPTION VALUE=January SELECTED>Jan</OPTION>
      <OPTION VALUE=February>Feb</OPTION>
      <OPTION VALUE=March>Mar</OPTION>
      <OPTION VALUE=April>Apr</OPTION>
      <OPTION VALUE=May>May</OPTION>
```

```
            <OPTION VALUE=June>Jun</OPTION>
            <OPTION VALUE=July>Jul</OPTION>
            <OPTION VALUE=August>Aug</OPTION>
            <OPTION VALUE=September>Sep</OPTION>
            <OPTION VALUE=October>Oct</OPTION>
            <OPTION VALUE=November>Nov</OPTION>
            <OPTION VALUE=December>Dec</OPTION>
        </SELECT>  
        <INPUT ID=txtYear NAME=txtYear SIZE=4 MAXLENGTH=4 ></INPUT>
        <BR>
        <INPUT TYPE='button' VALUE='Check Form'
            onclick="cmdValidate_onclick()"
            NAME='cmdValidate'>
    </FORM>
    </BODY>
    </HTML>
```

Our form, as shown below, now consists of the following elements: a text box to obtain the date, a select box with months listed, and another text box to obtain the year:

The Day and Year text boxes have had their maximum length set to 2 and 4 characters respectively to prevent values that are too large causing an overflow.

The top of our changed `cmdValidate_onclick()` function obtains the date part values entered or selected by the user:

```
var day = document.frmValidate.txtDay.value;
var month =
    document.frmValidate.cboMonth[document.frmValidate.cboMonth.
    selectedIndex].value;
var year = document.frmValidate.txtYear.value;
```

We then pass these to the `validator` object's `isValidDate()` method in our `if` statement and it returns `true` if valid and `false` otherwise:

```
if (validator.isValidDate(day,month,year))
{
    alert("Valid form");
}
else
{
    alert("Invalid form");
}
```

We can try whatever values we like – only valid dates will get through.

Valid Date of Birth

Just because a date is valid, it doesn't necessarily mean the information range is valid. If we are asking the user to enter their date of birth and they enter 1 Jan 3000, the likelihood is that it has been entered incorrectly. In this section, we are going validate birth dates by adding another method, isValidDateOfBirth() to our Validate class:

```
Validate.prototype.isValidDateOfBirth = function(day, month, year)
{
   var isValid = true;
   var nowDate = new Date();
   year = parseInt(year);
   dateOfBirth =  new Date(day + " " + month + " " + year);
   if (!this.isValidDate(day,month,year))
   {
      isValid = false;
   }
   else if (dateOfBirth > nowDate || (year + 140) < nowDate.getFullYear())
   {
      isValid = false;
   }

   return isValid;
}
```

In our new method, we first create a new Date object with today's date, ensure year is an integer, and finally create another Date object whose value is passed as the date of birth.

Using isValidDate() method of the this class, we check that the date is valid before checking in the second if statement that the date of birth is not in the future or more than 140 years before today. Finally, we return the result of our checks.

We just need to alter one line of our TestDate.html page's cmdValidate_onclick() method. We are changing isValidDate to isValidDateOfBirth so we can test our new method:

```
function cmdValidate_onclick()
{
   var day = parseInt(document.frmValidate.txtDay.value);
   var month =
document.frmValidate.cboMonth[document.frmValidate.cboMonth.selectedIndex].value;
   var year = document.frmValidate.txtYear.value;

   if (validator.isValidDateOfBirth(day,month,year))
   {
      alert("Valid form");
   }
   else
   {
   alert("Invalid form");
   }
}
```

Validating Credit Card Details

We will use the following strategies to validate credit card details:

❑   Ensure expiry date is valid.

❑   Check only numbers in the credit card number.

❑ Check the number of digits is valid for a given card type.

❑ Use the **Luhn** formula to check the validity of entered credit card numbers. This is a special algorithm that can be applied to most credit card numbers to check that the number would be valid.

We can only check that the details given could be a valid credit card. It is only via server-side programming that we can check the credit card account actually exists.

Let's start by adding a method to check credit card expiry dates:

```
Validate.prototype.isValidCreditCardExpiry = function(expiresMonth, expiresYear)
{
    var isValid = true;
    var nowDate = new Date();
    if (expiresMonth < (nowDate.getMonth() + 1) && expiresYear <=
        nowDate.getFullYear())
    {
        isValid = false;
    }
    else if (expiresYear < nowDate.getFullYear())
    {
        isValid = false;
    }


    return isValid;
}
```

In the method, we create a new `Date` object which, because we pass no value to the constructor, will default to contain today's date. In the first `if` statement we check if the expiry month and year are less than the current month and year. If that is the case, we set `isValid` to `false`. This catches cases where the expiry year is the current year, but the month is earlier than the current month. Note we add 1 to the value returned by `getyear()`, because in JavaScript months start at zero, so January is month zero, February is month one, and so on. In the second `if` statement, we check to see if the expiry year is before the current year, and if that is the case, `isValid` is set to `false`.

We'll now create a method that checks the validity of the credit card number, `isValidCreditCardNumber()`. This checks that the information entered by the user only contains numbers and spaces:

```
Validate.prototype.isValidCreditCardNumber = function(cardNumber, cardType)
{
    var isValid = false;
    var ccCheckRegExp = /[^\d ]/;
    isValid = !ccCheckRegExp.test(cardNumber);

    return isValid;
}
```

So far, our method is similar to the format checking of `isOnlyNumeric()`, except that it also allows spaces. The RegExp object's `test()` method checks for invalid characters – we reverse its return value and store the result in `isValid`.

Next, let's add the checking for credit card only numbers and that the number of digits is valid for a given card type. Each type of credit card has a specific number of digits, and always starts with certain numbers. The table below shows details for three common cards:

Card Type	Prefix	Number of Digits
Visa	4	13,16
Mastercard	51-55	16
American Express	34,37	15

You can find more information on card formats at:http://www.beachnet.com/~hstiles/cardtype.html.

We'll now translate these card rules into code:

```
Validate.prototype.isValidCreditCardNumber = function(cardNumber, cardType)
{
   var isValid = false;
   var ccCheckRegExp = /[^\d ]/;
   isValid = !ccCheckRegExp.test(cardNumber);

   if (isValid)
   {
      var cardNumbersOnly = cardNumber.replace(/ /g,"");
      var cardNumberLength = cardNumbersOnly.length;
      var lengthIsValid = false;
      var prefixIsValid = false;
      var prefixRegExp;

      switch(cardType)
      {
         case "mastercard":
            lengthIsValid = (cardNumberLength == 16);
            prefixRegExp = /^5[1-5]/;
            break;

         case "visa":
            lengthIsValid = (cardNumberLength == 16 ||cardNumberLength == 13);
            prefixRegExp = /^4/;
            break;

         case "amex":
            lengthIsValid = (cardNumberLength == 15);
            prefixRegExp = /^3(?:4|7)/;
            break;

         default:
            prefixRegExp = /^$/;
            alert("Card type not found");
      }

      prefixIsValid = prefixRegExp.test(cardNumbersOnly);
      isValid = prefixIsValid && lengthIsValid;
   }

   return isValid;
}
```

The new code is all contained inside the `if` statement that checks whether the number was valid so far. Our first job is to remove all the spaces the user may have entered between the digits. We have used a regular expression in the `replace()` method, but instead of creating a RegExp object and assigning its reference to a variable and passing that, we have instead created the regular expression in the method call.

With the spaces removed we then store the number of digits, `length`, in the card number. It is in the `switch` statement that we use the differing parameters of each card to check validity. Under each case, we set `lengthIsValid` to the Boolean result of comparing the `cardNumberLength` to the number of digits it should be. We also set `prefixRegExp` to a regular expression that will match the correct first few characters of the card number specific to a card type.

After the switch, we use the RegExp created to test if the card number's prefix matches that which is specific to the card. Finally, `isValid` is the result of `prefixIsValid` and `lengthIsValid` – both must be valid for `isValid` to be set to true.

The final part of our credit card number validation is to check that the number itself could be a valid credit card number. The **Luhn Formula**, also known as **Modula 10** or **Mod 10**, when applied to a credit card number, tells us whether that could be a valid number. Obviously, it doesn't guarantee that the number is actually in use, only that it could be used.

The basic formula is:

1. Start with the second digit from last. Moving to the first digit double each alternate digit.

2. Take the results of the doubling and add each of the digits together then add to the running total.

3. Add all the non-doubled digits together.

4. Add the value of the doubled digits and the value of the non-doubled digits together.

5. Take the value calculated in step 4 above and calculate the remaining amount when it is divided by 10. If the remainder is zero then it's a valid number, otherwise it's invalid.

So, if our number was:

4221 3456 1243 1237

Step 1:

Would be to double the alternate digits (highlighted in bold below) starting from the second from last digit:

4221 3456 1243 1237

$(3 * 2)$ $(1 * 2)$ $(4 * 2)$ $(1 * 2)$ $(5 * 2)$ $(3*2)$ $(2 * 2)$ $(4 * 2)$

Which is :

6, 2, 8, 2, 10, 6, 4, 8

Step 2:

Add each of the individual digits together:

$6 + 2 + 8 + 2 + (1 + 0) + 6 + 4 + 8 = 37$

Step 3:

Add all the non-doubled digits together:

4221 3456 1243 1237

$2 + 1 + 4 + 6 + 2 + 3 + 2 + 7 = 27$

Step 4:

Add the results of steps 2 and 3 together:

$37 + 27 = 64$

Step 5:

Find the remainder of the result in step 4 divided by 10:

64 modulus 10 = 4

The remainder after 64 has been divided by 10 is 4, meaning the credit card number is invalid. If it had been 0 it would indicate a valid credit card number.

Lets put this into code and add it to our isValidCreditCardNumber() method:

```
Validate.prototype.isValidCreditCardNumber = function(cardNumber, cardType)
{
   var isValid = false;
   var ccCheckRegExp = /[^\d ]/;
   isValid = !ccCheckRegExp.test(cardNumber);

   if (isValid)
   {
      var cardNumbersOnly = cardNumber.replace(/ /g,"");
      var cardNumberLength = cardNumbersOnly.length;
      var lengthIsValid = false;
      var prefixIsValid = false;
      var prefixRegExp;

      switch(cardType)
      {
         case "mastercard":
            lengthIsValid = (cardNumberLength == 16);
            prefixRegExp = /^5[1-5]/;
            break;

         case "visa":
            lengthIsValid = (cardNumberLength == 16 || cardNumberLength ==
            13);
            prefixRegExp = /^4/;
            break;

         case "amex":
            lengthIsValid = (cardNumberLength == 15);
            prefixRegExp = /^3(4|7)/;
            break;

         default:
            prefixRegExp = /^$/;
            alert("Card type not found");
      }

      prefixIsValid = prefixRegExp.test(cardNumbersOnly);
      isValid = prefixIsValid && lengthIsValid;
```

```
        }

        if (isValid)
        {
            var numberProduct;
            var numberProductDigitIndex;
            var checkSumTotal = 0;

            for (var digitCounter = cardNumberLength - 1; digitCounter > 0;
                digitCounter--)
            {
                checkSumTotal += parseInt(cardNumbersOnly.charAt(digitCounter));
                digitCounter--;

                numberProduct = new String((cardNumbersOnly.charAt(digitCounter) * 2));
                for (var productDigitCounter = 0;
                    productDigitCounter < numberProduct.length;
                    productDigitCounter++)
                {
                    checkSumTotal +=
                    parseInt(numberProduct.charAt(productDigitCounter));
                }

            }

            isValid = (checkSumTotal % 10 == 0);

        }

        return isValid;
    }
```

First, we check if isValid is true (if all other checks so far proved satisfactory). After our variable declarations, we have the main for loop that will go through the credit card number a digit at a time starting with the last digit (the furthest digit to the right) and moving to the first. In this loop we do a number of things. Firstly, we add a digit's value to a running total. Then we double the next digit along. We then take the digits forming the result of doubling and add the digits together in the inner loop. The result of this addition is then added to the running total. The loop continues by moving to the next digit to the left and this continues until we reach the first digit.

Here are the steps in our outer and inner loops as implemented in the code:

1. Extract the character whose position is specified by digitCounter, from the string in cardNumbersOnly.

2. Add this number to our running total, which is kept in the variable checkSumTotal.

3. Decrement the character counter, so we move on to the next character to the left.

4. Extract the next character, convert it to a number and then double it. This is all done on one line and this product is stored in variable numberProduct.

5. Convert the product calculated in step 4 above to a string

6. Loop through each digit in the product string, convert to an integer, and add to the running total. This is our inner loop. So if the character extracted in step 4 was 8, its product would be 16, and we'd add 1 and then 6 to our running total.

7. Decrement the digit counter and move to step 1.

If we think back to the explanation of the Luhn formula, our approach is out of step in that we are not doing step 1, then 2 and so on, but instead merging steps 1 – 4, and doing it on a digit by digit basis and keeping a running total. It amounts to exactly the same thing, but reduces the number of loops required.

Once we have our result, we find its **modulus 10**, which is the remainder left over when the running total is divided by ten – if it's zero, we have ourselves a valid credit card number, otherwise it's invalid. We set isValid to the result of the Boolean expression comparing the remainder to zero – if true it's valid, if false it's invalid.

We need to create a new test page to check our code works. Call it TestCard.html:

```
<HTML>
<HEAD>
<TITLE>Document Title</TITLE>
    <SCRIPT src="Validate.js"></SCRIPT>
    <STYLE>
    BODY
    {
        FONT-FAMILY: Verdana,'Arial Black';
        FONT-SIZE: 10pt;
        BACKGROUND-COLOR: white;
    }

    H1
    {
        FONT-FAMILY: Verdana,'Arial Black';
        FONT-SIZE: 21pt;
        COLOR: darkorange;
    }

    DIV { MARGIN: 15px }
    </STYLE>
    <SCRIPT LANGUAGE='JavaScript'>

    function getSelectedRadioValue(radioGroup)
    {
        var selectedRadioValue = "";
        var radIndex;
        for (radIndex = 0; radIndex < radioGroup.length; radIndex++)
        {
            if (radioGroup[radIndex].checked)
            {
                selectedRadioValue = radioGroup[radIndex].value;
                break;
            }
        }

        return selectedRadioValue;
    }

    function cmdCheckIsValid_onclick(theForm)
    {
        var isValid = true;
```

```
        var validator = new Validate();
        var selectedMonth =
        theForm.cboExpMonth.options[theForm.cboExpMonth.selectedIndex].value;
        var selectedYear =
        theForm.cboExpYear.options[theForm.cboExpYear.selectedIndex].value;
        if (validator.isValidCreditCardExpiry(selectedMonth,selectedYear) ==
        false)
        {
            isValid = false;
            alert("Invalid Expiry Date");
        }
        else
        {
            var cardType = getSelectedRadioValue(theForm.radCardType);
            var cardNumber = theForm.txtCardNumber.value;
            isValid = validator.isValidCreditCardNumber(cardNumber, cardType)
            if (!isValid)
            {
                alert("Invalid Card Number");
            }
            else
            {
                alert("Form Ok");
            }
        }
    }

    </SCRIPT>

</HEAD>
<BODY>
    <H3><P ALIGN='CENTER'>Please enter your credit card details below. </P> </H3>
    <FORM NAME='frmCCDetails'>
        <DIV>
            Credit Card Number:
            <BR>
            <INPUT TYPE='TEXT' NAME='txtCardNumber' MAXLENGTH='20'>
        </DIV>

        <DIV>
            Credit Card Type
            <BR>
            Visa <INPUT NAME='radCardType' TYPE='radio' VALUE='visa'>
            Mastercard <INPUT NAME='radCardType' TYPE='radio' VALUE='mastercard'>
            American Express<INPUT NAME='radCardType' TYPE='radio' VALUE='amex'>
        </DIV>

        <DIV>
            Card Expiry Date

            <SELECT NAME='cboExpMonth" SIZE="1">
                <OPTION VALUE='01'>01</OPTION>
                <OPTION VALUE='02'>02</OPTION>
                <OPTION VALUE='03'>03</OPTION>
                <OPTION VALUE='04'>04</OPTION>
                <OPTION VALUE='05'>05</OPTION>
                <OPTION VALUE='06'>06</OPTION>
                <OPTION VALUE='07'>07</OPTION>
                <OPTION VALUE='08'>08</OPTION>
```

```
                    <OPTION VALUE='09'>09</OPTION>
                    <OPTION VALUE='10'>10</OPTION>
                    <OPTION VALUE='11'>11</OPTION>
                    <OPTION VALUE='12'>12</OPTION>
                </SELECT>
                <SELECT NAME='cboExpYear' SIZE='1'>
                    <OPTION VALUE='2001'>2001</OPTION>
                    <OPTION VALUE='2002'>2002</OPTION>
                    <OPTION VALUE='2003'>2003</OPTION>
                    <OPTION VALUE='2004'>2004</OPTION>
                    <OPTION VALUE='2005'>2005</OPTION>
                    <OPTION VALUE='2005'>2006</OPTION>
                </SELECT>
            </DIV>
        </DIV>
        <INPUT NAME='reset' type='reset' value='Clear Form'>
        <INPUT NAME='cmdCheckIsValid' type='button' VALUE='Is Form Valid?'
        onclick='cmdCheckIsValid_onclick(document.frmCCDetails)'>

    </FORM>
</BODY>
</HTML>
```

There's a lot of HTML, but the example itself is fairly simple. The form looks like this:

When the **Is Form Valid?** button is clicked, the contents of the form are validated according to the following criteria:

❑   Is the expiry date valid?

❑   Does the card type selected correspond with the number entered?

❑   Is the number entered a valid card number?

The first function in our script is the `getSelectedRadioValue()` function which returns the value of the user selected radio button in a group, the group being passed in the functions only parameter. On the client side, to obtain the value of the radio button selected by the user, we need to loop through each radio button in the group until we hit on one that's been selected and get its value. Unlike select boxes, there is no `selectedIndex` property to tell us what the user has chosen:

```
function getSelectedRadioValue(radioGroup)
{
   var selectedRadioValue = "";
   var radIndex;
   for (radIndex = 0; radIndex < radioGroup.length; radIndex++)
   {
      if (radioGroup[radIndex].checked)
      {
         selectedRadioValue = radioGroup[radIndex].value;
         break;
      }
   }

   return selectedRadioValue;
}
```

Turning to our `cmdCheckIsValid_onclick()` function:

```
function cmdCheckIsValid_onclick(theForm)
{
   var isValid = true;
   var validator = new Validate();

   var selectedMonth =
   theForm.cboExpMonth.options[theForm.cboExpMonth.selectedIndex].value;
   var selectedYear =
   theForm.cboExpYear.options[theForm.cboExpYear.selectedIndex].value;
   if (validator.isValidCreditCardExpiry(selectedMonth,selectedYear) ==
      false)
   {
      isValid = false;
      alert("Invalid Expiry Date");
   }
```

`cmdCheckIsValid_onclick` has one parameter, `theForm`, which references the form object of the form whose data we will be checking. In the first few lines shown above, we create a new object instance of our `Validate` class, which we'll be using to do all the validation. Having obtained the values of the credit card expiry month and year, we then use the `isValidCreditCardExpiry()` method of the `validator` object to check it is correct. If it's not correct, we let the user know, otherwise we move onto the `else` part of our `if` statement where the credit card number is checked:

```
   else
   {
      var cardType = getSelectedRadioValue(theForm.radCardType);
      var cardNumber = theForm.txtCardNumber.value;
      isValid = validator.isValidCreditCardNumber(cardNumber, cardType);
      if (!isValid)
      {
         alert("Invalid Card Number");
      }
      else
      {
         alert("Form Ok");
      }
   }
}
```

We get the card type selected and card number entered by the user. We then set `isValid` to the return value from the validate object's `isValidCreditCardNumber()` method. If `isValid` is not `true`, we let the user know something is wrong with their credit card number. Otherwise, we let them know the form details are valid.

That completes our look at the `Validate` class. Using it in your own web pages is very easy and because it's a class, it's easy to extend and add new types of data to validate. In the next section we'll extend the class to simplify and automate some of the coding involved in form validation.

Extending the Validate Class

Until now, we have seen how to validate single input elements. If we had 100 such elements in a form, then calling the appropriate method from the validate class for each of them would be extremely cumbersome and make the code difficult to maintain. It would defeat the entire purpose of separating the presentation from the logic. Therefore, we need to have a single entry point in the code validation block.

Here we are talking about good coding practices. They will eventually lead to a better code. The context in which we use the `input` tag is not known by the JavaScript engine. We therefore need a method in which the JavaScript engine can identify at runtime whether or not a field was compulsory and the validation rules for the same.

In this section, we'll look at a way of automating many aspects of form checking using our `Validate` class. It allows us to add details of the type of data a form element must contain, and whether that element must be filled in by the user. Using just a single method call of our `Validate` class, the form will be checked and any elements that have been filled incorrectly will be highlighted for the user to change. Below is an example of the form we'll be using, where the user has failed to correctly complete any of the elements before clicking the Continue button:

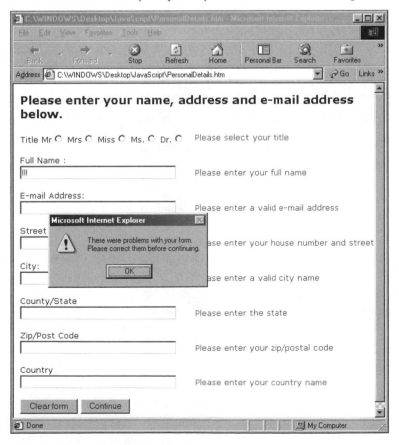

Overview of How it Works

In this section, we'll be adding a new method to our Validate class called checkFormValid(). This method will go through each form element in turn and check to see whether:

❑ It is a mandatory form element and if so, it has been filled in

❑ The information entered is valid with the specified data type

If either of these conditions are not met then the checkFormValid() method will display a red error message next to the form element. The method will also return whether the form was valid (that all compulsory elements were filled in and all data matched the specified type). Note that this method uses DHTML, so a version 4+ browser is required.

The first question is: how will our method know whether a form element is compulsory, and what type of data it should contain?

If you look at one of the element definitions shown below, you'll get a good idea:

```
<INPUT NAME='txtFullName_compulsory_alphabetic'
MAXLENGTH='150' CLASS='TextBox' >
```

If you look at the name given to the element, as well as the usual form element name, there is the suffix _compulsory_alphabetic appended to the name.

Our checkFormValid() method uses information inside the name of the element to determine if the element is compulsory and what information it is designed to garner from the user. If we want an element to be filled in by the user, we add _compulsory to the end of the element name. If we want to specify a specific type of information, we write underscore and the name of the information, in this case _alphabetic.

If we want a form element to be compulsory and specify the data type then we just add them one after the other like so: _compulsory_alphabetic. We need to make sure we get the order correct, so first specify if the element is compulsory, and then specify the type of data; _alphabetic_compulsory is not valid.

If we don't want a form element to be compulsory, but the user does enter data and we want to check that it's valid, we would write: _notcompulsory_alphabetic.

If we don't want a form element to be part of the automatic validation process then we simply leave off both the _compulsory and the data type parts.

In addition, we can also add _compulsory to radio button groups where we want to ensure that one of the buttons has been selected by the user. As we set their value, we don't check radio button groups for data type validity.

In the table below, we have a list of possible data type identifiers, the method of the Validate class used to check the data, and a description of the data matched:

Identifier	Method of Validate class Used	Description
_alphanumeric	isOnlyAlphaNumeric	Data must contain letters, numbers or spaces.
_alphanumeric nospace	isOnlyAlphaNumericNoSpace	Data must contain only letters and numbers, no spaces allowed.

Identifier	Method of **Validate** class Used	Description
_alphabetic	isOnlyAlphabetic	Data must contain only letters or spaces.
_numeric	isOnlyNumeric	Data must contain only numbers.
_integer	isValidInteger	Data must contain valid integer number.
_floatingpoint	isValidFloatingPoint	Data must contain valid floating point number.
_age	isValidAge	Data must be valid age - number characters within range 1-140.
_password	isValidPassword	Data must only contain letters and numbers and must contain between 8 and 16 characters in length.
_telephone	isValidTelephoneNum	Data should match valid international telephone number. Area code and subscriber number part compulsory, international dialing code and extension number optional.
_postcode	isValidPostalCode	Data must be in valid format for US ZIP code or UK postcode.
_email	isValidEmail	Data must be in valid format for e-mail address.

Looking at the table, we can see certain types of data are not listed For example, there are no identifiers for validating dates, credit card expiry dates, or credit card numbers. This is because those data types usually rely on more than one form element. For example, with a credit card number, the validity of the number depends on the card type entered, as well as the card number entered. To avoid making things too complex, we have not attempted to check data that is dependent on more than one form element.

You might wonder why we have used name as a way of describing the data inside an element, and whether it is compulsory, rather than adding a property to the form element itself. The main reason is backwards compatibility. While IE4+ and Netscape 6 allow us to define extra properties inside the HTML tag, Netscape 4 does not. It will allow us to add them later in the page, but this separates the element's definition from the validation details.

We mentioned earlier that when an element is either not filled in and is compulsory or contains invalid data, the checkFormValid() method will display a message next to the element. Let's see how it does this.

For each element in our form we must include a hidden DIV element containing the error message to be displayed. We may not want to position elements on the page absolutely, so in the examples the form element and the error-displaying DIV are both wrapped inside an outer DIV that acts as a container. We can then specify the position of the error DIV relative to the outer container DIV, but don't need to make the outer DIV absolutely or relatively positioned. Indeed, if we did that, then we'd need to change our Navigator 4 code (so that Navigator 4 can access the DIV we need to position it either relatively or absolutely).

Here's an example of this:

```
<DIV>Full Name :
   <BR>
   <INPUT NAME='txtFullName_compulsory_alphabetic' MAXLENGTH='150'
   CLASS='TextBox'>
   <DIV ID='FullNameError' NAME='FullNameError' CLASS='FormElementError'>
      Please enter your full name
   </DIV>
</DIV>
```

However, we still have the question of how the `checkFormValid()` method accesses the correct error `DIV` and displays it.

Again, it's down to a naming convention. The form element must start with a three-letter identifier, such as `txt` for a text box, `pwd` for a password element or `cbo` for a drop down combo box. You can use whatever identifiers you like, as long as they are three characters long and at the start of the name. You may even wish to change the code and have no identifiers. The `id` of the error `DIV` must contain the name of the associated form element, but without the three-letter identifier or the compulsory and data type identifiers, and with the word `Error` at the end. Based on the form element example above, we have our element with the name `txtFullName_compulsory_alphabetic` and the error `DIV` id being `FullNameError` (the `FullName` part of the element but without the `txt` at the front, the `_compulsory_alphabetic` at the end and with the word `Error` added.

Let's now add the `checkFormValid()` method and supporting functions to the `Validate` class.

Making the Extensions

Lets add the new code to the end of our `Validate.js` class file. The code is quite lengthy, so we'll describe each method under its own heading here. You can download the code file from http://www.wrox.com/.

checkFormValid Method

This is the key method that starts off validation of a form. It has two parameters: the form to be checked, and the document object of the page containing the form. We'll use the document object to access the error `DIV`s. At the top of the method, we have our variable declarations – notice the three regular expressions which will be used later to check the names of elements to see if they need checking, and what data they should contain:

```
var isWholeFormValid = true;
var isValid = true;
var theElement;
var isToBeValidatedElementRegExp = /(_Compulsory)|(_NotCompulsory)/i;
var isCompulsoryRegExp = /(_Compulsory)/i;
var validDataTypeRegExp = /_[a-zA-Z]+$/i;
var invalidDataType;
var elementName;
var errorDivId;
var isCompulsoryElement;
var isToBeCheckedElement;
var isTextBoxElement;
```

Then comes the main `for` loop that will loop through each element in the form. We start at the top of the loop by using the regular expressions we mentioned above to check if the element is compulsory and also if the element needs its data checking for validity. Remember, a compulsory element is any element with `_compulsory` in the name, and an element to be checked for data validity is one with `_compulsory` or `_notcompulsory` in the name followed by `_datatype`.

If we find an element to be validated, then in the `if` statement we first set `errorDivId` to the name of the associated `DIV` with the error message inside. Remember, the error `DIV`'s id is the same as the name of the form element, but without the first three characters, excluding anything after the underscore and with `Error` added at the end of the id. The error `DIV` will be used to display an error message if it turns out that the field is compulsory and has not been filled in, or a data type has been specified and the field contains invalid data. We don't know yet whether the data is valid, so in the final line below we hide the error `DIV`. Why do this? When the page first loads all the error `DIV`s will be hidden, as specified by the style sheet. When the user submits the form, it is checked and the error `DIV` of any invalid elements is shown. When the user corrects the errors and trys again, we want to make sure that all previous errors are hidden, so we re-check the form and show error messages only for those elements that if there are any,that are still invalid:

```
for (var formElementCounter = 0; formElementCounter < theForm.length;
formElementCounter++)
{
    theElement = theForm.elements[formElementCounter];
    elementName = new String(theElement.name);

    isCompulsoryElement = isCompulsoryRegExp.test(elementName);

    isToBeValidatedElement = isToBeValidatedElementRegExp.test(elementName);

    if (isToBeValidatedElement)
    {
        errorDivId = new String(theElement.name);
        errorDivId = errorDivId.slice(3,errorDivId.indexOf("_")) + "Error";
        this.hideErrorDiv(errorDivId,theDocument);
```

Next, we need to decide whether the element is a text box type element – this includes the text box, password box, and file elements. If it's a text element of some sort, we first check its validity by calling the `isTextElementValid` method of the `Validate` class. We'll see how this method works shortly. If `isValid` has not been set to true, then we display the error `DIV` by calling the `showErrorDiv` method of this class, hence the `this` keyword. We also set variable `isWholeFormValid` to `false`, and this will be the value returned by the `isFormValid()` method, indicating that one or more elements has invalid data or was not completed when it should have been:

```
isTextBoxElement =  theElement.type == "text" ||
    theElement.type == "password" ||
    theElement.type == "file";

if ( isTextBoxElement )
{
    isValid = this.isTextElementValid(
        theElement,
        theDocument,
        validDataTypeRegExp,
        isCompulsoryElement);

    if ( !isValid )
    {
        this.showErrorDiv(errorDivId,theDocument);
        isWholeFormValid = false;
    }
}
```

In the `else` part of the `if` statement that is checking for a text box, we check to see if this is a radio button element. If it is a radio button, we check to see if this is a compulsory element. If that is also true, then we need to get a reference to the radio button group as a whole rather than to an individual element within it. We do this by getting the name of the element and then using that with the form's elements array (included in the code below):

```
else if (theElement.type == "radio")
{

    if (isCompulsoryElement)
    {
        elementName = theElement.name;
        theElement = theForm.elements[theElement.name];
        isValid = this.isOneRadioButtonInGroupSelected(theElement);
```

We pass this reference to the `isOneRadioButtonInGroupSelected()` method of this class, (the `Validate` class), which will loop through and check that one element has been selected, returning `true` if it has, and `false` otherwise. In one of our previous examples, we saw that getting the index of the selected radio buttons needed an iteration over an array of radio buttons, and this is exactly what this method does.

If `isValid` is `false`, (no radio button selected), we show the applicable error `DIV` by calling the `showErrorDiv()` method of this class, passing it the `errorDivId` and the document of the page containing the form. We set `isWholeFormValid` to `false`, and as with the text box code, this is the same variable that determines what value, true or false, that `isFormValid()` will return:

```
if (isValid == false)
{
    this.showErrorDiv(errorDivId,theDocument);
    isWholeFormValid = false;
}
```

We then come to a `do...while` loop whose purpose is to simply move the `formElementCounter` on to the next element past those in the radio button group we've already checked. Radio buttons in a group have the same name so we just need to keep looping until the name changes or we reach the end of the form. This is required because the `length` property of the form elements only returns the total number of tags, without regard to their name, so this would even apply to a combo box. At the end of the loop, we decrement the `formElementCounter` by one. This is to compensate for the fact that when the main `for` loop re-iterates it increments the `formElementCounter` by one. Otherwise, because we are already pointing to the next element due to our `while` loop, we would skip an element that may need validating.

```
        do
        {
            formElementCounter++;
            theElement = theForm.elements[formElementCounter];
        }
        while (theElement.name == elementName && formElementCounter <
            theForm.length) formElementCounter--;
    }
```

Finally, at the end of the method, we return our findings as to whether the form was completely valid or not:

```
return isWholeFormValid;
```

isTextElementValid Method

It is in this method that the actual checking of an individual text element is done. The method, shown below, takes three parameters: the element object, a RegExp object that we'll use to obtain the data type information from the name, and finally whether this element is compulsory:

```
Validate.prototype.isTextElementValid = function(
    theElement,
    validDataTypeRegExp,
    isCompulsoryElement)
{

    var isValid = true;
    var validDataType;

    if (isCompulsoryElement && theElement.value == "")
    {
        isValid = false;
    }
    else
    {
        validDataTypeRegExp.exec(theElement.name);
        validDataType = new String(RegExp.lastMatch);
        validDataType = validDataType.toLowerCase();
        isValid = this.isElementDataValid(theElement.value,validDataType);
    }

    return isValid;
}
```

Inside the method, we check to see if the element is compulsory and if the element contains no value. If this is the case, isValid is set to false. Otherwise, we continue to check whether the information entered by the user is valid for the data type format specified. The naming conventions we have used should now be clear. We execute the regular expression on the element name and obtain the results of the lastMatch to get the value of the data type. We set this to lowercase to avoid problems with _IsValidEmail and _isvalidEmail being treated differently.

Finally, we set isValid to the value returned by isElementDataValid() method of this class which does the actual data validity checking. Then isValid is returned to the calling function to indicate the validity of the element checked.

isElementDataValid Method

This method is basically one big switch statement in which we call the relevant data validation method of our Validate class based on the validDataType parameter. This parameter contains the data type defined in the form element's name. The methods called are those we created earlier in the chapter to validate various types of data. If we wanted to extend our automatic checking, then we need only create the validation method that will check it, and then add a relevant data type name to this method:

```
Validate.prototype.isElementDataValid = function(elementValue, validDataType)
{
    var isValid = false;
    switch (validDataType)
    {

        case "_alphanumeric":
            isValid = this.isOnlyAlphaNumeric(elementValue);
            break;
```

```
        case "_alphanumericnospace":
            isValid = this.isOnlyAlphaNumericNoSpace (elementValue);
            break;

        case "_alphabetic":
            isValid = this.isOnlyAlphabetic(elementValue);
            break;

        case "_numeric":
            isValid = this.isOnlyNumeric(elementValue);
            break;

        case "_integer":
            isValid = this.isValidInteger(elementValue);
            break;

        case "_floatingpoint":
            isValid = this.isValidFloatingPoint(elementValue);
            break;

        case "_age":
            isValid = isValidAge(elementValue);
            break;

        case "_password":
            isValid = isValidPassword(elementValue);
            break;

        case "_telephone":
            isValid = isValidTelephoneNum(elementValue);
            break;

        case "_postcode":
            isValid = this.isValidPostalCode(elementValue);
            break;

        case "_email":
            isValid = this.isValidEmail(elementValue);
            break;

        default:
            alert("Error unidentified element data type");
    }

    return isValid;
}
```

isOneRadioButtonInGroupSelected Method

This method loops through the radio group passed as a parameter and checks to see if any radio button in the group has been checked. We set isValid to the value of each radio button as we loop through. If at any point it is true, and a radio button has been checked, we break out of the loop. If it is never true, then isValid remains at its initialization value of false. As we said earlier, checking if a radio button is selected requires an iteration over an array, unlike a select list where the index of the clicked item is passed as a parameter to the event handler.

```
Validate.prototype.isOneRadioButtonInGroupSelected = function(theElement)
{

    var radioCounter;
    var isValid = false;
    for (radioCounter = theElement.length - 1; radioCounter >= 0; radioCounter--)
    {

        isValid = theElement[radioCounter].checked;
        if (isValid)
        {
            break;
        }
    }

    return isValid;

}
```

showErrorDiv Method

We can access an element using its ID to change its properties dynamically. To show the error, we use its visibility property. The syntax for different browsers is different because they support DOM in a different fashion, but the basic idea remains the same – runtime modification to the contents and/or attributes of any element.

This method displays the error DIV. The method takes two parameters, the id of the error DIV and the document object of the page containing the form:

```
Validate.prototype.showErrorDiv = function ( errorDescripDivId,
    theDocument)
{
    if (document.layers)
    {
        theDocument.layers[errorDescripDivId].visibility = "visible";
    }
    else if (document.all)
    {
        theDocument.all(errorDescripDivId).style.visibility = "visible";
    }
    else
    {
        theDocument.getElementById(errorDescripDivId).style.visibility =
            "visible";
    }
}
```

Because IE4+, Netscape 4 and Netscape 6 access elements in a page differently, we have a series of if statements with the correct means of changing the DIV's visibility based on what each browser supports. Netscape 4 uses layers, so if document.layers is not null, the first if statement will evaluate to true. IE4+ supports document.all whereas Netscape 6 does not, so we use that in the second if statement to make sure that only IE attempts to execute the IE code. Finally, we have worked on the assumption that if nothing else has worked it must be Netscape 6 and its DOM-based getElementById method that will work, although you may wish to alter this to cover the less common browsers like Opera. This method will also work on IE5, but for simplicity, let's stick with the document.all method for all IE browsers. If you expect visitors to have browsers supporting none of these techniques, then you would have to add the specific code or spot them in advance and not use the automatic form validation.

hideErrorDiv Method

This is identical to the showErrorDiv in every respect except that it hides the DIV by setting its visibility style property to hidden:

```
Validate.prototype.hideErrorDiv = function (errorDescripDivId, theDocument)
{
   if (theDocument.layers)
   {
      theDocument.layers[errorDescripDivId].visibility = "hidden";
   }
   else if (document.all)
   {
      theDocument.all(errorDescripDivId).style.visibility = "hidden"
   }
   else
   {
      theDocument.getElementById(errorDescripDivId).style.visibility =
      "hidden"
   }
}
```

Using the Validate Class

Let's use our new form checking techniques in an example. We also use the Validate class in the Shopping Cart case study in Chapter 22. The HTML page below is available as PersonalDetails.html in the code download for this chapter:

```
<HTML>
<HEAD>
   <SCRIPT src="Validate.js"></SCRIPT>
   <STYLE>

      DIV.FormElementError
      {
         POSITION: relative;
         LEFT: 280px;
         TOP: -20px;
         COLOR: red;
         VISIBILITY: hidden;
      }

      INPUT.TextBox
      {
         WIDTH: 250px;
      }

      BODY
      {
         FONT-FAMILY: Verdana,'Arial Black';
         FONT-SIZE: 10pt;
         BACKGROUND-COLOR: white;
      }

      H1
      {
         FONT-FAMILY: Verdana,'Arial Black';
         FONT-SIZE: 21pt;
```

```
                COLOR: darkorange;
            }
        </STYLE>
        <SCRIPT>

            function cmdSubmit_onclick()
            {
                var validator = new Validate();

                if (validator.checkFormValid(document.frmCustomer, window.document))
                {
                    alert("No problems with the form data");
                }
                else
                {
                    alert("There were problems with your form.\n"
                        + "Please correct them before continuing.");
                }


            }

        </SCRIPT>

    </HEAD>
    <BODY>

        <H3>
            Please enter your name, address and e-mail address below.<BR>
        </H3>
        <FORM name="frmCustomer">

            <!-- Title -->
            <DIV>
                Title
                Mr<INPUT NAME="radTitle_compulsory" TYPE="radio"  VALUE="Mr">
                Mrs<INPUT NAME="radTitle_compulsory" TYPE="radio" VALUE="Mrs">
                Miss<INPUT NAME="radTitle_compulsory" TYPE="radio" VALUE="Miss">
                Ms.<INPUT NAME="radTitle_compulsory" TYPE="radio" VALUE="Ms.">
                Dr.<INPUT NAME="radTitle_compulsory" TYPE="radio" VALUE="Dr.">
                <DIV  ID="TitleError" CLASS="FormElementError">
                    Please select your title
                </DIV>
            </DIV>

            <!-- Full Name -->
            <DIV>Full Name :
                <BR>
                <INPUT NAME="txtFullName_compulsory_alphabetic" MAXLENGTH="150"
                CLASS="TextBox" >
                <DIV  ID="FullNameError" CLASS="FormElementError">
                    Please enter your full name
                </DIV>
            </DIV>

            <!-- Email -->
            <DIV>
                E-mail Address:
                <BR>
                <INPUT NAME="txtEmail_compulsory_email" CLASS="TextBox" MAXLENGTH="75" >
                <DIV ID="EmailError" CLASS="FormElementError">
```

```
                Please enter a valid e-mail address
         </DIV>
   </DIV>

   <!-- Street -->
   <DIV>
      Street:
      <BR>
      <INPUT NAME="txtStreet_compulsory_alphanumeric" CLASS="TextBox"
      MAXLENGTH="75" >
      <DIV ID="StreetError" CLASS="FormElementError">
         Please enter your house number and street name
      </DIV>
   </DIV>

   <!-- City -->
   <DIV>
      City:
      <BR>
      <INPUT NAME="txtCity_compulsory_alphanumeric" CLASS="TextBox"
      MAXLENGTH="50" >
      <DIV ID="CityError" CLASS="FormElementError">
         Please enter a valid city name
      </DIV>
   </DIV>

   <!-- County/State -->
   <DIV>
      County/State
      <BR>
      <INPUT NAME="txtLocality_notcompulsory_alphanumeric" CLASS="TextBox"
      MAXLENGTH="50" >
      <DIV ID="LocalityError" CLASS="FormElementError">
         Please enter the state
      </DIV>
   </DIV>

   <!-- Post/Zip Code -->
   <DIV>
      Zip/Post Code
      <BR>
      <INPUT NAME="txtPostalCode_compulsory_postcode" CLASS="TextBox"
      MAXLENGTH="15" >
      <DIV ID="PostalCodeError" CLASS="FormElementError">
         Please enter your zip/postal code
      </DIV>
   </DIV>

   <!-- Country -->
   <DIV>
      Country
      <BR>
      <INPUT NAME="txtCountry_compulsory_alphabetic" CLASS="TextBox"
      MAXLENGTH="50" >
      <DIV ID="CountryError" CLASS="FormElementError">
         Please enter your country name
      </DIV>
   </DIV>

<TD COLSPAN="2">
   <INPUT TYPE="reset" NAME="cmdReset" VALUE="Clear form">
   <INPUT TYPE="button" NAME="cmdSubmit" VALUE="Continue"
   onClick="cmdSubmit_onclick()">
```

```
    </FORM>

</BODY>
</HTML>
```

Our form looks like that below and contains eight elements, all of which need to be checked, yet our code to do the checking is just a few lines!

At the top of the page, inside the HEAD element, we include our Validate class's code:

```
<SCRIPT SRC="Validate.js"></SCRIPT>
```

The next important thing to look at is the style class definition for the error DIVs:

```
DIV.FormElementError
{
    POSITION: relative;
    LEFT: 280px;
    TOP: -20px;
    COLOR: red;
    VISIBILITY: hidden;
}
```

This ensures that the DIV's are positioned relatively inside the outer DIV, which we'll see shortly, enabling Navigator 4 to access them. Visibility is set to hidden so the error messages do not display when the page is first loaded – we want to give the user a chance of getting it right!

Next, we have the code that does the checking by calling our Validate class's checkFormValid() method. We can see that by including the code that is doing the checking inside a class contained in a .js file, we can keep the code in each of our pages nice and simple. If bugs are found in the validating code, we just need to change our Validate class, rather than every single page on our website that does validation:

```
function cmdSubmit_onclick()
{
   var validator = new Validate();

   if (validator.checkFormValid(document.frmCustomer, window.document))
   {
      alert("No problems with the form data");
   }
   else
   {
      alert("There were problems with your form.\n"
         + "Please correct them before continuing.")
   }

}
```

Let's now look at how we've defined the form elements. We'll look at just two of them, the radio button group and one text box. The rest follow the same principles, so let's start with the radio button group:

```
<DIV>
   Title
   Mr<INPUT NAME='radTitle_Compulsory' TYPE='radio'  VALUE='Mr'>
   Mrs<INPUT NAME='radTitle_Compulsory' TYPE='radio' VALUE='Mrs'>
   Miss<INPUT NAME='radTitle_Compulsory' TYPE='radio' VALUE='Miss'>
   Ms.<INPUT NAME='radTitle_Compulsory' TYPE='radio' VALUE='Ms.'>
   Dr.<INPUT NAME='radTitle_Compulsory' TYPE='radio' VALUE='Dr.'>
   <DIV  ID='TitleError' CLASS='FormElementError'>
      Please select your title
   </DIV>
</DIV>
```

We've put the whole group, including the descriptive text and the error DIV, inside an outer DIV. This is so that when the error DIV is positioned relatively, it is relative to the containing DIV and not the whole page. It means that we don't have to position the outer DIV relatively or absolutely, although we can if we want, with the proviso that for Netscape 4 we would have to make changes to the showErrorDiv and hideErrorDiv methods of our Validate class. In this case, the inner DIV for Netscape 4 would become part of the outer DIV's document and not the current page's document.

Next, we have the definition of the radio buttons. Each is named radTitle_compulsory. The _compulsory ensures that the one of the radio buttons is selected by the user. If we didn't want it checked, radTitle would suffice. Also note that the name starts with a three-letter prefix, in this case rad. This must be included as our Validate class relies on the fact that the first three letters can be ignored when working out the name of the error DIV.

Finally for this element, we have its error DIV. The id must contain the Title part from the name of the associated radio group and have Error added to the end. We've set the DIV's class to the FormElementError style class to ensure the element is positioned relative and starts off hidden. Inside the DIV is a simple text error message, but we can have what we like in there, an image for example.

Let's now look at the definition for the e-mail address element:

```
<DIV>
   E-mail Address:
   <BR>
   <INPUT NAME='txtEmail_compulsory_email' CLASS='TextBox' MAXLENGTH='75' >
   <DIV ID='EmailError' CLASS='FormElementError'>
      Please enter a valid e-mail address
   </DIV>
</DIV>
```

The principles applied to the radio button apply here, except now we define the type of information the text box can hold. Again, the element, its label, and the error DIV are enclosed in an outer DIV. The element's name this time is txtEmail_compulsory_email. This will tell the form checking code that the text box must be completed and the information it contains must correspond to a valid e-mail address format. If we changed it to txtEmail_email, then the form checker will ignore the element completely and won't validate the information. It relies on the fact that elements to be validated have either _compulsory or _notcompulsory in their names.

We'll just briefly mention one other of the INPUT elements, the text box that lets the user enter their state or county:

```
<DIV>
   County/State
   <BR>
   <INPUT NAME='txtLocality_notcompulsory_alphanumeric' CLASS='TextBox'
   MAXLENGTH='50' >
   <DIV ID='LocalityError' CLASS='FormElementError'>
      Please enter the state
   </DIV>
</DIV>
```

Note that we've made this one optional by adding _notcompulsory to the name. The user can choose to fill it in, but if they do they must enter only alphanumeric characters. We can do this with this type of data as it specifies only what characters are allowed and not the pattern of characters the user input must fit. Therefore, _notcompulsory won't work with the e-mail data type, because that data type specifies a pattern of characters, for example: me@medomain.com or someone.else@this.domain.co.uk. This pattern does not include a blank box, so _notcompulsory will still lead to the data checking part finding it invalid. We could of course change our regular expression in the e-mail checking method to make a blank entry valid.

Validation without JavaScript

If the user has an older browser which does not support JavaScript, or a browser which supports it but has JavaScript turned off, how can we ensure data entered by the user is valid?

Without JavaScript, we're quite limited in what we can check. We can take steps such as setting the maxlength in the HTML tags of text and password boxes. Our main data validation in these circumstances will be server-side validation. In fact, even if client-side validation is carried out, it is important to include server-side validation to prevent malicious attacks on the server by posting direct to the server with massive amounts of data or incorrect data in an attempt to make it fall over, for example. If the server supports JavaScript, then with just a little modification we could use the Validate class for checking form data server-side.

Summary

In this chapter, we've looked at form validation that goes beyond just checking that forms are completed, and checks the format of difficult patterns of data such as e-mail addresses and telephone numbers. We've been aided greatly in this by the use of regular expressions, which help make complex pattern matching fairly simple.

We also created a class specifically for validating form data. This class can easily be added to a web page with just one line and makes our pages easier to handle. It also means that our form validation coding can be centralized. If we later improve it, the improvements are instantly reflected throughout the web pages that use it without us needing to do extra work. The class is designed to be easily extensible so that as we come across different types of data that need validating, changes are quick and easy to make. Finally, we extended the class so that it validates a whole form in response to our calling just one method. We'll be seeing the Validate class in Chapter 22, a case study of a Shopping Cart application.

Pro JavaScript 2nd Edition

17

Making Pages Dynamic

Dynamic HTML (DHTML) has never had a rigorous definition, as it began life largely as a marketing term used by various browser vendors to promote technologies that became available with fourth generation versions of their products. DHTML basically involves dynamism on the *client*. Through the use of technologies such as the Document Object Model (DOM), Cascading Style Sheets (CSS), and client-side scripting, web documents can have changes made to them in real time, without the need to make additional trips back to the server.

> **Before reading this chapter, we recommend that you read the chapters that cover Object-Orientated Programming, DOM, CSS and DHTML.**

Prior to DHTML, most content on the web was static and unchanging. Version 3 browsers did allow content to be modified in a simplistic way such as changing background colors, form processing, and image swapping, while more enhanced features could be performed by adding plug-ins to pages.

The next generation, version 4 browsers, enhanced the capabilities of JavaScript with (DHTML). This allowed more advanced abilities such as enriched styling effects, visibility and positioning. However, the differences between the browser implementations of DHTML increased and cross-browser/platform issues became more apparent as programmers tried to use the more advanced features in each browser. This meant that a programmer had little choice but to identify the browser and version, and write code specifically for the browser in which it was to run. This meant that two or more different scripts were required, or a lot of `if...else` statements were needed so that scripts were compatible on different browsers.

It's ironic that HTML, CSS, core JavaScript, and now DOM are all standardized languages, yet there has been so much disparity between DHTML written for one browser compared to another. However, rather than a language, the DOM is an application programming interface (API) that defines methods and properties for accessing and editing elements within a document. It is this DOM API that has begun to standardize the way that DHTML will be written in the future, thus reducing cross-browser incompatibility.

Both IE 5+ and Netscape 6+ browsers are now embracing DOM and have embarked on implementing DOM APIs within their browsers. Though both major browsers are far from implementing the DOM in full, and there are many differences, some features are consistent in both implementations that can help the programmer write more efficiently, more quickly and achieve more dynamic effects.

> **Care should be taken when attempting to create a DOM compliant script. If we restrict ourselves to the W3C DOM, we may lack important functionality such as properties introduced by IE (`offsetLeft`/`offsetWidth`, `scrollHeight`, `scrollLeft`, `innerHTML`), which were subsequently implemented by Netscape 6, but are not part of the W3C DOM specification.**

The aim of this chapter is to show different examples of DHTML effects and how they are achieved using the latest DHTML techniques. We will see that many cross browser issues are largely removed, with the exception of the browser event models and backwards compatibility with older browser, versions. The chapter will focus on three main areas:

❑ Displaying content dynamically, with examples showing how to dynamically display, show and hide content

❑ Navigational elements, with examples of dynamic navigational elements

❑ Functional widgets with examples of portable self-contained code

Simple Dynamic Effects

Content in a HTML document comes in three main forms: textual, graphical and plug-ins. Mainly, DHTML is only concerned with the textual and graphical content. Since most content was static before DHTML, the only way to show new content was to open up a new browser window at a different location. This could be done either with a completely new window, or in a frame window that is part of a frameset. In the earlier browsers JavaScript added the ability to dynamically display new content via the use of the following functionalities:

❑ location changing

❑ popup windows

❑ writing to the document

❑ form manipulation

Version 4 browsers for the first time used DHTML, increased JavaScript's capabilities beyond simply accessing a few basic properties. DHTML allowed JavaScript to create dynamic effects within a document, such as repositioning elements either relative to another element, or absolutely within a window. It also enabled us to change font, border, and background styles either in response to events raised by the user or programmatically. The event models allowed more detailed information to be captured, such as the x and y co-ordinates of the mouse location.

We will now cover a few basic and simple dynamic effects.

Changing Location

The `location` property of `window` objects can be changed by JavaScript so that a window, whether the top, a child or a popup window, can display the content from another document. This always results in a document being replaced by another document, which although useful at times, is very limited and more suited to navigation. Hence, the most prolific use of this property can be seen in navigational effects such as selection boxes, which allow a user to select an option and jump to a page with information relevant to that particular selected option:

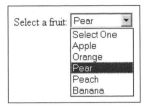

Clicking on an option in the selection box will raise an onChange event for the selection object. Adding an onChange event handler to the selection object will capture this event, and JavaScript can then identify the selected option and jump to a location defined by the OPTION VALUE.

```
<!-- Selector.htm -->
<FORM NAME="myForm">
Select a fruit:
<SELECT NAME="fruit"
        onChange="window.location=this[this.selectedIndex].value">
   <OPTION SELECTED>Select One
   <OPTION VALUE="apple.html">Apple
   <OPTION VALUE="orange.html">Orange
   <OPTION VALUE="pear.html">Pear
   <OPTION VALUE="peach.html">Peach
   <OPTION VALUE="banana.html">Banana
</SELECT>
</FORM>
```

The code above shows how we could implement this navigational effect. The first option has the SELECTED attribute as a default and forces the user to select an alternative option. Clicking on any other option raises an event that is captured by the onChange event handler of the selection object.

Each option of the SELECT element has a value that represents a HTML document. It is this value that needs to be obtained to set the window location to jump to. The JavaScript code attached to the event handler does exactly that. The this keyword is a reference to the selection object itself. Selection objects have a property called selectedIndex that stores the index number of the option that was selected by a user. We can reference the options of a select object by using an array syntax. The selectedIndex property can be used to access the correct option of the selection object and this value is used to set the window.location property, causing the window to jump to a new location.

Occasionally, we may find that this type of navigational effect will, rather than jump to a new page within the same browser window, popup a new smaller window. In this instance it is best to call a JavaScript function from the selection element's onChange event handler. When the user clicks on an option, the onChange event will trigger and the function call will popup a window containing a document from the URL in the OPTION VALUE.

The only drawback is that the option selected remains selected, and if for some reason the user has closed the popup window and they want to open it again, they must first select another option. The code below shows how to avoid this. First, change the onChnage event handler for the SELECT element so that it calls a function and passes a reference to the function for the selection element:

```
<SELECT NAME="fruit" onChange = "jumpToLocation(this)">
```

The jumpToLocation() function below then obtains the value of the selected option and stores it in a variable called docURL. Then the selectedIndex property of the selection element is set to equal 0 (the first option in the list is selected, and thus resets the selection object). JavaScript can then use the URL reference stored in the variable docURL to popup a window with this URL displayed. Having reset the selection element, the user can now reselect the same option over and over again:

```
function jumpToLocation(selector)
{
    var docURL = selector[selector.selectedIndex].value;
    selector.selectedIndex = 0

    //Insert popup code here
}
```

Popup Windows

Popping up new windows can be achieved using the open() method of window objects. The window object is the top-level, default object, and because the existence of the current window is assumed, we do not have to reference the name of the window when we call its methods and assign its properties. Referencing the methods and properties of another window does require a reference to the other window.

> In event handlers, we must specify **window.open()** instead of simply using **open()**. Due to the scope of static objects in JavaScript, a call to **open()** without specifying an object name would be equivalent to **document.open()**.

The open() method allows customized windows to be opened with different features, such as status bar, size, and showing/hiding menus. The general format for using the open() method is

```
open("someURL", "windowTarget", "features")
```

. SomeURL can be any valid URL, windowTarget provides the window name to use in the TARGET attribute of a FORM or A tag, and features is a comma-delimited list of features for the window. The standard options and values that can be used are listed below:

- ❑ toolbar[=yes|no]|[=1|0]
- ❑ location[=yes|no]|[=1|0]
- ❑ directories[=yes|no]|[=1|0]
- ❑ status[=yes|no]|[=1|0]
- ❑ menubar[=yes|no]|[=1|0]
- ❑ scrollbars[=yes|no]|[=1|0]
- ❑ resizable[=yes|no]|[=1|0]
- ❑ width=pixels
- ❑ height=pixels

We may use any subset of these options, separating each option with a comma, but we do not put spaces between the options. The Boolean values of the options can be yes or 1 to use the feature, and no or 0 to not use the feature. The width and height *pixels* value is a positive integer specifying the dimension of the window in pixels.

Popup windows are great for showing new content to a user, often as a complement to the content in the parent window. Though this is a useful functionality, it does have drawbacks. For instance, by changing the document location, only whole documents can be displayed. Also, the user may get annoyed from too many popup windows cluttering their desktop, and tracking all the open windows can be tricky for the programmer. The code below shows an example of how to use a popup window to display a color chooser widget (we can of course provide any URL to other HTML documents), with all the chrome effects removed:

```
var jsc = open("jscolor.html", "color",
"toolbar=no,scrollbars=no,location=no,directories=no,resizable=0,width=275,height=
133")
```

In this example, we have several features explicitly turned off by setting the feature values to no or 0. By default, features are only displayed if their values are explicitly set to yes or 1. Therefore, the code above can be replaced with the following:

```
var jsc = open("jscolor.html", "color", "width=275,height=133")
```

Notice the open() method returns a reference to the newly opened window. Use this variable when referring to the popup window's properties, methods, and containership.

Dynamic Writing

Finer and more granular control of dynamic content display can be achieved through the use of the write() method of the document object. A variable is used to store a string, including HTML, which is built up depending on the rules encoded within a script, and written out to the document by passing the variable to the write() method. Real life examples include writing out the contents of a shopping cart, including the total value with or without tax.

The document.write() method improves the ability to dynamically write content. The following example shows a page that will write the date that the file was last modified as the page is loading:

```
<!-- DocumentDate.htm -->
<HTML>
<BODY>
This document was last modified:
    <SCRIPT>
        document.write(document.lastModified)
    </SCRIPT>
</BODY>
</HTML>
```

Alternatively, we could write to a document after it has loaded. The big drawback in doing this is that the original document is completely overwritten. However, the previous documents do exist in the windows history object and can be returned to by using the browser's back button.

The following example creates a page with two links. The first link calls the openWin() function, which opens a HTML file in a popup window and stores a reference to this new window in the global variable pageSelect. This variable is used by the writeToWindow() function, which is called by the second link, to access the document object of this popup window and write to it.

The first line of the writeToWindow() function generates a string of the content including HTML tags, and concatenates into the string the numeric value of the global variable i (incrementing i each time the function is called). Before this line can be written to the document of the popup window, the document needs to be prepared to receive new content. The open() method opens a stream to collect the output of the write() method. If a document exists in the target window, the open() method clears all the current content. End writing to the document by using the close() method:

```
<!-- DocumentWrite.htm -->
<HTML>
<HEAD>
<SCRIPT>
var pageSelect
var i = 0
function openWin()
{
    pageSelect = open("selector.html", "color", "width=275,height=133")
}

function writeToWindow()
{
```

```
      var htmlStr = "This page has been written to<BR>" + i++ + "<BR>times."
      jsc.document.open()
      jsc.document.write(htmlStr)
      jsc.document.close()
   }
   </SCRIPT>
   </HEAD>
   <BODY>
      <A HREF="JavaScript:openWin()">Open a window</A><BR>
      <A HREF="JavaScript:doIt()">write to the window</A>
   </BODY>
   </HTML>
```

Documents in Documents

Rather than linking to a document, an author may sometimes wish to embed it directly into a primary HTML document. HTML 4 provides a non-programmatic solution that uses the IFRAME, available to IE 4+ and Netscape 6+ browsers. (Netscape 4 browsers used their proprietary and now deprecated LAYER tag).

The IFRAME is similar to a frame within a frameset, but exists as a window within a document. IFRAMEs improved dynamic content display, thus allowing supplementary documents to be viewed within a single document without losing any current content or having to use additional popup windows. With some careful design, IFRAMEs can fit seamlessly into a main document. The HTML code below will insert an IFRAME into a document with no border, so that it is displayed seamlessly within the flow of the surrounding content, by using the FRAMEBORDER attribute set to 0 (a border can be added by setting this attribute to 1). The document to be displayed in the IFRAME is referenced by the SRC attribute. If the SCROLLING attribute is set to auto, scroll bars are added to the IFRAME if necessary. Alternatively, we can set the SCROLLING attribute to no or yes, indicating whether the scroll bars should always be present or not:

```
<IFRAME SRC="somedoc.html" FRAMEBORDER=0 SCROLLING="auto" NAME="extra"></IFRAME>
```

JavaScript can load new content into the IFRAME using the location property of the IFRAME window, or by using the write() method of the document within the window.

With Netscape 4 browsers, a layer is similar to having a document within a document, unlike the IFRAME that is more akin to a window within a document. The content of a layer can be rewritten using the write() method of the document object. The write() method can display any number of expressions, including numerics, strings, or logicals. With Netscape 4, we have to wait for the BODY onload event to fire before we can write to any layer and then we can only write to one layer at a time.

The writeToLayer() function in the example below accepts two arguments. The first is the ID name of the layer and the second is a string. The first line uses the with statement to establish the document property of the layer as the default object for the set of statements within the code block that follows. This means the document.layers[lyrID].document is not required before the open(), write(), and close() methods. These three methods open the layers document, write to it, and then close it:

```
<!-- NS4 Write To Layer.htm -->
<HTML>
<HEAD>
<TITLE>Write To Layer Example</TITLE>
<STYLE>
   #fred
   {
      position:absolute;
      top:100px;
      left:100px;
      width:200px;
```

```
        height:auto;
        background-color:#f0f0f0;
    }
</STYLE>
<SCRIPT>
    function writeToLayer(lyrID, html)
    {
        with (document.layers[lyrID].document) {
            open();
            write(html);
            close();
        }
    }

    function changeLayer()
    {
        writeToLayer("fred", "<BR>New Content has been <BR>inserted");
    }
</SCRIPT>
</HEAD>

<BODY>
    <DIV ID='fred'>Some content</DIV>
    <A HREF='JavaScript:changeLayer()'>Click Me</A>
</BODY>
</HTML>
```

This is a Netscape only example, though it is not compatible with version 6. As we will see in the next section, IE 5 and Netscape 6 browsers were the first browsers to start implementing DOM, so a DOM solution is required to dynamically change the content of positioned elements within these browsers. Note that the layer in this example has been positioned absolutely; Netscape 4 contains bugs that mean that if the layer is positioned relatively, the layer will not resize to cope with the dimensions of the new content and the hyperlinks are not clickable.

Stacking Order

The use of layers has been lost with Netscape 6. Instead we now habe **positioned elements**, which were standardized as part of the CSS 2 Recommendation (see Chapter 8, CSS for further details on CSS). DHTML allows a positioned element to be sized and positioned relative to another element within a document, or absolutely positioned within the current browser window.

When more than one positioned element is in use, a zIndex can be set to place the layers above and below each other, known as the stacking order. Elements with higher zIndex values will be placed nearer the top of the stack.

Accessing Content

IE 5+ and Netscape 6+ herald a completely new mechanism for dynamic content display by the implementation of DOM. By using DOM, JavaScript can now insert or replace content at any location within a document. It can even completely rebuild a document, without the need to overwrite content or reload a new page in the current window, a child window or popup window.

The DOM provides several methods and properties that make life much simpler for the programmer to access and dynamically change content within elements and documents. Although there are a number of cross-browser issues due in part to the fact that browsers are not fully DOM compliant, there are methods and properties that are cross-browser compatible, and therefore essential for JavaScript programmers to master.

627

document.getElementById()

A powerful method to note is `document.getElementById()` that can search through the `document` tree and find an element that matches the named ID supplied as an argument. If a HTML tag with an ID is not present, we cannot access it using this method and it will give JavaScript errors at runtime. The same effect was previously achieved for Netscape 4 browsers by accessing `document.layers[layerNameorId]`, or in IE using `document.all[layerNameorId]` to obtain a reference to the positioned element.

It is important to mention that all HTML tags can have an ID attribute and, therefore using this method allows access to all HTML elements within the document. The code snippet below shows how we might access the element defined by `<DIV ID="myDiv">...</DIV>` within the document:

```
var divEl = document.getElementById("myDiv")
```

getElementsByTagName()

A second useful method is `getElementsByTagName()`. This will search through an element tree and return a collection of elements as an array that matches a tag name supplied as an argument. The code snippet below shows an example of how we might obtain an array of all the `DIV` elements within the document.

```
var divEls = document.getElementsByTagName("DIV")
```

These two methods can also be used together. The example code below shows how we might create a reference to a table, with an ID equal to `myTable`, and then extract as an array a collection of all the row elements within that table:

```
var tableEl = document.getElementById("myTable")
var rowEls = tableEl.getElementsByTagName("TR")
```

The DOM specification provides a much better approach to accessing the rows and cells of a table. Table elements possess a `rows` property that is a reference to an array of row elements within the table. Furthermore, each row element has a `cells` property that is a reference to an array of cell elements within the index row.

In the code snippet below, the first line produces an array of row elements in the table `myTable`, and stores them in `rowEls`. The second line uses `rowEls` to store an array of all the cells in the third row of a table and stores them in the `row3Cells` variable. The last line uses `row3Cells` to retrieve the fifth cell of the third row of a table and stores it in the `cell` variable:

```
var rowEls = document.getElementById("myTable").rows
var row3Cells = rowEls[3].cells
var cell = row3Cells.cells[5]
```

Knowing this, we may be able to figure out that each cell element and its content can be obtained very easily using two loops (an inner and outer loop). Assuming a table only contains textual content, the following code could be used to extract the content from each cell:

```
var rowEls = document.getElementById("myTable").rows
for (var i = 0; i < rowEls.length; i++)
{
   for (var j = 0; j < rowEls[i].cells.length; j++)
   {
      var txt = rowEls[i].cells[j].firstChild.nodeValue
      //do something with the cell value stored in the txt variable
   }
}
```

The JavaScript code above stores an array of rows from a table called myTable in the variable rowEls. Two for loops are then used to iterate through each cell element within the table. The outer loop iterates through the rows of the table and the inner loop iterates through each cell in a particular row.

The actual text content is not stored in the cell element itself; textual content is stored in a special element called a **text node**. If a cell only contains text content, then the cell will possess one child element (a text element), which stores actual content. The firstChild property of the elements provides a reference to the first child node of this element. In our example, the first child element is the text element that holds the content. There is also a nodeValue property for text elements that will provide access to the actual text content stored in the element. So, the content of the cell is obtained using the firstChild.nodeValue property of cell elements. The value of the cells content is stored in a variable txt ready for further processing.

innerHTML

An extremely useful property is innerHTML, which provides read/write access to content stored within an element. As the name suggests, innerHTML provides access to both textual and/or HTML mark up within an element. The following example shows how both the getElementById() method and the innerHTML property can be used together to retrieve and set the contents of an element within a document:

```
<!-- Write To Layer.htm -->
<HTML>
<HEAD>
<TITLE>DOM Test example</TITLE>
<SCRIPT>
    function callHTML()
    {
        alert(document.getElementById("item1").innerHTML)
    }

    function writeHTML()
    {
        var el = document.getElementById("item1");
        el.innerHTML = "new content to display in the DIV";
    }
</SCRIPT>
</HEAD>

<BODY>
    <DIV ID="item1">
        Content Block <I>trying out <B>DOM</B> examples</I>. Will it work?
    </DIV>
    <A HREF="javascript:callHTML()">InnerHTML Test</A>
    <A HREF="javascript:writeHTML()">Write Test</A>
</BODY>
</HTML>
```

Clicking on InnerHTML Test will display the content within the item1 DIV tag in an alert box. Clicking on Write Test will dynamically replace the current content of the DIV element with the new text, so if we click on InnerHTML Test again, the alert dialog will display the new contents of the DIV element.

> **innerHTML is not part of the DOM specification. It was first introduced in IE 4 browsers. Netscape introduced these properties in Netscape 6 to enable developers to write cross browser code (IE 4+, Netscape 6+).**

`innerHTML` allows both HTML and text content to be retrieved and set. A similar property, `innerText`, was introduced with IE 4, and only allows text content to be retrieved and set, ignoring all HTML mark up. `innerText` is also not part of the DOM Recommendation and, unlike `innerHTML`, not supported by Netscape browsers.

Although they are both powerful properties, because they are part of the IE DOM API and not the DOM Recommendation, they cannot be guaranteed to work in other DOM browsers that follow the W3C DOM Recommendation. Therefore, it would be useful to create some functions for the latest browsers that mimic these properties using DOM methods and properties.

The first function we will create will allow us to remove the content of an element and replace it with plain text, equivalent to setting the `innerText` property of an element in IE. This function is called `setInnerText` and accepts two arguments: the element that will store the text and the actual text to insert into the element.

The first part of the function uses a `while` loop to test if the element, `el`, has any child nodes using the `hasChildNodes()` method. If the element does have child nodes, then the loop executes. DOM provides a `removeChild()` method that removes a child element from an element. Each time the loop executes, the `firstChild` element is removed until all the child elements are removed. Then `hasChildNodes()` returns `false` and the loop exits. Having removed all the child elements, the function then creates a new text node element, using the `createTextNode()` method of the document object and passes the `txt` argument to this method. The text node is then appended to the element as a child element and the text is displayed in the element within the document:

```
function setInnerText(el, txt)
{
    while (el.hasChildNodes())
    {
        el.removeChild(el.firstChild)
    }
        var txtNode = document.createTextNode(txt)
        el.appendChild(txtNode)
}
```

This function is now as easy to use as the non-standard `innerText` property. The code snippet below shows how we could use the function to remove any content in a `DIV` element and replace it with some new plain text:

```
var myDiv = document.getElementById("myDiv")
setInnerText(myDiv, "some new content to display")
```

Being able to set the text content of an element provides the first functionality of the `innerText` property. The next function, `getInnerText()` provides the second piece of functionality, allowing the text content of all the child nodes to be retrieved as one single string.

This function accepts a single argument – the element from which to extract the text content. This is a little bit more difficult to get to grips with because it is a recursive function (it calls itself to do part of its work). The first part of the function uses an `if` statement to test if an element has any child nodes. If not, the function simply returns the node value and the function exits.

If the node does have child elements, a loop is used to iterate through each child element and attempt to extract the textual content from these nodes. Firstly, a variable `s` is defined that will store the string of text that is extracted from the child elements of the containing element. The `childNodes` property of elements is an array containing each child element and the length of this array is used to control the number of times the loop executes.

An `if` statement is used to check that each child element has its own set of child elements. If this is the case, it is passed in another call to the `getInnerText()` function (this is the recursive part), and the whole process is repeated for the child element. Eventually, when a child element is reached that does not have any more child elements, the recursive call to `getInnerText()` will return a string that is concatenated to the `s` variable.

If a child element in the `for` loop doesn't have any child elements, the value of the node is obtained and again concatenated to the `s` variable. A ternary operator is used to check that the `nodeValue` property has a value and is not null. If it does have a value it is concatenated to the variable `s` or an empty string is concatenated. When the loop exits, the value stored in the `s` variable is returned, thus returning only the text content of a containing element:

```
function getInnerText(el)
{
   if (!el.hasChildNodes())
   {
      return el.nodeValue
   }
   var s = ""
   for (var i = 0; i < el.childNodes.length; i++)
   {
      if (el.childNodes[i].hasChildNodes())
         s += getInnerText(el.childNodes[i])
      s += (el.childNodes[i].nodeValue) ? el.childNodes[i].nodeValue : ""
   }
   return s
}
```

The code snippet below shows how we could use the function to obtain any content a `DIV` element may contain and return that content as a plain string without any HTML markup:

```
var myDiv = document.getElementById("myDiv")
var txt = getInnerText(myDiv)
```

Functions can also be created to set or extract all the text content of an element including HTML. The `setInnerHTML()` function will allow new content marked up in HTML to replace the content of an element. The function accepts three arguments; the first argument `el` is the element whose content is to be changed. A second argument, `html`, is a string of marked up content to be inserted into the element and `dontClear` is a boolean value indicating whether the element's content should be removed.

The first part of the `setInnerHTML()` function uses a `while` loop to remove all the child nodes of the element if it has child elements and the `dontClear` argument equals `false`. After the execution of the `while` loop, three variables are created to store the positions within the `html` string argument. These are the first occurrence of each of the character(s) of a HTML tag (`<`), the start of a counter tag (`</`), and the end of either a tag or a counter tag (`>`). These variables will be used to identify the first occurrence of either a tag or counter tag in HTML, and mark the start and end characters of the mark up. If `html` does not contain any of these three features, `-1` will be stored in the respective variables.

The last section of this function consists of several `if"`..."`else` statements that will break up the string in the `html` argument and create the child elements to be inserted. If `tagIdxStart` is equal to `-1` there are no HTML tags present in the `html` string argument and must therefore contain only text elements. Therefore, a text element is created and the value of the `html` argument is stored in the element. The text element is then appended to the `el` argument.

If the `counterTagIdxStart` variable is equal to the `tagIdxStart` variable, the start of a HTML counter tag has been identified as the first piece of HTML mark up. If this is true, the variable `tagIdxEnd` stores the index position of the last character of the counter tag. The `html` argument will represent a string that may contain an initial piece of text or 0 or more characters, followed by a counter tag and 0 or more characters.

The first line of this `if` block calls the `setInnerHTML()` function, passing as arguments `el`, a string of 0 or more characters that exists before the counter tag, and `true`. The `true` value prevents the `while` loop from removing any nodes that have been added to the `el` element. When this string is passed, it only contains text ,and the function creates a text node and appends it to the element that is passed. When a counter tag is reached, no new elements need to be appended to the `el` argument, and node structure moves up to the parent node. A second call to `setInnerHTML()` is made, this time passing a reference to the sibling's parent element, a sub string of `html` from the first character after the counter tag to the last character of `html`, and again `true`.

Finally, the `else` block is executed if the `counterTagIdxStart` variable is not equal to the `tagIdxStart` variable, and therefore a HTML tag must have been identified as the first piece of mark up in the `html` argument. Similar to the counter tag scenario, if a HTML tag is found, there may be 0 or more characters before the tag. The first line of the code block extracts the sub string before the tag and passes it along with `el` and `true` to the `setInnerHTML()` function. This sub string only contains text, so the function creates a text element and appends it to the element passed to the function.

After this call to `setInnerHTML()`, a sub string of `html` is stored in the `tagName` variable that represents the name of the tag and a new child element is created of that tag name, using the `createElement()` method of the `document` object. This child element is then appended to the parent element `el`. Once the new child element is created, the sub string of characters after the tag characters is sent as an argument in another call to the `setInnerHTML()` function. Before this can happen, a test is made to check if a `BR` or `HR` element was created. Elements of type `BR` do not contain child nodes, so in this instance, rather than pass the newly created child element to `setInnerHTML()`, the parent element.el is passed. Conversely, if the newly created child element is not a `BR` element, then this child element is passed to the `setInnerHTML()` function with the sub string after the start tag:

```
function setInnerHTML(el, html, dontClear)
{
    while (el.hasChildNodes() && !dontClear)
    {
        el.removeChild(el.firstChild)
    }

    var tagIdxStart = html.indexOf("<")
    var counterTagIdxStart = html.indexOf("</")
    var tagIdxEnd = html.indexOf(">")

    if (tagIdxStart == -1)
{
        var txtNode = document.createTextNode(html)
        el.appendChild(txtNode)
    }
    else if (counterTagIdxStart == tagIdxStart)
    {
        setInnerHTML(el, html.substring(0, tagIdxStart), true)
        setInnerHTML(el.parentNode, html.substring(tagIdxEnd+1), true)
    }
    else
    {
        setInnerHTML(el, html.substring(0, tagIdxStart), true)
        var tagName = html.substring(tagIdxStart+1, tagIdxEnd)
        var node = document.createElement(tagName)
        el.appendChild(node)
        if (tagName == "BR" || tag == "HR")
            setInnerHTML(el, html.substring(tagIdxEnd+1), true)
        else
            setInnerHTML(node, html.substring(tagIdxEnd+1), true)
    }
}
```

The code snippet below shows how we could use the function to replace the content of a `DIV` element with new HMTL content. Notice that the third boolean argument does not have to be passed to the function. Its omission means the `dontClear` argument is undefined, and this allows the `while` loop of the `setInnerHTML()` function to execute, even though `false` hasn't been explicitly passed as the argument value:

```
var myDiv = document.getElementById("myDiv")
var txt = setInnerHTML(myDiv, "new<BR>content goes <B>here</B>")
```

The final function, `getInnerHTML()`, that will replace `innerHTML` completes the set DOM functions. This function returns a string representing the HTML source code that would be required to create the mark up content inside an element. A variable `s` is first created that will store the content as it is extracted from the element and its child elements.

An `if`"..."`else` statement is used to test if the element argument has child nodes. If it does not, then the node value is concatenated to the `s` variable and the function returns the `s` variable. If the element argument does contain child elements, a `for` loop is used to iterate through each child element. An `if` statement is used to test if the child element has child elements itself and if so is passed in a recursive call to the `getInnerHTML()` function. The value return from this call to `getInnerHTML()` is stored in the `ns` variable that is used in the next line to create the HTML representation of this node. Concatenated to the `s` variable is the element's HTML name inside angled brackets (creating the HTML tag), followed by the value of `ns` and the element's HTML name inside angle brackets with the first angled bracket followed by a forward slash (creating the counter tag).

If a child element does not have any child elements, an `if` statement checks to see if the element's name is either `BR` or `HR` and `if` concatenates the name of this element between angle brackets to create the `BR` or `HR` tag. The last line of the loop checks if the child element has any text content, and if so concatenates this to the `s` variable. Then our function exits once the loop iterates through all the child elements and returns the value of the `s` variable:

```
function getInnerHTML(el)
{
   var s = ""
   if (el.hasChildNodes())
   {
      for (var i = 0; i < el.childNodes.length; i++)
      {
         if (el.childNodes[i].hasChildNodes())
         {
            var ns = getInnerHTML(el.childNodes[i])
            s += ("<"+el.childNodes[i].nodeName+">" + ns + "</"+
                   el.childNodes[i].nodeName + ">")
         }
         if (el.childNodes[i].nodeName == "BR" ||
             el.childNodes[i].nodeName == "HR")
              s += "<" + el.childNodes[i].nodeName + ">"
         s += (el.childNodes[i].nodeValue) ? el.childNodes[i].nodeValue : ""
      }
      else
      {
      s += el.nodeValue
      }
   return s
}
```

The code snippet below shows how we could use the function to obtain any content a `DIV` element may contain and return that content as a string with any HTML markup:

```
var myDiv = document.getElementById("myDiv")
var txt = getInnerHTML(myDiv)
```

Both these functions can now be used to obtain and replace text content within an element in a document, and therefore replace the usage of innerText and innerHTML properties in IE 5+ and provide the same functionality in Netscape 6+ browsers.

getInnerHTML() and setInnerHTML() functions are not quite as powerful as the innerHTML property. The getInnerHTML() function will obtain the attributes for an element and display them in the returned HTML source. Also, the setInnerHTML() function will break if HTML tags have attributes included, because such features have not been programmed in. We can extend these functions further to include the ability to identify and add attributes by making use of the createAttribute() of the document, the attribute's array property of elements and the name and value properties of attribute elements that the DOM Recommendation supplies.

Armed with these new mechanisms for dynamically writing content to elements within a document, the previous Netscape 4-specific example we looked at earlier for writing to a positioned element can be modified to work in Netscape 6 and IE 4+ browsers by replacing the writeToLayer() function in NS4 Write To Layer.htm with the two functions below and importing the DOM function in the DOMFunctions.js file:

```html
<!-- NS4andDom Write To Layer.htm -->
<HTML>
<HEAD>
<TITLE>Write To Layer Example</TITLE>
<STYLE>
    #fred
    {
        position:absolute;
        top:100px;
        left:100px;
        width:200px;
        height:auto;
        background-color:#f0f0f0;
    }
</STYLE>
<SCRIPT SRC="DOMFunctions.js"></SCRIPT>
<SCRIPT>
function clientSniffer()
{
    var agent = navigator.appName
    this.isIE = function()
    {
        return (agent == "Microsoft Internet Explorer" && document.all)
    }
    this.isNS = function() { return (agent == "Netscape") }
    this.getVersion = function()
    {
        if (this.isNS()) return parseInt(navigator.appVersion)
        if (this.isIE())
        {
        var vIdx = navigator.appVersion.indexOf("MSIE ") + ("MSIE ").length
        return parseInt(navigator.appVersion.substring(vIdx, vIdx+3))
        }
        return 0
    }
    this.isDOM = function()
    {
        return document.getElementById ? true : false
    }
}

function writeToLayer(lyrID, html)
{
```

```
    var cs = new clientSniffer()
    if (cs.isDOM())
    {
    setInnerHTML(document.getElementById(lyrID), html)
    }
    else
    {
       if (cs.isNS())
       {
          with(document.layers[lyrID].document) {
             open()
             write(html)
             close()
          }
       }
       else
       {
          document.all[lyrID].innerHTML = html
       }
    }
}

function changeLayer()
{
    writeToLayer("fred", "<BR>New Content has been <BR>inserted")
}
</SCRIPT>
</HEAD>

<BODY>
    <DIV ID='fred'>Some content</DIV>
    <A HREF='JavaScript:changeLayer()'>Click Me</A>
</BODY>
</HTML>
```

Note that we have had to include a client sniffer to identify the browser version. We will use the client sniffer code in any further examples that require its inclusion.

The clientSniffer() function is a constructor to create an object that possesses several methods to identify the browser that it is currently executing in. The isDOM() method identifies a browser as being DOM compliant if the browser supports the document.getElementById property. The isIE() and isNS() methods identify whether IE or Netscape is being used. Each of these three methods returns true or false depending on the browser type. The fourth method, getVersion(), returns an integer number indicating the major version of the browser. This client sniffer has been written for IE and Netscape – we may wish to extend it further to test for other browser features or to cope with additional browsers, such as Opera.

If we do not have to worry about version 4 and earlier Netscape or IE browsers, then the amount of code can be dramatically decreased. The client sniffer is no longer required, and the writeToLayer() function can be reduced to the code below:

```
function writeToLayer (lyrID, html)
{
    setInnerHTML(document.getElementById(lyrID), html)
}
```

The getElementByID() method is now more generic, being able to write to any element within the document possessing an ID. In reality, we probably would not create a function for this sole purpose, but rather incorporate the body of this function into another function, saving the overhead of calling an extra function.

Code that utilizes DOM and the non-standard cross-browser properties is useful for displaying content in new generation browsers We will now cover many DHTML examples using these methods and properties.

Houdini Tricks

Having discussed several mechanisms for displaying content to the user that was not initially present when a web document loads, we should now see how DHTML has become easier and more flexible in the latest browsers to insert content without cross browser compatibility issues. Let's take this information and have a look at some real life examples of making content within web pages more dynamic for later browsers.

The following examples will use a combination of traditional DHTML techniques and show improvements with DOM. Since the examples will be using DOM, all will be Netscape 6 IE 5+ compatible, but not backwards compatible with earlier browsers unless stated.

Rotating Adverts

Many web sites use banner adverts to generate revenue. The advert graphics are delivered in several different ways, such as a single unchanging image per page, or an IFRAME sized exactly to the banner's dimensions that is refreshed approximately every 15-30 seconds. Using DHTML, an alternative method is available for rotating banners within the same page.

The idea is to preload a number of images and then swap the images after a period of time. By clicking on the adverts the user can go to the associated web site. We can also add mailto URLs or a JavaScript function using a JavaScript URL. Take a look at the code below that could be used to create the banner advert rotations:

```javascript
// AdRotator.js

function imgCache(src, w, h)
{
    if (!document.images || src == null || src=="") return
    var img = (w && h) ? (new Image(w, h)) : (new Image())
    img.src = src
    return img
}

function AdRotator(target, dt)
{
    //Private Variables
    var adverts = new Array()
    var ptr = 0
    var panel = null
    var time = dt || 15000
    var globalIdx = 0

    if (window["showAdvert"])
{
    globalIdx = showAdvert.length
    }
    else
    {
    showAdvert = new Array()
}

//Global Function array
    showAdvert[globalIdx] = function()
        {
            if (ptr >= adverts.length) ptr = 0
            panel.src = adverts[ptr][0].src
```

```
            panel.AREF = adverts[ptr][1]
            ptr++
    }

//Public Methods
    this.addAdvert = function(src, w, h, link)
        {
            var i = adverts.length
            adverts[i] = new Array(2)
            adverts[i][0] = imgCache(src, w, h)
            adverts[i][1] = link
        }

    this.run = function()
        {
            if (!target || target == "") return
            if (!panel) panel = document.getElementById(target)
            showAdvert[globalIdx]()
            setInterval("showAdvert[" + globalIdx + "]()", time)
        }
    }
```

`imgCache()` is used here as a utility function to preload the banner images that will be used in the ad rotator. The subsequent code creates an `AdRotator` object that is used to rotate the images for the adverts.

The `AdRotator` constructor accepts two arguments, `target` and `dt`, of which `target` must be supplied when creating a new instance of this object. The `target` argument will be used to accept a string representing the ID name of the `IMG` element that will be used to display each banner in succession. `dt` will accept a number that will represent the number of milliseconds to display the banner advert.

When the `AdRotator` constructor is called to create a new object, the private class member variables are initialized. The time variable is set to be either the value of dt that is supplied as an argument or if dt is null, a default value of 15000 milliseconds is used.

After initializing the private class member variables, an `if...else` statement is used to test if a global variable called `showAdvert` exists, which should store an array. If `showAdvert` does exist, the private variable `globalIdx` is set to equal the current size of the array that it stores; if the global variable does not exist, it is created and a new array is stored in it.

After a new `AdRotator` object is created the banner images and URL references must be stored. The `adverts` variable stores an array, which will hold these references for each advert. The public method `addAdvert()` is used to populate the `adverts` array with image and URL references by accepting four arguments: an image source, width, height, and a URL link. The first line creates a variable `i` that indicates the position in the array to be populated next and then a new array of two elements is created within this array at index `i`.

The `src`, `w` and `h` arguments are passed on to the `imgCache()` function, which in turn returns a reference to the image that is preloaded and stores it in the first element of the sub array. The URL reference is then stored in the second element of the sub array.

To set the Ad Rotator running a public method called `run` is available. This method checks to see if the constructor was passed to the value of the `target` and, if not returns from (exits) the function immediately and no further action occurs. With the `target` argument supplied, a reference to the element is created and stored in the `panel` variable, using the DOM method `getElementById()`. Next, the global function `showAdvert[globalIdx]()` is called to show the first advert immediately. This has a slightly different syntax to what we may normally be used to – the function is stored within an element of an array.

The global array variable showAdvert holds functions necessary to rotate each advert. Each time a new AdRotator object is created, the function to rotate the adverts is stored in this global array at the index stored in the variable globalIdx. Each new object stores its own function in the next position of the array.

Within the advert rotation function the private variable ptr stores a number indicating the position in the adverts array of the next image to be displayed. The function showAdvert[globalIdx]() first checks the value of ptr, and if its value is greater than or equal to the length of the adverts array, is reset back to 0 so that the first image in the array can be accessed again (hence the advert's loop). The ptr variable is then used to access the adverts array for the next advert to be displayed. The source property of the panel element is set to the source property of the image stored in the first sub array element, which allows the new image to be displayed, similar to an image roll over. The next line of code then sets a property for the panel element called AREF to equal the URL reference stored in the second element of the sub array. Finally, the last line of code increments the ptr variable by 1, ready for the next time showAdvert[globalIdx]() is called.

Having made sure the first image in the adverts array has been displayed, the last line of the run() method sets an interval timer that calls the showAdvert[globalIdx]() function after a number of milliseconds stored in the private variable time. Using the interval timer requires showAdvert[globalIdx]() to be represented by the string "showAdvert[" + globalIdx + "]()". If a call to the actual function within the array was used instead of the string representation, setInterval() will execute the function within the showAdvert array immediately and only once.

The following block of HTML code shows how to use this Advert Rotator code. The code above has been put into a separate file called AdRotator.js and loaded using the SRC property of the SCRIPT element. The BODY section contains an image with an onClick event handler, allowing it to be clickable. The IMG tag has been supplied with a default image, and the ID attribute set, is this image element that will be used to display the rotating banners:

```
<!-- AdRotator.htm -->
<HTML>
<HEAD>
<TITLE>Banner Ad Example</TITLE>
<SCRIPT SRC='AdRotator.js'></SCRIPT>
   <SCRIPT>
   function win_load()
     {
        var AdRot = new AdRotator("banner", 5000)
        AdRot.addAdvert("cdbanner.gif", 468, 60,
           "http://www.chimeradigial.com")
        AdRot.addAdvert("emailad.gif", 468, 60,
           "mailto:enquireies@chimeradigital.com")
        AdRot.addAdvert("jsad.gif", 468, 60, "http://www.wrox.com")
        AdRot.addAdvert("matica.gif", 468, 60, "http://www.matica.com")
        AdRot.run()
     }
   </SCRIPT>
</HEAD>
   <BODY onload='win_load()'>
      <IMG SRC='cdbanner.gif' WIDTH='468' HEIGHT='60' ID='banner'
         onClick='window.location=this.AREF'>
   </BODY>
</HTML>
```

When the page loads, the win_load() function is called by the onLoad event handler. The win_load() function creates a new AdRotator object, which is stored in the AdRot variable and has passed the ID name of the IMG element and the number 5000 to represent the 5 seconds for which each image should be displayed. The next four lines simply add the details for the banner images, by calling the addAdvert() method of the AdRotator object. Finally, the last statement calls the run() method of the object and the banner images are displayed sequentially in a loop.

When a user clicks on one of the adverts, the `OnClick` event handler sets the `window.location` property to the URL value of the `AREF` property of the image that was created by the `AdRotator` object. If the property has a value, the window location is updated, and the page jumps off to the relevant web site.

Although this code has been used here for rotating banner adverts, it can be used equally well for animations. If each image used is a frame of an animation and the interval time decreased, it is possible to create very smooth animation transitions.

Scrolling Marquees

Content and events are often promoted in web sites through the use of scrolling text banners or marquees. An old and often annoying trick is to scroll the text in the browser window status bar. This is ineffective because users may not notice the text in this area, or it can be difficult to read if other processes in the browser are trying to write to this area at the same time.

IE has a proprietary `MARQUEE element` for producing scrolling text. If we try using it in Netscape, the text simply sits static.

This example will use a cross browser solution to create a DHTML effect that performs a similar task to `MARQUEE`. JavaScript code is implemented to scroll text in the right to left direction and hold the text at the far left position for a set period of time before doing the same for the next message:

```
<!-- marquee.htm -->
<HTML>
<HEAD>
<TITLE>Scrolling Marquee Example</TITLE>
<STYLE>
    #myMarquee
    {
        width:200px;
        background-color:#c0c0c0;
        overflow:hidden;
    }
    #myMessage
    {
        position:relative;
        right:200px;
        font-weight:bold;
        color:#3030b0;
    }
</STYLE>
<SCRIPT SRC='DOMFunctions.js'></SCRIPT>
<SCRIPT SRC='Marquee.js'></SCRIPT>
<SCRIPT>
    function win_load()
    {
        var marq = new Marquee("myMarquee", "myMessage", 7)
        marq.addMessage("Message <B>one</B> scrolling")
        marq.addMessage("Message <I>two</I> following")
        marq.addMessage("Message <B><I>three</I></B> comes next")
        marq.addMessage("Message 4 is last")
        marq.run()
    }
</SCRIPT>
</HEAD>
<BODY onload='win_load()'>
    <DIV ID='myMarquee'><SPAN ID='myMessage'></SPAN></DIV>
</BODY>
</HTML>
```

The first point to note is that the code used to create the marquee effect is located in an external file and a Marquee object is created after the page loads. Additional DOM functions created earlier in this chapter are imported from another DOMFunctions.js file. Having created a Marquee object, the messages to be displayed are added to the object and then a run method of the object is called to start the text messages scrolling.

The BODY section contains a DIV element with an inner SPAN element. A style sheet is used to fix the width of the DIV element to 200 pixels and position the SPAN element relative to the DIV element 200pixels from the left-hand side of the DIV element. By setting the overflow style property of the DIV element to hidden only the region of the SPAN element within the DIV element bounds will be displayed. So, initially the SPAN element is positioned outside the bounds of the DIV element and is not visible.

The SPAN element will contain the actual message that will be scrolled. The trick here is not to scroll the text itself but to scroll the SPAN element containing the text in order to give the appearance that the text is scrolling. The DIV element acts as a container for the SPAN element with a fixed width and a background color set.

The JavaScript code for this scrolling effect is imported into the HTML page from the Marquee.js file. To create the marquee effect a single object is used. The constructor code below defines a class to create a Marquee object and accepts three arguments. The divPanel and spanPanel arguments are the ID names of the SPAN and DIV elements in the BODY section of the HTML code. The third argument, dt, defines the time (in seconds) that the message should be visible for, which includes the amount of time it takes to scroll the message. Both the divPanel and spanPanel arguments must be supplied, and if a value is not supplied for dt, then a default value of 10 seconds is used:

```
// Marquee.js
function Marquee(divPanel, spanPanel, dt)
{
   //Private Variables
   var sPanel = null, dPanel = null
   var msgs = new Array()
   var ptr = 0
   var rDT = 75
   var swapTime = (dt*1000) || 10000
   var currentTime = swapTime
   var sX = null
   var offset = 0
   var globalIdx = 0

   //Test the global array variable showMessage exists
   if (window["showMessage"]) {
   globalIdx = showMessage.length
   }
   else
   {
   showMessage = new Array()
   }

   //Store element scrolling function in a global array
   showMessage[globalIdx] = function()
   {
      if (currentTime >= swapTime)
         reset()
      if (sPanel.offsetLeft >= 2)
      {
         sPanel.style.left = (sPanel.offsetLeft - offset) + "px"
      }
      currentTime += rDT
   }
}
```

```
    //Private Methods
var reset = function()
{
    currentTime = 0
    if (sX == null)
    {
        sX = (sPanel.offsetLeft)
        var aniFrames = (swapTime - 2000) / rDT
        offset = sX / aniFrames
    }
    sPanel.style.left = (sX + "px")
    if (ptr >= msgs.length) ptr = 0
        setInnerHTML(sPanel, msgs[ptr++])
}

//Public Methods
this.addMessage = function(str)
{
    msgs[msgs.length] = str
}

this.run = function()
{
    if (divPanel == "" || spanPanel == "") return
    dPanel = document.getElementById(divPanel)
    sPanel = document.getElementById(spanPanel)
    setInterval("showMessage[" + globalIdx + "]()", rDT)
}
}
```

When a new Marquee Object is instantiated several private class member variables are initialized. Then an if"..."else statement is used to test if a global variable called showMessage exists, which should store an array. If showMessage does exist, the variable globalIdx is set to equal the current size of the array that it stores, otherwise it is created and a new array stored in it.

After a new object has been created, the messages to be scrolled are stored in the object by passing the messages to the addMessage() method of the object. This method stores the messages in the msgs array, each new message being added in a new position at the end of the array.

Once all the messages have been added, the Marquee object is ready to scroll them and, for this action to occur, the run() method is called. The first line of this method checks to see if the ID names of the DIV and SPAN elements have been supplied and if not exits the method immediately. Having passed this check, references to each of the elements are stored in the variables dPanel and sPanel. Finally, this method uses an interval timer to call the element scrolling function showMessage[globalIdx](), in a similar fashion to the use of showAdvert[globalIdx]() in the Rotating Adverts example. The interval time between each call to showMessage[globalIdx]() is set by the rDT variable. The rDT variable is also used to increment the currentTime variable, which is used to track the length of time each message is displayed.

The showMessage[globalIdx]() function first checks to see if the currentTime variable is greater than or equal to the swapTime variable and if so, the reset() method is called. The value of the constructor argument dt, which stores the total number of seconds that a message should be displayed (including the time it takes to scroll a message), is multiplied by 1000, and the resulting value stored in the swapTime variable. The swapTime variable therefore, holds the number of milliseconds to scroll and display the text message and to see if current message needs to be replaced with the next message.

When the `Marquee` object is initialized, the `currentTime variable` is set to equal the value of `swapTime` and therefore the `reset()` method is called the first time `showMessage[globalIdx]()` is called. Each time `showMessage[globalIdx]()` is called, the `currentTime` variable is incremented by the value of `rDT`, and therefore stores the time that a message has currently been displayed in milliseconds.

The first time the `reset()` method is called the value of the variable `sX` is null. By testing the value of `sX` in this first call to `reset()` allows `sX` to be set to equal the left (x co-ordinate) position of the `SPAN` element that can be accessed by the `offsetLeft` property of the element. Note that initially this is just outside the `DIV` element visible area, set by the style sheet. This variable is then used in subsequent calls to move the `SPAN` element containing the message so that it is positioned back to its initial position outside the `DIV` element where it is invisible, as the `overflow` style property of the `DIV` element is set to hidden.

After setting the `sX` variable, the value of the `offset` variable is calculated, which will store the number of pixels to move the `SPAN` element each time. The value of `offset` is calculated firstly by finding the number of iterations required to move the `SPAN` element to the left. In this example, the number of iterations is calculated so that the message will also stay static for 2 seconds and is stored in the `aniFrames` variable. To calculate the `offset` value is then a simple case of dividing the distance value stored in `sX` by the number of iterations stored in `aniFrames` to give the distance to move the layer each frame.

Having set the `sX` and `offset` variable, the `reset()` method resets the value of the `currentTime` variable back to 0, ready for the next round of incrementing. The `SPAN` element is then repositioned back outside the `DIV` element's display area by setting its `style.left` property to the initial starting position stored in the `sX` variable, thus hiding the element. Finally, the method checks the value of the `ptr` variable, setting it back to 0 if its value becomes greater than or equal to the length of the `msgs` array. With a valid value for the `ptr` variable, the method finally sets the content of the `SPAN` element to the next valid message, using the earlier created DOM `setInnerHTML()` function, and the `SPAN` element is ready to be scrolled with the next message.

Having determined whether `reset()` should be called or not, the message containing the `SPAN` element needs to be moved. To move this element, the `left` style property is set to the value of the element's `offsetLeft` property minus the value stored in the `offset` variable, making the element move right to left. Finally, the `currentTime` variable is incremented by `rDT`, and once the value of `currentTime` is greater than or equal to the value of `swapTime`, the `reset()` method is called again.

> **offsetLeft**, like the **innerHTML** property is not part of the DOM specification. IE 4
> first introduced it, along with analogous properties **offsetRight**, **offsetWidth**
> and **offsetHeight**, which hold the numerical values of the **right**, **width** and
> **height** properties of an element. Netscape introduced these properties in its version 6
> browser to enable developers to write cross browser code (IE 5+ and NN 6+).

Dynamic Displays

By using the `visibility` style property, whole blocks of content can be made visible or invisible. The drawback of this property is that when the element is made invisible, it retains its dimensions in the viewable document, and the web developer is left with a nasty blank space. A solution to this problem is to resize the invisible element so that its dimensions are set to zero. However, if we want to make the content visible again we would have to store the initial dimensions of the element in variables, retrieve them and resize the element back to the original size.

A more elegant and efficient solution to the problem is to use the `display` style property. This style property defines an element's `box` type and hence its visual appearance. If unfamiliar with this property, the values of the property we really need to know are `none`, `inline` and `block` (see Chapter 8, for more information about CSS properties).

In Netscape 6 and IE 4+, setting the `display` style property to `none` removes an element from the visual display of the document in the browser window and the space that would normally be taken up by the content is no longer visible. Inline elements are those elements of the source document that do not form blocks of content. (SPANs and Bs, for example). Block-level elements are those elements of the source document that are formatted visually as blocks (Ps and DIVs, for example).

Using the `display` style property to hide content allows more content to be inserted into a document and made visible at appropriate times. There are two main ways to achieve this effect. We can either copy content out of a hidden element and insert it into another visible element,or by changing the `display` property of a hidden element to either `block` or `inline`. The next two sections will show examples of both these techniques.

Hidden Messages

In the past, when a web site author has wanted to provide the user with further information, they often placed small messages in the browser window status bar. An alternative solution is to display the message in the document itself. As we've already seen, JavaScript can happily insert content into elements and a similar technique can be used here. However, this time the content will be extracted from another hidden element within the page and then inserted into the element, where it is displayed. The following function can be used to achieve this:

```
function showContent(elFromID, elToID)
{
    var to = document.getElementById(elToID)
    if (elFromID)
    {
        var from = document.getElementById(elFromID)
        setInnerHTML(to, getInnerHTML(from))
    }
    else
    {
        setInnerHTML(to, "")
    }
}
```

The `showContent()` function accepts two arguments that are the ID names of the elements from which to extract the content and where to subsequently insert the content. The first line stores a reference to the element where the content will be inserted. The next line tests to see if `elFromID` is supplied. If it is, a reference to the element from where to extract the content is made, and then the content of this element is copied to the element where it will be displayed. If the `elFromID` argument has not been supplied, the element that displays the content has all of its content removed by setting its `innerHTML` property to an empty string.

Let's have a look at an example of this in action where blocks of content contained in the page are hidden and can be copied from one hidden element to another visible element. By placing a mouse cursor over a list element, a piece of content will appear in an area next to the link. Take the mouse off the link and the area becomes blank. Putting the mouse over a different link causes a different piece of content to appear:

```
<!-- Hidden Messages.htm -->
<HTML>
<HEAD>
<TITLE>Hidden Messages Example</TITLE>
<STYLE>
    DIV { display:none; }
</STYLE>
<SCRIPT SRC='DOMFunctions.js'></SCRIPT>
<SCRIPT>
    function showContent(elFromID, elToID)
    {
        var to = document.getElementById(elToID)
```

```
              if (elFromID)
              {
                  var from = document.getElementById(elFromID)
                  setInnerHTML(to, getInnerHTML(from))
              }
              else
              {
                  setInnerHTML(to, "")
              }
          }
      </SCRIPT>
      </HEAD>
      <BODY>
          <TABLE>
          <TR>
              <TD>
                  <OL>
                  <LI>
                      <A HREF='#'
                          onMouseOver="showContent('refA', 'content')"
                          onMouseOut="showContent(null, 'content')">
                          Item A
                      </A>
                  <LI>
                      <A HREF='#'
                          onMouseOver="showContent('refB', 'content')"
                          onMouseOut="showContent(null, 'content')">
                          Item B
                      </A>
                  <LI>
                      <A HREF='#'
                          onMouseOver="showContent('refC', 'content')"
                          onMouseOut="showContent(null, 'content')">Item C</A>
                  </OL>
              </TD>
              <TD VALIGN='top' ID='content'></TD>
          </TR>
          </TABLE>
          <DIV ID='refA'>
              This is some hidden text waiting to be displayed
          </DIV>
          <DIV ID='refB'>
              This is a second hidden block of text waiting to be displayed
          </DIV>
          <DIV ID='refC'>
              This is the last hidden text block to be displayed
          </DIV>
      </BODY>
      </HTML>
```

Note the three DIV elements at the bottom of the code. Their display property has been set to none by the style sheet so that they are not rendered in the browser's window.

A list of items is visible on the page each with onMouseOver and onMouseOut event handlers to capture the mouse events. When the mouse is moved over the list element the showContent() function is called. Each time it passes the ID name of the DIV element from which to retrieve the content and the ID name of the TD element in which to show the content. The if statement is included in the showContent() function to check that the value of the first argument is not null. If not, content is copied from a hidden element and inserted into the table cell, else the content of the table cell is cleared by setting it to empty string (""). Removing the mouse from over the list element, null is passed as the first argument to showContent(), forcing any content that was displayed to be removed.

An alternative mechanism to achieve the same effect for this example would be to change the `display` style property of the individual `DIV` elements. This is a simpler and more efficient approach than copying and inserting content. The HTML code below shows the `DIV` elements have now been moved into the right hand table cell and this table cell no longer requires an ID attribute. The arguments passed to the `showContent()` function have been modified; the first argument is always the ID name of the element of interest and the second argument is a boolean value indicating whether to display or hide the content. The full example in the code download is `Alt Hidden Messages.htm`.

```
<TABLE>
    <TR>
        <TD>
            <OL>
            <LI onMouseOver="showContent('refA', true)"
                onMouseOut="showContent('refA', false)">
                    Item A
            <LI onMouseOver="showContent('refB', true)"
                onMouseOut="showContent('refB', false)">
                    Item B
            <LI onMouseOver="showContent('refC', true)"
                onMouseOut="showContent('refC', false)">
                    Item C
            </OL>
        </TD>
        <TD VALIGN="top">
            <DIV ID="refA">
                This is some hidden text waiting to be displayed
            </DIV>
            <DIV ID="refB">
                This is a second hidden block of text waiting to be displayed
            </DIV>
            <DIV ID="refC">
                This is the last hidden text block to be displayed
            </DIV>
        </TD>
    </TR>
</TABLE>
```

The `showContent()` function now simply accesses an element's `display` style property, whose ID name is provided by the `elID` argument, and sets it to either `'block'` (displays the element) or `'none'` (hides the element), depending on the boolean value of the `isDisplayed` argument:

```
function showContent(elID, isDisplayed)
    {
        document.getElementById(elID).style.display = (isDisplayed) ? 'block' :
'none'
    }
```

Although this example shows only a single line message, in reality there is no limit to how much we could hide, other than the limitations that the browser may impose. It could be perfectly feasible to have two or three pages 'stuffed' into a single HTML document. When a user navigates to another page, they're actually viewing a section of content that was already present but previously hidden. The great advantage to this is that although the user has a larger initial download, viewing the hidden content is virtually instantaneous.

A drawback is that although a new page of content may be displayed, because it is not actually a new document, the browser history does not update. If a user clicks the back button of the browser, rather than using the navigation in place on the page, they may unwittingly go to a completely different page. It is therefore important to design the layout of the document in such a way that it makes it obvious that these are pages within a document and not separate documents.

Content Management

The ability to show and hide blocks of content is extremely useful, not only on a front end web site to provide added information to users but also on back end content management systems. Web content management procedures enable the design, authoring, review, approval, conversion, storage, testing, and deployment of web site content. Once in service, content needs to be maintained, monitored, upgraded, and eventually retired and archived. Comprehensive end-to-end content management also consists of sophisticated reporting and analysis components.

Web based content management systems often need to display a large amount of information for a particular piece of content or certain areas of a web site. For example, a web page that shows a video clip, or flash animation may have other information associated with it, such as an age rating, reviews, headlines, and what page it belongs to. For site structure and pages, associated information includes where a page fits within the web site's document structure, what content goes within a page, or whether the page live on the site. This information can be large and often each section of information associated with a piece of content will be display on separate pages. Each page allows an editor to view the current data associated with the piece of content and edit that data. Putting each section of information on a separate page may logically separate the sections, but it can be a time consuming process to navigate to the relevant section and edit the data, not to mention the time it takes to download each page.

A far quicker and better system is to present all the data on a single page, which would mean a large but single download. As the information can be large, the page will also be large and a lot of scrolling can be required. Therefore, showing and hiding blocks of data can make a content management page more user friendly. In the following screenshots, the first screenshot shows a simple page with three headings. The first heading informs an editor when the element of content was created and by whom. The next two headings indicate sections that are available for viewing and editing:

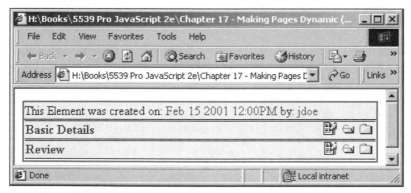

If a user clicks on the open folder icons associated with the section heading, the content will appear for that section and similarly will disappear if the closed folder icon is clicked:

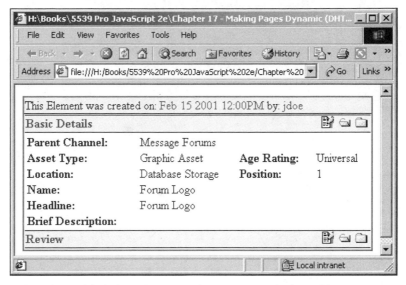

Alternatively, the user could click on the pen and paper icon, which could open a popup window that contains a form for editing that section of content (note this feature is not implemented in this example though could be if required).

The effect is achieved by changing the display style property of each table. Each section consists of a table. The first row of the table contains the section heading and the icons. The second row contains a nested table with the relevant content to the section, and it is this nested table whose display property is changed to hide or view the associated data.

The HTML code below shows the section of code to create the Review section in the above example. The full code is available in the Content Management.htm file in the code download.

```
<TABLE WIDTH='100%' CELLSPACING='0'>
   <TR CLASS='greyBar'>
      <TH CLASS='tlTitle'>
         <SPAN STYLE='color:#d00000'>Review</SPAN>
      </TH>
      <TH CLASS='tlTitle' STYLE='text-align:right'>
         <A HREF='#'>
            <IMG NAME='EditContent' SRC='edit.gif' ALT='Edit Details'
               WIDTH='16' HEIGHT='16' HSPACE='3' BORDER='0'>
         </A>
         <A HREF='JavaScript:expandTable('Review', true)'>
            <IMG NAME='ShowDetails' SRC='open.gif' ALT='Show Details'
               WIDTH='15' HEIGHT='15' BORDER='0'>
         </A>
         <A HREF='JavaScript:expandTable('Review', false)'>
            <IMG NAME='HideDetails' SRC='close.gif' ALT='Hide Details'
               WIDTH='16' HEIGHT='15' HSPACE='3' BORDER='0'>
         </A>
      </TH>
   </TR>
   <TR>
      <TD COLSPAN='2'>
         <TABLE width='100%' BGCOLOR='#ffffff' border='0' CELLSPACING='0'
            CELLPADDING='0' ID='Review' STYLE='display:none;'>
            <TR VALIGN='top'>
```

```
                    <TH COLSPAN='2' CLASS='nob'>
                        Review:
                    </TH>
                    <TD COLSPAN='2' ALIGN='left'>
                        No review description present
                    </TD>
                </TR>
            </TABLE>
        </TD>
    </TR>
</TABLE>
```

Looking at the code above, we can see that there is a main table, a nested table, and some styling information. Note that the inner table `display` style property is set to `none`, so that initially the nested table will not be displayed, and also the two image links with the JavaScript URLs that call the `expandTable()` function.

Only this single function is required to achieve the effect and the code for the function can be seen below. This function accepts two arguments: the first is the `ID` name of the table, and the second is a boolean value to indicate whether the table is to be visible (`true`) or hidden (`false`):

```
function expandTable(whichTable, show)
{
    document.getElementById(whichTable).style.display = (show) ? "block" : "none"
}
```

When the function is called, the `display` style property is accessed and its value set to `block`, making it visible, or `none` to make it invisible. Although the `expandTable()` function is used here to show and hide tables, it will function equally well for any element, as in the previous example's modified `showContent()` function.

> **Strictly speaking, we should have set the `display` style property on the nested table to `table` in order to be compliant with the CSS2 Recommendation. Unfortunately, IE doesn't recognize this display value and raises a JavaScript error if used. Hence, we have used `block` to allow the example to work in both IE 5 and Netscape 6.**

Multiple Forms Become One Form

Using the same technique in the previous system, it should be fairly obvious that the same effect can be achieved with forms. Multiple page forms such as some laborious registration forms are often an annoyance and users and they may leave without completing the form. There are occasions when long forms are necessary, but waiting for each section page to download can be tiresome and time consuming.

A much better idea is to have the whole form on a single page. Form elements can still be separated as if they were on separate pages, but instead are hidden in tables or DIVs. The advantage for the user is that they can see every section of a form that needs to be filled in and the overall time for completion of the form will be less.

From the server programming point of view, it is far better to receive all the information in one go, as would be the case with a form that is split up in this way. There is only one form submitted and processed at the server side because there is only one submit button at the end. Having a form in multiple pages results in each separate page having to be submitted. If the user does not complete all pages of the form, the server will receive incomplete information that wastes server memory and processor time. Additionally, if the form information is passed straight on to a database after each page is transmitted back to the server, transaction management will be made difficult.

Navigational Elements

DHTML's ability to show and hide content can be useful to provide extra help for users in the form of added information to clickable elements and menu systems. More information may also be displayed in a smaller area, removing the need for the user to scroll through long pages of content. This section will show several examples of enhancing the navigation of content within a document.

Tool Tips

One of the simplest methods to convey extra information to users about an element of content within a page is to use the TITLE attribute of HTML tags. The TITLE attribute allows an alternative description to be added to elements, which appears as a tool tip for an element, similar to adding the ALT attribute to IMG tags. The TITLE attribute was introduced with HTML 4 and is available with most elements.

The following provides an example of adding extra information to elements by using the TITLE attribute to a paragraph and anchor tag:

```
<!-- simple tool tip.htm -->
<HTML>
    <P TITLE='This is a paragraph'>
        Simple demonstration of Tool Tips
        <A HREF='#' TITLE='Click for more information'>
            Click me
        </A>
    </P>
</HTML>
```

Placing the mouse cursor over the paragraph will display the text supplied with the TITLE attribute of the paragraph in a tool tip. Similarly, placing the mouse over the link will display a tool tip with the text supplied with the TITLE attribute of the anchor.

Although not a DHTML trick, it is useful and removes the need for fiddly DHTML solutions. Unfortunately, when we supply a TITLE attribute for an element, the tool tip only displays as a single line. Inserting a new line character \n doesn't work, and the characters are also displayed as normal text. Instead we can use the decimal reference &#10 to create a new line within the tool tip.

Unfortunately, this method only works with IE 5+ and not Netscape 6. Netscape converts the new line characters to a single "|" character. Currently, the only solution to produce multiple line tool tips in Netscape 6 is to use layers. Furthermore, because the TITLE attribute was introduced with HTML 4, this technique for producing tool tips is not available to Netscape 4 browsers.

DHTML can be used to dynamically change the value of the TITLE attribute, and therefore create dynamic tool tips. The HTML source below shows the same code as the previous example with an ID attribute set for the paragraph:

```
<!-- dynamic tool tip.htm -->
<HTML>
<HEAD>
<SCRIPT>
    function writeToolTip(elID, tip)
    {
        document.getElementById(elID).setAttribute('title', tip)
    }
</SCRIPT>
</HEAD>
<BODY>
    <P TITLE='This is a paragraph' ID='mypara'>
        Simple demonstration of Tool Tips
```

```
            <A HREF="JavaScript:writeToolTip('mypara', 'You tested this example')"
               TITLE='Click for more information'>
               Click me
            </A>
        </P>
    </BODY>
</HTML>
```

In this example, clicking on the link will call the `writeToolTip()` function, passing it the ID name of the paragraph and some new text to replace the current value of the TITLE of the paragraph. The function for this effect is very simple and involves setting the TITLE attribute to a new value using the DOM `setAttribute()` method. This DOM method accepts two arguments; the first is the name of the element attribute and the second is the value the attribute needs to be set which in this case is the value of the `tip` argument.

Custom Tool Tips

We previously saw how to dynamically write content to a positioned element. Positioned elements are useful because they can be positioned with a document relative to another element or their x and y co-ordinate values can be set absolutely within the browser window. They therefore present the best mechanism to create custom tool tips. Also, because JavaScript can write to the positioned element and include HTML code, they can be made more visually stimulating by adding styling properties and images.

The 'layer' writing code we produced earlier is compatible with both IE 4+ and Netscape 4 & 6. We can therefore modify this code and use it to produce tool tips that will function across browsers.

In the Custom tooltip.htm example, a tool tip is displayed when a user moves their mouse over an image link and disappears after the mouse moves off the link. Also, the tool tip is positioned next to the mouse icon and therefore next to the element that the tip text refers to. Although we use an image link here, there is no reason why another event driven mechanism couldn't be used. Let us have a look at the HTML code for this example first:

```
<!-- Custom tooltip.htm -->
<HTML>
<HEAD>
<TITLE>Tool Tip Example</TITLE>
<STYLE>
    #tipLyr
    {
        position:absolute;
        left:5px;
        top:5px;
        width:100px;
        background-color:#7DCFC2;
        font-size:x-small;
        padding:2px;
        visibility:hidden;
    }
    .nsLyr
    {
        background-color:#7DCFC2;
        font-size:x-small;
        width:100px;
        padding:2px;
    }
</STYLE>
<SCRIPT SRC="DOMFunctions.js"></SCRIPT>
<SCRIPT SRC="clientSniffer.js"></SCRIPT>
<SCRIPT>
var cs = new clientSniffer();
```

```
function displayTip(elID, show, evt, tiptext)
{
   if (cs.isDOM())
   {
      var popMenu= document.getElementById(elID)
      setInnerHTML(popMenu, tiptext)
      popMenu.style.left = (cs.isNS()) ? (evt.clientX + 5) + "px": (event.clientX
+ 5) + "px"
      popMenu.style.top = (cs.isNS()) ? (evt.clientY + 5) + "px": (event.clientY
+ 5) + "px"
      popMenu.style.visibility = "visible"
      popMenu.style.visibility = (show) ? "visible" : "hidden"
   }
   else
   {
      var el = (cs.isNS()) ? document.layers[elID] : document.all[elID]
      if (cs.isNS()) {
         with(el.document)
         {
            open()
            write("<TABLE BORDER=1><TR><TD CLASS='nsLyr'>")
            write(tiptext)
            write("</TD></TR></TABLE>")
            close()
         }
      }
      else
      {
         el.innerHTML = tiptext
      }
      el.moveTo(evt.pageX + 10, evt.pageY + 10)
      el.visibility = (show) ? "show" : "hide"
   }
}
</SCRIPT>
</HEAD>
<BODY>
   <FORM>
   <TABLE>
   <TR>
      <TH>Name:</TH>
      <TD>
         <INPUT TYPE="text" NAME="username" VALUE="">
      </TD>
      <TD>
         <A HREF="#"
            onmouseover="displayTip('tipLyr', true, event, 'Enter your username.
It should be at least 6 characters long and is case sensitive')"
            onmouseout="displayTip('tipLyr', false, event, '')">
            <IMG SRC="help.gif" WIDTH=20 HEIGHT=20 BORDER=0 ALT="help">
         </A>
      </TD>
   </TR>
   </TABLE>
   </FORM>
   <DIV ID="tipLyr"></DIV>
</BODY>
</HTML>
```

An empty DIV element with an ID attribute set will be used to show the tool tip text. The element is positioned absolutely to the browser window origin, 5 pixels from the left and top, with its visibility property set to hidden.

The visibility style property is used rather than the display property because Netscape 4 does not recognise the display style property, so to use it would cause this example to break in this browser. Other style information for the layer and text appearance is included and, by changing these style sheet properties, the tool tips can be customised to fit into any web page. There is also a second style sheet class called nsLyr, which contains much of the same styling information as the layer. It will be clear why this class is present when we discuss the JavaScript code but for now simply realise it is there for Netscape 4 browsers.

The anchor tag link uses an onMouseOver/onMouseOut event to display/hide the tool tip. Each time these events are raised, the displayTip() function is called. The function is passed the name of the layer ID, a boolean value whether to show (true) or hide (false) the layer, the event for the mouse so that the mouse x and y co-ordinates can be captured and finally, the text that should be displayed. Note that for IE the event does not need to be passed to the displayTip() function because it is a global variable, though for Netscape it does.

The JavaScript code is similar to the code present earlier in the chapter for writing to layers. The client sniffer code uses the same class as in previous examples, but rather than creating a new instance of the clientsniffer object each time the displayTip() function is called, an object has been created that is stored in the global variable cs. This is more efficient, because creating an object is a costly operation.

The clientsniffer object is used by the displayTip() to differentiate between the three main browsers because the event handling is different between Netscape and IE, and changing the visibility is different between Netscape 4 and the DOM browsers. The first line of this function simply creates a reference to the DIV element that will display the tip text and the code is then forked using an if statement. The code in the if block is used for DOM capable browsers (Netscape 6 and IE 5+) and the else block by Netscape and IE 4 browsers. Each block effectively performs the same operations: it writes the tip text to the DIV element, positions the DIV element next to the mouse cursor and then sets the visibility of the DIV element to visible or hidden.

When writing to the DIV element with Netscape 4, the tip text is written inside a table. This is required because Netscape will attempt to write the text on a single line and resize the layer to accommodate this line. Wrapping the text in a table helps avoid this problem and the table cell that contains the text has the nsLyr class applied.

To locate the mouse position, IE and Netscape use different approaches. With IE the x and y co-ordinates are extracted from a global event variable called event. With Netscape browsers the same co-ordinates are retrieved from the evt argument that was passed to the function. Also, note that the event object properties that store the x and y position have different names for the browsers. The x and y co-ordinate properties are called x and y for IE 4, pageX and pageY for Netscape 4, and clientX and clientY for IE 5+ and Netscape 6. Netscape 4 provided the very handy layer method moveTo() that accepts x and y values and moves the DIV element to that position on screen. Unfortunately, the DOM browsers do not have this ability so the DIV element has to be positioned by individually setting left and top style properties.

Now Netscape 6 is more standards compliant, it uses the same code as IE to change the style visibility property of the DIV element. However, because Netscape 4 did not use the standard syntax, the proprietary values show and hide must be used.

Tabbed Panels

Tab panels are a useful form of navigation for moving between different sets of related information such as multiple sections of a form. The example for this section builds on the previous Content Management example where blocks of content were shown and hidden.

The screenshots below shows a page with three tabs: Details, Search, and Help. Clicking on any of the tabs will allow a different panel of information to be displayed and the tab itself will be highlighted:

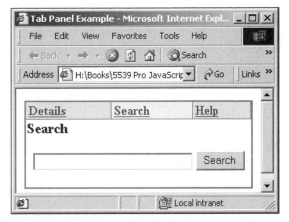

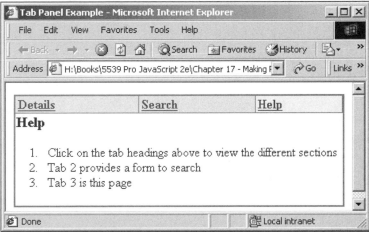

The code below shows how to set up the tab panels. There is a table used as the layout manager, with each of the tab headings located in the first table row and the content panel area located in the next row, which spans across the whole table.

The style sheet added provides the borders and colors for the elements of the tab panel. The display style property for all DIVs has been set to none, so that all content is initially hidden when the page loads. Note the two classes inactiveTab and activeTab. Initially, all the tabs will be inactive and so this style class is applied to each of the three tabs. When a tab is selected, JavaScript will dynamically change the style class of the element to the activeTab class and thus the active element will be highlighted to a light green color.

Each row of the table has been provided with an ID so that the child elements within each row can be accessed easily. Similarly, each TH and DIV element has their ID attribute set so that individual elements can be accessed and their properties altered. It is important to note that the custom CONNECT attribute of TH tags is not part of the HTML Recommendation and has been made up for the purpose of this example. The CONNECT attribute is used to connect a tab with a DIV element, and its value holds the ID name of the connected DIV element:

```
<!-- Tabbed Panels.htm -->
<HTML>
<HEAD>
<TITLE>Tab Panel Example</TITLE>
<STYLE>
```

```
     TABLE
     {
        border-width:2px;
        border-style:solid;
        border-color:#707070;
     }

     TH, TD { text-align:left; color:#000080; }

     .inactiveTab
     {
        border-bottom-width:1px;
        border-bottom-style:solid;
        border-bottom-color:#707070;
        border-right-width:1px;
        border-right-style:solid;
        border-right-color:#707070;
        padding-left:3px;
        background-color:#ffd0d0;
     }

     .activeTab
     {
        border-bottom-width:1px;
        border-bottom-style:solid;
        border-bottom-color:#707070;
        border-right-width:1px;
        border-right-style:solid;
        border-right-color:#707070;
        padding-left:3px;
        background-color:#d0ffd0;
     }

     DIV { display:none; }
</STYLE>
<SCRIPT>
function clearTabs()
{
   var tabs = document.getElementById("tabBar").cells
   for (var i = 0; i < tabs.length; i++)
   {
        tabs[i].className = "inactiveTab"
   }
   var contentDivs =
     document.getElementById('contentArea').getElementsByTagName("DIV")
   for (var i = 0; i < contentDivs.length; i++)
   {
     contentDivs[i].style.display = "none"
   }
}

function showPanel(selectedTab)
{
   clearTabs()
   var tabEl = document.getElementById(selectedTab)
   tabEl.className = "activeTab"
   var con = tabEl.getAttribute('CONNECT')
   document.getElementById(con).style.display = "block"
}
</SCRIPT>
</HEAD>
<BODY>
```

```
<TABLE BORDER=0 WIDTH="100%" CELLPADDING=1 CELLSPACING=0 ALIGN="center">
    <TR ID="tabBar">
        <TH ID="tab1" CONNECT="details" CLASS="inactiveTab">
            <A HREF="JavaScript:showPanel('tab1')">
                Details
            </A>
        </TH>
        <TH ID="tab2" CONNECT="search" CLASS="inactiveTab">
            <A HREF="JavaScript:showPanel('tab2')">
                Search
            </A>
        </TH>
        <TH ID="tab3" CONNECT="help" CLASS="inactiveTab">
            <A HREF="JavaScript:showPanel('tab3')">
                Help
            </A>
        </TH>
    </TR>
    <TR ID="contentArea">
        <TD COLSPAN=3>
            <DIV ID="details">
                <H3>Details</H3>
                Some information can be presented here
            </DIV>
            <DIV ID="search">
                <H3>Search</H3>
                <FORM>
                     
                    <INPUT TYPE="text" VALUE="" NAME="queryString" SIZE=30>
                    <INPUT TYPE="submit" VALUE="Search">
                </FORM>
            </DIV>
            <DIV ID="help">
                <H3>Help</H3>
                <OL>
                    <LI>Click on the tab headings above to view the different
                        sections
                    <LI>Tab 2 provides a form to search
                    <LI>Tab 3 is this page
                </OL>
            </DIV>
        </TD>
    </TR>
</TABLE>
</BODY>
</HTML>
```

Each tab heading is a link. Clicking on them calls the showPanel() function and passes the ID name of the tab selected as an argument.

The first statement of the showPanel() function calls the clearTabs() function, which hides all the DIVs in the panel content area and sets all the tab elements' style class to the inactiveTab class. To do this, the clearTabs() function first creates an array of all the TH elements within the first row (which has the ID tabBar) and stores the array in the tabs variable. Table row elements contain the cells property, which is an array providing access to each table cell element within that row.

A for loop is then used to iterate through each element of the array and the class name for each TH element is set to the inactiveTab class. In a similar fashion, the child DIV nodes of the TD content area are stored as an array in the contentDivs variable, except this time the getElementsByTagName() method has been used. A for loop is used again to iterate through the child nodes and the display style property for each DIV is set to none to hide their content.

Once the tab panel has been reset, a reference is created to the TH tab element that was clicked, using the argument of the function. The style class for this element is set to the activeTab class so that the tab highlights and the value of the custom attribute CONNECT is retrieved and stored in the con variable. Remembering that the value of this attribute stores the ID name of the DIV element the tab is connected to, a reference to the DIV element is created and the style property of this element is set to block so that its content is visually rendered.

Although the style class names have been changed here for highlighting the clicked tab, there is no reason why this example cannot be expanded upon to use an image roll over for the tabs themselves.

When is a Link Not a Link?

In the latest browsers, clickable elements may not necessarily be a link, as with the tab headings in the previous example or a form button. Almost every type of HTML element can now accept event handlers, such as onClick, onMouseOver, and onMouseOut. If a clickable element, such as a TD, TH, P, DIV or SPAN looks like other content within a page and there is no added styling, the user may never know that an element is clickable, unless information elsewhere tells them so.

If we attach event handlers to elements then it is a good idea to alter the style properties of the element to reflect this and therefore make it more intuitive for the user to realise that the element is clickable. The following style sheet defines two style classes: one called active and one inactive. The inactive class can be used as the default mouse out state style and the active class as the mouse over state style. By swapping the style classes as a mouse moves over an element the font color will change from blue to red and the mouse cursor will change to a hand icon. The pointer value of the cursor style property is defined by the CSS2 Recommendation and works with Netscape 6. Unfortunately, IE does accept the standard pointer value but rather uses its own value of hand to create the same effect.

> Note that setting the **cursor** style property to **pointer** in IE 5 browsers can cause JavaScript errors to be raised because it does not use the CSS2 specified value.

```
<STYLE>
   .active { color:#800000; cursor:pointer; }
   .inactive { color:#000080; cursor:default; }
</STYLE>
```

This style sheet could be used within a HTML page, like the code below. The inactive class is applied to the SPAN tag as a default. The onMouseOver and onMouseOut event handlers then swap the className associated with the SPAN, creating a look and feeling similar to a standard hyperlink.

```
<SPAN ID="myEl" CLASS="inactive"
   onClick="somefunction()"
   onMouseOver="this.className='active'"
   onMouseOut="this.className='inactive'">
   This is not a link but is clickable
</SPAN>
```

In this example the event handlers have been coded into the HTML tag, though there is no reason why they cannot be attached programmatically. The onClick handler is used to call a function, removing the need for using JavaScript URLs with a hyperlink. We can also use the onClick event handler to jump directly to another document using the code 'window.location=somedoc.html'. So the answer to the question 'When is a link not a link?' is when it is a clickable element.

Functional Widgets

Widgets are stand-alone pieces of code that can be "dropped" into a web page and function without any tweaking. We've already seen two examples: the AdRotator and the Marquee classes. In the remainder of this chapter, several more example widgets will be shown and discussed, each compatible and functioning identically in both IE 5 and Netscape 6.

Sorting Table Data

Many sites today present various forms of tabular data such as price lists and event schedules. The data presented will be delivered either ordered or unordered. Data that is sorted in numerical or alphabetical order and presented on a web page as soon as it loads is almost always sorted by software executed at the server, or the page has been hard coded.

Sorting tabular data on a web page at the client-side has never been easy. Until DOM was available, only two techniques were possible. The first was to store all the table data into an array, sort the arrays and then use the document.write() method to write the sorted table data out as the page is loading. The alternative was to write out the tabled data into a layer. Thanks to DOM, we are now able to write cross-browser code to traverse through a table's tree structure and access the data in each table cell, order them, and republish the sorted data back into the same table.

If we open up the file table sort.htm we will see a rather innocuous table with data that is completely unordered.

Clicking on the heading cell at the top of either column will cause the table to be sorted using the data in that particular column. One of the main things to note in the code below is that the TH cells have an onClick event handler and THEAD and TBODY tags have been added to define the table heading and table body. When triggered, the event handler calls the sortColumn() method of an object ts, and a reference to the clicked TH element is passed to the method:

```
<!-- table sort.htm -->
<HTML>
<HEAD>
<TITLE>Sorting Table Data</TITLE>
<STYLE>
    TH { color:#0000d0; cursor:pointer; text-decoration:underline; }
</STYLE>
<SCRIPT SRC="TableSorter.js"></SCRIPT>
<SCRIPT>
    var ts = new TableSorter()
</SCRIPT>
</HEAD>
<BODY>
    <TABLE BORDER=1>
        <THEAD>
            <TR>
                <TH onClick="ts.sortColumn(this)">Column A</TH>
                <TH onClick="ts.sortColumn(this)">Column B</TH>
                <TH onClick="ts.sortColumn(this)">Column C</TH>
            </TR>
        </THEAD>
        <TBODY>
            <TR>
                <TD>9</TD><TD>C</TD><TD>cat</TD>
            </TR>
            <TR>
                <TD>3</TD><TD>A</TD><TD>mouse</TD>
            </TR>
```

```
        <TR>
            <TD>5.4</TD><TD>j</TD><TD>zebra</TD>
        </TR>
        <TR>
            <TD>1</TD><TD>Z</TD><TD>dog</TD>
        </TR>
        <TR>
            <TD>6</TD><TD>e</TD><TD>moose</TD>
        </TR>
        <TR>
            <TD>5.2</TD><TD>m</TD><TD>goose</TD>
        </TR>
    </TBODY>
  </TABLE>
 </BODY>
</HTML>
```

As we can see, the `ts` object is a custom `TableSorter` object. It's simple to create a new `TableSorter` object, as can be seen above the constructor requires no arguments.

The screenshot below shows the table after clicking on the Column A:

Column A	Column B	Column C
1	Z	dog
3	A	mouse
5.2	m	goose
5.4	j	zebra
6	e	moose
9	C	cat

Note that `ID` attributes have not been used in this example. Therefore, this `TableSorter` object is completely generic and will sort almost any table of data. Tables must define the table body section using the `TBODY` tag and there must be more than one row in the table. In this example, the sorting mechanism is capable of sorting data in a lexigraphic order. When sorting letters alphabetically, an upper case letter is not equivalent to a lower case letter and always precedes the lower case letter, hence sorting Column B results in upper case letters sorted before lower case.

The JavaScript code below shows the `TableSorter` constructor. Instantiating this class creates an object with one private function and one public function:

```
// TableSorter.js
function TableSorter()
{
   //Private Methods
   var compare = function(a, b) {
       if (a.toLowerCase() < b.toLowerCase())
           return -1
       if (a.toLowerCase() > b.toLowerCase())
           return 1
       return 0
   }
}
```

```
    var getTableBodies = function(tableEl)
    {
        var parentEl = tableEl.parentNode
        while (parentEl.nodeName != "TABLE")
        {
            parentEl = parentEl.parentNode
            if (parentEl.nodeName == "BODY") return null
        }
        return parentEl.tBodies
    }

    //Public Methods
    this.sortColumn = function(clickedCol)
    {
        var tableBodyEls = getTableBodies(clickedCol)
        if(tableBodyEls && tableBodyEls[0].rows.length <= 1) return
        var columnData = new Array(tableBodyEls[0].rows.length)

        for (var i = 0; i < tableBodyEls[0].rows.length; i++)
        {
            columnData[i] =
tableBodyEls[0].rows[i].cells[clickedCol.cellIndex].firstChild.nodeValue
        }
//      columnData.sort(compare)
        columnData.sort()

        for (var i = 0; i < columnData.length; i++)
        {
            for (var j = 0; j < tableBodyEls[0].rows.length; j++)
            {
                if (columnData[i] ==
tableBodyEls[0].rows[j].cells[clickedCol.cellIndex].firstChild.nodeValue)
                {
                    tableBodyEls[0].appendChild(tableBodyEls[0].rows[j])
                        break
                }
            }
        }
    }
}
```

The entry point to this object is the public method `sortColumn()`, which accepts a reference to a table cell element as an argument, in this case a TH element. The first task of this method is to produce an array of objects that represent the body elements of the table. To do this the method `getTableBodies()` is called passing the `clickedCol` argument to the method and the returned array of table body objects is stored in the `tableBodyEls` variable.

The `getTableBodies()` method traverses up the node structure of the table until the TABLE node is found, which is the root node for the table. The method first creates a variable `parentEl`, which stores the parent node of the clicked element. In this case, the `parentNode` of the clickable elements is the TR element. The method then uses a `while` loop to continue iterating up the node structure until the TABLE element is reached. With each pass through the loop the node name of each element is tested. If at any point the node name equals BODY, an error has occurred and `null` is returned, or if the node name of the element is TABLE the loop exits. Exiting the loop after finding an element whose node name is TABLE means `parentEl` contains a reference to the table node and an array of `table body` objects is returned using the `tBodies` property of table elements.

Having obtained an array of objects that represent the table bodies, the sortColumn() method checks to see if tableBodyEls is equal to null. In other words, the table contains more than a single row of data in the TBODY section of the table. Note there is only one table body section in this table and the tableBodyEls array contains only a single element, so tableBodyEls[0] gives access to this body section. We may wish to modify this if we use a table with more than 1 table body section.

A variable, columnData, is then created to store an array that is equal in size to the number of rows in the table's body section. This array will be used to store the raw data for the column to be sorted. Table body elements possess a property called rows that is an array providing access to each row in this section of the table. A for loop is used to iterate through each of the elements of the tableBodyEls[0].rows array. Each row element possesses a property called cells that is an array providing access to each cell in a table row. The first child element of a table cell is a text element, which in turn has a property called nodeValue that stores the actual textual content of the cell. Each pass through the loop uses the firstChild.nodeValue property of cell elements to extract the data from the cell of the same column that was clicked. The cellIndex property of table cells provides a numerical reference to the cell in a row. Using clickedCol.cellIndex with the cells array or each row, the correct cell element in the cells array is accessed and its content extracted before being stored in the columnData[i] array.

Having extracted the column data to be sorted from the table and stored it in columnData, this array is now ready to be sorted. Being an array, columnData possesses a sort() method that we can use to sort the data within the array. With the data sorted by the sort() method, all that remains is to rearrange the rows in the table into the correct order.

The final part of the sortColumn() method achieves this by using an outer loop to iterate through the columnData array. The inner loop is used to iterate through each row in the table and on each time through the loop, check if the data in columnData[i] is equal to the content in the cell of the clicked column in this row. If they are equal, the table row element is appended to the table body element, using the appendChild() method. This removes the table row from its current position and moves it to be the last row of the table. After moving the row, a break statement is used to stop the inner loop returning back to the outer loop. The rows are appended in turn according to the order of the data in the columnData array so when the outer loop ends, the table rows are in their correctly ordered positions.

This object could be made more generic by adding a comparison function to sort the data of the columnData array. The sort() method will accept the name of a function to use for testing comparisons between the elements of an array and sort them according to the return value of the compare() function. The function below shows an example that allows the table data to be sorted, while not accounting for the case of the data:

```
var compare = function(a, b)
{
    if (a.toLowerCase() < b.toLowerCase())
        return -1
    if (a.toLowerCase() > b.toLowerCase())
        return 1
    return 0
}
```

A single line of the sortColumn() method then needs to be modified so that the call to the sort method of the columnData array uses the compare() function:

```
columnData.sort(compare)
```

If the compare() function returns a value less than 0, b is sorted to a lower index than a. If the return value is greater than 1, b is sorted to a higher index than a. If 0 is returned, a and b are unchanged with respect to each other. The compare() method could be modified to cope with other forms of data such as currencies.

What's The Time?

The ability to tell the time has been available ever since JavaScript was first released. The simplest method for displaying the time has been to create a new Date object, extract and format the hours, minutes and seconds, and then use document.write() to write out the time as the page loads. Though this works well, the time is not updated unless the page is refreshed. To create a simple cross-browser dynamic clock, the solution has been to update the value of a form element, such as a text box. Although this method works well, DOM provides the latest solution.

A clock that uses DOM can dynamically update the time within any HTML element and style sheet information allows the visual formatting of the display. The screenshot below shows how a DOM clock might look.

Monday, September 10th 2001
4:06:13 P.M.

A further advantage of DOM is that the additional buttons that would have been required with traditional DHTML effects are no longer needed to alter the properties of the clock. For example, if the user wanted to have the time displayed as a 24 hour display rather than a traditional 12 hour clock, all they need do is click on the time display and the time format will change from a 12 to 24 hour clock. In this example, that is exactly what happens.

The code below is used as a layout manager for the content and initializing the JavaScript code. The style sheet information is used to apply the visual elegance to the elements of the clock. A DIV element is used as a placeholder to show the date and time for the clock. When the page loads, the clockOn() function is called, which creates a new Clock object, passing the ID name of the DIV element to the constructor. An interval timer is then used to continuously call the displayTime() method of the clock object every 500 milliseconds, which displays the time in the document:

```
<!-- clock.htm -->
<HTML>
<HEAD>
<TITLE>Date Time Utility</TITLE>
<STYLE>
.chronos
    {
        background-color:#6b6bcd;
        color:#ffffff;
        width:250px;
        padding:2px;
        text-align:center;
        font-family:serif,monospace;
        font-weight:bold;
        cursor:pointer;
    }
</STYLE>
<SCRIPT SRC="clock.js"></SCRIPT>
<SCRIPT>
    var clock
    function clockOn()
    {
        clock = new Clock("timeDisplay")
        setInterval("clock.displayTime()", 500);
    }
</SCRIPT>
</HEAD>
<BODY onload="clockOn()">
    <DIV CLASS="chronos" ID="timeDisplay"></DIV>
</BODY>
</HTML>
```

Take a look at the `Clock` class constructor code below, which outlines several properties and methods required for the clock to function. Two variables, `daysOfWeek` and `monthsOfYear` are created outside of the constructor function and attached as public properties of the `Clock` class using the `prototype` property (see Chapter 3, *JavaScript OOP Techniques* for more details regarding the `prototype` property). Similarly, an external function, `dayNumberString()`, is created and attached as a public method again making use of the `prototype` property. These two properties and method are declared externally because they could be used by other code, without the need to create a new instance of the `Clock` class (they have global scope since they belong to the `window` object and can be accessed using `window.propName`). They are attached to the Clock's `prototype` property too, because their functionality is related to the clock's functionality:

```javascript
// clock.js
function Clock(display)
{
    //Private Varibales
    var clockFace = true
    var timeDisplayEl

    //Public Methods
    this.displayTime = function()
    {
        timeDisplayEl.nodeValue = this.getTime()
    }

     this.getDate = function()
    {
        var d = new Date()
        var yr = d.getFullYear()
        var today = (daysOfWeek[d.getDay()] + ", "
            + monthsOfYear[d.getMonth()] + " "
            + d.getDate()
            + this.dayNumberString(d.getDate()) + " " + yr)
        return today
    }

    this.getTime = function()
    {
        var d = new Date()
        var hours = d.getHours()
        var minutes = d.getMinutes()
        var seconds = d.getSeconds()
        var timeValue = ""

        if (clockFace)
            timeValue = ((hours > 12) ? (hours - 12) : hours)
        else
            timeValue += ((hours < 10) ? "0" : "") + hours
            timeValue += ((minutes < 10) ? ":0" : ":") + minutes
            timeValue += ((seconds < 10) ? ":0" : ":") + seconds
        if (clockFace)
            timeValue += ((hours >= 12) ? " P.M." : " A.M.")
        return timeValue
    }

    this.setClockFace = function() { clockFace = !clockFace }
    this.init = function()
    {
        var displayEl = document.getElementById(display)
        var dateNode = document.createElement("SPAN")
        var txtNode = document.createTextNode(this.getDate())
        dateNode.appendChild(txtNode)
        dateNode.style.cursor = "default"
```

```
            displayEl.appendChild(dateNode)
            var brNode = document.createElement("BR")
            displayEl.appendChild(brNode)
            var timeNode = document.createElement("SPAN")
            timeNode.style.fontSize = "medium"
            timeNode.style.fontFamily = "monospace"
            timeNode.onclick = this.setClockFace
            timeDisplayEl = document.createTextNode(this.getTime())
            timeNode.appendChild(timeDisplayEl)
            displayEl.appendChild(timeNode)
        }
        this.init()
}

var daysOfWeek = new Array("Sunday", "Monday", "Tuesday", "Wednesday", "Thursday",
"Friday", "Saturday")
var monthsOfYear = new Array("January", "February", "March", "April", "May",
"June", "July", "August", "September", "October", "November", "December")

function dayNumberString(dayNumber)
{
    switch(dayNumber)
    {
        case 1:
        case 21:
        case 31:
            return "st"
        case 2:
        case 22:
            return "nd"
        case 3:
        case 23:
            return "rd"
        default:
            return "th"
    }
}

Clock.prototype.daysOfWeek = daysOfWeek
Clock.prototype. monthsOfYear = monthsOfYear
Clock.prototype.dayNumberString = dayNumberString
```

As the HTML source code showed, to create a new Clock object the constructor is passed the ID name of the DIV element where the date and time are to be displayed. The last line of the Clock constructor calls a method called init(), which initializes the clock. The first line of the init() method creates a reference to the DIV element using the arguments to the constructor. Next, a new SPAN element is created dynamically called dateNode, using the DOM method createElement() and will be used to display the current date. The cursor style property of this element is set to default to remove the mouse pointer icon that would be inherited from the DIV element. Then a text node is created using createTextNode() and its initial text content is set to the formatted current date that is returned by the getDate() method. This text node is attached to the dateNode element, which is in turn attached to the DIV element within the document, and thus displays the current date.

With the date now displayed, a new BR element is created and attached to the DIV element so that the next piece of content inserted into the DIV element appears on a new line. All that remains is to create an element to insert the time display. As with the date, a new SPAN element, called timeNode is created and this time various style properties are set for the element over-riding the properties that would otherwise be inherited from the DIV element when it is attached. An onClick event handler is also attached, so that when a user clicks on this element the setClockFace() method is called. This method toggles the display between 12 and 24 hour clocks. The setClockFace() method simply changes the boolean variable clockFace to equal the opposite value of its current value.

A text node is created next, and attached to the timeNode SPAN element, whose initial content is set to the current time retrieved from the getTime() method. This text node is stored in the private variable timeDisplayEl, so that it can be accessed easily at a later stage by the displayTime method. Finally, the SPAN element is attached to the DIV element and the current time is displayed.

The init() method has dynamically created new elements within the document that would be equivalent to writing the following HTML code within the DIV tags of the document:

```
<SPAN>dateStr</SPAN>
<BR>
<SPAN STYLE="font-family:medium; font-size:medium; cursor:pointer"
    onClick="clock.setClockFace()">timeStr</SPAN>
```

Each time the interval timer calls the displayTime() method, the returned value from the getTime() method is used to set the text content of the text node. The getTime() method performs a similar function to the getDate() method, but for the time components of the current date. That is, a new Date object is created each time the method is called, the time elements such as seconds, minutes and hours are extracted, formatted and a string representation of the time is returned. The text is updated by setting the nodeValue property of the text node referenced by the timeDisplayEl private variable. This removes the need for the non-standard innerHTML property of HTML elements.

Note that if the clock runs past midnight, the date is not changed to reflect the new day. If we require this functionality we have to check the current time and update the date display as necessary. Storing a reference to the text node that holds the content for the date, equivalent to the timeDisplayEl will provide us with easy access to the node so that it can be updated.

Drag and Drop

In many games and business applications, a mouse can be used to click on an object and drag it to a new location within the application window. There are very few examples available on the web of how to create code to drag elements around on a web page and drop them at a completely different location within the page. This example will produce a self-contained piece of code to do exactly this.

The HTML source for this example requires two IMG tags to be inserted in the BODY section. Both images are absolutely positioned initially on the page using a simple style sheet. Each image has an ID attribute set and an onMouseDown event handler is attached to the allowDrag() method of an object called dragger. The allowDrag() method is passed a reference to the element itself, using the this keyword, and a reference to the mouse event is passed as the second argument, using the event keyword.

```
<!-- drag.htm -->
<HTML>
<HEAD>
<STYLE type='text/css'>
    #batton { position:absolute; left:20px; top:20px; }
    #ball { position:absolute; left:10px; top:10px; }
</STYLE>
```

```
<SCRIPT SRC='drag.js'></SCRIPT>
<SCRIPT SRC='clientsniffer.js'></SCRIPT>
<SCRIPT>
   var cs = new clientSniffer()
   var dragger = new dragObject()
</SCRIPT>
</HEAD>
<BODY>
   <img src='baton.gif' width='40' height='7' ID='batton'
      onmousedown='dragger.allowDrag(this, event)'>
   <img src='ball.gif'width='20' height='20' ID='ball'
      onmousedown='dragger.allowDrag(this, event)'>
</BODY>
</HTML>
```

We know that the event model in Netscape and IE are different and this example is dependent on event objects, therefore a client sniffer object will be required to differentiate between the two browsers. A second object called dragger is created that allows objects to be dragged when the mouse is pressed down on an element.

This is all that is required within the HTML page, except for two JavaScript source files that are imported, which contain the code for the clientSniffer and dragObject class constructors. The following code outlines the JavaScript code to implement a dragObject class:

```
// drag.js
function dragObject()
{
   var el = null

//Private Methods
   var DRAG_begindrag = function(e)
   {
      var btn = cs.isNS() ? e.button : event.button
      if (btn <= 1)
      {
         document.onmousemove = DRAG_drag
         document.onmouseup = DRAG_enddrag
         el.DRAG_dragging = true
      }
      return true
   }

   var DRAG_drag = function(e)
   {
      if (el.DRAG_dragging == true)
      {
         var evtX = cs.isNS() ? e.clientX : event.clientX
         var evtY = cs.isNS() ? e.clientY : event.clientY
         el.style.left = (evtX -  el.offsetWidth / 2) + "px"
         el.style.top = (evtY -  el.offsetHeight / 2) + "px"
         return false
      }
      else
         return true
   }

   var DRAG_enddrag = function(e)
   {
      el.DRAG_dragging = false
      el = null
      document.onmousemove = null
      document.onmouseup = null
```

```
      return true
   }

//Public Methods
   this.allowDrag = function(dragEl, e)
   {
      el = dragEl
      DRAG_begindrag(e)
   }
}
```

Each time the mouse is pressed down over one of the image elements, the `allowDrag()` method of the dragger object is called and references to the element which captured the mouse event and the mouse event itself are passed to it. Although this example uses `IMG` elements, we could just as easily use most other elements such as `DIV`, `P`, `SPAN`, and `TABLE`.

The first line of the `allowDrag()` method sets a private variable, `el`, equal to the element to be dragged and then passes the event onto the private method `DRAG_begindrag()`. The `DRAG_begindrag()` method first tests to see if the left-hand mouse button was pressed down. If so, the `document` event handlers for `onMouseMove` and `onMouseUp` are attached to the `DRAG_drag()` and `DRAG_enddrag()` methods. The `DRAG_drag()` method is used to drag the element around the browser window and when the mouse button is raised, the `DRAG_enddrag()` method clears up after the dragging action.

A `DRAG_dragging` property of the dragged element is set to `true` and this property is used by the `DRAG_drag()` method to determine if the element is currently being dragged or not. Initially, the element will not have a `DRAG_dragging` property, so it is created. Finally, the function returns `true` to indicate the event has been handled correctly.

The `document` now has two event handlers attached to methods of the dragger object. If the mouse is moved while the left-hand button is pressed down the `DRAG_drag()` function is called, or if the mouse button is released the `DRAG_enddrag()` function is called. The `DRAG_drag()` function first checks to see if the element is in drag mode and if it is, obtains the co-ordinates of the mouse cursor x and y location and moves the element so that it is centred at the same position. The function then returns `false` to indicate that we have not finished handling the event, or `true` if the `DRAG_dragging` property is set to `false` indicating that there is no further action required and the event has been handled.

When the user has finished dragging the element around a page they will release the left mouse button and the `onMouseUp` event handler for the document will call the `DRAG_enddrag()` function. This function simply detaches the `document` event handlers by setting them to `null`. The `DRAG_dragging` property of the element is set to `false` to indicate that it is no longer being dragged and the function returns `true` to indicate that the event has been handled.

The `DRAG_drag()` function is the main function that allows the element to be dragged around the browser window. If we modify this function we could restrict the movement of the element. For example, if we only extract the x co-ordinate of the mouse location and set the element's `left` style property, the element can only be dragged horizontally. Alternatively, extending the `dragObject()` Class we could store data that provides a bounding area, so that the element can only be dragged within this area and not outside.

Movement

Another aspect to dynamic pages is creating objects that can move automatically. In languages like Java or C/C++, a thread, which allows more than one piece of code to be executed within a single process after a period of inactivity, is commonly used to move objects. JavaScript doesn't have threads, but we have already seen objects that use the `setInterval()` function inside objects that effectively act like threads (look back at the `AdRotator` and `Marquee` objects).

In this example, we will see how to create an object that will move an element on the page and the movement will be restricted to a bounding area. The example will take the form of moving a ball image within a box. Each time the ball hits a boundary wall it will change direction so that its movement remains inside the bounding area.

The HTML code for this example is very simple; a DIV element is used to create the bounding box area and an image is used for the ball. A style sheet is used to define the dimensions of the DIV element, named gameField, and the background color and border of this element. The style sheet also absolutely positions the IMG element so that it initially lies within the bounds of the DIV element:

```
<!-- movement.htm -->
<HTML>
<HEAD>
<STYLE type='text/css'>
    #gameField
    {
        width:300px;
        height:300px;
        background-color:#f0f0ff;
        border-width:2px;
        border-color:#000000;
        border-style:solid;
    }
    #ball
    {
        position:absolute;
        left:40px;
        top:160px;
    }
</STYLE>
<SCRIPT SRC='moveObj.js'></SCRIPT>
<SCRIPT>
    function win_load()
    {
        var m = new moveObj('ball', 'gameField')
        m.setSpeed(50)
        m.setDirection(3, 3)
        m.run()
    }
</SCRIPT>
</HEAD>
<BODY onLoad='win_load()'>
    <DIV ID='gameField'></DIV>
    <IMG SRC='ball.gif' NAME='ball' WIDTH='20' HEIGHT='20' ID='ball'>
</BODY>
</HTML>
```

Once the page has loaded an object needs to be created that will move the ball image, so a function called win_load() is attached to the onLoad event handler. This function creates a moveObj object passing the ID names of the both the IMG and DIV elements as arguments. Having created the object, the setSpeed() and setDirection() methods are called to set the properties for moving the ball image. Finally, the run() method is called and the ball is set moving.

The JavaScript code is imported from an external file, and the constructor code can been seen below:

```
// moveObj.js
function moveObj(elID, boundingBox)
{
    if (!elID || !boundingBox) return
    //Private Variables
```

```
      var movableEl = null
      var bounds = null
      var dX = 3
      var dY = 3
      var dT = 75
      var globalIdx = 0

      if (window["autoMove"])
      {
         globalIdx = autoMove.length
      }

else
      {
         autoMove = new Array()
      }

      autoMove[globalIdx] = function()
      {
      var x = movableEl.offsetLeft + dX
      var y = movableEl.offsetTop + dY
      if (x < bounds.offsetLeft
          || x > bounds.offsetLeft+bounds.offsetWidth-movableEl.offsetWidth)
         dX = -dX
      if (y < bounds.offsetTop
          || y > bounds.offsetTop+bounds.offsetHeight-movableEl.offsetHeight)
         dY = -dY
      moveEl(x, y)
      }

      //Private Methods
      var moveEl = function(x, y)
      {
         var minX = bounds.offsetLeft
         var maxX = bounds.offsetLeft + bounds.offsetWidth
         var minY = bounds.offsetTop
         var maxY = bounds.offsetTop + bounds.offsetHeight
         var eX = Math.max(minX, Math.min(maxX-movableEl.offsetWidth, x))
         var eY = Math.max(minY, Math.min(maxY-movableEl.offsetHeight, y))
         movableEl.style.left = eX + "px"
         movableEl.style.top = eY + "px"
      }

      //Public methods
      this.setDirection = function(x, y)
      {
         dX = x
         dY = y
      }

      this.setSpeed = function(t)
      {
         dT = t
      }

      this.run = function()
      {
         movableEl = document.getElementById(elID)
         bounds = document.getElementById(boundingBox)
         setInterval("autoMove[" + globalIdx + "]()", dT)
      }
}
```

When a new object is created the constructor initially checks to see that both arguments are present and if they are not, the constructor exits and no further action occurs. The constructor is comprised of several properties and methods.

The public method setDirection() is used to set the number of pixels in the x and y direction and the ball element is moved and stored in the dX and dY private variables. The setSpeed() direction is used to set the interval time in milliseconds between each movement and stored in the dT variable. If these methods are not called, each of the variables is set to a default value when the object is created.

The run() method starts the 'ball rolling'. References to the ball image and DIV element are created and stored in the movableEl and bounds variables respectively. Finally, an interval timer is created and at each dT time interval, the autoMove[globalIdx]() function is called.

The autoMove() function takes the x and y co-ordinates of the movableEl and increments these values by the values stored in the dX and dY variables. The new values for the x and y location of the movable image are then tested to check that they do not fall outside the bounds of the DIV element. If they do, the value of dX and/or dY is set equal to the negative value. For example, if dX was 3 previously, it now becomes -3 and vice versa. This allows the direction of the ball movement to be reversed as it hits a wall. Hitting the left and right wall causes the value dX to be changed, and hitting the top and bottom walls causes the dY value to changed. Finally, the new x and y co-ordinate values for the movable element are passed to the moveEl() method.

The moveEl() method is responsible for the actual movement of the ball. The first four lines obtain, from the bounding DIV element, the values for the minimum and maximum x and y values within which the movable element can be located. The values of the x and y arguments to the function are then tested against the minimum and maximum x and y values. The variable eX then stores either minX, x or maxX (the movableEl width), by using a combination of the Math.min() and Math.max() methods. These methods accept any numerical arguments and either return a minimum, for Math.min(), or maximum argument value, for Math.max(). Note that the maxX value has the width of movableEl taken away so that the right hand side of the element will be next to the right hand wall of the bounds. The same operation is executed for the y co-ordinate and stored in the eY variable. Finally, the function sets the left and top location of the variable to the variables eX and eY.

This object simply creates the effect of a ball bouncing around inside a box. Each time the ball hits a wall, it bounces off in the opposite direction. As there are no events to handle, a client sniffer is not required this time. To give the ball different physical properties we can modify the autoMove[globalIdx]() method adding extra code to make the ball spin when it hits the wall, for example.

Pong

This final example will use the two previous widgets for drag and drop along with movement to create the basics of the game called Pong. In this classic game, a baton can be moved by a player to hit a ball. The objective is not to let the ball move behind the baton.

We already have all three elements to the game. The drag and drop section shows how to create an element that a user can drag around (the baton in this case). The last section, movement, shows how to implement a field of play (the bounding area) and how to create an object that moves automatically:

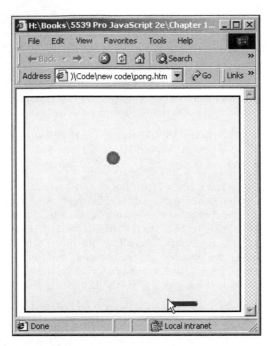

The HTML code for the body section of this example basically combines the body sections of the previous two examples as below. The only difference this time is the `dragObject()` function now accepts two arguments, the second argument being the ID name of the DIV element. The `dragObject()` function will require this so that the dragged element does not move outside the `gameField` area:

```
<DIV ID='gameField'></DIV>
<IMG SRC='baton.gif' WIDTH='40' HEIGHT='7'
    ID='baton' onmouseover='dragObject(this, 'gameField')'>
<IMG SRC='ball.gif' WIDTH='20' HEIGHT='20' ID='ball'>
```

Similarly, a style sheet is used that is a combination of the style sheets from the previous examples:

```
#gameField
{
    position:absolute;
    width:300px;
    height:300px;
    left:10px;
    top:10px;
    border-width:2px;
    border-color:#000000;
    border-style:solid;
    background-color:#f0f0ff;
}
#baton
{
    position:absolute;
    left:150px;
    top:290px;
}
#ball
{
```

```
     position:absolute;
     left:30px;
     top:30px;
}
```

No prizes for guessing that the JavaScript for the page is also a combination of the JavaScript from the previous two sections. Again, we need to include a client sniffer for the drag and drop code, so that the events in Netscape and IE can be handled correctly. Note that the `moveObj()` constructor in this example now accepts three arguments. The third argument is the ID name of the `baton` element. This element will be needed by the moving element to test if it has hit it or not. The `onLoad` event handler has the `win_load()` function attached, so the ball will only start moving once the page has finished loading:

```
var cs = new clientSniffer()

function win_load()
{
    var m = new moveObj('ball', 'gameField', 'baton')
    m.setSpeed(50)
    m.setDirection(3, 3)
    m.run()
}
```

Drag Modifications

The `dragObject()` constructor function code hardly changes; an extra variable called `bounds` is required that stores a reference to the `DIV` element that will define the bounding area in which the baton must exist. The ID name of the `DIV` element is supplied as an argument to the constructor:

```
function dragObject(boundBox)
{
    if (!boundBox) return
    var bounds = document.getElementById(boundBox)

    //private function go here
}
```

The `DRAG_drag()` method requires a small modification to ensure the baton doesn't move outside the bounding box area. The code for this is identical to the code in the previous example to keep the ball from moving outside the bounding area, with the exception that the code for moving in the y-direction has been removed so that the element can only be dragged horizontally:

```
DRAG_drag = function(e)
{
    var evtX = cs.isNS() ? e.clientX : event.clientX
    if (el.DRAG_dragging == true)
    {
        var minX = bounds.offsetLeft
        var maxX = minX + bounds.offsetWidth
        el.style.left = Math.max(minX, Math.min(maxX-el.offsetWidth, evtX))
        return false
    }
    else
        return true
}
```

Movement Modifications

The class constructor for `moveObject()` needs slightly more modifying than the drag code, requiring a new private variable and two new private functions. The `clash` variable is added and the public method `run()` is modified to store a reference in this variable to the baton. Remember, the ID name is passed to the constructor as the third argument to the constructor, `clashItemID`:

```
function moveObj(elID, boundingBox, clashItemID)
{
   if (!elID || !boundingBox) return
   var movableEl = null
   var bounds = null
   var clash = null
   var dX = 3
   var dY = 3
   var dT = 75
   var timerID = null
   var globalIdx = 0

   if (window["autoMove"])
   {
      globalIdx = autoMove.length
   }

else
   {
      autoMove = new Array()
   }

   //Global, Private + public methods go here

   this.run = function()
   {
      movableEl = document.getElementById(elID)
      bounds = document.getElementById(boundingBox)
      clash = document.getElementById(clashItemID)
      timerID = setInterval("autoMove[" + globalIdx + "]()", dT)
   }
}
```

The `autoMove[globalIdx]()` function is modified to detect if the ball element hits the baton or if it has gone behind the baton. An `if` statement calls the `isAClash()` function to test if the new location ball will clash with the baton If not, the `moveEl()` function is called and the ball moves, else if a clash does occur, the value of the `dY` variable is reversed and no movement occurs this time. The final `if` statement checks to see if the ball element is behind the baton by calling the `isBehind()` method. If the ball has gone behind, the interval timer is cleared and the ball element stops moving:

```
autoMove[globalIdx] = function()
{
   var x = movableEl.offsetLeft + dX
   var y = movableEl.offsetTop + dY
   if (x < bounds.offsetLeft || x > bounds.offsetLeft+bounds.offsetWidth-
movableEl.offsetWidth)
      dX = -dX
   if (y < bounds.offsetTop || y > bounds.offsetTop+bounds.offsetHeight-
movableEl.offsetHeight)
      dY = -dY
   if (!isAClash(x, y))
      moveEl(x, y)
   else
```

```
        dY = -dY
   if (isBehind(y)) clearInterval(timerID)
}
```

The `isAClash()` method tests to see if the ball will hit the baton (whether they clash), and if so return `true`, else return `false`. This method is passed new x and y co-ordinates for the ball element. A clash will occur (`true` is returned) if:

❑ the y value top edge of the baton is less than the value of the bottom edge of the ball

❑ the x value of right-hand edge of the ball is greater than the value of the left-hand edge of the baton

❑ the x value of the left-hand edge of the ball is less than the value of the right-hand edge of the baton

The `isBehind()` method checks to see if the ball is behind the baton (whether the player missed the ball), and returns `true` if behind or `false` otherwise. The method is passed, only the new y value of the ball. The vertical centre of the ball and baton is calculated and if the y value of the centre of the ball is greater than the value of the centre of the baton, the ball must be behind the baton:

```
var isAClash = function(x, y)
{
   return (clash.offsetTop < y + movableEl.offsetHeight &&
      + movableEl.offsetWidth > clash.offsetLeft &&
      x < clash.offsetLeft+clash.offsetWidth )
}

var isBehind = function(y)
{
   var ec = y + movableEl.offsetHeight / 2
   var cc = clash.offsetTop + clash.offsetHeight / 2
   return (ec > cc)
}
```

With the modifications added to the drag and movement code we now have the basics for a game of Pong. With a little bit of extra work, we can develop the game further by adding a score board, extra balls, or increasing the speed at which the ball moves. If we try to increase the ball speed, we do not try to change the interval timer, but increase the value of the `dX` and `dY` private variables each time the ball is hit.

Summary

The most interesting aspect to DHTML now is its power to manipulate elements within a document and alter a multitude of different features in a platform independent fashion. DHTML is not any one language, and in fact is not a language at all, but rather a means of producing dynamic effects within a web page. It is reliant on several other technologies such as HTML, CSS, JavaScript, and now DOM, each with their own uses. We can think of this family of technologies in the following way:

❑ HTML is a good, albeit basic layout manager, providing structural definition for content

❑ CSS is a very powerful visual enhancement manager and also a more sophisticated layout manager than HTML

❑ JavaScript is the engine that drives the co-ordinate responses to human and programmatic event based actions

❑ DOM is an accessibility manager allowing JavaScript access to manipulate content, structure and styling information, independently of the platform in which it runs

Throughout this chapter we have seen several different examples for creating DHTML effects. Now that the latest browsers adhere much more strongly to the latest standards for HTML, CSS, JavaScript, and DOM, code can be written once and run (almost) anywhere, and thus is very portable. This makes writing DHTML code much easier and quicker because the amount of coding required is much less.

This portability of code written using the latest DHTML techniques means that the requirements for producing client sniffing code has by and large been removed for the latest browsers. However, if we need code to be backwards compatible with older browsers we will still need to identify the browser and fork our code to cope with the deprecated methodologies of these older browsers.

By introducing and standardizing DOM, writing DHTML code has become more coherent. Although DOM has not been fully implemented by the browsers, and there are differences between browsers, careful use of DOM can still produce very powerful effects.

DHTML is now powerful enough to produce some of the simple effects that previously had to be created using plug-ins such as activeX controls or Java. DHTML will never be able to replace these plug-in technologies – after all, that's not its intention or purpose. However, it can remove some of the need for the effects that previously had to be created by these plug-in technologies and thus allow programmers using these technologies to concentrate on more worthwhile projects.

Pro JavaScript 2nd Edition

18

Internet Explorer Filters

Microsoft IE 5.5+ running in a 32 bit Windows environment supports a variety of special visual effects that you can use to create styled content, which Microsoft called filters when they were first introduced. The filters only work with IE browsers when used on the Windows platform, so the focus of this chapter will be of more interest to Windows users. None of these effects work on MSIE on non-Windows platforms. Nor do they work on other manufacturers browsers on any platform. Therefore, they aren't really safe for deployment unless you are using them within an Intranet where you have total control over the browsers being used to view them.

We have a short example showing browser detection at the end of the chapter if you need a fragment of code to test the browser type and version. That can then be used to conditionally execute any filter modification scripts.

You can use a great deal of the filter capabilities without ever writing any JavaScript. They are already very powerful, even when defined in a straightforward document source form or within <META> tags. Because the MSIE browser parses and stores all document content in a script accessible object model, you can locate and operate on the objects that it uses to represent the filters.

Microsoft implemented filters as an extension of their CSS support while at the same time, the Scalable Vector Graphics (SVG) working group were developing filter effects for use with SVG images. Therefore, the two applications of filters are somewhat related. However, they are implemented and described in a quite different way.

Scalable Vector Graphics are a way to draw graphical content using lines, rectangles, and specific placement of character glyphs. It allows the document to be treated as a free form canvas with items being drawn with vectors rather than image pixmaps. Because the images are drawn with vectors, they can be scaled to reveal more detail as they are zoomed to a larger scale. The filter effects are applied to SVG drawing primitives to add shadows and blur effects, and the work currently underway should yield some generally useful capabilities that can be applied outside of the SVG framework. The SVG filters are also applied using the filters property of a CSS style object.

Using the filters in your web pages can really make your content stand out from the rest of the crowd, and their use is becoming more popular as people discover that they are not as complicated to deploy as they thought. Meanwhile, new filters have been introduced, and those existing filters have been modified and enhanced for IE 5.5+ to provide better performance.

The following three broad categories of visual filter effect are supported:

❏   Static filters can be used to enhance the visual display effect of an object as it is rendered on screen. These are applied through an extended CSS interface. By using JavaScript timeout loops, you can also use the static filters as animated effects by altering one property of the filter continuously. However, transitional filters are generally better at this.

❏   Transitional filters control the change from one display to another in a timed fashion, but can be used as static filters by freezing them at a fixed point in the transition. Transitions can also be manually activated under JavaScript control by means of the Apply() and Play() methods and when executed, the transition will reveal the new display content.

❏   Procedural filters render a 2D surface according to a shading algorithm, and are considered to be a special case of the static filters.

The static effects can be applied to content within the page and the dynamic transition effects are used when modifying page content or navigating from page to page. It is certainly better to use a static filter effect to create a shadowed text than it is to download a GIF image, as you can avoid consuming a large amount of bandwidth that way.

We will assume here that you are using MSIE 5.5+ on a Windows 32 bit platform. This is because prior to that release, the filters were a little more primitive and the older syntax is now deprecated.

Due to the limited availability of these filters, we will avoid making the examples more complicated with the addition of any browser detection code. This is reasonable within an Intranet deployment, where you would likely control the deployed version of any browsers. If you intend to use these filters on an open access Internet web site, you should be detecting users of browsers other than MSIE 5.5+ on Window 32 bit operating systems and providing an alternative. Many of the examples will cause a crash on Netscape, and some will also not work on earlier versions of MSIE.

What are Filters?

Filters are a set of multimedia effects that can be applied to individual elements on a web page or to a whole page. A limited set of filters was first introduced with IE 4, but was radically overhauled during the version 5.5 upgrade. In fact, the changes were so extensive that version 4.0 filter functionality should be considered obsolete, and you should avoid implementing any of the legacy filters that have been replaced by the more flexible version 5 filters.

At present, filters are typically implemented as COM components registered in the Windows registry when the browser is installed. Later on, when a more standardised approach becomes popular, they may be implemented in a variety of other ways, perhaps as plug-ins of some kind.

Filters are applied through the CSS interface although, as they are a specialised part of the browser functionality, they were not covered in Chapter 8 on CSS. They are attached through the filter property of a style object or the filters[] collection of an HTML element object. This fragment of HTML shows how a filter is applied to an image tag:

```
<Element STYLE='filter:filtername(properties)'>
```

Assuming that you have located the object representing the HTML element and have stored it in myElement, you would access the filter in one of these ways:

```
myCSSSource = myElement.style.filter;
myFilterObject = myElement.filters[0];
```

If you are prepared to add some JavaScript, the filters become very powerful indeed. You can go some considerable way beyond what is possible without using filters. We shall explore those possibilities some more shortly.

Multimedia Visual Effects

Visual filters extend the W3C standardized CSS level 2 support by the addition of a `filter` property to the `style` object. In the chapter about JavaScript access to CSS, we explore many ways in which you can operate on the properties of the `style` object. To use those techniques with filters, simply access the source text of a filter definition as a string that is accessible at:

```
myElement.style.filter
```

This provides a means to add a CSS text string to describe the transition or static effect.

There are fundamentally two kinds of filters:

❑   Static effects that are intended to modify the appearance of an on-screen object

❑   Dynamic effects that are intended for use as an interstitial effect between two discrete states for the web page. The dynamic effects can be frozen at a specified state during the transition so they can also be used as a static effect.

Certain effects can be accomplished with some degree of scripting, but many go way beyond what is possible even with complex and sophisticated script implementations.

Creating some of these effects with scripting might actually be far more work than simply applying the filter affects as CSS style rules. Web content developers from an artistic design background are more likely to easily assimilate CSS styling based techniques than they are to develop robust and well-engineered JavaScript code. So, there are many subtle advantages to this approach.

Although the number of available colors in the display palette is not usually an issue these days, filters will generally work best if your display can cope with 256 colors or more. Fewer than 256 colors will severely degrade the appearance of the visual effect.

Defining a Simple Filter

You can apply a filter by putting a textual description of the effect into the `filter` property. There are several ways to accomplish this. The textual description resembles a function call, but it is parsed by the filter engine in the browser and is neither CSS nor JavaScript source. This can be a little bit confusing when you are trying to get filters to work for the first time. The parsing process in MSIE determines the location of the filter executable code by inspecting the registry reference defined as a `progid` value. It then binds that code to the drawing mechanisms in the browser.

The simplest way to add a filter is by putting its declaration into the STYLE attribute of an HTML element. The example below actually adds two filters:

```
<!-- Example_01.htm -->
<HTML>
<BODY>
<IMG SRC='cold.gif' WIDTH='50%'
    STYLE='filter:progid:DXImageTransform.Microsoft.MotionBlur(strength=50)
```

```
              progid:DXImageTransform.Microsoft.BasicImage(rotation=2, mirror=1);'>
</BODY>
</HTML>
```

The example illustrates how to blur the image and then flip it over in a vertical direction. Note how the filters are cascaded, but there is no dividing semi-colon. That is because the semi-colon is significant within the CSS parser and the filters, therefore, need to be expressed as well formed function calls, but separated from one another by spaces. Experimenting with these filter strings reveals that you can omit the brackets and parameters so this does work:

```
STYLE='filter:progid:DXImageTransform.Microsoft.MotionBlur'
```

This is not recommended, however as it is not the documented way to use the filter effects. Oddly enough, the function arguments are specified as name=value pairs, which is not the usual way that function arguments are presented. This does have the advantage however that they are somewhat self-documenting as you use them.

Filters and Layout

Note that in the previous example the <IMG> tag has a WIDTH attribute specified. Filters will only work if some CSS layout is defined on the target object. This is a potential pitfall when getting filters to work for the first time. You have to either define a WIDTH, HEIGHT (or both), or set the CSS position attribute to absolute to enable filters. This is quite easy to do by adding STYLE attributes or applying a STYLE class to the elements.

Setting absolute positioning may not be an option for your required page layout, in which case providing a dummy WIDTH value that can safely be exceeded will be sufficient.

Some objects, such as images and tables, already have layout defined implicitly. You can also impart layout to an element by setting its contentEditable property to the value true. Here is a short example that does that without using JavaScript:

```
<HTML>
<BODY>
   <DIV CONTENTEDITABLE="true">Edit this content<DIV>
</BODY>
</HTML>
```

The following variation defines the <DIV> block, but does not set its contentEditable property. The <SCRIPT> fragment checks the ContentEditable state, and makes it editable if the content is read only:

```
<!-- Example_02.htm -->
<HTML>
<BODY>
   <DIV ID="CONTENT">Edit this content</DIV>
   <SCRIPT LANGUAGE="JavaScript">
      myObject = document.getElementById("CONTENT");
      if(!myObject.isContentEditable)
      {
         alert("Content is not editable - making it editable now.");
         myObject.contentEditable = true;
      }
   </SCRIPT>
</BODY>
</HTML>
```

A small caveat is that if an object has position controls (and hence has filters active), those filters will be inactive if the object is nested inside an element that does not have position or layout controls activated. You should make sure that the outermost element has absolute positioning enabled. Here is an object that has position controls that are inhibited:

```
<HTML>
<BODY>
    <DIV ID="NO_POS_CONTROL">
        <DIV STYLE="position: absolute">Cannot filter this content</DIV>
    </DIV>
</BODY>
</HTML>
```

In the next case, all <DIV> blocks inside the outermost one inherit the position control, but are stacked one above the other because they don't each have a position:absolute clause in their style definitions. Rather, the position value is inherited:

```
<HTML>
<BODY>
    <DIV STYLE="position: absolute">
        <DIV>Can filter this content</DIV>
        <DIV>and this content too</DIV>
    </DIV>
</BODY>
</HTML>
```

The presence of the string 'progid:DXImageTransform.Microsoft.' is shown in all the examples that Microsoft publishes. It is necessary when defining the filters within CSS style attributes. The shorter form invokes some older legacy filter code and is now deprecated. The longer form will only work on the MSIE version 5.5 browser.

The prefixing 'progid:DXImageTransform.Microsoft.' string is constructed from several components. The general form for this prefix when creating your own filters is:

```
progid:filter-type.Companyname.filtername(props)
```

The filter-type for all the built-in transforms that are supplied with MSIE is DXImageTransform. Because they are supplied with MSIE, obviously the company name is Microsoft. The filtername and its properties depend on the filter you want to invoke.

If filters are implemented in a cross platform manner, or if the W3C defines them as part of the formal CSS specification one day, this prefix might well disappear because it invokes a proprietary Microsoft architecture. The SVG proposal suggests that filters will be invoked with a URL() function call being defined as the content of the style object's filter property.

Beware that the older IE 4 browser supports WIDTH and HEIGHT properties on <DIV> and <SPAN> elements, but some other elements cannot have layout properties assigned. The following element types cannot have filters applied to them under any circumstances:

❑ OBJECT elements

❑ EMBED elements

❑ APPLET elements

❑ SELECT and OPTION form elements

❑ TR, THEAD, TBODY, and TFOOT table elements

If the filtered element does not have layout constraints, the filter effect is ignored. This is a specific limitation of the filter implementation in MSIE, and may not be a limitation when a W3C standardized filter architecture is developed. At present, this is necessary so that the filter can work within a pixmap region that is finite and limited to the width and height of the filtered element. So, if your filters appear to be correctly set up but are still not working, check that the element has layout properties.

Another important thing to remember is that the older version 4 filters cannot change the size of the element they are filtering. If you do not allow large enough margins around the object to let the filter do its work, the original bounding box will clip the effect. The version 5 filters work differently and can expand the margins of a container. We give an example of this near the end of the chapter. Sometimes, it is necessary to encapsulate objects in further nested levels of <DIV> or <SPAN> elements to create some margin space, or to enlarge the margins of the target element itself. This is especially important with shadow and glow effects.

Filters and the Object Model

The IE browser creates a filter object that reflects the properties and attributes that control a single filter. A filter object is created for every filter, meaning that the more filters we use, the more memory it is going to consume on the client.

You can either operate on the filter objects which are accessible from the filters[] collection belonging to an element, or on the CSS source text stored in the filter property of the style object belonging to the element.

The filter object controls a visual effect that is used when the display is updated as the result of a change to the content of an element. Within the filter description string, certain property and method names may be common to several filters, but may not do the same thing in each case:

```
<HTML>
<BODY>
<IMG SRC='cold.gif' WIDTH='50%'
    STYLE='filter: progid:DXImageTransform.Microsoft.BasicImage(mirror=1)
        progid:DXImageTransform.Microsoft.BasicImage(rotation=2, mirror=1);'>
</BODY>
</HTML>
```

In the example, both invocations of the BasicImage filter have a mirror property. The first flips in the horizontal axis, while the second applies to the vertical axis.

Ideally, you should access the filter objects via the filters[] collection because you may have the same filter type repeated for a cascading effect, and you need to be sure that you are addressing the right one. Alternatively, you can access it as a property of the style object associated with the element, but that yields a source text version and not an object representation.

When using the filters in the context of the style object, this string must preceed the function name for each filter: 'progid:DXImageTransform.Microsoft.'

Some less sophisticated filters seem to work without this prefix, but they will behave as they did with IE 4. That may yield a different appearance for the final effect than it would if the IE 5.5 filter was invoked.

If you use the DirectX SDK available from Microsoft, you can manufacture your own special filter effects. Once these are registered, you would likely replace the word 'Microsoft' with your own company name. In all our examples, we are assuming you will use just the filters provided by Microsoft. These are then built into IE and they are always available.

In IE 4, the technique was to apply the filters directly as properties of the filter object that belongs to HTML element objects themselves. The following example demonstrates this:

```
<!-- Example_03.htm -->
<HTML>
<BODY>
    <P ID="PARA" STYLE="filter:Shadow()">Some text</P>
    <SCRIPT LANGUAGE="JavaScript">
        myElement = document.getElementById("PARA");
        myFilter = myElement.filters(0);
        myFilter.Shadow(… someAttributes …)
    </SCRIPT>
</BODY>
</HTML>
```

Generally, however, the syntax for accessing a filter definition now is:

```
myFilterSrc = myElement.style.filter;
myFilter    = myElement.filters(anIndex);
myFilter    = myElement.filters.item(anIndex);
myFilter    = myElement.filters.item(aProgidString);
myFilter    = myElement.filters[anIndex];
```

Note that one of the above accessors to the filters yields the source string rather than a `filter` object, where anIndex is a reference to an element in a collection and aProgidString is the complete filter name minus its `progid:` prefix and lacking any brackets. For example:

```
myFilter    = myElement.filters.item("DXImageTransform.Microsoft.Alpha");
```

Given our earlier example of an image with some filter effects, here is some example JavaScript for locating the relevant `filter` objects:

```
<!-- Example_04.htm -->
<HTML>
<HEAD>
<SCRIPT>
function checkFilters()
{
    var myBasicImage = document.images[0].filters.item(0);
    alert(myBasicImage);

    var myAlpha = document.images[0].filters[1];
    alert(myAlpha);

    var myBlur =
document.images[0].filters.item("DXImageTransform.Microsoft.MotionBlur");
    alert(myBlur);

    var myAllFilters = document.images[0].style.filter;
    alert(myAllFilters)
}
</SCRIPT>
</HEAD>
<BODY>
<IMG SRC="cold.gif" WIDTH="50%"
    STYLE="filter:progid:DXImageTransform.Microsoft.MotionBlur(strength=50)
        progid:DXImageTransform.Microsoft.BasicImage(rotation=2, mirror=1);">
<SCRIPT>
    checkFilters();
</SCRIPT>
</BODY>
</HTML>
```

The value in myAllFilters is like the CSS source text with each filter cited in a separate line. The others yield filter objects that are very opaque.

The Element.filters Collection

There are a variety of ways to access the filters belonging to an HTML element object. Each object that represents an HTML element has a filters property that yields a collection object, containing a list of filters. This collection contains all the filters associated with an element, and because it is a collection, you can operate on the individual filters in it.

This line of script will access the first filter belonging to an object pointed at by the variable myObject. The example enables the filter:

```
myObject.filters.item(0).enabled = true;
```

So, a filter object is considered to be a child of the element to which it is applied. This is because the object representing a filter can only be located by examining the filters[] collection belonging to the HTML Element object to which the filter is applied.

As the filters on an object are reflected into objects, you can operate on those filter objects as you would with other objects. They don't actually expose much in the way of an interface for the JavaScript programmer. The only enumerable property of a filter object is its enabled state that can be set to true or false as needed. Some examples in other reference sources have suggested that the filter objects support named properties according to the range of name=value parameters the filter function supports. We shall look at that possibility in a little while, when we examine the filter object.

If you make an enumerator for the filters[] collection, you don't see any entries having numeric index values as their names, but you do see a list of progid: values.

We can use indexed or associative access techniques to find the filter objects in the collection:

```
<!-- Example_05.htm -->
<HTML>
<HEAD>
<SCRIPT>
function switchOn()
{
   myImg.filters.item(0).enabled = true;
   myImg.filters.item(1).enabled = true;
   myImg.filters.item(2).enabled = true;
}

function switchOff()
{
   myImg.filters.item("DXImageTransform.Microsoft.BasicImage").enabled = false;
   myImg.filters.item("DXImageTransform.Microsoft.Alpha").enabled = false;
   myImg.filters.item("DXImageTransform.Microsoft.Blur").enabled = false;
}
</SCRIPT>
</HEAD>
<BODY>
<IMG SRC='cold.gif' ID= myImg
   STYLE=
'filter: progid:DXImageTransform.Microsoft.BasicImage(rotation=2, mirror=1)
   progid:DXImageTransform.Microsoft.Alpha(opacity=50)
   progid:DXImageTransform.Microsoft.Blur(strength=100);
   position: absolute'>
<BR></BR><BR></BR><BR></BR>
<FORM>
```

```
      <INPUT TYPE="BUTTON" VALUE="DISABLE" onClick="switchOff();">
      <INPUT TYPE="BUTTON" VALUE="ENABLE" onClick="switchOn();">
   </FORM>
   </BODY>
   </HTML>
```

Note that the image has an absolute position defined. This prevents the buttons from moving up and down as the transforms are enabled and disabled.

In the example, the filters are accessed as a numeric entry in the `filters[]` collection and using the associative names. There may be a risk involved with the associative name technique if the same filter is applied several times in different ways, so the numeric indexing may be better. For example, if we add an extra `BasicImage()` filter on the image to apply a further rotation effect, we cannot be sure which one we are referring to with the line:

```
   myImg.filters.item("DXImageTransform.Microsoft.BasicImage").enabled = false;
```

The numeric technique may also be more appropriate if the particular filter is defined at run time by script, in which case you may not know the associative name at all.

Some filters have common properties and methods. The `color` property is obviously likely to be quite popular, and transition filters all support the `Apply()` and `Play()` method calls.

The style.filter String

As Microsoft has implemented filters as an extension to the CSS support in IE, you can also access filters through the styling object model. So, another way to access the filter definition is like this:

```
   myObject.style.filter
```

This property is a string value that contains the CSS filter value. You can modify this directly from script to change the filtering being applied to the element. When you modify this property, a screen-refreshing trigger is generated that causes the browser to redraw the affected portion of the screen with the new filters being used.

So by way of an example, lets define a `<DIV>` block with a simple filter and then modify it from the script so that the contents of our `<DIV>` block should be displayed with a wavy pattern effect:

```
   <!-- Example_06.htm -->
   <HTML>
   <BODY>
   <DIV ID='myDiv' STYLE='position:absolute;
   filter:progid:DXImageTransform.Microsoft.Wave(strength=2)'>
   This is my div
   </DIV>
   </BODY>
   </HTML>
```

Now with a fragment of JavaScript we can append an additional filter to it by inserting the following code after the `<DIV>` block:

```
   <SCRIPT>
   myDiv.style.filter += " progid:DXImageTransform.Microsoft.Blur(strength=2)"
   </SCRIPT>
```

We just performed a string concatenate and wrote the new string back to the CSS filter string property. Note that because we concatenated the new filter, we included a space character to delimit the filters. If we wanted to take a filter out, the scripting could get quite complex, so this trick is good for adding a single filter effect, but is somewhat unwieldy when managing filters on a larger scale.

It is better to use the `filters[]` collection and access the individual filters through the object model. That way, you can switch them on and off one at a time. Trying to create a new `filter` object and add it to the `filters` collection is not recommended practice, as the collection is not designed to be edited in that way.

A better technique is to define all the possible filters in the style sheet so they are permanently attached to the element, but set their `enabled` state property to `false`. Then from script, you can selectively enable them as you need to by setting that property value to `true`.

Filter Object Property Access

With many objects in the browser implementations of JavaScript, you can set up an enumeration loop to inspect the object properties. We used that technique in Chapter 9 on DOM to examine the DOM and CSS structures inside the browser. However, when you try this with a `filter` object, the only thing that is displayed is the `enabled` property. Even so, we may be able to modify some of the attributes of a filter by changing property values that belong to the `filter` object. The names of the properties of the filter objects are based on the `name=value` arguments that are appropriate for each kind of filter.

Let's test out this hypothesis with an example:

```
<!-- Example_07.htm -->
<HTML>
<HEAD>
<SCRIPT>
function trackMouse()
{
    var myOpacity;
    var myFilter;

    myOpacity = event.x/4;
    myFilter = myImage.filters.item(0);

    myFilter.opacity = myOpacity;
    myOutput.innerText = myOpacity;
}
</SCRIPT>
</HEAD>
<BODY onMouseMove='trackMouse()'>
    <IMG ID='myImage'
        SRC='hot.gif'
        STYLE='filter:progid:DXImageTransform.Microsoft.Alpha(opacity=50)'>
    <BR>
    Move mouse left and right to change the image opacity.<BR>
    <BR>
    The new opacity value is: <SPAN ID='myOutput'></SPAN><BR>
</BODY>
</HTML>
```

It works! So, as long as we are careful with the values we specify, we can modify the filters using the familiar object model techniques that we use with DOM and CSS.

Let's just skip through the code to see that we understand what its doing. The `<SCRIPT>` block contains a definition for the `trackMouse()` function. This is attached to the `mouseMove` event handler hook so that it is called whenever the mouse is moved within the document area. Since it is attached to the `<BODY>` object, it is available to all parts of the document. The `<IMG>` tag has an `opacity` filter attached via its `STYLE` tag attribute. By accessing the image object via its `ID` value, and then traversing its `filters[]` collection, we can locate the object that represents the filter for the image. Modifying its `opacity` property according to the mouse movement, using the event properties containing the `X` co-ordinate, links the mouse movement to the opacity of the image. Moving the mouse triggers a filter update, which in turn causes the screen to be refreshed with the image being drawn at its new opacity value.

Procedural Effects

Put simply, this is a means of space filling an area within an HTML element object using a shading algorithm. This can be a useful way of making web page downloads much smaller, because you specify an algorithm to fill a space rather than a pixel image map. In this example, we draw a heading using an image tag to request a text block having a shadowed appearance:

```
<HTML>
<BODY>
   <IMG SRC='heading_text.gif'>
   <P>A paragraph of text placed under the heading.</P>
</BODY>
</HTML>
```

The same thing can be accomplished without the need to download the image file:

```
<!-- Example_08.htm -->
<HTML>
<BODY>
<DIV STYLE="width:100%;
   font-size:36px;
   font-weight:bold;
   filter:progid:DXImageTransform.Microsoft.dropshadow(OffX=2, OffY=2,
Color='#AAAAAA', Positive='true')">
   A Heading Text
</DIV>
<P>A paragraph of text placed under the heading.</P>
</BODY>
</HTML>
```

The table lists the static procedural filter function names. They are a special case of the static filters because they render the background effect from scratch rather than modify the foreground appearance of an element object:

Filter	Effect
AlphaImageLoader()	Loads an image and applies crop, scale and blending as it is drawn
Gradient()	Fills an area with a horizontal or vertical gradient

These procedural shaders compute the alpha channel transparency and the pixel color of the area in RGB co-ordinates.

The procedural effects are applied to the background of an element object or to an otherwise empty element object. If you define a <DIV> block and give it some layout controlling values such as WIDTH and HEIGHT, you can then define a gradient fill to occupy the area of that <DIV> block.

Example: AlphaImageLoader()

An Alpha Image Loader uses what is called an Alpha channel to control the blending of an image. An Alpha channel contains a value that controls the percentage of blending between two image sources. Sometimes, that alpha blending can be controlled by a pixmap that allows the blend percentage to be applied differentially across the surface of the image. In simpler implementations, a single percentage value indicates a blend value that is applied across the entire image surface.

Below is an example of the `AlphaImageLoader()` filter being applied to an image. The filter in MSIE provides some scaling and cropping capabilities as well as a blend percentage. You can choose to scale, crop or display as normal once the example is running. Each time you click on the button, the effect steps through a series of transformations applying each one in turn. Note that this only works on MSIE 5.5:

```
<!-- Example_09.htm -->
<HTML>
<BODY BGCOLOR="gray">
<SCRIPT>
var theState = 0;

// Cycle the sizingMethod property to size the image.
function changeState(oObj)
{
    switch(theState)
    {
        case 0:
            theState = 1;
            CONTAINER.filters(0).sizingMethod = "image";
            oObj.innerText = 'Scale to fit';
            break;
        case 1:
            theState = 2;
            CONTAINER.filters(0).sizingMethod = "scale";
            oObj.innerText = 'Crop to fit';
            break;
        case 2:
            theState = 0;
            CONTAINER.filters(0).sizingMethod = "crop";
            oObj.innerText = 'Normal';
            break;
    }
}
</SCRIPT>
<DIV ID='CONTAINER'
    STYLE='position:absolute; left:140px; height:50px; width:50px;
filter:progid:DXImageTransform.Microsoft.AlphaImageLoader(SRC='cold.gif',
sizingMethod='scale');' >
</DIV>
<BUTTON onclick='changeState(this);'>Scale to fit</BUTTON>
</BODY>
</HTML>
```

Note that the background color of the <BODY> tag is set to gray so you can see the sizing effect on the image against a darker background.

Example: Gradient()

The `Gradient()` procedural surface generator describes a gradient fill effect. A gradient effect is a gradual blending between two colors across the surface of an imaging rectangle. The pixels at one side are defined to be the starting color, while those at the opposite edge are the finishing color, and in between they are proportionally blended between the two.

When you run `Example_10.htm`, which is available for download from `http://www.wrox.com`, you can turn the gradient behind the image on and off and select the two alternative gradient types.

Static Filter Effects

Static effects are applied to an element object and are rendered with the object as it is displayed. This lets you draw some interesting glowing and shadowed effects without the need to download images to accomplish them. These filters are used to define the appearance of an HTML Element object. Here is an example that doesn't require any scripting at all that makes the image partly transparent:

```
<!-- Example_11.htm -->
<HTML>
<BODY>
    <IMG SRC='cold.gif'
        STYLE='filter:progid:DXImageTransform.Microsoft.Alpha(opacity=20)'>
</BODY>
</HTML>
```

Next is an example that lays an opaque rectangle over the image and places a caption text on top. You might use this on a broadband delivery system to simulate TV production techniques.

```
<!-- Example_12.htm -->
<HTML>
<HEAD>
<STYLE>
.tvpicture { width:320px; height:240px; }
.captionBox
{
    position:         absolute;
    top:              200px;
    left:             10px;
    width:            300px;
    height:           35px;
    background-color: black;
    filter:           progid:DXImageTransform.Microsoft.Alpha(opacity=20)
}
.captionText
{
    color:        red;
    position:     absolute;
    top:          205px;
    left:         10px;
    width:        300px;
    font-size:    14pt;
    font-weight:  bold;
    text-align:   center;
    filter:       progid:DXImageTransform.Microsoft.Alpha(opacity=100)
}
</STYLE>
</HEAD>
<BODY>
    <IMG SRC='cold.gif' CLASS='tvpicture'>
    <DIV CLASS='captionBox'></DIV>
    <P CLASS='captionText'>CAPTION TEXT HERE</P>
</BODY>
</HTML>
```

The table below lists the static visual filters supported in IE 5.5. They modify the appearance of an object, and therefore have to be applied to an element of some kind.

Filter	Effect
Alpha()	Opaque blending
BasicImage()	Various image processing convolution effects
Blur()	Blurring of the target object
Chroma()	Masking with a chroma key
Compositor()	Applying one image over the tope of another without obscuring the first
DropShadow()	Adding a drop shadow effect
Emboss()	Similar to the PhotoShop embossed effect
Engrave()	The opposite of an embossed effect
Glow()	A surrounding glow effect round the element
Light()	A light source modeller
MaskFilter()	Masking effects
Matrix()	Image rotation, stretch, scale, and shear effects
MotionBlur()	Motion blurring effect
Shadow()	Make the object appear as if it is a shadow
Wave()	A weird distortion effect

These are deprecated filters that were available with version IE 4 and have now been superseded. The reference tables in the appendices show the mapping of old filter names to new filter functionality:

Filter	Effect
FlipH()	Horizontal flip
FlipV()	Vertical flip
Grayscale()	Remove color information
Invert()	Invert all color values
Mask()	Mask out portions of the image
Xray()	Weird inversion effect just showing edge detail

Some of these may not be available with all versions of the IE browser. Refer to the appendices for details.

Note that, although the Compositor() filter is classified as a static effect, it is implemented as a transition filter, and should be placed last after all other static filters when multiple filters are used.

Next, we will exercise a few simple examples to illustrate basic static filter set-up.

Example: Alpha()

This is related to the AlphaImageLoader() filter we described earlier. In this case, the filter simply controls the overall opacity of the image. By modifying the opacity with an interval timer, we can get objects to fade in and out on the screen. This is quite an attractive way to accomplish a transition effect, although there are other ways to accomplish a fade with a transition filter, which we shall examine later.

This example uses the `Alpha()` filter to make a button gently blink on the screen:

```
<!-- Example_13.htm -->
<HTML>
<HEAD></HEAD>
<BODY onLoad="pulsateButton()">
<INPUT ID="MYBUTTON" TYPE="button" VALUE="Button"><BR>
<SCRIPT>
var theOpacity = 99;
var theIncrement = 2;

function pulsateButton()
{
   theOpacity += theIncrement;
   myFilter = "Alpha(opacity="+theOpacity+")";
   document.all.MYBUTTON.style.filter = myFilter;
   if((theOpacity > 100) || (theOpacity < 50))
   {
      theIncrement *= -1;
   }
   setTimeout("pulsateButton()", 5);
}
</SCRIPT>
</BODY>
</HTML>
```

In this example, we are using the IE 4 syntax, which is still supported in IE 5.5. If you use the older version 4 syntax, however the filters behave according to the version 4 implementation. This affects the way the edges of the filtered area are clipped. The clipping is improved in version 5.5 but, to use that new clipping algorithm, you must invoke the new version of the filter. For some filters such as this `Alpha()` effect, the clipping is irrelevant.

Example: Various Static Filters

To exercise a variety of filters, you can construct a test harness and select them with a popup menu. With the addition of a little script, you can test a variety of effects before using the one you think yields the most appropriate visual appearance.

In `Example_14.htm`, which is available in the code download from `http://www.wrox.com`, we'll define an array of filters that we'll apply based on the value of a listbox when it changes. This is a useful framework for experimenting with different filter settings and comparing the effects they provide.

Example: Matrix()

Matrix arithmetic is used in computer graphics to control image rotations and stretches. Applied in a 2x2 matrix, the transformations can control an image in a 2D plane. A 3x2 matrix can simulate 3D within a 2D surface, and a full 3x3 matrix provides transformation of an object in full 3 dimensional space.

By applying matrix transforms, you can rotate or stretch an image. Depending on whether you stretch the image before or after rotation, you will accomplish either a simple scaling effect or a shearing effect.

You may need to apply several transformations to accomplish the final positioning and orientation that you desire. The origin of the image is placed at one corner, and the image may need to be shifted so that the origin is placed in the centre of the object, then it can be rotated, and shifted back to its original position. Note that when you perform the origin shift, the object can be rotated about its centroid rather than its top left corner. This is important if you are trying to spin an object and keep it within a framed area.

The scaling and shearing effects look like this. First, we apply a scaling in the horizontal axis, then rotate the object and scale it in the vertical following by a reverse rotate back to its original orientation.

The `Matrix()` filter provides a way to accomplish very complex rotations and transformation effects on an image. It uses matrix arithmetic to compute the transforms. Although this only happens in 2D, the transforms are related to the mathematical formulae that are used in 3D graphics imaging.

`Example_15.htm`, also available in the code download from `http://www.wrox.com`, demonstrates this.

Example: Light()

The last example of the use of static filters (`Example_16.htm`, available for download) illustrates how the filters are extremely powerful when combined with JavaScript. In this example, we define a stack of filters to create an ambient lighting effect and a point source of light that resembles a torch beam. We also place some black text into the darkened "room". As we move the light source around with use of the mouse, it creates the effect of a torch shining down a smoky corridor and back-lights the black text.

Transition Effects

A transition effect takes a static filter effect and implements an interval timer that applies the filter every few milliseconds. Each time the filter is applied, one or more of its control parameters is modified incrementally. The time-varying changes create the animated effect. You can simulate this by modifying a static effect with some script, but by implementing transitions, Microsoft saves us a lot of trouble by building event trackers that carefully watch the screen updates. This makes transitions very easy to set up.

These are used to create an interstitial effect as a page's contents are replaced with that of another. They can be used without a page transition, and are useful when moving objects around or making them visible again after hiding them:

Filter	Effect
`Barn()`	Creates the effect of a pair of barn doors opening or closing.
`Blinds()`	A Venetian blind effect.
`CheckerBoard()`	Squares are filled in like a chequer board. Black squares first, then white.
`Fade()`	A dissolving fade from one image to the other.
`GradientWipe()`	A wipe with a soft edge.
`Inset()`	Another wipe effect.
`Iris()`	Like an opening iris on a camera.
`Pixelate()`	A pixellation effect. Quite gross if you make large pixels.
`RadialWipe()`	A wipe like a radar screen.
`RandomBars()`	Vertical bars sliding down the screen.
`RandomDissolve()`	A dissolve effect applied pixel by pixel.
`Slide()`	Slide one image on from the side.
`Spiral()`	A rotating wipe effect.
`Stretch()`	One image is pushed into the edge of the screen.
`Strips()`	Like random bars.
`Wheel()`	As if the image is wiped on with the spokes of a wagon wheel.
`Zigzag()`	A wipe effect that wipes alternately in opposite directions.

A transition can be applied to anything that is likely to cause the screen display to change. Obviously, if you change the image source URL for an <IMG> tag, then that image will be updated to acquire the new image content and display it to the user. A transition effect can make that appear quite attractive. Note the later discussion on optimizing synchronous and asynchronous event tracking and the use of the onReadyStateChange event handler. That can make the control of an image replacement transition much more effective.

Controlling the visibility property of the style object lets you perform transition effects directly from script, but it will likely be easier with the Alpha() filter.

When a transition is executed, the filter completes its display update, and the event-triggering mechanisms fire an onFilterChange event. If you attach a handler to that event hook, it will be called when the filter completes, so you can initiate a new filter. In this way, you can chain transition filter effects to run in a sequential fashion.

By inspecting the event object, you can determine the source element object whose appearance was modified and the filter that was used to handle the transition. The filter object we require is referenced by the srcFilter property.

Earlier on, we established that simply modifying the filter string of a style object or one of the items in the filters[] collection of an element object would trigger a filter update on-screen. Modifying the displayed elements would also trigger a transition effect. We also noted that rapid on-screen updates might be needed to take account of filter completion before applying another change, otherwise the screen would not yield the desired effect. This suggests that it is going to be difficult to apply a change to several filters or update several elements at once.

Microsoft has anticipated that need and provided us with the Apply() and Play() methods on filter objects. When you call the Apply() method, the transition activity is suspended while you apply a series of changes to the display. When all the changes are complete, calling the Play() method unlocks the transition, which can then perform all the updates collectively. If required, you can also stop a transition by calling its Stop() method.

You can also apply a transition as if it were a static effect by specifying a percentage of the transition to execute. If you specify 50%, then a dissolve effect will execute exactly half the blending, and will appear to be a stationary effect. This is done with the percentage=value filter function argument.

Note that the old blendTrans() and revealTrans() filters originally implemented in IE 4 are now replaced by new transition filters in IE 5.5.

Example: Compositor()

This filter provides many ways to composite one image on top of another. In the following example, the two images are drawn so that they overlap. When the button is clicked, the compositing filter is activated. If you deploy code that uses this filter, you should ensure you have browser version detection code to prevent the filter loader script from throwing errors in browser prior to MSIE 5.5:

```
<!-- Example_17.htm -->
<HTML>
<HEAD>
</HEAD>
<BODY bgcolor=gray onload='loader()'>
<BUTTON onClick='filterThing()'>Click me</BUTTON>
<BR>
<DIV ID='CONTAINER'
STYLE='filter:progid:DXImageTransform.Microsoft.Compositor(function=20);
position:absolute; height:300px; width:300px'>
   <IMG SRC='cold.gif' STYLE='position:absolute; left:50; top:50;'>
</DIV>
```

```
<SCRIPT>
function loader()
{
   CONTAINER.filters.item(0).Apply();
   CONTAINER.innerHTML = HIDDEN.innerHTML;
   CONTAINER.filters.item(0).Play();
}

function filterThing()
{
CONTAINER.filters.item('DXImageTransform.Microsoft.Compositor').Function = 2;
}
</SCRIPT>
<DIV ID='HIDDEN' STYLE='display:none'>
   <IMG SRC='cold.gif' STYLE='position:absolute; left:50; top:50;'>
   <IMG SRC='hot.gif'  STYLE='position:absolute; left:70; top:70;'>
</DIV>
</BODY>
</HTML>
```

Example: Various Transition Filters

This is another test harness like the one we developed for static filters. In this case, we are exercising transition filter effects. You can add some more or change the parameters quite easily in this one if you want to experiment a little more. This example is functionally similar to the one showing various static filters. In this case, the select popup lets you choose a transition effect that you then have to activate manually. Example_18.htm is available for download.

Page to Page Transitions

The most likely way you will use transition effects is to ease the user from one page to another with an interstitial effect placed between the two pages. A dissolve or wipe is quite effective in this respect. You can then create web-based experiences that are very similar to that you might accomplish otherwise with a multimedia presentation.

Until now, we have attached our filters to elements within the page and have applied transition effects only when those items within the page have changed. Applying the transitions across the whole page as it loads a new one requires a different approach to setting up the transition altogether.

To do this, we define some <META> tags in the <HEAD> portion of the document. This has the benefit that non-compliant browsers will ignore the effect altogether. In the <META> tag, we can select any of the available transition effects, and we can determine whether it is an exit transition as we depart from this page, or an entry transition as we load and display it when it is linked from elsewhere.

We show an example of how to use this <META> tag driven transition filter effect shortly. Let's just look a little closer at the way the <META> tags are structured first. The <META> tags are constructed with name=value pairs that define an identifier and a value. It is essentially an indefinite name=value pair, encapsulated in two name=value pairs having predefined names, like this:

```
<META http-equiv='identifier' CONTENT='value for identifier'>
```

The identifiers we are interested in for these page-to-page transitions are:

❑   Page-Enter

❑   Page-Exit

❑   Site-Enter

❑   Site-Exit

So, we can apply transitions between pages within our web site, when other web sites link to us, or when we link away to other sites.

Example: <META> Page Filter

In this example, we set up a slide effect as a transition and attach it to the page using the <META> tag. When this page is entered or exited, one of the transition effects comes into play. The first <META> tag sets up a transition that looks like a set of blinds being opened. This happens as the page is opened. The second <META> tag causes the page to slide off the screen when a new page is requested.

The values we put in the CONTENT="" tag attribute are any series of transition filters that we've already seen used with HTML tags in their STYLE="" tag attribute:

```
<!-- Example_19.htm -->
<HTML>
<HEAD>
<META http-equiv='Page-Enter'
CONTENT='progid:DXImageTransform.Microsoft.Blinds(Duration=4)' />
<META http-equiv='Page-Exit'
CONTENT='progid:DXImageTransform.Microsoft.Slide(Duration=2,slideSTYLE='HIDE')' />
</HEAD>
<BODY SCROLL="AUTO">
Page of text with transition on entry and exit.
</BODY>
</HTML>
```

Note in this example, the <META> tag is closed in an XML like manner. Microsoft implicitly recommends this practice by using it in their own examples, although the browser may not care whether you adhere to the formatting rules or not. Also, the auto scroll setting in the <BODY> tag prevents the scroll bar from being wiped across the page when the slide effect comes into play.

Events and Filters

There is a subtle relationship between events and filters. You can greatly enhance what is possible by adding JavaScript support for your filters and then ensuring that JavaScript interacts correctly with the events triggered by the browser. We shall describe the more esoteric events in more detail in a little while, but in the meantime, the following code illustrates how to trigger an image filter as the result of a mouse click on the image. Clicking on the image causes it to fade away using a transition effect:

```
<!-- Example_20.htm -->
<HTML>
<HEAD>
<SCRIPT>
function vanish()
{
   myImage.filters.item(0).Apply();
   myImage.filters.item(0).Transition = 12;
   myImage.style.visibility = 'hidden';
   myImage.filters.item(0).Play(5);
}
</SCRIPT>
</HEAD>
<BODY>
Click on the image to start the filter.<BR>
<IMG ID='myImage' SRC='cold.gif'
   STYLE='position: absolute; top:50px; left:50px; filter:revealTrans()'
```

```
           onClick='vanish()'>
    </BODY>
    </HTML>
```

The code is essentially very simple. We define some style properties, one of which is a filter value using the revealTrans() filter. Because we have created a filter, the filters collection on the image object will yield an object that represents that filter. Using the Apply() method, we can suspend screen updates while we modify several aspects of the appearance. This prevents each one of them triggering its own individual screen update. Then when we are ready, we release the filter so it can do its work by calling the Play() method. By encapsulating all of this in a function and attaching it to the onClick handler for the image, we can trigger the filter effect by clicking on the image.

Two important events to consider are onFilterChange and onReadyStateChange. The first event is triggered when a transition filter has completed its screen update, and the second happens when an asynchronous screen update is finished.

Your filters can be triggered within event handlers for all kinds of circumstances, such as when something is clicked on, or the mouse rolls over an object. Using JavaScript to initiate a trigger will eventually lead to an onFilterChange event being triggered. If the handler for that event also initiates another filter, a recursive loop might be created. You may need to add code to break that cycle, otherwise things may get out of control.

Some code for inhibiting filters while one is currently in progress is shown in the next example, where an image is active for clicking and triggers a cross-fade to another image. By storing the run state in a global variable and resetting it only when the onFilterChange event is triggered for the image object, we can lock out any subsequent clicks on that image until the transition is complete. Here's how it's done:

```
<!-- Example_21.htm -->
<HTML>
<HEAD>
<SCRIPT>
var myRunFlag   = false;
var myImages    = new Array();
var mySelection = 0;

myImages[0] = "cold.gif";
myImages[1] = "hot.gif";

function swopImages()
{
   if (!myRunFlag)
   {
      myRunFlag = true;
      SampleID.filters.item(0).Apply();
      SampleID.src = myImages[mySelection];
      SampleID.filters.item(0).Play(2)

      mySelection = (mySelection + 1) % 2;
   }
}
</SCRIPT>
<SCRIPT for="SampleID" event="onfilterchange">
   myRunFlag = false;
</SCRIPT>
</HEAD>
<BODY>
<IMG ID='SampleID' SRC='hot.gif'
     STYLE='filter:progid:DXImageTransform.Microsoft.Fade()'
```

```
      onclick='swopImages()'>
<BR>Click image for Transition to Fade.
<BR>Clicking again too soon will be ignored.
<BR>Image only changes when no transition is in force
</BODY>
</HTML>
```

When the example is loaded into an MSIE 5.5 browser, the run flag is set `false` by default. The two images are loaded into the cache so that any display effects happen rapidly and are not subject to network delays while they are fetched from the server.

The image tag has the `Fade()` filter attached to its CSS filter property. Because it is a transition filter, nothing happens unless the disposition of the image is changed. That is accomplished with the `swopImages()` function when it is triggered by a click event. That happens when the mouse clicks on the image. The `swopImages()` function checks the value of `myRunFlag`. If it is `false`, no filters are currently being executed. So, the transition is suspended while the image source is exchanged, and the transition is then released with the `Play()` method so it can display the new image. Before letting the transition run, the `myRunFlag` is set to `true` so as to block any subsequent clicks on the image. The event handler associated with the `onFilterChange` event is fired once the transition is complete. That is the only time we know it is safe to reset the `myRunFlag` to allow any subsequent clicks to trigger another transition.

The `<SCRIPT for="..." event="...">` construct only works on version 4 upwards of MSIE. We stated at the outset that the filter coverage in this chapter assumes version 5.5 of MSIE. However, for portability, you may prefer to use another technique for attaching the event handler. The `onFilterChange` script item might be implemented directly in the `<IMG>` tag by adding this HTML tag attribute:

```
onFilterChange="myRunFlag = false;"
```

Note in particular the way that a `<SCRIPT>` block is associated with an event and an object using its `FOR=" "` and `EVENT=" "` HTML tag attributes. This is subtle, but extremely useful if you know that your pages will only be used on MSIE 4+ browsers. Because this is non-standard, it won't work on non-MSIE browsers.

Optimizing Static Filter Design

As you apply more filters, you are asking the CPU to do quite a lot of work on a pixel-by-pixel basis. This can consume significant amounts of memory, since off-screen pixel maps need to be maintained. The CPU is also moving a lot of memory around, so is going to "sweat" a bit.

Filters that require transparency calculations generally consume more computing resource than non-transparent effects. This is because every pixel needs to be conditionally tested either for a value that is interpreted as being transparent, or against a mask which is stored in another pixmap. That mask may be an alpha channel that means the transparency effect may be proportional to the value in the corresponding pixel. Written in pseudo code, an alpha channel transparency calculation would go like this on a per pixel basis:

1. Determine source image pixel value

2. Determine destination's current pixel value

3. Determine transparency or alpha channel percentage value

4. Multiply the red, green and blue values of the source pixel individually by the alpha channel percentage

5. Multiply the red, green, and blue values individually by 100% minus the alpha channel percentage

6. Add the two proportional values together, still keeping the red, green, and blue components separate

7. Store the new value in the destination pixel

Compared with simply copying one pixel into another, you can see that this is a lot more computation. These transparency calculations are required for the following filters:

❑ Shadow

❑ Compositor

❑ Drop Shadow

❑ Glow

❑ Mask Filter

❑ Blocks of text with no background defined

❑ GIF89a images with no background color

Another good optimizing technique is to identify a parent object higher up the DOM tree and apply the filter to that, rather than independently filter its child objects. You need to ensure that the parent node has its CSS position attribute set to absolute or it has some position control attribute such as a `WIDTH` setting if any of its child objects are absolutely positioned. For example:

```
<!-- Example_22.htm -->
<HTML>
<BODY>
<IMG SRC="cold.gif"
   STYLE="filter:progid:DXImageTransform.Microsoft.Alpha(opacity=20)">
<BR></BR>
<IMG SRC="cold.gif"
   STYLE="filter:progid:DXImageTransform.Microsoft.Alpha(opacity=20)">
<BR></BR>
<IMG SRC="cold.gif"
   STYLE="filter:progid:DXImageTransform.Microsoft.Alpha(opacity=20)">
</BODY>
</HTML>
```

Here is the optimized version:

```
<!-- Example_22a.htm -->
<HTML>
<BODY>
<DIV STYLE="width:100%;
   filter:progid:DXImageTransform.Microsoft.Alpha(opacity=20)">
   <IMG SRC="cold.gif">
   <BR></BR>
   <IMG SRC="cold.gif">
   <BR></BR>
   <IMG SRC="cold.gif">
</DIV>
</BODY>
</HTML>
```

The optimization may give better performance or it may simplify your code that updates filters so that it only needs to operate on one filter instead of three. It is extremely difficult to measure the effects of this optimization. Speed improvements will be most noticeable with a complex filter being used on a slower machine.

The trade off is that the pixmap requirements for filtering all three images in this example are at least 3 times as much for the optimized version whereas for unoptimized version there is an opportunity for it to use less off-screen memory to calculate the filtered effect.

You may have overlapped elements that have a shadow effect that needs to indicate some kind of z-depth ordering appearance. Grouping all of them together and applying the shadow all at once may destroy the 3D effect you are trying to achieve and make them all appear to be in the same z-plane.

This all goes to show that using filters effectively requires some thought and occasionally a few tradeoffs.

Optimizing Asynchronous Changes

You should also consider the implications if you call for synchronous or asynchronous changes. Synchronous changes are where a method is called or an element is changed and control is returned to your script only when that change has been completed. The asynchronous change is where the browser says "OK, I'll get on with this – you carry on doing something else". Your script has delegated responsibility for completing the task, but is not really aware of it having been completed unless it spends a great deal of time polling and checking. That kind of "busy-waiting" is tedious and not a very good use of CPU resources, making your scripting quite unwieldy.

A good example of a synchronous operation might be modifying the innerHTML of an element object. It requires what is apparently just a simple assignment from JavaScript. However, that then triggers an HTML parsing process and a screen update to render the result. Control may be returned to the script before the parsing and screen update is complete. Successful interlocking between the completion of that screen update and your next script driven change may be essential.

An example of an asynchronous operation would be to change the SRC="" attribute of an <IMG> tag. The browser returns control, but spawns off a separate thread of activity to go and request the image from the web server. The value in the SRC property of the IMG object has changed synchronously, but the image update on screen almost certainly has not (unless the image was already cached locally).

You can code around this by trapping the onReadyStateChange event by means of a handler being attached to the IMG object. Eventually, the readyState property of the IMG object will be set to the value complete. That will only happen when the filter or behavior action that invoked the change has finished executing. This is not quite the same as an onLoad event, which is triggered when an image load is completed.

Locally, caching the images can greatly alleviate these kinds of issues and there is an example in Chapter 17, *Making Pages Dynamic* (DHTML and DOM) that illustrates this by way of the time honored image replacement technique.

Here is an example that applies these techniques. It switches between two images very rapidly, just giving the screen time to update before triggering the next switchover. You can run this with a delay of 1 millisecond to get the images to flicker as fast as possible, but this severely punishes the CPU. Try modifying the time value in the example and reloading the document again to adjust the update speed. Beating up your system with 1 millisecond event timers separating screen redraws within a browser environment may eventually crash the operating system with a "Blue Screen of Death", because a web browser is not optimized to cope with that sort of treatment:

```
<!-- Example_23.htm -->
<HTML>
<HEAD>
<SCRIPT LANGUAGE="JavaScript">
function checkReadyState()
{
    var myImage = document.getElementById("PIC");
    if (myImage.readyState == "complete")
```

```
      {
         setTimeout("switchImage()", 500);
      }
   }

   function switchImage()
   {
      var myImage = document.getElementById("PIC");
      window.status = myImage.src;
      if(myImage.src.indexOf("cold.gif") > 0)
      {
         myImage.src = "hot.gif";
      }
      else
      {
         myImage.src = "cold.gif";
      }
   }
   </SCRIPT>
   </HEAD>
   <BODY>
   <IMG ID="PIC" SRC="cold.gif" onReadyStateChange="checkReadyState()">
   </BODY>
   </HTML>
```

Optimizing Transition Filters

When designing complex transitions, you need to take account of processing limitations, because the browser is running in a multiple threaded process space. Your scripts may call for screen updates far more often than the CPU can accommodate. Either your later changes will not be honored or the browser may interrupt a change in process to handle the new one. The effects will be somewhat jerky and tend to only display the final state of all the accumulated renderings.

Fortunately, IE generates a trigger event that you can use to hold up your changes until the browser has caught up. This is the onFilterChange event and you can attach a handler to it that will be called when the filter has completed its rendering.

So, your most important consideration is timing. The onReadyStateChange event handler and the onFilterChange handler will both help to determine when a transition is fully complete. We examined the onReadyStateChange event handler just now. Let's try out a similar experiment with the onFilterChange event handler:

```
<!-- Example_24.htm -->
<HTML>
<HEAD>
<SCRIPT LANGUAGE="JavaScript">
function checkFilter()
{
   var myImage = document.getElementById("PIC");
   setTimeout("switchImage()", 500);
}

function switchImage()
{
   var myImage = document.getElementById("PIC");
   window.status = myImage.src;
   myImage.filters.item(0).Apply();
   if(myImage.src.indexOf("cold.gif") > 0)
   {
```

```
            myImage.src = "hot.gif";
         }
         else
         {
            myImage.src = "cold.gif";
         }
         myImage.filters.item(0).Play(2);

      }
   </SCRIPT>
   </HEAD>
   <BODY onLoad="switchImage()">
   <IMG ID="PIC"
         STYLE="filter:progid:DXImageTransform.Microsoft.RadialWipe(duration=2,
   wipestyle=clock)"
         SRC="cold.gif" onFilterChange="checkFilter()">
   </BODY>
   </HTML>
```

Transition filters should be placed after static filters when you are using multiple effects on a single object. Certain filters are considered to be transition filters, although their effect is basically static. The `Compositor()` filter is one such item.

There are certain artifacts that you need to be aware of when activating a transition effect. These come into play in particular when you move or reshape/resize an element.

If an element is moved before invoking the transition with its `Play()` method, then the original appearance of the object will be moved to the new location and then the transition effect is applied. It will not treat the old and new positions as key frames, and will not perform a "tweening" operation to mutate and translate at the same time. This example applies the radial wipe to the image which is moved as part of the transition:

```
<!-- Example_25.htm -->
<HTML>
<HEAD>
<STYLE TYPE="text/css">
IMG
{
   filter: progid:DXImageTransform.Microsoft.RadialWipe(duration=2,
wipestyle=clock);
   top: 100px;
   left: 100px;
   position: absolute;
}
</STYLE>
<SCRIPT LANGUAGE="JavaScript">
function checkFilter()
{
   var myImage = document.getElementById("PIC");
   setTimeout("switchImage()", 500);
}

function switchImage()
{
   var myImage = document.getElementById("PIC");
   window.status = myImage.src;
   myImage.filters.item(0).Apply();
   if(myImage.src.indexOf("cold.gif") > 0)
   {
      myImage.src = "hot.gif";
      document.styleSheets[0].rules[0].style.left = "200px";
   }
```

```
      else
      {
         myImage.src = "cold.gif";
         document.styleSheets[0].rules[0].style.left = "100px";
      }
      myImage.filters.item(0).Play(2);
}
</SCRIPT>
</HEAD>
<BODY onLoad="switchImage()">
   <IMG ID="PIC" SRC="cold.gif" onFilterChange="checkFilter()">
</BODY>
</HTML>
```

In the same way, if the size is changed, perhaps clipping or stretching the object, that spatial change will be applied in one go at the start of the transition.

Working round these limitations with transitional filters is virtually impossible. Although you can freeze them and modify the freeze point with JavaScript (use the percent property of the filter object), the prior and final states are not preserved, so you cannot easily modify the percentage a second time without switching the images back again.

Running static filters in interval based loops may provide a good enough effect. This example moves an image and fades it in as it moves across the screen:

```
<!-- Example_26.htm -->
<HTML>
<HEAD>
</HEAD>
<BODY onLoad="moveAndFade()">
<INPUT ID="MYBUTTON" TYPE="button" VALUE="Button" STYLE="position:absolute">
<BR>
<SCRIPT>
var theOpacity = 99;
var theIncrement = 2;

function moveAndFade()
{
   theOpacity += theIncrement;
   myFilter = "Alpha(opacity="+theOpacity+")";
   document.all.MYBUTTON.style.filter = myFilter;
   document.all.MYBUTTON.style.left = theOpacity + "px";
   if((theOpacity > 100) || (theOpacity < 1))
   {
      theIncrement *= -1;
   }
   setTimeout("moveAndFade()", 5);
}
</SCRIPT>
</BODY>
</HTML>
```

Portability and Filters

As we have stated earlier, filters are presently only available on MSIE running in a 32 bit Windows environment. In defence of Microsoft, they have put the specification for filters forward as a proposed, standard for W3C to evaluate. The CSS working group (in which Microsoft also participated) evaluated the proposal but decided not to proceed with it since the SVG working group had already defined a quite sophisticated and elegant way to add filter effects to vector graphics. This explains why the SVG standards are referred to in the W3C CSS level 3 work in progress summary, even though they operate under a different group.

702

The filter mechanisms that are being developed as part of the SVG standard support a variety of the static effects that we are likely to want. At this stage it is not yet clear what the position will be on transition effects, but we may be able to simulate them with JavaScript driven SVG object models. When the SVG group has completed its work, the CSS working group may then revisit the filter requirements to try to establish the best way to integrate the use of SVG filters for static and dynamic transition use. One suggested possibility, is to assign a `url(aSrc)` function call to the `filter` property of the `style` object. The `aSrc` argument value would refer to an SVG supplied filter.

These standards are currently undergoing a lot of revision and development, and it will be some time before they are finished and available as a recommendation. Even then, the browser manufacturers will need to implement the capabilities in their products. In the meantime, the `filter` property of the `style` object should be considered to be a reserved name and, if you do deploy Microsoft proprietary filters in your web site, there is a risk that they will be non-compliant with the eventual outcome.

Some related work on transition effects is also being developed within the SMIL working group. Microsoft is part of this initiative too, as you would expect, but has implemented the SMIL support within something it calls HTML+TIME.

Internet Explorer 4.0 Filters

The syntax for defining the filters has radically altered since IE 4. The IE 5.5 filter implementation has also changed the names of the filters and added new ones. Let's just examine the differences between the two filter definition formats.

Here is a typical version 4.0 filter definition similar to those we have seen before:

```
<Element STYLE='filter:filtername(properties)' >
```

This is what it becomes in version 5.5:

```
<Element STYLE='filter: progid:DXImageTransform.Microsoft.filtername(properties)'
>
```

IE 5.5 does allow you to omit the programmatic identifier (`progid:`) and only specify the filter name in a version 4.0 compatible way. However, this invokes a somewhat different handling of the filter and the appearance may differ. The most noticeable effect is in the way that margins around an element are treated in IE 4 versus the way that IE 5.5 treats them. IE 4 functionality does not compensate for the larger area occupied by an element when an effect such as glow is applied. The glow may be clipped by the original bounding rectangle of the object. IE 5.5 extends the margin so that the effect is not clipped in the same way. Invoking a filter using IE 4 syntax produces an IE 4 compliant appearance even in IE 5.5 and so you should use the correct syntax. This margin expansion applies to the following effects: `Shadow`, `DropShadow`, and `Glow`

Here is an example that shows the effect:

```
<!-- Example_27.htm -->
<HTML>
<HEAD>
</HEAD>
<BODY bgcolor=cadetblue>
<DIV STYLE="position:absolute">
    <DIV>Not filtered</DIV><BR></BR>
    <DIV STYLE="width:100%; filter:Glow(color=lightgreen, strength=20)">
        Version 4 glow effect</DIV><BR></BR>
    <DIV STYLE="width:100%;
        filter:progid:DXImageTransform.Microsoft.Glow(color=lightgreen,
strength=20)">
        Version 5 glow effect</DIV>
```

```
      </DIV>
      </BODY>
      </HTML>
```

IE 5.5 also enhances the color attribute, so an alpha value can be defined. In IE 4, color values are specified in the form:

```
      myColor = '#RRGGBB';
```

In IE 5.5, this form is allowed as well:

```
      myColor = '#AARRGGBB';
```

If you are upgrading some filter support from the earlier version, refer to http://msdn.microsoft.com/library/default.asp?url=/workshop/author/filter/filters.asp to see how the old filter names map to the new ones.

The version IE 4 RevealTrans() filter maps to the IE 5.5 filters in a more complex fashion. It has over twenty different variants, some of which are implemented as variants of the Iris() filter, while others are members of the new Blinds() filter. The mapping is summarized in the following table. The idx column is the index number of the transition within the version 4 RevealTrans() functionality. You specify the index rather than the symbolic name of the filter in that scenario.

Browser Version Detection

We expect that you will be running these examples on MSIE 5.5+, unless we explain that the example shows some effect in an earlier browser. Running the examples in an earlier browser is likely to throw an error of some kind due to the filters not being supported. Browser detection code is largely ignored to keep the examples as simple and focused as possible. You can add the browser detection and version checking code demonstrated in Example_28.htm (available for download) where appropriate to avoid attempting to execute scripts on incompatible browsers.

Browser detectors normally check for the navigator global variable as it refers to the navigator object. Microsoft points at the same object with the clientInformation global variable. Testing for the existence of this proprietary variable is a good way to eliminate a lot of browsers that do not support MSIE filters. To use this browser test you can do an early exit from an event handler with this fragment of JavaScript.

Clearly, if you condition out large blocks of script code, what you leave behind to be executed by other browsers must be viable on its own and not depend on the code that was conditionally executed within the if() block having been used.

Summary

So, we have explored the Microsoft implementation of filters. At present, it is proprietary and not at all portable, so it needs to be used only when you know that your users will have browsers that are capable of taking advantage. For example in an Intranet situation.

It is not recommended that you put filters into web pages that are likely to be used on non-MSIE browsers unless you take precautions to avoid any related JavaScript being executed in browsers that do not support the filter capabilities.

Filters have changed significantly enough that the legacy version 4 filters should not be used and you should mandate that your users are running MSIE version 5.5 or higher if they are to benefit from the filters.

For further information about the MSIE filters, the best and most complete source is the MSDN web site. The location is http://msdn.microsoft.com/library/default.asp?url=/workshop/author/filter/filters.asp.

19

Extension of Core and Browser Objects

Whether you belong to the school that says that JavaScript is truly "object-oriented", or the one that says it's merely "object-based", you'll have to agree that by now, JavaScript certainly makes profuse use of objects. In preceding chapters of this book, we've already had the opportunity to work with a number of these that are provided either as core features of the language itself, or by the browser environment. We won't break a great deal of new theoretical ground here; instead, we'll concentrate on applying a few key concepts that are often overlooked. Many of the example scripts we'll present here will be quite short and simple. However, their use can make the developer's job much easier by making scripts modular, more legible, and more easily customized.

In this chapter, we will:

- ❑ Provide a basic review of JS objects, prototypes, and inheritance

- ❑ Demonstrate techniques for extending objects from the ECMA core and those native to browsers

- ❑ Show how using these techniques can help simplify some of the developer's common tasks in a fashion that lends itself easily to code reusability and further extensibility

- ❑ Supply or suggest convenience methods for use with Arrays, Dates, and other core objects

- ❑ Demonstrate how object extensions can be used to supply ECMA-compliant methods (see Chapter 24, *ECMAScript 4*), where a particular browser or other environment lacks them, or implements them poorly

- ❑ Look at ways to make existing DHTML scripts compatible with newer browsers, and DOM-compliant scripts accessible to older browsers

❑ Provide self-contained examples that can be inserted into a desired web page, or used across an entire site, using script library (.js) files – this is one of our primary objectives, and a large portion of this chapter will be taken up with describing the libraries that are available for download from the Wrox web site

❑ Suggest further uses to which object extension techniques can be put, and refer the reader to additional resources for more information about them and examples of their application

A Short Review

In this section, we'll briefly refresh your memory concerning a few key aspects of JavaScript objects necessary for an understanding of the remainder of this chapter. For a more detailed explanation, review Chapter 3, *JavaScript OOP Techniques*.

A Simple Extension Example

By now, the reader should be familiar with the basics of JavaScript objects: an object is a compound datatype that can hold as many units and types of data as we desire or require, in order to accomplish a given task. For example, we could create an object with the following:

```
var aDog={name:"José",breed:"Chihuahua"};
```

In other words, we've created an object roughly mimicking a dog, whose name is "José" and whose breed is "Chihuahua." These are available to the programmer using dot-notation: `aDog.name` and `aDog.breed`.

Unlike some programming languages, JavaScript permits us to add new properties to an object at any time, either when we are first implementing it, or when using it in a script. The one exception to this is in Internet Explorer versions 4 and above, where we can prevent the accidental or unintended creation of new properties of `document` or its dependent objects, by setting the `document.expando` property to `false`. The `expando` property of the Document object can also be accomplished by setting `update="false"` in the `<BODY>` tag of the HTML document. For more information, see Cliff Wooton's *JavaScript Programmer's Reference*, (Wrox Press, ISBN 1-861000-459-1) or David Flanagan's *JavaScript, The Definitive Guide* (O' Reilly, ISBN 1-56592-392-8). Once created, an object property will persist for the lifetime of the object, unless we use the `delete()` operator on the property first (available in JavaScript 1.3 and above). So it's an easy task to add more information about José the Chihuahua, as the need arises. After our initial encounter with him, we can write:

```
aDog.disposition="vicious";
aDog.reactionTime=0.5;
aDog.favoriteSnack="trouser leg";
```

Let us suppose that we need to represent José's ability to vocalize a greeting. That is, we wish to add behavior to the object representing José that models José's vocalization. We can take advantage of the fact that, in JavaScript, a function is a perfectly acceptable datatype, and assign one to our object in much the same way:

```
aDog.greet=function(){document.write("<EM>Grrrrrrr!</EM>");}
```

We can verify this information about José by writing and executing:

```
document.write("Name: " + aDog.name + "<BR>");
document.write("Breed: " + aDog.breed + "<BR>");
document.write("Disposition: " + aDog.disposition + "<BR>");
document.write("Reaction time: " + aDog.reactionTime + " sec.<BR>");
```

```
document.write("Favorite snack: " + aDog.favoriteSnack + "<BR>");

aDog.greet();
```

We have modeled José pretty well, and should we need to improve our description of him, we can do so easily, either by updating the value of an existing property, or by assigning a new one. Now, let's suppose that we encounter another, kinder, gentler representative of the canine species. We start out describing him with:

```
var aNicerDog={name:"Penny",breed:"Cattle Dog"};
aNicerDog.disposition="friendly";
```

We realize that we're going to be doing some repetition to duplicate what we've already accomplished on behalf of the less-deserving José, and that this will grow increasingly cumbersome as we meet more dogs. Eventually, we're going to wind up with a pack of objects that are very similar, yet not programmatically connected. The disadvantages of this will become apparent when we need to add a new property or method to all of them.

Using the Prototype Property

Fortunately, JavaScript is not only very flexible with regard to modifying objects singly, but it's quite easy to update them in groups as well. All that's required is a little foresight and planning, and some knowledge of JavaScript inheritance. Without going to deeply into the technicalities (for which you're encouraged to refer to the chapter already cited above), let's demonstrate how we'd do this for our furry friends above. What we need to do is to create a blueprint that tells us how to build Dogs. First, we define a function object that will allow us to model a generic Dog:

```
function Dog(name,breed,disposition,reactionTime,favoriteSnack)
{
    this.name=name;
    this.breed=breed;
    this.disposition=disposition;
    this.reactionTime=reactionTime;
    this.favoriteSnack=favoriteSnack;
}
```

Remember that the this keyword always refers to the current object, that is, the object within whose scope we are currently operating. Now we can define a couple of dogs compactly using the new keyword and our function as a constructor:

```
var jose=new Dog("José","Chihuahua","vicious",0.5,"trouser leg");
var Martin=new Dog("Martin","Cattle Dog","friendly",1.5,"Milkbones");
var ringo=new Dog("Ringo","Dachshund","friendly",3.0,"Sausages");
```

Now, after we've reported what we know about these objects and otherwise interacted with them, we discover that it would really be good if they would give us some advance notice about their behavior toward us by giving an appropriate greeting when we meet them. Rather than defining a greet() method separately for each dog, however, we can define one for all instances of dog by making use of the Dog object's prototype property. As you may recall, each JavaScript object has a prototype whose properties it inherits. This means that all derived objects also inherit any properties that have been assigned to the prototype of the parent object. That is, when we create a new instance of an object using its constructor function, the instance inherits the properties belonging to the prototype property of the original object, and the prototype chain of the instance is searched for properties:

```
Dog.prototype.greet=Dog_greet;

function Dog_greet()
{
   if (this.disposition=="friendly")
      document.write(this.name + " wags tail.<BR>");
   else
      document.write(this.name + " says, <EM>Grrrrrrr!</EM><BR>");
}
```

Note that since we're assigning this function as a property to the prototype of the Dog object constructor, the this keyword continues to refer to that object; this means we can test properties of the object to which the function is assigned, from within the function. In this case, we're testing the value of the Dog's disposition property and modifying the output representing its greeting behavior accordingly. We can check the results by writing:

```
jose.greet();
Martin.greet();
ringo.greet();
```

The output from which is:

José says, Grrrrrrr!
Martin wags tail.
Ringo wags tail.

Advantages

While the preceding example may be a bit silly, the underlying principles behind it are anything but trivial. Extension of objects through prototyping can be a very powerful tool. It allows us to accomplish a number of tasks that are clearly to our advantage.

Simplicity

For our dog object above, we could have written a standalone greet() function that takes the name and disposition of a dog as arguments and called it as greet("Ringo","friendly"). This, however, is a lot more cluttered than the way in which we actually did it. Put simply, there are plenty of opportunities for programmers to make typographical and other errors without adopting practices that increase their chances of doing so.

Sensibility

We could also have written a standalone greet() function that takes an instance of Dog as an argument and calls it as greet(aDog). However, when you think about it, this isn't very natural, as we usually think of the dog expressing a greeting, and not of a greeting being expressed via a dog. There is nothing preventing us from doing so, of course, but that's not how we normally think of this. aDog.greet() looks and acts much more like the natural-language subject-verb word order we're accustomed to using in everyday English speech. We also find it easier to use methods that describe by name any mathematical or other common functions, than to attempt to remember how to write the functions themselves.

Extensibility

Suppose that later on we acquire some new additions to our menagerie that aren't of the canine persuasion, and discover that we have need of several instances of a Cat object. This object will also need a method that performs for it what the greet() method does for our Dog object. If we're using a standalone function for dogs, then we'll need to give the new function a different name, for example, Cat_greet(). Still later, we acquire some birds, model them as instances of a Bird object, and a pattern begins to emerge: greet() (or even Dog_greet()), Cat_greet(), Bird_greet() – requiring us to use different method names to perform what's essentially the same function for a variety of similar objects. Even if the internal workings of these functions differ, the manner in which they're called, the results, and the way in which we use those results can be the same. Using prototypes allows us to override a method, that is, to define the method to behave differently, according to the type of object it's attached to. That is, having defined a greet() method for all animals, we could redefine greet() only as it applies to dogs, while leaving its definition untouched as it relates to other instances of Animal. Alternatively, we could decide that all these creatures, being creatures, are also Animal objects, the said object having a greet() method that all of these objects inherit from it (shown by writing Animal.prototype.greet=Animal_greet;). In JavaScript, we would show this relationship by writing Dog.prototype=new Animal() to indicate that every new instance of Dog inherits all methods and properties of an Animal via the Animal object's prototype property. Of course, we could define additional properties and methods for dogs that would apply only to dogs, without affecting other animals such as cats or birds.

Compatibility

Object extension is a helpful technique in making it possible to write single scripts that will work in otherwise incompatible browsers. We can also use it to create a compatibility layer for enabling older browsers to perform well with scripts written for more recent user agents, as well as for implementing W3C and other standards. We'll provide examples using the Level 1 Document Object Model as well as providing support for a number object methods defined in ECMA-262 version 3. In the latter case, object extension is not only helpful – it's completely necessary.

Efficiency

In addition, and even more importantly in an active application development environment, we aren't required to rewrite previous methods, object definitions, or code making use of these, in order to give our objects increased capabilities. This makes it easier for us to augment our previous work without having to reinvent the wheel. It also reduces the amount of code and data that must be sent to the client.

Core Objects

We'll start this section off with an example where we create a new method prototype for the Array object, which will be made available to every new array we might create.

Example Using a Built-in JavaScript Object

By definition, every JavaScript Function object has a prototype property, and the constructor functions of built-in objects are no exception. Core objects are not in any way special, other than that they are already provided to us, and we're not required to define them before using them. Let's suppose we're writing a script in which we're required to find the element with the highest value from each of several arrays containing numbers. We can write a function that acts upon a single array, or we can write a function that will take an array (we'll use the same array named myArray defined above) as an argument:

```
var myArray=[7,15,-4,3,-1,0,6,23];

function getArrayMaximum(anArray)
{
```

```
            var maximumValue=anArray[0];

            for(var counter=anArray.length-1;counter>0;counter--)
            {
                if(anArray[counter]>maximumValue) maximumValue=anArray[counter];
            }

            return maximumValue;
        }

        document.write("Maximum value is " + getArrayMaximum(myArray) + ".<BR>");
```

Of course, what's true for dogs, is also true for arrays, at least when we're dealing with them as programming objects. Where a function takes an object as a parameter, and we're liable to use this function in conjunction with several instances of that object, it only makes sense to write the function as a method of that object:

```
    function Array_getMaximum()
    {
        var maximumValue=this[0];

        for(var counter=this.length-1;counter>0;counter--)
        {
            if (this[counter]>maximumValue)
            {
                maximumValue=this[counter];
            }
        }

        return maximumValue;
    }

    Array.prototype.getMaximum=Array_getMaximum;
    document.write("Maximum value is " + myArray.getMaximum() + ".");
```

We are re-using the same myArray as before. Once this is done, we can use the method with any array of any size. In fact, we're not even limited to arrays whose elements are numbers. It will retrieve the highest value String object, if the array contains strings.

The code we used in the examples above can be found in the files jose.html, dogs.html, and array_maximum.html.

One further word of explanation before we delve into the libraries: you'll find all of these files named according to the objects that they extend. For example, the library containing extensions for the Array object is called Array.js, the one containing Number object extensions is named Number.js, and so on. We'll list the extensions, the source code for each extension, describe what it does, define any parameters it requires, and note any other information relevant to its use. Some of the extensions may require that another one of the libraries is also available to scripts employing it; we'll note these dependencies where applicable.

Array

The following array methods can be found in the file Array.js, unless otherwise stated.

getRandomElement()

Returns a randomly selected element from any array.

Parameters

None.

Return Value

An array element.

Code

```
Array.prototype.getRandomElement=Array_getRandomElement;
function Array_getRandomElement()
{
    return this[Math.floor(Math.random()*this.length)];
}
```

getMaximum() / getMinimum()

Return the value of the (first) array element with the greatest or least value. Note that these methods can be used effectively with string elements, and that the usual rules for ordering these apply.

Parameters

None.

Return Value

Returns the array element with the greatest or smallest value.

Code

Complete code can be found in `Array.js`:

```
Array.prototype.getMaximum=Array_getMaximum;
function Array_getMaximum()
{
    var maximumValue=this[0];

    for (var counter=1;counter<this.length;counter++)
    {
        if (this[counter]>maximumValue) maximumValue=this[counter];
    }

    return maximumValue;
}
```

search() / binarySearch() / binarySearchRecursive()

We've also included implementations of some common array search algorithms in the `Array.js` source code file. These functions find the (first) index within an array of a given value.

Parameter

The sought-for value.

Return Value

Returns an array index value (hence an integer).

Code

The complete code can be found in `Array.js`:

```
Array.prototype.search=Array_search;
function Array_search(find)
{
    var intIndex;
    for(intIndex=this.length-1;
```

```
        intIndex>=0 && this[intIndex] != find; intIndex--);
    return intIndex;
}

Array.prototype.binarySearch=function(find){
    return this.binarySearchRecursive(find, 0, this.length - 1);}
```

push() / pop() / splice() / shift() / unshift()

The above methods were supported in Netscape 4, but not extremely well, as these weren't yet part of the ECMA standard when it was first released. These five methods should be familiar to those having been exposed to Perl. The push() and pop() methods add or remove items to the end of an array. shift() removes an element from the front of an array, while unshift() adds one. The splice() method removes a section of an array and returns it as a new array.

Parameters
- push() takes a list of items to add to the end of the array, resizing it as it goes
- pop() takes no parameters
- splice() takes the start index, the number of items to remove from the array, followed by any further items to replace the elements removed
- shift() take no parameters
- unshift() takes a list of items to add to the start of an array

Return Values
- push() returns the length of the new array
- pop() returns the new last element in the array
- splice() returns the new array spliced from the current array
- shift() returns the element removed from the start of the array
- unshift() returns the new length of the array

Code
The code can be found in Array.js:

```
if (!Array.prototype.push || Array(6,6,6,6).push(4) != 5)
    Array.prototype.push=Array_push;
function Array_push(items)
{
    for(var counter=0; counter<arguments.length; counter++)
    {
        this[this.length]=arguments[counter];
    }
    return this.length;
}

if (!Array.prototype.shift) Array.prototype.shift=Array_shift;
function Array_shift()
{
    var oldFirstValue=this[0];
    for (var counter=0; counter<this.length-1; counter++)
    {
        this[counter]=this[counter+1];
```

```
        }
        delete this[this.length-1];
        this.length--;
        return oldFirstValue;
}
```

toLocaleString()

Gets an implementation-dependent string representation of an `Array` object. In this case, we merely set its return value equal to the value already returned by the Array's `toString()` method.

Parameters

None.

Return Value

A locale-specific, implementation-dependent string representation of an Array.

Code

```
if (!Array.prototype.toLocaleString)
    Array.prototype.toLocaleString = Array.prototype.toString;
```

getSum()

Sums all the elements in array.

Parameters

None.

Return Value

The sum of all elements in an array. Presumed to be used on numeric arrays; string values will cause the array elements to be concatenated, rather than added.

Code

```
Array.prototype.getSum=Array_getSum;
function Array_getSum()
{
    var sumTotalOfArray=this[0];
    for(var counter=1; counter<this.length; counter++)
        sumTotalOfArray += this[counter];
    return sumTotalOfArray;
}
```

getAverage()

Gets the average value from a set of (numeric) array elements. Presumes that all array values will be numbers.

Parameters

None.

Return Value

Numeric average (mean) of the array element values (a floating point number); if the array is not numeric, then it returns NaN.

Dependencies

Requires the `Array_getSum()` method described above.

Code

```
Array.prototype.getAverage=function(){
    return this.getSum()/this.length;}
```

Date

The latest version of the ECMAScript standard provides a number of methods for this object intended to make the task of representing dates easier. Unfortunately, these are implemented only in version 5.5 and newer browsers. The following Date methods can be found in the file Date.js, unless otherwise stated.

toDateString()

Returns an implementation-dependent and human-readable representation of the date portion of the Date object.

Parameters
None.

Return Value
A string value representing the date: for example, Thu Aug 23 2001.

Code

```
if (!Date.prototype.toDateString )
{
    Date.prototype.toDateString = function ()
    {
        var DayOfWeek = ["Sun", "Mon", "Tue", "Wed", "Thu", "Fri", "Sat"];
        var Month = ["Jan", "Feb", "Mar", "Apr", "May", "Jun", "Jul", "Aug",
            "Sep", "Oct", "Nov", "Dec"];

        return (DayOfWeek[this.getDay()] + " " + Month[this.getMonth()] + " "
            + this.getDate() + " " + this.getFullYear());
    };
}
```

toTimeString()

Returns a convenient form of the Date representing the time in the current time zone. The exact form of the string is expected to be implementation-dependent.

Parameters
None.

Return Value
A string value.

Code
Can be found in Date.js.

toLocaleDateString()

Provides an implementation-dependent representation of the date portion of a Date object, the representation is expected to conform to the norms for the host environment's current locale. Currently, it just prototypes the toDateString() method. The code can be found in Date.js.

Parameters

None (developers should not make their implementation dependent upon any input parameters, as this may change in future revisions of ECMA-262).

Return Value

A string value.

toLocaleTimeString()

Provides an implementation-dependent representation of the time portion of a Date object; this representation is expected to conform to the norms for the host application's current locale. This function can be found in `Date.js`, and currently prototypes just the `toTimeString()` method.

Parameters

None (this is subject to change in future versions of the ECMAScript standard; programmers are advised not to make their implementation dependent on any input parameters).

Return Value

A string value.

toTimeDate()

Creates a customizable representation of the time and/or date; see below.

Parameters

A format string (see below)

- ❏ a – "am" or "pm" (lower case)
- ❏ A – "AM" or "PM" (upper case)
- ❏ a/A omitted: 24-hour time
- ❏ d – day of the month, no zeroes (1-31)
- ❏ D – day of month, leading zeroes (01-31)
- ❏ h – hours, no leading zero
- ❏ H – hours with leading zero
- ❏ I – minutes (leading zeroes always included) ("05")
- ❏ m – month, numeric, no zero ("8")
- ❏ M – month, numeric, leading zero ("08")
- ❏ n – month, text, short ("Aug")
- ❏ N – month, text, long ("August")
- ❏ o – English ordinal suffix, textual, 2 characters; in other words"th", "nd" [lowercase letter "O"] ("3rd")
- ❏ S – seconds (leading zeroes always shown)
- ❏ w – day of the week, short ("Fri")
- ❏ W – day of the week, long ("Friday")
- ❏ w/W omitted: no weekday is displayed

❑   y – 2-digit year ("01") [merely truncates 4-digit year]

❑   Y – 4-digit year ("2001")

The arguments to this function are entered as a string with a space separating the time and date. Whatever separator is used within these groups, is duplicated in the output. A space is inserted after each element in the date group, except when the date itself is followed by a comma, in which case a space is inserted following the comma. Within the date, the order of the arguments is duplicated. Omitted arguments are ignored, except as indicated above.

For example:

```
myDate=new Date();
```

The date, for these examples, is Friday August 3rd, 2001:

```
myDate.toTimeDate("h:I:Sa W,Ndo,Y");
```

Output is 9:20:30pm Friday, August 3rd, 2001:

```
myDate.toTimeDate("H.I D-M-y");
```

Output is 21.20 03-08-01

Here's a UNIX-style date (YYYY-MM-DD):

```
myDate.toTimeDate("Y-M-D");
```

Output is 2001-08-03

It should also be noted, that we've eliminated some of the arguments where duplicate methods of Date that were already present or where it was felt that there would not be much demand, for example, "Swatch Internet Time." We have also made some other changes to make this method's arguments a little simpler and more consistent.

Return Value

A formatted string representation of the Date object it is called from. Non-space formatting characters are preserved in the output. A few examples can be seen above. If this function is called with no arguments at all, it will return an empty string.

Dependencies

This function requires the String_contains() and String_isAlphaNumeric() methods found in String.js:

It is modeled loosely on the PHP date() function (see http://www.php.net/manual/en/function.date.php for the original). Note that we have no need for the optional timestamp argument present in the PHP version, since the Date object itself supplies this information to the method.

Code

```
Date.prototype.toTimeDate=Date_toTimeDate;

function Date_toTimeDate(format)
{
   // of course we declare a boatload of variables
   var output="";
   var uCaseFormat=format.toUpperCase();
```

```
    var lCaseFormat=format.toLowerCase();

    var myTime="";
    var myDate="";

    var myHours,myMinutes,myAmPm;
    var mySeconds="";
    var myWeekDay,myDate,myMonth,myYear;

    var separator="";

    var myTimeFormat="";
    var myDateFormat="";

    var timeFormat="";
    var dateFormat="";
```

The `toTimeDate()` method is easily localized, merely by updating the strings used in the following four arrays:

```
    var shortDays=["Sun","Mon","Tue","Wed","Thu","Fri","Sat"];
    var longDays=["Sunday","Monday","Tuesday","Wednesday",
      "Thursday","Friday","Saturday"];

    var shortMonths=["Jan","Feb","Mar","Apr","May","Jun",
      "Jul","Aug","Sep","Oct","Nov","Dec"];
    var longMonths=["January","February","March","April","May","June",
      "July","August","September","October","November","December"];
```

First, we need to ask whether or not the format string contains a space. If it does, then we assume that we're formatting both the time and the date:

```
    if(format.contains(" "))
    {
       myTimeFormat=format.split(" ")[0];
       myDateFormat=format.split(" ")[1];
    }
```

Otherwise, we test to see if the string contains either one time-formatting or date-formatting code:

```
    else
    {
       if(uCaseFormat.contains("H") || uCaseFormat.contains("I") ||
         uCaseFormat.contains("S"))
       {
          myTimeFormat=format;
       }
       else
       {
          myDateFormat=format;
       }
    }
```

We process the time-formatting characters, one at a time. We assume that we'll find any combination of time codes, so long as those they're used in the following order: hours/minutes/seconds – AM/PM/24. In other words, any element of the time can be omitted, but the remaining characters are expected to follow the order given:

```
    if (myTimeFormat!="")
    {
       // get the hours here
```

```
        timeFormat=myTimeFormat.toUpperCase();
        if (timeFormat.contains("H"))
        {
            myHours=this.getHours();
            if (timeFormat.contains("A"))
            {
                // set am/pm/12/24 formatting; 24 is default
                if(myHours>12)
                {
                    myHours-=12;
                    myTime += myTimeFormat.contains("a")?"pm":"PM";
                }
                else
                {
                    myTime += myTimeFormat.contains("a")?"am":"AM";
                }
            }
            if (myTimeFormat.contains("H") && myHours<10)
                    myHours="0"+myHours;
            separator=timeFormat.charAt(timeFormat.indexOf("H")+1);
```

We pass any non-whitespace, non-alphabetic characters as they are found, and assume that these are present as formatting characters. We check each character separately, so it's entirely possible to format a time such as 6/25:45, if that's what is desired:

```
            if (separator!=" "&&separator!="A")myHours+=separator;
        }

        // get minutes
        if(timeFormat.contains("I"))
        {
            myMinutes=this.getMinutes();
            if(myMinutes<10)
                myMinutes="0" + myMinutes;
            separator=timeFormat.charAt(timeFormat.indexOf("I")+1);
            if(separator != " " && separator != "A")
                myMinutes += separator;
        }

        // get seconds
        if(timeFormat.contains("S"))
        {
            mySeconds=this.getSeconds();
            if (mySeconds<10)
                mySeconds="0" + mySeconds;
        }
        myTime=myHours + myMinutes + mySeconds + myTime+" ";
    }
```

Here's where we format the date. We merely process the characters as they come, without regard for any order in which we find them. We want to space between any two parts of the date that don't have a formatting character already between them, and not place any spaces adjacent to formatting characters except for the comma, which we wish to pad with a single space to the right:

```
    // format the date substring here
    if (myDateFormat != "")
    {
        myDate="";
        var tempDate="";
        var myChar="";
```

```
for (var counter=0; counter<myDateFormat.length; counter++)
{
```

As we work through the date formatting string, we pass on any non-whitespace, non-alphabetic characters, as above, and assume that they are formatting characters. Otherwise, we put each character through the "is it a...?" chain of `if` statements:

```
var prevChar=myChar;
myChar=myDateFormat.charAt(counter);
var nextChar=counter<format.length ? myDateFormat.charAt(counter+1)
  : null;

// if the current character's not a formatting character
if(myChar.isAlphaNumeric())
{
   // day of the month
   if (myChar=="d" || myChar=="D")
      tempDate=this.getDate();
   if (myChar=="d" && temp<10)
      tempDate="0"+temp;

   // month (number)
   if (myChar=="m" || myChar=="M" || myChar=="n" || myChar=="N")
      tempDate=this.getMonth();
   if (myChar=="m" || myChar=="M")
      tempDate++;
   if(myChar=="M"&&temp<10)
      tempDate="0" + tempDate;

   // number (name)
   if (myChar=="n")
      tempDate=shortMonths[tempDate-0];
   if(myChar=="N")
      tempDate=longMonths[tempDate-0];

   // get the appropriate ordinal suffix
   if(myChar=="o")
   {
```

If we find the character denoting an ordinal number for the date, we get the last digit of the day of the month. We then add the appropriate 2-character suffix according to its value:

```
var switchDate=this.getDate()+"";
switch (switchDate.charAt(switchDate.length-1))
{
   case "1":
      tempDate += "st";
      break;

   case "2":
      tempDate += "nd";
      break;

   case "3":
      tempDate += "rd";
      break;
```

```
            default:
                tempDate += "th";
                break;
        }
    }
```

Finally, we check to see if the current formatting character is a "w" or "W," meaning that the day of the week is added to the temp string, which we'll add to the date output string after completing the processing of the current character:

```
if (myChar=="w"||myChar=="W")
    tempDate = this.getDay();
if (myChar=="w")
    tempDate = shortDays[tempDate];
if (myChar=="W")
    tempDate = longDays[tempDate];

// get the year
if (myChar=="y" || myChar=="Y")
    tempDate = this.getFullYear() + "";
if (myChar=="y")
    tempDate = temp.substr(tempDate.length-2,tempDate.length-1);
```

If the next character isn't a formatting character, and it's not the ordinal switch, we pad with a space:

```
            if (nextChar.isAlphaNumeric() && nextChar != "o")
                tempDate += " ";
        }
        else
        {
            tempDate=myChar;
        }
```

At the end of the loop, we pad the comma with a space, then add the `tempDate` value to the date output string, and clear the `tempDate` value before we get the next character in the format string:

```
        // pad commas with a space
        if (myChar==",")
            tempDate += " ";

        myDate += tempDate;

        tempDate=undefined;
    }
}
output = myTime +" " + myDate;
return output;
}
```

For an example that demonstrates and tests several different formatting strings, see the accompanying `Date_toTimeDate.html` file.

isLeapYear()

Tests to determine if the Date object is for a date falling within a leap year.

Parameters

None.

Returns

true if the year is divisible by 4, unless divisible by 100, except when divisible by 400; otherwise it returns false.

Code

```
Date.prototype.isLeapYear=Date_isLeapYear;
function Date_isLeapYear()
{
   var theYear = this.getFullYear();
   var returnValue=false;
   if ((theYear%4==0 && theYear%100!=0) || theYear%400==0)
      returnValue=true;
   return returnValue;
}
```

daysInMonth()

This Date method finds the number of days in a month, for a given month and year.

Parameters

None.

Return Value

An integer value: 28-31 (the number of days in a month).

Dependencies

Date_isLeapYear(); earlier (pre-JS1.2) browsers also require the Date.getFullYear() method, which we've also supplied here, as the older getYear() method is not Y2K-compliant. Our implementation will yield the correct four-digit year for any date since 1000, except in the case of IE 3, which does not recognize any dates prior to 1970.

Code

The code can be found in Date.js.

Function

We will only create two new methods of the Function object here: apply(), and call(), for those non-ECMA compliant browsers that do not have them already.

apply() & call()

These are ECMA-compliant replacements for the like-named Function object methods that are found in those browsers that don't implement them correctly (those prior to IE 5.5 and Netscape 6). The principal differences between the two are that additional arguments to apply() are optional, and that its length property is 1, whereas the length of call() is considered to be 2.

The apply() method takes two arguments, the first of these being an object, the second being an optional array of arguments. The function for which the method is called is applied to the object, as though the object were the value of the this keyword present in the body of the function. The arguments making up the second parameter passed to apply() are passed as arguments to the calling function. In other words, this method allows us to call any function as a method of any object. Note that this method is supported in Netscape 4 onwards.

Parameters

An object for applying to the function for which the function is called; arguments to be passed to the object (optional in the case of the apply() method).

Return Value

The value returned by the function for which it is called.

Code

Found in the `Function.js` file.

Note that while Internet Explorer 4 supports the `slice()` method of the Array object invoked in the current method, the implementation is not reliable. If this is an issue for your application, be sure to include the `Array_slice()` method provided above; `slice()` is implemented correctly in Netscape 4 and above. In the case of both the `apply()` and `call()` methods, if the object passed as the first argument is either null or undefined, the global object is instead passed as the `this` value of the function for which the method is called.

Math

The following `Math` methods can be found in the file `Math.js` unless stated otherwise.

factorial()

This common mathematical function is useful in physics and statistical applications. The factorial of an integer N is defined as the product of all integers between itself and 1, inclusive, and is written as N!. For example, 6! is equal to 6*5*4*3*2*1 = 720. 0! is defined as being equal to 1, and the factorial of a negative number is undefined.

Parameters

An integer, the maximum value for which is likely to be implementation-dependent.

Return Value

An integer (the factorial of the number for which it is called).

Code

```
Math.factorial=Math_factorial;

function Math_factorial(anInteger)
{
   var returnValue;
   if (anInteger<0)
      returnValue=-1;
   else if (anInteger<2)
      returnValue=1;
   else
   {
      var tempValue=1;
      for(var count=1;count<anInteger;count++)
         tempValue*=(count+1);
      returnValue=tempValue;
   }
   return returnValue;
}
```

Note that the maximum allowable value for `aNumber` will vary between implementations, being determined as that `Math.factorial(aNumber)<=Number.MAX_VALUE`. The maximum allowable value for `aNumber` is 171. If the browser follows the ECMA standard, `Number.MAX_VALUE`, is equal to 1.797693148623157E+308 – any result greater than this is represented simply as `Number.POSITIVE_INFINITY`.

Number

The following `Number` methods can be found in the file `Number.js` unless otherwise stated.

isOdd() / isEven()

Tests a number for oddness/evenness.

Parameters

None.

Return Value

A Boolean value (`isOdd()` returns `true` if the number is odd, `isEven()` `true` if it is even; otherwise both return `false`).

Code

```
Number.prototype.isOdd=function(){
    return (this%2==0)?false:true};
Number.prototype.isEven=function(){
  return (this%2==0)?true:false};
```

Several ECMAScript-defined methods for Number are not correctly implemented or even present in pre-5.5/6.0 browsers.

toLocaleString()

This just maps to the Number object's `toString()` method.

Code

The code for this method can be found in the `Number.js` file.

toFixed() / toExponential() / toPrecision()

These methods are part of the ECMA 3.0 standard, and are present in Internet Explorer 5.5 and above, and in Netscape 6.0 and above, but not in earlier version of these browsers. The first of these truncates a decimal to the stated number of digits. This is a much more sophisticated implementation than the typical rounding mechanism of the type...

```
roundedValue = parseInt(value*100)/100;
```

...which is often seen in scripts on the Web. We should note that it is dependent upon another example of object extension, the `Window.error` object – the definition of which may be found in the accompanying `Window.js` file. Please note that there are potential compatibility problems with older browsers due to the use of features not supported before JavaScript 1.4 and 1.5, such as the `throw` keyword and the `instanceof` operator. These features are necessary for full ECMA 3.0 compliance. However, there is no simple ECMA-compliant workaround for older browsers. While it is potentially an interesting intellectual challenge to provide some sort of emulation such as an `instanceof()` method, it is doubtful that developers under the time and other pressures of a production environment are going to be terribly interested in pursuing these. The solution that we suggest for circumstances where there may be users of older user agents is to break the ECMA compliance in favor of a mechanism that won't break the older browsers. For example, instead of invoking `Window.error`, simply use an `alert()` displaying an appropriate error message.

Parameters

The number of digits of precision desired.

Return Value

A representation of the number using the stated number of digits

❏   `toFixed()` truncates the value

❏   `toExponential()` returns an exponential representation of the number, to the stated number of digits

❏   `toPrecision()` returns either an exponential or a fixed representation containing the total stated number of digits of precision

Dependencies

The `Window.error` object, found in `Window.js`.

Code

These three ECMA methods help redress a lack often encountered by beginning JavaScript programmers in earlier web browsers: namely, that there were few simple built-in methods for formatting numbers:

```
Number.prototype.toFixed=Number_toFixed;
Number.prototype.toExponential=Number_toExponential;
Number.prototype.toPrecision=Number_toPrecision;

function Number_toFixed(fractionDigits)
{
    var numberOfFractionDigits,valueOfNumber,tempValue,exponent,sign
    var logTen,count,digit,returnValue,numberOfZeroes;
    numberOfFractionDigits=parseInt(fractionDigits);
    valueOfNumber=Number(this); // x
    sign=tempValue="";
    exponent=1;

    if (isNaN(numberOfFractionDigits))
        numberOfFractionDigits=0;
    if (numberOfFractionDigits<0 || numberOfFractionDigits>20)
    {
        // Section that will cause errors on older browsers
        if (window.Error)
        {
            var err=new Error("The number of fractional digits is out of "
                + "range.");
            err.name="RangeError";
            throw err;
        }
        else
            returnValue=1/q; //forces an error state, as q is undefined
        // End of problem section
    }
```

Recalling what we said above on ECMA compliance, we could replace the problematic error-handling routine between the comments with something like `alert("Sorry! The number of fractional digits is out of range")`, which does not strictly adhere to the specification, but is usable by older browsers. Similar amendments can be made throughout the methods we have supplied:

```
    else
    {
        if (isNaN(valueOfNumber))
        {
```

```
                returnValue="NaN";
        }
        else
        {
            if (valueOfNumber<0)
                sign="-", valueOfNumber *= -1;
            if(valueOfNumber >= Math.pow(10,21))
            {
                returnValue=sign + valueOfNumber.toString();
            }
            else
            {
                exponent=Math.floor(valueOfNumber *
                    Math.pow(10,numberOfFractionDigits));
                exponent += Math.round(Math.abs(valueOfNumber *
                    Math.pow(10,numberOfFractionDigits)-exponent));
                logTen=Math.floor(Math.log(exponent)/Math.LN10);
                while(logTen>-1)
                {
                    digit=Math.floor(exponent/Math.pow(10,logTen));
                    tempValue += digit;
                    exponent -= digit*Math.pow(10,logTen);
                    logTen--;
                }
                if (numberOfFractionDigits==0)
                {
                    returnValue=sign += tempValue;
                }
                else
                {
                    logTen=tempValue.length;
                    if (logTen <= numberOfFractionDigits)
                    {
                        count = numberOfFractionDigits + 1-logTen;
                        while (count>0)
                        {
                            count--
                            numberOfZeroes += "0";
                        }
                        // the value in the second one is returned
                        tempValue=numberOfZeroes + tempValue;
                        logTen = numberOfFractionDigits + 1
                    }
                    returnValue=sign +
                        tempValue.substring(0,logTen-numberOfFractionDigits) +
                        "." + tempValue.substring(logTen-numberOfFractionDigits);
                }
            }
        }
    }
    return returnValue;
}
```

The code for the other methods can be found in the `Number.js` file.

Both `Math` and `Number` lend themselves to additional extension. Some other possibilities for the `Number` object might include `isPrime()`, `isFactorOf()`, `allFactorsOf()`, and `isDivisibleBy()`. Some common mathematical functions might lend themselves better to one object or the other, depending upon your needs and preferences. For example, functions to calculate the greatest common denominator or least common multiple of two numbers might work better, for example, as `Math.getLCD(myNumber,yourNumber)` or as `myNumber.getLCD(yourNumber)`, depending upon your requirements, circumstances, and preferences.

727

Object

The following Object methods code demonstrations can be found in the file Object.js unless stated otherwise.

toLocaleString()

This method basically serves as an alias for the Object object's toString() method.

Parameters

None (note: this is expected to change in future versions of the ECMA standard).

Return Value

A String representation of the object.

hasOwnProperty()*

This differs from the hasProperty() method in that the object's property chain is not considered.

Parameters

A property name (method processes as string).

Return Value

true if the object has a property of the given name, otherwise false.

Code

```
if (!Object.prototype.hasOwnProperty)
   Object.prototype.hasOwnProperty = Object_hasOwnProperty

function Object_hasOwnProperty(propertyName)
{
   var undefined;
   var returnValue=true;
   if (this[propertyName] + "" == "undefined")
   {
      returnValue=false;
   }
   else if (!(this.constructor.prototype.[propertyName] + "" ==
      "undefined") && (this.constructor.prototype[propertyName] ==
      this[propertyName]
   {
      var oldConstructorValue = this.constructor.prototype[propertyName];
      this.constructor.prototype[propertyName] = undefined;
      if (this[propertyName] + "" == "undefined")
         returnValue=false;
      this.constructor.prototype[propertyName] = oldConstructorValue;
   }
   return returnValue;
}
```

String

The following String methods can be found in the file String.js, unless stated otherwise.

contains()

Tests to see if a given string or character is found in the current String.

Parameters

The string (character) to be found.

Return Value

Boolean `true` if the search string is found, otherwise `false`.

Code

```
String.prototype.contains=String_contains;

function String_contains(aChar)
{
    return (this.indexOf(aChar)!=-1);
}
```

isAlpha()

Tests the `String` to determine if it consists entirely of Latin alphabet characters.

Parameters

None.

Return Value

A Boolean `true` value unless a non-alphabet character is encountered, in which case it returns `false`.

Code

The code, which just matches against a regular expression, can be found in `String.js`, as can all of the methods in this section.

isNumeric()

Tests the String to see if it represents a number value.

Parameters

None.

Return Value

A Boolean `true` if the `String` represents a number, otherwise `false`.

isAlphaNumeric()

Tests the `String` to determine whether it contains only alphanumeric characters.

Parameters

None.

Return Value

`true` if the string contains only alphanumeric characters, otherwise `false`

isWhiteSpace()

Determines that the `String` contains only one or more whitespace characters.

Parameters

None

Return Value

Boolean `false` if the `String` contains at least one whitespace character, otherwise `true`.

Code

```
String.prototype.isWhiteSpace=String_isWhiteSpace;

function String_isWhiteSpace()
{
    return (this.match(/\S/)!=null);
}
```

containsWhiteSpace()

Tests the String on which it is called to see if it contains any whitespace characters.

Parameters

None.

Return Value

true if at least one whitespace character is encountered in the String; otherwise it returns Boolean false.

Code

```
String.prototype.containsWhiteSpace=String_containsWhiteSpace;

function String_containsWhiteSpace()
{
    return (this.match(/\s/)!=null);
}
```

validateAsDateString()

This method expects a 6-digit string of numbers that it attempts to validate as a date in mmddyy format (for example 072598). We are dealing with a two-digit year, therefore, the year is assumed to fall in the range 1970-2069.

Dependencies

Date_daysInMonth()

Parameters

None.

Return Value

Boolean true if the string represents a date in mmddyy format, otherwise false.

localeCompare()

Compares the string against a second one, and returns a numeric result based on the outcome of the comparison.

Parameters

A string to compare with the one for which the method is being called.

Return Value

1 if the calling string is greater, –1 if it is less than the string passed to the method as a parameter, and 0 if the two are same.

Code

```
String.prototype.localeCompare=String_localeCompare;

function String_LocaleCompare(that)
```

```
{
    var returnValue=0;
    var thisArg = String(this);
    var thatArg = String(that);
    if(thisArg<thatArg)
        returnValue=-1;
    else if(thisArg>thatArg)
        returnValue=1;
    return returnValue;
}
```

toLocaleLowerCase() / toLocaleUpperCase()

These two methods produce implementation-dependent lower-case and upper-case representations of a string. We've aliased them to the `toLowerCase()` and the `toUpperCase()` methods, respectively. Of course, if your application or environment requires it, you can override these with your own methods.

Parameters

None.

Returns

See above.

Browser Objects

We can extend browser objects, as well as objects that are core to the language itself. The creative developer is not limited to those presented here. For instance, a pair of `get()` and `set()` methods for cookies (that is, instances of an extended `document.cookie` object) could prove quite useful.

Window

In client-side JavaScript, the `Window` object really serves two different functions. In part, it represents the window as a document container and the visible dimensions of the web browser on the viewer's screen. It also serves as the `Global` object. The following `Window` methods can be found in the file `Window.js`, unless stated otherwise.

Window Dimensions

One problem that occurs time and again in cross-browser scripting is determining window and document dimensions in a manner that's consistent between different browsers. This is not always possible with any degree of certainty. However, there is at least one point of convergence – the interior dimensions of the browser window, which correspond with the visible dimensions of the document within the window. We are discounting the possibility of the browser window being placed partially off the user's screen here. We use object methods to determine which family of browsers we are dealing with, and branch accordingly:

Property name	Netscape property	Internet Explorer property
window.innerWidth	window.innerWidth	document.body.clientWidth
window.innerHeight	window.innerHeight	document.body.clientHeight

innerWidth / innerHeight

The `innerWidth` property gets the inner width of the view port, whereas the `innerHeight` property gets the inner height of the view port.

Parameters

None,

Return Value

Value in pixels (integer),

Code

```
if (!window.innerWidth)
    window.innerWidth=document.body.clientWidth;
if (!window.innerHeight)
    window.innerHeight=document.body.clientHeight;
```

Global Object Methods

undefined

The special undefined property, which is used to indicate a property for which a value has not yet been assigned:

```
var undefined;
window.undefined=undefined;
```

decodeURI()

This and the following methods are used for encoding and decoding Uniform Resource Identifiers, whose precise syntax can be found in RFC-2396 (see http://www.ietf.org/rfc/rfc2396.txt). What's important to our immediate purposes here, is that URIs may contain only characters that are included in one of the following groups:

❑   The alphabetic characters a-z or A-Z

❑   The decimal digits 0-9

❑   A number in hexadecimal format (preceded by the % character)

❑   The URI marks: "¬", "_", ".", "!", "~", "*", "'" (, and)

❑   The reserved URI characters: ";", "/", "?", ":", "@", "&", "=", "+", and ","

When a character to be included in a URI is not included in the above groups, or if it is a reserved character, but is not intended to have the special meaning usually assigned to one, it must be encoded into what amounts to a hexadecimal representation (actually a string representation of a hexadecimal number prefixed with a % or percent sign) of its UTF-8 equivalent. Perhaps the most common example of this occurs when information that's been typed into a form text input or text area needs to be passed to another page or sent to a server-side script for processing. Something must be done, for instance, with space characters, because otherwise both the browser and the server are liable to consider it to be at the end of the URI string.

Readers are encouraged to consult the comments contained in the source code that's included for the methods in the Window.js file, for more complete descriptions of the encoding and decoding algorithms.

The decodeURI() method decodes a URI-encoded string. Reserved characters are assumed to retain their special meaning and are not decoded.

Parameters

A string, which is presumed to be a valid URI.

Return Value

A string representing the decoded URI.

encodeURI()

Takes a string representing a URI but containing disallowed characters and encodes it into RFC-2369 compliant format. As with the previous method, the string is assumed to represent a complete URI, and so reserved characters are not encoded.

Parameters

A string representing a URI but containing characters outside the range given above.

Return Value

A complete URI with all characters encoded that require it

decodeURIComponent()

Processes a URI component, that is, a string representing a portion of a URI demarcated by one or two reserved characters and encodes all characters requiring it. For this reason, any reserved characters contained within the string to be encoded are presumed to be intended as literal characters, and are therefore encoded.

Parameters

A string representing an encoded component of a URI.

Return Value

The decoded input string.

encodeURIComponent()

Processes a string that is presumed to be an encoded URI component; the encoding algorithm operates upon all characters in the string.

Parameters

A string presumed to be a URI component.

Return Value

The URI-encoding of the input string.

Forms

Debugging and validation functions are the mainstay of client side web forms programming, and so it seems sensible to write some of these as methods of Form objects and elements. These will make extensive use of the methods developed for the String object, and will be dependent upon inclusion of the String.js file in order to function.

report()

A function that reports all form element types, names, and values, such as that presented as a bookmarklet in Chapter 9, could possibly be adapted as a prototyped method of Form in those browsers, which actively support this object. One might consider using a method of this type to override the Form object's built-in toString() method.

validate()

This is a further refinement and extension of the form reporting method. One scheme we've envisioned, would encode the desired type of data into each form field's name using a designated prefix, such as txt_ for text, int_ for an integer, phn_ for a telephone number, and so on, in a variant of Hungarian notation. For example, a simple address form could contain:

```
<FORM ACTION='mycgi.cgi' onSubmit='return this.validate()'>
   <INPUT TYPE='text' NAME='mix_Street'></INPUT>
   <INPUT TYPE='text' NAME='alp_City'></INPUT>
   <INPUT TYPE='text' NAME='sta_State'></INPUT>
   <INPUT TYPE='text' NAME='int_Zip'></INPUT>
</FORM>
```

To validate the form, we loop through all of its elements, checking type, then the prefix we've added to each of the names:

```
var els=this.elements;  //  "this" is the current form

for(var i=0;i<els.length;i++)
{
   var prefix=(els[i].name).split("_")[0]; // strip off the prefix
   switch(prefix)  //  each case corresponds to a prefix/datatype
   {               //  against which we wish to validate
      case "int":
         // validate as integer; validation method returns
         // a Boolean value
         break;

      case "alp":
         //  validate as alphabetic; return a Boolean
         break;
         //  etc

      default:
         //  default action, probably return true
   }
}
```

Sooner or later, we will finish looping through the form's elements and the method will return a Boolean true or false value to the calling form's onSubmit handler. If true is returned, then the form will be submitted, if false, then it will not, and the user will have the opportunity to correct the erroneous input before attempting to resubmit. One way that we could enhance this method would be to return the affected form element's name, type prefix, or index number; we could then use this information to get a type- or element-specific error, set focus on the offending element, clear its input, and so on.

Applications for Dynamic HTML

In this final section, we cover the various ways we can make the use of DHTML and the DOM more standardized by creating new methods.

Compatibility with the W3C DOM

We can extend the Netscape 4+ and Internet Explorer 4+ document objects to provide support for some, if not all of the Level 1 DOM document methods.

getElementById()

Gets the element whose ID is passed to the method. This is an instance method of document.

Parameters

A string ID value.

Return Value

An HTML element object (actually a Layer object in Netscape 4).

Code

You can view the complete source code for the Document-extension functions in the file `Document.js`; we sketch out what it does here. The function is implemented via a `makeDOM1Compliant()` function that is called when the page loads. First, the function of the same name is called, which in turn does the work of calling the other methods. Tests are made for the support of proprietary fourth generation object models. For IE 4, we map the function to the `document.all` collection; for Netscape 4, it's `document.layers`. For Netscape 4, we also map the element's `style` properties onto the element itself, where IE 4 and DOM-compliant browsers have `myElement.style.property`, Netscape 4 generally has `myElement.property`, but we alias it as `myElement.style.property` via a dummy `style` property.

We should note here that Netscape versions 4 and above support a means for us to track changes to an object property and to trigger a response to the change when it occurs – both our `makeDOM1Compliant()` function and the layer simulation script sketched out below make use of it. The `watch()` method of the `Object` object, takes as arguments: a property name to be tracked, a function to be executed when a change in the property value is detected, and a value to be passed to this function. We use this method to get and set an analogue to `innerHTML` for Netscape 4, since it doesn't offer native support for this property (another convenient use for `watch()` is to use it to keep properties from being changed by always returning the same value back to the property being watched).

We also emulate a `CSSInlineStyle ()` object (as `style`) to some degree for Netscape 4, but its capabilities are extremely limited in comparison with that supported by Internet Explorer 4 and above, as well as by Netscape 6 and Opera 5. We attempt to make these fail as gracefully as possible where we run up against the limitations of the browser without generating fatal errors; however, failing silently is not the same thing as success. In addition, the user is reminded that there are style properties that are simply not accessible by scripting in the version 4 browsers – Netscape 4.x especially. Even allowing for the difference in the object hierarchy caused by `style` – or rather, its non-support in Netscape 4.x – the correspondence between property names is far from perfect. For instance, Netscape 4 uses `left` and `top` (numbers), while IE 4 prefers `pixelLeft` and `pixelTop`, or `offsetLeft` and `offsetTop` (string values). Netscape layers don't support `width` and `height` properties. There's also a good case for creating a global, cross-browser `Event` object, using the W3C's DOM Level 2 Recommendation as a basis for one's implementation.

A complete cross-browser scripting library will have to take these differences in nomenclature and implementation into account. These are much too numerous to discuss in detail here. We merely suggest a possible starting point. For additional information, the reader is directed to Chapter 10, *Dynamic HTML*.

We can also provide additional methods to make certain tasks easier.

getElementsByClassName()

This is a utility method for retrieving all the elements in a page with a given style class. This method only works in browsers that support the `getElementsByTagName()` method, which we do not attempt to implement here.

Parameters

A string representation of the sought-after `className`.

Return Value

An array of all HTML element objects whose `className` property value matches the value passed to the method.

Code

Found in `Document.js`.

This is a convenience function for browsers that already support Level-1 DOM methods. The function takes as its argument a string value (the name of the desired class), and returns an array of all the named HTML elements in a document that share the same HTML `class` attribute:

```
function document_getElementsByClassName(elClassName)
{
   //  create an array to hold the returned elements
   classElements=new Array();
```

The algorithm is straightforward; we check the className property of each document node that corresponds to a tag element within the body of the page:

```
elementList=document.getElementsByTagName("body")[0].childNodes.length;
for(var count=0;count<elementList;count++)
{
   thisNode=document.getElementsByTagName("body")[0].childNodes[count];
```

For Netscape 6 compatibility, we must exclude any nodes of type TEXT_NODE ...

```
if(currNode.nodeName!="#text")
{
```

...before checking to see if it has the named style class assigned to it:

```
var currClassName=currNode.className;
```

According to the CSS Level 2 specification, a className attribute may contain either a single valid identifier or a comma-separated list of such identifiers. So we split the value using a space as the delimiter (and therefore the parameter supplied to the split() method) and check each of the elements of the resulting array for a match (if the value contains no spaces, the method returns an array of length 1 whose single element is the original string, so no harm done):

```
var currClassNames=currClassName.split(" ");
var match=false;
for(var count=0;count<currClassNames.length;count++)
{
   if(currClassNames[count]==elClassName)
   {
      match=true;
      break;
   }
}
```

If we have a match, we break from the loop, as there's no need to search for any more matches in the className property of the current element, and we push that element onto the classNames array:

```
}
if(match)
   classElements.push(currNode);
   }
}
```

Finally, having checked all the elements in the document, we return the classNames array, which consists only of those elements having the desired className:

```
return classElements;
}
```

Since the document object has no prototype, we assign this method directly to the document element itself after checking to make sure that it supports DOM element methods:

```
if(document.getElementByTagName)
   document.getElementsByClassName = Document_getElementsByClassName;
```

Backwards Compatibility with Older Scripts

In addition to making patches for older web browsers in order to support newer JavaScript or DOM standards, it is also quite possible to write scripts for newer browsers for added compatibility with legacy code making use of outmoded features. One example of this is the Geckonnection Layer Simulator Library, available from http://www.DHTMLplanet.com, which allows Netscape 6/Mozilla to run some scripts on web pages containing <LAYER> tags and scripts making use of the Netscape 4 DOM. It does so by creating its own `layers` array, and grafting it onto `document`, then setting the property values of these elements from those of the corresponding <LAYER> tags; for example:

```
document.layers=new Array();
layerArray=document.getElementsByTagName("LAYER");
lLength=layerArray.length;

for(var count=0;count<lLength;count++)
{
    layerTag=layerArray.item(count);

    top=layerTag.getAttribute("top");
    left=layerTag.getAttribute("left");
    name=layerTag.getAttribute("name");
    id=layerTag.getAttribute("id");
    // etc.
```

Then it creates new corresponding DIV elements and maps the properties of the former to equivalent properties of the latter:

```
newDiv=document.createElement("DIV");
newDiv.setAttribute("name",name);
newDiv.setAttribute("id",id);
// etc.

styleStr="position:absolute"
styleStr += "; left:" + left + "; top:" + top;
// etc.
newDiv.setAttribute("style",styleStr);
```

Finally, we replace the old `layer` elements with the new DIVs:

```
layerParent=layerTag.parentNode;
layerParent.insertBefore(newDiv,layerTag);
layerParent.removeChild(layerTag);
}
```

Of course, we must also be sure to repeat the process for any of the layer tag's children.

As this volume was going to press, the Netscape Developer site had just released a new Layer Emulation API for Netscape 6/Mozilla. This API has some advantages over the Geckonnection libraries, as it supports more of the Layer object's properties and methods; however, it does not attempt to dispose of the LAYER elements via script as does the Geckonnection script, stating that Mozilla does not recognize them at all. This is not quite the case – in fact, one can offer the following HTML page to Mozilla or Netscape 6.1:

```
<HTML>
<HEAD>
   <SCRIPT TYPE='text/javascript'>
      function main()
      {
         var myLayer=document.getElementsByTagName("LAYER")[0];
```

```
            alert(myLayer.innerHTML);

            var myBlarg=document.getElementsByTagName("BLARG")[0];
            alert(myBlarg.innerHTML);
        }
</SCRIPT>
</HEAD>
<BODY onLoad='main();'>
    <LAYER>
        <B>Hi!</B> I'm some content inside a LAYER tag.
    </LAYER>
    <BR>
    <BLARG>
        <B>Hey!</B> I'm some content inside a BLARG tag.
    </BLARG>
</BODY>
</HTML>
```

Either one of these browsers (but no version of MSIE through 5.5) will regard the nonstandard tag as a scriptable element, and will run the example quite happily:

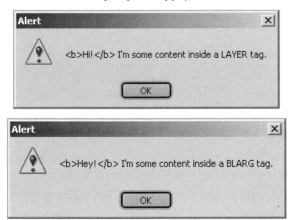

We're starting to run into constraints imposed by time, length, and topic, so we will leave further investigation of this area to the reader, who is invited to view the DevEdge article in question. See the Reference and Resources section links to this and other articles and other resources.

Summary

We've reviewed the basics of object extension in JavaScript, observed how it's entirely possible – even useful – to extend objects that are part of the language core or the browser environment. We've examined some applications of this technique. These include:

- ❑ Use of object extension for making code more reusable, portable, and easy to understand
- ❑ Convenience methods for implementing mathematical and other functions for Arrays and Numbers, and formatting options for Dates and Strings
- ❑ Correcting poor or missing implementations in some browsers with regard to ECMA-compliant object methods and properties

❑ Bridging the gaps between differing DOM implementations, either by enabling older browsers to use newer, more standards-compliant scripts (or fail gracefully where it's not possible to add the required functionality), or by making newer browsers able to cope with older scripts and markup

❑ Providing sample and example code, much of which can simply be "dropped into" HTML pages or referenced via the SCRIPT tag's SRC property and put immediately to use (there are some additional files in the archive which we haven't discussed here, and we hope that the reader will investigate these as well, and put them to use where applicable)

❑ Pointing the reader to further examples

By no stretch of the imagination have we made an exhaustive study of the subject, which could easily be made the subject of an entire book. We hope we have provided some useful information, code, links to more resources, and ideas that readers will be able to implement and develop further in their own applications!

Web Resources

❑ http://www.ecma.ch/ecma1/STAND/ECMA-262.HTM
ECMA Scripting Standard (download PDF or PostScript versions)

❑ http://www.webreference.com/js/tips/991216.html
Generic JS object extension

❑ http://www.i5ive.com/article.cfm/javascript/43835/
Another "generic" article on the subject

❑ http://www.webtechniques.com/archives/1999/11/junk/
JS component building

❑ http://www.dhtmlplanet.com/layer/
Documentation for the Geckonnection Layer Simulation scripts mentioned in the text is available here.

❑ http://developer.netscape.com/evangelism/docs/api/layer-emulation/
Netscape's Layer Emulation API for Mozilla and Netscape 6

❑ http://www.insidedhtml.com/tips/functions/ts18/page1.asp
Extends the Window object to create a cross-browser and backwards-compatible setInterval() method

❑ http://www.arch.vuw.ac.nz/papers/bbsc303/assign2/javascript_zen/zen_092.html
Creating and using a JS database object (first of three parts)

❑ http://www.ietf.org/rfc/rfc2396.txt
Text of RFC-2396 (August 1998) "Uniform Resource Identifiers (URI): Generic Syntax" referred to in the discussion of the URI-related methods in this chapter

❑ http://webfx.eae.net/dhtml/ieemu/
Emulating the MSIE DHTML feature set in Netscape 6/Mozilla using JavaScript 1.5 getter and setter methods – a work in progress. Note that this site is accessible only to browsers supporting the W3C DOM.

Printed Resources

❑ Meyers & Nahkimovsky, *JavaScript Objects* (Wrox Press, 1998)

❑ World Wide Web Consortium, *Document Object Model Level 1 Specification* (iUniverse, 2000)

Section Five

Case Studies

In this section, you'll see how the ideas covered so far work in practice, with some in-depth real-world case studies. The applications covered here illustrate some of the variety of applications that you may come across in your career.

The first case study is an audio-visual console on a news site, which not only demonstrates handling multimedia, but also the use of multiple frames, and how to cope with scripting between them. The second is a news ticker from the same site. Here you'll see how even with a small dynamic effect, we need to consider many different cross-browser issues. The third case study illustrates a typical e-commerce site, and discusses the various aspects of developing the client-side of a shopping cart application. Finally, we'll look at a complex dynamic HTML application, which is used to create an interactive online family tree.

Pro JavaScript 2nd Edition

BBC News Online Audio-Video Console

During the summer of 1999, the BBC News Online web site (http://news.bbc.co.uk/) launched an audio-video console that was designed to be a showcase for an increased amount of streamed video and audio. As a TV broadcaster, of course, the BBC has access to many hours of audio and video every day, and so this kind of re-purposing of existing resources is an attractive proposition.

The project had been experimented with for some time, and the graphic designers had built some interesting prototype visual models. However, it soon became apparent that a design led approach might well be appropriate for the general look and overall functionality, but the proposition required a more software-engineered approach to its implementation.

You can go and look at this project online and see it working. It's being updated via a large content management system that is at the core of the News Online service. That means that journalists are able to create new stories and videos and populate the indexes without ever needing to write any HTML or JavaScript themselves.

To enable you to experiment with the video console yourself, the original development sources have been packaged to run from your local hard disk without the need for a web server. There are, of course, some limitations to this approach, and you may want to substitute your own video sources to get it fully working. It would not be polite to simply refer to internal streamed video assets in the News Online service from your own development code. Taking a snapshot, so to speak, also gives us the opportunity to correct some minor shortcomings in the deployed version so that your experiments will work more satisfactorily on the newer version 6 Netscape Navigator browser. That browser did not exist when the console was developed and the plans at News Online are to radically overhaul the console in the near future, so the currently deployed version might only receive some minor adjustments in the meantime.

The changes necessary to support Netscape Navigator version 6 are enumerated near the end of the chapter, and have been included in the example source kit.

Why it was Built the Way it was

In this chapter, before looking at how some of the functionality is implemented, we need to understand why it needed to be done the way it was. Inevitably, you have to compromise an initially simple and elegant design, because of browser and platform limitations. Sometimes, a technique that works well and looks good from the code point of view, has to be reworked as it exposes a bug on one particular platform. It is important to bear that in mind when we look at someone else's code. It may be that your clever approach to the problem would work on your browser and platform of choice, but nowhere else. That is fine for a deployment on a constrained basis, but you will find you need to throw away many good designs to achieve portability if that is what you need.

The console is launched by a fragment of JavaScript that opens a new window, sized specifically to contain the console and devoid of any unnecessary window furniture. Here is an example of the launch button as it appears on the right hand side of the News Online front page:

Here is an illustration of how the final console design appears when you click on the launcher button:

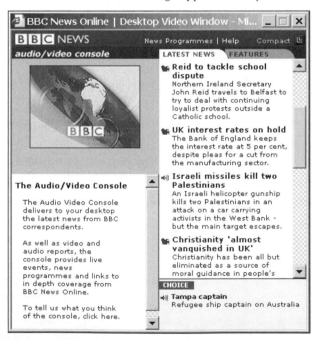

When we do illustrate fragments of JavaScript, they will be simplified just to show the principle involved. There are some areas where the producers have enhanced the JavaScript and HTML for reasons of ease of publishing and they are not fundamental to understanding this project or for creating your own version of it. In any case, you can access the source used at the site itself quite easily by turning off the JavaScript interpreter in your browser, and then loading the console HTML source text one frame at a time. By turning off the browser, you prevent any onLoad handlers being invoked. It also stops any rollover or onClick code from executing. This allows you to save the HTML source of the page more easily.

If you prefer of course, you can download the ZIP archive from the Wrox web site. This contains a slightly different set of sources that have been modified to work as a tutorial exercise. Certain file names at News Online need to be named the way they are, because they are generated by the publishing pipeline in the content management system. Various graphic components are managed as site wide furniture assets, and so that imparts a certain discipline to file names and SRC=" " parameter values that is unhelpful when experimenting with your own copy of the console.

Several things appear to happen at once, because of the multiple framed nature of this console. Frames call functions belonging to one another via the functions in the top-level frameset. The frames are described in the order that they become active during loading, or according to the events that occur when a video item is clicked on to trigger a video playback.

Setting out the Requirements

Given that the problem was already complex from the outset, some of the design constraints also raised a challenge. Consider these requirements that were specified. The console must:

- Potentially be able to play any format of video (QuickTime, Real, and Windows Media) on demand, with the player selected on a per clip basis. In the end, most of the currently delivered media is Real Player compatible.

- Must work in Internet Explorer and Netscape Navigator. Now we would mandate that it should work up to MSIE 5.5 and 6 as well as Navigator 6. In 1999, that was not the case though.

- Should work on as early a version of the browsers as possible. Explorer 3 was considered unworkable and very rapidly declining in usage so the version 4 was considered to be a baseline. Even so, that precluded some more sophisticated scripting techniques, such as any useful DOM based traversal. Navigator 4 was deemed to be viable and at the time there was no prospect of a version 5 let alone a version 6.

- Must work on Macintosh and Windows platforms.

- Should look and operate identically on all platforms.

- Be able to cope with 4:3 and 16:9 wide screen aspect ratio.

- Indicate which clip is playing.

- Load a story text with the video clip.

- Support at least two tabbed panels of clip menus.

- Support a continuously scrolling live content window.

- Display similar controls regardless of the player.

- Not display the player manufacturer logo any more than necessary.

- Be resizable to a minimal version as well as the full sized one.

None of these requirements are mutually exclusive, but some of them are quite challenging to deal with. In addition, an early requirement that was dropped allowed for the user to select their preferred player and for the console to remember that value. That implied that the console must be able to maintain some session state data.

In the early days, several other implementations were looked at. By its very nature, the design of a web page is transparent to the professional web developer. Simply by viewing the source of several other consoles, some grasp of the complexity involved can be had without the need to waste time coding and rejecting unworkable scenarios. For example, a really quite highly functional and sophisticated console was implemented by CNN in late 1998/early 1999, using layers and included JS files as a means of coping with cross platform difficulties. This was not inherently bad, but certainly mitigated against some of the features we wanted to implement.

745

From a software-engineering point of view, it was quite clever. You need consider the kind of hacks and tricks that streaming media players must use to place moving video into the video display. Putting multiple video streams into <LAYER> tags in a web page sets the alarm bells ringing and instinctively that feels dangerous. In any case, it only works in Netscape 4, and you need to find some similar structure that works on MSIE, for example, <DIV> blocks. Even so, hiding video windows is very difficult. Sometimes, the only way to make them invisible is to set them to a 1 x 1 pixel sized area, but you still have a small unsightly dot on the screen.

Certain areas of coding to do with screen display rely on critical timing and memory management. It is quite difficult to get them right and a plug-in media player has to somehow operate on some screen real estate that is owned by the browser application. Just try dragging a browser window while the video is playing to see examples of video frames left behind and screen updates lagging, until the browser gives up some processor idle time to the media player to track the relocated parent window. It's often not pretty, and is very prone to crashing. Some of the issues involved with coding such consoles were covered in Chapter 6.

That suggests that any video we might want to incorporate into a web page needs to be treated with the greatest respect, and any enclosing HTML and controlling JavaScript needs to be written very carefully. The areas that are most dangerous, are to do with implicitly modifying the display hardware. Partially obscuring the video window or making frames too small so the video getting clipped, causes some severe problems at a low level in the video driver software. Sometimes there are limitations such as video rectangles having to be placed on 8 or 16 pixel grid locations, because of the Direct Memory Access (DMA) needs of the video player. This can be even more of an issue if the window size also needs to be a multiple of 8 or 16, because the graphical design needs to be changed. Thankfully, more recent innovations in video player architecture mandate these restrictions far less often.

Obtaining the Source Code

If you go to the main front page at http://news.bbc.co.uk/, you will see a large button on the right hand side, which loads the console (see previous screenshot).

If we view the source of that front page, we can then trace the JavaScript call that creates the pop-up window and loads the console. If we then copy that URL, we can open a normal browser window and load the components of the video console manually, one frame at a time. It is not very difficult. You might want to temporarily turn off the JavaScript interpreter in your browser while you load the pages. This will avoid the frame contents complaining that they cannot access the required code they need in their onLoad() handlers. It will also inhibit the precautions against bookmarking internal console pages. Those are short fragments of code that check to see if the correct frameset configuration is being used, and displays an error message if it isn't.

The Example Source Kit

If you want to experiment with the console, a kit of source and image assets is available from the Wrox web site. You can access this kit at http://www.wrox.com/.

That code was originally the initial release of the console before it was deployed into the News Online publishing system. For reasons of making it more useful in the context of this book, it has been modified to simplify document locations and paths and to correct the most serious portability issues that were raised with the release of Netscape Navigator version 6. Any copyrighted media has also been removed and out of courtesy to News Online, calls to their media server have been normalized back to a reference to dummy media files in the source kit. This means you must do some configuration of these sources to point at viable media streams on your own server, before the full functionality is available to you. Most of the console functionality works without the need to do that however, and you can use the live deployed console at News Online in any case, so this is not going to provide much of a limitation.

Before discussing how the console works, let's just summarize the various component source items in that collection:

Asset	Description
Launcher.html	The page containing anchors that launch a variety of different consoles that share the same frame content, but are configured differently using their frameset constructions.
console	The document sources for the console files are all in this folder.
console/hack_error.htm	The error page displayed when you load console components outside of their frameset.
console/old_browser.htm	A file containing some help in case an old browser is being used.
console/vod.css	The CSS style sheet shared by any necessary frames to control the appearance of the console.
console/vod_home.htm	The outer frameset for the normal console. This also has all the session state and globally shared code.
console/vod_mini.htm	A frameset for a smaller console.
console/vod_tiny.htm	A frameset for a miniature console.
console/header_normal.htm	Contents of the banner header frame in the large console.
console/header_mini.htm	Contents of the banner header frame in the small console.
console/header_tiny.htm	Contents of the banner header frame in the miniature console.
console/features.htm	Menu frame contents for when features tab is active.
console/latest_news.htm	Menu frame contents for when latest news tab is active.
console/menu_default.htm	Menu frame default contents. This is in case there is no tab selected.
console/menu_mini.htm	The smaller console does not have tabs, so it only requires a single menu page.
console/live_default.htm	The scrolling live frame content is stored in this file.
console/legend_default.htm	A mostly empty file with some small fragments of JavaScript for maintaining the legend frame.
console/player_debug.htm	A debugging player module which is helpful for monitoring the global state of things. Not used in production.
console/player_default.htm	A default player frame content for when the console is initially loaded.

Table continued on following page

Asset	Description
console/player_mac_ie4_rpm.htm	The player specifically for Macintosh MSIE 4 upwards playing a Real Media file. Only a couple of these player examples are listed, there are many combinations according to the browsers, platforms and media you want to support,
console/player_mac_nav4_rpm.htm	Macintosh, Navigator 4, Real Media.
console/player_mac_nav6_rpm.htm	Macintosh, Navigator 6, Real Media.
console/player_win_ie4_rpm.htm	Windows MSIE 4 upwards, Real Media player.
console/player_unsupported.htm	Player frame contents for when the console runs on a new platform, but there is no supported player available.
console/story_default.htm	Default story frame content when the console is loaded.
console/story_example.htm	A dummy story example. This is linked to all clips in the example source set, although you would expect to publish a uniquely different story for each clip.
console/help_page.htm	A help page that can be toggled on and off, and which is placed in the story page when requested. It supports a part of the story frame API sufficient to toggle help mode off if it is selected before choosing a story.
controls	A directory containing various image assets for use when building custom controls for the players. There are spacers and rollover highlighted versions of pause, play, stop buttons, and volume widgets.
images	Various items of display furniture, such as small video or audio icons, bullets, and live banner graphics. The tab graphics are here too.
media	These are placeholder files for you to put in your own media. These are simply something that can be placed into the various places in the example source so we can indicate a dummy clip reference. The same items are always referred to in every clip example, but like the stories, you would expect to define a different target for each clip.
media/example.asx	A dummy Windows Media Player file.
media/example.gif	A dummy GIF file used as a poster image for audio clips.
media/example.mov	A dummy QuickTime movie.
media/example.rpm	A dummy Real Media reference file.

Laying the Foundations

As a general policy, the producers at BBC News Online do not like to use framesets. Instead, much formatting and layout control is accomplished with tables. Actually, this general dislike of framesets is quite common, and possibly due to framesets receiving some bad-press in the past, due to some browsers having problems navigating, such sites using forward and back buttons. In much the same way, cookies are also much maligned, because people were worried that malicious code could be executed on the client machine, or files could be deleted. Neither is a bad thing, though, and these concerns have really been removed in the more recent browsers, so you should not disregard the use of a technique simply because other people have expressed an opinion. If it is appropriate to use it, then we should do so.

Certain aspects of the console design would allow tables to be used, but this would mean that each click would load a fresh page, nothing would be persistent, and we won't be able to use any part of the page to store persistent information. Also, given the need to support three video formats, two browsers, and two platforms, that if there is any platform specific code required then twelve different versions of the page would need to be published. This is again something that instinctively seems wrong. Somehow, the content and the framework need to be separated so that there is only one set of platform specific HTML, and one instance of each item of content.

It is very clear that a frameset approach is really quite optimal for solving a lot of the difficulties that the console presents. For example, setting aside one single frame for the video player means we can abstract all the issues regarding player, browser and platform into a set of player documents that are selected according to the environment we find we are using. This means each of those can be designed as if the only platform under consideration is the one it is selected for. No further conditional code is necessary inside the player frame. Because we generically construct the name of the player file using a loader script, it works in all browsers and doesn't need any browser specific code either. This is a neat trick, because it places the browser selection at a neat boundary point and uses the file system as a 'switch ... case ... ' mechanism.

Another area that is greatly helped by the frameset approach, is the story frame. If we bound that to the player frame, we would have to publish a different version of the story page for each platform combination. Using frames we only need one. The tabbed frame becomes quite easy to implement, as does the separate scrolling live frame that would be hard to isolate any other way, and ensure that the scrolling only happened within a clipping rectangle.

Here is the frameset layout showing how the console is broken into rectangular fragments. These are chosen on a functional basis:

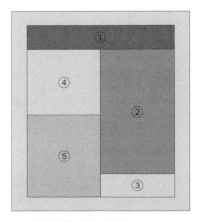

There are six frames in all:

- **Heading**. It holds the banner and is unchanging throughout the session, unless the console size button is clicked on. It also contains the tabs to indicate which of two alternative sets of content have been selected for the menu frame.

- **Menu**. This frame contains a menu of links to clips. In the current implementation, there are two alternative panels, but they are functionally identical. Their content is generated dynamically using a template. We'll examine how that template works shortly.

- **Live**. This is the live scrolling frame. Its content too is dynamic. It also contains links to clips, and like the clips in the menu frame, these can be clicked on to request the video or audio clip to be played.

- **Legend**. When the video clip is changed, a short text is placed into this frame. Using a separate frame greatly assisted with some problems that caused the player to shift up and down with legend text replacements on some browsers.

- **Player**. This is the player window. This is the one place where the code needs to be specifically designed to play a clip of a particular type and run in a particular environment (browser and operating system).

- **Story**. This is an area that can be loaded with some relevant story text or some additional images. This could be updated by embedding event data into the video clips. We'll cover that at the end of the chapter, because the techniques for managing that were only discovered when the console was already deployed.

The containing frameset is also essentially a component of this console. It is quite important because it is where the Session State store lives.

Implementation Decisions

See Launcher.html for details.

Now that the decision to use frames has been made, the various parts of the console can be mapped to the different frames. If it is possible, we do not want to have to test for browser versions and implement any code that is platform dependant unless we really have to. Occasionally, we are going to need to do that, as is the case with the live scrolling frame, but the console design is intended to minimize the need for that as far as possible.

In fact, it works out that the video player frame is really the only place that any serious platform dependent code is necessary, but we can pull a useful trick to simplify that. We'll look at how that is done when we talk about the containing frameset.

We want to control how the console looks, we want to define the size of the window it lives in, and we need to turn off any unnecessary furniture to avoid the window being resized. This fragment of JavaScript is used to open the new console window and request the main frameset to be loaded into it:

```
function launch_console()
{
    clickpop=window.open("console/vod_home.htm","clickmain",
                    "toolbar=0,location=0,status=0,menubar=0,
                    scrollbars=0,resizable=0,top=100,
                    left=100,width=420,height=390");
}
```

Note that Netscape Navigator is very picky about the format of the open() method and really does not like there to be any space characters in the list of window adornments. In the News Online web site, a few simple browser checks are actually carried out prior to calling this function, and an error page is presented if the detected browser type is incompatible.

Aside from that, most of the remaining design issues can be discussed on a frame-by-frame basis. One important point though, is that while JavaScript does not enforce the truly object oriented public/private access to methods and properties, we can still apply good object oriented style by hiding private data structures within the frames. This means, that they are exposed through an API and no frame has any knowledge of the private data within the other sibling frames. It helps with the maintenance of the code if we can compartmentalize it like this. However, clicking on a link in one frame can (and does) invoke some activity in other frames by calling accessor methods implemented as function calls. This is particularly relevant to the video player frame, the containing frameset, and to callbacks that set status values in several frames.

Click and Play

Before analyzing the code, it may help to walk through the functional process of what's involved. When the console loads, the scripts in the main frameset document construct a persistent session store and hold it in the JavaScript scope of that frameset document. They also provide some useful utility functions that can be called from the child frames.

Probably the most important aspect of those utilities, is that they can be called from any child frame, and will then delegate tasks to other child frames without the original calling child frame ever needing to know about other frames in the frameset. This helps to isolate the frames from one another and make it easier to add functionality.

This technique is used to its greatest effect when a video clip is played. Available clips are presented to the user in anchor tags containing a URL in their HREF="" tag attribute that calls a fragment of JavaScript which executes the playClip() function in the parent frameset. A set of parameters are passed to this function when it is called, and they are used to configure the console for the requested clip. So these anchors can be placed in any part of the console and call upward to the top level.

The playClip() function performs the following actions:

❑ All the parameters are saved in the globally available session store so that subsequent actions can enquire any details they need.

❑ The aspect ratio of the requested clip is calculated to see if any scaling needs to take place to maximize use of the available area.

❑ The aspect ration selects either horizontal or vertical scaling according to the slope of the clip's aspect ratio vs. the slope for the containing player frame's aspect ratio.

❑ Then the playClip() function checks to see if we need to change the clip. If a request has come in for the same one, we can keep the set up as it is, otherwise, we need to load a new player module.

❑ Then a call is made down into any child frames that may list video clips. This sets the indicators to flag that the clip is selected and playing.

❑ The player plug-in is alerted that a new video clip is required with a changeClip() call down into the player frame. This may rewrite some HTML with some DHTML techniques, or it may talk to the plug-in directly. The exact details depend on the plug-in and the platform as to how simple or complex this procedure is, but playClip() never knows the difference.

❑ Finally, the legend text above the clip is updated with a short text.

❑ At this point, the video or audio should be playing.

Now we'll examine all of the component part of that process in more detail.

The Containing Frameset

See files `vod_home.htm`, `vod_mini.htm` and `vod_tiny.htm` for details.

The main frameset controls the layout of the console. That is accomplished through simple HTML tag attributes. To simplify the HTML in the example, the following HTML tag attributes are omitted, but should be applied to all the frames. You will see that is the case if you inspect the example sources (`vod_home.htm`):

```
FRAMEBORDER='0'
BORDER='0'
FRAMESPACING='0'
MARGINHEIGHT='0'
MARGINWIDTH='0'
```

Here is the main part of the frameset in `vod_home.htm`. A similar structure is maintained in `vod_mini.htm` and `vod_tiny.htm` as well:

```
<FRAMESET ROWS='41,*' onLoad='setDefaults();'>
   <FRAME SRC='console_banner.htm' NAME='headerFrame'
      SCROLLING='no'></FRAME>
   <FRAMESET COLS='216,*'>
      <FRAMESET ROWS='170,*'>
         <FRAME SRC='console_player_default.htm' NAME='playerFrame'
            SCROLLING='no'></FRAME>
         <FRAME SRC='console_story_default.htm' NAME='storyFrame'
            SCROLLING='auto'></FRAME>
      </FRAMESET>
      <FRAMESET ROWS='*,1,75'>
         <FRAME SRC='console_blank.htm' NAME='headlinesFrame'
            SCROLLING='auto'></FRAME>
         <FRAME SRC='console_live.htm' NAME='liveFrame'
            SCROLLING='no'></FRAME>
      </FRAMESET>
   </FRAMESET>
</FRAMESET>
```

The layout is simplified, and there is a divider frame that inserts a black line between `headlinesFrame` and `liveFrame`, which has been removed for clarity.

So that the session state can be stored in this frameset, an accessor API is implemented with a library of functions that are called from documents in other frames. For every internal variable that the frameset needs to hold for the session, there is a corresponding `setXXX()` and `getXXX()` method, where `XXX` is the name of that variable. For example, the `setRealClipHeight()` accessor method also sets another dependant value. You can also check the incoming values for validity and split them into several other component values if necessary. Because the console is self-contained, this is not enforced in this application, but there was the possibility that we might expose the API more widely, and that is when the accessor-based checking becomes more useful.

Here is a `setXXX()` accessor that range-checks a value. You can make your checks much more complicated if necessary. Input checking like this, can simplify the code later on when you use the values, since you know they are already valid:

```
function setXXX(aString)
{
   if(aString > 120)
   {
```

```
    XXX = 120;
   }
   else
   {
      XXX = aString;
   }
}
```

Sometimes, you can introduce convenient getXXX() methods that behave as if a variable of that name exists, even though the result is constructed on the fly. This completely hides the internal variables, which you should avoid accessing directly with scripts running in other frames.

Here is the accessor that returns the value with some additional work, perhaps for use with a CSS style object for example:

```
function getXXX()
{
   return XXX + "px";
}
```

Another reason why accessor methods are a good idea, is that a script is supposed to run within the scope chain of its containing page. That means the values you pass in, will be assigned to variables in the scope chain of the frameset. Variables defined in that scope chain will remain intact, even if the frame that defined the value was then replaced and needs to retrieve the value again. This provides a persistent storage mechanism that can maintain session state in the client until the main enclosing frameset itself is disposed of.

These accessor functions are implemented to set global session variables in the Audio Video console. Aside from the one that sets all initial defaults (the setDefaults() function), there are corresponding getXXX() calls to obtain the current value, as shown in the table:

Set Accessor	Purpose
setClipHeight()	The visible clip height.
setClipIndex()	ID value for the clip so it can be referred to individually.
setClipLegend()	Store the legend text for the clip being setup.
setClipMode()	Clip mode can be one of static, audio or video.
setClipName()	URL value for the clip minus its file type.
setClipPoster()	The URL for an image to be displayed as a poster frame while the video is being loaded or in place of a video when the clip mode is static or audio.
setClipState()	The clip state indicates whether the clip is playing, paused or stopped. However this does depend on good interlocking callbacks from the players and this is not always reliable.
setClipStory()	Define the URL of a story page that can be loaded into the story frame.
setClipType()	File type for the clip that can be appended to the ClipName to make a complete URL or can be tested on its own.
setClipWidth()	The visible clip width to allow for clips to be resized onscreen.

Table continued on following page

Set Accessor	Purpose
setFrameWidth()	Defines the width of the HTML frame containing the video in pixels.
setHelpState()	Set the current help state.
setOldClipName()	When changing a clip, some nasty onscreen artifacts can be hidden if the user is clicking on the same clip as was used previously. This stores the previous clip name so it can be compared with the requesting clip name.
setOldClipStory()	When changing a clip, some nasty onscreen artifacts can be hidden if the user is clicking on the same clip as was used previously. This stores the previous clip story so it can be compared with the requesting clip story.
setRealClipHeight()	The actual height of a clip being set up for playback.
setRealClipWidth()	The actual width of a clip being set up for playback.
setVideoFrameHeight()	Video player height default value.
setVideoFrameWidth()	Defines the width of the video player by default.
setVolumeLevel()	Define the required playback volume level.

All of these set accessors take a single string argument. Most will simply store the value that is passed in the argument.

The RealClipWidth and ClipWidth variables are provided so that the window can be scaled to preserve the aspect ratio, but we still retain the original values in case we need them later. The player can scale clip sizes up and down, but if we need to position the clip centrally, we need to know the aspect ratio so that the picture is not distorted or offset when it is scaled and padded with spacers. The setClipWidth and setClipHeight are really intended for internal use. In the playback handler, we perform a calculation and modify theClipWidth and theClipHeight leaving theRealClipWidth and theRealClipHeight unchanged. They have to be modified together so that the picture shape is not changed.

Many of these are called during the console start up, and the remainder are generally called during the playClip() action. Here is the fragment of initialization code called during the console startup:

```
function setDefaults()
{
   setFrameWidth("200");

   setVideoFrameWidth("188");
   setVideoFrameHeight("120");

   setClipMode("static");
   setClipIndex("0");
   setClipName("");
   setClipType("");
   setClipWidth(theVideoFrameWidth);
   setClipHeight(theVideoFrameHeight);
   setClipPoster("../images/vod_logo.jpg");
   setClipLegend(" ");
   setClipStory("story_default.htm");
   setClipState("Stop");
```

```
        setVolumeLevel("3");
        setHelpState("OFF");
        setRealClipWidth(theVideoFrameWidth);
        setRealClipHeight(theVideoFrameHeight);

        setOldClipStory(getClipStory());
    }
```

In addition to those detailed above, the `getClipURL()` function is a convenience function call that concatenates several values and returns a single string. The `playClip()` function call, covered in more detail below, is the most complex of all, and is a parameterized and generic play clip handler that is called by clicking on buttons in any frame. It then forms an appropriate call sequence for functions belonging to the video player frame. If necessary, it loads an appropriate player wrapper if the one it requires is not currently active.

The following action functions are necessary to support custom video controllers. They are called by the input elements that contain the custom control graphics. These can be placed in any frame, and you can create a separate frame to build the controllers in if you wish, or you can embed the controllers in the player frame. By calling back to the top-level frame, the redirection back to the player frame is then globally available to any part of the console. In the present implementation, they are not used for Real Player as the default controllers are used there, and JavaScript control of the other players was somewhat limited in 1999. Although there are no signs of a W3C standardization initiative on media players, maybe some time in the future the QuickTime, Real, and Windows Media players will all support sufficient JavaScript functionality to use custom controls. These mechanisms can then be used to present all the players with the same look and feel. The user would then be unaware of which player is being used.

Action handler	Purpose
`actionPlay()`	Call the Play handler in the public API of the player frame. Placing the handler in the top-level frameset allows us to set indicators if we want to.
`actionPause()`	Call the player frame's pause handler.
`actionStop()`	Stop the video playing.
`actionVolume1()`	Set the volume to preset level 1. There are six separate handlers here in case we need to do something non linear and platform dependant with the volume levels. It simplifies the code that could get quite complex if we needed a switch statement to select which one of the 6 levels to use. Each player has a different range of volume settings. Although there are six levels, volume setting 0 is effectively a mute level.

The utility function `getPluginWrapper()` determines which player to invoke. To do that, it looks at the platform, current browser type and the file extension of the clip. Those are obtained with the `getBrowserType()`, `getPlatform()` and `getClipType()` functions. Because these are contained in the main frameset, they are available to all the child frames without needing to be duplicated in every frame.

For now, we'll just be aware of the existence of these functions in the main frameset and we'll deal with their specific functionality as we work through the child frames and the functionality they call in the main frameset.

The Play Clip Handler

This is the most important function in the main frameset document. It mediates all A/V clip playback and handles requests to play clips from any frame in the console. Aside from this player function, none of the other frames need have any detailed knowledge of the player plug-in or how it works.

The parameters are detailed in the following table:

Parameter	Description
aClipMode	Defines the kind of clip to be played and is one of audio|video|static. An audio clip has no moving video, but the console is able to display a poster image, while the clip is being played. The video value is used when there is moving picture and audio. A static clip just has a poster image, a story text, but no audio or video.
aClipIndex	The ID for the clip and its image indicator object. This allows us to call back to all frames that list video clips and tell them that this is the ID being played. There is code in the story, live, and menu frame documents that searches the list of images for the indicator icon and changes it from grey to maroon.
aClipName	The URL for the media file on the server (minus the file type extension). The file type is stripped off because we need it as a separate parameter. It was easy to do this as part of the News Online dynamic publishing system that creates the content for these pages. This is better than trying to finding the file extension at the end of a URL with JavaScript code that can lead to ambiguities.
aClipType	The file type from the URL. It will likely be one of ram, asf, or mov. This is concatenated back to the clip name to be passed to the player plug-in. However, it is also used to construct the name of a document containing the correct plug-in for the clip being requested.
aClipWidth	The width of the clip in pixels. This allows us to expand or shrink the clip to fit.
aClipHeight	The height of the clip in pixels. Given the width and height, we can also perform an aspect ratio calculation to maximize the clip within the available space.
aClipPoster	The URL for the poster image for this clip. This can be placed as an initial image if there is some delay in accessing the clip, and is also used when the clip is an audio only or static clip.
aClipLegend	The legend text for this clip. This text is placed underneath the poster/video clip rectangle in the player frame.
aClipStory	The URL for the story frame for this clip. This is loaded into storyFrame when the clip is played. We could build callbacks into the video clip to modify this frame content while the clip is playing.

Here is the playClip() function. It uses a lot of values that were defined during startup and others that are passed as parameters when it is called:

```
function playClip(aClipMode, aClipIndex, aClipName, aClipType,
                  aClipWidth, aClipHeight, aClipPoster,
                  aClipLegend, aClipStory)
{
   var myAspectRatio;
   var myScaleFactor;

   // Save old values to test against new request
   setOldClipStory(getClipStory());
   setOldClipName(getClipName());

   // Store new request data using accessors
   setClipMode(aClipMode);
   setClipIndex(aClipIndex);
```

```
    setClipName(aClipName);
    setClipType(aClipType);
    setRealClipWidth(aClipWidth);
    setRealClipHeight(aClipHeight);
    setClipPoster(aClipPoster);
    setClipLegend(aClipLegend);
    setClipStory(aClipStory);
    setClipState("Stop");

    // Calculate aspect ratio of the frame
    myAspectRatio = getRealClipWidth() / getRealClipHeight();

    // Work out whether to scale for H or V fitting
    if (myAspectRatio > (theVideoFrameWidth/theVideoFrameHeight))
    {
        // Horizontal
        if(getRealClipWidth() > theVideoFrameWidth)
        {
            myScaleFactor = theVideoFrameWidth/getRealClipWidth();
            setClipWidth(theVideoFrameWidth);
            setClipHeight(getRealClipHeight()*myScaleFactor);
        }
    }
    else
    {
        // Vertical
        if(getRealClipHeight() > theVideoFrameHeight)
        {
            myScaleFactor = theVideoFrameHeight/getRealClipHeight();
            setClipWidth(getRealClipWidth()*myScaleFactor);
            setClipHeight(theVideoFrameHeight);
        }
    }

    // Optionally load the story frame and set any clip indicators required
    if(getOldClipStory() == getClipStory())
    {
        storyFrame.check_live_play_item();
    }
    else
    {
        storyFrame.location.href = getClipStory();
    }

    // Call back to all frames to play the clip and set the indicators
    if (theClipMode!="static")
    {
        playerFrame.changeClip();
        headlinesFrame.switch_on_an_icon(getClipIndex());
        liveFrame.switch_on_an_icon(getClipIndex());
    }
}
```

The main purpose of this is to store the clip parameters, calculate the clip playback window size, invoke the correct player plug-in by loading the required player frame document, and set the indicators.

The player selection is based on the platform value (mac or win), the browser and version (nav4, ie4 upwards, and now in the example kit nav6). The clip type determines the plug-in that is used in the player page. Using these components, we can construct a document name algorithmically, and load it into the player frame. After that, we don't need to write platform or browser conditional code, because that choice has been made up front.

Below, is the script source for the functions that select and load the correct player into the video player frame. It comprises a group of functions that determine browser type, platform type, and player type based on the clip's file type extension in its URL:

```
// --- Work out which player plug-in to use ---
function getPluginWrapper()
{
   if ((getPlatform()    == "other") ||
       (getBrowserType() == "other") ||
       (getBrowserType() == "nav")   ||
       (getBrowserType() == "ie")
       )
   {
      // Flag an unsupported player because we have not gotten back a
      // value for a browser that we have a player for. The browser
      // test function also returns nav4, ie4.
      return "player_unsupported.htm";
   }

   return "player_" + getPlatform() + "_" + getBrowserType() + "_" + getClipType()
+ ".htm";
}

// --- Work out what platform we are on ---
function getPlatform()
{
   var myUserAgent;

   myUserAgent = navigator.userAgent.toLowerCase();

   if ( (myUserAgent.indexOf("win") != -1)   ||
        (myUserAgent.indexOf("16bit") != -1) )
   {
      return "win";
   }

   if (myUserAgent.indexOf("mac") != -1)
   {
      return "mac";
   }

   if (myUserAgent.indexOf("x11") != -1)
   {
      return "unx";
   }

   return "other";
}

// --- Work out what sort of browser we are using ---
function getBrowserType()
{
   var myUserAgent;
   var myMajor;

   myUserAgent    = navigator.userAgent.toLowerCase();
   myMajor        = parseInt(navigator.appVersion);

   if ( (myUserAgent.indexOf('mozilla')    != -1) &&
        (myUserAgent.indexOf('spoofer')    == -1) &&
        (myUserAgent.indexOf('compatible') == -1) &&
        (myUserAgent.indexOf('opera')      == -1) &&
```

```
            (myUserAgent.indexOf('webtv')      == -1) )
{
   if (myMajor > 3)
   {
      return "nav4";
   }
   // Old version of Navigator
   return "nav";
}

if (myUserAgent.indexOf("msie") != -1)
{
   if (myMajor > 3)
   {
      return "ie4";
   }
   // Old version of MSIE
   return "ie";
}

// Not recognised at all
return "other";
}
```

The Video Player Frame

See **player_debug.htm, player_default.htm, player_mac_ie4_rpm.htm, player_mac_nav4_rpm.htm, player_win_ie4_rpm.htm, player_unsupported.htm** and **player_win_nav4_rpm.htm** for details.

The content of this frame is initially filled with a blank placeholder document with a logo design in an image. We cannot know which of the available player wrapper pages to load here until we know what kind of video clips is going to be played.

This frame is extremely platform dependent. In exploring how to embed a video playback plug-in and connect JavaScript to it, the constraints meant that there would have to be platform dependent decisions being made throughout the code in a number of places. This would make it very difficult to maintain.

Instead, the technical design allowed that decision to be made once on receipt of the user's click on a video link. Then, a set of parameters describing the clip can be sent to a single API function that can select a platform specific URL and load that page into the frame. This approach is extremely useful, because the design of the player can then concentrate on the specifics of that unique combination of player plug-in, platform, and browser type (and even browser version if necessary).

The values representing the browser type, platform, and file type of the video clip's URL, are concatenated to form the URL of a player wrapper page. Here are a few of the combinations that are used to support the Real Video plug-in:

❑   player_mac_ie4_rpm.htm

❑   player_mac_nav4_rpm.htm

❑   player_win_ie4_rpm.htm

❑   player_win_nav4_rpm.htm

In the light of where we are in 2001, these choices look quite restrictive. Note, however, that this is a case study of an application that was built and deployed in 1999, and the video-streaming world was a very different place back then. At that time, QuickTime supported absolutely no JavaScript access until right after we deployed the console. Windows Media Player was one of the most unstable pieces of code apart from when it was running in Windows, and even then it wasn't even close to the capabilities of Real Player. So Real Player G2 was really the only game in town, although we could see the potential of the other players.

That has all matured somewhat, and there are certainly things we would tackle in QuickTime with wired sprites and suchlike that Real and Windows Media do not support. SMIL is just now becoming solidly standardised at version 2.0, and things could change quite a lot before we are far into the year 2002.

We will discuss each of these specific players from the point of view of any special considerations for that platform, browser, and plug-in later on.

The browser platform and video format tests are purposely contrived to be as small a set as we can manage, but adding a new browser version, such as Netscape Navigator 6, still requires that we provide even more player documents.

The deployed console requires that the browser version checker returns the values nav4 or ie4. All other values are deemed to be unsupported. The example source kit adds support for a nav6 case.

All of them respond to a public API that is identical. The API is provided as dummy function in those player modules that don't support all the required functionality. Here is a summary of the public API in the player modules:

API function	Description
changeClip()	Change to a new clip rewriting or doing whatever DHTML is necessary
publicPlay()	Play current clip
publicPause()	Pause current clip
publicStop()	Stop current clip
publicSetVolume(level)	Set volume (range 0-5) - not widely supported yet

Because the entire public API is supported in all player modules, they can be driven from the same playClip() function in the top most frameset document. It is through that function, that all of the video hyper-links in the other frames communicate with the player frame.

The API handlers take care of differences between players, such as, sometimes the play and pause functionality is supported in a single call. If that is the case, you need to manage state really carefully so that you know what the video plug-in is doing. Real Player supports some enquiry functions that you can use to see if it is possible to stop, play or pause a clip. These aren't supported in other players though. Changing the source URL for a clip works in some plug-ins and not others. All of these differences are hidden behind this API.

It was necessary to make certain compromises and design choices based on the player plug-ins and the recommendations from the companies that provided them. There are also limitations with early player versions, and the basic design dates back to mid 1999 when player plug-ins were somewhat more primitive than they are now.

We wanted to separate the controller area from the video display rectangle. Otherwise, the size of the controllers keeps changing when the video size is adjusted. Ideally, all controllers should look the same, but they don't. When QuickTime eventually did support JavaScript calls, we found that we could build a custom controller that looked the same on Windows Media Player and QuickTime.

We could not effect the level of control of Real Player from JavaScript that we wanted,therefore the controller for that player has been implemented as an additional <EMBED> style plug-in. This is okay however because Real Video plug-ins work cooperatively and it is designed to allow you to link multiple controllers and video players together. The developer documentation for the player is available at the Real Networks web site, but tends to move around with each release. It is fairly easy to locate by exploring the developer area.

All of this means that for the time being the QuickTime and Windows Media players don't look the same as the Real Player, and in fact the QuickTime and Windows Media players controllers don't easily fit the screen geometry we have defined. For now however all of the video being served is Real Video, therefore, the limitations are not too problematic.

The Video Player Frame (IE4 Win)

> See player_win_ie4_rpm.htm for details.

The most significant problem with this player is that Microsoft and Real Networks recommend quite strictly that you use an <OBJECT> tag to place the plug-in into a page. The Windows platform and the MSIE browser do not implement the <EMBED> tag very reliably (at least in earlier versions) and it's not HTML 4.01 compliant anyway.

This leads to some significant problems. The main one, is that you cannot communicate playback changes from JavaScript to a plug-in that is inside an <OBJECT> tag. The Real Networks manual states that you cannot change the src property with the ActiveX version of its plug-in. You can with its <EMBED> compatible one, but that's no good for the video playback window. This means you cannot take advantage of the mechanisms that Real provides for changing the URL of a video clip, without having to reload the page.

On the other hand, to create a custom controller, we had to use <EMBED> tags to create the necessary plug-in items. It all gets highly inelegant, and really looks a mess by the time it's finished (and that word is used in a very relative sense). The painful part of this as a developer, is that originally it all started very clean, neat, and tidy. The carbuncles grow on these implementations as you discover broken or missing functionality and, when you are trying to control video plug-ins from JavaScript, it exposes all of the worst aspects of every browser and plug-in.

The design calls for much more parameterization of the clip playback and we certainly want to accommodate a mixed collection of 16:9 and 4:3 aspect ratio clips. This means that height and width also need to be adjusted on a clip-by-clip basis. We also want to avoid filling up the file system on our server with unnecessary duplicated player files where the only difference is a URL and size parameter. So, the decision was made to use document.write() to generate the HTML containing the <OBJECT> tag. Then, at least at the expense of clearing and rewriting the entire page of HTML, we can significantly alter the contents of the <OBJECT> tag.

Getting this working at all, took a very long time with many failed experiments along the way. There is no easy way to access the <OBJECT> internals from JavaScript. The entire page needs to be written out, because during tests, it was found we could not use innerHTML or outerHTML mechanisms to modify the HTML object structures to create a new <OBJECT> tag. The only way that worked on all versions of the Internet Explorer browser from 4 upwards (as of 1999), is the technique we have used here. Now that we are several revisions further on with browsers and plug-ins, a fresh start may result in something more functional.

The consequence of this, is that the object that represents the <OBJECT> tag containing the plug-in, is not as tightly bound to the page as it would be if totally static HTML were used to describe it. The effect of this, is that if you drag the window, there is a noticeable lag while the browser figures out where the video rectangle is located. This is especially bad when the video is playing.

Here is just that fragment of JavaScript that creates the <OBJECT> tag inline:

```
<SCRIPT LANGUAGE='JavaScript'>
   var myTargetURL;
   var myObjectWidth;
   var myObjectHeight;

if (top.getClipName())
{
   myTargetURL = top.getClipURL();

   if (top.getClipMode() == "video")
   {
      myObjectWidth  = top.getClipWidth();
      myObjectHeight = top.getClipHeight();
      myPlayerObject = '';
   }
   else
   {
      document.write("<IMG SRC='" + top.getClipPoster() + "' BORDER='0' "
         +"WIDTH='" + top.getClipWidth() + "' HEIGHT='"
         + top.getClipHeight() + "' ALT=''></IMG>");
   }

   document.write("<OBJECT ID='videoScreen' WIDTH='" + myObjectWidth
      + "' HEIGHT='" + myObjectHeight
      + "' CLASSID='clsid:CFCDAA03-8BE4-11cf-B84B-0020AFBBCCFA'>");
   document.write("<PARAM NAME='controls' VALUE='ImageWindow'>");
   document.write("<PARAM NAME='backgroundcolor' VALUE='grey'>");
   document.write("<PARAM NAME='console' VALUE='Clip1'>");
   document.write("<PARAM NAME='nolabels' VALUE='true'>");
   document.write("<PARAM NAME='loop' VALUE='false'>");
   document.write("<PARAM NAME='reset' VALUE='false'>");
   document.write("<PARAM NAME='autostart' VALUE='true'>");
   document.write("<PARAM NAME='maintainaspect' VALUE='true'>");
   document.write("<PARAM NAME='nologo' VALUE='true'>");
   document.write("<PARAM NAME='backgroundcolor' VALUE='#DDDDDD'>");
   document.write("<PARAM NAME='src' VALUE='" + myTargetURL + "'>");
   document.write("</OBJECT>");
}
</SCRIPT>
```

The Video Player Frame (IE4 Mac)

See **player_mac_ie4_rpm.htm** for details.

There are issues on the Macintosh where Internet Explorer does not support many of the mechanisms that are found on the PC. On the Macintosh, using Real Video, we must use the <EMBED> tag.

On the Macintosh, there is such support as there is for the <OBJECT> tag in MSIE, actually crashes the machine. We have to create a different player module with new HTML and JavaScript, because, although it behaves in a functionally similar way, the <EMBED> tags are syntactically different. Here, is the fragment of code that writes the <EMBED> tag:

```
document.write("<EMBED ");
document.write("NAME='videoScreen' ");
document.write("SRC='" + theVideoToPlay + "' ");
document.write("WIDTH='" + theVideoWidth + "' ");
document.write("HEIGHT='" + theVideoHeight + "' ");
document.write("CONTROLS='ImageWindow' ");
```

```
              document.write("LOOP='false' ");
              document.write("BACKGROUNDCOLOR='#DDDDDD' ");
              document.write("AUTOSTART='true' ");
              document.write("MAINTAINASPECT='true' ");
              document.write("CONSOLE='Clip1' ");
              document.write("LOOP='false' ");
              document.write("NOLOGO='true' ");
              document.write(">");
```

Some optimization of JavaScript means that as a whole the page looks different, but the functionality is similar to that on the Windows version.

The Video Player Frame (Nav4 Win)

See `player_win_nav4_rpm.htm` for details.

Because we can more effectively control the <EMBED> plug-ins from JavaScript in Netscape Navigator, we can actually create a much better user experience on this platform. Of course, Netscape has nil support for <OBJECT> tags. There is a greater similarity with Netscape Navigator across all platforms. Although the public API needs to be available in all players so that the calls from external functions can be resolved without error, in this browser, they also work, rather than simply return with no action being taken. Here is the code for the public API on this player wrapper:

```
//- public api -

// PUBLIC API: Change to a new clip
function changeClip()
{
   // During testing some instabilities suggested we should stop
   // a clip from playing before closing its window. Later, that
   // seemed to have gone away so this call to stopClip() is
   // commented out but left here in case it is needed.
   // stopClip();
   window.location.href = self.top.getPluginWrapper();
}

// PUBLIC API: Play current clip
function publicPlay()
{
   if (document.videoScreen.CanPlay())
   {
      document.videoScreen.DoPlay();
   }
}

// PUBLIC API: Pause current clip
function publicPause()
{
   if (document.videoScreen.CanPause())
   {
      document.videoScreen.DoPause();
   }
}

// PUBLIC API: Stop current clip
function publicStop()
{
```

```
    if(document.videoScreen.CanStop())
    {
        document.videoScreen.DoStop();
    }
}

// PUBLIC API: Set volume (range 0-5)
function publicSetVolume(level)
{
    document.videoScreen.SetVolume(level*20);
}
```

Note that we can access the <EMBED> object by its name, and that the actions on the player plug-in test to see if they can be called before calling them. The audio level is also scaled, so that we can pass a value in the range 0-5 to all players.

The Video Player Frame (Nav4 Mac)

See **player_mac_nav4_rpm.htm** for details.

In fact, the Macintosh player is very similar to the Windows player for Navigator and Real Video. Oddly enough, the least popular platform and browser combinations are actually the most portable and, yet it is the most popular platform and browser that are least portable of all.

The Video Player Frame (Other Plug-Ins)

See **player_mac_ie4_asx.htm, player_mac_ie4_mov.htm, player_mac_nav4_asx.htm, player_mac_nav4_mov.htm, player_win_ie4_asx.htm, player_win_ie4_mov.htm, player_win_nav4_mov.htm,** and **player_win_nav4_asx.htm** for details.

Similar tricks need to be played to cope with the other plug-ins for Windows Media and QuickTime. At the time this software was being developed (summer 1999), the QuickTime plug-in would not support any kind of interaction with JavaScript but that has been rectified in a later revision.

Windows Media Player performs very well on Windows platforms and poorly everywhere else. The controller is not as flexible at the Real Player controller, and cannot be as effectively resized. On the other hand, Microsoft has tried to integrate with JScript, although this support is not likely to be platform independent.

The player plug-ins are improving all the time and there are other alternatives to the main three. SMIL compliant plug-ins are likely to offer some improvements, but there continue to be reliability problems with them at present.

The Story Frame

See **story_default.htm** and **story_example.htm** for details.

The idea here, is to augment the video being played with some additional story based content or related links. Like the live and tabbed menu frames, you can place links in here that call the playClip() function. That might result in the story frame being replaced. All three frames will be called back to set their active playing video indicator and they must all support the same public API.

There are no significant additional items of code in this frame.

The Banner Frame

See **header_mini.htm**, **header_tiny.htm**, and **header_normal.htm** for details.

The behavior of the banner frame is concerned mainly with the handling of the tabs for the lists of video clips. Currently, there are two pages of clips, and so two tabs are required. The control structures within the page are data driven, and so adding another tab is quite easy.

The menu switching is accomplished with the setMenuState() function. This enumerates through the images for all of the supported tabs. By default, it turns them off unless it encounters the one which matches the requested menu. In that case, it turns it on. Given that we are supporting only two menus, we should only pass the value 1 or 2. This is defined in theTabCount, and you will see that theTabPaths array only has two items in it:

```
// --- Tab setup
var theDefaultMenuState = 1;  // Default active tab
var theTabCount = 2;  // Indicate how many tabs are handled in this page
var theImageBase = 10;  /* Base image number for first tab
                          (Only change if you add images) */

// Add more paths to tabs here
var theTabPaths = new Array(theTabCount+1);
theTabPaths[1]  = "console_latest_news.htm";
theTabPaths[2]  = "console_features.htm";

// Set the requested menu state
function setMenuState(menuState)
{
    for (var myEnumerator=1; myEnumerator<theTabCount+1; myEnumerator++)
    {
        if (myEnumerator==menuState)
        {
          document.images[(theImageBase+myEnumerator)].src = "furniture_tab_"
              + (myEnumerator) + "_on.gif";
        }
        else
        {
          document.images[(theImageBase+myEnumerator)].src = "furniture_tab_"
              + (myEnumerator) + "_off.gif";
        }
    }
    top.headlinesFrame.location.href = theTabPaths[menuState];
}
```

Once the images representing the current state of each tab has been set, we can use the Menu State to index the array of tab paths to load the appropriate content into the menu frame.

There are a couple of other active links in this banner frame. These are implemented as JavaScript calls, because one is used to compact the console into a smaller window and the others to call up help pages.

765

The compact button calls a function that lives in the main frameset document which resizes the window in a browser-specific manner and then reloads the smaller console. That smaller version of the console contains a complementary piece of code to revert back to the larger console.

The Menu Panel Frame

> See `features.htm`, `latest_news.htm`, `menu_default.htm`, and `menu_mini.htm` for details.

The menu state handled in the banner frame determines the contents of this frame. There are two possible choices in the current implementation. In the example code, we called these `features` and `latest news`. The document content that is loaded in each case is named consistently with that. They are functionally identical, having been built dynamically from the same template. They are essentially a set of links to video clips, which are parameterized into function calls to a clip player function in the topmost frameset document. That player function can be called from any frame in the console, and it provides a central place where all clip playback is mediated. That means it can ensure that the current clip is stopped when a new one is called, and avoids duplicating player control calls all over the place.

These functions are provided to set and clear the playback indicators beside each clip. There are several functions and they are not always used in each frame they appear in. However, it was considered worthwhile implementing the same consistent API in all of the frames that might require this indicator functionality. So the features, latest news, live, and story documents all support a common API, which can be called from within the `playClip()` function in the global handler.

Here is a summary listing of the API:

Function	Description
switch_off_all_icons()	Sets all of the indicator icons in the receiving page to their unhighlighted state.
switch_on_an_icon()	Given an ID value, any indicators having that ID will be set to the highlighted state.
check_live_play_item()	After requesting the current ID value from the global session store, that value is used to highlight the indicator with the corresponding ID. All indicators are cleared down first.

Normally, the indicators are shown in a muted color, but change to a highlighted appearance when the associated clip is being played. This switching is accomplished by defining the NAME=" " attributes of the <IMG> tags. It is possible that a page may contain no matching indicators. Because we use the NAME=" " attribute of the image, there could be more than one matching indicator in the page but that is content dependant:

```
// --- Load time session check for live item
function check_live_play_item()
{
    var myClipIndex;

    myClipIndex = top.getClipIndex();

    if(myClipIndex != "0")
    {
switch_on_an_icon(myClipIndex);
```

```
      }
   }

   // --- Reset play icons to known off state
   function switch_off_all_icons()
   {
      var myHeadlineCount;

      myHeadlineCount  = document.images.length;

      for(var counter=0; counter < myHeadlineCount; counter++)
      {
         document.images[counter].src =
            document.images[counter].src.replace(/_on.gif/g, "_off.gif");
      }
   }

   // --- Switch on a play icon
   function switch_on_an_icon(anID)
   {
      var myImageSource;
      switch_off_all_icons();

      myImageSource = document.images[anID];

      if(myImageSource != null)
      {
         document.images[anID].src =
            myImageSource.src.replace(/_off.gif/g, "_on.gif");
      }
   }
```

For these to work they depend on the HTML for each link being carefully constructed to look like this. Any indicator images must have a filename that finishes with the string '_off' and no non-indicator images should contain that string or the '_on' string in their SRC attribute:

```
<IMG border=0 name='ID_112233' SRC='furniture_video_off.gif'>
<A HREF='javascript:void top.playClip("video", "ID_112233",
   "console_my_video_clip", "rpm", "160", "120",
   "furniture_vod_logo.jpg", "", "stories_1332668.htm");'>
   Click here
</A>
```

Note the correspondence between the NAME="" attribute of the <IMG> tag, and the index parameter being passed to playClip(). That value is passed back to the icon switch functions to 'green' the right image.

Any frame in the console can support these playback calls, as long as it also supports the icon switching call backs for the playClip() function to access. The reason they are located in the frame they are used in is so that they can present a consistent API, but if necessary have special functionality to deal with different page layouts. If we moved the functionality out to the calling frame, we would break one of the good object oriented rules where the calling frame would have to have knowledge of the internal structure of the target page.

The Live Scrolling Frame

See **live_default.htm** for details.

The requirements in the original design called for a list of live-streamed video feeds to be presented. However, it was not necessary to occupy a large amount of screen display real estate, and the number of items being listed could vary from time to time. So a gently scrolling list was implemented. This is placed into the live frame. For this list to scroll continuously, we need to create a loop that moves the content and then waits for a time-out and moves it again.

Implementing an endless and smooth scrolling list presented several problems. The difficulty arises when you have fully scrolled the list as far as you can, and you want to return to the original unscrolled position so you can start another cycle. This would give the appearance of the page content running in a continuous loop with no obvious join.

There is no easy way to measure the height of some content in a page reliably. This means that when the content has fully scrolled up, we have no easy way to detect that, reset the position and start scrolling again.

We can work around this by placing the items into a table making sure that all the rows are a fixed height. We also need to duplicate the first item and copy it to the end of the list. If we don't, then the last item in the list will scroll up the page, and we will have no way of scrolling the first item onto the bottom of the page without a disjoint or jump scroll appearance. By copying the first item, when that copy reaches a position just one pixel short of the top edge, we can jump back to the genuine first item. If it is scrolled exactly to the top edge, the fact that we have jumped from the end of the list back to the beginning, is hidden completely.

This is what you see in the visible part of the frame:

This, however, is what is in the document:

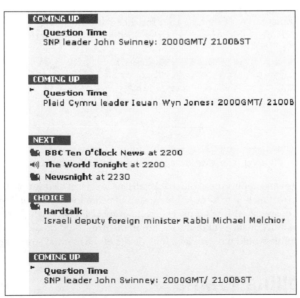

Note the text wrapping happens because of the frame width, but this is allowed for in the table cell height. See that the first item is duplicated at the end of the page, so we can gracefully scroll the page back to zero at the end. The right time to do this scroll back is calculated by knowing the height of each table cell and the number of items in the scrolling list.

The item count is passed in a hidden form field. If you own the publishing process, you can easily define this from JavaScript if you prefer. In 1999, the News Online content publishing system did not have access to the internals of <SCRIPT> tags and could only publish HTML and not JavaScript. The simplest solution at that time was to add a fragment of HTML like this:

```
<FORM method=post NAME="properties" action="/2">
<INPUT TYPE=HIDDEN NAME="storycount" VALUE="2">
</FORM>
```

So the total scrolling distance is:

```
((item height in pixels) * (item count + 1)) - 1 pixel
```

Note that we add 1 to the itemCount, because the list has an item duplicated and that needs to be taken account of in the value passed from the publishing system or here in the JavaScript.

Implementing this live scrolling frame also threw up some browser differences. For a start, on Netscape Navigator, you cannot scroll a page unless you make its scroll-bar visible. Internet Explorer does not demand that. This means we must wrap the table within a <LAYER> tag. Internet Explorer will ignore that, but it is necessary for Netscape Navigator version 4.

The other important difference is that Netscape Navigator and Internet Explorer scroll in the opposite direction when you increment the scroll value. This means that we must have browser detection somewhere, so that we can make the scrolling positive or negative. This can be managed quite effectively by using an eval() function to execute some code that is manufactured algorithmically.

Note the global variable called theRefreshCycles that is set to the value 10. This is incremented in the scroller code and when the threshold value is reached, we force a page reload by setting the href for the frame to itself. This ensures that the live scrolling list is refreshed every now and then, and it picks up changes quite soon after they are placed on the server. You may want to adjust that threshold value according to the effects it has on server loading when many thousands of people have your scrolling page on display. That test and reload is done with this line of code:

```
self.location.href = self.location.href;
```

Here is the rest of the code that manages the scrolling:

```
// --- Create global variables
var theScrollValue;
var theMaxScroll;
var theCycleCount;
var theItemHeight;
var theRefreshCycles;

// --- Start the scroller running on body load completed
function startScroller()
{
    var myScrollHandler;
    var myHeadlineCount;

    switch_on_an_icon(top.getClipIndex());

    theItemHeight    = 75;
    theRefreshCycles = 10;
    theCycleCount    = 0;
    theScrollValue   = 0;

    myHeadlineCount=parseInt(document.properties.storycount.value) + 1;
```

```
    theMaxScroll = (myHeadlineCount*theItemHeight);

    myScrollHandler = top.getBrowserType() + "_scrollPage()";
    eval(myScrollHandler);
}

// --- Browser specific scroller (IE)
function ie4_scrollPage()
{
    self.scrollTo(0,theScrollValue);
    theScrollValue++;

    if(theScrollValue == theMaxScroll)
    {
        theCycleCount++;
        theScrollValue = 0;
    }

    if(theCycleCount == theRefreshCycles)
    {
        theCycleCount=0;
        self.location.href = self.location.href;
    }

    setTimeout("ie4_scrollPage()", 75);
}

// --- Browser specific scroller (Navigator)
function nav4_scrollPage()
{
    self.document.layer1.moveTo(0,-theScrollValue);
    theScrollValue++;

    if(theScrollValue == theMaxScroll)
    {
        theCycleCount++;
        theScrollValue = 0;
    }

    if(theCycleCount == theRefreshCycles)
    {
        theCycleCount=0;
        self.location.href = self.location.href;
    }

    setTimeout("nav4_scrollPage()", 50);
}
```

The whole process is initiated when the <BODY> is closed and the onLoad event is triggered.

If you look carefully at the startup function, you should see that it walks through the document to pick up the number of items in the list. This is necessary to allow your publishing system to pass a value through when it makes the list of items longer or shorter. Without this, you would have to have a fixed number of items.

Here is the table structure containing several items with their playClip() calls embedded into the anchors:

```
<TABLE CELLPADDING=0 CELLSPACING=0 BORDER=0>

<TR>
  <TD VALIGN=TOP>
    <TABLE CELLPADDING=0 CELLSPACING=0 BORDER=0>
```

```
        <TR ALIGN=LEFT>
          <TD COLSPAN=2>
            <IMG SRC="../images/live.gif" NAME="LIVE" WIDTH=62
              HEIGHT=13 BORDER=0>
          </TD>
        </TR>
        <TR>
          <TD VALIGN=TOP>
            <IMG NAME="460773" BORDER=0
              SRC="../images/audio_off.gif" HSPACE=2 VSPACE=2><BR>
            <IMG HEIGHT=1 WIDTH=20 SRC="../images/nothing.gif">
          </TD>
          <TD>
            <A href="javascript: void top.playClip('audio', '460773',
'../media/example', 'rpm', '160', '120', '../media/example.gif', 'Story 1 audio 1
caption', 'story_example.htm');" CLASS="headline">
              Headline 1</A><BR>
            <A href="javascript: void top.playClip('audio', '460773',
'../media/example', 'rpm', '160', '120', '../media/example.gif', 'Story 1 audio 1
caption', 'story_example.htm');" CLASS="summary" >
              Summary 1</A>
          </TD>
        </TR>
      </TABLE>
      </TD>
      <TD>
        <IMG HEIGHT=75 WIDTH=1 SRC="../images/nothing.gif">
      </TD>
</TR>

<TR>
  <TD VALIGN=TOP>
  <TABLE CELLPADDING=0 CELLSPACING=0 BORDER=0>
    <TR ALIGN=LEFT>
      <TD COLSPAN=2>
        <IMG ALT SRC="../images/live.gif" NAME="LIVE" WIDTH=62
          HEIGHT=13 BORDER=0>
      </TD>
    </TR>
    <TR>
      <TD VALIGN=TOP>
        <IMG NAME="460785" BORDER=0 SRC="../images/audio_off.gif"
          HSPACE=2 VSPACE=2><BR>
        <IMG HEIGHT=1 WIDTH=20 SRC="../images/nothing.gif">
      </TD>
      <TD>
        <A href="javascript: void top.playClip('audio', '460785',
'../media/example', 'rpm', '160', '120', '../media/example.gif', 'Audio 1 story 2
caption', 'story_example.htm');" CLASS="headline">
          Headline 2</A><BR>
        <A href="javascript: void top.playClip('audio', '460785',
'../media/example', 'rpm', '160', '120', '../media/example.gif', 'Audio 1 story 2
caption', 'story_example.htm');" CLASS="summary" >
          Summary 2</A>
      </TD>
    </TR>
  </TABLE>
  </TD>
  <TD>
    <IMG HEIGHT=75 WIDTH=1 SRC="../images/nothing.gif">
  </TD>
</TR>
```

771

```
<TR>
  <TD VALIGN=TOP>
  <TABLE CELLPADDING=0 CELLSPACING=0 BORDER=0>
    <TR ALIGN=LEFT>
      <TD COLSPAN=2>
        <IMG ALT SRC="../images/live.gif" NAME="LIVE" WIDTH=62 HEIGHT=13
          BORDER=0>
      </TD>
    </TR>
    <TR>
      <TD VALIGN=TOP>
        <IMG NAME="460773" BORDER=0 SRC="../images/audio_off.gif"
          HSPACE=2 VSPACE=2><BR>
        <IMG HEIGHT=1 WIDTH=20 SRC="../images/nothing.gif">
      </TD>
      <TD>
        <A href="javascript: void top.playClip('audio', '460773',
'../media/example', 'rpm', '160', '120', '../media/example.gif', 'Story 1 audio 1
caption', 'story_example.htm');" CLASS="headline">
        Headline 1</A><BR>
        <A href="javascript: void top.playClip('audio', '460773',
'../media/example', 'rpm', '160', '120', '../media/example.gif', 'Story 1 audio 1
caption', 'story_example.htm');" CLASS="summary" >
        Summary 1</A>
      </TD>
    </TR>
  </TABLE>
  </TD>
  <TD>
    <IMG HEIGHT=75 WIDTH=1 SRC="../images/nothing.gif">
  </TD>
</TR>

</TABLE>
```

Note that we add 1 to the value, because we know the first item has been repeated.

The Function Library

Because the console is designed to run in a frameset and the individual frames are quite dysfunctional on their own, we want to make sure the frames are running in the right context.

There are several ways in which you can test whether you are inside a frameset or a standalone frame. This is the simplest and appears to work well for this application. It is used in several important frames to ensure they are loaded correctly:

```
// --- Check for loading outside of frameset
if (document.location == top.location)
{
    document.location.href = "console_error.htm";
}
```

It simply compares the location object of the current document with that belonging to the one in the topmost frame of the frameset. If they are the same object then we are not correctly framed so the browser is redirected to an error page. Maybe you could just as effectively redirect to the main frameset document instead.

In the console, there is sometimes a need to link from the story text associated with a clip out to a story page in the main News Online site. This needs to create a larger window (or use the existing one) without affecting the console. The gotoNews() function is used:

```
function gotoNews(newsID)
{
   var newsWindow;

   newsWindow = window.open(SRC="… News URL here …", "newsWindow" ,
      "toolbar=1,location=1,menubar=1,scrollbars=1,resizable=1,status=1");

   newsWindow.focus();
}
```

Note that the URL is passed in from outside and that the window takes the user focus when the function exits.

Video Driven Event Data

There is a constant evolution of functionality. SMIL playback is an interesting area worth investigating, but current plug-ins do not support multiple video streams in SMIL documents very effectively. That is a pity, because a SMIL player could provide most of the functionality we need within the video window, and we may be able to avoid frames and most of the JavaScript. Because SMIL is XML based, authoring tools for XML may help in creating the content for it. SMIL 2.0 has just been completed and standardised, and so this may become a more useful way to build portable event driven presentations.

QuickTime wired movies may be an alternative. It may be possible to embed some kind of events into the movie so that functionality in the console can be called back. Windows Media Player has been significantly enhanced for use with JavaScript. There is a more complete object model available and you can 'skin' the player more easily.

Real Video supports the insertion of URLs at time-coded intervals. These were originally intended to call back to the browser to request that it loads a page using the `http:` request method. However, you can use callbacks that route through the `javascript:` request method. If you carefully manage the player so that any callbacks will be routed to a function that you have built in, then you can dynamically alter the console behavior according to the video being played. This is a very interesting area and worthy of much further investigation.

Inserting these events into a video is quite simple. You create a time-line file with the event time and the URL, and then run the `RMMERGE` utility to join that event stream to the movie. Then, when the movie is played back, the events are sent to the browser to be activated. Simple `http:` events will spawn a new window. You can, however, include `javascript:` events to call any supported functions in the player window. The `RMMERGE` tool is available as part of the developer kit and, if you perform a web search, you will locate various interesting university projects that are using this technique.

Even though it is possible to generate these events and merge them with a live stream, the support documentation from Real Networks suggests that using SMIL is their preferred approach. All the same, this functionality appears to still be available, but has not been widely exploited.

Netscape Navigator 6 changes

Throughout this chapter, we have trod a thin line between describing a historical artifact and resisting the temptation to completely rework it and bring it up to date with the latest technology.

This is probably quite representative of many currently deployed applications. There is a need to perform some small upgrades but a complete reworking is out of the question on commercial or resource grounds. Despite the justifiable protestations of a few users who are enthusiastic about a minority web browser (and there are several that are extremely good products), it simply is not realistic to devote many developer months of effort, for an audience that is less than half a percent of your user base. It seems a harsh line to take, but it makes sense given the amount of work and the availability of resource to apply to it.

However, there are often some small changes you can make that will alleviate the pain for these users and it's helpful to look at this audio | video console in that light. To be sure it is due for an upgrade but the likely outcome of that will be a totally redesigned solution bearing little resemblance to the current model. That would be an opportunity to address the needs of these minority web browser users.

So, is there anything we can do in a minimal sense to make the current version work reasonably well on Netscape Navigator 6? The example source kit that you can download from Wrox (http://www.wrox.com) has already had these minor changes added, but we'll describe them here. Let's deal with them file by file.

In files vod_home.htm, vod_mini.htm, and vod_tiny.htm the browser detection is enhanced to add a nav6 output case. The new code is highlighted here:

```
function getBrowserType()
{
   var myUserAgent;
   var myMajor;

   myUserAgent   = navigator.userAgent.toLowerCase();
   myMajor       = parseInt(navigator.appVersion);

   if( (myUserAgent.indexOf('mozilla')    != -1) &&
       (myUserAgent.indexOf('spoofer')    == -1) &&
       (myUserAgent.indexOf('compatible') == -1) &&
       (myUserAgent.indexOf('opera')      == -1) &&
       (myUserAgent.indexOf('webtv')      == -1)
     )
   {
      if (myMajor > 4)
      {
         return "nav6";
      }
      if (myMajor > 3)
      {
         return "nav4";
      }
      return "nav";
   }

   if (myUserAgent.indexOf("msie") != -1)
   {
      if (myMajor > 3)
      {
         return "ie4";
      }
      return "ie";
   }

   return "other";
}
```

In the live frame, the live_default.htm file requires some important changes to get the scrolling working. The structure in the HTML where there is a <LAYER> tag enclosing the scrollable area, needs an additional <DIV> tag, like this:

```
<BODY>
<DIV ID="NAV6DIV" STYLE="position:absolute">
<LAYER TOP=0 LEFT=0 NAME="layer1">
<TABLE CELLPADDING=0 CELLSPACING=0 BORDER=0>

... Content omitted here ...
```

```
</TABLE>
</LAYER>
</DIV>

<FORM method=post NAME="properties">
<INPUT TYPE=HIDDEN NAME="storycount" VALUE="2">
</FORM>

</BODY>
```

Note that we set the CSS positioning to absolute, so we can scroll it and we give it a unique ID so we can find it. To support that, we define an additional global variable at the top of the script and use getElementById() to make a reference to the <DIV> block:

```
var theScrollObject;
```

Now add some code to the startScroller() function to store a reference to the <DIV> block.

```
function startScroller()
{
   var myScrollHandler;
   var myHeadlineCount;

   if(top.getBrowserType() == "nav6")
   {
      theScrollObject = document.getElementById("NAV6DIV");
   }

   switch_on_an_icon(top.getClipIndex());

   theItemHeight    = 75;
   theRefreshCycles = 30;
   theCycleCount    = 0;
   theScrollValue   = 0;

   myHeadlineCount  = document.properties.storycount.value;

   theMaxScroll     = myHeadlineCount * theItemHeight;

   myScrollHandler = top.getBrowserType() + "_scrollPage()";
   eval(myScrollHandler);
}
```

Because we need to control the scrolling by adjusting the CSS position of a <DIV> block, we need a special Navigator 6 scrolling control function:

```
function nav6_scrollPage()
{
   theScrollObject.style.top = -theScrollValue;

   theScrollValue++;

   if(theScrollValue == theMaxScroll)
   {
      theCycleCount++;
      theScrollValue = 0;
   }

   if(theCycleCount == theRefreshCycles)
   {
```

```
        window.location.href = window.location.href;
    }

    setTimeout("nav6_scrollPage()", 100);
}
```

This scroller is very similar to the MSIE scroller, but note that scrolling is still in a reverse direction with respect to MSIE, and the whole <DIV> based approach is necessary, because Navigator 6 still requires an active and visible scrollbar before you can scroll the content of a page. Hiding the scrollbar prevents the page from being scrolled even with JavaScript. Note that we use a CSS style accessor to locate the top edge with the scrolling value.

Also in the live_default.htm file, the icon switcher requires a change, because it can share the ie4 branch of the code as it no longer supports layers, and therefore, the images are in the one single document plane. The changes are to a conditional test in the switch_off_all_icons() function, and similar changes in switch_on_an_icon():

```
function switch_off_all_icons()
{
    var myHeadlineCount;
    var myEnumerator;

    if((top.getBrowserType() == "ie4") ||
       (top.getBrowserType() == "nav6"))
    {
        myHeadlineCount  = document.images.length;
        for(myEnumerator=0; myEnumerator<myHeadlineCount; myEnumerator++)
        {
          document.images[myEnumerator].src =
            document.images[myEnumerator].src.replace(/_on.gif/g, "_off.gif");
        }
    }
    else
    {
        myHeadlineCount  = document.layers["layer1"].document.images.length;
        for(myEnumerator=0; myEnumerator<myHeadlineCount; myEnumerator++)
        {
            document.layers["layer1"].document.images[myEnumerator].src =
document.layers["layer1"].document.images[myEnumerator].src.replace(/_on.gif/g,
"_off.gif");
        }
    }
}


function switch_on_an_icon(anID)
{
    var myEnumerator;
    var myImageCount;
    var myImageSource;

    switch_off_all_icons();

    if((top.getBrowserType() == "ie4") ||
       (top.getBrowserType() == "nav6"))
    {
        myImageCount = document.images.length;
    }
    else
    {
```

```
        myImageCount = document.layers["layer1"].document.images.length;
    }

    for(myEnumerator=0; myEnumerator<myImageCount; myEnumerator++)
    {
        if((top.getBrowserType() == "ie4") ||
           (top.getBrowserType() == "nav6"))
        {
            if(document.images[myEnumerator].name == anID)
            {
                myImageSource = document.images[myEnumerator];
            }
        }
        else
        {
            if(document.layers["layer1"].document.images[myEnumerator].name == anID)
            {
                myImageSource =
                    document.layers["layer1"].document.images[myEnumerator];
            }
        }

        if(myImageSource != null)
        {
            myImageSource.src =
                myImageSource.src.replace(/_off.gif/g, "_on.gif");
        }
    }
}
```

In the `legend_default.htm` file, we need a small change to locate the correct object to have its `innerHTML` changed. Here is a minimal `nav6` related change for that:

```
function changeLegend()
{
    var myLegendHTML;

    myLegendHTML = "<CENTER><FONT FACE=\"ARIAL\" SIZE=1>" + top.getClipLegend() +
"</FONT></CENTER>";

    if(top.getBrowserType() == "nav4")
    {
        document.legend_text_layer.document.write(myLegendHTML);
        document.legend_text_layer.document.close();
    }
    else if(top.getBrowserType() == "nav6")
    {
        mySpan = document.getElementById("legend_text_span");
        mySpan.innerHTML = myLegendHTML;
    }
    else
    {
        document.all.legend_text_span.innerHTML = myLegendHTML;
    }
}
```

Given the enhanced capabilities of newer browsers and the extent to which the older ones have declined, we could justify a much more rigorous reengineering of the console, but these few changes are sufficient to keep things working until we can replace the console with a new application.

The code that invokes the player, the function getPluginWrapper(), is unchanged. However, without modification, it will require a set of players with the following names to be provided:

- ❑ player_mac_nav6_asx.htm
- ❑ player_mac_nav6_mov.htm
- ❑ player_mac_nav6_rpm.htm
- ❑ player_win_nav6_asx.htm
- ❑ player_win_nav6_mov.htm
- ❑ player_win_nav6_rpm.htm

Adding 6 more player modules means we have rather more duplication than is preferable for ease of maintenance. In the next major overhaul, some kind of lookup mechanism can be constructed, so we need only provide the minimum number of player modules, and they can then be shared between several browser/platform/plug-in configurations.

Summary

In this chapter, we have seen how it is possible using JavaScript to bring the multimedia world and the plain HTML world together to create fantastic effects. This case study is based on a real-life news web site of the BBC, and we have shown how we can use JavaScript to allow the various different web browsers to be able to view the various multimedia contents in a standard way.

In terms of portability, the least popular platforms seem to provide a high degree of portability between them but the dominant platform is significantly different.

We find that to get the console operating in the correct way on Netscape Navigator 6, we only need to apply some quite minimal changes to the code.

Pro JavaScript 2nd Edition

The BBC News Online Ticker

In this chapter, we are going to review an application of JavaScript in the creation of a news ticker. This is the one used on the front page of the BBC News Online web site at http://www.bbc.co.uk/news. Here is a screenshot showing the ticker at the top of the middle column:

This was originally designed and implemented in 1999 at a time when the installed base of browsers was somewhat different to what is available now. When it was being developed, certain design choices were made, which now need to be readdressed given the progress that has been made since then. When the ticker was first implemented, these were considered to be the important criteria:

❑   It should work on IE without requiring Java.

❑   It should work on IE across all platforms (principally Windows and Macintosh).

❑   It must use an existing data feed which was driving the Java applet without requiring additional editorial work to create a new data feed.

❑   Some of the required dynamism was known to be unavailable in Netscape 4.x, so could continue to use the Java applet.

❑   DOM wasn't nearly standardized and deployed enough to use.

❑   It must not use an additional frame.

❑   Netscape 6 was not available.

❑   The market share of Netscape was declining and the future expectation was that usage of that browser would diminish and potentially vanish altogether.

From the viewpoint of 2001, we now need to reevaluate those objectives and consider some changes to the original design criteria:

❑ Netscape 6 and Opera now both support `IFRAME` tags, rendering our IE-only selection mechanism less than perfect.

❑ The JavaScript code that was carefully written (and compromised) to address the portability issues of IE across its various platforms needs to be revised somewhat to work on Opera and Netscape 6.

❑ DOM standardization is much improved but regrettably, much of it is still non-portable due to the way the browsers treat whitespace and empty text nodes in the object model.

The early part of this chapter, will describe how the ticker works, its internals, and why it was implemented the way it was. It is necessary to discuss the compromises you need to make when building a real world JavaScript application like this.

At the outset, you begin with a somewhat ideal implementation that works fine on a single platform and browser. As you test the code on more platforms and browser versions, you gradually reveal more deficiencies in the browsers, meaning that you need to modify code until it works on both old and new browsers and whatever platforms that browser is supported by. In the end, you arrive at a code base that is somewhat less pretty than that which you started with. Also, there are all sorts of extra code fragments and sub-optimal coding techniques that become necessary.

That's roughly where we are with the live deployed ticker as it is on the News Online site. It works on the platforms and browsers it was originally intended for, but new browsers are available which mandate some corrective code to enable the ticker to run on them as well.

Things have moved on and usage statistics tell, us that Netscape 4.x usage is still declining, while Netscape 6 usage is very small, but increasing. It is not yet a serious challenger to Microsoft, but it has the potential to gain significant market share. Opera browser usage is also small, but increasing, indicating that some people are considering alternatives to the Microsoft browser. We have a long way to go however before IE is no longer the dominant force in browser usage.

In the latter parts of this chapter, rather than simply review the ticker application as it was designed in 1999, we'll try to bring it up to date by remodeling the basic implementation so that it works with a wider variety of contemporary browsers.

Why do it in JavaScript?

One of the popular uses of *Java* is to build animated effects that can be embedded into a web page. Many applets provide button rollovers and menu handlers, or are used for news headline scrolls and tickers.

The major problem with all of this, is that there is a certain penalty involved in deploying these applets. The problem is that for many browser and platform combinations, the time taken for the Java Virtual Machine (JVM) to start up can be a nuisance. Also, if the applet requires a later version of the JVM, then that has to be installed as well. In its worst-case scenario, the JVM start-up can completely suspend the page loading and drawing process, meaning that the user can sometimes stare at an empty or unchanging screen for 30 seconds or more.

Using frames can alleviate this, but can still be frustrating. So, the challenge is to create a news ticker using JavaScript. It needs to be dynamically data driven and start-up very quickly.

When we look at an example like this, there is a temptation to suggest that there must surely be a very simple solution. We will see though that the result is something that did evolve from a simple solution, but has become complex as a necessity. The complexity comes from discovering shortcomings in the support of dynamic effects on different versions of browsers. Different platforms also exhibit failure modes that force us to code round the problem, sometimes in a sub-optimal way.

Simplicity is possible if you can bind your target audience with code that works on a very restricted platform and browser combination. However, portability dictates that we need to go the other way and accommodate many versions of many browsers on many platforms. That clearly must add complexity given the current state of the JavaScript and DOM implementations.

The Platform Issue

Right away, we bump into some difficult problems. Any dynamic effects are not likely to be browser independent. This kind of dynamism on Netscape prior to version 6, is going to rely on layers and may not be feasible at all, (that's assuming we are going to totally disregard browsers earlier than Netscape 4). With layers, we might be able to create some dynamic effects, but that would have to take place within the main content area of the page. Constraining the boundaries of the layer to fit exactly the right location and size, were also considered to be quite a difficult problem to solve in the context of the News Online front page where the ticker was intended to be used. On those grounds, and also being aware that even in 1999 layers were already considered a deprecated feature, we decided not to attempt to provide Netscape 4.x JavaScript driven tickers. We already had the Java ticker that was working on Netscape anyway.

On IE, we had Dynamic HTML techniques available to us to replace the content of a tagged block of HTML marked-up text.

Looking at the traffic figures for the BBC News Online site, we established at the outset that Netscape 4 accounted for less than 15% of the traffic. Most of our traffic was attributable to IE. This itself was quite a shock, as it clearly indicates the extent to which Microsoft now dominates the browser marketplace and the extent to which Netscape have lost market share.

Looking again at the figures 2 years on, Netscape 6 penetration is still very small at around 0.3% (as of summer 2001). Making special provision for Netscape 6, is very hard to justify from a commercial or resource allocation point of view. In the meantime, Netscape 4 browsers are rapidly declining in use. Arguably, the Holy Grail of a single platform is mostly within reach at the expense of it all being under Microsoft's control. Even that is a vain hope, because IE is implemented quite differently on Macintosh and Windows, and will only be available on platforms that Microsoft sees commercial benefit in supporting. There is no long-term alternative other than approaching the problem from a standards-driven perspective. In 1999, that was not viable, but it is now looking more attractive.

All of this dictated the design goal of getting this ticker working on IE and basically disregarding the other browsers since they could continue to use the Java applet, albeit with the 30 second delay for the Java VM.

Insetting the Ticker Into the page

We need to find a way to embed the ticker into a page so that our target browser invokes the JavaScript version, while any others call in the Java version.

Remember, that this decision was being made in 1999 when only IE supported the IFRAME tag and all other browsers ignored it. Yes, we did expect that other browsers might implement it in the future and now that future has arrived, we will review this later on in the chapter, when we develop a new ticker for contemporary browsers. For now, we are looking at the live deployed ticker.

The `IFRAME` tag was assembled in such a way as to call in the ticker HTML document only on IE. The other browsers would ignore the `IFRAME` tag and see the HTML contained within it. This fragment of HTML is taken from the News Online front page:

```
<IFRAME SRC='/ticker/ticker.stm' WIDTH='315' HEIGHT='30'
    SCROLLING='no' FRAMEBORDER='0'>
    <APPLET CODE='ticker.class' CODEBASE='/java/'
        WIDTH='300' HEIGHT='50'>
      <PARAM NAME='bgcolor'      VALUE='255,255,255'></PARAM>
      <PARAM NAME='linkcolor'    VALUE='255,0,0'></PARAM>
      <PARAM NAME='textcolor'    VALUE='0,0,0'></PARAM>
      <PARAM NAME='SectionID'    VALUE='252'></PARAM>
      <PARAM NAME='LanguageID'   VALUE='3'></PARAM>
      <PARAM NAME='RegionID'     VALUE='-1'></PARAM>
      <PARAM NAME='SubRegionID'  VALUE='-1'></PARAM>
    </APPLET>
</IFRAME>
```

Conveniently, IE ignores the HTML between the `IFRAME` and `/IFRAME` tags, while still implementing the `IFRAME`. Netscape ignores the `IFRAME` tags and sees the `APPLET` element inside. The applet parameters are not important to us here and are provided to allow the tickers to be customized for different language variants of News Online.

So, the ticker runs within a frame that is placed at the top of the page (or wherever we like).

How It Works

The workings are fairly simple:

❑   Test that we are running in the correct browser

❑   Initialize any data structures

❑   Construct an interval timer that plays out the ticker text

❑   On each cycle, pick up a new headline and play it out

❑   After a pre-defined number of cycles, reload the ticker page

We will now take a closer look at these steps to consider the design choices and compromises that were made.

Browser Test

During the initial page loading, several functions are declared, and a browser test forces a redirect to an alternative ticker written in Java if the browser is other than IE or older than IE 4. Here is the fragment of JavaScript code that carries out the test and redirect:

```
// --- Check for old browser and force load the applet
theBrowserVersion = parseInt(navigator.appVersion);

if (theBrowserVersion < 4)
{
  location.href = "/ticker/ticker_applet.252.htm";
}
```

Remember, that this is assumed to only be running on IE. Now that Opera and Netscape 6 support `IFRAME` tags, this browser test requires some modification. The smallest change we could make to the ticker script, is to test for non-IE browsers here and force the applet to load, but that's not a very nice way to solve the problem. It is far better to get the ticker to work on those other browsers instead.

Ticker Startup

Once the BODY is fully loaded, we can trigger the ticker start-up. It is important to wait until this time, because we need the BODY loading to be complete, so that we can extract the story text from the DIV blocks at the end of the page.

The ticker startup is called like this:

```
<BODY onLoad="startTicker();">
```

Here, is that startup function code:

```
// --- Only run for V4 browsers (check browser again here -
//    some old browsers won't do this inline)
    function startTicker()
    {
        theBrowserVersion = parseInt(navigator.appVersion);

        if (theBrowserVersion < 4)
        {
            location.href = "/ticker/ticker_applet.252.htm";
            return;
        }

// ------ Check and fixup incoming data block
        if(!document.body.children.incoming.children.properties)
        {
            document.all.incoming.innerHTML = "… default data …";
        }

// ------ Set up initial values - behavior
        theCharacterTimeout = 50;
        theStoryTimeout     = 5000;
        theWidgetOne        = "_";
        theWidgetTwo        = "-";

// ------ Set up initial values - content
        theStoryState       = 1;
        theItemCount        = document.all.itemcount.innerText;
        theCurrentStory     = -1;
        theCurrentLength    = 0;
        theLeadString       = "  …  ";
        theSpaceFiller      = "     …  <BR><BR><BR>";

// ------ Begin the ticker
        runTheTicker();
    }
```

Due to some browsers that support IFRAME tags not also supporting the earlier inline browser test and redirect, we also do that again here to catch them. This is mostly for the benefit of preventing IE 3 browsers from trying to run the ticker.

The next fragment of code checks that the data in the DIV blocks actually exists. This is a work around for a problem that occurred in the publishing system where an empty data feed was routed to the server. It resulted in the DIV blocks being present, but containing no data. This tests for that and reconstructs some default data if necessary. The code has been simplified to save a little space.

There are two blocks of global variable initialization. They are separated simply, because one set describes how the ticker works, while the other relates to the ticker data. The values in those variables control the ticker as follows:

Variable	Purpose
theCharacterTimeout	This is the time in milliseconds between drawing one character and the next. The value is used to determine the delay before calling the next cycle of the ticker.
theStoryTimeout	When a headline is complete, this delay in milliseconds determines how long the story dwells on the screen, before the next story begins to tick out.
theWidgetOne	The bouncing golf ball effect requires two characters to be alternately appended to the end of the ticker. This is the first.
theWidgetTwo	This is the other golf ball effect character. The two characters need to differ in their perceived shape. One needs to be elevated while the other needs to be low down. An underscore and a minus sign work quite well together. A more gross effect can be obtained with an underscore and an asterisk. You could experiment with HTML character entities as well.
theStoryState	The story state indicates whether we are currently playing out the headline text as a ticker, or whether it is completed.
theItemCount	The total number of stories available is stored here.
theCurrentStory	This determines which one of several stories is the one currently being played out.
theCurrentLength	The current ticker length enumerator variable.
theLeadString	In the News Online ticker, we must indent the text to avoid overwriting the 'Latest:' text that is part of the background. That spacer must be a series of HTML character entities that represent non-breaking-spaces. This is important, so that the mouse can enter and click on any part of the ticker.
theSpaceFiller	The as yet unfilled part of the ticker must also be filled with non-breaking space characters so that it can be clicked on.

The last line in the ticker startup function runs the first cycle of the ticker.

Main Run Loop

Each time the ticker cycles, the main run loop invokes this function:

```
// --- The basic rotate function
   function runTheTicker()
   {
      if(theStoryState == 1)
      {
         setupNextStory();
      }

      if(theCurrentLength != theStorySummary.length)
      {
         drawStory();
      }
```

```
        else
        {
            closeOutStory();
        }
    }
```

The `StoryState` indicates whether we need to set up the next story. That involves fetching its headline text and determining the URL value and headline length.

If we are not already at the end of the headline (`currentLength = headline length`), then we draw the story, taking into account that we must append one more character than we did last time. If we are at the end of a headline, we must close out the story. This draws the headline text without the golf ball effect.

Data import

Setting up the story involves the least portable part of this application. Due to the constraints imposed on the ticker design, the textual data must be embedded within the same file as the ticker script so it is loaded as a single document. The workflow processes that involve a team of journalists entering headline data via a client on a database, and that data being published as a data feed imposed this constraint. The format and presentation of that data feed was immutable, because it is used to feed several other processes, but we were able to pass it through a filter and convert it into something we could use. Unfortunately, that something was not JavaScript, but HTML structured with `DIV` blocks. That fragment of HTML is then inserted into a template ticker file with a server-side include. This is illustrated in the following diagram, which shows the critical parts of the process that are used by the ticker:

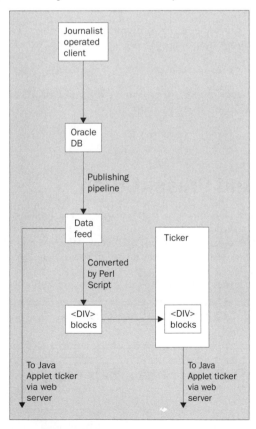

The story array is traversed one item at a time and having obtained the story text, we construct the HTML to be placed inside the DIV block containing the anchor which the user will click on to go to the story. We use the innerHTML property to change the content of the anchor object. Each cycle round the loop, we construct a longer text until the entire string is inserted. At that time, we wait for a few seconds before indexing to the next story. The story is indexed with the global variable called theCurrentStory and the ticker text is sub-stringed with the global variable called theCurrentLength.

We'll skip the details of that traversal and extraction for a little while, because there are several alternative ways to accomplish it and we'll review them all in due course shortly. We'll also not go into great detail on the sub-string extraction and ticker drawing because we'll also cover that when we come to build our new ticker later on. That part of the ticker functionality at least should be fine. The portability issues are really all to do with extracting the story data from its container.

On the whole, this functionality is not very complex and is based on time-outs, as you might expect. The large string full of non-breaking spaces is necessary to fill the IFRAME. There may be a more optimal way to build that string with a for() loop, but all of the techniques for iteratively concatenating a single   entity would in fact cause a memory leak due to the fresh instantiation of a string to contain the concatenation on each loop. Perhaps the non-breaking spaces could have been put into the HTML portion of the page and extracted, but there didn't seem to be any benefit and there was certainly no space saving there either.

The key to this is the setTimeout() method, which is a very useful facility. A similar and related method can be used to call a function periodically, which is the setInterval() method. That method would not be appropriate here, because we want to change the duration of the timeout when we have completed the drawing of a story.

There are two ways we call setTimeout() to invoke the next loop. The first, is when we are still intending to tick out some more text. In the drawStory function, we call setTimeout() like this:

```
setTimeout("runTheTicker()", theCharacterTimeout);
```

The other case is when we close out a story to remove the golf ball. It's very similar, but uses a different global variable to yield the longer timeout value:

```
setTimeout("runTheTicker()", theStoryTimeout);
```

Visual Effects and Presentation

To create the effect of an old-fashioned golf ball teletypewriter, the last character of the headline string is alternately replaced by an underscore (_) or a hyphen (-). You can experiment with using other characters to make the effect more obvious, but this seems effective and reasonably subtle. Using an asterisk instead of the hyphen, makes the effect much more noticeable.

Here is how two adjacent characters are painted in with the golf ball effect:

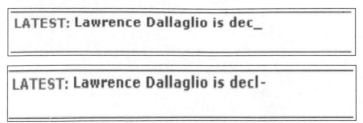

To determine which of the two characters to use, we perform a modulo 2 operation on the length of the output string to yield either a value of 1 or 0. This can then be used to select one or other of the widget characters. The code in the ticker is used inline, but can be wrapped in a function that returns one or other character. We'll use a function like this later on in our new ticker design:

```
function makeWidget()
{
    if((theCurrentLength % 2) == 1)
    {
        return theWidgetOne;
    }
    else
    {
        return theWidgetTwo;
    }
}
```

The string that is stored in the innerHTML of the target object needs to be constructed with the minimum amount of string construction/destruction possible. This is because garbage collection on some browsers does not reuse memory that is freed up by discarded strings until the page is cleared. The content of the ticker is manufactured when needed and is not stored in a string variable at all:

```
target.innerHTML = theLeadString + theStorySummary.substring(0,theCurrentLength) +
makeWidget() + theSpaceFiller;
```

Styling the Output

The appearance can be controlled with some simple CSS style settings at the top of the file. We just need to create a style for the anchor and define the hover effect. Here is the CSS style to define just those attributes:

```
<STYLE TYPE='text/css'>
    <!--
        A
        {
            font-family: Verdana, Arial, Helvetica, sans-serif;
            font-size: 11px;
            line-height: 11px;
            text-decoration: none;
            color: #333366;
            font-weight: bold;
        }

        A:hover
        {
            color: #CC3300;
        }
    -->
</STYLE>
```

Issues Regarding Screen Updates

During the development of the ticker algorithm, some important pitfalls were found. These were especially problematic with the IE browser on the Macintosh.

Initially, the headline item was composed simply of the text that was visible. This meant that the clickable text in the A tag did not cover the entire frame. It was constantly being replaced to create the animated effect, therefore there was some degree of object construction and destruction going on.

If at the same time the mouse was being rolled over the headline, an event was being generated to indicate mouseOver. This edge detection is fine, as long as the objects being monitored are static and non-moving. Destroying the object that the mouse has just entered, even though another is created, causes some problems to the event handling mechanism, which has some kind of memory handle on the object that was originally rolled over.

Since that object no longer exists, the browser rapidly becomes very confused when the mouseOver event is handled. IE on the Macintosh simply cannot cope with this and the whole thing crashes catastrophically.

The same object boundary problems with mouseOver events were in evidence when the text string "LATEST:" was placed in front of the link but outside the A tag. This is why a background graphic containing that text is placed in the BODY tag. Some leading non-breaking spaces are used to indent the text in the anchor but are included inside the A tag. Some additional trailing non-breaking spaces are also included in the A tag to ensure the clickable object covers the entire area of the frame. Even so, word wrapping comes into play and there is some uncertainty about the right hand edge of the object, though this does not seem to cause as much of a problem.

Memory Leaks and Garbage Collection

In the early trials, a great deal of string concatenation and construction/destruction took place. The visible string was assembled one character at a time on each cycle of the ticker loop. Amazingly, this could consume 50K of memory every few seconds and before long, massive amounts of memory were being used up. This is because JavaScript does not properly clean up its 'Auto Release Pool' until the page is reloaded.

The final version of the ticker uses the sub-stringing capabilities of JavaScript to slice out an increasingly longer portion of the text string and performs no persistent string concatenation. There is evidence on some platforms that a very small memory leak may occur, which is much better than the original version. It would be nice to eliminate these leaks altogether. By way of illustration, the following approach leaks massively:

```
myString = "";
for(iii=0; iii<10; iii++)
{
    myString = myString + "A";
    document.write(myString);
}
```

By contrast, this approach leaks hardly at all, although it appears to waste space by assigning content to myString at the outset:

```
myString = "AAAAAAAAAA";
for(iii=0; iii<10; iii++)
{
    document.write(myString.substring(0,iii));
}
```

Every few minutes, the whole ticker page can be reloaded to avoid any small memory leaks becoming a problem. This was originally done within the JavaScript code based on a count of the number of headlines that had been played out. That has now been removed, and happens courtesy of the main page being reloaded by the browser.

This reloading also has the added benefit that the ticker headline list is likely to be refreshed very soon after the master copy on the web server has been updated. It isn't a perfect synchronization but it's good enough. Usage patterns from the web server logs indicate that people don't stay on the front page for very long before going to read a story and then coming back again. If they do leave the page on display for long periods, then an automated page refresh ensures the ticker is updated periodically. There is a trade off in setting the update period too short. If many hundreds of thousands of users have the front page on display with the ticker, shortening the update time causes a measurable increase in traffic and web server loading.

These memory-leaking problems were observed to be far worse on Windows than on the Macintosh version of IE. This may be due to a variety of reasons dependant on how the underlying memory management is implemented. The Macintosh system software is known to implement a particularly effective garbage collection and memory compacting scheme. Segments of memory within the application heap are moved when necessary to collect all the free space into one contiguous block. While this happens, the memory manager also frees up any purgeable space to keep things neat and tidy.

Our Updated Ticker Design Specification

Let's outline our design criteria for the new ticker implementation:

❑   It should run on as many platforms as possible.

❑   Perhaps the code can be simpler than before.

❑   Passing the data to the ticker should be the most efficient technique and not be limited by the workflow constraints imposed by BBC News Online.

❑   Can we add any functional enhancements to the ticker?

❑   Can we find a better event detection mechanism that does not crash browsers with mouseOver/mouseOut boundary conditions?

❑   Can we place some HTML inside the IFRAME tag that avoids the need for the APPLET tag?

❑   Pose and answer the question "Does DOM standardization really help us in solving a problem like this?"

In our new implementation, lets also simplify things by removing the background graphic and see if we can streamline the main run loop.

Passing Data to the Ticker

Before proceeding with the coding of our new ticker design, we need to choose a means by which we shall import the story headline and URL into the scripting environment.

Passing data to a JavaScript execution context from a back end database is actually quite difficult to do in a portable manner. Probably because of the security implications, it is not possible to request a URL and access its data content as a text string within a variable. It would be useful to have a facility to do something like:

```
myVar = getURL('http://www.abc.com/mydata.txt');
```

This would be great even if there were a limitation, such as the file having to be on the same server that the script came from. It is certainly possible to do it with Java, because the applet we replaced in News Online does that very thing. However, the whole point of this JavaScript implementation is to eliminate the applet, so we can't really use a Java applet as a delegate to fetch the data for us.

Microsoft provides some non-portable solutions to this problem with IE 5, such as the download behavior or an ActiveX control for loading content. Both have the 'same server' restriction but are otherwise fully functional to load a text file into a string variable. However, neither of them work in Netscape or Opera.

There are several portable approaches, each having advantages and disadvantages:

❑ Hidden fields inside a form

❑ Textual content in a hidden frame or layer

❑ Building a document structure from nested DIV blocks

❑ DOM navigation of document structures

❑ XML data islands

❑ JavaScript code inserted or included into the document

We can experiment with some examples that illustrate each of these to discover their limitations.

Hidden Fields

The limiting factor with hiding fields inside a form is that there is no structure implied and it is simply a one-dimensional array of strings. Another disadvantage (although you may not consider it a problem), is that it must be embedded within the same page. You can add structure by embedding mark-up within the data, but that needs to be parsed out somehow. You could carefully hide executable JavaScript in these form fields and then use the eval() function to call it into your script. Here is an example that extracts some hidden JavaScript and uses that technique to insert the text into a DIV block at the top of the page:

```
<HTML>
<SCRIPT LANGUAGE="JavaScript">


function init()
{
    // Locate form element containing the script
    myHiddenScript = document.forms.HiddenData.Content.value;

    // Execute the hidden script data
    eval(myHiddenScript);

    // Locate the target DIV block
    myTarget = document.getElementById("TextBox");


    // Store the values extracted from the script
    myTarget.innerHTML = myData1 + "<HR>" + myData2 + "<HR>" + myData3;
}
</SCRIPT>

<BODY onLoad='init()'>
<DIV ID='TextBox'>
</DIV>
<FORM NAME='HiddenData'>
<INPUT TYPE='HIDDEN' NAME='Content'
VALUE='myData1='Hidden Text String one';
        myData2='Hidden Text String two';
        myData3='Hidden Text String three';'>
</FORM>
</BODY>
</HTML>
```

This is fairly portable. The insertion in `DIV` blocks limits how far back in browser versions you can go, but pulling things out of hidden form fields should work with very old browsers since access to forms data and the `eval()` function have been around for a long time.

Hidden Frames and Layers

This technique passes textual content in a hidden frame or layer. Layers are already risky, because they are deprecated. Hidden frames are a good solution although there is a flaw that we'll consider in a moment. At News Online, the HTML design authorities mandated that we should not use additional frames on the front page. That effectively ruled out that technique, even though it would be a fairly optimal approach. The downside, is that you need to hide the frame somewhere. The same JavaScript `eval()` trick would work though.

There's another more serious shortcoming in this technique, which is to do with the way web browsers load pages and web servers respond to simultaneous requests. The outcome of that, is that you simply cannot be sure when that frame containing the hidden data is loaded. The necessary tricks to set synchronization flags require `onLoad` handlers in the data frame and the ticker, which both call functions in the parent frameset container. That's guaranteed to be loaded, because otherwise the child frames wouldn't have been requested. You can then set semaphores to indicate loading is complete and then access the data conditionally on those semaphores being set. It's all a bit too uncertain and any connection failures and loading errors can cause even more problems.

DOM Navigation

DOM navigation of document structures has been proven to be unworkable. Both IE and Netscape 6 provide the same API to the document content. Unfortunately, they treat whitespace and empty `textNodes` differently, and so the `childNodes` collections that might have been useful for walking down the tree are of no use, because none of the index values correlate between browsers. Indeed, IE on the Macintosh and Windows platforms are even further apart than the Macintosh versions of IE and Netscape 6.

Setting those problems aside, it's quite desirable to use DOM techniques to extract content from within the same document that the `SCRIPT` tag is located.

If only the DOM implementations provided a way to examine the child nodes of an object in a consistent manner, this would be a really useful technique, because the structured `DIV` block approach is widely supported. The biggest problem with DOM is that the interstitial text between each `DIV` tag is treated differently in IE and Netscape. In fact, IE on Macintosh and Windows platforms are significantly different. This means that the `childNodes` collection on each platform puts the child `DIV` blocks in completely different index locations in the collections. You can fix this by manually filtering the `childNodes` collections to discard all the `textNodes`. That way you could walk down the `childNodes` tree.

The DOM situation is under development and the DOM Level 2 traversal and range module provides the necessary filters, node iterators and tree walking capabilities that we currently lack. Without these, the DOM implementations are really so incomplete as to only provide marginal help over and above what we had with DHTML.

Structured DIV Blocks

Building a document structure from nested `DIV` blocks has the same disadvantage of needing to be statically included in the same document, although that can be done with a server-side include. It has the major advantage of providing structure. There are limitations, such that the `ID` values need to be unique and HTML 4 compliant in their naming conventions. That may cause problems with generating ID names algorithmically, so they can be fetched more easily.

So, here is an example data block formatted with DIV tags and showing how to build a simple childNodes filter that produces consistently the same list of childNodes on all browsers:

```
<HTML>
<BODY>
    <DIV ID='Level0' STYLE='display:none'>
    <DIV ID='Level1'>
    <DIV ID='Level2'>
        Content
    </DIV>
    </DIV>
    </DIV>

<SCRIPT LANGUAGE="JavaScript">
    var myArray = new Array();
    var ii;
    var jj;

// Get a reference to the top level <DIV>
myObject = document.getElementById("Level0");

// Filter the childNodes collection
jj = 0;
for(ii=0; ii<myObject.childNodes.length; ii++)
{
    if(myObject.childNodes[ii].id)
    {
        myArray[jj] = myObject.childNodes[ii];
    }
}

// Display filtered childNodes
document.write(myArray.length);
document.write("<BR>");
document.write("<BR>");
for(ii=0; ii<myArray.length; ii++)
{
    document.write(myArray[ii]);
    document.write(" : ");
    document.write(myArray[ii].id);
    document.write("<BR>");
}
</SCRIPT>
</BODY>
</HTML>
```

In the News Online ticker, the DIV blocks are structured so that the content is a collection of several story headline texts and the associated links where we can see a page full of text about the story. The additional meta-data is just an item count, so we know how many stories there are. We could store other meta-data too. We could store some controls for the ticker speed, and how often it should be reloaded.

The entire story content and meta-data tree is also enclosed in a single top-level DIV block. This is helpful, because we can set the style of the block so its display: property makes the DIV block invisible. That's also shown in this simpler example. Without that, the content of the DIV blocks would be visible.

On a site, such as News Online, the news story data for the ticker is published into a separate file and a server-side include is used to insert it into the outgoing response from the web server.

An Alternative Using XML Data Islands

XML data islands are supported by IE 5+ and can be accessed easily from JavaScript but this is not yet available on other browsers in a portable manner.

The XML data island is created with the XML tag. The navigation mechanism is different to that normally used. We would usually expect to build a tree of nodes using ID values assigned as HTML tag attributes. This XML navigation technique uses tag names for navigation and is a lot more powerful.

Here, is an example of a block of XML in the middle of a HTML document:

```
<XML ID='myBlock'>
   <METADATA>
      <OWNER>Wrox</OWNER>
      <DATATYPE>Example</DATATYPE>
      <ABSTRACT>This is an example block of text.</ABSTRACT>
   </METADATA>
</XML>
```

Individual nodes in that so-called data island can be accessed through this XMLDocument property. The object returned by this property responds to the selectSingleNode() method. The argument to this is the slash-separated path to the node within the document you are looking for. The slash-separated values are the XML tagnames used to construct the document.

In this example, they all begin with the string "METADATA", and since the document only contains one layer inside that, all nodes can be reached with the following strings:

❑   METADATA/OWNER

❑   METADATA/DATATYPE

❑   METADATA/ABSTRACT

Given that our XML block has an ID value of "myBlock", this line of script code should yield a reference to an object that encapsulates the ABSTRACT node:

```
myBlock.XMLDocument.selectSingleNode("METADATA/ABSTRACT")
```

Having accessed the DOM node you want, its content can be examined by looking at its text property.

The example code illustrates this concept as it might be assembled together in a simple page:

```
<HTML>
<BODY>
<!-- Create an XML island -->
<XML ID='myBlock'>
   <METADATA>
      <OWNER TYPE='PUBLISHER'>Wrox</OWNER>
      <DATATYPE>Example</DATATYPE>
      <ABSTRACT>This is an example block of text.</ABSTRACT>
   </METADATA>
</XML>

<SCRIPT LANGUAGE="JavaScript">
// Get the XML island block
myXMLBlock = document.getElementById("myBlock");

// Get the DOM document
myXMLDocument = myXMLBlock.XMLDocument;
```

```
    // Find the node
    myNode = myXMLDocument.selectSingleNode("METADATA/ABSTRACT");

    // Display the text in the node
    alert(myNode.text);

    // Now access node attributes and content
    myOwner = myXMLDocument.getElementsByTagName('OWNER')[0];
    alert(myOwner.getAttribute('TYPE') + ': ' + myOwner.text);

</SCRIPT>
</BODY>
</HTML>
```

That lets us have some very convenient access to textual data, but this is only available in Windows-based versions of IE 5+. We can still accomplish largely the same effect with DIV blocks. We can at least build some structure and give them unique ID values.

Inserted and Included JavaScript Code

JavaScript code inserted into the document using an include mechanism, is an ideal solution for getting the data feed into the ticker. At News Online, we found that the data coming from the existing feed could not be changed because other systems depended on it. The format of data was such that valid and syntactically correct JavaScript could not be generated reliably due to the placement of certain quote characters. That won't be a problem for us here as we develop a ticker design from scratch and this is likely to be the approach we shall adopt for our optimally designed ticker.

Here is an example of how we can accomplish this. It is amazingly simple, which also makes it a very attractive option.

Save this fragment of script in a file called data.js:

```
var myData1 = "String one";
var myData2 = "String two";
var myData3 = "String three";
```

Now we can include that file using a <SCRIPT SRC=""> tag:

```
<HTML>
<SCRIPT SRC="data.js"></SCRIPT>
    <SCRIPT LANGUAGE="JavaScript">
    function init()
    {
        // Locate the target DIV block
        myTarget = document.getElementById("TextBox");

        // Store the values extracted from the script
        myTarget.innerHTML = myData1 + "<HR>" + myData2 + "<HR>" + myData3;
    }
    </SCRIPT>
<BODY onLoad='init()'>
<DIV ID='TextBox'>
</DIV>
</BODY>
</HTML>
```

The really neat thing about this approach, is that it factors the ticker code and the data into separate files, and the data in the included file can be rendered from a publishing system quite independently of the ticker software.

Implementing Our New Ticker Design

We need a way to include our ticker into a page. The `IFRAME` technique was good, and although it doesn't work on some older Netscape browsers, we can work around that. We can put in some kind of link that takes the user to a static page containing the headlines. Assuming we are driving this all from a content management system, creating the page containing the headlines should be fairly easy.

So, first of all, here is the code that you need to place into your page to include the ticker:

```
<HTML>
<BODY>
<IFRAME SRC='ticker.html' WIDTH='315' HEIGHT='60'
        SCROLLING='no' FRAMEBORDER='0'>
        <A HREF='headlines.html'>Click here for headlines</A>
</IFRAME>
</BODY>
</HTML>
```

The content of the `ticker.html` file is a combination of HTML, JavaScript, and CSS style control. Here is the main HTML structure with the CSS and JavaScript blocks condensed so you can see the overall layout:

```
<HTML>
<HEAD>
   <STYLE TYPE='text/css'>
      … CSS Styles here …
   </STYLE>
   <SCRIPT SRC="data.js">
   </SCRIPT>
   <SCRIPT LANGUAGE="JavaScript">
      … Ticker execution script here …
   </SCRIPT>
</HEAD>
<BODY onLoad='startTicker();'>
<A ID='Anchor' HREF='/' target=_top></A>
</BODY>
</HTML>
```

In the `HEAD` section, there is a `STYLE` block and two independent `SCRIPT` blocks.

The CSS block is for styling control. The two separate `SCRIPT` blocks are provided to abstract the executable ticker code from the data. The data block is included from a separate file so your content management system can publish new ticker data without having to republish the ticker code. We talked about this a little while ago when we discussed different ways of passing data to the ticker.

The `BODY` of the document is very simple; it's just the `anchor` tag. We set as a criterion the simplification of the design if it was possible. This is a much simpler `BODY` than the original News Online ticker.

The CSS styling is necessary to give us control over the hovering appearance, and to give us a way to eliminate the underscore that the browser automatically places on a link. This reveals a small bug in the Netscape 6 CSS object model, which requires that implemented CSS style properties must be specified, otherwise the rules are not created. This results in an empty `cssRules` collection and crashes the browser:

```
A
{
   display: none;
}
```

The following instantiates a rule and the browser works fine:

```
A
{
   text-decoration: none;
}
```

Here is the content of the STYLE block in the HEAD section of our new ticker:

```
<STYLE TYPE='text/css'>
A
{
   text-decoration: none;
}

A:hover
{
   text-decoration: none;
}
</STYLE>
```

Note that we only define the text-decoration: property. All the others will be defined from script, having located the style object that each of these rules instantiates. You could define more default values here and set up fewer properties in the script.

The first SCRIPT block contains the ticker data:

```
<SCRIPT SRC="data.js">
</SCRIPT>
```

Note that it includes an external file. This provides a good way to integrate things with your content management system. It also separates content from functionality. In this implementation, we can also control rather more of the stylistic appearance than we could with the original BBC News Online ticker. Here is the content of the data.js file. The story texts and URLs have been shortened to save space here:

```
// Control parameters
var theCharacterTimeout = 50;
var theStoryTimeout     = 5000;
var theWidgetOne        = "_";
var theWidgetTwo        = "-";
var theWidgetNone       = "";
var theLeadString       = "LATEST: ";

// Styling parameters
var theBackgroundColor  = "white";
var theForegroundColor  = "#333366";
var theFontFamily       = "Verdana, Arial, Helvetica, sans-serif";
var theFontSize         = "11px";
var theLineHeight       = "11px";
var theFontWeight       = "bold";
var theTextDecoration   = "none";
var theHoverColor       = "#CC3300";

// Content parameters
var theSummaries = new Array();
var theSiteLinks = new Array();

var theItemCount = 4;

theSummaries[0] = "This is the stext for story 1";
theSiteLinks[0] = story1.htm";
```

```
theSummaries[1] = "Here is story 2.";
theSiteLinks[1] = "/newsid_1405000/1405821.htm";

theSummaries[2] = "Story three has its headline here";
theSiteLinks[2] = "./Story3.html";

theSummaries[3] = "This is headline number four";
theSiteLinks[3] = "/stories/Four.htm";
```

The variable names should be fairly obvious. The control variables are similar to the ones that existed before, except that we can access them externally. There is an additional widget value that is placed at the end of the text, only when the story headline is complete. The leading string is also defined here instead of requiring a background image.

The CSS style property names are reflected in the variables that contain their values. These are assigned to the appropriate properties belonging to the style objects for the A rule, the A:hover rule and the document body object. This will become apparent shortly when we walk through the code.

The second SCRIPT block contains the functional code that makes the ticker work. This is much simpler than the original design we looked at. We'll work through the various components in there, starting with the more basic ones first.

It is necessary to construct a series of non-breaking spaces separated by breaking spaces so that they can be placed on the end of the anchor text so as to completely fill the IFRAME. This helps the UI to be a little more responsive and because of memory leak avoidance, this was done as a constant in the BBC ticker. Here it is created with a small function. There might be a memory leak due to the string concatenations, but because this is called only once it should not cause a serious problem. Here is the function that builds the space filler:

```
function buildSpaceFiller(aCount)
{
   var myResult = "";

   for(var ii=0; ii<aCount; ii++)
   {
      myResult = myResult + "  ";
   }

   return myResult;
}
```

We need to generate a widget character to create an animated golf ball effect, while the text 'teletypes' out. This function does the same job as the earlier example with one difference. Here we also return a special widget if we are at the end of the line which allows us to place a trailing symbol on the output if we want to. That could be done with a small IMG item. Here is the widget generator:

```
function whatWidget()
{
   if(theCurrentLength == theStorySummary.length)
   {
      return theWidgetNone;
   }

   if((theCurrentLength % 2) == 1)
   {
      return theWidgetOne;
   }
   else
   {
```

```
            return theWidgetTwo;
    }
}
```

There are just two functions left to describe. One starts the ticker after initializing all the style settings, while the other is the ticker `run` loop that calls itself with the `setTimeout()` function. Let's look at the start up function first:

```
function startTicker()
{
    // Define run time values
    theCurrentStory    = -1;
    theCurrentLength   = 0;
    theSpaceFiller     = buildSpaceFiller(200);


    // Locate base objects
    theAnchorObject    = document.getElementById("Anchor");

    // Locate style sheet objects
    theStyleSheet = document.styleSheets[0];


    // Fix the missing cssRules property for MSIE
    if(!theStyleSheet.cssRules)
    {
        theStyleSheet.cssRules = theStyleSheet.rules;
    }

    // Locate the style objects we want to modify
    theBodyStyle   = document.body.style;
    theAnchorStyle = theStyleSheet.cssRules[0].style;
    theHoverStyle  = theStyleSheet.cssRules[1].style;

    // Apply data driven style changes
    theBodyStyle.backgroundColor = theBackgroundColor;

    theAnchorStyle.color = theForegroundColor;
    theAnchorStyle.fontFamily = theFontFamily;
    theAnchorStyle.fontSize = theFontSize;
    theAnchorStyle.lineHeight = theLineHeight;
    theAnchorStyle.fontWeight = theFontWeight;
    theAnchorStyle.textDecoration = theTextDecoration;

    theHoverStyle.color = theHoverColor;

    // Fire up the ticker
    runTheTicker();
}
```

First, we call the `spaceFiller` and define some initial default values. Then we locate the `anchor` object using the `getElemerntById()` method. We then locate the `styleSheets` collection for the document and fix it up to correct the missing `cssRules` property on IE browsers.

Following that fix, we can then locate the `style` objects for the two CSS rules in the `STYLE` tags, one for all `anchor` elements, and the other for the pseudo element that applies style to anchors when they are being hovered over. We also locate the `style` object for the document body.

Having located all of these `style` objects, we now assign values to various properties, using the variables that were defined in the included content file (`data.js`).

Finally, we call the main ticker `run` loop to start things rolling.

Here is the code for that main animation function:

```
function runTheTicker()
{
    var myTimeout;

    // Go for the next story data block
    if(theCurrentLength == 0)
    {
        theCurrentStory++;
        theCurrentStory      = theCurrentStory % theItemCount;
        theStorySummary      = theSummaries[theCurrentStory];
        theTargetLink        = theSiteLinks[theCurrentStory];
        theAnchorObject.href = theTargetLink;
    }

    // Stuff the current ticker text into the anchor
    theAnchorObject.innerHTML = theLeadString +
theStorySummary.substring(0,theCurrentLength) + whatWidget() + theSpaceFiller;

    // Modify the length for the substring and define the timer
    if(theCurrentLength != theStorySummary.length)
    {
        theCurrentLength++;
        myTimeout = theCharacterTimeout;
    }
    else
    {
        theCurrentLength = 0;
        myTimeout = theStoryTimeout;
    }

    // Call up the next cycle of the ticker
    setTimeout("runTheTicker()", myTimeout);

}
```

This is much simpler than the earlier version. Several unnecessary variables are eliminated and all state preservation is accomplished using `theCurrentLength` value. Several duplicate fragments of code have been eliminated by moving the widget generator into a function as well as by pulling common code outside of the conditional test for whether we are at the end or in the middle of a line of ticker playout.

As we have totally eliminated all the DOM `childNodes` problems, this now works fine on IE and Netscape 6, although there are still some necessary functionalities missing from the Opera browser's JavaScript implementation that prevents the ticker from running.

Summary

We have examined a working case history of a ticker being used in a very busy site. We've learned that the design criteria that seemed reasonable in 1999, do not hold up over time and this gives us some cause for concern. We might make similar judgement calls now and still encounter similar problems with browsers because we did not anticipate their behavior. Hopefully, the continuing standards creation and evolution will address those issues and in time they will be less severe. A standards-based approach is probably the safest course.

We have looked at several alternative ways to solve our problems, and have designed a far better ticker. Around the time this book is published, that new ticker (or something similar to it), will be in daily use on the BBC News Online web site.

So, returning to our new design criteria, let's see if we have satisfied our original goals:

- ❑ It now runs on more platform/browser combinations than it did before.

- ❑ The code is most definitely simpler and is about half the length it was before.

- ❑ We now have a really optimum data passing mechanism and it could still be integrated into the workflow of a content management process.

- ❑ We have added significant style control functionality.

- ❑ We didn't find a better event control mechanism, but the behavior appears to be stable and doesn't crash.

- ❑ We have replaced the need for the APPLET by allowing the user to call an external page of headlines. We could replace that with all of the ticker headlines in place, but that might change the geometry of the page.

- ❑ DOM standardization does not really help us in solving a problem like this, because DOM is not nearly complete enough to be useful. We really need traversal and range to be implemented, or we have to write filter scripts to eliminate unwanted text nodes from the child node collections.

Pro JavaScript 2nd Edition

Shopping Cart Application

In this chapter, we will be developing an online shopping cart that does everything apart from take the money from your credit card. By the end of the chapter, a shopping cart class and a couple of supporting classes will have been created, which you can drop into your own pages for an instant shopping basket addition to your e-commerce web site. We'll only be looking at the client-side of things in this chapter, so our product lists won't be generated from database information, When an item is purchased, no deduction from stock in the database will be made – all things a full e-commerce system would do. Our system will, however, take us from the user adding an item to their basket, to displaying the contents of their basket and on to the checkout and actually buying the items, although as we mentioned, we won't be dealing with the server-side credit card transactions and database updating.

The shopping cart class has been designed to be easy to modify to allow you to make it fit your particular requirements. You may well want to extend it further and add extra features.

We'll start by taking an overview of the system in terms of what we want to achieve, what our web site is going to look like and how on a higher technical level the application works. Then we will turn to the task of actually creating the system, first by building the basic web site, and then by creating the JavaScript classes that will provide the shopping cart and checkout functionality and adding these to the web site.

Overview

We will be adding our shopping cart application to a fake online music web site called MusicMad.com. This will simply provide a framework on which to insert our code so that we can see it in action. We'll start in this section by looking at some of the aims of the system, then we'll look at a site map of MusicMad.com to give a better idea of what we'll be creating, and finally we'll take a technical overview of how we'll be doing things.

Goals

Before we start, we need to work out certain details, things like what we'd like our application to do. We have two sets of people we're looking to please. First and foremost is the visitors to our web site, our customers. We need to ensure that the visit to our web site is a pleasant and painless one. The easier it is to look at goods and purchase them, the the more likely the customer is to do so. Goal number one should be a user-friendly web site.

The second set of people we are catering for developers, more than likely that's us. By this we mean that the code we create must be easily extensible. It's likely that in the future more features will be added to the web site and refinements made to existing features, all of which means a developer going back over the code and making the changes. That developer might be us, so let's make our life easy by making the code easily extensible. This is goal number two.

User Friendliness

It may sound mercenary, but at the end of the day the primary aim of any e-commerce system is to extract money from the customer in exchange for some goods or services. We want to make this as easy, painless, and efficient as possible. The fewer barriers in the way of the customer buying something, then the more likely it is that they will reach the stage where we take money from them. A customer abandoning an online purchase part way through is very common. With this in mind, our aims should be to make it easy for a customer to:

❏ Add an item to the basket

❏ See what items they've selected so far

❏ Alter items selected – delete or update item quantities

❏ Go straight to the checkout and buy the items

❏ Leave the web site, close down the browser, and come back another day and not to have to re-select their items

❏ Enter their personal and credit card details quickly and easily at the checkout in a nice logical manner

❏ See a summary of what they will be buying as confirmation before going ahead and committing themselves to the order

❏ See a confirmation that the orders been placed and is on its way

In addition to being user friendly, we also want to make it user system friendly – that is, design the system to work with what are currently the most commonly used browsers, including Netscape Navigator 4+ and Internet Explorer 4+.

Extensibility

We've seen above how important it is to make life easy for the customer, but it's also important to make life easy for the developers. The aim of our system is that it will be re-used repeatedly in different circumstances. It's likely, therefore, that while it suits selling CDs, books, and so on, it would need to be adapted for other goods. Even if this were not the case, we are likely to want to extend and improve the system over time. Our aims should therefore, be that the system is easily:

❏ Incorporated in different situations

❏ Modifiable without the need for a complete re-write

❏ Extendable - it should provide firm foundations on which to build

Screen Flow

Shown below is a series of screenshots showing the screen flow from the home page, to adding an item, to going to the checkout, entering customer details, seeing the final order summary, and finally reaching the order completed page. The complete code for this site and the chapter can be downloaded from the usual place at http://www.wrox.com. This shopping cart application can also be seen online at http://pawilton.com/projs/musicmad/MusicMad.htm.

Shown above is the initial home page, `MusicMad.htm`, which is a frameset defining page that loads `top_menu.htm` into the top frame and `home.htm` into the lower frame. The top menu bar allows the user to view their basket, go to the checkout, or go to one of the music categories. The main page itself has links to the music categories.

If the user clicks the easy listening category, then he or she will be taken to the screen shown below. This contains details of CDs available to buy under that category. Clicking Add to Basket adds one item to the basket:

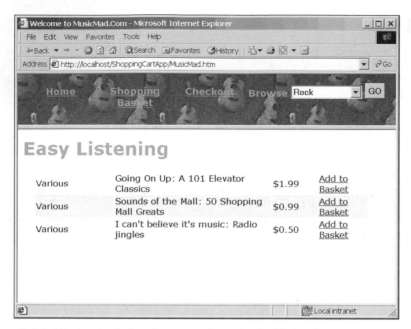

The user can click Add to Basket link in the screen above for the "Going On Up: 101 Elevator Classics"
CD. We add the item to their basket as shown in the screen below. This displays a summary of the basket
including the final price. To change quantities of an item, the user changes the value in the Quantity text box
and clicks Update Quantities. Setting the value to zero removes the item from the basket.

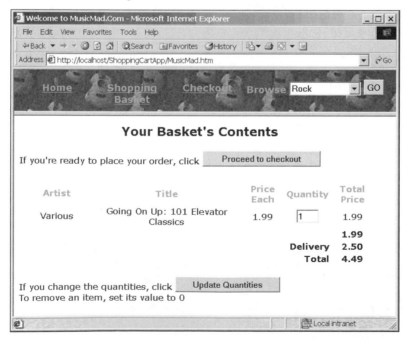

If the user clicks the Proceed to checkout button in the screen above, they are then directed to the main checkout screen shown below. Here, they have the option to change the items in the basket, continue shopping, or click Next to start entering their information:

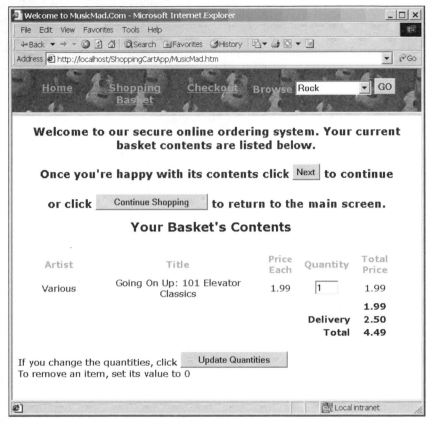

Users click Next to enter their information and are taken to the screen below where they can enter their personal details necessary to completion of the order. All the form elements are validated using client-side script to prevent the user forgetting to enter a value or entering a value incorrectly:

If the user clicks Continue, they are taken to the credit card page. In a live situation, this would be over some sort of secure link, such as **Secure Sockets Layer** (SSL), to ensure hackers could not intercept and read the information sent. Again, all details are validated so only valid card numbers and expiry dates are allowed:

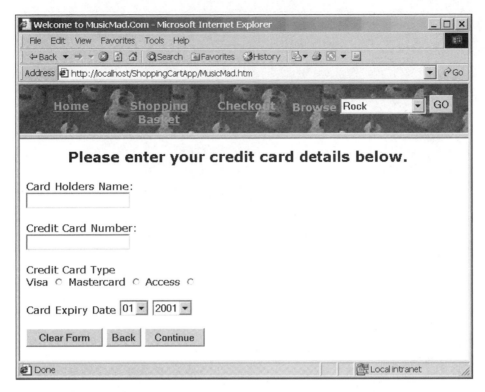

When the user clicks Continue in the screen above, they are taken to a final order summary screen where everything to do with their order is displayed, with the final amount, payment method, and delivery address being particularly important. This gives the user a chance to double check what they've entered, which ensures things are less likely to go wrong and the order reaches the customer. The credit card number is clearly fake, and only got through because the code was changed to allow the screen to be viewed:

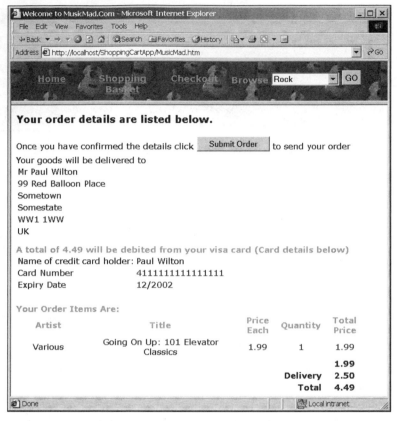

The user can then confirm their order and click Submit Order; this completes the online order and a suitable order completion screen is shown as below:

Technical Overview

To help make the code easily extensible and simple to add to web pages, the vast majority of the code has been split into five JavaScript classes contained in four separate `.js` files. We'll see that outside these classes there is very little code, and this helps keep our pages simple and manageable. As the code is centralized in one place, if we make a change to a method of our classes, it's automatically reflected in all the pages that use it.

The five classes are the `ShoppingBasket`, `ShoppingItem`, `Validate`, `Customer`, and `CreditCard` classes. Note that both `ShoppingBasket` and `ShoppingItem` are in the same `.js` file, `ShoppingBasket.js`. The class names give away their purpose, and we will look at them in much more detail in the next section. We instantiate objects based on these classes in the top frame of the web site, which never gets unloaded. This way the information we store about the goods in the basket, the customer, or their credit card, are not lost as the user moves from page to page. This has the advantage that we don't need to use cookies to store the basket – instead, variables inside the `ShoppingBasket` class hold the details. If, however, the user's browser does support cookies, then we make use of them to store the basket so that if the user leaves our web site, closes down the browser, and returns at another time, then we can still restore the basket.

Creating the Shopping Cart Application

We've talked enough about the shopping cart application, so now let's start to create the pages and code. We'll start by creating the basic web pages to which we'll add our code. Then we'll move on to the JavaScript classes, which we'll code up a class at a time and add them to our pages.

Creating the Basic Web Pages

As the HTML of the pages is simple and really just a framework for us to hang our code on, we'll create them without much detailed comment. They are available in the code download from http://www.wrox.com/, and are contained in a sub-folder named Bare Bones. The files contain only the HTML shell we need to start with, and which we will add to throughout the chapter. The completed files are available in the folder called Final Product.

We'll start with the pages that form the basics of the site:

❑ `Musicmad.htm`. This page defines the frames into which we load our other pages. It's in this page that the global web site accessible instances of objects based on our five classes will be created. As this page is always loaded and it's the pages within the frames that change as the user navigates the web site, any variables declared in this frame will remain in existence for the duration of the user's visit.

❑ `top_menu.htm`. This is the page that goes in the top frame. It provides links to the checkout, shopping basket, and the two music categories.

❑ `home.htm`. This is the default home page that appears in the bottom frame.

❑ `RockListing.htm`. This page is the one that lists all the CDs we have for sale in the rock category. In a full e-commerce system, this page would be created dynamically based on data from a database. However, for the purposes of our application, the CDs available are hard coded. We'll see later how they become added to the shopping basket.

❑ `EasyListeningListing.htm`. This is the easy listening category full of wonderful classics, which we create using the same principles as above.

❑ `viewbasket.htm`. This page will be used to display the contents of a shopping basket, with the HTML being written into the page using the `ShoppingBasket` class that we'll create later. Note the empty DIV tags, which will be used later, by our JavaScript, to display the shopping basket contents by writing the HTML into the DIV.

❑ emptybasket.htm. If the basket is empty, then we need a page for that. We have a couple of links to our music categories to encourage the user to browse the web site, and hopefully fill their basket. We could have just one page to display both a shopping basket and an empty basket warning, but it has been separated into two to keep things simple and easily maintainable.

The final few pages deal with a user who has filled their basket and clicked to go to the checkout and buy the goods:

❑ checkout_frame.htm. This page is another frameset defining page that splits the first checkout page to be displayed in the lower of our current two frames. The top frame will give the user options to continue with the checkout and fill in the necessary details for a purchase or continue shopping. The lower frame will display the basket and allow the user to make final modifications to quantities if they so wish before continuing with the ordering process.

❑ checkout.htm. This is the page to go in the top frame of the checkout frame set.

❑ checkoutbasket.htm. This is the page that goes in the bottom checkout frame.

❑ PersonalDetails.htm. If the user has decided they are happy with their basket and now wants to start the online ordering, they then come to this page below where they are asked for their personal details necessary for the order.

❑ CheckoutCredit.htm. Once the user has filled in the personal details form they can click Continue to move onto this page, where we get those all-important credit card details. Again, if this were a live shopping application we would need to make sure the user's card details were kept secure by using SSL.

❑ CheckoutConfirm.htm. Once they've entered their card details correctly and clicked Continue, they are taken to the final summary page where all the details of their order gathered are displayed as final confirmation before submitting the order.

❑ OrderComplete.htm. Finally, the user clicks to Submit Order and is taken to this page, which displays an order complete message.

Finally, we have our .css style sheet, which defines style classes for the whole web site. This page is called WebsiteGlobalStyle.css.

We've now completed the basic HTML for our web site, and in the next sections we'll be adding to this skeleton and creating the online shopping application. We'll start by concentrating on creating the shopping basket functionality, first be adding and deleting items, then displaying the basket, and finally we'll see how to save its contents for a later user session. With the shopping part of the application out the way, we'll then turn to the all-important paying for the goods part, the checkout. Here we'll see how to efficiently collect the user's information, such as personal and address details, then we'll obtain their credit card details. At the end we'll display a final summary so the user can feel sure that what they are agreeing to buy is actually what they want. After this point the server-side transactions would take place, monies would be debited, and goods would be detailed for sending. As we're not looking at the server-side aspect, we'll simply have a page thanking them for their order.

Creating the Shopping Basket

In this section, we're going to create the classes linked to the shopping basket functionality of the web site. Once we've created the two classes, we'll then update our web page and add the code necessary to use the classes to provide the shopping basket for the web site, but not the purchasing functionality as that would have to be provided by server-side code.

The ShoppingItem Class

The ShoppingItem class is very simple. Its purpose is to store a single item and its details, such as artist, description, quantity, and price. It also stores the unique reference ID that each item has. It's only used by the ShoppingBasket class, which has an array of object instances of the ShoppingItem class with each representing an item in the user's basket.

As we'll see shortly, the code consists of the class constructor and various methods for getting or setting values of an item, such as quantity and description. Why use methods for this, rather than simply accessing the properties of the class directly? JavaScript is a very easygoing language; it's untyped and it let's us add properties to objects simply by using the property name. This may make things easy, but it also allows errors to emerge that are difficult to track down. For example, our ShoppingItem class has the itemArtist property. We could set it like this:

```
myShoppingItemInstance.itemArtist = "REM";
```

Then get the value like this:

```
alert(myShoppingItemInstance.itemArtist);
```

Everything is fine, unless we make a typing error and try this:

```
myShoppingItemInstance.itemArtst = "REM";
```

Difficult to spot, stops the code working, and produces no error message. When we do this:

```
alert(myShoppingItemInstance.itemArtist);
```

Nothing appears as we've not set that property, we set the property with a typo, which JavaScript has kindly added to our object for us.

However, JavaScript is much more strict about methods. If we call a method on an object that doesn't exist then we'll get an error. So, by using methods to get and set the properties and not setting them directly, we are making life easier for ourselves as any mistakes in the names of methods will have JavaScript's interpreter alerting us to the source of the problem.

Let's start by creating our ShoppingItem class, first by creating the constructor:

```
// ShoppingBasket.js
function ShoppingItem(itemRefId, itemArtist, itemDesc, itemPrice, itemQty)
{
    this.itemRefId = itemRefId;
    this.itemArtist = itemArtist;
    this.itemDesc = itemDesc;
    this.itemPrice = itemPrice;
    this.itemQty = itemQty;
}
```

When we create a new object instance of our class, we need to pass the five arguments to its constructor, which is used to set the various item properties. The this keyword refers to the object instance of this class. So this.itemRefId will refer to that object instance's itemRefId property. For our CD web site, each item has five attributes, a unique reference ID, artist name, description, and price. We also have the quantity the customer has ordered.

Now we have the task of creating the methods, which will get or set the values of the five properties. They all follow the same pattern with just changes of name, so we'll look at the first one in more detail than the others:

```
ShoppingItem.prototype.getItemRefId = function()
{
    return this.itemRefId;
}

ShoppingItem.prototype.setItemRefId = function(itemRefId)
{
    this.itemRefId = itemRefId;
}
```

We use the prototype property to specify we want to add a method to the ShoppingItem class. That way all objects instantiated, based on this class, will have the method specified, in this case the getItemRefId and setItemRefId methods. We set the method to reference the function object we create straight after. We could create the function earlier and then specify that the method refers to it; there's no right or wrong way. However, this way is preferred as we save ourselves, and other pages using the code, the trouble of polluting the namespace with all the otherwise globally defined functions. Remember from earlier chapters that functions, like most things in JavaScript, are objects themselves. We're simply saying that the getItemRefId property of the prototype property of the ShoppingItem class should refer to the function object.

The first method has no parameters; that is, the function we create has no parameters, but simply returns the itemRefId. The second method has one parameter, the itemRefId we want the object's itemRefId property setting to. We simply set the value, but in the setItemRefId method we could additionally do validity checks or calculations.

The remaining get and set methods for the other properties are shown below:

```
ShoppingItem.prototype.getItemArtist = function()
{
    return this.itemArtist;
}

ShoppingItem.prototype.setItemArtist = function(itemArtist)
{
    this.itemArtist = itemArtist;
}

ShoppingItem.prototype.getItemDesc = function()
{
    return this.itemDesc;
}

ShoppingItem.prototype.setItemDesc = function(itemDesc)
{
    this.itemDesc = itemDesc;
}

ShoppingItem.prototype.getItemPrice = function()
{
    return this.itemPrice;
}

ShoppingItem.prototype.setItemPrice = function(itemPrice)
{
    // convert to number then set itemPrice
    this.itemPrice = Number(itemPrice);
}

ShoppingItem.prototype.getItemQty = function()
{
    return this.itemQty;
```

```
    }

    ShoppingItem.prototype.setItemQty = function(itemQty)
    {
        // convert to number then set itemQty
        this.itemQty = Number(itemQty);
    }
```

Create a file called `ShoppingBasket.js` and place the code in there. We'll also be adding the `ShoppingBasket` class to this file next, which is why we've called the file `ShoppingBasket.js`. The `ShoppingBasket` is the important class, `ShoppingItem` is a class it relies on and that is why we'll include it in the same file. Although strictly speaking the class could have a separate file, its purpose is so intertwined with the `ShoppingBasket` class that it's worth keeping the two together.

The ShoppingBasket Class

Now we turn to our core class, as far as our shopping cart application is concerned. The `ShoppingBasket` class provides all the methods and stores all the information necessary for our online shopping basket. As we'll see later, the object instance of this class will be created in the `Musicmad.htm` page, the frameset page that remains loaded throughout the visitor's browsing of the web site. This means any information stored in the class object remains in existence until the user either closes the browser or goes to another web site. However, even if they do either of these things we have code that persists the shopping basket's contents by using cookies, if the user has enabled them in his or her browser. If the user comes back within three months, then the basket is recreated by using the saved cookie information.

We'll start by creating the methods to add and delete items to the basket. Then we'll write the methods to display the basket's contents and allow the user to update the quantities. Next, we'll add some methods that will be necessary for the final checkout, when we need to display a summary of the basket. Finally, we'll look at how we can save and load the basket. As we do all this, we'll update the web site's pages so we can see things develop as we go along.

The Constructor

Before we can start generating our methods, we need to create the class constructor. Add the following to `ShoppingBasket.js`:

```
    function ShoppingBasket()
    {
        this.items = new Object();
        this.numItems = 0;
        this.deliveryCost = "2.50";
    }
```

It doesn't take any arguments, but just carries out some initialization of the object's properties. We begin by setting the `items` property to a new `Object` object. The `Object` object is the top-level object from which all JavaScript objects inherit their methods and properties, the mother of all objects as it were. We won't be adding any methods or properties to the object store in items, but will simply use it as a type of collection, or associative array that will hold the `ShoppingItem` objects that make up the user's basket. JavaScript has two ways of accessing properties of an object. The first is by using the property's name after a dot:

```
    myObject.myProperty;
```

The second is via square brackets, the same way arrays operate and are accessed, remember these are also objects in JavaScript:

```
myObject["myProperty"];
```

In the second method, we're passing a string in the square brackets that contains the name of the property. What we'll be doing in our code is storing each basket item in the items object as properties, but using the square brackets method to store and access them, with the unique item reference ID as the property name. We'll see more on this shortly. The advantage with the first way of accessing properties is speed, because we access the property directly, though the speed difference is normally too small to matter. With the second method using square brackets, JavaScript has to do a bit of processing first to work out which property we mean. Generally speaking, the first method is preferred, as well as being more efficient it's also more readable. However the advantage of the second way is that we can determine at run time, that is as the code is executed, which property we want to access. This ability to change the property being accessed at run time is the main advantage of the second method.

In the final two lines of the constructor, we initialize the numItems and deliveryCost variables. Property numItems will be used to keep track of how many items we have in the basket. The deliveryCost property contains the cost of delivery for the items, and it is used when creating the summary of costs. We've used a string rather than a number here, as we use the property to concatenate onto a HTML summary of the basket. However, it's easy enough to convert it to a number when the time comes.

Adding and Removing Shopping Basket Items

Next, we'll create a method that will add a new item to the shopping basket. This code snippet should be attached to ShoppingBasket.js:

```
ShoppingBasket.prototype.addItem = function(itemRefId, itemArtist, itemDesc,
    itemPrice, itemQty)
{
    if (typeof(this.items[itemRefId]) == "undefined")
    {
        this.items[itemRefId] = new ShoppingItem(itemRefId, itemArtist,
            itemDesc, itemPrice, itemQty);
        this.numItems++;
    }
    else
    {
        this.items[itemRefId].setItemQty(itemQty);
    }
}
```

At the top of the method we check to see that the item is not already in the basket. If it is not already in the item's associative array, the type of value returned using itemRefId is undefined, and then we know there is no current item with the same unique reference ID. We create a new ShoppingItem object and pass the item details to the constructor. This object is added to the items array, and the numItems property is updated to reflect the new addition to the basket.

If the item was already in the basket, then instead of adding it again, we update the quantity of the existing item. Deleting an item from the shopping basket is even easier:

```
ShoppingBasket.prototype.deleteItem = function(itemRefId)
{
    if (typeof(this.items[itemRefId]) != "undefined")
    {
        delete this.items[itemRefId];
        this.numItems--;
    }
}
```

We check that the item does actually exist, as we did in the addItem() method, then we use the delete operator to remove the property from the items object, with the reference ID contained in itemRefId. Then we decrement numItems to note the change.

Let's update our web site to incorporate the new methods, we won't need the deleteItem method until later, so we'll see addItem used.

First, we need to alter the Musicmad.htm page so that we incorporate our .js script and create a new object based on the ShoppingCart class. The changes are to the top of the page, and are shown below:

```
<!-- MusicMad.htm -->
<HTML>
<HEAD>
    <TITLE>Welcome to MusicMad.Com</TITLE>
    <SCRIPT LANGUAGE='JavaScript' SRC='ShoppingBasket.js'></SCRIPT>
    <SCRIPT LANGUAGE='JavaScript'>
        // Global Variables
        var myBasket = new ShoppingBasket();
    </SCRIPT>
</HEAD>
```

We add the .js file using the SRC attribute on the SCRIPT element, and then in the second script block, we declare the myBasket variable and set it to reference a new object instance of our ShoppingBasket class.

The next pages that need changing are the RockListing.htm and EasyListeningListing.htm pages. To the link next to each item listed that says **Add to Basket**, we'll add the onClick event handler. Once we've completed one, the rest follow the same pattern, so we'll look at the first change in more detail.

Open the RockListing.htm page and make the changes shown below:

```
<!-- RockListing.htm -->
<HTML>
<HEAD>
    <LINK REL='stylesheet' HREF='WebsiteGlobalStyle.css'>
</HEAD>
<BODY>
    <H1>Rock</H1>
    <DIV ALIGN='center'>
    <TABLE>
    <TR CLASS='ProductListStyle1'>
        <TD CLASS='Artist'>
            Radiohead
        </TD>
        <TD CLASS='Title'>
            Kid A
        </TD>
        <TD CLASS='Price'>
            $12.99
        </TD>
        <TD CLASS='AddToBasket'>
            <A HREF='ViewBasket.htm'
                onClick='window.parent.myBasket.addItem(
                    "RK1234", "Radiohead", "Kid A", 12.99, 1)'>
                Add to Basket
            </A>
        </TD>
    </TR>
    <TR CLASS='ProductListStyle2'>
        <TD CLASS='Artist'>
```

```
           Radiohead
       </TD>
       <TD CLASS='Title'>
           Ok Computer
       </TD>
       <TD CLASS='Price'>
           $12.99
       </TD>
       <TD CLASS='AddToBasket'>
           <A HREF='ViewBasket.htm'
               onClick='window.parent.myBasket.addItem(
                   "RK1236", "Radiohead", "Ok Computer", 12.99, 1)'>
               Add to Basket
           </A>
       </TD>
   </TR>
   <TR CLASS='ProductListStyle1'>
       <TD CLASS='Artist'>
           REM
       </TD>
       <TD CLASS='Title'>
           Automatic for the People
       </TD>
       <TD CLASS='Price'>
           $10.99
       </TD>
       <TD CLASS='AddToBasket'>
           <A HREF='ViewBasket.htm'
               onClick='window.parent.myBasket.addItem(
                   "RK1235", "REM", "Automatic for the People", 10.99, 1)'>
               Add to Basket
           </A>
       </TD>
   </TR>
   </TABLE>
   </DIV>
</BODY>
</HTML>
```

Let's look at the change to the first item, Radiohead's Kid A CD:

```
       <TD CLASS='AddToBasket'>
           <A HREF='ViewBasket.htm'
               onClick="window.parent.myBasket.addItem(
                   "RK1234", "Radiohead", "Kid A", 12.99, 1)'>
               Add to Basket
           </A>
       </TD>
```

With the hyperlink, we've added code to the onClick event handler that calls the addItem method of the object referenced in the myBasket variable in the Musicmad.htm top frameset-defining page. The onClick event handler's code will be called before the actual link is followed and ViewBasket.htm is loaded. This is vital, as we need to add the item first before displaying the basket's contents. In the onClick we call addItem() and pass it the details of the item in the method's parameters, which are the unique item reference ID, the name of the artist, description of the item, its price, and finally the quantity to be added, which we've set to 1. In a full e-commerce web site that included the server-side code, we'd most likely generate the onClick part dynamically with the item properties being drawn from a database of stock. For our client-side only example, we just hard code them.

The changes for the remaining items follow the same pattern; the item details only change to reflect the CD's details. Let's now change the `EasyListeningListing.htm` page in a similar manner:

```
<!-- EasyListeningListing.htm -->

    ...

        <TR CLASS='ProductListStyle1'>

            ...

        <TD CLASS='AddToBasket'>
            <A HREF='ViewBasket.htm'
                onClick='window.parent.myBasket.addItem(
                    "EL1234", "Various",
                    "Going On Up: 101 Elevator Classics",
                    1.99, 1)'>
                Add to Basket
            </A>
        </TD>

            ...

        <TR CLASS='ProductListStyle2'>

            ...

        <TD CLASS='AddToBasket'>
            <A HREF='ViewBasket.htm'
                onClick='window.parent.myBasket.addItem(
                    "EL1235", "Various",
                    "Sounds of the Mall: 50 Shopping Mall Greats",
                    0.99, 1)'>
                Add to Basket
            </A>
        </TD>

            ...

        <TR CLASS='ProductListStyle1'>

            ...

        <TD CLASS='AddToBasket'>
            <A HREF='ViewBasket.htm'
                onClick='window.parent.myBasket.addItem(
                    "EL1236", "Various",
                    "I can&#39t believe it&#39s music: Radio jingles",
                    0.50, 1)'>
                Add to Basket
            </A>
        </TD>
```

So that we can select the categories using the drop down combo box, let's also change the `top_menu.htm` page, and add some code. First, let's alter the SELECT element's definition and add an onChange event handler that will call a function to change the category displayed:

```
              <SELECT NAME='cboBrowse' SIZE='1'
                  onChange='selectMusicListing()'>
                  <OPTION VALUE='RockListing.htm'>
                      Rock
                  </OPTION>
                  <OPTION VALUE='EasyListeningListing.htm'>
                      Easy Listening
                  </OPTION>
              </SELECT>
```

Next we need to add the event handler for the cmdGo button that is to the right of the select control:

```
<INPUT TYPE="button" VALUE="GO" ID=cmdGo NAME=cmdGo
      onclick="selectMusicListing()">
```

This also calls the selectMusicListing() function, it's useful where the main frame and the select control get out of sync. For example, the select control has the rock option chosen, but the user has moved onto a different page, for example the basket page, and wants to go back to the rock category, the select controls change event is not going to fire if they simply select rock again so instead the user needs to click the Go button.

Now we need to create the selectMusicListing() function we're using in the onChange event handler. In the page's <HEAD>, add a script block and the following code:

```
<SCRIPT LANGUAGE='JavaScript'>
    function selectMusicListing()
    {
        var sURL = document.frmMenu.cboBrowse
          .options[document.frmMenu.cboBrowse.selectedIndex].value;
        window.parent.fraMain.location.href = sURL;
    }
</SCRIPT>
```

We can now go to the Music Mad web site and click the category links and add items. Unfortunately, the shopping basket page just displays an error, as we've not yet added the code to generate a shopping basket, so let's do that next.

Displaying the Basket's Contents and Updating Quantities

So we can actually see if the add basket methods working let's turn to the code that displays the current contents of the shopping basket. The method will be relying on a function named fix() that we need to create first and add to our ShoppingBasket.js file:

```
ShoppingBasket.prototype.fixDecimalPlaces = function
  (fixNumber, decimalPlaces)
{
    var lDiv = Math.pow(10,decimalPlaces);
    fixNumber = new String((Math.round(fixNumber * (lDiv)))/lDiv);

    var zerosRequired;
    var decimalPointLocation = fixNumber.lastIndexOf(".");
    if (decimalPointLocation == -1)
    {
        fixNumber = fixNumber + ".";
        zerosRequired = decimalPlaces;
    }
    else
    {
        zerosRequired = decimalPlaces -
```

```
            (fixNumber.length - decimalPointLocation - 1);
    }

    for (; zerosRequired > 0; zerosRequired--)
        fixNumber = fixNumber + "0";

    return fixNumber;
}
```

This function is a utility function that fixes a number passed as the first argument to the number of decimal places specified in the second argument. We'll use it to stop the final summary of costs returning numbers like 1.995 – we just want two decimal places for all the price figures.

The function starts by raising setting 1Div as 10 to the power of the number of decimal places. We then use this on the second line to multiply our fixNumber so that all the numbers we want to keep after the decimal place are moved to the left of the decimal point. For example, if our fixNumber was 2.379 and we want it fixed to two decimal places:

❑   1Div would equal 100 (2 to the power of 10)

❑   fixNumber * (100) is 237.9

❑   round(237.9) gives 238

238 is then divided down again using 1Div which gives 2.38, and this is our number rounded and fixed to two decimal places. However, the code continues because what if we have the number 2.3 and want it fixing to two decimal places – this would be 2.30 but with our code, fixNumber, after the second line will equal 2.3.

It's the code on the remaining lines that add any necessary zeros. It does this by first working out how many zeros are required. If the number was a whole number, in other words it had no decimal point at all, then we simply need to pad out the number with the number of zeros as specified by decimalPlaces. If there is a decimal point and let's say we asked for 2 decimal places, then in the **else** part of the **if** statement all we need do is see how many characters there are after the decimal point, and make up a shortfall by adding zeros. This gives us the number of characters after the decimal point:

```
    var decimalPointLocation = fixNumber.lastIndexOf(".");
```

So subtracting this number from the required number of digits after the decimal point gives us the number of zeros to add:

```
    else
    {
        zerosRequired = decimalPlaces -
            (fixNumber.length - decimalPointLocation - 1);
    }
```

In our example fixNumber.length will be 3, and variable decimalPointLocation, which we set earlier, will be 1, so 3 -1 - 1 is 1. Variable decimalPlaces - 1 is 1; we need one zero adding to the end.

The for loop that comes after, loops round and adds a zero onto the number, if any. The number is actually a string, because we did fixNumber = new String... on the second line as that's the only way we can concatenate zeros using + rather than simply adding zero to the total.

On the final line, we return fixNumber as a string and leave the calling functions to do any necessary conversion. This way numbers such as 1.00 will keep their .00; converted to a floating point number it would simply become 1.

Now let's turn to the method that will generate the HTML to display the user's basket. The method will be called from within our `viewbasket.htm`, `checkoutbasket.htm`, and `checkoutconfirm.htm` pages. The method goes through the shopping basket's items and generates a string with a HTML table inside it detailing the contents of the shopper's current basket. The pages will simply write the contents of this HTML out to a `DIV`, though we could use `document.write()` or write it to somewhere other than a `DIV`. The pages `viewbasket.htm` and `checkoutbasket.htm` will require a basket that the user can use to update quantities or even remove items completely. This is our updateable basket. The final checkout summary screen in `checkoutconfirm.htm` does not want to be updateable, it's there simply to re-assure the user before they commit themselves to the purchase that they have the details of the order correct. We'll talk about this in more detail later in the chapter, so now let's turn to the `getBasketHTML()` method shown below, and add it to `ShoppingBasket.js`:

```
ShoppingBasket.prototype.getBasketHTML = function(isBasketUpdateable)
{
   var basketHTML = "";

   // Final summary screen basket not updatable so no need for form
   if (isBasketUpdateable)
   {
      basketHTML = "<FORM NAME=basketForm>";
   }

   // Create shopping basket table head
   basketHTML += "<TABLE CLASS=BasketTable><TR CLASS=HeadTR>";
   basketHTML += "<TH class=BasketHeading>Artist</TH>";
   basketHTML += "<TH class=BasketHeading>Title</TH>";
   basketHTML += "<TH class=BasketHeading>Price Each</TH>";
   basketHTML += "<TH class=BasketHeading>Quantity</TH>";
   basketHTML += "<TH class=BasketHeading>Total Price</TH></TR>";

   var basketItem;
   var basketTotalCost = 0;
   var itemTotalCost = 0;

   // Loop through each item in basket and create HTML table cells
   // with items details
   for (basketItem in this.items)
   {
      // Artist Title Cell
      basketHTML += "<TR><TD ALIGN=CENTER CLASS=Artist>";
      basketHTML += this.items[basketItem].getItemArtist();
      basketHTML += "</TD>";

      // Description Cell
      basketHTML += "<TD ALIGN=CENTER CLASS=Title>";
      basketHTML += this.items[basketItem].getItemDesc();
      basketHTML += "</TD>";

      // Price Cell
      basketHTML += "<TD ALIGN=CENTER CLASS=Price>";
      basketHTML += this.items[basketItem].getItemPrice();
      basketHTML += "</TD>";

      // Qty Cell
      basketHTML += "<TD ALIGN=CENTER CLASS=Price>";

      // Updateable basket requires input box to allow user to
      // enter new quantity
      if (isBasketUpdateable)
      {
```

```
        basketHTML += "<INPUT TYPE=text SIZE=2 MAXLENGTH=2 NAME='" +
            this.items[basketItem].getItemRefId() + "' ";
        basketHTML += "VALUE=" + this.items[basketItem].getItemQty();
        basketHTML += ">";
    }
    else
    {
        basketHTML += this.items[basketItem].getItemQty();
    }
    basketHTML += "</TD>";

    // Keep running total of baskets total cost
    itemTotalCost = this.items[basketItem].getItemQty() *
        this.items[basketItem].getItemPrice();
    basketTotalCost += itemTotalCost;

    // Total Item Price
    basketHTML += "<TD ALIGN=CENTER class=Price>";
    basketHTML += this.fixDecimalPlaces(itemTotalCost, 2);
    basketHTML += "</TD>";

    basketHTML += "</TR>";
}

// Final Cost Summary
basketHTML += "<TR><TD COLSPAN=4 ALIGN=RIGHT class=BasketSummary"
    "STYLE='padding-top: 10px'>";
basketHTML += "Sub Total</TD>";
basketHTML += "<TD ALIGN='CENTER' CLASS= "
    + "'BasketSummary STYLE='padding-top: 10px'>";
basketHTML += this.fixDecimalPlaces(basketTotalCost,2)
basketHTML += "</TD></TR>"
basketHTML += "<TR><TD COLSPAN=4 ALIGN=RIGHT "
    +"CLASS='BasketSummary'>Delivery</TD>";
basketHTML += "<TD  ALIGN=CENTER class=BasketSummary>"
    + this.deliveryCost + "</TD></TR>";
basketHTML += "<TR><TD COLSPAN=4 ALIGN=RIGHT "
    + "CLASS='BasketSummary'>Total</TD>";
basketHTML += "<TD ALIGN=CENTER class=BasketSummary>"
basketHTML += this.fixDecimalPlaces(basketTotalCost +
                                    Number(this.deliveryCost), 2);
basketHTML += "</TD></TR></TABLE>";

if (isBasketUpdateable)
{
    basketHTML += "<P>If you change the quantities, click ";
    basketHTML += "<INPUT NAME='Submit' TYPE='submit' "
        +"VALUE='Update Quantities' ";
    basketHTML += "onClick='updateBasket()'>";
    basketHTML += "<BR>To remove an item, set its value to 0"
        +"</P></FORM>";
}
return basketHTML;
}
```

The HTML this method creates is an HTML table where each row contains details of the product, its price, and quantity in the basket. At the end of the table is a summary of the order cost, including a sub total of the items, the cost of delivery, and a final total for the order. An example screen is shown below:

This is what the method generates, including the **Update Quantities** button. Let's look at how it generates the HTML.

First, the method has one parameter, `isBasketUpdateable`, which is either `true` if the basket should be updateable by the user, or `false` it's not. If it's an updateable basket, then the table is placed inside a form and the quantities are displayed in text boxes, which the user can change. In addition, a button is displayed, **Update Quantities**, which the user clicks when they've made changes and want to apply them. If it's not updateable, instead of using a form and having input boxes, the shopping basket is text only inside the HTML table, with no update button at the bottom.

Following the `if` statement, which writes a form tag if the basket is updateable, we have the code that generates the headings at the top of the table:

```
basketHTML += "<TABLE CLASS=BasketTable><TR CLASS=HeadTR>"
basketHTML += "<TH class=BasketHeading>Artist</TH>"
basketHTML += "<TH class=BasketHeading>Title</TH>";
basketHTML += "<TH class=BasketHeading>Price Each</TH>"
basketHTML += "<TH class=BasketHeading>Quantity</TH>"
basketHTML += "<TH class=BasketHeading>Total Price</TH></TR>"
```

Now we're ready to start looping through the contents of the basket and generating the table rows with details of each item in the basket. The `for` loop above does this:

```
for (basketItem in this.items)
{

}
```

We've used a `for..in` loop, which will loop through each item in the item's associative array, each item in that array being an object of class `ShoppingItem`. In the following lines, we build the HTML by accessing the item details stored in each `ShoppingItem` object instance in the items array, and store the HTML inside `basketHTML`. When we come to generate the `quantity` cell, we check the `isBasketUpdateable` variable. If it's `true` then we write a text box with the quantity in. If it's `false`, we just write plain HTML, as we need a non-updateable version of the basket for the final summary page of the checkout.

As we're going though each item, we're calculating the total cost of that row (number of items ordered multiplied by the price of an item), and displaying that. We also keep a running total of the total cost of the items in variable `basketTotalCost`.

We've created our rows with details of individual products in the basket, now we generate the summary of basket cost:

```
basketTotalCost = Number(this.fixDecimalPlaces(basketTotalCost,2));
// Cost Summary
basketHTML += "<TR><TD COLSPAN=4 ALIGN=RIGHT class=BasketSummary
```

```
            STYLE='padding-top: 10px'>"
    basketHTML += "Sub Total</TD>"
    basketHTML += "<TD ALIGN='CENTER' CLASS= "
        + "'BasketSummary STYLE='padding-top: 10px'>"
    basketHTML += basketTotalCost + "</TD></TR>"
    basketHTML += "<TR><TD COLSPAN=4 ALIGN=RIGHT "
        +"CLASS='BasketSummary'>Delivery</TD>"
    basketHTML += "<TD  ALIGN=CENTER class=BasketSummary>"
        + this.deliveryCost + "</TD></TR>"
    basketHTML += "<TR><TD COLSPAN=4 ALIGN=RIGHT "
        + "CLASS='BasketSummary'>Total</TD>"
    basketHTML += "<TD ALIGN=CENTER class=BasketSummary>"
        + (basketTotalCost + (1 * this.deliveryCost))
    basketHTML += "</TD></TR></TABLE>"
```

This adds rows for sub total, delivery cost, and total basket cost to the end of the table. Note that `basketTotalCost` uses the `fixDecimalPlaces()` method we created earlier, as JavaScript, due to rounding errors, can leave the result as 1.99000000002.

Finally, if the basket is to be updateable we create a button to click to make the update. When clicked the button calls a function named `updateBasket()`, which we need to make sure is in any page we use the basket. On the last line, we return the HTML we've generated for writing into the page:

```
    if (isBasketUpdateable)
    {
        basketHTML += "<P>If you change the quantities, click ";
        basketHTML += "<INPUT NAME='Submit' TYPE='submit' "
            +"VALUE='Update Quantities' ";
        basketHTML += "onClick='updateBasket()'>";
        basketHTML += "<BR>To remove an item, set its value to 0"
            +"</P></FORM>";
    }
    return basketHTML;
```

Before we can use our new methods, we need to create a method called `isEmpty()` to add to `ShoppingBasket.js`, which as the name suggests will return `true` if the basket is empty or `false` otherwise:

```
ShoppingBasket.prototype.isEmpty = function()
{
    if (this.numItems < 1)
    {
        return true;
    }
    else
    {
        return false;
    }
}
```

We'll be using this to check that when the user clicks to go to the View Basket page, there is something to actually view; if not, we'll direct them to the `EmptyBasket.htm` page. The code simply checks to see how many items there are, and returns the result based on that.

Now let's change our web pages to make use of the new methods. First, let's change `viewbasket.htm` as shown below:

```
<!-- viewbasket.htm -->
<HTML>
<HEAD>
```

```
    <LINK REL='stylesheet' HREF='WebsiteGlobalStyle.css'>
    <SCRIPT LANGUAGE='JavaScript'>
        var gMusicMadPage = null;

        function window_onload()
        {
            gMusicMadPage = window.parent;

            if (typeof(gMusicMadPage.myBasket) == "undefined")
            {
                window.location.replace("musicmad.htm");
            }
            else
            {
                if (gMusicMadPage.myBasket.isEmpty())
                {
                    window.location.href = "emptybasket.htm";
                }
                else
                {
                    var basketHTML = window.parent.myBasket.getBasketHTML(true);
                    gMusicMadPage.writeInnerHTML(window.document,
                        "basketDisplayDiv", basketHTML);
                    gMusicMadPage.myBasket.saveBasket();
                }

                // Force NN4 to show scroll bars
                if (document.layers)
                {
                    document.height = document.basketDisplayDiv.top +
                        document.basketDisplayDiv.document.height;
                }
            }
        }
    </SCRIPT>
</HEAD>
<BODY ONLOAD='window_onload()'>
    <DIV ALIGN='CENTER'>
        <H3>
            Your Basket's Contents
        </H3>
    </DIV>
    <FORM METHOD='POST' NAME='frmItems'>
        <P ALIGN='left'>
            If you're ready to place your order, click
            <INPUT TYPE='Button' NAME='cmdCheckout'
                VALUE="Proceed to checkout"
                onClick='window.location.href="checkout_frame.htm"'>
        </P>
    </FORM>
    <DIV ID='basketDisplayDiv'
        STYLE='position: absolute; left: 10px; top: 125px;'>
         
    </DIV>
</BODY>
</HTML>
```

In the new script block added to the top of the page, we first have a global page variable
gMusicMadPage, which is initialized as null. We'll be using this to store a reference to the window
object of the MusicMad.htm page.

Then comes the `window_onload` function, which is called when the window loads, using the event handler in the `<BODY>`. The first thing the function does is set `gMusicMadPage` to this page's parent window, and then checks that the `myBasket` variable in that frame does exist (not null). We want to ensure that this page is loaded inside the frameset defined by `Musicmad.htm` and contains our `basket` object, because we'll be using functions and variables contained inside that page. If it does not exist, we load the top frame with `Musicmad.htm`.

If the correct parent exists, then we check to see if the basket contains items. If it's empty, we change the currently loaded page to the `emptybasket.htm` page. Otherwise, we set variable `basketHTML` to the HTML returned by the `getBasketHTML()` method we just created, passing `true` to indicate that the basket is updateable. Then we use the `writeInnerHTML()` function in the `MusicMad.htm` page to actually write the HTML to `basketDisplayDiv`. We will actually create the `writeInnerHTML()` function shortly. It takes three parameters, the `document` object of the page that will have the DHTML written to it, the `ID` of the tag that will have its inner HTML changed, and finally the HTML to be written to that tag.

On the last line of the `window_onload()` function we have:

```
// Force NN4 to show scroll bars
if (document.layers)
{
   document.height = document.basketDisplayDiv.top +
      document.basketDisplayDiv.document.height;
}
```

This may seem a little odd. Its purpose is to force Netscape 4 to show scroll bars by setting the height of the `document` to the `height` of the `basketDisplayDiv` DIV. Due to a bug in Netscape, without this code it will never show scroll bars, even if the basket's contents scrolls off the bottom of the page. To test for Netscape 4, we've used `document.layers`. If it's not null, that is if it's a browser that supports layers (which is only Netscape 4), then we know we need to set the document size.

Save `viewbasket.htm` and now let's add the `writeInnerHTML()` function to the `MusicMad.htm` page:

```
<!-- MusicMad.htm -->
<HTML>
<HEAD>
   <TITLE>Welcome to MusicMad.Com</TITLE>
   <SCRIPT LANGUAGE='JavaScript' SRC='ShoppingBasket.js'></SCRIPT>
   <SCRIPT LANGUAGE='JavaScript'>
      function writeInnerHTML(documentContainingTag,tagId, HTML)
      {
         var htmlElement;
         if (document.layers)
         {
            htmlElement = documentContainingTag.layers[tagId].document;
            htmlElement.open();
            htmlElement.write(HTML);
            htmlElement.close();
         }
         else if (document.all)
         {
            htmlElement = documentContainingTag.all(tagId);
            htmlElement.innerHTML = HTML;
         }
         else if (document.documentElement)
         {
            htmlElement = documentContainingTag.getElementById(tagId);
            htmlElement.innerHTML = HTML;
         }
      }
```

```
        // Global Variables
        var myBasket = new ShoppingBasket();
    </SCRIPT>
</HEAD>
<FRAMESET BORDER=5 ROWS='100,*' NAME='frasetMain'>
    <!-- MenuBar Top Frame -->
    <FRAME SCROLLING='NO' SRC='top_menu.htm' NAME='fraTop' NORESIZE></FRAME>
    <!-- Main area where most of the displaying of information occurs -->
    <FRAME SCROLLING='AUTO' SRC='home.htm' NAME='fraMain' NORESIZE></FRAME>
</FRAMESET>
</HTML>
```

The purpose of this function is to allow cross browser compatible DHTML. Netscape's version 4 browser uses layers in its DHTML. Changing HTML inside a layer requires that we open it, write our HTML to the tag's layer's document, then close the layer's document. If `document.layers` is not null, then it means layers are supported, which is the test we use to see if we are using Netscape 4. The tag to be acted upon is referenced by `htmlElement`, which is set to the document object of the tag with an ID specified in `tagId` in the `document` object, passed in the first parameter of our function.

IE4+ uses `document.all`, followed by the tag name, followed by the `innerHTML` property for changing the HTML inside a tag. Again, we just set `htmlElement` to reference the tag and then set its `innerHTML` to the HTML parameter passed to the function.

Finally, we have the Netscape version 6 way, which uses `getElementById()` method of the `document` object to set `htmlElement` to the tag due to have its `innerHTML` changed before setting the `innerHTML` to the HTML parameter passed.

Save `Musicmad.htm` and load it into the browser. We should now be able to add items and go to the shopping basket, although we can't yet update the quantity or go to the checkout.

Let's update the `top_menu.htm` page and add code that takes us to view the shopping basket:

```
<!-- top_menu.htm -->
<HTML>
<HEAD>
    <LINK REL='stylesheet' HREF='WebsiteGlobalStyle.css'>
    <STYLE>

        ...

    </STYLE>
    <SCRIPT LANGUAGE='JavaScript'>
        function selectMusicListing()
        {
            var sURL = document.frmMenu.cboBrowse
                .options[document.frmMenu.cboBrowse.selectedIndex].value;
            window.parent.fraMain.location.href = sURL;
        }
        function linkViewBasket_onClick()
        {
            if (parent.myBasket.isEmpty())
            {
                // Empty basket - go to empty basket page
                window.parent.fraMain.location.href = "emptybasket.htm";
            }
            else
            {
                // basket has contents - display basket page in main frame
                window.parent.fraMain.location.href = "viewbasket.htm";
            }
```

```
                return true;
            }
    </SCRIPT>
    <BASE TARGET='fraMain'></BASE>
</HEAD>
<BODY>
    <TABLE>
        <TR ALIGN='CENTER'>
            <TD VALIGN='TOP' WIDTH='140'>
            <A HREF='home.htm'>
                Home
            </A>
            </TD>
            <TD VALIGN='TOP' WIDTH='140'>
                <A HREF='' NAME='linkViewBasket'
                    onClick="linkViewBasket_onClick(); return false;">
                    Shopping Basket
                </A>
            </TD>
    ...
        </TR>
    </TABLE>
</BODY>
</HTML>
```

We've added the onClick event handler to the view basket's hyperlink so that it will call the linkViewBasket_onClick() function in the script block above. This function checks to see if the basket is empty using the ShoppingBasket class's isEmpty method we recently created. If it is empty, we navigate the bottom frame to the emptybasket.htm page; otherwise, we go to the viewbasket.htm page. Note that the onClick event handler returns false, this is to stop the link from being followed and changing the page loaded, whereas we are simply using the link for its click event.

Updating the Basket Quantities

We can view the basket, but we still can't change and update the quantities of each item required. So, let's add this functionality to the ShoppingBasket class by adding two new methods, setQty() and updateBasketWithForm().

We'll start by adding the setQty() method to the ShoppingBasket.js file:

```
ShoppingBasket.prototype.setQty = function(itemRefId, itemQty)
{
    if (itemQty < 1)
    {
        this.deleteItem(itemRefId);
    }
    else
    {
        this.items[itemRefId].setItemQty(itemQty);
    }
}
```

The method uses two arguments, the reference ID of the item to have its quantity changed, and the quantity into which to change it. If the new item quantity is less than 1, then we remove the item from the basket altogether using the classes deleteItem() method we created earlier in this section. Otherwise, we access the associate array of ShoppingItem objects inside the items property of this class and using the unique item reference Id, we set the quantity to the new value.

Updating the quantity of each item in the basket is done via the form displaying the shopping basket, with a text box showing the quantity for each item that the user can change and click an update button to keep the changes. We need a method that will go through each item in the shopping basket form, and update the quantities in our shopping basket, and that method is the `updateBasketWithForm()` method shown below:

```
ShoppingBasket.prototype.updateBasketWithForm = function(basketForm)
{
   var itemRefId;
   var numFormElements = basketForm.length;
   var basketFormElements = basketForm.elements;
   for (var elementIndex = 0; elementIndex < numFormElements;
      elementIndex++)
   {
      if (basketFormElements[elementIndex].type == "text")
      {
         itemRefId = basketFormElements[elementIndex].name;
         itemQty = parseInt(basketFormElements[elementIndex].value);
         if (!isNaN(itemQty))
         {
            this.setQty(itemRefId,itemQty);
         }
      }
   }
}
```

The method takes a `form` object as its only argument, the `form` object with the details of item quantities. The method consists of a `for` loop which goes through each element on the form. The form only consists of text boxes with quantities, and a button for the user to click to update the form. So when an element of type text is found, we know we have a text box containing a quantity. The name of the text box is important because it contains the item reference ID we need to access the relevant item whose quantity needs updating in our shopping basket. We then check that what the user entered for a quantity is a valid number (is not a NaN), and if so, make the update to the item's quantity using the `setQty()` method we just created.

Let's make the changes to the `viewbasket.htm` page so it will allow us to update the quantities:

```
<!-- viewbasket.htm -->
<HTML>
<HEAD>
   <LINK REL='stylesheet' HREF='WebsiteGlobalStyle.css'>
   <SCRIPT LANGUAGE='JavaScript'>
      var gMusicMadPage = null;

      function window_onload()
      {
         ...
      }

      function updateBasket()
      {
         var basketForm;
         if (document.layers)
         {
            basketForm =
               document.layers['basketDisplayDiv'].document.basketForm;
         }
         else
         {
            basketForm = document.basketForm;
         }
```

```
                    gMusicMadPage.myBasket.updateBasketWithForm(basketForm);
                    gMusicMadPage.myBasket.saveBasket();

            }
        </SCRIPT>
    </HEAD>
        ...
    </HTML>
```

The change is the addition of the `updateBasket()` function. Remember in our basket creating method, `getBasketHTML()`, we create an update button that calls the function `updateBasket()`.

The function starts by checking for the `document.layers` property – if that's not `null`, then this must be a layers supporting browser such as Netscape 4. We need to do this check, because our form is inside an absolutely positioned `DIV`. The `basketDisplayDiv` where the basket HTML is written to, has its style set with absolute positioning to enable Netscape 4 to write to the document of the layer representing the element.consequently, however, Netscape 4 considers the basket form inside the `DIV` not to be part of our page's document, but contained within the document of the layer representing the `DIV`. This is in contrast to Netscape 6 and IE4+ where the form is just considered part of our current page's document. So in the Netscape 4 part of the `if` statement, we set the `basketForm` variable to reference the layer's document's form. For IE and Netscape 6 we just set the variable to reference `document.basketForm`.

Next, we use the reference to the `myBasket` variable containing an object instance of our `ShoppingBasket` class in the parent window to call the `updateBasketWithForm()` method and pass the correct basket form. Remember that `gMusicMadPage` was set to reference the correct variable in the window's `onload` event. Then we save the shopping basket so that if the user leaves the web site, or closes their browser, then their basket will be preserved for their return, as long as cookies are turned on. We've not created the `saveBasket()` method of the `ShoppingBasket` class, so we will do that in the next section.

Saving and Loading the Basket

To allow the user to go away and think about their purchases and return later without needing to add the items again to their basket, we've created the `saveBasket()` method, which is called whenever the shopping basket is changed, and the `loadBasket()` method that is called when the user arrives at the site's home page. We'll start by creating the `saveBasket()` method:

```
ShoppingBasket.prototype.saveBasket = function()
{
    if (!this.isEmpty())
    {
        var basketDetails = "";
        var cookieExpires;

        for (basketItem in this.items)
        {
            basketDetails += this.items[basketItem].getItemRefId() + "`";
            basketDetails += this.items[basketItem].getItemArtist() + "`";
            basketDetails += this.items[basketItem].getItemDesc() + "`";
            basketDetails += this.items[basketItem].getItemPrice() + "`";
            basketDetails += this.items[basketItem].getItemQty() + "¬";
        }

        basketDetails = basketDetails.substring(0,basketDetails.length - 1);

        basketDetails = escape(basketDetails);
        var nowDate = new Date();
        nowDate.setMonth(nowDate.getMonth() + 3);
        cookieExpires = nowDate.toGMTString();
```

```
        document.cookie = "MusicMadBasket=" + basketDetails
            + ";expires=" + cookieExpires + ";";
    }
    else
    {
        document.cookie = "MusicMadBasket= "
            + ";expires=Sat,01 Jan 2000 00:00:00";
    }
}
```

This needs to be added to the `ShoppingBasket.js` file. The method starts by checking that the basket is not empty, there is no point looping through empty basket! If it does contain items, then we use a `for..in` loop to loop through each `ShoppingItem` object in the item's associate array. As we go through each item, we obtain its details and add them to the `basketDetails` string, which will be used later when setting the cookie value. We delimit each of the item's details with a "`" character and each item itself with a "¬"; these are unlikely to appear in details of our items so we should be safe using them as delimiters. We need to delimit details and items for when we recreate the basket in the load function, as we're saving the whole basket as one long string. This looping to obtain the details is very similar to how we built up the shopping basket HTML in the `getBasketHTML()` method.

Once we've finished looping through the item's associative array building up the details in the `basketDetails` string, we then lop off the last "¬" at the end of the string. Why? Well when we come to split the string again in the `loadBasket()` method we don't want the last "¬" in there otherwise the string will be split there as well, and we'll end up with an empty item, for example if basketDetails was:

item1¬item2¬item3¬

In addition, this string was split at the point of each ¬ when the array would have four elements containing item1, item2, item3, and an empty element. To avoid all this we have removed the last character in this line:

```
basketDetails = basketDetails.substring(0,basketDetails.length - 1);
```

`substring()` here will return all the characters, from the first to the second to last character, effectively removing the ¬ at the end of the string.

Now that we have all the right information in our `basketDetails` variable, we need to convert it to the escape value of `basketDetails`. This changes all the characters, such as spaces and punctuation, that can't be stored directly in a cookie and converts them to their character set number equivalent. So a space becomes `%20`, the "%" sign indicates it's a special character code, and the `20` is the hexadecimal number representing a space in ASCII. When we load the basket back in, we will unescape the values to return them to normal.

Finally, we need to generate a date for the cookie expiry date. We want the basket to expire in three months' time so we use the `Date` object to get the current date, set the month to the current month + 3 and set `cookieExpires` to the GMT string version of the date. On the last line, we set our cookie.

If the basket was empty, then we simply clear the cookie by setting the value of `MusicMadBasket` to nothing and expiring it by setting it to a date that has passed, any date will do as long as its in the past, 1 Jan 2000 is an arbitrary selected by me.

Before we look at the `load()` method, we first need to create a cookie reading method called `getCookieValue()`:

```
ShoppingBasket.prototype.getCookieValue = function(cookieName)
{
    var cookieValue = document.cookie;
```

```
   var cookieRegExp = new RegExp("\\b" + cookieName + "=([^;]+)");
   cookieValue = cookieRegExp.exec(cookieValue);

   if (cookieValue != null)
   {
      cookieValue = cookieValue[1];
      cookieValue = unescape(cookieValue);
   }

   return cookieValue;
}
```

This needs adding to the `ShoppingBasket.js` file. Browser cookies can only be read in one block; `document.cookie` returns all the cookies for that web site and not a specific cookie, so to get our shopping items cookie we need to create a method that gets an individual cookie. Once we have that individual value containing just our shopping items, it can be used by methods, such as our `loadBasket()` method which will `unescape()` it, split it, and extract the individual items

The method's only argument is the name of the cookie whose value we want. On the first line of the method, we get all the cookies. Then we create a regular expression that will match our cookie. The first part of the regular expression, `\\b` will match a word boundary. If we had two cookies named `Name` and `FirstName` and the `FirstName` cookie happened to be first, then searching for a cookie called `Name` would match `FirstName`; with `\\b`, this won't happen. Then we match the name of the cookie. Following this, we have an equals sign and then a regular expression group that will match any character except a semicolon (`;`), as a semi-colon indicates the end of a cookie value. We've used a capturing group, because this will capture the characters of the value and only the value and can be easily accessed using the special array returned by the `exec()` method. As we see on the next line the `exec()` method is used and this either returns `null` if no match found, or an array containing in element zero the whole match, in other words the cookie name and value, and in array element 1 just characters matched by the capturing group, in other words the cookie value we are after. We just `unescape()` the value and then return it at the end of the function.

Let's turn to the `loadBasket()` method, where we use the `getCookieValue()` method and recreate the user's shopping basket:

```
ShoppingBasket.prototype.loadBasket = function()
{
   var basketItems;
   var basketItemNum;
   var itemDetail;
   var itemRefId = "";
   var itemArtist = "";
   var itemDesc = "";
   var itemPrice = "";
   var itemQty = "";

   var basketDetails = this.getCookieValue("MusicMadBasket");
   if (basketDetails != null)
   {
      basketItems = basketDetails.split('¬');

      for (basketItemNum in basketItems)
      {
         basketItem = basketItems[basketItemNum];
         basketItem = basketItem.split('`');

         itemRefId = basketItem[0];
         itemArtist = basketItem[1];
         itemDesc =basketItem[2];
         itemPrice = basketItem[3];
```

```
            itemQty = basketItem[4];
            this.addItem(itemRefId,itemArtist,itemDesc,itemPrice, itemQty);
        }
    }
}
```

Our first task is to obtain the previous basket contents stored in the cookie named `MusicMadBasket`. This cookie will contain all of the basket's items in one long string, which we will split shortly. We then split the string based on the "¬" character. When we saved the basket with the `saveBasket()` method, we delimited each item with a "¬" and now we use that to generate an array, where each element contains one item (one CD). We then loop through this array with a `for...in` loop. Within this loop we split each array element, but this time with the "`" character. Again in the `saveBasket()` method we delimited each detail of an item, such as artist name, price, quantity, with the "`" character. By splitting the item with "`", we can access its individual details, and using the `addItem()` method, add it to the shopping basket.

That completes the code for the `saveBasket()` and `loadBasket()` methods, and we've already seen `saveBasket()` used in the `viewbasket.htm` page so we now just need to add the `loadBasket()` method to the `MusicMad.htm` page, the first page loaded when the user visits our web site:

```
var myBasket = new ShoppingBasket();
myBasket.loadBasket();
```

It has been added to the line below the `mybasket` variable declaration in the main `<SCRIPT>` tag in the `<HEAD>` section. Save the change to `Musicmad.htm`.

That completes the shopping basket part of the web site. It's now time to turn to the checkout side of things.

Creating the Checkout

We've created the functionality that allows the user to fill their basket with goodies and see what goodies are contained in the basket. Now it's time to let them spend their money, by adding the checkout functionality.

We'll start by making a few additions to the web site to display the basket at the start of the checkout stage to give the user the opportunity to make last minute changes to basket quantities. Then we will look at the `Validate` class and see how it can be used to check what the user enters is actually valid. Then we'll look at the `Customer` and `CreditCard` classes, which store details of the customer and their credit card. Finally, we'll create the final order summary screen prior to the user actually committing to buying the goods.

Creating the Checkout Basket

We'll be changing the `checkoutbasket.htm` page so it's virtually identical to the `viewbasket.htm` page. The main difference between the two is that the `checkoutbasket.htm` page doesn't need a button to take the user to the checkout as we're already there:

```
<!-- checkoutbasket.htm -->
<HTML>
<HEAD>
    <LINK REL=stylesheet HREF="WebsiteGlobalStyle.css">
    <SCRIPT LANGUAGE='JavaScript'>
        var gMusicMadPage

        function window_onload()
        {
            gMusicMadPage = window.parent.parent;

            if (gMusicMadPage.myBasket == null)
```

```
                {
                    window.location.replace("musicmad.htm");
                }
                else
                {
                    if (gMusicMadPage.myBasket.isEmpty())
                    {
                        window.parent.location.href = "emptybasket.htm";
                    }
                    else
                    {
                        var basketHTML = gMusicMadPage.myBasket.getBasketHTML(true);
                        gMusicMadPage.writeInnerHTML
                            (window.document,"basketDisplayDiv", basketHTML);

                        // force NN4 to show scroll bars
                        if (document.layers)
                        {
                            document.height = document.basketDisplayDiv.top +
                                        document.basketDisplayDiv.document.height;
                        }
                    }
                }
            }

            function updateBasket()
            {
                var basketForm;

                if (document.layers)
                {
                    basketForm =
                        document.layers['basketDisplayDiv'].document.basketForm;
                }
                else
                {
                    basketForm = document.basketForm;
                }

                gMusicMadPage.myBasket.updateBasketWithForm(basketForm);
                gMusicMadPage.myBasket.saveBasket();
            }
        </SCRIPT>
    </HEAD>
    ...
</HTML>
```

The change is similar to that with the viewbasket.htm page. We have added two JavaScript functions: one that runs when the page loads, and the other to update the basket. The code is virtually identical to the viewbasket.htm page except that because this page is in the lower frame of the checkout frameset, itself inside the lower frame of the musicmad.htm frameset, we have to access the ShoppingBasket class object in the parent.parent window and not the parent window:

```
        gMusicMadPage = window.parent.parent;
```

Other than that, the code is identical.

We've already added the code for the Proceed to Checkout button in the viewbasket.htm page, but we've not just added the same code to the top_menu.htm page's Checkout link, so let's do that now:

```
<!-- top_menu.htm -->
<HTML>
<HEAD>
    <LINK REL=stylesheet HREF="WebsiteGlobalStyle.css"></LINK>
    <STYLE>
        ...
    </STYLE>

    <SCRIPT LANGUAGE='JavaScript'>
        function selectMusicListing()
        {
            var sURL = document.frmMenu.cboBrowse
                .options[document.frmMenu.cboBrowse.selectedIndex].value;
            window.parent.fraMain.location.href = sURL;
        }

        function linkCheckout_onClick()
        {
            if (parent.myBasket.isEmpty())
            {
                // Empty basket - go to empty basket page
                window.parent.fraMain.location.href = "emptybasket.htm";
            }
            else
            {
                // something in basket to buy - so go to checkout
                parent.fraMain.location.href = "Checkout_frame.htm";
            }
            return true;
        }

        function linkViewBasket_onClick()
        {
            ...
        }
    </SCRIPT>
    <BASE TARGET="fraMain"></BASE>
</HEAD>
<BODY>
    <TABLE>
        <TR ALIGN='CENTER'>
            <TD VALIGN='TOP' WIDTH='140'>
                <A HREF='home.htm'>
                    Home
                </A>
            </TD>
            <TD VALIGN='TOP' WIDTH='140'>
                <A HREF='' NAME='linkViewBasket'
                    onClick='linkViewBasket_onClick(); return false;'>
                    Shopping Basket
                </A>
            </TD>
            <TD VALIGN='TOP' WIDTH='140'>
                <A HREF='' NAME='linkCheckout'
                    onClick='linkCheckout_onClick(); return false;'>
                    Checkout
                </A>
            </TD>

            ...
```

```
    </TR>
  </TABLE>
 </BODY>
</HTML>
```

We've added an onClick event handler to the checkout hyperlink and created the linkCheckout_onClick() function that it calls. This function checks that the basket is not empty, and if it is the user is taken to the emptybasket.htm page. Otherwise, they are taken to the checkout frameset page. Note that the onClick event handler returns false to stop the link itself being followed, we're just using the link's onClick event, and not using it as a normal hyperlink.

The final change, before we can go to the checkout without error messages appearing, is in the checkout.htm page. This page loads the top checkout frame and displays buttons allowing the user to move to the next stage of the checkout, or continue shopping for more goods:

```
<!-- checkout.htm -->
<HTML>
<HEAD>
   <LINK REL='stylesheet' HREF='WebsiteGlobalStyle.css'>
   <STYLE>
      BODY
      {
         FONT-SIZE: 12pt;
         COLOR: darkblue;
         FONT-WEIGHT: bolder;
         TEXT-ALIGN: center;
      }
   </STYLE>

   <SCRIPT LANGUAGE='JavaScript'>
      var gMusicMadPage = null;

      function window_onload()
      {
         gMusicMadPage = window.parent.parent;

         if (gMusicMadPage.myBasket == null)
         {
            window.location.replace("musicmad.htm");
         }
      }

      function cmdNext_onClick()
      {
         if (window.parent.parent.myBasket.isEmpty())
         {
            alert("Your basket is empty  - click continue shopping "
               + "to fill it up with our excellent bargains");
         }
         else
         {
            // go to page 2 of checkout process
            window.parent.location.href="personaldetails.htm";
         }
         return true;
      }
   </SCRIPT>
</HEAD>
<BODY onLoad='window_onload()'>
   Welcome to our secure online ordering system.
```

```
Your current basket contents are listed below.
<FORM>
    Once you're happy with its contents, click
    <INPUT NAME='cmdNext' TYPE='button' VALUE='Next'
        onClick='cmdNext_onClick()'>
    to continue <BR></BR> or click
    <INPUT NAME='cmdBrowse' TYPE='button' VALUE='Continue Shopping'
        onClick='window.parent.location.href="home.htm"'>
    to return to the main screen.
</FORM>
</BODY>
</HTML>
```

We've added two functions and event handlers to the buttons and the `<BODY>` tag. To the cmdBrowse button, we've added onClick event handler to take the user to the home page. To the cmdNext button, we've added an event handler to call the cmdNext_onClick() function.

Before we look at the cmdNext_onClick() function let's look at the window_onLoad() function. This firstly sets the variable gMusicMadPage to the window's parent's parent, the Musicmad.htm page's window containing the myBasket variable. If the myBasket variable is null, we replace the current page with the Musicmad.htm page, just in case the user has loaded this page directly rather than it being loaded within the frameset.

The cmdNext_onClick() function, as you might expect, navigates the user to the next stage in the checkout process, which is obtaining their personal details. However, before it does that, it checks that the basket is not empty. The user may have arrived at the checkout basket page with a full basket, but if they updated all the quantities to zero and left an empty basket then there would be no point in continuing with the checkout process. We alert them to that fact and suggest they fill their basket with lots of bargains! Otherwise, they are taken to the next stage.

The web site is now at a point where we can see almost everything working. All that's still unfinished are the obtaining personal details, obtaining credit card details, and displaying a checkout final summary. Before we add that functionality, however, we will take a brief look at the Validate class.

The Validate Class

The Validate class is the same Validate class that we created in Chapter 16 on form validation. Its purpose is form validation, and it contains a number of methods that validate different types of data and a method will go through a form and Validate each text box and radio button marked as needing validation. As we discussed the class and its use in detail in Chapter 16, we'll not be examining it here. However, it will be included in the code download for this chapter.

Using the Validate Class in Our Web Pages

Before we do use the Validate class, we need to add an extra function to the Musicmad.htm page:

```
function getSelectedRadioValue(radioGroup)
{
    var selectedRadioValue = "";
    var radIndex;
    for (radIndex = 0; radIndex < radioGroup.length; radIndex++)
    {
        if (radioGroup[radIndex].checked)
        {
            selectedRadioValue = radioGroup[radIndex].value;
            break;
        }
    }
```

```
            return selectedRadioValue;
        }
```

This can be added to the existing script block which contains our `writeInnerHTML()` function. We've included it in the `MuiscMad.htm` page as that allows any page on our web site to access it. We could have included it in our `Validate` class, but as its purpose is not form validation and as the `Validate` class can be used without it, it's best to keep it separate. In fact, if we had more data extracting functions like this, we could have a class just for them, for example a `FormData` class. As we have just the one function, it seems a lot of effort creating a class just for it alone. Now let's turn to using our `Validate` class.

First, we need to include the `Validate` code in our `Musicmad.htm` page by adding a `<SCRIPT>` tag with a `SRC` attribute pointing to our `Validate.js` file:

```
<!-- Musicmad.htm -->
<HTML>
<HEAD>
    <TITLE>Welcome to MusicMad.Com</TITLE>
    <SCRIPT SRC='ShoppingBasket.js'></SCRIPT>
    <SCRIPT SRC='Validate.js'></SCRIPT>
```

Now we need to declare a variable and set it to reference a new object instance of our `Validate` class:

```
    // Global Variables

    var myBasket = new ShoppingBasket();
    myBasket.loadBasket();
    var validator = new Validate();
```

We've finished with the `Musicmad.htm` page for now and need to open the `PersonalDetails.htm` page. Add the script block to the top of the page as shown:

```
<!-- PersonalDetails.htm -->
<HTML>
<HEAD>
    <LINK REL=stylesheet HREF="WebsiteGlobalStyle.css">
    <STYLE>
        H4.FormElementDescription
        {
            FONT-SIZE: 11pt;
        }
        INPUT.TextBox
        {
            width: 250px;
        }
    </STYLE>

    <SCRIPT LANGUAGE='JavaScript'>
        function cmdSubmit_onclick()
        {
            if (parent.validator.checkFormValid(document.frmCustomer,
              window.document))
            {
                window.location.href = "CheckoutCredit.htm";
            }
            else
            {
                alert("There were problems with your form.\n"
                    + "Please correct them before continuing.");
            }
        }
```

```
        </SCRIPT>
    </HEAD>
    <BODY>
```

The code uses the `Validate` class object referenced in the `validator` variable in the window's parent (`Musicmad.htm`). It calls the `checkFormValid()` method that will go through each form element in the form object passed in the first argument and check those elements that need validating. Those form elements that require validation are those that have a name with `_compulsory` followed by a `_` character and the type of data the element should hold. For example, `_email` if it's an e-mail address, or `_alphabetic` for the customers name. Radio buttons, in this case the radio buttons to select the customers formal title, also have `_compulsory` after the name to indicate that one of them must be selected by the user. Chapter 16 discusses how the `Validation` class works in much more detail. You'll also notice that each element has a `DIV` HTML element following it with an error message. This will be made visible by the `checkFormValid()` method if there is an error with the element or made invisible if it's OK. It uses this page's `document` object, which we pass as the methods second argument, to do the visibility change.

The `checkFormValid()` function returns `true` if the form is valid, and we navigate the user to the next page, the credit card details page, if this is the case. Otherwise, we display an alert box informing the user that there were problems that need to be corrected before continuing.

We need to make a few last changes to the page. We need to add the `onClick` event handlers to the `cmdPrevious` button, which navigates to the previous page. We also need to add an `onClick` event handler to the `cmdContinue` button, which calls the `cmdSubmit_onclick()` function we just created:

```
        <INPUT TYPE='reset' NAME='cmdReset'
            VALUE='Clear form'>
        <INPUT TYPE='button' NAME='cmdPrevious' VALUE='Back'
            onClick='window.location.href="checkout_frame.htm"'></INPUT>
        <INPUT TYPE='button' NAME='cmdSubmit' VALUE='Continue'
            onClick='cmdSubmit_onclick()'></INPUT>
    </FORM>
```

We can now save the `PersonalDetails.htm` page, and then load the `CheckoutCredit.htm` page to make changes shown below:

```
<!-- CheckoutCredit.htm -->
<HTML>
<HEAD>
<TITLE>Document Title</TITLE>
    <LINK REL='stylesheet' HREF='WebsiteGlobalStyle.css'></LINK>
    <SCRIPT LANGUAGE='JavaScript'>

        function cmdContinue_onclick(theForm)
        {
            var isValid = true;
            // check credit card expiry date is valid
            var selectedMonth =
                theForm.cboExpMonth.options[theForm.cboExpMonth.selectedIndex]
                .value;

            var selectedYear =
                theForm.cboExpYear.options[theForm.cboExpYear.selectedIndex]
                .value;

            if (parent.validator.isValidCreditCardExpiry
                (selectedMonth,selectedYear) == false)
            {
                isValid = false;
```

```
                    parent.validator.showErrorDiv("CardExpiryError",
                        window.document);
                }
                else
                {
                    parent.validator.hideErrorDiv("CardExpiryError",
                        window.document);
                }

                if (parent.validator.checkFormValid(document.frmCCDetails,
                    window.document) == false)
                {
                    isValid = false;
                }
                else
                {
                    var cardType =
                        parent.getSelectedRadioValue(theForm.radCardType_Compulsory);

                    var cardNumber =
                        theForm.txtCardNumber_Compulsory_Alphanumeric.value;

                    if (parent.validator.isValidCreditCardNumber(cardNumber,
                        cardType) == false)
                    {
                        parent.validator.showErrorDiv("CardNumberError",
                            window.document);
                            isValid = false;
                    }
                }

                if (isValid)
                {
                    window.location.href = "CheckoutConfirm.htm";
                }
                else
                {
                    alert("There were problems with your form.\n" +
                        "Please correct them before continuing.");
                }
            }
        </SCRIPT>
    </HEAD>
```

We've added a SCRIPT block inside the HEAD with a function that checks the form before allowing the user to continue onto the next page.

We start by checking the credit card's expiry date. The Validate class provides the isValidCreditCardExpiry() method to do this for us. We can therefore use the validator variable in the parent frame, which contains an object instance of this class, to do the checking. All we need do is obtain the month and year selected by the user in the cboExpMonth and cboExpYear select boxes.

If isValidCreditCardExpiry() returns false, then we set the isValid variable to false and display the error DIV in our page that is next to the expiry select elements. Again, the Validate class provides the showErrorDiv() method to do that for us, we just pass it the ID of the DIV and the document object for this page. If there is no problem with the expiry date, then we make sure the error DIV is hidden.

Next, we use the checkFormValid() method of the Validator class object referenced in parent.validator to check the elements of the form that have _compulsory after their name. This includes the txtCardHolderName_Compulsory_Alphabetic text box, and the radio button group for selecting card type. The textbox has _Alphabetic after its name to tell the checkFormValid() method that only letters are allowed as valid characters in that element.

If the result of checkFormValid() is false, then isValid is set to false, otherwise we then go on to check that the credit card number is valid. Again, the Validator class provides the validity checking. This time the isValidCreditCardNumber() method does the checking of the card number passed in the first argument. The second argument is the card type that the user selected in the radio button group. The isValidCreditCardNumber() method not only ensures that the characters are valid, (only numbers and spaces) and that it's the correct length for a given card type, but also employs an algorithm that can determine whether a number would be an acceptable number for a given card type. Of course, just because a card number is valid, it doesn't necessarily mean the credit card number has actually been allocated to someone – that requires server-side code for validation.

In the final if statement, if the form has checked out as valid, we go to the final summary page of the checkout. If it is invalid, we let the user know and ask them to fix the problems before continuing.

Before we leave this page, we need to add the onClick event handlers to the buttons:

```
<INPUT NAME='reset' TYPE='reset' VALUE='Clear Form'>
<INPUT NAME='cmdPrevious' TYPE='button' VALUE='Back'
    onClick='history.back()'>
<INPUT NAME='cmdContinue' TYPE='button' VALUE='Continue'
    onClick='cmdContinue_onclick(document.frmCCDetails)'>
```

That completes the changes to CheckoutCredit.htm for now, although we'll be revisiting it shortly. Before we alter the final summary screen, we will look at the Customer and CreditCard classes.

The Customer Class

We're using the Customer class to represent a customer. Each object instance of the class represents a customer. It stores information about the customer, such as their personal details, and it has a method that will be used in creating the final summary screen in the checkout process. Like the ShoppingItem class, we use methods to access its properties rather than access them directly. Again, this is to avoid difficult to debug typing errors when using property names. The class stores the following information about the customer, the same information we obtain in the personal details page:

❑   Title

❑   Full Name

❑   Street Address

❑   City

❑   Locality (state/county)

❑   Postal Code (zip/post code)

❑   Country

❑   E-mail address

For each of these we have a property, and for each property there is a get and set method.

The advantage of representing a customer as a class is that it keeps related data in the same place and makes it easy to extend functionality. If we wanted the customer's telephone number to be stored, we simply add the relevant property and methods to the class.

Let's turn to creating the code.

Creating the Customer Class

The `Customer`'s class code is shown below, and needs to be saved to a file called `Customer.js`:

```
// Customer.js
function Customer() {}

Customer.prototype.getCustomerDetailsSummary = function()
{
   var summaryHTML = "Your goods will be delivered to "
      + "<TABLE CLASS='Summary'>";
   summaryHTML += "<TR><TD>" + this.getTitle() + " " + this.getFullName()
      + "</TD></TR>";
   summaryHTML += "<TR><TD>" + this.getStreet() + "</TD></TR>";
   summaryHTML += "<TR><TD>" + this.getCity() + "</TD></TR>";
   summaryHTML += "<TR><TD>" + this.getLocality() + "</TD></TR>";
   summaryHTML += "<TR><TD>" + this.getPostalCode() + "</TD></TR>"
   summaryHTML += "<TR><TD>" + this.getCountry() + "</TD></TR>";
   summaryHTML += "</TABLE>"

   return summaryHTML;
}

Customer.prototype.setTitle = function(title)
{
   this.title = title;
}

Customer.prototype.getTitle = function()
{
   return this.title;
}

Customer.prototype.setFullName = function(fullName)
{
   this.fullName = fullName;
}

Customer.prototype.getFullName = function()
{
   return this.fullName;
}

Customer.prototype.setEmail = function(email)
{
   this.email = email;
}

Customer.prototype.getEmail = function()
{
   return this.email;
}

Customer.prototype.setStreet = function(street)
{
   this.street = street;
}

Customer.prototype.getStreet = function()
{
```

```
      return this.street;
   }

   Customer.prototype.setCity = function(city)
   {
      this.city = city;
   }

   Customer.prototype.getCity = function()
   {
      return this.city;
   }

   Customer.prototype.setLocality = function(locality)
   {
      this.locality = locality;
   }

   Customer.prototype.getLocality = function()
   {
      return this.locality;
   }

   Customer.prototype.setPostalCode = function(postalCode)
   {
      this.postalCode = postalCode;
   }

   Customer.prototype.getPostalCode = function()
   {
      return this.postalCode;
   }

   Customer.prototype.setCountry = function(country)
   {
      this.country = country;
   }

   Customer.prototype.getCountry = function()
   {
      return this.country;
   }
```

The majority of the class consists of the `get` and `set` methods for each property. They all follow the same pattern. First is a `set` method, which has one argument, the value the property is to be set to. Then we set the property using the `this` keyword to refer to this class, and then the name of the property. The `get` method is even simpler; it returns `this.propertyname`.

At the top of the class, after the empty constructor method, we have the `getCustomerDetailsSummary()` method, which generates an HTML table of details of the customer, their name and address. This will be used shortly in the final summary screen. We build up the HTML in the `summaryHTML` variable and use the `get` methods to access this class's properties.

Creating a Customer Object

We need to create an instance of the `Customer` class in `Musicmad.htm`. First, we need to add the `.js` file to the `Musicmad.htm` page and under `Validate.js` is a good place:

```
<SCRIPT SRC='ShoppingBasket.js'></SCRIPT>
<SCRIPT SRC='Validate.js'></SCRIPT>
<SCRIPT SRC='Customer.js'></SCRIPT>
```

Then we need to declare a variable and initialize it to reference a new object instance of the Customer class, this needs to be added to the MusicMad.htm page along with our other global variables:

```
// Global variables

        var myBasket = new ShoppingBasket();
        myBasket.loadBasket();
        var validator = new Validate();
        var thisCustomer = new Customer();
```

We'll be using this variable shortly, but first let's look at the CreditCard class.

The CreditCard Class

This class represents the customer's credit card. Like the Customer class, it has various properties with each property being accessed by set and get methods. Also like the Customer class, it has a method to generate the HTML to display a summary of the credit card details.

Creating the Credit Card Class

The CreditCard class code is shown below and needs to be saved in the file CreditCard.js:

```
// CreditCard.js
function CreditCard() {}

CreditCard.prototype.getCreditCardDetailsSummary = function()
{
    var summaryHTML = "<TABLE CLASS='Summary'>";
    summaryHTML += "<TR><TD>Name of credit card holder: </TD>";
    summaryHTML += "<TD>" + this.getCardHolderName() + "</TD></TR>";
    summaryHTML += "<TR><TD>Card Number</TD>";
    summaryHTML += "<TD>" + this.getCardNumber() + "</TD></TR>";
    summaryHTML += "<TR><TD>Expiry Date</TD>";
    summaryHTML += "<TD>" + this.getCardExpires() + "</TD></TR>";
    summaryHTML += "</TABLE>";

    return summaryHTML;
}

CreditCard.prototype.setCardType = function(cardType)
{
    this.cardType = cardType;
}

CreditCard.prototype.getCardType = function()
{
    return this.cardType;
}

CreditCard.prototype.setCardHolderName = function(cardHolderName)
{
    this.cardHolderName = cardHolderName;
}

CreditCard.prototype.getCardHolderName = function()
{
    return this.cardHolderName;
}

CreditCard.prototype.setCardNumber = function(cardNumber)
{
    this.cardNumber = cardNumber;
```

```
   }

   CreditCard.prototype.getCardNumber = function()
   {
      return this.cardNumber;
   }

   CreditCard.prototype.setCardExpires = function(cardExpires)
   {
      this.cardExpires = cardExpires;
   }

   CreditCard.prototype.getCardExpires = function()
   {
      return this.cardExpires;
   }
```

Creating a CreditCard Object

We need to create an instance of the `CreditCard` class in `Musicmad.htm`. First, we need to add the `.js` file to the `Musicmad.htm` page:

```
<SCRIPT SRC='ShoppingBasket.js'></SCRIPT>
<SCRIPT SRC='Validate.js'></SCRIPT>
<SCRIPT SRC='Customer.js'></SCRIPT>
<SCRIPT SRC='CreditCard.js'></SCRIPT>
```

Then we need to declare a variable and initialize it to reference a new object instance of the `CreditCard` class:

```
//Global variables

var myBasket = new ShoppingBasket();
myBasket.loadBasket();
var validator = new Validate();
var thisCustomer = new Customer();
var customerCreditCard = new CreditCard();
```

In the next section, we'll update the `PersonalDetails.htm` and `CheckoutCredit.htm` pages and, using the `Customer` and `CreditCard` classes to store the customer and credit card information, we are ready for our final checkout screen.

Keeping Track of Customer and Credit Card Details

As we obtain the customer and credit card details on separate pages to the final checkout page, we need some way to store them temporarily. We achieve this via the object instances of the `Customer` and `CreditCard` classes that were created in the `Musicmad.htm` frameset-defining page that will keep this information safe until the final stage.

Let's start by altering `PersonalDetails.htm`. We need to update the `cmdSubmit_onclick()` method as below:

```
function cmdSubmit_onclick()
{
   if (parent.validator.checkFormValid(document.frmCustomer,
      window.document))
   {
      var customer = parent.thisCustomer;
      var form = document.frmCustomer;

      // get value of title radio button
      var titleValue;
```

```
            titleValue = parent.getSelectedRadioValue
                (form.radTitle_Compulsory);
            customer.setTitle(titleValue);
            customer.setFullName
                (form.txtFullName_compulsory_alphabetic.value);
            customer.setEmail(form.txtEmail_compulsory_email.value);
            customer.setStreet
                (form.txtStreet_compulsory_alphanumeric.value);
            customer.setCity(form.txtCity_compulsory_alphanumeric.value);
            customer.setLocality
                (form.txtLocality_compulsory_alphanumeric.value);
            customer.setPostalCode
                (form.txtPostalCode_compulsory_postcode.value);
            customer.setCountry(form.txtCountry_compulsory_alphabetic.value)

            window.location.href = "CheckoutCredit.htm";
        }
        else
        {
            alert("There were problems with your form.\n"
                + "Please correct them before continuing.");
        }
    }
```

At the top, we declare the `Customer` and `form` variables, and point them to the `Customer` object `thisCustomer` in the parent frame (`Musicmad.htm`) and `form` object of this page. Doing this just helps shorten the code and make it a little more readable. To get the value of the title selected we use the `getSelectedRadioValue()` function we created in `Musicmad.htm` earlier in the chapter. Then the remaining changes use the `Customer` object's `set` methods to set the various properties to store the customer information entered in the form by the user. Those are the only changes so we can save `PersonalDetails.htm` and turn to `CheckoutCredit.htm`.

In `CheckoutCredit.htm` it's the `cmdContinue_onclick()` function that needs to be altered, so that before the next page is loaded we make a note of the card details entered by the user. This time we store them in the `customerCreditCard` variable in the parent window, which contains a `CreditCard` class object. Again, it's via the `set` methods of that class that the details are stored in the object's properties:

```
        function cmdContinue_onclick(theForm)
        {

            ...

            if (isValid)
            {
                parent.customerCreditCard.setCardType(cardType);
                parent.customerCreditCard.setCardHolderName
                    (theForm.txtCardHolderName_Compulsory_Alphabetic.value);
                parent.customerCreditCard.setCardNumber(cardNumber);
                parent.customerCreditCard.setCardExpires(selectedMonth + "/"
                    + selectedYear)

                window.location.href = "CheckoutConfirm.htm";
            }
            else
            {
                alert("There were problems with your form.\n"
                    + "Please correct them before continuing.")
            }
        }
```

That completes the changes to `CheckoutCredit.htm`, our next task for this chapter is to add the code that will display a summary of the order and customer details and enable these details to be passed server-side, although we won't actually do any server-side processing.

Displaying the Checkout Summary Screen

Before we alter the `CheckoutConfirm.htm` page we need to add two more methods to the `ShoppingBasket` class.

In our final screen, we have a sentence that says, "Your credit card will be debited..." and an amount that will be debited from the customer's card. We need a function that will return the total cost of the order plus delivery charge, and that's exactly what `getTotalIncDelivery()` shown below does:

```
ShoppingBasket.prototype.getTotalIncDelivery = function()
{
   var basketTotalCost = 0;
   var basketItem;
   var itemTotalCost = 0;

   for (basketItem in this.items)
   {
      itemTotalCost = this.items[basketItem].getItemQty() *
         this.items[basketItem].getItemPrice();
      basketTotalCost += itemTotalCost;
   }

   basketTotalCost += Number(this.deliveryCost);
   basketTotalCost = this.fixDecimalPlaces(basketTotalCost,2);
   return basketTotalCost;
}
```

This code needs to be added to `ShoppingBasket.js`. The code keeps the running total in `basketTotalCost` and starts by looping through each item in the customer' basket and totaling the cost. Remember that each `ShoppingItem` object representing a single item is stored in the items array property of the `ShoppingBasket` class. Finally, we add the delivery cost, which we convert from a string to a number using the `Number()` method, and return this total to the user fixed to two decimal places.

Next, we must add the `getHiddenInputHTML()` method. The purpose of this is to write HTML elements of type hidden into the page. These hidden HTML elements contain all the details of items in the basket so that when the form is submitted to the server, the page receiving the form post can process it server-side. Currently, the order details are only available client-side:

```
ShoppingBasket.prototype.getHiddenInputHTML = function()
{
   var hiddenInputHTML = "";
   var basketItem;

   for (basketItem in this.items)
   {
      // Ref
      hiddenInputHTML += "<INPUT TYPE='hidden' NAME='";
      hiddenInputHTML += this.items[basketItem].getItemRefId() + "_RefId'";
      hiddenInputHTML += " VALUE=" + this.items[basketItem].getItemRefId();
      hiddenInputHTML += ">";

      // Qty
      hiddenInputHTML += "<INPUT TYPE='hidden' NAME='";
      hiddenInputHTML += this.items[basketItem].getItemRefId() + "_Qty'";
      hiddenInputHTML += " VALUE=" + this.items[basketItem].getItemQty();
```

```
        hiddenInputHTML += ">";
    }

    return hiddenInputHTML;
}
```

As with the basket display code, the method loops through each ShoppingItem object in the item's array. It obtains the item details and generates the HTML required to create hidden text boxes in the page, with details of each CD in the basket. We write out two hidden text boxes per item; the first will hold the items reference id, and the second will hold the quantity. These are the only details that would need to be passed to the server side for processing to take place. Most databases have a unique reference id for each item, so should be no need to specify details and descriptions to specify a particular item, just the reference id.

If rather than using CGI, ASP, PHP or some other server-side scripting language in a page, you're using a Java applet, then you may wish to use alternative methods of getting the information to the server, for example by setting properties in the applet.

Let's alter the CheckoutConfirm.htm page to add the final summary display. First, we'll add a script block in the HEAD. At the top of the script block is an if statement which checks to see if the basket is empty, but how can it possibly be empty? Well, if the user has completed the order, then clicks their browser back button they will be taken to this page but with an empty basket and no customer or credit card details, which would cause our code to fail. We, therefore check for an empty basket and navigate the page the emptybasket.htm if it's empty. We need to do it here before any other code in the page executes as the rest of the page's code relies on a basket with items and Customer and CreditCard objects with details of the customer and their credit card.

Next in the script block is a function called window_onload() that will be connected to the onLoad event handler of the window:

```
<SCRIPT LANGUAGE='JavaScript'>

    if (parent.myBasket.isEmpty())
    {
        window.location.href = "emptybasket.htm";
    }

    function window_onload()
    {
        var customerSummaryHTML =
            parent.thisCustomer.getCustomerDetailsSummary();
        parent.writeInnerHTML(window.document,'divAddressSummary',
            customerSummaryHTML);

        var cardSummaryHTML =
            parent.customerCreditCard.getCreditCardDetailsSummary();
        parent.writeInnerHTML(window.document,'divCreditCardSummary',
            cardSummaryHTML);

        var cardDebitSummaryHTML = "A total of ";
        cardDebitSummaryHTML += parent.myBasket.getTotalIncDelivery();
        cardDebitSummaryHTML += " will be debited from your ";
        cardDebitSummaryHTML += parent.customerCreditCard.getCardType();
        cardDebitSummaryHTML += " card (Card details below)";
        parent.writeInnerHTML(window.document,'divAmountSummary',
            cardDebitSummaryHTML);

        var orderItemsSummaryHTML = parent.myBasket.getBasketHTML(false);
        parent.writeInnerHTML(window.document,'divBasketSummary',
            orderItemsSummaryHTML);
```

```
            // To force NN4 to show scroll bars
            if (document.layers)
            {
                document.height = document.divBasketSummary.top +
                document.divBasketSummary.document.height;
            }
        }
    }
    </SCRIPT>
</HEAD>
```

This function is concerned with creating summaries of the order. There are five absolutely positioned DIVs in the page: into the first, divAddressSummary, we write the delivery details; into the second, divAmountSummary, we write the amount to be charged to the credit card; into the third, divCreditCardSummary, the card details; into the fourth, divOrderItemsAre, is only for formatting purposes and holds a title; and into the fifth and final one, divBasketSummary, we write details of the order items. The summary methods of the Customer and CreditCard classes provide the address and card summaries. The amount to be debited comes from the getTotalIncDelivery() method of the ShoppingBasket class and the final order items summary also comes from the getBasketHTML() method - the same one that created the displayed basket, except this time the parameter isUpdateable is passed as false. We use the writeInnerHTML() method in Musicmad.htm in each case to perform the DHTML writing.

Our next change to the CheckoutConfirm.htm page is to the <BODY> tag:

```
<BODY onLoad='window_onload()'>
```

We've added the onLoad event handler that will call our window_onload() function. Now we need to add a script block after the hidden input boxes, which will set their values to those entered by the user and stored in Musicmad.htm's thisCustomer and customerCreditCard variables, containing references to objects of class type Customer and CreditCard respectively:

```
<!-- Credit Card Details -->
<INPUT TYPE='HIDDEN' NAME='txtCardHolderName' VALUE=''></INPUT>
<INPUT TYPE='HIDDEN' NAME='txtCardNumber' VALUE=''></INPUT>
<INPUT TYPE='HIDDEN' NAME='txtCardType' VALUE=''></INPUT>
<INPUT TYPE='HIDDEN' NAME='txtCardExpires' VALUE=''></INPUT>

<SCRIPT LANGUAGE='JavaScript'>
    var form = document.frmOrder;

    form.txtTitle.value = parent.thisCustomer.getTitle();
    form.txtFullName.value = parent.thisCustomer.getFullName();
    form.txtEmail.value = parent.thisCustomer.getEmail();
    form.txtStreet.value = parent.thisCustomer.getStreet();
    form.txtCity.value = parent.thisCustomer.getCity();
    form.txtLocality.value = parent.thisCustomer.getLocality();
    form.txtPostalCode.value = parent.thisCustomer.getPostalCode();
    form.txtCountry.value = parent.thisCustomer.getCountry();

    form.txtCardHolderName.value =
        parent.customerCreditCard.getCardHolderName();
    form.txtCardNumber.value = parent.customerCreditCard.getCardNumber();
    form.txtCardType.value = parent.customerCreditCard.getCardType();
    form.txtCardExpires.value =
        parent.customerCreditCard.getCardExpires();

    document.write(parent.myBasket.getHiddenInputHTML());
</SCRIPT>
```

```
<!-- Summarize Order details -->
<H4>Your order details are listed below.</H4>
<P>Once you have confirmed the details click
```

On the last line of the script, we use our `ShoppingBasket` class's `getHiddenInputHTML()` method to generate the necessary hidden input elements that contain the details of every item in the customer's basket and write it out to the page using `document.write()`.

We just need to add the `onClick` event handler to the `cmdSubmit` button and we're finished with this page:

```
<INPUT TYPE='button' NAME='cmdSubmit'
    onClick='window.location.href = "OrderComplete.htm"'
    VALUE='Submit Order'> to send your order
```

Why do use the `window.location.href` to go to the next page, why not submit the form? Well, if this was a server as well as a client-side application then we would. However, as we have concentrated solely on the client-side, any forms need to be posted to a server-side handler, for example an ASP page or CGI script. If they are not then it's likely an error will occur as the server. When you come to use the shopping cart application then you will need to change this line so it submits the form, for example by changing the button to a submit button and removing the `onClick` event handler:

```
<INPUT TYPE='submit'
    NAME='cmdSubmit'
    VALUE='Submit Order'> to send your order
```

That's the `CheckoutConfirm.htm` page complete – now we have just the order completion to do as the final task for this chapter.

Order Complete

Normally, at the point of submitting the order, we would start our server-side processing of the order. This would include the credit card transaction, notifying someone to process the order items and ship them out, and any necessary changes to database data. Our `checkoutconfirm.htm` page has posted all the form information to this page so it's all ready for server-side scripting to collect the posted data and use it. However, as we are not looking at the server-side aspect of things in this book, we just have one last task – to clear the customer's basket. Now they've ordered the items it's unlikely they will want to return and find their basket still fuller.

First, we need to add one final method to the `ShoppingBasket` class so open the `ShoppingBasket.js` file and add the following:

```
ShoppingBasket.prototype.clearBasket = function()
{
    this.items = new Object();
    this.numItems = 0;
    document.cookie = "MusicMadBasket= ; expires=1 Jan 2000 00:00:00";
}
```

The `clearBasket()` method sets the items property to a new object, and in the process ends our reference to the old object and basket items. We set the `numItems` to zero and finally clear the cookie that saves the basket contents.

Next, we need to add one final function to the `MusicMad.htm` page. Load that page into your editor, and add the following function the script block:

```
function resetShoppingApp()
{
    myBasket.clearBasket();
```

```
    thisCustomer = new Customer();
    customerCreditCard = new CreditCard();
}
```

This function will clear the basket, using the function we created above, then reset the variables `thisCustomer` and `customerCreditCard` to new objects, ready for the customer to start over and place a new order.

Now save the file, load `OrderComplete.htm`, and change it as shown below:

```
<!-- OrderComplete.htm -->
<HTML>
<HEAD>
    <LINK REL='stylesheet' HREF='WebsiteGlobalStyle.css'>
    <TITLE>Order Complete</TITLE>
</HEAD>
<BODY onLoad='window.parent.resetShoppingApp()'>
    <H1>Order Completed Successfully</H1>
    <H4>Your order will be with you shortly</H4>
    <H4>Thanks for shopping with MusicMad.Com</H4>
    <H4><A HREF='home.htm'>Home Page</A></H4>
</BODY>
</HTML>
```

We added the `onload` event handler to the `<BODY>` tag so that when the window load event fires we call the function `resetShoppingApp()` that we just added to the `MusicMad.htm` page, this page's parent. Now if the customer wants to place another order right away then they do so with a clean sheet. That completes all the changes to the shopping cart application.

Summary

In this chapter, we have looked at many of the client-side aspects of creating an e-commerce system. Some of the points covered in the chapter include:

❑   We talked about the importance of making any e-commerce system easy for the user to use. The fewer obstacles we put in the way of a user seeing something they want, the more likely we are to make a successful sale.

❑   Our shopping cart application needs to be easy to include in a web site and easily extensible, therefore we chose to create it as a JavaScript class based system. We kept all class source code inside .js files that we include in a page using the `<SCRIPT>` tag and setting the `SRC` property to the location of the .js file.

❑   Our application consists of five classes: `ShoppingItem`, `ShoppingBasket`, `Validate`, `Customer`, and `CreditCard`. Each of these classes represents an aspect of our online shopping application.

❑   The `ShoppingItem` class represents a single shopping item. It stores all the necessary details for one item, details of which we can read and write using get and set methods for each property. We learnt that using accessor methods to access an object's properties meant there was less likelihood of errors due to misnamed properties. JavaScript will allow us to access a non-existent property with no complaint, however attempting to access a non-existent method leads to an error being notified.

❑   The `ShoppingCart` class represents everything to do with the shopping basket part of our online application, for example adding items to a shopping basket, deleting items, displaying a list of all the items in the basket, and so on. This class even allows us to pass a `form` object to it and have the basket updated automatically.

- ❏ The `Validate` class deals with client-side validation of data entered into forms by the user. We talked about it in depth in Chapter 16: *Form Validation*. It also automates much of the form checking with a method that will check all the form elements in a form. This automated form checker uses the name given to a form element to decide whether the element needs to be checked, if it's compulsory and what type of information it should contain. The class also had other methods that allowed us to verify things like a user's credit card number, though it can only check if the information could be valid, not that it is valid. For example, the number may be in a valid format and fit an algorithm for checking it, but that does not mean that a credit card company has actually issued the number or that it hasn't been stolen or lost, etc.

- ❏ The `Customer` class is the Customer objectified. It allows us to store the details of a customer, again using accessor methods `get` and `set`, and it provides a method for generating a summary of the customer's information, used on the final checkout screen.

- ❏ The `CreditCard` class represents the users credit card details. We can store and retrieve the customer's card details inside it, using `get` and `set` accessor methods. Like the `Customer` class, it also provides a method to generate a summary of the credit card details entered by the user.

The web site created in this chapter could, as it stands and with some minor modifications, be used as an online shopping application. All that needs to be added is the code to deal with the server-side aspects of e-commerce system, for example processing the credit card details and notifying someone of the order details. The final page in the checkout part of the web site, `CheckoutConfirm.htm`, currently doesn't post its data but simply navigates to an order completed page. This page simple needs changing so that it posts the data to your server-side application for processing. This might be to a CGI component or if you're using Microsoft IIS it might be to an ASP page, the choice is yours. The server-side page would need to check the data, process the card details and ensure the warehouse is notified of the order for sending to the customer. It would need to deal with issues such as what happens if parts of the order are for items out of stock or if the customer's credit card is not valid.

Currently, the web site has hard-coded details of products into static HTML pages. For a real system, with any significant amount of goods for sale, we would really want to generate the product details dynamically, most probably by retrieving information about stock and stock levels from a database.

It's also likely that you would want to improve on the web site, but to keep the chapter manageable it's been kept to just the basics. However, for your particular needs there are bound to be many possible changes and additions. You may even wish to simply use the classes and add these to your web site and make use of the functionality they provide.

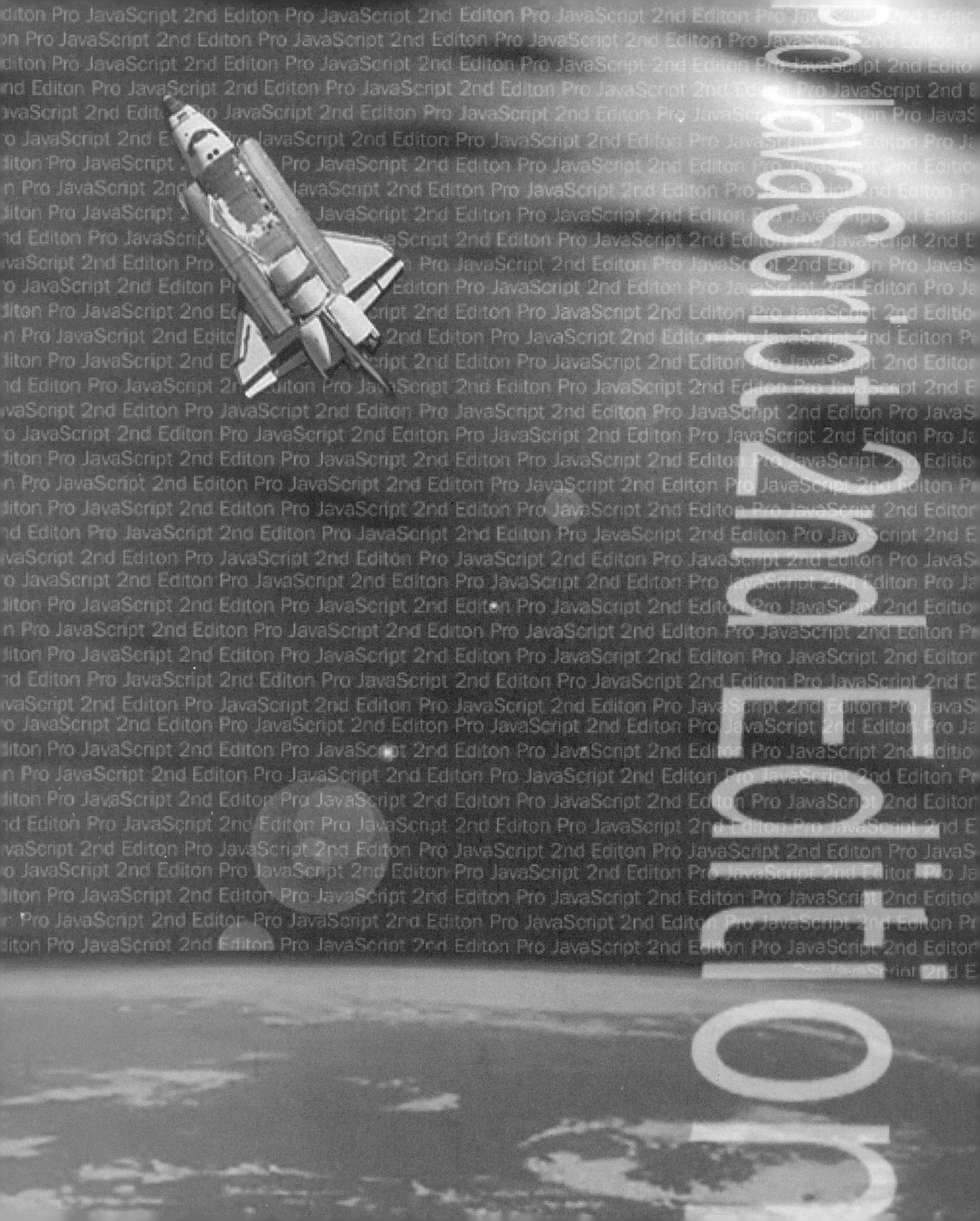
Pro JavaScript 2nd Edition
Pro JavaScript 2nd Editon

Creating a JavaScript Family Tree Photo Album

Now that we've had a look at much of the potential of JavaScript, now seems like an appropriate time to see how this all works in practice and to apply our knowledge to an interesting project. In this chapter, we will look at a case study that uses JavaScript to create a Family Tree Photo Album. The album will allow us to manage and display photographs of our current family, as well as ancestors, over the Internet.

We will start (as all projects should!) by considering the specific requirements of the application. Then we will discuss alternative design approaches and tradeoffs. Finally, we will examine in detail the code of the implementation. In fact, we will look at three different implementations of the project within this chapter.

One feature of this case study is that all the programming logic will be coded in JavaScript, with a little help from the browser's object model, DHTML, and Java. By the end of this project, we will have hands-on experience of:

- ❑ Working with JavaScript and DHTML to dynamically modify a web page
- ❑ Creating a reusable tree controller using only JavaScript and DHTML for IE based browsers
- ❑ Using JavaScript to assist in submitting a form through e-mail, without server-based CGI
- ❑ Simulating the operation of a cross-browser compatible modal dialog box using JavaScript
- ❑ Embedding a Java applet into a web page and interfacing it to work with JavaScript
- ❑ Understanding why one may want to integrate standard XML parsers in JavaScript programs
- ❑ JavaScript integration of an industry standard XML parser and the use of W3C DOM interfaces to access an XML document
- ❑ Writing JavaScript code that will work on the latest versions of both Netscape and Microsoft browsers (Netscape 6.1, Netscape 4.7, IE 6.0 and IE 5.5)
- ❑ Implementing a tree controller that works with version 4.x and later browsers

Before we can proceed further, let's take a quick look at how the application that we're building will actually work.

The Photo Album Application

This is how we want our Family Tree Photo Album to look when it's completed:

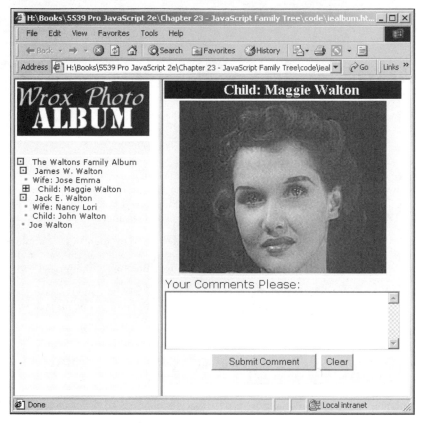

The user will typically:

❏ Navigate through the family tree by clicking on the left pane, collapsing or expanding sub-trees

❏ View the photograph of a family member by clicking on his or her name in the tree

❏ Submit a comment to the webmaster on any family member picture

The page will consist of two frames:

❏ A Tree Controller Page (the left-hand frame), which will allow the user to navigate through the family tree

❏ A Photo Display Page (on the right), where the picture of the family member will appear, and where the user will be given the chance to send a comment to the webmaster

When a user submits a comment, they should get a chance to confirm the message before it is sent.

Requirements of the Project

Other requirements for the project are that:

- ❏ The application should work with the current versions of major browsers (IE 6.0, IE 5.5, Netscape 6.1 and Netscape 4.75) on Win32 platforms.

- ❏ No CGI (server side processing) support will be available; comments will have to be submitted via e-mail.

Implementation Strategy

We will actually be working through three different versions of the project. In the first version, we will work with IE 6/5/4 and the DHTML that it supports. This will illustrate some of the power of the Microsoft object model and its implementation of DHTML. Next, we will be modifying the IE version of the album to use the XML parser that is built into IE 5 and 6. This second version will illustrate how we can make practical use of XML to simplify data driven applications (under which this photo album can be classified). In addition, we will use the W3C DOM support of IE 5 and 6 in this version of our application.

When we've got the application running smoothly in IE, we will look at the problems that must be overcome to build a cross-browser version of the page. In the third and final version, we will be building the application using JavaScript only. It will make use of a tree controller library that has cross browser support. This version will work with both IE 4+ and Netscape 4+, and will also give us a chance to see how JavaScript can be put to good use building a relatively complex cross-browser application.

Here is a table that summarizes the three versions of the application that we will create:

Version	Description	Compatible Browsers
1	Maximizes on IE specific object model and DHTML capabilities	IE 4.x and up
2	Uses XML to describe the photograph data and uses the W3C DOM support for page manipulation	IE 5+, with support for W3C DOM and XML standards
3	Uses JavaScript only and a cross platform library to manage the application	IE 4+, and Netscape 4+

Note that for this specific project, there is no requirement to handle Macintosh or UNIX clients since we know ahead of time that all users accessing the application will be on Win32 clients.

Designing the Application

All of our application versions will share the same basic design; only the implementation (and coding) differs. The basic problems that we must solve in the application are to:

- ❏ Implement a tree controller that graphically displays hierarchical data

- ❏ Dynamically change the picture and title displayed in the Photo Display Page when the user clicks on a tree controller link

- ❏ Display a pop-up modal dialog box

- ❏ Submit comments via e-mail from a form on the page

A Tree Controller Displaying Hierarchical Data

Our approach here is to introduce a simple XML-based description language to describe the family tree data. Next, we create a mini-parser that scans this description and builds the actual graphic tree for the controller. We will call our description language the **mini-Hierarchical Data Markup Language (mHDML)**. The figure below illustrates this process:

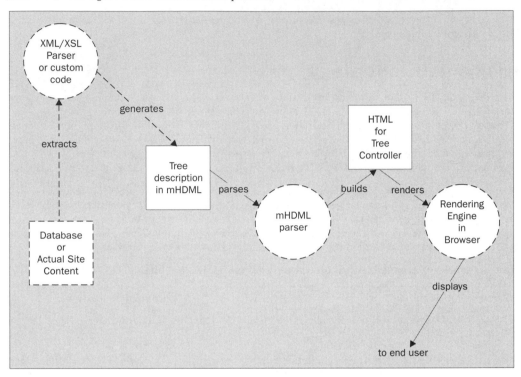

Additional flexibility is provided by the option of generating the actual mHDML on the fly using a server-based custom process via server-side XML/XSL (see Chapter 7, *HTML, XML and XHTML* for details on XML and XSL). This allows the tree display to vary as the actual server content changes, such as if new family members are added. Another possibility might be to update the mHDML description whenever content changes, instead of generating the file on the fly. This latter approach saves on the XSL processing required on the server-side; only once per change in content rather than once every page access.

Changing Pictures and Titles Dynamically

To change the picture and title displayed on the Photo Display frame, there are at least two possible approaches (see Chapter 10, *Dynamic HTML* for more on DHTML image manipulations):

❑ Directly modify the attributes of the associated DIV and IMG tags, causing the browser's rendering engine to display the new data

❑ Send data for a new title and a new image to JavaScript code within the Photo Display frame, and get the JavaScript code to generate the actual HTML to display that new data (using Document.write as detailed in Chapter 10)

We will be using both methods; the first one in our first two IE-specific implementations and the second in the last cross browser version.

Displaying a Modal Dialog Box

If the browser supports display of a modal dialog, it will be easy to achieve this. In our Microsoft-specific solution, we will use IE 6/5/4 support for modal dialogs. However, Netscape browsers do not support modal dialog boxes directly in any reliable cross-platform manner (although Netscape 6 on Win32 systems does support a restrictive modal dialog option). To ensure backwards compatibility with all supported browsers, we will emulate the behavior of a modal dialog box by repeatedly setting the focus. We will design a solution in a way that will work with both Netscape and IE browsers.

Submitting a Form Using E-mail

Fortunately, the ability to send e-mail via the default mail client software is a standard feature of both lea ding browsers. The general approach is to use a `mailto` URL via a specific `ACTION` attribute in the `FORM` tag:

```
<FORM NAME='myform' ACTION='mailto:lsing@working.com'
      ENCTYPE='text/plain' METHOD='post'>
```

The form data will be submitted as e-mail to the recipient (in this case, `lsing@working.com`), in `"text/plain"` or unencoded format. You will have to change the e-mail address in the source code during testing so that you will receive the test e-mail yourself, instead of the webmaster or systems administrator.

Obviously, the system must be configured to send e-mail via a default mail client for this to work properly. All of the browser versions that we need to be compatible with come with suitable default e-mail client applications. We will assume for our discussion that these default e-mail applications are used. When a user selects the "complete install" of IE 6, the Outlook Express client is the default application for sending and receiving e-mail. Part of the installation is a wizard that guides the user through mail server configuration. After installing the complete Netscape 6, start the mail application using **Tasks | Mail**, and then use the mail application's **Edit | Mail/News Account Settings** to configure your server settings. In Netscape 4.x, configure the **Mail & Newsgroups** setting under **Edit | Preferences**. In earlier versions of the browsers, the actual method of configuration may vary.

The Family Tree

The diagram below shows the family tree that we will be working with. It belongs to a fictitious family called the Waltons:

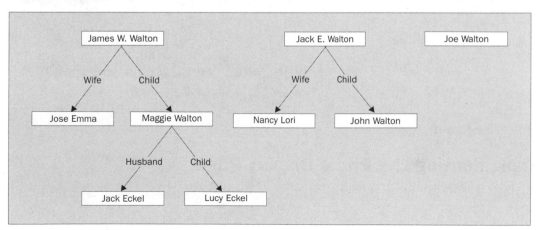

The associated picture files of each family member are:

Name	JPG file
James W. Walton	WALT1.JPG
Jose Emma	WALT2.JPG
Maggie Walton	WALT3.JPG
Jack Eckel	WALT4.JPG
Lucy Eckel	WALT5.JPG
Jack E. Walton	WALT6.JPG
Nancy Lori	WALT7.JPG
John Walton	WALT8.JPG
Joe Walton	WALT9.JPG

These picture files can be found in the code download for this chapter, available at
http://www.wrox.com.

An Internet Explorer Specific DHTML Application

As we stated earlier, our first solution will be created using IE 6, but will also be tested to ensure
compatibility with IE 5.5, and even version 4.01. It makes extensive use of JavaScript and DHTML.

The Main Application Frame

The main application page is called `iealbum.html` and can be found with the source code on the
Wrox web site. It contains just a frameset, which links to two other HTML pages: `ietree.html` for the
tree control page, and `iepage.html` for the Photo Display frame. A third page, called `iedlg.html` is
used for a modal dialog when the user submits a comment from the Photo Display page. Splitting up the
page into frames in this way enables us to take a "divide and conquer" approach to development:

```
<HTML>
    <HEAD>
    </HEAD>
    <FRAMESET COLS='210,*'>
        <FRAME SRC='ietree.html' NAME='treectrl' ALIGN='left' MARGINWIDTH=0
               SCROLLING='auto'>
        <FRAME SRC='iepage.html' NAME='albpage' MARGINWIDTH=0
               SCROLLING='auto'>
    </FRAMESET>
</HTML>
```

Implementing the Photo Display Page

The Photo Display Page, or `iedlg.html` consists of three general areas:

❑   Title area

❑   Picture area

❑   Comments form

We will build a table to manage the layout of the three areas; each area will occupy one cell in the table. We will use a DIV tag to mark out the title area, giving it a custom white-on-black format using CSS styling and providing us with the ability to change its content dynamically later on (see Chapter 8, *CSS* for more coverage of CSS styles). The picture area simply consists of an IMG element, whose SRC attribute we will modify when we want to display different photos. The comment form is a standard FORM element. We will create a custom SUBMIT button handler for this form. Clicking the submit button will launch a modal dialog box confirming the message.

Creating a Modal Dialog Box

Creating a modal dialog box is simple using DHTML in IE. It can be accomplished through the showModalDialog() method of the window object. The syntax for this method is:

```
var returnValue = window.showModalDialog(URL, Args, Options);
```

The above components are described below:

Component Name	Description
returnValue	A value returned by the dialog box. It is returned by setting the returnValue property of the window object, that represents the dialog box.
URL	The URL for the page to be displayed within the dialog box.
Args	A variable containing the arguments to be passed into the dialog box. The dialog box page can access this via the window.dialogArguments property.
Options	A string, in style sheet format, controlling the width, height, placement, and appearance of the window. It can contain: dialogWidth, dialogHeight, dialogTop, dialogLeft, center, help, resizable and status attributes.

The modal dialog displayed by this command is an actual Win32 application modal dialog box. This ensures that the parent browser window cannot get focus back unless the dialog is closed.

Passing Data into Modal Dialog Boxes

The source code for the Photo Display page is in the iepage.html file. Let's examine it in detail. The first section of script code contains the showform() function. This function prepares the arguments for passing into the modal dialog box, and then it displays the dialog via the showModalDialog() method:

```
<HTML>
   <HEAD>
      <SCRIPT LANGUAGE='JScript'>
         function showform()
         {
             var myArgs=new Array(2);
             myArgs[0]=document.all.cmttxt.value;
             myArgs[1]=document.all.showpic.src;

             var result=showModalDialog("iedlg.html", myArgs,
                 "dialogHeight:250px;dialogWidth:300px;status:no;help:no;");
         }
      </SCRIPT>
   </HEAD>
```

The variable `myArgs` is the array containing the arguments that are to be passed into the dialog box. The first item contains the comment entered by the user. This is taken from the `TEXTAREA` element called `cmttxt`, where the user will enter any comments. The second item is the name of the image file for the photo being displayed when the comment was entered. This name is available from the `SRC` attribute of our `IMG` tag. Note that the URL of the page displayed inside the dialog, the first parameter in the `showModalDialog()` call, is that for the `iedlg.html` page. We will examine the code for this page shortly.

Designing the Page Layout

In the next part of the Photo Display page, we design the customized heading for the page. This part of the code places the actual text for the title, initially set to **The Waltons Family Album**, within a `DIV` tag called `picTitle`. When a user clicks on a selection from the tree controller, the controller will use DHTML to modify this title directly:

```
<BODY STYLE='font-size:8pt;font-family:Verdana,Arial,Helvetica;'>
   <TABLE WIDTH='300' BORDER='0' ALIGN='left'>
      <TR><TD bgcolor='black'>
         <CENTER>
            <DIV ID='picTitle' STYLE='color:white; font-size:16pt;
                                      font-weight:bold;
                                      font-family:Times,Times Roman;'>
               The Waltons Family Album
            </DIV>
         </CENTER>
      </TD></TR>
```

Similar to the way in which the title was changed, the tree controller will also be able to modify the `SRC` attribute of the `IMG` tag directly when the user clicks on a selection.

```
<TR><TD BGCOLOR='lightyellow'>
   <CENTER>
      <IMG NAME='showpic' SRC='album.gif' width='300' height='250'>
   </CENTER>
</TD></TR>
```

Adding a Message Confirmation Dialog

The comment form is designed for processing entirely in JavaScript. It does not submit the form to the server with the `GET` or `POST` method, as traditional forms do. Instead, when the **Submit Comment** button is pressed, the `showform()` function is called to display the modal dialog. We will design the dialog box to look like this:

This dialog is used to confirm the message, and allow the user to enter their name before actually sending the message:

```
    <TR><TD BGCOLOR='lightyellow'>
        <FORM NAME='comment'>
            Your Comments Please:<BR>
            <TEXTAREA NAME='cmttxt' COLS='40' ROWS='5'></TEXTAREA><BR>
    </TD></TR>
    <TR><TD BGCOLOR='lightyellow'>
        <CENTER>
            <INPUT TYPE='button' ONCLICK='showform()'
                    VALUE='Submit Comment'>
            <INPUT TYPE='reset' VALUE='Clear'>
        </CENTER>
    </FORM>
    </TD></TR>
</TABLE>

</BODY>
</HTML>
```

That wraps it up for the Photo Display page. There is very little JavaScript code, apart from the showform() function for displaying the modal dialog box. Let us now turn our attention to the design of the page that will represent this dialog box.

Implementing the Modal Dialog Box

The code for the Modal Dialog page is in the iedlg.html file in the source code. This technique is important, so let's examine this code line by line:

```
<HTML>
    <HEAD>
        <TITLE>Confirm Message</TITLE>
        <SCRIPT LANGUAGE='JScript'>
            function delayClose() {
                setTimeout("top.close()",8000);
                return true;
            }
```

In the HEAD section, we first define a function called delayClose(), called when the dialog box is closed. There is a good reason why we need this function.

Recall that the message entered by the user will be submitted via e-mail. When a form is not submitted to the server via a GET or POST transaction, IE will not close the form or transfer to another page. This means that we must explicitly implement the behavior that we want. In this case, we want to give the application some time to send the e-mail, and then close the window (our modal dialog box).

Inside delayClose(), we use the JavaScript setTimeout() function to schedule a piece of JavaScript code to be executed at some time in the future. Here, it schedules the close() method of the top window to execute after 8000 ms, or 8 seconds later.

delayClose() always returns true, since it will be used within as an onsubmit event handler later. This enables the submission to occur successfully.

Escaping Quotes in JavaScript Generated Forms

The next function we define in the HEAD section is the escQuote() function to escape quotation marks in the comment text. To understand why this function is necessary, we need to understand better how the message entered on the Photo Display page ends up in the e-mail message sent from the Confirm Message modal dialog box. This diagram shows the process our code will follow, from the user entering a comment, to an e-mail being sent to the webmaster:

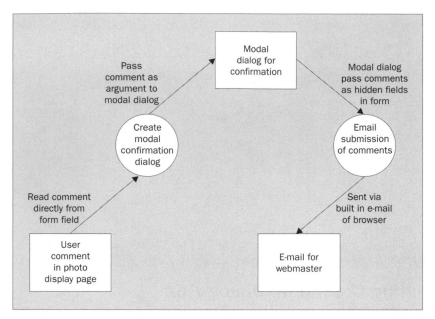

We can see that the argument passed into the modal dialog box is used to create part of the HTML confirmation page where the message is re-displayed. In fact, it is also used to create HTML for two hidden fields within the modal dialog box form. Conceptually, the code that will generate these two hidden fields will look something like this:

```
<SCRIPT>
   document.write("<INPUT NAME='pic' TYPE='hidden' VALUE='" +
                  window.dialogArguments[1] + "'>");
   document.write("<INPUT NAME='mesg' TYPE='hidden' VALUE='" +
                  window.dialogArguments[0] + "'>");
</SCRIPT>
```

Note how the hidden INPUT tags are made part of the HTML document. In particular, notice that the mesg field value (window.dialogArguments[0]) is written inside a pair of single quotes. This field value must not include an embedded single quote, otherwise the generated HTML code will not be syntactically correct. For this reason, we have written a JavaScript function called escQuote() to replace any embedded single quotes with an asterisk (*). We cannot use the standard JavaScript escape()/unescape() functions because the resulting message text will be e-mailed using the "text/plain" unencoded data type. These asterisks will not be replaced at the client-side, but may be unescaped on the receiver's side if desired. Here's our implementation of the escQuote() function:

```
function escQuote(inStr)
{
   var tpArray = inStr.split("'");
   var escMsg;
   if (tpArray.length > 1)
      escMsg = tpArray.join("*");
   else
      escMsg = inStr;
   return escMsg;
}
</SCRIPT>
</HEAD>
```

The `escQuote()` function demonstrates the powerful methods provided by the JavaScript `String` object. We can replace all the single quotes within a string with asterisks by simply calling the `split()` method. This removes the quotes and separates the string into an array of tokens, followed by a `join()` method that glues the array of tokens back using the new asterisk separator. Note that we could have used JavaScript's regular expression support (in other words, an alternative would be to use the versatile `replace()` method of the `String` object).

Argument Data Inside a Modal Dialog Box

The next part of the modal dialog page redisplays the message entered, so that users can confirm that this is really the message they want to send. This is done by accessing the `dialogArguments` array which passed in as a parameter. The argument array is the second parameter of the original `showModalDialog()` call:

```
<BODY BGCOLOR='lightyellow' STYLE='font-size:12;
    font-family:Verdana,Arial,Helvetica;' SCROLL='no'>
  <TABLE WIDTH=100%>
    <TR>
      <TD>
        Your Message:<BR>
      </TD>
    </TR>
    <TR>
      <TD bgcolor='white' valign='top' height='120'
        style='font-size:10;font-family:courier;'>
        <SCRIPT>
          document.write(window.dialogArguments[0]);
        </SCRIPT>
      </TD>
    </TR>
```

Submitting Form Information Via E-mail

Next comes the actual form that we will submit via e-mail. In the `FORM` tag, notice the `ACTION='mailto...'` attribute used to specify e-mail processing. The `ENCTYPE` attribute is included to ensure that the transmitted message is not escaped for special characters, but transmitted as unfiltered text instead. The `METHOD='post'` attribute must be included to ensure the form is submitted properly:

```
    <TR>
      <TD>
        <BR>
        <FORM NAME='myform'  ACTION='mailto:lsing@working.com'
            ENCTYPE='text/plain' METHOD='post' ONSUBMIT='delayClose()'>
          Name:  
          <INPUT NAME='myname' TYPE='text'><BR>
          <SCRIPT>
            document.write("<INPUT NAME='pic' TYPE='hidden' VALUE='" +
                          window.dialogArguments[1] + "'>");
            document.write("<INPUT NAME='mesg' TYPE='hidden' VALUE='" +
                          escQuote(window.dialogArguments[0]) + "'>");
          </SCRIPT>
          <INPUT TYPE='SUBMIT' VALUE='Send Comment Now'>
          <INPUT TYPE='button' VALUE='Cancel' ONCLICK='top.close()'>
        </FORM>
      </TD>
    </TR>
  </TABLE>
</BODY>
</HTML>
```

We have already seen why we have to include the `delayClose()` function. Here it is hooked in so that the modal dialog box will close a few seconds after the user has submitted the message. We see here the generation of the two hidden fields required for form submission. Note the use of the `escQuote()` function on the actual message within the `mesg` hidden field.

A Final Word On Our Choice of Mechanism for Submitting Feedback

The use of `mailto` URL for submitting feedback is certainly effective for this case study, and it has the benefit of being a client-side only mechanism that is usable across different browsers. One of our initial requirements is that there should be no special server-side support and therefore, any sort of CGI based solution will not be appropriate. Unfortunately, this technique can be difficult to manage/support if the client base all have different default mail clients installed, or if designers have security concerns that e-mail may be sent unknowingly on the user's behalf. When such issues arise, we could consider proprietary extensions that require special support. For example, Javamail provides a more reliable and secure means of accomplishing the same thing.

There are built-in measures that make the activities of the `mailto` URL mechanism quite explicit. To ensure the user realizes that a scripted application is sending e-mail on a user's behalf, the browser typically shows a security warning.

Furthermore, if you are using Netscape 6.x browsers, the default mail client will not automatically send the e-mail message. Instead, the client will start at the compose message mode, with the information from the `mailto` URL filled in. This is Netscape's chosen way of dealing with the potential security problem associated with `mailto` URL.

This completes our coverage of the modal dialog box page. We will now look at the most complex page in the entire project, `ietree.html`, which implements the tree controller.

A Tree Controller in Pure JavaScript

A tree controller displays hierarchical data in a graphical tree form, similar to the way in which Windows Explorer displays directories and files. The user can expand and collapse the various levels of the tree to increase or reduce the level of detail respectively. For our sample family tree, a completely collapsed tree includes the text "The Waltons Family Album" adjacent to a '+' icon.

If we expand the tree controller to its full level of details by clicking all the + icons, we will see the complete family tree.

By clicking on any link displayed, the tree controller will change the picture displayed on the Photo Display page.

Rendering Collapsing Tree Elements

To graphically display the collapsing tree elements, we need the following:

❑ Small icons that will indicate the state/type of the tree nodes (whether it is expanded or collapsed, whether it has children or not)

❑ A way to show and hide the tree nodes dynamically

We will use these three small graphic icon GIF files to display the state of the tree elements:

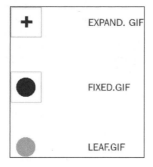

A single tree node will always consist of one of these graphics, followed by a string to be displayed.

In HTML, we will mark off the icons and the text inside a SPAN tag. Using this approach will allow us to work on the combined graphics and text as a single unit. In particular, it allows us to control the visibility of the entire element. Here is an example of how it appears conceptually in HTML:

```
<SPAN><IMG SRC='expand.gif'>  Waltons Family</SPAN>
```

To show the actual level of the tree, we can use a varying number of spaces before the display of the image within the SPAN. We will be constructing these indentations programmatically later on. For example, the HTML content of a second level element may be:

```
<SPAN>    <IMG SRC='fixed.gif'>  Sam Walton</SPAN>
```

See Chapter 10, *Dynamic HTML* for more details about using this versatile tag in conjunction with DHTML.

Dynamic Attributes and Mouseover Animation

We use IE's ability to dynamically define and create attributes to help us implement mouseover animation. As the user moves the cursor over the selectable elements that are displayed in the tree control, each element will change color. This creates a "flashing effect" when the mouse is moved over the selection The item will either be displayed in "dark" black or "bright" red. In order to implement this effect, we need to persist information on each element that supports it. The information we want to keep is:

❑ Whether an element should be mouseover animated

❑ The current state of an element: dark or bright

We will keep this information so that we can use one single set of event handlers for the entire document. Within the event handler, we will be checking these attribute values to determine what action to perform if any. Using dynamically created attributes, we can add a marker attribute to the SPAN tag to mark a specific element as eligible for mouseover animation. We will use a new FLASHER attribute. Using such a dynamic attribute will enable us to stop certain elements flashing if the need arises (by leaving out the attribute). Now, a typical second level element may have the following HTML:

```
<SPAN FLASHER>    
   <IMG SRC='fixed.gif'>  Sam Walton
</SPAN>
```

One unique benefit of DHTML is the ability to define our very own custom attributes (such as FLASHER). We can use the element.getAttribute() method to check the value or existence of these custom attributes.

In implementing the actual mouseover animation, we use a CSS class to format the small-font red (or black) characters. By switching the class associated with an element in JavaScript, we can cause the tree element to flash. This doubles as a way to keep track of the current brightness of a flashing element. We can use the CSS class to mark a flashing element as either "dark" or "bright". The second level element with this improvement will end up with:

```
<SPAN CLASS='dark' FLASHER>    
   <IMG SRC='fixed.gif'>  Sam Walton
</SPAN>
```

Last but not least, if we need to be able to react to mouse clicks on these elements, we can simply make the inner content a hyperlink. For example:

```
<SPAN CLASS='dark' FLASHER>    
   <IMG SRC='fixed.gif'>  
   <A href='http://www.mynode.com/~samw/'>Sam Walton</A>
</SPAN>
```

If we need more flexible event handling than simply transferring to a URL, we can use an ONCLICK handler:

```
<SPAN CLASS='dark' FLASHER>    
   <IMG SRC='fixed.gif' ONCLICK='clickHandler()'>   Sam Walton
</SPAN>
```

Note that we restrict the ONCLICK event handler here within the IMG tag because clicking the icons that will cause the tree to expand or collapse. Clicking on the text itself will instead cause the picture to change in the Photo Display page.

Use of Cascading DIV and SPAN Elements

The actual expanding and collapsing tree branches are implemented using cascading (or nested) DIV tags. We are going to take advantage of the ability of Microsoft's rendering engine to perform repeated layout immediately after the visibility of a branch has been modified via the CSS display:none style attribute.

Conceptually, a collapsed tree branch looks like this:

```
<SPAN CLASS='dark' FLASHER>... visible top level branch ...</SPAN>
<DIV ID='out1d' STYLE='display:none'>
  <SPAN CLASS='dark' FLASHER>...hidden sub level branch/leaf...</SPAN>
  <SPAN CLASS='dark' FLASHER>...hidden sub level branch/leaf...</SPAN>
  ...more hidden sub level branch/leaf...</DIV>
```

An expanded tree element can be expressed as:

```
<SPAN CLASS='dark' FLASHER>... visible top level branch ...</SPAN>
<DIV ID='out1d'>
  <SPAN CLASS='dark' FLASHER>...visible sub level branch/leaf...</SPAN>
  <SPAN CLASS='dark' FLASHER>... visible sub level branch/leaf...</SPAN>
  ...more visible sub level branch/leaf...</DIV>
```

Notice how we can expand or collapse a branch simply by changing the display:none STYLE attribute of the enclosing DIV tag. This can easily be done through the JavaScript code. If a DIV in the tree has the display:none style, it will be invisible. To collapse a branch:

```
document.all.out1d.style.display = "none";
```

Removing the display:none style will make the DIV visible again. Therefore, to expand a branch:

```
document.all.out1d.style.display = "";
```

While the technique detailed above can be used to expand and collapse a single tree branch, it can also be used to expand and collapse multiple nested tree branches. These other branches can include other collapsible tree branches as well, thus "nested". Therefore, in the general case, this is how a final collapsible tree may look in DHTML:

```
<SPAN CLASS='dark' FLASHER>  
   <IMG SRC='expand.gif'>  Collapsable Main
</SPAN>
<DIV ID='firslev' STYLE='display:none'>
   <SPAN CLASS='dark' FLASHER>    
      <IMG SRC='expand.gif'>  Another Level
   </SPAN>
   <DIV ID='seclev' STYLE='display:none'>
      <SPAN CLASS='dark' FLASHER>      
         <IMG SRC='leaf.gif'>  Inner Level
      </SPAN>

      <!-- ... more nested levels ... -->

   </DIV>
   <DIV>
      <SPAN CLASS='dark' FLASHER>  
         <IMG SRC='leaf.gif'>  A Standalone Level
      </SPAN>
      <!-- ... more collapsing elements ... -->

   </DIV>
</DIV>
```

If we orchestrate carefully the collapsing and expanding of these elements with changing the GIF icons and the end user's mouse clicks (via onClick event handlers), we can directly provide the tree controller functionality in JavaScript. We will see how this is done in code very shortly.

Enhancing the Tree Controller Algorithm

Before we move on to some actual code, we have one last problem that needs some consideration, and that is how to structure the data for our family tree. Of course, one way would be to hard-code the tree according as above, with collapsing DIV elements. There are two disadvantages to this approach:

❑   Any change in the data can be difficult and error prone, because structured data is mixed hopelessly within HTML

❑   The resulting tree controller is good only for this application, and we will have to hard-code all over again should we need to use the controller for another application

The Need for a Flexible Pictures Description Language

If we only have a language that can simply describe the tree data that we need to display to the tree controller, the problem would be solved. As well as describing the tree structure of the data, this language must also allow us to associate the appropriate behavior with "what to do" when the user selects the specific tree element. Those familiar with XML (see Chapter 7, *HTML, XML and XHTML* for details) will see that this is very close to the motivation for XML. However, we do not need the expressive power of the full XML language for our purposes. Lacking a prefabricated solution, we strike out and invent our own simple description language, and leverage IE's object model (and ability to provide access to user-defined tags) to create our own parser.

A Simple Description Language

Keeping things as straightforward as possible, we want our mini-markup language to look like this:

```
<LVL0 ITEXT='desc text' IURL='action' ITARGET=''></LVL0>
  <LVL1 ITEXT= 'desc text' IURL='action' ITARGET=''></LVL1>
  ...
    <LVLn ...></LVLn>
  ...
  <LVL1 ITEXT='desc text' IURL='action' ITARGET=''></LVL1>
```

We can see above how each successive level of the tree is marked out by a LVLn tag. LVL0 is the outer-most level and each lower level is collapsible within its parent. For example, all the LVL2 elements immediately following a LVL1 element are collapsible within the LVL1 element, and so on.

This allows us to describe the exact hierarchical relationship between the elements. The data itself is embedded in the tags as the custom attribute, ITEXT. We have done this in order to facilitate parsing using JavaScript. The associated behavior is specified via the IURL and ITARGET dynamic attributes. During parsing, these attributes can be easily accessed by the parser using the element.getAttribute() method.

Since the specification for HTML 3+ requires that unknown tags be left alone by the browser, we can embed the entire tree description into the body of the document. Should we ever want to reuse the tree controller, all we will need to do is replace this description.

Pseudo-code for Parser Algorithm

A new data description language would be pretty useless without a way to parse and use the data. Thanks to IE's ability to access every element of a HTML page (including custom elements) through its object model and its ability to define and access dynamic attributes, creating our parser based on this capability is actually quite a simple exercise.

Examining the mini-language that we have just defined, and matching it with the cascading DIV and SPAN HTML code that we must generate, we see the following patterns:

❑ For every transition from a lower LVL to the next higher LVL tag, we must generate an open DIV immediately after the SPAN for the element. This reflects a new collapsible branch of the tree, potentially with more sub-branches nested inside.

❑ For every transition from a higher LVL to a lower LVL, we must generate one or more /DIV closing tags after generating the SPAN for the higher-level element. This represents the end of a collapsible branch of tree (potentially nested further).

❑ For every element with the same LVL as the previous one, we simply generate the corresponding SPAN. This represents a leaf on the tree.

The first and second of these patterns above will require us to be able to "look ahead" at least one LVL tag, or always remember the last LVL tag. This is necessary in order to positively identify a "transition" between levels. For example, if we notice a LVL1 tag following a LVL0 tag, we know to create a new collapsible branch. If we notice a LVL1 tag following a LVL2 tag, we know to close the collapsible LVL2 branch. For the sake of simplicity, since we will be scanning the tags from beginning to end, we will always choose to remember the last LVL tag in order to detect such transitions.

Here is the final pseudo-code for our parser:

```
prevLevel = null;
current level = 0;
loop through all the <LVL> tags in the description;
   if (prevLevel = null)
```

```
      {
         // store the initial element information
         set prevLevel = <LVL> tag;
         set current level to <LVL> tag's level;
         skip to loop condition check;
      }

      if (<LVL> tag  > current level)
      {
         generate the previous level <SPAN>
         generate an open <DIV>
         set current level to <LVL> tag
      }
      else
      {
         generate the previous level <SPAN>
         if (<LVL> tag < current level)
            {
            generate as many </DIV> as necessary
            set current level to <LVL> tag
            }
      }
   end loop;
   // process the last element
   repeat loop operation one more time by using a <LVL0> tag
```

We will see the actual JavaScript implementation of this pseudo-code shortly.

Implementing the Tree Controller

You will find the implementation of the entire tree controller in the `ietree.html` file in the source code. Let's take a detailed line-by-line look at how the above algorithm is implemented.

CSS Stylesheet-Based mouseOver Animation

First, we must define the CSS attributes for the brightness of the display elements used during `mouseOver` animation. We can see the `bright` class has red lettering, while the `dark` class has black lettering. We set a small font size and a hand-shaped cursor for SPAN elements. This will ensure that all our displayed text will be in a small font, since all our displayed text inside an element is inside SPAN tags, as we explained earlier:

```
<HTML>
   <HEAD>
      <STYLE>
         SPAN {cursor: hand ; font-size: 8pt; font-
family:Verdana,Arial,Helvetica;}
         .bright {color: red ; font-size: 8pt; font-
family:Verdana,Arial,Helvetica;}
         .dark {color: black ; font-size: 8pt; font-
family:Verdana,Arial,Helvetica;}
      </STYLE>
```

Defining State Variables for Tree Controller

Next, we will implement the parser. The parser will use a number of variables to maintain the state of the parsing activity. Of specific importance here is the `builtHTML` string variable, which will hold the entire HTML page that we will generate during the parsing process. The approach we take in creating the tree controller is:

❑ To build the HTML code describing the entire controller by parsing the data and generating the `builtHTML` string.

❑   To create dynamic content consisting of the entire `builtHTML` string by replacing the `innerHTML` property of a `DIV` within an `ONLOAD` event handler for the document (see Chapter 10, *Dynamic DHTML* for more details on this technique).

This approach, rather than adding elements as we parse, has two advantages:

❑   We avoid the unpleasant flickering of the tree controller display that occurs when elements are added one at a time

❑   We speed up the generation process for the tree controller by rendering the HTML only once

```
<SCRIPT LANGUAGE='JScript'>
   var curLevel = 0;
   var prevElement = null;
   var prevLevel;
   var prevID;
   var builtHTML = "";
```

Coding the Hierarchical Data Markup Language Parsing Logic

The code for our parser is contained in a function called `MakeTree()`. You can compare it to the pseudo-code covered earlier to understand how it works. By iterating through the `document.all` collection from the browser's object model, we have access to every tagged element inside the HTML document, including our custom `LVL` elements in the mHDML language:

```
function MakeTree() {
   var coll = document.all;
   var level;
   var id;
   var tagBegin;
```

We speed up the tag scanning process somewhat by starting at the `BODY` tag, at `document.body.sourceIndex+1` in the `for` loop below. This ensures that we are only parsing the mHDML language portion:

```
for (var i=document.body.sourceIndex+1; i<coll.length; i++)
```

For each tag that we find, we take the fourth character, indicating its level and convert it to a numeric value:

```
{
   switch (coll[i].tagName.substring(0,3)) {
      case "LVL":
         level = parseInt(coll[i].tagName.charAt(3));
         break;
      default:
         level = -1;
   }
}
```

We call `addElem()` with the level and element information, for each `LVL` tag. The first non-`LVL` tag encountered will end the parsing:

```
   if (level!=-1) {
      id = i;
      addElem(coll[i], level, id);
   }
}
addElem(prevElement,0, prevID);
divWrap();
//   document.all.Debug.outerText = MyTree.innerHTML;
}
```

Notice that the core operation of the loop is factored out into the `addElem()` function. This is necessary to facilitate the same operation for the final element (see the pseudo-code).

The commented-out code is for debugging. We will have more to say about this shortly.

Generating Cascading DIV and SPAN HTML Code

The `addElem()` function contains the guts of the level detection and tree generation mechanism. It performs the one-behind processing as we defined in our earlier pseudo-code. Notice how all the HTML code for the cascading `DIV` and `SPAN` elements are concatenated together in the `builtHTML` string variable:

```
function addElem(el, level, id)
```

Here is where we store the first level of the associated "one level behind" information, as per our pseudo-code:

```
{
    if (prevElement == null)
    {
        prevElement = el;
        prevLevel = level;
        prevID = id;
        return;
    }
```

Next, we generate a geometric progression of indentation using hard spaces. Each successive level will have more whitespace indentations:

```
    var s = "";          // generate indentation
    var cs = " ";
    for (var j=0; j<prevLevel; j++)
        s = s + cs;
```

Here, we detect if there is a level change. If there is a level change, we construct the appropriate `builtHTML` string for update on the tree display. Note that the `DIV` and the corresponding `expand.gif` IMG tag are both generated with associated IDs, with the `DIV` having an ID that has an extra "D" at the end. This will make the `DIV` easier to locate when a mouse click is detected:

```
    if (level > curLevel)
    {
        builtHTML += "<SPAN STYLE='cursor:hand' CLASS='dark'  IURL='"
                  + prevElement.getAttribute('IURL')
                  + "' FLASHER>"
                  + s
                  + "<IMG SRC='expand.gif' ID='OUT"
                  + prevID.toString()
                  + "' CLASS='collapsible' >   "
                  + prevElement.getAttribute('ITEXT')
                  + "<BR></SPAN>"
                  + "<DIV ID='OUT"
                  + prevID.toString()
                  + "D' STYLE='display:none'  >";
        curLevel = level;
    }
    else
    {
        builtHTML += "<SPAN STYLE='cursor:hand'  CLASS='dark' IURL='"
                  + prevElement.getAttribute('IURL')
                  + "' FLASHER>"
                  + s
                  + "<IMG SRC='leaf.gif'> "
                  + prevElement.getAttribute('ITEXT')
```

```
                    + "<BR></SPAN>";
        if (level < curLevel)
        {
            for (var tplev = level; tplev < curLevel; tplev++)
                builtHTML += "</DIV>";
            curLevel = level;
        }
    }
```

Finally, we store the one level behind data again for the next iteration:

```
    prevElement = el;
    prevLevel = level;
    prevID = id;
}
```

Adding Dynamic Contents Using DHTML

To close off any pending open DIV tags at the very end of the parse, we will write a function named divWrap(). Another very important purpose of this function is actually to render our builtHTML string. We have a DIV placeholder in the document body called MyTree that is initially blank. By inserting the builtHTML string into this DIV, the tree control is immediately rendered. We perform this task by setting the innerHTML property of the MyTree element:

```
function divWrap() {
    while (curLevel > 0)
    {
        builtHTML +=      "</DIV>";
        curLevel--;
    }
    document.all.MyTree.innerHTML=builtHTML;
}
```

The next few functions in the source code are event handlers, which we will cover later, since they do not relate directly to the rendering of the tree controller.

Data in Our Mini Hierarchical Data Markup Language

The next portion of the file contains the BODY of the document. Note that the ONLOAD event handler is specified to be the MakeTree() function. This will ensure that the controller will be constructed properly once the page has finished loading.

The description of the family tree data is inserted right here. Using the custom LVL tags, we define the structure of the data for the tree. Notice how we have also embedded the behavioral information of which .gif file to display for each element, via the IURL dynamic attribute:

```
<BODY  ONLOAD='MakeTree()'>

<LVL0  ITEXT='The Waltons Family Album' IURL='album.gif' ITARGET=''></LVL0>
    <LVL1  ITEXT= 'James W. Walton' IURL='walt1.jpg' ITARGET=''></LVL1>
        <LVL2  ITEXT='Wife: Jose Emma' IURL='walt2.jpg' ITARGET=''></LVL2>
        <LVL2  ITEXT='Child: Maggie Walton' IURL='walt3.jpg' ITARGET=''></LVL2>
            <LVL3  ITEXT='Husband: Jack Eckel' IURL='walt4.jpg' ITARGET=''></LVL3>
            <LVL3  ITEXT='Grand child: Lucy Eckel' IURL='walt5.jpg'
                ITARGET=''></LVL3>
    <LVL1  ITEXT='Jack E. Walton'  IURL='walt6.jpg' ITARGET=''></LVL1>
        <LVL2  ITEXT='Wife: Nancy Lori' IURL='walt7.jpg' ITARGET=''></LVL2>
        <LVL2  ITEXT='Child: John Walton' IURL='walt8.jpg' ITARGET=''></LVL2>
    <LVL1  ITEXT='Joe Walton'  IURL='walt9.jpg' ITARGET=''></LVL1>
```

Creating Placeholders for Dynamic Contents

Now we get on to the real start of the displayed HTML page. At the top, we have a logo, and the tree controller will be inside the DIV at the bottom. Initially, it is completely blank. Once we have executed our parser on the data description, the DIV ID=MyTree element will be filled up with the HTML code representing the tree controller:

```
<TABLE WIDTH='95%' BORDER='0' ALIGN='left'>
   <TR><TD>
      <IMG SRC='Logo.gif'>
   </TD></TR>
   <TR><TD BGCOLOR='lightyellow'> </TD></TR>
   <TR><TD WIDTH='200' HEIGHT='340' VALIGN='top' BGCOLOR='lightyellow'>
   <DIV ID=MyTree>
   </DIV>
```

Debugging Dynamic Content Pages

When creating dynamic content, it is sometimes difficult to determine what went wrong if things do not display as expected. It is useful if we can see what our code actually generates. A useful debug technique is to define a placeholder in text form for displaying the raw HTML text that is generated. We have included a DIV ID=Debug element for exactly this purpose. If you uncomment the debug line in the MakeTree() function, this area will be filled with the actual generated HTML from the parser. When enabling debugging, it is useful to load the ietree.html file directly into the browser instead of going through iealbum.html. Examining this generated HTML text will enable you to locate problems quickly:

```
<DIV ID=Debug>
</DIV>
</TD></TR>
</TABLE>
```

See Chapter 13, *Error Handling, Debugging and Troubleshooting* for a comprehensive coverage of JavaScript debugging techniques.

Handling Mouse Clicks for Collapsing Elements

The next portion of the code sets the document level event handlers for the page. The onclick event handler is assigned to a function named clickHandler(), the onmouseover handler is MakeBright(), and the onmouseout handler is MakeDark(). The document is the entire tree controller, since the page contains nothing else:

```
<SCRIPT LANGUAGE='JScript'>
   document.onclick = clickHandler;
   document.onmouseover = MakeBright;
   document.onmouseout = MakeDark;
</SCRIPT>

</BODY>
</HTML>
```

Now, we will examine the event handlers themselves. These functions are the ones we omitted earlier when we were examining the HEAD section of the page. In clickHandler(), we determine if the .gif icon of one of the tree elements has been clicked on. These icons are all assigned the attribute CLASS="collapsible" upon generation for easy identification. If such an icon is clicked on, we toggle the display attribute of its style to show or hide its associated DIV tree. The DIV elements in the tree all have element ID set equal to the associated expansion icon IMG ID, concatenated with the letter "D" which helps to make them easy to locate. We also swap the .gif file accordingly (between the square with a + inside and the square with a dot inside):

```
function clickHandler() {
    var colId, colElem ;
    var tpURL;
    elem = window.event.srcElement;

    if (elem.className == "collapsible") {

        colId = elem.id + "D";
        colElem = document.all(colId);

        if (colElem.style.display == "none") {
            colElem.style.display = "" ;
            elem.src = "fixed.gif" ;
        } else {
            colElem.style.display = "none" ;
            elem.src = "expand.gif" ;
        }
    }
}
```

Handling Mouse Clicks for Photo Display and Title Changes

If the user has clicked on the text of one of the FLASHER elements, the mouse click will be associated with the SPAN element. Since the element should have been highlighted during the mouseOver animation, we can check simply whether the element belongs to the bright class. Processing the click involves changing the photo and title on the Photo Display page. We do this by extracting the file name to be displayed from the IURL dynamic attribute. Additionally, we set the SRC attribute of the IMG tag and the innerText property of the title DIV tag in the iepage.html frame:

```
    if (elem.className == "bright")
    {
        with (parent.frames[1].document.all)
        {
            showpic.src = elem.getAttribute("IURL");
            picTitle.innerText = elem.innerText;
        }
    }
}
```

Helper Routines for Dynamic mouseOver Animation

MakeBright() and MakeDark() are two helper routines used to assist in highlighting and darkening the selectable element creating mouseover animation. They are hooked up to the MOUSEOVER event for the document. Inside the function, a check is made to ensure the element involved has the FLASHER attribute. If so, we will change the CSS class associated with the element, causing its appearance to change:

```
function MakeBright()
    {
    el = event.srcElement ;
    if (el.getAttribute("FLASHER") != null) {
        el.className = "bright" ;
    }
}

function MakeDark() {
    el = event.srcElement ;
    if (el.getAttribute("FLASHER") != null) {
        el.className = "dark";
```

```
      }
  }

  </SCRIPT>
  </HEAD>
```

This concludes our coverage of the code for the version 1 solution. We are now ready to test the application.

Testing the Family Tree Photo Album

You can test the photo album application by opening the `iealbum.html` file inside your IE6 (or IE 5.5, or 4.x) browser. Here are some suggestions for testing/exploration:

❑ Expand and collapse the elements in the tree controller

❑ Move the mouse around the elements in the tree controller, and see the mouseover animation

❑ Click on a family member and see the title and photo displayed change

❑ Fill in a comment and submit it to see the argument passing and modal dialog handling

❑ Confirm and submit the comment from the modal dialog to see the delayed close routine and e-mail based submission of the form

❑ Enter a comment that contains a single quote and read the confirmation of the message to see what happened

❑ Modify or create your own tree control by changing the data description

Once you're satisfied that everything is working as specified, let us explore an enhancement to our Family Album application.

XML Enabling the Family Tree Photo Album

In the Family Album application, our mHDML markup language is loosely based on XML styled syntax and we designed a custom mini-parser for using JavaScript. Since IE now includes an XML parser as part of its distribution, we will now explore how to parse our mHDML using this standard mechanism. This second version of our project will use XML parser and W3C DOM interfaces available for IE JavaScript programming.

One disadvantage of using the latest standards, is that support for them in browsers is only just beginning to mature. Usage of this application will be restricted to users on a Win32 platform with IE 6, or IE 5.x with the latest MSXML parser update installed.

Benefits of Using a Standard XML Parser

By incorporating the use of the standard XML parser and the W3C DOM, we gain the following advantages:

❑ The ability to separate out the mHDML description as a separate `pics.xml` file, making it easier to maintain (or generate).

❑ Leveraging the ready made XML parser that is available by substantially saving the work required in parsing and also ensuring that support will be available far into the future.

❑ The mHDML can evolve as new requirements surface, with no need to radically modify an *ad hoc* parser (such as in our JavaScript implementation).

❑ Standardized (and often portable) access to document element via DOM Level 1 Core interfaces.

❑ Utilize XML as a standard that enables us to transition the application forward with new platform enhancements. For example, the Tree Controller is ready for incorporation as a client side JavaScript component under the new Microsoft .NET infrastructure).

The diagram below shows the new architecture for our application:

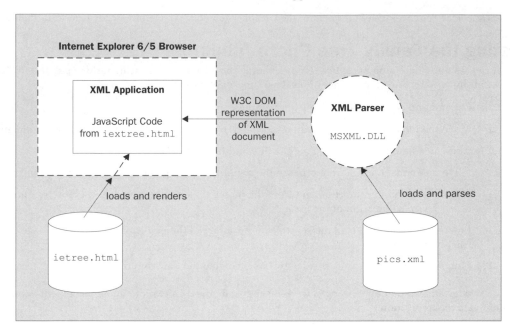

We now have a separate XML file that specifies the elements in the Photo Album. Our JavaScript Family Photo Album application will use the XML description, through the XML parser, to build the tree. In this case, the XML parser for IE 6 is housed in a standalone file (MSXML.DLL) that is installed with the distribution. MSXML.DLL has a different version-numbering scheme than the browser (since HTML and XML are evolving on different tracks – see Chapter 7, *HTML, XML and XHTML* for more information).

If you open the `pics.xml` file with IE, you can explore its content:

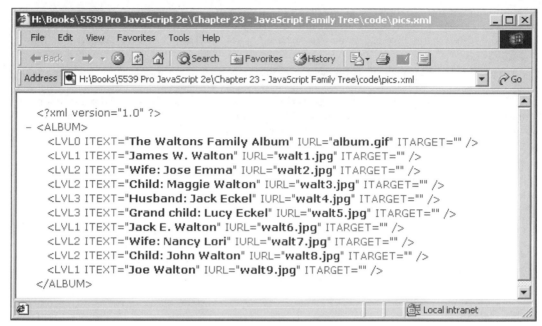

It is obvious that it has the same content as the embedded mHDML. We have added an enclosing root ALBUM element, and the `<?xml version="1.0" ?>` declaration to ensure the document complies with the XML standard.

Adding MSXML Parsing to Applications

We will now modify the `ietree.html` file to use the MSXML parser. The modified file can be found in `iextree.html`. Most of the modifications are in the `MakeTree()` function, since the old parser logic was embedded there.

The new `MakeTree()` function is reproduced below:

```
function MakeTree() {

    var pictureDOM;
    var rootNode;
    var picList;

    pictureDOM = new ActiveXObject("Msxml.DOMDocument");
    pictureDOM.async = false;
    pictureDOM.load("pics.xml");
```

In the code above, we use the Microsoft supplied `ActiveXObject()` extension to create an instance of the MSXML parser. The `async` property is set to `false`, which will cause the script to wait for the completion of the loading of the XML document. Otherwise, premature access of the DOM before the document is loaded may cause an error condition to occur. The loading is performed next via the `load()` method. At this point, `pictureDOM` is pointing to the XML tree representation of `pics.xml`, and we are ready to access all the other elements using the standard W3C DOM.

Accessing XML Document Elements Using DOM Level 1 Core Interfaces

Continuing our examination of the MakeTree() function, we use DOM interfaces to reference the documentElement (ALBUM) via the rootNode variable. Next, we retrieve a DOM NodeList interface and store it in picList. picList now can be used to access all the children of ALBUM:

```
rootNode = pictureDOM.documentElement;
picList = rootNode.childNodes;
```

At this point, we can go through the picList (children of ALBUM) one by one and parse them as we did previously. This time, we will use standard DOM interfaces to access the elements instead. Note that the code for level detection is identical to the previous version:

```
for (i=0; i<picList.length; i++)
{
    currentNode = picList[i];
    switch (currentNode.nodeName.substring(0,3)) {
        case "LVL":
            level = parseInt(currentNode.nodeName.charAt(3));
            break;
        default:
            level = -1;
    }
    if (level!=-1) {
        id = i;
        addElem(currentNode, level, id);
    }
}
addElem(prevElement,0, prevID);
divWrap();
//   document.all.Debug.outerText = MyTree.innerHTML;
}
```

Those are all the modifications necessary to incorporate the XML parser. We now need to modify the iealbum.html page to include this new iextree.html instead. We have created a new iexalbum.html page just for this purpose:

```
<HTML>
    <FRAMESET COLS='210,*'>
        <FRAME SRC='iextree.html' NAME='treectrl' ALIGN='left' MARGINWIDTH='0'
        SCROLLING='auto'>
        <FRAME SRC='iepage.html' NAME='albpage' MARGINWIDTH='0'
        SCROLLING='auto'>
    </FRAMESET>
</HTML>
```

This concludes all the changes that we need to make in order to incorporate MSXML parsing and W3C DOM access.

Testing the XML Driven Version

You can try out the new iexalbum.html application on IE 6 (or IE 5.5 as long as you have the latest MSXML update installed). Even though it now utilizes the MSXML parser and DOM interface, the operation is exactly the same as the previous JavaScript only version. Now, two questions come into mind:

❑ Why did we not use MSXML right off the bat to create our application, instead of using an *ad hoc* JavaScript-based parser?

The key problem here is compatibility. In fact, MSXML is not reliably available and usable with IE older than the version 5 release. The approach we have taken will work with all of the IE 4 level browsers as well. If you **only** work with IE 5 level browsers or beyond, you can feel free to use MSXML in your own projects.

❑   If this is standard XML and standard W3C DOM, and we know that Netscape 6 is highly standards compliant, does this mean that we can use the same code for Netscape 6?

Unfortunately, no! The way an XML parser is instantiated, and the way an XML document is loaded into the browser for processing are not yet standardized (for example, `pictureDOM.load()` in the `MakeTree()` function). Furthermore, in the DHTML manipulation and the page rendering processes, we have used IE only features that are not W3C DOM complaint, so will simply not work in Netscape.

What Doesn't Work in Netscape?

There are more than enough differences between Netscape and Microsoft's versions of Dynamic HTML to ensure that our IE-specific Photo Album application will not work on Netscape browsers. We will look at some of the more important differences that affect us here:

❑   While supporting the `SPAN` tag, visibility toggle, and fine positioning, the page rendering engines prior to Gecko (Netscape 6) do not re-execute when element attributes are changed. This makes the collapsing and expanding action of the tree controller extremely difficult to implement across Netscape browser versions.

❑   Prior to Netscape 6, the browser object model does not uniformly expose every non-HTML, user-defined tag as an object accessible from JavaScript.

❑   Netscape has no built-in support for creating modal dialog boxes from JavaScript that are reliable across multiple versions.

❑   Microsoft has implemented many JavaScript extensions specific to Microsoft browsers that make programming DHTML easier.

Getting the Photo Album to work by tweaking the code we have already written is close to impossible. Instead, we must reconsider our implementation strategy with a goal towards creating a cross-browser solution.

A Version 6, 5, 4.x Cross-Browser Application

We will overcome the differences between the browsers one at a time. The two most prominent problems that we must solve involve creating a cross-browser tree controller and catering for cross-browser modal dialogs.

To create a cross-browser tree controller, we will need to either write new code or find an existing library code to use. Fortunately, such a library does exist for both IE and Netscape.

Using the Netscape Collapsible List Library

Netscape provides a library of JavaScript functions that does essentially what we have done in our tree controller, except that it works with the DHTML on all current versions of Netscape browsers (Netscape 6 and Netscape 4.x). This is especially useful, since the Netscape 4.x series of browsers has a rendering engine that cannot display incremental changes. As a result, a solution is to use the deprecated `LAYER` tag to carry out the "collapsing" of the tree elements. The Netscape Collapsible List library that we will use will automatically detects 4.x level browsers and uses the `LAYER` tag accordingly. As a bonus, this library also works with IE 6/5/4.x using `DIV` tags. You can find the library code at this URL:

http://developer.netscape.com/evangelism/tools/xbCollapsibleLists/xbCollapsibleLists.js

The information on how to use this library is located at:

http://developer.netscape.com/evangelism/tools/xbCollapsibleLists/

As the use of the library depends on two other libraries and a couple of `.gif` files (to use as icons for the tree nodes), be sure to consult the link above for the latest usage information. Using this library greatly simplifies our coding for the tree controller. Essentially, we only need to create the list structures required and the library code takes care of the positioning, rendering, and event handling for us. Compared to our custom code, the library has the following minor disadvantages:

❑ The library does not handle mouseover animation, and it cannot be added easily

❑ The list management and rendering routine is quite slow, especially if the list is large

❑ The library does not support parsing of a generic list description language and hard coding is required

Let's take a look at the code of our solution, created using this library.

The Main Frame Document

The main HTML document is called `xbalbum.html`, and again contains just a frameset with two frames:

```
<HTML>
    <HEAD>
    </HEAD>
    <FRAMESET COLS='325,*'>
        <FRAME SRC='xbtree.html' NAME='treectrl' ALIGN='left' MARGINWIDTH='0'
            SCROLLING='auto'>
        <FRAME SRC='xbdpage.html' NAME='albpage' MARGINWIDTH='0'
            SCROLLING='auto'>
    </FRAMESET>
</HTML>
```

Note that we are now using `xbtree.html` for the tree control, and `xbdpage.html` for the photo display page.

Creating the Tree Controller

The tree controller code, as in all our versions is confined to one HTML file, which in this case is `xbtree.html`.

The `xbCollapsibleLists.js` file contains the actual library, but it is dependent on the Universal Browser Sniffer library (`ua.js`), as well as the Cross Browser Style Library (`xbStyle.js`). These are available from:

Library	Location
ua.js	http://developer.netscape.com/evangelism/tools/practical-browser-sniffing/
xbStyle.js	http://developer.netscape.com/evangelism/docs/api/xbStyle/

The collapsible list library requires `ua.js` to detect browser versions and uses different code accordingly. It is also dependent on `xbStyle.js` to perform cross-browser formatting and transformation. Therefore, we must also include these two dependent libraries:

```
<HTML>
   <HEAD>
      <SCRIPT LANGUAGE='JavaScript1.2' SRC='ua.js'></SCRIPT>
      <SCRIPT LANGUAGE='JavaScript1.2' SRC='xbStyle.js'></SCRIPT>
      <SCRIPT LANGUAGE='JavaScript1.2'
       SRC='xbCollapsibleLists.js'></SCRIPT>
```

The main logic for creating the list to be displayed is contained within a function called `init()`. This is the ONLOAD handler for our tree controller, similar to our `MakeTree()` function in the first version. The function first tests for the browser version and gives a warning if the browser is not at least version 4.0:

```
<SCRIPT LANGUAGE='JavaScript1.2'>

function init() {
   if(parseInt(navigator.appVersion) < 4) {
      alert('You need a 4.0+ browser to run this.');
      return;
   }
```

Next, we need to set the variables containing the height and width of each row within our tree. Here, we are using a height of 23 pixels, and a width depending on the size of the window. Here we cater for Netscape browsers that will return `window.innerWidth` with an "undefined" value. We also set the color of the list elements to white (#ffffff), and only the top-level element to `visible`

```
      var height = 23;
      var width;
      if (typeof window.innerWidth != 'undefined')
      width = window.innerWidth - 5;
   else
      width = document.body.clientWidth - 5;

      var backColor = "#ffffff";
      var visible = true;
      var leafVisible = false;
```

In the next large section of the code, we will create the sub-lists for our family tree data and attach them one at a time to the list or sub-list with which they are associated. Each sub-list is exactly equivalent to a collapsible DIV section in the first version of the application. The `addList()` method is used to attach a sub-list to an existing list or sub-list. A higher level element can be associated with each sub-list during the `addList()` call. This is identical to the SPAN associated with each collapsible DIV. The following section of code sets up the complete tree:

```
nsTree = new List(visible, width, height, backColor);

mySub = new List(leafVisible, width, height, backColor);
```

First, we create the top-level lists:

```
nsTree.addList(mySub, "The Waltons Family Album");
```

Next, we create the-sub level lists:

```
mySub2 = new List(leafVisible, width, height, backColor);
```

The leaves are added here:

```
mySub2.addItem("<A HREF='dpage.html?walt2.jpg&Wife%3a%20Jose%20Emma' "+
            "TARGET='albpage'>Wife: Jose Emma</A>");

mySub.addList(mySub2, "<A HREF='dpage.html?walt1.jpg&James%20W.%20Walton' "+
                "TARGET='albpage'>James W. Walton<A>");
```

This is another branch with more leaves:

```
mySub3 = new List(leafVisible, width, height, backColor);

mySub3.addItem("<A HREF='dpage.html?walt4.jpg&Husband%3a%20Jack%20Eckel' "+
            "TARGET='albpage'>Husband: Jack Eckel</A>");

mySub3.addItem("<A
            HREF='dpage.html?walt5.jpg&Grand%20child%3a%20Lucy%20Eckel'"+
            "TARGET='albpage'>Grand child: Lucy Eckel</A>");

mySub2.addList(mySub3, "<A HREF='dpage.html?walt3.jpg&Child%3a%20Maggie%20"+
                "Walton' TARGET='albpage'>Child: Maggie Walton</A>");
```

And the final branch with its leaves:

```
mySub4 = new List(leafVisible, width, height, backColor);

mySub4.addItem("<A HREF='dpage.html?walt7.jpg&Wife%3a%20Nancy%20Lori' "+
            "TARGET='albpage'>Wife: Nancy Lori</a>");

mySub4.addItem("<A HREF='dpage.html?walt8.jpg&Child%3a%20John%20Walton' "+
            "TARGET='albpage'>Child: John Walton</A>");

mySub.addList(mySub4, "<A HREF='dpage.html?walt6.jpg&Jack%20E.%20Walton' "+
                "TARGET='albpage'>Jack E. Walton</A>");

mySub.addItem("<A HREF='dpage.html?walt9.jpg&Joe%20Walton' "+
            "TARGET='albpage'>Joe Walton</A>");
```

Since there is no parser available, we have encoded the IURL information directly into the item as a hyperlink with an extended URL. This will enable the user to click directly on the link to the change the picture being displayed.

Extended URL Hyperlinks

The extended URL we create simulates a CGI GET query by adding a question mark (?) at the end of the URL and a set of argument values afterwards. One valid URL may be:

```
http://www.walt.com/dpage.html?walt1.jpg&Title
```

The page being loaded, dpage.html in the Photo Display page frame can then examine its own URL and pull the argument values in the query. It can then use this information to generate HTML code that will display the corresponding picture and title.

Something to be careful of here is that the parameters after the question mark must not contain blanks or other special characters. Instead, it should be an escaped URL. This means that blanks and certain special characters must be replaced by their hex encoded equivalent and as %xx where xx is the hexadecimal value for the character.

Escaping Special Characters for Extended URLs

We can see the escaping of special characters for the form GET URLs. Here is the decoding for the special characters that we have used in the code:

Character	Code
space	%20
:	%3a

Compared to the previous Tree Controller page, this one is barren. The JavaScript library has taken much of the complexity out of the equation.

Setting Fonts Used in Lists/Sub-lists

To change the default font, the setFont() method must be called for each list or sub-list that is created. The next section of code changes the font for the entire list to small blue type:

```
nsTree.setFont("<FONT FACE='Verdana,Arial,Helvetica' COLOR='blue' "+
            "SIZE=-1><BOLD>","</BOLD></FONT>");

mySub.setFont("<FONT FACE='Verdana,Arial,Helvetica' COLOR='blue' "+
            "SIZE=-1><BOLD>","</BOLD></FONT>");

mySub2.setFont("<FONT FACE='Verdana,Arial,Helvetica' COLOR='blue' "+
            "SIZE=-1><BOLD>","</BOLD></FONT>");

mySub3.setFont("<FONT FACE='Verdana,Arial,Helvetica' COLOR='blue' "+
            "SIZE=-1><BOLD>","</BOLD></FONT>");

mySub4.setFont("<FONT FACE='Verdana,Arial,Helvetica' COLOR='blue' "+
            "SIZE=-1><BOLD>","</BOLD></FONT>");
```

The very last part of the init() function simply creates the tree by calling the build() method. The two parameters specify the x and y co-ordinates in pixels relative to the top-left corner of the current window. In this case, we use y=95 to position the control below the logo:

```
    nsTree.build(8,95);
}
</SCRIPT>
```

Apart from specifying the ONLOAD event handler, the rest of the xbtree.html file contains style information and the fixed DIV elements that are necessary for IE compatibility. The library requires that one of these lItemx elements be created for each level of the list. In our case, we have nine levels, so we have created items 0 to 8:

```
    <STYLE TYPE='text/css'>
        #lItem0 { position:absolute; }
        #lItem1 { position:absolute; }
        #lItem2 { position:absolute; }
        #lItem3 { position:absolute; }
        #lItem4 { position:absolute; }
        #lItem5 { position:absolute; }
        #lItem6 { position:absolute; }
        #lItem7 { position:absolute; }
        #lItem8 { position:absolute; }
    </STYLE>
</HEAD>

<BODY ONLOAD='init();'>
    <IMG WIDTH='191' HEIGHT='79' SRC='Logo.gif'>
    <DIV ID='lItem0' NAME='lItem0'></DIV>
    <DIV ID='lItem1' NAME='lItem1'></DIV>
```

```
      <DIV ID='lItem2' NAME='lItem2'></DIV>
      <DIV ID='lItem3' NAME='lItem3'></DIV>
      <DIV ID='lItem4' NAME='lItem4'></DIV>
      <DIV ID='lItem5' NAME='lItem5'></DIV>
      <DIV ID='lItem6' NAME='lItem6'></DIV>
      <DIV ID='lItem7' NAME='lItem7'></DIV>
      <DIV ID='lItem8' NAME='lItem8'></DIV>
  </BODY>

  </HTML>
```

Simulating A Modal Dialog Box

The lack of usable native modal dialog support for Netscape browsers means that we must simulate modal dialog behavior using standard HTML dialogs. The `window.open()` method can be used for creating such a dialog. In order to simulate modal behavior, we must ensure that the parent browser window will not steal the focus away from the dialog.

One way to simulate a modal dialog box is to use `setTimeout()` to create a timer that will regularly set focus back to the dialog window. This actually will not work as intended. The main reason is that there are form elements within the modal dialog that can receive focus. When the timer sets the focus to the dialog window, the form element that the user is interacting with will lose focus. While this will maintain the dialog in focus all the time, it will also create an endless lockup loop.

To get around this problem, we can add a variable to the dialog. This variable will be set in the `ONFOCUS` handler of each active form element. Since the variable tracks which HTML control has the focus at any given time, the timer can then set the focus back to the element that was in focus.

This technique works relatively well across Netscape versions. We do not need this simulation for IE versions, since we already have an implementation that works well from the previous versions of the project.

The New Photo Display Page

You can find the new Photo Display Page as `dpage.html` in the source code. Let us take a look at how this page will decode the extended URL and generate the appropriate title and picture links.

Extracting Values from the Extended URL

The script code right at the beginning of the page will decode the extended URL. First and foremost, the entire URL (including all the information in the query) will be available through the browser's object model via the `document.location` property.

Note that the `ua.js` browser sniffer library is included here. We will be using it to differentiate between IE and Netscape versions and use the appropriate implementation of the modal dialog box:

```
<HTML>
   <HEAD>
       <SCRIPT LANGUAGE='JavaScript1.2' SRC='ua.js'></SCRIPT>
```

Here, `resize.js` is a JavaScript fix for Dynamic HTML rendering problems with Netscape 4.0x browsers during resizing. It ignores browser versions that do not exhibit the resize bug. The code can be downloaded from:

http://developer.netscape.com/docs/technote/dynhtml/toolbar/resize.js

We did not need this "fix" in the `xbtree.html` file, because the `xbStyle.js` library used there has the logic built into it:

```
<SCRIPT LANGUAGE='JavaScript1.2' SRC='resize.js'></SCRIPT>
<SCRIPT LANGUAGE='JavaScript1.2'>
```

We assign the full URL to a string array called `tpstr`, and then call the `String` object's `split` method with `"?"` as the argument. This places the query string (if there is one) in the second element of the resulting array, or `paramList[1]`:

```
var urlList;
var tpstr = new String(document.location);
var paramList = tpstr.split("?");
var mytitle; var mygif;
```

The next part of the code will set a variable called `mytitle` to the title we want to display and a variable called `mygif` to the name of the `.gif` file to display. We will use the default values of `"Walton Family Album"` and `"album.gif"` if no parameters are found. Note how we need to split up the title and `.gif` parameters, and unescape the title (which might contain hex code representing blanks and special characters):

```
if (paramList.length > 1)
{
   urlList = paramList[1].split("&");
   mytitle = unescape(urlList[1]);
   mygif = urlList[0];
}
else
{
   mytitle = "Walton Family Album";
   mygif = "album.gif";
}
```

Escaping Quotes in Generated HTML Code

Next comes a function that we are already familiar with, `escQuote`. It is needed here for the same reason as in the previous version of the application: when we generate the hidden fields in the modal dialog box form, we need to make sure it does not contain any single quotes. Again, it replaces any single quotes (`'`) with an asterisk (`*`). To be compatible with Netscape's `mailto` URL syntax, we will also be using the JavaScript `escape()` function to replace special characters with their hex equivalent later.

Using Focus Shift to Simulate Modal Dialog for Netscape Browsers

The `showform()` function in this version uses the sniffer library to determine the browser type, and then branches to the appropriate modal dialog code. In fact, the sniffer library documentation shows that the following useful variables are set:

Variable Name	Useful Values
navigator.version	A floating point numeric value indicating the version.
navigator.org	The organization that produce the browser. It is 'netscape' for all Netscape browsers.
navigator.family	Some useful values are 'ie4' for IE 4 and above, or 'gecko' for Netscape browsers using the Gecko engine, or 'nn4' for Netscape browsers using the older engine.

Here is the code for the `showform()` function:

```
function showform()
{
```

We can see that it detects IE 4 or above, and uses the same modal dialog handling code as we used previously. The code simply uses the `showModalDialog()` call on the `iedlg.html` page.

```
if ((navigator.version >= 4) && (navigator.family=="ie4")) {
    var myArgs=new Array(2);
    myArgs[0]=document.all.cmttxt.value;
    myArgs[1]=document.all.showpic.src;

    var result=showModalDialog("iedlg.html", myArgs,
    "dialogHeight:250px;dialogWidth:300px;status:no;help:no;");
}
```

Next, if it is not IE 4+, we test it to make sure it is from Netscape and is at least a version 4 browser. In this case, the `window.open()` method is used instead of the `showModalDialog()` method, since this method is not available on Netscape browsers:

```
else  if((navigator.version >= 4) && (navigator.org="netscape")) {

var mywin= window.open("", "newwin", "resizable=no,width=300,height=250");
```

It is important to note that the `window.open()` function actually returns a reference to the newly created window, which we will assign to a variable called `mywin`. The fact that we can maintain a reference (in the parent window) to the newly created child window allows us to do something not possible with the `showModalDialog()` method. We will see what this is in the next section.

Generating Dialog Content Dynamically With document.write()

We will not have a separate HTML file for the modal dialog form. Instead, we will have the code generate the form right inside `dpage.html`. There is no need to figure out how to pass parameters into the modal dialog, since we `write()` the data right into the HTML. Note how we break up the `SCRIPT` tag using string concatenation within `document.write()`.

```
with (mywin.document)
{
    open();
    write("<HTML><HEAD><SCRI" + "PT>var myElem = self; "+
        "setTimeout('setmyfocus()',500);");
```

The `setmyfocus()` function is generated here:

```
write("function setmyfocus() { ");
write("myElem.focus(); setTimeout('setmyfocus()',500);}");
write("</SCRI" + "PT><TITLE>Verify Comment</TITLE></HEAD>");
```

Followed by the comment submission box itself, we reprint the message within the box giving the user a chance to verify their comment:

```
write("<BODY BGCOLOR='lightyellow' STYLE='font-size:12;font-
family:Verdana,Arial,Helvetica;' SCROLL=no>");
    write("<TABLE WIDTH=100%><TR><TD>Your Message:<BR>");
    write("</TD></TR><TR><TD bgcolor='white' valign='top' height=120 style='font-
size:10;font-family:courier;'>");
    write(document.forms[0].elements[0].value);
```

Netscape's Support for `mailto` URL

Note that we are generating the `mailto` URL slightly differently, which fits in with Netscape's support for the `mailto` URL. Under Netscape, we can create a `mailto` URL and supply the recipient's address, subject and body of the message.

The next section of code illustrates how this is done in the form called `myform` that appears in the simulated modal dialog box:

```
    write("</TD></TR><TR><TD><BR><FORM NAME='myform'
ACTION='mailto:singontheroad@aol.com?Subject=From%20your%20JavaScript%20Picture%20
Album&Body=" + escape(document.forms[0].elements[0].value) + "%20%20pic%20is%20" +
escape(mygif) + "' ENCTYPE='text/plain' METHOD='post' >");
```

In the code above, the `mailto` URL contains a "?" right after the destination e-mail address. It can then include additional key/value pairs separated by the "&". The value should be passed through the JavaScript `escape()` function to replace restricted characters with their hex equivalent (%20 for space, %0a%0d for carriage return, and so on.).

Finally, we generate the rest of the simulated modal dialog box, including the code that tracks the element that has focus (in the `myElem` variable) and repeatedly set focus there using the `setTimeout()` call upon loss of focus. We will see this generated code in the next section:

```
    write("Name:  <BR><INPUT NAME='myname' TYPE='text'
ONFOCUS='myElem=this'><BR>");
    write("<INPUT TYPE='hidden' NAME='pic' VALUE='" + mygif +"'>");
    write("<INPUT TYPE='hidden' NAME='mesg' VALUE='" +
escQuote(document.forms[0].elements[0].value) + "'>");
```

The code below will close the simulated modal dialog after a 10 second delay for submission of e-mail. You may want to adjust the timeout value in `setTimeout()`:

```
    // onsubmit does not work reliably with e-mail on NS4.61
    write("<INPUT TYPE='submit' VALUE='Send Comment Now' "
        + "ONFOCUS='myElem=this' "+
        "ONCLICK='setTimeout(\"self.close(); return true\",10000)'>");
    write("<INPUT TYPE='button' VALUE='Cancel' ONFOCUS='myElem=this' "+
        "ONCLICK='self.close()'></FORM>");
    write("</TD></TR></TABLE>");
    write("</BODY></HTML>");
    close();
    }
}
</SCRIPT>
</HEAD>
```

Maintaining Focus on a Modeless Window

It's now time to take a detour and examine the HTML code for rendering the dialog box; this is the very same HTML that we `document.write()` into the dialog. The first part sets up the timer that will repeatedly set focus to the window, simulating modal behavior. Notice that the focus is set to a variable called `myElem`:

```
<HTML>
    <HEAD>
        <SCRIPT>
            var myElem = self;
            setTimeout('setmyfocus()',500);");
            function setmyfocus() {
```

```
            myElem.focus();
            setTimeout('setmyfocus()',500);
        }
    </SCRIPT>
```

The next part repeats the message entered so that the user can confirm it:

```
        <TITLE>Verify Comment</TITLE>
    </HEAD>
    <BODY BGCOLOR='lightyellow' STYLE='font-size:12;
                font-family:Verdana,Arial,Helvetica;'
        SCROLL=no>
    <TABLE WIDTH='100%'>
        <TR><TD>Your Message:<BR>
        </TD></TR>

        <TR><TD bgcolor='white' valign='top' height='120' style='font-
            size:10;
            font-family:courier;'>
            ...message entered by user...
        </TD></TR>
```

Next comes our form. Notice how every element in the form has an ONFOCUS handler that updates the myElem variable. This is necessary to ensure that focus is set to the correct element by the timer.

From a purist's point of view, the dialog is not actually modal. It is still possible for the user to quickly type something into the main browser window or to click one of its elements. Assuming that your user is vicious and attempts to beat your 0.5 second timer, you may have some problems with this implementation. In practice, the implementation is more than adequate to simulate modal behavior when using versions of the Netscape browser. There is no need for this when we are using IE browsers, since they support modal dialog natively:

```
        <TR><TD><BR>
            <FORM NAME='myform'
    ACTION='mailto:singontheroad@aol.com?Subject=From%20your%20JavaScript
    %20Picture%20Album&Body=" + escape(document.forms[0].elements[0].value) +
    "%20%20pic%20is%20" + escape(mygif) + "' ENCTYPE='text/plain' METHOD='post'>
```

The code above creates the mailto URL using the string "From your JavaScript Picture Album" (in the subject), message to be sent (in the body), and with the name of the picture in the mygif variable appended to the body:

```
        Name:  <BR>
        <INPUT NAME='myname' TYPE='text' ONFOCUS='myElem=this'><BR>
        <INPUT TYPE='hidden' NAME='pic' VALUE='...GIF Name...'>
        <INPUT TYPE='hidden' NAME='mesg'
            VALUE='...Quote Escaped Message...'>
```

The values of the two hidden fields, pic and mesg, are readily available within this frame, so we simply use document.write() to write the values in:

```
        <INPUT TYPE='submit' VALUE='Send Comment Now'
            ONFOCUS='myElem=this'
            ONCLICK='setTimeout("self.close(); return true",10000)'>
        <INPUT TYPE='button' VALUE='Cancel' ONFOCUS='myElem=this'
            ONCLICK='self.close()'>
```

Note that we do not use ONSUBMIT, but ONCLICK to start a timer before the dialog window is closed. Using ONSUBMIT to submit e-mail is not reliable for Netscape 4.61. Hooking the event handler for the ONCLICK event will work for all supported Netscape versions.

Generating Title and Picture Display

Since we have already set the mytitle and mygif variables, it is a simple matter to generate the HTML code with document.write() to display the correct title and image:

```
<BODY  STYLE='font-size:8pt;font-family:Verdana,Arial,Helvetica;'>

  <TABLE WIDTH='300' BORDER='0' ALIGN='left'>
    <SCRIPT LANGUAGE='JavaScript'>
       document.write("<TR><TD BGCOLOR='black'>");
    </SCRIPT>
```

The rest of the code supports changing the SRC of an IMG tag:

```
        <CENTER>
          <DIV ID='picTitle' STYLE='color:white;font-size:16pt;'+
                'font-weight:bold; font-family:Times,Times Roman;'>
           <SCRIPT>
              document.write(mytitle);
           </SCRIPT>
          </DIV>
        </CENTER></TD></TR>
        <TR><TD BGCOLOR='lightyellow'>
          <CENTER>
           <SCRIPT>
              document.write("<IMG ID='showpic' SRC='" + mygif +
                            "' WIDTH='300' HEIGHT='250'>");
           </SCRIPT>
          </CENTER>
        </TD></TR>
```

Comments Form with Confirmation Dialog

The final section of this page contains a form where users can add comments. This is exactly the same as in the first version. When the user clicks the **Send Comment** button, the showform() function is called to display the confirmation modal dialog box:

```
        <TR><TD BGCOLOR='lightyellow'>
          <FORM NAME='comment'>
            Your Comments Please :<BR>
            <TEXTAREA NAME='cmttxt' COLS='40' ROWS='5'></TEXTAREA><BR>
        </TD></TR>
        <TR><TD BGCOLOR='lightyellow'>
          <CENTER>
            <INPUT TYPE='button' VALUE='Send Comment' ONCLICK='showform()'>
            <INPUT TYPE='reset' VALUE='Clear'>
          </CENTER></FORM>
        </TD></TR>
     </TABLE>
  </BODY>
</HTML>
```

That's all the coding we need for our second version, so it's time to test the application with 4.x and 5.x browsers.

To test the cross-browser compatibility of this version of the Photo Album Application, you could try the example on IE 4.0x/5.0x/5.5+ and Netscape 4.0x/4.75+. Check the collapsible lists, test that the photos change when you select different members of the family tree and try out the modal dialog box.

Caveat: File URL Differences Between IE Versions

When testing the application, you should be hosting the pages off a server. While it is possible to test with IE 6 or 5.x by directly opening the file, some versions of IE 4.x may not handle the `location.href` and `location.href.search` properties properly with file-based URLs. In fact, you will not get any parameters after the question mark in an extended URL. This will result in no change on the Picture Display page when a link is clicked on the Tree Controller page. If you test pages from a web server, even if the server is local, this will not be a problem.

Summary

We have discovered the hard way that in real life, cross-browser JavaScript programming is much more difficult than we would like it to be. With every new version of browser and scripting technology release, a new Pandora's box of incompatibilities and problems is opened. The good news is that this evolution will ensure proficient JavaScript developers a long and prosperous career ahead of them; the bad news is that a project sometimes never seems to finish.

Even in this age of W3C DOM compatibility, programming using Microsoft Dynamic HTML in IE 4, 5 and 6 browsers can still lock us out of any compatibility with Netscape-based browsers (the key issues being the additional flexibility offered by DHTML, and the support for 4.x level browser that does not support W3C DOM). However, if we can restrict our design goals to only provide compatibility with Microsoft browsers, the task becomes quite easy. Creating our tree controller entirely in JavaScript for IE was quite straightforward once we had worked out the design.

We discovered that JavaScript libraries are available, and that several of the libraries from Netscape are actually cross-browser compatible, albeit requiring at least a 4.x level browser. These libraries are excellent tools when compatibility is required with a wide range of browsers (from 4.x to 6.x level). Using the browser sniffer library from this collection, we created code that will use native support of the modal dialog box where available (in IE) and simulated the code if necessary (when using Netscape browsers).

The very bottom line is that JavaScript is not just a simple "glue" or "play" programming language, but one that can be used to create sophisticated and complex applications – with a little help.

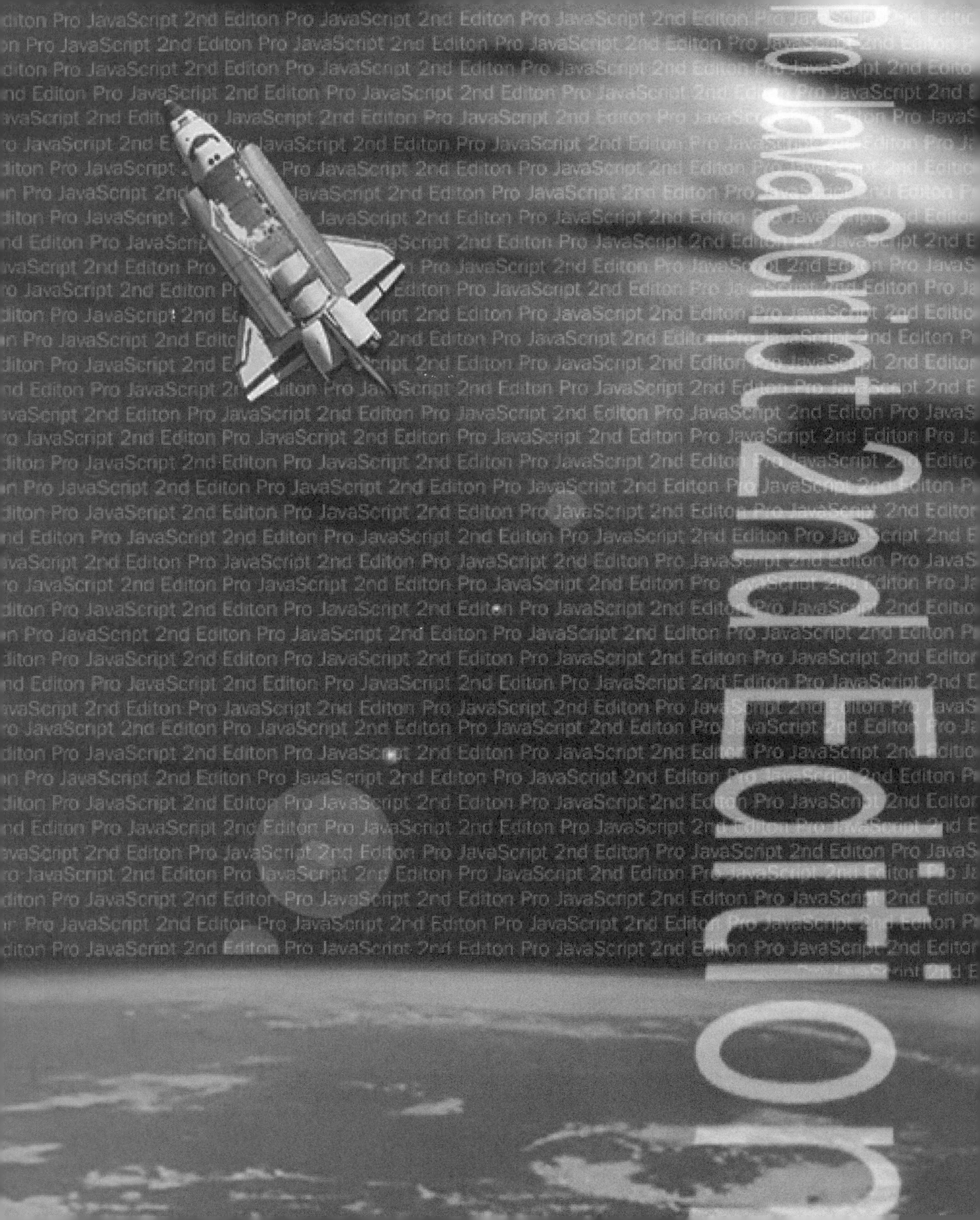
Pro JavaScript 2nd Edition
Pro JavaScript 2nd Editon

Section Six

Current JavaScript Developments

In this final part of the book, we focus on where JavaScript may be heading in the future, and give you some idea of the kind of technologies you may be dealing with over the next few years.

We start by examining ECMAScript, the standardized version of JavaScript, and look in detail at the proposal for the next version of the language. In the final chapter, we have an overview JScript.NET, the latest version of JScript from Microsoft. We'll see how this fits in with their .NET strategy and web services.

Pro JavaScript 2nd Edition

24

ECMAScript 4

This chapter discusses ECMAScript Edition 4 and what new abilities it will bring to the JavaScript language. ECMAScript is the formal standard behind the JavaScript language. At the time of editorial, much of the technologies discussed in this chapter aren't available in any JavaScript implementations. Also, some of the details could change before it is finalized. However, that being said, most of the functionality will remain the same and we will discuss in the following sections:

❑   The relationship between ECMAScript and JavaScript, and what ECMAScript is

❑   A brief history of JavaScript as it relates to ECMA

❑   JavaScript 2.0 from Netscape, and how it is a superset of ECMAScript Edition 4

❑   ECMAScript Edition 4 and what new features are covered

❑   What is important about the ECMAScript specifications and how each edition is backwards compatible

❑   Some useful online references so that you can keep up-to-date with this nascent technology

ECMAScript == JavaScript?

Today, when we look for information on JavaScript out on the Web, some of the information we find is confusing, to say the least. We find articles that say that JavaScript and ECMAScript is the same thing, or that one is replacing the other. Neither statement is accurate, but as we'll see, JavaScript and ECMAScript have been very closely tied together from their beginnings.

ECMAScript is not the new JavaScript, nor is it the old JavaScript, nor does it replace JavaScript or any other scripting language. It is a specification for scripting languages. Just as the beans in a collection of beans that do useful things in a Web application, such as suites of JavaBean components for chemistry or for crossword puzzles, are **implementations** of Sun's JavaBean specification, so JavaScript is an implementation of the ECMAScript specification.

> **ECMAScript is the international standard specification for an object-oriented scripting language that performs computations and manipulates objects in a host environment.**

ECMAScript is not a scripting language in itself, but is a basis for the creation, or implementation, of scripting languages. When run in a host environment, for example in a web browser, these scripting language implementations must combine with the level of support provided for them in the browser to provide a complete and consistent programming environment together. After all, the host environment provides the document object model (DOM), objects such as windows and documents, which a scripting language implementation manipulates.

ECMAScript is only a specification therefore it defines the core portion of the scripting language and leaves a lot of leeway for implementation differences when client-side and server-side implementations are created. Often, as we know all too well in the browser-scripting world, implementations differ in the way they support a concept or provide a feature that is an extension to the specification. In addition, host environment DOMs differ too, which leads to cross-browser compatibility headaches. As newer editions of ECMAScript have been adopted, and are reflected in implementations such as Netscape's JavaScript and Microsoft's JScript, it is important to make sure that the edition support we need is provided in our targeted web browsers. This gives the best consistent web page results for all our web site visitors.

JavaScript Origins and ECMAScript

In 1994, just a few months after Netscape Communications Corp. was founded, there existed LiveScript. LiveScript was the scripting language invented by Netscape for use in its new Navigator web browser, among other things. The name change from LiveScript to JavaScript came about in December 1995 as a marketing alliance was formed between Netscape Communications and Sun Microsystems. Both wanted to take advantage of the growing Java name recognition at the time and web developers' interest in client-side scripting. JavaScript 1.0 officially appeared in the Netscape Navigator 2.0 version, which became generally available in January 1996.

During the same timeframe, Microsoft recognized that this browser scripting capability was becoming a much-wanted feature. Microsoft added both VBScript (similar to BASIC and Visual Basic in syntax) and JScript (similar to C++ and Java in syntax) capability to its Internet Explorer 3 Web browser in order to keep it competitive. The JScript 1.0 scripting language introduced in Internet Explorer 3 was functionally and syntactically very much the same as the first JavaScript version. Internet Explorer is still the only major web browser that supports VBScript for browser scripting.

How is ECMAScript Related?

The next version of JavaScript, known as JavaScript 1.1, became available in Navigator 3. In late 1996, Netscape Communications Corp. proposed JavaScript 1.1 to the ECMA for consideration as the computer industry scripting language standard.

> **The ECMA was founded in 1961 as the European Computer Manufacturers Association. It was established to fill a need for the development of standardized computer operational formats in the computer industry. In 1994, the organization changed its name to the more descriptive: "ECMA – European Association for Standardizing Information and Communication Systems", and has been known since then simply as ECMA. As of June 2001, ECMA ordinary members were Alcatel, Apple, Avaya, Canon, Compaq, Dell, Ericsson, Fujitsu/ICL, Hewlett-Packard, Hitachi, IBM, Intel, Lucent Technologies, Microsoft, NCR, NEC, Netscape, Network Appliance, Oki Europe Ltd., Openwave, Panasonic, Philips, Pioneer Electric, Ricoh, Siemens, Sony, Sun, Tenovis, Toshiba, and Xerox.**

Due to this, the ECMA's Technical Committee on Programming and Scripting Languages, TC39 for short, was formed and it took up the proposal. The mission of TC39 at its creation was to develop the ECMAScript language specification standard.

Recently, TC39 has begun considering two other proposals for standards not directly related to scripting languages and so have formed three Task Groups within itself. The first is the Dynamic Scripting Language Task Group, or TG1, and TG1 considers proposals for complementary or additional scripting language technology that may be important to the future direction of ECMAScript. At this time, TG1 consists of representatives from Alcatel, Callscan, Compaq, Hewlett-Packard, IBM, Microsoft, Netscape, and Sun. The other two task groups are TG2 and TG3. TG2 is for the C# language proposal, and TG3 is for the Common Language Infrastructure, or CLI, which deals with support for C#, ECMAScript, and other modern language standards across a common platform.

At first TC39 had to consider the existing similar scripting language implementations from Microsoft and Borland, as well as Netscape's, for the scripting language standard it was creating. The resulting first edition of the ECMAScript specification, known as ECMAScript Edition 1, was adopted by the ECMA in June 1997. ECMAScript Edition 1 became the scripting language specification that reflected the implementations available at the time: JavaScript 1.1, JScript 1.0, and the scripting language in Borland's IntraBuilder development environment.

To further solidify ECMAScript's position as the international scripting language industry standard, ECMAScript was then submitted to the ISO/IEC JTC1, and was approved by that organization as International Standard ISO/IEC 16262 in April 1998.

> *The International Organization for Standardization (ISO) is a worldwide federation of national standards bodies, established in 1947. ISO's mission is to promote the development of standardization and related ... and to developing cooperation in the spheres of intellectual, scientific, technological and economic activity. ISO's work results in international agreements, published as International Standards.*

> *The International Electrotechnical Commission (IEC) is the international standards and conformity assessment body for all fields of electrotechnology.*

> *IEC signed an initial agreement with ISO in 1976 and ten years later, the two bodies established the Joint Technical Committee 1 (JTC1) to cover standards in the field of information technology.*

Subsequently, ECMAScript Edition 2 was quickly adopted by the ECMA for the tidying-up purpose of matching the editorial changes made to the specification during its ISO/IEC adoption.

Why We Need ECMAScript

ECMAScript was never intended to be a static specification. As scripting language implementations of ECMAScript are developed, new features in the implementations are developed, and those can be nominated for inclusion in the next version of the specification. Even as it grows, however, ECMAScript is a minimum required set that must be implemented in a scripting language that claims conformance. A host environment providing a scripting language that conforms to a particular edition of the ECMAScript specification (ECMAScript Editions 2 or 3 at this time) assures a developer that the minimum specified functionality is available for use.

If we want to use **extensions**, or functionality provided by a scripting language beyond the minimum required set, it is best to do some checking before actually using the extensions during script execution to make sure support for them is available in the host environment where the script is running. Sometimes we can do this by asking the browser what version it is. Sometimes we can ask the scripting language what version it is. In addition, sometimes we can do object checking to see if the extension itself is present. Not always, however, so sometimes we must to stick with the ECMAScript minimum level of functionality and test everything everywhere if it is important that our web pages behave consistently across all host environments that support scripting.

JavaScript Evolution and ECMAScript Edition 3

JavaScript 1.3 and JScript 3.0 (in Internet Explorer 4.0) both implemented browser scripting that conformed to the ECMAScript Edition 2 specification,. both browsers provided extensions to their scripting language implementations however, and as we just noted, this is an area where inconsistencies in browser behavior can arise, as extensions used in a script in one browser, may not be available in another browser when that same script is run. Examples of this in JavaScript 1.3 are the `call()` and `apply()` methods for the Function object, extensions that may or may not have been implemented similarly in other scripting languages, since they are not defined in the ECMAScript Edition 2 specification.

One major feature of ECMAScript Edition 2 is the use of Unicode support for internationalization. The scripting language's host environment must also support Unicode to ensure the correct display of literal Unicode characters and Unicode escape sequences in scripts.

ECMAScript Edition 3 was adopted by the ECMA in December 1999, and it is the current edition of the specification. The ECMAScript Edition 3 document is available for download from the ECMA web site (www.ecma.ch/ecma1/stand/ecma-262.htm), and hard copies may be obtained there as well. This third edition of the ECMAScript specification includes many additions and enhancements, most of which resulted from the extensions beyond ECMAScript Edition 2 that were implemented in JavaScript 1.3 and JScript 3.0. Areas where future growth of the scripting specification is expected are defined in ECMAScript Edition 3 as well.

Some major features of ECMAScript Edition 3 are:

❑ Structured exception handling, where runtime errors are reported as exceptions to a console instead of popping up alert boxes, and `try/catch` is available for error handling.

❑ Number formatting: (`Number.prototype.toFixed`, `Number.prototype.toExponential`, and `Number.prototype.toGeneral`).

❑ Strict equality operators `===` and `!==`, which perform equality comparisons only on operands of the same type.

❑ Regular expressions, which are patterns used to match character combinations in strings. This is a good example of an extension to ECMAScript Edition 1, implemented in JavaScript 1.3 that was subsequently added to the specification in Edition 3.

Some hosting environments where ECMAScript conformance in a scripting language implementation is provided (ECMAScript Edition 2 unless otherwise noted) are:

❑ Navigator 4.06+, Navigator and Communicator 4.5x, 4.6x, 4.7x, all from Netscape Communications

❑ Netscape version 6.1, from Netscape Communications, conforms to ECMAScript Edition 3

❑ Internet Explorer 4.0 and up, Internet Information Server 4.0 and up, and Windows Scripting Host 1.0, all from Microsoft

❑ Internet Explorer 5.5, from Microsoft conforms to ECMAScript Edition 3

❑ Opera 5, a Web browser from Opera Software

❑ Rhino (C-based) and Spidermonkey (Java-based); both are projects that implement JavaScript's core language (no objects or methods for manipulating HTML documents are provided) from the Mozilla Organization. Conform to ECMAScript Edition 3

❑ Mozilla, an open-source web browser from the Mozilla Organization, conforms to ECMAScript Edition 3

The following table outlines which versions of JScript and JavaScript are conforming implementations of ECMAScript at this time:

JavaScript Version	ECMAScript (version) Compliant?	JScript Version	ECMAScript (version) Compliant?
1.0	No	1.0	No
1.1	No	2.0	No
1.2	Yes (1)	3.0	Yes (1)
1.3	Yes (2)	4.0	Yes (1)
1.4	Yes (2)	5.0	Yes (2)
1.5	Yes (3)	5.5	Yes (3)

JavaScript 2.0, What's Next?

The JavaScript 2.0 proposal document is available on Netscape's web site (www.mozilla.org/js/language/js20.html). It's a good idea to visit this site from time to time to keep up with the latest changes. Notice that the proposal calls itself "experimental", and there's a good reason – this is a big next step! This work-in-progress JavaScript version is a lot more than just adding a few more features, as signaled by the symbolic jump in version numbering from 1.5 to 2.0.

The JavaScript 2.0 proposal is a re-write of the language specification and a re-development of the interpreter engine. Features such as classes, types, strictness, and static compilation of source code in addition to interpretation are proposed for addition to JavaScript 2.0. Given these big changes, backward compatibility with, or preservation of, the traditionally dynamic, loosely-typed, interpreted versions available to date is a major factor in determining where and how far the changes to JavaScript 2.0 can go.

Compile vs. Interpret

The source code of programming language implementations must be compiled, interpreted, or both before a computer can run it as machine code. If we search the Web for "compiled AND interpreted", we'll see many very detailed discussions on whether or not every language is interpreted at some level. For our purposes, the 30,000-foot view is fine – most languages require one *or* the other, and some require one *and then* the other. The line between the two basic methods is becoming less distinct, as we'll see here in JavaScript, and later with JScript.NET. Perl is another popular language implementation that goes through the same thing. Language designers today are trying to work out how to have the advantages of both in a single, sensible programming language.

As with most things in life, there are advantages and disadvantages to each way of doing it. Interpreted language programs, including scripts, are simple and quick to change, but require the same interpretation time overhead every time they are run. Run a script ten times, and it is interpreted ten times. Compiled languages run faster because they don't have that interpretation time overhead at run-time, but they have more and stricter programming rules and regulations to ensure that the compiler has the information it needs when it needs it during compilation. Run a compiled program ten times, and it doesn't take any additional compilation time.

JavaScript and JScript are two of many languages that are considered interpreted; the interpreter engine of the host environment (whatever its platform happens to be) changes one source statement at a time into machine code, which is then executed before the next statement is interpreted. Even if some pre-processing is done for things like function declarations, the process is still: statement after statement; parse it, do it, parse it, do it. Statement 23 doesn't know a thing about what's going to happen in statement 24 and beyond and doesn't care; it only knows the state of things after statement 22. Long ago, the BASIC programming language was the usual, interpreted introduction to programming for beginning programmers. Nowadays, that introduction is more likely to be a little interpreted script in the context of a HTML web page.

C++ is a language that has always been compiled; a compiler, separately from but aware of the run-time environment for the program, compiles the source code into an object code module for execution later. Some compilers are designed to make two passes through the code, looking for and remembering information in later parts of the code that it uses in the second pass through to "fill in the blanks" in earlier parts of the code and optimizing what has already compiled. Executable object code is most familiar to us as `.exe` or `.dll` files. These executables run fast because they don't have to be recompiled at every execution. Development is more rigid and complicated because any change in the source code requires a recompilation to get the change into the executable for testing.

A few language implementations, like Java and Python, are compiled into some form of portable **bytecode** at a time before the program runs and then the bytecode is interpreted at run-time. In some implementations, this is called 2-stage interpretation. Bytecode isn't human-readable, and it isn't machine code either. It is interpreted by a software virtual machine, such as the Java Virtual Machine, at run-time, and interpretation of bytecode is usually fast, but even this shorter runtime overhead is incurred every time the program is executed.

Class vs. Prototype

Object-oriented programming languages are either class-based or prototype-based. Class-based languages are often seen as strict and rigid, while prototype-based languages are often considered too flexible and relaxed. JavaScript 2.0 is just one project in the programming world trying to get the best of both methodologies into one language. JScript.Net is another, and so is Perl 6.0. If we search the Web, we can find many articles and papers with ideas for how to combine the methodologies in ways that keep the advantages of both and leave the disadvantages behind. Still though, the design point dilemmas that all these language implementation designers are actively working on have not yet been fully resolved, so we'll use rather generic code in examples we provide here.

A class is the definition of all the properties that characterize a set of objects; all objects created from this class must match this template. It is like a dictionary or look up table which contains a list of objects, methods, and properties, and by making an object part of that class, it inherits all of the objects, methods, and properties of that class.

A prototype is an existing object whose properties are used when defining another object. JavaScript is prototype-based, and Chapter 3 covers that well. A prototype is what it sounds like. By creating a prototype of an object, we can specify that we want all further instances of an object to possess all of the same properties of the prototyped object. Therefore, we can say that using prototypes, we create objects that are similar to other objects.

ECMAScript Edition 4, What's Next?

ECMAScript Edition 4 is also a work-in-progress in concert with JavaScript 2.0 and has been so since August 2000 when the initial version of the proposal was quite literally carved out of Netscape's JavaScript 2.0 working document. The ECMA's TC39/TG1 meets regularly, in person, and electronically, to discuss and make decisions on ECMAScript Edition 4 revision issues. The Technical Committee intends to have ECMAScript Edition 4 finalized and ready for adoption by the ECMA in 2002. The ECMAScript Edition 4 proposal document is available on Netscape's web site (www.mozilla.org/js/language/es4.html). Just as with the JavaScript 2.0 proposal, it's a good idea to visit the site if you're interested in keeping up-to-date with changes.

Netscape, with its upcoming JavaScript 2.0 implementation, and Microsoft, with its upcoming JScript.Net implementation, are obviously major forces behind the proposed changes in the specification. Another influence is a new programming language called **Spice**, developed by designers at Hewlett-Packard. Spice combines extensible cascading style rules from Cascading Style Sheets (CSS) with object-oriented scripting from the JavaScript implementation of ECMAScript. Some of the Spice extensions beyond ECMAScript Edition 3 are now being considered for inclusion in ECMAScript Edition 4.

Since Netscape intends that JavaScript 2.0 continue to be a "slight superset" of the ECMAScript Edition 4 specification, we'll consider them the same for our look here at some of the proposed changes. Near the end, we'll talk about what is in JavaScript 2.0 that isn't in ECMAScript Edition 4.

The ECMAScript Edition 4 proposal itself states that ECMAScript Edition 4 is intended to be backwards compatible with almost all scripts written with ECMAScript Edition 3 and earlier compliant scripting languages. A similar compatibility statement is made in the JavaScript 2.0 proposal document, regarding JavaScript 1.5 and earlier. The biggest challenge presented by the proposals, it seems, is how to add the desired changes without damaging the features that made scripting languages so popular in the first place.

Keeping the Old Functionality

Two of the best advantages of browser scripting are its development flexibility and its relatively relaxed usage rules, which make it easier for non-programmers and faster for programmers to write, test, and publish scripts. These advantages were two of the reasons why browser scripting became so popular when it was first introduced all those years ago.

Development flexibility comes from the fact that, for web browsers, scripts are served up in source code form by a web server along with the HTML web page and interpreted by the browser with no previous static compilation step. A change to the script is available to all just as soon as the Web page containing the change is published to the web server. As far as relaxed usage rules go, ECMAScript implementations to date deliberately "help" script programmers by not strictly enforcing correct line-ending syntax and strict variable typing in situations where the scripting language interpreter can work out what is meant.

While it is not the stated intention of TC39/TG1 and the ECMAScript Edition 4 designers to turn it into a specification for a complete programming language, much of what constitutes a complete object-oriented programming language can be found in the ECMAScript Edition 4 proposal. This represents a real change in the way scripting programmers will find themselves thinking about the objects they manipulate in scripts in the future.

Adding the New Functionality

Some of the major new features of the ECMAScript Edition 4 proposal are:

❑   Class definition syntax, both static and dynamic

❑   Types for program and interface documentation

❑   Machine types such as `int32` for integration with other programming languages, such as Java and C#

❑   `private`, `internal`, `public`, `external`, and user-defined access controls

❑   Invariant declarations

❑   Introspection facilities

❑   Overridable basic operators such as + and [ ]

❑   `Packages and versions`

We'll look at the reasons for each and some examples shortly. The examples are written in a rather generic code form deliberately here, because not all the details are finalized yet – we are at a time of editorial looking at a work-in-progress, after all. The proposal continues to be updated quite often.

There are, of course, other new features in the proposal, such as strict mode and directives, but they are still very much the subjects of discussion and debate at this time, so the best place to get the latest information on them is the specification web site itself. Just remember for now that the proposed changes are related to the goal of making ECMAScript-compliant implementations modular, more robust, more secure, and better at integrating with other programming languages.

Class Definition Syntax

Up to this point, ECMAScript-compliant scripting language implementations use prototype-based object creation and management. Any object can be the prototype for a new object, so an object becomes a prototype simply because that's the way the script developer uses it. New objects can be created by using the constructor of a prototypical object as a template for a new object, which is then created with the initial properties of the prototype specified. Let's define a `car` function object:

```
function car()
{
    this.wheels = "aluminum";
    this.color = "pearl white";
    this.engine = "V8";
    this.headlights = "halogen";
}
```

All we have to do to create a couple of car objects is:

```
car1 = new car();
car2 = new car();
```

We can do anything with `car2` that we can with `car1` because they are both `car` objects. Changes to the properties of the constructor, made by changing its function object, result in the same changes in all the objects created from it in a script, because each object contains a pointer to the constructor from which it was created. This ability to change an object's properties as the interpretation and execution of the script progresses is what makes scripting dynamic.

Now, in the class-based world, we don't start with a function object, we start with a class. A class is an object too, but it can't be used like objects in the prototype-based world. Let's define the Automobile class:

```
// Define the Automobile class
class Automobile
{
    // Constructor
    public function Automobile(w:String, c:String, e:String, h:String)
    {
        wheels = w;
        color = c;
        engine = e;
        headlights = h;
    }
    var wheels:String;
    var color:String;
    var engine:String;
    var headlights:String;
}
```

We don't have an instantiated object yet, just the definition of a class. An instance is an object that is an **instantiation** of a class; it is the literal, runtime object in a program that is created based on a class definition. In ECMAScript Edition 4, instances are called objects. This may be confusing since classes are objects too, but here we'll call instances, objects, and we'll call classes, classes.

Typically, each class definition has special methods for creating and destroying objects created from it. The method that constructs or creates the object is called the constructor, and the method that destructs or destroys the object is called the destructor. In some class-based programming languages, default constructors and destructors are provided if a class doesn't explicitly define them.

So, let's use our explicitly defined constructor method `Automobile()` to create an object. We do this by calling `new` in this way:

```
// Construct an object from the Automobile class
car1 = new Automobile("aluminum", "pearl white", "V8", "halogen");
```

Now we have a class definition and an object constructed from that class, two different kinds of things.

Let's say that the `car1` object is like the pearl white 2002 Lincoln Navigator SUV. That SUV was constructed at the factory from a blueprint much more complicated than our `Automobile` class definition. We can't drive the blueprint, only automobiles constructed from it. At the same time, the factory doesn't use an existing automobile to construct other automobiles; it must have a blueprint.

Therefore, in class-based programming languages, an instance cannot be created from another instance; only a class can be used to create an instance. A class can't be used as an instance, either. An instance has the properties named in its parent class definition at the time it is instantiated, and those properties don't change during program execution just because someone changes the definition of the parent class in the source code. An object in a compiled class-based script is frozen, or **static**. ECMAScript Edition 4 provides this class-based mechanism as well as ways to implement prototype-based object creation. It will be up to developers to use conforming implementations to produce scripts that are class-based, prototype-based, or a mix of the two.

Inheritance works differently in class-based languages than in prototype-based languages. A class inheriting from its parent class in a **hierarchy** is a **subclass** of the parent class. The parent class is called the **superclass**. No instance can be part of a class hierarchy, only classes can. With prototypical inheritance, on the other hand, an object may be the prototype from which other objects inherit their characteristics. We can define subclasses of our `Automobile` class to make it easier for us to create different kinds of `car` objects. Here's the `Pickup` subclass definition:

```
// Define the Pickup subclass
class Pickup extends Automobile
{
    var bedStyle:String;
    // Constructor
    public Pickup(w:String, c:String, e:String, h:String, b:String)
    {
        super(w, c, e, h);
        bedStyle = b;
    }
}
```

Here the keyword `super` always refers to the superclass, `Automobile` in this case, which is passed the four required parameters. Only pickup truck objects need the property `bedStyle`, so making `Pickup` a subclass of `Automobile` makes it easier to manage the various properties of it and the subclasses of `Automobile` we might want to define, such as `Sportscar` or `SUV`. Creating a Pickup object goes like this:

```
// Construct an object from Pickup subclass
truck = new Pickup("aluminum", "pearl white", "V8", "halogen", "long_wide");
```

A `truck` object has all the properties of a `car` object, plus `bedStyle`.

A subclass can use polymorphism to change characteristics that it inherited from its superclass without changing the interface to that characteristic. The fact that there is no change to the interface, which is a method's name and the parameters it requires, is what makes it different from function overloading. Let's add a method and two more properties to our superclass definition so that our objects can "move":

```
// Define the Automobile class
class Automobile
{
    var wheels:String;
    var color:String;
    var engine:String;
    var headlights:String;
    var speed:Integer;
    var rate:Integer;
    public function Automobile(w:String, c:String, e:String, h:String)
    {
        wheels = w;
        color = c;
        engine = e;
        headlights = h;
        speed = 0;
        rate = 0;
    }
    public function accelerate(r:Integer):Integer
    {
        rate = r;
        if (speed == 0)
            speed = 10;
        else
            speed = speed * rate;
        return(speed);
    }
}
```

Now all objects constructed from `Automobile` can `accelerate` and have `speed`. Objects we create, based on the `Pickup` class, can accelerate, but not as quickly as car objects. We define that difference in the `Pickup` subclass like this:

```
// Define the Pickup subclass, Automobile is its superclass
class Pickup extends Automobile
{
    var bedStyle:String;
    public function Pickup(w:String, c:String, e:String, h:String, b:String)
    {
        super(w, c, e, h);
        bedStyle = b;
    }
    // use this accelerate method instead of the one in Automobile
    public override function accelerate(r:Integer):Integer
    {
        rate = r/2;                  // half the rate
        if (speed == 0)
            speed = 5;               // half the starting speed
        else
            speed = speed * rate;
        return(speed);
    }
}
```

Notice that both `accelerate()` methods have the same name and the same number and type of parameters. Both methods are invoked the same way. Starting with `speed=0`, however `car.accelerate(1)` returns 10 and `truck.accelerate(1)` returns 5. The `accelerate()` method in the `Pickup` subclass hides the `accelerate()` method in the `Automobile` superclass.

Having to define classes and subclasses and then construct objects from them is quite a bit different from the function object behavior of prototyping and prototype inheritance chains, but that prototyping flexibility will still be available in ECMAScript Edition 4. The proposed specification permits a programmer to add dynamic properties to an object after it is constructed from a class, if the class definition permits it. Defining our `Automobile` class with the `dynamic` attribute gives this permission. We can then add the `trunkSize` property to the instance of `Automobile` that we call `car2`:

```
// Define the Automobile class; allow adding dynamic properties
// to objects constructed from this class
dynamic class Automobile
{
    var wheels:String;
    //etc.
}

// Construct an object from the Automobile class
car2 = new Automobile("aluminum", "pearl white", "V8", "halogen");

// Add a dynamic property to the object
car2.trunkSize = "large";
```

Objects constructed from a class defined with the `fixed` attribute may not have dynamic properties, and so they behave more like instances constructed from class definitions in other class-based languages like Java. Therefore, if we don't want to allow dynamic property addition for our class, we must define it like this:

```
// Define the Automobile class; forbid adding dynamic properties
// to objects constructed from this class
fixed class Automobile
{
    var wheels:String;
    //etc.
}
```

The property names defined by a class are called its **members**. Members of a class cause properties to be constructed when an object is constructed from that class definition.

Even though ECMAScript Edition 3 has no concept of class definitions, it is possible to write scripts where the objects' relationships form de facto classes by association. So why specify a formal class-based architecture?

Class-based languages provide stability and reliability when code is packaged for others to use. This feature supports the goal of modularity. Modularity means that a chunk of script that performs a particular task can be packaged somehow and made into a module, so that other programmers can find and use the module just as it is without having to know everything about the details of what's inside. All a developer needs to know is where to find it, a description of what it can do and how to use it.

Classes that might be defined and packaged in Austin, Texas can be used by programmers anywhere to reliably create objects that are what we intended them to be. We can provide a package of classes as a source code library, or a compiled runtime library, or both. We can ensure reliability if we define our classes as fixed and provide only compiled code so that the source code isn't available for alteration; all objects constructed from them would then be the same every time that compiled scripts using them are run. There would be no need to trace back through an object's prototype-based inheritance chain in a script to understand the properties of that object at any given point.

Polymorphism is a powerful object-oriented programming language feature. It adds flexibility to class-based object creation to make packages and classes more useful. A word of caution is in order, though. Through programming mistakes or deliberate maliciousness, classes with polymorphism implemented can result in unpleasant surprises for the programmer constructing objects from them. It pays to make sure that a method being called actually does under the covers what is expected.

Types

The definition of what a type is has been generalized more broadly than the defined types found in ECMAScript Edition 3. A programming language can be strongly typed, such as Java, where every variable in a program is required to have its type declared or the program won't compile. ECMAScript is not specified as strongly typed, but the capability to write a strongly typed script is provided. It is up to the conforming implementations of the specification to decide if the implementation is strong or loosely typed.

The description here is deliberately less detailed than in the ECMAScript Edition 4 proposal itself, so refer to the document on the Web if you want to be sure you have the latest updates. This is one area especially where the TC39/TG1 is still making decisions.

Let's begin with a value. A value is an entity that can be stored in a variable, passed to a function, or returned from a function. A **type** is a set of values. For example, we can define the rainbow type to be the set with member values "red, orange, yellow, green, blue, indigo, violet".

A value can be a member of multiple sets, but must only have one type. Let's also define the watercolor type to be the set with member values "red, yellow, blue, black, white". The value "red" is a member of both sets. When it comes time to use the value "red" in a script, however the type for "red" must be either rainbow or watercolor; it can't be both and it must consistently be one or the other.

Every type represents a set of values but not every set of values is represented by a type. The set of values "chartreuse, magenta, cyan" may or may not have a type definition to go with it, and that's okay. Every type is also itself a value, and can be stored in a variable, passed to a function, or returned from a function. We can define the colors type to be the set of member values "rainbow, watercolor" if we choose.

There is a **type hierarchy**, where:

❑ The type Object is the **supertype** of all types

❑ All types except Object are **subtypes** of Object

❑ A variable with type Object can hold any value

❑ The set containing no values is of the type Never

❑ Never is the subtype of all types

Therefore, all types can be placed somewhere in the type hierarchy between and including Object and Never. Object is not a new concept in ECMAScript or JavaScript, but Never is. The proposal says, "...the types Never and Void are different and serve different purposes. When used as a return type, Never describes the inability to return from a function, while Void states that the function returns, but the value returned is not useful (it's always undefined)".

Object and Never, along with Void, Null, Boolean, Integer, Number, Character, String, Function, Array, ConstArray, ConstArray[t], DynamicArray[t], StaticArray[t] , and Type, are the predefined types in the ECMAScript Edition 4 proposal at this time. Machine types are an optional, special set of types, which we'll look at next.

Strong typing assures that variables in a script or program have explicitly declared types; this cuts down on incidences of the kind of bugs caused by automatic type conversions. This also contributes to the goal of robustness because it eliminates the cause of these bugs. String-to-number and number-to-string conversions are the source of most conversion errors in JavaScript and other loosely typed implementations.

Another advantage of strong typing is that it makes more optimized code compilation possible. ECMAScript Edition 4 is expanding in the direction of providing the ability to compile source code separately from running the compiled program, and those compilers can be designed for better performance on strongly typed source code containing particular datatypes.

Strong typing can also be thought of as a form of enforced script documentation. If you must explicitly declare the type for all of your variables, it makes for easier review and cleaner update of scripts you produce. It also improves the understandability of class definitions, and so makes it easier to use the contents of packages correctly, which contributes to the goal of modularity. Scripts are more maintainable with strong typing because there is no ambiguity about what the variables in the script are supposed to be.

Machine Types

Machine types provide the definition of additional low-level types for use in scripts where integration with other programming languages is required. Implementations that support machine types can provide faster, Java-style integer operations for communicating with other programming languages for performance-critical code. Variables can be explicitly declared using these defined types. Using machine types can ensure that data passed between a script and another software application is passed accurately.

The proposed machine types are named (and correspond to) `int8` (byte), `uint8` (ubyte), `int16` (short), `uint16` (ushort), `int32` (int), `uint32` (uint), `int64` (long), and `uint64` (ulong). These are not intended to substitute for Number and Integer for general scripting purposes.

Correspondingly, the words `boolean`, `byte`, `char`, `double`, `int`, `long`, and `short` that are reserved words in ECMAScript Edition 3 will not be reserved words in ECMAScript Edition 4.

Providing machine types in the ECMAScript specification will enable scripting language implementations to adapt correctly to interfaces to other software applications. Whether the applications have interfaces implemented as APIs or as class abstractions, machine types will make it possible for ECMAScript-compliant implementations to integrate better with other languages and their various operating system/hardware environments.

Access Controls

Access controls, also called access modifiers, are a kind of attribute for a property definition in a class that describes who is authorized to see or use that property in an object constructed from that class. "Who" in this case means objects constructed from other classes in the script.

A **namespace** is a new concept in ECMAScript Edition 4 that is needed because of the addition of classes and packages. It is a name for the territory, or scope involved, for a class or package. JScript.Net has implemented namespaces as a specification extension already, but JavaScript has not. Be sure to check the ECMAScript Edition 4 proposal web site for the latest changes on this topic – what the concept is actually going to be called and how it will work is still actively being debated at this time.

In the picture showing the contents of a package called `package1`, the bubbles all represent different namespaces. The member `myVar` in `class1` is in the namespace of `class1` and the member `ourVar` in `class4` is in the namespace of `class4`. All four classes in `package1` are within the namespace of `package1`:

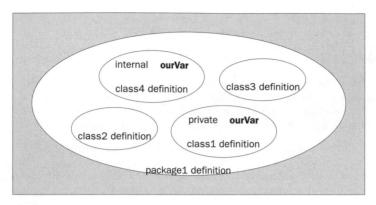

A property that may be accessed only by methods in its class's namespace is given the `private` attribute. In `package1`, only other properties defined in `class1`, the class where the property `myVar` is defined, can see and use it, because `myVar` has the `private` attribute:

```
// Define the class1 class
public class class1
{
    private var myVar:String;
    // etc.
}
```

A property that can be accessed by methods of objects constructed from its class and from other classes in its package's private namespace is given the `internal` attribute. In `class4` of `package1`, the property `ourVar` can be seen and used by properties in all of the classes in `package1`, but not by properties in classes defined in other packages, because it has the `internal` attribute:

```
// Define the class4 class
// Allow ourVar to be accessed by methods defined in class1,
// class2, class3, and class4 in package 1
public class class4
{
    internal var ourVar:String;
    // etc.
}
```

A `public` property can be accessed by properties of objects anywhere in the script, even as an unqualified variable by other packages, which is where it is different from an `explicit` property. The `explicit` attribute can be used to add class and property definitions to `package1` without having them conflict with definitions with the same names in other packages that import `package1`. This prevents an `explicit` property from being accessed as an unqualified variable when a package is imported.

JavaScript already provides `public` and `private` access controls for variables and methods, but these apply to prototype-based objects in the current JavaScript implementation. In the specification, however, these two access controls, along with `internal` and `explicit`, are the four pre-defined access controls in the ECMAScript Edition 4 proposal that apply to property definitions for classes. An ECMAScript Edition 4-compliant implementation may define and use its own access controls and other attributes as well.

Here again is a change contributing to the goals of modularity and robustness. By controlling the definitions of our classes and packages, and the exposure of our properties to other properties, we can ensure that the behavior of objects constructed from our classes is what we intend it to be – not only for our use in our scripts, but also for other programmers using our classes and packages in their scripts.

Invariant Declarations

Invariant declarations are attributes or modifiers that, when applied to properties or classes, make them unchangeable. When a class definition is modified with the `final` attribute, for example, it means that the class cannot be sub-classed; extending it is not permitted:

```
// Define the Automobile class, final - no sub-classing allowed
final class Automobile
{
   var wheels:String;
   //etc.
}
```

```
// define the Pickup subclass - THIS WON'T COMPILE, not allowed
class Pickup extends Automobile
{
   var bedStyle:String;
   public function Pickup(w:String, c:String, e:String, h:String, b:String)
   {
      super(w, c, e, h);
      bedStyle = b;
   }
      // etc.
}
```

Since the basic purpose of sub-classing is to create a new class definition based on an existing one, the `final` attribute locks a class down so that no other class can be based on it. Making a class final automatically makes all the methods in it final too.

If there's only one method in a class definition that we need to define as final, that individual method can be given the `final` attribute. This makes that one method non-overridable without preventing the ability to override other methods in the same class:

```
// Define the Automobile class, sub-classing is allowed
class Automobile
{
   var wheels:String;
   var color:String;
   var engine:String;
   var headlights:String;
   var speed:Integer;
   var rate:Integer;
   public function Automobile(w:String, c:String, e:String, h:String)
   {
      wheels = w;
      color = c;
      engine = e;
      headlights = h;
      speed = 0;
      rate = 0;
   }
   // final - overriding this method is not allowed
   final public function accelerate(r:Integer):Integer
   {
      rate = r;
      if (speed == 0)
         speed = 10;
      else
         speed = speed * rate;
      return (speed);
```

```
      }
   }

   // Define the Pickup subclass - this is allowed
   // since the superclass does not have the final attribute
   class Pickup extends Automobile
   {
      var bedStyle:String;
      public function Pickup(w:String, c:String, e:String, h:String, b:String)
      {
         super(w, c, e, h);
         bedStyle = b;
      }
      // Override the superclass's method with this one
      // THIS WON'T COMPILE - overriding accelerate() in Automobile
      /// is not allowed
      public function accelerate(r:Integer):Integer
      {
         rate = r/2;                 // half the rate
         if (speed == 0)
            speed = 5;               // half the starting speed
         else
            speed = speed * rate;
         return(speed);
      }
   }
}
```

Invariant declarations provide a way to ensure robustness and security in a programming language, which are both goals of the ECMAScript Edition 4 proposal. Class definitions in packages can be locked down, or frozen, as tightly as required by a particular application's security needs.

Beyond that, methods that must always behave exactly the same way in any instance constructed from the class definition to which they belong or any subclasses derived from that class can be defined with the final attribute. This ensures dependability in critical functional areas of the class and its package.

Introspection Facilities

Introspection facilities in a programming language provide a way to enumerate, or to list, object characteristics at runtime. In other words, it is a feature that gives objects the ability to respond to query at run-time and makes them inform us about themselves.

In ECMAScript Edition 4, this feature will be available only from objects constructed from class definitions and not from those created from prototypes. Querying an object constructed from a class definition may tell us what type of object it is, what its attributes are, the names of its methods, and other information. Design decision details have not been finalized; however so for the latest information, check the web site.

Introspection is valuable in object-oriented languages since, as we've seen, the way a class is defined determines the access other objects have to the properties of the objects constructed from it. Objects that are carefully designed to protect their members may still allow inspection of those members by other objects. Introspection makes it easier to use classes in packages from various sources, which enhances a language's modularity without compromising security or reliability.

Overridable Basic Operators

This feature is the major difference between ECMAScript Edition 3 and 4, as far as expressions are concerned. In ECMAScript Edition 4, most expression operators, such as + and [], can be overridden. There is a list in the proposal of which basic operators may be overridden. The overriding of operators is permitted only within the context of a class definition.

> Before December 2000, the ECMAScript Edition 4 proposal used the word "overload" instead of "override" to describe this feature.

When overriding an operator in a class, at least one operand for the operator must be of that class. A brief example, based on one found in the proposal, for how this looks when overriding the + operator in a class definition for complex numbers is:

```
public class Complex
{
    // ...
    // An override for +
    operator function "+" (a:Complex, b:Complex):Complex
    {
        return new Complex(x: a.x+b.x, y: a.y+b.y);
    }
    // Another override for +
    operator function "+" (a:Complex, b:Number):Complex
    {
        return new Complex(x: a.x+b, y: a.y);
    }
}
```

We could define more + overrides here as long as we follow this rule: in each operator override method in a class, at least one of the operands in the method must be derived from that class. This means that in our example, at least one of the operands in each of the two override functions shown must be of the Complex class, or of a subclass, whose superclass is Complex. Both of the methods comply with this rule, since the first method has two Complex operands, and the second method has one Complex operand and one Number operand.

Remember that the definition of what operator is overridden is contained in the class. The resulting plus sign behavior changes are seen in action when addition of a Complex object constructed from the class is performed in a script. Here, the + operator does two different things depending on the types of the two operands used with it. It's easy to use; once we've constructed objects from the Complex class; using the operator in both defined ways, the two code lines look the same:

```
ComplexSum1 = aComplex + anotherComplex;ComplexSum2 = aComplex + aNumber;
```

Without operators that can be overridden, we have to define two methods in the class instead to do the work properly, for example:

```
public class Complex
{
    // ...
    public function addComplexComplex(a:Complex, b:Complex):Complex
    {
        return new Complex(x: a.x+b.x, y: a.y+b.y);
    }
    //
    public function addComplexNumber(a:Complex, b:Number):Complex
    {
        return new Complex(x: a.x+b, y: a.y);
    }
}
```

Then the two equivalent code lines look like this:

```
ComplexSum1 = addComplexComplex(aComplex, anotherComplex);
ComplexSum2 = addComplexNumber(aComplex, aNumber);
```

While doing it this way gets the same job done, notice a couple of things:

❑ What happens in these two lines is not so plainly understandable as the two lines earlier with the overridden operator. This is a disadvantage when the developer who has to maintain the script wasn't the author, for example.

❑ If the class is sub-classed, overriding the methods is more awkward and maybe not even practical because neither the name of the function nor the type and number of its parameters can be changed.

The ability to override basic operators can provide a lot of flexibility for the development of applications. Additionally, having this feature in the specification gives scripting language implementations the freedom and a framework within which to define specific overridden operators themselves. It avoids having to expand the specification itself to cover the many possible definitions there would be if the feature weren't available.

Packages

ECMAScript Edition 4 proposes to provide a packaging mechanism, including library and version functionality. In Java, for example, a **package** is a library or container for classes and interfaces; it is simply a standardized way to organize them. The contents of a package are usually related in some way. A good example of a Java package is `java.util`, a collection of utility classes. In addition, Microsoft's MFC (Microsoft Foundation Classes) class library has been around since the early days of C++ object-oriented programming.

As packages are updated over time, classes in them could be added, renamed, or even deleted. Versioning is a way to handle this gracefully, meaning that scripts depending on the content of a package at a particular version can explicitly require that package version. Package developers can and do change the content of a package and still provide for backward compatibility with prior versions. Added classes can be marked as belonging to the updated version only and so aren't even visible to programs using the prior version. Changed classes can be identified in the same way so that either the prior or the updated class will be visible to a program, but not both.

Why should the ECMAScript Edition 4 proposal specify a packaging mechanism? Again, it's that goal of modularity. Packages of useful classes could be made available for inclusion in scripts, maybe as pre-compiled library packages called at run-time or as included source files. Packages can be made available in versions that indicate changes over time. A package could also be tailored for different platforms, for example a Windows version and an AIX version.

Using classes from packages to create a script would be like using pre-fabricated fence panels to build a fence. We could nail up every single board ourselves (write every line of every task in the script) or we could quickly put up fence panels that someone else had built (construct our objects from the classes to perform those same tasks). The pre-fabricated fence, and the modularized script, would go together more quickly and with fewer chances of error.

JavaScript 2.0 > ECMAScript Edition 4

Remember, it is JavaScript 2.0's intention to be a slight superset of ECMAScript Edition 4. Well, the primary specification extension that makes JavaScript 2.0 different is interfaces. An **interface** is a grouping of method definitions (without implementations) and constant values. An interface defines a set of behaviors that can be implemented by any class regardless of its position in a class hierarchy. Every interface is also a type and a value.

If we wanted to be able to organize our car and truck objects, and any other objects in a JavaScript 2.0 program, an interface could help us do that. A `Collection` interface might be written like this:

```
interface Collection
{
    Number MAXIMUM 100;        // a constant value
```

```
    void add(Object obj);      // some methods
    void delete(Object obj);
    Object find(Object obj);
    Number currentCount();
}
```

Notice that the methods don't actually define what they do, they just define the method names and parameters. Also, notice that there's no mention of the `Automobile` class or any other class in the interface definition.

To use this `Collection` interface in a script to organize our objects, we apply the interface to the class definitions like so:

```
// Define the CarShow class; implement the Collection interface
public class CarShow implements Collection
{
    String location;
    //etc.
    void add(Object obj)
    {
        // your code here
    }
    void delete(Object obj)
    {
        // your code here
    }
    Object find(Object obj)
    {
        // your code here
    }
    Number currentCount()
    {
        // your code here
    }
}
```

When a class definition implements an interface, the class must provide implementations for all of the methods in the interface. The interface defines things that the class must be able to do, and it is up to the class to define the action(s) performed in the methods. Here the `CarShow` class must provide the actions in the `add()`, `delete()`, `find()`, and `currentCount()` methods.

Backwards Compatibility

When all is said and done, the determining factors in the successful adoption of ECMAScript Edition 4 implementations once they are available will be:

❑   The final level of backwards compatibility with existing implementations conforming to ECMAScript Edition 3 – the intention is to provide backwards compatibility, but when the time actually comes, will most old scripts run reliably or not?

❑   The rate at which script developers get themselves educated;

❑   Correspondingly, the rate at which developers using the new implementations begin producing compiled, class-based programs with strong typing rather than continuing to produce prototype-based scripts with loose typing.

At this time, according to the JavaScript 2.0 proposal, the compatibility issues between JavaScript 1.5 and JavaScript 2.0 are:

❑ Commas are now significant inside brackets, so expr[expr, expr] should be replaced by expr[(expr, expr)].

❑ The post-increment and post-decrement operators (++ and --) return the value of the operand rather than the value of the operand converted number. The code var s = "5"; var y = s++ will store "5" in y instead of 5. The new value of s is still 6, just as in JavaScript 1.5.

❑ Uses of the identifiers as, is, namespace, and use need to be renamed or escaped with _ because these are now reserved words.

❑ JavaScript 2.0 drops the wrapper classes Boolean, Number, and String. Boolean, Number, and String now refer to classes that have primitive Booleans, numbers, and strings as instances. The methods of these new classes correspond to the methods of JavaScript 1.5's wrapper classes. The results of calling new on Boolean, Number, or String are now implementation-defined, so an implementation may choose to retain the wrappers for compatibility with JavaScript 1.5, but it is not required to do so.

❑ JavaScript 2.0 permits but does not require implementations to allow array indices greater than 4294967295 (2^{32}-1). Any code that relies on indices that may be greater than 4294967295, may not work on some platforms.

❑ Code that modifies the standard JavaScript 1.5 objects, such as Object and String, may not work. The specification does not detail why this may be the case.

❑ JavaScript 2.0 defines additional global constants, which may clash with top-level identifiers in programs.

❑ Invalid JavaScript 1.5 code may parse as valid JavaScript 2.0 code. JavaScript 1.5 programs that rely on getting exceptions for such formerly invalid code may not work.

For applications such as browsers where 100% compatibility is needed, scripts will be assumed to be written in JavaScript 1.5 unless explicitly marked as being JavaScript 2.0, through either an HTML or XML attribute or by including a use ecmascript(4) or use javascript(2) statement.

ECMAScript, It's a Good Thing

ECMAScript, JavaScript, and JScript go back a long way together, relatively speaking. ECMAScript and its various conforming implementations keep growing and evolving, as is expected, but the whole point of having industry standards, and a specification for a scripting language in particular, is to keep the implementations growing in the same direction in some sort of orderly fashion. For developers, this makes for easier maintenance and development long-term, and simplifies keeping skills up-to-date. Those skills can also more widely applicable in the job market rather than having to be narrowly focused on one implementation alone.

Granted, it's probably difficult for a scripting language provider such as Netscape or Microsoft to resist tailoring its ECMAScript-conforming implementation to a particular host environment, especially when that host environment is a widely available web browser. The science and philosophy of programming language design move forward based on research and experience.

The vast majority of scripting language consumers (like us and the companies we program for who use scripts to make money in the business world), need quick, consistent, cross-browser, cross-platform results in minimal time with simple maintenance. Look at it this way:

❑ IF a company has a business Web site

❑ AND that web site includes browser scripting

❑ AND it is important to develop and maintain the web site quickly and efficiently

❑ AND it is important that all of the potential customers coming to the web site have the same good experience, hopefully leading them to do business with the company

❑ THEN it is important to use a scripting language that conforms to the ECMAScript specification when building the web site, along with using the features in Web browsers that complement that same specification

Let's hope that scripting language designers continue to produce conforming implementations of ECMAScript and that host environment providers continue to support those implementations, even as ECMAScript ventures out into the class-based, strict, compiled part of our world in its Edition 4.

Summary

In this section, we have provided an overview of the ECMAScript Edition 4 specification and some details of its predecessors and JavaScript languages that will implement it in the future. Browsers are starting to converge on the upcoming edition 4 as it has matured enough for browser makers to keep all the existing functionality, while complying with the standard. All ECMAScript editions are backwards compatible too so any existing ECMAScript compliance can be left alone. So in summary, we have covered:

❑ What ECMAScript is

❑ The origins of JavaScript, and its convergence with ECMAScript

❑ The reasoning behind the ECMAScript specifications

❑ JavaScript 2.0 and what's different

❑ ECMAScript Edition 4 and what is kept, and added:

 ❑ Classes
 ❑ Types
 ❑ Access Controls
 ❑ Invariant Declarations
 ❑ Introspection Facilities
 ❑ Overridable Operators
 ❑ Packages

❑ How JavaScript 2.0 is a superset of ECMAScript 4

This chapter should have given enough information and references to enable you to learn about the next editions of JavaScript as they conform to the ECMAScript specifications. Various web references are given below, and the next chapter details JScript.NET (Microsoft's implementation of ECMAScript Edition 4 into their .NET strategy) in some detail.

Web References

Here are several online references that you might find very useful:

ECMAScript Edition 3 specification	www.ecma.ch/ecma1/stand/ecma-262.htm
ECMAScript Edition 4 proposal	www.mozilla.org/js/language/es4.html
Rhino project	www.mozilla.org/rhino/

Table continued on following page

Spidermonkey project	www.mozilla.org/js/spidermonkey/
JavaScript 2.0 proposal	www.mozilla.org/js/language/js20.html
JScript	msdn.microsoft.com/scripting/jscript/
VBScript	msdn.microsoft.com/scripting/vbscript/
JavaBean specification	java.sun.com/products/javabeans/
Free ECMAScript Interpreter (FESI)	home.worldcom.ch/jmlugrin/fesi/
ECMAScript binding for SVG DOM	www.w3.org/TR/2000/CR-SVG-20000802/ecmascript-binding.html
Spice	www.w3.org/TR/1998/NOTE-spice-19980123.html
Danny Goodman's JavaScript Pages	Great cross-browser support information here: www.dannyg.com/javascript/

Pro JavaScript 2nd Edition

.NET, Web Services, JScript.NET, and JavaScript

A fairly large change to the JavaScript language is coming, and this chapter is looking at the role JavaScript has to play in this latest change. The change we're talking about is web services, and in this chapter, that mostly means the version of web services that Microsoft has included in its .NET strategy. Microsoft's .NET strategy changes many other things as well, many directly relevant to the client side JavaScript programmer, so we'll have a look at some of these as well.

In this chapter we'll give an introduction to:

❑   What .NET is

❑   What JScript.NET is (and is not)

❑   Some specific .NET technologies such as Visual Studio.NET and ASP.NET and how these impact the JavaScript program

❑   What web services are

❑   The role a web browser can play in the world of web services

❑   How we can use client side JavaScript to access web services

Microsoft and .NET

One of the problems with explaining .NET is that it's such a large, all encompassing initiative; it can be difficult to explain one part of it without reference to another part. We'll attempt to explain it as best we can, but Wrox Press also publish a number of books on the .NET strategy, and you might be best turning to one of those if you are completely lost.

One of the key features of .NET is Web Services, which we'll look at in more depth later in this chapter. For now, I'll just say it's a way for an application to access functions exposed by another application over the Internet. While the applications that use Web Services, often referred to as consumers, can be on any platform, and the server providing the web service can be on any platform, this chapter will be focusing on creating web services using Microsoft's .NET technologies on the Windows 32 bit platform. While the consumer of the Web Service is truly platform independent, the server that provides the web service must be running Windows NT4.0 or later. There are several other vendors who are working aggressively towards providing a web services platform, most notably Sun and IBM. However, at time of writing Microsoft arguably has the most defined and sophisticated web services offering, so that's what we'll be looking at. Samples in this chapter were developed on Release candidate 1 of Windows XP with Beta 2 of the Microsoft.NET framework SDK. To run the samples yourself, you'll need to be running Windows NT4.0 or later, with IIS4 or later, and Beta 2 of the Microsoft.NET framework SDK installed. Visual Studio.NET is also helpful, especially if you want to start taking the ideas in this chapter and taking them to the next level, but far from essential. If you don't have access to such a system, check out the end of this chapter for some alternatives to having to install this software.

What is .NET?

According to Microsoft:

> ".NET is Microsoft's platform for XML Web services, the next generation of software that connects our world of information, devices and people in a unified, personalized way.
>
> The .NET platform enables the creation and use of XML-based applications, processes, and Web sites as services that share and combine information and functionality with each other by design, on any platform or smart device, to provide tailored solutions for organizations and individual people."

That may sound like marketing gobbledygook at first (and maybe to some extent it is), but it's not a bad description of Web Services. From a developer's perspective, .NET is a radical change – in many ways it's really a whole new way of thinking about things. It's a huge subject, and there are already many books written about it, so we can only hope to skim the surface here. There are many things we cannot cover in this chapter due to limitations on the space available, and huge subjects we can only introduce in one sentence (after all, this is a JavaScript book).

The key to the whole .NET strategy is the .NET framework. At its core is a software layer, which abstracts away most of the underlying Windows API. It handles all of the hard, day to day work that programmers have to deal with and presents it as a set of base classes which we can access, and leave them do the hard work. Let's have a look at a few key points, especially ones that are of concern to JavaScript developers.

Distributed Computing

.NET has been designed from the ground up with the Internet in mind, and particularly the concept of distributed computing. This is an idea where we have multiple applications running in different parts of the network – be it a server room, your intranet, or across the world via the Internet; all working together cooperatively and contributing their specialized functions to build an application where the whole is greater than the sum of the parts. Simple Object Access Protocol (**SOAP**) is the glue that holds all these applications together. We'll look more at the idea of distributed computing and SOAP (which is built on top of XML) later in the chapter when we talk about Web Services – the key to enabling applications to run in a distributed in environment. We'll develop a few web services using JScript.NET later on so you can get a really good feel for how they work, and how you can use your JavaScript skills in this new world.

Class Library

The .NET framework includes an incredibly comprehensive class library, similar to the packages in Java or the STL in C++, although many people say the .NET class library is more comprehensive than either of these, or indeed any other class library ever created. The functionality offered is very rich and broad reaching. Much of the common plumbing code that can be so time consuming to write, but we seem to spend so much our time writing and re-writing, has already been written and exposed in the class library. The developer who can get a good grasp on the .NET class library should see their productivity skyrocket.

Language Independence and the CLR

As a JavaScript programmer, it's easy to feel left out, in developer circles. The C++ programmers sometimes look down their noses at us, a little. While JavaScript is great for developing scripts quickly, we can't currently write a proper application in JavaScript, and there are performance issues compared with compiled languages!

Things have changed. .NET introduces the Common Language Runtime. All code in the .NET framework is compiled into an intermediate language. Everything, included JScript.NET, is compiled. Don't worry, however, about your days of high productivity being over. If you use JScript.NET for the sort of things you are used to doing with JScript, for example creating server side code, the compilation is transparent and happens behind the scenes. On the other hand, if you want to write a full-blown application and compile it as an executable, or compile JScript.NET components to use in web pages, you can.

C++, Visual Basic.NET, JScript.NET, and Microsoft's new language, C# (pronounced C Sharp), are all supplied out of the box by Microsoft as CLR compliant languages. VBScript has been dropped and VBScript users are expected to migrate to Visual Basic.NET instead. In addition, third parties are making around 30 other languages available for the CLR, including Perl and COBOL! Believe it or not, there really is a Cobol.NET, although I don't think too many web developers will be using it. All languages are compiled to the intermediate language, which is then converted to machine code by the CLR. As all code, regardless of the language it was written in, is ultimately compiled to an intermediate language, there is effectively no difference between languages at run-time, so performance of all languages is largely the same.

The CLR is designed such that languages can communicate completely with each other without barriers. We can have a JScript.NET module calling a C++ module, or a Visual Basic.NET class, as if it were all written in the same language. You can also do cross language debugging. As a result, choosing your language in the .NET world has been described as being "largely a lifestyle choice" – although your project manager might disagree!

More About JScript.NET

Microsoft has introduced a radically updated version of JavaScript along with the .NET framework, JScript.NET. Before you start thinking that Microsoft has made JavaScript their own, think again. JScript.NET is the first mainstream implementation of ECMAScript Edition 4, the latest version of the language developed by the standards body that oversees JavaScript, ECMA. Several companies, including Netscape, sit on the committee, and Netscape are planning their own implementation of ECMAScript 4, which they are calling JavaScript 2.0. Netscape choosing after all these years to finally give a whole version number to JavaScript correctly suggests that ECMAScript 4 is a radical reworking of the language and adds many new features. They've also been careful to make sure that it's backwards compatible, and to the best of my knowledge they've achieved this 100%. More details of ECMAScript 4 were given in the previous chapter.

ECMAScript 4 introduces many, new features. Arguably, the two most significant features are the introduction of strong typing and classes. For those not familiar with these two concepts, strong typing means that when we declare a variable, we explicitly say what type it is – perhaps a string or an integer. This gives both performance and code manageability advantages. Classes allow object oriented programming using techniques similar to those enjoyed by C++, Java, and C# developers. Although we touch on JScript.NET in this chapter, most of the examples can be tested in current versions of JScript.

JScript.NET and Web Browsers

There's a good reason why not all of the code in this chapter has been written for JScript.NET. The reason is that JScript.NET does not work in web browsers, yet. As JScript.NET is completely built on top of the CLR, JScript.NET can't be supported until the CLR is supported in the browser, and at this point it isn't. This means we could do our web page scripting in any .NET language – scripting pages in Visual Basic or C# will be possible, or even in COBOL, if the client machine has this language installed! It should be easy enough to tell whether the user has the CLR installed. This is the user agent of Internet Explorer on the author's development machine:

Mozilla/4.0 (compatible; MSIE 6.0b; Windows NT 5.1; .NET CLR 1.0.2914)

When the time comes, it will be relatively easy to tell not only whether they have the CLR available, but also what version they have, allowing us to easily make programmatic decisions about whether to use the features provided by the CLR.

Visual Studio.NET

A critical component to the .NET framework is Visual Studio.NET. Many of you might have used Visual Studio 6, and especially Visual Interdev 6, which is a fairly popular integrated development environment (IDE) for creating ASP pages. Visual Studio.NET has changed a little. In keeping with the whole concept of a universal CLR, it now has an integrated IDE. So, there are no separate IDEs as in Visual Studio 6 – it's all one program. Note that we definitely don't need Visual Studio.NET to create .NET applications. We can create all our applications in Notepad if we wish; Visual Studio.NET simply adds a lot of features that will increase productivity. With time, some good third party IDEs should appear.

Visual InterDev offers some fairly neat features to web developers. First of all is HTML code completion. For users of Allaire's HomeSite, this is old news, but Visual Interdev 6 users may get excited about this:

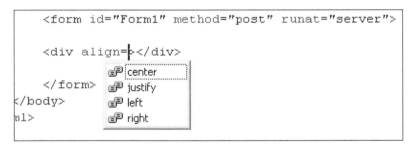

You can see that it has popped down a list of valid values for the `align` attribute. Microsoft calls this feature Intellisense, and while Visual Studio 6 has Intellisense for scripting, it doesn't do it for HTML. This is not only a time saver and a great memory jogger when we forget the name of an attribute, but it also ensures that we spell things correctly. There are few things more frustrating than debugging some code only to find the problem was due to a simple misspelling.

It also offers script completion. I personally find this a great way to explore the language. Few people can know or remember every part of the language, so this is a great memory jogger and a way to encourage exploration of the language:

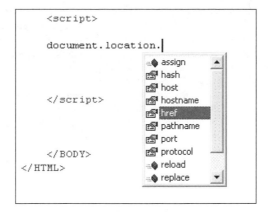

If you click inside any HTML element, the properties window (if you have it open) automatically shows something like this:

It shows the properties of the object complete with intelligent, object sensitive drop downs. Note that we don't *have* to use Visual Studio.NET to develop JScript.NET applications; as mentioned earlier, all we need is a text editor such as Notepad and the .NET framework installed. I'm sure you can see that from the examples above, there are productivity gains to be had from using it, so it's really up to you.

ASP.NET

This isn't an ASP book and this isn't an ASP chapter; however, while we are on the subject of .NET technologies, there are two key technologies that should be of extreme interest to client side JavaScript developers.

The first of these is server side processing of client side events. Traditionally, handling client side events has fallen well into the domain of the JavaScript developer. While it has always been possible to handle events on the server, it is often a lot of hassle and simply not worth it. For example, if we want to respond to a user clicking a button or checking a text box (perhaps to ask for further information based on their selection), we typically have two choices. One is to handle it with JavaScript in the way you are probably used to, which is pretty straightforward. We typically bind an event to the object, such as `<INPUT TYPE='button' onClick='myAction()'>` and handle the action in the `myAction()` function. The other way is to submit the page to the server using a form POST, GET, or a REDIRECT, which passes on the information via a query string. We can then write a new server page and present the result. ASP.NET introduces the concept of processing client events on the server. While it is basically the second scenario we have just discussed, it suddenly becomes much easier, and looks very similar to traditional client side form handling.

Take a look at this example, `clientserverevent.aspx`:

```
<HTML>
<SCRIPT LANGUAGE='JScript' RUNAT='server'>
   function CalcAge_Click(Src : Object, E : EventArgs) : void
   {
      var iAge : int = parseInt(Age.Text);
      if (iAge < 18)
      {
         Message.Text = iAge + " is quite young";
      }
      else
      {
         Message.Text = "It's all downhill from " + iAge;
      }
   }
</SCRIPT>
<BODY>
   <FORM ACTION='controls3.aspx' RUNAT='server' ID='Form1'>
      How old are you:
      <asp:textbox ID='Age' RUNAT='server' ></asp:textbox>
      <asp:button text='Enter' onclick='CalcAge_Click' RUNAT='server'
         ID='Button1'></asp:button>
      <BR>
      <asp:label ID='Message' RUNAT='server'></asp:label>
   </FORM>
</BODY>
</HTML>
```

When this page is loaded, ASP.NET converts all the server controls into their client side HTML equivalents. So:

```
<asp:button text='Enter' onClick='CalcAge_Click' RUNAT='server'
   ID='Button1'></asp:button>
```

Will become:

```
<INPUT TYPE='submit' NAME='Button1' VALUE='Enter' ID='Button1' />
```

After ASP.NET has parsed it. It's also worth noting that the .NET framework attempts to detect which version of JavaScript the client supports and generates code that is appropriate on that client.

At first glance, the code in the page seems like straightforward HTML and JavaScript. The thing to take note of is that the form is constructed from what are called ASP.NET server controls such as `asp:button`. Also note the extensive use of the `RUNAT='server'` attribute. This attribute means that ASP.NET interprets and manages these controls on the server, offering the rich functionality we are discussing here. One more last thing to watch for is the page after the results. Look at this:

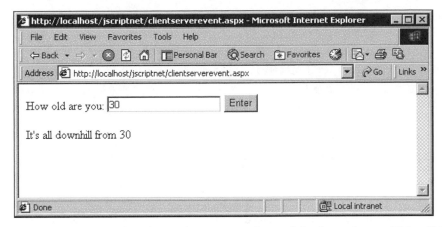

The key thing to note here is that, despite having just submitted the form, the age 30 is still in the text input box. As this form is being managed by ASP.NET on the server, as determined by the RUNAT='server' attribute, ASP.NET actually maintains the state of the form between pages. Once again, not rocket science, but it used to be difficult work to do this at all, now it's almost no work;

So what are the repercussions of this? It's only speculation, but it has suddenly become very trivial to manage traditional client side issues on the server. As server side code is almost always more reliable, easier to test, and has no cross browser issues, I would envisage organizations implementing ASP.NET will use a lot less client side JavaScript than they used to. There is a downside to this solution, as a page refresh is required, which increases server load and bandwidth usage, but given the potential saving in time and money on development, server side processing of client events can become very attractive. This is especially the case for low to medium traffic sites where the increased bandwidth and server load are less of an issue. This has a pretty big impact on you as a JavaScript programmer, especially if you don't have server side skills.

For those skeptics who have been burnt by software which produces very suspect or bloated HTML, I reassure you that the code outputted is extremely clean with no bloat and most of the attributes of the server controls map directly to their client side equivalents, leaving you in control.

The second major impact on JavaScript programmers that we are looking at is similar in some ways to the first. Form validation is truly the bread and butter work of JavaScript programmers, and ASP.NET takes the drudgery out of validation. We won't show any examples here as, while they are easy to use, they are a little more involved than the above example (although they follow the exact same principles of server controls as above) and we couldn't do them justice in less than 2 or 3 pages. The key point is we can add complex, highly customizable validation rules to our forms using just a few lines of server-side code. This is an amazing productivity boost, and should save many hours of programming.

A Beginner's Guide to Web Services

We have already spoken briefly above about distributed computing and Web Services. Web Services are such an important development, they need a more in depth explanation. Most of the rest of this chapter is about Web Services and how you can use them via JavaScript.

In essence, Web Services are a simple idea once some time has been spent understanding them. Web Services provide the ability for an application to execute a subroutine on another computer, regardless of location. This is similar to what CORBA, RPC, and DCOM were intending to do, but if you've been following that battle, you'll realize that they never quite lived up to the potential of the promises. If you need more explanation, let's think of this in terms of JavaScript.

Being a JavaScript programmer (or at least an aspiring one), you've written some JavaScript that calls a function elsewhere on the page that returns a result, which you use:

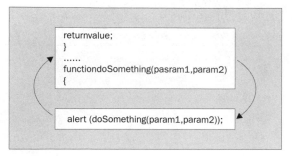

So, from one part of your script, you're calling another part in the same script. Likewise, most JavaScript programmers have called a function contained in a linked .js file. So, from your page you are calling a function in another document:

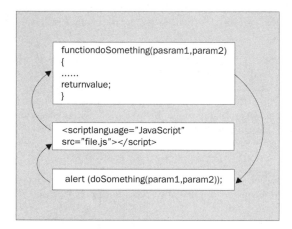

In some cases, you might not necessarily own that .js file. Perhaps you are using a .js file provided by a third party company. They can change the content of the .js file as often as they like, but as long as the function name stays the same, the arguments you pass to it are the same, and the type of result is the same; the inner workings are of little consequence to you.

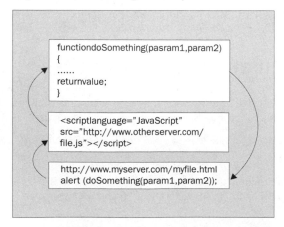

Think of Web Services as being able to call a function on a completely different server, which can be located anywhere on the Internet, or your intranet. The Web Services can be called from any application, by any language; it's not in any way restricted to JavaScript in a web browser. The code behind the Web Services can, and usually will, be unknown to you, but as long as the location is the same, the service is the same, the methods you call are the same, and the nature of the results is the same. The Web Service could be five lines of Visual Basic, 100 000 lines of C++ talking to a SQL Server database, or even COBOL talking to XML – it makes no difference to you, and in most cases you will not even know how it works, just as long as you get your result.

At its absolute core, this chapter is about helping you to understand what is happening in this diagram, and how to actually do it using client side JScript.

True Independence

One of the best things, maybe *the* best thing about Web Services is that they are completely language, platform, and environment agnostic. The lingua franca of Web Services is SOAP. Any system that can utilize SOAP is a candidate to be used in a web service. If you have a Web Service written in Visual Basic running on Windows .NET Server, and you want to access it from a Perl script running on Linux, there's no problem. As long as everyone is talking SOAP, everyone can continue talking to everyone else. Due to this, over the next year or two, you'll be seeing a lot of companies making Web Services available for all kinds of things. So, even though in this chapter we are calling Web Services from JavaScript, the language the Web Service is written in is irrelevant, and in real world cases, we'll usually never even know what language the Web Service is in.

Internet Explorer as a Web Service Consumer

So far, there has been much talk on .NET and Web Services; it's now time to see some action. As previously discussed, any application can consume a web service, but we are going to concentrate on using a web browser as a consumer. For an application to be able to consume a web service, it needs to meet two requirements: it needs to have access to an XML parser and can make HTTP responses and requests, which are the basic requirements for a SOAP client. Internet Explorer, from version 5 onwards, meets both these requirements and so makes an excellent candidate for a Web Service consumer. Internet Explorer 4 has only very limited XML support, and Netscape 4 has none. Netscape 6/Mozilla does have XML support, and Mozilla actually has a SOAP module. This makes it the ideal candidate, in theory at least, for being a web services consumer. Unfortunately, for whatever reason, the SOAP module is *not* included in standard builds of the Mozilla browser, the only way to get it in is to do your own build, or use a browser built on the Gecko engine that does have SOAP support. I'm not aware of any, and this chapter isn't going to get into writing a SOAP client from scratch. So, given the negligible number of Gecko-based browsers with SOAP support, we won't be looking at Netscape 6 as a Web Services consumer.

In reality, SOAP can be used with protocols other than HTTP. For example, a SOAP client that works over FTP is quite possible. However, .NET Web Services, and most other SOAP applications, are designed to work with SOAP over HTTP, and the W3C SOAP standard, while acknowledging the possibility of other protocols, assumes the use of HTTP, and so does this chapter.

SOAP is a whole subject in itself, and while it's not enormously complex, getting into the depths of SOAP is beyond the scope of this chapter. Fortunately, we don't need to learn SOAP. If you are programming web services in the .NET framework, especially if you are using Visual Studio.NET, all the hard work is handled for you. In fact, if you work in Visual Studio.NET, it's possible to go your whole life without ever seeing any SOAP (although you may need to close your eyes in a few places where it is displayed for information purposes). To support Internet Explorer, Microsoft has written a **WebService** behavior, which is essentially a SOAP client. Being a behavior file, it is easy to attach to and use in your own web pages. You can download the `WebService` behavior from: http://msdn.microsoft.com/downloads/samples/internet/behaviors/library/webservice/. You can also get more detailed instructions about it than we cover here, from: http://msdn.microsoft.com/workshop/author/webservice/overview.asp. We will go through it thoroughly enough for you to be able to confidently use it in real world applications.

If you are interested in doing more research into SOAP, the W3C's web site is a good place to start, their page for SOAP 1.2 can be found at http://www.w3.org/TR/soap12/. If you are interested in finding how to use Microsoft's SOAP toolkit to add SOAP functionality to existing Windows applications, have a look at http://msdn.microsoft.com/soap/.

Creating Our First Service

Let's do some coding. First of all, we'll create a simple web service that converts miles to kilometers. It takes one argument, miles, as an integer. Its return value is kilometers, as a double:

```
<%@ WebService Language='JScript' Class='Conversion' %>

import System;
import System.Web.Services;

public class Conversion extends WebService
{
    WebMethodAttribute public function con(miles : int) : double
    {
        return miles * 1.60943;
    }
}
```

Save this as a text file called `distance.asmx`. Web Services have the `.asmx` extension, but they are mostly like other ASP.NET pages (which have `.aspx` as their extension).

While this book is not about JavaScript on the server, let's have a quick look at a few interesting things in this code sample. You have probably noticed the `Language='JScript'` at the start of the document. That's the first surprise: this is JScript, Microsoft's version of JavaScript. That's probably a bit scary to some of you who don't recognize half the code in there. The difference is that this is JScript.NET, Microsoft's latest incarnation of JavaScript, or more specifically, ECMAScript v4. We spoke about JScript.NET at the beginning of the chapter.

The next two lines import two essential libraries in order for web services to work. Importing is a bit like a `#include` in C++. Next, we create a class. JScript.Net introduces the concept of classes. While JavaScript has been able to create objects for quite a while, it's always been a little convoluted, and even more misunderstood. ECMAScript 4 brings JavaScript into line with most other modern languages by supporting classes. With features like these in JScript.NET, combined with the CLR, there is a pretty compelling argument that you could do *all* your coding, be it for web pages or anything else, with JScript.NET.

The next interesting feature is where we see `miles : int`. This is an example of the ECMAScript 4 strong typing we spoke about earlier. Our language has grown up into a fine looking mature language. Strong typing is optional, but using it can give performance benefits, not to mention more solid programming practice. The .NET framework defines a collection of standard types, and JScript.NET supports all of the compulsory types. This is a real world demonstration of some of the principles that were discussed in the previous chapter on ECMAScript 4.

Testing the Web Service

With the wonders of .NET technology, if we put this file on a server, which has Microsoft's Internet Information Server (IIS) installed, as well as the .NET framework, and open it in a browser via HTTP, we get this:

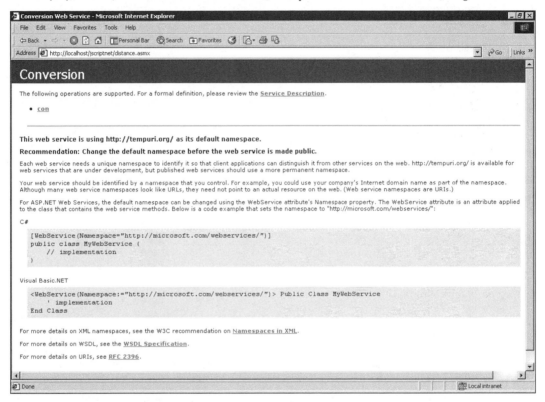

It's quite remarkable. With only eight lines of code, ASP.NET generates this page with various interesting pieces of information about the Web Service. Even more useful however is that it actually builds an implementation of the Web Service. If we click on the link to con, near the top of the screen, we get the screen shown overleaf:

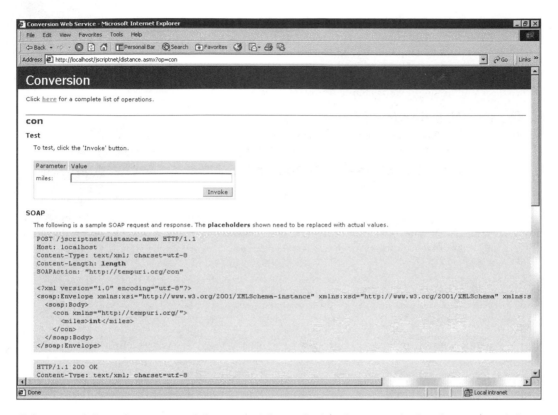

It has parsed the code, recognized the name of the method (only one method in this case), and the parameter it expects. Of course, when there are multiple methods and parameters, it generates the appropriate information for them. There's also a collection of samples of different HTTP requests valid to invoke the Web Service.

This interface makes testing a breeze. It becomes much easier to tell if a bug is occurring in the service or in the consumer, as there is a reference client built for us automatically. In fact, just to complete our walkthrough of building a simple service, let's have a look at what happens if we use this test interface to invoke our service. If we type in 10 and click Invoke, a new browser window is opened containing this XML document:

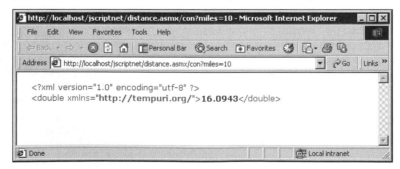

This contains the return value of our Web Service, so we now know that 10 miles is 16.0943 kilometers. Now, let's create a client that can consume this service.

Using the Web Service Behavior

As we mentioned before, the easiest way to consume a Web Service in Internet Explorer is to use the Web Service behavior. So let's do that. First thing we need to do is to include the behavior. This would normally be done by attaching a behavior to specific page elements via a style sheet, using code similar to this:

```
.myClass
{
   background-color: #F1F1F1;
   behavior: url(myBehavior.htc);
}
```

In our case, however we don't want the behavior associated with a specific element, but we do want an ID, which we can use to reference the behavior. To do that, we can just attach it using a gratuitous style, like this:

```
<DIV ID='service' STYLE='behavior: url(webservice.htc)'
   onResult='conResults()'></DIV>
```

As the DIV object has now inherited all the attributes (such as the methods and properties) of the behavior, we give it an id so we can conveniently reference those attributes later. Remember, if you are using a behavior hosted in another domain, there are security considerations and the user may get prompted with a security alert, so you want to host the behavior from the same domain as the page using the behavior in most cases. We also bind the onResult event which is created by the behavior to the conResults() function. We'll look at this shortly.

Next, let's create a simple input box so the user can enter the number of miles they want, and a button which can then click and do the serious stuff:

```
Enter the value in miles:
<INPUT TYPE='text' ID='miles'></INPUT>
<BR>
<INPUT TYPE='button' VALUE='Convert to Kilometers'
   onClick='doConversion()'></INPUT>
```

The useService() and callService() Methods

Once the user has entered the value and clicked on the button, we start the real work, which is buried away in a function called doConversion(). Let's look at it:

```
var iCallID = 0;

function doConversion()
{
   var iMiles = parseInt(document.all["miles"].value);
   service.useService("distance.asmx?WSDL", "Conversion");
   iCallID = service.Conversion.callService("con",iMiles);
}
```

There are a few things happening here. Let's go through them step by step. First of all, we get our miles from the text box and convert it from a string to an integer. In a live application, we would need error handling code here of course.

Next thing we do, is identify our web service and map it to a memorable name. Here's where things start to get interesting. Remember that service is the ID of our DIV, which we attached the behavior to. So here, we are calling the useService() method of that behavior. The useService() method allows us to specify the Web Service we will be using, and give it a more memorable name that we can use to reference that service. In this case, our service resides at distance.asmx, and the memorable name we have given to it is Conversion. It is recommended, although it is not essential, that the memorable name match the name of the class that contains the methods we are calling.

You have probably noticed the ?WSDL at the end of the URL. WSDL stands for Web Services Description Language. WSDL is an XML format that describes the Web Service. Getting into WSDL is beyond the scope of this chapter, and you don't need to know about it to use the code in this chapter. It mostly falls into the same category as SOAP, as it's handled behind the scenes in most cases. As WSDL has been submitted to the W3C, you can find out more about it on the W3C site at http://www.w3.org/TR/wsdl.

Moving on, let's have a look at the next method: the callService() method. The usage of this method is:

```
iCallID = id.FriendlyName.callService([CallbackHandler], "MethodName",
    Param1, Param2, ...);
```

We use the id of the object that has the behavior attached, a DIV called service in the case of this example. The FriendlyName is the memorable name that we gave the web service we are planning to use and have identified earlier. Next, we can define an optional call back handler. This allows us to define a function that will handle the results received from the Web Service. We will be looking at callback handlers in the second example. In this example, we are using the onResult event, and so we do not need to define a call back handler here. MethodName is where the name of the method that you will be using in the web service is defined. Although we have not looked at it, Web Services, like any class, can have multiple methods. You can then pass along whatever parameters the method is expecting. It's also worth mentioning at this point that callService() uses asynchronous calls by default. While it is possible to use synchronous calls, given the nature of distributed applications with their statelessness and often-high latency, asynchronous calls are usually a safer choice.

As the callService() method is asynchronous, a unique identifier is returned and stored in the variable iCallID in order to match the result with the method call.

So, let's look at our particular instance:

```
iCallID = service.Conversion.callService("con", iMiles);
```

service is the ID of our behavior (via the DIV), and Conversion is the memorable name of the specific Web Service we are using, distance.asmx in this case. We are calling the con() method of the Web Service, and passing iMiles as a parameter. iCallID contains our unique identifier so we can later identify this particular instance of callService() over any other that we may have.

The Result Object

Let's have a look at the conResults() function, which handles the result from the Web Service:

```
function conResults()
{
    var dKM = event.result.value;
    var sAnswer = "Your answer is " + dKM + " Kilometers";
    document.all.displayResults.innerHTML = sAnswer;
}
```

conResults is called by the onResult event, which we bound in the DIV object that hosts the behavior. When the onResult event calls conResults, it automatically passes an event object. The event object has a few interesting properties available, including one to expose the result object we are using above. The result object is interesting to us, and has a few useful properties. They are listed below:

Property	Description
error	A Boolean created after using the callService method, indicating the presence of an error
id	The unique id that corresponds to the value returned by the matching callService method call
raw	Exposes the raw SOAP data packet returned by the web service after invocation of the callService method
value	Returns the value or values of the method call

There is also a single object available, the errorDetail object, which has its own properties: code, raw, and string. We will look at this some more in the next example, and will go through an example of how to use it.

In the conResults() function, we get the value from the result object that has been passed to the function. We then use some simple DHTML to present the result to the user – the distance in kilometers, as returned by the Web Service.

Putting It All Together

If you have been following along as we built up this page bit by bit, you should have something like this:

```
<HTML>
<HEAD>
    <TITLE>Conversions R Us</TITLE>
    <SCRIPT LANGUAGE='JScript' TYPE='text/javascript'>
        var iCallID = 0;

        function doConversion()
        {
            var iMiles = parseInt(document.all["miles"].value);
            service.useService("distance.asmx?WSDL", "Conversion");
            iCallID = service.Conversion.callService("con",iMiles);
        }

        function conResults()
        {
            var dKM = event.result.value;
            var sAnswer = "Your answer is " + dKM + " Kilometers";
            document.all["displayResults"].innerHTML = sAnswer;
        }
    </SCRIPT>
</HEAD>
<BODY>
    <DIV ID='service' STYLE='behavior: url(webservice.htc)'
        onResult='conResults()'></DIV>
    Enter the value in miles: <INPUT TYPE='text' ID='miles'></INPUT>
    <BR>
    <INPUT TYPE='button' VALUE='Convert to Kilometers'
        onClick='doConversion()'></INPUT>
    <DIV ID='displayResults'></DIV>
</BODY>
</HTML>
```

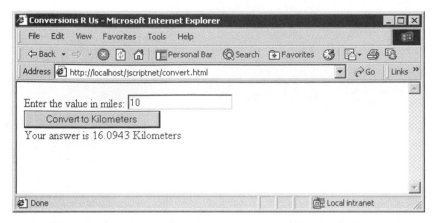

If we were using this technology in a real environment, we would probably also put in some code to make sure the Web Service behavior was not accessed until the behavior was fully loaded. The easiest way to do this is to simply wait until the onLoad event has been fired.

E-Commerce Web Service

You should understand the basics now, and have a big picture idea of how things hang together. Let's move onto a more complex example, which shows a way you might use a Web Service in reality. The example is still simplistic in places, and has little error checking or validation, except where directly relevant to the issues we are discussing, but it serves as a good demonstration.

This example is an online widget supplies shop, "Widgets R Us". They have their own web site from which we can order from their wide range of quality widgets. However, they also expose their ordering facility as a Web Service: their web site is just one consumer of this ordering service. One of the parameters the Web Service expects is a customer ID. Supplying this ID means we will be provided with a price list that is customized for our company. As our company is a big widget buyer, we get significantly better than retail prices. In the real world, we would want to use a password or some other form of authentication to implement the appropriate security.

So, our job is to write a page for our company intranet that allows people to purchase widgets using the data personalized for our company. If appropriate, we could also choose to implement business logic that is specific to our company, such as enforcing credit limits, and so on One of the great things about Web Services is since we are developing our own front end to someone else's back end, we can add as much logic as we want without getting involved in changing the core service.

Let's start by having a look at the Web Service offered. This is another area where Web Services are great. Remember when we wrote our simple Web Service earlier, and when we looked at it in a web browser, all these informational pages were automatically generated? We of course have the same thing available to us. This makes the Web Services, to an extent, self-documenting. In fact, when we get into some of the more advanced parts of creating and using Web Services, we'll discover some technologies that allow us to not only communicate with a Web Service depending on what it says it can do, but with other technologies (such as UDDI). UDDI allows us to actually programmatically find that Web Service in the first place. The point is that we know what is expected from us.

The Methods

Let's have a look at the methods exposed:

Method Name	Parameters required	Result
GetWidgets()	customerID as integer	XML node
OrderWidgets()	XML node	Boolean

GetWidgets() takes our customerID as a parameter, as we discussed earlier, allowing personalized responses. It returns an XML node containing a stock list. The XML looks like this:

```
<widgets>
    <widget>
        <name>Super widget</name>
        <sku>SW-4283</sku>
        <price>9.99</price>
    </widget>
    ...
</widgets>
```

OrderWidgets takes an XML node that contains our order and simply returns a Boolean to inform us whether the order was successful –a true return value indicates success. It could, as an alternative, take a few parameters containing arrays perhaps, but Widgets R Us chose XML. It's not the most sophisticated service in the world, but it serves our purpose. The return node is returned to the web service in this format:

```
<order>
    <item>
        <sku>WL-2601</sku>
        <quantity></quantity>
    </item>
    <item>
        <sku>EW-6738</sku>
        <quantity>2</quantity>
    </item>
    ...
</order>
```

The Process

Let's look at the flow of our code:

- ❑ Link to the Web Service behavior via a <DIV>, as in the last example

- ❑ Define a memorable name for the GetWidgets() method and call the service, passing along our customer ID

- ❑ The results are handled via a call back handler, getWidgetsResult(); more on call back handlers later

- ❑ After checking for errors, getWidgetsResult() loops through the XML and dynamically produces an order form

- ❑ When the customer has completed their order, placeOrder() is called, which converts the order into an XML node

- ❑ It then defines a memorable name for the Web Service, based on the OrderWidgets() method and called the service, passing the XML node along

- ❑ We check for errors and display a success or failure message to the user

All that gives us a regular HTML page that successfully consumes a web service, all in less than 100 lines, which is not a bad day's work.

Creating the Order Form

We start of by defining and then calling our Web Service much as we did in our previous example:

```
function getWidgets()
{
    var customerID = 16;
    service.useService("widgetorder.asmx?WSDL", "ListWidgets");
    iCallID = service.ListWidgets.callService(getWidgetsResult,
        "GetWidgets", customerID);
}
```

The difference between this code and our earlier simpler example is the use of a callback handler instead of the onResult event. As we are using a different method, using the onResult event becomes a little more complex. We could put some logic in the event handler which checks the value of iCallID and handles the event correctly, but that could just be a recipe for disaster, especially when we are using callService() in multiple places in our document. While there are certainly instances where using the onResult event in a page with multiple service calls is appropriate, I prefer the callback handler in most cases mainly for simplicity. The callback handler, getWidgetsResult() in this case, is a function that is called when the callService() method receives a response from the remote Web Service. It's designed to be called specifically for this method, rather than being a generic handler.

So, let's look at getWidgetsResult:

```
function getWidgetsResult(result)
{
    if (result.error && iCallID==result.id)
    {
        var sError = "There is an error\n";
        sError += "Code: " + result.errorDetail.code + "\n";
        sError += "String: " + result.errorDetail.string + "\n";
        sError += "Raw: " + result.errorDetail.raw  + "\n";
        alert(sError);
    }
    else if (iCallID==result.id)
    {
        var sOutput = "";
        var oXML = result.value;
        var oWidgets = oXML.getElementsByTagName("widget");

for (var count=0; count < oWidgets.length; count++)
        {
            sOutput += "<INPUT TYPE='TEXT' SIZE='2' ID='";
            sOutput += oWidgets[count].getElementsByTagName("sku")[0].text;
            sOutput += "'></INPUT> ";
            sOutput += oWidgets[count].getElementsByTagName("name")[0].text;
            sOutput += " : $";
            sOutput += oWidgets[count].getElementsByTagName("price")[0].text;
            sOutput += "<BR>";
        }
        document.all["displayResults"].innerHTML = sOutput;
    }
}
```

First thing we do is to check out the error property. If for some reason the Web Service failed (perhaps server problems at the web service end, or a problem with the parameters passed, or any other of a number of problems), we need to take appropriate action. We also need to check that iCallID==result.id so we can be sure that we are handling the correct instance of callService() – remember that iCallID is a global variable in this script as it is declared outside a script block, so we always know its latest value. We haven't covered the error property or the errorDetail object, so let's have a look at these in a bit more detail.

error and errorDetail

First, let's clarify that the `error` property and `errorDetail` object are both exposed by the `result` object. The `error` property is simply a Boolean that indicates whether an error occurred or not. Sometimes, just knowing an error occurred will be enough. Often however we'll want to know more about the nature of the error. For this, we look to the `errorDetail` object. The properties on the `errorDetail` object are shown in the table:

Property Name	Description
code	A machine-readable error code that corresponds to a specific invocation of the `callService()` method. It simply returns the string "Client" or "Server".
raw	This returns the raw SOAP packet returned by the Web Service.
string	A human-readable error message. This is what you probably want to display to your users (if anything).

Using the code displayed above, this is an example of the sort of error message returned. This particular case was the result of the Web Service not working (I deliberately introduced a simple syntax error in order to break the service):

Back to our code snippet above, We check if there is an error by looking at the `error` property of the `result` object. We also check to make sure the caller ID matches the ID we are working with, and then format and display the error message. If we were working on a large page with multiple Web Services making near-simultaneous calls, management of the caller ID would become extremely important – especially if we were using the `onResult` event rather than callback handlers as we are here.

If the call had no error, we then take a walk through the XML returned, use it to dynamically construct a form, and then output it into a placeholder `<DIV>` tag. That's basically all there is to creating our form.

To digress slightly, this is one of the great reasons to use behaviors. Despite the fact that we have just over 2000 lines of code in the behavior managing our SOAP requests, and so on we can remain completely oblivious to it, and just focus on the bare minimum amount of code needed to get the job done. The fact that almost all the code that we write in this example is presentation and very application specific logic is a good thing, and shows that we are doing a good job of code re-use.

Processing the Order Form

Once the user has decided on what widgets they want, they click on the **Place Order** button and things start to get interesting again. The order button calls the `placeOrder()` function and passes along the Form object:

```
<INPUT TYPE='BUTTON' VALUE='Place Order'
   onClick='placeOrder(this.form)'></INPUT>
```

941

As there is a reasonably large amount of data to send back to our Web Service, Widgets R Us have decided they want to receive the data as a XML node. The first part of `placeOrder()` displays the user a status message and creates a new XMLDOM object:

```
document.all.status.innerHTML="Placing your order...";
var oOrder = new ActiveXObject("Microsoft.XMLDOM");
var sXML = "<order>";

for (count=0; count<(oForm.length-1); count++)
{
    sXML += "<item>";
    sXML += "<sku>" + oForm[count].id + "</sku>";
    sXML += "<quantity>" + oForm[count].value + "</quantity>";
    sXML += "</item>";
}

sXML += "</order>";
oOrder.loadXML(sXML);
```

We have chosen a slightly unusual way to create this XML. The more conventional method would be to use the `createElement()` and `createNode()` methods. While that's certainly a completely valid way to do it, this method is easier, more intuitive, and more readable. We create the XML as a string, and then load it into the XML object via the `loadXML()` method. The downside to doing it this way is that the `loadXML()` method is not currently part of the W3C Recommendation and is only supported in Internet Explorer 5 and above. As this is also true for behaviors, this is clearly an IE5+ specific solution so it's not a problem here, but something worth bearing in mind if looking to expand this code beyond its intended purpose. However, the use of the `new ActiveXObject` declaration restricts us to MS Windows platforms as well. Different methods would need to be used to make it cross-platform.

So, once we have our completed XML, we need to pass this back to the Web Service:

```
service.useService("widgetorder.asmx?WSDL", "PlaceOrder");
iCallID = service.PlaceOrder.callService(getOrderResults,
    "OrderWidgets", oOrder);
```

In this code, we define a new callback handler, `getOrderResults()`. This very straightforward function simply checks for errors and displays the appropriate message to the user:

```
function getOrderResults(result)
{
    if (!(result.value) || (result.error && iCallID==result.id))
    {
        document.all.status.innerHTML =
            "Order failed. Please try again later.";
    }
    else
    {
        document.all.status.innerHTML = "Order was placed successfully.";
    }
}
```

The completed page from start to end should look like this, `buywidgets.html`:

```
<HTML>
<HEAD>
    <TITLE>Widget Orders</TITLE>
    <SCRIPT LANGUAGE='JScript' TYPE='text/javascript'>
        var iCallID = 0;
```

```
function getWidgets()
{
   var customerID = 16;
   service.useService("widgetorder.asmx?WSDL", "ListWidgets");
   iCallID = service.ListWidgets.callService(getWidgetsResult,
      "GetWidgets",customerID);
}

function getWidgetsResult(result)
{
   if (result.error && iCallID==result.id)
   {
      var sError = "There is an error\n";
      sError += "Code: " + result.errorDetail.code + "\n";
      sError += "String: " + result.errorDetail.string + "\n";
      sError += "Raw: " + result.errorDetail.raw  + "\n";
      alert(sError);
   }
   else if (iCallID==result.id)
   {
      var sOutput = "";
      var oXML = result.value;
      var oWidgets = oXML.getElementsByTagName("widget");

      for (var count=0; count<oWidgets.length; count++)
      {
         sOutput += "<INPUT TYPE='TEXT' SIZE='2' ID='";
         sOutput +=
            oWidgets[count].getElementsByTagName("sku")[0].text;
         sOutput += "'></INPUT> ";
         sOutput +=
            oWidgets[count].getElementsByTagName("name")[0].text;
         sOutput += " : $";
         sOutput +=
            oWidgets[count].getElementsByTagName("price")[0].text;
         sOutput += "<BR>";
      }
      document.all["displayResults"].innerHTML = sOutput;
   }
}

function placeOrder(oForm)
{
   document.all.status.innerHTML = "Placing your order...";
   var oOrder = new ActiveXObject("Microsoft.XMLDOM");
   var sXML = "<order>";

   for(count=0; count<(oForm.length-1); count++)
   {
      sXML += "<item>";
      sXML += "<sku>" + oForm[i].id + "</sku>";
      sXML += "<quantity>" + oForm[i].value + "</quantity>";
      sXML += "</item>";
   }

   sXML += "</order>";
   oOrder.loadXML(sXML);

   service.useService("widgetorder.asmx?WSDL", "PlaceOrder");
   iCallID = service.PlaceOrder.callService(getOrderResults,
      "OrderWidgets", oOrder);
}
```

```
     function getOrderResults(result)
     {
        if (!(result.value) || (result.error && iCallID==result.id))
        {
          document.all.status.innerHTML =
           "Order failed. Please try again later.";
        }
        else
        {
          document.all.status.innerHTML =
             "Order was placed successfully.";
        }
     }
   </SCRIPT>
</HEAD>
<BODY onLoad='getWidgets()'>
    <DIV ID='service' STYLE='behavior: url(webservice.htc)'></DIV>
    <H1>
      Place your widget orders
    </H1>
    <FORM ID='orderForm'>
      <DIV ID='displayResults'></DIV>
      <BR>
      <INPUT TYPE='button' VALUE='Place Order'
         onClick='placeOrder(this.form)'></INPUT>
    </FORM>
    <DIV ID='status'></DIV>
</BODY>
</HTML>
```

That's it!. We have successfully created a page that retrieves data from a Web Service, uses that data, and returns the data. That Web Service could be physically located anywhere in the world, and there is relatively little information you need to know about it in order to use it constructively. As always, the complete code for this Web Service, and all other code in this chapter, can be downloaded from http://www.wrox.com. We've also included a mock up widgetorder.asmx file in the downloadable code for this chapter. While it has no business logic in it, it will happily accept calls and return appropriate results that are needed to make this example work. Of course, it's written in JScript.NET. Those interested in writing their own JScript.NET Web Services might find this a good starting place, as it's a simple shell, which is just waiting for you to add appropriate business logic to it.

Taking it Further

One of the problems with this chapter is that to get the examples working, we need to be running a Microsoft web server, running Windows NT4.0 or later, with the .NET framework installed. Some people might not be willing or able to do this for whatever reason. If you are in this situation, but are still keen to experiment, there are a few possible solutions to this:

❑ Microsoft has made its www.microsoft.com search engine Web Service available for the public to use. We could modify the examples above to use this service, or look at some of their examples. These are at http://dotnet.microsoft.com/.

❑ At time of writing, when the .NET framework is in Beta 2, several web-hosting companies are offering experimental .NET hosting services. One particular service of interest is the free web host, Brinkster (http://www.brinkster.com/). They have been very committed to the Microsoft platform in general, and seem to be on the bleeding edge when it comes to .NET web hosting. They have a range of accounts which support .NET, including a basic free account.

❑ http://www.asp.net/ has an extensive collection of links to sites offering information about .NET in general, mostly focused on ASP.NET. Several of these have information on .NET web hosting services. There is also Wrox's own ASPToday.com, which has articles on .NET.

Summary

While the examples we have looked at in this chapter are relatively simple, if the idea of Web Services is new to you, then we strongly encourage you to think about them as you go about your day-to-day work. Some of the best applications of Web Services aren't necessarily immediately obvious, but think about how often you have trouble accessing a piece of information or a particular API on another system – even if it is on the same machine or the same local network. Or think how often you have to make modifications to the user interface of a particular application to meet a very specific need. These are all areas where Web Services may make your life easier, and as you think about it and let it sink into your head, you'll start to realize the multitude of ways this can change the way you work. Think about that enough, and you'll start to think about the whole concept of massively distributed applications, where many companies work together to create integrated systems where the platform *is* the Internet.

Now we have reached the end of the book. We have covered numerous aspects of JavaScript technology and what objects and methods are available to what browser. Apart from learning how to manipulate standard HTML and DHTML, we have learned good coding practices, how to define prototypes for methods on existing and new objects, how to manipulate cookies and images, and much more. We've ended with this introduction into the next phase of JavaScript as put forward by Microsoft. We hope that this book has served its purpose and has enabled you to solve any coding problems you might have had.

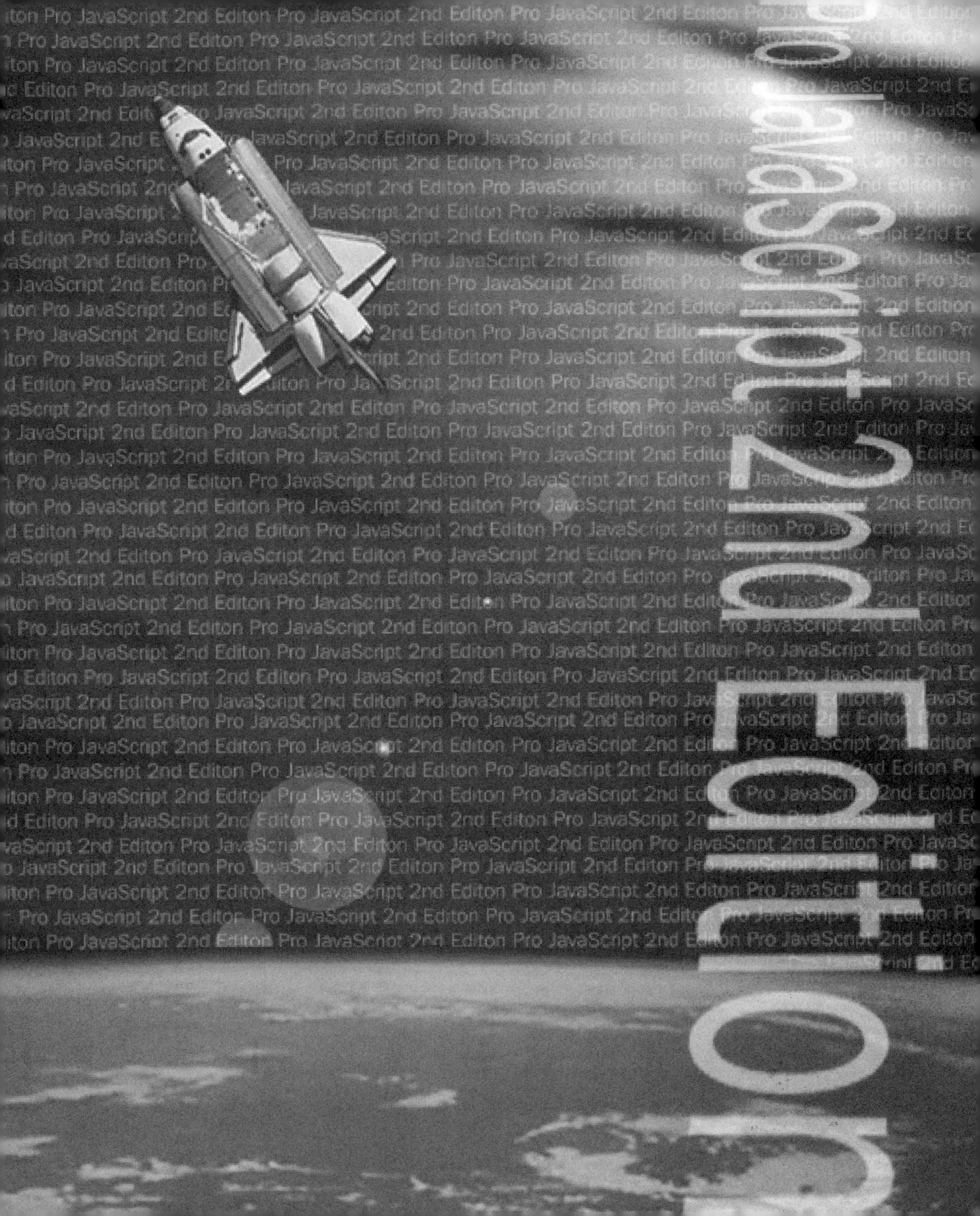
Pro JavaScript 2nd Edition

Functions, Statements, and Operators

This appendix contains the core JavaScript functions, operators, and constructs. In here, and later appendices, we shall also detail in which version of JavaScript each of these items first appeared.

Delimiters

The delimiters are considered punctuation, which has meaning according to the context in which it is used.

Operator	Example	Description
( )	myFunction()	Function arguments delimiter
.	myObject.property	Object property delimiter
[ ]	myArray[index]	Array element delimiter
{ }	{ ... code ... }	Code block delimiter
,	aFunction(a, b, c)	Argument delimiter
;	a = b+c; for(a=0;a<10;a++)	Statement delimiter
//	// This is a comment	Comment delimiter
/* ... */	/* This is a comment spanning several lines of source */	Comment delimiter, not terminated by newline characters.

Operators

Most of the operators have been available since the very earliest JavaScript version 1.0 interpreters. Items introduced at later versions are noted in the descriptive texts. Operators have an order of precedence. This is summarized in the precedence rules table.

Unary Operators

Unary operators have only a single operand and they are typically placed in front of (prefixing) the operand to which they apply.

Operator	Example	Description
+	+myValue	Convert the operand to a numeric value
-	-myValue	Convert the operand to a numeric value and negate it
~	~negator	Convert the operand to a 32-bit integer and perform a bitwise complement on it
!	!bitPattern	Convert the operand to a Boolean value and reverse its value

Prefix Operators

These are the prefix operators, which are also members of the unary operator classification. They operate on the value before it is used.

Operator	Example	Description
++	++index	Increment the operand by 1 before using it
--	--index	Decrement the operand by 1 before using it

Postfix Operators

The postfix operators are placed after an operand to modify its behavior. These are also members of the unary operator category since they only apply to a single operand. They operate on the value after it has been used.

Operator	Example	Description
++	index++	Increment the operand after using it
--	index--	Decrement the operand after using it

Arithmetic Operators

Additive operators include add, subtract, and simple increment or decrement operations. Multiplicative operators include multiply, divide, and remainder. The special compound assignment operators are also related to this set.

Operator	Example	Description
+	c = a + b	Add a to b and return the sum
-	c = a - b	Subtract b from a and return the difference

Operator	Example	Description
*	c = a * b	Multiply a by b and return the product
/	c = a / b	Divide a by b and return the quotient
%	c = a % b	Remainder after dividing a by b

Relational Operators

Relational operators are used to build logical expressions where the relative value of two operands is being compared. This is probably for use in defining a branching structure. Beware that some of these look confusingly similar to compound assignment operators, but they are not.

The strictly equal and not equal operators (=== and !==) were introduced at version 1.3 of JavaScript but have always been present in the JScript interpreter. JavaScript 1.4 suggests that comparing objects with == should be avoided and that a JSObject.equals() method should be used instead. Some strange behavior is noted with == and != operators in JavaScript 1.2. Neither used type conversion before returning a value. Several keyword operators were introduced at later versions and these are noted in the text.

Operator	Example	Description
==	a == b	Equal to. Returns Boolean true if a is equal to b.
===	a === b	Identically equal to. Returns Boolean true if a is identically equal to b in value and data type.
!=	a != b	Not equal to. Returns Boolean true if value of a is NOT equal to value of b.
!==	a !== b	Not identically equal to. Returns Boolean true if a is NOT identically equal to b either in value or type.
<	a < b	Less than. Returns Boolean true if value of a is less than that of b.
<=	a <= b	Less than or equal to. Returns Boolean true if value of a is less than or equal to that of b.
>	a > b	Greater than. Returns Boolean true if value of a is greater than that of b.
>=	a >= b	Greater than or equal to. Returns Boolean true if value of a is greater than or equal to that of b.

Logical Operators

Logical operators appear to be similar to relational operators but they perform a Boolean operation on the two operands. Logical operators are used to construct relational expressions that are more complex, as a rule. There are circumstances where logical operations fail if either of the operands does not evaluate to a sensible logical value. These type conversions are summarized in Appendix C.

Operator	Example	Description
&&	a && b	Logical AND. Returns Boolean true if both a and b have the Boolean value true.

Table continued on following page

Operator	Example	Description
`||`	`a || b`	Logical OR. Returns Boolean `true` if either of a or b has the Boolean value `true`.
`!`	`!a`	Logical NOT. Returns Boolean `true` only if a has the Boolean value `false`.
`in`	`property in object`	Returns Boolean `true` if named `property` is present as a member of `object`.
`instanceof`	`obj instanceof type`	Returns Boolean `true` if the referred to object, `obj`, is of the specified object `type`.

Assignment Operators

The assignment operators copy the expression to the right into the destination argument to the left. The compound versions of these behave as if the LValue and RValue are two operands either side of a binary operator, but the result is assigned to the left hand operand. It must therefore be an LValue even though the right hand operand may be an LValue or RValue. An example of an RValue is a constant while an LValue is a variable or property reference. This is illegal:

```
CONSTANT += INCREMENTOR;
```

You must recast that sort of expression as:

```
VARIABLE = CONSTANT + INCREMENTOR;
```

However, this would be valid:

```
VARIABLE += INCREMENTOR;
```

Operator	Example	Description
`=`	`a = b`	Simple assignment to an LValue
`+=`	`a += b` `a = a + b`	Add and assign to an LValue
`-=`	`a -= b` `a = a - b`	Subtract and assign to an LValue
`*=`	`a *= b` `a = a * b`	Multiply and assign to an LValue
`/=`	`a /= b` `a = a / b`	Divide and assign to an LValue
`%=`	`a %= b` `a = a % b`	Remainder and assign to an LValue

Object Operators

Object operators are generally also classed as unary operators since they tend to operate only on a single object.

Operator	Example	Description
new	new Object() new obj(params)	Invokes an object constructor, returning a new instance of the class. Initializing values may be passed in the brackets.
delete	delete object.property	Used to delete a property from an object, if it can be deleted.
in	for (myEnum in anObject)	Returns a list of properties of an object that can be enumerated. (See also logical operators.)
this	this this.property this.method()	A reference to self. Intended for use in functions that are attached as object methods.
export	export property export function	Provides a way for Netscape Navigator to export objects, properties, and methods for use by other scripts. Only works for signed scripts.
import	import obj.prop import obj.func	Provides a way for Netscape Navigator to import objects, properties, and methods that have been exported by other scripts.

String Operators

String operators perform operations on string operands. If necessary, the arguments will be converted to strings beforehand. However, these operators overload the arithmetic operators and so type conversion can be subtle and not what you expect. It is generally governed by the operand's content value and by the type of the left operand.

Operator	Example	Description
+	c = a + b	Concatenates a and b and returns a string containing both. This is invoked instead of numeric addition if the left operand is a string. The right operand is converted to a string if necessary.
+=	a += b	Concatenates b onto a. This is invoked instead of numeric addition if the left operand is a string. The right operand is converted to a string if necessary.

Miscellaneous Operators

Object operators are generally also classed as unary operators since they tend to operate only on a single object.

Operator	Example	Description
typeof	typeof myValue	Returns a string containing a textual description of the operand type.

Table continued on following page

Operator	Example	Description
void	void myExpr	Regardless of the result of evaluating the expression that is being operated on, this will always yield the undefined value.
?:	expr ? a : b	Conditional, ternary operator. If expr is true, the result of evaluating a is returned, otherwise b is evaluated and returned instead.
,	expr1, expr2	Comma operator. Where you would normally evaluate just one expression, you can evaluate several. However only the result of the last one will be returned. The results of the others will be discarded.

Bitwise Operators

These operators perform a bit-by-bit logical operation on the two operands. They should not be confused with the logical operators. These are most likely used for setting and clearing bits and making bit mask values. The special compound assignment operators are also related to this set. These operators have not been covered in this book, as they haven't been useful in any application within the previous pages.

Operator	Example	Description
&	c = a & b	Bitwise AND. Returns a bit pattern where bits in the result are set to 1 only if both corresponding bits in a and b are also 1.
|	c = a | b	Bitwise OR. Returns a bit pattern where bits in the result are set to 1 if either of the corresponding bits in a and b are 1.
^	c = a ^ b	Bitwise XOR – exclusive OR. Returns a bit pattern where bits in the result are set to 1 if either but not both of the corresponding bits in a and b are 1.
~	c = ~a	Bitwise complement – NOT. Returns a bit pattern where all the bits in a are switched from 1 to 0 and vice versa.
<<	c = a << b	Bitwise left shift. Returns a bit pattern equivalent to value a shifted left by b positions. The right side is filled with zero bits.
>>	c = a >> b	Bitwise signed right shift. Returns a bit pattern equivalent to value a shifted right by b positions. The left side is filled with zero bits.
>>>	c = a >>> b	Bitwise unsigned right shift. Returns a bit pattern equivalent to value a shifted right by b positions. The left side is filled with the sign bit.

Operator Precedence

Operators at the top of the list are evaluated first when the evaluation nesting level is identical:

Operator	Description	Associativity
()	Grouping operator	L-R
[]	Array index delimiter	L-R

Operator	Description	Associativity
.	Property accessor	L-R
++	Postfix increment	L-R
--	Postfix decrement	L-R
!	Logical NOT	R-L
~	Bitwise NOT	R-L
++	Prefix increment	R-L
--	Prefix decrement	R-L
-	Negation operand	L-R
delete	Delete a property from an object	R-L
new	Invokes an object constructor	R-L
typeof	Determines the type of a value	R-L
void	Always yields the undefined value.	R-L
*	Multiply	L-R
/	Divide	L-R
%	Remainder	L-R
+	Convert the operand to a numeric value	L-R
+	Add	L-R
-	Subtract	L-R
+	Concatenate string	L-R
<<	Bitwise shift left	L-R
>>	Bitwise shift right	L-R
>>>	Bitwise shift right (unsigned)	L-R
<	Compare less than	L-R
<=	Compare less than or equal to	L-R
>	Compare greater than	L-R
>=	Compare greater than or equal to	L-R

Table continued on following page

Operator	Description	Associativity
`in`	Property is in object	L-R
`instanceof`	Object is instance of another object	L-R
`==`	Compare equal to	L-R
`!=`	Compare NOT equal to	L-R
`===`	Compare identically equal to	L-R
`!==`	Compare identically NOT equal to	L-R
`&`	Bitwise AND	L-R
`^`	Bitwise XOR	L-R
`|`	Bitwise OR	L-R
`&&`	Logical AND	L-R
`||`	Logical OR	L-R
`?:`	Conditional execution	R-L
`=`	Assign	R-L
`*=`	Multiply and assign	R-L
`/=`	Divide and assign	R-L
`%=`	Remainder and assign	R-L
`+=`	Add and assign	R-L
`-=`	Subtract and assign	R-L
`<<=`	Bitwise shift left and assign	R-L
`>>=`	Bitwise shift right and assign	R-L
`>>>=`	Bitwise shift right (unsigned) and assign	R-L
`&=`	Bitwise AND and assign	R-L
`|=`	Bitwise inclusive OR and assign	R-L
`^=`	Bitwise XOR and assign	R-L
`,`	Argument delimiter	L-R
`;`	Empty statement	L-R
`{ }`	Delimit code block	L-R

Language Constructs

The JavaScript language has surprisingly few statement keywords. Some of these keywords behave like operators, and so they have been covered earlier in this appendix. A few relate to the flow of control and declaration of variables and functions.

Declarative Statements

Statement	Example	Description

var	`var myValue;`
	
	`var myNum = 5;`
	
	`var A, B, C = 6;`
		Declares and optionally initializes a variable. The scope of the variable depends on where it is declared. Declaration is implicit if this process is omitted.

function	`function`
	`example(a,b,c)`
	
	`{`
	
	   `... some code ...`
	
	`}`
	
	`function`
	`example(a,b,c)`
	
	`{`
	
	   `return (a * b *`
	`c);`
	
	`}`
		Creates a function object containing the source text.
		
		The `return` statement is optional but must be included if the function is to return a value.
		
		Functions referred to by object properties can be designed to work as methods and use the `this` keyword to refer to the owning object instance.

Branch Control

Statement	Example	Description

if ...	`if (someCondition)`
	`{`
	   `... some code ...`
	`}`
		If `someCondition` yields the Boolean `true` value when it is evaluated, then the block of code in braces is executed.

if ...
else ...
	`if (someCondition)`
	`{`
	   `... some code ...`
	`}`
	`else`
	`{`
	   `... some code ...`
	`}`
		If `someCondition` yields the Boolean `true` value when it is evaluated, then the block of code in braces is executed.
		
		If it is `false`, then the alternative block of code is used.

Table continued on following page

Statement	Example	Description

if ...
else if
...
	```if (someCondition)```
	
	```{```
	
	    ```... some code ...```
	
	```}```
	
	```else if```
	```(someCondition)```
	
	```{```
	
	    ```... some code ...```
	
	```}```
		If `someCondition` yields the Boolean `true` value when it is evaluated, then the block of code in braces is executed.
		
		If it is `false`, the second condition is tested to see if the next block should be executed.
		
		An optional `else` handler can be used in case neither condition yields `true`.

continue	```while (aCondition)```
	
	```{```
	
	    ```if (aCondition)```
	
	    ```{```
	
	        ```continue;```
	
	    ```}```
	
	    ```... some code ...```
	
	```}```
		The `continue` will halt the current loop and resume at the next iteration of a `for`, `while`, or `do` loop.

break	```while (someCondition)```
	
	```{```
	
	    ```if (aCondition)```
	
	    ```{```
	
	        ```break;```
	
	    ```}```
	
	    ```... some code ...```
	
	```}```
		The `break` will exit out of the innermost containing loop (`do`, `while`, or `for`) and can be used to prevent `switch` cases from dropping through into the next `case`.

return
...
	```function```
	```example(a,b,c)```
	
	```{```
	
	    ```return (a + b +```
	```c);```
	
	```}```
		Functions need not have a `return` statement but no value will be returned otherwise. More than one `return` can be used in a function if necessary so that several conditionally different `return` statements can be supported.

Statement	Example	Description

switch ...
case ...
default ...
	switch (someValue)
	{
	    case one:
	        ... *code* ...
	        break;
	
	    case two:
	        ... *code* ...
	        break;
	
	    default:
	        ... *code* ...
	        break;
	}
		The value is evaluated and the appropriately matching case is selected. The code at that case label is executed. Generally, there will be a break at the end of that code but there need not be and the code can drop through into the next case clause.

Loop Control

Statement	Example	Description

for ...	for (a=0; a<100; a++)
	{
	    ... *some code*
	    ...
	}
		The iterative loop is set up with the three control parameters. The first is the initialization instruction, the second is the test, which must be true for the loop to iterate, and the third is the incrementor, which is performed at the end of each cycle.

	for (;;)
	{
	    ... *some code*
	    ...
	}
		All three items are optional and the second loop example is one that will loop forever and requires some operation to force a break to be executed in the body of the loop.

for ... in ...	for (myEnum in anObject)
	{
	    ... *some code*
	    ...
	}
		If the properties of an object are marked as being enumerable, then this loop structure will visit each one, storing the name of the property in the myEnum variable. The loop is cycled once for each enumerable property.

Table continued on following page

Statement	Example	Description

`while ...`	`while (aCondition)`
	`{`
	   `... some code ...`
	`}`
		This loop will continue cycling while the condition returns `true`.
		
		This version tests the condition before executing a cycle.

`do ...`
`while ...`
	`do`
	`{`
	   `... some code ...`
	`}`
	`while(someCondition)`
		Although it looks structurally different, this loop is very similar to the `while` loop. The difference is that the condition is tested at the end of each cycle.
		
		It must continue to return `true` for the loop to cycle again.

Scope Control

Statement	Example	Description

`with`	`with (myObject)`
	`{`
	   `... some code ...`
	`}`
		The scope chain that the script is executing in will be extended by adding the cited object to the bottom of the chain. Until the code block is exited, all method and property calls will be passed first to that object before handing them up the scope chain.

Exception Handling

Neither of these exception-handling facilities was available prior to JavaScript 1.4 and JScript 5.0.

Statement	Example	Description
`throw ...`	`throw "exception";`	This statement provides a means to manually `throw` an exception.

`try...`
`catch...`
`finally...`
	`try`
	`{`
	   `... some code ...`
	`}`
	`catch`
	`{`
	   `...exception handling...`
	`}`
	`finally`
	`{`
	   `...clean up code...`
	`}`
		The code in the first block is executed and if an exception of any kind is thrown, control will be passed to the `catch` block.
		
		At the end, regardless of which code block was executed, the `finally` block will be executed.

Built-in JavaScript Functions

JavaScript provides some useful built-in utility functions. They are implemented as methods belonging to the global object. The language versions they first appeared in are indicated in the table below:

Constant	Example	Description	JavaScript	JScript
`escape(str)` `escape(str, flag)`	`v = escape(":");`	Converts dangerous characters into safe character codes preceded by a percent sign so that values can be transmitted inside a URL. The optional flag indicates whether to encode plus signs or not.	1.0	1.0
`unescape(str)`	`s = unescape ("%28");`	The complement of the `escape()` function.	1.0	1.0

`eval(src)`	`s = "v = 1 + 2";`
	 `eval(s);`
	 `alert(v);`
		Executes the code passed in the string argument, and returns the result.	1.0	1.0

`isFinite(num)`	`if (!isFinite(x))`
	 `   return`
	 `Infinity;`
		Tests to see if the number is a finite value.	1.3	3.0

`isNaN(num)`	`if (isNaN(x))` `alert("Error");`	Tests to see if the number is an error value.	1.1	1.0
`Number(value)`	`n = Number ("100");`	Converts the argument to a valid number using the built-in type conversion rules.	1.2	2.0
`String(value)`	`s = String(n)`	Converts the argument to a valid string using the built-in type conversion rules.	1.2	2.0
`Boolean(value)`	`b = Boolean ("true")`	Converts the argument to a valid Boolean value using the built-in type conversion rules.	1.2	2.0
`parseFloat(str)`	`f = parseFloat ("2.76");`	Parses a string into a floating-point numeric value.	1.0	1.0
`parseInt (str, radix)`	`I = parseInt ("FF", 16);`	Parses a string into an integer format, possibly carrying out base conversion at the same time. This is the complement of the `NumbertoString()` method. The radix is optional.	1.0	1.0

Reserved Words

The following are reserved words in JavaScript. Avoid using them for variable, function, or prototype declarations:

abstract	else	instanceof	switch
boolean	enum	int	synchronized
break	export	interface	this
byte	extends	long	throw
case	false	native	throws
catch	final	new	transient
char	finally	null	true
class	float	package	try
const	for	private	typeof
continue	function	protected	var
debugger	goto	public	void
default	if	return	volatile
delete	implements	short	while
do	import	static	with
double	in	super	

Pro JavaScript 2nd Edition

B

Objects, Methods, and Properties

The standard core JavaScript language provides some basic objects for manipulating common data types. Some implementations provide other additional objects as part of their core functionality but the following should be available in all implementations. The implementation-specific objects are summarized later.

The interpreter works hard to hide the fact that it changes primitives into objects and back again as it needs to. We can assign a literal value to a variable and it will remain a primitive until we start to operate on it as an object, at which time it is magically changed without us needing to do anything. We can manually force this conversion as well if we wish.

The JavaScript and JScript versions each of these first appeared in are indicated in the following tables. At the end of this appendix is also a list of built-in functions in JavaScript with details of the versions of the language in which they first appeared. Below are two tables relating JavaScript and JScript versions to the Netscape or Internet Explorer version. In the JScript table, as JScript is a component available in any browser and for other MS applications, versions 2.0 and 4.0 only appeared in IIS 3.0 and Visual Studio 6.0 respectively.

JavaScript Version	Netscape Browser Version
1.0	2.0
1.1	3.0
1.2	4.0 - 4.05
1.3	4.06-4.5
1.4	6.x

JScript Version	Internet Explorer Version
1.0	3.0
2.0	N/A
3.0	4.0
4.0	N/A
5.0	5.0
5.5	5.5

Object

This is the generic object. The basic Object class was available from JavaScript 1.0 and JScript 3.0. The properties and methods of the master Object are generally inherited by all other classes of objects in the implementation. However, many properties and methods will be overridden at the sub-class level. Unless indicated otherwise, assume that all these properties and methods are available to all other objects in JavaScript.

Construction

```
// Create a new empty object
myObject = new Object();
```

Properties

Name	Description	JavaScript	JScript
constructor	A reference to an object that can be used with the new operator to create new instances of this kind of object.	1.1	3.0
prototype	A reference to the prototype for this class of object. Adding new properties and methods to this object extends the behavior of all instances of this object type.	1.3	3.0

Methods

Syntax	Description	JavaScript	JScript
hasOwnProperty(aName)	Checks for the existence of a named property belonging to the receiving instance. Returns a Boolean result of true if the property is a member of the object instance.	1.5	5.5
isPrototypeOf(anObject)	Returns a Boolean true value if the receiver is a direct ancestor of the object in the argument.	1.5	5.5
propertyIsEnumerable(aProp)	Returns a Boolean true value if the named property is enumerable and therefore may be visited in a for (...in...) loop.	1.5	5.5
toLocaleString()	Returns a string primitive version of the object considering the present locale during the translation.	1.5	5.5
toSource()	Returns a string describing the object contents.	1.3	3.0
toString()	Returns a string representation of the object. Not necessarily the same as the results of toSource().	1.0	3.0

Syntax	Description	JavaScript	JScript
unwatch()	Disconnects the Netscape property watcher. Not supported in JScript.	1.2	X
valueOf()	The primitive numeric value of an object. Results are implementation and object dependent.	1.1	3.0
watch()	A Netscape-specific facility for watching for changes to object properties. Not supported in JScript.	1.2	X

Array

This is a collection of objects in a sequence. Individual elements can be accessed either by index position or by using an associative name. This is only available as an object as it cannot be represented as a primitive value. This object was introduced in JavaScript 1.1 and JScript 2.0.

Construction

```
// Create an empty array
myEmptyArray = new Array();

// Create an empty array of specified size
myTenArray   = new Array(10);

// Create a three-element array and initialize the values
myFullArray  = new Array("a", "b", "c");

// Create a simple array literal
var myArray = [100, 1.34, "String text", true, { prop:100 }];

// Create a nested multi-dimensional array
var matarray = [[1,0], [0,1]];

// JavaScript expression in arrays
var exprarray = [Math.random()*10, Math.random()*100];

// Sparse array
var sparse = [100, , , , , 1000];
```

Properties

Name	Description	JavaScript	JScript
index	When the String.match() method is used to make only a single match (the g attribute was not used) then the array returned will have this additional index property.	1.2	5.5

Table continued on following page

Name	Description	JavaScript	JScript
input	This `input` property is also present on the array returned by a `String.match()` when a single match is requested.	1.2	5.5
length	The number of items in the array.	1.1	2.0

Methods

Syntax	Description	JavaScript	JScript
concat(items...)	The result of this method is a new array consisting of the original array, plus the concatenation.	1.2	3.0
join() join(aSeparator)	Concatenate array elements to make a string. The optional separator string is used between the items in the output.	1.1	2.0
pop()	Pop items off the end of an array like a FILO stack.	1.2	5.5
push(items...)	Pushes items onto the end of an array like a FILO stack.	1.2	5.5
reverse()	Reverse the order of array elements.	1.1	2.0
shift()	Pull off a stack whose access is FILO from the start rather than the end.	1.2	5.5
slice(start) slice(start, end)	Slice out a sub-array from the receiving array. The end value is optional and a negative start value counts back from the last item in the array.	1.2	3.0
sort(aComparator)	Sort the array using an optional comparison function called to determine the sequencing of a pair of items in the array.	1.1	2.0
splice(start, aCount, items...)	Insert the new items at the start, replacing count items.	1.2	5.5

Syntax	Description	JavaScript	JScript
toLocaleString()	Returns a string primitive version of the array, considering the present locale during the translation.	1.5	5.5
toSource()	Output an array formatted as an Array literal contained in a string.	1.3	3.0
toString()	Return a string primitive version of an Array object.	1.1	2.0
unshift(items...)	Push onto a stack whose access is FILO from the start rather than the end.	1.2	5.5
valueOf()	Returns the contents of the array converted to a native primitive value.	1.1	2.0

Boolean

This is a logical value container. The value can be either `true` or `false`. Boolean data is available as either an object or a primitive value. This object was introduced in JavaScript 1.1 and JScript 2.0.

Construction

```
// Create a new empty Boolean object
myBoolean = new Boolean();

// Create and initialize a Boolean object
myTrue   = new Boolean(true);

// Create and initialize a Boolean object with type conversion
myFalse  = new Boolean("false");

// Create a Boolean primitive that can be type converted later
myBoolean = true;
```

Properties

These are the same as the `Object` properties above.

Methods

Syntax	Description	JavaScript	JScript
toSource()	Returns a string describing the object contents as a literal	1.3	X
toString()	Returns the Boolean value as a string	1.1	2.0
valueOf()	Returns the primitive value of the object	1.1	2.0

Date

This object is a date value container. Dates need to be instantiated using the `Date()` constructor to be used. The value can be converted to a time in milliseconds from the base time, but is otherwise not available as a primitive value.

Construction

```
// Make a Date object containing the current time.
myDate = new Date();

// Make a Date object and initialize with a millisecond time
myDate = new Date(940000000000);

// Make a Date object and init by parsing a string
myDate = new Date("Jan 1, 2001");

// Make a Date object and initialize some of its values
myDate = new Date(2001, 07, 24);

// Make a Date object and initialize all of its values
myDate = new Date(Y, M, D, HH, MM, SS, mS)
```

Properties

Name	Description	JavaScript	JScript
length	The `length` property always returns the value 7 for a `Date` object. It represents the maximum number of arguments accepted.	1.2	3.0

Methods

Syntax	Description	JavaScript	JScript
getDate()	Return the day number within a month for a date/time.	1.0	1.0
getDay()	Return the weekday number for a date.	1.0	1.0
getFullYear()	Return the full year for a date.	1.3	3.0
getHours()	Return the hours component of a time.	1.0	1.0
getMilliseconds()	Return the milliseconds component of a time.	1.3	3.0
getMinutes()	Return the minutes component of a time.	1.0	1.0
getMonth()	Return the month component of a date.	1.0	1.0
getSeconds()	Return the seconds component of a time.	1.0	1.0

Syntax	Description	JavaScript	JScript
getTime()	Return the time component of a date/time. The value is in milliseconds since base time.	1.0	1.0
getTimezoneOffset()	Return the time zone offset from UTC measured in minutes.	1.0	1.0
getUTCDate()	Return the day number within a month for a UTC date/time.	1.3	3.0
getUTCDay()	Return the weekday number for a UTC date.	1.3	3.0
getUTCFullYear()	Return the full year for a UTC date.	1.3	3.0
getUTCHours()	Return the hours component of a UTC time.	1.3	3.0
getUTCMilliseconds()	Return the milliseconds component of a UTC time.	1.3	3.0
getUTCMinutes()	Return the minutes component of a UTC time.	1.3	3.0
getUTCMonth()	Return the month component of a UTC date.	1.3	3.0
getUTCSeconds()	Return the seconds component of a UTC time.	1.3	3.0
getVarDate()	A special date format for use with ActiveX objects. Only supported by JScript on Windows platforms.	X	3.0
getYear()	Return a 2-digit non-Y2K-compliant year for a date/time.	1.0	1.0
parse(aString)	A class based factory method for converting strings to Date objects.	1.0	1.0
setDate(aDay)	Set the day number within a month of a date/time object.	1.0	1.0
setFullYear(Y, M, D)	Set the full year value of a date/time object. Month and day values are optional.	1.3	3.0
setHours(H, M, S, mS)	Set the hours of a date/time object. All but the hours argument are optional.	1.0	1.0
setMilliseconds(mS)	Set the milliseconds component of a time.	1.3	3.0

Table continued on following page

Syntax	Description	JavaScript	JScript
setMinutes(M, S, mS)	Set the minutes component of a time. All but the minutes argument are optional.	1.0	1.0
setMonth(month, day)	Set the month number of a date/time object. The day argument is optional.	1.0	1.0
setSeconds(S, mS)	Set the seconds component of a time. The milliseconds value is optional.	1.0	1.0
setTime(aTime)	Set the time value based in milliseconds since the base time.	1.0	1.0
setUTCDate(aDay)	Set the day number within a month of a UTC date/time object.	1.3	3.0
setUTCFullYear(Y, M, D)	Set the full year value of a UTC date/time object. Month and day values are optional.	1.3	3.0
setUTCHours(H, M, S, mS)	Set the hours of a UTC date/time object. All but the hours argument are optional.	1.3	3.0
setUTCMilliseconds(mS)	Set the milliseconds component of a UTC time.	1.3	3.0
setUTCMinutes(M, S, mS)	Set the minutes component of a UTC time. All but the minutes argument are optional.	1.3	3.0
setUTCMonth(month, day)	Set the month number of a UTC date/time object. The day argument is optional.	1.3	3.0
setUTCSeconds(S, mS)	Set the seconds component of a UTC time. The milliseconds value is optional.	1.3	3.0
setYear(year)	Set a non-Y2K-compliant year number of a date/time object.	1.0	1.0
toDateString()	The value of the Date object is presented just as a date.	1.5	5.5
toGMTString()	Convert a Date object to a string containing a GMT time.	1.0	1.0
toLocaleDateString()	The value of the Date object is presented just as a date considering the present locale.	1.5	5.5
toLocaleString()	Convert a Date object to a string with the locale-specific time.	1.0	1.0

Syntax	Description	JavaScript	JScript
toLocaleTimeString()	The time component of the Date object is presented just as a time, considering the present locale.	1.5	5.5
toSource()	Output a date formatted as a Date literal contained in a String.	1.3	3.0
toString()	Return a string primitive version of a Date object.	1.1	1.0
toTimeString()	The time component of the Date object is presented just as a time.	1.5	5.5
toUTCString()	Convert a Date object to a string with UTC time.	1.3	3.0
UTC(Y, M, D, HH, MM, SS, mS)	A class-based factory method for converting numeric values to Date objects.	1.0	1.0
valueOf()	Returns a number that is the date and time value for the receiving Date object.	1.1	2.0

Error

Error objects are used as part of the exception handling of the JavaScript environment. They are of most use during a try...catch... structure, where we can check the various properties of the Error object to find out about the exception that has just occurred.

Construction

Under normal circumstances, the implementation will manufacture these objects as needed. A reference to the object is passed as the first argument to a catch() block in a try...catch... structure. We can construct new instances if we need them.

```
// No parameters specified; object needs to initialized later
myError = new Error()

// Only the error number is specified
myError = new Error(aNumber)

// An error number and a text string are specified
myError = new Error(aNumber, descriptionString);

// Define using constants
myError = new Error(1000, "My own error code");
```

Properties

Name	Description	JavaScript	JScript
description	A property that corresponds to the description argument in the constructor function.	X	5.0
message	A property that corresponds to the description argument in the constructor function. The message and description properties are the same thing.	1.5	5.5
name	The name of an error object can be accessed with this property. It will likely be one of the following unless we assign our own name value to this property: EvalError, RangeError, ReferenceError, SyntaxError, TypeError, URIError	1.5	5.5
number	A property that corresponds to the number argument in the constructor function.	1.5	5.0
code	This is specified in DOM as a property that carries the DOM exception code values. These exception codes are listed in another table below.	X	X

DOM Exception Codes

Below are the exception code values contained within the code property above:

Value	Exception	DOM Level
0	UNSPECIFIED_EVENT_TYPE_ERR	2
1	INDEX_SIZE_ERR	1
2	DOMSTRING_SIZE_ERR	1
3	HIERARCHY_REQUEST_ERR	1
4	WRONG_DOCUMENT_ERR	1
5	INVALID_CHARACTER_ERR	1
6	NO_DATA_ALLOWED_ERR	1
7	NO_MODIFICATION_ALLOWED_ERR	1
8	NOT_FOUND_ERR	1
9	NOT_SUPPORTED_ERR	1
10	INUSE_ATTRIBUTE_ERR	1
11	INVALID_STATE_ERR	2

Value	Exception	DOM Level
12	SYNTAX_ERR	2
13	INVALID_MODIFICATION_ ERR	2
14	NAMESPACE_ERR	2
15	INVALID_ACCESS_ERR	2

Methods

Method	Description	JavaScript	JScript
toString()	The return value of this method is a string-formatted representation of the Error object.	1.5	5.0

Function

This object is a function code container. This is only available as an object. When a reference to a function is stored in an object property, it becomes a method either of that instance or of the class, if it is associated with the prototype.

Construction

```
// Declare a function object with a source literal
function myFunction(anArg)
{
    ... Some code ...
}

// Create a new empty Function
myFunc = new Function();

// Create a new empty function with some interface specification
myFunc = new Function(args...);
```

Properties

Name	Description	JavaScript	JScript
arguments	A reference to an Arguments object containing the passed in argument values.	1.1	2.0
arguments.callee	A reference to the body of the owning function.	1.2	5.5
arguments.caller	A reference to the function that called this function. See the Function.caller property.	1.2	2.0
arguments.length	The actual number of arguments passed to the function when it was called.	1.1	2.0

Table continued on following page

Name	Description	JavaScript	JScript
arity	The typical or maximum number of arguments expected by a function call. Use with caution.	1.2	3.0
caller	A reference to the caller of the function.	2.0	1.0
length	The number of arguments expected by a function call.	1.1	1.0

Methods

Name	Description	JavaScript	JScript
apply(target) apply (target, args)	If we want to force a particular function implementation to be used on a target object, we can locate the one we want and pass it an object on which to operate. The optional arguments are passed as an array.	1.3	5.5
call(target) call (target, args)	This is similar to the apply() method, which passed the arguments as an array. This passes them as a comma, separated list in a string.	1.3	5.5
toSource()	Returns a string primitive version of the function source text.	1.3	3.0
toString()	The result of calling this method is to obtain the source text of the function definition unless it is a host-implemented function.	1.1	2.0
valueOf()	Same as calling toString(). (Usually.)	1.1	2.0

Math

The Math object is provided as a container for some utility functions. Although these are implemented as methods, they don't operate on the Math object. Likewise, the properties belonging to the object are intended to be symbolic names for constant values and should not be modified. There is a constructor property in some implementations but this is not to facilitate instantiation of new Math objects. It does provide a way to access the prototype so that the Math object can be extended.

Construction

```
// Simple mathematical functions - the following calculates a tangent
var tangent=Math.tan(number)
```

Properties

These static constants often occur in mathematics:

Constant	Description	Approx Value	JavaScript	JScript
E	The numeric value for Euler's constant, the base of natural logarithms	2.718	1.0	1.0
LN10	The natural logarithm of 10	2.302	1.0	1.0
LN2	The natural logarithm of 2	0.693	1.0	1.0
LOG10E	The base 10 logarithm of E	0.434	1.0	1.0
LOG2E	The base 2 logarithm of E	1.442	1.0	1.0
PI	The value of Pi, the ratio of the circumference of a circle to its diameter	3.142	1.0	1.0
SQRT1_2	The square root of 1/2	0.707	1.0	1.0
SQRT2	The square root of 2	1.414	1.0	1.0

Methods

These are all the utility functions that contained within the `Math` object that require arguments.

Function	Description and Return Value	JavaScript	JScript
abs(num)	The absolute value of a positive or negative number: num	1.0	1.0
acos(num)	The inverse cosine of num	1.0	1.0
asin(num)	The inverse sine of num	1.0	1.0
atan(num)	The inverse tangent of num	1.0	1.0
atan2(num1, num2)	The inverse tangent of the slope of the two arguments, num1, and num2	1.0	1.0
ceil(num)	The value of num rounded up to the next integer value	1.0	1.0
cos(num)	The cosine of num	1.0	1.0
exp(num)	This function returns the exponential function of num (e raised to the power of the argument, where e is the base of the natural logarithms)	1.0	1.0
floor(num)	The value of num rounded down to the next integer	1.0	1.0
log(num)	The natural logarithm of num	1.0	1.0

Table continued on following page

Function	Description and Return Value	JavaScript	JScript
`max(num1, num2, ...)`	The maximum of the two or more input arguments is returned	1.0	1.0
`min(num1, num2, ...)`	The minimum of the two or more input arguments is returned	1.0	1.0
`pow(val, power)`	The result of raising a value, `val`, to the power of `power`	1.0	1.0
`random()`	Generate a pseudo-random value	1.0	1.0
`round(num)`	Rounds to the nearest integer value to `num`	1.0	1.0
`sin(num)`	The sine of the passed in value, `num`	1.0	1.0
`sqrt(num)`	The square root of `num`	1.0	1.0
`tan(num)`	The tangent of `num`	1.0	1.0

Number

This contains a numeric value. This can be expressed as a primitive or an object. This first appeared in JavaScript 1.1 and JScript 2.0.

Construction

```
// Create an empty Number object
myNumber = new Number();

// Create an initialize a Number object
_myValue  = new Number(100);

// Create a Number primitive that can be type converted later
myNumber = 1000;
```

Properties

Name	Description	JavaScript	JScript
`MAX_VALUE`	The largest number value that can be represented.	1.1	2.0
`MIN_VALUE`	The smallest number value that can be represented.	1.1	2.0
`NaN`	A value that represents an error when a numeric value cannot be realized.	1.1	2.0
`NEGATIVE_INFINITY`	The negative infinity value.	1.1	2.0
`POSITIVE_INFINITY`	The positive infinity value.	1.1	2.0

Methods

Syntax	Description	JavaScript	JScript
toExponential (aDigits)	Returns the number in an exponential format representation with the specified number of digits after the decimal point.	1.5	5.5
toFixed(aDigits)	Returns the number in a fixed format representation with the specified number of digits after the decimal point	1.5	5.5
toLocaleString()	Returns a string primitive version of the object, considering the present locale during the translation.	1.5	5.5
toPrecision (aDigits)	Converts a number to a string automatically selecting fixed or exponential notation. The argument value indicates how many digits after the decimal point.	1.5	5.5
toSource()	Returns the object value formatted as a Number literal contained in a String.	1.3	3.0
toString(aRadix)	Returns the numeric value as a string converted according to the specified radix. This is useful for converting values to hex and other number bases. Refer to parseInt() for a complementary function.	1.1	2.0
valueOf()	Returns the numeric value of the object as a Number primitive.	1.1	2.0

RegExp

This object is a container for regular expressions. The RegExp object provides some persistent storage for the expression so that the JavaScript can operate on it once the match has been made.

Construction

```
// Create a new specific RegExp object
myRegExp = new RegExp("Sm[iy]th", "g");

// Create a RegExp from a literal
myRegExp = /Sm[iy]th/g;
```

Properties

Name	Description	JavaScript	JScript
$1...$9	Up to 9 matches can be placed in parenthesis and recalled later.	1.2	3.0
global	Indicates whether the global flag (g) was used in the regular expression.	1.2	3.0

Table continued on following page

Name	Description	JavaScript	JScript
ignoreCase	Indicates whether the ignore case flag (i) was used in the regular expression.	1.2	5.5
index	The character position of the first match in the target string. Only supported by JScript.	X	3.0
input	The target string against which the regular expression is being matched. Can also be accessed as the $_ property	1.2	3.0
lastIndex	The starting position in the target string for the next match attempt.	1.2	3.0
lastMatch	The most recent characters to have been matched. Can also be accessed associatively as the RegExp["$&"] entry.	1.2	5.5
lastParen	If parentheses are specified in the regular expression and if any suitable matches occurred, this will hold the most recent one. Can also be accessed associatively as the RegExp["$+"] entry.	1.2	5.5
leftContext	The sub-string to the left of the most recent match. Can also be accessed associatively as the RegExp["$`"] entry.	1.2	5.5
multiline	Indicates whether multiple line searching is to be applied. Can also be accessed associatively as the RegExp["$*"] entry.	1.2	5.5
rightContext	The sub-string to the right of the most recent match. Can also be accessed associatively as the RegExp["$'"] entry.	1.2	5.5
source	The source text of the regular expression being used for matching.	1.2	3.0

Methods

Name	Description	JavaScript	JScript
compile(pattern) compile(pattern, attribs)	Compiles the regular expression from the source text. The attributes are combinations of ignore case (I), global match (g), or multiline mode (m).	1.2	3.0
exec() exec(string)	Executes a search in the target string using the regular expression. Omitting the string applies the match against the same as the previous exec() call.	1.2	3.0
test(string)	Tests for a match in the passed in string parameter.	1.2	3.0
toSource()	Returns the source text for the regular expression. Not supported by JScript.	1.3	X

Name	Description	JavaScript	JScript
toString()	Converts the RegExp object into a string.	1.2	3.0
valueOf()	Returns the primitive value of the regular expression object.	1.2	3.0

String

This object contains a sequence of characters. This can be expressed as a primitive or an object.

Construction

```
// Create an empty string object
myString  = new String();

// Create an init a String object
myString0 = new String("ABCDEF");

// Make a string from another object
myString1 = anotherObject.toString();

// Make a string using a literal
myString = "XYZ";
```

Properties

Name	Description	JavaScript	JScript
length	The length of the string measured in characters	1.0	1.0

Methods

Syntax	Description	JavaScript	JScript
anchor(aName)	Encapsulate the string within an <A NAME='aName'> tag context.	1.0	1.0
big()	Encapsulate the string within a <BIG> tag context.	1.0	1.0
blink()	Encapsulate the string within a <BLINK> tag context.	1.0	1.0
bold()	Encapsulate the string within a <B> tag context.	1.0	1.0
charAt(index)	Return the character at the index position within the string.	1.0	1.0
charCodeAt(index)	Return the Unicode value of the character at the index position.	1.2	3.0

Table continued on following page

979

Syntax	Description	JavaScript	JScript
concat(string2)	A method for concatenating string2 to the receiver as opposed to the concatenate operator.	1.2	3.0
fixed()	Encapsulate the string within a <TT> tag context.	1.0	1.0
fontcolor(aColor)	Encapsulate the string within a <FONT COLOR='aColor'> tag context.	1.0	1.0
fontsize(aSize)	Encapsulate the string within a <FONT SIZE='aSize'> tag context.	1.0	1.0
fromCharCode (aCode...)	A class-based factory method for converting a series of numeric character codes to a String object.	1.2	3.0
indexOf(search) indexOf(search, position)	Return the numeric position where the search string is found starting at the optional position if specified.	1.0	1.0
italics()	Encapsulate the string within an <I> tag context.	1.0	1.0
lastIndexOf(search) lastIndexOf(search, position)	Search from right to left and returns the numeric position where the search string is found starting at the optional position if specified.	1.0	1.0
link(aUrl)	Encapsulate the string within an <A HREF='aUrl'> tag context.	1.0	1.0
localeCompare (aString)	A locale-sensitive string comparison between the receiver and the referenced string.	1.5	5.5
match(aPattern)	Search a string using a regular expression and return the matches in an array.	1.2	3.0
replace (aPattern, aReplace)	Search a string using a regular expression and replace the matches.	1.2	3.0
search(aPattern)	Search a string using a regular expression.	1.2	3.0
slice(start) slice(start, end)	Return a sub-string sliced out of the original. The end is optional and if omitted implies the end of the string.	1.0	3.0
small()	Encapsulate the string within a <SMALL> tag context.	1.0	1.0
split(aPattern) split(aSeparator) split(aSeparator, aCount)	Split a string and store the components in an array. The count value is optional.	1.1	3.0
strike()	Encapsulate the string within a <STRIKE> tag context.	1.0	1.0

Syntax	Description	JavaScript	JScript
sub()	Encapsulate the string within a <SUB> tag context.	1.0	1.0
substr(start) substr(start, length)	Return a sub-string extracted from the original.	1.0	3.0
substring(start) substring(start, end)	Extract a portion of a string.	1.0	1.0
sup()	Encapsulate the string within a <SUP> tag context.	1.0	1.0
toLocaleLowerCase()	Convert a string to all lower case using a locale-sensitive character mapping.	1.5	5.5
toLocaleUpperCase()	Convert a string to all upper case using a locale-sensitive character mapping.	1.5	5.5
toLowerCase()	Convert a string to all lower case.	1.0	1.0
toSource()	Output a string formatted as a String literal contained in a string.	1.3	3.0
toString()	Return the string primitive value of the object.	1.1	2.0
toUpperCase()	Convert a string to all upper case.	1.0	1.0
valueOf()	Return the string primitive value of the object.	1.1	2.0

Window

The global object in a web browser is an alternative reference to the window object. All of the properties and methods of the window object are available without needing to add the window. prefix to the property or method reference.

JavaScript can be hosted in a variety of contexts. The most popular is within a web browser. Typically, this will be the Microsoft Internet Explorer browser or the Netscape browser. There are other browsers but they tend to support a strict W3C standards based behavior, which is a subset of the IE or Netscape functionality.

Construction

New windows are instantiated automatically as the browser opens new frames and contexts for the window object, so we would not expect to instantiate them ourselves with a constructor.

Properties

Name	Description	JavaScript	JScript
clientInformation	Another name for the navigator property	X	3.0
clipboardData	An object containing data that represents the contents of the clipboard	X	5.0
closed	A property value that is Boolean true if the window is closed	1.1	3.0
crypto	A reference to a Crypto object for security encoding	1.2	X
defaultStatus	A property containing the text displayed in the status bar.	1.0	1.0
dialogArguments	The arguments passed to a model dialog in a showModalDialog() call	X	3.0
dialogHeight	The height of a modal or modeless dialog window	X	3.0
dialogLeft	The left edge of a modal or modeless dialog window	X	3.0
dialogTop	The top edge of a modal or modeless dialog window	X	3.0
dialogWidth	The width of a modal or modeless dialog window	X	3.0
document	A reference to the document object that is contained in the window	1.0	1.0
event	During event handling, MSIE stores a reference to an event object in this variable	X	3.0
external	Reference to an external object outside of the interpreter	X	5.0
frame	This is another name for self and window	X	5.0
frameRate	An indication of the frame rate for the current display	1.2	X
history	This property returns a history object for this window	1.1	3.0
innerHeight	The height of the window inside the frame	1.2	X
innerWidth	The width of the window inside the frame	1.2	X
java	A reference to the Java package object that is the root of the java.* Packages tree	1.1	X
length	The number of frames in the window	1.0	3.0
location	A reference to the location object that represents the URL of the current window content	1.0	1.0
locationbar	A reference to an object that represents the location bar	1.2	X
menubar	A reference to an object that represents the menu bar	1.2	X

Name	Description	JavaScript	JScript
name	The name of the window either from the `<FRAME>` tag, the `window.open()` method call, or an assignment to this property	1.0	1.0
navigator	A reference to a `navigator` object that describes the browser	1.0	3.0
netscape	A reference to the Java package object that is the root of the `netscape.*` Packages tree	1.1	X
offscreenBuffering	A property that controls off-screen buffering effects	1.2	3.0
opener	A reference to the window that contained the link that opened this one	1.1	3.0
outerHeight	The height of the window including the frame	1.2	X
outerWidth	The width of the window including the frame	1.2	X
Packages	A top-level Java `Package` object that is the root of a tree of Java packages	1.1	X
pageXOffset	The amount that a window has been scrolled to the right.	1.2	X
pageYOffset	The amount that a window has been scrolled downwards.	1.2	X
parent	A reference to the parent window in a framed pane	1.0	1.0
personalbar	A reference to an object that represents the personal preferences bar	1.2	X
pkcs11	Part of the Netscape security manager	1.2	X
returnValue	The return value for a modal dialog window	X	3.0
screen	A reference to a `screen` object that the window is being displayed in	1.2	3.0
screenLeft	The left edge of the screen	X	5.0
screenTop	The top edge of the screen	X	5.0
screenX	The X co-ordinate of the window within the screen display	1.2	X
screenY	The Y co-ordinate of the window within the screen display	1.2	X
scrollbars	A reference to an object that represents the scroll bar	1.2	X
secure	A flag indicating that a window was loaded from a secure source	1.2	X
self	A reference to the window itself	1.0	1.0
sidebar	A reference to an object that represents the sidebar frame in Netscape Navigator version 6.0	1.4	X

Table continued on following page

Name	Description	JavaScript	JScript
status	A property containing the text displayed in the status bar	1.0	1.0
statusbar	A reference to an object that represents the status bar	1.2	X
sun	A reference to the Java package object that is the root of the sun.* Packages tree	1.1	X
toolbar	A reference to an object that represents the tool bar	1.2	X
top	The topmost window in a framed hierarchy	1.0	1.0
window	Another name for the self property	1.0	1.0

Methods

Name	Description	JavaScript	JScript
alert(string)	Present an alerting dialog box.	1.0	1.0
atob(base64)	A string containing base 64 encoded data to be converted to a binary form.	1.2	X
attachEvent (event, handler)	Attaches an event handler to the event hook for the receiving object.	X	5.0
back()	A method that mimics the user clicking on the Back button.	1.2	X
blur()	Send a blur event to the window object.	1.1	3.0
btoa(binary)	A block of binary data contained in a string that will be encoded into base 64 form.	1.2	X
captureEvents (eventMask)	Part of the Netscape Navigator event propagation complex.	1.2	X
clearInterval (intervalID)	Cancel a previous setInterval() timer that caused a function to be called periodically.	1.2	3.0
clearTimeout (timeoutID)	Clear a previously established setTimeout() function call.	1.0	1.0
close()	Close the window for the receiving global object.	1.0	1.0
confirm(string)	Present a confirmation dialog box.	1.0	1.0
detachEvent(event)	A means of detaching events from windows and documents that were previously attached with the attachEvent() method.	X	5.0

Name	Description	JavaScript	JScript
disableExternal Capture()	Part of the Netscape Navigator 4 event propagation complex.	1.2	X
enableExternal Capture()	Part of the Netscape Navigator 4 event propagation complex.	1.2	X
execScript (source, language)	Execute a script on behalf of a window. The language argument is optional.	X	3.0
find()	This duplicates the behavior of the [FIND] button on the Netscape Navigator button bar.	1.2	X
focus()	Send a focus event to the window.	1.1	3.0
forward()	Mimic the effect of the user clicking on the [FORWARD] button.	1.2	X
handleEvent(event)	Pass an event to the appropriate handler for the window.	1.2	X
home()	This duplicates the behavior of the Home button on the Netscape Navigator button bar.	1.2	X
moveBy(x, y)	Move the window by a specified distance.	1.2	3.0
moveTo(x, y)	Move the window to a specific location.	1.2	3.0
navigate(aURL)	Load a new URL into the window.	X	3.0
open(aURL, aName, aFeatures, aFlag)	A means of creating new windows under script control.	1.0	1.0
print()	This duplicates the behavior of the Print button on the Netscape Navigator button bar.	1.2	5.0
prompt (string, default)	Present a text input prompt box with a default button highlighted.	1.0	1.0
releaseEvents (eventMask)	Part of the Netscape Navigator 4 event propagation complex.	1.2	X
resizeBy(x, y)	Resize the window by a specified amount.	1.2	3.0
resizeTo(x, y)	Resize the window to specified dimensions.	1.2	3.0
routeEvent(event)	Part of the Netscape Navigator 4 event propagation complex.	1.2	X
scroll(x, y)	This is equivalent to the scrollTo() method but has been retained for backwards compatibility.	1.1	3.0
scrollBy(x, y)	Scroll the document in the window by a specific amount.	1.2	3.0

Table continued on following page

Name	Description	JavaScript	JScript
scrollTo(x, y)	Scroll the document in the window to a specific location.	1.2	3.0
setHotkeys(aFlag)	Activate or deactivate keyboard shortcuts for this window.	1.2	X
setInterval(src, time, args, lang)	Schedule a function to be executed at regular intervals. The arguments and language parameters are optional.	1.2	3.0
setResizable (aFlag)	Enable or inhibit the window resize capability.	1.2	X
setTimeout(src, time, args, lang)	Schedule a function to be executed after some period has elapsed. The arguments and language parameters are optional.	1.0	1.0
setZOptions (value)	Define the window stacking behavior.	1.2	X
showHelp(aURL)	Display the help window.	X	3.0
showModalDialog(URL, args, opts)	Display a modal dialog. The features argument is optional.	X	3.0
showModelessDialog (aURL, args, opts)	Display a modeless dialog window. The features argument is optional.	X	5.0
stop()	This duplicates the behavior of the Stop button on the Netscape Navigator button bar.	1.2	X

Collections

Name	Description	JavaScript	JScript
frames[]	A collection of objects, each one representing a frame within this window	1.2	3.0

Implementation Specific Objects – Microsoft

Both Microsoft and Netscape have implemented objects supported within the core of their interpreters that are not portable. We summarize them here, starting with Microsoft.

ActiveXObject

The JScript interpreter introduced the ActiveXObject type at version 3.0 so that it could interact with the Windows ActiveX extensions. The objects behave according to the Active X component they encapsulate and they are typically used for creating external resources, such as a Word Document for example.

Construction

```
// Make a Word Document wrapped as an ActiveXObject
myDoc = new ActiveXObject("MSWord.Document");
```

Properties

The supported properties depend on what the ActiveX component does. The appropriate properties of the ActiveX component should be reflected as JavaScript accessible properties.

Methods

Whatever appropriate function calls the ActiveX components supports should be reflected as JavaScript methods.

Enumerator

This is a convenient way of enumerating through the items in a collection. However, its functionality is easily replaced by a `for` loop and an indexing variable. For portability reasons, that is the recommended alternative.

Construction

```
// Make an empty Enumerator object
myEnum  = new Enumerator();

// Make an enumerator that encapsulates a collection
myEnum  = new Enumerator(document.forms);
```

Properties

Same as the `constructor` property in the `Object` object. The `prototype` property, however, is not accessible for scripting.

Methods

Syntax	Description	JScript
atEnd()	A method that returns a Boolean flag indicating the end of the collection.	3.0
item() item(index) item(selector) item(selector, index)	A reference to the current item in the collection or to an indexed item. This method returns the object from the collection that the enumerator is currently accessing if no arguments are specified. A selector that matches a subset of the collection can be used with an optional index starting position.	3.0
moveFirst()	Reset the enumerator to point at the first item in the collection.	3.0
moveNext()	Move the enumerator to the next item in the collection.	3.0

VBArray

Sometimes the JScript interpreter needs to exchange information with the VBScript interpreter. This can be accomplished with the `VBArray` object introduced at version 3.0 of JScript. The constructor takes a VB array as its argument value. From JScript you need to call a Visual Basic function to return an array as its result.

Construction

```
// Make an array in VBScript and import it into JScript
<SCRIPT LANGUAGE='VBScript'>
   function getArray()
      dim arrVB(1)
      arrVB(0) = 100
      arrVB(1) = 250
      getArray = arrVB
   End function
</SCRIPT>

<SCRIPT LANGUAGE='JavaScript'>
   var vbArr = new VBArray(getArray());
</SCRIPT>
```

Properties

There are no properties, only methods.

Methods

Name	Description	JScript
dimensions()	A method for requesting the number of dimensions or axes of the VB array.	3.0
getItem(idx1, idx2, ...)	An accessor method for retrieving items from the array. You can list as many items as you like.	3.0
lbound(axis)	A method that returns the index position of the first element in the VBArray for the specified axis.	3.0
toArray()	A conversion method for creating a JScript array object from a VBArray object.	3.0
ubound(axis)	A method that returns the index position of the last element in the VB array for the specified axis.	3.0

Implementation Specific Objects – Netscape

Here are the objects specific to the Netscape browsers.

JavaArray

Netscape introduced the JavaArray object at version 1.1 of JavaScript to enable the exchange of data between JavaScript and Java. Objects of this type are created by method calls on Java objects that return an array.

Construction

You would not normally expect to construct these objects in JavaScript but rather get them because of calling an object method.

```
// Example JavaArray creation
myJavaArray = myWindow.Packages;
```

Properties

Name	Description	JScript
length	The number of elements in the Java array	1.1

Methods

Name	Description	JScript
toString()	Prior to JavaScript version 1.4, this returns a string describing the object class. From version 1.4 of JavaScript, the behavior is overridden by that of the java.lang.Object superclass, which provides its own toString() method. That obscures the one in the JavaScript's Object object that is an ancestor of the JavaArray object.	1.1

JavaClass

JavaScript 1.1 introduces the JavaClass object. This is a means of encapsulating access to a Java class from within the JavaScript interpreter. The objects are created by accessing the Java classes as elements of the Packages object.

Construction

```
// Create a reference to a Java class object
myJavaDate = Packages.java.util.Date;
```

Properties

The static fields of the Java class being encapsulated are presented as JavaScript accessible properties of this object. The specific property names depend on the source Java class being accessed.

Methods

The static methods of the Java class being encapsulated are presented as JavaScript accessible methods of this object. The specific method names depend on the source Java class being accessed.

JavaObject

This encapsulation of a Java instance object was introduced at version 1.1 of JavaScript. These objects are created when a Java method returns an object or by applying the new operator to a JavaClass object or Java class under the Packages hierarchy.

Construction

```
// Create an object via a reference to a Java class object
myObject = new Packages.java.util.Date;
```

Properties

The public properties of the Java class being instantiated are presented as JavaScript accessible properties of this object. That includes any that it inherits from its superclasses. The specific property names depend on the source Java class being accessed.

Methods

The public methods of the Java class being instantiated are presented as JavaScript accessible methods of this object. That includes any that it inherits from its superclasses or from `java.lang.Object`. The specific method names depend on the source Java class being accessed.

In addition, these standard methods are supported:

Name	Description	JScript
booleanValue()	Performs a conversion before returning a Boolean equivalent value for the object.	1.1
getClass()	Returns a string describing the Java class from which the source object was instantiated.	1.1
toString()	Prior to JavaScript version 1.4, this returns a string describing the object class. From version 1.4 of JavaScript, the behavior is overridden by that of the `java.lang.Object` superclass that provides its own `toString()` method. That obscures the one in the JavaScript's `Object` object that is an ancestor of the `JavaArray` object.	1.1

JavaPackage

At version 1.1 of JavaScript, Netscape introduced this encapsulation of the Java package so it could be accessed as an object from JavaScript. Packages are returned by walking the `Packages` tree without descending to leaf nodes, which are the actual class objects. Anything higher than that should return a `JavaPackage` object.

Construction

```
// Access a package within the Java environment
myPackage = Packages.java.util;
```

Properties

It returns package objects in a tree-like hierarchy arrangement.

Methods

There are no accessible methods for this object type.

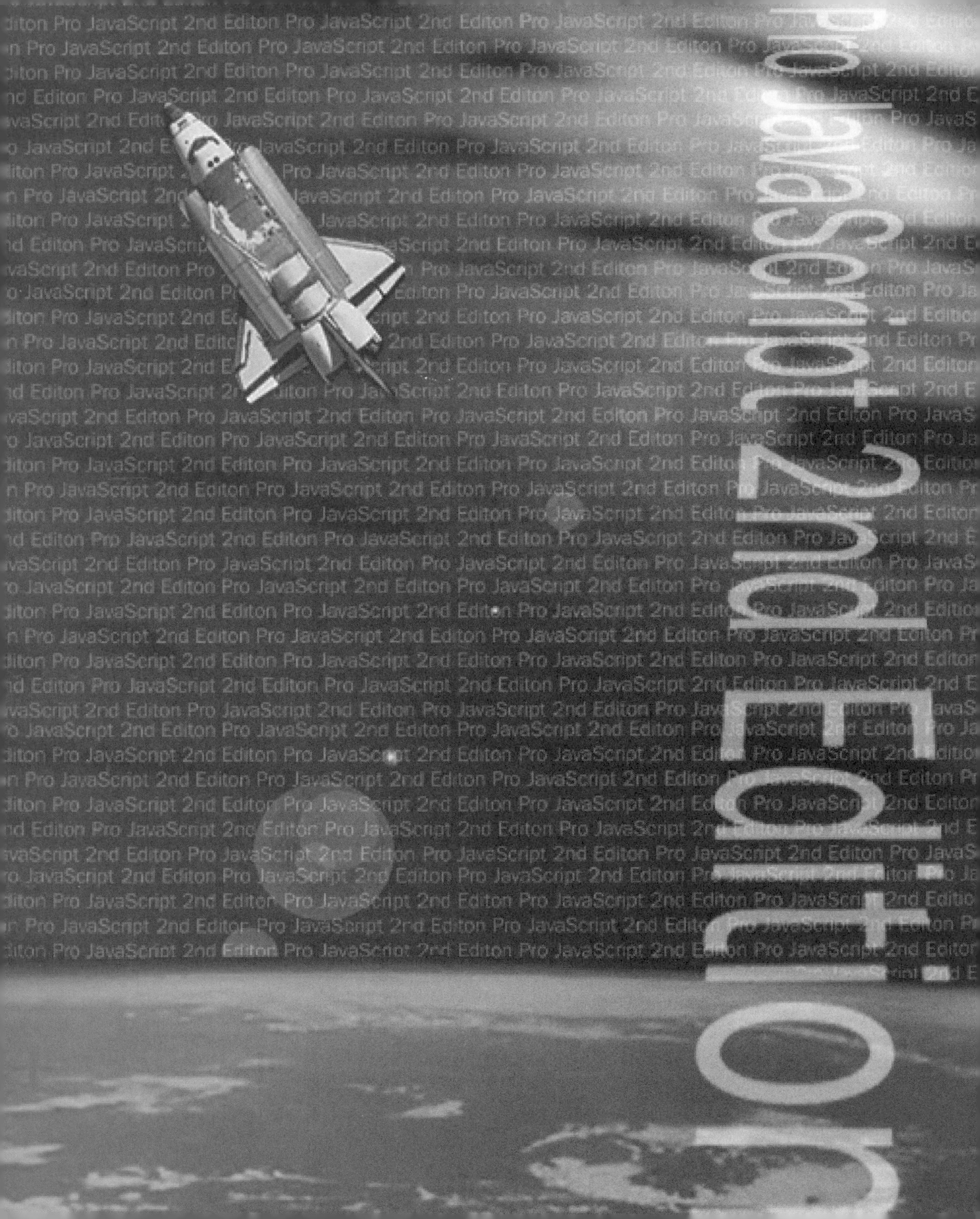
Pro JavaScript 2nd Edition
Pro JavaScript 2nd Editon

C

Data Types and Type Conversion

Core JavaScript supports a small but useful set of native data types. These are available as primitive values and as object classes of the same generic type.

During evaluation of expressions, the interpreter will need to convert from one data type to another. Sometimes values cannot be sensibly transformed. The various conversion rules are summarized in the type conversion tables.

Primitive Data Types

JavaScript provides three native primitive data types. These are also available as object classes.

Certain rules apply when converting from one data type to another. Refer to the type conversion tables for details.

Type	Example	Description
Boolean	`true` `false`	A logical value container. The value can be either `true` or `false`.
Number	`100` `-9.25`	A numeric value.
String	`"abcdef"` `myObject.toString()`	A sequence of characters.

Built-in Constants

There are three built-in constants provided by JavaScript, and it is important to know what these are for type conversion. They are built-in members of the Global object. These constants first appeared in JavaScript 1.3 and JScript 3.0.

Constant	Example	Description
Infinity	if (x>Number.MAXVALUE) return Infinity;	This is equivalent to the Number.POSITIVE_INFINITY constant.

NaN	if (error == true)
	
	result = NaN;
		This is equivalent to the Number.NaN constant. This should be used in preference for clarity of your source

undefined	if (v==undefined)
	
	v=100;
		A means of testing for undefined values.

Type Conversion

JavaScript can perform type conversion between different kinds of data; explicitly, or implicitly when a function or operator is expecting a certain primitive data type. Below are given the data types the data will be converted to and the values the data will take within that new data type.

Boolean

This is invoked by coercion due to evaluation context, or by use of the toBoolean() function implicitly during Boolean object instantiation, or explicitly by calling it from script.

Source value	Result
null	false
Undefined value	false
Non empty string	true
Empty string	false
0	false
1	true
NaN	false
Infinity	true
Negative infinity	true
Any other non-zero number	true
Object	true
Array	No direct Boolean equivalent – use intermediate conversion to another type
Function	true

Number

This is invoked by coercion due to evaluation context, or by use of the `toNumber()` function implicitly during `Number` object instantiation, or explicitly by calling it from script.

Source value	Result
`null`	0
Undefined value	NaN
Empty string	0
Numeric string	Numeric value of string
Non-numeric string	NaN
Boolean `true`	1
Boolean `false`	0
Object	Result of `Object.valueOf()`
Object lacking a `valueOf()` method	Result of conversion of result from `Object.toString()` method
Object without `toString()` or `valueOf()` methods	An error
Array	No direct numeric equivalent – use intermediate conversion to another type
Function	NaN

String

This is invoked by coercion due to evaluation context, or by use of the `toString()` method implicitly during `String` object instantiation, or explicitly by calling it from script.

Source value	Result
0	`"0"`
`null`	`"null"`
Undefined value	`"undefined"`
NaN	`"NaN"`
Infinity	`"Infinity"`
Negative infinity	`"-Infinity"`
Numeric value	That numeric value as a sequence of characters
Boolean `true`	`"true"`
Boolean `false`	`"false"`
Object	Result of `Object.toString()`

Source value	Result
Object lacking a `toString()` method	Result of conversion of result from `Object.valueOf()` method
Object without `toString()` or `valueOf()` methods	An error
Array	Individual elements joined by a comma
Function	Depends on implementation

Object

This is invoked by coercion due to evaluation context, or by use of the `toObject()` method implicitly during `Object` instantiation, or explicitly by calling it from script.

Source value	Result
`null`	An error
Undefined value	An error
Empty string	`String` object
Non-empty string	`String` object
`0`	`Number` object
`NaN`	`Number` object
`Infinity`	`Number` object
Negative infinity	`Number` object
Any other non-zero number	`Number` object
Boolean `true`	`Boolean` object
Boolean `false`	`Boolean` object

The typeof Operator

The `typeof` operator describes the data type of a piece of data. What it returns for each type is shown below:

Source type	Result string
`undefined`	`"undefined"`
`Infinity`	`"number"`
`NaN`	`"number"`
`null`	`"object"`
Boolean primitive	`"boolean"`

Source type	Result string
Number primitive	`"number"`
String primitive	`"string"`
`Boolean()` constructor	`"boolean"`
`Date()` constructor	`"string"`
`Number()` constructor	`"number"`
`RegExp()` constructor	`"undefined"`
`String()` constructor	`"string"`
`Boolean` object instance	`"object"`
`Date` object instance	`"object"`
`Math` object instance	`"object"`
`Number` object instance	`"object"`
`RegExp` object instance	`"object"`
`String` object instance	`"object"`
`Generic` object instance	`"object"`
Object not supporting a call interface	`"object"`
Object that supports a call interface	`"function"`
Other host objects	Implementation defined
`typeof` any value	`"string"`

Pro JavaScript 2nd Edition

D

Event Handlers

Event handling is a large and complex topic. It is gradually becoming more standardized due to the efforts of the DOM working group at the W3C, but there are many events available in the browsers that are not defined in the W3C standards. Internet Explorer in particular implements many non-standard events.

There are several aspects to consider here. The event itself is reflected in an `Event` object that is triggered by an action on an object with an attached event listener function. Element objects that can have event listeners attached are called **EventTarget** objects by the DOM specification. Event listeners are commonly called event handlers.

Event handling is inextricably bound up now with the DOM specification. Before that, it was already complex because certain event handling capabilities were supported differently in the IE and Netscape event models. DOM brings these all together in a somewhat unified fashion, but the browsers do not fully and completely support the DOM-specified behavior yet. In the meantime, while the browser manufacturers struggle to keep up, DOM has gone forward with some additional capabilities for supporting keyboard events in its Level 3 specification. Currently the state of play is to attempt to support DOM Level 1 document structures with event support at DOM Level 2.

Here we have documented a superset of the functionality in order to give complete coverage.

Compendium of Event Types

Here we summarize the currently implemented and standardized event names with a short description of when they are triggered. Their availability in the two major browsers is also summarized here.

Name	Description	JavaScript	JScript	DOM Level
onAbort	Called when image loading is aborted.	1.1	1.0	2
onAfterPrint	Called when printing has just finished.	X	5.0	X
onAfterUpdate	Called when an update is completed.	X	3.0	
onBack	Called when user has clicked on the Back button in the browser.	1.3	X	X
onBeforeCopy	Called immediately before a copy to the clipboard.	X	5.0	X
onBeforeCut	Called immediately before a cut to the clipboard.	X	5.0	X
onBeforeEditFocus	Called immediately before the edit focus is directed to an element.	X	5.0	X
onBeforePaste	Called immediately before the clipboard is pasted.	X	5.0	X
onBeforePrint	Called immediately before printing begins.	X	5.0	X
onBeforeUnload	Called immediately prior to the window being unloaded.	X	3.0	X
onBeforeUpdate	Called immediately before an update commences.	X	3.0	X
onBlur	Called when an input element loses input focus. Only valid for form elements.	1.1	3.0	2
onBounce	Triggered when a marquee element hits the edge of its element area	X	3.0	X
onChange	When edit fields have new values entered or a popup has a new selection, this event's handler can check the new value.	1.0	3.0	2
onClick	Called when the user clicks the mouse button on the Element object that represents the object on screen.	1.0	1.0	2

Name	Description	JavaScript	JScript	DOM Level
onContentReady	This event is called when the content of the element that the behavior is associated with has been loaded and parsed.	X	5.0	X
onContextMenu	Called for special handling for contextual menus.	X	5.0	X
onCopy	Called when a copy operation happens.	X	5.0	X
onCut	Called when a cut operation happens.	X	5.0	X
onDataAvailable	Called when some data has arrived asynchronously from an applet or data source.	X	3.0	X
onDataSetChanged	Called when a data source has changed the content or some initial data is now ready for collection.	X	3.0	X
onDataSetComplete	Called when there is no more data to be transmitted from the data source.	X	3.0	X
onDblClick	Called when the user double-clicks on an object.	1.2	3.0	X
onDocumentReady	This is a special event to signify that a document is loaded and ready for use.	X	5.0	X
onDOMActivate	Triggered when a DOM EventTarget is activated with a mouse click or key press.	X	X	2
onDOMAttrModified	Called when the attributes on a node have just been modified.	X	X	2
onDOMCharacterData Modified	Called when the data in a leaf text node has just been modified.	X	X	2
onDOMFocusIn	Triggered when a DOM EventTarget receives focus. This can be applied to non-form elements, unlike the focus event.	X	X	2

Table continued on following page

Name	Description	JavaScript	JScript	DOM Level
onDOMFocusOut	Triggered when a DOM EventTarget loses focus. This can be applied to non-form elements, unlike the blur event.	X	X	2
onDOMNodeInserted	Called when a DOM node is about to be added to the document.	X	X	2
onDOMNodeInsertedInto Document	Called when a DOM node has been added to the document.	X	X	2
onDOMNodeRemoved	Called when a DOM node is about to be removed from the document.	X	X	2
onDOMNodeRemovedFrom Document	Called when a DOM node has been removed from the document.	X	X	2
onDOMSubtreeModified	This is a general trigger for document changes. Other more specific events may also be triggered.	X	X	2
onDrag	Called when a drag operation happens.	X	5.0	X
onDragDrop	Called when some data has been dropped onto a window.	1.2	X	X
onDragEnd	Called when a drag ends.	X	5.0	X
onDragEnter	Called when a dragged item enters the element.	X	5.0	X
onDragLeave	Called when a dragged item leaves the element.	X	5.0	X
onDragOver	Called while the dragged item is over the element.	X	5.0	X
onDragStart	Called when the user has commenced some data selection with a mouse drag	X	3.0	X
onDrop	Called when a dragged item is dropped.	X	5.0	X
onError	Triggered if an error occurs when executing a script.	1.3	3.0	2

Name	Description	JavaScript	JScript	DOM Level
onErrorUpdate	Called when an error has occurred in the transfer of some data from a data source.	X	3.0	X
onFilterChange	Called if a filter has changed the state of an element or a transition has just been completed.	X	3.0	X
onFinish	Called when a marquee object has finished looping.	X	3.0	X
onFocus	Called when the form element is selected for entry. Only valid for form elements.	1.0	3.0	2
onForward	Called if the user has clicked on the **Forward** button in the browser.	1.3	X	X
onHelp	Called when the user has pressed the *F1* key or selected **Help** from the toolbar or menu.	X	3.0	X
onKeyDown	Called when a key is pressed.	1.2	3.0	3
onKeyPress	Pressing the key down and releasing it again elicits this event.	1.2	3.0	3
onKeyUp	Called when a key is released.	1.2	3.0	3
onLoad	Called when an object has completed loading.	1.0	1.0	2
onLoseCapture	Called when an element loses event-capturing permission.	1.2	X	X
onMouseDown	Called when the mouse button is pressed.	1.2	3.0	2
onMouseDrag	An event handler for mouse drag operations.	X	5.0	X
onMouseMove	Called when the mouse pointer is moved.	1.2	3.0	2
onMouseOut	Called when the mouse pointer leaves the active area occupied by the Element object that represents the object on screen.	1.1	3.0	2

Table continued on following page

Name	Description	JavaScript	JScript	DOM Level
onMouseOver	Called when the mouse pointer enters the active area owned by the object.	1.0	1.0	2
onMouseUp	Called when the mouse button is released.	1.2	3.0	2
onMove	Called if the browser window has been moved.	1.2	X	X
onPaste	Called when a paste operation happens.	X	5.0	X
onPropertyChange	Called when an object property is modified (similar to the Netscape watch() method).	X	5.0	X
onReadyStateChange	Called if an object in the window has changed its ready state.	X	3.0	X
onReset	Called if the user has clicked a reset button in a form	1.1	3.0	2
onResize	As the window is resized, this event is triggered.	1.2	3.0	2
onRowEnter	Called when the data in a field bound to a data source is about to be changed.	X	3.0	X
onRowExit	Called if the data in a field bound to a data source has been changed.	X	3.0	X
onRowsDelete	Called if some rows are about to be deleted from the database.	X	3.0	X
onRowsInserted	Called if some new data is being inserted into the database.	X	3.0	X
onScroll	Called if the window has been scrolled.	X	3.0	2
onSelect	Called if some textual content in the window has been selected.	1.0	3.0	2
onSelectStart	Called when a SELECT action is beginning.	X	3.0	X

Name	Description	JavaScript	JScript	DOM Level
onStart	Called when a marquee element is beginning its loop.	X	3.0	X
onStop	Called when a stop action occurs.	1.2	X	X
onSubmit	Called if the user has clicked on the submit button in a form.	1.1	3.0	2
onUnload	Triggered when the document is unloaded.	1.0	1.0	2

Ready States

Changes to the ready state will trigger an onReadyStateChange event in the MSIE browser. These values will then be reflected in the readyState property of the Element object whose ready state has just altered.

State	Description
uninitialized	The object is first instantiated, but it has not begun loading
loading	The object has commenced loading
loaded	The object has completed loading
interactive	The object is loaded but not closed, but is ready to handle interaction
complete	The object body has been closed and the loading is finished

DOM Event Types

Events can be classified into groups to allow sub-sets to be implemented. DOM Levels 2 and 3 specify the following event groupings. We cold probably classify many other events into these categories but that would be somewhat dangerous until the DOM standard adopts them.

Type	Name	DOM Level
HTMLEvent	abort	2
HTMLEvent	blur	2
HTMLEvent	change	2
HTMLEvent	error	2
HTMLEvent	focus	2
HTMLEvent	load	2

Table continued on following page

Type	Name	DOM Level
HTMLEvent	reset	2
HTMLEvent	resize	2
HTMLEvent	scroll	2
HTMLEvent	select	2
HTMLEvent	submit	2
HTMLEvent	unload	2
KeyEvent	onKeyDown	3
KeyEvent	onKeyPress	3
KeyEvent	onKeyUp	3
MouseEvent	click	2
MouseEvent	mousedown	2
MouseEvent	mousemove	2
MouseEvent	mouseout	2
MouseEvent	mouseover	2
MouseEvent	mouseup	2
MutationEvent	DOMAttrModified	2
MutationEvent	DOMCharacterDataModified	2
MutationEvent	DOMNodeInserted	2
MutationEvent	DOMNodeInsertedIntoDocument	2
MutationEvent	DOMNodeRemoved	2
MutationEvent	DOMNodeRemovedFromDocument	2
MutationEvent	DOMSubtreeModified	2
UIEvent	DOMActivate	2
UIEvent	DOMFocusIn	2
UIEvent	DOMFocusOut	2

Event Object

The event objects are instantiated by the event triggering mechanisms inside the browser. They are meant to carry auxiliary information about the event so that the handler can make use of it. Netscape creates a unique event object for each event, while Internet Explorer uses the same event object but updates its properties before calling each event handler. Because only one event handler can be running at a time within each execution context, this does not really pose a limitation.

Construction

You would not generally instantiate event objects yourself. DOM specifies some mechanisms for creating and initializing events that suggests that you could trigger your own events without necessarily throwing an exception. If you want to do that, you can use the `createEvent()` method belonging to the document and then the `initEvent()` method of the event object. Then you can use the `dispatchEvent()` method of the `EventTarget` to invoke the error handler.

You will find that accessing event objects is easier if you make sure they are passed in a consistent manner to the event handlers. MSIE simply expects you to access them via the event property of the global object. Netscape Navigator passes the event object as an argument to the event handler. This fragment of code shows how to ensure the event object is passed to the handler in both cases:

```
<HTML>
<BODY>
   <FORM NAME='myForm' ONSUBMIT='catchEvent(event)'>
      <INPUT TYPE='SUBMIT' VALUE='Click Me'>
   </FORM>
   <SCRIPT LANGUAGE='JavaScript'>
      function catchEvent(anEvent)
      {
         alert(anEvent.type);
      }
   </SCRIPT>
</BODY>
</HTML>
```

The return value of the handler function indicates to the browser whether it should consider the event fully dealt with or whether it needs to carry out some further default actions. To suppress this you should return `false`. By fault, if you do nothing, the handler will return `true`.

The DOM standard specifies a few additional properties and methods that are added to an event method when it is sub-classed into one of the specific DOM event types. These DOM event types are:

❑   HTMLEvent

❑   UIEvent

❑   MouseEvent

❑   MutationEvent

❑   KeyEvent

Properties

Note that not all of these are relevant to every type of event, and in some cases, they convey a value having a different meaning altogether.

Name	Description	JavaScript	JScript	DOM Level
altKey	A Boolean value that represents the state of the *Alt* key.	1.5	3.0	2

Table continued on following page

Name	Description	JavaScript	JScript	DOM Level
attrChange	Specified as part of the DOM MutationEvent support. It returns the mutation type. These types are listed in another table and are available symbolically as static constants.	1.5	X	2
attrName	Specified as part of the DOM MutationEvent support. It returns the name of an attribute that has been modified.	1.5	X	2
bubbles	A Boolean value that indicates whether the event can bubble or not.	1.5	X	2
button	The mouse button that was pressed to trigger the event.	1.5	3.0	2
cancelable	If the event can be canceled, then this flag will be set true.	1.5	X	2
cancelBubble	A flag that halts event bubbling in Internet Explorer browsers. Set this value to true on exiting from the event handler to cancel bubbling.	X	3.0	X
charCode	The character code of a key that was pressed to trigger the event relating to this object.	X	3.0	X
clientX	Horizontal mouse position relative to the web page.	1.5	3.0	2
clientY	Vertical mouse position relative to the web page.	1.5	3.0	2
ctrlKey	A Boolean value that represents the state of the *Ctrl* key.	1.5	3.0	2
currentTarget	A reference to the object whose listener is being called with the receiving Event object.	1.5	X	2
data	The URL of the data dropped into a window from a DragDrop event.	1.2	3.0	X
dataTransfer	A means of transferring drag and drop data via the Event object. This refers to a dataTransfer object.	X	5.0	X
detail	A DOM specified property belonging to the UIEvent sub-class. It provides some additional detailed information about the event, which is implementation-specific. For a Level 3 key event, this can indicate how many keystrokes arrived during a repetition.	1.5	X	2

Name	Description	JavaScript	JScript	DOM Level
eventPhase	Describes in what phase the event is currently being processed. See the DOM event phases table for potential values.	1.5	X	2
fromElement	The object that the mouse is moving from during a mouseOver event on another object.	X	3.0	X
height	The new height of a resized window or frame.	1.2	X	X
inputGenerated	A DOM Level 3 attribute that indicates whether any input was generated with a keystroke event. The value is Boolean. A true value indicates a visible character was entered.	X	X	3
keyCode	The code point for the key that was pressed in Internet Explorer.	X	3.0	X
keyVal	DOM Level 3 specifies that this is the Unicode value of the key if some input was generated.	X	X	3
layerX	The X-coordinate of the event within a layer. This is deprecated from version 6 of Netscape.	1.2	X	X
layerY	The Y-coordinate of the event within a layer. This is deprecated from version 6 of Netscape.	1.2	X	X
metaKey	A Boolean value in that represents the state of the *meta* key.	1.5	X	2
modifiers	A bit mask provided by Netscape and which contains a bit flag for each modifier key. See the Netscape modifier masks table for values.	1.2	X	X
newValue	Specified as part of the DOM MutationEvent support. It returns the new value that has just been defined by a modification.	1.5	X	2
numPad	Dom Level 3 specifies that this property should be true if the keystroke originated on the numeric keypad area.	X	X	3
offsetX	The X-coordinate of the event relative to its containing object.	X	3.0	X
offsetY	The Y-coordinate of the event relative to its containing object.	X	3.0	X
outputString	DOM Level 3 specifies that this is the string of characters generated by the keystroke event. This might be a single character or a longer string. It can also be empty.	X	X	3

Table continued on following page

Name	Description	JavaScript	JScript	DOM Level
pageX	Netscape horizontal mouse position relative to the web page.	1.2	X	X
pageY	Netscape vertical mouse position relative to the web page.	1.2	X	X
prevValue	Specified as part of the DOM MutationEvent support. It returns the old value that has just been replaced by a modification.	1.5	X	2
propertyName	The name of a property that was changed and which triggered an onPropertyChange event.	X	5.0	X
reason	An indication of the status of a data transfer.	X	3.0	X
relatedNode	Specified as part of the DOM MutationEvent support. It points at the node that has been mutated.	1.5	X	2
relatedTarget	An additional DOM-specified target element, which may be useful in handling the event. Typically, this might be a more formal way of specifying the fromElement as opposed to the currentElement.	1.5	X	2
repeat	If a keyboard can generate auto-repeating keystrokes then this is set true when a keystroke is an auto-repeat of a previous one.	X	5.0	X
returnValue	You may want to modify the return value for the event handler. By assigning a new value to this property, the returnValue of the event handler will be modified.	X	3.0	X
screenX	Horizontal position of mouse pointer when the event was triggered. The value is relative to the display screen measured in pixels.	1.2	3.0	2
screenY	Vertical position of mouse pointer when the event was triggered. The value is relative to the display screen measured in pixels.	1.2	3.0	2
shiftKey	A Boolean value that represents the state of the *shift* key.	1.5	3.0	2
srcElement	An IE-supported property containing the Element that is the event source.	X	3.0	X
srcFilter	A filter object representing the filter that triggered the onFilterChange event.	X	3.0	X

Name	Description	JavaScript	JScript	DOM Level
target	A property containing a reference to the object at which the event was directed.	1.2	X	2
timeStamp	A time value at which the event was triggered.	1.5	X	2
toElement	The object to which the mouse is moving.	X	3.0	X
type	Event type string. This is equivalent to the onEvent handler attachment property with the on prefix removed. In versions of Netscape prior to 6, a complex bit masking technique was used. Refer to the *Netscape Event Types* table for a list of mask values.	1.2	3.0	2
view	A DOM-specified property belonging to the UIEvent sub-class. This returns an AbstractView object representing the kind of document view currently in use. This functionality has not yet been fully implemented in browsers.	1.5	X	2
virtKeyVal	DOM Level 3 supports the use of key codes that have some virtual meaning and which may not have a Unicode equivalent character code point. The values specified here are listed in a table in the DOM Level 3 extensions section of this appendix.	X	X	3
which	The number of the mouse button or the code point value of a key that was pressed in Netscape. See the buttons table for details.	1.2	X	X
width	The new width of a resized window or frame.	1.2	X	X
x	In Internet Explorer, this is the horizontal position of mouse pointer when the event was triggered. The value is measured in pixels relative to the parent element. In Netscape, it is also used for the width value when a resize event happens. The mouse position value in other event types is measured relative to the layer the element resides in. However, Netscape 6 does not support layers and the position may be relative to the parent element in that case.	1.2	3.0	X
y	This is the vertical measurement corresponding to the x property. The same considerations apply regarding differences between Internet Explorer and Netscape.	1.2	3.0	X

DOM Mutation Event Types

The DOM mutation events can be classified according to the kind of mutation of the document that takes place. The value is available in the `attrChange` property of the event object. DOM suggests that the value is numeric according to these rules:

Value	Type
1	MODIFICATION
2	ADDITION
3	REMOVAL

DOM Event Phases

As events are tracked by DOM-compliant implementations, the various states of the event can be inspected by the event handler. This value is present in the `eventPhase` property of the event object. Symbolically named constants are available as static properties so you can test during script execution in a convenient manner.

```
if (event.eventPhase == event.AT_TARGET)
{
    ... some code ...
}
```

DOM suggests that the value is numeric according to these rules:

Value	Phase
1	CAPTURING_PHASE
2	AT_TARGET
3	BUBBLING_PHASE

Internet Explorer Key Code Modifier Masks

These are symbolic names for the bit-mask value in the property. They are available as constants from the `Event` object and are accessible as static properties of the current event object:

```
myMask = myEvent.ALT_MASK;
```

They can be used to mask out values against the `keyCode` property of the IE Event object like this:

```
myAltKey = myEvent.keyCode & Event.ALT_KEY;
```

Bit	Constant	Event type
2^0	ALT_MASK	The *Alt* key was held down while key was pressed
2^1	CONTROL_MASK	The *Ctrl* key was held down while key was pressed
2^2	SHIFT_MASK	The *shift* key was held down while key was pressed
2^3	META_MASK	The *meta* key was held down while key was pressed

Data Transfer reason Property

The reason property indicates data transfer success or failure with the following values:

Value	Meaning
0	The transfer was successful
1	The transfer was aborted prematurely
2	Some kind of error occurred during the transfer

Button Property – which

The which property indicates a button value with the following result codes:

Value	Meaning
1	The left button
2	The right button in a two button mouse
2	The middle button in a three button mouse
3	The right button in a three button mouse

Constants

These constants are defined as properties belonging to the Event class object. This means that they are statically defined. Some additional constants are defined in the DOM Level 3 extension table at the end of this appendix.

Name	Description	JavaScript	JScript	DOM Level
ABORT	A Netscape-defined symbolic name for the event triggered when a script execution is aborted with the stop() method.	1.2	X	X
ADDITION	A DOM-specified symbolic name for a mutation event type. The value can be tested against the contents of the attrChange property.	1.5	X	2
AT_TARGET	A DOM-specified constant that represents the at-target phase. You can compare for equality between this property and the eventPhase property to determine the current phase of the event in a DOM implementation. This indicates that the event has completed its capture phase and is about to return upwards on its bubbling phase.	1.5		2
BLUR	A Netscape-defined symbolic name for the event triggered when an element loses input focus.	1.2	X	X

Table continued on following page

Name	Description	JavaScript	JScript	DOM Level
BUBBLING_PHASE	A DOM-specified constant that represents the bubbling phase. You can compare for equality between this property and the eventPhase property to determine the current phase of the event in a DOM implementation.	1.5	X	2
CAPTURING_PHASE	A DOM-specified constant that represents the capturing phase. You can compare for equality between this property and the eventPhase property to determine the current phase of the event in a DOM implementation. During this phase, the event is still traveling down the DOM structure and has not yet reached the target.	1.5	X	2
CHANGE	A Netscape-defined symbolic name for the event triggered when an item in a select popup is changed.	1.2	X	X
CLICK	A Netscape-defined symbolic name for the event type representing a mouse button down and up event pair.	1.2	X	X
DBLCLICK	A Netscape-defined symbolic name for the event type representing a pair of mouse click events in close temporal proximity.	1.2	X	X
DRAGDROP	A Netscape-defined symbolic name for the event type triggered when some content is dragged and dropped onto the window.	1.2	X	X
ERROR	A Netscape-defined symbolic name for the event triggered by a script error.	1.2	X	X
FOCUS	A Netscape-defined symbolic name for the event triggered when an element receives input focus.	1.2	X	X
KEYDOWN	A Netscape-defined symbolic name for the event type representing a key down interaction.	1.2	X	X
KEYPRESS	A Netscape-defined symbolic name for the event type representing a key down and up event pair.	1.2	X	X
KEYUP	A Netscape-defined symbolic name for the event type representing a key release.	1.2	X	X
LOAD	A Netscape-defined symbolic name for the event triggered when an element or page has completed loading.	1.2	X	X

Name	Description	JavaScript	JScript	DOM Level
MODIFICATION	A DOM-specified symbolic name for a mutation event type. The value can be tested against the contents of the `attrChange` property.	1.5	X	2
MOUSEDOWN	A Netscape-defined symbolic name for the event type representing a mouse button click down interaction.	1.2	X	X
MOUSEMOVE	A Netscape-defined symbolic name for the event type representing a mouse position move.	1.2	X	X
MOUSEOUT	A Netscape-defined symbolic name for the event type representing a mouse pointer rolling out of an element.	1.2	X	X
MOUSEOVER	A Netscape-defined symbolic name for the event type representing a mouse pointer rolling over an element.	1.2	X	X
MOUSEUP	A Netscape-defined symbolic name for the event type representing a mouse button release.	1.2	X	X
MOVE	A Netscape-defined symbolic name for the event triggered when the window is moved.	1.2	X	X
REMOVAL	A DOM-specified symbolic name for a mutation event type. The value can be tested against the contents of the `attrChange` property.	1.5	X	2
RESET	A Netscape-defined symbolic name for the event triggered when form data is reset.	1.2	X	X
RESIZE	A Netscape-defined symbolic name for the event triggered when the window is resized.	1.2	X	X
SELECT	A Netscape-defined symbolic name for the event type triggered when a block of text is selected.	1.2	X	X
SUBMIT	A Netscape-defined symbolic name for the event triggered when form data is submitted.	1.2	X	X
UNLOAD	A Netscape-defined symbolic name for the event when a page is about to be discarded before loading another.	1.2	X	X

Netscape Event Types

These event type masks are used by Netscape prior to version 6 when determining the value in the type property of the incoming event object. The constant name defines a static property name belonging to the event object, which you can use in a symbolic manner from script to compare the event type values.

```
if (event.type == event.MOUSEDOWN)
{
   ... some code ...
}
```

Bit	Constant	Event type
2^0	MOUSEDOWN	The mouse button was pressed while the pointer was over the element
2^1	MOUSEUP	The mouse button was released while the pointer was within the extent region of the element
2^2	MOUSEOVER	The mouse has just moved over the extent region of the element
2^3	MOUSEOUT	The mouse has just moved out of the extent region of the element
2^4	MOUSEMOVE	The mouse was moved within the extent region of the element
2^5	undefined	Reserved for future use
2^6	CLICK	The element has been clicked on
2^7	DBLCLICK	The element has been double-clicked on
2^8	KEYDOWN	A key was pressed while the element had focus
2^9	KEYUP	A key was released while the element had focus
2^10	KEYPRESS	A key was pressed and released again while the element had focus
2^11	DRAGDROP	Some entity has been dragged over and dropped onto the element
2^12	FOCUS	The element has had input focus restored to it
2^13	BLUR	Window or input element has lost input focus
2^14	SELECT	An item in a pop-up menu was selected
2^15	CHANGE	The input element's value has changed
2^16	RESET	The [RESET] button within a <FORM> was clicked.
2^17	SUBMIT	The [SUBMIT] button within a <FORM> was clicked.
2^18	undefined	Reserved for future use
2^19	LOAD	An element (usually a <BODY> or <IMG>) has completed loading.
2^20	UNLOAD	The element (usually a <BODY>) is about to be unloaded.
2^21	undefined	Reserved for future use
2^22	ABORT	Image loading was aborted
2^23	ERROR	A script error has occurred
2^24	undefined	Reserved for future use
2^25	MOVE	The element (usually a Window) was moved
2^26	RESIZE	The element (usually a Window) was resized
2^27	undefined	Reserved for future use
2^28	undefined	Reserved for future use

Bit	Constant	Event type
2^29	undefined	Reserved for future use
2^30	undefined	Reserved for future use
2^31	undefined	Reserved for future use

Methods

Name	Description	JavaScript	JScript	DOM Level
getModifier (query)	DOM Level 3 introduces this means of querying whether a modifier key was pressed while the keystroke event was being generated. The valid keys for this query are signified in the table of virtual key codes listed at the end of this appendix.	X	X	3
initEvent (type, bubb, cancl)	An Event object initializer that must be called before dispatching the event object to an EventTarget. The type value indicates the event type, and it is specified as a string. The bubb and cancl arguments are flags that indicate whether the event will be allowed to bubble, and whether it can be canceled prematurely.	1.5		2
initKeyEvent (type, bubb, cancl, view, detail, output, keyVal, virtKey, input, numPad)	A KeyEvent object initializer that must be called before dispatching the event object to an EventTarget. The initUIEvent parameters are augmented with arguments that correspond to all the additional properties that a DOM Level 3 KeyEvent supports.	X	X	3
initMouseEvent (type, bubb, cancl, view, detail, screenX, screenY, clientX, clientY, ctrlKey, altKey, shiftKey, metaKey, button, relTarget)	A MouseEvent object initializer that must be called before dispatching the event object to an EventTarget. The initUIEvent parameters are augmented with arguments that correspond to all the additional properties that a MouseEvent supports.	1.5	X	2
initMutation Event(type, bubb, cancl, relNode, prevVal, newVal, attrName)	A MutationEvent object initializer that must be called before dispatching the event object to an EventTarget. The initEvent parameters are augmented by values that define the special MutationEvent properties.	1.5	X	2

Table continued on following page

Name	Description	JavaScript	JScript	DOM Level
initUIEvent (type, bubb, cancl, view, detail)	A UIEvent object initializer that must be called before dispatching the event object to an EventTarget. The initEvent parameters are augmented with a view parameter and a detail value. The view parameter is part of the DOM abstract viewing facility and the detail parameter is implementation-specific.	1.5	X	2
preventDefault()	A means of preventing the default behavior from being activated after the event returns to its dispatcher.	1.5	X	2
stopPropagation()	Prevents propagation of event handling via bubbling or capture techniques.	1.5	X	2

DOM Event Target Object Extensions

DOM event listeners can be attached to various other classes of objects. We shall discuss here only those properties and methods that enhance the API of these other classes. This is supported by Netscape version 6 and is expected to be available in the next major release of Internet Explorer.

Construction

There is actually no EventTarget class as such. An abstraction could be considered as a component of multiple inheritances for objects that support events. Objects that inherit this capability are likely to already be sub-classes from the Node object class within the overall DOM structure.

Properties

There are no additional properties for EventTarget enhanced objects.

Methods

Name	Description	JavaScript	JScript	DOM Level
addEvent Listener (type, func, flag)	The type parameter is a string primitive containing an event type name. The func parameter is an EventListener function (a.k.a. event handler) while the flag parameter is an indication of whether capture or bubbling event handling is to be used.	1.5	X	2
removeEvent Listener (type, func, flag)	The same parameter values that were used in the addEventListener() method must be used since they form a compound key to locate the relevant listener to be removed.	1.5	X	2
dispatchEvent (event)	Triggers an event under script control. You can manufacture your own event objects to be passed to this method.	1.5	X	2

DOM Extension to the Document Object

The DOM standard adds the `createEvent(type)` method to the `document` object. This allows the script developer to create a new event object and then dispatch it so that events can be triggered under script control. The following illustrates the use of a custom event. The sequence of operation is illustrated here with a fragment of pseudo-code.

```
//1. Define the handler
function myhandler(anEvent)
{
    alert("An attention event happened");
}

// 2. Locate the target
myTarget = some object in the document;

// 3. Attach the handler
myTarget.addEventListener("attention", myHandler, true);

// 4. Create your event object
myEvent = document.createEvent("attention");

// 5. Initialize the event object or an exception will be thrown
myEvent.initEvent("attention", true, true);

// 6. Dispatch the object to the target or one of its parents
myTarget.dispatchEvent(myEvent);
```

Note that these fragments of code need not necessarily reside in the same script block but they should be executed in this sequence otherwise the event will not be handled properly.

DOM Level 3 Key Event Additions

The DOM Level 3 event module is primarily concerned with adding more sophisticated keyboard event support.

Properties

The following properties are added at DOM Level 3 for the `KeyEvent` object, which is sub-classed from the `UIEvent` object:

- ❑ `outputString`
- ❑ `keyVal`
- ❑ `virKeyVal`
- ❑ `inputGenerated`
- ❑ `numPad`

Methods

The following properties are added at DOM Level 3 for the `KeyEvent` object, which is sub-classed from the `UIEvent` object:

- ❑ `getModifier()`
- ❑ `initKeyEvent()`

Constants

Many new constants have been defined to identify the keys being pressed. These are summarized in a table below and are defined as symbolically named static constants of the event object.

Virtual Key Codes

These represent virtual key codes and are not the physical key codes generated by the keyboard.

Symbolic name	Value	Description
DOM_VK_UNDEFINED	0x0000	No defined key type
DOM_VK_RIGHT_ALT	0x0012	Modifier key
DOM_VK_LEFT_ALT	0x0012	Modifier key
DOM_VK_LEFT_CONTROL	0x0011	Modifier key
DOM_VK_RIGHT_CONTROL	0x0011	Modifier key
DOM_VK_LEFT_SHIFT	0x0010	Modifier key
DOM_VK_RIGHT_SHIFT	0x0010	Modifier key
DOM_VK_META	0x009D	Modifier key
DOM_VK_BACK_SPACE	0x0008	Cursor move key
DOM_VK_CAPS_LOCK	0x0014	Modifier key
DOM_VK_DELETE	0x007F	Edit key
DOM_VK_END	0x0023	Cursor move key
DOM_VK_ENTER	0x000D	Edit key
DOM_VK_ESCAPE	0x001B	Edit key
DOM_VK_HOME	0x0024	Cursor move key
DOM_VK_NUM_LOCK	0x0090	Modifier key
DOM_VK_PAUSE	0x0013	Action key
DOM_VK_PRINTSCREEN	0x009A	Action key
DOM_VK_SCROLL_LOCK	0x0091	Action key
DOM_VK_SPACE	0x0020	Edit key
DOM_VK_TAB	0x0009	Edit key
DOM_VK_LEFT	0x0025	Cursor move key
DOM_VK_RIGHT	0x0027	Cursor move key
DOM_VK_UP	0x0026	Cursor move key
DOM_VK_DOWN	0x0028	Cursor move key
DOM_VK_PAGE_DOWN	0x0022	Cursor move key

Symbolic name	Value	Description
DOM_VK_PAGE_UP	0x0021	Cursor move key
DOM_VK_F1	0x0070	Function key
DOM_VK_F2	0x0071	Function key
DOM_VK_F3	0x0072	Function key
DOM_VK_F4	0x0073	Function key
DOM_VK_F5	0x0074	Function key
DOM_VK_F6	0x0075	Function key
DOM_VK_F7	0x0076	Function key
DOM_VK_F8	0x0077	Function key
DOM_VK_F9	0x0078	Function key
DOM_VK_F10	0x0079	Function key
DOM_VK_F11	0x007A	Function key
DOM_VK_F12	0x007B	Function key
DOM_VK_F13	0xF000	Function key
DOM_VK_F14	0xF001	Function key
DOM_VK_F15	0xF002	Function key
DOM_VK_F16	0xF003	Function key
DOM_VK_F17	0xF004	Function key
DOM_VK_F18	0xF005	Function key
DOM_VK_F19	0xF006	Function key
DOM_VK_F20	0xF007	Function key
DOM_VK_F21	0xF008	Function key
DOM_VK_F22	0xF009	Function key
DOM_VK_F23	0xF00A	Function key
DOM_VK_F24	0xF00B	Function key

Further support is being added in DOM Level 3 for event groups. This is not yet implemented in any browser and it may change somewhat before the standard is ratified completely. Therefore, we mention it here but adding any detailed coverage would be premature.

Pro JavaScript 2nd Edition

CSS Reference

Some of the CSS 3 additions are already implemented in Internet Explorer and we can see this where there is an apparently IE -specific feature not yet implemented in Netscape 6. At least working through the standards process ensures that ultimately the features will be supported in a portable way, but Internet Explorer still gains the advantage by implementing them while the standard is not yet ratified.

Further details about CSS 3 can be found at http://www.w3c.org/Style/CSS/current-work. In fact, many of the following explanations are almost direct copies of what can be found in the CSS tables at the W3C.

Objects

Here, we list the various objects we can manipulate that relate to CSS

The style Object

The following table lists all the properties found by inspecting style objects in Internet Explorer and Netscape 6. In addition, the properties described in the CSS 1 and CSS 2 standards documents have been noted. Information from the CSS 3 Working Group papers has also been added to show the likely additional properties that would be added if the CSS 3 standard were to be ratified according to the current state of the documentation. This, however, is likely to change – although probably only in minor details.

These properties represent the available CSS controls that can be placed in a rule and associated with a selector. We have not documented new CSS 3 selectors, pseudo-elements, or other values, as these are more likely to change and are not so much part of the JavaScript visible interface to a style object.

The CSS 2 standard refers to this as a CSS2Properties object, although the browsers merge in the properties that are classified as belonging to the CSSStyleDeclaration class as well.

Style Property	Description	Internet Explorer	Netscape	CSS
alignment Adjust	Precise alignment of inline level element. See the CSS 3 text module.	No	No	3
alignment Baseline	Alignment of an inline level element with respect to its parent. See the CSS 3 text module.	No	No	3
azimuth	Aural stylesheet property, not supported in any standard browser. Maybe supported in a speech browser in the future.	No	Yes	2
background	Shorthand property to set backgroundImage, backgroundColor, backgroundAttachment, backgroundPosition, backgroundRepeat.	Yes	Yes	1
background Attachment	If backgroundImage is specified, backgroundAttachment specifies whether the image is fixed in the view port of the document, or is scrolled with the document.	Yes	Yes	1
background Color	Specifies the background color. Default value of transparent lets the background of the parent element shine through.	Yes	Yes	1
background Image	Specifies a backgroundImage that is placed depending on backgroundPosition and repeated depending on backgroundRepeat.	Yes	Yes	1
background Position	Specifies the position of the backgroundImage, for instance: style.backgroundPosition = 'center bottom' to have the image center horizontally and put at the bottom vertically.	Yes	Yes	1
background PositionX	Specifies the horizontal position of the backgroundImage.	Yes	No	
background PositionY	Specifies the vertical position of the backgroundImage.	Yes	No	
background Repeat	Specifies whether the backgroudImage is not repeated, or is repeated horizontally and/or vertically.	Yes	Yes	1
baselineShift	Allows for super or subscript baseline shifting of inline level elements. See the CSS 3 text module.	No	No	3
behavior	Links the element with an HTC (HTML component), which encapsulates dynamic behavior (such as onMouseover/out) for the element.	5+	No	3
border	Shorthand property to set borderColor, borderWidth, and borderStyle.	Yes	Yes	1

Style Property	Description	Internet Explorer	Netscape	CSS
borderBottom	Shorthand property to set the color, width, and style of the bottom border.	Yes	Yes	1
borderBottom Color	Specifies the bottom border color.	Yes	Yes	2
borderBottom Style	Specifies the style of the bottom border; for example solid, dotted, dashed.	Yes	Yes	2
borderBottom Width	Specifies the width of the bottom border.	Yes	Yes	1
border Collapse	Applies to table elements – specifies a table's border model. See the CSS 2 specs for details.	Yes	Yes	2
borderColor	Shorthand property to set the borderTopColor, borderRightColor, borderBottomColor, and borderLeftColor.	Yes	Yes	1
borderInside	Applies to table elements, specifies a table's border model. See the CSS2 specs for details.	No	No	3
borderInside Color	Applies to table elements, specifies a table's border model. See the CSS2 specs for details.	No	No	3
borderInside Style	Applies to table elements, specifies a table's border model. See the CSS2 specs for details.	No	No	3
borderInside Width	Applies to table elements, specifies a table's border model. See the CSS2 specs for details.	No	No	3
borderLeft	Shorthand property to define borderLeftColor, borderLeftStyle, and borderLeftWidth.	Yes	Yes	1
borderLeft Color	Specifies the color of the left border.	Yes	Yes	2
borderLeft Style	Specifies the style of the left border, for example solid, dashed, dotted.	Yes	Yes	2
borderLeft Width	Specifies the width of the left border.	Yes	Yes	1
borderRight	Shorthand property for setting borderRightColor, borderRightStyle, and borderRightWidth.	Yes	Yes	1
borderRight Color	Sets the color of the right border.	Yes	Yes	2
borderRight Style	Sets the style of the right border.	Yes	Yes	2

Table continued on following page

Style Property	Description	Internet Explorer	Netscape	CSS
borderRight Width	Sets the width of the right border.	Yes	Yes	1
borderSpacing	For table with borderCollapse set to separate, this sets the spacing between table cell borders.	Yes	Yes	2
borderStyle	Shorthand property for setting borderTopStyle, borderRightStyle, borderBottomStyle, and borderLeftStyle.	Yes	Yes	1
borderTop	Shorthand property for setting borderTopColor, borderTopStyle, and borderTopWidth.	Yes	Yes	1
borderTop Color	Sets the color of the top border.	Yes	Yes	2
borderTop Style	Sets the style of the top border.	Yes	Yes	2
borderTop Width	Sets the width of the top border.	Yes	Yes	1
borderWidth	Shorthand property for setting borderTopWidth, borderRightWidth, borderBottomWidth, and borderLeftWidth.	Yes	Yes	1
bottom	For positioned elements sets the position of the bottom edge relative to the bottom edge of the containing element.	Yes	Yes	2
boxSizing	Specifies whether width/height determine the content box or the border box. With CSS 1 and CSS 2, width/height determine the content box, while with IE 4/5/5.5 on the Mac, the border box is determined. This isn't supported on IE for Windows.	Yes	No	3
captionSide	Sets the position of a table caption elements in relation to the table; for example at the top or bottom or left or right of the table.	Yes	Yes	2
clear	Specifies which side of a block-level element may not be adjacent to an earlier floating box.	Yes	Yes	1
clip	Sets the clipping region of a block-level element to a rectangular shape (with CSS 2).	Yes	Yes	2
color	Sets the text color.	Yes	Yes	1

Style Property	Description	Internet Explorer	Netscape	CSS
colorProfile	Some file formats contain embedded color profiles. This property tells you whether this is the case for the supplied image. IE 5/5.5 on Windows does not support this.	Yes	No	3
columnGap	The percentage gap between groups of columns, in a multi-column document. If there is a column rule between columns, then half the gap will appear on each side of the rule.	No	No	3
columnNumber	Specifies the number of columns in a multi-column document.	No	No	3
columnRule	This is a shortcut for columnRuleColor, columnRuleStyle, and columnRuleWidth.	No	No	3
columnRule Color	Sets the color of the rule/bar between columns.	No	No	3
columnRule Style	Sets the style of the rule/bar between columns – for example dashed	No	No	3
columnRule Width	Sets the width of the rule/bar between columns.	No	No	3
columns	Reference to all the column elements in a style sheet.	No	No	3
columnSpan	Allows us to specify that an elements spans two or more columns.	No	No	3
columnWidth	Specifies the optimum width of the column.	No	No	3
content	Used together with the :before and :after pseudo-elements to specify content inserted.	Yes	Yes	2
counterIncrement	Allows us to specify a counter and its increment.	Yes	Yes	2
counterReset	Resets the specified counter.	Yes	Yes	2
cssFloat	The corresponding CSS property is called float. As that is a reserved word in many programming languages, this property is according to DOM Level 2, which Netscape 6 implements scripted as cssFloat. IE 4+ on Windows implements it as styleFloat.	Yes	No	2
cssText	Read-only property that reflects the complete style declaration.	Yes	No	2
cue	Shortcut for cueAfter, and cueBefore. These elements only make sense in an aural browser.	No	Yes	2

Table continued on following page

Style Property	Description	Internet Explorer	Netscape	CSS
cueAfter	Indicates a sound file to play after an element has been rendered/spoken.	No	Yes	2
cueBefore	Indicates a sound file to play before an element has been rendered/spoken.	No	Yes	2
cursor	Sets the cursor on an element, for instance style.cursor = 'pointer', to have a hand. Note that IE 4/5/5.5 on Windows uses hand instead of pointer and is therefore not CSS-compliant.	Yes	Yes	2
direction	Specifies the writing direction, ltr for left to right or rtl for right to left.	Yes	Yes	2
display	Sets the display of an element to none, block, inline, or other value. For scripters, it is important to build collapsible lists by toggling style.display from none to ''.	Yes	Yes	1
dominant Baseline	See CSS 3 text module. Specifies the baseline for fonts. In Latin fonts, it is generally the bottom of the character, whereas in others, the tops of the characters might all be lined up instead.	No	No	3
elevation	Like the azimuth property, this is used to specify the spatial properties of some sound.	No	Yes	2
emptyCells	Specifies whether empty table cells are rendered or not. IE on Windows does not support this.	Yes	Yes	2
float	Use cssFloat instead.	No	No	1
styleFloat	It is the IE 4+ on Windows way to script the CSS property float.	Yes	No	
font	Shorthand property to set fontSize, fontStyle, fontFamily, and fontWeight.	Yes	Yes	1
fontFamily	Uses a comma-separated list of font names to specify the font to use. The first font in the list that is supported on the current system is used by the user agent.	Yes	Yes	1
fontSize	Sets the font size in pt or px or other units; for example style.fontSize = '12pt'.	Yes	Yes	1
fontSize Adjust	Allows us to adjust the aspect ratio of a replacement font. See the CSS 2 specs for details.	Yes	Yes	2
fontStretch	Selects a normal, condensed, or extended face from a font family.	Yes	Yes	2

Style Property	Description	Internet Explorer	Netscape	CSS
fontStyle	Sets a normal, italic, or oblique style of a font.	Yes	Yes	1
fontVariant	Sets normal or small-caps variant of a font.	Yes	Yes	1
fontWeight	Sets the font weight; how bold a font is to be rendered.	Yes	Yes	1
glyphOrientation Horizontal	Allows us to set the horizontal direction of a specific piece of text, relative to the primary text advance direction.	No	No	3
glyphOrientation Vertical	Allows us to set the vertical direction of a specific piece of text, relative to the primary text advance direction.	No	No	3
height	Sets the height of the content box (with NN 6 or CSS1 /2-compliant browser) and the height of the border box of an element with IE 4/5/5.5 on Windows.	Yes	Yes	1
kerningMode	Sets any special space between letters. It can be set to pair, where any letters that are paired together are given less space, or contextual, where spacing depends on context.	No	No	3
kerningPair Threshold	Sets the font size threshold with which kerning would be applied.	No	No	3
layoutGrid	A shortcut for the layoutGridChar, layoutGridLine, layoutGridMode, and layoutGridType properties. They are used in glyph tendering.	No	No	3
layoutGrid Char	Sets the horizontal grid size/width.	No	No	3
layoutGrid Line	Sets the vertical grid size/height.	No	No	3
layoutGrid Mode	Enables or disables the 2 dimensions of the grid.	No	No	3
layoutGrid Type	Specifies the type of grid: loose, strict, or fixed.	No	No	3
left	Sets the left coordinate of a positioned element relative to its parent.	Yes	Yes	2
length	Not a CSS property but a read-only property of the style object that gives the number of property: value declarations, for example <div style="color: green;" onClick="alert (this.style.length)"> shows 1 when clicked.	No	Yes	2
letterSpacing	Specifies the spacing behavior between words.	Yes	Yes	1

Table continued on following page

Style Property	Description	Internet Explorer	Netscape	CSS
lineBreak	Sets normal or strict line-break mode. Not supported yet in IE on the Mac.	Yes	No	3
lineHeight	Sets the height of inline elements.	Yes	Yes	1
listStyle	Shorthand property to set listStyleImage, listStylePosition, and listStyleType.	Yes	Yes	1
listStyle Image	Sets the list style image for list elements, that is an image replacing the usual bullet.	Yes	Yes	1
listStyle Position	Sets whether the list item marker is placed inside or outside the list item text box.	Yes	Yes	1
listStyleType	Sets the list style type for example disc, circle, square for unordered lists or decimal, lower-roman, lower-latin etc. for ordered lists.	Yes	Yes	1
margin	Shorthand property to set the marginTop, marginRight, marginBottom, and marginRight.	Yes	Yes	1
marginBottom	Sets the bottom margin.	Yes	Yes	1
marginInside	Alias for margin-left or margin-right, depending on the print medium. On this page, it would be margin-right, whereas on the facing page it would be margin-left.	No	No	3
marginLeft	Sets the left margin.	Yes	Yes	1
marginRight	Sets the right margin.	Yes	Yes	1
marginTop	Sets the top margin.	Yes	Yes	1
markerOffset	For marker elements, such as list counters, this sets the offset between the marker and the list item box.	Yes	Yes	2
marks	Sets crop or cross marks for printing only.	Yes	Yes	2
maxFontSize	If textAlignLast is size, then the fonts on the last line cannot be larger than the larger of fontSize and maxFontSize.	No	No	3
maxHeight	Sets a maximum height on an element.	Yes	Yes	2
maxWidth	Sets the minimum width on an element.	Yes	Yes	2
minFontSize	If textAlignLast is size, then the fonts on the last line cannot be smaller than the smaller of fontSize and minFontSize.	No	No	3
minHeight	Sets the minimum width on an element.	Yes	Yes	2

Style Property	Description	Internet Explorer	Netscape	CSS
minWidth	Sets the minimum width on an element.	Yes	Yes	2
MozBinding	Allows us to bind some content or behavior to an element. See http://www.mozilla.org/projects/xbl/xbl.html for details.	No	Yes	
MozOpacity	Sets the opacity of an element until the CSS 3 opacity property is implemented.	No	Yes	
opacity	Sets the opacity of an element.	No	No	3
orphans	Sets the minimum number of lines that must be left at the end of a paragraph when breaking the page. Not supported by IE on Windows.	Yes	Yes	2
outline	Shorthand property to set the outlineColor, outlineStyle, and outlineWidth. An outline is different from a border in not taking up layout space and in not necessarily being rectangular. These properties only appear to be available on the Mac.	Yes	Yes	2
outlineColor	Sets the color of the outline there is no way to set the color of individual sides of the outline – for example there is not outlineLeftColor, outlineTopColor etc.	Yes	Yes	2
outlineStyle	Sets the style of the outline.	Yes	Yes	2
outlineWidth	Sets the width of the outline.	Yes	Yes	2
overflow	Sets whether/how content is rendered that overflows the dimensions specified by width/height. Such content can be hidden or shown or scrollbars can be introduced to make it accessible.	Yes	Yes	2
padding	Shorthand property to set the paddingTop, paddingRight, paddingBottom, and paddingLeft. Padding sets the space between the border and the content.	Yes	Yes	1
paddingBottom	Sets the bottom padding.	Yes	Yes	1
paddingInside	Alias for paddingLeft or paddingRight, depending on context. On this page, paddingInside would be aliased to paddingLeft, and on the opposite page, it would be aliased to paddingRight.	No	No	3
paddingLeft	Sets the left padding.	Yes	Yes	1
paddingRight	Sets the right padding.	Yes	Yes	1

Table continued on following page

Style Property	Description	Internet Explorer	Netscape	CSS
paddingTop	Sets the top padding.	Yes	Yes	1
page	Sets a particular page for an element to print on. Not supported by IE on Windows.	Yes	Yes	2
pageBreak After	Sets a page break policy for printing; for example page-break-after: always.	Yes	Yes	2
pageBreak Before	Sets a page break policy for printing; for example page-break-before: avoid.	Yes	Yes	2
pageBreak Inside	Sets a page break policy for printing; for example page-break-inside: avoid. Not supported in IE on Windows.	Yes	Yes	2
parentRule	This is not a CSS property but a read-only property of style objects in DOM Level 2-compliant browsers. It points to the rule this declaration is contained in or is null for inline declarations.	No	Yes	
pause	Shorthand setting for pauseAfter and pauseBefore.	No	Yes	2
pauseAfter	Sets the pause after a word.	No	Yes	2
pauseBefore	Sets the pause before a word.	No	Yes	2
pitch	Specifies the average pitch of the speaking voice in hertz (Hz).	No	Yes	2
pitchRange	Specifies the variation from the average pitch. A pitchRange of 50% produces normal inflection.	No	Yes	2
pixelBottom	This and the following five functions are used to manipulate values using pixel values instead. It means we can write this.style.pixelLeft +=10;, instead of: this.style.left = (parseInt(this.style.left)+10) + "px";, for instance.	Yes	No	
pixelHeight	See pixelBottom above.	Yes	No	
pixelLeft	See pixelBottom above.	Yes	No	
pixelRight	See pixelBottom above.	Yes	No	
pixelTop	See pixelBottom above.	Yes	No	
pixelWidth	See pixelBottom above.	Yes	No	
playDuring	Indicates a sound to be played during speech.	No	Yes	2

Style Property	Description	Internet Explorer	Netscape	CSS
posBottom	This and the following properties are provided by IE to manipulate the positioning using the units already specified. For instance, if a `style='position: absolute, bottom 5cm'` attribute has been used, then using `style.posBottom+=5` would set the bottom position at 10cm.	Yes	No	
posHeight	See `posBottom`, above.	Yes	No	
position	Sets the position of an element to `static`, `absolute`, `relative`, or fixed.	Yes	Yes	2
posLeft	See `posBottom`, above.	Yes	No	
posRight	See `posBottom`, above.	Yes	No	
posTop	See `posBottom`, above.	Yes	No	
posWidth	See `posBottom`, above.	Yes	No	
punctuation Trim	Whether or not to trim punctuation at the start of the line so that it lines up with the starting characters on the lines before and after. If not trimmed, then the following characters line up with the characters above and below.	No	No	3
punctuation Wrap	Specifies whether punctuation is allowed in the margin area. Common in East Asian typography.	No	No	3
quotes	Sets the quote characters. Not supported by IE 5 on Windows.	Yes	Yes	2
richness	Specifies the richness, or brightness, of a voice.	No	Yes	2
right	Sets the right coordinate of a positioned element.	Yes	Yes	2
rubyAlign	These three set the `alignment`, overhang, and `position` of so-called ruby elements, which are annotational elements mostly used with Asiatic languages.	Yes	No	3
rubyOverhang	See `rubyAlign`, above.	Yes	No	3
rubyPosition	See `rubyAlign`, above.	Yes	No	3
script	Allows inline scripts within style sheets.	No	No	3
size	Only used in @page rules to set the relative or absolute page size for printing.	No	Yes	2
speak	Specifies if the text will be spoken.	No	Yes	2
speakHeader	Specifies if table headers are spoken before every cell.	No	Yes	2

Table continued on following page

Style Property	Description	Internet Explorer	Netscape	CSS
speakNumeral	Specifies if the individual numerals of a number are to be spoken, or if the number is spoken 'properly'.	No	Yes	2
speak Punctuation	Specifies how punctuation is spoken. Whether it is spoken literally, or whether the correct pauses are inserted into the speech instead.	No	Yes	2
speechRate	Specifies the speech rate or speed.	No	Yes	2
stress	Specifies how high certain peaks intonation are in speech.	No	Yes	2
styleFloat	The CSS property float is scriptable in IE on Windows as styleFloat.	Yes	No	
tabIndex	Replacement for the HTML 4 TABINDEX attribute.	No	No	3
tableLayout	Sets the table layout algorithm to fixed or automatic. Fixed is faster but requires width of table/table columns to be set.	Yes	Yes	2
textAlignLast	Specifies how the last line is aligned.	No	No	3
textCombine	Controls the creation of composite characters.	No	No	3
textJustify	Specifies the type of justification if text-align-justify is specified.	No	No	3
textJustify Trim	This sets the individual font blank space compression permissions for the text justification algorithm.	No	No	3
textKashida Space	Kashida is a typographic effect used in Arabic writing systems that allows character elongation at some carefully chosen points in Arabic.	No	No	3
textOverflow	Text overflow deals with the situation where some textual content is clipped.	No	No	3
textOverflow Ellipsis	Text overflow deals with the situation where some textual content is clipped.	No	No	3
textOverflow Mode	Text overflow deals with the situation where some textual content is clipped.	No	No	3
textOverline	Shortcut for the following three properties.	No	No	3
textOverline Color	The color of the over line.	No	No	3
textOverline Mode	Specifies whether the over line appears over just words or over words and whitespace.	No	No	3

Style Property	Description	Internet Explorer	Netscape	CSS
textOverline Style	Possible values are: none, solid, double, dotted, thick, dashed, dot-dash, dot-dot-dash, wave.	No	No	3
textSpace	Specifies whether whitespace is collapsed.	No	No	3
textUnderline	Shortcut for the following three properties.	No	No	3
textUnderline Color	Specifies the color of the underline.	No	No	3
textUnderline Mode	Specifies whether the underline appears only under words or under words and whitespace.	No	No	3
textUnderline Position	Possible values are before, or after.	No	No	3
textUnderline Style	Possible values are: none, solid, double, dotted, thick, dashed, dot-dash, dot-dot-dash, wave.	No	No	3
textWrap	Specifies whether text is wrapped when it reaches the flow edge of its containing block box.	No	No	3
textAlign	Sets the text alignment on block level-elements.	Yes	Yes	1
textDecoration	Shortcut to set textDecorationBlink, textDecorationLineThrough, textDecorationNone, textDecorationOverline, and textDecorationUnderline.	Yes	Yes	1
textDecoration Blink	IE provides individual Boolean properties to check or set the individual decorations. Note however that IE 5/5.5 on Windows doesn't render any blinking, whether this property is true or false.	Yes	No	
textDecoration LineThrough	Boolean property to check/set the line-through decoration.	Yes	No	
textDecoration None	Boolean property to check/set no decoration.	Yes	No	
textDecoration Overline	Boolean property to check/set over line decoration.	Yes	No	
textDecoration Underline	Boolean property to check/set the underline decoration.	Yes	No	
textIndent	Sets the indentation of the first line of a block level element.	Yes	Yes	1

Table continued on following page

Style Property	Description	Internet Explorer	Netscape	CSS
textJustify	If textAlign is set to justify, this allows us to set various modes of justification for non-western languages.	Yes	No	
textShadow	This CSS 2 property allows for shadow effects on text. It is however not supported in Netscape 6 or in IE 5/5.5 on Windows. However, with IE on Windows you can achieve such effects with filters.	No	No	2
textTransform	Sets text transformation like capitalize, uppercase, lowercase.	Yes	Yes	1
top	Sets top coordinate of a positioned element relative to its parent.	Yes	Yes	2
unicodeBidi	Sets, together with direction, the bi-directional layout of text.	Yes	Yes	2
verticalAlign	Sets vertical alignment of inline level and of table cell elements.	Yes	Yes	1
visibility	Sets the visibility of an element.	Yes	Yes	2
voiceFamily	Compare with font-family. Possible generic values are male, female, or child. Otherwise, specific voiceFamily names may be specified.	No	Yes	2
volume	Sets the volume of the speech used.	No	Yes	2
whiteSpace	Sets how whitespace in the element is handled.	Yes	Yes	1
widows	Sets the minimum number of lines that have to be left at the top of a page when breaking the page for printing.	Yes	Yes	2
width	In a CSS 1/2-compliant browser this sets the width of the content box of an element. With IE 4/5/5.5 on Windows, this sets the width of the border box of an element.	Yes	Yes	1
wordBreak	This property controls line-breaking behavior inside of words.	No	No	3
wordBreakCJK	See wordBreak, above.	No	No	3
wordBreak Inside	See wordBreak, above.	No	No	3
wordBreakWrap	See wordBreak, above.	No	No	3
wordSpacing	This sets any additional spacing between words.	IE 6	Yes	1
zIndex	Sets the stacking order of elements on the z-axis.	Yes	Yes	2

The CSSStyleSheet Object

This table summarizes the properties and methods belonging to a CSSStyleSheet object. These are the standard properties only. While we might exploit non-standard properties that belong to a style object quite effectively, exploiting non-standard properties of a CSSStyleSheet will likely lead to more problems. In Internet Explorer, this object is instantiated as a member of the styleSheet class so we should be careful when using class names of objects in portable code. These names differ from browser to browser, so we have indicated their names below. These inconsistencies could be taken care of using a bit of code such as:

```
if (!myStyleSheet.cssRules)
{
    myStyleSheet.cssRules = myStyleSheet.rules;
}
```

DOM Name	Description	Type
cssRules	This property is known as rules in IE for Windows and it is a collection of all the style sheet rules	Property
deleteRule(anIndex)	This method removes a specific rule at anIndex	Method
disabled	This property, if set to true, prevents this style object from being implemented	Property
href	Sets/Returns the location of the style sheet	Property
insertRule(<aRule>, <anIndex>)	Inserts a new rule into the style sheet at anIndex	Method
media	Returns the destination media for the style sheet	Property
owningNode	Returns the node that associates this style sheet with the document	Property
parentStyleSheet	Returns the style sheet that included this one within it, if it exists	Property
title	Returns the advisory title	Property
type	Type of document (such as text/css)	Property

The CSSStyleRule Object

This is a sub-class of the CSSRule object although the two classes are not presented separately for you to instantiate individually.

Name	Description	Type
type	Returns the type of rule. The table defining the constants for the return value is below.	Property
cssText	The parseable textual representation of the rule.	Property

Table continued on following page

Name	Description	Type
parentStyleSheet	Returns the style sheet that included this one within it, if it exists.	Property
selectorText	The textual representation of the selector for the rule set.	Property
style	The declaration block of this rule set.	Property

Type of Style Sheet Rule Constants

Constant	Description	Value
UNKNOWN_RULE	The rule is a CSSUnknownRule	0
STYLE_RULE	The rule is a CSSStyleRule	1
IMPORT_RULE	The rule is a CSSImportRule	2
MEDIA_RULE	The rule is a CSSMediaRule	3
FONT_FACE_RULE	The rule is a CSSFontFaceRule	4
PAGE_RULE	The rule is a CSSPageRule	5

The CSSMediaRule Object

This is a sub-class of the CSSRule object although the two classes are not presented separately for you to instantiate individually.

Name	Description	Type
type	Returns the type of rule. The table defining the constants for the return value is above in *Type of Style Sheet Rule Constants*.	Property
cssText	The parseable textual representation of the rule.	Property
parentStyleSheet	Returns the style sheet that included this one within it, if it exists.	Property
mediaTypes	A comma, separated list of media types for this rule. These are: all; aural (speech); braille (Braille tactile devices); embossed (paged Braille printers); handheld (small screen, monochrome, limited bandwidth devices); print (printed documents); projection (projected presentations); screen (color computer screens); tty (teletypes and terminals – fixed width display); tv (television-type – low resolution, limited scroll ability, sound).	Property
cssRules	A list of all CSS rules contained within the media block. This is known as rules in IE for Windows.	Property

Name	Description	Type
insertRule(<aRule>, <anIndex>)	Used to insert a new rule in the media block.	Method
deleteRule(<anIndex>)	Used to delete a rule from the media block.	Method

The CSSFontFaceRule Object

This is a sub-class of the CSSRule object although the two classes are not presented separately for you to instantiate individually.

Name	Description	Type
type	Returns the type of rule. The table defining the constants for the return value is above in *Type of Style Sheet Rule Constants.*	Property
cssText	The parseable textual representation of the rule.	Property
parentStyleSheet	Returns the style sheet that included this one within it, if it exists.	Property
style	The declaration-block of this rule (the part within the { } brackets).	Property

The CSSPageRule Object

This is a sub-class of the CSSRule object although the two classes are not presented separately for you to instantiate individually.

Name	Description	Type
type	Returns the type of rule. The table defining the constants for the return value is above in *Type of Style Sheet Rule Constants.*	Property
cssText	The parseable textual representation of the rule.	Property
parentStyleSheet	Returns the style sheet that included this one within it, if it exists.	Property
selectorText	The parseable textual representation of the page selector for the rule.	Property
style	The declaration-block of this rule (the part within the { } brackets).	Property

The CSSImportRule Object

This is a sub-class of the CSSRule object although the two classes are not presented separately for you to instantiate individually.

Name	Description	Type
type	Returns the type of rule. The table defining the constants for the return value is above in *Type of Style Sheet Rule Constants*.	Property
cssText	The parseable textual representation of the rule.	Property
parentStyleSheet	Returns the style sheet that included this one within it, if it exists.	Property
href	The location of style sheet to be imported.	Property
media	A list of media types for which this style sheet may be used.	Property
styleSheet	The style sheet referred to by this rule, if it has been loaded.	Property

The CSSUnknownRule Object

This is a sub-class of the CSSRule object although the two classes are not presented separately for you to instantiate individually.

Name	Description	Type
type	Returns the type of rule. The table defining the constants for the return value is above in *Type of Style Sheet Rule Constants*.	Property
cssText	The parseable textual representation of the rule.	Property
parentStyleSheet	Returns the style sheet that included this one within it, if it exists.	Property

Measurement Units

#	A hash precedes hex color triplet values	
%	A percentage of the containing element's value	
cm	Absolute measure of a centimeter	
deg	A value used for angular positioning of sound sources	

em	A floating point value indicating a fractional portion of the length of an em-dash in the current font
ex	A floating-point value used to multiply the height of a small x in the current font
Hz	A frequency value for aural style sheets
in	Absolute measure of an inch
kHz	A frequency value for aural style sheets
mm	Absolute measure of a millimeter
ms	A value in milliseconds (used for aural style durations)
pc	Absolute measure of a pica
pi	Absolute measure of a pica (possibly a misprint in some documentation)
pt	Absolute measure using a font point size
px	An integer value measured in pixels on the screen
s	A value in seconds (used for aural style durations)

Pro JavaScript 2nd Edition

F

DOM Reference

In this appendix, we list the various methods and properties related to the DOM. Compliant browsers make these methods of the document object.

DOM Node Types

You can distinguish one kind of node from another by examining its nodeType property. At DOM level 2, the Node class object has a set of constant values defined that can be used to test the type of specific nodes within the document. There are a range of different kinds of nodes, some reflecting the content of an element and others the text between the tags. Here is a list of the currently defined node types and the constants belonging to the Node class object that correspond to them. These are defined in the DOM Level 2 core specification:

Type	Constant	Description
1	ELEMENT_NODE	A generic element within the document. HTMLElement objects may reflect this value even though they are a sub-class of the element node.
2	ATTRIBUTE_NODE	Attribute nodes are a means of describing HTML tag attributes in an object-oriented manner.
3	TEXT_NODE	Text nodes are that document content between elements.
4	CDATA_SECTION_NODE	CDATA section nodes are a special case of the text nodes.
5	ENTITY_REFERENCE_NODE	Entity reference nodes are part of the XML support.

Table continued on following page

Type	Constant	Description
6	ENTITY_NODE	Entity nodes represent XML entities parsed from the source document.
7	PROCESSING_INSTRUCTION_NODE	Processing instruction nodes contain information for processing the document in an XML context.
8	COMMENT_NODE	Comment nodes are a special case of the text node.
9	DOCUMENT_NODE	A Document node is the top-level node where the DOM tree begins its structure. It is the root.
10	DOCUMENT_TYPE_NODE	Document type nodes provide a container for the <DOCTYPE> information that describes the DTD and document language.
11	DOCUMENT_FRAGMENT_NODE	Document fragment nodes are like a document root node but are used as a handle at the top of a section of the tree that has been taken out of its containing document context. For example if you cut several paragraphs from a document, the branches of the document containing those paragraphs can be attached to a document fragment node.
12	NOTATION_NODE	Notation nodes are used by the DTD handling mechanisms in XML based documents.

Whenever a DOM node is available, (for example. the `document` object), then there are a number of properties and methods available to it, which are detailed below.

Properties

Property	Description	DOM Level Introduced
nodeName	The value depends on the kind of node being examined. Element nodes place the HTML tag type that instantiated the object in this property. That is not the same value as the `NAME=" "` HTML tag attribute. Attribute objects have an HTML tag attribute name as their `nodeName` value. Others are assigned according to the type of node.	1
nodeValue	For attributes and Text node objects, this is the value or content of the attribute or Text node. For most other node types, this value is `null` apart from comments, processing instructions, and CDATA nodes. Comment nodes use this to store the text within the comment delimiters. `ProcessingInstruction` nodes store information about how to process the XML data in the document. CDATA nodes are containers to store XML content that may have markup embedded in them. They escape the content in such a way that it won't be accidentally parsed.	1

Property	Description	DOM Level Introduced
nodeType	The nodeType property determines the kind of node this object represents. However, in browser implementations, the object is instantiated as a sub-class of DOM Node object and its class type distinguishes how it actually behaves. Nevertheless, from the DOM perspective, if a subset of the properties is taken, the object can be seen as a simple DOM node.	1
parentNode	A reference to the node to whose childNodes collection this node belongs.	1
childNodes	A collection of node objects that are immediate children of the owning node.	1
firstChild	The first item in the childNodes collection.	1
lastChild	The last item in the childNodes collection.	1
previous Sibling	The node immediately before the current node in the childNodes collection belonging to their joint parent node.	1
next Sibling	The node immediately after the current node in the childNodes collection belonging to their joint parent node.	1
attributes	A collection of Attribute node objects belonging to this node.	1
owner Document	A reference to the root of the DOM tree structure.	1
baseURI	Returns the absolute base URI of this node.	3
text Content	Returns the text content of a particular node, ignoring all tagged content.	3

Methods

Method	Description	DOM Level Introduced
append Child(new)	Append a node to the receiving Node object's childNodes collection.	1
cloneNode (deep)	Clone an existing node, potentially copying recursively down into its own tree structure. Note that if we do clone a node, any attached event handlers associated with the node being copied will not be cloned with it. We will need to re-attach them if necessary.	1

Table continued on following page

Method	Description	DOM Level Introduced
has Attributes()	Return Boolean true if the Node has some attribute nodes belonging to it.	2
hasChild Nodes()	Return Boolean true if the Node owns any children.	1
insertBefore (aNode, target)	Insert a new node into the childNodes collection of the receiving node immediately before the indicated oldNode.	1
isSupported (feat, ver)	Test whether the DOM implementation implements a specific feature and that feature is supported by this node. The table detailing feat (Feature) and ver (Version) is show below.	2
normalize()	Normalize the node so that only markup separates text nodes.	1
removeChild (old)	Remove a node from the receiving node's childNodes collection.	1
replaceChild (new, old)	Replace an old node with a new one in the receiving nodes' childNodes collection.	1

isSupported Method

These are the parameters of the isSupported() method; it will return true if the required feature is supported.

Feature	Version	Description
CSS	2.0	DOM level 2 CSS support
CSS2	2.0	DOM level 2 support for CSS extended interfaces
Events	2.0	DOM level 2 event model
HTML	1.0	DOM level 1 HTML model
HTML	2.0	DOM level 2 HTML model
HTMLEvents	2.0	DOM level 2 HTML event support
KeyEvents	3.0	DOM level 3 key event support (part of Events)
MouseEvents	2.0	DOM level 2 mouse event support (part of Events)
MutationEvents	2.0	DOM level 2 mutation event support (part of Events)
Range	2.0	DOM level 2 text range module
StyleSheets	2.0	DOM level 2 StyleSheets module
Traversal	2.0	DOM level 2 document traversal module
UIEvents	2.0	DOM level 2 user interface event support (part of Events)
Views	2.0	DOM level 2 views module
XML	1.0	DOM level 1 XML extended interfaces
XML	2.0	DOM level 2 XML extended interfaces

DOM Document Node

DOM Document Node objects all support these properties and methods in addition to the basic Node properties and methods shown above.

Properties

Property	Description	DOM Level Introduced
doctype	The Document Type Declaration associated with this document.	1
implementation	The DOMImplementation object that handles this document	1
document Element	Shortcut to the root node of the document.	1
actual Encoding	An attribute specifying the actual encoding of the document.	3
encoding	An attribute specifying the encoding of the document as specified in an XML declaration.	3
standalone	An attribute specifying whether a document is standalone as specified in an XML declaration.	3
strictError Checking	Sets whether to enforce strict error checking. When set to false the implementation is free not to not test every possible error case and raise a DOMException. It is set to true by default.	3
version	An attribute that specifies, as part of an XML declaration, the version of the document.	3

Methods

DOM Document Node objects all support these methods in addition to the basic Node methods:

Method	Description	DOM Level Introduced
createElement (tagName)	Creates a new instance of an Element node based on the tag name provided. In a HTML context, there is the implication that this should suitably sub-class the created Element. The standard is ambiguous here and this method belongs to the Document node definition and not to the HTMLDocument node definition. The results may well be browser-specific since browsers support different class names.	1

Table continued on following page

Method	Description	DOM Level Introduced
createDocument Fragment()	Creates an empty DocumentFragment object.	1
createTextNode (aText)	Creates a new instance of a Text node containing the specified text as its data.	1
createComment (aTxt)	Returns an HTML comment containing aTxt.	1
createCDATA Section(aData)	Returns a CDATA section containing aData.	1
create Processing Instruction (aTarg,aData)	Returns a Processing Instruction, with aTarg being the target and aData being the data of the instruction.	1
createAttribute (aName)	Creates an attribute. This is then fastened to the relevant attribute using the setAttributeNode() method.	1
getElementsBy TagName (tagName)	Returns a collection of objects having been instantiated from the specified tag name.	1
importNode (aNode, aRecursive)	Imports a node from another childNodes collection potentially copying recursively down into its own tree structure.	2
getElementBy Id(anId)	This HTMLDocument extension locates an object according to its unique ID value. Therefore, it refers to a singular HTMLElement object.	2
getElementsBy Attribute Value(nsURI, lName, val)	Gets a list of attributes which have a specific value.	3
setAttribute Node(newAttr)	Adds a new attribute to an element.	1

DOM Element Node

The Element Nodes support all the capabilities of the fundamental DOM Node object. In addition, these properties specific to Element nodes are supported.

Properties

Property	Description	DOM Level Introduced
tagName	Returns the name of the Element node of which this property is a member	1

Methods

The following methods are added to the Element Node object over and above the basic Node methods:

Method	Description	DOM Level Introduced
getAttribute (aName)	Returns the attribute value of aName	1
setAttribute (aName, aValue)	Changes the value of the aName attribute to aValue	1
removeAttribute (aName)	Removes the aName attribute from this element	1
getAttribute Node(aNode)	Returns the attribute node of aNode	1
setAttribute Node(aNode)	Adds a new attribute to an element	1
removeAttribute Node(aNode)	Removes the attribute node of aNode	1
getElementsBy TagName(aName)	Returns a node list of all descendents with the given aName name	1
hasAttribute (aName)	Returns true if the attribute of the given aName exists in this element	2

DOM Attribute Node

Attribute Node objects support all the capabilities of the Node object. In addition, they also support the following properties and methods:

Properties

Property	Description	DOM Level Introduced
name	The name of the attribute	1
specified	If the attribute was explicitly given a value in this document, then this is set to true	1
value	The value of the attribute	1
ownerElement	Returns the element node that contains this attribute	2

Methods

Attribute Node objects also support the following methods:

Method	Description	DOM Level Introduced
getNamed Item(aName)	Returns a node by name from a collection of attributes. Not supported on MSIE 4 & 5.	1
setNamed Item(aNode)	Adds a node by name to a collection of attributes. Not supported on MSIE 4 & 5.	1
removeNamed Item(aName)	Removes a node by name from a collection of attributes. Not supported on MSIE 4 & 5.	1
item (anIndex)	Get the anIndex'th item from an attribute node.	1

DOM Character Data Node

All Character Data nodes support the properties and methods of the Node object. In addition, these special properties and methods, specific to the Character Data node are supported as well:

Properties

Property	Description	DOM Level Introduced
data	The character data of the Character Data node.	1
length	The number of 16-bit units (because each character in 16-bits long in UTF-16) that is available to the data property. In other words, the length of this node.	1

Methods

These methods are also specific to Character Data Nodes:

Method	Description	DOM Level Introduced
substring Data(off, nn)	Extracts a range of data from the node. off is the offset and says where to start from and nn is the number of 16-bit units, or characters, to extract from that point.	1
appendData (arg)	Appends the string, arg, to the end of the character data of the node.	1
insertData(o ff, arg)	Inserts a string, arg, into the specified starting position of off.	1
deleteData (off, nn)	Removes a range of characters from the node, starting from off, and counting nn characters forward.	1
replaceData (off, nn, arg)	Replaces a set of characters with the specified string, arg. The section replaced begins at off, and ends nn characters from that point.	1

These special capabilities of the Character Data Nodes are also inherited by Text Nodes, Comment Nodes, and CDATASection Nodes.

DOM Text Nodes

Text Nodes inherit all the capabilities of a Character Data Node, which in turn provides the capabilities inherited from the fundamental DOM Node object type. In addition, Text Node objects add the following property and method.

Properties

Property	Description	DOM Level Introduced
isWhitespace InElement Content	Specifies whether this node contains whitespace in element content. Often referred to as ignorable whitespace (almost exclusively indentation). This can only return true if a DTD or Schema is available to validate the document.	3

Methods

The following method is also added by the Text node sub-class:

Method	Description	DOM Level Introduced
splitText (off)	Breaks the text node into two nodes at the position specified by off. They are both kept in the tree as siblings.	1

DOM Comment Nodes

Comment nodes inherit the capabilities of Character Data and fundamental DOM Node objects. No special properties or methods are added at DOM Level 1.

DOM CDATA Section Nodes

CDATASection nodes inherit the capabilities of Text nodes. Therefore, they also have the capabilities of Character Data and fundamental DOM Node objects. No special properties or methods are added at DOM Level 1.

Index

A Guide to the Index

The index is arranged hierarchically, in alphabetical order, with symbols preceding the letter A. Most second-level entries and many third-level entries also occur as first-level entries. This is to ensure that users will find the information they require however they choose to search for it.

The ~ character is used to reduce the need to duplicate almost identical entries (e.g. getX/~Y means getX/getY).

Notes